THE WORLD OF PSYCHOLOGY

SECOND EDITION

Samuel E. Wood

Lindenwood College

Ellen Green Wood

*St. Louis Community College
Meramec*

ALLYN AND BACON

BOSTON   LONDON   TORONTO   SYDNEY   TOKYO   SINGAPORE

Vice President and Publisher, Social Sciences: Susan Badger
Executive Marketing Manager: Joyce Nilsen
Developmental Editor: Elizabeth Brooks
Editorial Assistant: Erika Stuart
Senior Editorial Production Administrator: Susan McIntyre
Editorial Production Service: Lifland et al., Bookmakers
Text Designer: Deborah Schneck
Photo Researcher: Laurel Anderson/Photosynthesis
Composition Buyer: Linda Cox
Manufacturing Buyer: Megan Cochran
Cover Administrator: Linda Knowles
Electronic Composition: Tim Ries

Library of Congress Cataloging-in-Publication Data

Wood, Samuel E.
    The world of psychology / Samuel E. Wood, Ellen Green Wood. — 2nd ed.
        p.   cm.
    Rev. ed. of: The world of psychology / Ellen R. Green Wood. c 1993.
    Includes bibliographical references and index.
    ISBN 0-205-16302-5
    1. Psychology.   I. Wood, Ellen R. Green.   II. Wood, Ellen R.
Green.   World of psychology.   III. Title.
BF121.W657   1996
150—dc20   95–36411
                                                            CIP

Printed in the United States of America
10 9 8 7 6 5 4 3 2 1   00 99 98 97 96 95

Credits appear on pages 759–761, which constitute a continuation of the copyright page.

About the Authors

Samuel E. Wood received his doctorate from the University of Florida. He has taught at West Virginia University and the University of Missouri–St. Louis and served on the doctoral faculty at both universities. He is currently adjunct professor of psychology at Lindenwood College; president of the Higher Education Center, a consortium of 13 colleges and universities in the St. Louis area; president and co-founder of the Higher Education Cable TV channel (HEC-TV) in St. Louis; and executive director of the Educational Opportunity Centers in metropolitan St. Louis.

Ellen Green Wood received her Ph.D. in educational psychology from St. Louis University, and currently teaches psychology at St. Louis Community College at Meramec. Previously she taught in the clinical experiences program in education at Washington University and the University of Missouri–St. Louis. In addition to her teaching, Dr. Wood has developed and taught seminars on critical thinking. In the area of distance learning, she received the Telecourse Pioneer Award from 1982 through 1988.

Together, Sam and Evie Wood have nearly 30 years of experience teaching introductory psychology to thousands of students of all ages, backgrounds, and abilities. *The World of Psychology* is the direct result of their teaching experience.

Dedication

We dedicate this book with love to our children:
Liane, Susan, and Alan
Bart and Julie

CONTENTS

CHAPTER 3

Sensation and Perception   79

States of
Consciousness   127

Learning   163

CHAPTER 13

CHAPTER 14

CHAPTER 15

CHAPTER 16

CHAPTER 17

PREFACE

Our goals for this book are the same as for the first edition: to introduce the world of psychology accurately and clearly to students in an interesting and memorable format. We have tried to present the principles of psychology using a clear and engaging writing style in a pedagogically sound learning format that is accessible and appealing to students.

We are also sensitive to the complexities of the teaching/learning process, having taught thousands of students their first course in psychology. Over the years we have witnessed tremendous changes in the field, in our students, and in ourselves as well. Thus, we sought to create a textbook that is sensitive to the changing needs of modern students and their professors and that will provide a context in which the readers may learn about psychology's past, its present, and its probable future.

To accomplish our goals, we set the following objectives:

To Maintain a Clear, Understandable Writing Style That Students Will Find Interesting

First and foremost, a textbook is a teaching instrument. It cannot be a novel; nor should it be an esoteric, academic treatise. A good psychology textbook must communicate clearly to a diverse audience of various ages and levels of academic ability. Our text is appealing to academically accomplished students, yet accessible to students whose academic skills are yet to be fully developed.

We seek to achieve this objective by explaining concepts in much the same way as we do in our own psychology classes. Throughout the text we have sought to ensure a flow and continuity by using a dialogic style that avoids abrupt shifts in thought. In addition, this text is filled with everyday examples pertinent to students' lives.

To Provide a Series of High-Interest Features That Will Appeal to Today's Students

Every chapter opens with a high-interest vignette to capture student interest and build motivation. We have also included three types of special features:

(1) *Applications* sections to show the practical applications of the principles of psychology; (2) *World of Psychology* sections to explore issues involving race, gender, and ethnic and cultural diversity; and (3) *Pioneers* sections to showcase selected figures in psychology and explore their human side, as well as their contributions to the field.

To Write a Textbook That Encourages Students to Become Active Participants in the Learning Process

Reading about psychology is not enough. Students should be able to practice what they have learned, where appropriate. Many of the principles we teach can be demonstrated, often without elaborate equipment and sometimes as the student reads. What better way to teach new material and make it fresh, interesting, and memorable than to have students demonstrate principles for themselves using an important and innovative element of the book: *Try It!* sections. The response to *Try It!* demonstrations from professors and students has been so positive that this feature now appears in every chapter. The *Try It!* sections personalize psychology and make it come alive.

Student involvement is also promoted through the extensive use of rhetorical questions and by casting the student in the role of the subject in selected studies (for example, as the "teacher" in the Milgram experiment). Thus, students who use *The World of Psychology* become active participants in the learning process rather than simply passive recipients of information.

To Promote and Nurture Critical Thinking

Critical thinking does not consist of being critical of all viewpoints other than our own. To live peacefully and productively in an increasingly diverse society, we must learn to develop an understanding and appreciation of conflicting viewpoints on the multitude of issues that divide us—psychological, social, economic, political, moral, and ethical.

Critical thinking is too important to leave to chance. The first *Applications* section, "Study Skills and Critical Thinking," provides students with an understanding of what critical thinking entails. In addition to promoting critical thinking throughout the text, we have also developed a systematic method of nurturing it. A *Thinking Critically* section appears at the end of each chapter and features three categories of critical thinking questions:

1. *Evaluation* questions teach students to think critically as they evaluate psychological theories, techniques, approaches, perspectives, and research studies.
2. *Point/Counterpoint* questions require students to comprehend, to analyze, and to formulate convincing arguments to support *both* sides of important issues in psychology.
3. *Psychology in Your Life* questions allow students to apply psychological principles and concepts to their own lives and the everyday world.

To Help Students Understand and Appreciate Human Diversity and More Fully Comprehend the Part Multicultural Issues Play in Modern Psychology

We remain dedicated to the goal of promoting understanding of human diversity, but we have changed our means of achieving it. Rather than emphasizing diversity in a separate chapter, as we did in the first edition, we have responded to reviewer preferences and have integrated our expanded coverage of diversity issues throughout the book. *World of Psychology* sections appear in 16 chapters and cover a wide range of multicultural issues. Among the new topics are "Bias in Psychological Research," "Cultural Differences in the Perception of Illusions," "Culture and Altered States of Consciousness," "Memory and Culture," "Expectations, Effort, and Academic Achievement—A Cross-Cultural Comparison," "Personality and Culture," and "Discrimination in the Workplace." In addition, human diversity has been considered in relation to dozens of other topics throughout the text.

To Achieve a Balance between Psychological Principles and Applications

To present psychological principles alone may leave students wondering what psychology has to do with their own lives. The second edition has expanded *Applications* sections at the end of every chapter to help students apply psychology to their personal lives

and to contemporary issues or problems in the larger cultural milieu. New *Applications* include "Handedness: Does It Make a Difference?" "How to Win the Battle against Procrastination," "Stimulating Creativity," "Eating Disorders—The Tyranny of the Scale," "Nonverbal Behavior—The Silent Language," and "Sexual Harassment."

In this edition, Chapter 17 is devoted exclusively to applied psychology. This chapter explores the major specialties in applied psychology: I/O, human factors, environmental, forensic, sports, and consumer psychology.

Finally, every chapter contains a critical thinking question, "Psychology in Your Life," that requires students to consider the many ways psychological principles can be applied to their own lives and to life in general.

To Be Current in Our Coverage While Preserving the Classic Contributions in Our Field

Advances in knowledge and research are occurring at an ever increasing pace, and modern authors must keep abreast. This edition introduces students to the most up-to-date research on many rapidly changing topics—including the DSM-IV, adolescent drug use, sexual behavior in the United States, aging and intellectual development, and genes and homosexuality. New text topics include:

Taste Sensitivities: Nontasters to Supertasters
Drug Use and Classical Conditioning
Recovering Repressed Memories
Computer Neural Networks
Vygotsky's Sociocultural View of Cognitive Development
Part-Time Jobs for Adolescents: A Positive or a Negative?
The "Big Five" Personality Factors

Yet we do not value newness for its own sake. We include, as well, studies that have stood the test of time, and we explore in depth the classic contributions to psychology.

To Give Students an Appreciation of Psychology's History and Its Pioneers and an Understanding That Psychology Is a Living, Growing, Evolving Science

A portion of Chapter 1 is devoted to psychology's history. But in our view, the history of psychology is best understood and appreciated in the context in which the contributions were made. Consequently, discussions of such topics as learning, memory, intelligence, emotion, and personality, for example, integrate the historical and recent research contributions to show how psychology has evolved up to the present day. In addition, we emphasize pioneers in psychology throughout the text—including B. F. Skinner, John B. Watson, Alfred Binet, Jean Piaget, Erik Erikson, Sigmund Freud, Karen Horney, and Hans Selye—in a special feature called *Pioneers*. We focus on the human qualities of the pioneers, their life struggles and successes along with with their contributions, to bring the history of psychology alive for students.

To Provide an Accurate and Thoroughly Researched Textbook That Features Original Sources

To accomplish our goal of introducing the world of psychology accurately and clearly, we have gone back to original sources and have read or reread the basic works of the major figures in psychology and the classic studies in the field. This has enabled us to write with greater clarity and assurance, rather than having to hedge or write tentatively when discussing what experts in the field have actually said. This book is one of the most carefully researched, the most up-to-date, and the most extensively referenced psychology textbooks available.

To Weave a Sound Pedagogical System throughout the Text and the Learning Package

The pedagogical system in *The World of Psychology* consists of the following components:

Learning Objective Questions. Learning objectives written in question form guide student reading, focusing attention on key information, provide a framework for the SQ3R approach, and assist students in preparing for exams.

Memory Checks. An average of six *Memory Checks* are interspersed throughout each chapter to encourage students to pause at the end of sections and test their comprehension of the material they have just read. In this edition, the *Memory Checks* now cover more completely the material emphasized in the Learning Objective Questions.

Review and Reflect Tables. We have expanded our use of summary tables, now called *Review and Reflect* tables, useful for reviewing and comparing various perspectives, theories, and other concepts.

Margin Glossary. A margin glossary provides a ready reference for important key terms that appear in boldface print in the text. All definitions also appear in the end-of-text glossary. Phonetic pronunciations are provided for more than 100 potentially hard-to-pronounce terms.

Chapter Summary and Review. The *Chapter Summary and Review* section provides answers to the learning objectives questions and lists the key terms, all of which are arranged according to the major headings in the chapter. This feature can be used both as a preview to the chapter and as a review in preparing for tests.

SQ3R. All of the above features support a modified SQ3R approach, which is explained to the student in the Applications section in Chapter 1: "Study Skills and Critical Thinking." SQ3R is a systematic approach to maximize learning, improve retention, and develop more effective study skills. SQ3R stands for "Survey, Question, Read, Recite, and Review."

To Continue to Meet the Needs of Students and Professors

In response to the valuable suggestions of our reviewers, we have made many additions, changes, and improvements, including the following:

Chapter 7, now entitled "Intelligence, Cognition, and Language" features expanded coverage of language, including the structure of language, animal language, language and thinking, and sexism in language.

In Chapter 9, Erikson's final four stages are discussed as a unit, rather than being presented separately throughout the chapter.

"Understanding Body Weight" and "Dieting" are now found in Chapter 10 along with "Hunger."

"Love" is presented with the other emotions in Chapter 10.

"Prejudice and Discrimination" is now presented in Chapter 16, "Social Psychology."

We have added an entirely new chapter, "Applied Psychology." It features coverage of I/O, human factors, environmental, forensic, sports, and consumer psychology.

Multicultural material is now more integrated throughout the book.

Chapter 14, "Psychological Disorders," now includes a discussion of the current DSM-IV classifications and descriptions.

Instructors can find complete, chapter-by-chapter listings of changes made in the new edition in the Instructor's Section of the *Annotated Instructor's Edition*.

To Provide Instructors with a Complete, Coordinated Teaching Package of the Highest Quality

The *Annotated Instructor's Edition* has been developed by Mark Garrison of Kentucky State University to encourage student involvement and understanding. It comprises two parts: the Instructor's Section bound into the front of the book, and the detailed annotations that appear in blue type in the margins of the text. The annotations include Lecture Examples, Demonstrations, Critical Thinking topics, Diversity Issues, and guides to using other ancillary materials such as transparencies, video disc segments, and CNN videos.

Accompanying the *Annotated Instructor's Edition* is a separate *Instructor's Resource Manual* (IRM), also prepared by Mark Garrison. It provides detailed instructions for all of the annotations as well as more than 150 ready-to-duplicate handouts.

The World of Psychology is also supported by a comprehensive computer-ready test item file, which we have co-written with Mark Garrison, to ensure that the items it includes are of the highest quality for users of our book. The Test Bank includes detailed explanations for answers to the more difficult questions to help students understand *why* an answer is incorrect.

Also available for instructors are a superb set of acetate transparencies, CNN videos, Allyn and Bacon's exclusive Video Disc series, an extensive video library,

and much more. Please see your Allyn and Bacon sales representative for more information about these and other ancillary materials.

To Provide Students with Top Quality, Innovative Supplements to Enhance Their Learning

The comprehensive and innovative *Study Guide Plus*, written by Joyce Bishop of Golden West College, accompanies the book. It features language enrichment, practice tests for each chapter, flash cards, graphics, and a variety of additional exercises based on SQ3R to help students learn the material. A separate booklet of additional practice tests is also available.

Core Concepts in Psychology: An Interactive CD-ROM is an exciting and revolutionary addition to the introductory psychology course. It offers students a unique chapter review format, enhanced with video, sound, and animations.

Sound Guide for Psychology is another exciting option for introductory psychology students. In an audiocassette format, it reinforces key text concepts and helps students review, rehearse, and take practice tests.

Additional student resources include *Studying Psychology: A Manual for Success*, by Robert T. Brown; *Evaluating Psychological Information: Sharpening Your Critical Thinking Skills*, by James Bell; *World of Psychology*, readings from the *Washington Post*; and *Psychology and Culture*, edited by Walter Lonner. Your Allyn and Bacon sales representative can tell you more about these and other supplements to accompany *The World of Psychology*, Second Edition.

ACKNOWLEDGMENTS

We are indebted to an incredible group of people at Allyn and Bacon for their contributions to *The World of Psychology*. First, we want to thank Susan Badger, Vice President and Social Sciences Publisher at Allyn and Bacon. We have met few people as exceptional as Susan. In addition to being a person of warmth and great personal magnetism, she personifies excellence in every aspect of her work. From the signing of our book to the completion of the second edition, we have benefited from her immense talent, expertise, keen insight, and

impeccable taste. She brings out the best in others, and we have never ended a meeting or phone conversation with her without a renewed feeling of enthusiasm for our work.

Long strings of superlatives would not do justice to Beth Brooks, our Development Editor. If we were to describe all of the qualities the ideal development editor should have, the list would fall far short of those Beth possesses. We have been blessed by her extraordinary professional skills and her exceptionally sound judgment through both editions. And competence is but one of Beth's attributes—she is an utter joy to work with and a person whom we both admire and love.

Although the production process that transforms a manuscript into a finished book is long and complex, our book was in the superbly capable hands of Susan McIntyre, Senior Editorial Production Administrator. Susan is a perfectionist who manages the many stages of the production process with great skill and precision. Fully aware of Susan's commitment to excellence, we were confident that all the parts of the process would come together smoothly. Jay Howland, our meticulous copyeditor, gave us the benefit of her useful suggestions, her intelligence, her expertise in the language, her firm grounding in psychology, and her attention to detail. She has contributed much to this book.

We were exceedingly fortunate to have had Jane Hoover, of Lifland et al., Bookmakers, skillfully and painstakingly guide and coordinate the tedious day-to-day activities of the production process. Jane is a consummate professional who read every word of the manuscript and scrutinized every figure and table to make sure they came together with clarity and precision.

We want to thank Laura Ellingson for expert administration of the review process and for her help in the preparation of our manuscript; Erika Stuart, Editorial Assistant, for her highly competent handling of many details of the project; and Laurie Runge for her very efficient library assistance.

Production is one component of a successful book; marketing is another. We want to express our deep appreciation to Sandi Kirshner, Vice President of Marketing, who brings to her craft infectious enthusiasm and creative insight, and who is a wellspring of innovative ideas. In our travels with Joyce Nilsen, Executive Marketing Manager for Psychology, we have seen firsthand her competence and learned the secret of her success. Joyce is a master of human relations with a rare ability to empathize with professors and sales representatives alike. She can truly understand their wants and needs and skillfully solve problems. We also extend our thanks to Lou Kennedy, Director of Advertising, for her outstanding role in developing the brochures, catalogs, and other materials for presenting the book and its ancillary materials.

No psychology text is considered complete without an accompanying package of ancillary materials. We are deeply grateful to Joyce Bishop of Golden West College for her outstanding and creative *Study Guide Plus,* for her extensive class testing of the text and learning package, and for her enthusiastic support of the book. Mark Garrison, of Kentucky State University, made many contributions. He prepared the excellent *Annotated Instructor's Edition* and the *Instructor's Re-*

source Manual. Mark also assisted us in preparing a completely new test bank for the second edition.

We are deeply indebted to Ward Moore, Senior Publisher's Representative, for initially bringing our manuscript to the attention of Allyn and Bacon. Ward is both a trusted colleague and a friend.

All of the professionals at Allyn and Bacon work hard to maintain a standard of excellence in producing fine books. This certainly includes Bill Barke, President of Allyn and Bacon, who has kept in close touch with our book from its inception. We extend our sincere appreciation to Bill for his confidence in us and for his commitment to this project.

Last but far from least, we want to express once again our gratitude and appreciation to Jane Blaffer Owen, who has been a source of encouragement, support, and inspiration through both editions of this book. Jane Owen symbolizes the values and ideals we admire most, and she has had a profound influence on our lives. She has afforded us the opportunity to write most of this book in one of her houses in New Harmony, Indiana, a setting that we love and that is so conducive to work. We also want to express our appreciation to Gary Gerard, Nancy McIntyre, and all of our friends at the New Harmony Inn and Red Geranium Enterprises for making our months in New Harmony so enjoyable, productive, and hassle-free.

To Our Reviewers

We want to thank the conscientious and knowledgeable reviewers whose suggestions have helped shape this book. First, we extend our sincere appreciation to three people who adopted and reviewed the entire first edition and provided us with a wealth of valuable feedback and helpful suggestions for fine-tuning our book:

Ann Brandt-Williams
Glendale Community College

Patricia Crane
San Antonio College

Harold Siegel
Rutgers University

In addition, we'd like to thank the students at Glendale, San Antonio, and Rutgers for their helpful feedback. We also want to thank Murray Preston-Smith of Houston Community College, who provided us with valuable suggestions.

The following professors generously agreed to review one or more chapters of manuscript:

George Armstrong
Bucks County Community College

Norma Baker
Belmont University

Michael L. Bell
Marlboro, MA

Joyce Bishop
Golden West College

Tim C. Bockes
Sul Ross State University

Ann Brandt-Williams
Glendale Community College

Ed Brady
Belleville Area College

Pat Crane
San Antonio College

Vern R. Dorschner
Brainerd Community College

Linda E. Flickinger
St. Clair County Community College

Sally Foster
Mira Costa College

Laura Freberg
California Polytechnic State University

Wayne Hall
San Jacinto College

Jack Hartnett
Virginia Commonwealth University

Barbara Honhart
Baker College of Flint

Stephen Hoyer
Pittsburg State University

Clixie L. Larson
Utah Valley Community College

John T. Long
Mt. San Antonio College

Maria Elena Lopez-Treviño
Mt. San Jacinto College

Rick Lowe
Salt Lake City Community College

Jesse B. Newkirk III
Grossmont College

Robert J. Pellegrini
San Jose State University

William E. Pelz
Herkimer County Community College

Harold Siegel
Rutgers University–Newark

Jonathan Stone
Dutchess Community College

Patti Thompson
Liberty University

Thomas Tutko
San Jose State University

June Vess
Liberty University

Ken Vincent
Houston Community College

Douglas Wessel
Black Hill State University

Diane E. Wille
Indiana University–South East

In addition, the following professors provided helpful survey responses:

Yukie Aida
Austin Community College–Rio Grande

Kristin Anderson
Houston Community College–Southwest

Elizabeth A. Baldwin
Austin Community College–Southwest

Joyce Bishop
Golden West College

Sandra Y. Boyd
Houston Community College–Central

Maria G. Cisneros-Solis
Austin Community College–Rio Grande

Michael R. Cline
J. Sargent Reynolds Community College

Herbert Coleman
Austin Community College–Rio Grande

Pat Crane
San Antonio College

Linda E. Flickinger
St. Clair County Community College

John H. Forthman
San Antonio College

Laura Freberg
California Polytechnic State University

Patricia Kennedy Furr
Austin Community College–Northridge

David Gersh
Houston Community College–Central

Irene Gianakos
Kent State University

Joanne C. Hsu
Houston Community College

Jennifer Jacobs
Indiana University–Southeast

Chris Jenkins-Burk
Sandhills Community College

Susan S. Maher
Austin Community College–Southwest

Duane G. McClearn
Elon College

Jim Mullen
Pierce College

Ramona Parrish
Guilford Technical Community College

Gary W. R. Patton
Indiana University of Pennsylvania

Robert J. Pellegrini
San Jose State University

Vicky Phares
University of South Florida

Paula Pile
Greensboro College

Murray Preston-Smith
Houston Community College–Southwest

George D. Ritchie
Guilford Technical Community College

Karen Saenz
Houston Community College

Rita S. Santanello
Belleville Area College

Joyce Schaeuble
Sacramento City College

Diane Silver
Austin Community College–Northridge

Jeanne Spaulding
Houston Community College–Northwest

L. K. Springer
Glendale Community College

Jean E. Stiles
Glendale Community College

Jonathan Stone
Dutchess Community College

Deborah Van Marche
Glendale Community College

Ken R. Vincent
Houston Community College–Northwest

Andrea Wagonblast
Bowling Green State University

Marie Waung
University of Michigan–Dearborn

Janet Wiegel-De Le Vère
Black Hawk College

Gordon Whitman
Sandhills Community College

Diane E. Wille
Indiana University Southeast

Joseph A. Zizzi
Mohawk Valley Community College

Finally, we extend our sincere thanks to the reviewers of the first edition, who offered comprehensive and valuable insight into what an introductory psychology text should be. The book could not exist without them.

Joyce Bishop
Golden West College

Allen Branum
South Dakota State University

Andre Cedras
Macomb Community College

Samuel Church
Fairmont State College

James Dooley
Mercy College

William Dwyer
University of Memphis

Thomas Fitzpatrick
Rockland Community College

Katherine Fuhs
J. Sargeant Reynolds Community College

Wayne Hall
San Jacinto College North Campus

Barbara Honhart
Baker College of Flint

Claire Lowder
Illinois Central College

Lynn McCutcheon
Northern Virginia Community College

James Nelson
Parkland College

Diane Owsley
Elizabethtown Community College

Gregory Pezzetti
Rancho Santiago College

Pennie Seibert
Boise State University

Pamela Stewart
Northern Virginia Community College

Thomas Tighe
Moraine Valley Community College

Rene Villa
Hillsborough Community College

Everett Wagner
San Antonio College

Phyllis Walrad
Macomb Community College

Patrick Williams
University of Houston–Downtown

1

INTRODUCTION TO PSYCHOLOGY

CHAPTER OUTLINE

Introduction to Psychology

Psychology: Science or Common Sense?

The Goals of Psychology

What Is a Theory?

Basic and Applied Research

Descriptive Research Methods

Naturalistic Observation: Caught in the Act of Being Themselves

Laboratory Observation: A More Scientific Look at the Subject

The Case Study Method: Studying a Few Subjects in Depth

Survey Research: The Art of Sampling and Questioning

The Experimental Method: Searching for Causes

Independent and Dependent Variables

Experimental and Control Groups: The Same Except for the Treatment

Control in the Experiment: Attempting to Rule Out Chance

Generalizing the Experimental Findings: Do the Findings Apply to Other Groups?

Potential Problems in Experimental Research

Advantages and Limitations of the Experimental Method

Other Research Methods

The Correlational Method: Discovering Relationships, Not Causes

Psychological Tests: Assessing the Subject

Meta-analysis: Combining the Results of Many Studies

Subjects in Psychological Research

Human Subjects in Psychological Research

World of Psychology: Bias in Psychological Research

The Use of Animals in Research

Ethics in Research: First and Foremost

The History of Psychology: Exploring Psychology's Roots

Wilhelm Wundt: The Founding of Psychology

Titchener and Structuralism: Psychology's Blind Alley

Functionalism: The First American School of Psychology

Behaviorism: Never Mind the Mind

Psychoanalysis: It's What's Down Deep That Counts

Gestalt Psychology: The Whole Is Greater Than the Sum of Its Parts

Humanistic Psychology: Looking at Human Potential

Cognitive Psychology: Focusing on Mental Processes

Psychology Today

Modern Perspectives in Psychology: Current Views on Behavior and Thinking

Psychologists at Work

Applications: Study Skills and Critical Thinking

Thinking Critically

Chapter Summary and Review

1

Do you remember what you were doing on June 17, 1994? You may have joined some 95 million other Americans—over 36 percent of the U.S. population—who watched all or part of the slow-speed police chase and arrest of O.J. Simpson, who was charged with the murders of Nicole Brown Simpson and Ronald Goldman. O.J., who ran to stardom as a football hero, who ran through airports in the famous Hertz TV commercials, was now making a desperate last run, holding a gun to his chin.

In a bizarre way, the slow-speed chase resembled the massive police escort you might see in a presidential motorcade. But rather than leading O.J., the celebrity, through a mass of cheering fans, the police were chasing O.J., the fugitive. Nevertheless, crowds gathered, waved, and cheered "Go, O.J., Go!" as the white Bronco led the police caravan down the freeway. And ever since that chase, more dramatic, more riveting than any movie scene, millions of Americans have been fascinated by the events that have unfolded in the "trial of the century."

Could the superstar O.J. Simpson, many people wondered, so highly esteemed, loved, and respected, have actually committed two such bloody and brutal murders? When the trial began in 1995, CNN carried it live, and the ratings skyrocketed, easily surpassing talk shows, game shows, and popular soap operas. It seemed as if the American public could not get enough.

Why were we so fascinated with the O.J. Simpson story? In part because the entire affair involved many issues in human behavior that psychologists study and research—race and racism, gender, sexual behavior and promiscuity, drug use, spousal abuse, obsessive jealousy, and murder. And the trial showcased other aspects of human behavior that you will study in *The World of Psychology*, such as the accuracy of memory. Do we remember events, both recent and remote, in vivid detail exactly as they happen, or do we "reconstruct" them and recollect partly truth and partly fiction? And how do we perceive events? Do different people perceive the same details in vastly different ways—especially if the individuals differ in race, gender, and/or social class? A self-confessed drug dealer who claimed to have sold large amounts of amphetamines to O.J. the night of the murders passed a series of lie detector tests. But are lie detector tests accurate and reliable? Can we be assured that those who pass lie detector tests are telling the truth and those who do not are lying?

The trial evoked other issues in psychology as well, ones involving motives, emotion, and the link between stress and illness. (One stressed-out prosecutor actually fell ill during the trial, and a juror had to quit because "she couldn't take it anymore.") Further, the trial demonstrated the various roles psychologists play in the legal system, from expert witnesses to jury consultants.

Never before have so many Americans slipped into the role of amateur psychologist at the same time, analyzing the motives of the defendant, the witnesses, the police, the lawyers, and the jurors. But the world of psychology you are about to enter asks questions, probes issues, and tests hypotheses that are far wider and deeper than those involving O.J. Simpson and the "trial of the century."

◆ Introduction to Psychology

When many people consider the field of psychology, they conjure up images of mental disorders and abnormal behavior. Psychologists do study the strange and unusual, but they are interested in the normal and commonplace as well.

Just what is psychology? Psychology has changed over the years, and so has its definition. In the late 1800s mental processes were considered to be the appro-

2

priate subject matter of psychology. Later there was a movement to restrict psychology to the study of observable behavior alone. Today the importance of both areas is recognized, and **psychology** is now defined as the scientific study of behavior and mental processes.

Answer true or false for each statement in the *Try It!* to see how much you already know about some of the topics we will explore in *The World of Psychology*. (You'll find the answers below.)

> **psychology:** The scientific study of behavior and mental processes.

Try It!

Indicate whether each statement is true (T) or false (F).

___ 1. Memory is more accurate under hypnosis.
___ 2. All people dream during a night of normal sleep.
___ 3. As the number of bystanders at an emergency increases, the time it takes for the victim to get help decreases.

___ 4. There is no maternal instinct in humans.
___ 5. Older adults tend to express less satisfaction with life in general than younger adults do.
___ 6. Eyewitness testimony is often unreliable.
___ 7. Children with high IQs tend to be less able physically than their peers.
___ 8. Creativity and high intelligence do not necessarily go together.
___ 9. When it comes to close personal relationships, opposites attract.
___ 10. The majority of teenagers have good relationships with their parents.

Psychology: Science or Common Sense?

When students begin their first course in psychology, they come with differing expectations of what psychology is all about. At first, many of them consider it more common sense than science. Will you be studying a collection of common-sense notions this semester? Or can we make a valid claim that psychology is a science?

For the *Try It!* common sense might have led you astray. All of the odd-numbered items are false, and all of the even-numbered items are true. So, common sense, alone, will not take you very far in your study of psychology.

Many people also believe that whether a field of study is considered a science depends upon the nature of its body of knowledge. Physics, for example, is a science, and so is chemistry. But neither qualifies as a science solely because of its subject matter. A science is a science not because of the nature of its body of knowledge, but because of the approach—the standards, methods, values, and general principles—employed in acquiring that body of knowledge. Psychology is considered a science because it uses scientific methodology in building and refining the body of knowledge we will explore in the chapters of this book.

The Goals of Psychology

> **?** *What are the four goals of psychology?*

The goals of psychology are the description, explanation, prediction, and control of behavior and mental processes. Psychological researchers always seek to attain one or more of these goals when they plan and conduct their studies.

Description is usually the first step in understanding any behavior or mental process and is, therefore, more important in a very new area of research or in the early stages of research. To attain this goal, researchers describe the behavior or

theory: A general principle or set of principles proposed in order to explain how a number of separate facts are related to one another.

basic research: Research conducted for the purpose of advancing knowledge rather than for its practical application.

applied research: Research conducted for the purpose of solving practical problems.

mental process of interest as accurately and completely as possible. A description tells *what* occurred.

The second goal, *explanation*, requires an understanding of the conditions under which a given behavior or mental process occurs. Such an understanding often enables researchers to state the causes of the behavior or mental process they are studying. But researchers do not reach the goal of explanation until their results have been tested, retested, and confirmed. The way researchers confirm an explanation is by eliminating or ruling out other competing explanations. An explanation tells *why* a given event or behavior occurred.

The goal of *prediction* is met when researchers can specify the conditions under which a behavior or event is likely to occur. Thus, if researchers can identify all the antecedent (prior) conditions required for a behavior or event to occur, then they can predict the behavior or event.

The goal of *control* is accomplished when researchers know how to apply a principle or change a condition to prevent unwanted occurrences or to bring about desired outcomes. A therapy could be designed to prevent anxiety attacks; a technique could be employed to improve memory.

What Is a Theory?

Any science has a well-established body of theory to guide its research, and psychology is no exception. A **theory** is a general principle or set of principles proposed in order to explain how a number of separate facts are related to one another. A theory enables researchers to fit many separate facts into a larger framework and thus imposes order on what otherwise would be a disconnected jumble of data. The value of a theory rests upon how well it accounts for the accumulated research findings in a given area and how accurately it can predict new findings.

A theory serves two important functions: (1) to organize facts—a necessary step toward arriving at a systematic body of knowledge—and (2) to guide research.

? *What is the difference between basic and applied research?*

Basic and Applied Research

The two types of research psychologists pursue to accomplish their goals are (1) basic, or pure, research and (2) applied research. The purpose of **basic research** is to seek new knowledge and to explore and advance general scientific understanding. Basic research explores such topics as the nature of memory, brain function, motivation, and emotional expression. It also searches for the causes of psychological disorders such as schizophrenia and depression, sleep and eating disorders, and others. Psychologists doing basic research usually seek to accomplish the first three goals—description, explanation, and prediction. Basic research is not intended to solve specific problems; nor is it meant to investigate ways to apply what is learned to immediate real-world problems. Yet, very often, the findings of basic research are used later in applied settings.

Applied research is conducted specifically for the purpose of solving practical problems and improving the quality of life. Applied research focuses on such concerns as methods to improve memory or increase motivation, therapies to treat psychological disorders, ways to decrease stress, and so on. Applied psychologists are primarily concerned with the fourth goal—control—because it specifies ways and means of changing behavior. In Chapter 17 you will learn more about some fields of applied psychology—industrial/organizational, human factors, environmental, forensic, sports, and consumer psychology.

Descriptive Research Methods

The goals of psychological research—description, explanation, prediction, and control—are typically accomplished in stages. In the early stages of research, descriptive research methods are usually the most appropriate. **Descriptive research methods** yield descriptions rather than identifying causes of behavior. Naturalistic observation, laboratory observation, the case study, and the survey are examples of descriptive research methods.

Naturalistic Observation: Caught in the Act of Being Themselves

Naturalistic observation is a research method in which the researchers observe and record behavior in its natural setting without attempting to influence or control it. Ethologists are researchers who study the behavior patterns of animals in their natural environment. They might observe their subjects through high-powered telescopes or from blinds that they build to conceal themselves.

Often human subjects are not aware that they are being observed. This can be accomplished by means of one-way mirrors, a technique researchers often use to observe children in nursery schools or special classrooms. You may have seen episodes of "60 Minutes," "20/20," or "Candid Camera" in which hidden cameras or tape recorders were used to gather information from unsuspecting subjects "caught in the act of being themselves."

The major advantage of naturalistic observation is the opportunity to study behavior in normal settings. Here behavior occurs more naturally and spontaneously than it would under artificial and contrived laboratory conditions. Sometimes naturalistic observation is the only feasible way to study certain phenomena that would be either impossible or unethical to set up in an experiment, such as how people typically react during disasters like earthquakes or fires.

Naturalistic observation has its limitations, however. Researchers must wait for events to occur; they cannot speed the process up or slow it down. And because they have no control over the situation, the researchers cannot reach conclusions about cause-and-effect relationships. Another potential problem in naturalistic observation is observer bias, which is a distortion in researchers' observations. Observer bias can result when researchers' expectations about a situation cause them to see what they expect to see or to make incorrect inferences about the behavior they observe.

Laboratory Observation: A More Scientific Look at the Subject

Another method of studying behavior involves observation that takes place not in its natural setting, but in the laboratory. There researchers can exert more control and use more precise equipment to measure

descriptive research methods: Research methods that yield descriptions of behavior rather than causal explanations.

naturalistic observation: A research method in which the researcher observes and records behavior in its natural setting, without attempting to influence or control it.

? *What is naturalistic observation, and what are some of its advantages and limitations?*

Jane Goodall, shown here with a chimp she named Freud, has conducted naturalistic observation of chimpanzees' behavior for over 30 years.

responses. Much of our knowledge about sleep, for example, has been gained by laboratory observation of subjects who sleep for several nights in a sleep laboratory or sleep clinic.

The Case Study Method: Studying a Few Subjects in Depth

What is the case study method, and for what purposes is it particularly well suited?

Another descriptive research method used by psychologists is the **case study**, or case history. In a case study, a single individual or a small number of persons are studied in great depth, usually over an extended period of time. A case study involves the use of observation, interviews, and sometimes psychological testing. The case study is exploratory in nature, and its purpose is to provide a detailed description of some behavior or disorder. This method is particularly appropriate for studying people who have uncommon psychological or physiological disorders or brain injuries. Often case studies emerge during the course of treatment of these disorders. You may have read the book or seen the movie *Sybil*, the case study of a young woman who had multiple personalities. Much of what we know about unusual psychological disorders such as multiple personality comes from the in-depth analyses provided by case studies.

In some instances the results of detailed case studies have provided the foundation for psychological theories. The theory of the famous Sigmund Freud is based primarily on case studies of his own patients.

Although the case study has proven useful in advancing knowledge in several areas of psychology, it has certain limitations. Researchers cannot establish the cause of observed behaviors in a case study. Moreover, because so few subjects are studied, researchers do not know how applicable, or generalizable, their findings may be to larger groups or to different cultures.

Survey Research: The Art of Sampling and Questioning

What are the methods and purposes of survey research?

Psychologists are interested in many questions that would not be possible to investigate using naturalistic observation or the case study. The **survey** is a method in which researchers use interviews and/or questionnaires to gather information about the attitudes, beliefs, experiences, or behaviors of a group of people. The results of carefully conducted surveys have provided much of the information available about the incidence of drug use, about sexual behaviors of particular segments of the population, and about the incidence of various mental disorders.

What is a representative sample, and why is it essential in a survey?

Selecting a Sample: More Than Numbers to Consider Researchers in psychology rarely conduct experiments or surveys using all members of the group they would like to study. For example, researchers interested in studying the sexual behavior of American women do not attempt to study every woman in the United States. Instead of studying the whole **population** (the entire group of interest to researchers and to which they wish to apply their findings), the researchers select a sample for study. A **sample** is a part of the population that is selected and studied in order to reach conclusions about the entire larger population of interest.

Perhaps you have seen a carton of Neapolitan ice cream that contains three separate flavors packed side by side—chocolate, strawberry, and vanilla. To properly sample the carton, a person would need a small amount of ice cream con-

case study: An in-depth study of one or a few subjects consisting of information gathered through observation, interview, and perhaps psychological testing.

taining all three flavors in the same proportions as in the whole carton—a representative sample. A **representative sample** is a sample that includes important subgroups in the same proportions as they are found in the larger population.

Selecting a representative sample is difficult, but expert organizations like Gallup and Roper can select relatively small samples and get an accurate view of the opinions of large groups of people. As far back as 1968, Gallup polled a mere 2,000 voters in the United States and predicted that Richard Nixon would get only 43 percent of the popular vote. When the final election results were reported, Nixon received 42.9 percent of the votes. And modern sampling and polling techniques are even more sophisticated than those of decades past.

The results of carefully conducted surveys have provided valuable information about a wide variety of human behaviors.

The Use of Questionnaires Researchers using the survey method rely on information gathered through questionnaires, interviews, or some combination of the two. Surveys that use questionnaires can be completed more quickly and less expensively than those involving interviews.

The largest survey ever taken of the sexual behavior of American women was conducted by *Cosmopolitan* magazine (Wolfe, 1981). About 106,000 women—3.5 percent of *Cosmopolitan* readers—completed and returned a questionnaire that had appeared in the magazine. Two-thirds of the respondents claimed to have had 5 to 25 sexual partners, and a high percentage reported having had intercourse with more than one partner on the same day. Do these results reflect the sexual behavior of American women in general?

The number of people who respond to a survey is not the most critical element. A researcher can generalize findings from a sample *only* if it is representative of the entire population of interest. The readers of *Cosmopolitan* magazine do not represent a cross section of American women but tend to be young, single, and relatively affluent. Furthermore, the response rate was only 3.5 percent of the readers. It is possible that women who *chose* to respond to the survey were more sexually active than the average reader. So questionnaires appearing in magazines and the phone-in surveys that TV viewers respond to are not scientific.

The Interview: A Better Way "The best survey research uses the personal interview as the principal method of gathering information" (Kerlinger, 1986, p. 379). Skilled interviewers asking well-worded questions of a carefully selected sample of subjects can provide accurate information.

When respondents feel comfortable with an interviewer, they feel freer to share personal information. Imagine that you are being interviewed about a sensitive subject such as sexual behavior. Will you be equally comfortable and truthful regardless of whether the interviewer is male or female? young, middle-aged, or old? of any racial or ethnic group? Christian or Jewish? middle class or working class? The validity or truthfulness of responses can be affected by personal characteristics of interviewers, such as their gender, age, racial and ethnic background, religion, social class, accent, and vocabulary.

In general, male interviewers obtain less information than do female interviewers. And people are most inhibited when they give personal information to interviewers who are the same age but of the opposite sex. Skilled survey researchers, therefore, must select interviewers who have personal characteristics that are appropriate for their subjects.

survey: A method in which researchers use interviews and/or questionnaires to gather information about the attitudes, beliefs, experiences, or behaviors of a group of people.

population: The entire group of interest to researchers and to which they wish to generalize their findings; the group from which a sample is selected.

sample: The portion of any population that is selected for study and from which generalizations are made about the larger population.

representative sample: A sample of subjects selected from the larger population in such a way that important subgroups within the population are included in the sample in the same proportions as they are found in the larger population.

Advantages and Disadvantages of Survey Research Surveys, if conducted properly, can provide highly accurate information about large numbers of people and can show changes in attitudes and behavior over time. Yet large-scale surveys can also be costly and time-consuming. Researchers must have expertise in many areas—in selecting a representative sample, constructing questionnaires, interviewing, and analyzing data.

The major limitation of the survey is that the respondents may provide inaccurate information. Subjects may give false information because of a faulty memory or a desire to please the interviewer (saying what they think the interviewer wants to hear). Subjects may have a tendency to present themselves in a good light (called the social desirability response), or they may even deliberately attempt to mislead the researcher.

Memory Check 1.1

1. Basic research is designed to solve practical problems. (true/false)

2. Researchers using naturalistic observation attempt to control the behavior being observed. (true/false)

3. Much knowledge about sleep and the human sexual response has been gained through:
   a. naturalistic observation.
   b. laboratory observation.
   c. the survey.
   d. the case study.

4. The case study is *not* useful for:
   a. learning about rare physical and psychological disorders.
   b. learning the consequences of rare brain injuries.

   c. supplying detailed descriptions of behavior that can provide the foundation for psychological theories.

   d. studying large numbers of people.

5. The survey is most useful when we wish to learn about:
   a. rare psychological and physical disorders.
   b. the behaviors, beliefs, or attitudes of a large group of people.
   c. how people react during natural disasters.
   d. how people respond under highly controlled conditions.

6. The most accurate surveys are those with the largest number of respondents. (true/false)

Answers: 1. false 2. false 3. b 4. d 5. b 6. false

? *What is the main advantage of the experimental method?*

experimental method: The research method in which researchers randomly assign subjects to groups and control all conditions other than one or more independent variables, which are then manipulated to determine their effect on some behavioral measure—the dependent variable in the experiment.

hypothesis: A prediction about the relationship between two or more variables.

The Experimental Method: Searching for Causes

The descriptive research methods (naturalistic observation, the case study, and the survey) are all well suited for satisfying the first goal of psychology—that of description. From descriptions, researchers may propose possible explanations for the behaviors they study. At some point researchers usually seek to determine the causes of behavior and various other psychological phenomena. What, for example, are the causes of depression, insomnia, stress, forgetting, and aggression?

The **experimental method**, or the experiment, is the *only* research method that can be used to identify cause–effect relationships. The experiment is designed to test a **hypothesis**—a prediction about a cause–effect relationship between two or more conditions or variables. A variable is any condition or factor that can be manipulated, controlled, or measured. One variable of interest to you is the grade you will receive in this psychology course. Another variable that probably interests you is the amount of time you will spend studying for this course. Do you suppose there is a cause–effect relationship between the amount of time students spend studying and the grades they receive?

Consider two other variables—alcohol consumption and aggression. Does the consumption of alcohol cause people to behave more aggressively? Alcohol consumption and aggressive behavior are often observed together. We can assume that there is likely to be more aggression among drinkers in a lively tavern than among a gathering of nondrinkers in a discussion group. But can we assume that the alcohol consumption itself causes the aggressive behavior?

Alan Lang and his colleagues (1975) conducted an experiment to determine if alcohol consumption itself increases aggression or if the beliefs or expectations about the effects of alcohol cause the aggressive behavior. Subjects in the experiment were 96 male college students who were classified as heavy social drinkers. Half the subjects were given plain tonic to drink; the other half were given a vodka-and-tonic drink in amounts sufficient to raise their blood alcohol level to .10, which in most states is the legal limit of intoxication. Subjects were assigned to four groups:

Group 1: Expected alcohol / Received tonic (only)
Group 2: Expected alcohol / Received alcohol (mixed with tonic)
Group 3: Expected tonic / Received alcohol (mixed with tonic)
Group 4: Expected tonic / Received tonic (only)

You might think that heavy social drinkers could detect the difference between plain tonic and a one-to-five mixture of vodka and tonic. But during pilot testing, drinkers could distinguish between the two with no more than 50 percent accuracy (Marlatt & Rohsenow, 1981).

After the subjects had consumed the designated amount, the researchers had a confederate—an accomplice who posed as a subject—purposely provoke half of the subjects by belittling their performance on a difficult task. All the subjects then participated in a learning experiment in which the same confederate posed as the learner. The subjects were told to administer an electric shock to the confederate each time he made a mistake on a decoding task. Each subject was allowed to determine the intensity and duration of the "shock." (Although the subjects believed they were shocking the confederate, no shocks were actually delivered.) The researchers measured the aggressiveness of the subjects in terms of the duration and the intensity of the shocks they chose to deliver.

What were the results of the experiment? As you might imagine, the subjects who had been provoked gave the confederate stronger shocks than the subjects who had not been provoked. But the subjects who drank the alcohol were not necessarily the most aggressive. Regardless of the actual content of their drinks, the subjects who thought they were drinking alcohol gave significantly stronger shocks, whether provoked or not, than the subjects who assumed they were drinking only tonic (see Figure 1.1 on page 10). The researchers concluded that it was the expectation of drinking alcohol, not the alcohol itself, that caused the subjects to be more aggressive. Evidently it was their thinking, not their drinking, that caused the aggression.

Independent and Dependent Variables

In all experiments there are two types of variables. First there are one or more **independent variables**—variables that the researcher manipulates in order to determine whether they cause any change in another behavior or condition. Sometimes the independent variable is referred to as the treatment. In the Lang experiment, there were two independent variables—the alcoholic content of the drink and the expectation of drinking alcohol.

> **independent variable:** In an experiment, the factor or condition that the researcher manipulates in order to determine its effect on another behavior or condition known as the dependent variable.

> *What is the difference between the independent variable and the dependent variable?*

FIGURE 1.1

Mean Intensity of Shock Chosen by Provoked and Unprovoked Subjects

In the Lang experiment, subjects who thought they were drinking alcohol chose to give significantly stronger shocks, whether provoked or not, than subjects who believed they were drinking only tonic. (Data from Lang et al., 1975.)

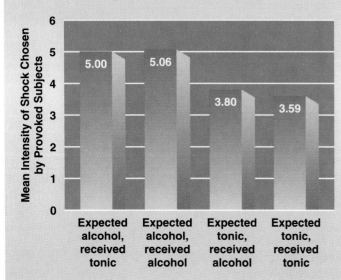
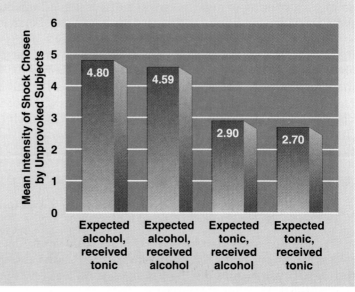

The second type of variable found in all experiments is the **dependent variable**. It is measured at the end of the experiment and is presumed to vary (increase or decrease) as a result of the manipulations of the independent variable(s). The dependent variable is presumed to depend on or to be affected by changes in the independent variable. In the Lang study, the dependent variable was the level of aggression. And the level of aggression was measured by the intensity and duration of the "shocks" the subjects chose to deliver to the confederate.

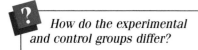

How do the experimental and control groups differ?

Experimental and Control Groups: The Same Except for the Treatment

Most experiments are conducted using two or more groups of subjects. There must always be at least one **experimental group**—a group of subjects who are exposed to the independent variable, or the treatment. The Lang experiment used three experimental groups:

Group 1: Expected alcohol/Received tonic (only)
Group 2: Expected alcohol/Received alcohol (mixed with tonic)
Group 3: Expected tonic/Received alcohol (mixed with tonic)

In most experiments it is desirable to have a **control group**—a group that is similar to the experimental group and used for purposes of comparison. The control group is exposed to the same experimental environment as the experimental group but is not given the treatment. The fourth group in the Lang study was not exposed to either of the two independent variables; that is, this group did not expect alcohol and did not receive alcohol. Because this group was similar to the experimental groups and was exposed to the same experimental environment, it should be considered a control group. In an experiment, all groups, including the control group, are measured on the dependent variable at the end of the experiment.

Control in the Experiment: Attempting to Rule Out Chance

By conducting the Lang experiment in a laboratory, the experimenters were able to control the environmental setting in order to rule out other factors that could conceivably have caused the aggressive responses. Frustration, pain, and extreme noise or heat are several conditions that can increase aggressive responses. Therefore, the researchers carefully controlled the environment so that none of these conditions was present. They varied only the independent variables: the subjects' expectations and the content of their drinks. That way, the researchers could be reasonably sure that the manipulation of the independent variables (alcohol and expectations) caused the differences in the degree of aggression among the groups.

Generalizing the Experimental Findings: Do the Findings Apply to Other Groups?

What should be concluded from the Lang experiment? Can you conclude that people in general tend to be more aggressive when they believe they are under the influence of alcohol? Before reaching such a conclusion, consider several factors: (1) The only subjects used in this experiment were male college students. You cannot be sure that the same results would have occurred if males of other ages or females had been used. (2) The subjects in this experiment were classified as heavy social drinkers. Would the same results have occurred if nondrinkers, moderate social drinkers, or alcoholics had been included? To apply this experiment's findings to other groups, researchers would have to replicate, or repeat, the experiment using different populations of subjects. (3) The amount of alcohol given to the students was just enough to bring their blood alcohol level to .10. You cannot be sure that the same results would have occurred if subjects had consumed more or less alcohol.

Potential Problems in Experimental Research

If an experiment is properly designed and conducted, the researcher should be able to attribute changes in the dependent variable to the manipulations of the independent variable. But several factors other than the independent variables can cause changes in the dependent variable and, therefore, destroy the validity of an experiment. Three of these potential problems are selection bias, the placebo effect, and experimenter bias. Researchers must design experiments to control for these and other problems that could invalidate their results.

Selection Bias: Bias from the Start Selection bias occurs when subjects are assigned to groups in such a way that systematic differences among the groups are present at the beginning of the experiment. If selection bias occurs, then differences at the end of the experiment may not reflect the manipulation of the independent variable but may be due to preexisting differences in the groups.

To control for selection bias, researchers must use **random assignment**. This process consists of selecting subjects by using a chance procedure (such as drawing the names of subjects out of a hat) to guarantee that all subjects have an equal probability of being assigned to any of the groups. Random assignment maximizes the likelihood that the groups will be as similar as possible at the beginning of the experiment. If there had been preexisting differences in the level of aggressiveness of subjects in Lang's alcohol experiment, random assignment should have spread those differences across groups.

dependent variable: The variable that is measured at the end of an experiment and is presumed to vary as a result of manipulations of the independent variable.

experimental group: In an experiment, the group of subjects that is exposed to the independent variable, or the treatment.

control group: In an experiment, a group that is similar to the experimental group and is exposed to the same experimental environment but is not exposed to the independent variable; used for purposes of comparison.

selection bias: The assignment of subjects to experimental or control groups in such a way that systematic differences among the groups are present at the beginning of the experiment.

random assignment: In an experiment, the assignment of subjects to experimental and control groups by using a chance procedure, which guarantees that all subjects have an equal probability of being placed in any of the groups; a control for selection bias.

What is selection bias, and what technique do researchers use to control for it?

What is the placebo effect, and how do researchers control for it?

The Placebo Effect: The Power of Suggestion (for the Subject)

Another factor that can influence the outcome of an experiment is the placebo effect. The **placebo effect** occurs when a subject's response to a treatment is due to the subject's expectations about the treatment rather than to the actual treatment itself. Suppose a drug is prescribed for a patient and the patient reports improvement. The improvement could be a direct result of the drug, or it could be a result of the patient's expectation that the drug would work. Studies have shown that sometimes remarkable improvement in patients can be attributed solely to the power of suggestion—the placebo effect.

The researcher must use a control group to test whether results in an experiment are due to the treatment or to the placebo effect. So subjects in the control group are given a fake treatment. In drug experiments, the control group is usually given a **placebo**—an inert, or harmless, substance such as a sugar pill or an injection of saline solution. To control for the placebo effect, researchers do not let subjects know whether they are in the experimental group (receiving the treatment) or in the control group (receiving the placebo). If subjects getting the real drug or treatment show a significantly greater improvement than the subjects who receive the placebo, then the improvement can be attributed to the drug rather than to the power of suggestion. In the Lang experiment, some subjects who expected alcohol mixed with tonic were given only tonic. The tonic without alcohol functioned as a placebo. This enabled the researchers to measure the effect of the power of suggestion alone in producing aggression.

The placebo effect can invalidate the results of experiments when researchers do not take into account the subjects' expectations. But what about the expectations of those who conduct the experiments—the researchers themselves?

What is experimenter bias, and how is it controlled?

Experimenter Bias: The Power of Suggestion (for the Experimenter)

The expectations of the experimenter are a third factor that can influence the outcome of an experiment. **Experimenter bias** occurs when researchers' preconceived notions or expectations become a self-fulfilling prophecy and cause the researchers to find what they expect to find. A researcher's expectations can be communicated to the subjects, perhaps unintentionally, through tone of voice, gestures, or facial expression. These communications can influence the subjects' behavior. Expectations can also influence a researcher's interpretation of the experimental results, even if no influence occurred during the experiment.

Robert Rosenthal (1973) tested the effect of teacher expectations on student test scores. A group of 100 students were assigned randomly to five mathematics classes. However, the math instructors were told that students had been assigned to their classes according to high or low ability in math. Even though math achievement scores for the five classes should have been about the same, those students who had been labeled as high in math ability outperformed the students who had been labeled low in math ability. It seems amazing that nothing more than a belief held by teachers or experimenters can make a difference in the actual performance of students or subjects. But more amazing is the finding that the subjects don't even have to be human. The effects of experimenter bias have been observed in research with animal subjects as well.

To control for experimenter bias, researchers must not know which subjects are assigned to the experimental and control groups. The identities of both the experimental and control subjects are coded, and their identities are not revealed to the researcher until after the research data are collected and recorded. (Obviously, someone assisting the researcher must know which subjects are in which group.) When neither the subjects nor the experimenter knows which subjects are getting the treatment and which are in the control group, the experiment

placebo effect: The phenomenon that occurs when a person's response to a treatment or response on the dependent variable in an experiment is due to expectations regarding the treatment rather than to the treatment itself.

placebo (pluh-SEE-bo): Some inert substance, such as a sugar pill or an injection of saline solution, given to the control group in an experiment as a control for the placebo effect.

experimenter bias: A phenomenon that occurs when the researcher's preconceived notions in some way influence the subjects' behavior and/or the interpretation of experimental results.

is using the **double-blind technique**. The double-blind technique is the most powerful procedure for studying cause-effect relationships.

Advantages and Limitations of the Experimental Method

The overwhelming advantage of the experiment is its ability to reveal cause-effect relationships. This benefit is possible because researchers are able to exercise strict control over the experimental setting. This allows them to rule out factors other than the independent variable as possible reasons for differences in the dependent variable. But often the more control the experimenter exercises, the more unnatural and contrived the research setting becomes and the less generalizable findings will be to the real world. When subjects know that they are participating in an experiment, their behavior may be different from what it would be in a more natural setting. When a natural setting is considered to be an important factor in a study, researchers may choose to use a field experiment—an experiment conducted in a real-life setting. Although some control over the experimental environment is sacrificed, the advantage is more natural behavior on the part of the subjects.

A major limitation of the experimental method is that in many areas of interest to researchers in psychology, this method is either unethical or not possible. Some treatments cannot be given to human subjects because their physical or psychological health would be endangered, or their constitutional rights violated.

> **double-blind technique:** An experimental procedure in which neither the subjects nor the experimenter knows who is in the experimental or control groups until after the results have been gathered; a control for experimenter bias.

Memory Check 1.2

1. The experimental method is the *only* research method that can be used to identify cause-effect relationships between variables. (true/false)

2. Which of the following statements is *not* true about a control group?
   a. It should be similar to the experimental group.
   b. It is exposed to the independent variable.
   c. At the end of the experiment, it is measured on the dependent variable.
   d. It is used for purposes of comparison.

3. Match the description with the appropriate term.
   ____ 1) a prediction about a relationship between two variables
   ____ 2) any condition that can be manipulated, measured, or controlled
   ____ 3) the variable measured at the end of the experiment
   ____ 4) the variable manipulated by the researcher

   a. independent variable
   b. variable
   c. hypothesis
   d. dependent variable

4. The placebo effect occurs when a subject responds according to:
   a. the hypothesis.
   b. the actual treatment.
   c. how other subjects behave.
   d. his or her expectations.

5. The results of an experiment can be influenced by the expectations of either the subjects or the researcher. (true/false)

6. Random assignment is used to control for:
   a. experimenter bias.
   b. the placebo effect.
   c. selection bias.
   d. subject bias.

Answers: 1. true 2. b 3. 1) c 2) b 3) d 4) a 4. d 5. true 6. c

Other Research Methods

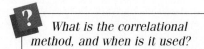
What is the correlational method, and when is it used?

The Correlational Method: Discovering Relationships, Not Causes

We know that researchers are interested in finding the causes of various psychological phenomena. Does stress cause illness? Does smoking cause cancer? Does heavy marijuana use cause students to lose interest in school and get lower grades? Researchers would like to have answers to these questions, but none of them can be researched using the experimental method. It is often illegal and always unethical to assign human subjects randomly to experimental conditions that could be harmful. For example, to find out if smoking marijuana causes a decline in academic achievement, no researcher would randomly assign high school students to an experimental study that would require students in the experimental groups to smoke marijuana. Can you imagine a principal notifying parents that their son or daughter had been chosen to smoke marijuana for 2 years in order to further scientific knowledge?

Much of our knowledge of the effects on human health of marijuana, cigarette smoking, or stress has been gained through experiments on animals or through other research methods. When, for ethical reasons, an experimental study cannot be performed to determine cause–effect relationships, the **correlational method** is usually used. This research method determines the correlation, or relationship, between two characteristics, events, or behaviors. A group is selected for study, and the variables of interest are measured for each subject participating in the study. For example, the variables might be the amount of marijuana previously used and grade point average. Then the researcher applies a statistical formula to obtain a correlation coefficient.

What is a correlation coefficient?

The Correlation Coefficient: How Variables Relate A **correlation coefficient** is a numerical value indicating the degree and direction of the relationship between two variables. A correlation coefficient ranges from +1.00 (a perfect positive correlation) to .00 (no relationship) to −1.00 (a perfect negative correlation). The sign of a correlation coefficient (+ or −) indicates whether the two variables vary in the same or opposite directions. A positive correlation indicates that two variables vary in the same direction. In other words, an increase in the value of one variable is associated with an increase in the value of the other variable. Or, a decrease in the value of one variable is associated with a decrease in the value of the other. There is a positive though weak correlation between stress and illness, for example. When stress increases, illness is likely to increase; when stress decreases, illness tends to decrease.

A negative correlation means that an increase in the value of one variable is associated with a decrease in the value of the other variable. Think of a negative correlation as a seesaw—when one variable goes up, the other goes down. There is a negative correlation between the number of cigarettes people smoke and the number of years they can expect to live. When cigarette smoking increases, the number of years someone lives tends to decrease, and vice versa.

The number in a correlation coefficient indicates the relative *strength* of the relationship between two variables—the higher the number, the stronger the relationship. Therefore, a correlation of −.85 is higher than a correlation of +.64, and a correlation of −.58 is equally strong as one of +.58. A correlation of .00 indicates that no relationship exists between the variables. Examples of variables that are *not* correlated are grade point average and height, and illness and shoe size.

correlational method: A research method used to establish the relationship (correlation) between two characteristics, events, or behaviors.

correlation coefficient: A numerical value that indicates the strength and direction of the relationship between two variables; ranges from +1.00 (a perfect positive correlation) to −1.00 (a perfect negative correlation).

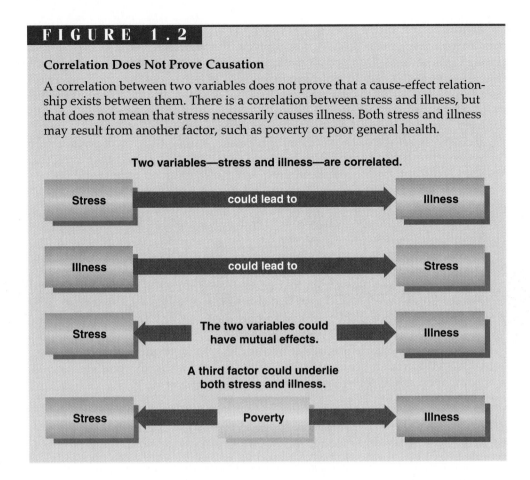

FIGURE 1.2

Correlation Does Not Prove Causation

A correlation between two variables does not prove that a cause-effect relationship exists between them. There is a correlation between stress and illness, but that does not mean that stress necessarily causes illness. Both stress and illness may result from another factor, such as poverty or poor general health.

Two variables—stress and illness—are correlated.

Stress — could lead to → Illness

Illness — could lead to → Stress

The two variables could have mutual effects.
Stress ← → Illness

A third factor could underlie both stress and illness.
Stress ← Poverty → Illness

Correlation and Prediction   Correlations are useful in making predictions. The stronger the relationship between the variables, the better able we are to predict the presence or absence of one variable by measuring the presence of the other. If correlations are high, they will be good predictors. A perfect correlation (+1.00 or −1.00) would enable you to make completely accurate predictions.

A correlation is more useful for predicting the probable performance of a group than for predicting that of an individual. Because there is a correlation between cigarette smoking and lung cancer, it can be predicted that a group of 1,000 nonsmokers will experience a lower incidence of lung cancer than a group of 1,000 two-pack-a-day smokers. But from the correlation coefficient alone you cannot accurately predict which individuals in the group will develop cancer.

The fact that there is a correlation between two variables does not mean that one variable causes the other. Only the experimental method allows us to reach conclusions about cause and effect. When two variables such as stress and illness are correlated, we cannot conclude that stress makes people sick. It might be that illness causes stress, or that a third factor such as poverty or poor general health causes susceptibility to both illness and stress, as shown in Figure 1.2.

Psychological Tests: Assessing the Subject

Psychologists have developed a wide range of tests for measuring intelligence, scholastic achievement, aptitudes, creativity, vocational interests, personality traits, and psychiatric problems. As a student, you have taken some of these tests—IQ tests, SAT or ACT, Iowa Test of Basic Skills or California Achievement Test, Kuder

Preference Test or Strong Interest Inventory, to name a few. Psychological tests are used in a variety of situations—in schools, in the workplace, and in therapeutic settings. These tests are used to evaluate or compare individuals, to measure changes in behavior, and to make predictions about behavior. Test results also provide information that can be used in educational decision making, personnel selection, and vocational guidance. But these psychological tests and every other test are useless instruments unless they have proven reliability and validity.

Reliability refers to the consistency of a test. A reliable test will yield nearly the same score time after time if the same person is tested and then retested. **Validity** is the ability of a test to measure what it is intended to measure. Just as a clock is a valid instrument for measuring time, so a psychological test must be able to measure accurately and adequately the specific area it is designed to measure—vocational aptitude, achievement, and so on. (Reliability and validity will be discussed in more detail in Chapter 7.)

Psychologists often use testing in conjunction with their research. Tests may be administered as part of the intensive study of an individual in a case study. And in an experiment, the dependent variable might be the score on a psychological test. For example, an educational psychologist who is experimenting with a new educational program might use an achievement test to compare the performance of experimental and control subjects.

Tests are also used in correlation studies. To determine the correlation between SAT scores and college grades, researchers statistically compare the SAT scores with the actual college grades of the subjects tested.

Meta-analysis: Combining the Results of Many Studies

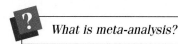
What is meta-analysis?

Psychology may claim to be a science only to the extent that its research data and findings are objective and reproducible. In fact, Schmidt (1992) claims that "contrary to widespread belief, no single primary study can resolve an issue or answer a question" (p. 1179). To verify research findings, it is necessary that studies be replicated. **Replication** is the repeating of studies with the same procedures, but with different subjects and preferably different investigators.

A scientific experiment is somewhat like a recipe or a set of exact instructions. It spells out in detail precisely what the researchers did, how they did it, who the subjects were, how they were selected, what conditions were in place, and what the researchers found. If the results of a study are scientifically valid, a careful replication of the study should yield similar results. When the same findings occur again and again, confidence grows that the findings are indeed genuine. When replications do not yield the same findings, researchers should be suspicious of their initial results and be willing to discard their belief in them.

But what if some replications find evidence of strong support for a hypothesis, some find weak support, others find no support, and still others find evidence to the contrary? Is there any way researchers can average or combine the results of all such studies and reach conclusions about what the weight of evidence shows in that particular area of research? Fortunately, yes.

Researchers have developed a powerful statistical technique known as meta-analysis. **Meta-analysis** is a complex statistical procedure that investigators can use to combine the results from many separate studies on the same topic in order to determine the strength of support for a hypothesis. For example, Janet Hyde and Marcia Lynn (1988) used meta-analysis to examine 165 studies reporting test results on verbal ability for about 1.5 million males and females. Their meta-analysis revealed no significant gender differences in verbal ability.

reliability: The ability of a test to yield nearly the same scores when the same people are tested and then retested using the same test or an alternate form of the test.

validity: The ability of a test to measure what it is intended to measure.

replication: The process of repeating a study with different subjects and preferably a different investigator to verify research findings.

meta-analysis: A complex statistical procedure used by researchers to combine the results from many studies on the same topic in order to determine the degree to which a hypothesis can be supported.

Some experts in the field are so enthusiastic about the potential of meta-analysis that they suggest that individual studies should be thought of only as sources of data that will eventually contribute to a future meta-analysis (Schmidt, 1992).

Review and Reflect Table 1.1 summarizes the different types of research methods we've discussed in this chapter.

Review and Reflect 1.1 *Research Methods in Psychology*

Method	Description	Advantages	Limitations
Naturalistic observation	Observation and recording of behavior in its natural setting. Subjects may or may not know that they are being observed.	Provides descriptive information. Can provide basis for hypotheses to be tested later. Behavior studied in everyday setting is more natural.	Researchers' expectations can distort observations (observer bias). Presence of researcher may influence behavior of subjects. Little or no control over conditions.
Laboratory observation	Observation under more controlled conditions where sophisticated equipment can be used to measure responses.	More control than naturalistic observation.	Possible observer bias. Behavior of subjects may be less natural than in naturalistic observation.
Case study	In-depth study of one or a few subjects using observation, interview, and/or psychological testing.	Source of information for rare or unusual conditions or events. Can provide basis for hypotheses to be tested later.	May not be representative of condition or event. Time-consuming. Subject to misinterpretation by researcher.
Survey	Interviews and/or questionnaires used to gather information about attitudes, beliefs, experiences, or behaviors of a group of people.	Can provide accurate information about large numbers of people.	Responses may be inaccurate. Sample may not be representative. Characteristics of interviewer may influence responses.
Experimental method	Random assignment of subjects to groups. Manipulation of the independent variable(s) and measurement of its effect on the dependent variable.	Enables identification of cause-effect relationships.	Laboratory setting may inhibit natural behavior of subjects. Findings may not be generalizable to the real world. In some cases, experiment is unethical.
Correlational method	Method used to determine the relationship (correlation) between two events, characteristics, or behaviors.	Can assess strength of relationship between variables. Provides basis for prediction.	Does not demonstrate cause and effect.
Psychological tests	Tests used for measuring intelligence, scholastic achievement, aptitudes, vocational interests, personality traits, psychiatric problems.	Provide data for educational and vocational decision making, personnel selection, research, and psychological assessment.	Tests may not be reliable or valid.
Meta-analysis	Statistical method of combining the results from many research studies to determine whether a hypothesis is supported.	Provides an overall estimate of the combined effects of many studies on the same topic.	Findings can be no more reliable than the research on which it is based.

Memory Check 1.3

1. A correlation coefficient shows a cause-effect relationship. (true/false)

2. Which of the following describes a negative correlation?
   a. When the value of one variable goes up, the value of the other variable goes down.
   b. When the value of one variable goes down, the value of the other goes down.
   c. When the value of one variable goes up, the value of the other goes up.
   d. When the value of one variable goes up or down, the value of the other variable remains unchanged.

3. Which of the following correlation coefficients indicates the strongest relationship?
   a. +.65   b. −.78   c. .00   d. +.25

4. Psychological tests are sometimes used in experiments or correlation studies. (true/false)

5. What is the term for a statistical procedure used to combine the results from many research studies to determine whether a specific hypothesis is supported?
   a. combinatorial analysis
   b. multiple analysis
   c. statistical summation
   d. meta-analysis

Answers: 1. false 2. a 3. b 4. true 5. d

Subjects in Psychological Research

Human Subjects in Psychological Research

"Modern psychology has been called 'the science of the behavior of the college sophomore'" (Rubenstein, 1982, p. 83). For practical reasons, the majority of studies with human subjects in the last 30 years have used college students. Students are a convenient group for college professors to study, and professors often encourage their participation by offering pay or points toward a course grade. Psychology studies have also used disproportionate numbers of males (Gannon et al., 1992) and of whites (Graham, 1992).

Heavy reliance on college students presents a problem. College students are a relatively select group in terms of age, socioeconomic class, and educational level. Thus, they are not representative of the general population. But how generalizable the findings of such studies are to the general population depends on the nature of the study. Studies that investigate basic psychological processes such as sensation, perception, and memory are likely to be relatively generalizable, because these processes probably function in similar ways in most adults. But with research on human social behavior, there is great cultural and individual variation and thus a problem in generalizing the results of studies with college students to other segments of the population.

To learn about some other sources of bias in psychological research, read the following World of Psychology section.

World of Psychology

Bias in Psychological Research

Several researchers have cited evidence of bias in psychological research, including gender bias (Gannon et al., 1992), racial bias, and age bias.

In their studies of gender bias in psychological research, Ader and Johnson (1994) report that over the decades, gender bias in the sampling and selection of research subjects has decreased. Yet they maintain that bias is still very much in evidence in reports of research findings and in discussion of single-sex studies. When conducting research in which all of the subjects are of one sex, these authors ask, why do researchers consider it important to specify the gender of the sample clearly when it is female, but not when the sample is exclusively male? Such a practice, say Ader and Johnson, reveals a "tendency to consider male participants 'normative,' and results obtained from them generally applicable, whereas female participants are somehow 'different,' and results obtained from them are specific to female participants" (pp. 217–218).

Investigating race bias, Sandra Graham (1992) reported finding a decline in research on African Americans in psychological journals. And prominent among the research articles that she did find was what she termed a methodological flaw—failure to include socioeconomic status—in research comparing white and African Americans. Graham points out that African Americans are overrepresented among those who are economically disadvantaged. She maintains that socioeconomic status should be incorporated into research designs "to disentangle race and social class effects" in studies that compare white and African Americans (p. 634).

Ageism is a continuing source of bias, too, especially in the language used in psychological research (Schaie, 1993). Even the titles of research on aging tend to focus heavily on loss, deterioration, decline, dependency, and so on. Moreover, researchers are too likely to understate the great diversity among the senior subjects they study. According to Schaie (1993), "Most research on adulthood shows that differences between those in their 60s and those in their 80s are far greater than those between 20- and 60-year-olds" (p. 50). Researchers should guard against descriptions or conclusions implying that all members of a given age group are defined by deterioration, forgetfulness, and deficits. Schaie also warns that researchers should be sensitive to offensive and insulting items such as the following test item contained in an Educational Testing Service kit:

Youth/Beauty/Life::Age/_____/Death

The correct answer, of course, is "ugliness," an ugly stereotype against the aged.

In planning and conducting psychological research, researchers need to consider many factors in addition to close adherence to scientific methodology. Important among these are the factors of sensitivity toward human differences and respect for the dignity of human subjects.

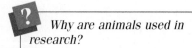

Why are animals used in research?

The Use of Animals in Research

Where would psychology be today without the laboratory rat, Pavlov's salivating dogs, the pigeon, and the many other species of animals used to advance scientific knowledge? Psychologists recognize the tremendous contributions that laboratory animals have made and continue to make to science, and most psychologists favor the use of animals in research. Animals are used in 7 to 8 percent of psychological experiments, and 95 percent of the animals used are rodents (American Psychological Association, 1984).

Why are animals used in research? There are at least six reasons. Animals are used in experimental studies because (1) they provide a simpler model for studying processes that operate similarly in humans; (2) researchers can exercise far more control over animal subjects and thus be more certain of their conclusions; (3) a wider range of medical and other manipulations can be used with animals; (4) it is easier to study the entire life span and multiple generations in some animal species; (5) animals are more economical to use and are available at the researchers' convenience; and (6) some researchers simply want to learn more about the animals themselves. Above all, many of the marvels of modern medicine would not be available today without the use of animals in research. "Every disease eliminated, every vaccine developed, every method of pain relief devised, every surgical procedure invented, every prosthetic device implanted—indeed, virtually every modern medical therapy is due, in part or in whole, to experimentation using animals" (Cohen, 1986, p. 868).

Most psychologists recognize that many scientific advances would not have been possible without animal research. Where do you stand on this issue?

Nevertheless, a storm of controversy surrounds the research use of animals. Animal rights advocates are becoming more militant in their efforts to stop animal research. They have broken into research laboratories, freed laboratory animals, destroyed research records, and wrecked laboratory equipment and other property. One animal rights group has demanded that all animal research studies be stopped immediately. Many activists are also against using animals for food, clothing, or any other purpose.

Very few psychologists favor these extreme views. The American Psychological Association has always supported the use of animals in research, and its code of ethics supports the humane treatment of animals. According to the association's guidelines governing animal research, researchers must do everything possible to minimize discomfort, pain, and illness in animal subjects (American Psychological Association, 1992b). Scientists are making great strides in improving the conditions under which animals are kept and used for research.

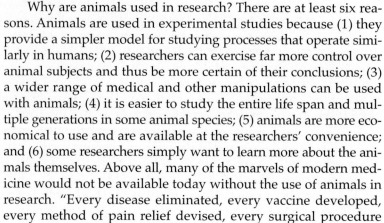

What are some ethical guidelines governing the use of human subjects in research?

Ethics in Research: First and Foremost

In 1992 the American Psychological Association adopted a new set of ethical standards governing research with human subjects. These standards safeguard the rights of experimental subjects while supporting the goals of scientific inquiry. The participation of subjects must be strictly voluntary, and there must be respect for confidentiality (Blanck et al., 1992). Also, subjects must be free to withdraw from the study at any time. The U.S. government has also adopted specific standards for researchers receiving federal funding. At a more local level, colleges and universities usually have ethics committees that must approve any research studies proposed by professors.

Most people would agree that research must be conducted to advance scientific knowledge and that research must be an ethical enterprise. But what about deception? Is it ethical for researchers to lie to their human subjects or otherwise mislead them in order to conduct their studies? The experimental study by Lang and his associates on alcohol and expectations involved deception. The subjects were told that they were delivering electric shocks to another human being, and some of the experimental groups were deceived about the alcoholic content of their drinks. But clearly, without deception, the study could not have been conducted, or the knowledge gained.

Can studies that use deception be justified on scientific grounds, as many psychologists believe? No, say other psychologists, who strictly oppose the use of deception under any circumstances. Diane Baumrind (1985) opposes research using deception because of the potential harm to the subjects. She also believes that such practices will damage the reputation of psychology and psychologists and cause people to lose confidence in the profession.

Even so, deception is used in many research studies, particularly in the field of social psychology. Today the American Psychological Association's code of ethical standards allows deception (1) if it is justified by the value of the potential findings, provided that equally effective procedures that do not involve deception cannot be used; (2) if subjects are not deceived about "physical risks, discomfort, or unpleasant emotional experiences" that might affect their willingness to participate; and (3) if subjects are debriefed as soon as possible after the experiment. The debriefing sessions provide subjects with information about the nature of the research and clear up any misconceptions they may have about what occurred during the study. Researchers want to ensure that the subjects understand that no other participants were actually harmed. In the Lang study, debriefing interviews informed subjects of the deception and revealed to them that no electric shocks were actually used. The subjects who had consumed alcohol were given a breathalyzer test to measure their blood alcohol levels, so that no subject left the laboratory impaired to any degree by alcohol.

Memory Check 1.4

1. Which of the following groups has *not* been overrepresented as subjects in psychological research?
   a. whites   b. males   c. females   d. college students

2. Psychologists are required to debrief subjects thoroughly after a research study when the study:
   a. violates subjects' rights to privacy.
   b. deceives subjects about the true purpose of the research.
   c. exposes subjects to unreasonable risk or harm.
   d. wastes taxpayers' money on trivial questions.

3. Investigators use animals in psychological research to learn more about humans. (true/false)

4. The American Psychological Association has guidelines for ethical treatment for human subjects but not for animal subjects. (true/false)

5. Which of the following has *not* been identified as a source of bias in psychological research, according to the text?
   a. age   b. gender   c. race   d. religion

Answers: 1. c   2. b   3. true   4. false   5. d

The History of Psychology: Exploring Psychology's Roots

If we were to trace the development of psychology from the beginning, we would need to stretch far back to the earliest pages of recorded history, even beyond the early Greek philosophers, such as Aristotle and Plato. People have always had questions about human nature, and they have always tried to understand human behavior. For centuries these questions were the subject of speculation and were considered to be in the realm of philosophy. Most professors who were teaching anything resembling psychology had their appointments in philosophy.

Wilhelm Wundt: The Founding of Psychology

What was Wundt's contribution to psychology?

It was not until experimental methods were applied to the study of psychological processes that psychology became recognized as a formal academic discipline. Three German physiologists—Ernst Weber, Gustav Fechner, and Hermann von Helmholtz—pioneered in the application of experimental methods to the study of psychological processes, and they profoundly influenced the early development of psychology.

Although a number of early researchers were contributing to the new field of psychology, Wilhelm Wundt is generally thought of as the "father of psychology." The establishment of his psychological laboratory in 1879 in Leipzig, Germany, is considered to be the official birth of psychology as a formal academic discipline (see Figure 1.3 on pages 24–25). Wundt's lectures attracted many people from Europe and the United States, some of whom became important figures in psychology. But the studies and experiments that Wundt, his associates, and his students performed in that early laboratory were very different from psychology as we know it today.

For Wundt, the subject matter of psychology was experience—the actual, immediate, conscious experiences of individuals. Wundt believed that mental experiences could be reduced to their basic elements, just as early chemists discovered water was composed of the basic elements hydrogen and oxygen (H_2O). In other words, Wundt was searching for the structure of conscious experience.

A conscious experience can be observed only by the person having that experience. Therefore, research on the experience necessarily involves self-observation or introspection. Introspection as a research method involves looking inward to examine one's own conscious experience—sensations, perceptions, thoughts, images, and feelings—and then reporting that experience. Wundt's advanced psychology students were rigorously trained in introspection. It is said that they had to introspect their way through some 10,000 separate practice experiences before their reports could be considered valid.

structuralism: The first formal school of psychology, aimed at analyzing the basic elements, or structure, of conscious mental experience through the use of introspection.

Wundt and his associates conducted experiments on reaction time and on attention span. They also studied the perception of a variety of visual, tactile, and auditory stimuli, including rhythm patterns using metronomes set at different speeds. Wundt published the results of countless experiments in the journal he founded. He wrote nearly 54,000 printed pages, yielding almost 80 volumes the size of this book. It would take you almost 5 years, reading 30 pages (about one chapter) every day, to read all that Wundt wrote, but we don't recommend it. Modern psychology, as you will discover, is far more fascinating than the psychology defined by Wundt and his followers.

Titchener and Structuralism: Psychology's Blind Alley

What were the goals and method of structuralism, the first school of psychology?

Wundt's most famous student, Englishman Edward Bradford Titchener, took the new field to the United States, where he set up a psychological laboratory at Cornell University. Although Titchener differed from Wundt on some points, he pursued similar goals. He gave the name **structuralism** to this first school of thought in psychology, which aimed at analyzing the basic elements, or the structure, of conscious mental experience.

Structuralism was most severely criticized for its primary method, introspection. Introspection was not objective, even though it involved observation, measurement, and experimentation. When different introspectionists were exposed to the same stimulus, such as the click of a metronome, they frequently reported different experiences. Even when the same person was exposed to exactly the same stimulus at different times, he or she would often report somewhat different experiences. Structuralism was not long considered to be a viable school of thought. Later schools of thought in psychology were established, in part, in reaction against structuralism, which collapsed with the death of its most ardent spokesperson, E. B. Titchener.

functionalism: An early school of psychology that was concerned with how mental processes help humans and animals adapt to their environments.

Functionalism: The First American School of Psychology

As structuralism was losing its influence in the United States in the early 1900s, a new school of psychology called functionalism was taking shape. **Functionalism** was concerned not with the structure of consciousness, but with how mental processes function, that is, how humans and animals use mental processes in adapting to their environment.

What was the goal of the early school of psychology known as functionalism?

An influential work of Charles Darwin, *On the Origin of Species by Means of Natural Selection* (1859), had a strong impact on the thinking of the leading proponents of functionalism. Darwin's ideas about evolution and the continuity of species were largely responsible for an increasing use of animal subjects in psychological experiments.

Another British thinker and a cousin of Charles Darwin was Sir Francis Galton. Galton did pioneering work in the study of individual differences and the role of genetic inheritance in mental abilities. In addition, he made a significant contribution in the areas of measurement and statistics. The correlation coefficient, discussed earlier, was his brainchild.

Darwin and Galton contributed important seeds of thought that helped give birth to the new school of psychology, but functionalism was primarily American in character and spirit. The famous American psychologist William James (1842–1910) was an advocate of functionalism even though he did much of his writing before this school of psychology appeared. James's best-known work is his highly regarded and frequently quoted textbook *Principles of Psychology*, published more than 100 years ago (1890). James taught that mental processes are fluid and that they have continuity, rather than a rigid or fixed structure as the structuralists suggested. James spoke of the "stream of consciousness," which he said functioned to help humans adapt to their environment.

Functionalism broadened the scope of psychology to include the study of behavior as well as mental processes. Functionalism also included the study of children, animals, and the mentally impaired. These groups were not subjects of study for the structuralists because they could not be trained to use introspection. Functionalism also focused on an applied, more practical use of psychology by encouraging the study of educational psychology, individual differences, and industrial psychology (adaptation in the workplace).

Behaviorism: Never Mind the Mind

Psychologist John B. Watson (1878–1958) looked at the study of psychology as defined by the structuralists and functionalists and disliked virtually everything he saw. In Watson's view the study of mental processes, the concepts of mind and consciousness, and the primary investigative technique of introspection were not

How did behaviorism differ from previous schools of psychology?

FIGURE 1.3 Some Milestones in the Development of Modern Psychology

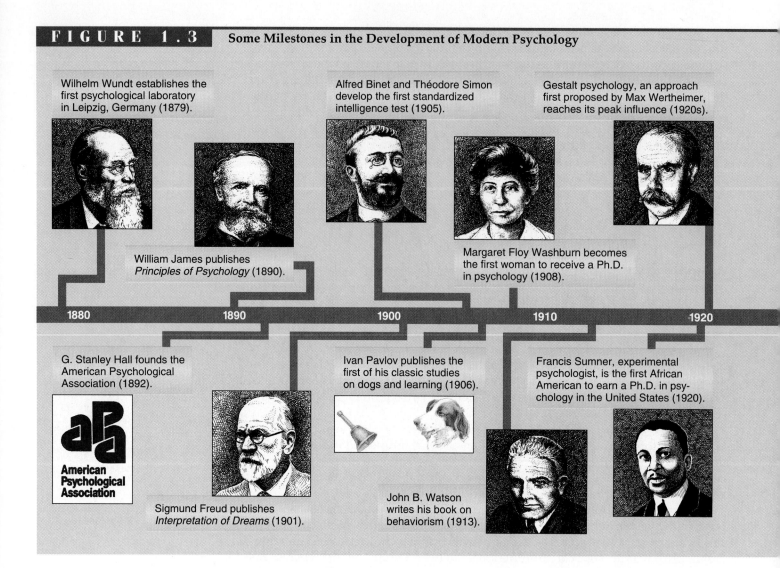

Wilhelm Wundt establishes the first psychological laboratory in Leipzig, Germany (1879).

Alfred Binet and Théodore Simon develop the first standardized intelligence test (1905).

Gestalt psychology, an approach first proposed by Max Wertheimer, reaches its peak influence (1920s).

William James publishes *Principles of Psychology* (1890).

Margaret Floy Washburn becomes the first woman to receive a Ph.D. in psychology (1908).

G. Stanley Hall founds the American Psychological Association (1892).

Ivan Pavlov publishes the first of his classic studies on dogs and learning (1906).

Francis Sumner, experimental psychologist, is the first African American to earn a Ph.D. in psychology in the United States (1920).

Sigmund Freud publishes *Interpretation of Dreams* (1901).

John B. Watson writes his book on behaviorism (1913).

---

scientific. Watson pointed out that each person's introspection is strictly individual. He further maintained that self-reflection and internal ruminations cannot be observed, verified, understood, or communicated in objective, scientific terms. In his article "Psychology as the Behaviorist Views It" (1913), Watson argued that all the strictly subjective techniques and concepts in psychology must be thrown out. Out with introspection, the study of consciousness, and other fuzzy mentalistic concepts. Watson did not deny the existence of conscious thought or experience. He simply did not view them as appropriate subject matter for psychology.

Watson proposed a radically new approach to psychology. This new school of psychology, called **behaviorism**, redefined psychology as the "science of behavior." Behaviorism confined itself to the study of behavior because it was observable and measurable and, therefore, objective and scientific. Behaviorism also emphasized that behavior is determined primarily by factors in the environment.

B. F. Skinner: Continuing the Behaviorist Tradition

Behaviorism soon became the most influential school of thought in American psychology. It is still a major force in modern psychology, in large part because of the profound influence of B. F. Skinner (1904–1990). Skinner agreed with Watson that concepts such as mind, consciousness, and feelings were neither objective nor measurable and,

behaviorism: The school of psychology founded by John B. Watson that views observable, measurable behavior as the appropriate subject matter for psychology and emphasizes the key role of environment as a determinant of behavior.

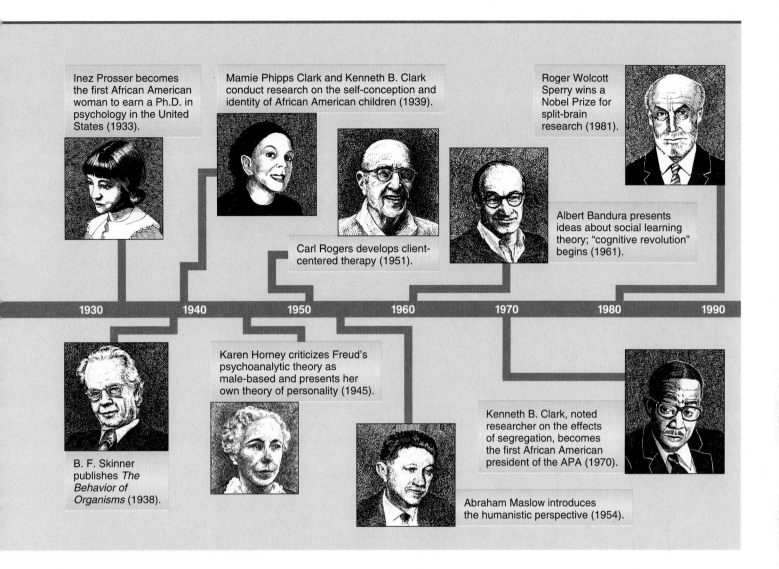

Inez Prosser becomes the first African American woman to earn a Ph.D. in psychology in the United States (1933).

Mamie Phipps Clark and Kenneth B. Clark conduct research on the self-conception and identity of African American children (1939).

Roger Wolcott Sperry wins a Nobel Prize for split-brain research (1981).

Carl Rogers develops client-centered therapy (1951).

Albert Bandura presents ideas about social learning theory; "cognitive revolution" begins (1961).

1930   1940   1950   1960   1970   1980   1990

Karen Horney criticizes Freud's psychoanalytic theory as male-based and presents her own theory of personality (1945).

Kenneth B. Clark, noted researcher on the effects of segregation, becomes the first African American president of the APA (1970).

B. F. Skinner publishes *The Behavior of Organisms* (1938).

Abraham Maslow introduces the humanistic perspective (1954).

therefore, were not the appropriate subject matter of psychology. Furthermore, Skinner argued that these concepts were not needed in order to explain behavior. We can explain behavior, he claimed, by analyzing conditions that were present before a behavior occurs and by analyzing the consequences that follow the behavior.

Skinner's research on operant conditioning emphasized the importance of reinforcement in learning and in shaping and maintaining behavior. Any behavior that is reinforced—followed by pleasant or rewarding consequences—is more likely to be performed again. Skinner's work has had a powerful influence on modern psychology.

Skinner always lamented the fact that "behavior has seldom been thought of as subject matter in its own right, but rather has been viewed as the mere expression or symptom of more important happenings inside the behaving person" (1987, p. 780). Because the strict behaviorist position of Skinner and others has ignored inner, mental processes like thoughts and feelings, behaviorism has been a continuing target of criticism. Today many behaviorists do not take as extreme a view. While they still emphasize the central importance of the study of behavior, they are also willing to consider what these mental processes contribute to an explanation of behavior.

What was the role of the unconscious in psychoanalysis, Freud's approach to psychology?

psychoanalysis (SY-ko-ah-NAL-ih-sis): The term Freud used for both his theory of personality and his therapy for the treatment of psychological disorders; the unconscious is the primary focus of psychoanalytic theory.

Psychoanalysis: It's What's Down Deep That Counts

Whereas the behaviorists completely rejected unobservable mental forces in explaining behavior, this is precisely where Sigmund Freud looked in formulating his theory. Freud emphasized the importance of unseen, unconscious mental forces as the key to understanding human nature and behavior.

Sigmund Freud (1856–1939), whose life and work you will study in Chapter 12, developed a theory of human behavior based largely on case studies of his patients. Freud's theory, **psychoanalysis**, maintains that human mental life is like an iceberg. The smallest, visible part of the iceberg represents the conscious mental experience of the individual. But underwater, hidden from view, floats a vast store of unconscious impulses, thoughts, wishes, and desires. Although people are not aware of them directly or consciously, these unconscious forces have the largest impact on behavior.

Freud believed that the unconscious is the storehouse for material that threatens the conscious life of the individual—disturbing sexual and aggressive impulses as well as traumatic experiences that have been repressed or pushed down to the unconscious. Once there, rather than resting quietly (out of sight, out of mind), the unconscious material festers and seethes, like "the bubbling, boiling brew in a cauldron," Freud wrote.

Freud's psychological theory does not paint a very positive or hopeful picture of human nature. He believed that we do not consciously control our thoughts, feelings, and behavior, but that they are determined by these unconscious forces that we cannot see and cannot control.

The overriding importance that Freud placed on sexual and aggressive impulses caused much controversy both inside and outside the field of psychology. The most notable of Freud's famous students—Carl Jung, Alfred Adler, and Karen Horney—broke away from their mentor and developed their own theories of personality. These three are often collectively referred to as neo-Freudians.

Freud's influence in the field of psychology is not nearly as strong as it once was, but he has had a tremendous impact on the popular culture. When they think of Freud, many people picture a psychiatrist using psychoanalysis with a patient on the familiar couch. The general public has heard of such concepts as the unconscious, repression, rationalization, and the Freudian slip. Such familiarity has made Sigmund Freud a larger-than-life figure rather than an obscure Austrian doctor resting within the dusty pages of history.

What is the emphasis of Gestalt psychology?

Gestalt psychology (geh-SHTALT): The school of psychology that emphasizes that individuals perceive objects and patterns as whole units and that the perceived whole is greater than the sum of its parts.

Gestalt Psychology: The Whole Is Greater Than the Sum of Its Parts

Gestalt psychology made its appearance in Germany in 1912, at almost the same time that John Watson launched behaviorism in the United States. The Gestalt psychologists objected to the central idea of structuralism, that we can best understand conscious experience by reducing it to its basic elements. **Gestalt psychology** emphasized that individuals perceive objects and patterns as whole units, and that the whole thus perceived is greater than the sum of its parts. The German word *Gestalt* roughly means "whole, form, or pattern."

The leader of the Gestalt psychologists was Max Wertheimer (1880–1943). To support the Gestalt theory, Wertheimer presented his famous experiment demonstrating the phi phenomenon. In this experiment two light bulbs are placed a short distance apart in a dark room. The first light is flashed on and then flashed off just as the second light is flashed on. As this pattern of flashing the lights on and off continues, an observer perceives something quite different from what is actually happening. The observer sees what looks like a single light moving back and forth from one position to another. Here, said the Gestaltists, is proof that perceptions do not all arise from independent sensations, as the structuralists claimed.

You have probably seen flashing neon lights that you perceived as figures moving back and forth; actually, separate lights are flashed on and off with precision timing, as in the phi phenomenon. We perceive wholes or patterns, not collections of separate and independent sensations.

Other prominent Gestalt psychologists were Kurt Koffka and Wolfgang Köhler. Today the Gestalt psychologists continue to exert their influence in the study of perception, which will be discussed in Chapter 3.

Humanistic Psychology: Looking at Human Potential

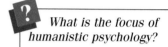

What is the focus of humanistic psychology?

Humanistic psychology emerged in part as a reaction against behaviorism and psychoanalysis, the two major forces in psychology in the United States. In fact, its leading proponent, Abraham Maslow, called humanistic psychology the third force in psychology. **Humanistic psychology** focuses on the uniqueness of human beings and their capacity for choice, growth, and psychological health. The humanists reject the behaviorist notion that people have no free will and are shaped and controlled strictly by the environment. Humanists also reject Freud's theory that people are determined and driven from within, acting and marching to the dark drums of the unconscious.

Maslow objected to Freud's pessimistic view of human potential and pointed out that Freud had based his theory primarily on data from his disturbed patients. Maslow and other prominent humanistic psychologists, such as Carl Rogers, emphasized a much more positive view of human nature. They maintained that people are innately good and that they possess free will. The humanists believe that people are capable of making conscious, rational choices, which can lead to growth and psychological health.

Maslow proposed a theory of motivation that consists of a hierarchy of needs. He considered the need for self-actualization (developing to one's fullest potential) to be the highest need on the hierarchy. Carl Rogers developed his client-centered therapy and, with other humanists, popularized encounter groups and other techniques that are part of the human potential movement.

> **humanistic psychology:** The school of psychology that focuses on the uniqueness of human beings and their capacity for choice, growth, and psychological health.
>
> **cognitive psychology:** A specialty that studies mental processes such as memory, problem solving, decision making, perception, language, and other forms of cognition; often uses the information-processing approach.

Cognitive Psychology: Focusing on Mental Processes

What is the focus of cognitive psychology?

Cognitive psychology is a specialty that focuses on mental processes such as memory, problem solving, concept formation, reasoning and decision making, language, and perception. Just as behaviorism developed in part as a reaction against the focus on mental processes that was characteristic of structuralism and functionalism, so cognitive psychology grew and developed partly in response to strict behaviorism. Ironically, several psychologists who were behaviorists during the 1950s provided the greatest impetus to the development of cognitive psychology (Viney, 1993).

Cognitive psychologists see humans not as passive recipients who are pushed and pulled by environmental forces, but as active participants who seek out experiences, who alter and shape them, and who use mental processes to transform information in the course of their own cognitive development.

Pervasive in the research of cognitive psychology is the information-processing approach. According to this approach, our brain processes information in sequential stages, or levels, in much the same way as a computer works. And some cognitive psychologists have extended their study of problem solving, decision making, and other human mental processes to artificial intelligence. In this research, sophisticated computers are used to simulate the intellectual processes of the human brain.

Moreover, unlike the early behaviorists, psychologists today *can* observe some mental processes directly. Thanks to modern brain-imaging techniques such as the PET scan, combined with sophisticated computer technology, researchers can observe the action (behavior) of specific clusters of brain cells (neurons) involved in carrying out various mental processes (Raichle, 1994b). Such mental activities as thinking, remembering, solving a problem, listening to a melody, speaking, viewing images and colors, and so on have all been "observed" and have provided a rich field of knowledge that cognitive psychologists use in their work.

Review and Reflect Table 1.2 summarizes the major schools of thought in psychology.

Review and Reflect 1.2 *Schools of Thought in Psychology*

School	Description
Structuralism Edward Titchener	The first formal school of psychology. Focuses on analyzing the basic elements or structure of conscious mental experience through the use of introspection.
Functionalism William James	The first American school of psychology. Concerned with the study of mental processes and their role in facilitating adaptation to the environment. Broadened the scope of psychology to include the study of behavior as well as mental processes, and the study of children, the mentally impaired, and animals.
Behaviorism John Watson B. F. Skinner	Views observable, measurable behavior rather than internal mental processes as the appropriate subject matter of psychology. Stresses the key roles of learning and the environment in determining behavior.
Psychoanalysis Sigmund Freud	Emphasizes the roles of unconscious mental forces and conflicts in determining behavior.
Gestalt psychology Max Wertheimer Kurt Koffka Wolfgang Köhler	Emphasizes that individuals perceive objects and patterns as whole units. The perceived whole is greater than the sum of its parts and is not best understood by analysis of its elemental parts (as suggested by the structuralists).
Humanistic psychology Abraham Maslow Carl Rogers	Focuses on the uniqueness of human beings and their capacity for choice, growth, and psychological health. Called the third force in psychology (behaviorism and psychoanalysis being the other two forces).
Cognitive psychology	Focuses on mental processes such as memory, problem solving, reasoning, and decision making, language, and perception. Uses information-processing approach.

Memory Check 1.4

1. Match the school of psychology with its major emphasis.
   ____ 1) the scientific study of behavior
   ____ 2) the perception of whole units or patterns
   ____ 3) the unconscious
   ____ 4) analysis of the basic elements of conscious mental experience
   ____ 5) the uniqueness of human beings and their capacity for conscious choice and growth
   ____ 6) the function of conscious mental experience
   ____ 7) the study of mental processes

   a. Gestalt psychology
   b. structuralism
   c. functionalism
   d. psychoanalysis
   e. humanistic psychology
   f. behaviorism
   g. cognitive psychology

2. Match the major figures with the appropriate school of psychology.
   ____ 1) James
   ____ 2) Freud
   ____ 3) Watson and Skinner
   ____ 4) Titchener
   ____ 5) Maslow and Rogers

   a. behaviorism
   b. structuralism
   c. functionalism
   d. psychoanalysis
   e. humanistic psychology

Answers: 1.1) f 2) a 3) d 4) b 5) e 6) c 7) g 2.1) c 2) d 3) a 4) b 5) e

Psychology Today

Modern Perspectives in Psychology: Current Views on Behavior and Thinking

> **?** *What are the seven major perspectives in psychology today?*

Modern psychologists are not easily categorized by a specific school of thought. There are no structuralists roaming the halls of psychology departments and, to our knowledge, no professors who call themselves functionalists. Today, rather than discussing schools of psychology, it is more appropriate to refer to psychological perspectives—points of view used for explaining people's behavior and thinking, whether normal or abnormal. Psychologists need not limit themselves to only one perspective or approach. Some take an eclectic position, choosing a combination of approaches to explain a particular behavior or psychological problem.

Psychologists who adopt the **biological perspective** emphasize the role of biological processes and heredity as the key to an understanding of behavior and thinking. To explain thinking, emotion, and behavior, both normal and abnormal, biologically oriented psychologists study the structures of the brain and central nervous system, the functioning of the neurons, the delicate balance of neurotransmitters and hormones, and the impact of genes. For example, we know that too much or too little of different neurotransmitters in the brain is related to various psychological disorders, such as schizophrenia and depression. Drugs already used in treating some of these disorders are designed to restore the brain's biochemical balance. Researchers and theorists who adopt the biological perspective are often referred to as physiological psychologists, psychobiologists, or neuropsychologists. The continuing development of medical technology in recent decades has spurred the research efforts of physiological psychologists, and many important findings in psychology have resulted from their work.

The psychoanalytic (psychodynamic) perspective in psychology is derived from the theory of Sigmund Freud. But the psychoanalytic approach has been

biological perspective: A perspective that emphasizes the role of biological processes and heredity as the key to understanding behavior.

psychoanalytic perspective (SY-ko-AN-il-IT-ik): A perspective initially proposed by Freud that emphasizes the importance of the unconscious and of early childhood experiences as the keys to understanding behavior and thought.

behavioral perspective: A perspective that emphasizes the role of environment in shaping behavior.

cognitive perspective: A perspective that emphasizes the role of mental processes that underlie behavior.

humanistic perspective: A perspective that emphasizes the importance of an individual's subjective experience as a key to understanding behavior.

evolutionary perspective: A perspective that focuses on how humans have evolved and adapted behaviors required for survival against various environmental pressures over the long course of evolution.

sociocultural perspective: A perspective that emphasizes social and cultural influences on human behavior and stresses the importance of understanding those influences when we interpret the behavior of others.

What are some specialists in psychology, and in what settings are they employed?

modified considerably over the past several decades by psychologists known as neo-Freudians. The **psychoanalytic perspective** emphasizes the role of unconscious motivation and early childhood experiences in determining behavior and thought.

The biological approach looks inward to physical and biochemical processes to explain behavior, and the psychoanalytic approach looks deeply inward to the unconscious. But the **behavioral perspective** looks in exactly the opposite direction—outward—emphasizing learning and the role of environmental factors in shaping behavior. What factors in the environment reinforce and thus maintain certain behaviors? According to the behaviorists, it is environmental factors that primarily shape behavior. Psychologists must analyze these environmental factors in order to understand the causes of behavior and to establish programs of behavior modification to change problem behaviors.

The **cognitive perspective** considers the role of mental processes to be key. We must know more than what precedes a response and what follows it in order to understand behavior. The cognitive approach maintains that a given stimulus does not simply cause a given response. Rather, the individual consciously perceives, remembers, thinks, organizes, analyzes, decides, and then responds. To explain behavior more fully, according to the cognitive psychologists, we must consider such cognitive processes as perception, thinking, memory, language, and others.

Humanistic psychologists reject with equal vigor (1) the pessimistic view of the psychoanalytic approach, that human behavior is determined primarily by unconscious forces; and (2) the behaviorist view that behavior is determined by factors in the environment. The **humanistic perspective** views humans as capable of making rational, conscious choices. It emphasizes the importance of people's own subjective experiences as the key to understanding their behavior. Less scientific and objective than many other approaches, the humanistic approach unashamedly admits the inherent subjective nature of its position.

The **evolutionary perspective** focuses on how humans have evolved and adapted behaviors required for survival in the face of various environmental pressures over the long course of evolution (Nisbett, 1990). Evolutionary psychologists study how inherited tendencies and dispositions in humans influence a wide range of behaviors—from how we select mates, to what level of intellectual performance we demonstrate, and even why we help others of our species. But most evolutionary psychologists recognize that our genes alone do not control our ultimate destiny. Our inherited tendencies are *not* set in concrete.

The **sociocultural perspective** emphasizes social and cultural influences on human behavior and stresses the importance of understanding those influences when we interpret the behavior of others. As when someone is quoted out of context and thus misunderstood, we may misinterpret actions or gestures of those from other cultures because we do not understand the cultural context in which they occur.

Review and Reflect Table 1.3 gives a brief summary of these seven perspectives in psychology today.

Psychologists at Work

We know that psychologists have many different orientations toward the practice of psychology. Some psychologists teach at colleges and universities; others have private clinical practices and counsel patients. Psychologists work in hospitals and other medical facilities, in elementary and secondary schools, and in business and industry. Wherever you find human activity, you will likely find psychologists. Figure 1.4 shows the settings in which psychologists work.

Review and Reflect 1.3 Modern Perspectives in Psychology

Perspective	Emphasis
Biological	The role of biological processes and structures, as well as heredity, in explaining behavior
Psychoanalytic	The role of unconscious motivation and early childhood experiences in determining behavior and thought
Behavioral	The role of environment in shaping and controlling behavior
Cognitive	The role of mental processes—perception, thinking, and memory—that underlie behavior
Humanistic	The importance of an individual's subjective experience as a key to an understanding of his or her behavior
Evolutionary	The roles of inherited tendencies that have proven adaptive in humans
Sociocultural	The roles of social and cultural influences on behavior

FIGURE 1.4

Where Psychologists Work

Psychologists work in a variety of settings. About 34 percent of psychologists work in colleges and universities, 24.5 percent work in hospitals and clinics, and 22 percent are in private practice. (Data from Howard et al., 1986.)

Schools (3.7%)
Government and business (13%)
Other (2.9%)
Private practice 22%
33.9%
24.5%
Hospitals and clinics
Colleges and universities

There are many specialties within the field of psychology. A few of them are briefly described here.

Clinical psychologists specialize in the diagnosis and treatment of mental and behavioral disorders. Some clinical psychologists also conduct research in these areas. Most clinical psychologists work in clinics, hospitals, and private practice, and many hold professorships at colleges and universities.

Counseling psychologists help people who have adjustment problems (marital, social, behavioral) that are less severe than those generally handled by clinical psychologists. Counseling psychologists may also provide academic or vocational counseling. Counselors usually work in a nonmedical setting such as a school or university, or they may have a private practice. About 56 percent of all psychologists in the United States may be classified as either clinical or counseling psychologists.

Physiological psychologists also called neuropsychologists, study the relationship between physiological processes and behavior. They study the structure and function of the brain and central nervous system, the role of the neurotransmitters and hormones, and other aspects of body chemistry to determine how physical and chemical processes affect behavior in both people and animals.

Experimental psychologists specialize in the use of experimental research methods. They conduct experiments in most fields of specialization in psychology—learning, memory, sensation, perception, motivation, emotion, and other areas as well. Some experimental psychologists study the brain and nervous system and how they affect behavior; their work overlaps with that of physiological psychologists. Experimental psychologists usually work in a laboratory, where they can exert precise control over the human or animal subjects being studied. Many experimental psychologists are faculty members who teach and conduct their research in college or university laboratories.

Psychologists work in a wide range of settings.

FIGURE 1.5

What Psychologists Do

Clinical psychologists make up the largest percentage of members of the American Psychological Association who work in the field of psychology. (Data provided by American Psychological Association, 1992a.)

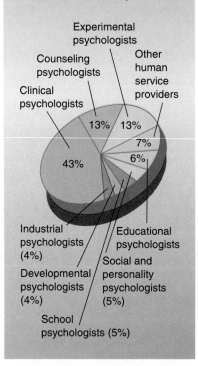

Developmental psychologists study how people grow, develop, and change throughout the life span. Some developmental psychologists specialize in a particular age group, such as infancy, childhood (child psychologists), adolescence, or old age (gerontologists). Others may concentrate on a specific aspect of human development such as physical, language, cognitive, or moral development.

Educational psychologists specialize in the study of teaching and learning. They may help train teachers and other educational professionals or conduct research in teaching and classroom behavior. Some help prepare school curricula, develop achievement tests, or conduct evaluations of teaching and learning. Some school psychologists are employed by elementary and secondary schools to diagnose learning problems, to test students, and to counsel students, teachers, and parents on school-related problems.

While most other psychologists are concerned with what makes the individual function, social psychologists investigate how the individual feels, thinks, and behaves in a social setting—in the presence of others. When you are alone in a room, your behavior is probably different from what it would be if another person entered. It would probably be different still if more and more people entered the room. Social psychologists study human behavior under a variety of conditions and in many different social situations.

Industry and business have found that expertise in psychology pays off in the workplace. Industrial/organizational (I/O) psychologists study the relationships between people and their work environments. These specialists can benefit employers by suggesting ways to increase productivity, decrease job turnover and absenteeism, and improve job-training programs, personnel selection, and evaluation of employees. I/O psychologists also try to increase employee morale, job satisfaction, and motivation. They are likely to work on improving the organizational structure, to advise management on effective techniques for supervision, and to design programs to enhance cooperation among employees and between workers and management.

Figure 1.5 shows the percentages of psychologists who work in the specialties discussed in this section. As you can see, psychology is an enormously broad and diverse field of study. We hope that you will enjoy your explorations in *The World of Psychology*.

Memory Check 1.5

Match the psychological perspective with its major emphasis.

_____ 1) the role of biological processes and heredity

_____ 2) the role of learning and environmental factors

_____ 3) the role of mental processes

_____ 4) the role of the unconscious and early childhood experiences

_____ 5) the importance of the individual's own subjective experience

_____ 6) the role of social and cultural influences

_____ 7) the role of inherited tendencies that have proved adaptive in humans

a. psychoanalytic
b. biological
c. behavioral
d. cognitive
e. humanistic
f. evolutionary
g. sociocultural

Answers: 1) b 2) c 3) d 4) a 5) e 6) g 7) f

APPLICATIONS   ·   APPLICATIONS   ·   APPLICATIONS

Study Skills and Critical Thinking

An effective system to maximize learning is an old one, the *SQ3R* method, developed more than 50 years ago by a teacher, Francis Robinson (1941). This book is organized to help you make use of *S-Q-R-R-R*, which stands for *Survey, Question, Read, Recite,* and *Review*. Instead of simply reading each chapter, you will learn and remember more if you faithfully follow *SQ3R*. Here is the process:

Survey. First scan the chapter you plan to read. Read the chapter outline, the opening vignette, and the topic headings and study questions. Glance at the illustrations. Then read the chapter summary. This process will give you an overview of the chapter.

Question. Before you actually read each section in the chapter, turn each topic heading into one or more questions. For some sections a study question is provided, but you can also add questions of your own. In other sections you alone supply the question. For example, one topic in this chapter is *Naturalistic Observation*. The two-part study question is "What is naturalistic observation, and what are some of its advantages and limitations?" You might add these questions: "How is naturalistic observation used? What kind of information does it provide?" Asking such questions helps to focus your reading.

Read. Read the information included in the first topic. As you read, try to answer the questions (the study question and your own questions). After reading the first topic, stop. If the topic is very long, or if the material seems especially difficult

or complex, you should stop after reading only one or two paragraphs. Now you are ready for the second *R*.

Recite. The second *R* means *recite*. After reading one topic, answer the topic questions. To further grasp the material, write a short summary of the topic. If you have trouble summarizing the topic or answering the questions, scan or read the topic again before trying another time.

When you have finished one topic, move on to the next topic (in this chapter, *Laboratory Observation*). You are back to the *Q* of *SQ3R*. Since no study question is provided, formulate your own. For example, you could ask: "What is laboratory observation? How does it differ from naturalistic observation?" With your questions in mind, read the topic and then recite, answering your questions or writing a brief summary as before.

Review. Periodically you will find a *Memory Check* that consists of a few questions about the preceding topics. Answer the questions and check your answers. If you make errors, quickly review the preceding material until you know the answers.

When you have finished the chapter, turn to the *Chapter Summary and Review* section. Review the *Key Terms*. If you don't know the meaning of a key term, turn to the page that has the term's definition in the margin. Next review each study question in the summary and answer it in your own words. The answers provided are given only as condensed reminders, and you should be able to expand on them.

Finally, look at the three *Thinking Critically* questions: *Evaluation, Point/Counterpoint,* and *Psychology in Your Life*. Answering these questions requires more than simple memorization. The critical thinking questions give you the chance to show

that you really understand the information presented in the chapter.

Study Habits That Pay Rich Dividends

- Select a quiet place, free of distractions, where you do nothing else but study. You can condition yourself to associate this environment with studying, so that entering the room or area will be your cue to begin work. Moreover, you will be less tempted to do other things while you are there.

- Research on memory has proven that spaced learning is more effective than massed practice (cramming). Instead of studying for 5 hours straight, try five study sessions of one hour each.

- The more active the role you play in the learning process, the more you will remember. Spend some of your study time *reciting* rather than *rereading* the material. One effective method is to use three-by-five index cards as flash cards. Write a key term on the front of each card. On the back, list information from the text and lecture pertaining to

continued

that term. You should also have an index card for each study question; write the answer on the back of the card. Use these cards to help you prepare for tests. Test yourself before your professor does.

- *Overlearning* means studying beyond the point where you can just barely recite the information you are trying to memorize. For best results, don't stop studying at this point. Spend more time reviewing the information again and again until it is firmly locked in memory. If you are subject to test anxiety, overlearning will help. The overlearned information is more likely to survive an attack of nerves.

- Forgetting takes place most rapidly within the first 24 hours after you study. No matter how much you have studied for a test, *always* review shortly before you take the test. Refreshing your memory will raise your grade.

- *Sleeping* immediately after you study will help you retain more of what you learned. If you can't study before you go to sleep, at least review before sleep what you studied earlier in the day. This is a good time to go through your index cards. (When you read Chapter 6, you will learn why sleep facilitates memory and why the other suggestions will help you remember more of what you study.)

Thinking Critically about Psychology

We live in the "information age," and we are bombarded daily with information on every conceivable subject and with attempts to influence our behavior as well—buy this product, vote for this political candidate. We are all consumers of information. And unless you know how to think critically, you may be consuming a great deal of false information and accepting it as factual. How can you sift through all of the information you encounter, pick out the true and useful, discard the false and misleading, and make intelligent decisions? In short, how can you learn to use critical thinking?

Critical thinkers are not all identical, but they share some importance characteristics.

- *They are independent thinkers.* Critical thinkers do not automatically accept and believe what they read or what they hear. They carefully analyze and evaluate the evidence and the reasoning presented. They are able to recognize manipulative emotional appeals, spot unsupported assumptions, and detect faulty logic.

- *They are willing to suspend judgment.* Critical thinkers do not leap to judgment; they seek out and assemble the most relevant and up-to-date information on all sides of an issue before taking a position.

- *They are willing to modify or abandon prior judgments, including deeply held beliefs.* When later evidence or experience contradicts their existing beliefs, critical thinkers will evaluate the new contradictory evidence. If they find it valid, they will modify their previous beliefs to accommodate it.

- *Critical thinkers consider not only the content of information, but its source as well.* A great deal of information about psychological research appears in newspapers and magazines and on television. Critical thinkers know that such reports are not primary sources, but rather secondary sources of information. Secondary sources present the observations, research and conclusions, and views of other people, although not always fully or accurately. Primary sources (from the horse's mouth, so to speak) are articles that appear in scholarly journals or books in which researchers describe in detail their own research studies. False or misleading information can be disseminated by either primary or secondary sources.

Evaluating Secondary Sources in Psychological Research

Some publications are more scientifically respectable than others—*Science News* and *Psychology Today* are more credible than *The National Enquirer* and *Cosmopolitan*. Science writers have more experience reading and understanding research and usually give more accurate reports of psychological research than general reporters do. Science writers tend to write more objectively than nonscience writers.

To evaluate the information in a secondary source, James Bell (1991) suggests that you must be able to answer three key questions: "Who says so? What do they say? How do they know?" (p. 36). To critically evaluate research, you need to know who conducted the study and the methodology used.

Critical thinkers determine: (1) whether the methodology used in the research would enable the authors to reach their conclusions, (2) whether those conclusions are logical, (3) whether they are supported by the data, and (4) whether there are alternative explanations for the findings.

Critical thinkers understand the difference between scientific and nonscientific research evidence. Testimonials and accounts of personal experience are nonscientific evidence. Testimonials most often appeal to emotions rather than intellect. "Hooked on Phonics" might *not* work for you!

Critical thinkers carefully consider the biases of writers and researchers. Do they have "axes to grind"? Are they expressing information that can be confirmed as factual or merely their own opinions?

Finally, critical thinkers do not accept the results of one study as definitive evidence. They want to know whether the research has been replicated and what other studies have been published on the subject. As a critical thinker, you would not modify your life based on one study you read. "One study does not a finding make" (Weeks, quoted in Schmitz, 1991, p. 44).

Thinking Critically

Evaluation

Consider the three major forces in psychology: behaviorism, psychoanalysis, and humanistic psychology. Which appeals to you most and which least, and why?

Point/Counterpoint

This chapter discussed deception in research and described a study that used deception to examine the effects of alcohol and expectations on aggres-

sion. Prepare convincing arguments to support each of these opinions:
a. Deception is justified in research studies.
b. Deception is not justified in research studies.

Psychology in Your Life

In this chapter you've learned something about experimental research and survey research. How can you use this new knowledge to evaluate research results you may read or hear about?

Chapter Summary and Review

Introduction to Psychology

What are the four goals of psychology?

The four goals of psychology are the description, explanation, prediction, and control of behavior and mental processes.

What is the difference between basic and applied research?

Basic research is conducted to advance knowledge rather than to discover any practical application. Applied research is conducted for the purpose of solving practical problems.

Key Terms

psychology (p. 3)
theory (p. 4)
basic research (p. 4)
applied research (p. 4)

Descriptive Research Methods

What is naturalistic observation, and what are some of its advantages and limitations?

In naturalistic observation, researchers observe and record the behavior of subjects in a natural setting without at-

tempting to influence or control it. Limitations include the researcher's lack of control over the observed situation, and the potential for observer bias.

What is the case study method, and for what purposes is it particularly well suited?

The case study is an in-depth study of one or several subjects through observation, interview, and sometimes psychological testing. It is particularly appropriate for studying people with rare psychological or physiological disorders.

What are the methods and purposes of survey research?

In survey research, investigators use interviews and/or questionnaires to gather information about the attitudes, beliefs, experiences, or behaviors of a group of people.

What is a representative sample, and why is it essential in a survey?

A representative sample is a sample of subjects selected from the population of interest in such a way that

important subgroups within the whole population are included in the same proportions in the sample. A sample must be representative for the findings to be applied to the larger population.

Key Terms

descriptive research methods (p. 5)
naturalistic observation (p. 5)
case study (p. 6)
survey (p. 6)
population (p. 6)
sample (p. 6)
representative sample (p. 7)

The Experimental Method: Searching for Causes

What is the main advantage of the experimental method?

The experimental method is the only research method that can be used to identify cause–effect relationships.

What is the difference between the independent variable and the dependent variable?

In an experiment an independent variable is a condition or factor manipulated by the researcher to determine its effect on the dependent variable. The dependent variable, measured at the end of the experiment, is presumed to vary as a result of the manipulations of the independent variable.

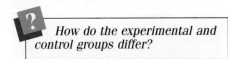
How do the experimental and control groups differ?

The experimental group is exposed to the independent variable. The control group is similar to the experimental group and is exposed to the same experimental environment but is not exposed to the independent variable.

What is selection bias, and what technique do researchers use to control for it?

Selection bias occurs when there are systematic differences among the groups before the experiment begins. Random assignment—the assignment of subjects to groups by means of a chance procedure—maximizes the probability that groups are similar at the beginning of the experiment.

What is the placebo effect, and how do researchers control for it?

The placebo effect occurs when a person's expectations influence the outcome of a treatment or experiment. To control for the placebo effect, the researcher must ensure that the subjects do not know if they are members of the experimental group (receiving the treatment) or of the control group (receiving the placebo).

What is experimenter bias, and how is it controlled?

Experimenter bias occurs when the researcher's expectations affect the outcome of the experiment. It is controlled by using the double-blind technique, in which neither the experimenter nor the subjects know which subjects are in an experimental group and which are in a control group.

Key Terms

experimental method (p. 8)
hypothesis (p. 8)

independent variable (p. 9)
dependent variable (p. 10)
experimental group (p. 10)
control group (p. 10)
selection bias (p. 11)
random assignment (p. 11)
placebo effect (p. 12)
placebo (p. 12)
experimenter bias (p. 12)
double-blind technique (p. 13)

Other Research Methods

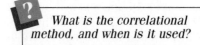
What is the correlational method, and when is it used?

The correlational method is used to determine the correlation or relationship between two variables. It is often used when an experimental study cannot be conducted because it is either impossible or unethical.

What is a correlation coefficient?

A correlation coefficient is a numerical value that indicates the strength and direction of the relationship between two variables.

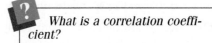
What is meta-analysis?

Meta-analysis is a complex statistical procedure researchers use to combine the results from many research studies on a particular topic in order to determine the degree to which a specific hypothesis can be supported.

Key Terms

correlational method (p. 14)
correlation coefficient (p. 14)
reliability (p. 16)
validity (p. 16)
replication (p. 16)
meta-analysis (p. 16)

Subjects in Psychological Research

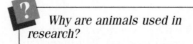
Why are animals used in research?

Animals are used because they provide a simpler model for studying sim-

ilar processes in humans, researchers can exercise more control over animals and use a wider range of medical and other manipulations, it is easier to study the entire life span and even several generations in some species, and animals are readily available and more economical to study.

What are some ethical guidelines governing the use of human subjects in research?

Subjects' participation must be strictly voluntary; there must be respect for confidentiality; subjects must be free to withdraw from the study at any time; and subjects must be debriefed as soon as possible after they participate.

The History of Psychology: Exploring Psychology's Roots

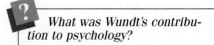
What was Wundt's contribution to psychology?

Wundt, considered the father of psychology, established the first psychological laboratory in 1879 and launched the study of psychology as a formal academic discipline.

What were the goals and method of structuralism, the first school of psychology?

Structuralism's main goal was to analyze the basic elements or structure of conscious mental experience through the use of introspection.

What was the goal of the early school of psychology known as functionalism?

Functionalism was concerned with how mental processes help humans and animals adapt to their environment.

How did behaviorism differ from previous schools of psychology?

Behaviorism, the school of psychology founded by John B. Watson, views observable, measurable behavior as the only appropriate subject matter for psychology. Behaviorism also emphasizes the environment as the key determinant of behavior.

 What was the role of the unconscious in psychoanalysis, Freud's approach to psychology?

According to Freud's theory of psychoanalysis, our thoughts, feelings, and behavior are determined primarily by the unconscious—the part of the mind that we cannot see and cannot control.

 What is the emphasis of Gestalt psychology?

Gestalt psychology emphasizes that individuals perceive objects and patterns as whole units and that the perceived whole is greater than the sum of its parts.

What is the focus of humanistic psychology?

Humanistic psychology focuses on the uniqueness of human beings and their capacity for choice, growth, and psychological health.

What is the focus of cognitive psychology?

Cognitive psychology is a specialty that focuses on mental processes such as memory, problem solving, concept formation, reasoning and decision making, language, and perception.

Key Terms

structuralism (p. 22)
functionalism (p. 23)
behaviorism (p. 24)
psychoanalysis (p. 26)
Gestalt psychology (p. 26)
humanistic psychology (p. 27)
cognitive psychology (p. 27)

Psychology Today

What are seven major perspectives in psychology today?

Seven major perspectives in psychology today are (1) the biological perspective, which emphasizes the role of biological processes and heredity as the keys to understanding behavior and thought; (2) the psychoanalytic perspective, which focuses on the role of the unconscious and early childhood experiences; (3) the behavioral perspective, which emphasizes learning and the role of environmental factors in shaping behavior; (4) the cognitive perspective, which stresses the role of the mental processes (perceiving, thinking, remembering, etc.); (5) the humanistic perspective, which emphasizes the importance of an individual's subjective experience; (6) the evolutionary perspective, which looks at the inherited tendencies that have proved adaptive in humans; and (7) the sociocultural perspective, which emphasizes the role of social and cultural influences on behavior.

What are some specialists in psychology, and in what settings are they employed?

There are clinical and counseling psychologists, physiological psychologists, experimental psychologists, developmental psychologists, educational and school psychologists, social psychologists, and industrial/organizational psychologists. Psychologists are found in many different settings—colleges and universities, elementary and secondary schools, medical settings, business and industry, and private practice.

Key Terms

biological perspective (p. 29)
psychoanalytic perspective (p. 30)
behavioral perspective (p. 30)
cognitive perspective (p. 30)
humanistic perspective (p. 30)
evolutionary perspective (p. 30)
sociocultural perspective (p. 30)

2

BIOLOGY AND BEHAVIOR

CHAPTER OUTLINE

The Neurons and the Neurotransmitters

The Neurons: Billions of Brain Cells

Neurotransmitters: The Chemical Messengers of the Brain

The Variety of Neurotransmitters

The Rate of Neural Firing and the Speed of the Impulse

Glial Cells: The Neurons' Helper Cells

The Central Nervous System

The Spinal Cord: An Extension of the Brain

The Brainstem: The Most Primitive Part of the Brain

The Cerebellum: A Must for Graceful Movement

The Thalamus: The Relay Station between Lower and Higher Brain Centers

The Hypothalamus: A Master Regulator

The Limbic System: Primitive Emotion and Memory

The Cerebral Hemispheres

The Lobes of the Brain

Specialization of the Cerebral Hemispheres

Functions of the Left Hemisphere: Language, First and Foremost

Functions of the Right Hemisphere: The Leader in Visual-Spatial Tasks

The Split Brain: Separate Halves or Two Separate Brains?

Discovering the Brain's Mysteries

The EEG and the Microelectrode

The CT Scan and Magnetic Resonance Imaging

The PET Scan and Other Imaging Techniques

Brain Damage: Causes and Consequences

Stroke

Head Injury

Recovering from Brain Damage

The Peripheral Nervous System

The Somatic Nervous System: For Sensing and Moving

The Autonomic Nervous System: Doing Its Job without Our Conscious Thought

The Endocrine System

The Pituitary Gland: The Master Gland, Small as a Pea

The Thyroid Gland: Balancing the Body's Metabolism

The Adrenal Glands: Necessary for Fight or Flight

The Pancreas: Our Insulin Factory

The Sex Glands: The Gonads

Applications: Handedness—Does It Make a Difference?

Thinking Critically

Chapter Summary and Review

On September 13, 1848, Phineas Gage, a 25-year-old foreman on a railroad construction crew, was using dynamite to blast away rock and dirt. Suddenly an unplanned explosion almost took Gage's head off, sending a 3½-foot-long, 13-pound metal rod under his left cheekbone and out through the top of his skull (as shown in the drawing).

Much of the brain tissue in Gage's frontal lobe was torn away, along with flesh, pieces of his skull, and other bone fragments. This should have been the end of Phineas Gage, but it wasn't. He regained consciousness within a few minutes and was loaded onto a cart and wheeled to his hotel nearly a mile away. He got out with a little help, walked up the stairs, entered his room, and walked to his bed. He was still conscious when the doctor arrived nearly 2 hours later.

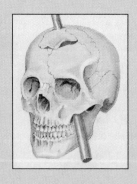

Gage recovered and returned home in about 5 weeks, but he was not the same man. Before the accident, he was described as a hard worker who was polite, dependable, and well liked. But the new Phineas Gage, without part of his frontal lobe, was found to be loud-mouthed and profane, rude and impulsive, and contemptuous toward others. He no longer planned realistically for the future and was no longer motivated and industrious, as he once had been. Gage lost his job as foreman and joined P. T. Barnum's circus as a sideshow exhibit at carnivals and county fairs. (Adapted from Harlow, 1848.)

Almost 150 years have passed since the heavy metal rod tore through Phineas Gage's brain. During that time we have learned much about the human brain—some of it puzzling and mysterious, all of it fascinating. How can the brain sustain such massive damage as in the case of Gage, who survived, while a small bullet fired through the brain in a number of different places can result in instant death? In this chapter you will learn how tough and resilient, yet how fragile and vulnerable this remarkable 3-pound organ really is.

In Chapter 1, our introduction to *The World of Psychology*, we defined psychology as the scientific study of behavior and mental processes. Before we can gain an understanding and an appreciation of our behavior and mental processes, we must first explore the all-important biological connection. Every thought we think, every emotion we feel, every sensation we experience, every decision we reach, every move we make—in short, all of human behavior—is rooted in a biological event. Therefore we follow our introduction to psychology with the study of biology and behavior. Our story begins where the action begins, in the smallest functional unit of the brain—the nerve cell, or neuron.

The Neurons and the Neurotransmitters

The Neurons: Billions of Brain Cells

What is a neuron, and what are its three parts?

neuron (NEW-ron): A specialized cell that conducts impulses through the nervous system and contains three major parts—a cell body, dendrites, and an axon.

All our thoughts, feelings, and behavior can ultimately be traced to the activity of **neurons**—the specialized cells that conduct impulses through the nervous system. Most experts estimate that there may be as many as 100 billion neurons in the brain (Fishbach, 1992). This would mean that you have about 20 times as many neurons as there are people living on the earth right now.

Neurons perform several important tasks: (1) Afferent (sensory) neurons relay messages from the sense organs and receptors—eyes, ears, nose, mouth, and skin—to the brain or spinal cord. (2) Efferent (motor) neurons convey signals from the brain and spinal cord to the glands and the muscles, enabling us to move. (3) Interneurons, thousands of times more numerous than motor or sensory neurons, carry information between neurons in the brain and between neurons in the spinal cord.

40

Anatomy of a Neuron: Looking at Its Parts   Although no two neurons are exactly alike, all are made up of three important parts: **cell body** (soma), dendrites, and axon. The cell body contains the nucleus and carries out the metabolic, or life-sustaining, functions of the neuron. Branching out from the cell body are the **dendrites**, which look much like the leafless branches of a tree (*dendrite* comes from the Greek word for "tree"). The dendrites are the primary receivers of signals from other neurons, but the cell body can also receive the signals directly.

The **axon** is the slender, tail-like extension of the neuron that sprouts into many branches, each ending in a bulbous-shaped axon terminal. The axon terminals transmit signals to the dendrites, to the cell bodies of other neurons, and to muscles, glands, and other parts of the body. In humans, some axons are short—only thousandths of an inch. Others can be up to a meter long—39.37 inches—long enough to reach from the brain to the tip of the spinal cord, or from the spinal cord to remote parts of the body. Figure 2.1 shows a neuron's structure.

The Synapse   Remarkably, the billions of neurons that relay signals back and forth to each other and to all parts of the body are not physically connected. The axon terminals are separated from the receiving neurons by tiny, fluid-filled gaps called synaptic clefts. The **synapse** is the junction where the axon terminal of a sending (presynaptic) neuron communicates with a receiving (postsynaptic) neuron across the synaptic cleft. There may be from 10 trillion (Levine, 1988) to perhaps 100 trillion synapses in the human nervous system (Pinel, 1990).

What is a synapse?

How big is 1 trillion? Numbers in the trillions are hard for us to conceptualize. It might surprise you to learn that it would take almost 32,000 years for 1 trillion seconds to pass. Now try to imagine the incredible complexity of your brain if there are from 10 trillion to 100 trillion synapses across which your neurons are passing and receiving messages.

If neurons are not physically connected, how do they communicate? How do they spread their messages throughout the brain, spinal cord, and every area of the body?

FIGURE 2.1

The Structure of a Neuron

Neurons have three important parts: (1) a cell body, which carries out the metabolic functions of the neuron; (2) branched fibers called dendrites, which are the primary receivers of the impulses from other neurons; and (3) a slender, tail-like extension called an axon, the transmitting end of the neuron, which sprouts into many branches, each ending in an axon terminal. The photograph shows human neurons greatly magnified.

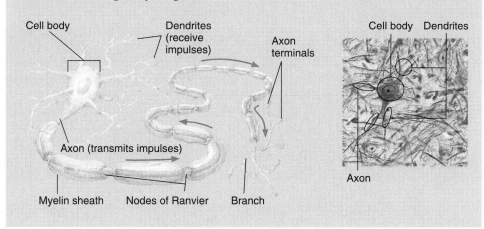

cell body: The part of the neuron, containing the nucleus, that carries out the metabolic functions of the neuron.

dendrites (DEN-drytes): The branchlike extensions of a neuron that receive signals from other neurons.

axon (AK-sahn): The slender, tail-like extension of the neuron that transmits signals to the dendrites or cell body of other neurons or to the muscles or glands.

synapse (SIN-aps): The junction where the axon of a sending neuron communicates with a receiving neuron across the synaptic cleft.

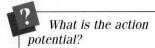

What is the action potential?

resting potential: The membrane potential of a neuron at rest, about −70 millivolts.

action potential: The firing of a neuron that results when the charge within the neuron becomes more positive than the charge outside the cell's membrane.

The Neural Impulse: The Beginning of Thought and Action   Researchers have known for about 200 years that cells in the brain, the spinal cord, and the muscles generate electrical potentials. These tiny electric charges play a part in all bodily functions. Every time we move a muscle, experience a sensation, or have a thought or a feeling, a small but measurable electrical impulse is present.

How does this biological electricity work? Even though the impulse that travels down the axon is electrical, the axon does not transmit it the way a wire conducts an electrical current. What actually moves through the axon is a change in the permeability of the cell membrane. This process allows ions (electrically charged molecules) to move through the membrane, into and out of the neuron. Bodily fluids contain certain types of chemical molecules known as ions, some with positive charges and others with negative charges. Like other living cells, every neuron is contained within its own thin skin, the cell membrane. Inside this membrane there are normally more negative than positive ions. When at rest (not firing), a neuron carries a negative electrical potential of about −70 millivolts ($70/1000$ of a volt) in comparison to the environment outside the cell. This slight negative charge is referred to as the neuron's **resting potential**.

When a neuron is sufficiently stimulated, its resting potential becomes disturbed. As a result, the cell membrane of the neuron changes its permeability. This causes more positive ions, particularly sodium, to flow into the cell and other ions to flow out. If the disturbance reaches a minimum intensity known as the threshold, the neuron's resting membrane potential is suddenly reversed. It becomes positive, to about +50 millivolts for about $1/1000$ of a second (Kalil, 1989). This sudden reversal of the resting potential is the **action potential**. The action potential operates according to the "all or none" law—the neuron either fires completely or does not fire at all. Immediately after the neuron reaches its action potential and fires, it returns to its resting potential until stimulated again. But its rest may be very short, because neurons can fire up to 1,000 times per second. Figure 2.2 illustrates the movement of positive ions across the cell membrane, which stimulates the neuron to its action potential.

FIGURE 2.2

The Action Potential

(a) When a neuron is at rest (not firing), the inside of the neuron has a slight negative electrical charge compared to the outside; this is referred to as the neuron's resting potential.
(b) When a neuron is stimulated, more positively charged particles flow into the cell, making the inside

suddenly positive compared to the outside of the cell. This sudden reversal is the action potential.
(c) Immediately after the neuron fires, some positive particles are actively pumped out of the cell.
(d) The neuron returns to its resting potential and is ready to fire again if stimulated.

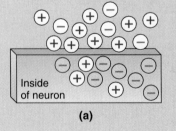
(a)

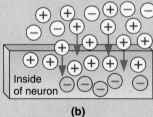
(b)

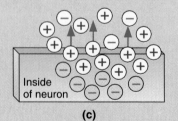
(c)

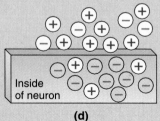
(d)

Neurotransmitters: The Chemical Messengers of the Brain

Once a neuron fires, how does it get its message across the synaptic cleft and on to other neurons? Messages are transmitted between neurons by one or more of a large group of chemical substances known as **neurotransmitters** (Hökfelt et al., 1984).

Where are the neurotransmitters located? Inside the axon terminal are many small, sphere-shaped containers with thin membranes called synaptic vesicles, which hold the neurotransmitters. (*Vesicle* comes from a Latin word meaning "little bladder.") When an action potential arrives at the axon terminal, synaptic vesicles move toward the cell membrane, fuse with it, and release their neurotransmitter molecules. This is shown in Figure 2.3.

The Receptor Sites: Locks for Neurotransmitter Keys Once released, neurotransmitters do not simply flow into the synaptic cleft and stimulate all the adjacent neurons. Each neurotransmitter has a distinctive molecular shape, and **receptor sites** on the surfaces of dendrites and cell bodies also have distinctive shapes. Neurotransmitters can affect only those neurons that contain receptor sites designed to receive molecules having their particular shape. In other words, each receptor site is somewhat like a locked door that only certain neurotransmitter keys can unlock (Restak; 1993).

What are neurotransmitters, and what role do they play in the transmission of signals from one neuron to another?

neurotransmitter (NEW-ro-TRANS-mit-er): A chemical that is released into the synaptic cleft from the axon terminal of the sending neuron, crosses the synapse, and binds to appropriate receptor sites on the dendrites or cell body of the receiving neuron, influencing the cell either to fire or not to fire.

receptor site: A site on the dendrite or cell body of a neuron that will receive only specific neurotransmitters.

FIGURE 2.3

Synaptic Transmission

Sending neurons transmit their messages to receiving neurons by electrochemical action. When a neuron fires, the action potential arrives at the axon terminal and triggers the release of neurotransmitters from the synaptic vesicles. Neurotransmitters flow into the synaptic cleft and move toward the receiving neuron, which has numerous receptor sites. The receptor sites will receive only neurotransmitters with distinctive molecular shapes that match them. Neurotransmitters influence the receiving neuron only to fire or not to fire.

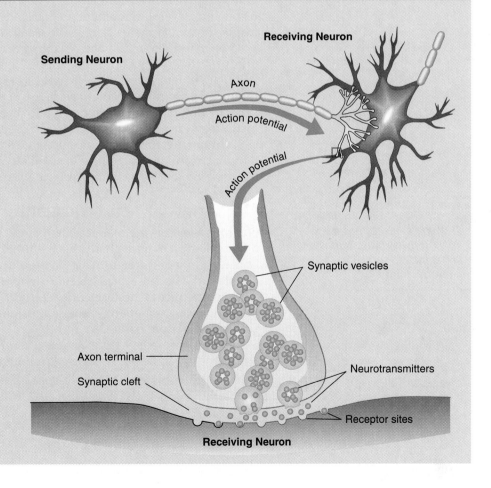

reuptake: The process by which neurotransmitter molecules are taken from the synaptic cleft back into the axon terminal for later use, thus terminating their excitatory or inhibitory effect on the receiving neuron.

acetylcholine: A neurotransmitter that plays a role in learning, memory, and rapid eye movement (REM) sleep and causes the skeletal muscle fibers to contract.

However, the process of neurotransmitters binding with receptor sites is not as fixed and rigid as keys fitting locks, or jigsaw puzzle pieces interlocking. Receptor sites in the brain are living matter; they can expand and contract their enclosed volume. Consequently, the interaction where the neurotransmitter and the receptor meet is controlled not by the direct influence of one on the other, but by their mutual influence on each other. In such a dynamic interplay, a certain neurotransmitter may be competing for the same receptor with another neurotransmitter of a slightly different shape. The receptor will admit only one of the competing neurotransmitters—the one that fits it most perfectly. Thus, a neurotransmitter may be received by a receptor at one time, but not at other times if another neurotransmitter molecule is present whose "affinity with the receptor is even stronger. As in dating and mating, what is finally settled for is always a function of what is available" (Restak, 1993, p. 28).

The Action of Neurotransmitters When neurotransmitters enter receptor sites on the dendrites or cell bodies of receiving neurons, their action is either excitatory (influencing the neurons to fire) or inhibitory (influencing them not to fire). Because a single neuron may synapse with thousands of other neurons at the same time, there will always be both excitatory and inhibitory influences on receiving neurons. For the neuron to fire, the excitatory influences must exceed the inhibitory influences of neurotransmitter substances by a sufficient amount (the threshold).

For many years researchers believed that each individual neuron responded to only one neurotransmitter. But it is now known that individual neurons may respond to several different neurotransmitters, suggesting a greater flexibility of response, even at the level of a single neuron.

You may wonder how the synaptic vesicles can continue to pour out their neurotransmitters, yet have a ready supply so the neuron can respond to continuing stimulation. First, the cell body of the neuron is always working to manufacture more of the neurotransmitter substance. Second, unused neurotransmitters in the synaptic cleft may be broken down into their component molecules and reclaimed by the axon terminal to be recycled and used again. Third, by an important process called **reuptake**, the neurotransmitter substance is taken intact back into the axon terminal, ready for immediate use. This terminates the neurotransmitter's excitatory or inhibitory effect on the receiving neuron.

What are some of the ways in which neurotransmitters affect our behavior, and what are some of the major neurotransmitters?

The Variety of Neurotransmitters

Neurotransmitters are manufactured in the brain, the spinal cord, the glands, and a few other parts of the body. Each kind of neurotransmitter affects the activity of the brain in a different way. Some neurotransmitters regulate the actions of glands and muscles; others affect learning and memory; still others promote sleep or stimulate mental and physical alertness. Some neurotransmitters orchestrate our feelings and emotions, from depression to euphoria, and others (endorphins) provide relief from pain.

To date, researchers have identified some 60 chemical substances manufactured by the body that may act as neurotransmitters (Greden, 1994). It was long believed that an individual neuron could secrete only one neurotransmitter. But more recently it has been demonstrated that some single neurons may secrete several different neurotransmitters (Changeux, 1993). Some neurotransmitters are always excitatory, others are always inhibitory, but some neurotransmitters can be either excitatory or inhibitory depending on the receptor with which they bind.

Acetylcholine The neurotransmitter **acetylcholine** (ACh) stimulates excitatory effects on the skeletal muscle fibers, causing them to contract so that we can move. But it has an inhibitory effect on the muscle fibers in the heart. How can the same neurotransmitter excite some postsynaptic membranes and inhibit others? In such cases it is not the neurotransmitter itself that produces the effect, but the different nature of the receptors on the postsynaptic (receiving) neuron that determines it.

Acetylcholine is involved in a variety of functions, including learning and memory, and in rapid eye movement (REM) sleep, during which dreaming occurs. Recent studies of acetylcholine and memory indicate that acetylcholine plays an excitatory role in stimulating the neurons involved in learning new information. At the same time, acetylcholine performs an inhibitory function in preventing "previously learned memories from interfering with the learning of new memories" (Hasselmo & Bower, 1993, p. 218).

The Monoamines An important class of neurotransmitters called monoamines includes four neurotransmitters—dopamine, norepinephrine (noradrenalin), epinephrine (adrenalin), and serotonin. Like acetylcholine, **dopamine** (DA) produces both excitatory and inhibitory effects and is involved in several functions, including learning, attention, and movement. A deficiency in dopamine is related to Parkinson's disease, a condition characterized by tremors and rigidity in the limbs. An oversensitivity to dopamine is thought to be related to some cases of schizophrenia, a severe psychotic disorder that you will learn more about in Chapter 14.

Norepinephrine (NE) has effects on eating habits (it stimulates the intake of carbohydrates) and on sleep (it plays a major role in alertness and wakefulness). Epinephrine affects the metabolism of glucose and causes the nutrient energy stored in the muscles to be released during strenuous exercise. Epinephrine also acts as a neurotransmitter in the brain but plays a minor role compared to norepinephrine.

Serotonin produces inhibitory effects at most of the receptors with which it forms synapses. It plays an important role in regulating mood, sleep, impulsivity, aggression, and appetite (Greden, 1994). In a weight-loss study, 176 patients were given fenfluramine, a drug that inhibits the reuptake of serotonin, thereby making more of it available at the synapses. Over a period of a year, the patients lost weight steadily. But, in general, when they stopped taking the drug over the next 12 months, the patients regained the weight they had lost (Bray, 1992a).

A deficiency in serotonin has been associated with such behaviors as suicide (Nordström et al., 1994) and impulsive violence (Sandou et al., 1994). Both serotonin and norepinephrine are related to positive moods, and a deficiency in the two has been linked to depression. Some antidepressant drugs relieve the symptoms of depression by blocking the reuptake of serotonin or norepinephrine, thus increasing the neurotransmitter's availability in the synapses.

Amino Acids Researchers believe that eight or more amino acids also serve as neurotransmitters. Two of particular importance are found more commonly than any other transmitter substances in the central nervous system. They are glutamate (glutamic acid) and GABA (gamma-aminobutyric acid). Glutamate is the primary excitatory neurotransmitter in the brain (Hyman, 1995). And researchers believe that it serves to initiate changes in synapses that are responsible for learning.

GABA is the main inhibitory neurotransmitter in the brain. An abnormality in the neurons that secrete GABA is believed to be one of the causes of epilepsy, a serious neurological disorder that produces seizures. Some of the GABA receptors will bind with tranquilizing drugs such as Valium and Librium, which lessen anxiety, relax muscles, promote sleep, and reduce seizure activity. Other GABA receptor sites bind with alcohol and barbiturates to increase neural inhibition and produce a calming effect, relaxation, and sleep.

Endorphins Over two decades ago, Candace Pert and fellow researchers (1974) demonstrated that a localized region of the brain contains neurons with receptors that respond to the opiates—drugs such as opium, morphine, and heroin. Later it

dopamine (DOE-pah-meen): A neurotransmitter that plays a role in learning, attention, and movement; a deficiency of dopamine is associated with Parkinson's disease, and an oversensitivity to it is associated with some cases of schizophrenia.

norepinephrine: A neurotransmitter affecting eating and sleep; a deficiency of norepinephrine is associated with depression.

serotonin: A neurotransmitter that plays an important role in regulating mood, sleep, aggression, and appetite; a serotonin deficiency is associated with anxiety, depression, and suicide.

Review and Reflect 2.1 *Major Neurotransmitters and Their Functions*

Neurotransmitter	Believed to Affect
Acetylcholine (ACh)	Movement, learning, memory, REM sleep
Dopamine (DA)	Learning, attention, movement
Norepinephrine (NE)	Eating and sleep
Epinephrine	Metabolism of glucose, energy release during exercise
Serotonin	Mood, sleep, appetite, impulsivity, and aggression
GABA	Neural inhibition in the central nervous system
Endorphins	Relief from pain, feelings of pleasure and well-being

was learned that the brain itself produces its own opiatelike substances, known as **endorphins**. Endorphins provide relief from pain and produce feelings of pleasure and well-being. (See Chapter 3 for more information on endorphins.)

When different types of opiate receptors are stimulated, a number of different effects are produced. One effect is relief from pain. Another is stimulation of certain "pleasure centers" whose neurons are involved in reinforcement, or reward; this effect is important for learning, and it helps explain the addictive properties of opiates.

Review and Reflect Table 2.1 summarizes the major neurotransmitters and their functions.

The Rate of Neural Firing and the Speed of the Impulse

How can we tell the difference between a very strong and a very weak stimulus?

Consider this important question: If a neuron only fires or does not fire, how can we tell the difference between a very strong and a very weak stimulus? a jarring blow and a soft touch? a blinding light and a dim one? a shout and a whisper? The answer lies in the number of neurons firing at the same time and their rate of firing (the number of times per second). A weak stimulus may cause relatively few neurons to fire, while a strong stimulus may trigger thousands of neurons to fire at the same time. Also, a weak stimulus may be signaled by neurons firing very slowly, while stronger stimuli may incite the neurons to fire hundreds of times per second. Normally the firing rate is much slower, but the ability of a neuron to change from resting to action potential so many times in a single second is difficult to imagine.

Once a neuron fires, how fast do you suppose the impulse travels down the length of the axon? Impulses travel at speeds from about 1 meter per second to approximately 100 meters per second (about 224 miles per hour). The speed of the impulse is related to the size of the axon. The larger, longer axons—those that reach from the brain through the spinal cord, and from the spinal cord to remote parts of the body—send impulses at a faster speed than neurons with smaller, shorter axons.

The most important factor in speeding the impulse on its way is the **myelin sheath**—a white, fatty coating wrapped around some axons that acts as insulation. If you look again at Figure 2.1 (on page 41), you will see that the coating has numerous gaps called nodes of Ranvier. These nodes cause the myelin sheath to look like links of sausage strung together. The electrical impulse is retriggered or

endorphins (en-DOOR-fins): Chemicals produced naturally by the brain that reduce pain and positively affect mood.

myelin sheath (MY-uh-lin): The white, fatty coating wrapped around some axons that acts as insulation and enables impulses to travel much faster.

regenerated at each node (or naked gap) on the axon. This speeds the impulse up to 100 times faster than impulses in axons without myelin sheaths.

Glial Cells: The Neurons' Helper Cells

Glial cells are specialized cells in the brain that form the myelin coating and perform many other important functions. *Glia* means "glue," and these cells hold the neurons together. Glial cells remove waste products such as dead neurons from the brain by engulfing and digesting them, and they handle other manufacturing, nourishing, and clean-up tasks. Glial cells serve another function when the brain is being formed and as it grows and develops. During this period of development, glial cells act as guides, taking the specialized neurons from where they are formed to where they will finally function (Rakic, 1988).

Glial cells are smaller than neurons but outnumber them about nine to one (Travis, 1994). And, remarkably, glial cells make up more than one-half the volume of the human brain. It is now known that glial cells interact with neurons in complex ways, and that they play a part in creating a more efficient brain (Abbott & Raff, 1991). Marian Diamond and others (1985) analyzed four small cubes of brain tissue from different parts of Albert Einstein's brain and comparable cubes from the brains of 11 people of average intelligence. They found that Einstein had about 73 percent more glial cells than the average person in one part of the left parietal lobe that is involved in analyzing information from various regions in the brain.

One type of glial cells, the astrocytes (star cells), perform more than support and clean-up tasks in the central nervous system. Nedergaard (1994) has demonstrated that astrocytes have functional neurotransmitter receptors and can communicate directly with neurons. This research, states Nedergaard, "challenges the general assumption that neurons alone are responsible for information processing in the central nervous system" (p. 1770).

glial cells (GLEE-ul): Cells that help to make the brain more efficient by holding the neurons together, removing waste products such as dead neurons, making the myelin coating for the axons, and performing other manufacturing, nourishing, and clean-up tasks.

Memory Check 2.1

1. The branchlike extensions of neurons that act as the *primary* receivers of signals from other neurons are the:
   a. dendrites.　　　c. glia.
   b. axons.　　　　　d. cell bodies.

2. The junction where the axon of a sending neuron communicates with a receiving neuron is called the:
   a. reuptake site.　　c. synapse.
   b. receptor site.　　 d. axon terminal.

3. When a neuron fires, neurotransmitters are released from the synaptic vesicles in the _____ terminal into the synaptic cleft.
   a. dendrite　　　　c. receptor
   b. cell body's　　　d. axon

4. The (resting, action) potential is the firing of a neuron that results when the charge within the neuron becomes more positive than the charge outside the cell membrane.

5. Receptor sites on the receiving neuron:
   a. receive any available neurotransmitter molecules.
   b. receive only neurotransmitter molecules of a specific shape.
   c. can only be influenced by neurotransmitters from a single neuron.
   d. are located only on the dendrites.

6. Which of the following substances cross the synaptic cleft and enter receptor sites on the dendrites and cell bodies of receiving neurons?
   a. sodium ions　　　c. neurotransmitters
   b. potassium ions　　d. synapse modulators

7. Endorphins, norepinephrine, dopamine, and serotonin are all examples of:
   a. hormones.　　　　c. neuropeptides.
   b. neurotransmitters.　d. neuromodulators.

Answers: 1. a　2. c　3. d　4. action　5. b　6. c　7. b

The Central Nervous System

We have discussed how neurons function individually and in groups through electrochemical action. But human functioning involves much more than the action of individual neurons. Collections of neurons, brain structures, and organ systems also must be explored. The nervous system is divided into two parts: (1) the **central nervous system (CNS)**, which is composed of the brain and the spinal cord, and (2) the peripheral nervous system, which connects the central nervous system to all other parts of the body (see Figure 2.4).

Now we will follow the spinal cord up through the brainstem and the other brain structures to the most distinctly human part of the brain—the cerebrum, with its incredible cortex. The peripheral nervous system will be discussed later in this chapter.

The Spinal Cord: An Extension of the Brain

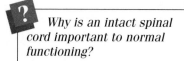

Why is an intact spinal cord important to normal functioning?

The **spinal cord** can best be thought of as an extension of the brain. Like the brain, it has gray matter as well as white matter and is loaded with glial cells. A cylinder of neural tissue about the diameter of your little finger, the spinal cord reaches from the base of the brain, through the neck, and down the hollow center of the spinal column. The spinal cord is protected by bone and also by spinal fluid, which serves as a shock absorber. The spinal cord literally links the body with the brain. It transmits messages between the brain and the peripheral nervous system. Thus, sensory information can reach the brain, and messages from the brain can be sent to the muscles, the glands, and other parts of the body.

Although the spinal cord and the brain usually function together, the spinal cord can act without help from the brain to protect us from injury. For example, the spinal reflex that causes you to withdraw your hand quickly from a hot stove is controlled by the spinal cord without the initial involvement of the brain. The

central nervous system (CNS): The brain and the spinal cord.

spinal cord: An extension of the brain, reaching from the base of the brain through the neck and spinal column, that transmits messages between the brain and the peripheral nervous system.

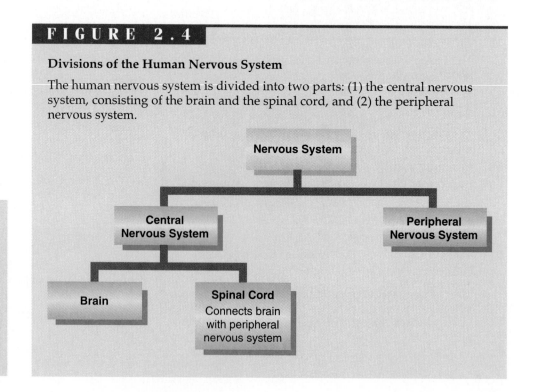

FIGURE 2.4

Divisions of the Human Nervous System

The human nervous system is divided into two parts: (1) the central nervous system, consisting of the brain and the spinal cord, and (2) the peripheral nervous system.

brain, however, quickly becomes aware and involved when the pain signal reaches it. At that point you might plunge your hand into cold water to relieve the pain.

The Brainstem: The Most Primitive Part of the Brain

What are the crucial functions handled by the brainstem?

The **brainstem** begins at the site where the spinal cord enlarges as it enters the skull. The brainstem includes the medulla, the pons, and the reticular formation, as shown in Figure 2.5. The brainstem handles functions that are so critical to our physical survival that damage to it is life-threatening. The **medulla** is the part of the brainstem that controls heartbeat, breathing, blood pressure, coughing, and swallowing. Fortunately, the medulla handles these functions automatically, so you do not have to decide consciously to breathe or remember to keep your heart beating.

Extending through the brainstem into the pons is another important structure, the **reticular formation**, sometimes called the reticular activating system (RAS). Find it in Figure 2.5. The reticular formation plays a crucial role in arousal and attention. Every day our sense organs are bombarded with stimuli, but we

FIGURE 2.5

Major Structures of the Human Brain

Some of the major structures of the brain are shown in the drawing, and a brief description of the function of each is provided. The brain stem contains the medulla, the reticular formation, and the pons.

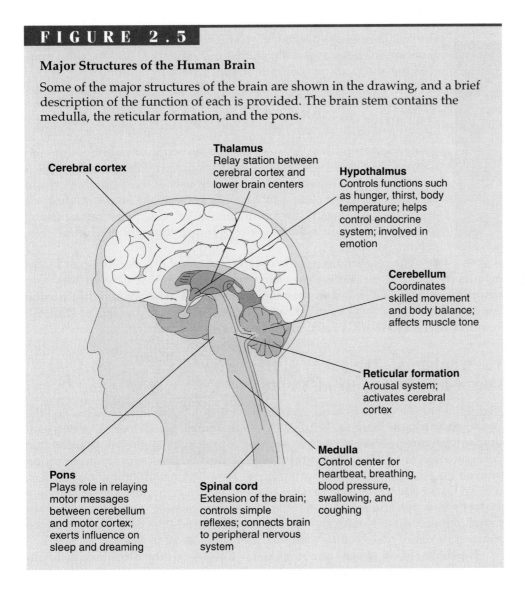

brainstem: The structure that begins at the point where the spinal cord enlarges as it enters the brain and that includes the medulla, the pons, and the reticular formation.

medulla (muh-DUL-uh): The part of the brainstem that controls heartbeat, blood pressure, breathing, coughing, and swallowing.

reticular formation: A structure in the brainstem that plays a crucial role in arousal and attention and that screens sensory messages entering the brain.

cerebellum (sehr-uh-BELL-um): The brain structure that executes smooth, skilled body movements and regulates muscle tone and posture.

thalamus (THAL-uh-mus): The structure, located above the brainstem, that acts as a relay station for information flowing into or out of the higher brain centers.

cannot possibly pay attention to everything we see or hear. The reticular formation screens messages entering the brain. It blocks some messages and sends others on to higher brain centers for processing.

The reticular formation also determines how alert we are. When it slows down, we doze off or go to sleep. But like an alarm clock, it also can jolt us into consciousness. Thanks to the reticular formation, important messages get through even when we are asleep. That is why parents may be able to sleep through a thunderstorm but will awaken to the slightest cry of their baby. (The next time you sleep through your alarm and are late for class, blame it on your reticular formation.)

Above the medulla and at the top of the brainstem is a bridgelike structure called the pons (a Latin word meaning "bridge"). The pons extends across the top front of the brainstem and connects to both the left and right halves of the cerebellum. The pons plays a role in body movement and even exerts an influence on sleep and dreaming. Hobson and McCarley (1977) report that the neurons in the pons begin firing rapidly just as a sleeper begins to dream.

? *What are the primary functions of the cerebellum?*

The Cerebellum: A Must for Graceful Movement

Cerebellum means "little cerebrum," and with its two hemispheres, the cerebellum resembles the large cerebrum, which rests above it (refer to Figure 2.5).

Current knowledge about the cerebellum suggests that its main functions are to execute smooth, skilled movements and to regulate muscle tone and posture (Lalonde & Botez, 1990). It guides the graceful movements of the ballet dancer and the split-second timing of the skilled athlete. But more typically, the cerebellum coordinates and orchestrates the series of movements necessary to perform many everyday activities without studied, conscious effort. It enables you to guide food from the plate to your mouth without stabbing yourself with a fork. People who have suffered damage to the cerebellum must concentrate very intently as they consciously and purposely perform each movement—pick up a fork, carefully locate the food with the fork, bring the food toward the mouth, and so on. Can you imagine trying to dance or carry on a dinner conversation without the help of the cerebellum?

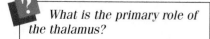

The major functions of the cerebellum are to execute smooth, skilled movements and to regulate muscle tone and posture.

The cerebellum has also been found to play a role in motor learning and in retaining memories of motor activities (Lalonde & Botez, 1990). And more recent evidence indicates that the cerebellum is also involved in mental imagery and even in some language and problem-solving tasks (Kim et al., 1994; Leiner et al., 1993). We will explore these functions more fully in Chapter 6.

? *What is the primary role of the thalamus?*

The Thalamus: The Relay Station between Lower and Higher Brain Centers

Above the brainstem lie two extremely important structures—the thalamus and the hypothalamus (refer back to Figure 2.5). The **thalamus**, which looks like two egg-shaped structures, serves as the relay station for virtually all the information that flows into and out of the higher brain centers. This includes sensory information from all the senses except smell. Incoming sensory information from the eyes, ears, skin, or taste buds travels first to parts of the thalamus or hypothalamus and then to the proper area of the cortex that handles vision, hearing, taste, or touch. Pain signals connect directly with the thalamus, which sends the pain message to the appropriate sensory areas of the cerebral cortex (Roland, 1992; Talbot et al., 1991).

The thalamus, or at least one small part of it, apparently affects our ability to learn new information, especially if it is verbal. This structure also plays a role in the production of language (Metter, 1991). Another function of the thalamus is the regulation of sleep cycles, which is thought to be accomplished in cooperation with the pons and the reticular formation. The synchronized firing of networks of neurons in one part of the thalamus has been observed during slow-wave (deep) sleep (Krosigk, 1993).

What a diverse range of activities this single brain structure performs. Now consider a much smaller structure, the hypothalamus.

The Hypothalamus: A Master Regulator

Nestled directly below the thalamus and weighing only about 2 ounces, the **hypothalamus** is, ounce for ounce, the most influential structure in the brain. It regulates hunger, thirst, sexual behavior, and a wide variety of emotional behaviors. The hypothalamus also regulates internal body temperature, starting the process that causes us to perspire when we are too hot and to shiver to conserve body heat when we are too cold. Some experts believe that the hypothalamus also regulates the biological clock—our body rhythms and the timing of our sleep/wakefulness cycle (Ginty et al., 1993). As small as it is, the hypothalamus maintains nearly all bodily functions except blood pressure, heart rhythm, and breathing.

The physiological changes in the body that accompany strong emotion are initiated by neurons concentrated primarily in the hypothalamus. You have felt these physical changes—sweaty palms, a pounding heart, a hollow feeling in the pit of your stomach, or a lump in your throat.

The electrical stimulation of parts of the hypothalamus has elicited some unusual reactions in animals. Long ago, researcher José Delgado (1969) implanted an electrode in a particular spot in the hypothalamus of a bull, specifically bred for bull fighting in Spain. Delgado stood calmly in the ring as the bull charged toward him. He then pressed a remote control box that stimulated an area of the bull's hypothalamus. The bull stopped abruptly in its tracks. (Fortunately for Delgado, the batteries in the remote were working.) Apparently, aggression in animals can be turned on or off by stimulating specific areas of the hypothalamus. Not only that, even the sensations of pleasure can be produced if the right place on the hypothalamus is stimulated (Olds, 1956).

The Limbic System: Primitive Emotion and Memory

The **limbic system** is composed of a group of structures in the brain, including the amygdala and the hippocampus, which are collectively involved in emotional expression, memory, and motivation. The **amygdala** plays an important role in emotion, particularly in response to aversive (unpleasant) stimuli (LeDoux, 1994). It is also prominently involved in various aspects of learning, such as learned fear responses, which help humans and other animals avoid dangerous situations and aversive consequences (LeDoux, 1993). Specifically, the amygdala helps us form associations between external events (including social actions) and the emotions related to those events (Aggleton, 1993).

The **hippocampus** is an important brain structure of the limbic system located in the interior temporal lobes (see Figure 2.6 on page 52). The hippocampus is essential in the formation of conscious memory (Squire, 1992). If your hippocampus were destroyed, you would not be able to store or recall any new information of a personal or cognitive nature. Yet memories already stored before destruction of the hippocampus would remain intact. The hippocampus also plays a role in the brain's internal representation of space in the form of neural "maps" that help us learn our way about in new environments and remember where we have been (Thompson & Best, 1990; Wilson & McNaughton, 1993). You will learn more about the central role the hippocampus plays in the formation of memories in Chapter 6.

What are some of the processes regulated by the hypothalamus?

hypothalamus (HY-po-THAL-uh-mus): A small but influential brain structure that controls the pituitary gland and regulates hunger, thirst, sexual behavior, body temperature, and a wide variety of emotional behaviors.

limbic system: A group of structures in the brain, including the amygdala and hippocampus, that are collectively involved in emotion, memory, and motivation.

What is the role of the limbic system?

amygdala (ah-MIG-da-la): A structure in the limbic system that plays an important role in emotion, particularly in response to aversive stimuli.

hippocampus (hip-po-CAM-pus): A structure in the limbic system that plays a central role in the formation of long-term memories.

FIGURE 2.6

The Principal Structures in the Limbic System

The amygdala plays an important role in emotion; the hippocampus is essential in the formation of conscious memory.

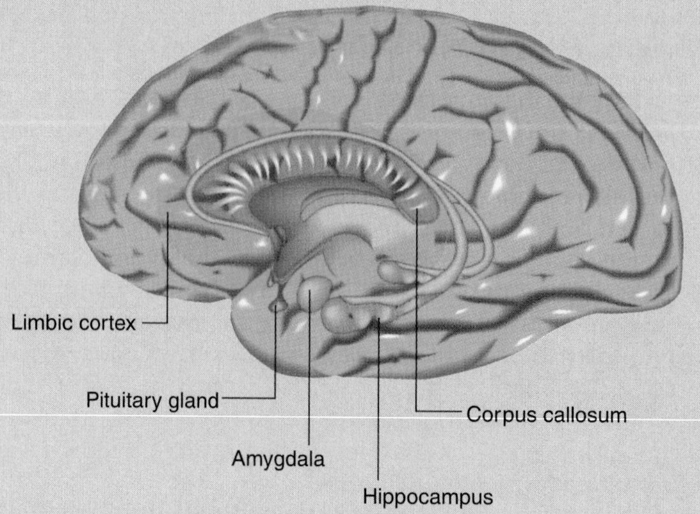

Limbic cortex

Pituitary gland

Amygdala

Corpus callosum

Hippocampus

Autopsies performed on patients suffering from the severe memory impairment of Alzheimer's disease have revealed extensive damage to neurons in the hippocampus (West et al., 1994). Alzheimer's disease is an insidious brain disease that develops gradually and continues to destroy neurons in brain areas that control memory. Former President Ronald Reagan announced in 1994 that neurological tests revealed he was in the early stages of Alzheimer's disease. You will learn more about Alzheimer's disease in Chapter 9.

Memory Check 2.2

1. The brain and the spinal cord make up the peripheral nervous system. (true/false)

2. The hypothalamus regulates all the following except:
   a. internal body temperature
   b. hunger and thirst
   c. coordinated movement
   d. sexual behavior

3. The hippocampus is the part of the limbic system primarily involved in the formation of memories. (true/false)

4. Match the brain structure with its description.
   ____ 1) connects the brain with the peripheral nervous system
   ____ 2) controls heart rate, breathing, and blood pressure
   ____ 3) consists of the medulla, the pons, and the reticular formation
   ____ 4) influences attention and arousal
   ____ 5) coordinates complex body movements
   ____ 6) serves as a relay station for sensory information flowing into the brain

   a. medulla
   b. spinal cord
   c. reticular formation
   d. thalamus
   e. cerebellum
   f. brainstem

Answers: 1. false 2. c 3. true 4. 1) b 2) a 3) f 4) c 5) e 6) d

The Cerebral Hemispheres

The most extraordinary and the most essentially human part of the magnificent 3-pound human brain is the cerebrum and its cortex. If you could peer into your skull and look down upon your own brain, you would see a structure that resembles the inside of a huge walnut (see Figure 2.7). Like a walnut, which has two matched halves connected to each other, the **cerebrum** is composed of two **cerebral hemispheres**—a left and a right hemisphere resting side by side. The two hemispheres are physically connected at the bottom by a thick band of nerve fibers called the **corpus callosum**. This connection makes possible the transfer of information and the coordination of activity between the hemispheres. In general, the right cerebral hemisphere controls movement and feeling on the left side of the body. The left hemisphere controls the right side of the body. In over 95 percent of people, the left hemisphere also controls the language functions (Hellige, 1990).

> **?** *What are the cerebral hemispheres, the corpus callosum, and the cerebral cortex?*

FIGURE 2.7

Two Views of the Cerebral Hemispheres

The two hemispheres rest side by side like two matched halves, physically connected by the corpus callosum, shown in (a). An inside view of the right hemisphere of the cerebrum and cerebellum is shown in (b).

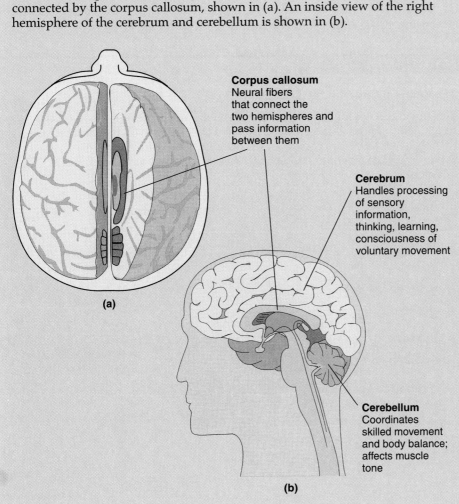

Corpus callosum
Neural fibers that connect the two hemispheres and pass information between them

Cerebrum
Handles processing of sensory information, thinking, learning, consciousness of voluntary movement

Cerebellum
Coordinates skilled movement and body balance; affects muscle tone

(a)

(b)

The two cerebral hemispheres show up clearly in this view looking down on an actual brain.

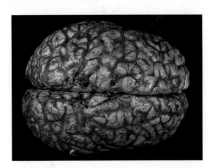

cerebrum (seh-REE-brum): The largest structure of the human brain, consisting of the two cerebral hemispheres connected by the corpus callosum and covered by the cerebral cortex.

cerebral hemispheres (seh-REE-brul): The right and left halves of the cerebrum, covered by the cerebral cortex and connected by the corpus callosum.

corpus callosum (KOR-pus kah-LO-sum): The thick band of nerve fibers that connects the two cerebral hemispheres and makes possible the transfer of information and the synchronization of activity between them.

The cerebral hemispheres have an outer covering of gray matter about ⅛ inch thick called the **cerebral cortex**. The cerebral cortex accounts for approximately 40 percent of the human brain's total weight. The cortex is primarily responsible for the higher mental processes of language, memory, and thinking. In humans the cortex is very large—about 2 feet by 3 feet—and is roughly three times the size of the cerebrum. For this reason, it does not fit smoothly around the cerebrum. Rather, it is arranged in numerous folds or wrinkles called convolutions. About two-thirds of the cortex is hidden from view in the folds. The cortex of less intelligent animals is much smaller in proportion to total brain size and, therefore, is much less convoluted.

The cerebral cortex contains three types of areas: (1) sensory input areas, where vision, hearing, touch, pressure, and temperature register; (2) motor areas, which control voluntary movement; and (3) **association areas**, which house our memories and are involved in thought, perception, and language.

The Lobes of the Brain

In each cerebral hemisphere there are four lobes—the frontal lobe, the parietal lobe, the occipital lobe, and the temporal lobe. Find them in Figure 2.8.

The Frontal Lobes: For Moving, Speaking, and Thinking Of the lobes in the brain, the frontal lobes are by far the largest. Beginning at the front of the brain, the **frontal lobes** extend to the top center of the skull. They contain the motor cortex, Broca's area, and the frontal association areas.

> **?** *What are some of the main areas within the frontal lobes, and what are their functions?*

cerebral cortex (seh-REE-brul KOR-tex): The gray, convoluted covering of the cerebral hemispheres that is responsible for higher mental processes such as language, memory, and thinking.

association areas: Areas of the cerebral cortex that house memories and are involved in thought, perception, learning, and language.

frontal lobes: The lobes that control voluntary body movements, speech production, and such functions as thinking, motivation, planning for the future, impulse control, and emotional responses.

FIGURE 2.8

The Cerebral Cortex of the Left Hemisphere

This illustration of the left cerebral hemisphere shows the four lobes: (1) the frontal lobe, including the motor cortex and Broca's area; (2) the parietal lobe, with the somatosensory cortex; (3) the occipital lobe, with the primary visual cortex; and (4) the temporal lobe, with the primary auditory cortex and Wernicke's area.

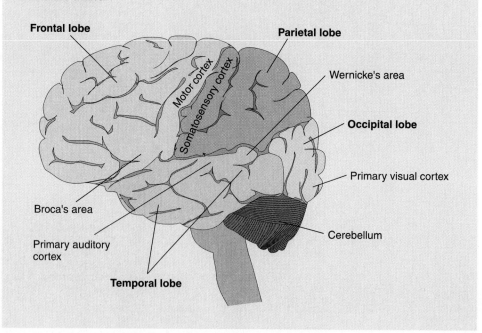

The Motor Cortex In 1870 two medical doctors, Fritsch and Hitzig, used a probe to apply a weak electrical current to the cortex of a dog. (The brain itself is insensitive to pain, so probing the brain causes no discomfort.) When the doctors applied electrical stimulation to various points along the rear of the frontal lobe, different parts of the dog's body moved. Fritsch and Hitzig had discovered the **motor cortex**—the area that controls voluntary body movement (refer to Figure 2.8). The right motor cortex controls movement on the left side of the body, and the left motor cortex controls movement on the right side of the body. Recent research, however, has established that the left motor cortex is involved with the control of voluntary movement on the left side of the body as well (Kim et al., 1993).

Examine Figure 2.9. Notice the motor homunculus, or "little man," drawn next to the cross section of the motor cortex. The body parts are drawn in proportion to the amount of motor cortex that controls each body part. The parts of the body that are capable of the most finely coordinated movements, such as the fingers, lips, and tongue, have a larger share of the motor cortex. Areas such as the legs and the trunk of the body, which are capable only of gross movement, have a smaller amount of motor cortex. The lower parts of the body are controlled primarily by neurons at the top of the motor cortex, while upper body parts (face, lips, and tongue) are controlled mainly by neurons near the bottom of the motor cortex. For example, when you wiggle your right big toe, a cluster of brain cells firing at the top of the left motor cortex is chiefly responsible for producing the movement.

What happens when part of the motor cortex is damaged? Depending on the severity of the damage, either paralysis or some impairment of coordination can result. Sometimes damage in the motor cortex causes the grand mal seizures of epilepsy.

motor cortex: The strip of tissue at the rear of the frontal lobes that controls voluntary body movement.

FIGURE 2.9

The Motor Cortex and the Somatosensory Cortex from the Left Hemisphere

The left motor cortex controls voluntary movement in the right side of the body. The left somatosensory cortex is the site where touch, pressure, temperature, and pain sensations from the right side of the body register. The more sensitive the body parts and the more capable they are of finely coordinated movements, the greater the areas of somatosensory cortex and motor cortex dedicated to those body parts. Note what large sections of cortex serve the head, face, hands, and fingers, and what small sections serve such large areas as the trunk, arms, and legs.

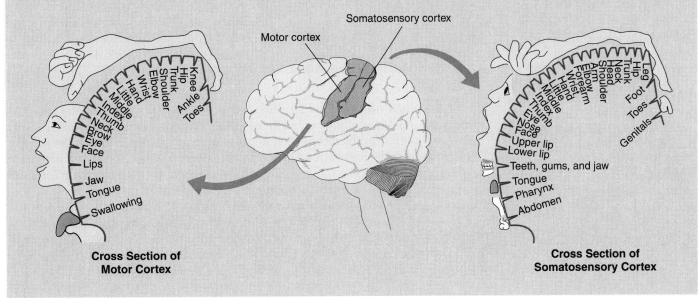

Cross Section of Motor Cortex

Cross Section of Somatosensory Cortex

Broca's area (BRO-kuz): The area in the frontal lobe, usually in the left hemisphere, that controls the production of speech sounds.

Broca's aphasia (BRO-kuz uh-FAY-zyah): An impairment in the ability physically to produce the speech sounds, or in extreme cases an inability to speak at all; caused by damage to Broca's area.

aphasia (uh-FAY-zyah): A loss or impairment of the ability to understand or communicate through the written or spoken word, which results from damage to the brain.

parietal lobes (puh-RY-uh-tul): The lobes that contain the somatosensory cortex (where touch, pressure, temperature, and pain register) and other areas that are responsible for body awareness and spatial orientation.

somatosensory cortex (so-MAT-o-SENS-or-ee): The strip of tissue at the front of the parietal lobes where touch, pressure, temperature, and pain register in the cerebral cortex.

This computer-generated image shows the likely path of the bar that tore through Phineas Gage's skull.

? *What are the primary functions of the parietal lobes in general and the somatosensory cortex in particular?*

Broca's Area In 1861 Paul Broca performed autopsies on two patients—one who had been totally without speech, and another who could say only four words (Jenkins et al., 1975). Broca found that both patients had damage in the left hemisphere, slightly in front of the part of the motor cortex that controls movement of the jaw, lips, and tongue. Broca was among the first scientists to demonstrate the existence of localized functions in the cerebral cortex (Schiller, 1993). He concluded that the site of damage, now called **Broca's area**, was the part of the brain responsible for speech production (refer back to Figure 2.8). Broca's area is involved in directing the pattern of muscle movement required to produce the speech sounds.

If Broca's area is damaged, **Broca's aphasia** may result. **Aphasia** is a general term for a loss or impairment of the ability to use or understand language, resulting from damage to the brain (Goodglass, 1993). Characteristically, patients with Broca's aphasia know what they want to say but can speak very little or not at all. So Broca's aphasia is primarily a deficit in producing language, not in understanding it (Maratsos & Matheny, 1994). If those with Broca's aphasia are able to speak, words are produced very slowly, with great effort, and are poorly articulated. One patient attempting to explain what he was doing in the hospital therapy program said, "nine o'cot, speech . . . two times . . . read . . . wr . . . ripe, er, rike, er, write" (Gardner, 1975, p. 61). Such patients, who cannot speak or who can speak only two or three words in a sequence, are often able, nevertheless, to sing songs that they had previously known. Singing is normally controlled by the right hemisphere, and words to familiar songs are already stored there (Albert & Helm-Estabrooks, 1988).

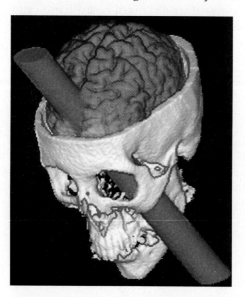

Frontal Association Areas Much of the frontal lobes consists of association areas that are involved in thinking, motivation, planning for the future, impulse control, and emotional responses (Stuss et al., 1992). Sometimes pronounced changes in emotional responses occur when the frontal lobes are damaged. Phineas Gage, discussed in the story that opened this chapter, is one case in which damage to the frontal lobes drastically altered impulse control and emotional responses. Using measurements from Gage's skull and modern brain-imaging techniques, researchers have been able to identify the probable location of the damage (Damasio et al., 1994).

The Parietal Lobes: Vital to Our Sense of Touch The **parietal lobes** lie directly behind the frontal lobes, in the top middle portion of the brain. The parietal lobes are involved in the reception and processing of touch stimuli. The front strip of brain tissue in the parietal lobes is the **somatosensory cortex**, the site where touch, pressure, temperature, and pain register in the cortex (refer back to Figure 2.8) (Stea & Apkarian, 1992). The somatosensory cortex also makes us aware of movement in our body and the positions of our body parts at any given moment.

Dusser de Bareene discovered the function of the somatosensory cortex in 1916 when he applied a small amount of strychnine to a number of points along a monkey's somatosensory cortex. The strychnine stimulated the neurons to fire. As he touched each point, the monkey scratched a different location on its skin. With this technique, de Bareene was able to map the monkey's somatosensory cortex.

If various points on your own somatosensory cortex were to be electrically stimulated, you would feel either a tingling sensation or a numbness in a corresponding part of your body. A person with damage to the somatosensory cortex of one hemisphere loses some sensitivity to touch on the opposite side of the body. If the damage is severe enough, the person might not be able to feel the difference between sandpaper and silk, or the affected part of the body might feel numb.

The two halves of the somatosensory cortex in the left and right parietal lobes are wired to opposite sides of the body. Also, cells at the top of the somatosensory cortex govern feeling in the lower extremities of the body. Drop a brick on your right foot, and the topmost brain cells of the left somatosensory cortex will fire and register the pain sensation. (Note, this is not a *Try It!* exercise.) Notice in Figure 2.9 the large somatosensory areas connected to sensitive body parts such as the tongue, lips, face, and hand, particularly the thumb and index finger. Observe the small amount of cortex connected to a large area such as the trunk of the body.

Under some circumstances, the organization of the somatosensory cortex may undergo change to accommodate unusual demands made upon it (Diamond et al., 1994). For example, among blind persons who must read by their sense of touch, the experienced Braille readers have a larger area of the somatosensory cortex dedicated to the fingertips they use for reading than to their other fingertips (Pascual-Leone & Torres, 1993).

Other parts of the parietal lobes are responsible for spatial orientation and our sense of direction. There are association areas in the parietal lobes that house our memory of how objects feel, a fact that explains why we can identify objects by touch. People with damage to these areas could hold a pencil, scissors, or a ball in their hand but not be able to identify the object by touch alone.

The Occipital Lobes: The Better to See You With

Behind the parietal lobes at the rear of the brain lie the **occipital lobes**, which are involved in the reception and interpretation of visual information (refer back to Figure 2.8). At the very back of the occipital lobes is the **primary visual cortex**, the site where vision registers in the cortex (Glickstein, 1988). If this site is stimulated with an electrical probe, the subject reports seeing flashes of light.

Each eye is connected to the primary visual cortex in both the right and left occipital lobes. Look straight ahead and draw an imaginary line down the middle of what you see. Everything to the left of the line is referred to as the left visual field and registers in the right visual cortex. Everything to the right of the line is the right visual field and registers in the left visual cortex. A person who sustains damage to one primary visual cortex will still have partial vision in both eyes.

The association areas in the occipital lobes are involved in the interpretation of visual stimuli. The association areas hold memories of past visual experiences and enable us to recognize what is familiar among the things we see. When these areas are damaged, people can lose their ability to identify objects visually, although they are still able to identify the same objects by touch or through some other sense.

The Temporal Lobes: Hearing's Here

The **temporal lobes**, located slightly above the ears, are involved in the reception and interpretation of auditory stimuli. The site in the cortex where hearing registers is known as the **primary auditory cortex** (Aitkin, 1990; Zatorre et al., 1992). When this area is stimulated with an electrical probe, the person hears bursts of sound. The primary auditory cortex in each temporal lobe receives sound inputs from both ears. Injury to one of these areas results in reduced hearing in both ears, and the destruction of both areas causes total deafness.

Wernicke's Area Adjacent to the primary auditory cortex in the left temporal lobe is **Wernicke's area**, which is the language area involved in comprehending the spoken word and in formulating coherent written and spoken language (refer back to Figure 2.8). In about 95 percent of people, Wernicke's area is in the left hemisphere. When you listen to someone speak, the sound registers first in the primary

---

occipital lobes (ahk-SIP-uh-tul): The lobes that contain the primary visual cortex, where vision registers, and association areas involved in the interpretation of visual information.

primary visual cortex: The area at the rear of the occipital lobes where vision registers in the cerebral cortex.

temporal lobes: The lobes that contain the primary auditory cortex, Wernicke's area, and association areas for interpreting auditory information.

primary auditory cortex: The part of the temporal lobes where hearing registers in the cerebral cortex.

? *What are the primary functions of the occipital lobes in general and the primary visual cortex in particular?*

? *What are the major areas within the temporal lobes, and what are their functions?*

Wernicke's area: The language area in the temporal lobe involved in comprehension of the spoken word and in formulation of coherent speech and written language.

Wernicke's aphasia: Aphasia resulting from damage to Wernicke's area, in which the patient's spoken language is fluent, but the content is either vague or incomprehensible to the listener.

auditory cortex. The sound is then sent to Wernicke's area, where the speech sounds are unscrambled into meaningful patterns of words. The same areas that are active when we listen to someone speak are also active in deaf individuals when they watch a person using sign language (Söderfeldt et al., 1994). Wernicke's area is also involved when we select the words to use in speech and written expression.

Wernicke's aphasia is a type of aphasia resulting from damage to Wernicke's area. Although speech is fluent and words are clearly articulated, the actual message does not make sense to others (Maratsos & Matheney, 1994). The content may be vague or bizarre and may contain inappropriate words, parts of words, or a gibberish of nonexistent words. One Wernicke's patient, when asked how he was feeling, replied, "I think that there's an awful lot of mung, but I think I've a lot of net and tunged in a little wheat duhvayden" (Buckingham & Kertesz, 1974). People with Wernicke's aphasia are not aware that anything is wrong with their speech.

Another kind of aphasia is auditory aphasia, or word deafness. It can occur if there is damage to the nerves connecting the primary auditory cortex with Wernicke's area. The person is able to hear normally but may not understand spoken language, as when you hear a foreign language spoken—you hear the sounds but have no idea what the speaker is saying.

In some cases the effects of aphasia on the language system are highly selective. For example, patients may be able to name objects they touch but not be able to name the same objects when they simply view them. Other patients are unable to understand words from a single category (such as body parts, animals, fruits, or vegetables) and yet have no problem at all with words in any other category. Some aphasia patients have trouble with the most common words in the language (such as *for*, *the*, *of*, and so on) but no problem with other longer and far less common words, while other patients have exactly the opposite problem (Goodglass, 1993).

The Temporal Association Areas The remainder of the temporal lobes consist of the association areas that house memories and are involved in the interpretation of auditory stimuli. For example, you have an association area where your memories of various sounds are stored, so you instantly recognize the sounds of running water, fire engine sirens, dogs barking, and so on. There is also a special association area where familiar melodies are stored.

Memory Check 2.3

1. What is the thick band of fibers connecting the two cerebral hemispheres?
   a. cortex
   b. cerebrum
   c. corpus callosum
   d. motor cortex

2. The ⅛-inch outer covering of the cerebrum is the:
   a. cerebral cortex.
   b. myelin sheath.
   c. cortex callosum.
   d. white matter.

3. Match the lobes with the brain areas they contain.
   ____ 1) primary auditory cortex, Wernicke's area
   ____ 2) primary visual cortex
   ____ 3) Broca's area, motor cortex
   ____ 4) somatosensory cortex

   a. frontal lobes
   b. parietal lobes
   c. occipital lobes
   d. temporal lobes

4. Match the specialized area with the appropriate description of function.
   ____ 1) site where hearing registers
   ____ 2) site where vision registers
   ____ 3) site where touch, pressure, and temperature register
   ____ 4) speech production
   ____ 5) voluntary movement
   ____ 6) formulation and understanding of the spoken and written word
   ____ 7) thinking, motivation, impulse control

   a. primary visual cortex
   b. motor cortex
   c. frontal association area
   d. primary auditory cortex
   e. somatosensory cortex
   f. Wernicke's area
   g. Broca's area

Answers: 1. c 2. a 3. 1) d 2) c 3) a 4) b 4. 1) d 2) a 3) e 4) g 5) b 6) f 7) c

Specialization of the Cerebral Hemispheres

Although they may look very much alike, the two cerebral hemispheres make different but complementary contributions to our mental and emotional life. Research has shown that some **lateralization** of the hemispheres exists; that is, each hemisphere is specialized, to some extent, to handle certain functions. Yet functions are usually not handled exclusively by one hemisphere; the two hemispheres always work together (Bradshaw, 1989; Efron, 1990).

Functions of the Left Hemisphere: Language, First and Foremost

In 95 percent of right-handers and in about 62 percent of left-handers, the **left hemisphere** handles most of the language functions, including speaking, writing, reading, and understanding the spoken word (Hellige, 1990). Even American sign language (ASL) used by deaf persons is clearly a left hemisphere function (Corina et al., 1992). From birth, in children of both sexes, the left hemisphere appears to be more attuned to language (Hahn, 1987). The left hemisphere is also specialized for mathematical abilities, particularly calculation, and it processes information in an analytical and sequential, or step-by-step, manner (Corballis, 1989). Logic is primarily a left hemisphere specialty (Levy, 1985).

The left hemisphere coordinates complex movements by directly controlling the right side of the body and by indirectly controlling the movements of the left side of the body. The left hemisphere accomplishes this by sending orders across the corpus callosum to the right hemisphere so that the proper movements will be coordinated and executed smoothly. Remember also that the cerebellum plays an important role in helping coordinate complex movements.

Functions of the Right Hemisphere: The Leader in Visual-Spatial Tasks

The **right hemisphere** is generally considered to be the hemisphere more adept at visual-spatial relations. Artists, sculptors, architects, and household do-it-yourselfers have strong visual-spatial skills. When you put together a jigsaw puzzle, draw a picture, or assemble a piece of furniture according to instructions, you are calling primarily on your right hemisphere.

The right hemisphere processes information holistically rather than part by part or piece by piece as the left hemisphere does (Corballis, 1989). Auditory, visual, and touch stimuli register in both hemispheres, but the right hemisphere appears to be more specialized than the left for complex perceptual tasks. Consequently, the right hemisphere is better at pattern recognition, whether of familiar voices, melodies, or visual patterns.

Although the left hemisphere is generally considered the language hemisphere, the right hemisphere also makes an important contribution to our understanding of language. According to Howard Gardner (1981), the right hemisphere is involved "in understanding the theme or moral of a story, in grasping metaphor . . . and even in supplying the punch line for a joke" (p. 74). Van Lancker (1987) points out that "although the left hemisphere knows best what is being said, the right hemisphere figures out how it is meant and who is saying it" (p. 13). It is the right hemisphere that is able to

lateralization: The specialization of one of the cerebral hemispheres to handle a particular function.

? *What are the main functions of the left hemisphere?*

left hemisphere: The hemisphere that controls the right side of the body, coordinates complex movements, and, in 95 percent of people, controls the production of speech and written language.

right hemisphere: The hemisphere that controls the left side of the body and that, in most people, is specialized for visual-spatial perception and for interpreting nonverbal behavior.

? *What are the primary functions of the right hemisphere?*

The right hemisphere of the brain is generally considered to be more adept at visual-spatial relations than the left hemisphere. Can you think of other examples of complex perceptual tasks?

understand familiar idiomatic expressions such as "He is turning over a new leaf." If the right hemisphere is damaged, a person can understand only the literal meaning of the statement.

To experience an effect of the specialization of the cerebral hemispheres, try your hand at the *Try It!*

Get a meter stick or yardstick. Try balancing it vertically on the end of your left index finger as shown in the drawing. Then try balancing it on your right index finger. Most people are better with their dominant hand—the right hand for right-handers, for example. Is this true for you?

Now try this: Begin reciting the ABCs out loud as fast as you can while balancing the stick with your *left* hand. Do you have less trouble this time? Why should that be? The right hemisphere controls the act of balancing with the left hand. However, your left hemisphere, though poor at controlling the left hand, still tries to coordinate your balancing efforts. When you distract the left hemisphere with a steady stream of talk, the right hemisphere can orchestrate more efficient balancing with your left hand without interference.

Creativity and intuition are typically considered right hemisphere specialties, but the left hemisphere shares these functions. The right hemisphere controls singing and seems to be more specialized for musical ability in untrained musicians (Kinsella et al., 1988). But in trained musicians, both hemispheres play important roles in musical ability.

Patients with right hemisphere damage may have difficulty with spatial orientation, such as in finding their way around even in familiar surroundings. They may have attentional deficits and be unaware of objects in the left visual field, a condition called unilateral neglect (Halligan & Marshall, 1994). Unilateral neglect patients may eat only the food on the right side of their plate, read only the words on the right half of a page, and even groom only the right half of their body.

The Right Hemisphere's Role in Emotion: Recognizing and Expressing Emotion   The right hemisphere is also more active in the recognition and expression of emotion (Borod, 1992). It even responds to the emotional message conveyed by another's tone of voice (Heilman et al., 1975). For example, a professor sarcastically says to a student who enters the class late, "Well, I'm so glad you could come today." A student with right hemisphere damage might respond only to the actual meaning of the words rather than the sarcastic tone.

Reading and interpreting nonverbal behavior, such as gestures and facial expressions, is primarily a right hemisphere task (Hauser, 1993). Look at the two faces in the *Try It!* (Jaynes, 1976).

Pick out the happy face and the sad face.

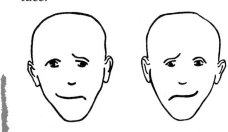

Even though the faces in the drawings are mirror images, right-handed people tend to see the face at the left as the happier face. When we look at a face, we are likely to perceive the emotional tone revealed by the part of the face to our left as we view it (McGee & Skinner, 1987). The right hemisphere processes information from the left visual field, so right-handed people tend to be more emotionally affected by the left side of the face as we view it.

The right hemisphere is involved in our own expression of emotion through our tone of voice and particularly our facial expression. The left side of the face, controlled by the right hemisphere, usually conveys stronger emotion than the right side of the face. Lawrence Miller (1988) describes the facial expressions and the voice inflection of people with right hemisphere damage as "often strangely blank—almost robotic" (p. 39).

Evidence also continues to accumulate that brain mechanisms responsible for negative emotions reside in the right hemisphere, while those responsible for positive emotions are located in the left hemisphere (Hellige, 1993).

The Split Brain: Separate Halves or Two Separate Brains?

The fact that the human brain is specialized for some functions—the left hemisphere for speech and the right hemisphere for visual-spatial abilities—does not mean that some people are left-brained, while others are right-brained. Unless the hemispheres have been surgically separated, they do not operate in isolation from each other and cannot be educated separately. The idea of the left or right hemisphere person is more fiction than fact; it sprang from the rich imagination of popular science writers. Such a notion is unscientific, even though it has served to heighten public interest in hemispheric specialization and neuroscience in general (Hellige, 1993). Even though each contributes its own important specialized functions, the cerebral hemispheres are always in intimate and immediate contact, thanks to the corpus callosum.

There have been rare cases where people have been born with no corpus callosum or have had their corpus callosum severed in a drastic surgical procedure called the **split-brain operation**. Neurosurgeons Joseph Bogen and Philip Vogel (1963) found that patients with severe epilepsy, suffering frequent and uncontrollable grand mal seizures, could be helped by surgery that severed their corpus callosum. In this way, the pulsing waves of neural activity that occur during a seizure could be confined to one hemisphere rather than spreading across the corpus callosum and involving the entire brain.

The split-brain operation surgically separates the hemispheres, making the transfer of information between them impossible. The patient is then left with two independently functioning hemispheres. The operation has been quite suc-

 What is the significance of the split-brain operation?

split-brain operation: An operation, performed in severe cases of epilepsy, in which the corpus callosum is cut, separating the cerebral hemispheres and usually lessening the severity and frequency of grand mal seizures.

cessful, completely eliminating the seizures in some patients. And the surgery causes no major changes in personality, intelligence, or behavior.

Research with split-brain patients by Roger Sperry (1964) and colleagues Michael Gazzaniga (1970, 1989) and Jerre Levy has expanded our knowledge of the unique capabilities of the individual hemispheres. Sperry (1968) found that when surgically separated, each hemisphere continued to have individual and private experiences, sensations, thoughts, and perceptions. However, most sensory experiences are shared almost simultaneously because each ear and eye has direct sensory connections to both hemispheres. For his work, Sperry won the Nobel Prize in Medicine in 1981.

Testing the Split-Brain Person Sperry's research revealed some fascinating findings. Look at Figure 2.10. In this illustration, a split-brain patient sits in front of a screen that separates the right and left fields of vision. If an orange is flashed to the right field of vision, it will register in the left (verbal) hemisphere. If asked what he saw, the patient will readily reply, "I saw an orange." Suppose that instead an apple is flashed to the left visual field and is relayed to the right (nonverbal) hemisphere. The patient will reply, "I saw nothing."

Why could the patient report that he saw the orange but not the apple? Sperry maintains that in split-brain patients, only the verbal left hemisphere can report what it sees. In these experiments, the left hemisphere does not see what is flashed to the right hemisphere, and the right hemisphere is unable to report verbally what it has viewed. But did the right hemisphere actually see the apple that was flashed in the left visual field? Yes, because with his left hand (which is controlled by the right hemisphere), the patient can pick out from behind a screen the apple or any other object shown to the right hemisphere. The right hemisphere knows

FIGURE 2.10

Testing a Split-Brain Person

Using special equipment, researchers are able to study the independent functioning of the hemispheres in split-brain persons. In this experiment a visual image (an orange), when flashed on the right side of the screen, is transmitted to the left (talking) hemisphere. When asked what he sees, the split-brain patient replies, "I see an orange." When an image (an apple) is flashed on the left side of the screen, it is transmitted only to the right (nonverbal) hemisphere. Because the split-brain patient's left (language) hemisphere did not receive the image, he replies "I see nothing." But he can pick out the apple by touch if he uses his left hand, proving that the right hemisphere "saw" the apple. (Based on Gazzaniga, 1983.)

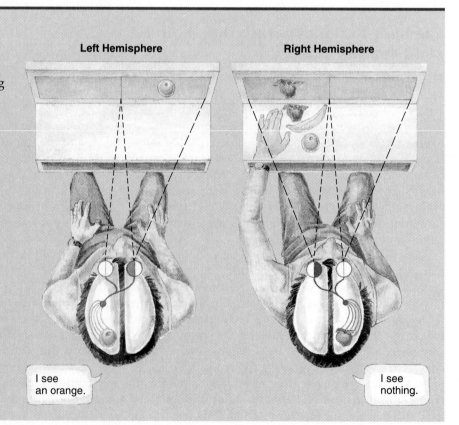

and remembers what it sees just as well as the left, but unlike the left hemisphere, the right cannot name what it has seen. (In these experiments, images must be flashed for no more than $1/10$ or $2/10$ of a second so that the subjects do not have time to refixate their eyes and send the information to the opposite hemisphere.)

Memory Check 2.4

1. Match the hemisphere with the specialized abilities usually associated with it.

   ____ 1) visual-spatial skills   a. right hemisphere

   ____ 2) speech   b. left hemisphere

   ____ 3) recognition and expression of emotion

   ____ 4) singing

   ____ 5) mathematics

2. Which of these statements is *not* true of the split-brain operation?

   a. It is used for people suffering from severe epilepsy.

   b. It provides a means of studying the functions of the individual hemispheres.

   c. It causes major changes in intelligence, personality, and behavior.

   d. It makes transfer of information between the hemispheres impossible.

Answers: 1.1) a 2) b 3) a 4) a 5) b 2. c

Discovering the Brain's Mysteries

As we have seen, the first attempts to discover the mysteries of the human brain were through autopsies, such as those performed by Paul Broca, and through clinical observations of the effects of brain injury and diseases. The next method of study was to insert electrical probes into live brains, as done by Fritsch and Hitzig in 1870.

Modern researchers need not rely solely on autopsies or wait for injuries to learn more about the brain. Today researchers are unlocking the mysteries of the human brain using electrical stimulation, the electroencephalograph (EEG), the microelectrode, and modern scanning devices such as the CT scan, magnetic resonance imaging (MRI), the PET scan, and others (Andreasen et al., 1992).

The EEG and the Microelectrode

Before 1924 there was no known way to measure the electrical activity in the brain. But in that year Austrian psychiatrist Hans Berger invented the electroencephalograph, a machine that amplifies a million times the electrical activity occurring in the brain. This electrical activity, detected by electrodes placed at various points on the scalp, provides the power to drive a pen across paper, producing a record of brain-wave activity called an **electroencephalogram (EEG)**. The **beta wave** is the brain-wave pattern associated with mental or physical activity. The **alpha wave** is associated with deep relaxation, and the **delta wave** with slow-wave (deep) sleep. Figure 2.11 (on page 64) shows the various brain-wave patterns and their associated psychological states.

A recent EEG computerized imaging technique shows the different levels of electrical activity occurring every millisecond on the surface of the brain. It can show an epileptic seizure in progress and can be used to study neural activity in

? *What are some methods that researchers have used to learn about brain function?*

electroencephalogram (EEG) (ee-lek-tro-en-SEFF-uh-lo-gram): A record of brain-wave activity made by the electroencephalograph.

beta wave (BAY-tuh): The brain wave associated with mental or physical activity.

? *What is the electroencephalogram (EEG), and what are three of the brain-wave patterns it reveals?*

alpha wave: The brain wave associated with deep relaxation.

delta wave: The brain wave associated with slow-wave (deep) sleep.

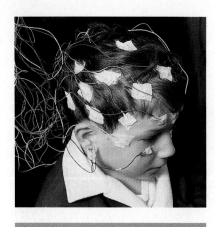

The electroencephalograph (EEG) uses electrodes placed on the scalp to amplify and record electrical activity in the brain.

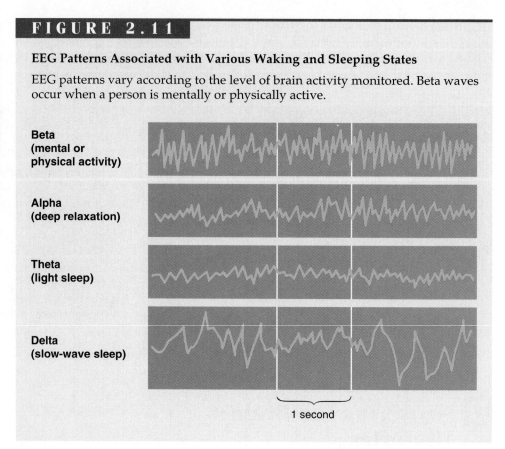

FIGURE 2.11

EEG Patterns Associated with Various Waking and Sleeping States

EEG patterns vary according to the level of brain activity monitored. Beta waves occur when a person is mentally or physically active.

Beta (mental or physical activity)

Alpha (deep relaxation)

Theta (light sleep)

Delta (slow-wave sleep)

1 second

people with learning disabilities, schizophrenia, Alzheimer's disease, sleep disorders, and other neurological problems.

While the EEG is able to detect electrical activity in different areas of the brain, it cannot reveal what is happening in individual neurons. The microelectrode can. A **microelectrode** is a wire so small that it can be inserted into a single neuron without damaging it. Microelectrodes can be used to monitor the electrical activity of a single neuron or to stimulate activity within it. Researchers have used microelectrodes to discover the exact functions of single cells within the primary visual cortex and the primary auditory cortex.

Since the 1970s, a growing number of brain-imaging techniques have been developed.

The CT Scan and Magnetic Resonance Imaging

The patient undergoing a **CT scan (computerized axial tomography)** is placed inside a large, doughnut-shaped structure where an X-ray tube encircles the entire head. The tube shoots pencil-thin X rays through the brain as it completes the circle. A series of computerized, cross-sectional images reveal the structures within the brain (or other parts of the body) as well as abnormalities and injuries, including tumors and old or more recent strokes.

Another technique, **MRI (magnetic resonance imaging)**, produces higher-resolution images without exposing patients to the hazards of X-ray photography (Potts et al., 1993). The MRI is a powerful diagnostic tool that can be used to find abnormalities in the central nervous system and in other systems of the body.

microelectrode: An electrical wire so small that it can be used either to monitor the electrical activity of a single neuron or to stimulate activity within it.

CT scan (computerized axial tomography): A brain-scanning technique involving a rotating X-ray scanner and a high-speed computer analysis that produces slice-by-slice, cross-sectional images of the structure of the brain.

magnetic resonance imaging (MRI): A diagnostic scanning technique that produces high resolution images of the structures of the brain.

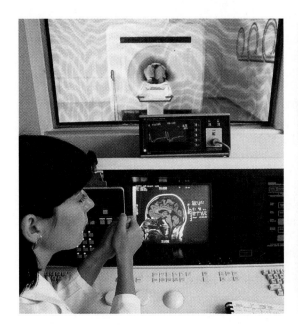

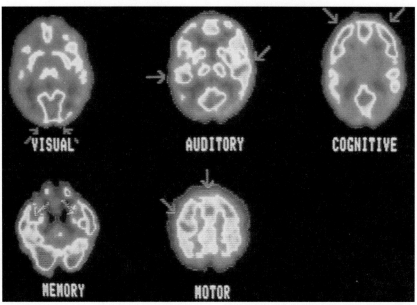

Although the CT scan and MRI do a remarkable job of showing what the brain looks like both inside and out, they cannot reveal what the brain is doing. But other technological marvels can.

The PET Scan and Other Imaging Techniques

The **PET scan (positron-emission tomography)** is a powerful instrument for identifying malfunctions that cause physical and psychological disorders and also for studying normal brain activity (Volkow & Tancredi, 1991). The PET scan can map the patterns of blood flow, oxygen use, and glucose consumption (the food of the brain). It can also show the action of drugs and other biochemical substances in the brain and other bodily organs.

Still, the PET scan can detect only *changes* in blood flow and in oxygen and glucose consumption as they occur in the various brain areas. But many parts of the brain are always active, even when a person is doing nothing observable. How do researchers separate the activity of specific brain locations responsible for seeing, speaking, reading, and so on from the other unrelated brain areas that are active at the same time? Thanks to sophisticated computers, researchers can subtract all other brain activity from the activity involved in the specific mental tasks subjects are performing (Raichle, 1994b).

One new application, functional MRI (fMRI), can image both brain structure and brain activity. It has several advantages over other imaging techniques: It requires nothing (radioactive or otherwise) to be injected into subjects. Its ability to image precise locations of activity clearly is better than PET's. And with the proper equipment, it is capable of ultrafast imaging (Cohen & Bookheimer, 1994).

There are still other imaging devices now available. SQUID (superconducting quantum interference device) images brain activity by measuring magnetic changes produced by the electric current neurons discharge when they fire. Another imaging marvel, MEG (magnetoencephalography), also measures magnetic changes produced by the electrical activity from firing neurons. MEG can image neural activity within the brain as rapidly as it occurs, much faster than PET or fMRI.

MRI (left) is a powerful tool for revealing what the brain looks like. Unlike PET scans, however, it cannot show us what the brain is doing. PET scans (right) show activity in specific areas of the brain.

PET scan (positron-emission tomography): A brain-imaging technique that reveals activity in various parts of the brain, based on the amount of oxygen and glucose consumed.

SQUID is a relatively new brain-imaging tool that measures magnetic changes in the brain.

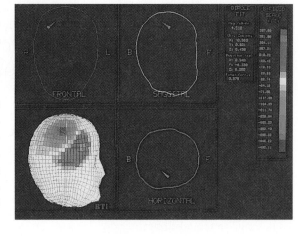

PET pioneer Marcus Raichle (1994a) believes that researchers will begin to use these imaging techniques in various combinations to yield more complete images of brain structure and function.

Brain Damage: Causes and Consequences

Let us recall the question we posed at the beginning of this chapter. How can the brain sustain such massive damage as in the case of Phineas Gage, who survived, while a small bullet fired into the brain in particular places can result in instant death? The precise location of a brain injury is the most important factor in determining whether a person lives or dies. Had the metal rod torn through Gage's brainstem, that would have been the end of him. Brain damage has many causes. Stroke, head injuries, diseases, tumors, and the abuse of drugs can leave people with a variety of disabilities.

Why is a stroke so serious?

Stroke

A stroke is the most common cause of injury to the adult brain and the third most common cause of death. Of some 500,000 people who suffer strokes each year

in the United States, about 150,000 die (Alberts et al., 1990). Another 100,000 to 150,000 are severely and permanently disabled (Zivin & Choi, 1991). Stroke patients may be left with impaired intellect, loss of coordination or sensation, or paralysis. About 25 percent of stroke survivors are left with aphasia.

Stroke occurs when the blood supply to a part of the brain is cut off, depriving that brain area of oxygen and glucose and thus killing many brain cells. Stroke can be caused by a blood clot, hardening of the arteries, or a cerebral hemorrhage brought on by high blood pressure. High doses of stimulants such as amphetamines and cocaine also increase the risk of stroke.

Head Injury

Intensive therapy can help patients recover some abilities lost because of brain damage due to stroke.

Each year more than 300,000 Americans survive injuries that leave them with significant brain damage (Chance, 1986). Impaired motor coordination and language ability are often the most obvious results of head injury. Even more devastating is the loss of intellectual functioning—concentration, memory, reasoning, judgment, and problem-solving and decision-making abilities. Social behavior is frequently affected, as in the case of Phineas Gage, who became irritable, verbally abusive, and irresponsible. The precise disability depends largely on the area of the brain that is affected and the severity of the damage.

stroke: A cardiovascular accident that occurs when the blood supply to the brain is cut off, killing many neurons; the major cause of damage to the adult brain.

Many people who suffer injuries to the head develop epilepsy—a chronic brain disorder that results in recurring seizures and frequently a loss or impairment of consciousness. Grand mal seizures are marked by convulsions and loss of consciousness. Petit mal seizures involve sudden lapses of consciousness lasting several seconds, during which the victim neither falls nor has a convulsion.

Recovering from Brain Damage

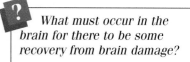

What must occur in the brain for there to be some recovery from brain damage?

Once neurons are completely destroyed, they are gone forever. We are born with our full supply of neurons, and those that are lost are never replaced. If neurons are damaged, however, they can sprout new dendrites and reestablish connections with other neurons to assume some of the functions of the brain cells that were lost. Axons, too, are able to regenerate and grow (Fawcett, 1992).

Some abilities lost through brain damage can be regained if areas near the damaged site take over the lost function. In the case of aphasia, the undamaged hemisphere can sometimes be trained to handle the language function but can rarely restore it to normal. The ability of the brain to reorganize and to compensate for brain damage is termed **plasticity**. Plasticity is greatest in young children before the hemispheres are completely lateralized (Bach-y-Rita & Bach-y-Rita, 1990). Some individuals who have had an entire hemisphere removed early in life because of uncontrollable epilepsy have been able to lead a near-normal intellectual life (Bower, 1988). In one case, a man with only one hemisphere carried a double major in college and graduated with honors.

plasticity: The ability of the brain to reorganize and compensate for brain damage.

Memory Check 2.5

1. The CT scan and MRI are used to:
   a. show the amount of activity in various parts of the brain.
   b. produce images of the structures within the brain.
   c. measure electrical activity in the brain.
   d. observe neural communication at synapses.

2. Which of the following reveals the electrical activity of the brain by producing a record of brain waves?
   a. electroencephalograph   c. PET scan
   b. CT scan   d. MRI

3. Which of the following reveals brain activity and function, rather than the structure of the brain?
   a. CT scan   b. EEG   c. PET scan   d. MRI

4. Match the brain-wave pattern with the state associated with it.

   ____ 1) slow-wave (deep) sleep   a. beta wave
   ____ 2) deep relaxation while   b. delta wave
          awake   c. alpha wave
   ____ 3) physical or mental activity

5. Which of the following is *not* true of stroke?
   a. Stroke is the main cause of injury to the adult brain.
   b. Stroke can cause paralysis and total loss of language ability.
   c. Stroke is caused when the blood supply to part of the brain is cut off.
   d. Although stroke causes many disabilities, it is not life-threatening.

6. Plasticity of the brain increases with age. (true/false)

Answers: 1. b 2. a 3. c 4. 1) b 2) c 3) a 5. d 6. false

◤The Peripheral Nervous System

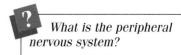

What is the peripheral nervous system?

The **peripheral nervous system (PNS)** is made up of all the nerves that connect the central nervous system to the rest of the body. Without the peripheral nervous system, the brain and spinal cord, encased in their bone coverings, would be isolated and unable to send information to or receive information from other parts of the body. The peripheral nervous system has two subdivisions—the somatic nervous system and the autonomic nervous system. Figure 2.12 (on page 68) shows the subdivisions within the peripheral nervous system.

peripheral nervous system (PNS) (peh-RIF-er-ul): The nerves connecting the central nervous system to the rest of the body.

FIGURE 2.12

The Human Nervous System

The nervous system is divided into two parts: the central nervous system and the peripheral nervous system. The diagram shows the relationships among the parts of the nervous system and provides a brief description of the functions of those parts.

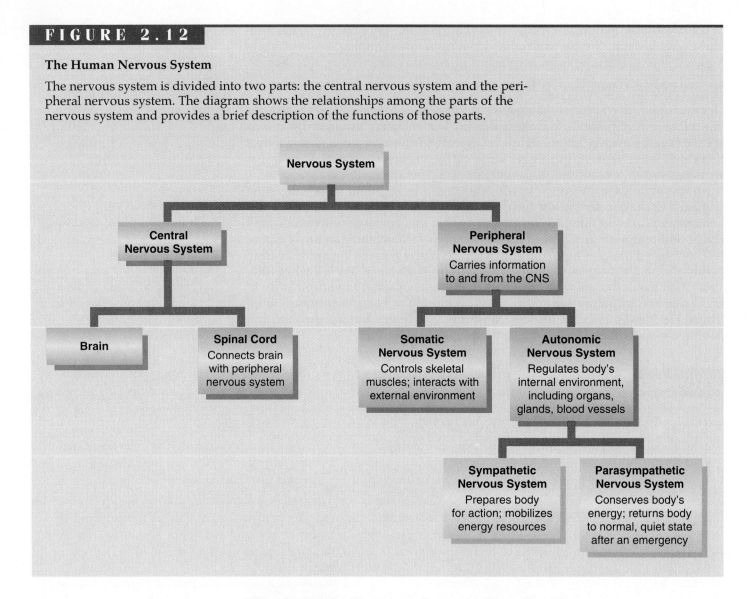

The Somatic Nervous System: For Sensing and Moving

The somatic nervous system consists of (1) all the sensory nerves, which transmit information from the sense receptors—eyes, ears, nose, tongue, and skin—to the central nervous system; and (2) all the motor nerves, which relay messages from the central nervous system to all the skeletal muscles of the body. In short, the nerves of the somatic nervous system make it possible for us to sense our environment and to move, and they are primarily under our conscious control.

> **?** *What are the roles of the sympathetic and parasympathetic nervous systems?*

The Autonomic Nervous System: Doing Its Job without Our Conscious Thought

The word *autonomic* is sometimes misread by students as "automatic," and that is not a bad synonym—because the autonomic nervous system operates quite well automatically, without our being conscious of it. It transmits messages between the central nervous system and the glands, the cardiac (heart) muscle, and the smooth muscles, which are not normally under voluntary control (such as those in the large arteries and the gastrointestinal system).

The autonomic nervous system is further divided into two parts—the sympathetic and the parasympathetic nervous systems. Any time you are under stress or faced with an emergency, the **sympathetic nervous system** automatically mobilizes the body's resources, preparing you for action. This physiological arousal produced by the sympathetic nervous system was named the fight-or-flight response by Walter Cannon. If an ominous-looking stranger started following you and quickened his pace as you turned down a dark, deserted street, your sympathetic nervous system would automatically set to work. Your heart would begin to pound, your pulse rate would increase rapidly, your breathing would quicken, and your digestive system would nearly shut down. The blood flow to your skeletal muscles would be enhanced, and all of your bodily resources would be made ready to handle the emergency—*run!*

But once the emergency is over, something must happen to bring these heightened bodily functions back to normal. The **parasympathetic nervous system** does just that. As a result of its action, your heart stops pounding and slows to normal, your pulse rate and breathing slow down, and your digestive system resumes its normal functioning. As shown in Figure 2.13 (on page 70), the sympathetic and parasympathetic branches act as opposing but complementary forces in the autonomic nervous system. Their balanced functioning is essential for health and survival.

The Endocrine System

We have seen how chemical substances called neurotransmitters exert their influence on the 100 billion or so neurons in the nervous system. There is another system in which chemical substances stimulate and regulate many other important functions in the body. The **endocrine system** is a series of ductless glands, located in various parts of the body, that manufacture and secrete chemical substances known as hormones (from the Greek root meaning "to excite"). A chemical substance is called a **hormone** if it is manufactured and released in one part of the body but has an effect on other parts of the body. Hormones are released into the bloodstream and travel throughout the circulatory system, but each hormone performs its assigned job only when it connects with the body cells having receptors for it. Some of the same chemical substances that are neurotransmitters act as hormones as well—norepinephrine and vasopressin, to name two. Figure 2.14 (on page 71) shows the glands in the endocrine system and their locations in the body.

The Pituitary Gland: The Master Gland, Small as a Pea

The **pituitary gland** rests in the brain just below the hypothalamus and is controlled by it (see Figure 2.14). The pituitary is considered to be the master gland of the body because it releases the hormones that "turn on," or activate, the other glands in the endocrine system—a big job for a tiny structure about the size of a pea. The pituitary also produces the hormone that is responsible for body growth. Too little of this powerful substance will make one a dwarf, while too much will produce a giant.

The Thyroid Gland: Balancing the Body's Metabolism

The thyroid gland rests in the front, lower part of the neck just below the voice box (larynx). The thyroid produces the important hormone thyroxin, which is responsible for keeping the body's metabolism in balance. In other words, thy-

sympathetic nervous system: The division of the autonomic nervous system that mobilizes the body's resources during stress, emergencies, or heavy exertion, preparing the body for action.

parasympathetic nervous system: The division of the autonomic nervous system that is associated with relaxation and the conservation of energy and that brings the heightened bodily responses back to normal following an emergency.

What is the endocrine system, and what are some of the glands within it?

endocrine system (EN-duh-krin): A system of ductless glands in various parts of the body that manufacture and secrete hormones into the bloodstream or lymph fluids, thus affecting cells in other parts of the body.

hormone: A substance manufactured and released in one part of the body that affects other parts of the body.

pituitary gland: The endocrine gland located in the brain and often called the "master gland," which releases hormones that control other endocrine glands and also releases a growth hormone.

FIGURE 2.13

The Autonomic Nervous System

The autonomic nervous system consists of (1) the sympathetic nervous system, which mobilizes the body's resources during emergencies or during stress, and (2) the parasympathetic nervous system, which is associated with relaxation and which brings the heightened bodily responses back to normal after an emergency. This diagram shows the opposite effects of the sympathetic and parasympathetic nervous systems on various parts of the body.

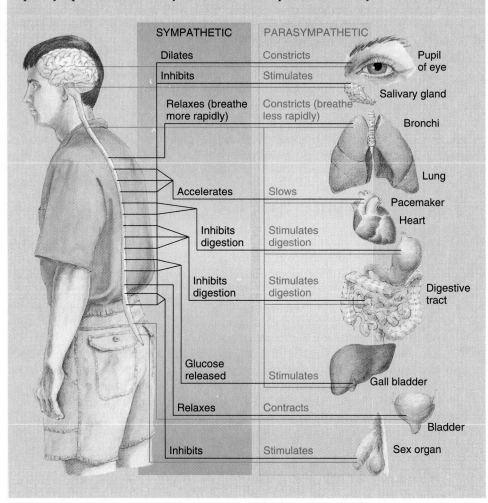

roxin regulates the rate at which we metabolize, or transform into energy, the food we eat. Too much thyroxin can result in hyperthyroidism, a condition in which people are nervous and excitable, find it hard to be still and relax, and are usually thin. Hypothyroidism, an underproduction of thyroxin, has just the opposite effect. An adult with hypothyroidism may feel sluggish, lack energy, and tend to be overweight.

The Adrenal Glands: Necessary for Fight or Flight

adrenal glands (ah-DREE-nal): A pair of endocrine glands that release hormones that prepare the body for emergencies and stressful situations and also release small amounts of the sex hormones.

Lower in the body are the two **adrenal glands**, which rest just above the kidneys as shown in Figure 2.14. The adrenal glands produce epinephrine and norepinephrine, two hormones that activate the sympathetic nervous system. The

FIGURE 2.14

The Endocrine System

The endocrine system is a series of glands, which manufacture and secrete hormones. The hormones travel through the circulatory system and have important effects on many bodily functions.

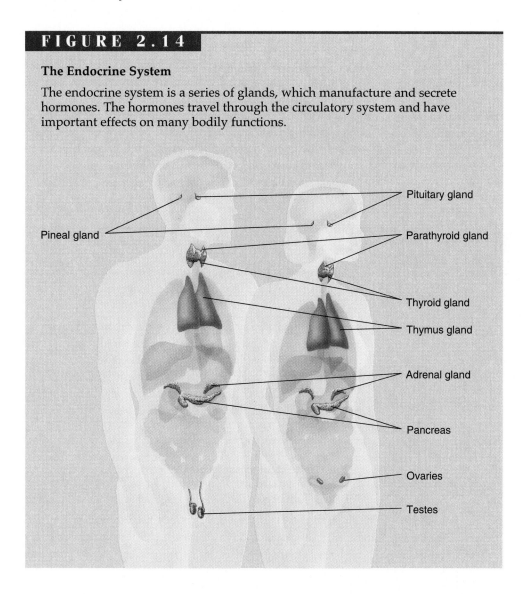

adrenal glands release the corticoids, which control the important salt balance in the body and also release small amounts of the sex hormones.

The Pancreas: Our Insulin Factory

Curving around between the small intestine and the stomach is the pancreas (see Figure 2.14). The pancreas regulates the body's blood sugar levels by releasing the hormones insulin and glucagon into the bloodstream. The pancreas also produces digestive enzymes. In people with diabetes, too little insulin is produced. Without insulin to break down the sugars we ingest, the level of blood sugar can get dangerously high. In hypoglycemia, the opposite effect occurs—too much insulin is produced, resulting in low blood sugar. Both conditions may be partly controlled by diet, but in many cases the diabetic must also take daily insulin injections.

The Sex Glands: The Gonads

The gonads are the sex glands—the ovaries in females and the testes in males (see Figure 2.14). Activated by the pituitary gland, the gonads release sex hormones that make reproduction possible and that are responsible for the secondary sex characteristics—pubic and underarm hair in both sexes, breasts in females, and facial hair and a deepened voice in males.

Androgens, the male sex hormones, influence sexual motivation. Estrogen and progesterone, the female sex hormones, help regulate the menstrual cycle. Although both males and females have androgens and estrogens, males have considerably more androgens, and females have considerably more estrogens. The sex hormones and their effects are discussed in more detail in Chapter 11.

Biology and behavior are intimately related. However, there is much more to the scientific study of behavior and mental processes than the biological connection can teach us. Other chapters in this text expand on other aspects of behavior and mental processes.

Memory Check 2.6

1. The _____ nervous system connects the brain and spinal cord to the rest of the body.
   a. central   c. somatic
   b. peripheral   d. autonomic

2. The _____ nervous system mobilizes the body's resources during times of stress; the _____ nervous system brings the heightened bodily responses back to normal when the emergency is over.
   a. somatic; autonomic
   b. autonomic; somatic
   c. sympathetic; parasympathetic
   d. parasympathetic; sympathetic

3. The endocrine glands secrete _____ directly into the _____.
   a. hormones; bloodstream
   b. enzymes; digestive tract
   c. enzymes; bloodstream
   d. hormones; digestive tract

4. Match the endocrine gland with the appropriate description.
   ____ 1) keeps body's metabolism in balance
   ____ 2) acts as a master gland that activates the other glands
   ____ 3) regulates the blood sugar
   ____ 4) makes reproduction possible
   ____ 5) releases hormones that prepare the body for emergencies

   a. pituitary gland
   b. adrenal glands
   c. gonads
   d. thyroid gland
   e. pancreas

Answers: 1. b 2. c 3. a 4. 1) d 2) a 3) e 4) c 5) b

APPLICATIONS · APPLICATIONS · APPLICATIONS

Handedness—Does It Make a Difference?

If you are left-handed, you are in good company. Alexander the Great, Michelangelo, Leonardo da Vinci, and Benjamin Franklin are among the better-known lefties of earlier centuries. Other famous lefties include Mark Twain, Albert Einstein, Babe Ruth, and Marilyn Monroe; among left-handers of more recent times are Martina Navratilova, Whoopi Goldberg, and Tom Cruise.

The majority of people—about 90 percent of the world's population—are right-handed. Evidently this has been true for at least 50 centuries (Coren & Porac, 1977). Left-handedness occurs more often in males than in females. People who are left-handed are generally also left-footed, and to a lesser extent left-eyed and left-eared as well. There is a difference in the motor control provided by the two hemispheres of the brain. Thus, in a person whose left hand is dominant, the right hemisphere is providing superior motor control for that hand.

Other animals, such as monkeys, also exhibit handedness, but there tends to be a more even distribution of right- and left-handedness in animal species other than humans. Scholars and scientists have long wondered why such a small percentage of humans are left-handed, and a number of possible explanations have been suggested.

Handedness: Inherited or Learned?

Some researchers propose a genetic cause (Annett, 1985; Levy & Nagylaki, 1972); others claim that handedness is learned (Blau, 1946; Collins, 1970). No theory yet proposed is able to explain all the facts, although there is strong evidence that there is a genetic element in handedness. Hepper and others (1990) found that a hand preference is already apparent in the womb. Of the fetuses they observed, 94.6 percent were sucking their right thumb, while only 5.4 percent were sucking their left thumb.

Geschwind and Behan (1982) found further evidence for a genetic contribution to handedness. According to Geschwind, a genetically based excess of testosterone, or an increased sensitivity to testosterone, slows the growth of the left hemisphere and thereby allows greater development of the right hemisphere, which may lead to left-handedness.

Differences: Left and Right

Investigators have identified a number of physiological differences between right-handed and left-handed people. On the average, the corpus callosum of left-handers is 11 percent larger and contains up to 2.5 million more nerve fibers than that of right-handers (Witelson, 1985). In about 60 percent of left-handers, language functions are controlled by the left hemisphere; in 25 percent, by the right hemisphere; and in about 15 percent, by both hemispheres. In general, the two sides of the brain are less specialized in left-handers (Hellige et al., 1994). Because of this characteristic, left-handers tend to experience less language loss following an injury to either hemisphere (Geschwind, 1979); and they are more likely to recover, because the undamaged hemisphere can more easily take over the speech functions.

In many respects, left-handed people are at a disadvantage. Geschwind and Behan (1982) found that left-handers are 12 times more likely than right-handers to stutter and have learning disabilities such as dyslexia. Left-handers are also 2½ times more likely to have autoimmune diseases such as allergies, and they are more likely to suffer from migraine headaches, epilepsy, mental retardation, depression, and other mental disorders. A disproportionate number of premature and low-birth-weight infants are left-handed. It has even been suggested that, on the average, left-handers have a shorter life span than right-handers (Coren & Halpern, 1991). This hypothesis is somewhat controversial, and research on the subject continues (Halpern & Coren, 1993; L. J. Harris, 1993).

Left in a Right-handed World

Left-handedness is also associated with a variety of positive traits. Benbow and Stanley (1983) found that over 20 percent of 12- and 13-year-olds with exceptionally high scores on the math portion of the SAT were left-handed. Left-handers are also overrepresented among musicians, artists, engineers, mathematicians, and major-league baseball players. And in the 1990s, it is clear that left-handedness is no barrier to being elected to the highest office in the land. In 1992, all three of the presidential candidates—Bill Clinton, George Bush, and Ross Perot—were left-handed.

Left-handers are five times more likely to suffer serious accidents than right-handers, and they are sometimes said to be clumsier than right-handers. This is probably because they must function in a world designed for right-handers (Coren, 1989). For example, the seats found in many college classrooms have a large writing surface at the end of the right arm, allowing right-handed people to rest their arms while writing. Left-handed people are cramped by this arrangement, which forces them to sit at an awkward angle

and keep both arms on the writing surface. In cars with a standard shift, the gear shift is located on the right side of the driver's seat. Most cameras are designed for right-handed people. The markings on measuring

cups, thermometers, and other measuring devices cannot be read unless the object is held in the right hand. On many musical instruments, the melody must be played by the right hand, which is assumed to have greater strength and dexterity. Table settings and doorknobs also assume right-handedness. The bias toward right-handedness even extends to feet: The arrangement of pedals in a car favors right-footed people.

Most left-handed people are able to adapt to these conditions. Some actually become ambidextrous as a result of using both hands for certain activities (working with tools, for example). Eating and writing, however, are rarely performed with the "other" hand. Fortunately some items—tools and sports equipment—are designed specifically for left-handers.

Most children show a consistent preference for one hand over the other by the age of 5; some, however, begin to rely on the use of one hand by 18 months. In earlier decades in the United States and in some other parts of the world today, efforts were made to train left-handed children to eat or write with their right hand. Today most experts on child development agree that it is harmful, if not futile, to interfere with the hand preference of a young child. It can cause emotional distress and may lead to speech or reading problems (Herron, 1980).

Thinking Critically

Evaluation

Using your knowledge about how the human brain has been studied in the past and today, point out the advantages and the disadvantages of the older investigative methods—the case study, the autopsy, the study of people with brain injuries or who have had brain surgery (including the split-brain operation). Follow the same procedure to discuss the more modern techniques—EEG, CT scan, MRI, and PET scan.

Point/Counterpoint

A continuing controversial issue is the ethical question of whether animals should be used in biological research. Review the chapter and find each

occasion in which animals were used to advance our knowledge of the brain. Using what you have read in this chapter and any other information you have acquired, prepare arguments to support both of the following positions:

a. The use of animals in research projects is ethical and justifiable because of the possible benefits to humankind.
b. The use of animals in research projects is not ethical or justifiable on the grounds of possible benefits to humankind.

Psychology in Your Life

How would your life change if you had a massive stroke in your left hemi-

sphere? How would it change if the stroke were in your right hemisphere? Which stroke would be more tragic for you, and why?

Chapter Summary and Review

The Neurons and the Neurotransmitters

 What is a neuron, and what are its three parts?

A neuron is a specialized cell that conducts messages through the nervous system. Its three main parts are the cell body, dendrites, and axon.

 What is a synapse?

A synapse is the junction where the axon terminal of a sending neuron communicates with a receiving neuron across the synaptic cleft.

 What is the action potential?

The action potential is the firing of a neuron that results when the charge within the neuron becomes more positive than the charge outside the cell's membrane.

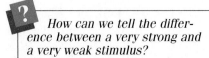 *What are neurotransmitters, and what role do they play in the transmission of signals from one neuron to another?*

Neurotransmitters are chemicals released into the synaptic cleft from the axon terminal of the sending neuron. They cross the synaptic cleft and bind to receptor sites on the receiving neuron, influencing the cell to fire or not to fire.

What are some of the ways in which neurotransmitters affect our behavior, and what are some of the major neurotransmitters?

Neurotransmitters regulate the actions of glands and muscles, affect learning and memory, promote sleep, stimulate mental and physical alertness, and influence our moods and emotions from depression to euphoria. Some of the major neurotransmitters are acetyl-

choline, dopamine, norepinephrine, serotonin, glutamate, GABA, and endorphins.

How can we tell the difference between a very strong and a very weak stimulus?

A strong stimulus will cause many more neurons to fire and to fire much more rapidly than a weak stimulus will.

Key Terms

neuron (p. 40)
cell body (p. 41)
dendrites (p. 41)
axon (p. 41)
synapse (p. 41)
resting potential (p. 42)
action potential (p. 42)
neurotransmitter (p. 43)
receptor site (p. 43)
reuptake (p. 44)
acetylcholine (p. 44)
dopamine (p. 45)
norepinephrine (p. 45)

serotonin (p. 45)
endorphins (p. 46)
myelin sheath (p. 46)
glial cells (p. 47)

The Central Nervous System

Why is an intact spinal cord important to normal functioning?

The spinal cord is an extension of the brain connecting it to the peripheral nervous system so that sensory information can reach the brain, and messages from the brain can reach the muscles and glands.

What are the crucial functions handled by the brainstem?

The brainstem contains (1) the medulla, which controls heartbeat, breathing, blood pressure, coughing and swallowing, and (2) the reticular formation, which plays a crucial role in arousal and attention.

What are the primary functions of the cerebellum?

The main functions of the cerebellum are to execute smooth, skilled movements and to regulate muscle tone and posture.

What is the primary role of the thalamus?

The thalamus acts as a relay station for information flowing into or out of the higher brain centers.

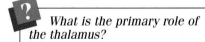

What are some of the processes regulated by the hypothalamus?

The hypothalamus controls the pituitary gland and regulates hunger, thirst, sexual behavior, body temperature, and a variety of emotional behaviors.

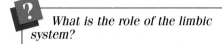

What is the role of the limbic system?

The limbic system is a group of structures in the brain, including the amygdala and the hippocampus, which are collectively involved in emotion, memory, and motivation.

Key Terms

central nervous system (p. 48)
spinal cord (p. 48)
brainstem (p. 49)
medulla (p. 49)
reticular formation (p. 49)
cerebellum (p. 50)
thalamus (p. 50)
hypothalamus (p. 51)
limbic system (p. 51)
amygdala (p. 51)
hippocampus (p. 51)

The Cerebral Hemispheres

What are the cerebral hemispheres, the corpus callosum, and the cerebral cortex?

The cerebral hemispheres are the two halves of the cerebrum, connected by the corpus callosum and covered by the cerebral cortex, which is responsible for higher mental processes such as language, memory, and thinking.

What are some of the main areas within the frontal lobes, and what are their functions?

The frontal lobes contain (1) the motor cortex, which controls voluntary motor activity; (2) Broca's area, which functions in speech production; and (3) the frontal association areas, which are involved in thinking, motivation, planning for the future, impulse control, and emotional responses.

What are the primary functions of the parietal lobes in general and the somatosensory cortex in particular?

The parietal lobes are involved in the reception and processing of touch stimuli. They contain the somatosensory cortex, where touch, pressure, temperature, and pain register.

What are the primary functions of the occipital lobes in general and the primary visual cortex in particular?

The occipital lobes are involved in the reception and interpretation of visual information. They contain the primary visual cortex, where vision registers in the cerebral cortex.

What are the major areas within the temporal lobes, and what are their functions?

The temporal lobes contain (1) the primary auditory cortex, where hearing registers in the cortex; (2) Wernicke's area, which is involved in comprehending the spoken word and in formulating coherent speech and written language; and (3) association areas, where memories are stored and auditory stimuli are interpreted.

Key Terms

cerebrum (p. 53)
cerebral hemispheres (p. 53)
corpus callosum (p. 53)
cerebral cortex (p. 54)
association areas (p. 54)
frontal lobes (p. 54)
motor cortex (p. 55)
Broca's area (p. 56)
Broca's aphasia (p. 56)
aphasia (p. 56)
parietal lobes (p. 56)
somatosensory cortex (p. 56)

occipital lobes (p. 57)
primary visual cortex (p. 57)
temporal lobes (p. 57)
primary auditory cortex (p. 57)
Wernicke's area (p. 57)
Wernicke's aphasia (p. 58)

Specialization of the Cerebral Hemispheres

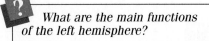 *What are the main functions of the left hemisphere?*

The left hemisphere controls the right side of the body, coordinates complex movements, and handles most of the language functions, including speaking, writing, reading, and understanding of the spoken word.

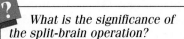 *What are the primary functions of the right hemisphere?*

The right hemisphere controls the left side of the body; is specialized for visual-spatial perception, singing, and interpreting nonverbal behavior; and is more active in the recognition and expression of emotion.

What is the significance of the split-brain operation?

In the split-brain operation a surgeon cuts the corpus callosum, which prevents the transfer of information between the hemispheres. Research on split-brain patients has extended our knowledge of the functions of the hemispheres.

Key Terms

lateralization (p. 59)
left hemisphere (p. 59)
right hemisphere (p. 59)
split-brain operation (p. 61)

Discovering the Brain's Mysteries

What are some methods that researchers have used to learn about brain function?

Researchers have learned about brain function from clinical studies of patients, through electrical stimulation of the brain, and from studies using the EEG, microelectrode, CT scan, MRI, and PET scan.

What is the electroencephalogram (EEG), and what are three of the brain-wave patterns it reveals?

The electroencephalogram (EEG) is a record of brain-wave activity. Three normal brain-wave patterns are the beta wave, alpha wave, and delta wave.

Key Terms

electroencephalogram (EEG) (p. 63)
beta wave (p. 63)
alpha wave (p. 63)
delta wave (p. 63)
microelectrode (p. 64)
CT scan (p. 64)
MRI (p. 64)
PET scan (p. 65)

Brain Damage: Causes and Consequences

 Why is a stroke so serious?

In the United States stroke is the most common cause of damage to the adult brain, is the third leading cause of death, and leaves many of its victims with paralysis and/or aphasia.

What must occur in the brain for there to be some recovery from brain damage?

For some recovery from brain damage to occur, (1) damaged neurons may sprout new dendrites and reestablish connections with other neurons, (2) areas near the damaged site may take over the lost function, or (3) the undamaged hemisphere may assume the lost language function (as in aphasia).

Key Terms

stroke (p. 66)
plasticity (p. 67)

The Peripheral Nervous System

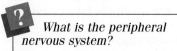 *What is the peripheral nervous system?*

The peripheral nervous system connects the central nervous system to the rest of the body. It has two subdivisions: (1) the somatic nervous system, which consists of the nerves that make it possible for us to sense and move; and (2) the autonomic nervous system.

What are the roles of the sympathetic and parasympathetic nervous systems?

The autonomic nervous system has two parts: (1) the sympathetic nervous system, which mobilizes the body's resources during emergencies or during stress; and (2) the parasympathetic nervous system, which is associated with relaxation and brings the heightened bodily responses back to normal after an emergency.

Key Terms

peripheral nervous system (p. 67)
sympathetic nervous system (p. 69)
parasympathetic nervous system (p. 69)

The Endocrine System

What is the endocrine system, and what are some of the glands within it?

The endocrine system is a system of glands in various parts of the body that manufacture hormones and secrete them into the bloodstream. The hormones then affect cells in other parts of the body. The pituitary gland releases hormones that control other glands in the endocrine system and also releases a growth hormone. The thyroid gland produces thyroxin, which regulates metabolism. The adrenal glands release epinephrine and norepinephrine, which prepare the body for emergencies and stressful situations; those glands also release small amounts of the sex hormones. The pancreas produces insulin and regulates blood sugar. The gonads are the sex glands, which produce the sex hormones and make reproduction possible.

Key Terms

endocrine system (p. 69)
hormone (p. 69)
pituitary gland (p. 69)
adrenal glands (p. 70)

3

SENSATION AND PERCEPTION

CHAPTER OUTLINE

Sensation: The Sensory World

The Absolute Threshold: To Sense or Not to Sense

The Difference Threshold: Detecting Differences

Signal Detection Theory

Transduction: Transforming Sensory Stimuli into Neural Impulses

Sensory Adaptation

Vision

Light: What We See

The Eye: Window to the Visual Sensory World

Color Vision: A Multicolored World

Hearing

Sound: What We Hear

The Ear: More to It Than Meets the Eye

Theories of Hearing: How Hearing Works

Bone Conduction: Hearing Sound Vibrations through the Bones

Hearing Loss: Kinds and Causes

Smell and Taste

Smell: Sensing Scents

Taste: What the Tongue Can Tell

Our Other Senses

The Skin Senses: Information from Our Natural Clothing

Pain: Physical Hurts

The Kinesthetic Sense: Keeping Track of Our Body Parts

The Vestibular Sense: Sensing Up and Down and Changes in Speed

Perception: Ways of Perceiving

The Gestalt Principles of Perceptual Organization

Perceptual Constancy

Depth Perception: Perceiving

What's Up Close and Far Away

Perception of Motion

Extraordinary Perceptions: Puzzling Perceptions

World of Psychology: Cultural Differences in the Perception of Illusions

Additional Influences on Perception

Bottom-Up and Top-Down Processing

The Role of Psychological Factors in Perception

Subliminal Persuasion and Extrasensory Perception

Subliminal Persuasion: Does It Work?

Extrasensory Perception: Does It Exist?

Applications: Noise and Hearing Loss—Bad Vibrations

Thinking Critically

Chapter Summary and Review

The man called S.B. had never seen a sunrise, a flower, a smile, or even his own face, for he had lost his sight in both eyes when he was only 10 months old. Despite his blindness, S.B. had managed to live a fairly full and happy life. He could get around on his own, cross streets, and even ride a bicycle with his friend's hand on his shoulder to guide him. He read Braille, and he loved to make things with tools in the small shed he used as a workshop.

All his life S.B. had wondered what it would be like to see. Then, when he was 50 years old, he learned that his useless, opaque corneas could be replaced through a cornea transplant. Finally the miracle of sight he had dreamed about would be a reality.

When the surgeon first removed the bandages from S.B.'s eyes, people and objects were little more than large blurs to him. But the operation was successful, and after a few days S.B. could see quite well. He could walk up and down the hospital corridors without using a cane or holding onto the wall. Soon he was able to see and recognize objects by sight that he already knew well by touch. But all was not well.

S.B. had difficulty recognizing unfamiliar objects and things he had never touched. He never learned to read by

sight, although he could recognize numbers and capital letters. S.B. had trouble perceiving distance. From the window of his hospital room he watched the cars and trucks pass in the street below. He thought his feet would touch the ground if he hung from the windowsill with his hands, yet his window was nearly 60 feet above the ground.

The ending of S.B.'s story is not a happy one. The world looked drab to him, and he was upset by the imperfections he saw. Objects he had once imagined to be perfect now had disappointing defects. He could no longer cross streets because seeing cars whizzing by terrified him. Often he would not even bother to turn on the lights at night, for he preferred to sit in his more comfortable world of darkness. As time passed, S.B. became more and more depressed and withdrawn. Within 3 years after the cornea transplant, he died. (Adapted from Gregory, 1978.)

> ? **What is the difference between sensation and perception?**

Are you surprised that the miracle in S.B.'s life, the gift of sight, turned out to be hardly a gift at all? The surgeons were able to give him the sensation of sight but, sadly, not the 50 years of visual perceptual experience he had missed.

Sensation and perception are intimately related in everyday experience, but they are not the same. **Sensation** is the process through which the senses detect visual, auditory, and other sensory stimuli and transmit them to the brain. **Perception** is the process by which sensory information is actively organized and interpreted by the brain. Sensation furnishes the raw material of sensory experience, while perception provides the finished product.

To a large extent we must learn to perceive, and people whose sight has been restored differ greatly in their ability to develop useful perception. S.B.'s life shows dramatically the great gap between receiving sensory information—sensation—and the ability to give it meaning, the process of perception. For many who regain their vision, it is truly a remarkable gift; but for others like S.B., gaining sight can be a major disappointment.

In this chapter we will explore the world of sensation, with a focus on the five primary senses—vision, hearing, touch, taste, and smell—along with such secondary senses as balance and pain. You will learn how the senses detect sensory information and how this sensory information is actively organized and interpreted by the brain. We begin with a closer look at sensation.

sensation: The process through which the senses pick up visual, auditory, and other sensory stimuli and transmit them to the brain; sensory information that has registered in the brain but has not been interpreted.

perception: The process by which sensory information is actively organized and interpreted by the brain.

Sensation: The Sensory World

Our senses serve as ports of entry for all information about our world. Virtually everything we call experience is detected initially by our senses. Yet it is amazing how little of this sensory world we actually sense. For example, we see only a thin slice of the vast spectrum of electromagnetic energy. With the unaided eye we cannot see microwaves, X rays, or ultraviolet light. We are unable to hear the

80

ultrasonic sound of a dog whistle, and our ears can detect a scant 20 percent of the sounds a dolphin or a bat can hear. Nor can we see the outline of a warm-blooded animal from its infrared heat pattern at night, but rattlesnakes and other pit vipers can. Yet all of these sensory stimuli exist in the real, physical world.

No matter which of our senses we select for comparison, humans are not at the top of the list for quality or sensitivity. Some animals have a superior sense of hearing (bats and dolphins); others have sharper vision (hawks); still others have a superior sense of smell (bloodhounds); and so on. Nevertheless, we humans have remarkable sensory abilities and superior abilities of perception.

The Absolute Threshold: To Sense or Not to Sense

What is the softest sound you can hear, the dimmest light you can see, the most diluted substance you can taste? What is the lightest touch you can feel, the faintest odor you can smell? Researchers in sensory psychology and psychophysics have performed many experiments over the years to answer these questions. Their research has established measures for the senses known as absolute thresholds. Just as the threshold of a doorway is the dividing point between being outside a room and inside, the **absolute threshold** of a sense marks the difference between not being able to hear a sound (or see a light) and being just barely able to hear it (or see it). Psychologists have arbitrarily defined this absolute threshold as the minimum amount of sensory stimulation that can be detected 50 percent of the time. The absolute thresholds established for the five primary senses in humans are (1) for vision, a candle flame 30 miles away on a clear night; (2) for hearing, a watch ticking 20 feet away; (3) for taste, 1 teaspoon of sugar dissolved in 2 gallons of water; (4) for smell, a single drop of perfume in a three-room house; and (5) for touch, a bee's wing falling a distance of 1 centimeter onto your cheek.

Important as it is, the absolute threshold, once crossed, says nothing about the broad range of sensory experiences. To sense or not to sense—that is the only question the absolute threshold answers. But read on—there are other questions to be answered.

The Difference Threshold: Detecting Differences

If you are listening to music, the very fact that you can hear it means that the absolute threshold has been crossed. But how much must the volume be turned up or down for you to notice a difference? Or, if you are carrying a load of books, how much weight must be added or subtracted for you to be able to sense that your load is heavier or lighter? The **difference threshold** is a measure of the smallest increase or decrease in a physical stimulus that is required to produce the **just noticeable difference (JND)**. The JND is the smallest change in sensation that we are able to detect 50 percent of the time. If you were holding a 5-pound weight and 1 pound were added, you could easily notice the difference. But if you were holding 100 pounds and 1 additional pound were added, you could not sense the difference. Why not? A pound is a pound, isn't it?

More than 100 years ago, researcher Ernst Weber observed that the JND for all our senses depends on a proportion or percentage of change rather than a fixed amount of change. This observation became known as **Weber's law**. A weight we are holding must increase or decrease by a ratio of $\frac{1}{50}$, or 2 percent, for us to notice the difference. According to Weber's Law, the greater the original stimulus, the more it must be increased or decreased for us to tell the difference.

> ? *What is the difference between the absolute threshold and the difference threshold?*

absolute threshold: The minimum amount of sensory stimulation that can be detected 50 percent of the time.

difference threshold: The smallest increase or decrease in a physical stimulus required to produce a difference in sensation that is noticeable 50 percent of the time.

just noticeable difference (JND): The smallest change in sensation that we are able to detect 50 percent of the time.

Weber's law: The law stating that the just noticeable difference (JND) for all our senses depends on a proportion or percentage of change in a stimulus rather than on a fixed amount of change.

signal detection theory: The view that detection of a sensory stimulus involves both discriminating a stimulus from background "noise" and deciding whether the stimulus is actually present.

The difference threshold is not the same for all the senses. We need a very large (⅕, or 20-percent) difference to detect some changes in taste. In contrast, if you were listening to music, you would notice a difference if a tone became slightly higher or lower in pitch by only one-third of 1 percent.

Aren't some people more sensitive to sensory changes than others? Yes, the difference thresholds for the various senses are not the same for all people. In fact, there are great individual differences. Expert wine tasters would know if a particular vintage was a little too sweet, even if it varied by only a fraction of the 20-percent change. Professionally trained musicians would know if they were singing or playing slightly out of tune long before the one-third of 1 percent difference in pitch appeared. Actually, Weber's law best fits people with average sensitivities, and sensory stimuli that are neither very strong (loud thunder) nor very weak (a faint whisper).

Signal Detection Theory

You may have realized that the classic methods in psychophysics for measuring sensory thresholds have a serious limitation. They focus exclusively on the physical stimulus—how strong or weak it is or how much the stimulus must change for the difference to be noticed. But even within the same individual, sensory capabilities are sharper and duller from time to time and under differing conditions. Factors that affect the ability of people to detect a sensory signal are, in addition to the strength of the stimulus, their motivation to detect it, their previous experience, and their expectation that it will occur, as well as their alertness or level of fatigue.

Another approach takes into account these factors. **Signal detection theory** is the view that the detection of a sensory stimulus involves both discriminating that stimulus from background "noise" and deciding whether the stimulus is actually present. Deciding whether a stimulus is present depends partly on the probability that the stimulus will occur and partly on the potential gain or loss associated with deciding that it is present or absent.

Suppose you were given the description of a cousin you had never seen before and were asked to pick her up at the gate when her plane arrived at the airport. Your task would be to scan a sea of faces for someone fitting the description and then to decide which of the several people who fit the description was actually your cousin. All the other faces and objects in your field of vision would be considered background noise. How sure you would have to be before you approached someone would depend on several factors—the embarrassment you might feel approaching the wrong person as opposed to the distress you would feel if you failed to find your cousin.

Signal detection theory has special relevance to people in many occupations—air traffic controllers, police officers, military personnel on guard duty, medical professionals, poultry inspectors, to name a few. Whether these professionals detect certain stimuli can have important consequences for the health and welfare of us all.

How are sensory stimuli in the environment experienced as sensations?

Transduction: Transforming Sensory Stimuli into Neural Impulses

You may be surprised to learn that our eyes do not actually see; nor do our ears hear. Our sense organs provide only the beginning point of sensation that must be completed by the brain. As you learned in Chapter 2, specific clusters of neurons in specialized parts of the brain must be stimulated for us to see, hear, taste, and so on. Yet the brain itself cannot respond directly to light, sound waves, odors, and tastes. How, then, does it get the message? The answer is through the sensory receptors.

All our senses are equipped with specialized cells called **sensory receptors**, which detect and respond to one type of sensory stimuli—light, sound waves, odors, and so on. Then, through a process known as **transduction**, the receptors change or convert the sensory stimulation into neural impulses, the electrochemical language of the brain. The neural impulses are then transmitted to their own special location in the brain, such as the primary visual cortex for vision or the primary auditory cortex for hearing. We experience a sensation only when the appropriate part of the brain is stimulated. Our sense receptors provide the essential link between the physical sensory world and the brain.

Sensory Adaptation

All of our senses are more receptive, more finely tuned, to changes in sensory stimuli than to sameness. After a time the sensory receptors grow accustomed to constant, unchanging levels of stimuli—sights, sounds, smells—so that we notice them less and less, or not at all. This process of becoming less sensitive to an unchanging sensory stimulus over time is known as **sensory adaptation**.

In going for a swim, when you first enter the water, the temperature receptors in your skin may vigorously signal "ice water." But gradually sensory adaptation occurs and the water feels comfortable. Similarly, you have undoubtedly noticed the distinctive odor of your home when you first walk through the door, but after a few minutes you are not aware of it. A continuous odor will stimulate the smell receptors to respond only for a while. Then, if there is no change in the odors, the receptors will steadily diminish their firing rate, and smell adaptation will occur. However, sensory adaptation is not likely to occur in the presence of very strong stimuli—the smell of ammonia, an ear-splitting sound, or the taste of rancid food.

sensory receptors: Specialized cells in each sense organ that detect and respond to sensory stimuli—light, sound, odors, etc.—and transduce (convert) the stimuli into neural impulses.

transduction: The process by which sensory receptors convert sensory stimulation—light, sound, odors, etc.—into neural impulses.

sensory adaptation: The process of becoming less sensitive to an unchanging sensory stimulus over time.

People who swim in icy water experience a degree of sensory adaptation, which helps their bodies adjust to the frigid temperature. What other examples of sensory adaptation can you think of?

Memory Check 3.1

1. The process through which the senses detect sensory information and transmit it to the brain is called (sensation, perception).

2. The point at which you can barely sense a stimulus 50 percent of the time is called the (absolute, difference) threshold.

3. The difference threshold is the same for all individuals. (true/false)

4. Which of the following is *not* true of sensory receptors?
   a. They are specialized to detect certain sensory stimuli.
   b. They transduce sensory stimuli into neural impulses.

c. They are located in the brain.
d. They provide the link between the physical sensory world and the brain.

5. The process by which a sensory stimulus is converted into a neural impulse is called _____.

6. Each morning when Jackie goes to work at the dry cleaners, she smells the strong odor of cleaning fluid. After she is there for a few minutes, she is no longer aware of it. What accounts for this?
   a. signal detection theory
   b. sensory adaptation
   c. transduction
   d. the just noticeable difference

Answers: 1. sensation 2. absolute 3. false 4. c 5. transduction 6. b

 **ision**

For most of us, vision is our most valued sensory experience, and it is the sense that has been most investigated. But, before looking at how we see, consider *what* we see. We cannot see any object unless light is reflected from it or given off by it.

Light: What We See

Light is one form of electromagnetic rays made up of tiny light particles called photons, which travel in waves. But light is only a small portion of the electromagnetic energies (see Figure 3.1). They range from the shortest cosmic rays, 10 trillionths of an inch, to the progressively longer X rays, ultraviolet rays, infrared rays, radar

FIGURE 3.1

The Electromagnetic Spectrum

The electromagnetic spectrum is composed of waves ranging in wavelength from many miles long (radio and other broadcast bands) to only 10 trillionths of an inch (cosmic rays). Our eyes can perceive only a very thin brand of electromagnetic waves known as the visible spectrum.

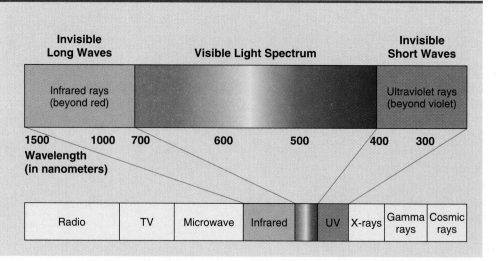

waves, microwaves, radio waves, and other broadcast bands whose waves are many miles long. The vast majority of these waves are either too long or too short for humans and other animals to see. Our eyes can respond only to a very narrow band of electromagnetic waves, a band called the **visible spectrum**.

The length of a light wave primarily determines the color we perceive. The shortest light waves we can see appear violet, and the longest ones we see are red. *What* we see is confined to the visible spectrum, but *how* we see depends on the many parts of the eye and brain that bring us the world of sight.

The Eye: Window to the Visual Sensory World

The eye is our most important sensory connection to the world. Vision provides most of the information on which our brain feeds. Look at the parts of the eye (shown in Figure 3.2), and next read the role each structure plays in vision.

The Cornea, Iris, and Pupil: Up Front in the Eye

The round, globe-shaped human eyeball measures about 1 inch in diameter. Bulging from its front surface is the **cornea**—the tough, transparent, protective layer covering the front of the eye. About the size of a dime, the cornea performs the first step in vision by bending the light rays inward. It herds the light rays through the pupil—the small, dark opening in the center of the iris.

The iris is the circular, colored part of the eye. Two muscles in the iris dilate and contract the pupil and thus regulate the amount of light entering the eye. Although the pupil never closes completely, in very bright light it can contract to the size of the head of a pin; in very dim light it can dilate to the size of a pencil

> **?** *How do the cornea, the iris, and the pupil function in vision?*

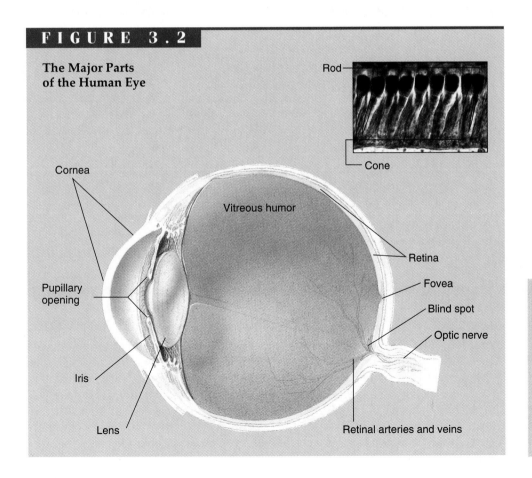

FIGURE 3.2

The Major Parts of the Human Eye

Labels: Rod, Cone, Cornea, Vitreous humor, Retina, Fovea, Blind spot, Optic nerve, Pupillary opening, Iris, Lens, Retinal arteries and veins

visible spectrum: The narrow band of electromagnetic rays, 380–760 nm in length, that are visible to the human eye.

cornea (KOR-nee-uh): The transparent covering of the colored part of the eye that bends light rays inward through the pupil.

eraser (Freese, 1977). We have no control over the dilation and contraction of our pupils; the motion is a reflex, completely automatic.

The pupils respond to emotions as well as light. When we look at someone or something highly desirable, our pupils dilate as if to take in more of the pleasing view (Hess, 1965). Pupils also dilate when we are frightened, telling a lie, or sexually aroused. Our pupil size is also related to mental effort—the more intense the mental activity, the larger our pupils become (Janisse & Peavler, 1974).

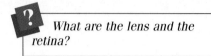

What are the lens and the retina?

From Lens to Retina: Focusing Images Suspended just behind the iris and the pupil, the **lens** is composed of many thin layers and looks like a transparent disc. The lens performs the task of focusing on objects closer than 20 feet. It flattens as it focuses on objects viewed at a distance, but it becomes more spherical, bulging in the center, as it focuses on close objects. This flattening and bulging action of the lens is known as **accommodation**. As we grow older, the lens loses some elasticity. Hence, it loses the ability to change its shape to accommodate for near vision, a condition called presbyopia ("old eyes"). This is why many people over age 40 must hold a book or newspaper at arm's length or use reading glasses to magnify the print. As a result of aging, disease, or injury, some people develop cataracts—a clouding of the lens that grows worse with time and can lead to blindness if not treated.

The lens focuses the image we see onto the **retina**—a membrane about the size of a small postage stamp and as thin as onion skin. The retina contains the sensory receptors for vision. The image projected onto the retina is upside down and reversed left to right. You can demonstrate this for yourself in the *Try It!*

Try It !

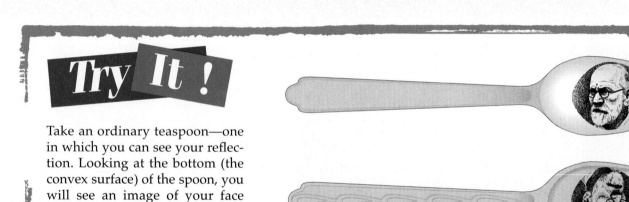

Take an ordinary teaspoon—one in which you can see your reflection. Looking at the bottom (the convex surface) of the spoon, you will see an image of your face that is right side up—the way the image enters the eye. Turn the spoon over and look at the inside (the concave surface), and you will see your face upside down and reversed left to right—the way the image appears on the retina. The brain, however, perceives images right side up.

In some people, the distance through the eyeball (from the lens to the retina) is either too short or too long for proper focusing. Nearsightedness (myopia) occurs when the lens focuses images of distant objects in front of, rather than on, the retina. A person with this condition will be able to see near objects clearly, but distant images will be blurred. Farsightedness (hyperopia) occurs when the focal image is longer than the eye can handle, as if the image should focus behind the retina (see Figure 3.3). The individual is able to see far objects clearly, but close objects are blurred. Both conditions are correctable with eyeglasses or contact lenses.

FIGURE 3.3

Normal Vision, Nearsightedness, and Farsightedness

In normal vision, an image is focused on the retina.

In nearsightedness (myopia), the image is focused in front of the retina.

In farsightedness (hyperopia), the image is focused behind the retina.

The Rods and Cones: Receptors for Light and Color At the back of the retina is a layer of light-sensitive receptor cells—the **rods** and the **cones**. Named for their shapes, the rods look like slender cylinders and the cones appear shorter and more rounded. There are about 120 million rods and 6 million cones in each retina.

The cones are the receptor cells that enable us to see color and fine detail in adequate light, but they do not function in very dim light. There are three types of cones, each particularly sensitive to one of three colors—red, green, or blue (Livingstone, 1988). The bipolar cells and the ganglion cells in the retina begin the work that the brain completes in computing the colors we perceive and analyzing the relative activity in the three types of cones (Nathans, 1989; Schnapf et al., 1987). You will read more about color vision later in this chapter.

If we were to plot an imaginary line through the middle of your pupil, the line would strike the center of the retina in the **fovea**, a small pit-like area about the size of the period at the end of this sentence (refer to Figure 3.2). When you look directly at an object, the image of the object is focused on the center of your fovea. The clearest point of your vision, the fovea is the part of the retina that you use for fine detail work.

Only $\frac{1}{50}$ of an inch in diameter, the fovea contains no rods but has nearly 50,000 cones tightly packed together. Recent anatomical evidence confirms that cones are most densely packed at the center of the fovea, but their density decreases sharply just a few degrees beyond the fovea's center and levels off more gradually to the periphery of the retina (Abramov & Gordon, 1994).

The rods respond to black and white, and they encode all other visible wavelengths but encode them in shades of gray instead of in color. More sensitive to light than the cones, the rods enable us to see in very dim light and provide us with night vision. A single rod can respond to the smallest possible quantity of light—a single photon (Stryer, 1987). Even though the rods are more sensitive to light and enable us to see in dim light, they do not provide the sharp, clear images that the cones make possible.

What happens to enable us to adapt to very different lighting conditions, from extremely dim to brightly illuminated? The answer lies primarily in a reddish-purple, light-sensitive pigment in the rods called rhodopsin. Exposure to light causes the molecules of rhodopsin to split apart and become bleached, making the rods less light-sensitive. In dim light or in the dark, the molecules gradually recombine and restore the rod's sensitivity to light.

Dark Adaptation Step from the bright sunlight into a darkened movie theater and at first you can hardly tell which seats are occupied and which are empty. After a few moments in the dark, your eyes begin to adapt and you can see dimly.

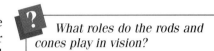

What roles do the rods and cones play in vision?

lens: The transparent structure behind the iris that changes in shape as it focuses images on the retina.

accommodation: The changing in shape of the lens as it focuses objects on the retina, becoming more spherical for near objects and flatter for far objects.

retina: The tissue at the back of the eye that contains the rods and the cones and onto which the retinal image is projected.

rods: The light-sensitive receptors in the retina that provide vision in dim light in black, white, and shades of gray.

cones: The receptor cells in the retina that enable us to see color and fine detail in adequate light, but that do not function in dim light.

fovea (FO-vee-uh): A small area of the retina, $\frac{1}{50}$ of an inch in diameter, that provides the clearest and sharpest vision because it has the largest concentration of cones.

dark adaptation: The eye's increasing ability to see in dim light; results from the recombining of molecules of rhodopsin in the rods and the dilation of the pupils.

optic nerve: The nerve that carries visual information from the retina to the brain.

Yet it takes about half an hour or more for your eyes to adapt completely. After complete **dark adaptation**, you can see light that is 100,000 times less bright than daylight. You may have thought that dark adaptation was a direct result of the dilation of your pupils, but this accounts for only a sixteenfold difference in your sensitivity to light. Dark adaptation cannot occur until the rhodopsin molecules in the rods recombine, restoring their sensitivity to light.

When you leave a movie theater, your eyes are dark adapted, but the return to the bright sunlight is a "blinding" experience. However, it takes only about 60 seconds, not half an hour, to become light adapted again.

In light adaptation, a reflexive action occurs; the pupils immediately become smaller, permitting less light to enter the eyes. And soon after you move from the dark into the light, the rods in your retinas become bleached—the rhodopsin molecules break apart, resulting in a great reduction in their sensitivity to light. But even though the rods, bleached by the bright light, are not functioning until they become light adapted, the ample light is sufficient to stimulate the cones so that they become fully functional.

What path does the neural impulse take from the retina to the primary visual cortex?

From the Retina to the Brain: From Visual Sensation to Visual Perception   The rods and cones are the receptors in the eye. They transduce or change light waves into neural impulses that are fed to the bipolar cells, which in turn pass the impulses along to the ganglion cells. The ganglion cells bundle together their some 1 million axonlike extensions in a pencil-sized cable that extends through the wall of the retina, leaving the eye on its way to the brain. Where the cable runs through the retinal wall, there can be no rods or cones, and so we are blind in that spot in each eye. After the cable leaves the retinal wall, it becomes known as the **optic nerve**. You can find your own blind spot if you perform the *Try It!*

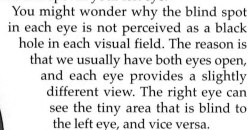

To locate your blind spot, hold this book at arm's length. Close your right eye and look directly at the magician's eyes. Now slowly bring the book closer, keeping your eye fixed on the magician. When the rabbit disappears, you have found the blind spot in your left eye.

You might wonder why the blind spot in each eye is not perceived as a black hole in each visual field. The reason is that we usually have both eyes open, and each eye provides a slightly different view. The right eye can see the tiny area that is blind to the left eye, and vice versa.

Leaving each eye at the blind spot, the optic nerve cables come together at the optic chiasma, a point where some of the nerve fibers cross to the opposite side of the brain. The visual fibers from the right half of each retina go to your right hemisphere, while visual fibers from the left half of each retina go to the left hemisphere. This switching is important because it allows visual information from a single eye to be represented on the primary visual cortex of both hemispheres of the brain. Furthermore, it plays an important part in depth perception.

From the optic chiasma, the optic nerve travels to the thalamus (specifically to its lateral geniculate nucleus). There it synapses with neural fibers that transmit the impulses to the primary visual cortex. Approximately one-fourth of the primary visual cortex is dedicated exclusively to analyzing input from the fovea, which, as we have seen, is a very small but extremely important part of the retina.

Mapping the Primary Visual Cortex and Discovering the Feature Detectors   During the last few decades, researchers have learned a great deal about how the primary visual cortex works to produce the sensation of vision. Much of the pioneering work in this field has been conducted by researchers David Hubel and Torsten Wiesel (1959, 1979; Hubel, 1963), who won a Nobel Prize for their work in 1981. Using cats as their subjects, Hubel and Wiesel placed a microelectrode in a single cell in the animal's visual cortex. They then flashed different patterns of lines on a screen in the cat's field of vision. They observed that the neurons appeared to be highly specialized, firing only in response to particular patterns of lines.

Hubel and Wiesel moved the tiny electrode carefully and precisely from cell to cell in order to map the visual responses over a sizable area of the cat's visual cortex. They found numbers of single neurons that respond only to lines and angles. One neuron, for example, would fire only when the cat saw a vertical line, while another neuron would respond only to a horizontal line. Other neurons were responsive to nothing but right angles, while some neurons were sensitive only to lines of a certain length. These neurons are known as **feature detectors**, and they are already coded at birth to make their unique responses. Neurons in the primary visual cortex respond not only to specific lines and angles but to several other features as well, including movement, texture, and color (Carlson, 1994).

But we see whole pictures, whole images, not collections of isolated features. Our ultimate visual perceptions are complete only when the primary visual cortex transmits millions of pieces of visual information to other areas in the brain, where they are combined and assembled into whole visual images.

Color Vision: A Multicolored World

Some light waves striking an object are absorbed by it, and others are reflected from it. We see only the wavelengths that are reflected, not those that are absorbed. Why does an apple look red? If you hold a red apple in bright light, light waves of all the different wavelengths are striking the apple, but more of the longer red wavelengths of light are reflected from the apple's skin. The shorter wavelengths are absorbed, so you see only the reflected red. Bite into the apple and it looks white. Why? We see white because, rather than being absorbed, all the wavelengths of the visible spectrum are reflected from the inside part of the apple. The presence of all visible wavelengths gives the sensation of white.

Our everyday visual experience goes far beyond the colors in the rainbow. We detect thousands of subtle color shadings. What enables us to make these fine color distinctions? Researchers have identified three dimensions that combine to provide the rich world of color we experience: (1) The chief dimension is **hue**, which refers to the actual color we view—red, green, and so forth. (2) **Saturation** refers to the purity of a color. A color becomes less saturated, or less pure, as other wavelengths of light are mixed with it. (3) **Brightness** refers to the intensity of the light energy we perceive. Figure 3.4 (on page 90) illustrates the dimensions of hue, saturation, and brightness.

feature detectors: Neurons in the brain that respond to specific features of a sensory stimulus (for example, to lines or angles).

hue: The property of light commonly referred to as color (red, blue, green, etc.), determined primarily by the wavelength of light reflected from a surface.

saturation: The degree to which light waves producing a color are of the same wavelength; the purity of a color.

brightness: The dimension of visual sensation that is dependent on the intensity of light reflected from a surface and that corresponds to the amplitude of the light wave.

? *What are the three dimensions that combine to provide the colors we experience?*

FIGURE 3.4

Hue, Saturation, and Brightness

Three dimensions combine to produce the rich world of color we experience. They are (1) hue, the actual color we see (blue, green, and so on); (2) saturation, the purity of a color; and (3) brightness, the intensity of the light energy reflected from a surface. The colors shown here are of the same hue but differ in saturation and brightness.

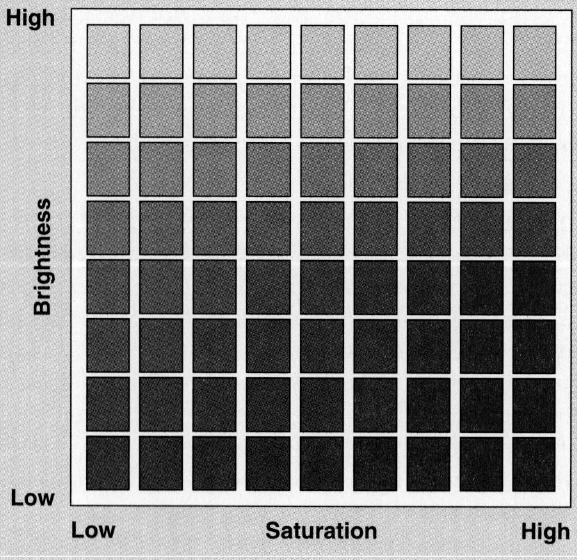

What two major theories attempt to explain color vision?

trichromatic theory: The theory of color vision suggesting that there are three types of cones, which are maximally sensitive to red, green, or blue, and that varying levels of activity in these receptors can produce all of the colors.

opponent-process theory: The theory that certain cells in the visual system increase their firing rate to signal one color and decrease their firing rate to signal the opposing color (red/green, yellow/blue, white/black).

Theories of Color Vision: How We Sense Color Two major theories have been offered to explain color vision, and both were formulated before the development of laboratory technology capable of testing them. The **trichromatic theory**, first proposed by Thomas Young in 1802, was modified by Hermann von Helmholtz about 50 years later. This theory states that there are three kinds of cones in the retina and that each kind makes its maximum chemical response to one of three colors—blue, green, or red—as shown in Figure 3.5. Research in the 1950s and the 1960s by Nobel Prize winner George Wald (1964; Wald et al., 1954) supports the trichromatic theory. Wald discovered that even though all cones have basically the same structure, the retina does indeed contain three kinds of cones.

The trichromatic theory alone, however, cannot explain how we are able to perceive such a rich variety of colors. Researchers now know that there must be color-coding processes that combine color information in a more complex way than occurs in the cones.

The other major attempt to explain color vision is the **opponent-process theory**, which was first proposed by physiologist Ewald Hering in 1878 and revised in 1957 by researchers Leon Hurvich and Dorthea Jamison. According to the opponent-process theory, the cells respond by increasing or decreasing their rate of firing when different colors are present. The red/green cells increase their firing rate when red is present and decrease it when green is present. The yellow/blue cells have an increased response to yellow and a decreased response to blue. Another type of cell increases its response rate for white light and decreases it in the absence of light. Think of the opponent-process theory as opposing pairs of cells on a seesaw. As one goes up, the other goes down, and vice versa. The relative firing positions of the three pairs of cells transmit color information to the brain.

Does the opponent process operate in the cones, or elsewhere? Researchers now believe that the cones pass on information about wavelength color to higher levels of visual processing. Researchers De Valois and De Valois (1975) proposed that the opponent processes might operate at the ganglion cells in the retina and in the higher brain centers rather than at the level of the receptors, the cones.

If you look long enough at one color in the opponent-process pair and then look at a white surface, your brain will give you the sensation of the opposite

FIGURE 3.5

Relative Sensitivity of the Three Types of Cones

Color vision is largely dependent on three types of cones. Each type responds maximally to a restricted range of wavelengths. The maximal response for one cone type is to short wavelengths of 450–500 nm (blue), for another type to medium wavelengths of 500–570 nm (green), and for another type to long wavelengths of 620–700 nm (red).

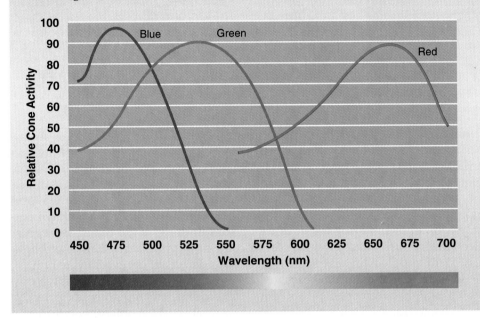

color—a negative **afterimage**. After you have stared at one color in an opponent-process pair (red/green, yellow/blue, black/white), the cell responding to that color tires and the opponent cell begins to fire, producing the afterimage. Demonstrate this for yourself in the *Try It!*

Stare at the dot in the green, black, and yellow flag for approximately 1 minute. Then shift your gaze to the dot in the blank rectangle. You will see the American flag in its true colors—red, white, and blue, which are the opponent-process colors of green, black, and yellow.

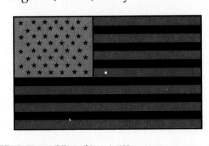

afterimage: The visual sensation that remains after a stimulus is withdrawn.

On the left a hot air balloon is shown as it would appear to a person with normal color vision; on the right is the same balloon as it would appear to a person with red-green color-blindness.

color blindness: The inability to distinguish some or all colors in vision, resulting from a defect in the cones.

Color Blindness: Weakness for Sensing Some Colors Not all of us see the world in the same colors. If normal genes for the three color pigments are not present, there will be some form of **color blindness**—the inability to distinguish some colors or, in rare cases, the total absence of color vision. Total color blindness affects only about 1 in 100,000 people (Nathans et al., 1989). We know what the world looks like to a color-blind person because of research with people who have normal vision in one eye but some form of color blindness in the other. Most color vision defects are actually weaknesses or color confusion, rather than color blindness. Many people who have some type of color defect are not even aware of it.

In order to have normal color vision, you must inherit a gene for blue pigment found on chromosome 7 and genes for red and green pigments carried on the X chromosome (Nathans, 1989). Some form of what is commonly referred to as red-green color blindness is found in about 8 percent of males, compared to less than 1 percent of females. The large difference is due to the fact that males have only one X chromosome.

Before leaving vision, let us dispel the myth that some mammals, especially dogs, generally lack color vision. Recent research confirms that some form of color vision is present in all species of mammals (Jacobs, 1993).

Memory Check 3.2

1. Match the parts of the eye with their descriptions.
   - _____ 1) the colored part of the eye
   - _____ 2) the opening in the iris that dilates and constricts
   - _____ 3) the transparent covering of the iris
   - _____ 4) the transparent structure that focuses an inverted image on the retina
   - _____ 5) the thin, photosensitive membrane at the back of the eye on which the lens focuses an inverted image

   a. retina
   b. cornea
   c. pupil
   d. iris
   e. lens

2. The receptor cells in the retina that enable us to see in dim light are the (cones, rods); the cells that enable us to see color and sharp images are (cones, rods).

3. Neural impulses are carried from the retina to the thalamus by the _____ and then relayed to their final destination, the _____.
   a. optic chiasma; primary visual cortex
   b. rods and cones; optic nerve
   c. optic nerve; primary visual cortex
   d. optic nerve; optic chiasma

4. Most people who are color-blind see no color at all. (true/false)

Answers: 1. 1) d 2) c 3) b 4) e 5) c 2. rods; cones 3. c 4. false

Hearing

Many years ago, the frightening science fiction movie *Alien* was advertised this way: "In space no one can hear you scream!" Although the movie was fiction, the statement is true. Light can travel through the vast nothingness of space, a vacuum, but sound cannot. In the following section, you will learn why.

Sound: What We Hear

Sound requires a medium through which to move, such as air, water, or a solid object. This fact was first demonstrated by Robert Boyle in 1660 when he suspended a ringing pocket watch by a thread inside a specially designed jar. When Boyle pumped all the air out of the jar, he could no longer hear the watch ring. But when he pumped the air back into the jar, he could again hear the watch ringing.

If you have attended a very loud rock concert, you not only heard but actually felt the mechanical vibrations. The pulsating speakers may have caused the floor, your seat, the walls, and the air around you to seem to shake or vibrate. You were feeling the moving air molecules being pushed toward you in waves as the speakers blasted their vibrations outward.

Frequency is an important characteristic of sound and is determined by the number of cycles completed by a sound wave in one second. The unit used to measure frequency, or the cycles per second, is known as the hertz (Hz). The pitch, how high or low the sound, is chiefly determined by frequency—the higher the frequency (the more vibrations per second), the higher the sound (see Figure 3.6). The human ear can hear sound frequencies from low bass tones of around 20 Hz up to high-pitched sounds of about 20,000 Hz. The lowest tone on a piano sounds at a frequency of about 28 Hz and the highest tone at about 4,214 Hz. Many

> **?** *What determines the pitch and the loudness of sound, and how is each quality measured?*

FIGURE 3.6

The Frequency and Amplitude of a Sound Wave

The frequency of a sound wave—the number of cycles completed per second—determines the pitch of the sound. Loudness is determined by amplitude—the energy or height of the sound wave.

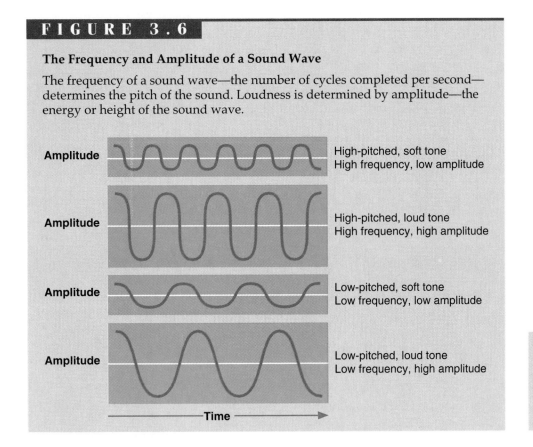

Amplitude — High-pitched, soft tone / High frequency, low amplitude

Amplitude — High-pitched, loud tone / High frequency, high amplitude

Amplitude — Low-pitched, soft tone / Low frequency, low amplitude

Amplitude — Low-pitched, loud tone / Low frequency, high amplitude

Time

frequency: Measured in the unit hertz, the number of sound waves or cycles per second, determining the pitch of the sound.

mammals—dogs, cats, bats, and rats—can hear tones much higher in frequency than 20,000 Hz. Amazingly, dolphins can respond to sounds up to 100,000 Hz.

The loudness of a sound is determined largely by a measure called **amplitude**. Amplitude depends on the energy of the sound wave (refer back to Figure 3.6). The force or pressure with which air molecules move chiefly determines loudness. We can measure the sound pressure level (loudness) of sounds using a unit called the bel, named for Alexander Graham Bell. Because the bel is a rather large unit, sound levels are expressed in tenths of a bel, or **decibels** (dB). The threshold of human hearing is set at 0 dB, which does not mean the absence of sound but the softest sound that can be heard in a very quiet setting. Each increase of 10 decibels makes a sound 10 times louder. A whisper is about 20 dB, but that is 100 times louder than 0 dB. A normal conversation, around 60 dB, is 10,000 times louder than a soft whisper at 20 dB. Figure 3.7 shows comparative decibel levels for a variety of sounds.

If pitch and loudness were the only perceptual dimensions of sound, we could not tell the difference between two instruments if both were playing exactly the same note at the same decibel level. A third characteristic of sound, **timbre**, refers to the distinct quality of a sound that distinguishes it from other sounds of the same pitch and loudness. Unlike the pure sound of a tuning fork, which has only one frequency, most sounds we hear consist of several different frequencies. The frequencies that form the sound pattern above any tone a musical instrument produces are called overtones, or harmonics. Overtones are not actually heard as tones, but they give musical instruments their characteristic quality of sound, or timbre. The rich, full sound of a French horn is due to the large number of overtones it produces. The almost pure sound of the flute is produced because relatively few overtones are generated above the notes sounded on that instrument.

amplitude: Measured in decibels, the magnitude or intensity of a sound wave, determining the loudness of the sound; in vision the *amplitude* of a light wave affects the brightness of a stimulus.

decibel (DES-ih-bel): A unit of measurement of the intensity or loudness of sound based on the amplitude of the sound wave.

timbre (TAM-burr): The distinctive quality of a sound that distinguishes it from other sounds of the same pitch and loudness.

FIGURE 3.7

Decibel Levels of Various Sounds

The loudness of a sound (its amplitude) is measured in decibels. Each increase of 10 decibels makes a sound 10 times louder. A normal conversation at 3 feet measures about 60 decibels, which is 10,000 times louder than a soft whisper of 20 decibels. Any exposure to sounds of 130 dB or higher puts a person at immediate risk for hearing damage.

Psychological Response	Decibel Scale	Example
Threshold of severe pain	140	
Painfully loud		Rock band at 15 feet
Prolonged exposure produces damage to hearing	120	Jet takeoff at 200 feet
		Riveting machine
	100	Subway train at 15 feet
Very loud		Water at foot of Niagara Falls
	80	Automobile interior at 55 mph
		Freeway traffic at 50 feet
	60	Normal conversation at 3 feet
		Quiet restaurant
Quiet	40	Quiet office
		Library
Very quiet	20	Whisper at 3 feet
Just audible		Normal breathing
Threshold of hearing	0	

The Ear: More to It Than Meets the Eye

The part of the body we call the ear plays only a minor role in human **audition**. In fact, even if your visible outer ears were cut off, your hearing would suffer very little. Let's learn how each part of the ear contributes to our ability to hear.

The Structure of the Ear: The Outer, Middle, and Inner Ears The oddly shaped, curved flap of cartilage and skin called the pinna is the visible part of the **outer ear** (see Figure 3.8). Inside the ear, your auditory canal is about 1 inch long, and its entrance is lined with hairs. At the end of the auditory canal is the eardrum (the tympanic membrane), a thin, flexible membrane about 1/3 inch in diameter. The eardrum moves in response to the sound waves that strike it.

The **middle ear** is no larger than an aspirin tablet. Inside its chamber are the ossicles, the three smallest bones in your body, each "about the size of a grain of rice" (Strome & Vernick, 1989). Named for their shapes, the three connected ossicles—the hammer, the anvil, and the stirrup—link the eardrum to the oval window (see Figure 3.8). The ossicles amplify the sound some 22 times (Békésy, 1957).

The **inner ear** begins at the inner side of the oval window on the base of the **cochlea**—a fluid-filled, snail-shaped, bony chamber. When the stirrup pushes against the oval window, it sets up vibrations that move the fluid in the cochlea back and forth in waves. The movement of the fluid sets in motion the thin basilar membrane that runs through the cochlea. Attached to the basilar membrane are about 15,000 sensory receptors called **hair cells**, each with a bundle of tiny hairs protruding from it. The tiny hair bundles are pushed and pulled by the motion of the fluid inside the cochlea. If the tip of the hair bundle is moved only as much as the width of an atom, an electrical impulse is generated, which is transmitted to the brain by way of the auditory nerve (Hudspeth, 1983).

> *How do the outer, middle, and inner ears function in hearing?*

FIGURE 3.8

Anatomy of the Human Ear

Sound waves pass through the auditory canal to the eardrum, causing it to vibrate and set in motion the ossicles in the middle ear. When the stirrup pushes against the oval window, it sets up vibrations in the inner ear. This moves the fluid in the cochlea back and forth and sets in motion the hair cells, causing a message to be sent to the brain via the auditory nerve.

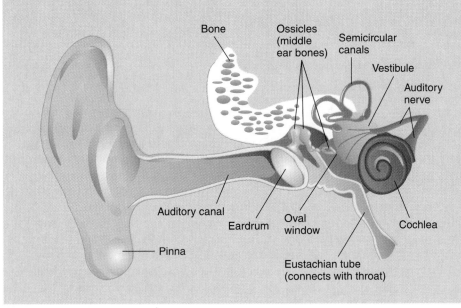

audition: The sensation of hearing; the process of hearing.

outer ear: The visible part of the ear, consisting of the pinna and the auditory canal.

middle ear: The portion of the ear containing the ossicles, which connect the eardrum to the oval window and amplify the vibrations as they travel to the inner ear.

inner ear: The innermost portion of the ear, containing the cochlea, the vestibular sacs, and the semicircular canals.

cochlea (KOK-lee-uh): The snail-shaped, fluid-filled organ in the inner ear that contains the hair cells (the sound receptors).

hair cells: Sensory receptors for hearing, found in the cochlea.

Having two ears, one on either side of the head, enables us to determine the direction from which sounds are coming (Konishi, 1993). Unless a sound is directly above, below, in front of, or behind us, it reaches one ear slightly before it reaches the other (Spitzer & Semple, 1991). The brain detects differences as small as 0.0001 second and interprets them, telling us the direction of the sound (Rosenzweig, 1961). The source of a sound may also be determined by the difference in intensity of the sound reaching each ear (Middlebrooks & Green, 1991).

Theories of Hearing: How Hearing Works

? What two major theories attempt to explain hearing?

In the 1860s Hermann von Helmholtz helped develop **place theory**, one of the two major theories of hearing. This theory holds that each individual pitch we hear is determined by the particular spot or place along the basilar membrane of the cochlea that vibrates the most. To test this theory, George von Békésy drilled holes in the cochleas of human cadavers and observed the effect of differently pitched sounds on the basilar membrane. He found that high-frequency sounds caused the basilar membrane to vibrate most at the beginning or base of the cochlea; lower-pitched tones caused the most vibration farther along the coil, nearer the tip of the basilar membrane (Békésy, 1957). More recent techniques have enabled researchers to observe the living basilar membrane, and their studies verify that different locations do indeed vibrate in response to differently pitched sounds (Ruggero, 1992). Even so, place theory cannot explain how we perceive the low frequencies below 150 Hz.

Another attempt to explain hearing is **frequency theory**. According to this theory, the hair cell receptors vibrate the same number of times per second as the sounds that reach them. Thus, a tone of 500 Hz would stimulate the hair cells to vibrate 500 times per second as well. Frequency theory seems valid for low- and medium-pitched tones, but it has a major problem with high-frequency tones. Individual neurons cannot fire more than about 1,000 times per second. Therefore, they could not signal to the brain the higher-pitched tones exceeding 1,000 Hz.

The volley principle was put forth to suggest that groups, or volleys, of neurons, if properly synchronized, could together produce the firing rate required for higher tones (Wever, 1949). Yet even with the help of the volley principle, frequency theory is not able to explain how we hear tones with frequencies higher than about 4,000 Hz. Today researchers believe that (1) frequency theory best explains how we perceive low frequencies, 150 Hz and below; (2) frequency theory supplements place theory in the 150- to 4,000-Hz range; and (3) place theory best accounts for how we perceive frequencies from 4,000 Hz to the highest frequencies humans are able to hear, about 20,000 Hz (Matlin & Foley, 1992).

Bone Conduction: Hearing Sound Vibrations through the Bones

The eardrum is not required for all of the sounds we hear. We also hear through **bone conduction**—the vibrations of the bones in our face and skull. When you click your teeth or eat crunchy food, you hear these sounds mainly through bone conduction. Some of these vibrations bypass the outer and middle ear and are transmitted directly to the cochlea. Find a watch that ticks, and place it between your teeth. Close your ears with your fingers. Listen and you will hear the ticking through bone conduction, without help from the outer and middle ear.

If you have heard a recording of your own voice, you may have considered it somewhat strange and very unlike your normal speaking voice. When you listen to your own voice as you are talking, you hear sound waves coming through the auditory canal *and* through bone conduction. But when you listen to a recording of your voice, there are no bone conduction vibrations in the sound you hear. This is the way your voice sounds to other people.

place theory: The theory that sounds of different frequency or pitch cause maximum activation of hair cells at certain locations along the basilar membrane.

frequency theory: The theory that hair cell receptors vibrate the same number of times as the sounds that reach them, thereby accounting for how variations in pitch are transmitted to the brain.

bone conduction: The transmission of vibrations along the bones of the skull or face directly to the cochlea.

Hearing Loss: Kinds and Causes

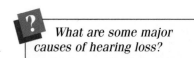

What are some major causes of hearing loss?

There are about 30 million people in the United States who have hearing problems (Catlin, 1986), and that number is growing rapidly (Dobbin, 1987). Hearing loss and deafness can be caused by disease, birth defects, injury, excessive noise, and old age. Conductive hearing loss, or conduction deafness, is usually caused by disease or injury to the eardrum or the bones of the middle ear, which prevents sound waves from being conducted to the cochlea. People with conductive hearing loss can usually be helped with a hearing aid that bypasses the middle ear and uses bone conduction to reach the cochlea.

Conventional hearing aids are useless instruments, however, for the people who suffer from neural hearing loss, or nerve deafness. With this disorder the eardrum and the middle ear may be intact, but some injury or deterioration of the inner ear prevents the transduction of sound waves into neural impulses. Many people over 60 (more men than women) suffer from gradual deterioration of the auditory nerve that results in a loss of hearing. But in contemporary society there are some indications that lifelong exposure to excessive noise may be more of a factor than aging in explaining hearing loss. Older persons in one culture, the Mabaan tribe in the Sudan in Africa, don't appear to suffer much hearing loss as they age. In fact, when hearing tests were conducted on Mabaan tribe members, some 80-year-old members could hear as well as 20-year-old people in industrialized countries. The Mabaan pride themselves on their sensitive hearing, and an important tribal custom is never to raise their voices. Even their festivals and celebrations are quiet affairs, featuring dancing and soft singing accompanied by stringed instruments rather than drums. The loudest sounds they usually hear in their everyday world are made by their own domestic animals like sheep or roosters (Bennett, 1990).

Researchers have long believed that when mammals suffer hair cell loss from the inner ear, it is irreversible. Three recent studies have demonstrated that mammal hair cells (rat cells, guinea pig cells, and human cells in culture) can be regenerated, although the newly regenerated cells are not functional (Forge et al., 1993; Lefebvre et al., 1993; Warchol et al., 1993). These findings offer hope that some day techniques will be developed that can enable mammals to recover some hearing function after auditory hair cell damage (Lefebvre et al., 1993).

Memory Check 3.3

1. Pitch is chiefly determined by _____; loudness is chiefly determined by _____.
   a. amplitude; frequency
   c. intensity; amplitude
   b. wavelength; frequency
   d. frequency; amplitude

2. Pitch is measured in (hertz, decibels); loudness is measured in (decibels, hertz).

3. Match the part of the ear with the structures it contains.
   ____ 1) ossicles
   ____ 2) pinna, auditory canal
   ____ 3) cochlea, hair cells
   a. outer ear
   b. middle ear
   c. inner ear

4. The receptors for hearing are found in the:
   a. ossicles.
   c. auditory membrane.
   b. auditory canal.
   d. cochlea.

5. The two major theories that attempt to explain hearing are:
   a. conduction theory and place theory.
   b. hair cell theory and frequency theory.
   c. place theory and frequency theory.
   d. conduction theory and hair cell theory.

6. According to the text, lifelong exposure to excessive noise may be more of a factor in hearing loss than aging is. (true/false)

Answers: 1. d 2. hertz; decibels 3. 1) b 2) a 3) c 4. d 5. c 6. true

Odors have a powerful ability to evoke memories and stir up emotions.

S mell and Taste

You have been reading how important are our abilities to sense light and sound. Now let's explore our chemical senses, smell and taste.

Smell: Sensing Scents

Consider what it would be like to live in a world without smell. "Not really so bad," you might say. "Although I could not smell flowers, perfume, or my favorite foods, I would never again have to endure the foul odors of life. It's a trade-off, so what's the difference?"

The difference is large indeed. Your ability to detect odors close at hand and at a distance is an aid to survival. You smell smoke and can escape before the flames of a fire envelop you. Your nose broadcasts an odor alarm to the brain when certain poisonous gases or noxious fumes are present. But the survival value of odor detection in humans does not stop there. Smell, aided by taste, is the last line of defense—your final chance to avoid putting spoiled food or drink into your body.

It is well known that odors alone have a powerful ability to call forth old memories and rekindle strong emotional feelings, even decades after events in our lives. This is not surprising when we consider that the olfactory system sends information to the limbic system, an area in the brain that plays an important role in emotions and memories as well.

The human olfactory system is capable of sensing and distinguishing 10,000 different odor molecules (Firestein, 1991) and more than 100,000 compounds (Dionne, 1988). But there are large individual differences in smell sensitivity. Although perfumers and whiskey blenders can distinguish about 100,000 odor compounds, the average person with training can distinguish from 10,000 to about 40,000 (Dobb, 1989). According to Rabin and Cain (1986), there is a twentyfold difference in individual sensitivity to smell, that is, in the threshold for various odors.

> **?** *What path does a smell message take on its journey from the nose to the brain?*

The Mechanics of Smell: How the Nose Knows Olfaction—the sense of smell—is a chemical sense. We cannot smell a substance unless some of its molecules vaporize—pass from a solid or liquid into a gaseous state. Heat speeds up the evaporation of molecules, which is why food that is cooking has a stronger and more distinct odor than uncooked food. When odor molecules vaporize, they become airborne and make their way up our nostrils to the olfactory epithelium. The **olfactory epithelium** consists of two 1-square-inch patches of tissue, one at the top of each nasal cavity, which together contain about 10 million receptor cells for smell. Figure 3.9 shows a diagram of the human olfactory system.

Have you ever wondered why dogs have a keener sense of smell than humans? Not only do most dogs have a large and long snout, but in some breeds the olfactory epithelium can be as large as the area of a handkerchief and can contain up to 200 million receptors for smell, 20 times the average number found in humans (Engen, 1982).

The olfactory receptors are different from all other sensory receptors. They are special types of neurons that both come into direct contact with sensory stimuli and reach directly into the brain. Unlike all other neurons, olfactory neurons have a short life span, less than 8 weeks, and they are continuously being replaced (Farbman, 1992). The axons of the olfactory receptor cells relay the smell message directly to the **olfactory bulbs**—two brain structures the size of matchsticks that rest above the nasal cavities (refer to Figure 3.9). From the olfactory bulbs, the message is relayed to different parts of the brain.

olfaction (ol-FAK-shun): The sensation of smell; the process of smell.

olfactory epithelium: Two 1-inch square patches of tissue, one at the top of each nasal cavity, which together contain about 10 million receptors for smell.

olfactory bulbs: Two matchstick-sized structures above the nasal cavities, where smell sensations first register in the brain.

FIGURE 3.9

The Olfactory Sense

Odor molecules travel up the nostrils to the olfactory epithelium, which contains the receptor cells for smell. Olfactory receptors are special neurons whose axons form the olfactory nerve. The olfactory nerve relays smell messages to the olfactory bulbs and on to other parts of the brain.

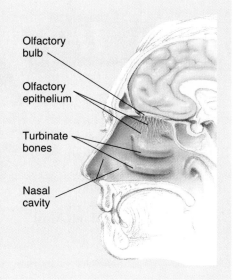

Olfactory bulb

Olfactory epithelium

Turbinate bones

Nasal cavity

Until recently, researchers were not sure whether there were many different types of olfactory receptors and the decoding of different odors took place primarily in the nose, or whether there were fewer different types of receptors and decoding was accomplished mainly in the brain. Researchers Buck and Axel (1991) have evidence that more than 100 different types of receptors exist, and the total may be even greater. Their work suggests that the olfactory receptor is the main site for the discrimination of odors.

The intensity of the smell stimulus—how strong or weak it is—is apparently determined by the number of olfactory receptors firing at the same time. The location, or spatial pattern, of the olfactory receptors that are firing is believed to transmit the nature of the scent to the olfactory bulb (Freeman, 1991).

Taste: What the Tongue Can Tell

A sizzling steak, hot buttered popcorn, chocolate cake—does your sense of taste alone tell you what these foods taste like? Surprisingly, no. **Gustation**, or the sense of taste, gives us only four distinct kinds of sensations—sweet, sour, salty, and bitter. When we say that a food tastes good or bad, we are actually referring to flavor—the combined sensory experience of the taste, smell, and touch. As we taste, we feel the texture and temperature of foods we put in the mouth. But most of the pleasure we attribute to our sense of taste is actually due to smell, which comes from odor molecules forced up the nasal cavity by the action of the tongue, cheeks, and throat when we chew and swallow.

Although aging typically is accompanied by a decline in the other senses, people lose very little of their ability to detect the four primary taste sensations as they age (Bartoshuk et al., 1986). When older people complain that food doesn't taste as good as it once did, the reason is usually a loss of smell rather than a failing sense of taste (Bartoshuk, 1989).

Even color can contribute to our sense of taste. In one study many subjects could not even recognize the taste of root beer when it was colored red (Hyman, 1983). And many common foods with similar textures cannot be identified by taste alone. Prove this for yourself by doing the *Try It!* (on page 100).

? *What are the four primary taste sensations, and how are they detected?*

gustation: The sensation of taste.

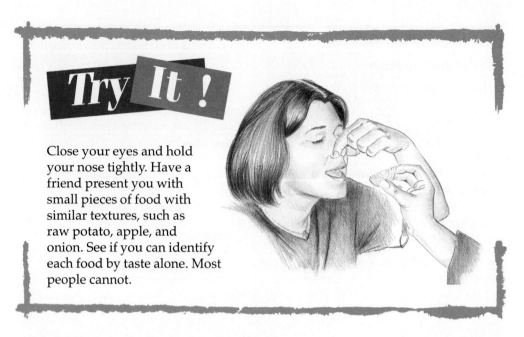

Try It !

Close your eyes and hold your nose tightly. Have a friend present you with small pieces of food with similar textures, such as raw potato, apple, and onion. See if you can identify each food by taste alone. Most people cannot.

The Taste Receptors: Taste Detectors   If you look at your tongue in a mirror, you will see many small bumps called papillae. There are four different types of papillae, and three of them contain **taste buds**, which cluster around the cracks and crevices between the papillae (see Figure 3.10). Each taste bud is composed of from 60 to 100 receptor cells, which resemble the petals of a flower (Kinnamon, 1988). Taste receptors are also found in the palate, in the mucus lining of the cheeks and lips, and in parts of the throat, including the tonsils (G. H. Parker, 1922). The life span of the receptor cells for taste is very short, only about 10 days, and they are continually replaced (Beidler & Smallman, 1965).

Taste buds are most densely packed on the tip of the tongue, less densely packed on the rear edges, and absent from the center of the tongue (Bartoshuk,

taste buds: The structures that are composed of 60 to 100 sensory receptors for taste.

FIGURE 3.10

The Tongue's Taste Buds

Taste buds are sensitive to only four tastes: bitter, sour, salty, and sweet. The vertical cross-section enlargement shows one of the papillae. The taste buds are in the small trenches around the papillae.

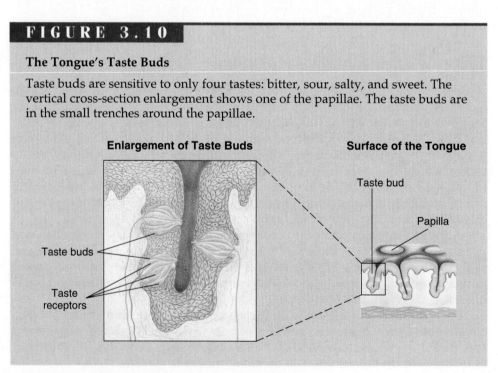

Enlargement of Taste Buds

Taste buds

Taste receptors

Surface of the Tongue

Taste bud

Papilla

1989). But taste is poorly localized, and taste sensations appear to come from all over the mouth. Even people with damage over large areas of the mouth are usually unaware of the loss of taste buds, because very intense sensations can be produced by rather small areas of normal tissue (Bartoshuk et al., 1987).

For many years textbooks included a "tongue map" showing the four basic tastes spatially distributed over different areas of the tongue. Supposedly, sweet taste sensations were perceived on the tip of the tongue, sour and salty tastes on the sides, and bitter tastes on the back. But the tongue map is an error that resulted from a mistranslation of a 1901 article written in German by a psychophysicist who worked in Wilhelm Wundt's laboratory. Researchers who have performed extensive spatial testing for the four taste sensations report that all four tastes can be detected by taste buds on all locations of the tongue (Bartoshuk & Beauchamp, 1994).

Taste Sensitivities: Nontasters to Supertasters   There are large differences among individuals in taste sensitivity and specific taste abilities that appear to be genetically determined. Recent research indicates that humans can be divided into three groups according to taste sensitivity for certain sweet and bitter substances—nontasters, medium tasters, and supertasters (Bartoshuk et al., 1992). Nontasters are unable to taste some sweet and bitter compounds, but they do taste most other substances, although with less sensitivity. Supertasters taste certain sweet and bitter compounds with far stronger intensity than other people. For example, supertasters tend to take only half as much sugar or saccharin as other people to sweeten their coffee or tea, yet such sweeteners as aspartame are perceived as having the same level of sweetness by supertasters and other tasters alike. Supertasters also suffer more from oral burn when they eat chili peppers, being supersensitive to its active ingredient, capsaicin (Karrer & Bartoshuk, 1991).

Researchers, using videomicroscopy, have actually counted the number of taste buds on the tongues of different individuals (Miller & Reedy, 1990). Not surprisingly, nontasters had the smallest number of taste buds per square centimeter, with an average of 96. Medium tasters averaged nearly twice as many taste buds at 184, and supertasters had more than four times as many taste buds, an average of 425. But the fact that supertasters do not taste all substances with greater intensity suggests that the number of taste buds alone does not explain general taste sensitivity.

Memory Check 3.4

1. The technical name for the process or sensation of smell is (gustation, olfaction).

2. The olfactory, or smell, receptors are located in the:
   a. olfactory tract.
   b. olfactory nerve.
   c. olfactory epithelium.
   d. olfactory bulbs.

3. The four primary taste sensations are _____, _____, _____, and _____.

4. Our ability to identify foods with similar textures is most influenced by our sense of (taste, smell).

5. Each (papilla, taste bud) contains from 60 to 100 receptor cells.

6. Taste receptor cells have a very short life span and are continually replaced. (true/false)

7. Supertasters have the same number of taste buds as medium tasters and nontasters. (true/false)

Answers: 1. olfaction 2. c 3. sweet, salty, sour, bitter 4. smell 5. taste bud 6. true 7. false

Our Other Senses

Other senses are our sense of touch (the tactile sense), our sense of balance (the vestibular sense), and our kinesthetic sense.

The Skin Senses: Information from Our Natural Clothing

? *How does the skin provide sensory information?*

Our own natural clothing, the skin, is the largest organ of the body. It performs many important biological functions while also yielding much of what we know as sensual pleasure. Your skin can detect heat, cold, pressure, pain, and a vast range of touch sensations—caresses, pinches, punches, pats, rubs, scratches, and the feel of many different textures, from silk to sandpaper.

The Mechanism of Touch: How Touch Works **Tactile** information is conveyed to the brain when an object touches and depresses the skin, stimulating one or more of the several distinct types of nerve cell receptors. These sensitive nerve endings in the skin send the touch message through nerve connections to the spinal cord. The message travels up the spinal cord and through the brainstem and the lower brain centers, finally reaching the brain's somatosensory cortex. Only then do we become aware of where and how hard we have been touched. Remember from Chapter 2 that the somatosensory cortex is the strip of tissue at the front of the parietal lobes where touch, pressure, temperature, and pain register.

If we examine the skin from the outermost to the deepest layer, we find a variety of nerve endings that differ markedly in appearance. Most or all of these nerve endings appear to respond in some degree to all different types of tactile stimulation.

If someone touched your skin with a sharp object like a toothpick, could you identify the exact spot where the toothpick was placed on your body? The *Try It!* may prove interesting.

Have someone touch the palm of your hand with two toothpicks held about 1½ inches apart. Do you feel one point or two? How far apart do the toothpicks have to be before you perceive them as two separate touch sensations? How far apart do they have to be on your face? on your forearm? on your fingers? on your toes? Which of these body parts are the most sensitive? Which are the least sensitive?

tactile: Pertaining to the sense of touch.

In the 1890s one of the most prominent researchers of the tactile sense, Max von Frey, discovered the two-point threshold that measures how far apart two points must be before we feel them as two separate touches. Figure 3.11 illustrates two-point thresholds for different body parts, showing the actual distance apart at which two-point discriminations can be made by most people.

FIGURE 3.11

The Two-Point Threshold

The two-point threshold measures how far apart two points must be to be felt as two separate touches. The drawing shows the average two-point thresholds for different parts of the body. The shortest bars on the graph indicate the greatest sensitivity; the longest bars, the least sensitivity. The thumb and fingers, being the most sensitive, have the lowest two-point thresholds (less than 5 mm). The calves, being the least sensitive body parts, have two-point thresholds of about 45 mm. (After Weinstein, 1968.)

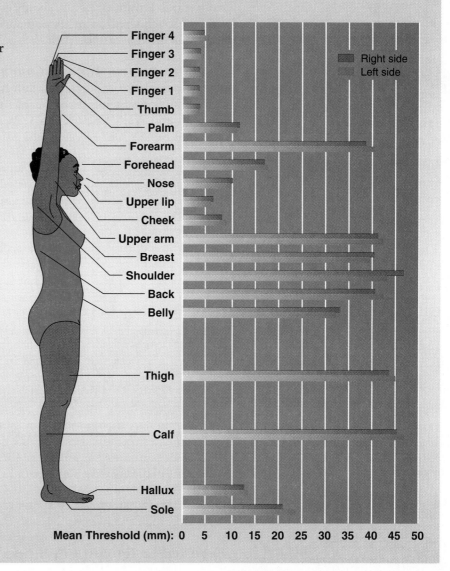

Pain: Physical Hurts

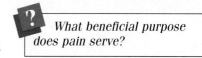

What beneficial purpose does pain serve?

Although our sense of touch brings us a great deal of pleasure, it delivers pain as well.

> He has never had a headache or a toothache, never felt the pain of a cut, a bruise, or a burn. If you are thinking, "How lucky!" you are completely wrong. His arms and legs are twisted and bent. Some of his fingers are missing. A large, bloody wound covers one of his knees, and his lips are chewed raw.
>
> A battered child? No. Born with a very rare genetic defect, he is totally insensitive to pain. He does not even notice a deep cut, a burn, or a broken bone when it happens, so he continues whatever he is doing and injures himself severely. (Adapted from Wallis, 1984.)

This story shows that pain functions as a valuable warning and protective mechanism. It motivates us to tend to our injuries, restrict our activity, and seek medical help if we need it. Pain also teaches us to avoid pain-producing circumstances in the future. Chronic pain, however, persists long after it serves any useful function and is itself a serious medical problem for some 50 to 55 million Americans (Edmund, 1990). The three major types of chronic pain are low-back pain, headache, and arthritis pain; and for its victims, chronic pain is like a fire alarm that no one can turn off.

 What is the gate-control theory of pain?

The Gate-Control Theory: Conducting Pains Great and Small Pain is probably the least understood of all the sensations. We are not certain how pain works, but one major theory seeks to explain it—the **gate-control theory** of Melzack and Wall (1965, 1983). They contend that there is an area in the spinal cord that can act like a "gate" and either inhibit pain messages or transmit them to the brain. Only so many messages can go through the gate at any one time. We feel pain when pain messages carried by the small, slow-conducting nerve fibers reach the gate and cause it to open. Large, fast-conducting nerve fibers carry other sensory messages from the body, and these can effectively tie up traffic at the gate so that it will close and keep many of the pain messages from getting through.

What is the first thing you do when you stub your toe or pound your finger with a hammer? If you rub or apply gentle pressure to the injury, you are stimulating the large, fast-conducting nerve fibers, which get their message to the spinal gate first and block some of the pain messages from the slower nerve fibers. Applying ice, heat, or electrical stimulation to the painful area also stimulates the large nerve fibers and closes the spinal gate.

The Lamaze relaxation technique, which can lessen the pain of childbirth, recognizes that pain has both cognitive and emotional components.

The gate-control theory also accounts for the fact that psychological factors, both cognitive and emotional, can influence the perception of pain. Melzack and Wall contend that messages from the brain to the spinal cord can inhibit the transmission of pain messages at the spinal gate and thereby affect the perception of pain. This explains why some people can undergo surgery under hypnosis and feel little or no pain. It also explains why soldiers injured in battle or athletes injured during games can be so distracted that they do not experience pain until some time after the injury.

 What are endorphins?

Endorphins: Our Own Natural Pain Relievers Americans spend more money trying to get rid of pain than for any other medical purpose. In fact, we spend over $40 billion each year on treatments for chronic pain ranging from over-the-counter medications to surgery and psychotherapy (Budiansky et al., 1987).

Our body produces its own natural painkillers, the **endorphins**, which block pain and produce a feeling of well-being. Endorphins are released when we are injured, when we experience stress or extreme pain, and when we laugh, cry, or exercise (Bolles & Fanselow, 1982; Terman et al., 1984). "Runner's high" and an elevated mood after exercising are often attributed to an increase in endorphin levels (Goldberg, 1988).

Some people release endorphins even when they only *think* they are receiving pain medication. When hospital patients recovering from surgery ask for pain medication, they are sometimes given, instead, a placebo in the form of a sugar pill or an injection of saline solution. Nevertheless, 35 percent of the patients who receive placebos report relief from pain (Melzack & Wall, 1983). Why? When patients believe that they have received a drug for pain, apparently that belief stimulates the release of their own natural pain relievers, the endorphins. How do we know?

The proof comes from another drug, **naloxone**, which blocks the action of endorphins. When naloxone is injected into patients, it binds to the endorphin

gate-control theory: The theory that the pain signals transmitted by slow-firing nerve fibers can be blocked at the spinal gate if fast-firing fibers get their messages to the gate first, or if the brain itself inhibits transmission of the pain messages.

endorphins (en-DOR-fins): Chemicals, produced naturally by the pituitary gland, that reduce pain and positively affect mood.

naloxone: A drug that blocks the action of endorphins.

receptor sites, thereby preventing the endorphins from having their pain-relieving effect (Fields, 1978). Joggers who normally experience runner's high will not experience it if they are injected with naloxone before they run, an indication that jogging stimulates the release of endorphins.

Acupuncture, the ancient Chinese technique for relieving pain, appears to work because the fine needles that are inserted at specific points on the body seem to stimulate the release of endorphins, thereby relieving pain. Evidence for this notion is provided by naloxone again, because when it is injected into patients, acupuncture has no effect (Hassett, 1980). But endorphins do not account for other methods of pain relief, such as meditation, relaxation, distraction, and hypnosis, which we will discuss in Chapter 4 (Hilgard & Hilgard, 1975; McCaul & Malott, 1984). The next time you experience pain, you may want to try out the texhniques in the *Try It!*

If you experience pain, you can try any of the following techniques for controlling it:

- Distraction can be particularly effective for controlling brief or mild pain. Generally, activities or thoughts that require a great deal of attention will provide more relief than passive distractions.
- Counterirritation—stimulating or irritating one area of the body in order to mask or diminish pain in another area—can be accomplished with ice packs, heat, massage, mustard packs, or electrical stimulation.
- Relaxation techniques such as the one described on page 144 are useful for reducing the stress and muscular tension that usually accompany pain.
- Positive statements can help you cope, whereas negative thoughts tend to increase your anxiety. For example, replace "I can't stand this anymore" with "I have had worse pain than this before, and I lived through it."
- Attention and sympathy from family members and friends should be kept at a moderate level; too much attention may prove to be so reinforcing that it serves to prolong pain.

The other two senses we will explore may seem minor, but they too make important contributions to our sensory world.

The Kinesthetic Sense: Keeping Track of Our Body Parts

The **kinesthetic sense** provides information about (1) the position of our body parts in relation to each other and (2) the movement in various body parts. This information is detected by receptors in the joints, ligaments, and muscles. The other senses, especially vision, provide additional information about body position and movement, but our kinesthetic sense works well on its own. Thanks to our kinesthetic sense, we are able to perform smooth and skilled body movements without visual feedback or a studied, conscious effort. A companion sense, the vestibular sense, involves equilibrium or the sense of balance.

What kind of information does the kinesthetic sense provide, and how is this sensory information detected?

kinesthetic sense: The sense providing information about relative position and movement of body parts.

> **?** *What is the vestibular sense, and where are its sensory receptors located?*

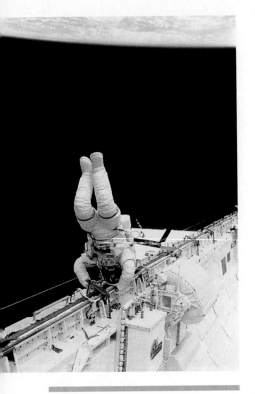

The vestibular sense provides information about the body's orientation in space. This astronaut is taking part in NASA research on working in a weightless environment, where the vestibular sense is severely impaired.

vestibular sense (ves-TIB-yu-ler): Sense that provides information about movement and our orientation in space through sensory receptors in the semicircular canals and the vestibular sacs, which detect changes in the movement and orientation of the head.

semicircular canals: Three fluid-filled tubular canals in the inner ear that provide information about rotating head movements.

The Vestibular Sense: Sensing Up and Down and Changes in Speed

Our **vestibular sense** detects movement and provides information about our orientation in space. The vestibular sense organs are located in the semicircular canals and the vestibular sacs in the inner ear. The **semicircular canals** sense the rotation of your head, such as when you are turning your head from side to side or when you are spinning around (see Figure 3.12). Because the canals are filled with fluid, rotating movements of the head in any direction send the fluid coursing through the tubelike semicircular canals. In the canals the moving fluid bends the hair cells, which act as receptors and send neural impulses to the brain. Because there are three canals, each positioned on a different plane, the hair cells in one canal will bend more than the hair cells in the other canals, depending on the direction of rotation.

The semicircular canals also play an important role in the stabilization of vision. If you move your head from side to side as you read, you can still read without losing your place. The compensatory eye movements are reflex actions that automatically move the eyes just exactly the right amount to provide a continuous, clear focus (Wallach, 1985b). The two fluid-filled vestibular sacs in your inner ear provide information about the orientation of your head. They contain hair cells that act as motion receptors, detecting the direction of head movement. The bending of the hair cells sets up a neural impulse telling the brain in which direction you are moving (D. E. Parker, 1980). The faster you accelerate in any direction, the more the hair cells bend.

The semicircular canals and the vestibular sacs signal only *changes* in motion or orientation. If you were blindfolded and had no visual or other external cues, you would not be able to sense motion once your speed reached a constant rate. For example, in an airplane you feel the takeoff and landing or sudden changes in speed. But once the pilot levels off and maintains about the same speed, your vestibular organs do not signal the brain that you are moving, even if you are traveling hundreds of miles per hour.

FIGURE 3.12

Sensing Balance and Movement

We sense the rotation of the head in any direction because the movement sends fluid coursing through the tubelike semicircular canals in the inner ear. The moving fluid bends the hair cell receptors—which, in turn, send the message to the brain.

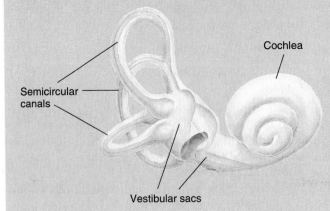

Semicircular canals

Cochlea

Vestibular sacs

Memory Check 3.5

1. Each skin receptor responds only to touch, pressure, warmth, or cold. (true/false)

2. The two-point threshold varies for different body parts. (true/false)

3. People would be better off if they could not feel pain. (true/false)

4. Match the substance with the appropriate description.

   ____ 1) a sugar pill or saline injection that is said to be a drug
   ____ 2) pain-relieving substances produced by the body
   ____ 3) a drug that blocks the action of endorphins
   ____ 4) thought to cause "runner's high"

   a. naloxone
   b. endorphins
   c. placebo

5. The (kinesthetic, vestibular) sense provides information about the position of our body parts in relation to each other and about movement in those body parts.

6. The receptors for the (kinesthetic, vestibular) sense are located in the semicircular canals and vestibular sacs in the (middle ear, inner ear).

Answers: 1. false 2. true 3. false 4. 1) c 2) b 3) a 4) b 5. kinesthetic 6. vestibular, inner ear.

Perception: Ways of Perceiving

In the first part of this chapter, you learned how the senses detect visual, auditory, and other sensory information and transmit it to the brain. Now we will explore **perception**—the process by which this sensory information is actively organized and interpreted by the brain. We *sense* sounds in hertz and decibels, but we *perceive* melodies. We *sense* light of certain wavelengths and intensities, but we *perceive* a multicolored world of objects and people. Sensations are the raw materials of human experiences; perceptions are the finished products.

We know that physical objects can be analyzed down to their smallest parts, even to the atoms that make up the object. But can perception be analyzed and understood in the same way—broken down into its smallest sensory elements? The answer is no, according to Gestalt psychology, a school of thought that began in Germany in the early 1900s.

The Gestalt Principles of Perceptual Organization

The Gestalt psychologists maintained that we cannot understand our perceptual world by breaking down experiences into tiny parts and analyzing them separately. When sensory elements are brought together, something new is formed. "The whole is greater than the sum of its parts," they insisted. The German word **Gestalt** has no exact English equivalent, but it roughly refers to the whole form, pattern, or configuration that we perceive.

How do we organize the world of sights, sounds, and other sensory stimuli in order to perceive the way we do? The Gestalt psychologists claimed that we organize our sensory experience according to certain basic principles of perceptual organization. The principles include the figure-ground relationship and other principles of perceptual grouping.

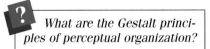

What are the Gestalt principles of perceptual organization?

perception: The process by which sensory information is actively organized and interpreted by the brain.

Gestalt (geh-SHTALT): A German word roughly meaning "form" or "pattern."

figure-ground: A principle of perceptual organization whereby the visual field is perceived in terms of an object (figure) standing out against a background (ground).

innate: Inborn, unlearned.

FIGURE 3.13

Reversing Figure and Ground

In this illustration, you can see a white vase as figure against a black background, or two black faces in profile on a white background. Exactly the same visual stimulus produces two opposite figure-ground perceptions.

Figure and Ground: One Stands Out   The **figure-ground** relationship is the most fundamental principle of perceptual organization and is, therefore, the best place to start analyzing how we perceive. As you view your world, some object (the figure) seems to stand out from the background (the ground).

Many psychologists believe that the figure-ground perceptual ability is **innate**, an ability that we do not have to learn. We know that figure-ground perception is present very early in life. It is also the first ability to appear in patients blind from birth who have received their sight as adults, as it was with S.B. We also know that figure-ground perception is not limited to vision. If you listen to a symphony orchestra or a rock band, the melody line tends to stand out as figure, while the chords and the rest of the accompaniment are heard as background. An itch or a pain would immediately get your attention, while the remaining tactile stimuli you feel would fade to ground.

How can we be sure that knowing the difference between figure and ground is achieved by the perceptual system rather than being part of the sensory stimulus itself? The best proof is represented by reversible figures, where figure and ground seem to shift back and forth between two equal possibilities, as shown in Figure 3.13.

Sometimes a figure or an object blends so well with its background that we can hardly see it. When there are no sharp lines of contrast between a figure and its background, a figure is camouflaged. For many animals, camouflage provides protection from predators.

Gestalt Principles of Grouping: Perceptual Arrangements   The Gestalt psychologists believed that when we see figures or hear sounds, we organize or integrate them according to the simplest, most basic arrangement possible. They proposed the following principles of grouping: similarity, proximity, continuity, and closure (Wertheimer, 1958).

Similarity   We tend to group visual, auditory, or other stimuli according to the principle of similarity. Objects that have similar characteristics are perceived as a unit. In Figure 3.14(a) dots of a similar color are perceived as belonging together to form horizontal rows on the left and vertical columns on the right. When we listen to music, we group the instruments and perceive them as units—the violins, trumpets, and so on—on the basis of similarity in sound.

Proximity   Objects that are close together in space or time are usually perceived as belonging together, because of a principle of grouping called proximity. Because of their spacing, the lines in Figure 3.14(b) are perceived as four pairs

FIGURE 3.14

Gestalt Principles of Grouping

Gestalt psychologists proposed four principles of perceptual grouping: similarity, proximity, continuity, and closure.

A B			
(a) Similarity	**(b) Proximity**	**(c) Continuity**	**(d) Closure**

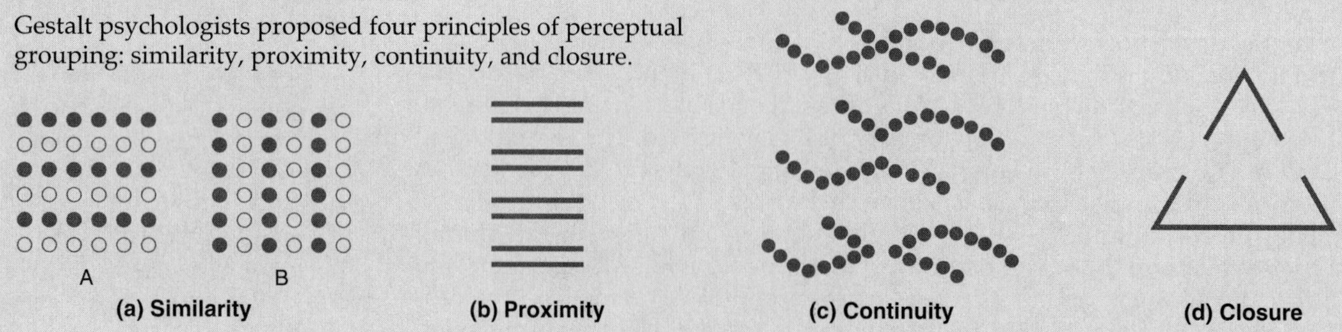

of lines rather than as eight separate lines. Musical notes sounded close together in time are perceived as belonging together to produce musical phrases.

Continuity The principle of continuity means that we tend to perceive figures or objects as belonging together if they appear to form a continuous pattern, as in Figure 3.14(c). When two singers sing or two instruments play in harmony, we perceive the notes in the melody line as belonging together, and the notes in the harmony line as belonging together, even if they converge on the same note and then cross over.

Closure The principle of closure attempts to explain our tendency to complete figures with gaps in them. Even though parts of the figure in Figure 3.14(d) are missing, we use closure and perceive it as a triangle. If you were listening to your favorite song on the radio and interference periodically interrupted it, you would fill in the gaps to perceive the whole song.

Perceptual Constancy

As we view people and objects from different angles and distances and under different lighting conditions, we tend to see them as maintaining the same size, shape, brightness, and color. We call this phenomenon **perceptual constancy**.

What is perceptual constancy, and what are its four types?

Size Constancy: When Smaller Means Farther Away When you say good-bye to friends and watch them walk away, the image they cast on your retina grows smaller and smaller until they finally disappear in the distance. But the shrinking-size information that the retina sends to your brain (the sensation) does not fool the perceptual system. As objects or people move farther away from us, we continue to perceive them as being about the same size.

This perceptual phenomenon is known as **size constancy**. We do not make a literal interpretation about the size of objects from the **retinal image**—the image projected onto the retina of objects in the visual field. If we did, we would believe that objects we see become larger as they approach us and smaller as they move away from us. Some evidence suggests that size constancy is learned. Recall that S.B. had trouble perceiving visual sensations he had never experienced. S.B. so grossly misjudged distances that he perceived the automobiles 60 feet below his hospital window as toy cars nearby.

Shape Constancy: Seeing Round as Round from Any Angle The shape or image of an object projected onto the retina changes according to the angle from which we view it. But our perceptual ability gives us **shape constancy**—the tendency to perceive objects as having a stable or unchanging shape regardless of changes in the retinal image resulting from differences in viewing angle. In other words, we perceive a door as rectangular and a plate as round from whatever angle we view them (see Figure 3.15 on page 110).

Brightness Constancy: Perceiving Brightness in Sunlight and Shadow
We normally see objects as maintaining a constant level of brightness regardless of differences in lighting conditions—a phenomenon known as **brightness constancy**. Nearly all objects reflect some part of the light that falls upon them, and we know that white objects reflect more light than black objects. However, a black asphalt driveway actually reflects more light at noon in bright sunlight than a white shirt reflects indoors at night in dim lighting. Nevertheless, the driveway still looks black and the shirt still looks white. Why? We learn to infer the brightness of objects by comparing them to the brightness of all other objects viewed at the same time.

perceptual constancy: The tendency to perceive objects as maintaining stable properties, such as size, shape, brightness, and color despite differences in distance, viewing angle, and lighting.

size constancy: The tendency to perceive objects as the same size regardless of changes in the retinal image.

retinal image: The image of objects in the visual field projected onto the retina.

shape constancy: The tendency to perceive objects as having a stable or unchanging shape regardless of differences in viewing angle.

brightness constancy: The tendency to see objects as maintaining the same brightness regardless of differences in lighting conditions.

color constancy: The tendency to see objects as maintaining about the same color regardless of differences in lighting conditions.

FIGURE 3.15

Shape Constancy

The door projects very different images on the retina when viewed from different angles. But because of shape constancy, we continue to perceive the door as rectangular.

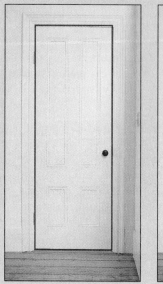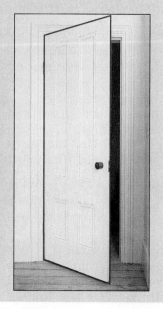

Color Constancy: When Colors Stay the Same in Sunlight or Shadow
Colors can change considerably under different lighting conditions. But when objects are familiar to us, they appear to look about the same color under different conditions of illumination. This is called **color constancy**. Like brightness constancy, color constancy depends on the comparisons we make between differently colored objects we view at the same time (Brou et al., 1986).

Imagine what a strange world you would live in if it were not for the perceptual constancies. If your brain made a literal interpretation of all retinal images,

Memory Check 3.6

1. Camouflage blurs the distinction between:
   a. sensation and perception.
   b. figure and ground.
   c. continuation and closure.
   d. proximity and similarity.

2. The Gestalt principle of (continuity, closure) refers to our tendency to complete figures with gaps in them.

3. Which of the perceptual constancies cause us to perceive objects as being different from the retinal image they project?
   a. brightness constancy and color constancy
   b. color constancy and shape constancy
   c. shape constancy and size constancy
   d. color constancy and size constancy

4. Which of the perceptual constancies depend on our comparing one object with other objects viewed under the same lighting conditions?
   a. brightness constancy and color constancy
   b. color constancy and shape constancy
   c. shape constancy and size constancy
   d. color constancy and size constancy

Answers: 1. b 2. closure 3. c 4. a

the familiar sizes, shapes, and colors you view would appear to change back and forth before your eyes. Fortunately, the perceptual constancies, so natural and commonplace, provide a stable perceptual world.

Depth Perception: Perceiving What's Up Close and Far Away

Depth perception is the ability to perceive the visual world in three dimensions and to judge distances accurately. We judge how far away from us are the objects we grasp and the people we reach out to touch. We climb and descend stairs without stumbling, and perform other visual tasks too numerous to list, all requiring depth perception.

Our depth perception ability is three-dimensional. Yet each eye is able to provide us with only a two-dimensional view. The images cast upon the retina do not contain depth; they are flat, just like a photograph. How, then, do we perceive depth so vividly?

Binocular Depth Cues: The Cues Only Two Eyes Reveal Some cues to depth perception depend on our two eyes working together. These are called **binocular depth cues**, and they include convergence and binocular disparity. **Convergence** occurs when our eyes turn inward as we focus on nearby objects—the closer the object, the greater the convergence. Hold the tip of your finger about 12 inches in front of your nose and focus on it. Now slowly begin moving your finger toward your nose. Your eyes will turn inward so much that they virtually cross when the tip of your finger meets the tip of your nose. Many psychologists believe that the tension of the eye muscles as they converge conveys information to the brain that serves as a cue for distance and depth perception.

Fortunately, our eyes are just far enough apart, about 2 ½ inches or so, to give each eye a slightly different view of the objects we focus on and, consequently, a slightly different retinal image. The difference between the two retinal images, known as **binocular disparity** (or retinal disparity), provides an important cue for depth and distance. The farther away from us the objects we view (up to 20 feet or so), the less the disparity or difference between the two retinal images. The brain integrates these two slightly different retinal images and gives us the perception of three dimensions (Wallach, 1985a). Ohzawa and others (1990) suggest that there are specific neurons in the visual cortex particularly suited to detecting disparity. Ordinarily we are not aware that each eye provides a slightly different view of the objects we see, but you can prove this for yourself in the *Try It!*

depth perception: The ability to see in three dimensions and to estimate distance.

binocular depth cues: Depth cues that depend on two eyes working together; convergence and binocular disparity.

? *What are the binocular depth cues?*

convergence: A binocular depth cue in which the eyes turn inward as they focus on nearby objects—the closer an object, the greater the convergence.

binocular disparity: A binocular depth cue resulting from differences between the two retinal images cast by objects at distances up to about 20 feet.

Hold your forefinger or a pencil at arm's length straight in front of you. Close your right eye and focus on the pencil. Now quickly close your left eye at the same time that you open your right eye. Repeat this procedure, closing one eye just as you open the other one. The pencil will appear to move from side to side in front of your face.

Now slowly bring the pencil closer and closer until it almost reaches your nose. The closer you bring the pencil, the more it appears to move from side to side. This is because there is progressively more disparity between the two retinal images as we view objects closer and closer.

Convergence and binocular disparity provide depth or distance cues only for nearby objects. Fortunately, each eye by itself provides cues for objects at greater distances.

What are seven monocular depth cues?

Monocular Depth Cues: The Cues One Eye Can Detect   Close one eye and you will see that you can still perceive depth. The visual depth cues perceived by one eye alone are called **monocular depth cues**. The following is a description of seven monocular depth cues, many of which artists have used to give the illusion of depth to their paintings.

- *Interposition.* Some psychologists consider interposition, or overlapping, to be the most powerful depth cue of all. When one object partly blocks our view of another, we perceive the partially blocked object as farther away.
- *Linear perspective.* Linear perspective is a depth cue in which parallel lines that are known to be the same distance apart appear to grow closer together or converge as they recede into the distance. Linear perspective was used extensively by Renaissance artists in the 1400s.
- *Relative size.* Larger objects are perceived as being closer to us, and smaller objects as being farther away, as shown in Figure 3.16. We know that most adults are between 5 and 6 feet tall, so when images of the people we view are two, three, or many times smaller than their normal size, we perceive them as being two, three, or as many times farther away.
- *Texture gradient.* Texture gradient is a depth cue in which near objects appear to have a sharply defined texture, while similar objects appear progressively smoother and fuzzier as they recede into the distance.
- *Atmospheric perspective.* Atmospheric perspective, sometimes called aerial perspective, is a depth cue in which objects in the distance have a bluish tint and appear more blurred than objects close at hand.
- *Shadow or shading.* When light falls on objects, shadows are cast. We can distinguish bulges from indentions by the shadows they cast. This ability appears to be learned (Hess, 1961).

Parallel lines appear to converge as they recede into the distance. This effect is known as linear perspective.

The texture of objects can provide depth cues. The flowers in the foreground appear sharp and well defined, while those in the distance are blurred and fuzzy.

FIGURE 3.16

Relative Size: A Monocular Depth Cue

If we assume that these playing cards are all the same size, we perceive the largest card as being closest and the smaller cards as being progressively farther away.

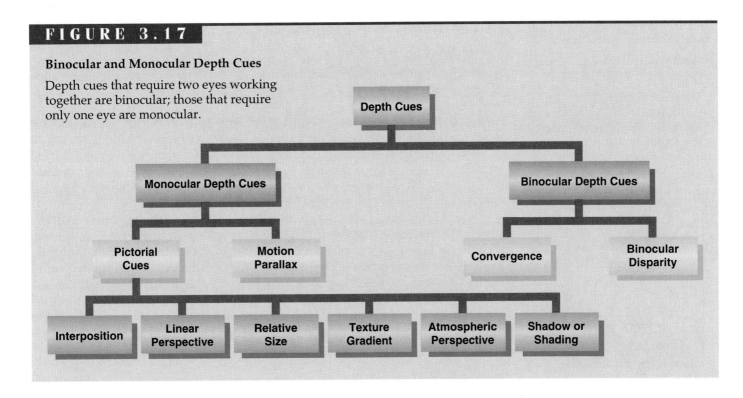

FIGURE 3.17

Binocular and Monocular Depth Cues

Depth cues that require two eyes working together are binocular; those that require only one eye are monocular.

- *Motion parallax.* When we ride in a moving vehicle and look out the side window, the objects we see outside appear to be moving in the opposite direction. The objects also seem to be moving at different speeds—those closest to us appear to be moving faster than objects in the distance. This phenomenon, called motion parallax, provides another monocular cue to depth perception. Objects very far away, such as the moon and the sun, appear to move in the *same* direction as we are moving.

Figure 3.17 summarizes the binocular and monocular depth cues.

Perception of Motion

When we focus and concentrate on visual and other sensory information, we must disregard a great deal. We fix our attention on the information that is important to us and ignore the rest. There is, however, one universal visual attention-getter: Movement gets our attention, and that of practically every other animal. We notice motion, usually regardless of where in our visual field it occurs. When objects do move in our field of vision, they project images that move across the retina, but this alone does not explain our perception of movement. We can perceive movement, that is, **apparent motion**, even when objects do not move at all.

If several stationary lights are flashed on and off in sequence, the light will actually appear to move from one spot to the next. This type of apparent motion, called the **phi phenomenon**, was first discussed by Max Wertheimer (1912), one of the founders of Gestalt psychology. How many neon signs have you seen that caused you to perceive motion? Neon lights don't move; lights simply flash on and off in a particular sequence.

When you watch a motion picture, you are seeing apparent motion. People and objects appear to be moving, but in reality you are seeing stroboscopic motion, a series of still pictures of successive phases of movement. The pictures are flashed in rapid succession to give the illusion of movement.

monocular depth cues (mah-NOK-yu-ler): Depth cues that can be perceived by only one eye.

apparent motion: The perception of motion when none is occurring (as in the phi phenomenon or in stroboscopic movement).

phi phenomenon: An illusion of movement occurring when two or more stationary lights are flashed on and off in sequence, giving the impression that the light is actually moving from one spot to the next.

FIGURE 3.18

"Old Woman/Young Woman" by E. G. Boring

The most famous ambiguous figure can be seen alternately as a young woman or an old woman depending on where your eyes fixate.

Extraordinary Perceptions: Puzzling Perceptions

Not only can we perceive motion that does not exist, but we perceive ambiguous figures, impossible figures, and illusions as well.

Ambiguous Figures: More Than One Way to See Them When we are faced for the first time with an ambiguous figure, we have no experience to call on. Our perceptual system is puzzled and tries to work its way out of the quandary by seeing the ambiguous figure first one way and then another, but not both at once. We never get closure with ambiguous figures that seem to jump back and forth beyond our control.

In some ambiguous figures, two different objects or figures are seen alternately. The best known of these, "Old Woman/Young Woman," by E. G. Boring, is shown in Figure 3.18. If you direct your gaze to the left of the drawing, you are likely to see an attractive young woman, her face turned away. But the young woman disappears when you suddenly perceive the image of the old woman. Such examples of object ambiguity offer striking evidence that our perceptions are more than the mere sum of sensory parts. It is hard to believe that the same drawing (the same sum of sensory parts) can convey such dramatically different perceptions.

Impossible Figures: This Can't Be At first glance, the pictures of impossible figures do not seem so unusual—not until we examine them more closely. Would you invest your money in a company that manufactured three-pronged tridents as shown in Figure 3.19? Such an object could not be made as pictured because the middle prong appears to be in two different places at the same time. However, this type of impossible figure is more likely to fool the depth-perception sensibilities of people from Western cultures. People in some African cultures do not represent three-dimensional visual space in their art, and they do not perceive depth in drawings that contain pictorial depth cues. These people see no ambiguity in drawings similar to the three-pronged trident, and they can draw the figure accurately from memory much more easily than people from Western cultures (Bloomer, 1976).

Illusions: False Perceptions An **illusion** is a false perception or a misperception of an actual stimulus in the environment. We can misperceive size, shape, or the relationship of one element to another. We need not pay to see illusions performed by magicians. Illusions occur naturally, and we see them all the time. An oar in the water appears to be bent where it meets the water. The moon looks much larger at the horizon than it does overhead. Why? One explanation of the moon illusion involves relative size. This idea suggests that the moon looks very

illusion: A false perception of actual stimuli involving a misperception of size, shape, or the relationship of one element to another.

FIGURE 3.19

The Three-Pronged Trident

This is an impossible figure because the middle prong appears to be in two places at the same time.

FIGURE 3.20

The Müller-Lyer Illusion

The two horizontal lines in (a) are identical in length. Although the two vertical lines in (b) are the same length, the line on the left seems to project forward and appears closer than the line on the right, which seems to recede in the distant corner. When two lines are the same length, the one perceived as farther away will appear longer. (Based on Gregory, 1978).

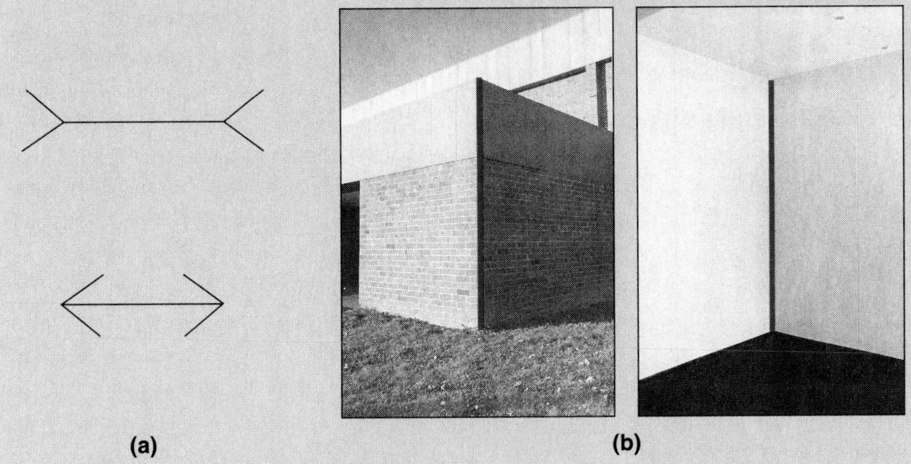

(a)　　　　　　　　　(b)

large on the horizon because it is viewed in comparison to trees, buildings, and other objects. When viewed overhead, the moon cannot be compared with other objects, and it appears smaller. People have been speculating about the moon illusion for 22 centuries and experimenting for 50 years to determine its cause, but there is still no agreement (Hershenson, 1989).

The Müller-Lyer Illusion　In Figure 3.20(a), which horizontal line is longer, the upper or the lower one? Although the two lines are the same length, the diagonals extending outward from both ends of the upper line make it look longer than the lower line, which has diagonals pointing inward. British psychologist R. L. Gregory (1978) has suggested that the Müller-Lyer illusion is actually a misapplication of size constancy. In Figure 3.20(b), the corner in the left-hand photo projects forward, toward the viewer, and is therefore perceived to be closer. The corner in the right-hand photo appears to be more distant because it seems to recede from the viewer. When two lines are the same length, the line we perceive to be farther away will look longer.

The Ponzo Illusion　The Ponzo illusion also plays an interesting trick on our estimation of size. Look at Figure 3.21. Which obstruction on the railroad tracks looks larger? You have undoubtedly guessed by now, contrary to your perceptions, that A and B are the same size. Again, our perceptions of size and distance, which we trust and which are normally accurate in informing us about the real world, can be wrong. If we saw two obstructions on real railroad tracks identical to the ones in the illusion, the one that looks larger would indeed be larger. So the Ponzo illusion is not a natural illusion but rather a contrived one. In fact, all these illusions are really misapplications of principles that nearly always work properly in our normal everyday experience.

FIGURE 3.21

The Ponzo Illusion

The two white bars superimposed on the railroad track are actually identical in length. Because A appears farther away than B, we perceive it as longer.

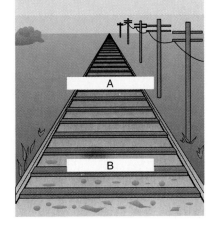

The culture in which people live is responsible to some extent for the illusions they perceive. Read the following World of Psychology section to learn about such cultural differences.

Cultural Differences in the Perception of Illusions

British psychologist R. L. Gregory believed that our susceptibility to the Müller-Lyer and other such illusions does not occur because of inborn ways of perceiving due to the structure of the human nervous system. Rather, he maintained that it probably results from our experiences with lines, edges, doors, corners, and rooms. In other words, there is a cultural explanation for illusions.

To test whether susceptibility to the Müller-Lyer and similar illusions is due to experience, Segall and others (1966) tested 1,848 adults and children from 15 different cultures in Africa, the Philippines, and the United States. Included were a group of Zulus from South Africa and a group of Illinois residents. The study revealed that "there were marked differences in illusion susceptibility across the cultural groups included in this study" (Segall, 1994, p. 137). Some tendency to see the illusion was reported for all the cultures, indicating a biological component, but experience was clearly a factor. Zulus, who have round houses and see few corners of any kind, are not fooled by the Müller-Lyer illusion. Illinois residents saw the illusion readily, while the Zulu tribespeople tended not to see it.

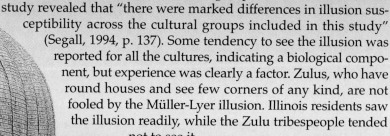

Some researchers suggested that race might offer an explanation for the cultural differences observed (Pollack, 1970). But a study by Stewart (1973) provides evidence to indicate that it is fundamentally culture, not race, that drives our perceptions of illusions. When two groups of schoolchildren from Illinois (60 African American and 60 white subjects) were tested with the Müller-Lyer and other illusions, no significant differences were found in susceptibility to the illusions. And in Zambia, researchers tested five different groups of black African schoolchildren using the same illusions. Children's tendency to see the illusions had nothing to do with race but was strongly influenced by culture. Those children who lived in areas where buildings consisted of angles, edges, corners, and doors were likely to be fooled by the illusions; those who lived in remote villages with primarily round houses were not.

Other research also indicates that perceptual illusions are strongly influenced by culture. Pedersen and Wheeler (1983) studied Native American responses to the Müller-Lyer illusion among two groups of Navajos. One group of Navajos, who lived in rectangular houses and had experienced corners, angles, and edges, tended to see the illusion. The other group of Navajos, like the Zulus, tended not to see it because their cultural experience consisted of round houses such as the one shown in the photo.

Other researchers found that everyday experience also influences susceptibility to the Ponzo illusion. Liebowitz and others (1969; Liebowitz & Pick, 1972) learned that residents of Guam are far less likely to be deceived by the Ponzo illusion than are American subjects. On Guam, there are no long expanded stretches of highways and no railways, and the irregular, hilly terrain of the island is home to a culture less susceptible to illusions that depend on depth cues.

Memory Check 3.7

1. Retinal disparity and convergence are two (monocular, binocular) depth cues.

2. Match the appropriate monocular depth cue with each example.

   ____ 1) one building partly blocking another
   ____ 2) railroad tracks converging in the distance
   ____ 3) closer objects appearing to move faster than far objects
   ____ 4) far objects looking smaller than near objects

   a. motion parallax
   b. linear perspective
   c. interposition
   d. relative size

3. The type of apparent motion we see in motion pictures is (motion parallax, stroboscopic motion).

4. An illusion is:
   a. an imaginary sensation.
   b. an impossible figure.
   c. a misperception of a real stimulus.
   d. a figure-ground reversal.

Answers: 1. binocular 2. 1) c 2) b 3) a 4) d 3. stroboscopic motion 4. c

Additional Influences on Perception

Why don't all people perceive sights, sounds, odors, and events in the same way? The reason is that our perceptions involve more than just the sensory stimuli themselves.

Bottom-Up and Top-Down Processing

Psychologists distinguish between two distinct information-processing techniques we use in recognizing patterns—bottom-up processing and top-down processing. **Bottom-up processing** begins with the individual components of a stimulus that are detected by the sensory receptors. The information is then transmitted to areas in the brain where it is combined and assembled into the whole patterns that we perceive.

bottom-up processing: Information processing in which individual components or bits of data are combined until a complete perception is formed.

In what types of situations do we rely more on bottom-up processing or top-down processing?

In **top-down processing**, on the other hand, past experience and knowledge of the context plays a role in forming our perceptions. In other words, what we perceive is more than the sum of the individual elements taken in by our sensory receptors. If you have ever tried to decipher a prescription written by your doctor (bottom-up processing), you may have been amazed that your pharmacist could fill it. But prior knowledge and experience enabled the pharmacist to use top-down processing.

Of course, we use both bottom-up and top-down processing when we form perceptions. In situations unfamiliar to us, we are likely to use bottom-up processing. In familiar situations where we have some prior knowledge and experience, we tend to use top-down processing.

The Role of Psychological Factors in Perception

We make perceptual judgments from our own individual point of reference. Other people are perceived as tall or short, young or old, depending on our own height or age. Words such as *intelligent, attractive, expensive, thin, successful, sensible, talented, rich, exciting, loud*, and so on are all measured from our own perceptual point of view. Our perceptions are also affected by our values, needs, interests, and emotions.

Our **perceptual set**—what we expect to perceive—determines, to a large extent, what we actually see, hear, feel, taste, and smell. If you ordered raspberry sherbet and it was colored green, would it still taste like raspberry, or might it taste more like lime? Once our expectations are set, we often bend reality to make it fit them. Psychologist David Rosenhan (1973) and some of his colleagues were admitted as patients to various mental hospitals with "diagnoses" of schizophrenia. Once admitted, they acted normal in every way. The purpose? They wondered how long it would take the doctors and the hospital staff to realize that they were not mentally ill. But the doctors and the staff members saw only what they expected to see and not what actually occurred. They perceived everything the pseudo-patients said and did, such as notetaking, to be symptoms of their illness. But the real patients were not fooled. They were the first to realize that the psychologists were not really mentally ill.

$\mathbf{S}$ ubliminal Persuasion and Extrasensory Perception

So far we have considered perceptions that are formed above the threshold of our awareness and perceptions that arise from our known sensory abilities. Can we be influenced by persuasive messages below our level of awareness, through subliminal persuasion? And are we able to gain information by some means other than our known sensory channels, through extrasensory perception?

Subliminal Persuasion: Does It Work?

Over 30 years ago, it was reported that moviegoers in a New Jersey theater were exposed to advertising messages flashed on the screen so briefly that they were not aware of them. An advertising executive, James Vicary, claimed that the words

---

[margin note] **?** *What are some psychological factors that affect our perceptions?*

[margin definitions]
top-down processing: Application of previous experience and conceptual knowledge to first recognize the whole of a perception and thus easily identify the simpler elements of that whole.

perceptual set: An expectation of what will be perceived, which can affect what actually is perceived.

[margin note] **?** *Is subliminal persuasion effective in influencing behavior?*

"Eat Popcorn" and "Drink Coca-Cola" were projected on the screen for only $\frac{1}{3000}$ of a second every 5 seconds during the movie. The purpose of the messages was to influence the audience to buy popcorn and Coca-Cola, not by getting their conscious attention, but by sending persuasive messages below their level of awareness, a technique called **subliminal persuasion**. During the 6-week period the messages ran, popcorn sales supposedly went up by 57.5 percent, and Coca-Cola sales rose by more than 18 percent (McConnell et al., 1958).

Technically, **subliminal perception** would be defined as the perception of sensory stimuli that are below the absolute threshold. But the subliminal persuasion experiment was limited to messages flashed so quickly that they could *never* be normally perceived at all. Can we actually perceive information that is completely below our level of awareness? Some people say that we can, and today subliminal persuasion is aimed at selling much more than popcorn and Coke. Subliminal self-help tapes, popularized by the New Age movement, are so popular that Americans now spend over $50 million a year on the tapes (Adams, 1991). There are tapes that claim to help people remedy virtually every ill (relieve depression, cure migraine headaches), solve every problem (reduce stress, quit smoking), and meet every need (increase confidence, gain peace of mind). Embedded in the recordings of soothing music or ocean waves lapping the shore are subliminal messages for those who want to lose weight ("I eat less"), reduce stress ("I am calm"), or improve their self-image ("I am capable").

Is subliminal persuasion in audiotapes effective? Researchers conducting double-blind studies have found that audiotapes that claimed to influence behavior with subliminal messages were no more effective in doing so than tapes containing unrelated subliminal messages or no subliminal messages whatsoever (Greenwald, 1992; Greenwald et al., 1991; Russell et al., 1991). But if subliminal persuasion does not influence behavior, why do some users insist that the tapes have helped them to quit smoking, lose weight, and so on? Evidently the change is due to the power of suggestion or the placebo effect, and not the power of the tapes. But just think of the many implications that would make life easier for psychology professors if subliminal persuasion really worked. Professors could revolutionize college life by entertaining students with interesting films, during which subliminal messages would be flashed every 5 seconds: "Study Psychology," "Read Psychology," and "Study Harder." If you watched enough movies, your friends and family might find it impossible to tear you away from your psychology books.

Extrasensory Perception: Does It Exist?

We know that perception refers to the process by which we organize and interpret sensory input. But is it possible to perceive information that does not come through the senses? Is there such a thing as **extrasensory perception (ESP)**—gaining information about objects, events, or another's thoughts through some means other than the known sensory channels? Can some people read minds or foretell the future? According to a 1990 Gallup poll, 49 percent of Americans believe in ESP (Gallup & Newport, 1990b). Extrasensory perception is part of a larger area of interest known as **parapsychology**, the study of psychic phenomena. Reported cases of ESP roughly fall into three categories—telepathy, clairvoyance, and precognition.

Telepathy means gaining awareness of the thoughts, the feelings, or the activities of another without the use of the senses—in other words, reading a person's mind. Clairvoyance means gaining information about objects or events without use of the senses, such as knowing the contents of a letter before opening it. Precognition refers to an awareness of an event before it occurs. Most of

subliminal persuasion: Sending persuasive messages below the recipient's level of awareness.

subliminal perception: Perceiving sensory stimulation that is below the absolute threshold.

extrasensory perception (ESP): Gaining awareness of or information about objects, events, or another's thoughts through some means other than the known sensory channels.

parapsychology: The study of psychic phenomena, including extrasensory perception (ESP).

What is extrasensory perception, and have the claims of psychics been verified scientifically?

the reported cases of precognition in everyday life have occurred while people were dreaming.

One researcher revealed the poor record of well-known psychics who made New Year's predictions for the *National Enquirer* between 1978 and 1985. Only two of their 425 predictions proved to be accurate (Strentz, 1986). But probably the most telling blow against precognition is the failure of any of these psychics to predict some of the most astounding world events of the century—the fall of the Berlin Wall in 1989, the breakup of the Soviet Union in 1991, the end of the Cold War, and the slaughter of hundreds of thousands of people in Rwanda.

Because psychic phenomena violate what we know about the real, measurable, physical world, scientists and skeptics naturally demand proof of their existence (Hansel, 1966, 1980; Randi, 1980). Time after time, investigators have discovered trickery when examining the claims of psychics who assert that they can read minds or contact and communicate with the dead. Uri Geller, well known for his ability to bend spoons and keys, to "read" the contents of sealed envelopes, and to perform other feats supposedly using his mind alone, was found to use magic tricks and fraud to deceive the public.

One professional magician, the Amazing Randi (1980), has gained popularity in exposing the fraudulent techniques used by Uri Geller and others who claim great powers or abilities (Yam, 1995). In 1980 Randi offered to pay $10,000 "to any person or group that can perform *one* paranormal feat of *any* kind under the proper observing conditions" (p. 3). To this day he has not found a single person able to demonstrate psychic ability under controlled conditions, although the offer still stands.

What is the truth about psychic phenomena? Either they exist but have not yet been proven, or they may exist but might not be verifiable under laboratory conditions, or they do not exist at all. What do you believe?

Earlier we noted that sensation and perceptions are so closely linked in everyday experience that it is hard to see clearly where one ends and the other begins. But in this chapter you have seen many examples of what is sensed and what is perceived. Our perceptual system is continuously trying to complete what we merely sense. We are always busy filling in, organizing, and making more complete perceptual sense out of the sensory parts that we are able to see, hear, touch, taste, and smell.

Memory   Check 3.8

1. In situations where we have some prior knowledge and experience, we are likely to rely more on (bottom-up, top-down) processing.

2. Perceptual set is most directly related to our:
   a. needs.   c. expectations.
   b. interests.   d. emotions.

3. Subliminal advertising has been proven effective in influencing consumers to buy products. (true/false)

4. Match the type of psychic phenomenon with the description:

   ____ 1) reading someone's mind
   ____ 2) gaining awareness of events before they occur
   ____ 3) gaining information about objects or events without the use of the senses

   a. clairvoyance
   b. precognition
   c. telepathy

5. Carefully controlled and repeatable laboratory experiments have proved the existence of extrasensory perception. (true/false)

Answers: 1. top-down 2. c 3. false 4. 1) c 2) b 3) a 5. false

Noise and Hearing Loss—Bad Vibrations

Hearing loss is increasing rapidly in the industrialized world, and the main reason for the increase is NOISE. Jet engines, power mowers, radios, firecrackers, motorcycles, chain saws, and other power tools are well-known sources of noise that can injure the ear. For centuries we have known that noise can cause hearing loss, but it was not until the early 1970s that the U.S. Congress passed legislation to protect employees in the workplace who are exposed regularly to hazardous noise.

Unfortunately, there are no laws outside of the workplace to protect us from hearing loss. And we are in more danger of losing our hearing off the job than at the work site. Without proper protection, recreational hunting, rock concerts, and some sports events can cause more damage to hearing than industrial noise.

Noisy Toys and Other Hazards

Exposure to hazardous noise can begin long before we are old enough to listen to a Sony Walkman, experience a rock concert, or attend a baseball game at a covered or domed stadium. Some babies and toddlers get an early start on hearing loss with a variety of toys on the market. Researchers Axelsson and Jerson (1985) tested seven squeaking toys that, at a distance of 10 centimeters, squeaked out pure sound levels loud enough to put toddlers at risk for hearing loss with only 2 minutes of daily exposure.

If older children play with toy weapons, noise-induced hearing loss can occur with only seconds of exposure. Researchers tested several toy weapons and found that, at a distance of 50 centimeters, the guns produced explosive sound levels ranging from 144 to 152 dB (Axelsson

& Jerson, 1985). All exceeded the 130-dB peak level that is considered the upper limit for exposure to short-lived explosive sounds if hearing loss is to be avoided.

Firecrackers pose a particular hazard if they explode close to the ear. In one study a number of firecrackers were tested at 3 meters, and sound levels were found to range from 130 dB to an unbelievable and highly dangerous 190 dB (Gupta & Vishwakarma, 1989).

The Destructive Effects of Noise

Explosions, gun blasts, and other extremely loud noises may burst the eardrum or may fracture or dislocate the tiny ossicles in the middle ear. Often these injuries can be repaired surgically, but noise injuries to the inner ear cannot. "Extremely intense sounds can rip the delicate sensory [hair] cells completely off the basilar membrane on which they normally sit, kill the cells, or merely injure them permanently" (Bennett, 1990, p. 3). During the filming of a Western movie, former President Ronald Reagan's hearing was damaged beyond repair by a single shot from a blank pistol fired too close to his ear. It doesn't take an explosion or years of exposure to noise to injure hair cells. Rock musician Kathy Peck lost 40 percent of her hearing in one evening after her band opened a stadium concert for Duran Duran.

Noise: How Much Is Too Much?

How can you tell when noise levels are high enough to jeopardize your hearing? You are putting yourself at risk if you have difficulty talking over the noise level, or if the noise exposure leaves you with a ringing

in your ears or a temporary hearing loss (Dobie, 1987).

Experts claim that exposure to noise of 90 dB (a lawn mower, for example) for more than 8 hours in a 24-hour period can damage hearing. For every increase of 5 dB, maximum exposure time should be cut in half—4 hours for 95 dB, 2 hours for 100 dB, and 1 hour for 105 dB. The Department of Labor considers 115 dB to be the maximum allowable level of exposure to steady sound levels (Catlin, 1986). And 120 decibels, what you would hear directly in front of the speakers at a rock concert, would immediately destroy some of the hair cell receptors.

In 1986 the rock group The Who entered the *Guiness Book of World Records* as the loudest rock band on record, blasting out deafening sound intensities that measured 120 decibels at a distance of 164 feet from the speakers. Unless their ears were protected, every person within that 164-foot radius probably suffered some irreversible hearing loss. And the band members? Pete Townshend of The Who has severely damaged hearing and, in addition, is plagued by tinnitus, an annoying condition in which there is a continuous ringing in the ears.

continued

In an article in *Rolling Stone*, Ted Nugent admitted his hearing problem. "My left ear is there just to balance my face, because it doesn't work at all" (Murphy, 1989, p. 101). In the same interview, Axl Rose of Guns N' Roses expressed less concern than his older fellow rock stars. If hearing loss results in the future, "that's the sacrifice I guess we'll have to make," he said. But there are other "sacrifices" that Rose and others in the rock industry might be less willing to make. In the early 1990s a rash of lawsuits were filed against rock musicians and promoters by fans complaining of tinnitus and hearing loss suffered after attending their concerts.

Protecting Yourself from Hearing Loss

What can you do to protect yourself from noise?

- If you must be exposed to loud noise, use earplugs (not the kind used for swimming) or earmuffs to reduce noise by as much as 15–30 dB (Dobie, 1987).

- If you must engage in an extremely noisy activity, such as cutting wood with a chain saw, limit periods of exposure so that stunned hair cells can recover.

- Keep the volume down on your Walkman-type radio or tape player. If the volume control is numbered 1 to 10, a volume above 4 probably exceeds the federal standards for noise. If you have a ringing in your ears, if sounds seem muffled, or if you have a tickling sensation after you remove your headset, you could have sustained some hearing loss.

- Begin humming before you are exposed to loud noise. Humming will set in motion the very tiny muscles in the middle ear that will dampen the sound and provide some measure of protection (Borg & Counter, 1989).

- Put your fingers in your ears or leave the scene.

Thinking Critically

Evaluation

Using what you have learned about the factors that contribute to hearing loss, prepare a statement indicating what the government should do to control noise pollution, even to the extent of banning certain noise hazards. Consider the workplace, the home, toys, machinery, rock concerts, and so on.

Point/Counterpoint

Recent polls indicate that nearly 49 percent of the people believe in ESP. Prepare a sound, logical argument supporting one of the following positions:

a. There is evidence to suggest that ESP exists.

b. There is no evidence to suggest that ESP exists.

Psychology in Your Life

Vision and hearing are generally believed to be the two most highly prized senses. How would your life change if you lost your sight? How would your life change if you lost your hearing? Which sense would you find more traumatic to lose? Why?

Chapter Summary and Review

Sensation: The Sensory World

> **?** *What is the difference between sensation and perception?*

Sensation is the process through which the senses pick up sensory stimuli and transmit them to the brain. Perception is the process by which this sensory information is actively organized and interpreted by the brain.

> **?** *What is the difference between the absolute threshold and the difference threshold?*

The absolute threshold is the minimum amount of sensory stimulation that can be detected 50 percent of the time. The difference threshold is a measure of the smallest increase or decrease in a physical stimulus that can be detected 50 percent of the time.

? How are sensory stimuli in the environment experienced as sensations?

For each of our senses, there are sensory receptors that detect and respond to sensory stimuli. Through a process known as transduction, the receptors convert sensory stimuli into neural impulses, which are then transmitted to their own special location in the brain.

Key Terms

sensation (p. 80)
perception (p. 80)
absolute threshold (p. 81)
difference threshold (p. 81)
just noticeable difference (p. 81)
Weber's law (p. 81)
signal detection theory (p. 82)
sensory receptors (p. 83)
transduction (p. 83)
sensory adaptation (p. 83)

Vision

? How do the cornea, the iris, and the pupil function in vision?

The cornea bends light rays inward through the pupil—the small, dark opening in the eye. The iris dilates and contracts the pupil to regulate the amount of light entering the eye.

? What are the lens and the retina?

The lens changes its shape as it focuses images of objects from varying distances on the retina, a thin membrane containing the sensory receptors for vision.

? What roles do the rods and cones play in vision?

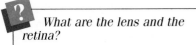

The cones detect color, provide our sharpest vision, and function best in high illumination. The rods enable us to see in dim light. Rods respond to black and white, and they encode all other visible wavelengths in shades of gray.

? What path does the neural impulse take from the retina to the primary visual cortex?

The rods and the cones transduce light waves into neural impulses that pass from the bipolar cells to the ganglion cells, whose axons form the optic nerve. At the optic chiasma, some of the fibers of the optic nerve cross to the opposite side of the brain, before reaching the thalamus. From the thalamus, the neural impulses travel to the primary visual cortex.

? What are the three dimensions that combine to provide the colors we experience?

The three dimensions are hue, saturation, and brightness.

? What two major theories attempt to explain color vision?

Two major theories that attempt to explain color vision are the trichromatic theory and the opponent-process theory.

Key Terms

visible spectrum (p. 85)
cornea (p. 85)
lens (p. 86)
accommodation (p. 86)
retina (p. 86)
rods (p. 87)
cones (p. 87)
fovea (p. 87)
dark adaptation (p. 88)
optic nerve (p. 88)
feature detectors (p. 89)
hue (p. 89)
saturation (p. 89)
brightness (p. 89)
trichromatic theory (p. 90)
opponent-process theory (p. 90)
afterimage (p. 91)
color blindness (p. 92)

Hearing

? What determines the pitch and the loudness of a sound, and how is each quality measured?

The pitch of a sound is determined by frequency, which is measured in hertz. The loudness of a sound is determined largely by the amplitude of a sound wave and is measured in decibels.

? How do the outer, middle, and inner ears function in hearing?

Sound waves enter the pinna, the visible part of the outer ear, and travel to the end of the auditory canal, causing the eardrum to vibrate. This sets in motion the ossicles in the middle ear, which amplify the sound waves. The vibration of the oval window causes activity in the inner ear, setting in motion the fluid in the cochlea and moving the hair cell receptors, which transduce the vibrations into neural impulses. The auditory nerve carries the neural impulses to the brain.

? What two major theories attempt to explain hearing?

Two major theories that attempt to explain hearing are place theory and frequency theory.

? What are some major causes of hearing loss?

Some major causes of hearing loss are disease, birth defects, aging, injury, and noise.

Key Terms

frequency (p. 93)
amplitude (p. 94)
decibel (p. 94)
timbre (p. 94)
audition (p. 95)
outer ear (p. 95)
middle ear (p. 95)
inner ear (p. 95)
cochlea (p. 95)
hair cells (p. 95)
place theory (p. 96)
frequency theory (p. 96)
bone conduction (p. 96)

Smell and Taste

 What path does a smell message take on its journey from the nose to the brain?

The act of smelling begins when odor molecules reach the smell receptors in the olfactory epithelium at the top of the nasal cavity. The axons of these receptors form the olfactory nerve, which relays the smell message to the olfactory bulbs. From there the smell message travels to other parts of the brain.

 What are the four primary taste sensations, and how are they detected?

The four primary taste sensations are sweet, salty, sour, and bitter. The receptor cells for taste are found in the taste buds on the tongue and in other parts of the mouth and throat.

Key Terms

olfaction (p. 98)
olfactory epithelium (p. 98)
olfactory bulbs (p. 98)
gustation (p. 99)
taste buds (p. 100)

Our Other Senses

How does the skin provide sensory information?

Nerve endings in the skin (the sensory receptors) respond to different kinds of stimulation, including heat and cold, pressure, pain, and a vast range of touch sensations. The neural impulses ultimately register in the somatosensory cortex.

What beneficial purpose does pain serve?

Pain can be a valuable warning and protective mechanism, motivating us to tend to an injury, to restrict our activity, and to seek medical help if needed.

What is the gate-control theory of pain?

Melzack and Wall's gate-control theory of pain holds that pain signals transmitted by slow-conducting fibers can be blocked at the spinal gate (1) if fast-conducting fibers get their message to the gate first, or (2) if the brain itself inhibits their transmission.

 What are endorphins?

Endorphins, released when we are stressed or injured, are the body's natural painkillers; they block pain and produce a feeling of well-being.

What is the vestibular sense, and where are its sensory receptors located?

The kinesthetic sense provides information about the relative position of body parts and movement of those body parts. The position or motion is detected by sensory receptors in the joints, ligaments, and muscles.

What kind of information does the kinesthetic sense provide, and how is this sensory information detected?

The vestibular sense provides information about movement and our orientation in space. Sensory receptors in the semicircular canals and in the vestibular sacs detect changes in the movement and orientation of the head.

Key Terms

tactile (p. 102)
gate-control theory (p. 102)
endorphins (p. 104)
naloxone (p. 104)
kinesthetic sense (p. 105)
vestibular sense (p. 106)
semicircular canals (p. 106)

Perception: Ways of Perceiving

 What are the Gestalt principles of perceptual organization?

The Gestalt principles of perceptual organization include the figure-ground relationship and four principles of perceptual grouping—similarity, proximity, continuity, and closure.

 What is perceptual constancy, and what are its four types?

Perceptual constancy is the tendency to perceive objects as maintaining the same size, shape, brightness, and color despite changes in lighting conditions or changes in the retinal image that result when objects are viewed from different angles and distances.

What are the binocular depth cues?

The binocular depth cues are convergence and binocular disparity, and they depend on both eyes working together for depth perception.

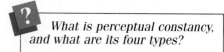 *What are seven monocular depth cues?*

The monocular depth cues, those that can be perceived by one eye, include interposition, linear perspective, relative size, texture gradient, atmospheric perspective, shadow or shading, and motion parallax.

Key Terms

perception (p. 107)
Gestalt (p. 107)
figure-ground (p. 108)
innate (p. 108)
perceptual constancy (p. 109)
size constancy (p. 109)
retinal image (p. 109)
shape constancy (p. 109)
brightness constancy (p. 109)
color constancy (p. 110)

depth perception (p. 111)
binocular depth cues (p. 111)
convergence (p. 111)
binocular disparity (p. 111)
monocular depth cues (p. 112)
apparent motion (p. 113)
phi phenomenon (p. 113)
illusion (p. 114)

Additional Influences on Perception

? *In what types of situations do we rely on bottom-up processing or top-down processing?*

We use bottom-up processing more in unfamiliar situations, top-down processing more in situations where we have some prior knowledge and experience.

? *What are some psychological factors that affect our perceptions?*

Our perceptions are affected by our own point of reference, by the value we attach to a stimulus, and by our perceptual set—what we expect to perceive.

Subliminal Persuasion and Extrasensory Perception

? *Is subliminal persuasion effective in influencing behavior?*

In experimental studies, subliminal persuasion has not been found to influence behavior.

? *What is extrasensory perception, and have the claims of psychics been verified scientifically?*

Extrasensory perception refers to gaining awareness of information about objects, events, or another's thoughts through some means other than known sensory channels. Experiments claiming to prove psychic phenomena have not been repeatable under carefully controlled conditions.

Key Terms

bottom-up processing (p. 117)
top-down processing (p. 118)
perceptual set (p. 118)
subliminal persuasion (p. 119)
subliminal perception (p. 119)
extrasensory perception (ESP) (p. 119)
parapsychology (p. 119)

4

STATES OF CONSCIOUSNESS

Shortly after 6:00 A.M. one day in March 1990, Northwest Airlines Flight 650, with 91 passengers on board, left Fargo, North Dakota, bound for St. Paul, Minnesota. The flight was uneventful, and the plane landed safely.

A safe landing doesn't usually make the news, but Flight 650 did. Upon arrival, all three members of the cockpit crew—the pilot, the first officer, and the second officer—were arrested. On the night before their early morning flight, all three had been out drinking until after midnight at a tavern across the street from their motel. Although there was no evidence that any of the three were drunk, tests confirmed the presence of alcohol in their blood. Having violated Federal Aviation Administration rules against drinking alcohol within 8 hours of flying, all three fliers lost their FAA licenses.

Several years before the Flight 650 incident, a Boeing 707 took off from New York en route to Los Angeles International Airport. The flight was scheduled to arrive at midnight. As the plane neared Los Angeles, the air traffic controllers were puzzled to see it maintaining its altitude

of 32,000 feet. The flight tower continued to issue clearances to land, but the plane passed over Los Angeles and was soon 50 miles out over the Pacific Ocean, still at a high altitude. The air traffic controllers were alarmed as the plane continued flying 100 miles westward over the Pacific, because its fuel supply was running low.

What was wrong with the pilots? They had used neither drugs nor alcohol but were responding naturally to their biological clocks, which were synchronized with New York time. In New York, it was 3:00 A.M.—a time when most of us feel an urgent need to sleep. And indeed the flight crew had succumbed to their urgent need. They were all sound asleep, cruising on automatic pilot. Finally the tower was able to awaken them by activating a series of chimes in the cockpit, and the pilots returned to Los Angeles with just enough fuel to land safely. (Coleman, 1986)

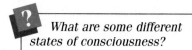

What are some different states of consciousness?

What Is Consciousness?

The crews of the two flights had problems because they were not flying in a state of ordinary waking consciousness. Consciousness is one of the most basic concepts in the study of psychology, and yet even today, it remains rather elusive. We may think of **consciousness** as a state of awareness—a continuous stream of perceptions, thoughts, feelings, or sensations of which we are aware from moment to moment.

Our ability to define and explain consciousness has increased little over the century since the first American psychologist, William James, likened consciousness to a flowing stream. This "stream of consciousness," he believed, was made up of a combination of attention and short-term memory. Today a number of researchers are launching an effort to study consciousness through scientific investigation. Among them is Francis Crick, who shared a Nobel Prize for discovering the structure of DNA in 1953. Crick argues that consciousness results from some underlying mechanism that combines attention and short-term memory, the same idea that William James put forth at the beginning of this century (Crick & Koch, 1992; Horgan, 1994).

As James imagined, consciousness moves and flows like a stream. It wanders, meanders, sometimes where we will it, and sometimes not. We control our flow of consciousness when we concentrate and focus our attention. At other times we do not control it, as images, thoughts, and feelings, like uninvited guests, may slip into the stream of consciousness and capture it temporarily.

Sigmund Freud extended the notion of consciousness as envisioned by James. Far beneath the stream of consciousness, Freud identified what he termed the unconscious, within which flow wishes, ideas, and impulses, primarily sexual and aggressive in nature, of which we are unaware. Freud advanced the notion of various levels of awareness in consciousness.

When we are at the highest level of consciousness, we are fully absorbed, and our thoughts are fixed on the details of our concentration, such as studying, tak-

consciousness: The continuous stream of perceptions, thoughts, feelings, or sensations that we are aware of from moment to moment.

ing an exam, learning a new skill, and so on. But at such times we are less conscious of other potentially competing stimuli, both external (the noise around us) and internal (whether we are hungry). Athletes at full concentration during a game may be oblivious to pains signaling potentially serious injuries.

A lower level of awareness involves such mental activities as daydreaming. Have you ever drifted off into a daydream while sitting in class? When your consciousness is tuned in to a daydream, your awareness of the world around you is tuned out, and it can be embarrassing if your professor calls on you when you are lost in a daydream. Yet most of us lower our level of awareness to daydreams quite often (Singer, 1975).

Still lower levels of awareness are the states of consciousness to which we descend when we sleep. We will now explore the various states of consciousness and examine the many ways in which consciousness may be altered. Ordinary waking consciousness can be altered by substances such as alcohol or drugs, and by focused concentration as in meditation and hypnosis. This chapter will explore these **altered states of consciousness**.

The most fundamental altered state is one in which we spend about one-third of our lives, the one we visit for several hours nearly every night—sleep.

Circadian Rhythms: Our 24-Hour Highs and Lows

What is a circadian rhythm, and which rhythms are most relevant to the study of sleep?

Do you notice changes in the way you feel throughout the day—fluctuations in your energy level, moods, or efficiency? Over 100 of our bodily functions and behaviors fluctuate regularly from a high to a low point over a 24-hour period (Dement, 1974). Called **circadian rhythms**, these daily fluctuations are controlled largely by the brain, apparently by the suprachiasmatic nucleus in the hypothalamus (Ginty et al., 1993; Ralph, 1989). Blood pressure, heart rate, appetite, secretion of hormones and digestive enzymes, sensory acuity, elimination, and even our body's response to medication all follow circadian rhythms (Hrushesky, 1994). Our learning efficiency and our ability to perform a wide range of tasks also ebb and flow according to these daily rhythms.

Two circadian rhythms of particular importance to the study of sleep are the sleep/wakefulness cycle and body temperature. Normal human body temperature can range from a low of about 97 or 97.5 degrees between 4:00 and 5:00 A.M. to a high of about 98.6 degrees between 5:00 and 8:00 P.M. People sleep best when their body temperature is lowest, and they are most alert when their body temperature is at its daily high point. Alertness also follows a circadian rhythm, one that is quite separate from the sleep/wakefulness rhythm (Monk, 1989). For most of us, alertness decreases between 2:00 and 5:00 P.M. and between 2:00 and 7:00 A.M. (Mitler et al., 1988). During the afternoon decrease in alertness, body temperature also dips (Barrett et al., 1993).

Are circadian rhythms strictly biological, or do environmental cues play a part? Researchers have already identified a gene that underlies circadian rhythms in the mouse (Takahashi & Hoffman, 1995; Vitaterna et al., 1994). And in experiments where people are placed in an environment with no cues indicating the time of day, most people naturally fall into a 25-hour schedule (Mistlberger & Rusak, 1989). But external stimuli—day and night, alarm clocks, job or school demands—cause us to modify our own biological clock's preference for a 25-hour rhythm in order to conform to a 24-hour schedule. Circadian rhythms are slightly disrupted each year when daylight saving time begins and

altered state of consciousness: A mental state other than ordinary waking consciousness, such as sleep, meditation, hypnosis, or a drug-induced state.

circadian rhythm (sur-KAY-dee-un): Within each 24-hour period, the regular fluctuation from high to low points of certain bodily functions.

ends. An even greater disruption occurs when people fly across a number of time zones or work rotating shifts.

Jet Lag: Where Am I and What Time Is It?

Suppose you fly from Chicago to London, and the plane lands at 12:00 midnight Chicago time, about the time you usually go to sleep. At the same time that it is midnight in Chicago, it is 6:00 A.M. in London, almost time to get up. The clocks, the sun, and everything else in London tell you it is early morning, but you still feel like it is 12:00 midnight. You are experiencing jet lag.

The problem is not simply the result of losing a night's sleep. You are fighting your own biological clock, which is synchronized with your usual time zone and not the time zone you are visiting (Graeber, 1989). It is difficult to try to sleep when your biological clock is telling you to wake up and feel alert. It is even harder to remain awake and alert when your internal clock is telling you to sleep.

There are people who experience a similar problem without the benefit of a trip to Europe or Asia. These people are shift workers.

Shift Work: Working Day and Night

About 6 percent of Americans are night-shift workers, and an additional 25 percent are engaged in various other patterns of shift work (Leger, 1994). The health care, data-processing, and transportation industries are the largest employers of shift workers. When people must work at night, there is a disruption in the rhythms of many bodily functions normally synchronized for efficient daytime functioning. These rhythm disruptions can cause a variety of physical and psychological problems.

Not surprisingly, shift workers complain of sleepiness and sleeping difficulties. Shift workers average 5.6 hours of sleep compared to 7.5 hours for workers on regular shifts (Hales, 1981). Forced to remain awake when their body temperature is low, they consume more caffeine. Trying to sleep when their temperature is high, they use more alcohol and sleeping pills (Gordon et al., 1986). Moreover, digestive problems such as appetite loss, diarrhea, and irregularity are common, because shift workers eat at times not in synchrony with the circadian rhythms governing appetite, elimination, and the secretion of digestive enzymes (Regestein & Monk, 1991; Vener et al., 1989).

What about performance on the job? Alertness and performance deteriorate if people work during **subjective night**, when their biological clock is telling them to go to sleep (Åkerstedt, 1990; Folkard, 1990). During subjective night, energy and efficiency reach their lowest point, reaction time is slowest, and productivity is diminished. From 75 to 90 percent of workers complain of sleepiness during the night shift, and many actually fall asleep during their shift (Leger, 1994). In one study of 1,000 locomotive engineers, 59 percent admitted that they dozed off on most night trips (Åkerstedt, 1988). So more than performance and productivity may suffer; safety also becomes a problem (Monk, 1990).

Many air, rail, marine, and highway accidents have occurred when the shift workers in charge suffered sleep loss and fatigue because of the disruption of their circadian rhythms (Lauber & Kayten, 1988). More errors in judgment and most accidents occur during the night shift. The failure of the nuclear reactor at Three Mile Island, the Russian nuclear disaster at Chernobyl, and even the Challenger disaster are thought to have occurred in part because workers on the night shift were in charge (Mitler et al., 1988). Figure 4.1 is a summary of the times of day when vehicular accidents occur.

What can be done to make shift rotation less disruptive? Rotating work schedules forward—from days to evenings to nights—and changing work shifts every

---

? *What are some problems experienced by people who work rotating shifts?*

What are the physical and psychological effects of disturbing the normal sleep/wakefulness cycle when a person works the night shift, as this printing press operator does?

subjective night: The time during a 24-hour period when your body temperature is lowest and when your biological clock is telling you to go to sleep.

FIGURE 4.1

Fatigue-Related Accidents Occurring at Various Times of the Day

Both the sleep/wakefulness cycle and alertness follow circadian rhythms. The rate of vehicular accidents is dramatically higher between 10 P.M. and 6 A.M., when sleepiness is greatest, and again between 2 P.M. and 4 P.M., when alertness typically decreases. (After Mitler et al., 1988.)

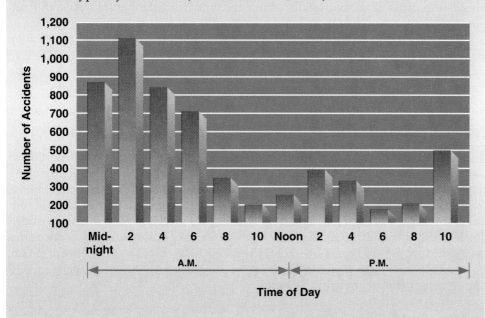

three weeks rather than every week have improved job satisfaction, health, and productivity of workers (Czeisler et al., 1982). Even exposure to appropriately timed bright light can reset the biological clock (Czeisler et al., 1990; Dawson & Campbell, 1991). Only a 4-hour exposure to bright light between midnight and 4:00 A.M. on one night improved performance and lessened sleepiness during the same period the following night (Thessing et al., 1994). Industries, police departments, and hospitals should seriously consider the research in this field to help workers adjust to shift changes.

Memory Check 4.1

1. Which of the following best defines consciousness?
   a. awareness   c. receptiveness
   b. wakefulness   d. rationality

2. The two circadian rhythms most relevant to the study of sleep are the sleep/wakefulness cycle and:
   a. blood pressure.   c. body temperature.
   b. secretion of hormones.   d. heart rate.

3. We sleep best when our body temperature is at the low point in our 24-hour cycle. (true/false)

4. Which is *not* characteristic of people who work rotating shifts?
   a. disturbed sleep
   b. digestive problems
   c. increased efficiency and alertness during subjective night
   d. greater use of caffeine, alcohol, and sleeping pills

5. For swing-shift workers, work schedules should be rotated from nights to evenings to days. (true/false)

Answers: 1. a 2. c 3. true 4. c 5. false

Sleep: That Mysterious One-Third of Our Lives

Over a lifetime, a person spends about 25 years sleeping. For decades sleep researchers argued about the function of sleep. Some believed sleep simply served a restorative function; others argued that it evolved to keep animals out of harm's way. But neither of these theories alone accounts for many of the research findings about sleep. For example, if you miss a night's sleep, why are you very sleepy during the middle of the night, but less so the next day? Today most sleep researchers believe that sleep should be viewed as a circadian rhythm that, in part, serves a restorative function (Webb, 1994). This view accommodates the variety of findings about sleep that we will explore in the following pages.

NREM and REM Sleep: Watching the Eyes

NREM sleep: Non–rapid eye movement sleep, consisting of the four sleep stages and characterized by slow, regular respiration and heart rate, an absence of rapid eye movements, and blood pressure and brain activity that are at a 24-hour low point.

Before the 1950s there was no understanding of what goes on during the state of consciousness we call sleep. Then, in the 1950s, several universities set up sleep laboratories where people's brain waves, eye movements, chin-muscle tension, heart rate, and respiration rate were monitored through a night of sleep. From analyses of their sleep recordings, known as polysomnograms, researchers discovered the characteristics of the two major categories of sleep. The two categories are NREM (non–rapid eye movement) sleep and REM (rapid eye movement) sleep. Figure 4.2 shows a sleep research subject whose brain activity, eye movement, and chin-muscle activity are being recorded.

How does a sleeper react physically during NREM sleep?

NREM Sleep: From Light to Deep Sleep in Stages   NREM (pronounced NON-rem) **sleep** is the sleep in which there are no rapid eye movements. It is often called "quiet sleep," because heart rate and respiration are slow and regular, there is little body movement, and blood pressure and brain activity are at their lowest points of the 24-hour period.

There are four stages of NREM sleep—Stages 1, 2, 3, and 4—with Stage 1 being the lightest sleep and Stage 4 being the deepest. You pass gradually rather

FIGURE 4.2

How Researchers Study Sleeping Subjects

Researchers study subjects in a sleep laboratory or sleep clinic by taping electrodes to the subject's head to monitor brain-wave activity, eye movements, and muscle tension. (After Dement, 1974.)

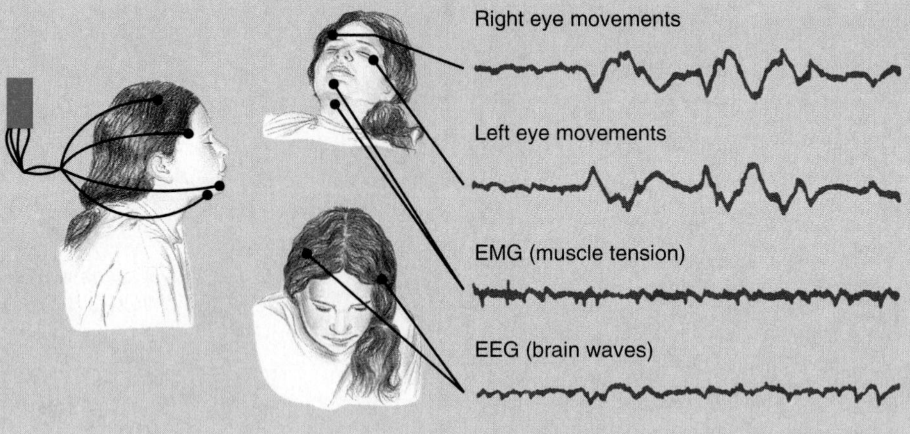

Right eye movements

Left eye movements

EMG (muscle tension)

EEG (brain waves)

FIGURE 4.3

Brain-Wave Patterns Associated with Different Stages of Sleep

By monitoring brain-wave activity with the EEG throughout a night's sleep, researchers have identified the brain-wave patterns associated with different stages of sleep. As sleepers progress through the four NREM stages, the brain-wave pattern changes from faster, low-voltage waves in Stages 1 and 2 to the slower, larger delta waves in Stages 3 and 4. Notice that the brain-wave activity during REM sleep is similar to that of the subject when awake. (After Hobson, 1989.)

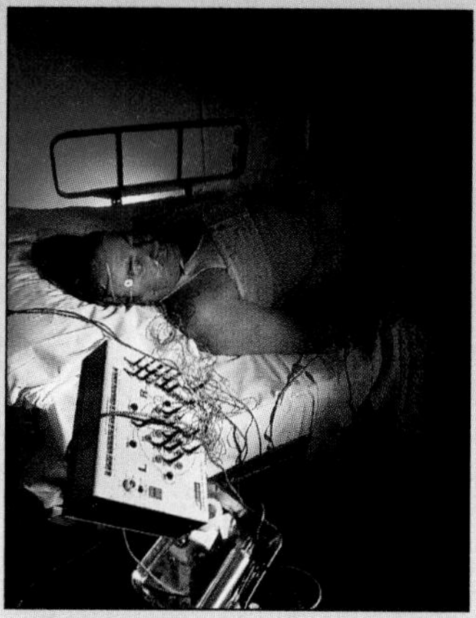

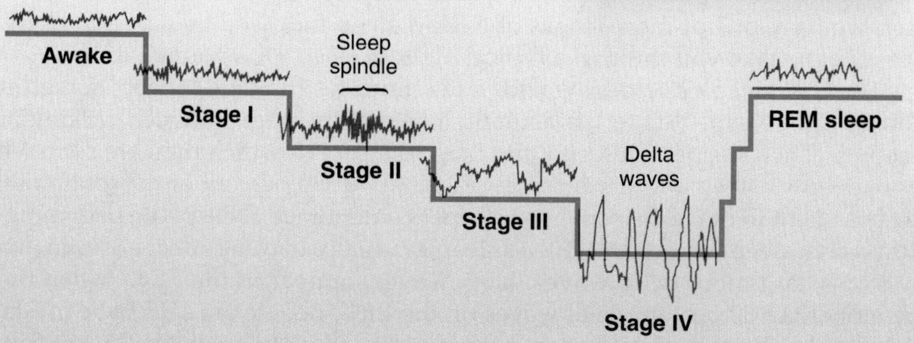

Awake

Stage I

Sleep spindle

Stage II

Stage III

Delta waves

Stage IV

REM sleep

than abruptly from one stage to the next. Each stage can be identified by its brain-wave pattern, as shown in Figure 4.3 (Hobson, 1989). Growth hormone is secreted primarily in Stage 3 and Stage 4 sleep.

REM Sleep: Rapid Eye Movements and Dreams Most of us envision sleep as a time of deep relaxation and calm. But **REM sleep**, sometimes called "active sleep," is anything but calm, and it constitutes 20 to 25 percent of a normal night's sleep in adults. During the REM state, there is intense brain activity, and our body reacts as if to a daytime emergency. Epinephrine (adrenaline) shoots into the system, blood pressure rises, and heart rate and respiration become faster and irregular. Ulcer patients may secrete 3 to 20 times as much stomach acid as during the day and may awaken with stomach pains (Webb, 1975). In contrast to this storm of internal activity, there is an external calm during REM sleep. The large muscles of the body—arms, legs, trunk—become paralyzed (Chase & Morales, 1990). Some researchers suggest that the reason for this paralysis is to prevent us from acting out our dreams.

If you observe a sleeper during the REM state, you can see the eyes darting around under the eyelids. In 1952 Eugene Azerinsky first discovered these bursts of rapid eye movements, and William Dement and Nathaniel Kleitman (1957) made the connection between rapid eye movements and dreaming. It is during REM periods that most of our vivid dreams occur. When awakened from REM sleep, 80 percent of subjects report dreaming (Carskadon & Dement, 1989).

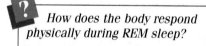

How does the body respond physically during REM sleep?

REM sleep: Sleep characterized by rapid eye movements, paralysis of large muscles, fast and irregular heart rate and respiration rate, increased brain-wave activity, and vivid dreams.

Almost from birth, regardless of the content of their dreams, males have a full or partial erection during REM sleep, and women experience vaginal swelling and lubrication. Because sleepers are more likely to awaken naturally at the end of a REM period than during the NREM stages of sleep, men usually wake up with an erection (Campbell, 1985). In males suffering from impotence, the presence of an erection during REM sleep indicates that the impotence is psychological; its absence indicates that the impotence is physiological in origin.

If you awaken during REM sleep and remain awake for several minutes, you will not go back into REM sleep for at least 30 minutes. This is why most of us have experienced the disappointment of waking in the middle of a wonderful dream and trying in vain to get quickly back to sleep and into the dream.

Sleep Cycles: The Nightly Pattern of Sleep

Many people are surprised to learn that sleep follows a fairly predictable pattern each night. We sleep in cycles. During each **sleep cycle**, which lasts about 90 minutes, we have one or more stages of NREM sleep followed by a period of REM sleep. Let us take you through a typical night of sleep for a young adult.

The first sleep cycle begins with a few minutes in Stage 1 sleep, sometimes called "light sleep." Stage 1 is actually a transition stage between waking and sleeping. Then sleepers descend into Stage 2 sleep, in which they are somewhat more deeply asleep and harder to awaken. About 50 percent of the total night's sleep is spent in Stage 2 sleep. Next sleepers enter Stage 3 sleep, the beginning of **slow-wave sleep** (or deep sleep). As sleep gradually becomes deeper, brain activity slows, and more **delta waves** (slow waves) appear in the EEG. When there are more than 50 percent delta waves on the EEG, people are said to be in **Stage 4 sleep**, the deepest sleep, when people are hardest to awaken (Carskadon & Rechtschaffen, 1989). Perhaps you have taken an afternoon nap and awakened confused, not knowing whether it was morning or night, a weekday or a weekend. If so, you probably awakened during Stage 4 sleep.

After about 40 minutes in Stage 4 sleep, brain activity increases and the delta waves begin to disappear. Sleepers ascend back through Stage 3 and Stage 2 sleep, then enter their first REM period, which lasts 10 or 15 minutes. At the end of this REM period, the first sleep cycle is complete, and the second sleep cycle begins. Unless people awaken after the first sleep cycle, they go directly from REM into Stage 2 sleep. They then follow the same progression as in the first sleep cycle, through Stages 3 and 4 and back again into REM sleep.

After the first two sleep cycles of about 90 minutes each (3 hours total), the sleep pattern changes and sleepers usually get no more Stage 4 sleep. From this point on, during each 90-minute sleep cycle, people alternate mainly between Stage 2 and REM sleep for the remainder of the night. With each sleep cycle, the REM periods (and therefore dreaming time) get progressively longer. At the end of the night, REM periods may last 30 minutes. Most people sleep about five sleep cycles (7½ to 8 hours) and on the average get about 1½ hours of slow-wave sleep and 1½ hours of REM sleep. Figure 4.4 shows the progression through NREM and REM sleep during a typical night.

Variations in Sleep: How We Differ

There are great individual variations in patterns of sleep, and the major factor contributing to this variation is age.

Sleep Changes over the Life Span: The Older We Get, the Less We Get
Infants and young children have the longest sleep time and the highest percentage of REM and slow-wave sleep, but they get even more REM sleep

---

What is the progression of NREM stages and REM sleep that a person follows in a typical night of sleep?

---

sleep cycle: A cycle of sleep lasting about 90 minutes and including one or more stages of NREM sleep followed by a period of REM sleep.

slow-wave sleep: Stage 3 and Stage 4 sleep; deep sleep.

delta wave: The slowest brain-wave pattern, associated with Stage 3 sleep and Stage 4 sleep.

Stage 4 sleep: The deepest NREM stage of sleep, characterized by an EEG pattern of more than 50 percent delta waves.

How do sleep patterns change over the life span?

FIGURE 4.4

The Typical Composition of Sleep Cycles for Young Adults

A typical night's sleep for young adults consists of about five sleep cycles of approximately 90 minutes each. Stage 4 sleep occurs during the first two sleep cycles. People spend progressively more time in REM sleep with each succeeding 90-minute cycle. (After Hartmann, 1967.)

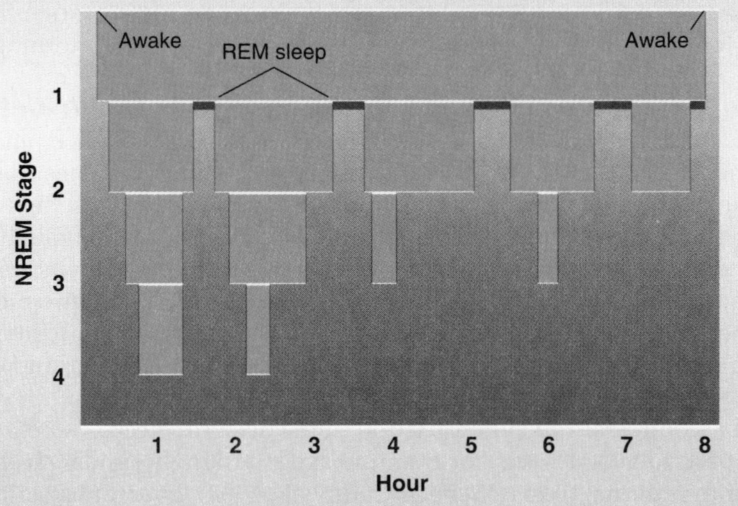

before birth. The fetus spends up to 80 percent of the time in REM sleep (Hobson, 1989).

Children from age 6 to puberty are the champion sleepers and wakers. They fall asleep easily, sleep soundly for $8\frac{1}{2}$ to 9 hours at night, and feel awake and alert during the day. From puberty to the end of adolescence, teenagers average about $7\frac{1}{2}$ hours and typically feel the need for more sleep regardless of how much they actually sleep (Strauch & Meier, 1988).

As adults age, the quality and quantity of sleep usually decrease (Monane, 1992). Older people have more difficulty falling asleep, and they typically have lighter sleep and more and longer awakenings than younger people (Buysse et al., 1991). They spend more time awake in bed but less time asleep, averaging about $6\frac{1}{2}$ hours of sleep (Prinz et al., 1990). Slow-wave sleep decreases with age and may be virtually absent in one's late 70s and 80s. The percentage of REM sleep stays about the same (Moran & Stoudemire, 1992).

Larks and Owls: Early to Rise and Late to Bed Some people awaken early every morning and leap out of bed with enthusiasm, eager to start the day. Others fumble for the alarm clock and push in the snooze button to get a few more precious moments of sleep. The early risers find it hard to keep from yawning after 10:00 P.M. and have an overwhelming urge to get to bed. But this is precisely the time that the night people come to life.

Sleep researchers have names for these two types—larks and owls—and there is a physical explanation for the difference in the way they feel. About 25 percent of people are larks, people whose body temperature rises rapidly after they awaken and stays high until about 7:30 P.M. Larks turn in early and have the fewest sleep problems. Then there are the 25 percent who are owls and the 50 percent who are somewhere in between. The body temperature of an owl gradually rises throughout the day, peaking in the afternoon and not dropping until later in the evening. Anderson and others (1991) tested subjects on memory tasks at 9:00 A.M., 2:00 P.M., and 8:00 P.M. The performance of the larks declined as the day progressed, while that of the owls improved. It is not surprising that larks have more difficulty than owls in adapting to night shifts. They are sleepier during their subjective night and are more likely to complain of difficulty sleeping (Hilliker et al., 1992).

"Larks see owls as lazy; owls see larks as party poopers" (Coleman, 1986, p. 15). Can an owl turn into a lark with a little self-discipline? The authors have tried in vain to accomplish this for years. Even when owls change their sleep schedule to match the early risers, they still *feel* like owls in the morning.

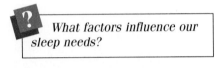

What factors influence our sleep needs?

How much sleep does the average person need? More than he or she gets, according to sleep researcher William Dement.

How Much Sleep Do We Need? More Than We Probably Get   Maybe you have wondered how much sleep you need in order to feel good, and perhaps you are hoping to find the answer in this chapter. When it comes to sleep, the expression "one size fits all" does *not* apply. Although adults average about 7½ hours of sleep daily with an extra hour on weekends, this is too much for some people and too little for others. Short sleepers are the 20 percent who require less than 6 hours of sleep; long sleepers are the 10 percent who require more than 9 hours. There seems to be a limit below which most of us cannot go. In one study, not a single subject could get by with less than 4½ hours of sleep, and 6½ hours appears to be the minimum most people require.

What accounts for the large variation in the need for sleep? Genetics appears to play a part. Identical twins, for example, have strikingly similar sleep patterns compared to fraternal twins (Webb & Campbell, 1983). Laboratory animals have even been bred to be short or long sleepers. But genetics aside, people need more sleep when they are depressed, under stress, or experiencing significant life changes such as changing jobs or schools. Increases in mental, physical, or emotional effort also increase our need for sleep (Hartmann, 1973). Contrary to popular opinion, the amount of activity required in an occupation does not affect the amount of sleep a person needs.

Do most Americans sleep enough? Not according to the well-known sleep researcher William Dement, who claims that we have "a national sleep deficit."

Memory Check 4.2

1. State the type of sleep—NREM or REM—that corresponds to each characteristic:

   ____ 1) paralysis of large muscles   a. REM
   ____ 2) slow, regular respiration   b. NREM
          and heart rate
   ____ 3) rapid eye movements
   ____ 4) penile erection and
          vaginal swelling
   ____ 5) vivid dreams

2. The average length of a sleep cycle in adults is:
   a. 30 minutes.   c. 90 minutes.
   b. 60 minutes.   d. 120 minutes.

3. After the first two sleep cycles, most people get equal amounts of deep sleep and REM sleep. (true/false)

4. Match the age group with the appropriate description of sleep.

   ____ 1) have most difficulty sleep-   a. infancy
          ing, most awakenings   b. middle
   ____ 2) sleep best at night; feel best   childhood
          during day   c. adolescence
   ____ 3) have highest percentage of   d. old age
          REM and deep sleep
   ____ 4) are usually sleepy during
          the day regardless of the
          amount of sleep at night

Answers: 1. 1) a 2) b 3) a 4) a 5) a 2. c 3. false 4. 1) d 2) b 3) a 4) c

Sleep Deprivation: How Does It Affect Us?

What is the longest you have ever stayed awake—two days, three days? According to the *Guinness Book of World Records*, Robert McDonald stayed awake 453 hours and 40 minutes (almost 19 days) in a 1986 rocking-chair marathon. Unlike McDonald, most of us have missed no more than a few consecutive nights of sleep, perhaps studying for final exams. If you have ever missed two or three nights of sleep, you may remember having had difficulty concentrating, lapses in attention, and general irritability. After 60 hours without sleep, some people even have minor hallucinations. Most people who try to stay awake for long periods of time will have **microsleeps**, 2- to 3-second lapses from wakefulness into sleep. You may have experienced a microsleep if you have ever caught yourself nodding off for a few seconds in class or on a long automobile trip.

What suffers most from prolonged sleep loss is the motivation to sustain performance. If a task is brief or interesting or demanding, we can do almost anything. But the problem is that we have difficulty making ourselves pay attention or work; we would rather be asleep. If you know you will be up for an extended period (more than 14 hours), taking as long a nap as possible beforehand will improve alertness and performance for the next 24 to 30 hours (Bonnet, 1991).

When people are deprived of REM sleep as a result of general sleep loss, illness, too much alcohol, or other drugs, they will make up for the loss by getting an increased amount of REM sleep after the deprivation (Vogel, 1975). This increase in the percentage of REM sleep to make up for REM deprivation is called a **REM rebound**. Because the intensity of REM sleep is increased during a REM rebound, nightmares often occur. But why do we need REM sleep?

The Function of REM Sleep: Necessary, But Why? The fact that newborns have such a high percentage of REM sleep has led to the conclusion that REM sleep is necessary for maturation of the brain in infants (G. Marks et al., 1995). But humans are not the only animals who dream. Researchers have been able to study REM sleep in other mammals, particularly rats and cats.

Animal studies provide strong evidence for a relationship between REM sleep and learning (Hennevin et al., 1995; Smith, 1995; Winson, 1990). Some studies have revealed that animals increase their REM sleep following learning sessions. Other studies have indicated that when animals are deprived of REM sleep after new learning, their performance on the learned task is impaired the following day. But depriving subjects of NREM sleep had no such effect in the studies.

Recent research has shown that REM sleep is involved in the consolidation of memories after human learning as well. Karni and others (1994) found that research subjects learning a new perceptual skill showed an improvement in performance, with no additional practice, 8 to 10 hours later if they had a normal night's sleep or if the researchers disturbed only their NREM sleep. Performance did not improve, however, in subjects who were deprived of REM sleep.

An opposite view is proposed by Francis Crick and Graeme Mitchison (1983, 1995). They suggest that REM sleep functions as mental housecleaning, erasing trivial and unnecessary memories and clearing overloaded neural circuits that might interfere with memory and rational thinking. In other words, they say, people dream in order to forget.

Dreaming: Mysterious Mental Activity While We Sleep

We humans have always been fascinated by our dreams. The vivid dreams we remember and talk about are **REM dreams**—the type that occur almost continu-

What happens when people are deprived of REM sleep? What function does REM sleep appear to serve?

microsleep: A momentary lapse from wakefulness into sleep, usually occurring when one has been sleep deprived.

REM rebound: The increased amount of REM sleep that occurs after REM deprivation; often associated with unpleasant dreams or nightmares.

REM dreams: A type of dream having a dreamlike and storylike quality and occuring almost continuously during each REM period; more vivid, visual, and emotional than NREM dreams.

How do REM and NREM dreams differ?

What do we dream about? REM dreams have a storylike quality and are more visual, vivid, and emotional than NREM dreams.

ously during each REM period. But there is also mental activity called **NREM dreams**, which occur during NREM sleep (Cavallero et al., 1992). REM dreams have a story-like or dreamlike quality and are more visual, vivid, and emotional than NREM dreams, which typically have a thoughtlike quality (Hobson, 1989; Webb & Cartwright, 1978). As the night wears on, our REM dreams become longer and more complex (Cipolli & Poli, 1992).

You may have heard that an entire dream takes place in an instant. Did you find that hard to believe? In fact, it is not true. Sleep researchers have discovered that it takes about as long to dream a dream as it would to experience the same thing in real life (Kleitman, 1960). Let's take a closer look at the dream state.

Dream Memories: We Remember Only a Few   Sleepers have the best recall of a dream if they are awakened during the dream; the more time that passes after the dream ends, the poorer the recall. If we awaken 10 minutes or more after a dream is over, we probably will not remember it. Even the dreams we remember upon awakening will quickly fade from memory unless we mentally rehearse them or write them down. Very few dreams are memorable enough to be retained very long. Although some people insist that they do not dream at all, sleep researchers say that all people dream unless they are drinking heavily or taking drugs that suppress REM sleep.

Would we be better off if we remembered more of our dreams? Probably not. If our dream memories were as vivid as our memories of real events, we might have difficulty differentiating between events that actually happened and those we merely dreamed about.

?   *In general, what have researchers found regarding the content of dreams?*

The Content of Dreams: Bizarre or Commonplace?   What do we dream about? You may be surprised to learn that dreams are less bizarre and less filled with emotion than is generally believed (Cipolli et al., 1993; Hall & Van de Castle, 1966; Snyder, 1971). Because dreams are notoriously hard to remember, the features that stand out tend to be those that are bizarre or emotional.

Sleep researchers generally agree that dreams reflect our preoccupations in waking life—our "fears, wishes, plans, hopes, and worries" (Hauri, 1982, p. 20). Most dreams have rather commonplace settings with real people, half of whom are known to the dreamer. In general dreams are more unpleasant than pleasant, and they contain more aggression than friendly interactions and more misfortune than good fortune. Some dreams are in "living color," while others are in black and white.

Table 4.1 lists the 20 most common dream themes among 250 college students. Although the study was conducted in 1958, a study today would probably yield similar results. Complete the *Try It!* (on the opposite page) and compare your dream themes with the results of the study shown in the table.

Some people are troubled by unpleasant recurring dreams. The two most common themes involve being chased or falling (Stark, 1984). People who have recurring dreams seem to have more minor physical complaints, greater stress, and more anxiety and depression than other people (Brown & Donderi, 1986). Is there anything that can be done to stop recurring dreams? Some people have been taught to use lucid dreaming to bring about satisfactory resolutions to their unpleasant recurring dreams.

Have you ever experienced a **lucid dream**—one during which you were aware that you were dreaming? If so, you are among the 10 percent who claim to have

NREM dreams: Mental activity occurring during NREM sleep that is more thoughtlike in quality than REM dreams are.

lucid dream: A dream during which the dreamer is aware of dreaming and is often able to influence the content of the dream while it is in progress.

TABLE 4.1   Common Dream Themes

Listed are the 20 most common dream themes reported by 250 college students and the percentage of students having each type of dream.

Type of Dream	Percentage of Students
Falling	83
Being attacked or pursued	77
Trying repeatedly to do something	71
School, teachers, studying	71
Sexual experiences	66
Arriving too late	64
Eating	62
Being frozen with fright	58
Death of a loved person	57
Being locked up	56
Finding money	56
Swimming	52
Snakes	49
Being dressed inappropriately	46
Being smothered	44
Being nude in public	43
Fire	41
Failing an examination	39
Flying	34
Seeing self as dead	33

Source: Griffith, Miyago, & Tago, 1958.

Try It!

On this list of 20 common dream themes, place a check mark next to each one you have dreamed about.

_____ Falling
_____ Being attacked or pursued
_____ Trying repeatedly to do something
_____ School, teachers, studying
_____ Sexual experiences
_____ Arriving too late
_____ Eating
_____ Being frozen with fright
_____ Death of a loved person
_____ Being locked up
_____ Finding money
_____ Swimming
_____ Snakes
_____ Being dressed inappropriately
_____ Being smothered
_____ Being nude in public
_____ Fire
_____ Failing an examination
_____ Flying
_____ Seeing self as dead

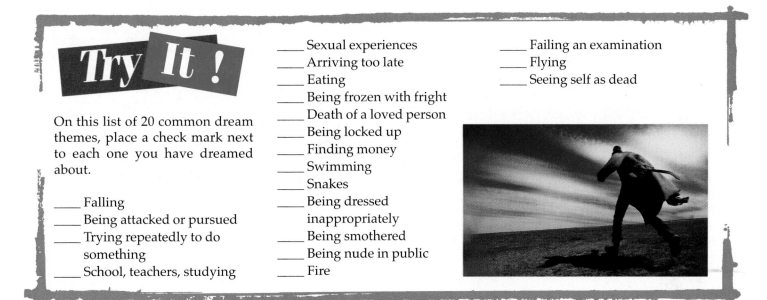

this ability. Many lucid dreamers are able to change a dream while it is in progress, and a few virtuosos claim to be able to dream about any subject at will (Gackenbach & Bosveld, 1989; La Berge, 1981).

Interpreting Dreams: Are There Hidden Meanings in Our Dreams?

Sigmund Freud believed that dreams function to satisfy unconscious sexual and aggressive wishes. Because such wishes are unacceptable to the dreamer, they have to be disguised and therefore appear in a dream in symbolic form. Freud (1900/1953a) claimed that objects like sticks, umbrellas, tree trunks, and guns symbolize the male sex organ; objects like chests, cupboards, and boxes represent the female sex organ. Freud differentiated between the manifest content of the dream—the dream as recalled by the dreamer—and the underlying meaning of the dream, called the latent content, which he considered more significant.

In recent years there has been a major shift away from the Freudian interpretation of dreams. Now there is a greater focus on the manifest content, the actual dream itself, rather than on searching for symbolic meanings that can be interpreted to reveal some underlying personal conflict. The symbols in dreams, when analyzed, are now perceived as being specific to the individual rather than as having standard or universal meanings for all dreamers. Furthermore, dreams are seen more as an expression of a broad range of the dreamer's concerns than as primarily an expression of sexual impulses (Webb, 1975).

J. Allan Hobson (1988) rejects the notion that nature would equip us with a capability and a need to dream dreams that would require a specialist to interpret. Hobson and McCarley (1977) advanced the activation-synthesis hypothesis of dreaming. This hypothesis suggests that dreams are simply the brain's attempt to make sense of the random firing of brain cells during REM sleep. But Hobson (1989) now believes that our dreams have psychological significance, nevertheless, because they are woven from our personal experiences, remote memories, and "associations, drives, and fears" (p. 5).

Memory Check 4.3

1. Which factor *least* affects the amount of sleep people need?
   a. their heredity
   b. their emotional state
   c. the amount of stress in their lives
   d. the amount of physical activity required in their occupation

2. Following REM deprivation, there is usually:
   a. an absence of REM sleep.
   b. an increase in REM sleep.
   c. a decrease in REM sleep.
   d. no change in the amount of REM sleep.

3. Which type of sleep seems to aid in learning and memory in humans and other animals?
   a. Stage 1
   b. Stage 2
   c. Stages 3 and 4
   d. REM sleep

4. Dream memories usually do not persist for more than 10 minutes after a dream has ended. (true/false)

5. Compared to REM dreams, NREM dreams are:
   a. more emotional.
   b. more visual.
   c. more thoughtlike.
   d. more vivid.

6. According to researchers, each of the following statements about the content of dreams is correct *except*:
   a. dreams are generally bizarre and filled with emotion.
   b. dreams generally reflect our waking preoccupations.
   c. dreams are generally more unpleasant than pleasant.
   d. dreams contain more aggression than friendly interactions.

Answers: 1. d   2. b   3. d   4. true   5. c   6. a

Sleep Disorders

So far our discussion has centered on a typical night for a typical sleeper. But one-third of American adults report sleep problems (Rosekind, 1992), and many children also experience sleep disturbances. Sleep problems range from mild to severe and from problems that affect only sleep to those that affect a person's entire life. Yet even today, medical schools, on average, provide less than 2 hours of instruction on sleep and sleep disorders (Rosen et al., 1993).

Parasomnias: Unusual Behaviors during Sleep

Parasomnias are sleep disturbances in which unusual behaviors and physiological states that normally occur only in the waking state take place during sleep or the transition from sleep to wakefulness.

Sleepwalking and Sleep Terrors: Stage 4 Sleep Disturbances
Sleepwalking (**somnambulism**) and **sleep terrors** are parasomnias that often run in families (Dement, 1974). They occur during a partial arousal from Stage 4 sleep in which the sleeper does not come to full consciousness. Most cases begin in childhood and are attributed primarily to a delayed development of the nervous system (Karacan, 1988). The disturbances are usually outgrown by adolescence.

Sleepwalking: Walking Around but Sound Asleep Cartoonists often depict sleepwalkers groping about with their eyes closed and their arms extended forward. But sleepwalkers actually have their eyes open with a blank stare, and rather than walking normally, they shuffle about. Their coordination is poor, and if they talk, their speech is usually unintelligible.

If an EEG recording were made during a sleepwalking episode, it would show a combination of delta waves, indicating deep sleep, and alpha and beta waves, signaling the waking state. Sleepwalkers are awake enough to carry out activities that do not require their full attention, but asleep enough not to remember having done so the following day. Sleepwalkers may get up and roam through the house, or simply stand for a short time and then go back to bed (Ferber, 1989; Karacan, 1988). Occasionally they get dressed, eat a snack, or go to the bathroom. The most important concern in sleepwalking is safety. Because of their reduced alertness and coordination, sleepwalkers are at risk of hurting themselves. They have been known to walk out windows, fall down stairs, and more.

Finally, let us dispel a myth about sleepwalking. You may have heard that it is dangerous to awaken a sleepwalker. This simply is not true.

Sleep Terrors: Screams in the Night Sleep terrors usually begin with a piercing scream. The sleeper springs up in a state of panic—eyes open, perspiring, breathing rapidly, with the heart pounding at two to four times the normal rate (Karacan, 1988). Episodes usually last from 5 to 15 minutes, and then the person falls back to sleep. If not awakened during a night terror, children usually have no memory of the episode the next morning. If awakened, however, they may recall a single frightening image (Hartmann, 1981).

Parents should not be unduly alarmed by sleep terrors in young children, but episodes that continue through adolescence into adulthood are more serious (Horne, 1992). Sleep terrors in adults often indicate extreme anxiety or other psychological problems (Kales et al., 1980).

Nightmares: The Worst of Dreams
Unlike sleep terrors, **nightmares** are very frightening dreams that occur during REM sleep and are likely to be remembered in vivid detail. The most common themes are being chased, threatened, or attacked.

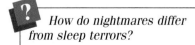

What are the characteristics common to sleepwalking and sleep terrors?

somnambulism (som-NAM-bue-lism): Sleepwalking that occurs during a partial arousal from Stage 4 sleep.

sleep terror: A sleep disturbance in which a person partially awakens from Stage 4 sleep with a scream, dazed and groggy, in a panic state, and with a racing heart.

nightmare: A very frightening dream occurring during REM sleep.

What is a sleep terror?

How do nightmares differ from sleep terrors?

Sleep researcher William Dement holds a dog that is experiencing a narcoleptic sleep attack. Much has been learned about narcolepsy through research with dogs.

 What are the major symptoms of narcolepsy?

narcolepsy (NAR-co-lep-see): A serious sleep disorder characterized by excessive daytime sleepiness and sudden, uncontrollable attacks of REM sleep.

sleep apnea: A sleep disorder characterized by periods when breathing stops during sleep and the person must awaken briefly in order to breathe; major symptoms are excessive daytime sleepiness and loud snoring.

What is sleep apnea?

Nightmares can be a reaction to traumatic life experiences (Hefez et al., 1987), and they are more frequent at times of high fevers, anxiety, and emotional upheaval. REM rebound during drug withdrawal or following long periods without sleep can also produce nightmares. Sleep terrors occur early in the night during Stage 4 sleep, while anxiety nightmares occur toward morning, when the REM periods are longest.

According to the American Psychiatric Association (1994), from 10 to 50 percent of children between ages 3 and 5 have nightmares severe enough to worry their parents. And about 50 percent of adults have occasional nightmares, which are nothing to be alarmed about. But frequent nightmares may be associated with psychological maladjustment (Berquier & Aston, 1992).

Sleeptalking (Somniloquy): Might We Reveal Secrets?   Do you sometimes talk in your sleep? Are you afraid that you might confess to something embarrassing, or reveal some deep, dark secret? Relax. Sleeptalkers rarely reply to questions, and they usually mumble words or phrases that make no sense to the listener. Sleeptalking can occur during any sleep stage, and is more frequent in children than in adults. There is no evidence at all that sleeptalking is related to a physical or psychological disturbance—not even to a guilty conscience (Arkin, 1981).

Major Sleep Disorders

Some sleep disorders can be so debilitating that they affect a person's entire life. These disorders are narcolepsy, sleep apnea, and insomnia.

Narcolepsy: Sudden Attacks of REM Sleep   Many people complain about having difficulty falling asleep, but a more serious problem is not being able to stay awake when we need to. **Narcolepsy** is an incurable sleep disorder characterized by excessive daytime sleepiness and uncontrollable attacks of REM sleep, usually lasting 10 to 20 minutes (American Psychiatric Association, 1994). People with narcolepsy—some 250,000 to 350,000 in the United States—are often unfairly stigmatized as lazy, depressed, and disinterested in their work.

Anything that causes an ordinary person to be tired can trigger a sleep attack in a narcoleptic—a heavy meal, sunbathing at the beach, or a boring lecture. A sleep attack can also be brought on by any situation that is exciting (such as love-making) or that causes a strong emotion (such as anger or laughter).

Narcolepsy is a physiological disorder caused by an abnormality in the part of the brain that regulates sleep (Mefford et al., 1983), and it appears to have a strong genetic component (Billiard et al., 1994; Partinen et al., 1994). Some dogs are subject to narcolepsy, and much has been learned about this disorder from research on canine subjects. Although there is no cure for narcolepsy, stimulant medications improve daytime alertness in most patients (Guilleminault, 1993; Mitler et al., 1994). Experts also recommend scheduled naps to relieve sleepiness (Mullington & Broughton, 1993).

Sleep Apnea: Can't Sleep and Breathe at the Same Time   Over 1 million Americans—mostly obese men—suffer from another dangerous sleep disorder, sleep apnea. **Sleep apnea** consists of periods during sleep when breathing stops, and the individual must awaken briefly in order to breathe (White, 1989). The major symptoms of sleep apnea are excessive daytime sleepiness and extremely loud snoring (as loud as a jackhammer), often accompanied by snorts, gasps, and choking noises.

A person with sleep apnea will drop off to sleep, stop breathing altogether, and then awaken struggling for breath. After gasping several breaths in a semi-awakened state, the person falls back to sleep and stops breathing again. People with severe sleep apnea may have as many as 800 partial awakenings to gasp for air. Alcohol and sedatives aggravate the condition (Langevin et al., 1992).

Severe sleep apnea can lead to chronic high blood pressure, heart problems, and even death (Fleury, 1992; Hillman, 1993). The favored treatment is the continuous positive airways pressure (CPAP) device, which delivers air through a mask worn over the nose at night (Aubert, 1992; Sériès et al., 1992).

Insomnia: When You Can't Fall Asleep   People with **insomnia** suffer distress and impairment in daytime functioning due to difficulty falling or staying asleep or to sleep that is light, restless, or of poor quality. Transient (temporary) insomnia, lasting 3 weeks or less, can result from jet lag, emotional highs (an upcoming wedding) or lows (losing a loved one or a job), or a brief illness or injury that interferes with sleep. Much more serious is chronic insomnia, which lasts for months or even years and plagues about 10 to 15 percent of the adult population (Morin et al., 1994). The percentages are even higher for women, the elderly, and people suffering from psychiatric and medical disorders (Moran & Stoudemire, 1992; Rosekind, 1992). Chronic insomnia may begin as a reaction to a psychological or medical problem but persist long after the problem is resolved.

In the Applications section at the end of this chapter, we examine some ways to overcome insomnia.

 What is insomnia?

insomnia: A sleep disorder characterized by difficulty falling or staying asleep or by light, restless, or poor sleep, and causing distress and impaired daytime functioning.

Memory Check 4.4

1. Sleepwalking and sleep terrors occur during a partial arousal from:
   a. Stage 1 sleep.
   b. Stage 2 sleep.
   c. Stage 4 sleep.
   d. REM sleep.

2. Sleepwalking episodes and sleep terrors are rarely recalled. (true/false)

3. Match the disorder with the description or associated symptom.
   ____ 1) sleep attacks during the day   a. narcolepsy
   ____ 2) cessation of breathing during   b. sleep
            sleep; loud snoring   apnea
   ____ 3) difficulty falling or staying   c. insomnia
            asleep   d. nightmare
   ____ 4) very frightening REM dream

Answers: 1. c   2. true   3. 1) a   2) b   3) c   4) d

Altering Consciousness through Concentration and Suggestion

 For what purposes is meditation used?

Sleep is an altered state of consciousness and a necessary one. We must sleep. But there are other forms of altered consciousness that we may enter only if we choose to do so. Meditation and hypnosis are two of these.

Meditation: Expanded Consciousness or Relaxation?

Meditation is a group of techniques that involve focusing attention on an object, a word, one's breathing, or body movement in order to block out all distractions and achieve an altered state of consciousness. Some forms of meditation—yoga, Zen, and transcendental meditation (TM)—have their roots in Eastern religions and are practiced by followers of those religions to attain a higher state of spiri-

meditation: A group of techniques that involve focusing attention on an object, a word, one's breathing, or body movement in order to block out all distractions and achieve an altered state of consciousness.

tuality. In the United States these approaches are often used to increase relaxation, reduce arousal, or expand consciousness.

Some meditators sit in a comfortable chair with eyes closed, both feet flat on the floor, and hands in the lap or simply resting on the arms of the chair. They might begin meditation by relaxing their muscles from the feet up, to achieve a deep state of relaxation. Other people concentrate on their breathing—slowly, rhythmically, in and out. In transcendental meditation, the meditator is given a mantra, a secret word (such as "om") assigned by the teacher. The meditator repeats the mantra over and over during meditation to block out unwanted thoughts and facilitate the meditative state. Dr. Herbert Benson (1975) suggests that any word or sound will do. Moreover, he claims that the beneficial effects of meditation can be achieved through simple relaxation techniques. Do the *Try It!* to experience Benson's relaxation response.

Find a quiet place and sit in a comfortable position.

1. Close your eyes.

2. Relax all your muscles deeply. Begin with your feet and move slowly upward, relaxing the muscles in your legs, buttocks, abdomen, chest, shoulders, neck, and finally your face. Allow your whole body to remain in this deeply relaxed state.

3. Now concentrate on your breathing, and breathe in and out through your nose. Each time you breathe out, silently say the word *one* to yourself.

4. Repeat this process for 20 minutes. (You can open your eyes to look at your watch periodically but don't use an alarm.) When you are finished, remain seated for a few minutes—first with your eyes closed, then with them open.

Benson recommends that you maintain a passive attitude. Don't try to force yourself to relax. Just let it happen. If a distracting thought comes to mind, ignore it and just repeat *one* each time you exhale. It is best to practice this exercise one or two times each day, but not within two hours of your last meal. Digestion interferes with the relaxation response.

What is hypnosis, and when is it most useful?

hypnosis: A trancelike state of concentrated, focused attention, heightened suggestibility, and diminished response to external stimuli.

Hypnosis: Look into My Eyes

Have you ever been hypnotized? Many people are fascinated by this unusual, somewhat mysterious altered state of consciousness. Other people doubt that it even exists.

Hypnosis is a trancelike state of concentrated and focused attention, heightened suggestibility, and diminished response to external stimuli. In the hypnotic state, people suspend their usual rational and logical ways of thinking and perceiving and allow themselves to experience distortions in perceptions, memories, and thinking. Under hypnosis people may experience positive hallucinations, in which they see, hear, touch, smell, or taste things that are not present in the environment. Or they may have negative hallucinations and fail to perceive those things that are present.

About 80 to 95 percent of people are hypnotizable to some degree, but only 5 percent can reach the deepest levels of trance (Nash & Baker, 1984). The ability to become completely absorbed in imaginative activities is characteristic of highly hypnotizable people (Nadon et al., 1991). Silva and Kirsch (1992) found that individuals' fantasy-proneness and their expectation of responding to hypnotic suggestions were predictors of hypnotizability.

Myths about Hypnosis: Separating Fact from Fiction

There are many misconceptions about hypnosis, some of which probably stem from its long and unfortunate association with stage entertainers. Have you ever believed one of these myths?

Hypnosis is a trancelike state of concentrated attention and heightened suggestibility. This hypnotherapist suggested to the subject that a balloon was tied to his right hand—and his arm raised accordingly.

- *Hypnotized subjects are not aware of what is going on during hypnosis.* Hypnotized subjects know where they are and what they are doing, and they are aware that they are in a trance. Because many subjects expect something far different, they often have difficulty believing that they were, in fact, hypnotized.

- *Subjects will violate their moral values under hypnosis.* Generally subjects under hypnosis will not behave contrary to their true moral values. If told to violate their values, they will simply come out of the trance.

- *Subjects can demonstrate superhuman strength and perform amazing feats under hypnosis.* Subjects are not stronger or more powerful under hypnosis.

- *Memory is more accurate under hypnosis.* Memory is *not* more accurate under hypnosis (Barnier & McConkey, 1992; Dinges et al., 1992). Hypnotized subjects supply more information and are more confident of their recollections, but the information is often inaccurate (Dywan & Bowers, 1983; Nogrady et al., 1985; Weekes et al., 1992).

- *Subjects under hypnosis will reveal embarrassing secrets.* Hypnosis is not like a truth serum. Subjects can keep secrets or lie under hypnosis.

- *Subjects under hypnosis can relive an event as it occurred when they were children and can function mentally as if they were that age.* Careful reviews of studies on hypnotic age regression have found no evidence to support this claim (Barber, 1962). "Although hypnotically regressed subjects may undergo dramatic changes in demeanor and subjective experience, their performance is not accurately childlike" (Nash, 1987, p. 50).

- *Subjects are under the complete control of the hypnotist.* Hypnosis is not something that is done to subjects. They retain the ability to break the trance.

Medical Uses of Hypnosis: It's Not Just Entertainment

Hypnosis has come a long way from the days when it was used mainly by stage entertainers. It is now recognized as a viable technique to be used in medicine, dentistry, and psychotherapy. Hypnosis is accepted by the American Medical Association, the American Psychological Association, and the American Psychiatric Association. Hypnosis has been particularly helpful in the control of pain (Hilgard, 1975; Kilstrom, 1985). It has also been used successfully to treat a wide range of disorders, including high blood pressure, bleeding, psoriasis, severe morning sickness, side effects of chemotherapy, and burns (Kelly & Kelly, 1985). Other problems that have responded well to hypnosis are asthma, severe insomnia, some phobias (Orne, 1983), and multiple-personality disorder (Kluft, 1992). Furthermore, there are recent studies suggesting that hypnosis can be useful in treating warts (Ewin, 1992), pain due to burns (Patterson et al., 1992), repetitive nightmares

(Kingsbury, 1993), and sexual dysfunctions such as inhibited sexual desire (Hammond, 1992) and impotence (Crasilneck, 1992).

For the most hypnotizable subjects, hypnosis can be used instead of a general anesthetic in surgery. In one operation "a surgeon cut through a woman's chest into her heart to enlarge one of its valves. Without chemical anesthesia, the woman was conscious and awake but suffered no pain" (Freese, 1980, p. 20).

Suppose you are overweight, or you smoke or drink heavily. Would a quick trip to a hypnotist rid you of overeating or other bad habits? Hypnosis has been only moderately effective in weight control and virtually useless in overcoming drug and alcohol abuse (Orne, 1983).

Critics' Explanations of Hypnosis: Is It Really What It Seems?

Because there is no reliable way to determine whether a person is truly hypnotized, some critics offer other explanations for behavior occurring during this state. One explanation is that subjects are simply acting out the role suggested by the hypnotist (Coe & Sarbin, 1977). Although some people claiming to be hypnotized may be role-playing, this theory does not adequately explain how people can undergo surgery with hypnosis rather than a general anesthetic (Kroger & Fezler, 1976).

Another idea is that behavior under hypnosis is no different from behavior of other highly motivated subjects. Barber (1970) found that "both hypnotic and waking control subjects are responsive to suggestions for analgesia [pain relief], age regression, hallucinations and amnesia if they have positive attitudes toward the situation and are motivated to respond" (p. 27).

Perhaps the best way to determine whether subjects are truly hypnotized or are deceiving the hypnotist is to give them a lie detector test while they are hypnotized. Kinnunen and others (1994) did just that. Using skin conductance response (SCR), they found that 89 percent of hypnotized subjects passed the test as being truly hypnotized. In contrast, only 35 percent of subjects who were trying to simulate being hypnotized were able to meet the criteria for truthfulness.

Memory Check 4.5

1. Which is *not* a proposed use of meditation?
   a. to promote relaxation
   b. to substitute for anesthesia during surgery
   c. to bring a person to a higher level of spirituality
   d. to alter consciousness

2. A special mantra is used in transcendental meditation. (true/false)

3. According to Dr. Herbert Benson, the beneficial effects of meditation cannot be duplicated with simple relaxation techniques. (true/false)

4. Which of the following statements is true of people under hypnosis?
   a. They will often violate their moral code.
   b. They are much stronger than in the normal waking state.
   c. They can be made to experience distortions in their perceptions.
   d. Their memory is more accurate than during the normal waking state.

5. For a moderately hypnotizable person, which use of hypnosis would probably be most successful?
   a. for relief from pain
   b. for surgery instead of a general anesthetic
   c. for treating drug addiction
   d. for improving memory

Answers: 1. b 2. true 3. false 4. c 5. a

World of Psychology

Culture and Altered States of Consciousness

In every culture around the world, and throughout recorded history, human beings have found ways to induce altered states of consciousness. Some means of inducing altered states in other cultures may seem strange and exotic to most of us. Entering ritual trances and experiencing spirit possession are forms of altered states of consciousness used in many cultures in the course of religious rites and tribal ceremonies. Possession and trances are normally part of public ceremonies but may require advance preparation in the form of purification rites and fasting (Ward, 1994). Typically, people induce ritual trance by flooding the senses with repetitive chanting, clapping, or singing; by whirling in circles until a dizzying speed is reached; or by burning strong, pungent incense.

In Singapore, Hong Kong, and Korea, temple mediums use ritual trances, as do shamans in Thailand and the Bantu people in South Africa (Ward, 1994). Closer to home, the voodoo practitioners in Haiti and other Caribbean countries use ritual trances to induce spirit possession.

The fact that so many different forms of altering consciousness are practiced by members of so many varied cultures around the world has led some experts to ask whether "there may be a universal human need to produce and maintain varieties of conscious experiences" (Ward, 1994, p. 60).

Whatever the method used to induce it, the experience of an altered state of consciousness can vary greatly from one culture to another. Mescaline, the psychedelic derivative from the mescal cactus, has long been used by some groups of Native Americans to produce hallucinations in their religious ceremonies. Others have also used peyote, another mescal derivative, but typically only to get high. Is the altered state of consciousness induced by either mescaline or peyote the same for Native Americans and for nonreligious recreational users? No, the descriptions of the hallucinatory experiences of these two cultural groups tend to be so different that they do not even seem to be taking the same substance (Ward, 1994). So in these two groups, at least, the culture and the motives, more than the substance itself, seem to define the quality of the altered state.

Altered States of Consciousness and Psychoactive Drugs

The altered states of consciousness we have examined thus far are natural ones. We will now explore psychoactive drugs, a wide range of substances that are used to modify natural consciousness. A **psychoactive drug** is any substance that alters mood, perception, or thought. Some of these drugs are legal, but most are not. When these drugs are approved for medical use only, they are called controlled substances.

Every year since 1975, the University of Michigan's Institute for Social Research has conducted surveys of drug use, and attitudes and beliefs about drug

psychoactive drug: A drug that alters normal mental functioning—mood, perception, or thought; if used medically, called a controlled substance.

use, among high school students and young adults. These surveys show that drug use among high school graduates had been falling continuously from 1980 to 1992. But as of 1993 the 12-year decline reversed itself and drug use was on the rise again, as shown in Figure 4.5. Researchers Johnston, O'Malley, and Bachman (1994) believe one reason for the increase may be that in 1992 and 1993 there was a decline in the perception of the harmfulness of certain drugs and less disapproval associated with their use. But the rates of drug use were not the same for all racial and ethnic groups in the United States. In fact, the survey revealed lower rates of use of alcohol, cigarettes, and virtually all **illicit drugs** (illegal drugs) among eighth-, tenth-, and twelfth-grade African American students than for their white or Hispanic counterparts.

Of all the industrial nations in the world, the United States has the highest rate of illicit drug use (Newcomb & Bentler, 1989). About 28 million Americans use illicit drugs (Jarvik, 1990), and 5.5 million are addicted to them (Holloway,

FIGURE 4.5

Results of a Survey on the Use of Alcohol, Marijuana, Cocaine, and Any Illicit Drug among High School Seniors

Shown for 1975 through 1993 are the percentages of high school seniors who reported using alcohol, marijuana, cocaine, or any illicit drug during the 30 days preceding the survey. After a decline in the use of marijuana and most illicit drugs from 1985 to 1992, drug use appeared to be increasing in 1993. (Data from Johnston, O'Malley, & Bachman, 1994.)

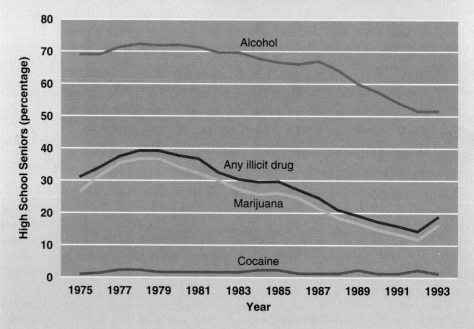

illicit drug: An illegal drug.

1991). But in terms of "damage to users, harm to society, or numbers of addicts," alcohol and tobacco are "our most serious problem drugs by far" (Goldstein & Kalant, 1990, p. 1516).

Why do so many Americans use psychoactive drugs? There are many reasons for taking drugs, and users often do not recognize their real motivation. Some people take drugs to cope with or relieve anxiety, depression, or boredom (Baker, 1988). Others use drugs just to feel good, for a thrill, or because of social pressures. Still others use psychoactive drugs for their medical benefits.

Peer influence is the factor most highly correlated with the use of illicit drugs, cigarettes, and alcohol by adolescents. According to Dinges and Oetting (1993), there is a "90 percent correspondence between an adolescent's use of particular drugs and the use of those exact drugs by friends" (p. 264). Table 4.2 summarizes the risk factors and protective factors associated with adolescent drug use and abuse.

TABLE 4.2 Risk Factors and Protective Factors for Adolescent Drug Use and Abuse

	Risk Factors	Protective Factors
Peer influences	Peers who are users and encourage use Peers who provide substances	Peers who are not users
Educational variables	Poor school performance Low educational aspirations	Good grades High educational aspirations
Social/family variables	Family conflict Family alcohol and/or drug abuse Lack of religious commitment	Positive family relationships Perceived sanctions against drug use Religious service attendance
Environmental variables	Extreme poverty Neighborhood disorganization Availability of drugs	
Psychological/ behavioral variables	Low self-esteem Antisocial behavior Need for excitement Poor impulse control Stressful life events Depression Anxiety Apathy and pessimism Alienation and rebelliousness	Self-acceptance Law abidance Perceived future opportunities

Source: Adapted from Hawkins, Catalano, & Miller, 1992; Jarvik, 1990; Newcomb & Bentler, 1989; and Newcomb & Felix-Ortiz, 1992..

What is the difference between physical and psychological drug dependence?

drug dependence (physical): A compulsive pattern of drug use in which the user develops a drug tolerance coupled with unpleasant withdrawal symptoms when the drug is discontinued.

drug tolerance: A condition in which the user becomes progressively less affected by the drug so that larger and larger doses are necessary to maintain the same effect.

withdrawal symptoms: The physical and psychological symptoms (usually the opposite of those produced by the drug) that occur when a regularly used drug is discontinued and that terminate when the drug is taken again.

drug dependence (psychological): A craving or irresistible urge for a drug's pleasurable effects.

How do stimulants affect the user?

stimulants: A category of drugs that speed up activity in the central nervous system, suppress appetite, and cause a person to feel more awake, alert, and energetic; also called "uppers."

Drug Dependence: Slave to a Substance

The trip from first use to abuse of drugs may be a long one or a very short one. Some drugs create a physical or chemical dependence; others create a psychological dependence. **Physical drug dependence** comes about as a result of the body's natural ability to protect itself against harmful substances by developing a **drug tolerance**. This means that the user becomes progressively less affected by the drug and must take larger and larger doses to get the same effect or high. Tolerance occurs because the brain adapts to the presence of the drug by responding less intensely to it. In addition, more enzymes are produced by the liver to break down the drug. The various bodily processes adjust in order to continue to function with the drug in the system.

Once drug tolerance is established, a person cannot function normally without the drug. If the drug is taken away, the user begins to suffer withdrawal symptoms. The **withdrawal symptoms**, both physical and psychological, are usually the exact opposite of the effects produced by the drug. For example, withdrawal from stimulants leaves a person exhausted and depressed; withdrawal from tranquilizers leaves a person nervous and agitated.

If physical dependence alone explained drug addiction, there would be no problem with drugs long thought to be physically nonaddictive. Also, once the period of physical withdrawal was over, the desire for the drug would end along with the withdrawal symptoms. But this is not the case. There is more to drug addiction than physical dependence. **Psychological drug dependence** is a craving or irresistible urge for the drug's pleasurable effects, and it is more difficult to combat than physical dependence.

Four factors influence the addictive potential of a drug: (1) how fast the effects of the drug are felt, (2) how pleasurable the drug's effects are in producing euphoria or in extinguishing pain, (3) how long the pleasurable effects last, and (4) how much discomfort is experienced when the drug is discontinued (Medzerian, 1991). The pleasurable effects of the most addictive drugs are felt almost immediately, and they are short-lived. For example, the intense, pleasurable effects of crack are felt in 7 seconds, and last only about 5 minutes. The discomfort after the pleasurable effects wear off is intense, so a user is highly motivated to take more of the drug. The abuse potential is higher if the drug is injected rather than taken orally, and higher still if it is smoked rather than injected.

Psychoactive drugs alter consciousness in a variety of ways. Let's consider the various alterations produced by the major categories of drugs: stimulants, depressants, and hallucinogens (or psychedelics).

Stimulants: Speeding Up the Nervous System

Stimulants, often called "uppers," speed up the central nervous system, suppress appetite, and can make a person feel more awake, alert, and energetic. Stimulants increase pulse rate, blood pressure, and respiration rate, and they reduce cerebral blood flow (Mathew & Wilson, 1991). In higher doses, stimulants make people feel nervous, jittery, and restless, and they can cause shaking or trembling and interfere with sleep.

No stimulant actually delivers energy to the body. Instead, a stimulant forces the body to use some of its own stored-up energy sooner and in greater amounts than it would naturally. When the stimulant's effect wears off, the body's natural energy is depleted, leaving the person feeling exhausted and depressed.

There are legal stimulants, such as caffeine and nicotine; controlled stimulants, such as amphetamines; and illegal stimulants, such as cocaine.

Caffeine: The Most Widely Used Drug Caffeine is the world's most widely used drug, and more than 85 percent of Americans ingest it daily in one form or another (Hughes et al., 1992). If you cannot start your day without a cup of coffee (or two, or more), you may be addicted to the stimulant caffeine. Coffee, tea, cola drinks, chocolate, and more than 100 prescription and over-the-counter drugs contain caffeine. They provide a mild jolt to the nervous system that perks us up, at least temporarily. Caffeine makes us more mentally alert and can help us stay awake. Many people use caffeine to lift their mood; but laboratory studies reveal that 1 hour after consuming medium or high doses of caffeine, subjects show significantly higher levels of anxiety, depression, and hostility (Veleber & Templer, 1984).

Nicotine: A Deadly Poison   Nicotine is a poison so strong that the body must develop a tolerance to it almost immediately—in only hours, in contrast to days or weeks for heroin, and usually months for alcohol. It is estimated that 46 million Americans smoke cigarettes (Sherman, 1994), and tobacco kills 434,000 Americans every year (Raloff, 1994). White adolescents smoke more than their African American, Asian, and Latino counterparts, and they are more likely to be influenced by peers who smoke (Landrine et al., 1994). The many health problems associated with smoking are discussed in Chapter 13.

Amphetamines: Energy to Burn—at a Price   **Amphetamines** are a class of stimulants that increase arousal, relieve fatigue, suppress the appetite, and give a rush of energy. In low to moderate doses, they may temporarily boost athletic and intellectual performance. A person becomes more alert and energetic, mildly euphoric, and usually more talkative, animated, and restless.

In high doses—100 milligrams or more—amphetamines can cause confused and disorganized behavior, extreme fear and suspiciousness, delusions and hallucinations, aggressiveness and antisocial behavior, even manic behavior and paranoia. The powerful amphetamine methamphetamine (known as "crank" or "speed") now comes in smokable form—"ice," which is highly addictive and can be fatal.

The withdrawal symptoms from amphetamines leave a person physically exhausted, sleeping for 10 to 15 hours or more, only to awaken in a stupor, extremely depressed and intensely hungry. Stimulants constrict the tiny capillaries and the small arteries. Over time, high doses can stop the blood flow, causing hemorrhaging and leaving parts of the brain deprived of oxygen. In fact, victims of fatal overdoses of stimulants usually have multiple hemorrhages in the brain.

Yet some stimulants have therapeutic benefits. According to the Standards of Practice Committee of the American Sleep Disorders Association (1994), "stimulants are the only effective treatment for the sleepiness of narcolepsy" (p. 348). Stimulants are also useful in treating attention deficit disorder (Kleven & Seiden, 1992).

Cocaine: Snorting White Powder, Smoking Crack   "Cocaine can make you feel brilliant, masterful, invulnerable. It can also kill you" (Gold, 1986).

Cocaine, a stimulant derived from coca leaves, can be sniffed as a white powder, injected intravenously, or smoked in the form of crack. The rush of well-being is dramatically intense and powerful, but it is just as dramatically short-lived. The euphoria lasts no more than 15 to 30 minutes and is followed by an equally intense **crash**, marked by depression, anxiety, agitation, and a powerful craving for more cocaine (Gawin, 1991).

Cocaine stimulates the reward or "pleasure" pathways in the brain, which use the neurotransmitter dopamine (Craine & Koob, 1993). With continued use, the reward systems fail to function normally, and the user becomes incapable of feeling any pleasure except from the drug (Gawin, 1991). The main withdrawal symptoms are psychological—the inability to feel pleasure and the craving for more cocaine (Gawin & Ellinwood, 1988).

amphetamines: A class of CNS stimulants that increase arousal, relieve fatigue, and suppress the appetite.

cocaine: A type of stimulant that produces a feeling of euphoria.

crash: The feelings of depression, exhaustion, irritability, and anxiety that occur following an amphetamine, cocaine, or crack high.

What effects do amphetamines have on the user?

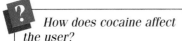
How does cocaine affect the user?

crack: The most potent, inexpensive, and addictive form of cocaine, and the form that is smoked.

hallucinogens (hal-lu-SIN-o-jenz): A category of drugs, sometimes called psychedelics, that alter perception and mood and can cause hallucinations.

Cocaine constricts the blood vessels, raises blood pressure, speeds up the heart, quickens respiration, and can even cause epileptic seizures in people who have no history of epilepsy (Pascual-Leone et al., 1990). Over time, or even quickly in high doses, cocaine can cause heart palpitations, an irregular heartbeat, and heart attacks (Lange et al., 1989). Even strong, young hearts sometimes cannot stand the strain of high doses of cocaine. In 1993 River Phoenix, a promising young actor, died from an overdose of cocaine combined with morphine.

Animals become addicted more readily to cocaine than to any other drug (Geary, 1987). Given unlimited access to cocaine, animals will lose interest in everything else—food, water, and sex—and will rapidly and continually self-administer cocaine. They die within 14 days, usually from cardiopulmonary collapse (Gawin, 1991). Cocaine-addicted monkeys will press a lever as many as 12,800 times to get one cocaine injection (Yanagita, 1973).

Crack, or "rock," has made cocaine affordable, even for the very poor. Not only the cheapest but the most dangerous form of cocaine, crack can produce a powerful dependency in several weeks. Dr. Jeffrey Rosecan, a drug abuse consultant to the National Football League, calls cocaine "the most addicting substance known to man"; and crack, he says, is "the most addicting form of the most addicting drug" (Lundgren, 1986, p. 7).

Memory Check 4.6

1. Which of the following does not necessarily occur with drug tolerance?
   a. The body adjusts to functioning with the drug in the system.
   b. The person needs larger and larger doses of the drug to get the desired effect.
   c. The user becomes progressively less affected by the drug.
   d. The user develops a craving for the pleasurable effects of the drug.

2. During withdrawal from a drug, the user experiences symptoms that are the opposite of the effects produced by the drug. (true/false)

3. Psychological dependence on a drug is more difficult to combat than physical dependence. (true/false)

4. Match the stimulant with the appropriate description.
   ____ 1) responsible for the most deaths
   ____ 2) used to increase arousal, relieve fatigue, and suppress appetite
   ____ 3) found in coffee, tea, chocolate, and colas
   ____ 4) snorted or injected
   ____ 5) most dangerous, potent, and addictive form of cocaine

   a. caffeine
   b. cigarettes
   c. amphetamines
   d. crack
   e. cocaine

Answers: 1. d 2. true 3. true 4. 1) b 2) c 3) a 4) e 5) d

What are the main effects of hallucinogens, and what are two psychoactive drugs classified as hallucinogens?

Hallucinogens: Seeing, Hearing, and Feeling What Is Not There

The **hallucinogens**, or psychedelics, are drugs that can alter and distort perceptions of time and space, alter mood, and produce feelings of unreality. Hallucinogens have been used in religious and recreational rituals and ceremonies in diverse cultures since ancient times (Millman & Beeder, 1994). As the name implies, hallucinogens also cause hallucinations, sensations that have no basis in external reality (Andreasen & Black, 1991; Miller & Gold, 1994).

Rather than producing a relatively predictable effect like most other drugs, hallucinogens usually magnify the mood of the user at the time the drug is taken. The hallucinogens we will discuss are LSD and marijuana.

LSD (Lysergic Acid Diethylamide): Mind Altering, Not Mind Expanding LSD is lysergic acid diethylamide, sometimes referred to simply as "acid." The average LSD "trip" lasts for 10 to 12 hours and usually produces extreme perceptual changes—visual hallucinations and distortions. Emotions can become very intense and unstable, ranging from euphoria to anxiety, panic, depression, or even suicidal thoughts and actions (Miller & Gold, 1994). LSD can cause bad trips that can be terrifying and leave the user in a state of panic. On occasion, bad LSD trips have ended tragically in accidents, death, or suicide. Sometimes a person who has taken LSD experiences a **flashback**, a brief recurrence of a trip that occurs suddenly and without warning. Flashbacks reportedly can occur for weeks, or even up to 5 years after LSD use. The use of marijuana and some other drugs may trigger these LSD flashbacks (Gold, 1994).

According to the National Institute on Drug Abuse (1993), 5.6 percent of high school students used LSD in 1992, a steady increase since 1988.

Marijuana: More Harmful Than We Once Believed About 20 million people in the United States use marijuana regularly, making it the most widely used illicit drug (Andreasen & Black, 1991). In general, **marijuana** tends to produce a feeling of well-being, promote relaxation, relieve inhibitions, and relieve anxiety. The user may experience an increased sensitivity to sights, sounds, and touch, as well as perceptual distortions and a perceived slowing of time.

THC (tetrahydrocannibinol), the ingredient in marijuana that produces the high, remains in the body long after it has been smoked. Even a week after use, 30 percent of the THC ingested is still in the system; 10 percent remains after 7 weeks (Jones & Jones, 1977). A person who smokes only one marijuana cigarette, or joint, every few weeks is never completely free of THC. Marijuana impairs attention and coordination and slows reaction time, and these effects make operating complex machinery such as an automobile dangerous, even after the feeling of intoxication has passed.

Marijuana can interfere with concentration, logical thinking, and the ability to form new memories. It can produce fragmentation in thought and confusion in remembering recent occurrences (Herkenham, 1992). Many of the receptor sites for marijuana are in the hippocampus, which explains why it affects memory (Matsuda et al., 1990). Chronic use of marijuana has been associated with loss of motivation, general apathy, and decline in school performance—referred to as the amotivational syndrome (Andreasen & Black, 1991).

Smoking marijuana can cause respiratory damage even faster than cigarette smoking (Tzu-Chin et al., 1988). Marijuana abuse affects the reproductive system in males, causing (1) a 20-percent impotence rate, (2) a 44-percent reduction in testosterone level (Kolodny et al., 1979), (3) a 30- to 70-percent reduction in sperm count, and (4) an abnormal appearance of sperm cells (Hembree et al., 1979). In women, failure to ovulate, other menstrual irregularities, and lower-birth-weight babies have been associated with heavy marijuana use (Hingson et al., 1982; Kolodny et al., 1979).

Even so, marijuana has some beneficial medical effects in treating the eye disease glaucoma (Restak, 1993) and in "controlling nausea and stimulating appetite in patients receiving chemotherapy for cancer or AIDS" (Herkenham, 1992, p. 30).

Marijuana, the most widely used illicit drug in the United States, has been associated with loss of motivation, general apathy, and decline in school performance.

? *What are some harmful effects associated with heavy marijuana use?*

LSD (lysergic acid diethylamide): A powerful hallucinogen with unpredictable effects ranging from perceptual changes and vivid hallucinations to states of panic and terror.

flashback: The brief recurrence, occurring suddenly and without warning at a later time, of effects a person has experienced while taking LSD.

marijuana: A hallucinogen with effects ranging from relaxation and giddiness to perceptual distortions and hallucinations.

THC (tetrahydrocannabinol): The principal psychoactive ingredient in marijuana and hashish.

? *What are some of the effects of depressants, and what drugs comprise this category?*

depressants: A category of drugs that decrease activity in the central nervous system, slow down bodily functions, and reduce sensitivity to outside stimulation; also called "downers."

alcohol: A central nervous system depressant.

Depressants: Slowing Down the Nervous System

Another class of drugs, the **depressants** (sometimes called "downers") decrease activity in the central nervous system, slow down body functions, and reduce sensitivity to outside stimulation. Within this category are the sedative-hypnotics (alcohol, barbiturates, and minor tranquilizers) and the narcotics, or opiates.

Alcohol: The Nation's Number One Drug Problem   Even though **alcohol** is a depressant, the first few drinks seem to relax and enliven at the same time. But the more alcohol consumed, the more the central nervous system is depressed. As drinking increases, the symptoms of drunkenness mount—slurred speech, poor coordination, staggering. Men tend to become more aggressive (Bushman & Cooper, 1990) and more sexually aroused (Roehrich & Kinder, 1991) but less able to perform sexually (Crowe & George, 1989). Excessive alcohol can cause a person to lose consciousness, and extremely large amounts can kill. People have died playing the party game of chug-a-lugging whiskey.

Alcohol is a problem substance responsible for much misery in the United States. We discuss the health consequences of alcohol abuse in detail in Chapter 13. The World of Psychology section indicates that culture affects patterns of alcohol use and abuse.

World of Psychology

The Use and Abuse of Alcohol

Human societies throughout recorded history have brewed and distilled alcohol and used it for recreational purposes, in religious rites, and for social celebrations. Alcohol has also been widely abused. There is great cultural variation in drinking habits and styles, and in attitudes toward alcohol. Moderate drinking is prevalent in some American ethnic groups, most notably Jewish, Greek, Chinese, and Italian (Colón & Wuollet, 1994; Peele, 1984). In these cultures alcohol is used primarily in the family or larger social settings where young people are gradually included. Alcohol is rarely used excessively and is controlled by cultural norms and social customs.

Alcohol use is rare or nonexistent among some religious groups in the United States, especially the Amish, Mennonites, and Mormons. The use of alcohol is forbidden for members of these three religions, as is the use of other psychoactive drugs (Trimble, 1994).

Culture, more than genes, seems to drive the patterns of use and abuse of alcohol. Certain genetic similarities have been found among Native Americans and Chinese Americans. Both groups are subject to a biological constitution in which their body metabolism has an exaggerated reaction to alcohol (Peele, 1984). Yet Native Americans have a high rate of alcoholism, while Chinese Americans have an unusually low rate.

According to a 1992 Gallup poll, 36 percent of Americans are total abstainers, and 64 percent define themselves as drinkers (McAneny, 1992). The poll further revealed that more men (72 percent) drink than women (57 percent), considerably more whites (66 percent) drink than nonwhites (50 percent), and more college graduates (78 percent) drink than high school graduates (65 percent).

Barbiturates: Sedatives That Can Kill in Overdose Barbiturates depress the central nervous system and, depending on the dose, can act as a sedative or a sleeping pill. People who abuse barbiturates become drowsy and confused, their thinking and judgment suffer, and their coordination and reflexes are affected (Henningfield & Ator, 1986). Barbiturates can kill if taken in overdose, and a lethal dose can be as little as only three times the prescribed dose.

The Minor Tranquilizers: Prescribed by the Millions The popular **minor tranquilizers**, the benzodiazepines, came on the scene in the early 1960s and are sold under the brand names Valium, Librium, Dalmane, and, more recently, Xanax (also used as an antidepressant). About 90 million prescriptions for minor tranquilizers are filled each year. Benzodiazepines are prescribed for several medical and psychological disorders, and they are rarely used recreationally (Woods et al., 1987). Alcohol and benzodiazepines, when taken together, are a potentially hazardous combination that can be fatal.

Narcotics: Drugs from the Opium Poppy **Narcotics** are derived from the opium poppy and produce both a pain-relieving and a calming effect. Opium affects mainly the brain and the bowel. It paralyzes the intestinal muscles, which is why it is used medically to treat diarrhea. If you have ever taken paregoric, you have had a little tincture of opium. Because opium suppresses the cough center, it is used in some cough medicines. Both morphine and codeine, two drugs prescribed for pain, are natural constituents of opium.

A highly addictive narcotic derived from morphine is **heroin**. Heroin addicts describe a sudden "rush," or euphoria, followed by drowsiness, inactivity, and impaired concentration. Withdrawal symptoms begin about 6 to 24 hours after use, and the addict becomes physically sick. Nausea, diarrhea, depression, stomach cramps, insomnia, and pain grow worse and worse until they become intolerable—unless the person gets another fix.

For years heroin sold on the street was 5 to 10 percent pure, but a newer kind called "China White" is up to 90 percent pure (Maas, 1994). China White is so pure that it can be smoked or snorted, but when people inject it, they run a risk of a lethal overdose. River Phoenix and Kurt Cobain have been among its casualties. Heroin has become popular in Hollywood, on college campuses, and at all levels of society. Its users in the United States number as many as 2 million, a fourfold increase from the late 1980s (Maas, 1994).

Review and Reflect Table 4.1 (on page 156) provides a summary of the effects and withdrawal symptoms of the major psychoactive drugs.

How Drugs Affect the Brain

Eating, drinking, and sexual activity are pleasurable, in large measure, because they result in the release of dopamine, a transmitter substance involved in reinforcement. Unfortunately, many substances that are abused also stimulate the release of dopamine and therefore reinforce continuing use of the drugs.

There is now ample evidence that dopamine is involved in the rewarding and motivational effects produced by stimulants such as amphetamine and cocaine (Di Chiara et al., 1992). Amphetamines affect dopamine transmission directly by stimulating the release of the neurotransmitter. Both cocaine and amphetamines slow the reuptake of dopamine at the synapses, and thus increase and prolong its reinforcing effects. Alcohol and nicotine also stimulate the release of dopamine in some areas of the brain, and this is what yields their pleasant, reinforcing effects.

> **?** *What are the general effects of narcotics, and what are several drugs in this category?*

> **barbiturates:** A class of addictive depressants used as sedatives, sleeping pills, and anesthetics; overdoses can cause coma or death.
>
> **tranquilizer (minor):** A central nervous system depressant that calms the user.
>
> **narcotics:** A class of depressant drugs that are derived from the opium poppy, and have pain-relieving and calming effects.
>
> **heroin:** A highly addictive, partly synthetic narcotic derived from morphine.

Review and Reflect   4.1   The Effects and Withdrawal Symptoms of Some Psychoactive Drugs

Psychoactive Drug	Effects	Withdrawal Symptoms
Stimulants		
Tobacco (nicotine)	Effects range from alertness to calmness; lowers appetite for carbohydrates; increases pulse rate and other metabolic processes	Irritability, anxiety, increased appetite
Caffeine	Produces wakefulness and alertness; increases metabolism but slows reaction time	Headache, depression
Amphetamines	Increase metabolism and alertness; elevate mood, cause wakefulness, suppress appetite	Fatigue, increased appetite, depression, long periods of sleep, irritability
Cocaine	Brings on euphoric mood, energy boost, feeling of excitement; suppresses appetite	Depression, fatigue, increased appetite, long periods of sleep, irritability
Hallucinogens		
Marijuana	Generally produces euphoria, relaxation; affects ability to store new memories	Anxiety, difficulty sleeping, decreased appetite, hyperactivity
LSD	Produces excited exhilaration, hallucinations, experiences perceived as insightful and profound	
Depressants		
Alcohol	First few drinks stimulate and enliven while lowering anxiety and inhibitions; higher doses have a sedative effect, slowing reaction time, impairing motor control and perceptual ability	Tremors, nausea, sweating, depression, weakness, irritability, and in some cases hallucinations
Tranquilizers (e.g., Valium, Xanax)	Lower anxiety, have calming and sedative effect, decrease muscular tension	Restlessness, anxiety, irritability, muscle tension, difficulty sleeping
Barbiturates (e.g., phenobarbital)	Promote sleep, have calming and sedative effect, decrease muscular tension, impair coordination and reflexes	Sleeplessness, anxiety; sudden withdrawal can cause seizures, cardiovascular collapse, and death
Narcotics		
Opium, morphine, heroin	Produce euphoria, relax muscles, suppress pain, cause constipation	Anxiety, restlessness, diarrhea, nausea, muscle spasms, chills and sweating, runny nose

Opiates such as morphine and heroin mimic the effects of the brain's own endorphins, which have pain-relieving properties and make us feel good. Research has shown that alcohol, barbiturates, and benzodiazepines (such as Valium and Librium) act upon GABA receptors (Harris et al., 1992). GABA, an inhibitory neurotransmitter, slows down the central nervous system. Thus, stimulating the release of GABA with alcohol or tranquilizers has a calming, sedating effect. If enough GABA is released, it can shut down the brain. This is why alcohol and tranquilizers together are such a potentially deadly duo.

Research on the neurobiology of drug and alcohol addiction continues to shed new light on the problem, and the work in progress may well point the way toward more effective means for dealing with addiction in our society.

Memory Check 4.7

1. Which category of drugs alters perception and mood and can cause hallucinations?
   a. stimulants
   b. more visual.
   c. hallucinogens
   d. narcotics

2. Which of the following is *not* associated with long-term use of marijuana?
   a. respiratory damage
   b. loss of motivation
   c. reproductive problems
   d. increased risk of heart attack and stroke

3. Decreased activity in the central nervous system is the chief effect of:
   a. stimulants.
   b. depressants.
   c. hallucinogens.
   d. narcotics.

4. Which of the following is a narcotic?
   a. cocaine
   b. heroin
   c. LSD
   d. Valium

5. Narcotics have:
   a. pain-relieving effects.
   b. stimulating effects.
   c. energizing effects.
   d. perception-altering effects.

6. Cocaine and amphetamines are highly rewarding because they increase the effect of the neurotransmitter:
   a. acetylcholine.
   b. GABA.
   c. dopamine.
   d. serotonin.

Answers: 1. c   2. d   3. b   4. b   5. a   6. c

APPLICATIONS • APPLICATIONS • APPLICATIONS

Battling Insomnia

As we saw in this chapter, insomnia is a sleep disorder in which a person has trouble falling or staying asleep or in which sleep is light, restless, or of poor quality. If you've ever experienced insomnia, you know the negative effects it can have on your state of mind and ability to function during the day.

What causes insomnia? Sleep researchers believe that most cases are psychological in origin. Some of the major causes include the following (Rosekind, 1992; Bootzin & Perlis, 1992):

- Psychological disorders such as depression, anxiety disorders, or alcohol or other drug abuse

- Medical problems such as chronic pain, breathing problems, or gastrointestinal disorders

- Circadian rhythm disturbances caused by shift work, jet lag, or a chronic mismatch between a person's body time and clock time

- Use of various drugs, such as prescription drugs, caffeine, nicotine, alcohol, tranquilizers, sleeping pills, and so on

- Poor sleep environment with conditions that may be too noisy, hot, cold, or bright

- Poor sleep habits, such as spending too much nonsleep time in bed, taking too many naps, or having irregular sleep times; or associating bedtime with the frustration of not being able to get to sleep

Sleeping Pills: Do They Help?

In desperation, many people resort to sleeping pills to help them fall asleep when insomnia becomes a problem. But do sleeping pills really work? In general, many leading authorities on sleep disorders believe that low-dose benzodiazepine *hypnotics*—drugs approved by the FDA for the treatment of insomnia—are effective and safe to use in treating transient (temporary) insomnia (Dement, 1992; Vogel, 1992; Walsh & Engelhardt, 1992). Short-term use of hypnotics for "a bout of stress-related insomnia or jet lag" is beneficial, according to Dement, and does not cause addiction or dependence. In fact, it may prevent

continued

an even more serious problem—chronic insomnia—from developing. It is important to note that hypnotics are usually *not* recommended for the treatment of chronic (long-term) insomnia, because they lose their effectiveness with prolonged use, and such use may lead to physical dependence (Bootzin & Perlis, 1992).

When insomnia disturbs a person's sleep, he or she may resort to a variety of sleep "aids," including tranquilizers, over-the-counter sleep products, and the most widely used one—alcohol. A few drinks at bedtime may get you to sleep faster, but there is a price to be paid: lighter sleep, more awakenings, and less sleep overall (Hartmann, 1988). Over-the-counter sleep aids are useless in serious cases of insomnia, because instead of actually inducing sleep, they simply cause grogginess (Kales et al., 1971). These products can be dangerous if taken in higher-than-recommended doses (Webb, 1975).

Help may be on the way for desperate insomniacs. Researchers Cravatt and others (1995) have discovered a previously unrecognized molecule in the cerebrospinal fluid of sleep-deprived cats. It effectively induced normal sleep in a group of laboratory rats. And a form of this molecule is found in the human brain.

Hints for a Better Night's Sleep

So what can you do to battle insomnia and improve the quality of your sleep? If you associate your bed with the frustration of being unable to fall asleep, here are some tips that can help you:

- Use your bed *only* for sleep. Don't read, study, write letters, watch television, eat, or talk on the phone from your bed.

- Leave the bedroom whenever you cannot fall asleep within 10 minutes. Go to another room and read, watch television, or listen to music. Don't return to bed for another try until you feel more tired. Repeat the process as many times as necessary until you fall asleep within 10 minutes.

- Establish a consistent, relaxing ritual that you follow each night just before bedtime. For example, take a warm bath, eat a small snack, brush your teeth, pick out your clothes for the next day, and so on.

- Set your alarm and wake up at the same time every day including weekends, regardless of how much you have slept. No naps are allowed during the day.

- Exercise regularly—but not within several hours of bedtime. (Exercise raises body temperature and makes it more difficult to fall asleep.)

- Establish regular mealtimes. Don't eat heavy or spicy meals close to bedtime. If you must eat then, try milk and a few crackers.

- Beware of caffeine and nicotine—they are sleep disturbers. Avoid caffeine within 6 hours and smoking within 1 or 2 hours of bedtime.

- Avoid wrestling with your problems when you go to bed. Try counting backward from 1,000 by twos. Or try a progressive relaxation exercise (see the *Try It!* on p. 144).

Thinking Critically

Evaluation

Suppose you have been hired by a sleep clinic to formulate a questionnaire for evaluating patients' sleep habits. List ten questions you would include in your questionnaire.

Point/Counterpoint

You hear much debate about the pros and cons of legalizing drugs. Present the most convincing argument possible to support each of these positions:

a. Illicit drugs should be legalized.

b. Illicit drugs should not be legalized.

Psychology in Your Life

You have been asked to make a presentation to seventh and eighth graders about the dangers of drugs. What are the most persuasive general arguments you can give to convince them not to get involved with drugs? What are some convincing, specific arguments against using each of these drugs: alcohol, marijuana, cigarettes, and cocaine?

Chapter Summary and Review

What Is Consciousness?

> [?] *What are some different states of consciousness?*

Various states of consciousness include ordinary waking consciousness, daydreaming, sleep, and altered states brought about through meditation, hypnosis, or the use of psychoactive drugs.

Key Terms

consciousness (p. 128)
altered state of consciousness (p. 129)

Circadian Rhythms: Our 24-Hour Highs and Lows

> [?] *What is a circadian rhythm, and which rhythms are most relevant to the study of sleep?*

A circadian rhythm is the regular fluctuation in certain body functions from a high point to a low point within a 24-hour period. Two rhythms most relevant to sleep are the sleep/wakefulness cycle and body temperature.

> [?] *What are some problems experienced by people who work rotating shifts?*

People working rotating shifts experience a disruption in their circadian rhythms that causes sleep difficulties, digestive problems, and lowered alertness, efficiency, productivity, and safety during subjective night.

Key Terms

circadian rhythm (p. 129)
subjective night (p. 130)

Sleep: That Mysterious One-Third of Our Lives

> [?] *How does a sleeper react physically during NREM sleep?*

During NREM sleep, heart rate and respiration are slow and regular, blood pressure and brain activity are at a 24-hour low point, and there is little body movement and no rapid eye movements.

> [?] *How does the body respond physically during REM sleep?*

During REM sleep, the large muscles of the body are paralyzed, respiration and heart rates are fast and irregular, brain activity increases, and rapid eye movements and vivid dreams occur.

> [?] *What is the progression of NREM stages and REM sleep that a person follows in a typical night of sleep?*

During a typical night, a person sleeps in sleep cycles, each lasting about 90 minutes. The first sleep cycle contains Stages 1, 2, 3, and 4, and REM sleep; the second contains Stages 2, 3, and 4, and REM sleep. In the remaining sleep cycles, the sleeper alternates mainly between Stage 2 and REM sleep, with each sleep cycle having progressively longer REM periods.

> [?] *How do sleep patterns change over the life span?*

Infants and young children have the longest sleep time and largest percentage of REM and slow-wave sleep. Children from age 6 to puberty sleep best. The elderly typically have shorter total sleep time, more awakenings, and a virtual lack of slow-wave sleep.

> [?] *What factors influence our sleep needs?*

Factors that influence our sleep needs are heredity, the amount of stress in our lives, and our emotional state.

> [?] *What happens when people are deprived of REM sleep? What function does REM sleep appear to serve?*

Following REM deprivation, people experience a REM rebound—an increase in the percentage of REM sleep. REM sleep appears to aid in learning and memory.

> [?] *How do REM and NREM dreams differ?*

REM dreams have a dreamlike, storylike quality and are more vivid, visual, and emotional than the more thought-like NREM dreams.

> [?] *In general, what have researchers found regarding the content of dreams?*

Dreams usually reflect the dreamer's preoccupations in waking life. They tend to have commonplace settings, to be more unpleasant than pleasant, and to be less emotional and bizarre than people tend to remember them.

Key Terms

NREM sleep (p. 132)
REM sleep (p. 133)
sleep cycle (p. 134)
slow-wave sleep (p. 134)
delta wave (p. 134)
Stage 4 sleep (p. 134)
microsleep (p. 137)
REM rebound (p. 137)
REM dreams (p. 137)
NREM dreams (p. 138)
lucid dream (p. 138)

Sleep Disorders

 What are the characteristics common to sleepwalking and sleep terrors?

Sleepwalking and sleep terrors occur during a partial arousal from Stage 4 sleep, and the person does not come to full consciousness. Episodes are rarely recalled. These disorders are typically found in children and outgrown by adolescence, and they tend to run in families.

What is a sleep terror?

A sleep terror is a parasomnia in which the sleeper awakens from Stage 4 sleep with a scream, dazed and groggy, in a panic state, and with a racing heart.

How do nightmares differ from sleep terrors?

Nightmares are frightening dreams that occur during REM sleep and are remembered in vivid detail. Sleep terrors occur during Stage 4 sleep, are rarely remembered, and often involve a single, frightening image.

What are the major symptoms of narcolepsy?

The symptoms of narcolepsy include excessive daytime sleepiness and sudden attacks of REM sleep.

What is sleep apnea?

Sleep apnea is a serious sleep disorder in which breathing stops during sleep and the person must awaken briefly to breathe. Its major symptoms are excessive daytime sleepiness and loud snoring.

 What is insomnia?

Insomnia is a sleep disorder that involves difficulty in falling or staying asleep, or sleep that is light, restless, or of poor quality.

Key Terms

somnambulism (p. 141)
sleep terror (p. 141)
nightmare (p. 141)
narcolepsy (p. 142)
sleep apnea (p. 142)
insomnia (p. 143)

Altering Consciousness through Concentration and Suggestion

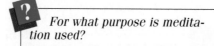 *For what purpose is meditation used?*

Meditation is used by some to promote relaxation and reduce arousal, and by others to expand consciousness or attain a higher level of spirituality.

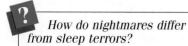 *What is hypnosis, and when is it most useful?*

Hypnosis, which has been used most successfully for the control of pain, is a trancelike state of consciousness characterized by focused attention, heightened suggestibility, and diminished response to external stimuli.

Key Terms

meditation (p. 143)
hypnosis (p. 144)

Altered States of Consciousness and Psychoactive Drugs

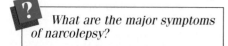 *What is the difference between physical and psychological drug dependence?*

With physical drug dependence, the user develops a drug tolerance so that larger and larger doses are needed to get the same effect. Withdrawal symptoms appear when the drug is discontinued and disappear when the drug is taken again. Psychological drug dependence involves an intense craving for the drug.

 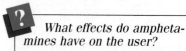 *How do stimulants affect the user?*

Stimulants speed up activity in the central nervous system, suppress appetite, and make a person feel more awake, alert, and energetic.

 What effects do amphetamines have on the user?

Amphetamines energize, increase arousal, and suppress the appetite; but with continued use they result in exhaustion, depression, and agitation.

How does cocaine affect the user?

Cocaine energizes, causes a feeling of euphoria, and is highly addictive. Heavy use can cause heart damage, seizures, and even heart attacks.

What are the main effects of hallucinogens, and what are two psychoactive drugs classified as hallucinogens?

Hallucinogens—LSD and marijuana—can alter perception and mood and cause hallucinations.

What are some harmful effects associated with heavy marijuana use?

There is some evidence that heavy marijuana use can cause memory problems, respiratory damage, loss of motivation, impotence, lowered testosterone level and sperm count, and irregular menstrual cycles.

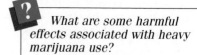 *What are some of the effects of depressants, and what drugs comprise this category?*

Depressants decrease activity in the central nervous system, slow down body functions, and reduce sensitivity to outside stimulation. Depressants include sedative-hypnotics (alcohol, barbiturates, and minor tranquilizers) and narcotics (opiates).

What are the general effects of narcotics, and what are several drugs in this category?

Narcotics, which include opium, codeine, morphine, and heroin, have both pain-relieving and calming effects.

Key Terms

psychoactive drug (p. 147)
illicit drug (p. 148)
physical drug dependence (p. 150)
drug tolerance (p. 150)
withdrawal symptoms (p. 150)
psychological drug dependence (p. 150)
stimulants (p. 150)
amphetamines (p. 151)
cocaine (p. 151)
crash (p. 151)

crack (p. 152)
hallucinogens (p. 152)
LSD (p. 153)
flashback (p. 153)
marijuana (p. 153)
THC (p. 153)
depressants (p. 154)
alcohol (p. 154)
barbituates (p. 155)
minor tranquilizers (p. 155)
narcotics (p. 155)
heroin (p. 155)

5

LEARNING

CHAPTER OUTLINE

Robert Wilson (not his real name) had it all. Born in 1960, he grew to be superior in every way—he was handsome, exceptionally bright and talented, and had an unusually charming personality. Robert completed his MBA at Harvard in 1985 when he was 25 years old, and he promptly joined a leading brokerage firm. He was ambitious and did little more than work for 2 years. Then in 1987 a senior executive with the firm who was 10 years older than Robert became his mentor and took him under his wing. Robert and his mentor were virtually inseparable at work and at play, and Robert was now on a fast track to the top.

At a party the mentor arranged, he and Robert, with some other executives, spent a long weekend with several young women. Robert was introduced to cocaine. He watched with fascination as his mentor and one of the young women took some white powder from a plastic bag and, with a razor blade, arranged it in neat lines on a mirror. They each snorted a couple of lines and seemed to enjoy it immensely.

"The first time I used cocaine, the feeling was great," said Robert. "A few days later, I wanted to do it again, and within 2 years I didn't want to do anything else. The craving was intense. The euphoria, the high, was something I could never get out of my mind. But when the high was over, I felt miserable. I would do anything to escape that feeling."

Within a short time cocaine took everything Robert had—his job, his friends, all his possessions, his self-esteem, his ambition, and finally his freedom. In 1991 he was convicted as a drug dealer and now sits in prison, far removed from the successful life he had planned.

What does cocaine addiction have to do with learning? Our opening story provides examples of the three basic types of learning that psychologists study—these are classical conditioning, operant conditioning, and observational learning. In classical conditioning, an association is learned between one stimulus and another. A **stimulus** is any event or object in the environment to which an organism responds (plural, *stimuli*). In Robert's case, certain environmental cues (parties, beautiful people, a good time, drug paraphernalia) became associated with cocaine. In operant conditioning, an association is formed between a behavior and its consequences—the snorting of cocaine and the feeling of euphoria that follows. In observational learning, we learn by observing the behavior of others and then may imitate that behavior. Observational learning occurred when Robert began to use cocaine after watching his mentor, his model, use it.

These three kinds of learning are powerful forces that influence human thought and behavior for good or for ill. Not only did they serve to initiate and maintain Robert's addiction, but the same principles of learning can help people break addictions and improve their lives, as you will learn.

Learning may be defined as a relatively permanent change in behavior, capability, or attitude that is acquired through experience and cannot be attributed to illness, injury, or maturation. Several parts of this definition warrant further explanation. First, defining learning as a "relatively permanent change" excludes temporary changes that could result from illness, fatigue, or fluctuations in mood. Second, by referring to changes that are "acquired through experience," we exclude some relatively permanent, readily observable changes in behavior that occur as a result of brain injuries or certain diseases. Also, there are observable changes as we grow and mature that have nothing to do with learning. For example, a young male at puberty does not *learn* to speak in a deeper voice, but his voice changes to a lower pitch because of maturation.

We cannot observe learning directly but must infer that it has occurred. We draw inferences from changes in observable behavior or in measurable capabilities and attitudes. Certainly much learning occurs that we are not able to observe or measure. As a student, you might have experienced occasions when you had learned more than your test scores reflected. But learning does not always result in a change in behavior. Often we learn or acquire a capability that we may not demonstrate until we are motivated to do so.

Learning is one of the most important topics in the field of psychology, and available evidence suggests that we learn through many different avenues. This

stimulus (STIM-yu-lus): Any event or object in the environment to which an organism responds; plural is *stimuli*.

learning: A relatively permanent change in behavior, capability, or attitude that is acquired through experience and cannot be attributed to illness, injury, or maturation.

chapter explores the three basic forms of learning—classical conditioning, operant conditioning, and observational learning.

Classical Conditioning

Classical conditioning is one of the simplest forms of learning, yet it has a powerful effect on our attitudes, likes and dislikes, and emotional responses. We have all learned to respond in specific ways to a variety of words and symbols. Adolf Hitler, the IRS, Santa Claus, and the American flag are just sounds and symbols, but they tend to evoke strong emotional responses because of their associations.

When you meet someone who has the same name as another person you like very much, the name may carry such a positive association that you like the new person from the start. The explanation for these feelings is simple—learning by association. We associate one thing with another—a positive or a negative attitude with a name, a particular gesture, a style of dress, or a manner of speaking. When we hear the name or observe the gesture, that single stimulus calls to mind the positive or negative association.

Our lives are profoundly influenced by the associations we learn through classical conditioning. We will now explore the work of Ivan Pavlov, whose research on the conditioned reflex in dogs revealed much of what we know about the principles of classical conditioning (sometimes referred to as respondent or Pavlovian conditioning).

Pavlov and Classical Conditioning

Ivan Pavlov (1849–1936) organized and directed research in physiology at the Institute of Experimental Medicine in St. Petersburg, Russia, from 1891 until his death 45 years later. There he conducted his classic experiments on the physiology of digestion, which won him a Nobel Prize in 1904. He was the first Russian to be so honored. Pavlov's study of the conditioned reflex in dogs brought him fame, and he pursued this research from about 1898 until the end of his career. His book *Conditioned Reflexes* is one of the classic works in psychology.

As with so many other important scientific discoveries, Pavlov's contribution to psychology came about quite by accident. To conduct his study of the salivary response, Pavlov made a small incision in the side of each dog's mouth. Then he attached a tube so that the flow of saliva could be diverted from inside the animal's mouth, through the tube, and into a container, where the saliva was collected and measured.

Pavlov's purpose was to collect the saliva that the dogs would secrete naturally in response to food placed inside the mouth. But he noticed that, in many cases, the dogs would begin to salivate even before the food was presented. Pavlov observed drops of saliva collecting in the container when the dogs heard the footsteps of the laboratory assistants coming to feed them. He observed saliva collecting when the dogs heard their feeding dishes rattling, or saw the attendant who fed them, or at the mere sight of their food. How could an involuntary

classical conditioning: A process through which a response previously made only to a specific stimulus is made to another stimulus that has been paired repeatedly with the original stimulus.

? *What was Pavlov's major contribution to psychology?*

Ivan Pavlov (1849–1936) earned fame by studying the conditioned reflex in dogs.

FIGURE 5.1

The Experimental Apparatus Used in Pavlov's Classical Conditioning Studies

In Pavlov's classical conditioning studies, the dog was restrained in a harness in the cubicle and isolated from all distractions. An experimenter observed the dog through a one-way mirror and, by remote control, presented the dog with food and other conditioning stimuli. A tube carried the saliva from the dog's mouth to a container where it was measured.

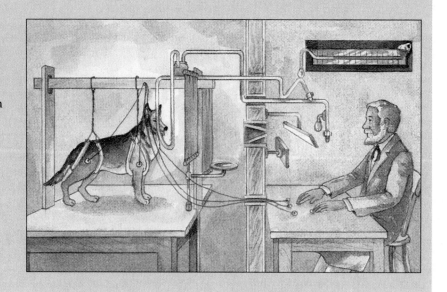

response such as salivation come to be associated with the sights and sounds involved in feeding? Pavlov spent the rest of his life studying this question, and the type of learning that he studied is known today as classical conditioning.

Pavlov's Laboratory: Leaving Nothing to Chance Pavlov was a meticulous researcher; he wanted an experimental environment in which he could carefully control all the factors that could affect the dogs during the experiments. To accomplish this, Pavlov planned and built a laboratory at the Institute of Experimental Medicine in St. Petersburg. Note how advanced the laboratory was, considering that it was built a century ago:

> The windows were covered with extra thick sheets of glass; each room had double steel doors which sealed hermetically when closed; and the steel girders which supported the floors were embedded in sand. A deep moat filled with straw encircled the building. Thus, vibration, noise, temperature extremes, odors, even drafts were eliminated. Nothing could influence the animals except the conditioning stimuli to which they were exposed. (Schultz, 1975, pp. 187–188)

The dogs were isolated inside soundproof cubicles and placed in harnesses to restrain their movements. From an adjoining cubicle, the experimenter observed the dogs through a one-way mirror. Food and other stimuli were presented and the flow of saliva measured by remote control (see Figure 5.1). What did Pavlov and his colleagues learn?

The Elements and Processes in Classical Conditioning

reflex: An involuntary response to a particular stimulus, like the eyeblink response to a puff of air or salivation to food placed in the mouth.

The Reflex: We Can't Help It A **reflex** is an involuntary response to a particular stimulus. Two examples are the eyeblink response to a puff of air and salivation to food placed in the mouth. There are two kinds of reflexes—conditioned and unconditioned. Think of the term *conditioned* as meaning "learned" and the term *unconditioned* as meaning "unlearned." Salivation in response to food is an unconditioned reflex because it is an inborn, automatic, unlearned response to a particular stimulus. Unconditioned reflexes are built into the nervous system.

When Pavlov observed that his dogs would salivate at the sight of food or the sound of rattling dishes, he realized that this salivation reflex was the result of learning. He called these learned involuntary responses **conditioned reflexes**.

The Conditioned and Unconditioned Stimulus and Response Pavlov (1927/1960) continued to investigate the circumstances under which a conditioned reflex is formed. He used tones, bells, buzzers, lights, geometric shapes, electric shocks, and metronomes in his conditioning experiments. In a typical experiment, food powder was placed in the dog's mouth, causing salivation. Dogs do not need to be conditioned to salivate to food, so salivation to food is an unlearned or **unconditioned response (UR)**. Any stimulus, such as food, that without learning will automatically elicit, or bring forth, an unconditioned response is called an **unconditioned stimulus (US)**.

Remember, a reflex is made up of both a stimulus and a response. Following is a list of some common unconditioned reflexes, showing their two components—the unconditioned stimulus and the unconditioned response.

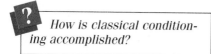

How is classical conditioning accomplished?

conditioned reflex: A learned reflex rather than a naturally occurring one.

unconditioned response (UR): A response that is invariably elicited by the unconditioned stimulus without prior learning.

unconditioned stimulus (US): A stimulus that elicits a specific response without prior learning.

conditioned stimulus (CS): A neutral stimulus that, after repeated pairing with an unconditioned stimulus, becomes associated with it and elicits a conditioned response.

conditioned response (CR): That response that comes to be elicited by a conditioned stimulus as a result of its repeated pairing with an unconditioned stimulus.

extinction: The weakening and often eventual disappearance of a learned response (in classical conditioning, the conditioned response is weakened by repeated presentation of the conditioned stimulus without the unconditioned stimulus).

Unconditioned Reflexes

Unconditioned Stimulus (US)	Unconditioned Response (UR)
food	→ salivation
onion juice	→ tears
heat	→ sweating
loud noise	→ startle
light in eye	→ contraction of pupil
puff of air in eye	→ blink
touching hot stove	→ hand withdrawal

Pavlov demonstrated that dogs could be conditioned to salivate to a variety of stimuli never before associated with food. During the conditioning or acquisition process, the researcher would present a neutral stimulus such as a musical tone shortly before placing food powder in the dog's mouth. The food powder would cause the dog to salivate. After pairing the tone and food many times, usually 20 or more, Pavlov found that the tone alone would elicit salivation (Pavlov, 1927/1960, p. 385). Because dogs do not naturally salivate in response to musical tones, he concluded that this salivation was a learned response. Pavlov called the tone the learned or **conditioned stimulus (CS)**, and salivation to the tone the learned or **conditioned response (CR)**. (See Figure 5.2 on page 168.)

In a modern view of classical conditioning, the conditioned stimulus can be thought of as a signal that the unconditioned stimulus will follow (Schreurs, 1989). In Pavlov's experiment the tone became a signal that food would follow shortly. So, the signal (conditioned stimulus) gives advance warning, and a person or animal is prepared with the proper response (conditioned response) even before the unconditioned stimulus arrives.

Extinction and Spontaneous Recovery: Gone but Not Forgotten After conditioning an animal to salivate to a tone, what would happen if you continued to sound the tone but no longer paired it with food? Pavlov found that salivation to the tone without the food would become weaker and weaker and then finally disappear altogether—a process known as **extinction**.

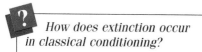

How does extinction occur in classical conditioning?

But extinction does not completely erase the conditioned response. Rather, the animal learns that the tone is no longer a signal that food will soon follow, and the old conditioned response is gradually inhibited or suppressed. Animals are better able to adapt to a changing environment if they have the ability to discard conditioned responses that are no longer useful or needed.

spontaneous recovery: The reappearance of an extinguished response (in a weaker form) when an organism is exposed to the original conditioned stimulus following a rest period.

generalization: In classical conditioning, the tendency to make a conditioned response to a stimulus similar to the original conditioned stimulus; in operant conditioning, the tendency to make the learned response to a stimulus similar to the one for which it was originally reinforced.

A child attacked by a dog can easily develop a long-lasting fear of all dogs, through the process of generalization.

 What is generalization?

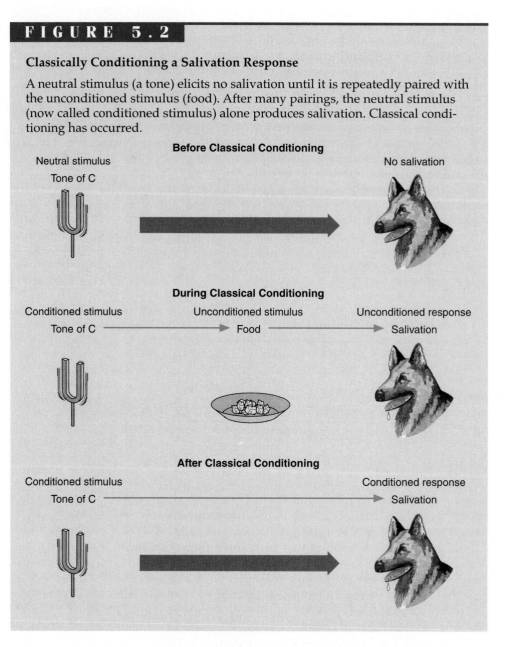

FIGURE 5.2

Classically Conditioning a Salivation Response

A neutral stimulus (a tone) elicits no salivation until it is repeatedly paired with the unconditioned stimulus (food). After many pairings, the neutral stimulus (now called conditioned stimulus) alone produces salivation. Classical conditioning has occurred.

Before Classical Conditioning

Neutral stimulus — Tone of C → No salivation

During Classical Conditioning

Conditioned stimulus — Tone of C → Unconditioned stimulus — Food → Unconditioned response — Salivation

After Classical Conditioning

Conditioned stimulus — Tone of C → Conditioned response — Salivation

How did Pavlov learn that the conditioned response, once extinguished, had not been permanently erased or forgotten? After the response had been extinguished, Pavlov allowed the dog to rest and then brought it back to the laboratory. Pavlov found that the dog would again salivate to the tone. Pavlov called this recurrence **spontaneous recovery**. But the spontaneously recovered response was weaker and shorter in duration than the original conditioned response. Figure 5.3 shows the processes of extinction and spontaneous recovery.

Generalization: Responding to Similarities   Assume that you have conditioned a dog to salivate when it hears the tone middle C on the piano. If in your experiment, you accidentally played the tone D or E, would that note produce salivation? Or would the dog not salivate to this slightly different tone? Pavlov found that a tone similar to the original conditioned stimulus will produce the conditioned response, a phenomenon called **generalization**. If you were as careful a researcher as Pavlov, you would observe that as you move farther away

FIGURE 5.3

Extinction of a Classically Conditioned Response

When a classically conditioned stimulus (the tone) was presented in a series of trials without the unconditioned stimulus (the food), Pavlov's dogs salivated less and less until there was virtually no salivation. But after a 20-minute rest, with one sound of the tone the conditioned response would reappear in a weakened form (producing only a small amount of salivation), a phenomenon Pavlov called spontaneous recovery. (Data from Pavlov, 1927/1960, p. 58.)

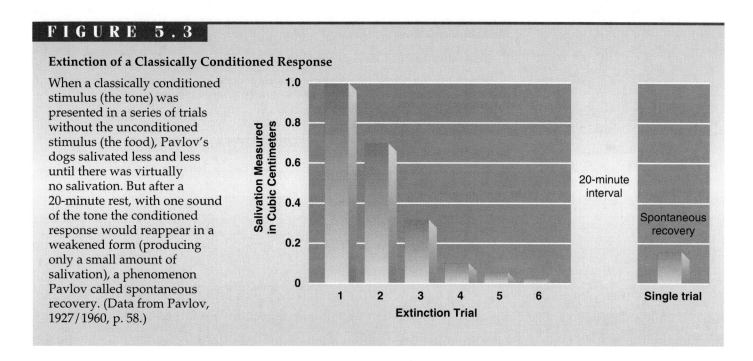

from the original tone, salivation would decrease. Eventually the tone would be so different that the dog would not salivate at all (see Figure 5.4 on page 170).

It is easy to see the value of generalization in everyday life. Suppose that as a child you had been bitten by a large, gray dog. You would not need to see exactly the same dog or one of the same breed or color coming toward you to experience fear. Your original fear would probably generalize to all large dogs of any description. Because of generalization, we do not need to learn a conditioned response to every stimulus that may differ only slightly from the original one. Rather, we learn to approach or avoid a range of stimuli similar to the one that produced the original conditioned response.

Discrimination: Learning That They're Not All Alike   Not only must we be able to generalize, we must also learn to distinguish between stimuli that may be very similar. Using the previous example of a dog being conditioned to a musical tone, we can trace the process of **discrimination**.

> *What is discrimination in classical conditioning?*

Step 1: The dog is conditioned to the tone C.

Step 2: Generalization occurs, and the dog salivates to a range of musical tones above and below tone C. The dog salivates less and less as the tone moves away from C.

Step 3: The original tone C is repeatedly paired with food. Neighboring tones are also sounded, but they are not followed with food. The dog is being conditioned to discriminate. Gradually, the salivation response to the neighboring tones is extinguished, while salivation to the original tone C is strengthened.

Conditioned Stimulus	Conditioned Response
Tone C ⟶	more salivation
Tones A, B, D, E ⟶	progressively less salivation

Step 4: Discrimination is achieved.

Conditioned Stimulus	Conditioned Response
Tone C ⟶	strengthened salivation response
Tones A, B, D, E ⟶	no salivation

discrimination: The learned ability to distinguish between similar stimuli so that the conditioned response occurs only to the original conditioned stimulus but not to similar stimuli.

FIGURE 5.4

Generalization in Classical Conditioning

Because of the phenomenon of generalization, a dog conditioned to salivate to middle C (the CS) on the piano also salivates to similar tones—but less and less so as the tone moves away from middle C.

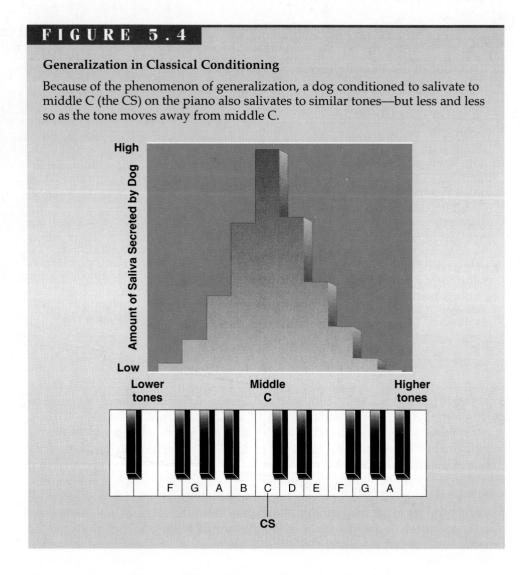

Like generalization, discrimination has survival value. Discriminating between the odors of fresh and spoiled milk will spare you an upset stomach. Discriminating between a rattlesnake and a garter snake could save your life.

Higher-Order Conditioning Classical conditioning would be somewhat limited in its effect on behavior if a conditioned response could be produced in only two ways: (1) by the pairing of a conditioned stimulus with an unconditioned stimulus, or (2) through generalization. Fortunately, classical conditioning can occur in another way—through higher-order conditioning. **Higher-order conditioning** takes place when a neutral stimulus is paired with an existing conditioned stimulus, becomes associated with it, and gains the power to elicit the same conditioned response. Let us assume that after Pavlov conditioned the dogs to salivate to a tone, he presented a light (a neutral stimulus) immediately before the tone a number of times. Then the light would become associated with the tone, and the dogs would learn to give the salivation response to the light alone.

Higher-order conditioning can account for many of our positive and negative feelings toward stimuli that we associate with certain people or situations. A student may develop an intense dislike of an algebra professor who has given him his first and only F in college. From then on he may get angry not only when he sees the professor but when he walks by her classroom or office, when he sees her car in the parking lot, or even when he hears the word *algebra*.

higher-order conditioning: Occurs when a neutral stimulus is paired with an existing conditioned stimulus, becomes associated with it, and gains the power to elicit the same conditioned response.

Memory Check 5.1

1. Classical conditioning was originally researched most extensively by _____.

2. The dog's salivation in response to a musical tone was a(n) (conditioned, unconditioned) response.

3. The gradual weakening and disappearance of a conditioned response—when the conditioned stimulus is presented repeatedly without the unconditioned stimulus—is termed:
   a. generalization.
   b. discrimination.
   c. extinction.
   d. spontaneous recovery.

4. Juanita had an automobile accident on a bridge and now becomes nervous whenever she has to cross any bridge. Which process accounts for this feeling?
   a. generalization
   b. discrimination
   c. extinction
   d. spontaneous recovery

5. Five-year-old Jesse was bitten by his neighbor's collie. He won't go near that dog but seems to have no fear of other dogs, even other collies. Which process accounts for his behavior?
   a. generalization
   b. discrimination
   c. extinction
   d. spontaneous recovery

Answers: 1. Ivan Pavlov 2. conditioned 3. c 4. a 5. b

John Watson, Little Albert, and Peter

Little Albert and the Conditioned Fear Response: Learning to Fear

John Watson believed that in humans all fears except those of loud noises and loss of support are classically conditioned. In 1919 Watson and his assistant, Rosalie Rayner, conducted a now famous study to prove that fear could be classically conditioned. The subject of the study, known as Little Albert, was a healthy and emotionally stable 11-month-old infant. When tested, he showed no fear except of the loud noise Watson made by striking a hammer against a steel bar near Albert's head. In this classic study, Watson tested whether he could condition Albert to fear a white rat by causing him to associate the rat with a loud noise.

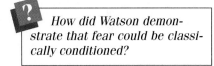

How did Watson demonstrate that fear could be classically conditioned?

Conditioned Stimulus	Unconditioned Stimulus	Unconditioned Response
white rat ⟶	loud noise ⟶	fear reaction

Conditioned Stimulus		Conditioned Response
white rat ⟶		fear reaction

Little Albert demonstrates that his fear of the white rat has generalized to a rabbit.

PIONEERS *John B. Watson (1878–1958)*

John B. Watson was born to a poor family on a farm near Greenville, South Carolina, in 1878. His mother was devoutly religious, while his father's three primary activities were said to be swearing, drinking, and chasing women. His father deserted the family when Watson was 13 years old, leaving him with a keen sense of loss. Watson did not see his father again for more than 30 years.

Although Watson was highly intelligent, he disliked school and was a poor student. He engaged in violent behavior and was arrested by the local authorities on two occasions. At age 15, however, Watson made a drastic change in his habits and his life. Managing to get accepted by Furman University, he worked his way through college and became a conscientious and successful student. Watson completed his Ph.D. in psychology at the University of Chicago in 1903. Five years later he accepted a professorship at Johns Hopkins University, where he pursued a productive career.

Watson advocated a new approach to psychology, restricting its scope to the study of observable, measurable behavior. He wanted nothing to do with concepts like "mind" and "consciousness," which he claimed were neither measurable nor observable. His new school of psychology was appropriately named *behaviorism*, and its principles were set down in his works "Psychology as the Behaviorist Views It" (1913), *Psychology from the Standpoint of a Behaviorist* (1919), and *Behaviorism* (1925). Watson believed that environmental influences primarily determine human behavior.

Regrettably, Watson's academic career in psychology was cut short. When his wife discovered that he was having an affair with his laboratory assistant, Rosalie Rayner, the resulting divorce suit created a national scandal, forcing him to resign his university position in 1920.

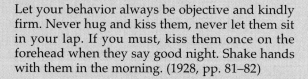

In 1921 Watson married Rosalie Rayner and began a new career in advertising. He was so successful that by 1930 he was making nearly $70,000 a year— a tremendous salary for the time. Watson revolutionized advertising and probably originated testimonial advertising by glamorous people (Cohen, 1979). The image of purity that Watson created for Johnson's Baby Powder more than 65 years ago is still widely known today.

Even without an academic affiliation, Watson continued his research and writing on infants and children. With the publication of his *Psychological Care of the Infant and Child* (1928), he became the leading authority on child rearing. Opposed to permissive parenting, Watson developed a strict, objective, unemotional program for parents. A sample of his advice follows:

> Let your behavior always be objective and kindly firm. Never hug and kiss them, never let them sit in your lap. If you must, kiss them once on the forehead when they say good night. Shake hands with them in the morning. (1928, pp. 81–82)

Watson initiated many important trends in psychology that continue today. He laid the groundwork for present-day behavior therapy techniques for removing fears, and he was a pioneer in the detailed study of infants and children. Through his research and writing, Watson freed psychology from its exclusively academic setting and made it a subject of great interest to the general public. He wrote articles for popular magazines such as *McCall's, Cosmopolitan, Collier's, Harper's,* and *The Nation.* One of the most colorful and influential figures in the field of psychology, John B. Watson died in 1958.

In the laboratory, Rosalie presented Little Albert with a white rat. As Albert reached for the rat, Watson struck a steel bar with a hammer just behind Albert's head. This procedure was repeated, and Albert "jumped violently, fell forward and began to whimper" (Watson & Rayner, 1920, p. 4). A week later, Watson continued the experiment, pairing the rat with the loud noise five more times. Then at the sight of the white rat alone, Albert began to cry.

When Albert returned to the laboratory 5 days later, the fear had generalized to a rabbit and, somewhat less, to a dog, a seal coat, Watson's hair, and a Santa Claus mask. After 30 days Albert made his final visit to the laboratory, and at this time his fears remained, although they were somewhat less intense. Watson concluded that conditioned fears "persist and modify personality throughout life" (Watson & Rayner, 1920, p. 12).

Although Watson had formulated techniques for removing conditioned fears, he apparently knew that Albert would be moving out of the city before they could be tried on him. Some of Watson's ideas for removing fears were excellent and laid the groundwork for therapies used today. One method consisted of conditioning a new association between the feared object and a positive stimulus. In Albert's case, candy or other food could have been given just as the white rat was presented. Another procedure was a modeling technique in which Albert could have observed other children playing happily with the white rat.

We cannot escape the conclusion that Watson showed a disregard for the welfare of Little Albert. Fortunately, the American Psychological Association now has strict ethical standards for the use of human and animal subjects in research experiments. The APA would not sanction such an experiment today.

Removing Peter's Fears: The Triumph of Cookies and Patience Some 3 years passed after Watson's experiment with Little Albert. Then Watson and a colleague, Mary Cover Jones (1924), found 3-year-old Peter, who, like Albert, was afraid of white rats. He was also afraid of rabbits, a fur coat, feathers, cotton, and a fur rug. Peter's fear of the rabbit was his strongest fear, and this became the target of Watson's fear-removal techniques.

Peter was brought into the laboratory, seated in a high chair, and given cookies to eat. A white rabbit in a wire cage was brought into the room but kept far enough away from Peter that it would not upset him. Over the course of 38 therapy sessions, the rabbit was brought closer and closer to Peter, who continued to enjoy his cookies. Occasionally some of Peter's friends were brought in to play with the rabbit at a safe distance from Peter so that he could see firsthand that the rabbit did no harm. Toward the end of Peter's therapy, the rabbit was taken out of the cage and eventually put in Peter's lap. By the final session, Peter had grown fond of the rabbit. What is more, he had lost all fear of the fur coat, cotton, and feathers, and he could tolerate the white rats and the fur rug.

So far we have considered classical conditioning primarily in relation to Pavlov's dogs and Watson's human subjects. How does classical conditioning occur in our everyday lives?

Classical Conditioning in Everyday Life

? What types of responses can be acquired through classical conditioning?

Do certain songs have special meaning because they remind you of a current or past love? Do you find the scent of a particular perfume or after-shave pleasant or unpleasant because it reminds you of a special person? Many of our emotional responses, whether positive or negative, result from classical conditioning (often higher-order conditioning). Neutral cues become associated with particular people, objects, locations, situations, or even words, and develop the power to elicit the same feeling as the original stimulus.

Fears and phobias largely result from classical conditioning. For example, many people who have had painful dental work develop a dental phobia. Not only do they come to fear the dentist's drill, but they develop anxiety in response to a wide range of stimuli associated with it—the dental chair, the waiting room, or even the building where the dentist's office is located.

Businesspeople wine and dine customers, hoping that they and their product or service will elicit the same positive response as the pleasant setting and fine food. Advertisers seek to classically condition us when they show products along with great-looking models or celebrities or in situations where people are enjoying themselves. They reason that if the "neutral" product is associated with

Classical conditioning has proved to be effective in advertising. Here a neutral product (fragrance) has been paired with a sexy image.

people, objects, or situations we particularly like, then in time the product will elicit a similarly positive response. Pavlov found that presenting the tone just before the food was the most efficient way to condition salivation. Television advertisements, too, are most effective when the products are presented *before* the beautiful people or situations are shown (van den Hout & Merckelbach, 1991).

You might want to see just how much the principles of classical conditioning are applied in TV advertising with the following *Try It!*

Some commercials simply give information about a product or place of business. Others attempt to classically condition the viewer to form a positive association. One night while you are watching TV, keep a record of the commercials you see. What proportion rely on classical conditioning? What are the kinds of cues (people, objects, or situations) with which the products are to be associated? Are the products introduced slightly before, during, or after these cues?

Classical Conditioning and the Immune Response   Research indicates that the immune system itself is subject to classical conditioning (Ader, 1985; Ader & Cohen, 1982, 1993). In the mid-1970s Robert Ader was conducting an experiment with rats, conditioning them to avoid saccharin-sweetened water. Immediately after drinking the sweetened water (which rats consider a treat), the rats were injected with a tasteless drug that causes severe nausea. The conditioning worked, and from that time on, the rats would not drink the sweet water, with or without the drug.

Attempting to reverse the conditioned response, Ader had to force-feed the sweetened water to the rats for many days; but later, unexpectedly, many of them died. Ader was puzzled, because the saccharin water was in no way lethal. Checking further into the properties of the tasteless drug (cyclophosphamide), Ader learned that it suppresses the immune system. A few doses of an immune-suppressing drug paired with sweetened water had produced a conditioned response; as a result, the sweet water alone continued to suppress the immune system, causing the rats to die. Ader and Cohen successfully repeated the experiment with strict controls to rule out other explanations. Later other researchers showed that classical conditioning could be used to suppress the immune system in order to prolong the survival of heart tissue transplants in mice (Grochowicz et al., 1991).

How far-reaching is the power of classical conditioning if neutral stimuli alone, such as sweetened water, can produce effects similar to those of powerful drugs? If classical conditioning can suppress the immune system, might it also be used to boost it, as well?

Drug Use and Classical Conditioning   Researchers are discovering that the effects of drug abuse and classical conditioning in combination can have potentially deadly consequences. All drugs produce their characteristic physiological effects. As a person continues to use a drug, the body partially protects itself by making adjustments that decrease the drug's effects. These adjustments enable the body to *tolerate* the drug. For example, among other things, opiates elevate skin temperature and decrease respiratory function, so the body compensates for these effects by lowering skin temperature and increasing the respiratory response. Over time a **drug tolerance** develops—that is, the user becomes progressively less affected by the drug and must take higher and higher doses to maintain the same effects.

If drug tolerance were solely a physiological phenomenon, then it wouldn't make any difference where or under what circumstances the addict took the drug. But it does make a difference. In many cases drug overdoses, some fatal ones, were taken, not where the addict habitually took the drug, but in unfamiliar surroundings—a hotel room, for example. Why should the same amount of a drug produce stronger physiological effects in an unfamiliar than in a familiar environment? The answer is classical conditioning. Here is how the process works.

Classical conditioning helps explain why certain environmental cues or social situations can lead to continued drug use.

Environmental cues associated with the setting where drugs are usually taken—the familiar surroundings, sights, sounds, odors, drug paraphernalia, and the familiar drug use ritual—can act as conditioned stimuli that become associated with the unconditioned stimulus, the drug itself (Dworkin, 1993; O'Brien et al., 1992). These cues signal to the user that the drug is on the way and initiate the compensatory mechanisms. The cues stimulate physiological effects that are primarily the opposite of the physiological effects of the drug and hence serve to protect the body from the drug. But if the user takes the usual dose of the drug in unfamiliar surroundings, the environmental cues that initiate these protective compensatory mechanisms are not present. Consequently, the effects of the drugs are more powerful—sometimes even fatal.

Through classical conditioning, the environmental cues associated with past drug use can also "evoke physiological changes (autonomic responses) that the experienced user interprets as drug-craving or withdrawal symptoms" (O'Brien et al., 1992, p. 400). Such symptoms are powerful forces and may lead the individual to seek out the drug and use it. This explains why drug counselors strongly urge recovering addicts to avoid any cues associated with their past drug use—the people, places, drug paraphernalia, and so on. Relapse is far more common in people who do not avoid the associated environmental cues.

Factors Influencing Classical Conditioning

There are four major factors that affect the strength of a classically conditioned response and the length of time required for conditioning.

1. The first factor is *the number of pairings of the conditioned stimulus and the unconditioned stimulus*. The number of pairings required varies considerably, depending on the individual characteristics of the person or animal being conditioned. But in general, the greater the number of pairings, the stronger the conditioned response.

2. The second factor is the *intensity of the unconditioned stimulus*. If a conditioned stimulus is paired with a very strong unconditioned stimulus, the conditioned response will be stronger and will be acquired more rapidly than if it is paired with a weaker unconditioned stimulus (Gormezano, 1984). Striking the steel bar with the hammer produced stronger and faster conditioning in Little Albert than if Watson had merely clapped his hands behind Albert's head.

3. The third and, according to Robert Rescorla (1967, 1988), the most important factor is *how reliably the conditioned stimulus predicts the unconditioned stimulus*. Rescorla has shown that classical conditioning does not occur automatically just because a neutral stimulus is repeatedly paired with an unconditioned stimulus. The neutral stimulus must also reliably predict the occurrence of the unconditioned stimulus. A smoke alarm that never goes off except in response to a fire will elicit more fear when it sounds than one that occasionally gives false alarms. A tone that is *always* followed by food will elicit more salivation than one that is followed by food only some of the time.

? *What are four factors that influence classical conditioning?*

drug tolerance: A condition in which the user becomes progressively less affected by a drug so that larger and larger doses are necessary to maintain the same effect.

taste aversion: The dislike and/or avoidance of a particular food that has been associated with nausea or discomfort.

4. The fourth critical factor in classical conditioning is *the temporal relationship between the conditioned stimulus and the unconditioned stimulus.* Conditioning takes place fastest if the conditioned stimulus occurs shortly before the unconditioned stimulus. It takes place more slowly or not at all when the two stimuli occur at the same time. Conditioning rarely takes place when the conditioned stimulus follows the unconditioned stimulus (Spetch et al., 1981; Spooner & Kellogg, 1947).

The ideal time between the presentation of the conditioned and the unconditioned stimuli is about ½ second, but this varies according to the type of response being conditioned. Some studies indicate that the age of the subject may also be a variable affecting the optimal time interval (Solomon et al., 1991). In general, if the conditioned stimulus occurs too long before the unconditioned stimulus, an association between the two will not form. One notable exception to this general principle is in the conditioning of taste aversions.

Classically Conditioned Taste Aversions

Experiencing nausea and vomiting after eating a certain food is often enough to condition a long-lasting *taste aversion.* A **taste aversion** is an intense dislike and/or avoidance of a particular food associated with nausea or discomfort. Taste aversions can be classically conditioned when the delay between the conditioned stimulus (food) and the unconditioned stimulus (nausea) is as long as 12 hours. Researchers believe that many taste aversions begin when we are between 2 and 3 years old, so we may not remember how they originated (Rozin & Zellner, 1985). Taste aversions are more likely to develop to "less preferred, less familiar foods," and they can be acquired even when people are convinced that the food did not cause the nausea (Logue, 1985). Once developed, taste aversions often generalize to similar foods (Logue et al., 1981). For example, an aversion to chili might include Sloppy Joes as well.

Research on conditioned taste aversions has led to the solution of practical problems such as controlling predators and helping cancer patients.

Controlling Predators by Conditioning Taste Aversions Plagued by wild coyotes attacking and killing their sheep, ranchers in the western United States tried to solve their problem simply by killing the coyotes. But Gustavson and others (1974) applied research on conditioned taste aversion in animals to spare the lambs and save the coyotes. They set out lamb flesh laced with lithium chloride, a poison that made the coyotes extremely ill but that was not fatal. The plan was so successful that after one or two experiences, the coyotes would get sick even at the sight of a lamb.

In a similar case, rangers at a national park became concerned about camper safety when a large pack of coyotes began scavenging food on the campgrounds. Psychologists again came to the rescue and laced a wide variety of camping foods with lithium chloride. After a few encounters with the tainted foods, the coyotes ended their visits to the campground, and even 2 years later, they had not returned (Cornell & Cornley, 1979).

Using Conditioned Taste Aversions to Help Cancer Patients Knowledge about conditioned taste aversion is useful in solving human problems as well. One unfortunate side effect of chemotherapy treatment in cancer patients is that nausea is often associated with foods eaten in the several hours preceding treatment (Bovbjerg et al., 1992). As a result, patients often develop taste aversions to normal foods in their diet. This can lead to a loss of appetite and weight at a time when good nutrition is particularly important.

Bernstein and others (1982; Bernstein, 1985) report a technique they used to help patients avoid aversions to desirable foods. A group of cancer patients were fed a novel-tasting, maple-flavored ice cream before chemotherapy. The nausea

Chemotherapy treatments can result in conditioned taste aversions, but providing patients with a "scapegoat" target for the taste aversion can help them maintain a proper diet.

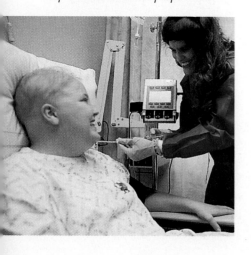

caused by the treatment resulted in a taste aversion to the ice cream. The researchers found that when an unusual or unfamiliar food becomes the "scapegoat," or target for taste aversion, other foods in the patient's diet may be protected, and the patient will continue to eat them regularly. So cancer patients should refrain from eating preferred or nutritious foods prior to chemotherapy. Instead, they should be given an unusual-tasting food shortly before treatment.

Some Limits to Classical Conditioning Pavlov believed that almost any neutral stimulus could serve as a conditioned stimulus. But in their research on taste aversion Garcia and Kelling (1966) found that there are exceptions to this notion. In a well-known study, rats were exposed to a three-way conditioned stimulus—a bright light, a clicking noise, and flavored water. For one group of rats, the unconditioned stimulus was an electric shock to their feet; for the other group, the unconditioned stimulus was either X rays or lithium chloride, either of which produces nausea and vomiting. The rats receiving the electric shock continued to prefer the flavored water over unflavored water, but they would not drink at all in the presence of the bright light or the clicking sound. The rats that were made ill avoided the flavored water at all times, but they would still drink unflavored water when the bright light and the clicking sound were present. The rats in one group associated electric shock only with the light and the sound. The rats in the other group associated nausea only with the flavored water.

Apparently animals are *prepared* to associate only certain stimuli with particular consequences (Seligman, 1970). Associating nausea with food or drink ingested beforehand has definite survival value, for rats as well as for humans. Sound and light do not produce nausea, so making such an association would not be adaptive. But electric shock, on the other hand, is likely to be accompanied by a light or a sound, so associating these stimuli would be adaptive.

Memory Check 5.2

1. In Watson's experiment on Little Albert, the white rat was the (conditioned, unconditioned) stimulus, and Albert's crying when the hammer struck the steel bar was the (conditioned, unconditioned) response.

2. Albert's fear of the white rat transferred to the rabbit, dog, fur coat, and mask. What process did this demonstrate?
   a. generalization   c. extinction
   b. discrimination   d. spontaneous recovery

3. In everyday life, which of the following are *not* acquired through classical conditioning?
   a. positive feelings   c. skills
   b. negative feelings   d. fears and phobias

4. Which of the following does *not* increase the strength of the conditioned response in classical conditioning?
   a. more pairings of the conditioned and the unconditioned stimuli
   b. presenting the conditioned stimulus a considerable time before the unconditioned stimulus

   c. increasing the intensity of the unconditioned stimulus
   d. always following the conditioned stimulus with the unconditioned stimulus

5. Which element in classical conditioning is the signal?
   a. unconditioned response
   b. unconditioned stimulus
   c. conditioned response
   d. conditioned stimulus

6. For classical conditioning to occur, the unconditioned stimulus should occur immediately after the conditioned stimulus and the two must be paired repeatedly. An exception to this statement is the conditioned
   a. salivation response.
   b. immune response.
   c. taste aversion.
   d. drug tolerance.

Answers: 1. conditioned, unconditioned 2. a 3. c 4. b 5. d 6. c

Operant Conditioning

Thorndike and the Law of Effect

What is Thorndike's major contribution to psychology?

Before Pavlov began his experiments with dogs, American psychologist Edward Thorndike (1874–1949) was designing and conducting experiments to study animal intelligence. Profoundly influenced by Darwin's theory of evolution, Thorndike attempted to answer questions about the nature of learning across animal species. He investigated **trial-and-error learning** in cats, dogs, chicks, and monkeys. In his best-known experiments, Thorndike would place a hungry cat in a puzzle box designed so that the animal had to manipulate a simple mechanism— pressing a pedal or pulling down a loop—to escape and claim a food reward just outside the box (see Figure 5.5).

The cat would first try to squeeze through the slats in the box; when these attempts failed, it would scratch, bite, and claw inside the box. In time, the cat would accidentally trip the mechanism, which would open the door and release it. Each time, after winning freedom and claiming the food reward, the cat was returned to the box. After many trials, through trial and error the cat learned to open the door almost immediately after being placed in the box.

From the puzzle-box experiments, Thorndike formulated several laws of learning, the most important being the law of effect. The **law of effect** states that the consequence, or effect, of a response will determine whether the tendency to respond in the same way in the future will be strengthened or weakened. Responses closely followed by satisfying consequences are more likely to be repeated (Thorndike, 1911/1970). Thorndike's law of effect formed the conceptual starting point for B. F. Skinner's work in operant conditioning.

Skinner and Operant Conditioning

How are responses acquired through operant conditioning?

Recall that in classical conditioning, the organism does not learn a new response. Rather, it learns to make an old or existing response to a new stimulus. Classically conditioned responses are involuntary or reflexive, and in most cases the person or animal cannot help but respond in expected ways.

Let's now examine a method for conditioning *voluntary* responses known as **operant conditioning**. Operant conditioning does not begin, as did classical con-

trial-and-error learning: Learning that occurs when a response is associated with a successful solution to a problem after a number of unsuccessful responses.

law of effect: Thorndike's law of learning, which states that connections between a stimulus and a response will be strengthened if followed by a satisfying consequence and weakened if followed by discomfort.

operant conditioning: A type of learning in which the consequences of behavior tend to increase or decrease that behavior in the future.

FIGURE 5.5

Thorndike's Puzzle Box

Cats placed in the puzzle box learned, through trial and error, to push the pedal and escape.

PIONEERS *Burrhus Frederic Skinner (1904–1990)*

Burrhus Frederic Skinner was born in 1904 in Susquehanna, Pennsylvania. He had an early interest in constructing mechanical devices and in collecting an assortment of animals, which he kept as pets. He was also fascinated with the complex tricks he saw trained pigeons perform at country fairs. These early interests were destined to play a major role in his later scientific achievements (Bjork, 1993).

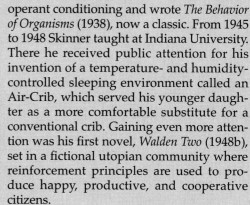

After graduating from college, Skinner attempted to become a writer, encouraged, in part, by a favorable comment on his work by the famous American poet Robert Frost. But after a laborious year trying his hand at writing in his parents' attic, Skinner concluded that he had nothing to say.

Skinner began to spend time reading the books of Pavlov and Watson and became so intrigued that he entered graduate school at Harvard in 1928. He completed his Ph.D. in psychology in 1931. Skinner described his years at Harvard this way:

> I would rise at six, study until breakfast, go to classes, laboratories, and libraries with no more than 15 minutes unscheduled during the day, study until exactly nine o'clock at night and go to bed. I saw no movies or plays, seldom went to concerts, had scarcely any dates and read nothing but psychology and physiology. (Skinner, 1967, p. 398)

It was precisely this unusual degree of self-discipline that enabled Skinner to become a tireless researcher and prolific writer. At his death he had 19 books to his credit and hundreds of journal articles (Holland, 1992; Lattal, 1992).

In 1936 Skinner joined the faculty at the University of Minnesota, where he conducted much of his research in operant conditioning and wrote *The Behavior of Organisms* (1938), now a classic. From 1945 to 1948 Skinner taught at Indiana University. There he received public attention for his invention of a temperature- and humidity-controlled sleeping environment called an Air-Crib, which served his younger daughter as a more comfortable substitute for a conventional crib. Gaining even more attention was his first novel, *Walden Two* (1948b), set in a fictional utopian community where reinforcement principles are used to produce happy, productive, and cooperative citizens.

In 1948 Skinner returned to Harvard and continued his research and writing. There he wrote *Science and Human Behavior* (1953), which provides a description of the process of operant conditioning.

In a later and highly controversial book, *Beyond Freedom and Dignity* (1971), Skinner was critical of society's preoccupation with the notion of freedom. He maintained that free will is a myth and that our behavior is always shaped and controlled by others—parents, teachers, peers, advertising, television. He argued that rather than leaving the control of human behavior to chance, societies should systematically shape the behavior of their members for the larger good.

Skinner seemed to have a talent for provoking controversy. Little controversy exists, however, about the significance of his research in operant conditioning. Skinner's long career ended when he died in 1990 at the age of 86, but his strong influence in shaping the direction of modern psychology will be felt for years to come.

ditioning, with the presentation of a stimulus to elicit a response. Rather, the response comes first, and then the consequence that follows tends to modify this response in the future. In operant conditioning, the consequences of behavior are manipulated to increase or decrease the frequency of a response or to shape an entirely new response. Behavior that is reinforced—followed by rewarding consequences—tends to be repeated. A **reinforcer** is anything that strengthens or increases the probability of the response it follows. Behavior that is ignored or punished is less likely to be repeated.

Operant conditioning permits the learning of a broad range of new responses. A simple response can be operantly conditioned if we merely wait for it to appear and then reinforce it. But this can be time-consuming. The process can be speeded up with a technique called shaping. Shaping also can be used to condition responses that would never occur naturally.

reinforcer: Anything that strengthens a response or increases the probability that it will occur.

How is shaping used to condition a response?

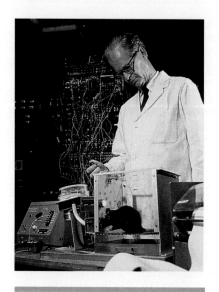

B. F. Skinner shapes a rat's bar-pressing behavior in a Skinner box.

Shaping Behavior: Just a Little Bit at a Time **Shaping** is a technique employed by B. F. Skinner that is particularly useful in conditioning complex behaviors. With shaping, rather than waiting for the desired response to occur and then reinforcing it, any movement in the direction of the desired response is reinforced, gradually guiding the responses closer and closer to the ultimate goal.

Skinner designed a soundproof operant-conditioning apparatus, commonly called a **Skinner box**, in which he conducted his experiments. One type of box is equipped with a lever, or bar, that a rat presses to gain a reward of food pellets or water from a dispenser. A record of the animal's bar-pressing is registered on a device called a cumulative recorder, also invented by Skinner.

Rats in a Skinner box are conditioned through shaping to press a bar for rewards. A rat may be rewarded first for simply turning toward the bar. The next reward comes only when the rat moves closer to the bar. Each step closer to the bar is rewarded. Next the rat must touch the bar to receive a reward; finally, the rat is rewarded only when it presses the bar.

Shaping—rewarding gradual **successive approximations** toward the terminal or desired response—has been used effectively to condition complex behaviors in people as well as other animals. Parents may use shaping to help their children develop good table manners, praising them each time they show an improvement. Teachers often use shaping with disruptive children, reinforcing them at first for very short periods of good behavior and then gradually expecting them to work productively for longer and longer periods. Through shaping, circus animals have learned to perform a wide range of amazing feats, and pigeons have learned to bowl and play Ping-Pong. You might even want to try shaping your own behavior using the *Try It!*

Use conditioning to modify your own behavior.

1. *Identify the target behavior.* It must be both observable and measurable. You might choose, for example, to increase the amount of time you spend studying.

2. *Gather and record baseline data.* Keep a daily record of how much time you spend on the target behavior for about a week. Also note where the behavior takes place and what cues (or temptations) in the environment precede any slacking off from the target behavior.

3. *Plan your behavior modification program.* Formulate a plan and set goals to either decrease or increase the target behavior.

4. *Choose your reinforcers.* Any activity you enjoy more can be used to reinforce any activity you enjoy less. For example, you could reward yourself with a movie after a specified period of studying.

5. *Set the reinforcement conditions and begin recording and reinforcing your progress.* Be careful not to set your reinforcement goals so high that it becomes nearly impossible to earn a reward. Keep in mind Skinner's concept of shaping—rewarding small steps to reach a desired outcome. Be perfectly honest with yourself and claim a reward *only* when the goals are met. Chart your progress as you work toward gaining more and more control over the target behavior.

Superstitious Behavior: Mistaking a Coincidence for a Cause
Sometimes a reward follows a response but the two are not related. Superstitious behavior occurs if an individual falsely believes that a connection exists between

an act and its consequences. A gambler in Las Vegas blows on the dice just before he rolls them and wins $1,000. On the next roll, he follows the same ritual and wins again. Although this rewarding event follows the ritual of blowing on the dice, the connection between the two is accidental.

Superstitious behavior is not confined to humans. Skinner (1948a) developed superstitious behavior in pigeons by giving food rewards every 15 seconds regardless of the pigeon's behavior. Whatever response the pigeons happened to be making was reinforced, and before long each pigeon developed its own ritual, such as turning counterclockwise in the cage several times or making pendulum movements with its head.

Extinction: Withholding Reinforcers We have seen that responses followed by reinforcers tend to be repeated and that responses no longer followed by reinforcers will occur less and less frequently and eventually die out. In operant conditioning, **extinction** occurs when reinforcers are withheld. A rat in a Skinner box will eventually stop pressing a bar when it is no longer rewarded with food pellets.

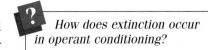
How does extinction occur in operant conditioning?

In humans and other animals, extinction can lead to frustration or even rage. Consider a child having a temper tantrum. If whining and loud demands do not bring the reinforcer, the child may progress to kicking and screaming. If a vending machine takes your coins but fails to deliver candy or soda, you might shake the machine or even kick it before giving up. It is what we expect and don't get that makes us angry.

The process of spontaneous recovery, which we discussed in relation to classical conditioning, also occurs in operant conditioning. A rat whose bar pressing has been extinguished may again press the bar a few times when returned to the Skinner box after a period of rest.

Generalization and Discrimination Skinner conducted many of his experiments with pigeons placed in a Skinner box specially designed for them. The box contained small illuminated disks that the pigeons could peck to receive bits of grain from a food tray. Skinner found that generalization occurs in operant conditioning. A pigeon reinforced for pecking at a yellow disk is likely to peck at another disk similar in color. The less similar a disk is to the original color, the lower the rate of pecking will be.

Discrimination in operant conditioning involves learning to distinguish between a stimulus that has been reinforced and other stimuli that may be very similar. We learn discrimination when our response to the original stimulus is reinforced but responses to similar stimuli are not reinforced. For example, to encourage discrimination, a researcher would reinforce the pigeon for pecking at the yellow disk but not for pecking at the orange or red disk.

There are certain cues that have come to be associated with reinforcement or punishment. For example, children are more likely to ask their parents for a treat when the parents are smiling than when they are frowning. The stimulus that signals whether a certain response or behavior is likely to be rewarded, ignored, or punished is called a **discriminative stimulus**. If a pigeon's peck at a lighted disk results in a reward but a peck at an unlighted disk does not, the pigeon will soon be pecking at the lighted disk but not at the unlighted one. The presence or absence of the discriminative stimulus, in this case the lighted disk, will control whether the pecking takes place.

Why do children sometimes misbehave with a grandparent but not with a parent, or make one teacher's life miserable yet be model students for another? The children may have learned that in the presence of some people, the discriminative stimuli, their misbehavior will almost certainly lead to punishment, but that in the presence of certain other people it may even be rewarded.

shaping: Gradually molding a desired behavior by reinforcing responses that become progressively closer to it; reinforcing successive approximations of the desired response.

Skinner box: A soundproof operant conditioning chamber with a device for delivering food and either a bar for rats to press or a disk for pigeons to peck.

successive approximations: A series of gradual training steps, with each step becoming more like the final desired response.

extinction: The weakening and often eventual disappearance of a learned response (in operant conditioning, the conditioned response is weakened by withholding reinforcement).

discriminative stimulus: A stimulus that signals whether a certain response or behavior is likely to be followed by reward or punishment.

Memory Check 5.3

1. Who researched trial-and-error learning using cats in puzzle boxes and formulated the law of effect?
   a. Watson
   b. Thorndike
   c. Skinner
   d. Pavlov

2. Operant conditioning has been researched most extensively by:
   a. Watson
   b. Thorndike
   c. Skinner
   d. Pavlov

3. Operant conditioning can be used effectively for all of the following *except*:
   a. learning new responses.
   b. learning to make an existing response to a new stimulus.
   c. increasing the frequency of an existing response.
   d. decreasing the frequency of an existing response.

4. Even though the B that Billy wrote looked more like a D, his teacher, Mrs. Chen, praised him because it was better than his previous attempts. Mrs. Chen is using a procedure called _____.

5. Which of the following processes occurs in operant conditioning when reinforcers are withheld?
   a. generalization
   b. discrimination
   c. spontaneous recovery
   d. extinction

Answers: 1. b 2. c 3. b 4. shaping 5. d

Reinforcement: What's the Payoff?

What is the goal of both positive reinforcement and negative reinforcement, and how is the goal accomplished with each?

Positive and Negative Reinforcement: Adding the Good, Taking Away the Bad   **Reinforcement** is a key concept in operant conditioning and may be defined as any event that strengthens or increases the probability of the response that it follows. There are two types of reinforcement, positive and negative. **Positive reinforcement**, roughly the same thing as a reward, refers to any *positive* consequence that, if applied after a response, increases the probability of that response. We know that many people will work hard for a raise or a promotion, salespeople will increase their efforts to get awards and bonuses, students will study to get good grades, and children will throw temper tantrums to get candy or ice cream. In these examples, the raises, promotions, awards, bonuses, good grades, candy, and ice cream are positive reinforcers.

Just as people engage in behaviors in order to get positive reinforcers, they also engage in behaviors to avoid or escape unpleasant conditions. Terminating an unpleasant stimulus in order to strengthen or increase the probability of a response is called **negative reinforcement**. If people find that a response successfully ends an aversive condition, they are likely to repeat it. People will turn on their air conditioner to terminate the heat, and they will get out of bed to turn off a faucet to avoid listening to the annoying "drip, drip, drip." Heroin addicts will do almost anything to obtain heroin to terminate their painful withdrawal symptoms. In these instances, negative reinforcement involves putting an end to the heat, the dripping faucet, and the withdrawal symptoms.

Responses that end discomfort and those that are followed by rewards are likely to be strengthened or repeated because *both* lead to a more desirable outcome. Some behaviors are influenced by a combination of positive and negative reinforcement. If you eat a plateful of rather disgusting leftovers to relieve intense hunger, then you are eating solely to remove hunger, a negative reinforcer. But if your hunger is relieved by a gourmet dinner at a fine restaurant, both positive and negative reinforcement will have played a role. Your hunger has been removed, and the delicious dinner has been a reward in itself.

How does positive and negative reinforcement affect your behavior? Complete the *Try It!* to find out.

reinforcement: An event that follows a response and increases the strength of the response and/or the likelihood that it will be repeated.

positive reinforcement: A reward or pleasant consequence that follows a response and increases the probability that the response will be repeated.

negative reinforcement: The termination of an unpleasant stimulus after a response in order to increase the probability that the response will be repeated.

Make a chart like the one shown below, and list all of your behaviors during the course of a day that were influenced by either positive or negative reinforcement. Also list the behaviors that were influenced by a combination of the two. During that day, were more behaviors positively or negatively reinforced?

Behavior	Positive Reinforcement	Negative Reinforcement	Combination
Ate breakfast Attended class			
Totals:			

Primary and Secondary Reinforcers: The Unlearned and the Learned

A **primary reinforcer** is one that fulfills a basic physical need for survival and does not depend on learning. Food, water, sleep, and termination of pain are examples of primary reinforcers. And sex is a powerful reinforcer that fulfills a basic physical need for survival of the species. Fortunately, learning does not depend solely on primary reinforcers. If that were the case, we would need to be hungry, thirsty, or sex starved before we would respond at all. Much observed behavior in humans is in response to secondary reinforcers. A **secondary reinforcer** is acquired or learned by association with other reinforcers. Some secondary reinforcers (money, for example) can be exchanged at a later time for other reinforcers. Praise, good grades, awards, applause, and signals of approval such as a smile or a kind word are all examples of secondary reinforcers.

Attention is a secondary reinforcer of great general worth. In order to obtain the reinforcers we seek from other people, we must first get their attention. Children vie for the attention of parents because they represent the main source of a child's reinforcers. But often parents reward children with attention for misbehavior and ignore their good behavior. When this happens, misbehavior is strengthened, and good behavior may be extinguished for lack of reinforcement.

Schedules of Reinforcement: When Will I Get My Reinforcers?

In conditioning rats, the experimenter reinforced each bar-pressing response with a food pellet. Reinforcing every correct response, known as **continuous reinforcement**, is the most efficient way to condition a new response. However, after a response has been conditioned, partial or intermittent reinforcement is more effective in maintaining or increasing the rate of response. **Partial reinforcement** is operating when some but not all responses are reinforced. In real life, reinforcement is almost never continuous. Partial reinforcement is the rule.

Partial reinforcement may be administered according to different **schedules of reinforcement**. Different schedules produce distinct rates and patterns of responses, as well as varying degrees of resistance to extinction when reinforcement is discontinued. The two basic types are the ratio and interval schedules. Ratio schedules require that a certain *number of responses* be made before one of the responses is reinforced. With interval schedules, a given *amount of time* must pass before a reinforcer is administered. These schedules are further subdivided into fixed and variable categories, as the following descriptions indicate.

---

primary reinforcer: A reinforcer that fulfills a basic physical need for survival and does not depend on learning.

secondary reinforcer: A neutral stimulus that becomes reinforcing after repeated pairings with other reinforcers.

continuous reinforcement: Reinforcement that is administered after every desired or correct response; the most effective method of conditioning a new response.

partial reinforcement: A pattern of reinforcement in which some portion, rather than 100 percent, of the correct responses are reinforced.

schedule of reinforcement: A systematic program for administering reinforcements that has a predictable effect on behavior.

? *What are the four major schedules of reinforcement, and which schedule yields the highest response rate and the greatest resistance to extinction?*

Seamstresses like those shown here are paid according to a fixed-ratio schedule. Since their earnings depend on the number of flags they complete, they are motivated to work quickly. Gamblers receive payoffs according to a variable-ratio schedule. They cannot predict when they will be reinforced, so they are highly motivated to keep playing.

fixed-ratio schedule: A schedule in which a reinforcer is given after a fixed number of correct responses.

variable-ratio schedule: A schedule in which a reinforcer is given after a varying number of nonreinforced responses based on an average ratio.

fixed-interval schedule: A schedule in which a reinforcer is given following the first correct response after a fixed period of time has elapsed.

The Fixed-Ratio Schedule On a **fixed-ratio schedule**, a reinforcer is given after a fixed number of nonreinforced responses. If the fixed ratio is set at 30 responses (FR-30), a reinforcer is given after 30 correct responses. Examples are payments to factory workers according to the number of units produced and to migrant farm workers for each bushel of fruit they pick.

The fixed-ratio schedule is a very effective way to maintain a high response rate, because the number of reinforcers received depends directly on the response rate. The faster people respond, the more reinforcers they earn. When large ratios are used, people and animals tend to pause after each reinforcement but then return to the characteristic high rate of responding.

The Variable-Ratio Schedule The pauses after reinforcement on a high fixed-ratio schedule do not occur with the variable-ratio schedule. On a **variable-ratio schedule**, a reinforcer is given after a varying number of nonreinforced responses based on an average ratio. With a variable ratio of 30 responses (VR-30), you might be reinforced one time after 10 responses, another after 50, another after 30 responses, and so on. You cannot predict exactly which responses will be reinforced, but in this example, reinforcement would average 1 in 30.

Variable-ratio schedules result in higher, more stable rates of responding than fixed-ratio schedules. Skinner (1953) reports that on this schedule "a pigeon may respond as rapidly as five times per second and maintain this rate for many hours" (p. 104). According to Skinner (1988), the variable-ratio schedule is useful because "it maintains behavior against extinction when reinforcers occur only infrequently. The behavior of the dedicated artist, writer, businessman, or scientist is sustained by an occasional, unpredictable reinforcement" (p. 174).

An insurance salesperson, working on a variable-ratio schedule, may sell policies to 2 clients in a row but have to contact 20 more prospects before making another sale. The best example of the seemingly addictive power of the variable-ratio schedule is found in the gambling casino. Slot machines, roulette wheels, and most other games of chance pay on a variable-ratio schedule. In general, it produces the highest response rate and the most resistance to extinction.

The Fixed-Interval Schedule On a **fixed-interval schedule**, a specific time interval must pass before a response is reinforced. For example, on a 60-second fixed-interval schedule (FI-60), a reinforcer is given for the first correct response that occurs 60 seconds after the last reinforced response. People working on salary are reinforced on the fixed-interval schedule.

Unlike ratio schedules, reinforcement on interval schedules does not depend on the number of responses made, only on the one correct response made after the time interval has passed. Characteristic of the fixed-interval schedule is a pause or a sharp decline in responding immediately after each reinforcement and a rapid acceleration in responding just before the next reinforcer is due.

As an example of this schedule, think of a psychology test as a reinforcer and studying for the test as the desired response. Suppose you have four tests scheduled during the semester. Your study responses will probably drop to zero immediately after the first test, gradually accelerate and perhaps reach a frenzied peak just before the next scheduled exam, then immediately drop to zero again, and so on. As you may have guessed, the fixed-interval schedule produces the lowest response rate.

The Variable-Interval Schedule Variable-interval schedules eliminate the pause after reinforcement typical of the fixed-interval schedule. On a **variable-interval schedule**, a reinforcer is given after the first correct response following a varying time of nonreinforced responses based on an average time. Rather than reinforcing a response every 60 seconds, for example, a reinforcer might be given after a 30-second interval with others following after 90-, 45-, and 75-second intervals. But the average time elapsing between reinforcers would be 60 seconds (VI-60). This schedule maintains remarkably stable and uniform rates of responding, but the response rate is typically lower than that of the ratio schedules, because reinforcement is not tied directly to the *number* of responses made.

Again, with another flight into fantasy, we could think of the psychology exam as the reinforcer and studying for the exam as the response. Rather than a regularly scheduled exam, however, we need pop quizzes to illustrate the variable-interval schedule. Because you cannot predict when a pop quiz will be given, your study responses will be more uniform and stable. Also, the response rate tends to be higher with shorter intervals and lower with longer ones. If your professor gives a pop quiz once a week on the average, your study response will be higher than if you average only one quiz per month. Review and Reflect Table 5.1 summarizes the characteristics of the four schedules of reinforcement.

The Effect of Continuous and Partial Reinforcement on Extinction

One way to understand extinction in operant conditioning is to consider how consistently a response is followed by reinforcement. On a continuous schedule, a reinforcer is expected without fail after each correct response. When a reinforcer is withheld, it is noticed immediately. But on a partial-reinforcement schedule, a reinforcer is not expected after every response. Thus, no immediate difference is apparent between the partial-reinforcement schedule and the onset of extinction.

When you put money in a vending machine and pull the lever but no candy or soda appears, you know immediately that something is wrong with the machine. But if you are playing a broken slot machine, you could have many nonreinforced responses before suspecting that the machine is malfunctioning.

Partial reinforcement results in a greater resistance to extinction than does continuous reinforcement. This result is known as the **partial-reinforcement effect**. There is an inverse relationship between the percentage of responses that have been reinforced and resistance to extinction. The lower the percentage of responses that are reinforced, the longer extinction will take when reinforcement is withheld. The strongest resistance to extinction that we can find occurred in one experiment in which pigeons were conditioned to peck at a disk. Holland and Skinner (1961) report that "after the response had been maintained on a fixed

variable-interval schedule: A schedule in which a reinforcer is given after the first correct response following a varying time of nonreinforcement based on an average time.

partial-reinforcement effect: The greater resistance to extinction that occurs when a portion, rather than all, of the correct responses are reinforced.

? *What is the partial-reinforcement effect?*

Review and Reflect 5.1 *Reinforcement Schedules Compared*

Schedule of Reinforcement	Response Rate	Pattern of Responses	Resistance to Extinction
Fixed ratio	Very high	Steady response with low ratio. Brief pause after each reinforcement with very high ratio.	The higher the ratio, the more resistance to extinction.
Variable ratio	Highest response rate	Constant response pattern, no pauses.	Most resistance to extinction.
Fixed interval	Lowest response rate	Long pause after reinforcement, followed by gradual acceleration.	The longer the interval, the more resistance to extinction.
Variable interval	Moderate	Stable, uniform response.	More resistance to extinction than fixed-interval schedule with same average.

punishment: The removal of a pleasant stimulus or the application of an unpleasant stimulus, which tends to suppress a response.

ratio of 900 and reinforcement was then discontinued, the pigeon emitted 73,000 responses during the first 4½ hours of extinction" (p. 124).

Parents often wonder why their children continue to nag in order to get what they want, even though the parents *usually* do not give in to the nagging. Unwittingly parents are reinforcing nagging on a variable-ratio schedule, which results in the most persistent behavior. This is why experts always caution parents to be consistent. If parents *never* reward nagging, the behavior will extinguish; if they give in occasionally, it will persist and be extremely hard to extinguish.

Memory Check 5.4

1. Negative reinforcement (increases, decreases) the likelihood of a response.

2. Many people take aspirin to terminate a painful headache. Taking aspirin is a behavior that is likely to continue because of the effect of (positive, negative) reinforcement.

3. (Partial, Continuous) reinforcement is most effective in conditioning a new response; afterward, (partial, continuous) reinforcement is best for maintaining the response.

4. Jennifer and Ashley are both employed raking leaves. Jennifer is paid $1 for each bag of leaves she rakes; Ashley is paid $4 per hour. Jennifer is paid according to the _____ schedule; Ashley is paid according to the _____ schedule.

   a. fixed-interval; fixed-ratio
   b. variable-ratio; fixed-interval
   c. variable-ratio; variable-interval
   d. fixed-ratio; fixed-interval

5. Which schedule of reinforcement yields the highest response rate and the greatest resistance to extinction?
   a. variable-ratio schedule
   b. fixed-ratio schedule
   c. variable-interval schedule
   d. fixed-interval schedule

6. Danielle's parents have noticed that she has been making her bed every day, and they would like this to continue. Because they understand the partial-reinforcement effect, they will want to reward her *every* time she makes the bed. (true/false)

Answers: 1. increases 2. negative 3. Continuous, partial 4. d 5. a 6. false

---

How does punishment differ from negative reinforcement?

Punishment: That Hurts!

In many ways **punishment** is the opposite of reinforcement. Punishment tends to lower the probability of a response by following it with an aversive or unpleasant consequence. And punishment can be accomplished by either adding an unpleasant stimulus or removing a pleasant stimulus. The added unpleasant stimulus might take the form of criticism, a scolding, a disapproving look, a fine, or a prison sentence. The removal of a pleasant stimulus might consist of withholding affection and attention, suspending a driver's license, or taking away a privilege such as watching television.

Students often confuse negative reinforcement and punishment. Unlike punishment, negative reinforcement increases the probability of a desired response by removing an unpleasant stimulus when the correct response is made (see the Review and Reflect Table 5.2 on page 188). "Grounding" can be used in either punishment or negative reinforcement. If teenagers fail to clean their room after many requests to do so, their parents could ground them for the weekend—a punishment. An alternative approach would be to use negative reinforcement—to tell them they are grounded *until* the room is clean. Which approach would be more effective?

What are some disadvantages of punishment?

The Disadvantages of Punishment: Its Downside Skinner always argued that punishment does not extinguish an undesirable behavior; rather, it suppresses that behavior when the punishing agent is present. But the behavior is apt to continue when the threat of punishment is removed and in settings where punishment is unlikely. There is ample empirical support for Skinner's argument. If punishment (imprisonment, fines, and so on) did extinguish criminal behavior, there would be fewer repeat offenders in our criminal justice system.

Another problem with punishment is that it indicates which behaviors are unacceptable but does not help people develop more appropriate behaviors. If punishment is used, it should be administered in conjunction with reinforcement or rewards for appropriate behavior.

The use of punishment has a number of other potential disadvantages. The person who is severely punished often becomes fearful and feels angry and hostile toward the punisher. These reactions may be accompanied by a desire to avoid or escape from the punisher and the punishing situation, or to find a way to retaliate. Many runaway teenagers leave home to escape physical abuse.

Punishment frequently leads to aggression. Those who administer physical punishment may become models of aggressive behavior—people who demonstrate aggression as a way of solving problems and discharging anger. Children of abusive, punishing parents are at greater risk than other children of becoming aggressive and abusive themselves (Widom, 1989b).

Alternatives to Punishment: There's More Than One Way to Change Behavior   Because of the many disadvantages of punishment, parents and teachers should explore alternative ways of handling misbehavior. Often the use of extinction and positive and negative reinforcement lead to the desired outcomes without the negative side effects of punishment.

Many psychologists believe that *removing the rewarding consequences of undesirable behavior* is the best way to extinguish a problem behavior. According to this view, parents should extinguish a child's temper tantrums not by punishment but by *never* giving in to the child's demands during a tantrum. A parent might best extinguish problem behavior performed merely to get attention by ignoring it and giving attention to more appropriate behavior. Sometimes, simply giving a rational explanation for why certain behaviors are not appropriate is all that is required to extinguish the behavior.

Using positive reinforcement such as praise will make good behavior more rewarding for children. This approach brings with it the attention that children want and need—attention that often only comes when they misbehave. And as we saw in our earlier example of grounding, negative reinforcement can often be more effective than punishment in bringing about desired outcomes.

It is probably unrealistic to believe that punishment can be dispensed with entirely. If a young child runs into the street, puts a finger near an electrical outlet, or reaches for a hot pan on the stove, a swift punishment may save the child from a potentially disastrous situation. Review and Reflect Table 5.2 (on page 188) summarizes the differences between reinforcement and punishment.

Making Punishment More Effective: Some Suggestions   Research has revealed several factors that influence the effectiveness of punishment: its *timing*, its *intensity*, and the *consistency* of its application (Parke, 1977). Punishment is most effective when it is applied during the misbehavior or as soon afterward as possible. Interrupting the problem behavior is most effective because it abruptly halts its rewarding aspects. The longer the delay between the response and the punishment, the less effective it is in suppressing the response (Camp et al., 1967). If punishment must be delayed, the punisher should explain to the perpetrator why the behavior was inappropriate.

What three factors increase the effectiveness of punishment?

Animal studies reveal that the more intense the punishment, the greater the suppression of the undesirable behavior (Church, 1963). But that does not mean that the severity of punishment should be the same for major and minor misbehaviors alike. The intensity of the punishment should match the seriousness of

Review and Reflect 5.2 *The Effects of Reinforcement and Punishment*

Reinforcement (Serves to increase or strengthen a particular behavior)	Punishment (Serves to decrease or suppress a particular behavior)
Adding a Positive **Positive Reinforcement** Presenting food, money, praise, attention, or other rewards.	**Adding a Negative** Delivering a pain-producing or otherwise aversive stimulus such as a spanking or an electric shock.
Subtracting a Negative **Negative Reinforcement** Removing or terminating some pain-producing or otherwise aversive stimulus such as an electric shock.	**Subtracting a Positive** Removing some pleasant stimulus or taking away privileges such as TV watching, use of automobile.

the misdeed. Ideally punishment should be the minimum necessary to suppress the problem behavior. Unnecessarily severe punishment is likely to produce the negative side effects mentioned earlier. But if the initial punishment is too mild, it will have no effect. What if the intensity of the punishment is gradually increased? The perpetrator will gradually adapt to it, and the unwanted behavior will persist (Azrin & Holz, 1966). At a minimum, if a behavior is to be suppressed, the punishment must be more punishing than the misbehavior is rewarding. In human terms, a $200 ticket is more likely to suppress the urge to speed than a $2 ticket.

To be effective, punishment must be applied consistently. A parent cannot ignore misbehavior one day and punish the same act the next. And both parents should react to the same misbehavior in the same way. An undesired response will be suppressed more effectively when the probability of punishment is high. Few people speed if they see a police car in the rear-view mirror.

Finally, punishment should not be administered in anger. The purpose of punishment must always be clearly understood. It is not to vent anger but rather to modify behavior. Punishment meted out in anger is likely to be more intense than necessary to bring about the desired result.

Learn about some cultural differences in the use of punishment in the following World of Psychology section.

World of Psychology

Culture and Punishment

Punishment has been used to control and suppress behavior throughout recorded history. And there are clear cultural differences in the ways in which punishment is viewed and administered. A widely publicized incident revealed sharp differences in concepts of crime and punishment between the United States and Singapore.

Michael Fay, an 18-year-old American living in Singapore, was arrested and charged with 53 counts of vandalism, including the spray painting of dozens of cars. He was fined approximately $2,000, sentenced to 4 months in jail, and received four lashes with a rattan cane. In justifying their system of punishment, the officials in Singapore were quick to point out that their city, about the same size as Los Angeles, is virtually crime-free—few murders, rapes, beatings, or robberies.

Among Americans, sentiment about the caning was mixed. Some viewed it as barbarous and cruel, as did Michael's parents. But many Americans (51 percent in a CNN poll) expressed the view that caning might be an effective punishment under certain circumstances. Even some American judges, 17 percent according to a survey in the July 1994 *American Law Journal*, considered caning to be a punishment worth considering by U.S. courts.

All crimes are punished harshly in Singapore—murder, rape, robbery, dealing drugs. It is even unlawful for residents and visitors alike to miss the urinal when relieving themselves. Although the culture of Singapore is severely repressive and restrictive by American standards, Singaporeans have succeeded in suppressing undesirable behavior by using the threat of harsh punishment and applying punishment swiftly and surely.

How far do you think a society should go in its use of punishment to suppress unlawful behavior?

Escape and Avoidance Learning

Learning to perform a behavior because it terminates an aversive event is called escape learning, and it reflects the power of negative reinforcement. Running away from a punishing situation and taking aspirin to relieve a pounding headache are examples of escape behavior. In these situations the aversive event has begun and an attempt is being made to escape it.

Avoidance learning depends on two types of conditioning. First, through classical conditioning, an event or condition comes to signal an aversive state. Drinking and driving may be associated with automobile accidents and death. Because of such associations, people may engage in behaviors to avoid the anticipated aversive consequences. Making it a practice to avoid driving with people who have had too much to drink is sensible avoidance behavior.

Many avoidance behaviors are maladaptive, however, and occur in response to phobias. Students who have had a bad experience speaking in front of a class may begin to fear any situation that involves speaking before a group. Such students may avoid taking classes that require class presentations or avoid taking leadership roles that necessitate public speaking. Avoiding such situations prevents them from suffering the perceived dreaded consequences. But the avoidance behavior is negatively reinforced and thus strengthened through operant conditioning. Maladaptive avoidance behaviors are very difficult to extinguish, because people never give themselves a chance to learn that the dreaded consequences probably will not occur, or they are greatly exaggerated.

Learned Helplessness

Humans and other animals can learn easily to escape and avoid punishing or aversive situations. But research on learned helplessness suggests that if we are exposed to repeated aversive events that we cannot escape or avoid, we may learn to do nothing—simply to sit or stand helplessly and suffer the punishment. **Learned helplessness** is a passive resignation to aversive conditions learned by repeated exposure to aversive events that are inescapable and unavoidable.

The initial experiment on learned helplessness was conducted by Overmeier and Seligman (1967), who used dogs as their subjects. Dogs in the experimental group were strapped, one at a time, into a harness from which they could not escape and were exposed to electric shocks. Later, these same dogs were placed

avoidance learning: Learning to avoid events or conditions associated with dreaded or aversive outcomes.

learned helplessness: The learned response of resigning oneself passively to aversive conditions, rather than taking action to change, escape, or avoid them; learned through repeated exposure to inescapable or unavoidable aversive events.

in a shuttle box with two experimental compartments separated by a low barrier. The dogs then experienced a series of trials in which a warning signal was followed by an electric shock. The floor on one side was electrified, and the dogs should have learned quickly to escape the electric shocks simply by jumping the barrier. Surprisingly, the dogs did not do so; they simply suffered as many shocks as the experimenter chose to deliver *as if* escape were impossible. Another group of dogs, the control group, had not previously experienced the inescapable shock, and they quickly learned to jump the barrier when the warning signal sounded and thus to escape the shock. Seligman reported that the group experiencing the inescapable shock were less active than normal, suffered loss of appetite, and showed other symptoms resembling those of depression.

Following his findings with animals, Seligman (1975) reasoned that humans, too, who have suffered painful experiences they could neither avoid nor escape may experience learned helplessness. Then, having experienced helplessness, they may simply give up and react to disappointment in life by becoming inactive, withdrawn, and depressed (Seligman, 1991).

Factors Influencing Operant Conditioning

What three factors, in addition to the schedule of reinforcement, influence operant conditioning?

You have learned that responses are acquired more quickly with continuous rather than partial reinforcement and that the schedule of reinforcement influences both response rate and resistance to extinction. Several other factors affect response rate, resistance to extinction, and how quickly a response is acquired.

The first factor is the *magnitude of reinforcement*. In general, as the magnitude of reinforcement increases, acquisition of a response is faster, the rate of responding is higher, and resistance to extinction is greater (Clayton, 1964). People would be motivated to work harder and faster if they were paid $30 for each yard mowed rather than only $10. Other research indicates that level of performance is also influenced by the relationship between the amount of reinforcement expected and what is actually received (Crespi, 1942). For example, your performance on the job would undoubtedly be affected if your salary were suddenly cut in half. Also, it might improve dramatically if your employer doubled your pay.

The second factor affecting operant conditioning is the *immediacy of reinforcement*. In general, responses are conditioned more effectively when reinforcement is immediate. One reason people become addicted to crack cocaine so quickly is because its euphoric effects are felt almost instantly (Medzerian, 1991). As a rule, the longer the delay in reinforcement, the more slowly a response is acquired (Capaldi, 1978; Perin, 1943). (See Figure 5.6.) Overweight people have difficulty changing their eating habits partly because of the long delay between their behavior change and the rewarding consequences of weight loss.

The third factor influencing conditioning is the *level of motivation* of the learner. If you are highly motivated to learn to play tennis, you will learn faster and practice more than if you have no interest in the game. Skinner found that when food is the reinforcer, a hungry animal will learn faster than a full animal. To maximize motivation, he used rats that had been deprived of food for 24 hours and pigeons that were maintained at 75 to 80 percent of their normal body weight.

Comparing Classical and Operant Conditioning: What's the Difference?

In summary, the processes of generalization, discrimination, extinction, and spontaneous recovery occur in both classical and operant conditioning. Both types of conditioning depend on associative learning. In classical conditioning, an association is formed between two stimuli—for example, a tone and food, a white rat and a loud noise, a product and a celebrity. In operant conditioning, the associa-

FIGURE 5.6

The Effect of Delay in Reinforcement on Conditioning of a Response

In general, responses are conditioned more effectively when reinforcement is immediate. The longer the delay in reinforcement, the lower the probability that a response will be acquired.

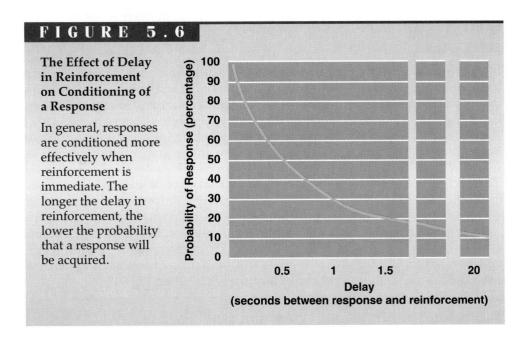

tion is established between a response and its consequences—studying hard and a high test grade, or, in the world of rats, bar pressing and food.

In classical conditioning, the focus is on what precedes the response. Pavlov focused on what led up to the salivation in his dogs, not on what happened after they salivated. In operant conditioning, the focus is on what follows the response. If a rat's bar pressing or your studying is followed by a reinforcer, that response is more likely to occur in the future.

Generally, in classical conditioning, the subject is passive and responds to the environment rather than acting on it. In operant conditioning, the subject is active and *operates* on the environment. Children *do* something to get their parents' attention or their praise. Review and Reflect Table 5.3 highlights the major differences between classical and operant conditioning.

Review and Reflect 5.3 *Classical and Operant Conditioning Compared*

Characteristics	Classical Conditioning	Operant Conditioning
Type of association	Between two stimuli	Between a response and its consequence
State of subject	Passive	Active
Focus of attention	On what precedes response	On what follows response
Type of response typically involved	Involuntary or reflexive response	Voluntary response
Bodily response typically involved	Internal responses: emotional and glandular reactions	External responses: muscular and skeletal movement and verbal responses
Range of responses	Relatively simple	Simple to highly complex
Responses learned	Emotional reactions: fears, likes, dislikes	Goal-oriented responses

What is biofeedback?

Biofeedback: Observable Evidence of Internal Processes

It was long believed that internal responses such as heart rate, brain-wave patterns, and blood flow were not subject to operant conditioning. We now know that when people are given very precise feedback about these internal processes, they can learn, with practice, to exercise control over them (Green & Green, 1977). **Biofeedback** is a way of getting information about our internal biological state. Biofeedback devices have sensors that monitor slight changes in these internal responses and then amplify and convert them into visual or auditory signals. Thus, subjects can *see* or *hear* evidence of internal physiological processes, and by trying out various strategies (thoughts, feelings, or images), they can learn which ones routinely increase, decrease, or maintain a particular level of activity.

Biofeedback has been used to regulate heart rate and to control migraine and tension headaches, gastrointestinal disorders, asthma, anxiety tension states, epilepsy, sexual dysfunctions, and neuromuscular disorders such as cerebral palsy, spinal-cord injuries, and stroke (Kalish, 1981; Miller, 1985, 1989).

What is behavior modification?

Behavior Modification: Changing Our Act

Behavior modification is a method of changing behavior through a systematic program based on the principles of learning—classical conditioning, operant conditioning, or observational learning (which we will discuss soon). Most behavior modification programs use the principles of operant conditioning.

Many institutions—schools, mental hospitals, homes for juvenile delinquents, prisons—have used behavior modification programs with varying degrees of success. Institutions are well suited to such techniques because they provide a restricted environment where the consequences of behavior can be more strictly controlled. Some institutions such as prisons or mental hospitals use a **token economy**—a program that motivates socially desirable behavior by reinforcing it with tokens. The tokens (poker chips or coupons) may later be exchanged for desired goods such as candy or cigarettes and privileges such as weekend passes, free time, or participation in desired activities. People in the program know in advance exactly what behaviors will be reinforced and how they will be reinforced. Token economies have been used effectively in mental hospitals to encourage patients to attend to grooming, to interact with other patients, and to carry out housekeeping tasks (Ayllon & Azrin, 1965, 1968). Although the positive behaviors generally stop when the tokens are discontinued, this does not mean that the programs are not worthwhile. After all, most people who are employed would probably quit their jobs if they were no longer paid.

Classroom teachers have used behavior modification to modify undesirable behavior and to encourage learning. "Time out" is a useful technique in which a child who is misbehaving is removed for a short time from sources of positive reinforcement. (Remember, according to operant conditioning, a behavior that is no longer reinforced will extinguish.)

Some research indicates, however, that it may be unwise to reward students for participating in learning activities they already enjoy. Reinforcement in these cases may lessen students' natural interest in the tasks, and when reinforcers are withdrawn, the natural interest may disappear (Deci, 1975; Lepper et al., 1973).

Behavior modification is used successfully in business and industry to increase profits and to modify employee behavior in health, safety, and learning. In order to keep their health insurance premiums down, some companies give annual rebates to employees who do not use up the deductibles in their health insurance plan. To reduce costs associated with automobile accidents and auto theft, insurance companies offer incentives in the form of reduced insurance premiums for

biofeedback: The use of sensitive equipment to give people precise feedback about internal physiological processes so that they can learn, with practice, to exercise control over them.

behavior modification: The systematic application of the learning principles of operant conditioning, classical conditioning, or observational learning to individuals or groups in order to eliminate undesirable behavior and/or encourage desirable behavior.

token economy: A program that motivates and reinforces socially acceptable behaviors with tokens that can be exchanged for desired items or privileges.

installing airbags and burglar alarm systems. To encourage employees to take company-approved college courses, some companies offer tuition reimbursement contingent on course grades. Many companies promote sales by giving salespeople special bonuses, trips, and other prizes for increasing sales.

One of the most successful applications of behavior modification has been in the treatment of psychological problems ranging from phobias to addictive behaviors. In this context, behavior modification is called behavior therapy, and this kind of therapy is discussed in Chapter 15.

Memory Check 5.5

1. Punishment is roughly the same as negative reinforcement (true/false)

2. Which of the following is *not* presented in the text as one of the major factors influencing the effectiveness of punishment?
   a. timing   c. intensity
   b. consistency   d. frequency

3. Punishment usually does *not* extinguish undesirable behavior. (true/false)

4. People often engage in behavior that is reinforcing in the short term but is not in their long-term interest. This reflects the influence of:
   a. the magnitude of reinforcement.
   b. their level of motivation.
   c. the immediacy of reinforcement.
   d. the schedule of reinforcement.

5. Recall what you have learned about classical and operant conditioning. Which of the following is descriptive of operant conditioning?
   a. An association is formed between a response and its consequence.
   b. The responses acquired are usually emotional reactions.
   c. The subject is usually passive.
   d. The response acquired is usually an involuntary or reflexive response.

6. Using sensitive electronic equipment to monitor physiological processes in order to bring them under conscious control is called _____.

7. Applying learning principles to eliminate undesirable behavior and/or encourage desirable behavior is called _____.

Answers: 1. false   2. d   3. true   4. c   5. a   6. biofeedback   7. behavior modification

Cognitive Learning

So far, we have explored relatively simple types of learning. In classical and operant conditioning, learning is defined in terms of observable or measurable changes in behavior. Behaviorists such as Skinner and Watson believed that learning through operant and classical conditioning could be explained without reference to internal mental processes. Today, however, a growing number of psychologists stress the role of mental processes. They choose to broaden the study of learning to include such **cognitive processes** as thinking, knowing, problem solving, remembering, and forming mental representations. According to cognitive theorists, these processes are critically important in a more complete, more comprehensive view of learning.

cognitive processes (COG-nuh-tiv): Mental processes such as thinking, knowing, problem solving, and remembering.

We will consider the work of three important researchers in the field of cognitive learning—Wolfgang Köhler, Edward Tolman, and Albert Bandura.

Learning by Insight: Aha! Now I Get It

Wolfgang Köhler (1887–1967), a German psychologist, studied anthropoid apes and became convinced that they behaved intelligently and were capable of prob-

What is insight, and how does it affect learning?

lem solving. In his book *The Mentality of Apes* (1925), Köhler describes experiments he conducted on chimpanzees confined in caged areas.

In one experiment, Köhler hung a bunch of bananas inside the caged area but overhead, out of reach of the apes; boxes and sticks were left around the cage. Köhler observed the chimps' unsuccessful attempts to reach the bananas by jumping up or swinging sticks at them. Eventually the chimps solved the problem by piling the boxes one on top of the other until they could reach the bananas.

In another experiment, Sultan, the brightest of the chimps, was given one short stick; beyond reach outside the cage was a longer stick and a bunch of bananas. After failing to reach the bananas with the short stick, Sultan used it to drag the long stick within reach. Then, finding that the long stick did not reach the bananas, Sultan finally solved the problem by fitting the two sticks together to form one long stick. With this stick, he successfully retrieved the bananas.

Köhler observed that the chimps sometimes appeared to give up in their attempts to get the bananas. However, after an interval, they returned and came up with the solution to the problem as if it had come to them in a flash of **insight**. They seemed to have suddenly discovered the relationship between the sticks or boxes and the bananas. Köhler insisted that insight, rather than trial-and-error learning, accounted for the chimps' successes, because they could easily repeat the solution and transfer this learning to similar problems.

Köhler's major contribution to learning is his notion of learning by insight. Learning by insight occurs when there is a sudden realization of the relationship between elements in a problem situation so that a solution becomes apparent. In human terms, a solution gained through insight is more easily learned, less likely to be forgotten, and more readily transferred to new problems than solutions learned through rote memorization (Rock & Palmer, 1990).

Latent Learning and Cognitive Maps: I Might Use That Later

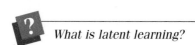
What is latent learning?

Like Köhler, Edward Tolman (1886–1959) differed with the prevailing ideas on learning. First, Tolman (1932) believed that learning could take place without reinforcement. Second, he differentiated between learning and performance. He maintained that **latent learning** could occur, that is, learning could occur without apparent reinforcement but not be demonstrated until the organism was motivated to do so. The following experiment by Tolman and Honzik (1930) supports this position.

Three groups of rats were placed in a maze daily for 17 days. The first group always received a food reward at the end of the maze. The second group never received a reward, and the third group did not receive a food reward until the 11th day. The first group showed a steady improvement in performance over the 17-day period. The second group showed slight, gradual improvement. The third group, after being rewarded on the 11th day, showed a marked improvement the next day and from then on, outperforming the rats that had been rewarded daily (see Figure 5.7). The rapid improvement of the third group indicated to Tolman that latent learning had occurred—that the rats had actually learned the maze during the first 11 days.

Skinner was still in graduate school in 1930, when Tolman provided this exception to a basic principle of operant conditioning—that reinforcement is required for learning new behavior. The rats in the learning group *did* learn something before reinforcement and without exhibiting any evidence of learning by overt, observable behavior. But what did they learn? Tolman concluded that the rats had learned to form a **cognitive map**, a mental representation or picture, of the maze but had not demonstrated their learning until they were reinforced.

In later studies, Tolman showed how rats quickly learn to rearrange learned cognitive maps and find their way through increasingly complex mazes with

insight: The sudden realization of the relationship between elements in a problem situation, which makes the solution apparent.

latent learning: Learning that occurs without apparent reinforcement but that is not demonstrated until sufficient reinforcement is provided.

cognitive map: A mental representation of an area.

FIGURE 5.7

Latent Learning

Rats in Group 1 were rewarded for running the maze correctly, while rats in Group 2 were never rewarded. Group 3 rats were rewarded only on the 11th day, and thereafter outperformed the rats in Group 1. The rats had "learned" the maze but were not motivated to perform until rewarded, demonstrating that latent learning had occurred. (From Tolman & Honzik, 1930.)

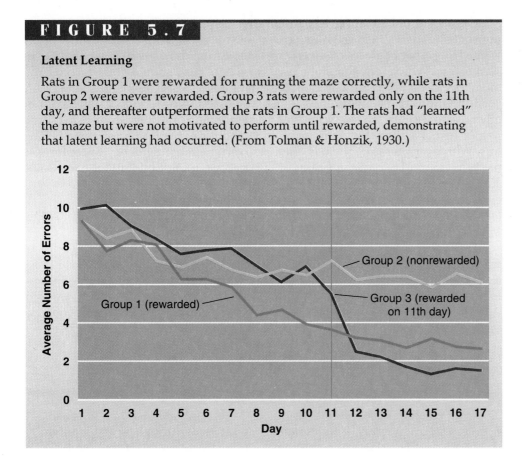

ease. The concepts of cognitive maps and latent learning have a far more important place in psychology today than was ever true in Tolman's lifetime.

Observational Learning: Watching and Learning

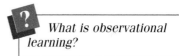

What is observational learning?

In our exploration of operant conditioning, you read how people and other animals learn by directly experiencing the consequences, positive or negative, of their behavior. But must we experience rewards and punishment firsthand in order to learn? Not according to Albert Bandura (1986), who contends that many behaviors or responses are acquired through observational learning. **Observational learning**, sometimes called **modeling**, results when we observe the behavior of others and note the consequences of that behavior.

The person who demonstrates a behavior or whose behavior is imitated is called the **model**. Parents, movie stars, and sports personalities are often powerful models. The effectiveness of a model is related to his or her status, competence, and power. Other important factors are the age, sex, attractiveness, and ethnicity of the model. Whether learned behavior is actually performed depends largely on whether the observed models are rewarded or punished for their behavior and whether the person expects to be rewarded for the behavior (Bandura, 1969a, 1977a).

We use observational learning to acquire new responses or to strengthen or weaken existing responses. Consider your attitudes, gestures, personality traits, good habits (or bad habits, for that matter), moral values, and food preferences. Do you share any of these with your parents? While you were growing up, their example probably influenced your behavior for better or worse. Look around the classroom, and observe the dress, hairstyles, and verbal patterns of the other students. Most people have been greatly influenced by observing others.

observational learning: Learning by observing the behavior of others and the consequences of that behavior; learning by imitation.

modeling: Another name for observational learning.

model: The individual who demonstrates a behavior or serves as an example in observational learning.

Observational learning is particularly useful when we find ourselves in unusual situations. Picture yourself as a guest at an elaborate state dinner at the White House. More pieces of silverware extend from the plate than you have ever seen before. Which fork should be used for what? How should you proceed? You might decide to take your cue from the First Lady—observational learning.

Inhibitions can be weakened or lost as a result of observing the behavior of others. Adolescents can lose whatever resistance they may have to drinking, drug use, or sexual activity by seeing or hearing about peers engaging in these behaviors. With peer pressure, there is often an overwhelming tendency to conform to the behavior and accept the values of the peer group. But inhibitions can also be strengthened through observational learning. A person does not need to experience the unfortunate consequences of dangerous behavior to avoid it. American teenagers in Singapore are not likely to carry out any act of vandalism after seeing Michael Fay caned for allegedly spray painting cars.

Fears, too, can be acquired through observational learning. A parent with an extreme fear of the dentist or of thunderstorms might serve as a model for these fears in a child. Observational learning is not even restricted to humans. Monkeys, for example, learn specific fears by observing other monkeys (Cook et al., 1985). And the octopus has been shown to learn some responses even faster by observing others of its species than through conditioning (Fiorito & Scotto, 1992).

Apply what you know about the three basic types of learning to do the following *Try It!*

Think about everything you did yesterday from the time you woke up until the time you went to sleep. List ten behaviors and indicate whether observational learning (OL), operant conditioning (OC), and/or classical conditioning (CC) played some role in the acquisition of each one. Remember, a behavior might originally have been learned by some combination of the three types of learning and then maintained by one or more of the types.

Behavior	Acquired through:			Maintained through:		
	OL	OC	CC	OL	OC	CC
Brushing teeth	X	X		X		

You probably learned to brush your teeth through a combination of observational learning (watching a parent demonstrate how to brush) and operant conditioning (being praised as your technique improved—shaping). Now that behavior is maintained through operant conditioning, specifically negative reinforcement (getting rid of the terrible taste in your mouth). Avoiding cavities and the scorn of everyone around you is an extra bonus.

Which kind of learning had the most checks on your chart?

Learning Aggression: Copying What We See   Albert Bandura suspected that aggressive behavior is particularly subject to observational learning and that aggression and violence depicted on television or in cartoons tend to increase aggression in children. His pioneering work has greatly influenced current thinking on these issues. In several classic experiments, Bandura demonstrated how children are influenced by exposure to aggressive models.

One study involved three groups of preschool children. Children in one group individually observed an adult model punching, kicking, and hitting a 5-foot inflated plastic "Bobo Doll" with a mallet, while uttering aggressive words such as "Sock him in the nose . . . ," "Throw him in the air . . . ," "Kick him . . . ," "Pow . . . " (Bandura et al., 1961, p. 576). Children in the second group observed a nonaggressive model who ignored the Bobo Doll and sat quietly assembling Tinker Toys. The control group was placed in the same setting with no adult present. Later, each subject was observed through a one-way mirror. Subjects exposed to the aggressive model imitated much of the aggression and also engaged in significantly more non-imitative aggression than either of the other groups. Subjects who had observed the nonaggressive model showed less aggressive behavior than the control group.

A further study compared the degree of aggression in children following exposure to (1) a live aggressive model, (2) a filmed version of the episode, and (3) a film depicting an aggressive cartoon character using the same aggressive behaviors in a fantasylike setting (Bandura et al., 1963). A control group was not exposed to any of the three situations of aggression. The groups exposed to aggressive models used significantly more aggression than the control group. The researchers concluded that "of the three experimental conditions, exposure to humans on film portraying aggression was the most influential in eliciting and shaping aggressive behavior" (p. 7).

Children can learn effectively by observing and imitating others.

Bandura's research provided the impetus for studying the effects of television violence and aggression in both cartoons and regular programming. Although there has been some consciousness raising about the negative impact of media violence, the amount of television violence is still excessive. The problem is compounded by the fact that the average family watches more than 7 hours of television each day. Watching excessive violence gives people an exaggerated view of the pervasiveness of violence in our society, while making them less sensitive to the victims of violence. Media violence also encourages aggressive behavior in children by portraying aggression as an acceptable and effective way to solve problems and by teaching new forms of aggression (Wood et al., 1991). But just as children imitate the aggressive behavior they observe on television, they also imitate the prosocial, or helping, behavior they observe. Programs like "Mister Rogers' Neighborhood" and "Sesame Street" have been found to have a positive influence on children.

Apparently many avenues of learning are available to humans and other animals. Thankfully, our capacity to learn seems practically unlimited. Certainly advances in civilization could not have been achieved without the ability to learn.

Memory Check 5.6

1. The sudden realization of the relationship between the elements in a problem situation that results in the solution to the problem is called (latent learning, insight).

2. Learning not demonstrated until one is motivated to perform the behavior is called:
   a. learning by insight.
   b. observational learning.
   c. classical conditioning.
   d. latent learning.

3. Hayley has been afraid of snakes for as long as she can remember, and her mother has the same paralyzing fear. Hayley most likely acquired her fear through:
   a. learning by insight.
   b. observational learning.
   c. classical conditioning.
   d. latent learning.

4. Match the researcher with the subject(s) researched.
   ____ 1) Edward Tolman
   ____ 2) Albert Bandura
   ____ 3) Wolfgang Köhler

   a. observational learning
   b. cognitive maps
   c. learning by insight
   d. latent learning

Answers: 1. insight 2. d 3. b 4. 1) b, d 2) a 3) c

APPLICATIONS · **APPLICATIONS** · **APPLICATIONS**

How to Win the Battle against Procrastination

From time to time, virtually everyone is plagued by procrastination—postponing, or putting off until some future time, an assignment they have been given or a task or activity they have decided to complete. Many people procrastinate only in certain areas of their lives, but for others procrastination is their defining lifestyle.

Procrastination is fueled when we yield to the temptation of immediate rewards at the expense of long-term benefit. In other words, procrastinators have difficulty suffering short-term pain for long-term gain. They often fail to consider the negative consequences of their procrastination or the positive consequences of working on the task at hand.

Procrastinators typically engage in self-deception, making and breaking promise after promise to themselves about when they will do their work. They also tend to magnify the difficulty of the task. The more painful, difficult, or boring they visualize the task to be, the more they dread it and the more they postpone getting started.

Types of Procrastinators

While it is true that all procrastinators suffer from the same general problem, the authors have identified four different types. Many procrastinators fit into more than one category. If you are a procrastinator, which type or types are you?

The Shameless Procrastinator. Shameless procrastinators are fully aware that they fritter away their time, and they don't care. They do it without guilt or remorse, without any rationalizations or excuses. Often considered to be "lazy," they openly procrastinate and escape into pleasure.

The Rationalizing Procrastinator. Rationalizing procrastinators have a long list of seemingly rational reasons for putting off a task until another time. Some dutifully schedule a specific time to work on a task, but when the time arrives, they find or manufacture reasons to reschedule the task for the next day or week. Claiming that they work better under pressure, rationalizing procrastinators often put off tasks until the very last minute. At other times they may insist that they can do a good job only if they are in the mood or seized with creative inspiration.

The Guilty Procrastinator. Guilty procrastinators are painfully aware that they waste much of their time. They regret it, feel guilty about it, and berate themselves for doing it, but they can't seem to stop. If their discomfort reaches a high enough level, the guilt may become more punishing than the task itself, and they may reluctantly tackle the task at hand.

The Busy Procrastinator. Busy procrastinators may not even realize that they procrastinate, for they are always busy at something. Unfortunately, the something is hardly ever completing the major task at hand. Before settling down to a major task or assignment, they may busily perform countless other tasks that could just as well be done later. They may do housecleaning, shop for groceries, mow the lawn, wash the car, or pay their bills early. Rather than escaping into pleasure like shameless procrastinators, they escape into ill-timed busyness, which seems to give them a sense of accomplishment.

Steps to Take in Overcoming Procrastination

Procrastinators of all types can profit from the following 10 steps for overcoming procrastination. We'll use studying as our example in each step.

- *Identify the environmental cues that habitually interfere with your studying.* What competing interests are most likely to cause you to put off studying or interrupt your studying—television, bed, refrigerator, telephone, friends, family members?

- *Select your work environment.* Select a place to study that you associate *only* with studying, preferably away from the distracting environmental cues you have identified. The library might be such a place.

- *Schedule your study time.* Schedule your study time in advance, maybe even the previous day, so your decisions about when to start work will not be ruled by the whim of the moment.

- *Get started.* The most difficult part is getting started. Plan your study time. Give yourself an extra reward for starting on time and, perhaps, a penalty for not starting on time. Let the clock rather than your mood be the signal to begin studyng. Once you begin, you will probably find that the work is not as distasteful as you had imagined.

- *Use visualization.* Because much procrastination results from the failure to consider its negative consequences, visualizing the consequences of *not* studying can be an effective tool for combating procrastination. Suppose you are considering going out of town with friends for the weekend instead of studying for a midterm test on Monday. Picture this! You walk into the classroom Monday morning unprepared; you know the answers to very few questions; you flunk the test. Visualize further the impact this will have on your final grade in the course and on your GPA. Now visualize the outcome if you stay home for the weekend and study. Picture how much better you will feel as you breeze through the test on Monday and get a high grade.

- *Become better at estimating how long it takes to complete an assignment.* Estimate how long it will take to complete an assignment, and then keep track of how long it actually takes. If you habitually underestimate the time involved, begin scheduling longer periods of time to accomplish your work.

- *Beware of jumping to another task when you reach a difficult part of an assignment.* This is a procrastination tactic designed to give you the feeling that you are busy and accomplishing something, but it is, nevertheless, an avoidance tactic.

- *Beware of preparation overkill.* Busy procrastinators may actually begin work on a scheduled task or assignment but spend hours preparing for the task rather than on the task itself. They may gather enough materials in the library to write a book rather than a five-page term paper. This enables them to postpone writing the paper.

- *Keep a record of the reasons you give yourself for postponing studying or completing important assignments.* If a favorite rationalization is "I'll wait until I'm in the mood to do this," count the number of times in a week you are seized with the desire to study. The mood to study typically arrives *after* you begin, not before.

- *Stop believing your own promises.* Procrastinators are notorious for breaking their own promises to get to work. How much confidence would you have in a friend who made promises to you but never followed through? Can you relate to any of these self-promises?

"I'll do this tomorrow." Why is tomorrow going to be a better day? You told yourself this yesterday, and now you are not following through.

"I'll go out with my friends, but only for a few hours." As a rule, does your time with friends turn out to be a few hours or a whole day or night?

"I'll get some sleep and set my alarm for 3:00 A.M. and then study." Are you usually able to get up at 3:00 A.M.? Is that really the ideal time for you to study? Research on sleep indicates that the middle of your subjective night is the worst time.

"I'll watch TV for a few minutes and then get back to studying." Does a few minutes often turn into several hours?

"I'll rest for a few minutes and clear my mind so I can think better." Does your ability to think really improve, or do you find that you are more tired than you realized and that you need to rest longer?

Don't procrastinate! Begin now! Apply the steps outlined here to gain more control over your behavior and win the battle against procrastination. A good source for finding other suggestions on this topic is the book *Overcoming Procrastination* by Albert Ellis and William J. Knaus (1977).

Thinking Critically

Evaluation

Outline the strengths and limitations of classical conditioning, operant conditioning, and observational learning in explaining how behaviors are acquired and maintained.

Point/Counterpoint

The use of behavior modification has been controversial. Prepare arguments supporting each of these positions:

a. Behavior modification should be used in society to shape the behavior of others.

b. Behavior modification should not be used in society to shape the behavior of others.

Psychology in Your Life

Think of a behavior of a friend, a family member, or a professor that you would like to change. Using what you know about classical conditioning, operant conditioning, and observational learning, formulate a detailed plan for changing the behavior of the target person.

Chapter Summary and Review

Classical Conditioning

What was Pavlov's major contribution to psychology?

Pavlov's study of the conditioned reflex provided a model of learning called classical conditioning.

How is classical conditioning accomplished?

During classical conditioning, a neutral stimulus (a tone) is presented shortly before an unconditioned stimulus (food), which naturally elicits or brings forth an unconditioned response (salivation). After repeated pairings, the conditioned stimulus (the tone) alone will elicit the conditioned response (salivation).

How does extinction occur in classical conditioning?

If the conditioned stimulus (tone) is presented repeatedly without the unconditioned stimulus (food), the conditioned response (salivation) becomes progressively weaker and eventually disappears.

What is generalization?

Generalization occurs when an organism makes a conditioned response to a stimulus similar to the original conditioned stimulus.

What is discrimination in classical conditioning?

Discrimination is the ability to distinguish between similar stimuli, so that the conditioned response is made only to the original conditioned stimulus.

How did Watson demonstrate that fear could be classically conditioned?

Watson showed that fear could be classically conditioned when, by presenting a white rat along with a loud, frightening noise, he conditioned Little Albert to fear the white rat.

What types of responses can be acquired through classical conditioning?

Positive and negative emotional responses (including likes, dislikes, fears, and phobias), conditioned immune responses, and conditioned drug tolerance in drug users are some types of responses acquired through classical conditioning.

What are four factors that influence classical conditioning?

Four factors influencing classical conditioning are (1) the number of pairings of conditioned stimulus and unconditioned stimulus, (2) the intensity of the unconditioned stimulus, (3) how reliably the conditioned stimulus predicts the unconditioned stimulus, and (4) the temporal relationship between the conditioned stimulus and unconditioned stimulus.

Key Terms

stimulus (p. 164)
learning (p. 164)
classical conditioning (p. 165)
reflex (p. 166)
conditioned reflex (p. 167)
unconditioned response (p. 167)
unconditioned stimulus (p. 167)
conditioned stimulus (p. 167)
conditioned response (p. 167)
extinction (p. 167)
spontaneous recovery (p. 168)
generalization (p. 168)
discrimination (p. 169)
higher-order conditioning (p. 170)
drug tolerance (p. 175)
taste aversion (p. 176)

Operant Conditioning

What is Thorndike's major contribution to psychology?

Thorndike formulated the law of effect, which formed the conceptual starting point for Skinner's work on operant conditioning.

How are responses acquired through operant conditioning?

Operant conditioning is a method for conditioning voluntary responses. The consequences of behavior are manipulated to shape a new response or to increase or decrease the frequency of an existing response.

How is shaping used to condition a response?

In shaping, rather than waiting for the desired response to be emitted, we selectively reinforce successive approximations toward the goal response until the desired response is achieved.

How does extinction occur in operant conditioning?

In operant conditioning, extinction occurs when reinforcement is withheld.

What is the goal of both positive reinforcement and negative reinforcement, and how is the goal accomplished with each?

Both positive reinforcement and negative reinforcement are utilized to strengthen or increase the probability of a response. With positive reinforcement the desired response is followed by a reward; with negative reinforcement it is followed by the termination of an aversive stimulus.

What are the four major schedules of reinforcement, and which schedule yields the highest response rate and the greatest resistance to extinction?

The four basic schedules of reinforcement are the fixed-ratio, variable-ratio, fixed-interval, and variable-interval schedules. The variable-ratio schedule provides the highest response rate and the most resistance to extinction.

 What is the partial-reinforcement effect?

The partial-reinforcement effect is the greater resistance to extinction that occurs when responses are maintained under partial reinforcement rather than under continuous reinforcement.

 How does punishment differ from negative reinforcement?

Punishment is used to decrease the frequency of a response; negative reinforcement is used to increase the frequency of a response.

What are some disadvantages of punishment?

Punishment generally suppresses rather than extinguishes behavior; it does not help people develop more appropriate behaviors. And it can cause fear, anger, hostility, and aggression in the punished person.

What three factors increase the effectiveness of punishment?

Punishment is most effective when it is given immediately after undesirable behavior, and when it is consistently applied and fairly intense.

What three factors, in addition to the schedule of reinforcement, influence operant conditioning?

In operant conditioning, acquisition of a response, response rate, and resistance to extinction are influenced by the magnitude of reinforcement, the immediacy of reinforcement, and the motivation of the organism.

 What is biofeedback?

Biofeedback involves the use of sensitive equipment to give people precise feedback about internal physiological processes so that they can learn, with practice, to exercise control over them.

 What is behavior modification?

Behavior modification involves systematically applying learning principles to individuals or groups in order to eliminate undesirable behavior and/or encourage desirable behavior.

Key Terms

trial-and-error learning (p. 178)
law of effect (p. 178)
operant conditioning (p. 178)
reinforcer (p. 179)
shaping (p. 180)
Skinner box (p. 180)
successive approximations (p. 180)
extinction (p. 181)
discriminative stimulus (p. 181)
reinforcement (p. 182)
positive reinforcement (p. 182)
negative reinforcement (p. 182)
primary reinforcer (p. 183)
secondary reinforcer (p. 183)
continuous reinforcement (p. 183)
partial reinforcement (p. 183)
schedule of reinforcement (p. 183)
fixed-ratio schedule (p. 184)
variable-ratio schedule (p. 184)
fixed-interval schedule (p. 184)
variable-interval schedule (p. 184)
partial-reinforcement effect (p. 185)

punishment (p. 186)
avoidance learning (p. 189)
learned helplessness (p. 189)
biofeedback (p. 192)
behavior modification (p. 192)
token economy (p. 192)

Cognitive Learning

 What is insight, and how does it affect learning?

Insight is the sudden realization of the relationship between elements in a problem situation that makes the solution apparent; this solution is easily learned and transferred to new problems.

 What is latent learning?

Latent learning occurs without apparent reinforcement, but it is not demonstrated in performance until the organism is motivated to do so.

 What is observational learning?

Observational learning is learning by observing the behavior of others, called models, and the consequences of that behavior.

Key Terms

cognitive processes (p. 193)
insight (p. 194)
latent learning (p. 194)
cognitive map (p. 194)
observational learning (p. 195)
modeling (p. 195)
model (p. 195)

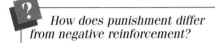

6

MEMORY

CHAPTER OUTLINE

Remembering

The Three Processes in Memory: Encoding, Storage, and Retrieval

The Three Memory Systems: The Long and the Short of It

The Levels-of-Processing Model: Another View of Memory

Measuring Memory

Three Methods of Measuring Memory

Hermann Ebbinghaus and the First Experimental Studies on Learning and Memory

Forgetting

The Causes of Forgetting

Prospective Forgetting: Forgetting to Remember

The Nature of Remembering and Forgetting

Memory as a Permanent Record: The Videocassette Recorder Analogy

Memory as a Reconstruction: Partly Fact and Partly Fiction

Eyewitness Testimony: Is It Accurate?

Recovering Repressed Memories: A Controversy

Unusual Memory Phenomena

World of Psychology: Memory and Culture

Factors Influencing Retrieval

The Serial Position Effect: To Be Remembered, Be First or Last But Not in the Middle

Environmental Context and Memory

The State-Dependent Memory Effect

Stress, Anxiety, and Memory: Relax and Remember

Biology and Memory

Brain Damage: A Clue to Memory Formation

Neuronal Changes in Memory: Brain Work

Improving Memory

Study Habits That Aid Memory

Applications: Improving Memory with Mnemonic Devices

Thinking Critically

Chapter Summary and Review

N o, no, not me. Not me!" cried Hen Van Nguyen in halting English. This unfortunate Vietnamese immigrant, on trial for murder, protested his innocence for 2 full days at the trial before it was discovered that he was not the real defendant. Before the trial, Nguyen had been charged with theft and was being held in a Georgia county jail. In the same jail was another Vietnamese man, who had been accused of stabbing to death the woman he lived with.

The jailer had mistakenly delivered the wrong man to the courtroom. Yet unbelievably, during the trial, two eyewitnesses identified Nguyen and swore that he had committed the murder. Even more astonishing, the defense attorney, who had met several times with his client to prepare his defense, sat with the wrong man in the courtroom and defended him for 2 days. The county sheriff remarked, "How the defense attorney did not know his client, I don't know." (Adapted from "Wrong Man Tried for Murder," 1985, p. 9A.)

In this case, the defense attorney, the sheriff, and the eyewitnesses were all members of a racial group different from Mr. Nguyen's. In another case, however, even though all seven eyewitnesses were of the same race as the suspect, they picked the wrong man. Look at the photographs. Do these two men look alike to you?

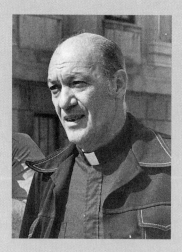

In a famous case in Delaware, a Catholic priest was arrested for a series of armed robberies. At his trial, 53-year-old Father Pagano was identified by seven eyewitnesses and probably would have been convicted if another man, Ronald Clouser, had not confessed to the robberies. The unbelievable part of this case is that the priest was bald and shorter, thinner, and 14 years older than the confessed robber, who had a full head of hair. (Adapted from Buckhout, 1979.)

Do these two cases simply reflect the rare and unusual in human memory, or are memory errors common occurrences? This and many other questions you may have about memory will be answered in this chapter. We will describe three memory systems: sensory, short-term, and long-term. You will learn how much information each system holds, for how long, and in what form. You will discover why virtually everyone finds it harder to remember names than faces. Is memory like a video recorder, in which the sights and sounds we experience are captured intact and simply played back in exact detail? Or do we "reconstruct" the past when we remember, leaving out certain bits and pieces of events that actually happened and adding others that did not?

Would you like to improve your memory? You will learn some techniques that can help you study more effectively, and some mnemonic devices (memory strategies) that can be used in practical ways every day as memory aids. Now read on . . . and remember.

R emembering

Our memory is the storehouse for everything we know. It enables us to know who and where we are when we awaken each morning. Memory provides the continuity of life—the long thread to which are tied our joys and sorrows, our knowledge and skills, our triumphs and failures, and the people and places that form our lives.

204

Most current efforts to understand human memory have been conducted within a framework known as the information-processing approach (Klatzky, 1984). This approach makes use of modern computer science and related fields to provide models that help us understand the processes involved in memory.

The Three Processes in Memory: Encoding, Storage, and Retrieval

What must occur to enable us to remember a friend's name, a fact from history, or an incident from our past? The act of remembering requires the successful completion of three processes: encoding, storage, and retrieval. The first process, **encoding**, involves transforming information into a form that can be stored in memory. Sometimes we encode information automatically, without any effort, but often we must do something with the information in order to remember it. For example, if you met someone named George at a party, you might associate his name with George Washington or George Bush. Such simple associations can markedly improve your ability to recall names and other information. The careful encoding of information greatly increases the chance that you will remember it.

The second memory process, **storage**, involves keeping or maintaining information in memory. For encoded information to be stored, some physiological change in the brain must take place—a process called **consolidation**. Normally consolidation occurs automatically, but if a person loses consciousness for any reason, the process can be disrupted and a permanent memory may not form. That is why a person who has been in a serious car accident could awaken in a hospital and not remember what has happened.

The final process, **retrieval**, occurs when information stored in memory is brought to mind. Calling George by name the next time you meet him shows that you have retrieved his name from memory. To remember, we must perform all three processes—encode the information, store it, and then retrieve it. Memory failure can result from the failure of any one of the three (see Figure 6.1).

Similar steps are required in the information processing of computers. Information is encoded (entered in some form the computer is able to use), then stored on disk, and later retrieved on the screen. You would not be able to retrieve the material if you had failed to enter it, if a power failure occurred before you could save what you had entered, or if you forgot which disk or file contained the needed information. Of course, human memory is far more complex than even the most advanced computer systems, but computer processing provides a useful analogy to memory, if not taken too literally.

> **?** *What three processes are involved in the act of remembering?*

encoding: Transforming information into a form that can be stored in short-term or long-term memory.

storage: The act of maintaining information in memory.

consolidation: The presumed process, believed to involve the hippocampus, by which a permanent memory is formed.

retrieval: The act of bringing to mind material that has been stored in memory.

FIGURE 6.1

The Processes Required in Remembering

The act of remembering requires the successful completion of three processes: encoding, storage, and retrieval. Memory failure can result from the failure of any one of the three processes.

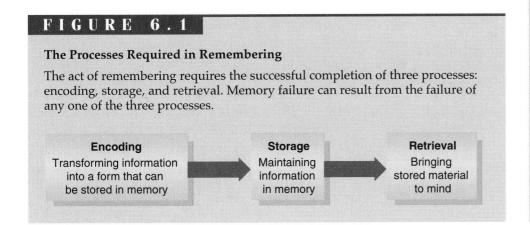

Encoding	Storage	Retrieval
Transforming information into a form that can be stored in memory	Maintaining information in memory	Bringing stored material to mind

FIGURE 6.2

The Three Memory Systems

According to the Atkinson-Schiffrin model, there are three separate memory systems: sensory memory, short-term memory, and long-term memory.

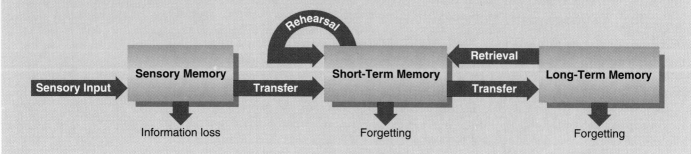

The Three Memory Systems: The Long and the Short of It

How are memories stored? According to one widely accepted view, the Atkinson-Shiffrin model, there are three different, interacting memory systems known as sensory, short-term, and long-term memory (Atkinson & Shiffrin, 1968; Broadbent, 1958). Considerable recent research in the biology of memory lends support to the model (Squire et al., 1993). We will examine each of these three memory systems, which are shown in Figure 6.2.

? *What is sensory memory?*

Sensory Memory: Images and Echoes As information comes in through the senses, virtually everything we see, hear, or otherwise sense is held in **sensory memory**, but only for the briefest period of time. Sensory memory normally holds visual images for a fraction of a second and sounds for about 2 seconds. Visual sensory memory lasts just long enough to keep whatever we are viewing from disappearing when we blink our eyes.

We know that a motion picture is a series of still pictures presented at the proper speed to create the illusion of movement. Our visual sensory memory retains one frame until the next one arrives, enabling us to see a flow of movement rather than discrete, still pictures. You can demonstrate visual sensory memory for yourself by doing the *Try It!*

To prove the existence of visual sensory memory, move your forefinger back and forth rapidly in front of your face. You will see what appears to be the blurred images of many fingers. This occurs because your sensory memory briefly holds a trace of the various positions that your finger occupies as it moves.

sensory memory: The memory system that holds information coming in through the senses for a period ranging from a fraction of a second to several seconds.

Exactly how long does visual sensory memory last? In 1740, Senger, a Swedish investigator, tried to answer this question. He attached a glowing ember to a rotating wheel and found that when he rotated the wheel rapidly, he could see a complete circle. When he rotated the wheel more slowly, he could see only a part of the circle. Senger then rotated the wheel at the exact speed that just allowed a complete circle to be perceived. He calculated the time of one revolution to be approximately $\frac{1}{10}$ of a second (Baddeley, 1982).

For a fraction of a second, glance at the three rows of letters shown below and then close your eyes. How many of the items can you recall?

X B D F

M P Z G

L C N H

Most people can recall correctly only four or five of the items when they are briefly presented. Does this indicate that visual sensory memory can hold only four or five items at a time? No. Researcher George Sperling (1960) knew that our visual sensory capacity should enable us to take in most or all of the 12 items at a single glance. Could it be that sensory memory is so short-lived that while we are reporting some items, others have already faded from sensory memory? Sperling thought of an ingenious method to test this notion. He briefly flashed 12 items to his subjects. Immediately upon turning the pattern off, he sounded a high, medium, or low tone that signaled the subjects to report *only* the top, middle, or bottom row of items. Before they heard the tone, the subjects had no way of knowing which row they would have to report. Yet Sperling found that when the subjects could view the letters for $^{15}\!/_{1000}$ to $\frac{1}{2}$ second, they could report correctly all the items in any row nearly 100 percent of the time. But the items fade from sensory memory so quickly that during the time it takes to report three or four of the items, the other eight or nine have already disappeared. Figure 6.3 shows the steps involved in Sperling's research study.

Sensory memory for sound is similar to that for vision. You have experienced auditory sensory memory when the last few words someone has spoken seem to

Sensory memory holds a visual image, such as a lightning bolt, for a fraction of a second—just long enough for us to perceive a flow of movement.

FIGURE 6.3

Sperling's Study of the Capacity of Sensory Memory

Sperling demonstrated that sensory memory holds more information than subjects are able to report completely because the visual afterimage fades so quickly. Sperling proved that subjects could retain 12 items in sensory memory but only long enough to report 4 items in the designated row. (Based on Sperling, 1960.)

Step 1 — Subjects fixate on a cross on the screen.

Step 2 — Subjects look at array of letters flashed on the screen for $\frac{1}{20}$ of a second.

X B D F	
M P Z G	
L C N H	

High tone (top row)
Medium tone (middle row)
Low tone (bottom row)

Step 3 — A high, medium, or low tone is sounded after $^{15}\!/_{1000}$ to $\frac{1}{2}$ second has elapsed.

Pitch of tone determines which row of letters the subjects will report.

Step 4 — "M, P, Z, G"

Subjects report letters.

echo briefly in your head. Auditory sensory memory lasts about 2 seconds, compared with a fraction of a second for visual sensory memory (Klatzky, 1980).

We have seen that an abundance of information in raw, natural form can be stored briefly in sensory memory. This brief period is just long enough for us to begin to process the sensory stimuli and to select the most important information for further processing in the second memory system—short-term memory.

> **?** *What are the characteristics of short-term memory?*

Short-Term Memory: Short Life, Small Capacity Whatever you are thinking about right now is in your **short-term memory** (STM). We use short-term memory when we carry on a conversation, solve a problem, or look up a telephone number and remember it just long enough to dial it.

Unlike sensory memory, which holds virtually the exact sensory stimulus, short-term memory usually codes information according to sound, that is, in acoustic form (Conrad, 1964). The letter T is coded as the sound "tee," not as the shape T. Short-term memory can also hold visual images and store information in semantic form (according to meaning) as well (Shulman, 1972).

The Capacity of Short-Term Memory Compared to sensory memory, which can hold vast amounts of information briefly, short-term memory has a very limited capacity—about seven (plus or minus two) different items or bits of information at one time. Test the capacity of your short-term memory in the *Try It!*

Try It !

Read aloud the digits in the first row (row a) at a steady rate of about two per second. Then, from memory, write them down on a sheet of paper.

Repeat the process, row by row.

a. 3 8 7 1
b. 9 6 4 7 3
c. 1 8 3 0 5 2
d. 8 0 6 5 9 1 7
e. 5 2 9 7 3 1 2 5
f. 2 7 4 0 1 9 6 8 3
g. 3 9 1 6 5 8 4 5 1 7

How well did you do in the *Try It*? Most people recall about seven items. This is just enough for phone numbers and the ordinary zip codes. (Nine-digit zip codes strain the capacity of most people.) When short-term memory is filled to capacity, **displacement** can occur. In displacement, each new, incoming item pushes out an existing item, which is then forgotten.

One way to overcome the limitation of seven or so bits of information is to use a technique that George A. Miller (1956) calls chunking. Chunking means organizing or grouping separate bits of information into larger units, or chunks. A chunk is an easily identifiable unit such as a syllable, a word, an acronym, or a number (Cowan, 1988). For example, the numbers 5 2 9 7 3 1 2 5 can be chunked 52 97 31 25, leaving the short-term memory with the easier task of dealing with four chunks of information rather than eight separate bits. Complete the *Try It!* on page 209 and see if chunking works for you.

Chunking is a very useful technique for increasing the capacity of short-term memory, but there are limits. Simon (1974) suggests that the larger the chunk, the fewer chunks we can remember.

The Duration of Short-Term Memory Items in short-term memory are lost very quickly, in less than 30 seconds, unless we repeat them over and over

short-term memory: The second stage of memory, which holds about seven (a range of five to nine) items for less than 30 seconds without rehearsal; working memory; the mental workspace we use to keep in mind tasks we are thinking about at any given moment.

displacement: The event that occurs when short-term memory is holding its maximum and each new item entering short-term memory pushes out an existing item.

Read the following letters individually at the rate of about one per second and then see if you can repeat them.

> N-F L-C-B S-U-S
> A-V-C R-F-B I

Did you have difficulty? Probably so, because there are 15 different letters.

Now try this:

> NFL CBS USA VCR FBI

Did you find that five chunks are easier to remember than 15 separate items?

to ourselves, silently or out loud, to retain them. This process is known as **rehearsal**. We rehearse telephone numbers that we have looked up to keep them in short-term memory long enough to dial the number. But short-term memory is easily disrupted. It is so fragile, in fact, that an interruption or a distraction can cause information to be lost in just a few seconds.

How long does short-term memory last if rehearsal is prevented? In a series of early studies, subjects were briefly shown three consonants, such as H, G, and L, and then asked to count backward by threes from a given number (738, 735, 732, and so on) (Peterson & Peterson, 1959). After intervals lasting from 3 to 18 seconds, subjects were instructed to stop their backward counting and recall the three letters. Following a delay of 9 seconds, the subjects could recall an average of only one of the three letters. After 18 seconds, there was practically no recall whatsoever. An 18-second distraction had completely erased the three letters from short-term memory (see Figure 6.4).

Short-Term Memory as Working Memory Allan Baddeley (1990, 1992) suggests that "working memory" is a more fitting term, because short-term memory is used as a kind of mental workspace to keep in mind the tasks we are working on or thinking about at any given moment. You would be using working memory if you mentally multiplied 124×9. Sometimes it is necessary to call up material from long-term memory while we carry out our mental activities (Goldman-Rakic, 1992). When we write a paper, for example, every word must

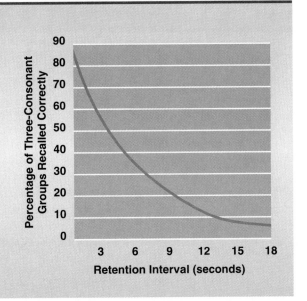

FIGURE 6.4

Results of the Peterson and Peterson Experiment

After briefly viewing groups of three consonants, subjects began counting backward by threes from a given number. The graph shows the percentage of letters subjects could recall after intervals of 3 to 18 seconds. At 18 seconds, recall was nearly zero. (From Peterson & Peterson, 1959.)

rehearsal: The act of purposely repeating information to maintain it in short-term memory or to transfer it to long-term memory.

first be retrieved from long-term memory and then held in short-term or working memory long enough for us to write it down.

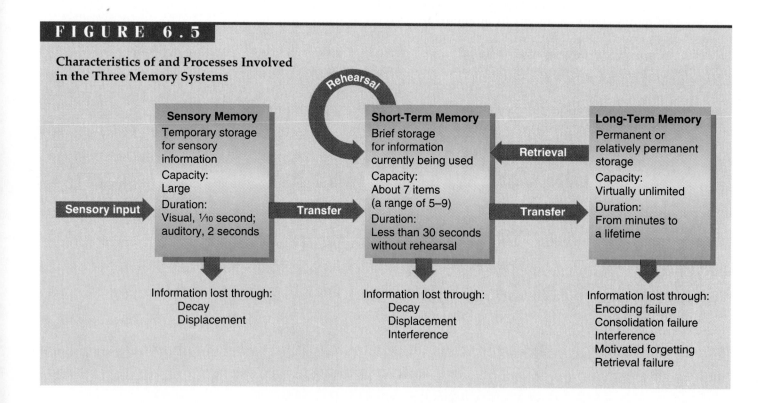

What is long-term memory, and what are its subsystems?

Long-Term Memory: As Long as a Lifetime   Some information from short-term memory makes its way into long-term memory. **Long-term memory** (LTM) is our vast storehouse of permanent or relatively permanent memories. There are no known limits to the storage capacity of long-term memory, and long-term memories last a long time, some of them for a lifetime.

When we talk about memory in everyday conversation, we are usually referring to long-term memory. Long-term memory holds all the knowledge we have accumulated, the skills we have acquired, and the memories of our past experiences. Information in long-term memory is usually stored in semantic form, although visual images, sounds, and odors can be stored there, as well.

But how does this vast store of information make its way from short-term memory into long-term memory? We seem to remember some information with ease, almost automatically, but other kinds of material require great effort. Sometimes, through mere repetition or rehearsal, we are able to transfer information into long-term memory. Your teachers may have used drill to try to cement the multiplication tables and other material in your long-term memory. This rote rehearsal, however, is not necessarily the best way to transfer information to long-term memory (Craik & Watkins, 1973). When you relate new information to the information already safely tucked away in long-term memory and then form multiple associations, you increase the chance that you will be able to retrieve the new information. Figure 6.5 summarizes the three memory systems.

long-term memory: The relatively permanent memory system with a virtually unlimited capacity.

Declarative Memory and Nondeclarative Memory   Some experts believe that there are two main subsystems within long-term memory—declarative memory and nondeclarative memory.

FIGURE 6.5

Characteristics of and Processes Involved in the Three Memory Systems

Rehearsal

Sensory input →

Sensory Memory
Temporary storage for sensory information
Capacity: Large
Duration: Visual, 1/10 second; auditory, 2 seconds

Transfer →

Short-Term Memory
Brief storage for information currently being used
Capacity: About 7 items (a range of 5–9)
Duration: Less than 30 seconds without rehearsal

← Retrieval
Transfer →

Long-Term Memory
Permanent or relatively permanent storage
Capacity: Virtually unlimited
Duration: From minutes to a lifetime

Information lost through:
Decay
Displacement

Information lost through:
Decay
Displacement
Interference

Information lost through:
Encoding failure
Consolidation failure
Interference
Motivated forgetting
Retrieval failure

Nondeclarative memory (also called implicit memory) consists of motor skills, habits, and simple classically conditioned responses (Squire et al., 1993). Motor skills are acquired through repetitive practice and include such things as eating with a fork, riding a bicycle, or driving a car. Although acquired slowly, once learned, these skills become habit, are quite reliable, and can be carried out with little or no conscious effort. For example, you probably use the keyboard on a computer without consciously being able to name the keys in each row from left to right.

Nondeclarative memory encompasses motor skills, such as dance movements, which once learned can be carried out with little or no conscious effort. Declarative memory stores facts, information, and personal life events, such as a trip to a foreign country.

Declarative memory (also called explicit memory) stores facts, information, and personal life events that can be brought to mind verbally or in the form of images and then declared or stated. Declarative memory is accessible to conscious awareness but is often unreliable (Squire et al., 1993). There are two types of declarative memory—episodic memory and semantic memory.

Episodic Memory and Semantic Memory **Episodic memory** is the subpart of declarative memory that contains the memory of events we have experienced personally (Tulving, 1985). It is somewhat like a mental diary, recording the episodes of our lives—the people we have known, the places we have seen, and the personal experiences we have had. According to Tulving (1989):

> The episodic system stores and makes possible subsequent recovery of information about personal experiences from the past. It enables people to travel back in time, as it were, into their personal past, and to become consciously aware of having witnessed or participated in events and happenings at earlier times. (p. 362)

A person would be using episodic memory to make these statements:

"Last summer I went to Florida on my vacation."
"I did the grocery shopping this morning."
"I took French in high school and Spanish in college."

Semantic memory, the second subpart of declarative memory, is our memory for general knowledge and is made up of general facts and information. In other words, semantic memory is our mental dictionary or encyclopedia of stored knowledge:

> George Washington was the first president of the United States.
> Dictionary is spelled d-i-c-t-i-o-n-a-r-y.
> 10 times 10 equals 100.

If you have ever played the board game Trivial Pursuit, you called on semantic memory almost exclusively to answer the questions. As a rule, the semantic facts you have stored are not personally referenced to time and place as episodic memories are. You probably do not remember exactly where and when you learned to spell *dictionary* or that 10×10 equals 100.

Figure 6.6 (on page 212) shows the subsystems of long-term memory.

nondeclarative memory: The subsystem within long-term memory that consists of skills acquired through repetitive practice, habits, and simple classically conditioned responses; also called *implicit memory*.

declarative memory: The subsystem within long-term memory that stores facts, information, and personal life experiences; also called *explicit memory*.

episodic memory (ep-ih-SOD-ik): The subpart of declarative memory that contains memories of personally experienced events.

semantic memory: The subpart of declarative memory that stores general knowledge; our mental encyclopedia or dictionary.

FIGURE 6.6

Subsystems of Long-Term Memory

Nondeclarative memory consists of motor skills acquired through repetitive practice, habits, and simple classically conditioned responses. Declarative memory can be divided into two subparts—episodic memory, which stores memories of personally experienced events, and semantic memory, which stores facts and information.

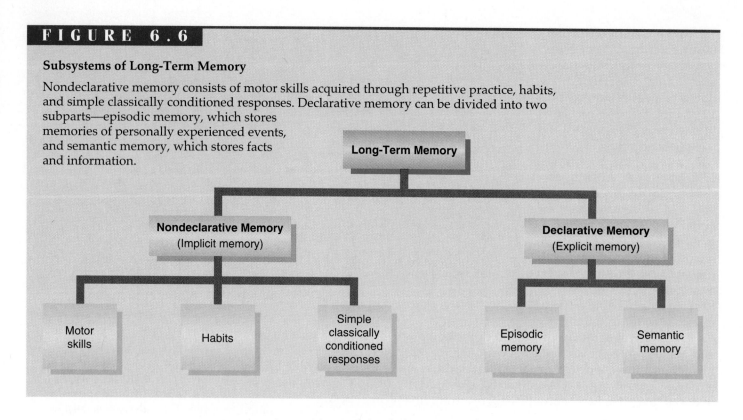

The Levels-of-Processing Model: Another View of Memory

Not all psychologists support the notion of three memory systems. Craik and Lockhart (1972) propose instead a **levels-of-processing model**. They suggest that whether we remember an item for a few seconds or a lifetime depends on how deeply we process the information. With the shallowest levels of processing, we are merely aware of the incoming sensory information. Deeper processing takes place only when we do something more with the information—when we form a relationship, make an association, or attach meaning to a sensory impression.

Craik and Tulving (1975) tested the levels-of-processing model. They had subjects answer *yes* or *no* to questions asked about words just before the words were flashed to them for 1/5 of a second. The subjects had to process the words: (1) visually (was the word in capital letters?); (2) acoustically (does the word rhyme with another particular word?); and (3) semantically (does the word make sense when used in a particular sentence?). Test yourself in the *Try It!*

levels-of-processing model: A single memory system model in which retention depends on how deeply information is processed.

1. Is the word *LARK* in capital letters? ____Yes ____No

2. Does the word *speech* rhyme with *sleet*? ____Yes ____No

3. Would the word *park* make sense in this sentence?

The woman passed a _____ on her way to work.

____Yes ____No

Wait a few minutes and see which words you can recall.

The test required shallow processing for the first question, deeper processing for the second question, and still deeper processing for the third question. Later the subjects were unexpectedly given a retention test to see whether deeper levels of processing would facilitate memory. Craik and Tulving report that the deeper the level of processing, the higher the accuracy rate of memory. But this conclusion would be equally valid for the three-system model.

Memory Check 6.1

1. Transforming information into a form that can be stored in memory is called _____; bringing the material that has been stored to mind is called _____.
   a. encoding; decoding
   b. consolidation; retrieval
   c. consolidation; decoding
   d. encoding; retrieval

2. Match the memory system with the best description of its capacity and the duration of time it holds information:
   ____ 1) sensory memory
   ____ 2) short-term memory
   ____ 3) long-term memory

   a. virtually unlimited capacity; long duration
   b. large capacity; short duration
   c. very limited capacity; short duration

3. Match each example with the appropriate memory system:
   ____ 1) semantic memory
   ____ 2) episodic memory
   ____ 3) nondeclarative memory
   ____ 4) working memory

   a. playing tennis
   b. remembering your high school graduation
   c. deciding what you will do tomorrow
   d. naming the presidents of the United States

4. Which subsystem of long-term memory does not require conscious awareness?
   a. episodic memory
   b. semantic memory
   c. nondeclarative memory
   d. declarative memory

Answers: 1. d 2. 1) b 2) c 3) a 3. 1) d 2) b 3) a 4) c 4. c

Measuring Memory

Three Methods of Measuring Memory

Psychologists have used three main methods to measure memory: recall, recognition, and the relearning method.

What are three methods of measuring retention?

Recall: Memory at Its Best In **recall** we must produce the required information by searching our memory without the help of **retrieval cues**. Trying to remember someone's name, recalling items on a shopping list, memorizing a speech or a poem word for word, and remembering appointments are all recall tasks. Test items such as essay and fill-in-the-blank questions require recall. Try to answer the following question:

The three processes involved in memory are _____, _____, and _____.

To recall, we must remember information "cold." A recall task may be made a little easier if cues are provided to jog our memory. Such cues might consist of providing the first letter of the required words for fill-in-the-blank questions. If you did not recall the three terms in the first question, try again with cued recall:

The three processes involved in memory are e _____, s _____, and r _____.

Sometimes serial recall is required; that is, information must be recalled in a specific order. This is the way you learned your ABCs, memorized poems, and

recall: A measure of retention that requires one to remember material with few or no retrieval cues, as in an essay test.

retrieval cue: Any stimulus or bit of information that aids in the retrieval of particular information from long-term memory.

learned any sequences that had to be carried out in a certain order. Often serial recall is easier than free recall—recalling the items in any order—because in serial recall, each letter, word, or task may serve as a cue for the one that follows.

We may fail to recall information in a memory task even if we are given many different retrieval cues, but this does not necessarily mean that the information is not in long-term memory. We still might be able to remember if a recognition test were used to measure memory.

Recognition: I've Seen That Before **Recognition** is exactly what the name implies. We simply recognize something as familiar—a face, a name, a taste, a melody. Multiple-choice, matching, and true/false questions are examples of recognition test items. Answer the following question:

Which of the following is *not* one of the processes involved in memory?

a. encoding   b. assimilation   c. storage   d. retrieval

Was this recognition question easier than the recall version? The main difference between recall and recognition is that a recognition task does not require you to supply the information but only to recognize it when you see it. The correct answer is included along with the other items in a recognition question.

Are you better at remembering faces than names? Have you ever wondered why? Actually the task involves recognition as opposed to recall. We must recall the name but merely recognize the face; and, as we have seen, recognition is easier than recall. Remembering faces would be considerably more difficult if we had to recall each feature of a person's face rather than simply recognize it as familiar. But are we better at recognizing faces than names? No. When recognition is the memory task, there is no difference in our ability to recognize faces and names (Faw, 1990).

The Relearning Method: Learning Is Faster the Second Time Around
There is yet another way to measure memory that is even more sensitive than recognition. With the **relearning method** (the savings method), retention is expressed as the percentage of time saved when material is relearned compared with the time required to learn the material originally. Suppose it took you 40 minutes to memorize a list of words, and 1 month later you were tested, using recall or recognition. If you could not recall or recognize a single word, would this mean that you had absolutely no memory of anything on the test? Or could it mean that the recall and the recognition methods of testing were not sensitive enough to pick up what little information you may have stored? How could we measure a remnant of this former learning? Using the relearning method, we could time how long it would take you to relearn the list of words. If it took 20 minutes to relearn the list, this would represent a 50-percent savings over the original learning time of 40 minutes. The percentage of time saved—the **savings score**—reflects how much material remains in long-term memory.

Often parents wonder if the time they spend reading to their young children or exposing them to good music has any lasting influence. Do some traces of such early exposure remain? Many years ago, H. E. Burtt (1932) carried out a unique relearning experiment on his 15-month-old son Benjamin to study this question. Every day Burtt read to his son three passages from Sophocles' *Oedipus Tyrannus* in the original Greek. He would repeat the same three passages for 3 months, and then read three new passages for the next 3 months. This procedure continued until Benjamin was 3 years old. Nothing more was done for 5 years until the boy reached the age of 8. Then Burtt tested Benjamin by having him memorize some of the passages read to him originally and some similar passages that he had never heard before. It took Benjamin 27 percent fewer trials to memorize the

recognition: A measure of retention that requires one to identify material as familiar, or as having been encountered before.

relearning method: Measuring retention in terms of the percentage of time or learning trials saved in relearning material compared with the time required to learn it originally; also called the savings method.

savings score: The percentage of time or learning trials saved in relearning material over the amount of time or number of learning trials required for the original learning.

original passages than the new passages. This 27 percent savings score suggests that a considerable amount of information remained in his memory for an extended period of time—information that could not have been detected through recall or recognition tests. Furthermore, the study suggests that even information we do not understand can be stored in memory. Between 15 months and 3 years of age, young Benjamin did not speak or understand Greek, yet much of the information remained in his memory for years.

Research strongly indicates that the relearning method is superior to recognition and recall in measuring fully what we have learned (Groninger & Groninger, 1980; Nelson, 1978). College students demonstrate this method each semester when they study for comprehensive final exams. Relearning material for the final exams takes less time than it took to learn the material originally.

Hermann Ebbinghaus and the First Experimental Studies on Learning and Memory

> **?** *What was Ebbinghaus's major contribution to psychology?*

Hermann Ebbinghaus (1850–1909) conducted the first experimental studies on learning and memory. In 1885 he published his findings in a small but important volume entitled simply *Memory*. Ebbinghaus realized that some materials are easier than others to understand and remember. To study memory objectively, he was faced with the task of selecting materials that would all be equally difficult to memorize. So he invented the **nonsense syllable**—a consonant-vowel-consonant combination that is not an actual word. Examples are LEJ, XIZ, LUK, and ZOH. The use of nonsense syllables largely accomplished Ebbinghaus's goal. But did you notice that some of the syllables sound more like actual words than others and would, therefore, be easier to remember?

Ebbinghaus (1885/1964) conducted his studies on memory using 2,300 nonsense syllables as his material and himself as his only subject. He carried out all his experiments at about the same time of day in the same surroundings, eliminating all possible distractions. Ebbinghaus memorized lists of nonsense syllables by repeating them over and over at a constant rate of 2.5 syllables per second, marking time with a metronome or a ticking watch. He repeated a list until he could recall it twice without error, a point that he called *mastery*.

Ebbinghaus recorded the amount of time or the number of trials it took to memorize his lists to mastery. Then, after different periods of time had passed and forgetting had occurred, he recorded the amount of time or number of trials needed to relearn the same list to mastery. Ebbinghaus compared the time or trials required for relearning with those of the original learning and then computed the percentage of time saved—the savings score. The percentage of savings represented the percentage of the original learning that remained in memory.

Ebbinghaus learned and relearned over 1,200 lists of nonsense syllables to discover how rapidly forgetting occurs (Slamecka, 1985). His famous curve of forgetting, shown in Figure 6.7 (on page 216), consists of savings scores at various time intervals after the original learning. The curve of forgetting shows that the largest amount of forgetting occurs very quickly, then gradually tapers off. If Ebbinghaus retained information as long as a day or two, very little more would be forgotten even a month later. But remember, this curve of forgetting applies to nonsense syllables. Meaningful material is usually forgotten more slowly.

What Ebbinghaus learned about the rate of forgetting is relevant for all of us. Do you, like most students, cram before a big exam? If so, don't assume that everything you memorize on Monday can be held intact until Tuesday. So much forgetting occurs within the first 24 hours that it is wise to spend at least some time reviewing the material on the day of the test. The less meaningful the material is to you, the more you will forget and the more necessary a review will be.

nonsense syllable: A consonant-vowel-consonant combination that does not spell a word; used to control for the meaningfulness of the material.

FIGURE 6.7

Ebbinghaus's Curve of Forgetting

After memorizing lists of nonsense syllables similar to those at left, Ebbinghaus measured his retention after varying intervals of time using the relearning method. Forgetting was most rapid at first, as shown by his retention of only 58 percent after 20 minutes and 44 percent after 1 hour. Then the rate of forgetting tapered off, with a retention of 34 percent after 1 day, 25 percent after 6 days, and 21 percent after 31 days. (Data from Ebbinghaus, 1913.)

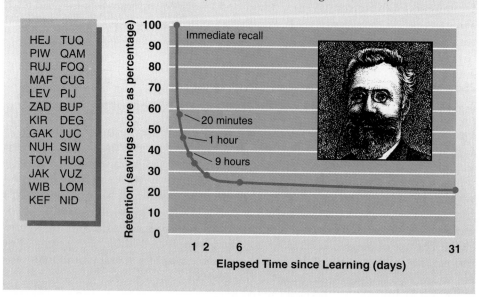

Memory Check 6.2

1. Which of the following methods is the most sensitive way of measuring retention and can detect learning when other methods cannot?
   - a. recall
   - b. recognition
   - c. relearning
   - d. retrieval

2. Who invented the nonsense syllable, conceived the relearning method for testing retention, and plotted the curve of forgetting?
   - a. George Sperling
   - b. H. E. Burtt
   - c. Frederick Bartlett
   - d. Hermann Ebbinghaus

3. The curve of forgetting shows that memory loss:
   - a. occurs most rapidly at first and then levels off to a slow decline.
   - b. begins to occur about 3 to 4 hours after learning.
   - c. occurs at a fairly steady rate over a month's time.
   - d. occurs slowly at first and increases steadily over a month's time.

4. Match all examples with the corresponding method of measuring retention:
   - ___ 1) identifying a suspect in a lineup
   - ___ 2) answering a fill-in-the-blank question on a test
   - ___ 3) having to study less for a comprehensive final exam than for the sum of the previous exams
   - ___ 4) answering questions on this Memory Check
   - ___ 5) reciting one's lines in a play

   - a. recognition
   - b. relearning
   - c. recall

Answers: 1. c 2. d 3. a 4. 1) a 2) c 3) b 4) a 5) c

Forgetting

Patient: Doctor, you've got to help me. I'm sure I'm losing my memory. I hear something one minute and forget it the next. I don't know what to do!
Doctor: When did you first notice this?
Patient: Notice what?

Most of us think of forgetting as a problem to be overcome, but forgetting is not all bad. Wouldn't it be depressing if you were condemned to remember in stark detail all the bad things that ever happened to you?

The Causes of Forgetting

There are many reasons why we fail to remember. Among them are encoding failure, consolidation failure, decay, interference, motivated forgetting, and retrieval failure.

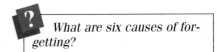
What are six causes of forgetting?

Encoding Failure: Never Entering Long-Term Memory
There is a distinction between forgetting and not being able to remember. Forgetting is the inability to recall something that you could recall previously. But often when we say we cannot remember, we have not actually forgotten. Our inability to remember may be a result of **encoding failure**—the information never entered our long-term memory in the first place. Of the many things we encounter every day, it is sometimes surprising how little we actually encode. Can you recall accurately, or even recognize, something you have seen thousands of times before? Read the *Try It!* to find out.

On a sheet of paper, draw a sketch of a U.S. penny from memory using recall. In your drawing, show the direction in which President Lincoln's image is facing and the location of the date, and include all the words on the "heads" side of the penny. Or try the easier recognition task and see if you can recognize the real penny in the drawings below.

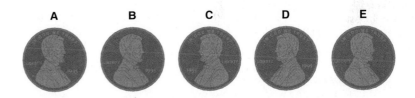

In your lifetime you have seen thousands of pennies, but unless you are a coin collector, you probably have not encoded the details of a penny. If you did poorly on this exercise, you have plenty of company. After studying a large group of subjects, Nickerson and Adams (1979) reported that few people could reproduce a penny from recall. In fact, only a handful of subjects could even recognize a drawing of a real penny when it was presented along with incorrect drawings. (The correct penny is labeled A in the *Try It!*)

In preparing for tests, do you usually assume a passive role? Do you merely read and reread your textbook and notes and assume that this process will eventually result in learning? If you don't test yourself by reciting the material, you may find that you have been the unwitting victim of encoding failure.

encoding failure: A cause of forgetting resulting from material never having been put into long-term memory.

consolidation failure: Any disruption in the consolidation process that prevents a permanent memory from forming.

retrograde amnesia (RET-ro-grade): A loss of memory for events occurring for a period of time preceding a brain trauma that caused a loss of consciousness.

decay theory: A theory of forgetting that holds that the memory trace, if not used, disappears with the passage of time.

What is interference, and how can it be minimized?

Consolidation Failure: Failing to Form a Permanent Memory Consolidation is the process by which a permanent memory is formed. When a disruption in this process occurs, a permanent memory usually does not form. **Consolidation failure** can result from anything that causes a person to lose consciousness—a car accident, a blow to the head, a grand mal seizure, or an electroconvulsive shock treatment given for severe depression. Memory loss of the experiences that occurred shortly before the loss of consciousness is called **retrograde amnesia** (Stern, 1981).

Decay: Fading Away with Time **Decay theory**, probably the oldest theory of forgetting, assumes that memories, if not used, fade with time and ultimately disappear entirely. The term *decay* implies a physiological change in the neural trace that recorded the experience. According to this theory, the neural trace may decay or fade within seconds, days, or much longer periods of time.

Today most psychologists accept the notion of decay, or fading of the memory trace, as a cause of forgetting in sensory and short-term memory but not in long-term memory. There does not appear to be a gradual, inevitable decay of the long-term memory trace. Harry Bahrick and others (1975) found that after 35 years subjects could recognize 90 percent of their high school classmates' names and photographs, the same percentage as recent graduates.

Interference: The Major Cause of Forgetting A major cause of forgetting that affects us every day is **interference**. Whenever we try to recall any given memory, two types of interference can hinder our efforts. Information or associations stored either before or after an item can interfere with our ability to remember it (see Figure 6.8). Interference can reach either forward or backward in time to affect memory. It gets us coming and going. Also, the more similar the interfering associations are to what we are trying to recall, the more trouble we have recalling the information (Underwood, 1964).

Proactive Interference Laura's romance with her new boyfriend, Todd, got off to a bad start when she accidentally called him Dave, her former boy-

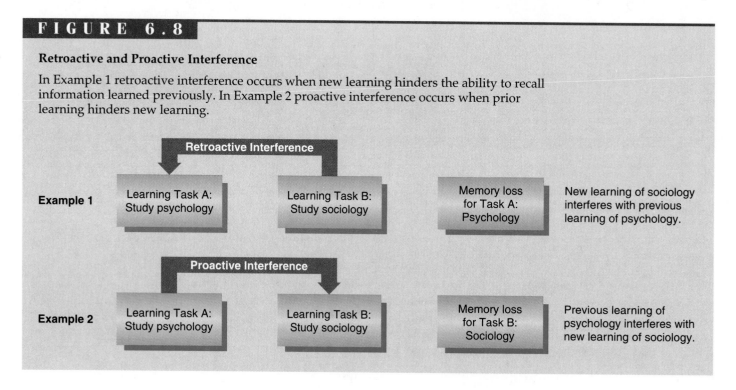

FIGURE 6.8

Retroactive and Proactive Interference

In Example 1 retroactive interference occurs when new learning hinders the ability to recall information learned previously. In Example 2 proactive interference occurs when prior learning hinders new learning.

Retroactive Interference

Example 1

Learning Task A: Study psychology → Learning Task B: Study sociology → Memory loss for Task A: Psychology → New learning of sociology interferes with previous learning of psychology.

Proactive Interference

Example 2

Learning Task A: Study psychology → Learning Task B: Study sociology → Memory loss for Task B: Sociology → Previous learning of psychology interferes with new learning of sociology.

friend's name. How many checks written early in January do you suppose have the wrong year? Such mistakes result from proactive interference. Proactive interference occurs when information or experiences already stored in long-term memory hinder our ability to remember newer information (Underwood, 1957). For example, when you drive a new car, it may take a while to feel comfortable with the new arrangement of the dashboard. Your earlier habits of responding to the old car's dashboard may interfere with your driving at first. This type of proactive interference is called negative transfer. One explanation for interference is the competition between old and new responses (Bower et al., 1994).

Retroactive Interference New learning or experience that interferes with our ability to remember information previously stored is called retroactive interference. The more similar the new learning or experience is to the previous learning, the more interference there is.

What can we do to minimize interference? You may be surprised to learn that of all the activities we engage in, sleep interferes with previous learning the least. In one of the earliest studies of the effect of interference on memory, four subjects memorized a list of nonsense syllables (Jenkins & Dallenbach, 1924). Two subjects memorized the list to mastery late in the evening and immediately went to bed. Two other subjects memorized the list to mastery earlier in the day and then went about their normal waking activities. The researchers compared the retention of the first two subjects after 1, 2, 4, and 8 hours of sleep with that of the second two subjects after 1, 2, 4, and 8 hours of being awake. They found that retention scores were much higher when sleep followed learning. Subjects who stayed awake 8 hours recalled about 10 percent of the nonsense syllables, while subjects who slept for 8 hours remembered 50 to 60 percent of the material.

What can you do to lessen the effects of retroactive interference on memory?

- When possible, study before going to sleep.
- If you can't study before going to sleep, at least review at that time the material you need to remember.
- Try not to study similar subjects back-to-back. Better yet, after studying one subject, take a short break before beginning the next subject.
- Schedule your classes so that courses with similar subject matter do not follow each other.

We have discussed ways to avoid forgetting, but there are occasions when we may need to avoid remembering—times when we want to forget.

Motivated Forgetting: Don't Remind Me Victims of rape or physical abuse, war veterans, and survivors of airplane crashes or earthquakes all have had terrifying experiences that may haunt them for years. These victims are certainly motivated to forget their traumatic experiences, but even people who have not suffered any trauma use **motivated forgetting** to protect themselves from experiences that are painful, frightening, or otherwise unpleasant.

With one form of motivated forgetting, suppression, a person makes a conscious, active attempt to put a painful, disturbing, anxiety- or guilt-provoking memory out of mind, but the person is still aware that the painful event occurred. With another type of motivated forgetting, **repression**, unpleasant memories are literally removed from consciousness, and the person is no longer aware that the unpleasant event ever occurred (Freud, 1922). People who have **amnesia** (memory loss) that is not due to loss of consciousness or brain damage have actually repressed the events they no longer remember. Motivated forgetting is probably used by more people than any other method to deal with unpleasant memories. It seems to be a natural human tendency to forget the unpleasant circumstances of life and to remember the pleasant ones (Linton, 1979; Meltzer, 1930).

interference: Memory loss that occurs because information or associations stored either before or after a given memory hinder our ability to remember it.

motivated forgetting: Forgetting through suppression or repression in order to protect oneself from material that is too painful, anxiety- or guilt-producing, or otherwise unpleasant.

repression: Removing from one's consciousness disturbing, guilt-provoking, or otherwise unpleasant memories so that one is no longer aware a painful event occurred.

amnesia: A partial or complete loss of memory resulting from brain trauma or psychological trauma.

Retrieval Failure: Misplaced Memories How many times have these experiences happened to you? You are with a friend when you meet an acquaintance, but you can't introduce the two because you cannot recall the name of your acquaintance. Or, while taking a test, you can't remember the answer to a question that you are sure you know. Often we are certain that we know something, but we are not able to retrieve the information when we need it. This type of forgetting is called retrieval failure.

Endel Tulving (1974) claims that much of what we call forgetting is really our inability to locate the information we seek. The information is in our long-term memory, but we cannot retrieve it. In his experiments, Tulving found that subjects could recall a large number of items they seemed to have forgotten if he provided retrieval cues to jog their memory. For example, odors often provide potent reminders of experiences from the past, and they can serve as retrieval cues for information learned when certain odors were present (Schab, 1990).

A common retrieval failure experience is known as the tip-of-the-tongue phenomenon (TOT) (Brown & McNeil, 1966). Surely you have experienced trying to recall a name, a word, or some other bit of information, knowing what you were searching for almost as well as your own name. You were on the verge of recalling the word or name, perhaps aware of the number of syllables and the beginning or ending letter of the word. It was on the tip of your tongue, but it just wouldn't quite come out.

Prospective Forgetting: Forgetting to Remember

Do you have trouble remembering appointments? Do you forget to mail birthday cards on time, pick up your clothes at the cleaners, pay your bills, or water your plants? If you do, you are not alone. In a study of everyday forgetting, Terry (1988) had 50 subjects keep a diary of the instances of forgetting that occurred each day. Of the 751 recorded instances of forgetting, most did not involve forgetting names, facts, or other information already known. Most instances involved prospective forgetting—forgetting to carry out some action.

Memory Check 6.3

1. Match the example with the appropriate cause of forgetting:

   ____ 1) encoding failure
   ____ 2) consolidation failure
   ____ 3) retrieval failure
   ____ 4) repression
   ____ 5) interference

   a. failing to remember the answer on a test until after you turn the test in
   b. forgetting a humiliating childhood experience
   c. not being able to describe the back of a dollar bill
   d. calling a friend by another's name
   e. waking up in the hospital and not remembering you had an automobile accident

2. To minimize interference, it is best to follow learning with:
   a. rest.
   b. recreation.
   c. sleep.
   d. unrelated study.

3. In older people, decay is the main cause of forgetting in long-term memory. (true/false)

4. According to the text, the major cause of forgetting is interference. (true/false)

Answers: 1. 1) c 2) e 3) a 4) b 5) d 2. c 3. false 4. true

The Nature of Remembering and Forgetting

Memory as a Permanent Record: The Videocassette Recorder Analogy

For hundreds of years people have speculated about the nature of memory. Aristotle suggested that the senses imprint memories in the brain like signet rings stamping impressions in wax. Sigmund Freud believed that all memories are permanently preserved, with some lying deep in the unconscious. Wilder Penfield (1969), a Canadian neurosurgeon, claimed that experiences leave a "permanent imprint on the brain . . . as though a tape recorder had been receiving it all" (p. 165). What would lead him to such a conclusion?

Penfield (1975) performed over 1,100 operations on patients with epilepsy. He found that when parts of the temporal lobes were stimulated with an electrical probe, 3.5 percent of patients reported flashback experiences, as though they were actually reliving parts of their past. After reviewing Penfield's findings, other researchers offered different explanations for his patients' responses. Neisser (1967) suggests that the experiences patients reported were "comparable to the content of dreams," rather than the recall of actual experiences (p. 169).

When people recall an event, such as a car accident, they are actually reconstructing it from memory by piecing together bits of information that may or may not be totally accurate.

Memory as a Reconstruction: Partly Fact and Partly Fiction

Other than Penfield's work, there is no research to suggest that memory works like a videocassette recorder, capturing every part of an experience exactly as it happens. Normally what we recall is not an exact replica of an event, according to Elizabeth Loftus, a leading memory researcher. Rather, it is a **reconstruction**—a memory that is pieced together from a few highlights, using information that may or may not be accurate (Loftus & Loftus, 1980). Recall is, even for those of us with the most accurate memories, partly truth and partly fiction. We supply what we *think* are facts to flesh out or complete those fragments of our experiences that we do recall accurately. This was the finding of another pioneer in memory research, Englishman Sir Frederick Bartlett.

? *What is meant by the statement "Memory is reconstructive in nature"?*

Sir Frederick Bartlett (1886–1969) Ebbinghaus explored memory by memorizing nonsense syllables under rigidly controlled experimental conditions. In contrast, Sir Frederick Bartlett studied memory using rich and meaningful material learned and remembered under more lifelike conditions. Bartlett (1932) gave his subjects stories to read and drawings to study, and at varying time intervals he had the subjects reproduce the original material. He found that accurate reports were rare. His subjects seemed to reconstruct the material they had learned, rather than actually remember it. They recreated the stories, making them shorter and more consistent with their own individual viewpoints. The subjects rationalized puzzling features of the stories to fit their own expectations; and they often changed details, substituting more familiar objects or events instead. Errors in memory increased with time, and Bartlett's subjects were not aware that they had partly remembered and partly invented. Ironically, the parts his subjects had created were often the very parts that they most adamantly claimed to have remembered.

? *What is Bartlett's contribution to our understanding of memory?*

reconstruction: A memory that is not an exact replica of an event but has been pieced together from a few highlights using information that may or may not be accurate.

Bartlett concluded that we systematically distort the facts and the circumstances of our experiences, and that we do not simply remember new experiences as isolated events. Rather, information already stored in long-term memory exerts a strong influence on how we remember new information and experiences. As Bartlett (1932) put it, "The past is being continually remade, reconstructed in the interest of the present" (p. 309).

? *What are schemas, and how do they affect memory?*

Schemas and Memory   Bartlett suggested that his subjects' inaccuracies in memory reflected their **schemas**—the integrated frameworks of knowledge and assumptions they had about people, objects, and events. Schemas aid us in processing large amounts of material, because they provide frameworks into which we can incorporate new information and experience. Schemas also provide association cues that can help us in retrieval.

Once formed, our schemas influence what we notice and how we encode and recall information. When we encounter new information or have a new experience related to an existing schema, we try to make it fit or be consistent with that schema. To accomplish this, we may have to distort some aspects of the information and ignore or forget other aspects. Some of the distorting and ignoring occurs as the material is being encoded; more can occur when we try to remember or reconstruct the original experience (Brewer & Nakamura, 1984).

Distortion in Memory   When we reconstruct our memories, we do not purposely try to distort the actual experience—unless, of course, we are lying. But all of us tend to omit some facts that actually occurred and to supply other details from our own imaginations. Distortion occurs when we alter the memory of an event or of our experience in order to fit our beliefs, expectations, logic, or prejudices.

The tendency toward systematic distortion of actual events has been proven many times. Demonstrate distortion in memory in the *Try It!*

Try It!   Read this list of words aloud at a rate of about one word per second. Then close your book and write down all the words you can remember.

| bed | awake | dream | comfort | eat | snore |
| rest | tired | wake | sound | night | slumber |

Now check your list. Did you "remember" the word *sleep*? Many people do, even though it is not one of the words on the list (Deese, 1959).

schemas: The integrated frameworks of knowledge and assumptions we have about people, objects, and events, which affect how we encode and recall information.

The *Try It!* shows that we are very likely to alter or distort what we see or hear to make it fit with what we believe *should* be true. All the words on the list are related to sleep, so it seems logical that *sleep* should be one of the words.

On the one hand, our tendency to distort makes our world more understandable and enables us to organize our experiences into our existing systems of beliefs and expectations. On the other hand, this tendency is often responsible for gross inaccuracies in what we remember. The most dramatic examples of systematic distortion often occur in eyewitness testimony.

Eyewitness Testimony: Is It Accurate?

When people say, "I ought to know—I saw it with my own eyes," we might accept their statement almost without question. After all, seeing is believing. Or is it?

Traditionally, eyewitness testimony has been viewed as reliable by the legal system in the United States and elsewhere (Brigham & Wolfskeil, 1983). Recall from our opening story Hen Van Nguyen and Father Pagano, both victims of faulty eyewitness identification. Are their cases just two isolated incidents? According to Elizabeth Loftus (1993a), there are a staggering number of wrongful convictions in the United States each year.

Studies on the accuracy of human memory suggest that eyewitness testimony is highly subject to error, and that it should always be viewed with caution (Loftus, 1979). Nevertheless, it does play a vital role in our justice system. Says Loftus (1984), "We can't afford to exclude it legally or ignore it as jurors. Sometimes, as in cases of rape, it is the only evidence available, and it is often correct" (p. 24).

Fortunately, eyewitness mistakes can be minimized. Eyewitnesses to crimes typically identify suspects from a lineup. If shown photographs of a suspect before viewing the lineup, eyewitnesses may mistakenly identify that suspect in the lineup because the person looks familiar. The familiarity may result from the mug shot, not from seeing the suspect at the scene of the crime.

The composition of the lineup is also important. Other subjects in a lineup must resemble the suspect in age, body build, and certainly in race. Even then, if the lineup does not contain the guilty party, eyewitnesses may identify the person who most resembles the perpetrator (Gonzalez et al., 1993). Eyewitnesses are less likely to make errors if a sequential lineup is used, that is, if the members of the lineup are viewed one after the other, rather than simultaneously (Loftus, 1993a). Some police officers and researchers prefer a "showup"—presenting only one suspect and having the witness indicate whether that person is the perpetrator. There are fewer misidentifications with a showup, but also more failures in making positive identifications (Wells, 1993).

Eyewitnesses are more likely to identify the wrong person if the person is of a different race. According to Egeth (1993), misidentifications are approximately 15 percent higher in cross-race than in same-race identifications. Misidentification is also somewhat more likely to occur when a weapon is used in a crime. The witnesses may pay more attention to the weapon than to the physical characteristics of the criminal (Ellis, 1984; Steblay, 1992).

Even questioning witnesses after a crime can influence what they later remember. Leading questions can change substantially a witness's memory of the event (Loftus, 1975). Misleading information supplied after the event can result in erroneous recollections of the actual event, a phenomenon known as the misinformation effect (Kroll et al., 1988; Loftus & Hoffman, 1989).

Witnessing a crime is highly stressful. How does stress affect eyewitness accuracy? Research suggests that eyewitnesses do tend to remember the central, critical details of the event even though their arousal is high, but the memory of peripheral details suffers (Burke et al., 1992; Christianson, 1992).

? *What conditions reduce the reliability of eyewitness testimony?*

Studies on the accuracy of human memory suggest that eyewitness testimony is highly subject to error and should be weighed critically.

Eyewitness identification poses another problem. There is little relationship between the confidence eyewitnesses have in their testimony and the accuracy of the testimony (Loftus, 1993a). When witnesses make incorrect identifications with great certainty, they can be highly persuasive to judges and jurors alike. "A false eyewitness identification can create a real-life nightmare for the identified person, friends, and family members. . . . False identifications also mean that the actual culprit remains at large—a double injustice" (Wells, 1993, p. 568).

Hypnosis for Eyewitnesses   Most of us have heard accounts of how eyewitnesses, when hypnotized, recalled important information about a crime. But research suggests that under controlled laboratory conditions, people do not show improved memory under hypnosis (Buckhout et al., 1981). Hypnotized subjects supply more information and are more confident of their recollections, but they supply more inaccurate information as well (Dywan & Bowers, 1983; Nogrady et al., 1985). Because subjects are much more confident of their memories after hypnosis, they are very convincing witnesses. Some critics of hypnosis oppose using it in court to aid eyewitness testimony, but believe that it can be a valuable investigative tool during the course of criminal investigations.

Recovering Repressed Memories: A Controversy

Since the late 1980s, thousands of people, most of them adult women under the age of 50, have come forward claiming to have been sexually abused as children. Given the fact that childhood sexual abuse is widespread and underreported, a growing number of claims of sexual abuse, including incest, should not be surprising. But many of these new claims are surprising because the accusers maintain that they had repressed all memory of the abuse until they underwent therapy or read a self-help book for survivors of childhood sexual abuse. Could people endure repeated episodes of childhood sexual abuse for years, selectively repress all memory of their abuse, and then recover the repressed memories as adults? Many psychologists are doubtful, but a growing number of therapists specialize in helping people recover repressed memories.

A best-selling book, *The Courage to Heal*, by Ellen Bass and Laura Davis, was published in 1988 as a self-help book for survivors of childhood sexual abuse. This book has become the "bible" for sex abuse victims and the leading "textbook" for some therapists who specialize in treating them. Bass and Davis not only seek to help survivors who remember having suffered sexual abuse; they reach out as well to other people who have no memory of any sexual abuse and try to help them determine whether they might have been abused. They suggest that "if you are unable to remember any specific instances . . . but still have a feeling that something abusive happened to you, it probably did" (p. 21). They offer a definite conclusion: "If you think you were abused and your life shows the symptoms, then you were" (p. 22). And they free potential victims of sexual abuse from the responsibility of establishing any proof: "You are not responsible for proving that you were abused" (p. 37). Other similar self-help books suggest that almost anything can be interpreted as a symptom of early sexual abuse—depression, loss of appetite, eating disorders, anxiety, sexual problems, problems with intimacy, phobias, low self-

> **?** *Does hypnosis improve the memory of eyewitnesses?*

As the debate over the existence of repressed memories continues, some—like Gary Ramona (left)—have fought back. Ramona went to court to accuse his daughter's therapist of using improper suggestions and drugs to implant false memories of molestation.

esteem, lack of motivation, feeling bad, feeling ashamed or powerless, and feeling the need to be perfect.

The critics of repressed-memory therapy claim that problems shown to have multiple causes, such as depression, eating disorders, sexual dysfunction, and others, should not be cited as symptoms to support the probability of abuse (Wakefield & Underwager, 1992). Also troubling is the possibility that patients looking for a cause of their problems might be inclined to accept an explanation so confidently put forth by the therapist. According to Loftus (1993b), "The therapist convinces the patient with no memories that abuse is likely, and the patient obligingly uses reconstructive strategies to generate memories that would support that conviction" (p. 528). Such therapists believe, however, that healing hinges on their patient's being able to recover these repressed memories.

Critics are especially skeptical of recovered memories of events that occurred in the first few years of life. According to Loftus (1994), "Not a single piece of empirical work in human memory provides support for the idea that adults have concrete episodic memories of events from the first years of their lives" (p. 443). In fact, most people have few if any memories from the second and third years of life, in part because the hippocampus, vital in the formation of declarative memories, is not fully developed. And neither are the areas of the cortex where memories are stored (Squire et al., 1993). Furthermore, young children, who are still limited in language ability, do not store memories in the categories that would be accessible to them later in life. The relative inability of older children and adults to recall events from the first few years of life is referred to as **infantile amnesia**.

Finally, critics charge that repressed memories of sexual abuse are suspect because they are usually recovered using hypnosis. And, as you have learned, hypnosis does *not* improve the accuracy of memory, only the confidence that what one remembers is accurate. Are recovered memories generally accurate?

An increasing number of former patients who recovered what they believed to be repressed memories of sexual abuse now deny that any abuse occurred (Jaroff, 1993). False accusations are apparently widespread, because a group of accused parents who deny the accusations against them have formed an organization known as the False Memory Syndrome (FMS) Foundation (Gutheil, 1993).

Strong evidence suggests that the memory of an event is not like a photograph or recording that sits awaiting retrieval, capable of being recalled intact. Rather, memory, like other brain functions, is fluid, plastic, and malleable. Even at its best, memory is a mixture of accurate recall and fragments of our own imagination.

Unusual Memory Phenomena

Flashbulb Memories: Extremely Vivid Memories

Most people over age 45 remember the assassination of President John F. Kennedy, and many claim to have unusually vivid memories of exactly when and where they received the news of the assassination. This type of extremely vivid memory is called a **flashbulb memory** (Bohannon, 1988). Brown and Kulik (1977) suggest that a flashbulb memory is formed when a person learns of an event that is very surprising, shocking, and highly emotional. You might have a flashbulb memory of when you received the news of the death or the serious injury of a close family member or a friend.

infantile amnesia: The relative inability of older children and adults to recall events from the first few years of life.

flashbulb memory: An extremely vivid memory of the conditions surrounding one's first hearing the news of a surprising, shocking, or highly emotional event.

A flashbulb memory is formed when a person learns of an event that is shocking and highly emotional, such as the bombing of the federal building in Oklahoma City. Where were you when you first heard the news of the bombing?

Pillemer (1990) argues that flashbulb memories do not constitute a different type of memory altogether. Rather, he suggests that all memories can vary on the dimensions of emotion, consequentiality (the importance of the consequences of the event), and rehearsal (how often people think or talk about the event afterwards). Flashbulb memories rank high in all three dimensions and thus are extremely memorable. Therefore, flashbulb memories should be the most accurate of any memories. But are they infallible? Hardly.

Several studies suggest that flashbulb memories are not as accurate as people believe them to be. Neisser and Harsch (1992) questioned university freshmen about the Challenger disaster the following morning. When the same students were questioned again 3 years later, one-third gave accounts that differed markedly from those given initially, even though they were extremely confident of their recollections. Weaver (1993) questioned students following the bombing of Iraq that signaled the beginning of the Gulf War and again 1 year later. He found that the accuracy of the students' accounts decreased, although confidence in their recollections had not.

Eidetic Imagery: Almost Like "Photographic Memory" Have you ever wished that you had a photographic memory? Perhaps you have heard of someone who is able to read a page in a book and recall it word for word. More than likely, that person has developed an enviable memory by learning and applying principles of memory improvement. Psychologists doubt that there are more than a few rare cases of a truly photographic memory that captures all the details of an experience and retains them perfectly. But some studies do show that about 5 percent of children apparently have something akin to photographic memory that psychologists call eidetic imagery (Haber, 1980). **Eidetic imagery** is the ability to retain the image of a visual stimulus, such as a picture, for several minutes after it has been removed from view and to use this retained image to answer questions about the visual stimulus (see Figure 6.9).

eidetic imagery (eye-DET-ik): The ability to retain the image of a visual stimulus several minutes after it has been removed from view.

FIGURE 6.9

Test for Eidetic Imagery

Researchers test children for eidetic imagery by having them stare for 30 seconds at a picture like the one in (a). A few minutes later, the drawing in (b) is shown to the children, who are asked to report what they see. Those with eidetic imagery usually claim that they see a face and describe the composite sketch in (c). The face can be perceived only if the subject retains the image of the first picture and fuses it with the middle drawing. (From Haber, 1980.)

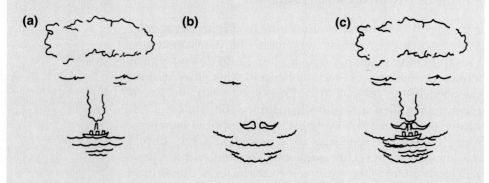

Children with eidetic imagery generally have no better long-term memory than others their age. And virtually all children with eidetic imagery lose it before adulthood. One exceptional case, however, is Elizabeth, a teacher and a skilled artist. She can project on her canvas an exact duplicate of a remembered scene in all its rich detail. Just as remarkable is her ability to retain visual images of words. "Years after having read a poem in a foreign language, she can fetch back an image of the printed page and copy the poem from the bottom line to the top line as fast as she can write" (Stromeyer, 1970, p. 77).

Some impressive memory abilities develop because of cultural needs, as the World of Psychology section describes.

World of Psychology

Memory and Culture

Sir Frederick Bartlett (1932) believed that memory operates within a social or cultural context and cannot be understood as a pure process. He stated that "both the manner and matter of recall are often predominantly determined by social influences" (p. 244).

Studying memory in a cultural context, Bartlett (1932) described the amazing ability of the Swazi people of Africa to remember the slight differences in individual characteristics of their cattle. One Swazi herdsman, Bartlett claimed, could remember details of every cow he had tended the year before. Such a feat is less surprising when we consider that the key component of traditional Swazi culture consists of the herds of cattle the people tend and depend upon for their living. Do the Swazi people have super powers of memory? Bartlett performed experiments comparing young Swazi men with young European men of comparable ages. Asked to recall a message consisting of 25 words, the Swazi young people had no better recall ability than the young Europeans.

Among many of the tribal peoples in Africa, the history of the tribe is preserved orally. Thus an oracle, or specialist, must be able to encode, store, and retrieve huge volumes of historical data (D'Azevedo, 1982). Elders of the Iatmul people of New Guinea are also said to have committed to memory the lines of descent for the various clans of their people stretching back generation upon generation (Bateson, 1982). The unerring memory of the elders for the kinship patterns of generations of their people are used to resolve disputed property claims (Mistry & Rogoff, 1994).

Barbara Rogoff, an expert in cultural psychology, maintains that such phenomenal, prodigious memory feats are best explained and understood in their cultural context (Rogoff & Mistry, 1985). The tribal elders perform their impressive memory feats because it is an integral and critically important part of the culture in which they live. Most likely, their ability to remember lists of nonsense syllables would be no better than your own.

Memory is not a pure process that exists apart from cultural context, social influences, or our individual interests. We remember what we are interested in, what we think about, and the daily transactions that occur in our cultural and social world.

Memory Check 6.4

1. What early memory researcher found that, rather than accurately recalling information detail by detail, people often reconstruct and systematically distort facts to make them more consistent with past experiences?
   a. Hermann Ebbinghaus
   b. Frederick Bartlett
   c. Wilder Penfield
   d. William James

2. Which of the following is *not* true of schemas?
   a. Schemas are the integrated frameworks of knowledge and assumptions we have about people, objects, and events.
   b. Schemas affect the way we encode information.
   c. Schemas affect the way we retrieve information.
   d. When we use schemas, our memories are accurate.

3. There are fewer errors in eyewitness testimony if:
   a. eyewitnesses are identifying a person of their own race.
   b. eyewitnesses view suspects' photos prior to a line-up.
   c. a weapon has been used in the crime.
   d. questions are phrased to provide retrieval cues for the eyewitness.

4. As a rule, people's memories are more accurate under hypnosis. (true/false)

5. The ability to retain a visual image several minutes after it has been removed is called:
   a. photographic memory.   c. eidetic imagery.
   b. flashbulb memory.   d. sensory memory.

Answers: 1. b 2. d 3. a 4. false 5. c

Factors Influencing Retrieval

Researchers in psychology have identified several factors that influence memory. We can control some of these factors, but not all of them.

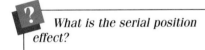
What is the serial position effect?

The Serial Position Effect: To Be Remembered, Be First or Last But Not in the Middle

If you were introduced to a dozen people at a party, you would most likely recall the names of the first few people you met and the last one or two, but forget more of the names in the middle. The reason is the **serial position effect**—the finding that for information learned in sequence, recall is better for items at the beginning and the end than for items in the middle of the sequence.

Information at the beginning of a sequence is subject to the **primary effect** and likely to be recalled because it already has been placed in long-term memory. Information at the end of a sequence is subject to the **recency effect** and has an even higher probability of being recalled because it is still in short-term memory. The poorer recall of information in the middle of a sequence occurs because that information is no longer in short-term memory and has not yet been placed in long-term memory. The serial position effect lends strong support to the notion of separate systems to short-term and long-term memory (Postman & Phillips, 1965).

Primacy and recency effects can also have an impact on information stored for longer periods of time (Roediger, 1991). For example, children learning their ABCs are likely to remember the first and last several letters of the alphabet better than many of the letters in the middle.

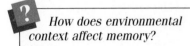
How does environmental context affect memory?

Environmental Context and Memory

Have you ever stood in your living room and thought of something you needed from your bedroom, only to forget what it was when you got there? Did the item come to mind when you returned to the living room? Some research reveals that we recall information better when we are in the same location—the same environmental context—as when the information was originally encoded.

Tulving and Thompson (1973) suggest that many elements of the physical setting in which we learn information are encoded along with the information and become part of the memory trace. If part or all of the original context is reinstated, it may serve as a retrieval cue. Then the information learned in that context may come to mind.

Godden and Baddeley (1975) conducted one of the early studies of context and memory with members of a university diving club. Subjects memorized a list of words when they were either 10 feet underwater or on land. They were later tested for recall of the words in the same or in a different environment. The results of the study suggest that recall of information is strongly influenced by environmental context (see Figure 6.10). Words learned underwater were best recalled underwater, and words learned on land were best recalled on land. In fact, when the scuba divers learned and recalled the words in the same context, their scores were 47 percent higher than when the two contexts were different.

Godden and Baddeley (1980) found that changes in context had no effect, however, when they measured memory using recognition rather than recall. Why? The original context provides retrieval cues that make recall easier. But in a recognition task, people have only to recognize the information as being familiar, so there is less need for the extra retrieval cues that the original context provides (Eich, 1980).

Going from 10 feet underwater to dry land is a rather drastic change in context, yet some researchers find the same effects even in more subtle context changes, such as going from one room to another. Steven Smith and others (1978) had students memorize lists of words in one room. The following day, students tested in the same room recalled 50 percent more words than those subjects tested in another room. Again there were no significant differences on recognition tests.

FIGURE 6.10

Context-Dependent Memory

Godden and Baddeley showed the strong influence of environmental context on recall. Scuba divers who memorized a list of words, either on land or underwater, had significantly better recall in the same physical context in which the learning had taken place. (Data from Godden & Baddeley, 1975.)

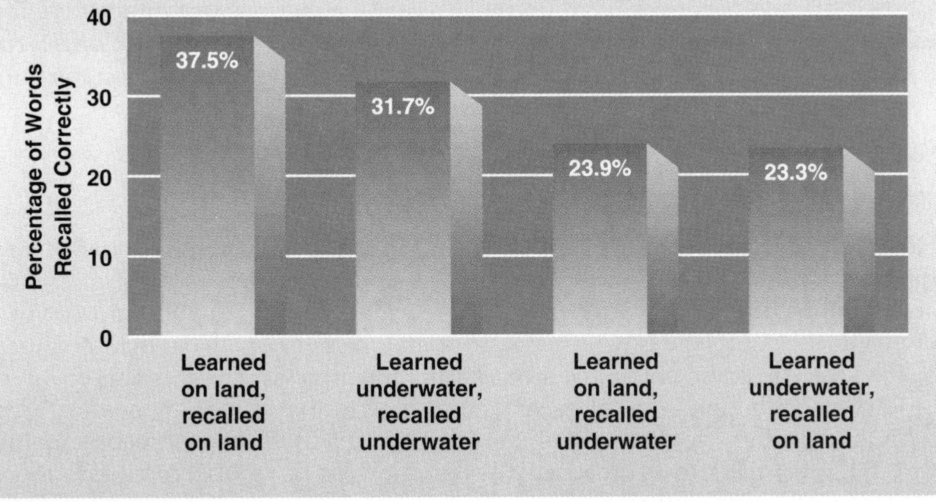

Bar chart — Percentage of Words Recalled Correctly (y-axis, 0 to 40):

Condition	Percentage
Learned on land, recalled on land	37.5%
Learned underwater, recalled underwater	31.7%
Learned on land, recalled underwater	23.9%
Learned underwater, recalled on land	23.3%

serial position effect: Upon presentation of a list of items, the tendency to remember the beginning and ending items better than the middle items.

primacy effect: The tendency to recall the first items on a list more readily than the middle items.

recency effect: The tendency to recall the last items on a list more readily than those in the middle of the list.

Smith (1979) also found that students who simply visualized the room in which they had learned the words could remember almost as much when tested in a different room as students who learned and were tested in the same room.

Not all studies have found that memory performance is enhanced when students learn and are tested in the same environment (Fernandez & Glenberg, 1985). Why? McDaniel and others (1989) reasoned that the more completely and carefully people encode material to be remembered, the less dependent they are on reinstating the original context. But people do not always carefully encode information and events to be remembered. This is why criminal investigators often bring eyewitnesses back to the crime scene or ask them to visualize it to help them recall more details of the crime.

The State-Dependent Memory Effect

What is the state-dependent memory effect?

If, as we have stated, the external environment can affect memory, might our internal state (happy or sad, intoxicated or sober) also influence our memory performance? The answer is yes. We tend to recall information better if we are in the same internal state as when the information was encoded. Psychologists call this the **state-dependent memory effect**.

Alcohol, Other Drugs, and Memory Some studies have shown a state-dependent memory effect for alcohol and drugs such as marijuana, amphetamines, and barbiturates (Eich, 1980). Subjects learned (encoded) material while sober or intoxicated, and later were tested in either the sober or intoxicated state. Recall was found to be best when the subjects were in the same state for both learning and testing (Weingartner et al., 1976). As in other studies, the state-dependent memory effect was evident for recall but not for recognition.

Mood and Memory Researchers have not been able to demonstrate reliably that recall is best if subjects are in the same mood (happy or sad) when they encode or learn material as when they try to recall it. However, some evidence does suggest that pleasant experiences are more likely to be recalled when people are in a happy mood, and negative experiences when people are experiencing a negative mood (Bower, 1992; Eich et al., 1994; Teasdale & Fogarty, 1979). Adults who are clinically depressed tend to recall more negative life experiences (Clark & Teasdale, 1982) and are likely to recall their parents as unloving and rejecting (Lewinsohn & Rosenbaum, 1987). But as depression lifts, the tendency toward negative recall reverses itself (Lloyd & Lishman, 1975).

Seidlitz and Diener (1993) found that recall of either positive or negative life events was influenced by subjective well-being (life satisfaction and long-term happiness), rather than by current mood (momentary happiness or unhappiness).

Stress, Anxiety, and Memory: Relax and Remember

Have you ever watched a TV quiz show and thought you could have easily won the prize? Would your memory work as well under the stress of cameras, lights, and millions of people watching as it does in the privacy and comfort of your own home? Psychologists who study stress and memory say that either too much or too little stress and emotional arousal can hinder memory performance.

People with high levels of general anxiety perform less well on memory tests than those with lower levels of anxiety (Loftus, 1980). Moreover, people going through great life stress—death of a loved one, loss of a job, divorce—do more poorly on tests of recent memories.

state-dependent memory effect: The tendency to recall information better if one is in the same pharmacological or psychological (mood) state as when the information was encoded.

Memory Check 6.5

1. When children learn the alphabet, they often learn "A, B, C, D . . ." and ". . . W, X, Y, Z" before learning the letters in between. This is called the:
   a. primacy effect.
   b. recency effect.
   c. serial position effect.
   d. state-dependent memory effect.

2. Recall is about as good when people visualize the context in which learning occurred as it is when recall and learning occur in the same context. (true/false)

3. Scores on recognition tests (either multiple-choice or true/false) will be higher if testing and learning take place in the same physical environment. (true/false)

4. Which best explains why drugs such as alcohol and marijuana can interfere with recall if the drugs are taken during learning but not during retrieval?
   a. the consistency effect
   b. the state-dependent memory effect
   c. context-dependent memory
   d. consolidation failure

5. Compared to nondepressed people, depressed people tend to have more sad memories. (true/false)

Answers: 1. c 2. true 3. false 4. b 5. true

Biology and Memory

Obviously our vast store of memories must exist physically somewhere in the brain. But where?

Brain Damage: A Clue to Memory Formation

Researchers are finding specific locations in the brain that house and mediate functions and processes in memory. One important source of information comes from people who have suffered memory loss resulting from damage to specific brain areas. One such person is H.M., a man who has had a major influence on our knowledge of human memory, not as a researcher but as a subject.

The Case of H.M. H.M. suffered from such severe epilepsy that, out of desperation, he agreed to a radical surgical procedure. The surgeon removed the site causing his seizures, including the front two-thirds of the hippocampus on both sides of the brain. It was 1953, and H.M. was 27 years old.

> After his surgery, H.M. remained intelligent and psychologically stable, and his seizures were drastically reduced. But unfortunately, the tissue cut from H.M.'s brain housed more than the site of his seizures. It also contained his ability to form new, conscious long-term memories. Though his short-term memory is still as good as ever and he easily remembers the events of his life stored well before the operation, H.M. suffers from **anterograde amnesia**. He has not been able to remember a single event that has occurred since the surgery over 40 years ago. And though H.M. turned 70 in 1996, as far as his conscious long-term memory is concerned, it is still 1953 and he is still 27 years old.
>
> Surgery affected only H.M.'s declarative, long-term memory—his ability to store facts, personal experiences, names, faces, telephone numbers, and the like. But researchers were surprised to discover that he could still form nondeclarative memories; that is, he could still acquire skills through repetitive practice although he could not remember having done so. For example, since the surgery, H.M. has learned to play tennis and improve his game, but he has no memory of having played. (Adapted from Milner, 1966, 1970; Milner et al., 1968)

What has the study of H.M. revealed about the role of the hippocampus in memory?

anterograde amnesia: The inability to form long-term memories of events occurring after a brain injury or brain surgery, although memories formed before the trauma are usually intact.

hippocampus (hip-po-CAM-pus): The brain structure in the limbic system involved in the formation of memories of facts, information, and personal experiences.

H.M.'s case was one of the first indications that the **hippocampus** (see Chapter 2) is involved in forming long-term memories. Other patients who have suffered similar brain damage show the same types of memory loss (Squire, 1992).

The hippocampus is needed for only a limited time after learning (Kim & Fanselow, 1992). It plays a continuing role during the process of reorganization and consolidation through which memories are finally stored in other areas of the cortex. Once stored, however, memories can be recalled independent of the hippocampus (Frackowiak, 1994; Squire & Zola-Morgan, 1991).

Just as H.M.'s case indicates that declarative and nondeclarative memories are processed and stored by different parts of the brain, a more recent case of amnesia suggests that different parts of the brain may be involved in episodic and semantic memory.

The Case of K.C. To support the distinction between semantic and episodic memory, Tulving and others (1988) report the case of K.C., who sustained a severe head injury from a motorcycle accident. K.C. suffered massive damage to his left frontal lobe and other parts of the brain as well.

> K.C.'s case is remarkable in that he cannot remember, in the sense of bringing back to conscious awareness, a single thing that he has ever done or experienced in the past. . . . This total absence of personal recollections makes K.C.'s case unique; no other reports exist of amnesiac patients who have been incapable of recollecting *any* personal happenings. (Tulving, 1989, p. 362)

Although his episodic memory was erased, K.C.'s semantic memory was largely spared. His storehouse of knowledge from fields such as geography, history, politics, and music is still large, enabling him to answer questions about many topics. Tulving concludes that episodic memory depends upon the functioning of parts of the frontal lobe. After studying patients with frontal lobe lesions, Janowsky and others (1989) suggest that the frontal lobes may play a special role in associating facts to the context in which they were learned.

We have described how researchers have identified and located some of the brain structures that play a role in memory. But what happens within these brain structures as they change, reshape, and rearrange to make new memories?

Neuronal Changes in Memory: Brain Work

Some researchers are exploring memory more minutely, by studying the actions of single neurons. Others are studying collections of neurons and their synapses, and the neurotransmitters whose chemical action begins the process of recording and storing a memory. The first close look at the nature of memory in single neurons was provided by Eric Kandel and his colleagues, who traced the effects of learning and memory in the sea snail *Aplysia* (Dale & Kandel, 1990). Using tiny electrodes implanted in several single neurons in the sea snail, the researchers mapped the neural circuits that are formed and maintained as the animal learns and remembers. They also discovered the different types of protein synthesis that facilitate short-term and long-term memory (Sweatt & Kandel, 1989).

But the studies of learning and memory in *Aplysia* reflect only simple classical conditioning, which is a type of nondeclarative memory. Other researchers studying mammals report that physical changes occur in the neurons and synapses in brain regions involved in declarative memory.

What is long-term potentiation, and why is it important?

Long-Term Potentiation: Prolonged Action at the Synapses As far back as the 1940s, Canadian psychologist Donald O. Hebb (1949) argued that the necessary neural ingredients for learning and memory must involve the enhancement of transmission at the synapses.

Today the most widely studied model for learning and memory at the level of the neurons meets the requirements of the mechanism Hebb described (Fischbach, 1992). It is called long-term potentiation (Cotman & Lynch, 1989; Stein et al., 1993). To potentiate means to make potent or to strengthen. **Long-term potentiation (LTP)** is an increase in the efficiency of neural transmission at the synapses that lasts for days or even weeks (Nguyen et al., 1994; Shuman & Madison, 1994). LTP is important because it may be the basis for learning and memory at the level of the neurons.

Long-term potentiation does not take place unless *both* the sending and receiving neurons are activated at the same time by intense high-frequency stimulation. Also, the receiving neuron must be depolarized (ready to fire) when stimulation arrives, or LTP will not occur. LTP is a common occurrence in the hippocampus, which, as you have learned, is essential in the formation of declarative memories (Eichenbaum & Otto, 1993).

If the changes in synapses produced by LTP are the same neural changes that take place in learning, then blocking or interfering with LTP should likewise interfere with learning. And it does. When Davis and others (1992) gave rats a drug that blocks NMDA receptors in sufficient doses to interfere with a spatial learning task, they discovered that LTP in the hippocampus was also disrupted.

It appears that long-term potentiation is also involved in causing structural changes in the neurons as Hebb had envisioned (Pinel, 1993). LTP at specific pathways in the hippocampus can alter dendritic spines, small structures on the dendrites of many neurons. Koch and others (1992) suggest that these dendritic spines may play a crucial role in initiating information storage in the brain, but not in actually retaining information.

Leading researchers now believe that LTP has the characteristics required of a process that is capable of forming memories (Cotman & Lynch, 1989). The final years of the twentieth century promise to yield exciting information about the neurochemical nature of learning and memory.

long-term potentiation: A long-lasting increase in the efficiency of neural transmission at the synapses.

Improving Memory

Study Habits That Aid Memory

There are no magic formulas for improving your memory. Remembering is a skill and, like any other skill, requires knowledge and practice. In this section we will show you several study habits and techniques that can improve your memory.

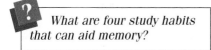
What are four study habits that can aid memory?

Organization: Everything in Its Place   We tend to retrieve information from long-term memory according to the way we have organized it for storage. Almost anyone can name the months of the year in about 12 seconds, but how long would it take to recall them in alphabetical order? The same 12 items, all well-known, are much harder to retrieve in alphabetical order, because they are not organized that way in memory. Try to organize items in alphabetical order, or according to categories, historical sequence, size, shape, or any other way that will make retrieval easier.

A telephone directory would be of little use to you if the names and phone numbers were listed in random order. In a similar way, you are giving your memory a task it probably will not accept if you try to remember large amounts of information in a haphazard fashion. Organizing material to be learned is a tremendous aid to memory. You can prove this for yourself by completing the *Try It!*

Have a pencil and a sheet of paper handy. Read the following list of items out loud and then write down as many as you can remember.

peas	ice cream	fish	perfume	bananas
toilet paper	onions	apples	cookies	ham
carrots	shaving cream	pie	grapes	chicken

If you organize this list, the items are much easier to remember. Now read each category heading and the items listed beneath it. Write down as many items as you can remember.

Desserts	Fruits	Vegetables	Meat	Toilet Articles
pie	bananas	carrots	chicken	perfume
ice cream	apples	onions	fish	shaving cream
cookies	grapes	peas	ham	toilet paper

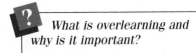

What is overlearning and why is it important?

overlearning: Practicing or studying material beyond the point where it can be repeated once without error.

Overlearning: Reviewing Again, and Again, and Again Do you still remember the words to songs that were popular when you were in high school? Can you recite many of the nursery rhymes you learned as a child even though you haven't heard them in years? You probably can because of **overlearning**.

Suppose that you wanted to memorize a list of words, and you studied until you could recite them once without error. Would this amount of study or practice be sufficient? Research suggests that we remember material better and longer if we overlearn it, that is, if we practice or study beyond the minimum needed to barely learn it (Ebbinghaus, 1885/1964). A pioneering study in overlearning by Krueger (1929) showed very substantial long-term gains for subjects who engaged in 50- and 100-percent overlearning (see Figure 6.11). Furthermore, overlearning

FIGURE 6.11

Overlearning

When material is learned only to the point of one correct repetition, forgetting is very rapid. Just 22 percent is retained after 1 day, 3 percent after 4 days, and 2 percent after 14 days. When subjects spend 50 percent more time going over the material, retention increases to 36 percent after 1 day, 30 percent after 4 days, and 21 percent after 14 days. (Data from Krueger, 1929.)

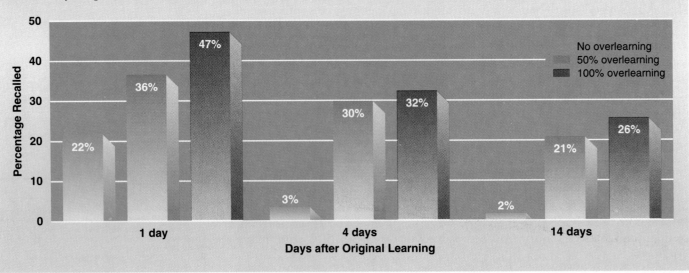

makes material more resistant to interference and is perhaps your best insurance against stress-related forgetting.

The next time you study for a test, don't stop studying as soon as you think you know the material. Spend another hour or so going over it, and you will be surprised at how much more you will remember.

Spaced versus Massed Practice: A Little at a Time Beats All at Once
We have all tried cramming for examinations, but spacing study over several different sessions generally is more effective than **massed practice**—learning in one long practice session without rest periods (Glover & Corkill, 1987).

You will remember more with less total study time if you space your study over several sessions. Long periods of memorizing make material particularly subject to interference and often result in fatigue and lowered concentration. Also, when you space your practice, you probably create a new memory that may be stored in a different place, thus increasing your chance for recall.

The spacing effect applies to learning motor skills as well as to learning facts and information. All music students can tell you that it is better to practice for half an hour each day, every day, than to practice many hours in a row once a week.

Recitation versus Rereading: Recitation Wins
Many students simply read and reread their textbook and notes when they study for an exam. Research over many years shows that you will recall more if you increase the amount of recitation in your study. For example, it is better to read a page or a few paragraphs and then recite or practice recalling what you have just read. Then continue reading, stop and practice reciting again, and so on. When you study for a psychology test and review the assigned chapter, try to answer each of the study questions. Then read the material that follows each question and check to see if you answered the question correctly. This will be your safeguard against encoding failure. Don't simply read each section and assume that you can answer the question. Test yourself before your professor does.

A. I. Gates (1917) tested groups of students who spent the same amount of time in study, but who spent different percentages of their time in recitation and rereading. His subjects recalled two to three times more if they increased their recitation time up to 80 percent and spent only 20 percent of their study time rereading.

> **massed practice:** One long learning practice session as opposed to spacing the learning in shorter practice sessions over an extended period.

Memory Check 6.6

1. The hippocampus is the brain structure involved in the formation of permanent memories of:
   a. motor skills.
   b. facts and personal experiences.
   c. motor skills, facts, and personal experiences.
   d. motor skills and personal experiences.

2. What is the term for the long-lasting increase in the efficiency of neural transmission at the synapses that may be the basis for learning and memory at the level of the neurons?
   a. long-term potentiation
   b. synaptic facilitation
   c. synaptic potentiation
   d. presynaptic potentiation

3. When studying for an exam, it is best to spend:
   a. more time reciting than rereading.
   b. more time rereading than reciting.
   c. equal time rereading and reciting.
   d. all of the time reciting rather than rereading.

4. Being able to recite a number of nursery rhymes from childhood is probably due mainly to:
   a. spaced practice.   c. mnemonics.
   b. organization.   d. overlearning.

Answers: 1. b 2. a 3. a 4. d

Improving Memory with Mnemonic Devices

We all use external aids to help us remember. Writing notes, making lists, writing on a calendar, or keeping an appointment book is often more reliable and accurate than trusting our own memory (Intons-Peterson & Fournier, 1986). But there are times, such as when you are taking a test, when you cannot rely on external prompts. What if you need information at some unpredictable time, when you do not have external aids handy?

Several *mnemonics*, or memory devices, have been developed over the years to aid memory (Bower, 1973; Higbee, 1977; Roediger, 1980). The different mnemonic techniques that we will explore are rhyme, the first-letter technique, the method of loci, the peg-word method, and the link method.

Rhyme

Many of us use rhymes to help us remember material that otherwise might be difficult to recall. Perhaps as a child you learned your ABCs by using a rhyming song:

A - B - C - D
E - F - G
H - I - J - K
L - M - N - O - P

You may repeat the verse "Thirty days hath September" when you try to recall the number of days in each month, or the saying "*i* before *e* except after *c*" when you are trying to spell a word. Rhymes are useful because they ensure that information is recalled in the proper sequence. Otherwise there is no rhyme.

The First-Letter Technique

Another useful technique is to take the first letter of each item to be remembered and form a word, a phrase, or a sentence with those letters (Matlin, 1989). For example, if you had to memorize the seven colors of the visible spectrum in their proper order, you could use the first letter of each color to form the name Roy G. Biv. Three chunks are easier to remember than seven different items.

**Red Orange Yellow Green
Blue Indigo Violet**

As a child taking music lessons, you may have learned the saying "*Every good boy does fine*" to remind you of the lines of the treble clef, and *F A C E* as a reminder of the spaces. To remember their license plate more easily, the authors think of the letters PCS as "poor civil servant."

The Method of Loci: "In the First Place"

The *method of loci* is a mnemonic device that can be used when you want to remember a list of items such as a grocery list, or when you give a speech or a class report and need to make your points in order without using notes. The word *loci* (pronounced loh'-sye) is the plural form of *locus*, which means "location" or "place." The use of loci as a memory aid may be the origin of the phrase "in the first place."

Figure 6.12 shows how to use the method of loci. Select any familiar location—your home, for example—and simply associate the items to be remembered with places there. Begin by picturing the first locus, for example, your driveway; the second locus, your garage; the third locus, the walk leading to your front door; and the fourth locus, perhaps the front hall closet. Progress through your house from room to room in an or-

FIGURE 6.12

The Method of Loci

Begin by thinking of locations, perhaps in your home, that are in a sequence. Then visualize one of the items to be remembered in each location.

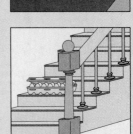

derly fashion. Visualize the first item or idea you want to remember in its place on the driveway, the second item in your garage, the third at your front door, and so on until you have associated each item you want to remember with a specific place. You may find it helpful to conjure up exaggerated images of the items that you place at each location (see Figure 6.12).

When you want to recall the items, take an imaginary walk starting at the first place—the first item will pop into your mind. When you think of the second place, the second item will come to mind, and so on.

Research suggests that the method of loci is very effective. In one study, college students memorized a different list of 40 nouns on each of four consecutive days. They visualized each word at specific locations on campus (Ross & Lawrence, 1968). When tested immediately after mem-

orizing each list, the average recall was 37 out of 40 words in the exact order in which they were memorized. Average recall one day later was 34 words, and average recall at the end of all four lists was 29 words per 40-word list.

The Pegword System

Figure 6.13 illustrates the **pegword system**, a mnemonic developed in

FIGURE 6.13

The Pegword System

Items to be recalled are each associated with a pegword using a mental image. (Based on Bower, 1973.)

Item Number	Pegword	Peg Image	Item to Be Recalled		Connecting Image
1	bun	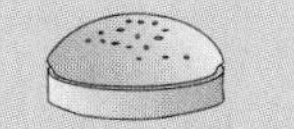	milk		*Milk* pouring onto a soggy hamburger *bun*
2	shoe		bread		A *shoe* kicking and breaking a brittle loaf of French *bread*
3	tree		bananas		Several bunches of *bananas* hanging from a *tree*
4	door		cigarette		Keyhole of a *door* smoking a *cigarette*
5	hive	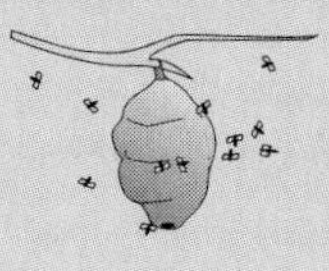	coffee		Pouring *coffee* into top of a bee *hive*

continued

England around 1879. It uses rhyming words:

one = bun	six = sticks
two = shoe	seven = heaven
three = tree	eight = gate
four = door	nine = wine
five = hive	ten = hen

Many children in English-speaking countries have learned these rhyming associations from the nursery rhyme "One, two, buckle my shoe—three, four, close the door." The rhyming words are memorized in sequence and then linked through vivid associations with any items you wish to remember in order.

For example, here are five items you might want to remember to buy at the store: grapefruit, laundry detergent, steak, eggs, and milk. Begin by associating the grapefruit with the bun (your first pegword) by picturing a big grapefruit sandwich. Next picture the shoe, the second pegword, filled with laundry detergent; then continue by associating each item on your list with a pegword. To recall the items, simply go through your list of pegwords and the associated word will immediately come to mind.

The Link Method: A Memory Chain

If you use the method of loci or the pegword method often, you may find that eventually new items get confused with old ones when the same locations or pegwords are used time after time. Another mnemonic device called the *link method* solves this problem. It, too, can be used to remember items in sequence forward or backward (Lorayne & Lucus, 1974). The link method does not require that you associate items with locations or key words that you have previously committed to memory. Rather, you simply link or associate the first item on the list with the second, the second with the third, and so on to the end of the list. This technique works best if you picture some unusual, vivid connection between each pair of items in the link. Items linked do not have to have any natural order or relationship, and you can link and remember 20 or more items almost as easily as you can link 5 or 10.

The Memory Book by Lorayne and Lucus (1974) lists 10 unrelated words to demonstrate the method:

1. airplane
2. tree
3. envelope
4. earring
5. bucket
6. sing
7. basketball
8. salami
9. star
10. nose

To memorize the items, link them together simply by picturing some unusual or bizarre connection between the words. For example, link the words in the following way:

1 to 2: Link airplane to tree. Imagine trees, not people, boarding the airplane.

2 to 3: Link tree to envelope. Picture gleaming white envelopes on the trees.

3 to 4: Link envelope to earring. Imagine loads of gold earrings spilling from the envelopes.

4 to 5: Link earring to bucket. See the earrings spilling into buckets.

5 to 6: Link bucket to sing. Imagine a choir singing with buckets over their heads.

Create your own links for items 6 through 10.

Now see if you can recall all 10 items in order. Begin with airplane and recall the exaggerated images you used to link the 10 items. Linking images works best if they are highly unusual and if there is action or movement in the images you create.

The human memory is truly amazing. We hope you will use the information we have shared with you to make your memory even more amazing.

Thinking Critically

Evaluation

Some studies cited in this chapter involved only one or a few subjects.

a. Select two of these studies and discuss the possible problems in drawing conclusions on the basis of studies using so few subjects.

b. Suggest several possible explanations for the researchers' findings other than those proposed by the researchers.

c. In your view, should such studies even be mentioned in a textbook? Why or why not?

Point/Counterpoint

Prepare an argument in favor of each of these therapeutic approaches for treating depression and eating disorders in patients who at the outset have no memory of childhood sexual abuse:

a. Attempting to recover repressed memories of childhood sexual abuse through hypnosis is useful.

b. Attempting to recover repressed memories of childhood sexual abuse through hypnosis can cause more harm than good.

Psychology in Your Life

Drawing upon your knowledge, formulate a plan that you can put into operation to help improve your memory and avoid the pitfalls that cause forgetting.

Chapter Summary and Review

Remembering

 What three processes are involved in the act of remembering?

Three processes involved in remembering are (1) encoding—transforming information into a form that can be stored in memory; (2) storage—maintaining information in memory; and (3) retrieval—bringing stored material to mind.

 What is sensory memory?

Sensory memory holds information coming in through the senses for up to several seconds, just long enough for us to begin to process the information and send some on to short-term memory.

 What are the characteristics of short-term memory?

Short-term (working) memory holds about seven unrelated items of information for less than 30 seconds without rehearsal. Short-term memory also acts as our mental workspace while we carry out any mental activity.

 What is long-term memory, and what are its subsystems?

Long-term memory is the permanent or relatively permanent memory system with a virtually unlimited capacity. Its subsystems are (1) declarative memory, which holds facts and information (semantic memory) along with personal life experiences (episodic memory); and (2) nondeclarative memory, which consists of motor skills acquired through repetitive practice, habits, and simple classically conditioned responses.

Key Terms

encoding (p. 205)
storage (p. 205)
consolidation (p. 205)
retrieval (p. 205)
sensory memory (p. 206)
short-term memory (p. 208)
displacement (p. 208)
rehearsal (p. 209)
long-term memory (p. 210)
nondeclarative memory (p. 211)
declarative memory (p. 211)
episodic memory (p. 211)
semantic memory (p. 211)
levels-of-processing model (p. 212)

Measuring Memory

 What are three methods of measuring retention?

Three methods of measuring retention are (1) recall, where information must be supplied with few or no retrieval cues; (2) recognition, where information must simply be recognized as having been encountered before; and (3) the relearning method, which measures retention in terms of time saved in relearning material compared with the time required to learn it originally.

 What was Ebbinghaus's major contribution to psychology?

Hermann Ebbinghaus conducted the first experimental studies of learning and memory. He invented the nonsense syllable, conceived the relearning method as a test of memory, and plotted the curve of forgetting.

Key Terms

recall (p. 213)
retrieval cue (p. 213)
recognition (p. 214)
relearning method (p. 214)
savings score (p. 214)
nonsense syllable (p. 215)

Forgetting

What are six causes of forgetting?

Six causes of forgetting are encoding failure, consolidation failure, decay, interference, motivated forgetting, and retrieval failure.

What is interference, and how can it be minimized?

Interference occurs when information or associations stored either before or after a given memory hinder our ability to remember it. To minimize interference, follow a learning activity with sleep, and arrange learning so that similar subjects are not studied back to back.

Key Terms

encoding failure (p. 217)
consolidation failure (p. 218)
retrograde amnesia (p. 218)
decay theory (p. 218)
interference (p. 218)
motivated forgetting (p. 219)
repression (p. 219)
amnesia (p. 219)

The Nature of Remembering and Forgetting

What is meant by the statement "Memory is reconstructive in nature"?

Our memory does not work like a videocassette recorder. We reconstruct memories, piecing them together from a few highlights and using information that may or may not be accurate.

What is Bartlett's contribution to our understanding of memory?

Sir Frederick Bartlett found that people do not recall facts and experiences detail by detail. Rather, they systematically reconstruct and distort them to fit information already stored in memory.

What are schemas, and how do they affect memory?

Schemas are the integrated frameworks of knowledge and assumptions we have about people, objects, and events; schemas affect how we encode and recall information.

What conditions reduce the reliability of eyewitness testimony?

The reliability of eyewitness testimony is reduced when witnesses view a photograph of the suspect before viewing the lineup, when members of a lineup are viewed at the same time rather than one by one, when the perpetrator is of a different race from the eyewitness, when a weapon has been used in the crime, and when leading questions are asked to elicit information.

Does hypnosis improve the memory of eyewitnesses?

Hypnotized subjects supply more information and are more confident of their recollections, but they supply more inaccurate information as well.

Key Terms

reconstruction (p. 221)
schemas (p. 222)

infantile amnesia (p. 225)
flashbulb memory (p. 225)
eidetic imagery (p. 226)

Factors Influencing Retrieval

What is the serial position effect?

The serial position effect is the tendency, when recalling a list of items, to remember the items at the beginning of the list (primacy effect) and the items at the end of the list (recency effect) better than items in the middle.

How does environmental context affect memory?

People tend to recall material more easily if they are in the same physical location during recall as during the original learning.

What is the state-dependent memory effect?

The state-dependent memory effect is our tendency to recall information better if we are in the same pharmacological or psychological state as when the information was learned.

Key Terms

serial position effect (p. 228)
primacy effect (p. 228)
recency effect (p. 228)
state-dependent memory effect (p. 230)

Biology and Memory

What has the study of H.M. revealed about the role of the hippocampus in memory?

The case of H.M. reveals that the hippocampus is essential in forming declarative memories but not in forming nondeclarative memories.

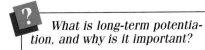 *What is long-term potentiation, and why is it important?*

Long-term potentiation is a long-lasting increase in the efficiency of neural transmission at the synapses. LTP is important because it may be the basis for learning and memory at the level of the neurons.

Key Terms

anterograde amnesia (p. 231)
hippocampus (p. 232)
long-term potentiation (p. 233)

Improving Memory

 What are four study habits that can aid memory?

Four study habits that can aid memory are organization, overlearning, the use of spaced rather than massed practice, and the use of a higher percentage of time reciting than rereading material.

What is overlearning, and why is it important?

Overlearning means practicing or studying material beyond the point where it can be repeated once without error. Material that is overlearned is remembered better and longer, and it is more resistant to interference and stress-related forgetting.

Key Terms

overlearning (p. 234)
massed practice (p. 235)

7

INTELLIGENCE, COGNITION, AND LANGUAGE

CHAPTER OUTLINE

The Nature of Intelligence

The Search for Factors Underlying Intelligence

Intelligence: More Than One Type?

Measuring Intelligence

Alfred Binet and the First Successful Intelligence Test

Pioneers: Alfred Binet

The Intelligence Quotient or IQ: Can a Number Capture It?

Intelligence Testing in the United States

Requirements of Good Tests: Reliability, Validity, and Standardization

The Range of Intelligence

The IQ Controversy: Brainy Dispute

The Uses and Abuses of Intelligence Tests

The Nature–Nurture Controversy: Battle of the Centuries

Intelligence: Is It Fixed or Changeable?

World of Psychology: Expectations, Effort, and Academic Achievement— A Cross-Cultural Comparison

Imagery and Concepts: Tools of Thinking

Imagery: Picture This— Elephants with Purple Polka Dots

Concepts: Our Mental Classification System (Is a Penguin a Bird?)

Problem Solving and Creativity

Approaches to Problem Solving: How Do We Begin?

Impediments to Problem Solving: Mental Stumbling Blocks

Artificial Intelligence

Creativity: Unique and Useful Productions

Language

The Structure of Language

Animal Language

Language and Thinking

Applications: Stimulating Creativity

Thinking Critically

Chapter Summary and Review

243

Who has the highest IQ score ever recorded on an intelligence test? The name of Albert Einstein quickly comes to mind and perhaps a host of other great thinkers of the past—mostly men. But the person with the highest IQ score ever recorded happens to be a woman.

Marilyn Mach, born in St. Louis, in 1946, scored an amazing 230 on the Stanford-Binet IQ test when she was a 10-year-old elementary school student. How high is a 230 IQ? The average Stanford-Binet IQ score is set at 100, and a score of 116—only about half as high as Marilyn Mach's lofty score—places a person in the top 16 percent of the population. Not only does Marilyn Mach have no peer when it comes to measured intelligence, she doesn't even have a competitor. Her score is nearly 30 points higher than that of her nearest rival.

Descended from the Austrian philosopher and physicist Ernst Mach, who did pioneering work in the physics of sound (Mach 1, Mach 2), Marilyn added her mother's maiden name and so as an adult became known as Marilyn Mach vos Savant. She completed about 2 years of college courses but has no college degree. Her primary intellectual interest is creative writing, and she has written 12 books and 3 plays. Her first published work was the Omni IQ Quiz Contest. Marilyn lives with her husband in New York, where she writes a newspaper column, lectures on intelligence, and pursues various other interests.

Now consider another person, Dr. Robert Jarvik, the world-famous inventor of the Jarvik artificial heart. Dr. Jarvik combined his medical knowledge and his mechanical genius to produce the world's first workable artificial heart. But his path wasn't easy. Unlike Marilyn Mach vos Savant,

Jarvik was a poor test taker. In fact, he scored too low on intelligence and admissions tests to be admitted to any medical school in the United States. Eventually, despite his low test scores, he was accepted by a medical school in Italy, where he completed his studies and received his M.D. degree. Then he returned to practice in the United States and made his contribution to medical science—a contribution that kept alive many gravely ill heart patients until a suitable heart transplant could be performed.

Perhaps, if Dr. Jarvik wishes, he can learn to score higher on IQ tests. His wife, Marilyn Mach vos Savant-Jarvik, might be willing to teach him.

Like Dr. Jarvik, many highly creative individuals have tested poorly in school. Some of the most prominent include the famous American inventor Thomas A. Edison; Winston Churchill, whose teachers thought he was mentally limited; and even the great Albert Einstein, who was labeled a dunce in math. We all have some notion of what intelligence is, and we have met people we believe to be more intelligent, and others we believe to be less intelligent, than we are.

In this chapter we will explore intelligence, thinking skills, creativity, and language. You will learn about the nature of intelligence and how it is measured. Where does our intelligence come from—our genes, experiences provided by our environment, or both? We will look at the extremes in intelligence—the mentally gifted and the mentally retarded. We will consider how we think and examine the approaches we use to solve problems. Finally, we will explore language.

First, let us ask the most obvious question: What is intelligence? Even experts in the field can't agree on an answer. Probably the most generally accepted definition was proposed by David Wechsler (1975): "Intelligence is the global capacity of the individual to act purposefully, to think rationally, and to deal effectively with the environment."

The Nature of Intelligence

The Search for Factors Underlying Intelligence

Is intelligence a single trait or capability? Is it many capabilities unrelated to each other? Are there certain common factors that underlie intelligence?

> ? *What factors underlie intelligence, according to Spearman, Thurstone, and Guilford?*

Spearman and General Intelligence: The g Factor English psychologist Charles Spearman (1863–1945) observed that people who are bright in one area are usually bright in other areas as well. In other words, they tend to be generally intelligent. Spearman (1927) came to believe that intelligence is composed of a general ability, or *g* **factor**, which underlies all intellectual functions.

Spearman arrived at his "*g* theory" when he found that there were positive relationships among scores on the subtests of intelligence tests. People who score high on one subtest tend to score high on the other subtests. Spearman theorized that this positive relationship meant that the tests were measuring something in common—that general ability was expressed to some degree in all of them. This, said Spearman, was evidence of the *g* factor—general intelligence.

But some of the correlations between subtests are higher than others. If the *g* factor alone defined the whole of what intelligence tests measure, then all of the correlations would be nearly perfect. Because they are not, some other abilities in addition to the *g* factor must be present. These other abilities Spearman named "*s* factors" for specific abilities.

Spearman concluded that intelligence tests tap a person's *g* factor, or general intelligence, and a number of *s* factors, or specific intellectual abilities. Spearman's influence can be seen in those intelligence tests, such as the Stanford-Binet, that yield one IQ score to indicate the level of general intelligence.

Thurstone's Primary Mental Abilities: Primarily Seven Louis L. Thurstone (1938), another famous researcher in testing, rejected Spearman's notion of general intellectual ability, or *g* factor. After analyzing the scores of many subjects on some 50 separate ability tests, Thurstone identified seven **primary mental abilities**: verbal comprehension, numerical ability, spatial relations, perceptual speed, word fluency, memory, and reasoning. He maintained that all intellectual activities involve one or more of these primary mental abilities. Thurstone and his wife, Thelma G. Thurstone, developed their Primary Mental Abilities Tests to measure these seven abilities.

Thurstone believed a single IQ score obscured more than it revealed. He suggested that a profile showing relative strengths and weaknesses on the seven primary abilities would provide a more accurate picture of a person's mental ability.

Guilford's Structure of Intellect: A Mental House with 180 Rooms Still another effort to shed light on the nature of intelligence is J. P. Guilford's **structure of intellect**. Guilford (1967) proposed that the structure of intelligence has three dimensions: mental operations, contents, and products.

When we think, we perform a mental operation or activity. According to Guilford, that mental operation can be cognition, memory, evaluation, divergent production, or convergent production. But we can't think in a vacuum; we must think about something. The something we think about, Guilford calls "contents," which can be visual, auditory, symbolic, semantic, or behavioral. The end result of bringing some mental activity to bear on some contents is a "product."

Guilford (1967) hypothesized that there are 120 different intellectual abilities, depending on how the different operations, contents, and products are combined in a task. Shortly before his death, however, Guilford (1988) expanded his theory

***g* factor:** Spearman's term for a general intellectual ability that underlies all mental operations to some degree.

primary mental abilities: According to Thurstone, seven relatively distinct abilities that singularly or in combination are involved in all intellectual activities.

structure of intellect: The model proposed by Guilford consisting of 180 different intellectual abilities, which involve all of the possible combinations of the three dimensions of intellect—mental operations, contents, and products.

FIGURE 7.1

Guilford's Structure of Intellect

Guilford's three dimensions of intellect—operations, contents, and products—may be arranged in various combinations to produce 180 separate factors of intellect.

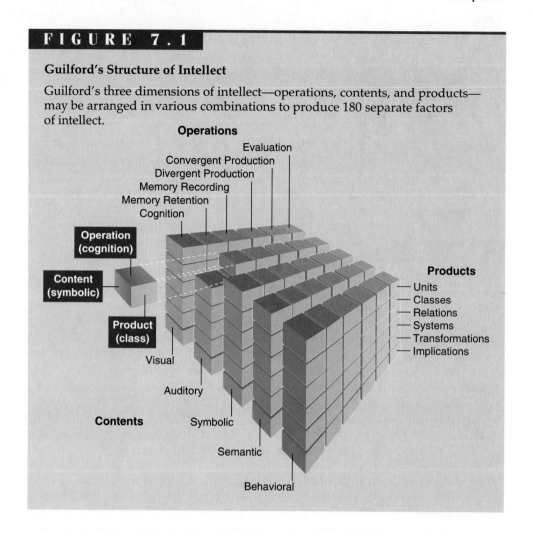

from 120 to 180 abilities, when he divided the operation of memory into two categories (memory recording and memory retention). See Figure 7.1.

Intelligence: More Than One Type?

Some theorists, instead of searching for the factors that underlie intelligence, propose that there are different types of intelligence. Two such modern theorists are Howard Gardner and Robert Sternberg.

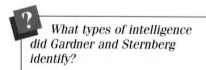

What types of intelligence did Gardner and Sternberg identify?

Gardner's Seven Frames of Mind: One Frame Is as Good as Another

Harvard psychologist Howard Gardner (1983) also denies the existence of a *g* factor. Instead he proposes seven independent and equally important forms of intelligence. Gardner's multiple intelligences are as follows:

1. *Linguistic* (language skills)
2. *Logical/mathematical* (math and quantitative skills)
3. *Musical*
4. *Spatial* (skills used by painters and sculptors to manipulate and re-create forms)
5. *Bodily kinesthetic* (body control and dexterity in handling objects)
6. *Interpersonal* (understanding the behavior and reading the moods, desires, and intentions of others)
7. *Intrapersonal* (understanding one's own feelings and behavior)

Gardner (1983) developed his theory by studying patients with different types of brain damage that affect some forms of intelligence but leave others intact. He also studied reports of people with savant syndrome—those who possess a strange combination of mental retardation and unusual talent or ability. Finally, Gardner considered how various abilities and skills have been valued differently in other cultures and periods of history.

Gardner's critics doubt that all seven frames of mind are of equal value in education and in life. Robert Sternberg (1985b) claims that "the multiple intelligences might better be referred to as multiple talents" (p. 1114). He asks whether an adult who is tone-deaf and has no sense of rhythm can be considered mentally limited in the same way as one who has never developed any verbal skills. But Sternberg is not merely a critic. He has developed his own theory of intelligence.

Sternberg's Triarchic Theory of Intelligence: The Big Three   Robert Sternberg uses the information-processing approach to understand intelligence. This approach involves a step-by-step analysis of the cognitive processes people use as they acquire knowledge and use it to solve problems.

Sternberg admits that when he was young he never did well on traditional intelligence tests. "I really stunk on IQ tests. I was just terrible," says Sternberg (Trotter, 1986, p. 56). Today he is one of the most respected theorists in the field.

Sternberg (1985a; 1986a) has formulated a **triarchic theory of intelligence**, which, as the term *triarchic* implies, proposes that intelligence consists of three main parts: the componential, the experiential, and the contextual (see Figure 7.2). The first part, the "componential," refers to the mental abilities most closely related to success on conventional IQ and achievement tests. Sternberg claims that traditional IQ tests tap only the componential aspect of intelligence.

The second part, the "experiential," encompasses creativity and insight, although creativity has not yielded easily to conventional measurement efforts. The third leg of the triarchic theory is "contextual," or practical, intelligence, which some might equate with common sense or "street smarts." People with high contextual intelligence are survivors who capitalize on their strengths and compensate for their weaknesses. They either adapt well to their environment, change the environment to help them succeed, or if necessary, find a new environment. People who have succeeded in spite of hardships and adverse circumstances probably have a great deal of contextual intelligence.

triarchic theory of intelligence: Sternberg's theory that intelligence consists of three parts—the componential, the contextual, and the experiential.

FIGURE 7.2

Sternberg's Triarchic Theory of Intelligence

According to Sternberg, there are three types of intelligence: componential, experiential, and contextual.

Componential Intelligence
Mental abilities most closely related to success on traditional IQ and achievement tests

Experiential Intelligence
Creativity and insight

Contextual Intelligence
Practical intelligence or "street smarts"

Memory Check 7.1

Match the theorist with the theory of intelligence.

___ 1) triarchic theory of intelligence

___ 2) seven primary mental abilities

___ 3) structure of intellect

___ 4) seven frames of mind

___ 5) the g factor

a. Spearman
b. Thurstone
c. Guilford
d. Sternberg
e. Gardner

Answers: 1) d 2) b 3) c 4) e 5) a

Measuring Intelligence

Alfred Binet and the First Successful Intelligence Test

What is Binet's major contribution to psychology?

The first successful effort to measure intelligence resulted not from a theoretical approach, but as a practical means of solving a problem in the schools of France. Around the turn of the century, the Ministry of Public Instruction in Paris was struggling with a problem—trying to find some objective means of sorting out children whose intelligence was too low for them to profit from regular classroom instruction. The ministry wanted to ensure that average or brighter children would not be wrongly assigned to special classes and that children of limited ability would not be subjected to the regular program of instruction. In 1903 a commission was formed to study the problem, and one of its members was French psychologist Alfred Binet.

The Intelligence Quotient, or IQ: Can a Number Capture It?

What does IQ mean, and how was it originally calculated?

Binet believed that children with a mental age 2 years below their chronological age were retarded and should be placed in special education classes. But there was a flaw in his thinking. A 4-year-old with a mental age of 2 is far more retarded than a 12-year-old with a mental age of 10. How could a similar degree of retardation at different ages be expressed?

German psychologist William Stern (1914) provided an answer. In 1912 he devised a simple formula for calculating an index of intelligence—the **intelligence quotient**, or **IQ**. He divided a child's mental age by his or her chronological age. Then, to eliminate the decimal, he multiplied the result by 100.

$$\frac{\text{Mental Age}}{\text{Chronological Age}} \times 100 = \text{IQ}$$

Here is how some IQs for 10-year-olds would be calculated:

$$\frac{14}{10} \times 100 = 1.40 \times 100 = \text{IQ } 140 \text{ (Superior IQ)}$$

$$\frac{10}{10} \times 100 = 1.00 \times 100 = \text{IQ } 100 \text{ (Normal IQ)}$$

$$\frac{6}{10} \times 100 = 0.60 \times 100 = \text{IQ } 60 \text{ (Below Normal IQ)}$$

intelligence quotient (IQ): An index of intelligence originally derived by dividing mental age by chronological age and then multiplying by 100.

PIONEERS *Alfred Binet (1857–1911)*

Alfred Binet was born on July 11, 1857, in Nice, France. Binet's father, a physician, and his mother, an artist, separated when Binet was young, and he was raised by his mother. Binet first studied law and then decided to follow the family tradition in medicine as had his father and both his grandfathers before him. However, his interests soon turned to psychology, and he did not complete his medical studies.

In 1890 Binet began making careful observations of the development of his two daughters—Alice, who was 2½ at the time, and Madeleine, age 4½. Struck by the differences in their reasoning ability and memory, Binet devised tests to measure various abilities in the girls. He had them memorize digits and words, match colors, copy drawings, perform reasoning tasks, and play other intellectual games. As he watched them develop, he observed that Alice could not perform many of the tasks that her older sister could complete with ease. But 2 years later, Alice was able to perform the same tasks as well as her older sister had earlier. This suggested to Binet that intelligence is developmental and progresses according to age. Perhaps tests could be constructed that would reveal what the average child could do at certain ages—5, 6, 7, and so on.

In 1903 Binet set to work on the task of developing an intelligence test that could make assessment more objective. With the help of his colleague, psychiatrist Theodore Simon, Binet began testing the schoolchildren of Paris in 1904. The two men used a wide variety of tests, some of which Binet had tried with his own daughters, and they kept only those items that discriminated well between older and younger children. Binet and Simon published their intelligence scale in 1905 and revised it in 1908 and again in 1911. The Binet–Simon Intelligence Scale was an immediate success.

Test items on the scale were structured according to increasing difficulty—with the easiest item first and each succeeding item becoming more and more difficult. Children went as far as they could, and then their progress was compared to others of the same age. A child with the mental ability of a normal 5-year-old could be said to have a mental level of 5. Binet established the concept that mental retardation and mental superiority are a function of the difference between chronological age (one's actual age) and mental age. An 8-year-old with a mental age of 8 is normal or average. An 8-year-old with a mental age of 5 is seriously deficient, while an 8-year-old with a mental age of 11 is mentally superior.

Binet, a prolific writer, authored nearly 300 published works—books, articles, reviews, and even four plays that were produced in the theaters of Paris (Siegler, 1992). In October 1911 Binet's career was ended abruptly by his untimely death at the age of 54. But his contribution—the idea of mental age and the publication of an individual intelligence test for measuring it—is still very much alive today.

It is interesting to note that Binet and Simon were totally against the use of an IQ score. They believed that it was impossible to represent human intelligence with a single number and that doing so was not only misleading but dangerous (Hothersall, 1984).

Intelligence Testing in the United States

The Stanford–Binet Intelligence Scale: A Famous IQ Test Lewis M. Terman, a psychology professor at Stanford University, published a thorough revision of the Binet–Simon scale in 1916. Terman revised and adapted the items for American children, added new items, and established new **norms**—standards based on the scores of a large number of people and used as bases for comparison. Terman's revision, known as the **Stanford–Binet Intelligence Scale**, was the first test to make use of Stern's IQ score (von Mayrhauser, 1992). Within 2½ years, 4 million children had taken the test.

The highly regarded Stanford–Binet is an individually administered IQ test for those aged 2 to 23. It contains four subscales—verbal reasoning, quantitative reasoning, abstract visual reasoning, and short-term memory. An overall IQ score

norms: Standards based on the range of test scores of a large group of people who are selected to provide the bases of comparison for those who take the test later.

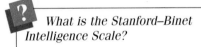
? *What is the Stanford–Binet Intelligence Scale?*

Stanford–Binet Intelligence Scale: An individually administered IQ test for those aged 2 to 23; Terman's adaptation of the Binet–Simon Scale.

deviation score: A test score calculated by comparing an individual's score to the scores of others of the same age.

Wechsler Adult Intelligence Scale (WAIS-R): An individual intelligence test for adults that yields separate verbal and performance (nonverbal) IQ scores as well as an overall IQ score.

What did Wechsler's tests provide that the Stanford–Binet did not?

is derived from scores on the four subscales, and the test scores correlate well with achievement test scores (Laurent et al., 1992).

Intelligence Testing for Adults: A Scale for All Ages Intelligence testing became increasingly popular in the United States in the 1920s and 1930s, but it quickly became obvious that the Stanford–Binet Intelligence Scale was not useful for testing adults. The original IQ formula could not be applied to adults, because at a certain age, maturity in intelligence is reached. According to the original IQ formula, a 40-year-old with the same IQ test score as the average 20-year-old would be considered mentally retarded, with an IQ of only 50. Obviously, something was wrong with the formula when applied to populations of all ages.

Today we still use the term *IQ*, but for adults, IQ is a **deviation score** derived by comparing an individual's score to scores of others the *same age* on whom the test was normed. The deviation score is a contribution of David Wechsler, another pioneer in mental testing.

The Wechsler Intelligence Tests: Among the Best In 1939 psychologist David Wechsler developed the first successful individual intelligence test for adults, designed for those age 16 and older. The original test has been revised, restandardized, and renamed the **Wechsler Adult Intelligence Scale (WAIS-R)** and is now one of the most commonly used psychological tests. The test contains both verbal and performance (nonverbal) subtests, which yield separate verbal and performance IQ scores as well as an overall IQ score. This test is a departure from the Stanford–Binet scale, which yields just one IQ score.

Wechsler also published the Wechsler Intelligence Scale for Children (WISC-R) and the Wechsler Preschool and Primary Scale of Intelligence (WPPSI), which is normed for children aged 4 to 6½. Table 7.1 describes the types of tasks found on the WISC-R.

TABLE 7.1 Typical Subtests on the WISC-R

Verbal Subtests		Performance Subtests	
Subtest	**Sample Items**	**Subtest**	**Description of Item**
Information	How many wings does a bird have?	Picture arrangement	Arrange a series of cartoon panels to make a meaningful story.
Digit span	Repeat from memory a series of digits, such as 3 1 0 6 7 4 2 5, after hearing it once.	Picture completion	What is missing from these pictures?
General comprehension	What is the advantage of keeping money in a bank?	Block design	Copy designs with blocks
Arithmetic	If 2 apples cost 15¢, what will be the cost of a dozen apples?		
Similarities	In what way are a lion and a tiger alike?		
Vocabulary	This test consists simply of asking, "What is a _____?" or "What does _____ mean?" The words cover a wide range of difficulty or familiarity.	Object assembly	Put together a jigsaw puzzle.
		Digit symbol	Fill in the symbols:

Group Intelligence Tests: Testing More Than One at a Time Administering individual intelligence tests such as the Stanford–Binet and the Wechsler is expensive and time-consuming. The tests must be given to one person at a time by a qualified professional. For testing large numbers of people in a short period of time on a limited budget, group intelligence tests are the answer. Group intelligence tests, such as the California Test of Mental Maturity, the Cognitive Abilities Test, and the Otis–Lennon Mental Ability Test, are now widely used.

Requirements of Good Tests: Reliability, Validity, and Standardization

What is meant by the terms reliability, validity, and standardization?

If your watch gains 6 minutes one day and loses 3 or 4 minutes the next day, it is not reliable. You want a watch that you can rely on to give the correct time day after day. Like a watch, an intelligence test must have **reliability**; the test must consistently yield nearly the same score when the same people are tested and then retested on the same test or an alternative form of the test. The higher the correlation between the two scores, the more reliable the test. A correlation coefficient of 1.0 would indicate perfect reliability. Most widely used tests, such as the Stanford–Binet and Wechsler tests and the Scholastic Assessment Test (SAT), boast high reliabilities of about .90.

Tests can be highly reliable but worthless if they are not valid. **Validity** is the ability or power of a test to measure what it is intended to measure. For example, a thermometer is a valid instrument for measuring temperature; a bathroom scale is valid for measuring weight. But no matter how reliable your bathroom scale, it will not take your temperature. It is valid only for weighing.

Aptitude tests are designed to predict a person's probable achievement or performance at some future time. Selecting students for admission to college or graduate schools is based partly on the predictive validity of aptitude tests, such as the Scholastic Assessment Test (SAT), American College Testing Program (ACT), and the Graduate Record Examination (GRE). How well do SAT scores predict success in college? Moderately at best. The correlation between SAT scores and the grades of college freshmen is about .40 (Linn, 1982).

Once a test is proven to be valid and reliable, the next requirement is **standardization**. There must be standard procedures for administering and scoring the test. Exactly the same directions must be given, whether written or oral, and the same amount of time must be allowed for every test taker. But even more important, standardization means establishing norms by which all scores are interpreted. A test is standardized by administering it to a large sample of people representative of those who will be taking the test in the future. The group's scores are analyzed, and then the average score, standard deviation, percentile rankings, and other measures are computed. These comparative scores become the norms used as the standard against which all other test scores are measured.

reliability: The ability of a test to yield nearly the same score when the same people are tested and then retested on the same test or an alternative form of the test.

validity: The ability of a test to measure what it is intended to measure.

aptitude test: A test designed to predict a person's achievement or performance at some future time.

standardization: Establishing norms for comparing the scores of people who will take a test in the future; administering tests using a prescribed procedure.

The Range of Intelligence

What are the ranges of IQ scores considered average, superior, and in the range of mental retardation?

When large populations are measured on intelligence or on physical characteristics such as height or weight, the test scores or results usually conform to the bell-shaped distribution known as the normal curve. The majority of the scores cluster around the mean (average). The farther scores deviate or move away from the mean, either above or below, the fewer scores there are.

The average IQ test score for all people in the same age group is arbitrarily assigned an IQ score of 100. On the Wechsler intelligence tests, approximately 50 percent of the scores are in the average range, between 90 and 110. About 68 percent of the scores fall between 85 and 115, and about 95 percent fall between 70 and 130. About 2 percent of the scores are above 130, which is considered superior, and about 2 percent fall below 70, in the range of mental retardation (see Figure 7.3 on page 252).

FIGURE 7.3

The Normal Curve

When a large number of test scores are compiled, they typically are distributed in a normal (bell-shaped) curve. On the Wechsler intelligence scales, the average or mean IQ score is set at 100. As the figure shows, about 68 percent of the scores fall between 15 IQ points (1 standard deviation) above and below 100 (from 85 to 115), and about 95.5 percent of the scores fall between 30 points (2 standard deviations) above and below 100 (from 70 to 130).

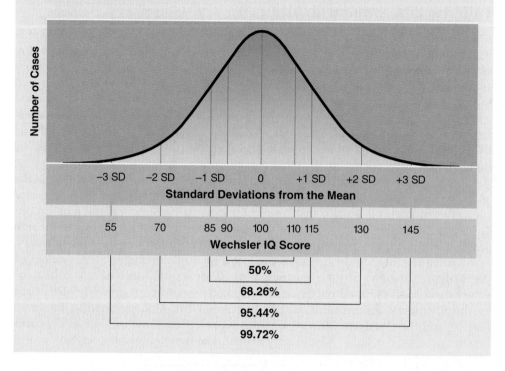

> **?** *According to the Terman study, how do the gifted differ from the general population?*

Terman's Study of the Gifted: 1,528 Geniuses and How They Grew In 1921 Lewis M. Terman (1925) launched a longitudinal study, now a classic, in which 1,528 gifted students were selected and measured at different ages throughout their lives. Tested on the Stanford–Binet, the subjects, 857 males and 671 females, had unusually high IQs, ranging from 135 to 200, with an average of 151. Terman assumed the Stanford–Binet measured innate intelligence and that IQ was fixed at birth (Cravens, 1992).

Terman's early findings put an end to the myth that mentally superior people are more likely to be physically inferior. Terman's gifted subjects excelled in almost all of the abilities he studied—intellectual, physical, emotional, moral, and social. Terman also exploded many other myths about the mentally gifted (Terman & Oden, 1947). For example, you may have heard the saying that there is a thin line between genius and madness. Actually Terman's gifted group enjoyed better mental health than the general population. Also, you may have heard that mentally gifted people are long on "book sense" but short on "common sense." In reality Terman's subjects were more likely to be successful in the real, practical world than their less mentally gifted peers. Terman (1925) concluded that "there is no law of compensation whereby the intellectual superiority of the gifted is offset by inferiorities along nonintellectual lines" (p. 16).

The Terman study still continues today, with most of the subjects in their 70s and 80s. In a report on Terman's subjects, Shneidman (1989) states the basic findings of the study—that "an unusual mind, a vigorous body, and a relatively well-adjusted personality are not at all incompatible" (p. 687).

Who Are the Gifted? Beginning in the early 1920s, the term *giftedness* was used to describe the intellectually superior—those with IQs in the upper 2 to 3 percent of the U.S. population. Today the term includes both the exceptionally creative and those excelling in the visual or performing arts.

Traditionally, special programs for the gifted have involved either acceleration or enrichment. Acceleration enables students to progress at a rate that is consistent with their ability. Students may skip a grade, progress through subject matter at a faster rate, be granted advanced placement in college courses, or enter college early. Enrichment programs aim to broaden students' knowledge by giving them special courses in foreign language, music appreciation, and the like, or by providing special experiences designed to foster advanced thinking skills.

The Mentally Retarded At the opposite end of the continuum from the intellectually gifted are the 2 percent of the U.S. population whose IQ scores place them in the range of **mental retardation**. Individuals are not classified as mentally retarded unless (1) their IQ score is below 70 and (2) they have a severe deficiency in everyday adaptive functioning—the ability to care for themselves and relate to others (Grossman, 1983). There are degrees of retardation from mild to profound. Individuals with IQs ranging from 55 to 70 are considered mildly retarded; from 40 to 55, moderately retarded; from 25 to 40, severely retarded; and below 25, profoundly retarded. Table 7.2 shows the level of functioning expected for various categories of mental retardation.

mental retardation: Subnormal intelligence reflected by an IQ below 70 and by adaptive functioning severely deficient for one's age.

? *What two criteria must one meet to be classified as mentally retarded?*

TABLE 7.2 Mental Retardation as Measured on the Wechsler Scales

Classification	IQ Range	Percentage of the Mentally Retarded	Characteristics of Retarded Persons at Each Level
Mild	55–70	90%	Are able to grasp learning skills up to 6th grade level. They may become self-supporting and can be profitably employed in various vocational occupations.
Moderate	40–55	6%	Probably are not able to grasp more than 2nd grade academic skills but can learn self-help skills and some social and academic skills. They may work in sheltered workshops.
Severe	25–40	3%	Can be trained in basic health habits; can learn to communicate verbally. Learn through repetitive habit training.
Profound	Below 25	1%	Rudimentary motor development; may learn very limited self-help skills.

Mentally retarded (1–3%)

Moderate, severe, and profound (10%)

90%

Mild

Total U.S. Population

Total Population of People with Mental Retardation

mainstreaming: Educating mentally retarded students in regular rather than special schools by placing them in regular classes for part of the day or having special classrooms in regular schools.

There are many causes of mental retardation, including brain injuries, chromosomal abnormalities such as Down syndrome, chemical deficiencies, lead poisoning, and hazards present during fetal development.

Before the late 1960s, mentally retarded children in the United States were educated almost exclusively in special schools. Since then there has been a movement toward **mainstreaming**—an attempt to educate mentally retarded students in regular schools. Mainstreaming may involve placing these students in classes with nonhandicapped students for part of the day or in special classrooms in regular schools.

Resources spent on training programs for the mentally retarded are proving to be sound investments. Such programs rely heavily on behavior modification techniques and are making it possible for some retarded citizens to become employed workers earning the minimum wage or better. Everyone benefits—the individual, the family, and society as well.

Memory Check 7.2

1. The first valid intelligence test was the:
   a. Stanford–Binet.   c. Wechsler.
   b. Binet–Simon.   d. Terman.

2. According to Stern's formula, what is the IQ of a child with a mental age of 12 and a chronological age of 8?
   a. 75   b. 150   c. 125   d. 100

3. The Stanford–Binet and Wechsler intelligence tests must be administered individually, rather than in groups. (true/false)

4. Wechsler developed intelligence tests for adults and children. (true/false)

5. The largest percentage of people taking an IQ test will score in the range from:
   a. 80 to 100.   c. 100 to 130.
   b. 90 to 109.   d. 65 to 90.

6. In his study of the gifted, Terman found that mentally superior individuals tend to be physically smaller and weaker. (true/false)

7. People are considered mentally retarded if they are clearly deficient in adaptive functioning and their IQ is below:
   a. 100.   b. 90.   c. 80.   d. 70.

8. A test that measures what it claims to measure has _____; a test that gives consistent results has _____.
   a. reliability; validity
   b. equivalence; reliability
   c. validity; reliability
   d. objectivity; validity

Answers: 1. a 2. b 3. true 4. true 5. b 6. false 7. d 8. c

The IQ Controversy: Brainy Dispute

The Uses and Abuses of Intelligence Tests

Intelligence testing has become a major growth industry. And many Americans have come to believe that a "magical" number—an IQ score, a percentile rank, or some other derived score—unfalteringly portrays a person's intellectual capacity, ability, or potential. In many cases, the score has served as the ticket of admission or the mark of rejection to educational and occupational opportunity.

For what are intelligence tests good and poor predictors?

Intelligence Test Scores: Can They Predict Success and Failure?

What can intelligence tests really tell us? IQ scores are fairly good predictors of academic achievement and success in school. The Stanford–Binet Intelligence Scale and the verbal scale of the Wechsler tests correlate highly with school grades. This is not surprising, since success in schoolwork and success on these intelligence tests both require the same set of skills—verbal and test-taking ability. But IQ tests and aptitude tests such as the SAT are far from infallible.

Is there a high correlation between IQ and success in life? Although the average IQ score of people in the professions (doctors, dentists, lawyers) tends to be higher than that of people in lower-status occupations, the exact relationship between IQ score and occupational status is not clearly understood. Among people of the same social class and level of education, IQ scores do not reliably predict comparative degrees of occupational success.

The Abuses of Intelligence Tests: Making Too Much of a Single Number

Abuses occur when scores on intelligence or aptitude tests are the only or even the major criterion for admitting people to various educational programs. Intelligence tests do not measure attitude and motivation, critical ingredients of success. Many people are admitted to educational programs who probably should not be, while others are denied admission who could profit from them and possibly make significant contributions to society. Consider Dr. Robert Jarvik, described at the beginning of this chapter.

Early categorization based solely on IQ scores can doom children to slow-track educational programs that are not appropriate for them. Many poor and minority children (particularly those for whom English is a second language) and visually or hearing impaired children have been dumped into special education programs. IQ tests predicted that they were not mentally able to profit from regular classroom instruction. There would be no problem if IQ test results were unfailingly accurate, but in fact they are not.

In some states IQ tests are banned altogether. In others it is now illegal to place children in classes for the mentally retarded based solely on their IQ scores without additional testing of their level of adaptive functioning in daily life. Mercer (1973) developed tests to measure performance on practical life skills, such as keeping score in baseball, reading a newspaper, and so on. She tested African-American and white students, all of whom had IQ scores under 70. Her results showed that on pass-fail tests on these skills, 95 percent of the African-American subjects passed, but none of the white subjects did. Such results may suggest that "IQ tests are measuring something fundamentally different for blacks and whites, at least for low scores" (Crane, 1994, p. 200).

Are minority children and those for whom English is a second language at a disadvantage when they are assessed on conventional tests? Attempts have been made to develop **culture-fair intelligence tests** designed to minimize cultural bias. The questions do not penalize individuals whose cultural experience or language differs from that of the middle or upper classes. See Figure 7.4 (on page 256) for an example of the type of test item found on a culture-fair test.

The Nature–Nurture Controversy: Battle of the Centuries

The most vocal area of disagreement concerning intelligence has been the **nature–nurture controversy**, the debate over whether intelligence is primarily the result of heredity or environment. Englishman Sir Francis Galton (1874) initiated this debate and coined the term. After studying a number of prominent families in England, Galton concluded that intelligence was inherited.

The nature–nurture controversy has raged for well over 100 years. Hereditarians like Galton claim that intelligence is largely inherited—the result of

What are some of the abuses of intelligence tests?

culture-fair intelligence test: An intelligence test that uses questions that will not penalize those whose culture differs from that of the middle or upper classes.

nature–nurture controversy: The debate over whether intelligence and other traits are primarily the result of heredity or environment.

How does the nature–nurture controversy apply to intelligence?

FIGURE 7.4

An Example of a Test Item on a Culture-Fair Test

This culture-fair test does not penalize test takers whose language or cultural experiences differ from those of the urban middle or upper classes. Subjects are to select, from the six samples on the right, the patch that would complete the pattern. Patch number 3 is the correct answer. (Adapted from the Raven Standard Progressive Matrices Test.)

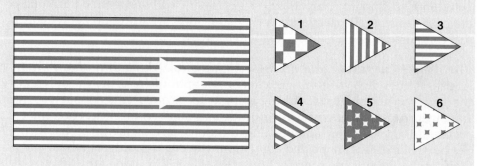

nature. Environmentalists, on the other hand, insist that it is influenced primarily by one's environment—the result of nurture. Most psychologists today agree that both nature and nurture contribute to intelligence, but they continue to debate the proportions contributed by each.

Behavioral Genetics: Investigating Nature and Nurture

Behavioral genetics is a field of research that investigates the relative effects of heredity and environment on behavior and ability (Plomin & Rende, 1991). Two of the primary methods used by behavioral geneticists are the twin study method, first used by Galton (1875) in his studies of heredity, and the adoption method.

In the **twin study method**, researchers study **identical twins** (monozygotic twins) and **fraternal twins** (dizygotic twins) to determine how much they resemble each other on a variety of characteristics. Identical twins have exactly the same genes because a single sperm cell of the father fertilizes a single egg of the mother, forming a cell that then splits and forms two human beings—"carbon copies." But fraternal twins are no more alike genetically than other siblings born to the same parents. In the case of fraternal twins, two separate sperm cells fertilize two separate eggs that happen to be released at the same time during ovulation.

Twins who are raised together, whether identical or fraternal, have similar environments. If identical twins raised together are found to be more alike than fraternal twins on a certain trait, then that trait is assumed to be more influenced by heredity. But if identical and fraternal twins from similar environments do not differ on a trait, then that trait is assumed to be influenced more by environment. The term **heritability** is an index of the degree to which a characteristic is estimated to be influenced by heredity. Figure 7.5 shows estimates of genetic and environmental factors contributing to intelligence.

In the **adoption method** behavioral geneticists study children adopted shortly after birth. By comparing their abilities and personality traits to those of their adoptive family members with whom they live and those of their biological parents whom they may never have met, researchers can disentangle the effects of heredity and environment (Plomin et al., 1988).

What is behavioral genetics, and what are the primary methods used in the field today?

behavioral genetics: A field of research that investigates the relative effects of heredity and environment on behavior and ability.

twin study method: Studying identical and fraternal twins to determine the relative effects of heredity and environment on a variety of characteristics.

identical twins: Twins with identical genes; monozygotic twins.

fraternal twins: Twins who are no more alike genetically than ordinary brothers and sisters; dizygotic twins.

FIGURE 7.5

Correlations between the IQ Scores of Persons with Various Relationships

The more closely related two individuals are, the more similar their IQ scores tend to be. Thus, there is a strong genetic contribution to intelligence. (Based on data from Bouchard & McGue, 1981; Erlenmeyer-Kimling & Jarvik, 1963.)

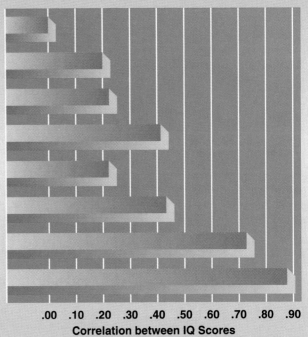

Unrelated persons, reared apart
Unrelated persons, reared together
Foster parent and child
Parent and child living together
Brothers and sisters, reared apart
Brothers and sisters, reared together
Identical twins, reared apart
Identical twins, reared together

.00 .10 .20 .30 .40 .50 .60 .70 .80 .90
Correlation between IQ Scores

A Natural Experiment: Identical Twins Reared Apart Minnesota—home of the twin cities and the Minnesota Twins—is also, fittingly, the site of the most extensive U.S. study of identical and fraternal twins. The Minnesota Center for Twin and Adoption Research has assembled the Minnesota Twin Registry, which in 1990 included some 9,200 twin pairs (Lykken et al., 1990).

Probably the best way to assess the relative contributions of heredity and environment is to study identical twins who have been separated at birth and raised apart. When separated twins are found to have strikingly similar traits, it is assumed that heredity has been a major contributor. When separated twins differ on a given trait, the influence of the environment is thought to be greater.

Since 1979 the Minnesota researchers headed by Thomas Bouchard have studied more than 100 sets of twins or triplets from many parts of the world who were reared apart. Comparing the similarity in IQ of identical twins reared together and apart, Bouchard and others (1990) concluded that *"general intelligence or IQ is strongly affected by genetic factors"* (p. 227). In four independent studies, primarily of middle-aged adults, a heritability of .70 was found, indicating that 70 percent of the variation in IQ can be attributed to genetic factors. Not all researchers agree with Bouchard's heritability estimate of intelligence. Combining data from a number of twin studies, Plomin and others (1994) found the heritability estimate for general intelligence to be .52.

Psychologists who consider environmental factors as the chief contributors to differences in intelligence take issue with Bouchard's findings. They claim that most separated identical twins are raised by adoptive parents who have been matched as closely as possible to the biological parents. This fact, the critics say, could account for the similarity in IQ. In response to their critics, Bouchard and others (1991) point out that studies comparing nonbiologically related siblings reared in the same home reveal that IQ correlations are close to zero by the time the subjects reach adolescence (Scarr & Weinberg, 1978; Teasdale & Owen, 1984).

How do twin studies support the view that intelligence is inherited?

heritability: An index of the degree to which a characteristic is estimated to be influenced by heredity.

adoption method: A method researchers use to study the relative effects of heredity and environment on behavior and ability in children adopted shortly after birth, by comparing them to their biological and adoptive parents.

Adoption studies reveal that children adopted shortly after birth have IQs more closely resembling those of their biological parents than those of their adoptive parents. The family environment has an influence on IQ early in life, but that influence seems to diminish. Twin and adoption studies indicate that as subjects reach adulthood, it is genes that are most closely correlated with IQ (Loehlin et al., 1988, 1989; McCartney et al., 1990; Plomin & Rende, 1991). Bouchard and others (1990) claim that "although parents may be able to affect their children's rate of cognitive skill acquisition, they may have relatively little influence on the ultimate level attained" (p. 225). But does this mean that the degree to which intelligence is inherited is the degree to which it is absolutely fixed and immune to environmental intervention?

> ? *What are Jensen's and Herrnstein and Murray's controversial views on race and IQ?*

Race and IQ: The Controversial Views of Jensen and of Herrnstein and Murray   Some studies over the past several decades have reported that, on the average, African Americans score about 15 points lower than whites on standardized IQ tests (Herrnstein & Murray, 1994; Jensen, 1985; Loehlin et al., 1975). In 1969 psychologist Arthur Jensen published an article in which he attributed the IQ gap to genetic differences between the races. Further, he claimed that the genetic influence on intelligence is so strong that the environment cannot make a significant difference. Almost immediately, Jensen's views on race and intelligence sent a shock wave through the scientific community.

Recently, Herrnstein and Murray (1994) added fresh fuel to the controversy with their book *The Bell Curve*. They argue that IQ differences among people and between groups explain how those at the top in U.S. society got there and why those at the lower rungs of society's ladder remain there. Herrnstein and Murray (1994) largely attribute the social ills of modern society—poverty, welfare dependency, crime, illegitimacy—to low IQ, which they imply is primarily genetic and largely immune to change by environmental intervention. Yet they offer their own estimate that 60 percent of IQ is genetically inherited, "which, by extension, means that IQ is about 40 percent a matter of environment" (p. 105). That 40 percent would seem to leave a lot of room for improvement.

The Bell Curve offers correlational data to show a relationship between IQ and many other variables—poverty, for example. Critics of *The Bell Curve* were quick to point out that correlational data cannot be used to conclude that low IQ causes poverty—or, for matter, that poverty causes low IQ (Kamin, 1995). Herrnstein and Murray's most ominous conclusion rests heavily on the notion that IQ is destiny and warns of castelike divisions in modern society based upon IQ. The highest 5 to 10 percent of the intelligence distribution will be even more firmly entrenched at the top of society, they write. And those with low IQs will remain a permanent underclass. But the frightening outcomes envisioned by Herrnstein and Murray are inescapable ones only to the degree that IQ is *not* affected by environmental factors.

Jensen's and Herrnstein and Murray's views run counter to the belief that an enriched, stimulating environment can overcome the deficits of poverty and cultural disadvantage and thus reduce the IQ deficit.

Is the Gap Due to Race Alone?   If average IQ differences were genetically determined by race, then the mean IQ scores of mixed-race individuals should fall somewhere between the mean scores for African-Americans and whites. But studies over the decades have not found such a relationship between IQ and mixed ancestry (Loehlin et al., 1973; Scarr et al., 1977). At the end of World War II, American soldiers stationed in Germany, both African American and white, fathered thousands of children with German women. Fifteen years later, Eyeferth (1961) randomly selected samples of these children. The mean IQs of the two groups were virtually identical. Having a white father conferred no measurable IQ advantage at all.

Intelligence: Is It Fixed or Changeable?

Probably the most important issue in intelligence is whether IQ is fixed or changeable. Clearly, the high degree of similarity in intelligence scores between identical twins reared apart makes a strong case for the powerful influence of genetics. But even Bouchard and his colleagues (1990) caution against trying to generalize their findings to people raised in disadvantaged environments. Moreover, they leave open the possibility that IQ may be enhanced in a more optimal environment.

The idea that a behavior or characteristic that is genetic in origin cannot be changed is a myth. According to Richard Weinberg (1989):

> Genes do not fix behavior. Rather, they establish a range of possible reactions to the range of possible experiences that environments can provide. . . . How people behave or what their measured IQs turn out to be or how quickly they learn depends on the nature of their environments *and* on their genetic endowments bestowed at conception. (p. 101)

Adoption Studies: Enriched Environments Boost IQs Several studies indicate that IQ test scores are not fixed but can be modified with an enriched environment. More than two decades ago, Sandra Scarr and Richard Weinberg (1976) studied 130 African American and interracial children who had been adopted by highly educated, upper-middle-class white families; 99 of the children had been adopted in the first year of life. The adoptees were fully exposed to middle-class cultural experiences and vocabulary, the "culture of the tests and the school" (p. 737).

How did the children perform on IQ and achievement tests? For these children, the 15-point black–white IQ gap was bridged by an enriched environment. Compared to an average IQ score of 90, which would be expected had these children been reared by their biological parents, the average IQ score of the 130 adoptees was 106.3. And their achievement test scores were slightly above the national average, not below. On the average, the earlier the children were adopted, the higher their IQs. The mean IQ score of the 99 early adoptees was 110.4, about 10 IQ points above the average for whites (see Figure 7.6).

Studies in France also show that IQ scores and achievement are substantially higher when children from lower-class environments are adopted by middle- and upper-middle-class families (Duyme, 1988; Schiff and Lewontin, 1986).

Changes in Standard of Living Further evidence that drastic changes in the environment can have major effects on intelligence stretches back more than half a century. In 1940, group IQ tests were given to 3,200 economically disadvantaged white children from 40 schools in the Appalachian Mountains of Tennessee. Their scores were compared to the scores of other children from the same area and of many from the same families, who had been tested 10 years earlier in 1930. From 1930 to 1940, the area had undergone tremendous improvements in economic, educational, and cultural conditions; and within this period, average IQ score had increased 11 points (Wheeler, 1942). The same gene pool, after a decade of continuing environmental enrichment, had raised its average IQ by 11 points, about three-fourths of a standard deviation—a major effect, by any measure.

Other evidence also suggests that environmental factors have a strong influence on IQ scores. Americans and similarly advanced populations all over the world have gained about 3 IQ points per decade over the past 50 years. James Flynn (1987b) analyzed 73 studies involving some 7,500 subjects ranging in age from 12 to 48 and found that "every Binet and Wechsler sample from 1932 to 1978 has performed better than its predecessor" (p. 225). The average IQ in Western industrialized nations is currently about 15 IQ points, or 1 standard deviation, higher than 50 years ago. In regard to the black–white IQ gap among U.S. adults,

What kinds of evidence suggest that IQ is changeable rather than fixed?

FIGURE 7.6

Mean IQ Scores of African American Adoptees

The 130 African American children adopted by upper-middle-class white families had a mean IQ score of 106.3, 6 points higher than the average for whites. But 99 of the 130 children who had been adopted early had a mean IQ score of 110.4. (After Scarr & Weinberg, 1976.)

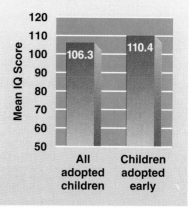

Children's environment—whether deprived or enriched—can have a significant effect on their IQ scores and future achievement.

Flynn (1987b) asserts that "the environmental advantage whites enjoy over blacks is similar to what whites (adults) of today enjoy over their own parents or grandparents of 50 years ago" (p. 226).

Researcher Ken Vincent (1991) presents data suggesting that while African American and white adults remain separated by about 15 IQ points, the gap is narrower in young children—about 7 or 8 IQ points. Vincent (1993) attributes the rapid mean gains by African American children to environmental changes in economic and educational opportunity.

We should not be surprised when enriched environments alter traits that are highly heritable. Consider the fact that American and British adolescents are 6 inches taller on average than their counterparts a century and a half ago (Tanner, 1962). Height has the same heritability (.90) today as it did in the mid-1800s. So this tremendous average gain in height of 6 inches is entirely attributable to environmental influences: better health, better nutrition, and so on. The highest heritability estimates for intelligence are far lower than those for height. It seems clear then that environmental influences have the power to affect intelligence and achievement.

The environmental influences that affect us for good or ill are transmitted to us through our culture. Are there identifiable cultural values related to academic achievement? The World of Psychology section explores this question.

World of Psychology

Expectations, Effort, and Academic Achievement— A Cross-Cultural Comparison

Stevenson and others (1986) compared the math ability of randomly selected elementary school children from three comparable cities—Taipei in Taiwan, Sendai in Japan, and Minneapolis in the United States. It was no contest. By the fifth grade, the Asian children were outscoring the students in the United States by about 15 points in math ability, roughly one standard deviation. And the Asian superiority held firmly from the highest to the lowest achievement levels. Of the lowest 100 students in math achievement, 67 were Americans; of the top 100, only 1 was. The Japanese children scored the highest of the three groups in fifth grade, and even the lowest-scoring Japanese classes did better than the top-scoring classes in the United States.

How do we explain such differences in achievement in children from different cultures? Researchers such as Jensen (1985) and Galton before him, and more recently Herrnstein and Murray (1994), would point to genetic differences; but there are other possibilities. Stevenson and others (1990) suggest that cultural, rather than genetic, differences may be a major factor in explaining the gap in math ability. Their study was conducted with first and fifth graders from the same three cities and included 1,440 students (480 from each of the three countries). The children were tested in reading and mathematics and interviewed along with their mothers. In a follow-up study 4 years later, the first graders (now fifth graders) were tested again, and again they and their mothers were interviewed.

The interviews revealed significant differences between the Asian and American cultures. Stevenson and others (1990) report that the Chinese and Japanese mothers considered academic achievement to be *the most important* pursuit of their children, whereas American parents did not value it as a central concern. The Asian, but not the American, families structured their home activities to promote academic achievement as soon as their first child started elementary school.

The Asian parents downplayed the importance of innate ability but emphasized the value of hard work and persistence (Stevenson, 1992). American parents, in contrast, believed more firmly in genetic limitations on ability and achievement. Such a belief has devastating effects, according to Stevenson, who states, "When parents believe success in school depends for the most part on ability rather than effort, they are less likely to foster participation in activities related to academic achievement" (p. 73). Also, American mothers tended to overestimate the cognitive abilities of their children, but the Chinese and Japanese mothers did not. Asian mothers held their children to higher standards while giving

FIGURE 7.7

Mothers' Satisfaction with Their Children's Academic Performance

Even though American students had by far the poorest achievement record of the children studied in the United States, Taiwan, and Japan, American mothers expressed much higher satisfaction with their children's academic performance than did mothers from the two Asian countries. (From Stevenson, 1992.)

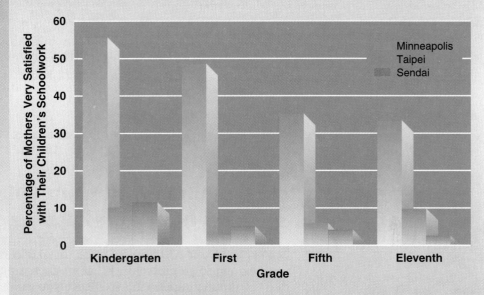

more realistic assessments of their children's abilities (see Figure 7.7).

In follow-up studies, Stevenson and others (1993) found that the achievement gap between Asian and American students persisted over a 10-year period. Differences in high-school achievement were explained in part by the fact that the American students spent more time working at part-time jobs and socializing than their Asian counterparts did (Fuligni & Stevenson, 1995). But do Asian students pay a psychological price for their stunning academic achievement? Are they more likely than students in the United States to be depressed, nervous, stressed, and heavily burdened by pressures to maintain academic excellence? A recent, large cross-cultural study comparing 11th-grade students from Japan, Taiwan, and the United States did find a correlation between achievement in mathematics and psychological distress—but, surprisingly, for the American students, not the Asian students (Crystal et al., 1994). Moreover, contrary to popular belief, adolescent suicide rates are lower in Japan than in the United States.

Why should high-achieving American students, but not Asian students, pay a price in terms of psychological distress? The researchers found that Asian teenagers typically enjoy support and encouragement for their academic achievement from family and peers alike. In contrast, high-achieving teenagers in the United States are torn between studying harder to excel academically and pursuing nonacademic social interests. Such interests may be strongly encouraged by their peers and often by parents who want their children to be "well-rounded."

Which of these two cultural tendencies is more likely to maximize the development of one's intellectual potential, whether large or modest? Perhaps the answer to the stunning record of academic achievement of Asian students lies not in their genes, but in the cultural values that nurtured them.

Memory | Check 7.3

1. IQ tests are good predictors of success in school. (true/false)

2. What field of research investigates the relative effects of heredity and environment on behavior and ability?
   a. genetics   c. biology
   b. behavioral genetics   d. physiology

3. Twin studies suggest that environment is stronger than heredity as a factor in shaping IQ differences. (true/false)

4. Jensen and Herrnstein and Murray claim that the black–white IQ gap is due primarily to:
   a. genetics.   c. discrimination.
   b. environment.   d. racism.

5. Several adoption studies have revealed that when infants from disadvantaged environments are adopted by middle- and upper-middle-class parents, their IQ scores are raised about 15 points. (true/false)

Answers: 1. true 2. b 3. false 4. a 5. true

Imagery and Concepts: Tools of Thinking

Whatever our IQ happens to be, we use certain skills and strategies when we think and solve problems. What are these tools of thinking?

In trying to prove his existence, the great French philosopher René Descartes (1596–1650) said, "I think, therefore I am." Unfortunately, he did not proceed to describe the act of thinking itself. All of us have an intuitive notion of what thinking is. We say, "I think it's going to rain" (a prediction); "I think this is the right answer" (a choice); "I think I will resign" (a decision). But our everyday use of the word *think* does not suggest the processes we use to perform the act itself. Sometimes our thinking is free flowing rather than goal-oriented. At other times, it is directed and aimed at a goal such as solving a problem or making a decision. Just how is the act of thinking accomplished? There is general agreement that at least two tools are commonly used when we think—images and concepts.

Imagery: Picture This—Elephants with Purple Polka Dots

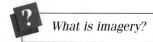

What is imagery?

Can you imagine hearing a recording of your favorite song or someone calling your name? Can you picture yourself jogging, walking, or kissing someone you love? In your imagination, can you smell ammonia or taste your favorite ice cream? The vast majority of us are able to produce mental **imagery**; that is, we can represent or picture a sensory experience in our mind. Albert Einstein is said to have done much of his thinking in images.

In a survey of 500 adults conducted by McKellar (1972), 97 percent said they had visual images; 93 percent reported auditory images (imagine your psychology professor's voice); 74 percent claimed to have motor imagery (imagine raising your hand); 70 percent, tactile or touch images (imagine rubbing sandpaper); 67 percent, gustatory images (imagine the taste of a dill pickle); and 66 percent, olfactory images (imagine smelling a rose). Visual imagery is certainly the most common, although auditory imagery is not far behind.

imagery: The representation in the mind of a sensory experience—visual, auditory, gustatory, motor, olfactory, or tactile.

Our images may be dimmer and less vivid than actual experiences, but images are not limited to time and space, size, or other physical realities. We can imagine ourselves flying though the air like an eagle, singing to the thundering applause of adoring fans, or performing all sorts of amazing feats. But normally our imaging is quite similar to the real world we are thinking about.

When we construct visual mental images, we may believe that we form the entire image all at once. But according to Stephen Kosslyn (1988), we do not. Rather, we mentally construct the objects we image, one part at a time. Studies with split-brain patients (discussed in Chapter 2) and normal subjects suggest that two types of processes are used in the formation of visual images. First, we retrieve stored memories of how parts of an object look, and then we use mental processes to arrange or assemble those parts into the proper whole. Both the left and right hemispheres participate in the processes of forming visual images. Try forming visual images as you do the *Try It!*

A. Picture an ant crawling on a newspaper about 3 feet away. How many legs does the ant have?

B. Picture an ant perched on the end of a toothpick right in front of your eyes. Does the ant have eyelashes?

In which mental picture is the ant larger, A or B? Which mental picture provides more detail of the ant? (After Finke, 1985.)

Kosslyn (1975, 1983) asked research subjects many questions like those in the *Try It!* and found that they answered questions concerning larger images about ⅕ second faster than questions about small images. It takes us slightly longer to zoom in on smaller images than on larger ones, just as it does when we actually look at real objects.

But what if we are forming new images rather than answering questions about large and small images already formed? Picture an elephant standing 2 feet away. Now picture a rabbit standing at the same distance. Which image took longer to form? Kosslyn (1975) discovered that it takes people longer to form large mental images than to conjure up small ones. It takes longer to view the elephant because there is more of it to view, and likewise more of it to image.

Not only do we form a mental image of an object, but we manipulate and move it around in our mind much as we would if we were actually holding and looking at the object (Cooper & Shepard, 1984). Shepard & Metzler (1971) asked eight subjects to judge some 1,600 pairs of drawings like the ones in Figure 7.8. Subjects had to rotate the objects in their imagination to see if they matched. In Figure 7.8 (a) and (b) the objects are a match; those in Figure 7.8 (c) are not. But the important finding is that the more the objects had to be rotated in imagery, the longer it took subjects to decide whether they matched. This is precisely what would happen if the subjects had rotated real objects—the farther they needed to be rotated, the longer it would take to make the decision.

Similarities in the Processes of Imaging and Perceiving

If we form mental images (visual, auditory, etc.) much as we actually perceive them, then is

FIGURE 7.8

Samples of Geometric Patterns in Shepard and Metzler's Mental Rotation Study

Mentally rotate one of the patterns in each pair—(a), (b), and (c)—and decide whether the two patterns match. Do you find that the more you have to rotate the objects mentally, the longer it takes to decide if they match? (From Shepard & Metzler, 1971.)

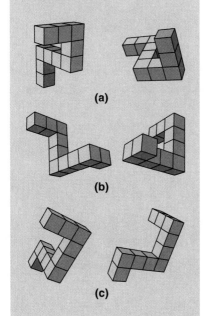

(a)

(b)

(c)

imaging subject to interference, just like our perceptions? Close your eyes, and form a mental image of your psychology professor. Now keep the visual image, and open your eyes. Doesn't the mental image fade or disappear as soon as you see a real object? If viewing an actual object interferes with a visual image, is the reverse also true? Will a vivid visual image interfere with a real object?

Yes, according to Craver-Lemley and Reeves (1992). In an earlier study, Segal and Fusella (1970) asked student subjects to form either a visual image of a tree or an auditory image of the sound of a typewriter. The researchers then made a faint sound on a harmonica or flashed a small, dimly lighted blue arrow, or did nothing at all. Subjects who were holding the visual image of a tree were more likely to miss seeing the blue arrow but more likely to hear the harmonica. But subjects imaging the sound of a typewriter had the opposite experience. They saw the arrow but missed the sound of the harmonica. This study suggests that the same mental processes are used in both perceiving and imaging. Furthermore, using the same processes *simultaneously* on two different tasks causes interference.

But not all researchers who study imagery and perception agree (Roland & Gulyás, 1994). There is agreement that certain higher-order visual areas in the temporal and parietal lobes are involved both in imagery and in perception (Moscovitch et al., 1994). But some researchers say that the primary visual cortex is not necessarily active during imaging unless a person is actually scrutinizing the features of some object stored in memory, as you did in the *Try It!* (Sakai & Miyashita, 1994). On the other hand, Kosslyn and Ochsner (1994; Kosslyn, 1994) claim that the primary visual cortex *is* also involved in most imaging. They believe that the same brain pathways are used both in perceiving and in imaging objects, although the pathways for imaging are activated in reverse order from the pathways for perceiving.

Concepts: Our Mental Classification System (Is a Penguin a Bird?)

? *What are concepts and how are they formed?*

Fortunately, thinking is not limited to conjuring up a series of pictures, sounds, touches, tastes, and smells. We humans are capable of conceptualizing as well. A **concept** is a label that represents a class or group of objects, people, or events that share common characteristics or attributes. Concepts are useful tools that help us to order our world and to think and communicate with speed and efficiency.

Imagine that you are walking down the street with a friend, and you see approaching in the distance a hairy, brown and white, four-legged animal with two eyes and two ears, its mouth open, its tongue hanging out, and a long, wagging tail. You simply say to your friend, "Here comes a dog." Thanks to our ability to use concepts, we are not forced to consider and describe everything in great detail before we make an identification. We do not need a different name to identify and describe every single rock, tree, animal, or situation we meet. *Dog* is a concept that stands for a family of animals that share similar characteristics or attributes, even though they may differ in significant ways. Whether Great Dane, dachshund, collie, Chihuahua, or any other breed, we recognize all these varied creatures according to our concept *dog*.

Household pet is a broader concept, which might include dog, cat, bird, goldfish, and so on. Although other creatures may take up residence in our house—cockroach, mouse, mosquito, housefly, or bedbug—they are not likely to fit our concept of household pet.

We have concepts of abstractions as well as of tangible objects and organisms. Love, beauty, and justice are abstract concepts, and we can identify and consider aspects of beauty and justice because we have formed concepts of them.

concept: A label that represents a class or group of objects, people, or events sharing common characteristics or attributes.

Also, we use relational concepts in our thinking—larger than, smaller than, older than, younger than, and so on—to compare individuals, objects, and ideas.

Concept Formation: Learning What Fits a Concept How do we acquire concepts, and how do we know what fits or does not fit a given concept? We can form concepts (1) from a formal definition of the concept, (2) by systematically memorizing a concept's common features, (3) through our experiences with positive and negative instances of the concept, (4) through the use of prototypes, or (5) through the use of exemplars.

Systematic or Formal Approaches Studies have been conducted and theories proposed to explain how we form concepts. Some theorists maintain that we approach concept formation in an active, orderly, and systematic way, rather than in a random, informal, haphazard fashion (Bruner et al., 1956). Sometimes we learn a concept from a formal definition or from a formal classification system used in the sciences and other disciplines. You surely have memorized several of these formal classification systems in biology, chemistry, English, or other courses you have taken.

Positive and Negative Instances We acquire many simple concepts through experiences with examples or positive instances of the concept. When children are young, parents may point out examples of a car—the family car, the neighbor's car, cars on the street, and pictures of cars in a book. But if a child points to some other type of moving vehicle and says "car," the parent will say, "No, that is a truck," or "This is a bus." "Truck" and "bus" are negative instances, or nonexamples, of the concept "car." After experience with positive and negative instances of the concept, a child begins to grasp some of the properties of a car that distinguish it from other wheeled vehicles.

Prototypes Eleanor Rosch (1973, 1978) argues that formal theories of concept formation, and the experiments on which they are based, tend to be rather artificial, contrived, and not related to our actual experience. She and her colleagues have studied concept formation in its natural setting and have concluded that in real life our thinking and concept formation are somewhat fuzzy, not clear-cut and systematic. Sometimes we identify objects based on a memorized list of features or attributes that are common to instances of a concept. But in addition, we are likely to picture a **prototype** of the concept—an example that embodies the most common and typical features of the concept.

What is your prototype for the concept *bird?* Chances are it is not a penguin, an ostrich, or a kiwi. All three are birds that cannot fly. A more likely bird prototype is a robin or perhaps a sparrow. Most birds can fly, but not all; most mammals cannot fly, but bats are mammals, have wings, and can fly. So not all examples within a concept fit it equally well. Nevertheless, the prototype most closely fits a given concept, and items and organisms belonging to the concept share more attributes with their prototype than with the prototype of any other concept.

The concepts we form do not simply exist in isolation. We form them in hierarchies. For example, the canary and the cardinal are subsets of the concept *bird;* at a higher level, birds are subsets of the concept *animal;* and at a still higher level, animals are a subset of the concept *living things.*

Exemplars The most recent theory of concept formation suggests that concepts are represented by their **exemplars**—individual instances, or examples, of a concept that we have stored in memory from our own experience (Estes, 1994). To decide whether an unfamiliar item belongs to a concept, we compare it with exemplars (other examples) of that concept.

A prototype is an example that embodies the most typical features of a concept. Which of the animals shown here best fits your prototype for the concept bird?

prototype: The example that embodies the most common and typical features of a concept.

exemplars: The individual instances of a concept that we have stored in memory from our own experience.

Memory Check 7.4

1. The two most common forms of imagery are:
   a. visual and motor.   c. visual and auditory.
   b. auditory and tactile.   d. visual and gustatory.

2. Our images are generally as vivid as the real thing. (true/false)

3. A prototype is the most _____ example of a concept.
   a. abstract   b. unusual   c. recent   d. typical

4. A label that represents a class or group of objects, people, or events that share common characteristics or attributes is called a(n):
   a. image.   c. positive instance.
   b. concept.   d. prototype.

5. A stork is an exemplar of the concept *bird*. (true/false)

Answers: 1. c 2. false 3. d 4. b 5. true

Problem Solving and Creativity

What are three problem-solving techniques, and how are they used?

Approaches to Problem Solving: How Do We Begin?

All of us are faced with a variety of problems that need to be solved every day. Many are simple and mundane, like what to have for dinner or what clothes to put on in the morning. But some of our problems are more far-reaching, such as what major to choose in college, what career to pursue, how to sustain or improve a relationship, or how to stretch our income from one paycheck to the next. Then there are the problems we meet in our schoolwork, which we must think through using problem-solving techniques. Among these techniques are trial and error, algorithms, and heuristics.

How would you go about solving the problem described in the *Try It!*?

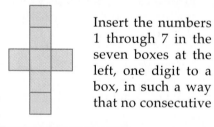

Insert the numbers 1 through 7 in the seven boxes at the left, one digit to a box, in such a way that no consecutive numbers will be next to each other horizontally, vertically, or diagonally. Several possible solutions can be found.

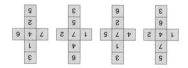

Answers:

Trial and Error: If at First You Don't Succeed . . .   How did you choose to solve the *Try It!* problem? Some people examine the problem carefully and devise a strategy—such as placing the 1 and the 7 in the middle boxes because each of these has only *one* forbidden consecutive number (2 and 6) to avoid. Many people, however, simply start placing the numbers in the boxes and then change them around when a combination doesn't work. In this approach, called **trial and error**, we try one solution after another, in no particular order, until we chance to hit upon the answer. Even nonhuman animals use trial and error.

Trial and error can be very time-consuming and perhaps even dangerous. Would you feel comfortable with a surgeon who operated on you using trial and error? You might not survive the errors to enjoy the solution. Of course, most of our problems are not life-or-death situations, and if all else fails in our efforts to solve a problem, we may be reduced to trial and error. But other techniques are far more effective and less time-consuming.

Applying Prior Knowledge: We Don't Have to Start from Scratch Rather than beginning with a haphazard, trial-and-error approach, it is best to reflect on a problem and see if you already have any knowledge that might help you find a solution. Some problems can be solved with only a little ready knowledge. The problem in the next *Try It!* is a good example.

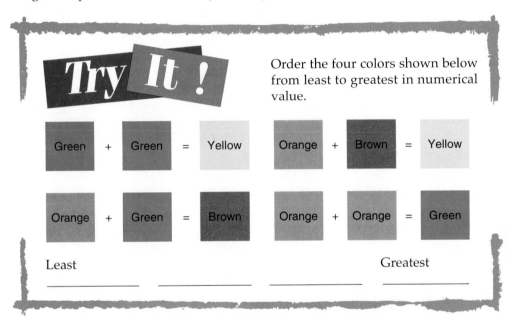

Order the four colors shown below from least to greatest in numerical value.

Green + Green = Yellow   Orange + Brown = Yellow

Orange + Green = Brown   Orange + Orange = Green

Least   Greatest

From the *Try It!* problem you can see that yellow is twice the value of green, and green is twice the value of orange. So yellow is four times the value of orange. Then you can see that brown is numerically greater than either orange or green, but less than yellow. Also you should know that both yellow and green must be even numbers, because any two odd numbers or any two even numbers will always equal an even number. The answer to the *Try It!* is that the colors are ordered from least value to greatest value as follows: orange, green, brown, and yellow.

Algorithms: Formulas That Can't Miss Another major problem-solving method is the algorithm (Newell & Simon, 1972). An **algorithm** is a systematic, step-by-step procedure that guarantees a solution to a problem of a certain type if the algorithm is appropriate and executed properly. Formulas used in mathematics and other sciences are algorithms. Another type of algorithm is a systematic strategy for exploring every possible solution to a problem until the correct one is reached. In some cases there may be millions or even billions or more possibilities that one would have to try before reaching a solution. Often computers are programmed to solve such problems, because with a computer an accurate solution is guaranteed and millions of possible solutions can be tried in a few seconds.

trial and error: An approach to problem solving in which one solution after another is tried in no particular order until a workable solution is found.

algorithm: A systematic, step-by-step procedure, such as a mathematical formula, that guarantees a solution to a problem of a certain type if the algorithm is appropriate and executed properly.

heuristic (hyu-RIS-tik): A problem-solving method that offers a promising way to attack a problem and arrive at a solution, although it does not guarantee success.

working backwards: A heuristic strategy in which a person discovers the steps needed to solve a problem by defining the desired goal and working backwards to the current condition.

means–end analysis: A heuristic problem-solving strategy in which the current position is compared with the desired goal, and a series of steps are formulated and taken to close the gap between them.

Many problems do not lend themselves to solution by algorithms, however. Suppose you were a contestant on "Wheel of Fortune," trying to solve this missing-letter puzzle: P_Y_ _OL_ _ _. An exhaustive search algorithm would be out of the question—even Vanna White's smile would fade long before the nearly 9 billion possibilities could be considered. An easier way to solve such problems is with the method of heuristics.

Heuristic Strategies in Problem Solving: Fast, But Not Infallible   A **heuristic** is a problem-solving method that does not guarantee success but offers a promising way to attack a problem and arrive at a solution. Chess players must use heuristics because there is not enough time in a lifetime to consider all of the moves and countermoves that would be possible in a single game of chess (Bransford et al., 1986).

We use heuristic techniques to eliminate useless steps and to take the shortest probable path toward a solution. The missing-letter puzzle presented earlier is easily solved through a simple heuristic approach that makes use of our existing knowledge of words (prefixes, roots, suffixes). Like any good contestant on the "Wheel of Fortune" quiz show, we can supply the missing letters and spell out PSYCHOLOGY.

Working Backwards   One heuristic that is effective for solving some problems is **working backwards**, sometimes called the backward search. In this approach we start with the solution, a known condition, and work our way backwards through the problem. Once our backward search has revealed the steps to be taken and their order, we can solve the problem. Try working backwards to solve the water lily problem in the *Try It!*

Water lilies double the area they cover every 24 hours. At the beginning of the summer there is one water lily on a lake. It takes 60 days for the lake to become covered with water lilies. On what day is the lake half covered?

Answer: The most important fact is that the lilies double in number every 24 hours. If the lake is to be completely covered on the 60th day, it has to be half covered on the 59th day.

Means–End Analysis   A popular heuristic strategy is **means–end analysis**, in which the current position is compared with a desired goal, and a series of steps are formulated and then taken to close the gap between the two (Sweller & Levine, 1982). Many problems are large and complex and must be broken down into smaller steps or subproblems before a solution can be reached. If your professor assigns a term paper, for example, you probably do not simply sit down and write it. You must first determine how you will deal with your topic, research the topic, make an outline, and then write the subtopics over a period of time. At last you are ready to assemble the complete term paper, write several drafts, and put the finished product in final form before handing it in.

Impediments to Problem Solving: Mental Stumbling Blocks

What are the two major impediments to problem solving?

Sometimes the difficulty in problem solving lies not with the problem but with ourselves. The two major impediments to problem solving are functional fixedness and mental set.

Functional Fixedness: Every Tool Has Only One Function Many of us are hampered in our efforts to solve problems in daily living because of **functional fixedness**—the failure to use familiar objects in novel ways to solve problems. We tend to see objects only in terms of their customary functions. Just think of all the items we use daily—tools, utensils, and other equipment—that help us perform certain functions. Often the normal functions of objects become fixed in our thinking so that we do not consider using them in new and creative ways.

Suppose you injured your leg and knew that you should apply ice to prevent swelling, but you had no ice cubes or ice bag in your refrigerator. Or what if you wanted a cup of coffee, but the decanter for your coffeemaker was broken? If you suffered from functional fixedness, you might come to the conclusion that there was nothing you could do to solve your problem at that moment. The solution? Rather than thinking about the object or utensil that you don't have, think about the function you need served in order to solve your problem. In the first instance, what you need is something very cold, not necessarily an ice bag or ice per se. A cold can of soda might be a temporary solution. In the second case, what you need is something to catch the coffee, rather than the specific glass decanter that came with the coffeemaker. Could you catch the coffee in some other type of bowl or cooking utensil, or even in a coffee mug?

Mental Set: But I've Always Done It This Way Another impediment to problem solving, similar to functional fixedness but much broader, is mental set. **Mental set** means that we get into a mental rut in our approach to solving problems, continuing to use the same old method even though another approach might be better. Perhaps we hit on a way to solve a problem once in the past and continue to use the same technique in similar situations, even though it is not highly effective or efficient. We are much more susceptible to mental set when we fail to consider the special requirements of a problem. Not surprisingly, the same people who are subject to mental set are also more likely to have trouble with functional fixedness when they attempt to solve problems (McKelvie, 1984).

functional fixedness: The failure to use familiar objects in novel ways to solve problems because of a tendency to view objects only in terms of their customary functions.

mental set: The tendency to apply a familiar strategy to the solution of a problem without carefully considering the special requirements of the problem.

Humans are not the only ones on the planet able to solve problems. We have seen that many animals can solve problems, and apparently modern machines can too.

Artificial Intelligence

What is artificial intelligence?

Computer intelligence that rivals or surpasses human intelligence has long been the stuff of which science fiction is made. You may remember Hal, the uncontrollable superintelligent computer from Arthur Clarke's novel or the movie based on it, *2001: A Space Odyssey*. Although the year 2001 is now only a few years away, no computer anything like the sinister Hal is on the horizon.

Nevertheless, amazing progress has been made in the field of artificial intelligence since the term was first used officially by researcher John McCarthy in 1956. **Artificial intelligence**, or AI, refers to computer systems that are programmed to simulate human thinking in solving problems and in making judgments and decisions. The first successful effort to program computers that could mimic human thinking was made by Allen Newell and Herbert A. Simon. They developed programs that could play chess as well as a human expert could (although not as well as master players).

Newell and Simon opened the door for artificial intelligence systems able to do far more than play chess like an expert. Now AI expert systems or programs are available that contain the collective knowledge and problem-solving strategies of the top experts in many different fields. The first of these expert systems was MYCIN, an expert diagnostician in the area of blood diseases and meningitis. Today there are expert systems in medicine, psychotherapy, space technology, military defense, weather prediction, and a variety of other sciences.

Expert programs have severe limitations, however. They "work in well-defined domains in which the systems' information, or knowledge base, is not extremely large. Typically, AI systems produce their answers based on no more than several hundred facts concerning the area of their expertise" (Hendler, 1994, p. 891). Outside of their area of expertise, these expert systems cannot function. Expert programs, then, are useful only as assistants to humans, not as expert systems that can stand alone.

How does the ability of computer systems compare with that of the human brain? These systems far surpass the human brain in their ability to (1) retrieve accurately massive amounts of material from a database, (2) make decisions about the data based on specific facts and rules that have been programmed into the system, and (3) carry out complex mathematical operations, all at lightning speed.

Computer Neural Networks Conventional computers have a single central processing unit that solves problems one step at a time. In contrast, parallel supercomputers contain a number of processors. A problem can be divided into parts and handled by the various processors simultaneously; this enables the job to be completed much more quickly.

The human brain resembles the parallel computer in that it can carry out many functions at the same time. Researchers are now devising computer systems based on their understanding of how neurons in certain parts of the brain are connected and how the connections develop (Buonomano & Merzenich, 1995; Hinton et al., 1995). Computer systems that are intended to mimic the human brain are called **neural networks**. Like those in the brain, connections in a computer neural network can be strengthened or weakened as a result of experience. Using neural networks, psychologists can test theories about how the brain works, and computer scientists can use the knowledge gained to develop new systems that better simulate the ability of the human brain.

For example, computer scientist Alex Waibel and colleagues used a neural network in their research on speech recognition. "Programmed to modify itself according to whatever signals come into the system, the speech recognizer actually 'learns' how to identify sounds and words" (Peterson, 1993, p. 245). Already there is a speech recognition system that can handle a 20,000-word vocabulary regardless of who the speaker is. But unlike a person, the computer system cannot understand the subtleties of language—tone of voice, quality of nonverbal behavior, or even level of politeness (Peterson, 1993). No computer can even approach the complexity and capability of the human brain.

artificial intelligence: Computer systems that simulate human thinking in solving problems and in making judgments and decisions.

neural networks: Computer systems that are intended to mimic the human brain.

Creativity: Unique and Useful Productions

Measuring Creativity: Are There Reliable Measures? **Creativity** can be thought of as the ability to produce original, appropriate, and valuable ideas and/or solutions to problems. But can creativity be measured? A number of efforts have been made to measure creativity, even though a clear definition of it has never been formulated. One well-known effort is that of J. P. Guilford, whose tests of divergent production have been used as measures of creativity. **Divergent production** is thinking aimed at producing one or more possible ideas, answers, or solutions to a problem rather than a single, correct response.

Obviously, creative thinking is divergent. But is the ability to think in divergent ways a sufficient condition for the production of creative thinking? No! All creative thought is divergent, but not all divergent thought is creative. Novelty is not synonymous with creativity. We are not surprised, then, to find that high scores on tests of divergent production do not have a very high correlation with creative production in real life. Guilford (1967) himself admitted that in studies of students from elementary through high school, the correlations of his divergent-production tests with actual creative production were not spectacular.

Other researchers have also tried to design tests to measure creative ability. Mednick and Mednick (1967) reasoned that the essence of creativity consists of the creative thinker's ability to fit ideas together that might appear remote or unrelated to the noncreative thinker. To measure creative ability they created the Remote Associates Test (RAT). Test your creativity with the *Try It!*

> **?** *What is creativity, and what tests have been designed to measure it?*

One indication of creativity may be the ability to make associations among several elements that seem only remotely related or unrelated. Test your ability to find associations for these 10 sets of words, which are similar to those on the Remote Associates Test. Think of a fourth word that is related in some way to all three of the words in each row. For example, the words *keeper*, *text*, and *worm* are related to the word *book* and become *bookkeeper*, *textbook*, and *bookworm*.

1. sales, collector, income
2. flower, room, water
3. red, shot, dog
4. ball, hot, stool
5. rock, man, classical
6. story, true, sick
7. news, plate, waste
8. stuffed, sleeve, sweat
9. class, temperature, bath
10. wrist, man, stop

Answers: 1. tax 2. bed 3. hot 4. foot 5. music 6. love 7. paper 8. shirt 9. room 10. watch

---

Mednick and Mednick point out that some studies show a relationship between high scores on the RAT and creative thinking in the workplace; other studies, however, have not found this relationship (Matlin, 1983).

Creativity and Intelligence: How Do They Relate? Is creativity related to intelligence? Research to date indicates that there is a modest correlation between creativity and IQ. Highly creative people tend to be well above average in intelligence, but in the upper IQ ranges (over 120) there seems to be little correlation between IQ and creativity (Barron & Harrington, 1981).

Remember the young geniuses studied by Lewis Terman? Not a single one of them has produced a highly creative work (Terman & Oden, 1959). No Nobel laureates, no Pulitzer prizes. Geniuses, yes; creative geniuses, no.

creativity: The ability to produce original, appropriate, and valuable ideas and/or solutions to problems.

divergent production: Producing one or more possible ideas, answers, or solutions to a problem rather than a single, correct response.

Memory Check 7.5

1. Which of the following is guaranteed, if properly applied, to result in the correct answer to a problem?
   - a. an algorithm
   - b. a heuristic
   - c. trial and error
   - d. applying prior knowledge

2. Working backwards and means–end analysis are examples of:
   - a. algorithms.
   - b. heuristics.
   - c. mental sets.
   - d. functional fixedness.

3. John uses a wastebasket to keep a door from closing. In solving his problem, he was not hindered by:
   - a. a heuristic.
   - b. an algorithm.
   - c. functional fixedness.
   - d. mental set.

4. One characteristic of good problem solvers is mental set. (true/false)

5. Artificial intelligence systems now surpass the problem-solving ability of experts in a number of fields. (true/false)

6. Divergent-production tests and the Remote Associates Test are used to measure:
   - a. imaging ability.
   - b. concept formation.
   - c. problem-solving ability.
   - d. creativity.

Answers: 1. a 2. b 3. c 4. false 5. false 6. d

Language

Without language, there would be no books to read, no papers to write, no lectures to endure. Not bad so far, you may be thinking. But consider, without language we would each live in a largely solitary and isolated world, unable to communicate or receive any information. But thanks to language, we can profit from the experience, the knowledge, and the wisdom of others and can benefit others with our own. Not confined to time and space, language makes available the wisdom of the ages from every corner of the world. Truly, language is one of the most important capabilities of the human species. Whether spoken, written, or signed, it is our most important tool of thought. What are the components and the structure of this most amazing tool of human communication called language?

The Structure of Language

> ? **What are the four important components of language?**

Psycholinguistics is the study of how language is acquired, produced, and used and how the sounds and symbols of language are translated into meaning. Psycholinguists devote much effort to the study of the structure of language and the rules governing its use. The structure and rules governing language involve four different components—phonemes, morphemes, syntax, and semantics.

psycholinguistics: The study of how language is acquired, produced, and used, and how the sounds and symbols of language are translated into meaning.

phonemes: The smallest units of sound in a spoken language.

Phonemes   The smallest units of sound in a spoken language are known as **phonemes**. Phonemes form the basic building blocks of a spoken language. Three phonemes together form the sound of the word *cat*—the *c* (which sounds like *k*), *a*, and *t*. Phonemes do not sound like the single letters of the alphabet as we recite them, *a-b-c-d-e-f-g*, but like the sounds of the letters as they are used in words, like the *b* in *boy*, the *p* in *pan*, and so on. The sound of the phoneme *c* in the word *cat* is different from the sound of the phoneme *c* in the word *city*.

Letters combined to form sounds are also phonemes, such as the *th* in *the* and the *ch* in *child*. The same sound (phoneme) may be represented by different letters in different words, as the *a* in *stay* and the *ei* in *sleigh*. And, as we saw with *c*, the same letter can serve as different phonemes. The letter *a*, for example, can be sounded as four different phonemes as in *day*, *cap*, *watch*, and *law*.

How many phonemes are there? About 100 or so different sounds could serve as phonemes, but most languages have far fewer. English uses about 45 phonemes, while some languages may have as few as 15 and others as many as 85 (Solso, 1991). Though phonemes are the basic building blocks of language, they alone, with a few exceptions, do not provide language with meaning. For meaning, we must move to the next component of language, the morphemes.

Morphemes Morphemes are the smallest units of meaning in a language. In almost all cases in the English language, a morpheme is made of two or more phonemes. But a few phonemes also serve as morphemes, such as the article *a* and the personal pronoun *I*. Many words in English are single morphemes—*book, word, learn, reason,* and so on. In addition to root words, morphemes may also be prefixes (such as *re* in *relearn*) or suffixes (such as *ed* to show past tense—*(learned)*. The single morpheme *reason* becomes the two-morpheme *reasonable*. Another morpheme—the prefix *un*—added to *reasonable* will reverse its meaning—*unreasonable*. The letter *s* gives a plural meaning to a word and is thus a morpheme. The morpheme *book* (singular) becomes the two-morpheme *books* (plural).

So morphemes, singly and in combination, form the words in a language and provide meaning. But sounds and single words alone are not enough. A language also requires rules for structuring or putting together words in orderly and meaningful fashion. This is where syntax enters the picture.

Syntax Syntax is the aspect of grammar that specifies the rules for arranging and combining words to form phrases and sentences. An important rule of syntax in English is that adjectives usually come before nouns. So we refer to the residence of the U.S. President as the White House. But in Spanish the noun usually comes before the adjective, and speakers would say, *"la Casa Blanca,"* or "the House White." So the rules of word order, or syntax, differ from one language to another. In English, we ask, "Do you speak German?" But speakers of German would ask, *"Sprechen sie Deutsch?"* or "Speak you German?"

Semantics Semantics refers to the meaning we derive from morphemes, words, and sentences. The same word can have different meanings depending on how it is used in sentences: "I don't mind." "Mind your manners." "He has lost his mind."

"Loving to read, the young girl read three books last week." In this example, the word *read* is pronounced two different ways and in one case is in the past tense.

Language is a universal human phenomenon, yet there is great diversity in the way language is used around the world—there are some 6,000 spoken languages (Berreby, 1994). But however it is spoken, written, signed, and otherwise used, language is one of the most complex human capabilities. Is language confined to the human species?

Animal Language

Ask people what capability most reliably sets humans apart from all other animal species, and most will answer language. And for good reason. As far as we know, humans are the only species to have developed this rich, varied, and complex system of communication. But even though they have never developed language, could our nearest cousins, the chimpanzees, learn to master its rudiments and complexities if humans taught them? The earliest attempts to answer this question date back more than 60 years. Psychologists Winthrop and Luella Kellogg (1933) took a baby chimpanzee into their home to raise along with their

morphemes: The smallest units of meaning in a language.

syntax: The aspect of grammar that specifies the rules for arranging and combining words to form phrases and sentences.

semantics: The meaning or the study of meaning derived from morphemes, words, and sentences.

How does language in trained chimpanzees differ from human language?

FIGURE 7.9

Sarah's Symbols

A chimpanzee named Sarah learned to communicate using plastic chips of various shapes, sizes, and colors to represent words in an artificial language developed by her trainer, David Premack.

son who was about the same age. Although she learned some human habits, the chimp was never able to utter any sounds resembling language.

Later another couple, Cathy and Keith Hayes (1951) raised a chimp named Vicki in their home, but they, too, failed to teach the chimp to speak. Although Vicki learned to make roughly articulated sounds resembling "mama," "papa," "cup," and "up," the raspy sounds were produced only with great difficulty. Such failures are not surprising, because the vocal tract in chimpanzees and the other apes is not adapted to human speech.

Researchers next turned to sign language. Psychologists Allen and Beatrix Gardner (1969) took in a 1-year-old chimp named Washoe and taught her sign language. Washoe learned signs for objects, and certain commands and concepts such as "flower," "give me," "come," "open," and "more." By the end of her fifth year she had mastered about 160 signs (Fleming, 1974). Washoe learned to sign requests to her trainer such as "you, me go out please." And once, on seeing a swan in the water, she signed, "water bird." But it is unclear whether Washoe creatively named the "water bird" or was separately signing two different objects, the water and the bird.

Psychologist David Premack (1971) taught another chimp, Sarah, to use an artificial language he developed. It consisted of magnetized metal-backed plastic chips of various shapes, sizes, and colors, as shown in Figure 7.9. Premack used operant conditioning techniques to teach Sarah, who learned to select the plastic chip representing a fruit and place it on a magnetized language board. The trainer would then reward Sarah with the fruit she had requested. Later, Sarah had to add the name of her trainer, Mary, and select chips that symbolized "Mary apple." Still later, rewards would come only when Sarah identified herself as well and signaled "Mary give apple Sarah."

Sarah mastered the concepts of similarities and differences, and eventually she could signal whether two objects were the same or different with nearly perfect accuracy (Premack & Premack, 1983). She even performed well on part–whole relationships and could match such things as half an apple and a glass half filled with water. Even more remarkable, Sarah could view a whole apple and a cut apple and, even though she had not seen the apple being cut, could match the apple with the utensil needed to cut it—a knife.

At the Yerkes Primate Research Center at Emory University, a chimp named Lana participated in a computer-controlled language training program. She learned to press keys imprinted with geometric symbols that represented words in an artificial language called Yerkish. Researcher Sue Savage-Rumbaugh (1986; Rumbaugh, 1977) varied the location, color, and brightness of the keys, so Lana had to learn which symbols to use no matter where they were located. One day her trainer Tim had an orange that she wanted. Lana had available symbols for many fruits—apple, banana, and so on—but none for an orange. Yet there was a colored symbol for the color orange. So Lana improvised and signaled, "Tim give apple which is orange." Impressive!

But the most impressive performance to date is that of one pygmy chimpanzee, Kanzi, who developed an amazing ability to communicate with his trainers without any formal training. During the mid-1980s, researchers had taught Kanzi's mother to press symbols representing words. Her progress was not remarkable; but her infant son Kanzi, who stood by and observed her during training, was learning rapidly (thanks to observational learning, which we discussed in Chapter 5). When Kanzi had a chance at the symbol board, his performance quickly surpassed that of his mother and of every other chimp the researchers had tested.

Kanzi demonstrated an advanced understanding (for chimps) of spoken English and could respond correctly even to new commands, such as "Throw your ball to the river," or "Go to the refrigerator and get out a tomato" (Savage-Rumbaugh, 1990; Savage-Rumbaugh et al., 1992). By the time Kanzi was 6 years old, a team of researchers who worked with him had recorded more than 13,000 "utterances" and reported that Kanzi could communicate using some 200 different geometric symbols (Gibbons, 1991). Kanzi could press symbols to ask someone to play chase with him and even ask two others to play chase while he watched. Also, if Kanzi signalled someone to "chase" and "hide," it mattered greatly to him that his first command, "chase," be done first (Gibbons, 1991).

Kanzi was not merely responding to nearby trainers whose actions or gestures he might have copied. He could respond just as well when requests were made over earphones so no one else in the room could signal to him purposely or inadvertently.

Do such seemingly remarkable feats indicate that chimps are capable of using anything close to human language? Impressive as Kanzi's accomplishments seem to be, Premack firmly maintains that it is unlikely that animals are capable of language. They can be taught to signal, to choose, and to solve some problems, but none of these amazing tricks suggest grammatical competence. A language cannot be structured without some understanding of syntax. Mere strings of words spoken, written, or signed do not amount to language unless they are structured grammatically. A language is flexible and provides many ways to convey the same information. Not bound by space and time, by the here and now, language enables us to communicate about the past, present, and future, to express ideas, both concrete and abstract, and to converse about relationships.

From their studies of communication among chimps and other animals, researchers have gained useful insights into the nature of language. The pygmy chimp Kanzi is skilled in using a special symbol board to communicate.

Clearly chimpanzees can learn to string together requests. But these are constructions, not sentences. The difference between a construction—"Mary give apple Sarah"—and a sentence (a fundamental requirement of human language) was captured by the philosopher Bertrand Russell. Someone once asked Russell if apes might ever learn to speak. He is said to have answered that he would be persuaded if a member of the species could demonstrate understanding of a sentence such as "My father was poor but honest" (quoted in Restak, 1988, p. 202).

Language and Thinking

If language is unique to humans, then does language drive human thinking? Does the fact that you speak English mean that you reason, think, and perceive your world differently than someone who speaks Spanish, or Chinese, or Swahili? According to one hypothesis presented some 40 years ago, it does.

Benjamin Whorf (1956) put forth his **linguistic relativity hypothesis** suggesting that the language a person speaks largely determines the nature of that person's thoughts. According to this hypothesis, our worldview would be constructed primarily by the words in our language. As proof, Whorf offered his classic example. The languages used by the Eskimo people have a number of different words for snow, "*apikak*, first snow falling; *aniv*, snow spread out; *pukak*, snow for drinking water," while the English-speaking world has but one word, *snow* (Restak, 1988, p. 222). Whorf claimed that such a rich and varied selection of words for snow enabled Eskimos to think differently about it than do people whose languages lack specific words for various snow conditions. But do the Eskimos perceive snow differently because they have so many words for it? Or do they have so many words for snow because they perceive it differently? No matter what language you speak, you can perceive and think about snow according to whether it is falling or on the ground, powdery or slushy, fluffy or packed, without specific words for those conditions.

What is the linguistic relativity hypothesis, and is it supported by research?

linguistic relativity hypothesis: The notion that the language a person speaks largely determines the nature of that person's thoughts.

Cognitive psychologist Eleanor Heider Rosch (1973) tested Whorf's hypothesis. If language determines thinking, she reasoned, then people whose language contains many names for colors should be better at thinking about and discriminating among colors than people whose language has only a few color names. Her subjects were English-speaking Americans and the Dani, members of a remote tribe in New Guinea whose language has only two names for colors—*mili* for dark, cool colors and *mola* for bright, warm colors. How would the Dani perform compared to the English-speaking subjects in perceiving, discriminating, and remembering colored chips of many different hues?

Rosch showed subjects from both groups single-color chips of 11 colors—black, white, red, yellow, green, blue, brown, purple, pink, orange, and gray—for 5 seconds each. Then, after 30 seconds, she had subjects select the 11 colors they had viewed from a larger group of 40 color chips. If Whorf's hypothesis was accurate, she reasoned, the American subjects would perform with far greater accuracy than the Dani subjects, for whom brown, black, purple, and blue are all *mili*, or dark. But this was not the case. Rosch found no significant differences in the performance of the Dani and the American subjects in discriminating, remembering, or thinking about the 11 basic colors.

Rosch's study did not support the linguistic relativity hypothesis. And neither did a larger study of 98 different languages by Berlin and Kay (1969). They found a consistent pattern in establishing names for colors in all the cultures they studied. Cultures with only two color names, such as the Dani, use dark and light, or black and white. As additional color names are added, they appear in the same order across the cultures studied. In cultures with three color names, red is the third color. Then come green and yellow (in either order), and then blue, brown, purple, pink, orange, and gray. It appears, then, that cultures throughout the world think about colors in much the same way regardless of the language they speak. And all cultures have the same priorities for naming colors, even though some cultures use many names and others few.

Benjamin Whorf appeared to go too far in suggesting that our language determines how we think. But let us not go too far in the opposite direction and assume that language has little influence on how people think. Humans think both without language (as in imagery) and with language. A large and rich vocabulary is one of our most important tools for thinking. And there is a strong, consistent correlation between one's vocabulary and one's performance on most of the widely accepted tests for measuring intelligence.

Sexism in Language The words we use matter a great deal. Consider the generic use of the pronoun *he* to refer to people in general. If your professor says, "I expect each student in this class to do the best he can," does this announcement mean the same to males and females? Not according to research conducted by Gastil (1990) in which subjects read sentences worded in three different forms. Perform Gastil's experiment yourself by completing the *Try It!*

After reading each of these three sentences, pause and jot down any image that comes to mind.

1. The average American believes he watches too much television.
2. The average American believes he/she watches too much television.
3. Average Americans believe they watch too much television.

Whether you are male or female, the odds are high that you imaged a male after reading the first sentence in the *Try It!* Other studies confirm that the generic *he* is not interpreted very generically. It is interpreted heavily in favor of males (Hamilton, 1988; Henley, 1989; Ng, 1990).

It is true that we can think without language. We can use imagery, picture steps in a process, think kinesthetically in terms of body movements, and so on. Yet, language remains a critically important tool of thought. Language increases our ability to think abstractly, to grasp and formulate concepts, to reason by analogy, to solve problems, to express our ideas with greater clarity and, if we are poetic, with greater beauty. One of the most important educational activities students can undertake is to add words to their vocabulary, an undertaking that will pay rich dividends.

Memory Check 7.6

1. Match the component of language with the appropriate description.
   _____ 1) the smallest units of meaning
   _____ 2) the meaning derived from phonemes, morphemes, and sentences
   _____ 3) grammatical rules for arranging and combining words to form phrases and sentences
   _____ 4) the smallest units of sound in a spoken language

   a. syntax
   b. morphemes
   c. semantics
   d. phonemes

2. Communication in trained chimpanzees approaches human language in form and complexity. (true/false)

3. The linguistic relativity hypothesis is not supported by research. (true/false)

Answers: 1. 1) b 2) c 3) a 4) d 2. false 3. true

APPLICATIONS · APPLICATIONS · APPLICATIONS

Stimulating Creativity

The famous American inventor Thomas Edison had a habit of dozing in a chair with his arms hanging over the sides. In each hand he held a ball bearing, and on the floor beneath his hands were pie plates. When he entered the pleasant, dreamy state that lies somewhere between waking and sleeping, his hands would relax and he would drop the bearings. The sound of the bearings striking the pie plates would wake him, and he would write down any ideas that came to him while dozing.

Edison was taking advantage of what is termed the hypnagogic state, a state of consciousness in which dreams and reality mix and people are especially likely to have creative ideas and insights. But you don't need to be half asleep to make contact with your creative side. It can happen while you are exercising, meditating, taking a shower, or playing an instrument. What happens, apparently, is a kind of "letting go," a surrender to the creative spirit that lives in all of us.

It is this willingness to let go, to go with the flow, that results in what is often called inspiration. When inspiration happens, time seems to pass much more slowly—or more quickly—and one becomes totally absorbed in the creative activity, tuned in, oblivious to distractions. This inspired state can be seen in the expression on the face of a figure skater performing a routine flawlessly or a violinist playing a concerto with mastery. It can also be seen in children playing.

continued

You don't have to be an athlete or a musician or a child to experience inspiration. You may be walking through the woods, thinking of nothing, when the solution to a problem that has been bothering you for days or weeks suddenly pops into your head. The creative insight seems to come out of nowhere, but in reality it is the final step in a process that has been going on since you first became aware of the problem. You may not have realized it, but you have been engaging in creative problem solving all along.

Stages in Creative Problem Solving

There are four basic stages in the creative problem-solving process: *preparation*, in which you search for information that may help you solve the problem; *incubation*, or letting the problem "sit" while you digest the relevant information; *illumination*, in which the answer comes to you, seemingly "out of nowhere"; and *translation*, or transforming your new insight into useful action. The incubation stage, perhaps the most important part of the process, takes place in the unconscious. That is why we often tell someone who is trying to solve a problem to "sleep on it." It is also the reason why solutions may come to us when we are daydreaming or letting our thoughts wander aimlessly—or dozing, like Thomas Edison.

Keys to Creativity

The key to creativity is flexibility and openness to new possibilities. Creativity involves trying out new approaches, going beyond the routine or conventional, and, most important, questioning assumptions. It involves willingness to make mistakes. For the creative person, a mistake is something to learn from, not something to be avoided at all costs. Mistakes provide valuable information. If you are afraid of making a mistake, you'll miss out on the

information that could be gained from it. In fact, research has shown that creative people tend to make more mistakes than less imaginative people, mainly because they make more attempts, try more experiments, come up with more ideas to be tested.

Humor is a key ingredient of creativity. Groups whose members joke a lot, kid around, and laugh easily and often have been found to be more creative than groups whose members interact more formally. Also important is the absence of anxiety or self-consciousness. That is why brainstorming groups do not allow any criticism or judgment of the ideas proposed by participants, no matter how wild or off-the-wall they may seem.

Becoming More Creative

Creativity is certainly not limited to certain "special" people who are naturally gifted with flair and imagination. Everyone has some potential for creativity. What can you do to become more creative? Psychologists have suggested a variety of techniques for stimulating creativity. The first step is to be flexible and open to new possibilities. You need to free your thoughts from arbitrary restraints. Learn to avoid mental set— the failure to consider alternative solutions to common problems. Also be alert to the tendency toward self-censorship. Ignore the inner voice that tells you something couldn't possibly work or that you will look silly if you make a mistake.

Perhaps the best way to stimulate creative thinking is to relax. Go for a walk, take a long shower, sit in a comfortable chair and daydream, lie on the beach. Relaxing gives the unconscious mind a chance to play with ideas and combine them in new ways. The result may be a flash of insight like the one that led Archimedes to leap from his bath and exclaim "Eureka!" (Greek for "I've found it!") when he figured out why heavy objects float in water.

It's important to "tune in" to your own creativity and to have confidence in it. The more you develop the habit of thinking of yourself as a creative person, the more likely you will be to come up with creative ideas and solutions to problems.

For some people, becoming creative means focusing more directly on areas in which they have a special interest. Suppose you enjoy cooking or photography, for example. By setting small challenges for yourself, you can go beyond simply cooking a

tasty meal or taking good pictures; you can start inventing new recipes or photographing conventional subjects in new and original ways. The more you stretch yourself beyond the routine, the more creative you will become.

Another way to stimulate your creative side is to try consciously to change your normal routine. Have lunch at a different time. Take a different route to school. Seek out someone you never talk to and strike up a conversation with him or her.

Don't ask yourself why you're making the change; just do it for the sake of change.

Also try looking at ordinary things from a different perspective. As you go through your everyday routines, look around you and notice the patterns made by clouds, the way raindrops catch the morning light, the expressions on the faces of people you pass on the street, the perfect roundness of oranges at a fruit stand—whatever catches your eye (or your ear or any other sense, for that matter). Your world will seem more vivid, and you will find yourself gaining new insights and coming up with some original ideas. (Adapted from *The Creative Spirit*, by D. Goleman, P. Kaufman, and M. Ray, 1992, New York: Dutton.)

Thinking Critically

Evaluation

Which of the theories of intelligence best fits your notion of intelligence? Why?

Point/Counterpoint

Prepare an argument supporting each of the following positions:

a. Intelligence tests should be used in the schools.

b. Intelligence tests should not be used in the schools.

Psychology in Your Life

Give several examples of how tools of thinking (imagery and concepts) and problem-solving strategies (algorithms and heuristics) can be applied in your educational and personal life.

Chapter Summary and Review

The Nature of Intelligence

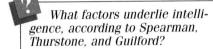 *What factors underlie intelligence, according to Spearman, Thurstone, and Guilford?*

Spearman believed that intelligence is composed of a general ability (*g* factor), which underlies all intellectual functions, and a number of specific abilities (*s* factors). Thurstone points to seven primary mental abilities, which singly or in combination are involved in all intellectual activities. Guilford's model, the structure of intellect, consists of 180 different intellectual abilities that involve all of the possible combinations of the three dimensions of intellect—mental operations, contents, and products.

 What types of intelligence did Gardner and Sternberg identify?

Gardner believes that there are seven independent and equally important types of intelligence. Sternberg's triarchic theory of intelligence identifies three: the componential (conventional intelligence), the experiential (creative intelligence), and the contextual (practical intelligence).

Key Terms

g factor (p. 245)
primary mental abilities (p. 245)
structure of intellect (p. 245)
triarchic theory of intelligence (p. 247)

Measuring Intelligence

 What is Binet's major contribution to psychology?

Binet's major contribution to psychology is the concept of mental age and a method for measuring it—the intelligence test.

 What does IQ mean, and how was it originally calculated?

IQ stands for intelligence quotient, an index of intelligence originally derived by dividing a person's mental age by his or her chronological age and then multiplying by 100.

What is the Stanford–Binet Intelligence Scale?

The Stanford–Binet Intelligence Scale is a highly regarded individual intelligence test for those aged 2 to 23. It yields one overall IQ score.

What did Wechsler's tests provide that the Stanford–Binet did not?

David Wechsler developed the first successful individual intelligence test for adults, the Wechsler Adult Intelligence Scale (WAIS-R). His tests for adults, children, and preschoolers yield separate verbal and performance (nonverbal) IQ scores as well as an overall IQ score.

What is meant by the terms reliability, validity, and standardization?

Reliability is the ability of a test to yield nearly the same score each time a person takes the test or an alternative form of the test. Validity is the power of a test to measure what it is intended to measure. Standardization refers to prescribed procedures for administering a test and to established norms that provide a means of evaluating test scores.

What are the ranges of IQ scores considered average, superior, and in the range of mental retardation?

Fifty percent of the U.S. population have IQ scores ranging from 90 to 109; 2 percent have scores above 130, considered superior; and 2 percent have scores below 70, in the range of mental retardation.

According to the Terman study, how do the gifted differ from the general population?

Terman's longitudinal study revealed that, in general, the gifted enjoy better physical and mental health and are more successful than their less gifted counterparts.

What two criteria must one meet to be classified as mentally retarded?

To be classified as mentally retarded, one must have an IQ score below 70 and show severe deficiencies in everyday adaptive functioning.

Key Terms

intelligence quotient (IQ) (p. 248)
norms (p. 249)
Stanford–Binet Intelligence Scale (p. 249)
deviation score (p. 250)
Wechsler Adult Intelligence Scale (WAIS-R) (p. 250)
reliability (p. 251)
validity (p. 251)
aptitude test (p. 251)
standardization (p. 251)
mental retardation (p. 253)
mainstreaming (p. 254)

The IQ Controversy: Brainy Dispute

For what are intelligence tests good and poor predictors?

IQ tests are good predictors of success in school but not good predictors of occupational success among people of the same social class and level of education.

What are some of the abuses of intelligence tests?

Abuses occur when IQ tests are the only criterion for admitting people to educational programs, for tracking children, or for placing them in classes for the mentally retarded. Many people claim that IQ tests are biased in favor of the urban middle or upper class.

How does the nature–nurture controversy apply to intelligence?

The nature–nurture controversy is the debate over whether intelligence is primarily the result of heredity or environment.

What is behavioral genetics, and what are the primary methods used in the field today?

Behavioral genetics is the field that investigates the relative effects of heredity and environment on behavior and ability. The twin study method and the adoption method are the primary methods used.

How do twin studies support the view that intelligence is inherited?

Twin studies provide evidence that intelligence is primarily inherited because identical twins are more alike in intelligence than fraternal twins, even if they have been reared apart.

What are Jensen's and Herrnstein and Murray's controversial views on race and IQ?

These researchers claim that the black–white IQ gap is due to genetic differences between the races that are too strong to be changed significantly through environmental intervention.

What kinds of evidence suggest that IQ is changeable rather than fixed?

Several adoption studies have revealed that when infants from disadvantaged environments are adopted by middle- and upper-middle-class parents, their IQ scores are higher on average than would otherwise be expected. Also, IQ scores have been rising steadily over the past 50 years in western industrialized nations, presumably because of increases in the standard of living and educational opportunities.

Key Terms

culture-fair intelligence test (p. 255)
nature–nurture controversy (p. 255)
behavioral genetics (p. 256)
twin study method (p. 256)
identical twins (p. 256)
fraternal twins (p. 256)
heritability (p. 256)
adoption method (p. 256)

Imagery and Concepts: Tools of Thinking

 What is imagery?

Imagery is the representation in the mind of a sensory experience—visual, auditory, gustatory, motor, olfactory, or tactile.

 What are concepts, and how are they formed?

Concepts are labels that represent classes or groups of objects, people, or events sharing common characteristics or attributes. We can form a concept (1) from a formal definition of the concept, (2) by systematically memorizing features or attributes common to members of a concept (as in formal classification systems), (3) through our experiences with positive and negative instances of the concept, (4) through the use of prototypes, or (5) through the use of exemplars.

Key Terms

imagery (p. 262)
concept (p. 264)
prototype (p. 265)
exemplars (p. 265)

Problem Solving and Creativity

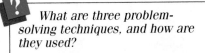 *What are three problem-solving techniques, and how are they used?*

Trial and error is an unsystematic problem-solving technique by which we try one solution after another until we hit on one that works. An algorithm is a step-by-step procedure that guarantees a solution, such as a mathematical formula or a systematic exploration of every possible solution. A heuristic method such as working backwards or means–end analysis does not guarantee success but offers a promising way to solve a problem.

 What are the two major impediments to problem solving?

Two major impediments to problem solving are functional fixedness and mental set.

 What is artificial intelligence?

Artificial intelligence is a field of research in which computer systems are programmed to simulate human thinking in solving problems and in making judgments and decisions.

 What is creativity, and what tests have been designed to measure it?

Creativity is the ability to produce original, appropriate, and valuable ideas and/or solutions to problems. Two tests used to measure creativity are divergent-production tests and the Remote Associates Test.

Key Terms

trial and error (p. 267)
algorithm (p. 267)
heuristic (p. 268)
working backwards (p. 268)
means–end analysis (p. 268)
functional fixedness (p. 268)
mental set (p. 269)
artificial intelligence (p. 270)
neural networks (p. 270)
creativity (p. 271)
divergent production (p. 271)

Language

 What are the four important components of language?

The four important components of language are (1) phonemes, the smallest units of sound in a spoken language; (2) morphemes, the smallest units of meaning; (3) syntax, grammatical rules for arranging and combining words to form phrases and sentences; and (4) semantics, the meaning derived from phonemes, morphemes, and sentences.

 How does language in trained chimpanzees differ from human language?

Chimpanzees do not have a vocal tract adapted to speech, and their communication using sign language or symbols consists merely of constructions strung together and not sentences.

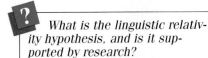 *What is the linguistic relativity hypothesis, and is it supported by research?*

The linguistic relativity hypothesis suggests that the language a person speaks largely determines the nature of the person's thoughts, but this theory is not supported by research.

Key Terms

psycholinguistics (p. 272)
phonemes (p. 272)
morphemes (p. 273)
syntax (p. 273)
semantics (p. 273)
linguistic relativity hypothesis
 (p. 275)

8

CHILD DEVELOPMENT

CHAPTER OUTLINE

Developmental Psychology: Basic Issues and Methodology

Controversial Issues in Developmental Psychology

Approaches to Studying Developmental Change

Heredity and Prenatal Development

The Mechanism of Heredity: Genes and Chromosomes

The Stages of Prenatal Development: Unfolding According to Plan

Negative Influences on Prenatal Development: Sabotaging Nature's Plan

Physical Development and Learning in Infancy

The Neonate: Seven Pounds of Beauty?

Perceptual Development in Infancy

Learning in Infancy

Motor Development in Infancy

Emotional Development in Infancy

Temperament: How and When Does It Develop?

The Formation of Attachment

The Father–Child Relationship

Piaget's Theory of Cognitive Development

The Cognitive Stages of Development: Climbing the Steps to Cognitive Maturity

Pioneers: Jean Piaget

An Evaluation of Piaget's Contribution

Vygotsky's Sociocultural View of Cognitive Development

Language Development

The Stages of Language Development: The Orderly Progression of Language

Theories of Language Development: How Do We Acquire It?

Socialization of the Child

Erikson's Theory of Psychosocial Development

The Parents' Role in the Socialization Process

World of Psychology: Cultural Values and Academic Achievement

Peer Relationships

Television as a Socializing Agent: Does It Help or Hinder?

Applications: What Kind of Care Is Best for Your Child?

Thinking Critically

Chapter Summary and Review

North of Kampala, Uganda, in Africa, the jungle is dark and dense, lush with a rich variety of exotic plant life and an abundance of animal species. But civil war disturbed the peace and beauty of Uganda for many years, and brutal massacres claimed the lives of many men, women, and children.

In 1984 Ugandan soldiers retreating through the jungle came upon one of the strangest sights they had ever seen. They were accustomed to the large tribes of monkeys living in the jungle, hopping, chattering, and leaping from place to place and avoiding humans who alarmed them. But with one tribe of monkeys, they saw a larger creature unlike the others, who was playfully hopping around with them. Intrigued, they came closer and were amazed to discover that this strange creature was a human child.

The soldiers captured the young boy and brought him to an orphanage in Kampala, Uganda. Here staff members named him Robert, estimated him to be between 5 and 7 years old, and were amazed by his behavior. He squealed and grunted but could not speak. He didn't walk normally but jumped from one place to another the way a monkey would.

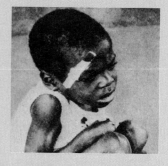

He scratched people when they approached him; he ate grass or any other edible thing he could find. And he did not sit but squatted when he was not moving around. Small for his age, Robert was only 2½ feet tall when he was found and weighed only 22 pounds. One staff member at the orphanage said that Robert always looked miserable: No one ever saw a smile on his face.

Foreign relief workers stationed in Uganda at the time were afraid that other children might be living as wild creatures in the jungle where Robert was found. They suspected this because hundreds of orphaned children had been discovered wandering around in nearby villages after the civil war ended. Those who studied Robert's case believed that his parents had been slaughtered when he was about 1 year old. Somehow he had managed to escape the massacre and make his way deep into the jungle.

Genetically, Robert is fully as human as any other human, but for most of his young life he was "adopted" by a monkey tribe whose members nurtured him as though he were one of their own. Developmental psychologists are intrigued by cases like Robert's because they show the profound effect that extreme environmental conditions can have on the course of human development.

Developmental Psychology: Basic Issues and Methodology

Developmental psychology is the study of how we grow, develop, and change throughout the life span. Some developmental psychologists specialize in a particular age group along the continuum from infancy, childhood, and adolescence to old age. Others may concentrate on a specific area of interest such as physical development, language or cognitive development, or moral development.

Controversial Issues in Developmental Psychology

Developmental psychologists must consider several controversial issues as they pursue their work.

developmental psychology: The study of how humans grow, develop, and change throughout the life span.

nature–nurture controversy: The debate concerning the relative influences of heredity and environment on development.

1. *To what degree do heredity and environment influence development?* For centuries thinkers have debated the influences of heredity and environment on development—a debate called the **nature–nurture controversy**. Some thinkers have taken the nature side in the debate, believing that our abilities are determined almost exclusively by heredity and are transmitted to us through our genes. Others have taken the nurture position, maintaining that our environment—the circumstances in which we are raised—determines what we become. Today the debate is not about nature *versus* nurture, but about the degree to which each influences various aspects of development.

Obviously heredity imposes some limits on what we can become. The best possible home environment, education, and nutrition cannot produce an Einstein. However, parental neglect, poor nutrition, ill health, and lack of education can prevent even the brightest among us from becoming the best that our genes would allow. Robert, devoid of all human contact, suffered such extreme deprivation that he failed to develop in ways most characteristically human. But surely nature and nurture are not opposing forces in the course of our development. They are partners and together wield their shared influence in forging and shaping us into the persons we become (Plomin et al., 1994).

2. *Is development continuous or does it occur in stages?* Physical growth during middle childhood is usually gradual, continuous, and cumulative. Children change quantitatively as they grow taller, heavier, and stronger. Are other aspects of development—cognitive and moral development, for example—best understood in terms of gradual, continuous, cumulative change? Or does change in some aspects of development occur in spurts in the form of stages, with one stage *qualitatively* different from the next? We will explore two stage theories in this chapter—Piaget's theory of cognitive development and Erikson's theory of psychosocial development.

3. *To what extent are personal characteristics stable over time?* In various chapters we will be discussing whether certain personal traits (intelligence, aggression, and aspects of temperament, for example) tend to be stable or changeable over time. How do developmental psychologists study changes over the life span?

Approaches to Studying Developmental Change

Developmental psychologists use the longitudinal study and the cross-sectional study to investigate age-related changes. A **longitudinal study** is one in which the same group of subjects is followed and measured at different ages, and it may take years to complete. There are some drawbacks to the longitudinal study. It is time-consuming and expensive, and subjects may drop out of the study, possibly leaving the researcher with a biased sample.

A **cross-sectional study** is a less expensive and less time-consuming method in which researchers compare groups of subjects of different ages on various characteristics to determine age-related differences. But in the cross-sectional study, differences found in age groups are based on group averages, and so this approach is not able to provide answers to some questions. For example, it could not be used to determine if the temperament of individuals is stable over time. Moreover, there may be certain relevant differences in groups of subjects that have to do less with the subjects' ages than with the eras in which they grew up. Figure 8.1 (on page 286) illustrates the longitudinal and cross-sectional studies.

Development is a fascinating and remarkable process that begins even before birth, and we will trace its course from the very beginning.

Heredity and Prenatal Development

The Mechanism of Heredity: Genes and Chromosomes

Genes are the biological blueprints that determine and direct the transmission of all of our hereditary traits. Genes are segments of DNA located on each of the rod-shaped structures called **chromosomes**, which are found in the nucleus of the body cells. Normal body cells, with two exceptions, have 23 pairs of chromosomes (46 chromosomes in all). The two exceptions are the sperm cells and the mature egg cells, which each have 23 single chromosomes. At conception the sperm adds its 23 single chromosomes to the 23 of the egg. This union forms a

longitudinal study: A type of developmental study in which the same group of subjects is followed and measured at different ages.

cross-sectional study: A type of developmental study in which researchers compare groups of subjects of different ages on certain characteristics to determine age-related differences.

genes: Within the chromosomes, the segments of DNA that are the basic units for the transmission of hereditary traits.

? *What are two types of studies developmental psychologists use to investigate age-related changes?*

? *How are hereditary traits transmitted?*

chromosomes: Rod-shaped structures in the nuclei of body cells, which contain all the genes and carry all the hereditary information.

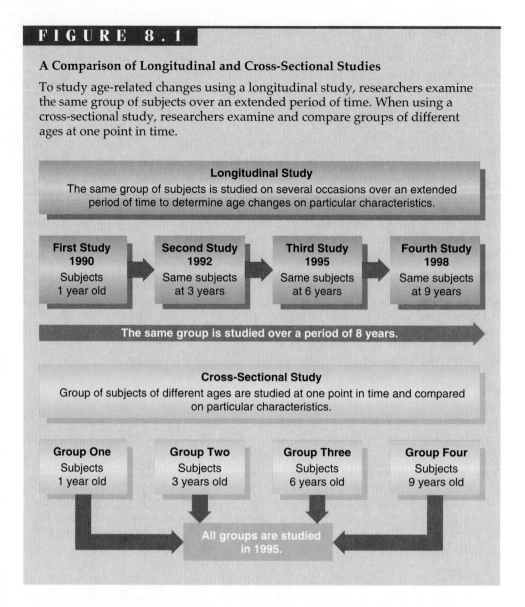

FIGURE 8.1

A Comparison of Longitudinal and Cross-Sectional Studies

To study age-related changes using a longitudinal study, researchers examine the same group of subjects over an extended period of time. When using a cross-sectional study, researchers examine and compare groups of different ages at one point in time.

Longitudinal Study
The same group of subjects is studied on several occasions over an extended period of time to determine age changes on particular characteristics.

First Study 1990	Second Study 1992	Third Study 1995	Fourth Study 1998
Subjects 1 year old	Same subjects at 3 years	Same subjects at 6 years	Same subjects at 9 years

The same group is studied over a period of 8 years.

Cross-Sectional Study
Group of subjects of different ages are studied at one point in time and compared on particular characteristics.

Group One	Group Two	Group Three	Group Four
Subjects 1 year old	Subjects 3 years old	Subjects 6 years old	Subjects 9 years old

All groups are studied in 1995.

sex chromosomes: The 23rd pair of chromosomes, which carries the genes that determine one's sex and primary and secondary sex characteristics.

dominant gene: The gene that is expressed in the individual.

recessive gene: A gene that will not be expressed if paired with a dominant gene but will be expressed if paired with another recessive gene.

period of the zygote: Lasting about 2 weeks, the period from conception to the time the zygote attaches itself to the uterine wall.

prenatal: Occurring between conception and birth.

single cell called a zygote, thus providing the full 46 chromosomes (23 pairs), which contain about 100,000 genes—all of the genetic information needed to make a human being.

Twenty-two of the 23 pairs of chromosomes are matching pairs, called autosomes, and each member of these pairs carries genes for particular physical and mental traits. The 23rd pair are called **sex chromosomes** because they carry the genes that determine a person's sex; primary and secondary sex characteristics; and other sex-linked traits, such as red-green color blindness, male pattern baldness, and hemophilia.

The sex chromosomes of females consist of two X chromosomes (XX), while males have an X chromosome and a Y chromosome (XY). The egg cell always contains an X chromosome. Therefore the sex of a child will depend on whether the egg is fertilized by a sperm carrying an X chromosome, which produces a female, or a sperm carrying a Y chromosome, which produces a male. Half of a man's sperm cells carry an X chromosome, and half carry a Y.

In some cases a single gene from each pair of chromosomes provides the genetic influence for a particular trait. In many other cases, such as intelligence, height, and weight, a number of genes collectively produce the genetic influence

FIGURE 8.2

Gene Transmission for Hair Color

This figure shows all the possible combinations in children when both parents carry a gene for brown hair (B) and a gene for blond hair (b). The chance of their having a blond-haired child (bb) or a brown-haired child (BB) is 25 percent in each case. There is a 50 percent chance of having a brown-haired child who carries both the dominant gene (B) and the recessive gene (b).

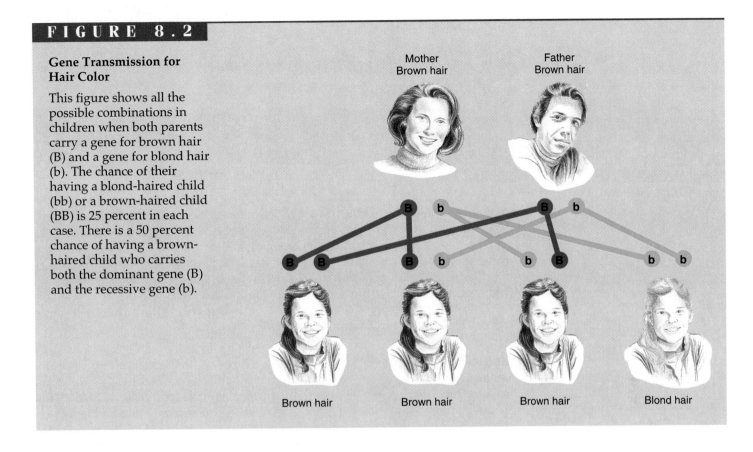

for a particular trait or ability. The Human Genome Project is aimed at identifying the functions of all of the genes and locating them on the chromosomes. Its ultimate goal is to decipher the complete instructions for making a human being.

Dominant and Recessive Genes: Dominants Call the Shots When two different genes are transmitted for the same trait, one is usually a **dominant gene**, causing the dominant trait to be expressed in the individual. The gene for brown hair, for example, is dominant over the gene for blonde hair. A person having one gene for brown hair and one gene for blonde hair will have brown hair. And, of course, two dominant genes will produce brown hair (see Figure 8.2).

The gene for blond hair is recessive. A **recessive gene** will be expressed if it is paired with another recessive gene. Therefore, blond-haired people have two recessive genes for blond hair. A recessive gene will *not* be expressed if it is paired with a dominant gene. Yet a person with such a pair can pass either the recessive gene or the dominant gene along to his or her offspring.

The Stages of Prenatal Development: Unfolding According to Plan

Conception occurs the moment a sperm cell fertilizes the ovum (egg cell), forming the single-celled zygote. Conception usually takes place in one of the fallopian tubes, and within the next 2 weeks the zygote travels to the uterus and attaches itself to the uterine wall. During this 2-week period, called the **period of the zygote**, rapid cell division occurs. At the end of this first stage of **prenatal** development, the zygote is only the size of the period at the end of this sentence.

The second stage is the period of the **embryo**, when the major systems, organs, and structures of the body develop. Lasting from week 3 through week

When are dominant or recessive genes expressed in a person?

What are the three stages of prenatal development?

embryo: The developing human organism during the period (week 3 through week 8) when the major systems, organs, and structures of the body develop.

This sequence of photos shows the fertilization of an egg by a sperm (left), an embryo at 7 weeks (middle), and a fetus at 22 weeks (right).

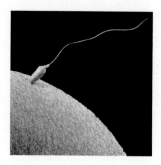 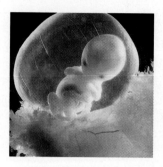 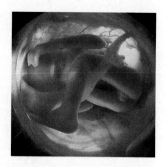

8, this period ends when the first bone cells form. Only 1 inch long and weighing 1/7 of an ounce, the embryo already resembles a human being, with limbs, fingers, toes, and many internal organs that have begun to function.

The final stage of prenatal development, called the period of the **fetus**, lasts from the end of the second month until birth. It is a time of rapid growth and further development of the structures, organs, and systems of the body. Table 8.1 describes the characteristics of each stage of prenatal development.

This is how life begins for most of us, with a single egg fertilized by a single sperm. But what occurs in multiple births?

Multiple Births: More Than One at a Time In the case of **identical twins (monozygotic twins)**, one egg is fertilized by one sperm, but the zygote splits and develops into two embryos with identical genetic codes. Thus, identical twins are always of the same sex. This splitting of the zygote seems to be a chance occurrence accounting for about 4 in 1,000 births.

Fraternal twins (dizygotic twins) develop when two eggs are released during ovulation and are fertilized by two different sperm. The two zygotes develop into two siblings who are no more alike genetically than ordinary brothers and sisters. The likelihood of fraternal twins increases if there is a family history of multiple births, if the mother is between ages 35 and 40, or if the mother has recently stopped taking birth control pills. Also, fertility drugs often cause the release of more than one egg. Triplets, quadruplets, and quintuplets can develop when multiple eggs are released during ovulation, when one or more eggs split before or after fertilization, or with any combination of these events.

fetus: The developing human organism during the period (week 9 until birth) when rapid growth and further development of the structures, organs, and systems of the body occur.

identical (monozygotic) twins: Twins with exactly the same genes, who develop after one egg is fertilized by one sperm, and the zygote splits into two parts.

fraternal (dizygotic) twins: Twins, no more alike genetically than ordinary siblings, who develop after two eggs are released during ovulation and fertilized by two different sperm.

TABLE 8.1 Stages of Prenatal Development

Stage	Time after Conception	Major Activities of the Stage
Period of the zygote	1 to 2 weeks	Zygote attaches to the uterine lining. At 2 weeks, zygote is the size of the period at the end of this sentence.
Period of the embryo	3 to 8 weeks	Major systems, organs, and structures of the body develop. Period ends when first bone cells appear. At 8 weeks, embryo is about 1 inch long and weighs 1/7 of an ounce.
Period of the fetus	9 weeks to birth (38 weeks)	Rapid growth and further development of the body structures, organs, and systems.

Negative Influences on Prenatal Development: Sabotaging Nature's Plan

? *What are some negative influences on prenatal development, and during what time is their impact greatest?*

Teratogens are agents in the prenatal environment that can have a negative impact on prenatal development, causing birth defects and other problems. A teratogen's impact depends on both its intensity and the time during prenatal development when it is present. Most negative influences—drugs, illnesses, and environmental hazards such as X rays or toxic waste—have the most devastating consequences during the first 3 months of development (the first trimester). During this time there are **critical periods** when certain body structures develop. If drugs or infections interfere with development during a critical period, the structure or body part will not form properly, nor will it develop later (Kopp & Kaler, 1989).

Exposure to risks during the second trimester of pregnancy—the fourth to sixth month—are more likely to result in various types of intellectual and social impairments than to cause physical abnormalities.

Prenatal malnutrition can harm the developing embryo and fetus and can have particularly severe effects on the brain development during the final trimester. The belief that a baby can get all the nutrition it needs from the mother regardless of her diet is simply not true. A woman should have proper nutrition and take appropriate multivitamin supplements before as well as during pregnancy (Bendich & Keen, 1993).

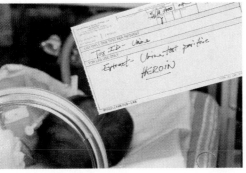

Infants exposed to drugs such as heroin in the prenatal environment often suffer severe and lasting physical and developmental complications.

The Hazard of Drugs: What the Pregnant Mother Takes, the Baby Gets, Too Many drugs cross the placental barrier and directly affect the unborn child. Consequently, both prescription and nonprescription drugs (for example, aspirin, nose sprays, laxatives, douches, reducing aids, baking soda, and vitamin supplements) should be taken only with the consent of a doctor (Apgar & Beck, 1982). Some prescription drugs, such as certain antibiotics, tranquilizers, and anticonvulsants, are known to cause specific damage in the unborn.

Heroin, Cocaine, and Crack The use of heroin, cocaine, and crack during pregnancy has been linked to miscarriage, prematurity, low birth weight, physical defects, and fetal death. Infants prenatally exposed to cocaine often suffer severe and lasting physical and developmental complications (Christmas, 1992). Cocaine use by the father at the time of conception also can be harmful because tiny specks of cocaine can bind to sperm and "piggyback" their way into the zygote (Yazigi et al., 1991).

Most people realize that pregnant women should not take hard drugs, but fewer people are aware of the potential dangers of alcohol and cigarettes.

Alcohol Few mothers would think of giving their newborns beer, wine, or hard liquor. But this is precisely what they are doing when they drink alcohol during pregnancy. Alcohol crosses the placental barrier, and alcohol levels in the fetus almost match the levels in the mother's blood (Little et al., 1989). And alcohol can alter brain development throughout pregnancy (Streissguth et al., 1989). Women who drink heavily during pregnancy risk having babies with **fetal alcohol syndrome**. Babies with this syndrome are mentally retarded and abnormally small and have facial, organ, and limb abnormalities (Becker et al., 1990; Cooper, 1987). Some children prenatally exposed to alcohol have fetal alcohol effects— some of the characteristics of fetal alcohol syndrome but in less severe form.

Streissguth and others (1989) reported that well-educated, middle-class women who consumed 1.5 ounces of alcohol daily had children who at age 4 averaged 5 IQ points lower than children of women who drank less. Moderate drinking also had adverse affects on fine and gross motor development in 4-year-

teratogens: Harmful agents in the prenatal environment, which can have a negative impact on prenatal development or even cause birth defects.

critical period: A period that is so important to development that a harmful environmental influence can keep a bodily structure or behavior from developing normally.

fetal alcohol syndrome: A condition, caused by maternal alcohol intake during pregnancy, in which the baby is born mentally retarded, abnormally small, and with facial, organ, and limb abnormalities.

low-birth-weight baby: A baby weighing less than 5.5 pounds.

preterm infant: An infant born before the 37th week and weighing less than 5.5 pounds; a premature infant.

old children (Barr et al., 1990). Women should abstain from drinking alcohol altogether during pregnancy. In addition, there is now some evidence that when men ingest large amounts of alcohol, changes in sperm cells occur that can inhibit conception or cause complications in development (Cicero, cited in Dryden, 1994).

Smoking Smoking decreases the amount of oxygen and increases the amount of carbon monoxide crossing the placental barrier. The embryo or fetus is exposed to nicotine and several thousand other chemicals as well. Smoking increases the probability that a baby will be premature or of low birth weight (McDonald et al., 1992). Women smoking one pack per day are at three times the risk for premature birth. Smoking is also associated with higher rates of spontaneous abortion (Armstrong et al., 1992), sudden infant death syndrome (Slotkin et al., 1995), stillbirth, and infant mortality. And Olds and others (1994) found that 3- and 4-year-old children of mothers who smoked 10 cigarettes a day or more during pregnancy scored 4 IQ points lower, on average, than children of nonsmokers.

Low-Birth-Weight Babies: Newborns at High Risk The infant mortality rate in the United States is about 8.9 per 1,000 live births. The rate is 7.3 per 1,000 for white infants and more than twice as high—17.6 per 1,000—for African American infants (U.S. Bureau of the Census, 1994). Sixty-five percent of these deaths occur in the 6 to 7 percent who are **low-birth-weight babies**—babies weighing less than 5.5 pounds. Infants of this weight born at or before the 37th week are considered **preterm infants**. The smaller and more premature the baby, the greater the risk (Lukeman & Melvin, 1993). The handicaps of prematurity range from subtle learning and behavior problems, in babies closer to normal birth weight, to "severe retardation, blindness, hearing loss, and even death," in the smallest newborns (Apgar & Beck, 1982, p. 69).

Poor nutrition, poor prenatal care, smoking, drug use, and maternal infection all increase the likelihood of having a low-birth-weight baby with complications. But even with good prenatal care and nutrition and no drug use, 14 to 17 year olds appear to be at higher risk of having very small babies (Ward et al., 1995).

Memory Check 8.1

1. The cross-sectional study takes longer to complete than the longitudinal study. (true/false)

2. In humans, genes are located on how many pairs of chromosomes?
   a. 22   b. 23   c. 44   d. 46

3. Females have an X and a Y chromosome. (true/false)

4. A dominant gene will not be expressed if the individual carries:
   a. two dominant genes for the trait.
   b. one dominant and one recessive gene for the trait.
   c. two recessive genes for the trait.
   d. either one or two dominant genes for the trait.

5. Fraternal twins are no more alike genetically than ordinary brothers and sisters. (true/false)

6. Match the stage of prenatal development with its description.
   ____ 1) first 2 weeks of life
   ____ 2) rapid growth and further development of body structures and systems
   ____ 3) formation of major systems, organs, and structures

   a. period of the fetus
   b. period of the embryo
   c. period of the zygote

7. Negative influences such as drugs, illnesses, and environmental hazards cause the most devastating consequences during the _____ trimester.
   a. first   c. third
   b. second   d. second or third

Answers: 1. false 2. b 3. false 4. c 5. true 6. 1) c; 2) a; 3) b 7. a

Physical Development and Learning in Infancy

The Neonate: Seven Pounds of Beauty?

Although **neonates** (newborn babies) may be beautiful to their parents, they do not yet resemble the babies who pose for the Gerber or Johnson & Johnson baby ads. Newborns measure about 20 inches long, weigh about 7½ pounds, and have a head one-quarter the length of the body. They arrive with dry and wrinkled skin, a rather flat nose, and an elongated forehead—the temporary result of the journey through the birth canal. Nevertheless, newborns come equipped with an impressive range of **reflexes**—built-in responses to certain stimuli that are needed to ensure survival in their new world.

Reflexes: Built-In Responses Sucking, swallowing, coughing, and blinking are some important behaviors that newborns can perform right away. They will move an arm, a leg, or other body part away from a painful stimulus, and they will try to remove a blanket or a cloth placed over their face, which might hamper breathing. Stroke a baby on the cheek and you will trigger the rooting reflex—the baby's mouth opens and actively searches for a nipple. Neonates also have some reflexes that serve no apparent function, and these reflexes are believed to be remnants of our evolutionary past. As the brain develops, behaviors that were initially reflexive, controlled by the lower brain centers, gradually come under the voluntary control of the higher brain centers. The presence of these reflexes at birth and their disappearance between the second and fourth months provide researchers with a means of assessing development of the nervous system.

Perceptual Development in Infancy

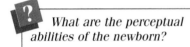

What are the perceptual abilities of the newborn?

The five senses, although not fully developed, are functional at birth, and the newborn already has preferences for certain odors, tastes, sounds, and visual configurations. Hearing is much better developed than vision in the neonate and is functional even before birth (Busnel et al., 1992). Newborns are able to turn their head in the direction of a sound (Javel, 1980; Spezzano & Waterman, 1977), and they show a general preference for female voices. Shortly after birth, infants prefer their own mother's voice to that of an unfamiliar female (DeCasper & Fifer, 1980), although a preference for the father's voice over a strange male voice does not develop until later. Newborns are able to discriminate among and show preferences for certain odors and tastes (Bartoshuk & Beauchamp, 1994; Leon, 1992). They show a favorable response to sweet tastes and are able to differentiate between salty, bitter, and sour solutions. Newborns are also sensitive to pain (Porter et al., 1988) and are particularly responsive to touch, reacting positively to stroking and fondling.

Robert Fantz (1961) made a major breakthrough when he realized that the interest of babies in an object can be gauged by the length of time they fixate on it. Infants' visual preferences can be assessed with eye-tracking devices that measure what a baby looks at and for how long. This and other techniques have shown that newborns have clear preferences and powers of discrimination, and even memory recognition and learning ability.

Vision: What Newborns Can See At birth, vision is about 20/150 (Dayton et al., 1964). Newborns focus best on objects about 9 inches away, and they can follow a slowly moving object. Infants 22 to 93 hours old already indicate a preference for their own mother's face over that of an unfamiliar female (Field et al.,

neonate: Newborn infant up to 1 month old.

reflexes: Inborn, unlearned, automatic responses to certain environmental stimuli (examples: coughing, blinking, sucking, grasping).

visual cliff: An apparatus used to test depth perception in infants and young animals.

habituation: A decrease in response or attention to a stimulus as an infant becomes accustomed to it.

? *What types of learning occur in the first few days of life?*

When placed on the visual cliff, most infants older than 6 months will not crawl out over the deep side, indicating that they can perceive depth.

1984). At 1 to 2 months, infants can see all or almost all of the colors adults see (Clavadetscher et al., 1988), but they prefer red, blue, green, and yellow (Bornstein & Marks, 1982).

The famous **visual cliff** experiment was devised to study depth perception in infants and other animals. Gibson and Walk (1960) designed an apparatus consisting of "a board laid across a sheet of heavy glass, with a patterned material directly beneath the glass on one side and several feet below it on the other" (p. 65). This arrangement made it appear that there was a large drop off, or "visual cliff," on one side. When 36 babies aged 6 to 14 months were placed on the center board, most could be coaxed by their mothers to crawl to the shallow side, but only three would crawl onto the deep side. Gibson and Walk concluded that most babies "can discriminate depth as soon as they can crawl" (p. 64).

Using the visual cliff, Campos and others (1970) found that 6-week-old infants had distinct changes in heart rate when they faced the deep side of the cliff, but no change when they faced the shallow side. The change in heart rate indicated interest and showed that the infants could perceive depth.

Learning in Infancy

When are babies first capable of learning? If you say from the moment of birth, you may be underestimating them. We know that learning begins even before birth, because infants' experiences in the womb can affect their preferences shortly after birth. DeCasper and Spence (1986) had 16 pregnant women read *The Cat in the Hat* to their developing fetuses twice a day during the final 6½ weeks of pregnancy. A few days after birth the infants could adjust their sucking on specially designed, pressure-sensitive nipples to hear their mother reading either *The Cat in the Hat* or *The King, the Mice, and the Cheese*, a story they had never heard before. Which story did the infants prefer? You guessed it—by their sucking behavior they showed a clear preference for the familiar sound of *The Cat in the Hat*.

Researchers have demonstrated both classical conditioning and operant conditioning in infants in the first few days of life (Lipsitt, 1990). The simplest evidence of learning in infants is the phenomenon of **habituation**. When presented with a new stimulus, they respond with a general quieting, their heart rate slows, and they fixate on the stimulus. But when infants become accustomed to the stimulus, they stop responding—that is, they habituate to it. Later, if the familiar stimulus is presented along with a new stimulus, they will usually pay more attention to the new stimulus, indicating that they remember the original stimulus but prefer the new one. Memory can be measured by (1) the speed with which habituation occurs and (2) the relative amounts of time infants spend looking at or listening to a new and an old stimulus.

Swain and others (1993) demonstrated that 3-day-old newborns could retain in memory for 24 hours a speech sound that had been presented repeatedly the day before. When the same sound was repeated the following day, the babies quickly showed habituation by turning their head away from the familiar sound and toward a novel sound. And infants 2 to 3 months old can form memories of their past experience lasting for days and even longer as they get older (Rovee-Collier, 1990).

Amazing as it may seem, babies only 42 minutes old can imitate gestures such as sticking out the tongue or opening and closing the mouth (Meltzoff & Moore, 1977). And infants averaging 42 hours in age can imitate head movements (Meltzoff & Moore, 1989). A study by Meltzoff (1988) demonstrated observational learning in 14-month-olds. After watching an adult on television handling "a novel toy in a particular way," the babies were able to imitate the behavior when presented with the toy 24 hours later. Perhaps parents should be more particular about the TV programs their babies watch.

Motor Development in Infancy

Babies undergo rapid change during the first few years of life. Some changes are due to maturation, others to learning. **Maturation** occurs naturally according to the infant's own genetically determined, biological timetable of development. Many motor milestones, such as sitting, standing, and walking (shown in Figure 8.3) are primarily a result of maturation and ultimately depend on the growth and development of the central nervous system. But the rate at which these milestones are achieved is delayed when an infant is subjected to extremely unfavorable environmental conditions such as severe malnutrition or maternal and sensory deprivation. Cross-cultural research reveals that in some African cultures in Uganda and Kenya, mothers use special motor training techniques that enable their infants

> **?** *What is the primary factor influencing attainment of the major motor milestones?*

FIGURE 8.3

The Progression of Motor Development

Most infants develop motor skills in the sequence shown in the figure. The ages indicated are only averages, so normal, healthy infants may develop any of these milestones a few months earlier or several months later than the average.

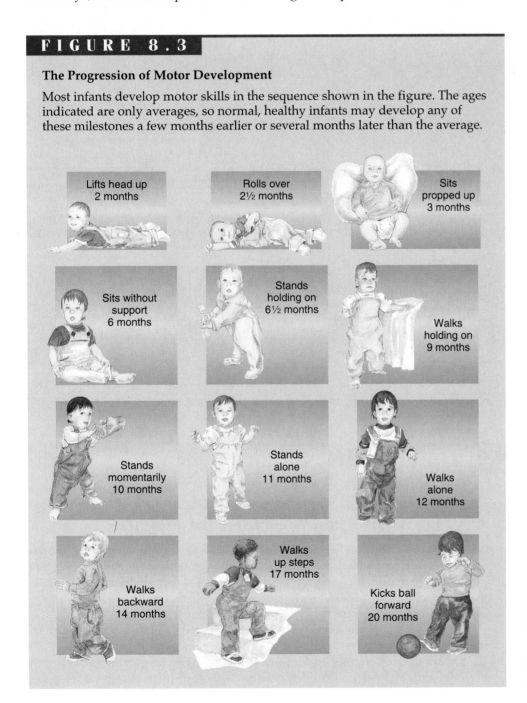

Lifts head up
2 months

Rolls over
2½ months

Sits
propped up
3 months

Sits without
support
6 months

Stands
holding on
6½ months

Walks
holding on
9 months

Stands
momentarily
10 months

Stands
alone
11 months

Walks
alone
12 months

Walks
backward
14 months

Walks
up steps
17 months

Kicks ball
forward
20 months

maturation: Changes that occur according to one's genetically determined, biological timetable of development.

to attain some of the major motor milestones earlier than most infants in the United States (Kilbride & Kilbride, 1975; Super, 1981). But speeding up the attainment of motor skills has no lasting impact on development. Babies will walk, talk, and be toilet trained according to their own developmental schedule.

Although infants follow their own individual timetable, there is a sequence in which the basic motor skills usually appear. Physical and motor development proceeds from the head downward to the trunk and legs, so babies lift their heads before they sit, and they sit before they walk. Development also proceeds from the center of the body outward—trunk to shoulders to arms to fingers. Thus control of the arms develops before control of fingers.

The second process affecting development is learning, but learning cannot take place until particular areas of the brain mature. In other words, the child must be physically and neurologically *ready* to learn.

Memory Check 8.2

1. Compared to a neonate, the number of reflexes you possess is:
   a. much larger.   c. the same.
   b. slightly larger.   d. smaller.

2. Which of the following statements about infant sensory development is *not* true?
   a. Vision, hearing, taste, and smell are all fully developed at birth.
   b. Vision, hearing, taste, and smell are all functional at birth.
   c. Infants can show preferences in what they want to look at, hear, taste, and smell shortly after birth.
   d. Hearing is better developed at birth than vision.

3. Classical and operant conditioning and observational learning occur in the first few days of life. (true/false)

4. Two-month-old Michael likes to look at the soft, multicolored ball in his crib, but the new black-and-white ball has recently gained his attention. Habituation has occurred, meaning that
   a. Michael has gotten used to a stimulus (the multicolored ball).
   b. Michael no longer remembers the stimulus he has seen previously.
   c. Michael has a short attention span.
   d. a complex form of learning has taken place.

5. The primary factor influencing the attainment of the major motor milestones is:
   a. experience.   c. learning.
   b. maturation.   d. habituation.

Answers: 1. d   2. a   3. true   4. a   5. b

E motional Development in Infancy

What is temperament, and what are the three temperament types identified by Thomas, Chess, and Birch?

temperament: A person's behavioral style or characteristic way of responding to the environment.

Temperament: How and When Does It Develop?

Maria is usually cheerful, easygoing, and adaptable. John is always on the go, and he sticks with a problem until it is solved, but he gets upset easily. Their parents say the two children have always been that way. Are babies born with an individual behavior style or characteristic way of responding to the environment, which is referred to as **temperament**?

The New York Longitudinal Study was undertaken in 1956 to investigate temperament and its effect on development. Thomas, Chess, and Birch (1970) studied 2- to 3-month-old infants and followed them for 10 years using observation, interviews with parents and teachers, and psychological tests. They found that "children do show distinct individuality in temperament in the first weeks of life independently of their parents' handling or personality style" (p. 104). Three general types of temperament emerged from the study.

"Easy" children—40 percent of the group—had generally pleasant moods, were adaptable, approached new situations and people positively, and established regular sleep, eating, and elimination patterns. "Difficult" children—10 percent of the group—had generally unpleasant moods, reacted negatively to new situations and people, were intense in their emotional reactions, and showed irregularity of bodily functions. "Slow-to-warm-up" children—15 percent of the group—tended to withdraw, were slow to adapt, and were "somewhat negative in mood." The remaining 35 percent of the group were too inconsistent to categorize.

Thomas and others (1970) believe that "personality is shaped by the constant interplay of temperament and environment" (p. 102). Although the environment can intensify, diminish, or modify these inborn behavioral tendencies, "the original characteristics of temperament tend to persist in most children over the years" (p. 104). Activity level seems to show the most consistency over time (Goldsmith et al., 1987; Korner et al., 1985). Researchers conducting twin studies (Emde et al., 1992; Plomin et al., 1990) and adoption studies (Braungart et al., 1992) have found a genetic influence on activity level and on other aspects of temperament such as mood/extraversion, inhibition to the unfamiliar (shyness), and task orientation.

The Formation of Attachment

Human newborns are among the most helpless and dependent of all animal species and cannot survive alone. Fortunately, infants form a strong **attachment** to their mothers or primary caregivers. Because their attachment is a two-way affair, the word "bonding" has been used to describe this mutual attachment (Brazelton et al., 1975).

What precisely is the glue that binds caregiver (usually the mother) and infant? For decades people believed that an infant's attachment to its caregiver was formed primarily because the caregiver provides the nourishment that sustains life. However, a series of classic studies conducted by Harry Harlow on attachment in rhesus monkeys suggests that physical nourishment alone is not enough to bind infants to their primary caregivers.

Attachment in Infant Monkeys: Like Humans in So Many Ways Harry Harlow found that the behavior of monkeys deprived of mothering was not unlike that of children raised in orphanages. Motherless monkeys would "sit in their cages and stare fixedly into space, circle their cages in a repetitive stereotyped manner and clasp their heads in their hands or arms and rock for long periods of time" (Harlow & Harlow, 1962, p. 138).

To investigate systematically the nature of attachment and the effects of maternal deprivation on infant monkeys, Harlow constructed two **surrogate** (artificial) monkey "mothers." One was a plain wire-mesh cylinder with a wooden head; the other was a wire-mesh cylinder that was padded, covered with soft terry cloth, and fitted with a somewhat more monkeylike head (see the photograph on page 296). A baby bottle could be attached to either surrogate mother for feeding.

Newborn monkeys were placed in individual cages where they had equal access to a cloth surrogate and a wire surrogate. The source of their nourishment (cloth or wire surrogate) was unimportant. "The infants developed a strong attachment to the cloth mothers and little or none to the wire mothers" (Harlow & Harlow, 1962, p. 141). Harlow found that it was contact comfort—the comfort supplied by bodily contact—rather than nourishment that formed the basis of the infant monkey's attachment to its mother.

What did Harlow's studies reveal about maternal deprivation and attachment in infant monkeys?

attachment: The strong affectionate bond a child forms with the mother or primary caregiver.

surrogate: Substitute; someone or something that stands in place of.

Harlow found that infant monkeys developed a strong attachment to a cloth-covered surrogate mother and little or no attachment to a wire surrogate mother—even when the wire mother provided nourishment.

? *According to Bowlby, when does the infant have a strong attachment to the mother?*

separation anxiety: The fear and distress shown by toddlers when their parent leaves, occurring from 8 to 24 months and reaching a peak between 12 and 18 months.

The monkeys formed the same type of attachment to the cloth mother as normal monkeys did to their real mothers. In both cases monkeys would cling to their mothers many hours each day and "run to them for comfort or reassurance when they are frightened" (Harlow, 1959, p. 73). If the cloth mother was not present when unfamiliar objects were placed in the cage, the monkey would huddle in the corner, clutching its head, rocking, sucking its thumb or toes, and crying in distress. But when the cloth mother was present, it would first cling to her and then explore and play with the unfamiliar objects.

If the infant monkeys were placed with the cloth mother for the first 5½ months of life, their attachment was so strong that it persisted even after an 18-month separation. Their attachment to the cloth mother was almost identical to the attachment normal monkeys have to their real mother, but their emotional development was not. They would not interact with other monkeys and they showed inappropriate aggression. Their sexual behavior was grossly abnormal, and they would not mate. If impregnated artificially, they became terrible mothers whose behavior ranged from ignoring their babies to violently abusing them (Harlow et al., 1971). The only aspect of development not affected was learning ability.

The Necessity for Love Harlow's research reveals the disastrous effects of maternal deprivation on infant monkeys. Human infants, too, need love in order to grow physically and psychologically. Between 1900 and 1920 in the United States, the majority of infants under 1 year old who were placed in orphanages did not survive, even with adequate food and medical care (Montagu, 1962). Usually kept in cribs, the sides draped with sheets, these unfortunate infants were left to stare at the ceiling. Lacking a warm, close, personal caregiver and the all-important ingredient love, the infants who survived their first year failed to gain weight and grow normally—a condition known as deprivation dwarfism (Gardner, 1972). And they were severely retarded in their mental and motor development (Spitz, 1946). For their very survival, infants need to become attached to someone. That someone can be nearly anyone, but it is most often the mother. Is the emotional bond between mother and infant present at birth?

The Development of Attachment in Humans A strong emotional attachment between mother and infant is not present at birth but develops gradually. The mother holds, strokes, and talks to the baby, and responds to the baby's needs, and the baby gazes at and listens to the mother and even moves in synchrony with her voice (Condon & Sander, 1974; Lester et al., 1985). The baby's responses reinforce the mother's attention and care. Even crying can promote attachment, because the mother is motivated to relieve the baby's distress and she feels rewarded when she is successful. Much like Harlow's monkeys, babies cling to their mothers, and when they are old enough to crawl, they use locomotion to stay near them. Young Robert, described at the beginning of this chapter, may have become attached to a mothering monkey that adopted him into her tribe.

John Bowlby (1951), a leading theorist on attachment, believes that to grow up mentally healthy, infants and young children "should experience a warm, intimate, and continuous relationship" with their mother or permanent mother substitute that is mutually satisfying and enjoyable (p. 13). The infant's attachment to the mother develops over time and is usually quite strong by age 6 to 8 months (Bowlby, 1969). According to Bowlby, attachment behavior serves the evolutionary function of protecting the infant from danger (Bretherton, 1992).

Once the attachment has formed, infants show **separation anxiety**—fear and distress when the parent leaves them. Occurring from about age 8 to 24 months, separation anxiety peaks between ages 12 and 18 months (Fox & Bell, 1990). Toddlers who previously voiced no distress when their parents left them with a babysitter may now scream when their parents leave.

At about 6 or 7 months of age, infants develop a fear of strangers called **stranger anxiety**, which increases in intensity until 12½ months and then declines in the second year (Marks, 1987b). Stranger anxiety is greater in an unfamiliar setting, when the parent is not close at hand, and when a stranger abruptly approaches or touches the child. Interestingly, stranger anxiety is not directed at unfamiliar children until ages 19 to 30 months (P. K. Smith, 1979).

Stranger anxiety and separation anxiety in infants are not just Western phenomena. They are found in Israeli kibbutzim and in cultures as diverse as those of the Kung bushmen, rural Ganda, Navajo, and Guatemalan Maya (Super, 1981).

stranger anxiety: A fear of strangers common in infants at about 6 months and increasing in intensity until about 12½ months, and then declining in the second year.

Ainsworth's Study of Attachment: The Importance of Being Securely Attached In a classic study of mother–child attachment, Mary Ainsworth (1973, 1979) observed mother–child interactions in the home during the infants' first year and then again at age 12 months in a laboratory procedure called the Strange Situation. Based on infants' reactions to their mothers after two brief separations, Ainsworth identified three patterns of attachment—secure, ambivalent, and avoidant. She related these patterns to how sensitive, responsive, and accepting the mothers had been toward their infants during home observations the previous year.

What are the three attachment patterns identified by Ainsworth?

Securely attached infants (65 percent of the sample) were distressed when they were separated from their mothers. They eagerly sought to reestablish contact after separation, and then showed an interest in play. The securely attached infants used their mothers as a safe base of operation from which to explore, much as Harlow's monkeys had done when unfamiliar objects were placed in their cages. Securely attached infants were the most responsive, obedient, and content, and they cried less than babies who were less strongly attached (Ainsworth et al., 1978). The mothers of securely attached infants had been the most sensitive, accepting, affectionate, and responsive to their cries and needs (Isabella et al., 1989; Pederson et al., 1990). This finding contradicts the notion that mothers who respond promptly to an infant's cries end up with spoiled babies who cry more.

Infants with an ambivalent attachment (10–15 percent of the group) both approached and then tried to avoid their mothers when they returned after the separations. These mothers had been inconsistent in their responsiveness to their babies, attending to them only when they were in the mood rather than when the child needed them.

Infants with the weakest attachment, classified as avoidant attachment (20–25 percent of the sample), actually avoided contact when they were reunited with their mothers. These mothers had shown little affection and had been generally unresponsive to their infants' needs and cries.

Securely attached infants are likely to grow up to be more sociable, more effective with peers, more interested in exploring the environment, and generally more competent than less securely attached infants (Masters, 1981). Furthermore, their interactions with friends tend to be more harmonious and less controlling (Park & Waters, 1989).

Secure attachment is the most common type across cultures. However, cross-cultural research has revealed a higher incidence of insecure attachment patterns in Israel, Japan, and West Germany than in the United States (Collins & Gunnar, 1990). Ainsworth's procedure, may not be valid for all cultures.

The Father–Child Relationship

What are the typical differences in the ways mothers and fathers interact with their children?

Mother–child rather than father–child relationships have been the traditional focus of research. But this is changing because of the greater child-rearing responsibility some fathers are assuming. Fathers can be as responsive and competent as mothers when they voluntarily assume child-rearing responsibilities (Parke et al., 1972), and their attachments can be just as strong. Yet even when attachment to both parents is strong, infants in the first year tend to go to their mother for comfort when they are in distress (Hartup, 1989).

Differences exist in the types of activities children share with their mothers and fathers and in both the frequency and extent of their interactions (Collins & Gunnar, 1990). In the United States, as well as in many other cultures around the world, mothers spend more time in caretaking—feeding, bathing, changing—and fathers generally spend more time playing with their infants (Bronstein, 1984; Lamb, 1987). Mother play and father play also seem to differ. Fathers engage in more exciting and arousing physical play, while mothers tend to talk more to their children, provide toys, and play more conventional games with them.

When the mother and the father have a good relationship, fathers tend to develop a more intense and positive relationship with the infant (Lamb & Elster, 1985) and to maintain it in middle childhood (Brody et al., 1986).

Memory Check 8.3

1. Which statement best describes Thomas, Chess, and Birch's thinking about temperament?
   a. Temperament develops gradually as a result of parental handling and personality.
   b. Temperament is inborn and is not influenced by the environment.
   c. Temperament is inborn but can be modified by the family and the environment.
   d. Temperament is set at birth and is unchangeable.

2. Infants raised with adequate physical care but without the attention of a close, personal caregiver often become mentally and/or physically retarded. (true/false)

3. Which of the following was *not* true of infant monkeys raised with surrogate mothers?

   a. They showed inappropriate aggression.
   b. They would not interact with other monkeys.
   c. Their learning ability was impaired.
   d. They became abusive mothers.

4. A strong attachment between infant and mother usually occurs shortly after birth. (true/false)

5. Ainsworth found that most infants had a secure attachment. (true/false)

6. The most common type of interaction most fathers have with their infant is in the context of caregiving—feeding, changing, and bathing. (true/false)

Answers: 1. c   2. true   3. c   4. false   5. true   6. false

Piaget's Theory of Cognitive Development

How does a child's mind differ from an adult's? Thanks to the work of Swiss psychologist Jean Piaget, we have gained insights into the cognitive, or mental, processes of children—how they think, perceive, and gain knowledge about the world.

Piaget maintained that children are active participants in their own cognitive development. Unlike empty vessels that can be filled with knowledge, children discover and construct knowledge through their own activity. According to Piaget, cognitive development begins with a few basic **schemas**—cognitive structures or concepts used to identify and interpret objects, events, and other information in the environment. Confronted with new objects, events, experiences, and information, children try to fit them into their existing schemas, a process known as **assimilation**. But not everything can be assimilated into the existing schemas. If children call a stranger "Daddy" or the neighbor's cat "doggie,"

schema: Piaget's term for a cognitive structure or concept used to identify and interpret information.

assimilation: The process by which new objects, events, experiences, or information are incorporated into existing schemas.

assimilation is not appropriate. When parents and others correct them, or when they discover for themselves that something cannot be assimilated into an existing schema, children will use a process known as accommodation. In **accommodation**, existing schemas are modified or new schemas are created to process new information. It is through the processes of assimilation and accommodation, then, that schemas are formed, differentiated, and broadened.

The Cognitive Stages of Development: Climbing the Steps to Cognitive Maturity

> ? *What were Piaget's claims regarding his stages of cognitive development?*

Piaget formulated a comprehensive theory that systematically describes and explains how intellect develops (Piaget, 1963b, 1964; Piaget & Inhelder, 1969). He claimed that cognitive development occurs in four stages, which differ not according to the knowledge children have accumulated, but in the way they reason. Each stage reflects a qualitatively different way of reasoning and understanding the world. The stages occur in a fixed sequence in which the accomplishments of one stage provide the foundation for the next stage. Although children throughout the world seem to progress through the stages in the same order, there are individual differences in the rate at which they pass through them. And the rate is influenced by a child's level of maturation and experience. The transition from one stage to another is gradual, not abrupt, and children often show aspects of two stages at the same time during these transitions.

The Sensorimotor Stage (Ages Birth to 2 Years) In the first stage, the **sensorimotor stage**, infants gain an understanding of the world through their senses and their motor activities (actions or body movements), hence the name *sensorimotor*. An infant's behavior, which is mostly reflexive at birth, becomes increasingly complex and gradually evolves into intelligent behavior. At this stage, the intelligence is one of action rather than of thought, and it is confined to objects that are present and events that are directly perceived. The child learns to respond to and manipulate objects, and to use them in goal-directed activity.

> ? *What is Piaget's sensorimotor stage?*

At birth, infants are incapable of thought, and they are unable to differentiate themselves from others or from the environment. Living in a world of the here and now, infants are aware that objects exist only when they can actually see them. Take a stuffed animal away from a 5-month-old and it ceases to exist as far as the child is concerned. At this age, out of sight is always out of mind.

The major achievement of the sensorimotor period is the development of **object permanence**, which is the realization that objects (including people) continue to exist even when they are out of sight. This concept develops gradually and is complete when the child is able to represent objects mentally in their absence. This marks the end of the sensorimotor period.

accommodation: The process by which existing schemas are modified and new schemas are created to incorporate new objects, events, experiences, or information.

sensorimotor stage: Piaget's first stage of cognitive development (ages birth to 2 years), culminating with the development of object permanence and the beginning of representational thought.

object permanence: The realization that objects continue to exist even when they are no longer perceived.

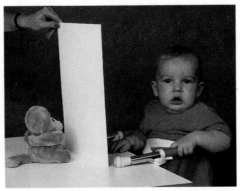

According to Piaget, in the sensorimotor stage children learn object permanence—the understanding that objects continue to exist even when they are out of sight.

> **?** What cognitive limitations characterize a child's thinking during the preoperational stage?

preoperational stage: Piaget's second stage of cognitive development (ages 2 to 7 years), characterized by rapid development of language and thinking governed by perception rather than logic.

conservation: The concept that a given quantity of matter remains the same despite rearrangement or change in its appearance, as long as nothing has been added or taken away.

centration: A preoperational child's tendency to focus on only one dimension of a stimulus and ignore other dimensions.

The Preoperational Stage (Ages 2 to 7 Years) The **preoperational stage** is a period of rapid development in language. Children become increasingly able to represent objects and events mentally with words and images. Now their thinking is no longer restricted to objects and events that are directly perceived and present in the environment. Evidence of representational thought is the child's ability to imitate the behavior of a person who is no longer present (deferred imitation). Other evidence is the child's ability to engage in imaginary play using one object to stand for another, such as using a broom to represent a horse.

Although thinking at the preoperational stage is more advanced than at the previous stage, it is still quite restricted. Thinking is dominated by perception, and children at this stage exhibit egocentrism in thought. They believe that everyone sees what they see, thinks as they think, and feels as they feel.

At this stage children also show animistic thinking, believing that inanimate objects such as a tree, the sun, and a doll are alive and have feelings and intentions as well (Piaget, 1960, 1963a). That explains why 2-year-old Kate says "hello" to her food before she eats it, and why 3-year-old Meghan shows distress when her brother throws her doll into her toy box. Children also believe that all things, even the moon and clouds, are made for and usually by people.

The preoperational stage is so named because children are not yet able to perform mental operations (manipulations) that follow logical rules. Children at this stage are not aware that a given quantity of matter (a given number, mass, area, weight, or volume of matter) remains the same if it is rearranged or changed in its appearance, as long as nothing has been added or taken away. This concept is known as **conservation**.

If you know a child of preschool age, try the conservation experiment illustrated in the following *Try It!*

Show a preschooler two glasses of the same size and then fill them with the same amount of juice. After the child agrees they are the same, pour the juice from one glass into a taller, narrower glass. Now ask the child if the two glasses have the same amount of juice, or if one glass has more than the other. Children at this stage will insist that the taller, narrower glass has more juice, although they will quickly agree that you neither added juice nor took it away.

PIONEERS — Jean Piaget (1896–1980)

Born in Neuchatel, Switzerland, in 1896, Jean Piaget made his professional debut in his small, French-speaking hometown at the tender age of 10. Bright beyond his years and keenly interested in biology, Piaget volunteered to work without pay as a laboratory assistant, helping the director of a museum of natural history conduct his experiments on mollusks (snails, oysters, clams, and the like). The museum director, an expert on mollusks, soon died, so Piaget wrote his own descriptions of the experiments and had them published.

Piaget's scientific papers came to the attention of many scientists, and soon a letter came offering him a job in Geneva, Switzerland, as curator of a natural history museum. But Piaget had to refuse the offer, for he was only 11 years old.

Piaget continued to study and publish his writings, and at age 22 he finished his Ph.D. in the natural sciences at the University of Neuchatel. Not sure what he wanted to do with his life, Piaget began to turn his interest to another field—psychology—and went to Paris to continue his studies at the Sorbonne.

About a year later Theodore Simon (who worked with Alfred Binet to create the first IQ test) offered Piaget a job. Piaget's work was to test French schoolchildren in order to standardize mental test items. The work seemed boring to Piaget at first, but it was destined to open the door to a distinguished career, which consumed the rest of his professional life. Strangely, it was the children's wrong answers on the test items that captured Piaget's interest. He observed that the wrong responses were not just random mistakes; instead, they seemed to reflect an unusual logic or reasoning that was systematic and shared by most children of similar ages.

Piaget had discovered a new field of research, and he began studying patterns of thinking and logical reasoning in children. His articles on the subject resulted in the offer of a new position as director of studies at the Rousseau Institute for Child Study and Teacher Training in Geneva. Still only 24, Piaget accepted the job, and his long, pioneering career was launched.

Using hundreds of children as subjects, including his own three children, Piaget studied the development of thinking and reasoning and language concepts in children. His books, which were based on his research, made him world-famous by the time he was 30 years old. Piaget's contribution to our knowledge of children's thinking and cognitive development is without equal in developmental psychology.

Centration and irreversibility are two restrictions in children's thinking that lead them to wrong conclusions. **Centration** is the tendency to focus on only one dimension of a stimulus and ignore the other dimensions. For example, in the *Try It!* the child focused on the tallness of the glass and failed to notice that it was also narrower. At this stage, taller means more.

Preoperational children have not developed **reversibility** in thinking—the realization that after any change in the shape, position, or order of matter, it can be returned mentally to its original state. The preoperational child in the *Try It!* cannot mentally return the juice to the original glass and realize that once again the two glasses of juice are equal.

reversibility: The realization that any change in the shape, position, or order of matter can be reversed mentally.

The Concrete Operations Stage (Ages 7 to 11 or 12 Years)

In the third stage, the **concrete operations stage**, children gradually overcome the obstacles to logical thought associated with the preoperational period. Their thinking is less egocentric, and they come to realize that other people have thoughts and feelings that may be different from their own. Children acquire the ability to carry out mentally the operations essential for logical thought. They can now decenter

? *What cognitive abilities do children acquire during the concrete operations stage?*

concrete operations stage: Piaget's third stage of cognitive development (ages 7 to 11 years), during which a child acquires the concepts of reversibility and conservation and is able to apply logical thinking to concrete objects. (p. 301)

their thinking, that is, attend to two or more dimensions of a stimulus at the same time. They can also understand the concept of reversibility, which is crucial in problem solving. Finally, during this stage children acquire the concept of conservation.

Children at this stage, however, are able to apply logical operations only to concrete problems that they can perceive directly. They cannot apply these mental operations to verbal, abstract, or hypothetical problems. Surprisingly, the concepts of conservation of number, substance (liquid, mass), length, area, weight, and volume are not all acquired at once. They come in a certain sequence and usually at the ages shown in Figure 8.4.

FIGURE 8.4

Piaget's Conservation Tasks

Pictured here are several of Piaget's conservation tasks. The ability to answer correctly develops over time according to the ages indicated for each task. (From Berk, 1991.)

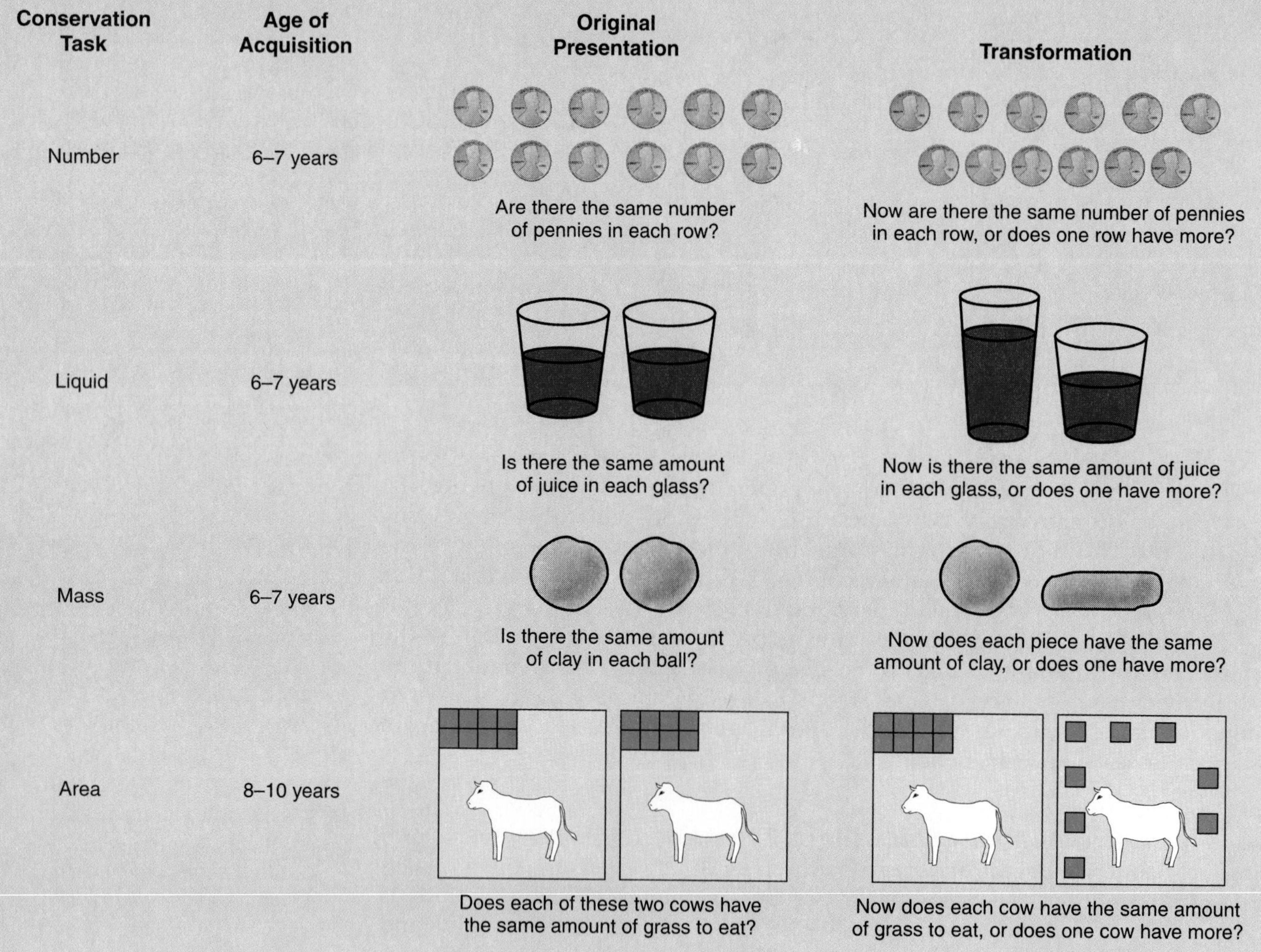

Conservation Task	Age of Acquisition	Original Presentation	Transformation
Number	6–7 years	Are there the same number of pennies in each row?	Now are there the same number of pennies in each row, or does one row have more?
Liquid	6–7 years	Is there the same amount of juice in each glass?	Now is there the same amount of juice in each glass, or does one have more?
Mass	6–7 years	Is there the same amount of clay in each ball?	Now does each piece have the same amount of clay, or does one have more?
Area	8–10 years	Does each of these two cows have the same amount of grass to eat?	Now does each cow have the same amount of grass to eat, or does one cow have more?

The Formal Operations Stage (Ages 11 or 12 Years and Beyond) The **formal operations stage** is the fourth and final stage of cognitive development. At this stage adolescents can apply reversibility and conservation to abstract, verbal, or hypothetical situations and to problems in the past, present, or future. Teenagers can comprehend abstract subjects such as philosophy and politics. They become interested in the world of ideas, and they begin to formulate theories.

Not all people attain full formal operational thinking (Kuhn, 1984; Neimark, 1981), but high school math and science experience seems to facilitate it (Sharp et al., 1979). Failure to achieve formal operations has been associated with below-average scores on intelligence tests (Inhelder, 1966).

Review and Reflect Table 8.1 provides a summary of Piaget's four stages.

> **?** *What new capability characterizes the formal operations stage?*

> **formal operations stage:** Piaget's fourth and final stage, characterized by the ability to apply logical thinking to abstract problems and hypothetical situations.

Review and Reflect 8.1 *Piaget's Stages of Cognitive Development*

Stage		Description
Sensorimotor (0 to 2 years)		Infants experience the world through their senses, actions, and body movements. At the end of this stage, toddlers develop the concept of object permanence and can mentally represent objects in their absence.
Preoperational (2 to 7 years)		Children are able to represent objects and events mentally with words and images. They can engage in imaginary play (pretend), using one object to represent another. Their thinking is dominated by their perceptions, and they are unable to consider more than one dimension of an object at the same time (centration). Their thinking is egocentric; that is, they fail to consider the perspective of others.
Concrete operational (7 to 11 or 12 years)		Children at this stage become able to think logically in concrete situations. They acquire the concepts of conservation and reversibility, can order objects in a series, and can classify them according to multiple dimensions.
Formal operational (11 or 12 years and beyond)		At this stage, adolescents learn to think logically in abstract situations, learn to test hypotheses systematically, and become interested in the world of ideas. Not all people attain full formal operational thinking.

An Evaluation of Piaget's Contribution

Although Piaget's genius and his monumental contribution to our knowledge of mental development are rarely disputed, his methods and some of his findings and conclusions have been criticized (Halford, 1989). It now seems clear that children are more advanced cognitively and adults less competent cognitively than Piaget believed (Flavell, 1985, 1992; Mandler, 1990; Siegler, 1991).

Piaget was limited in the information he could gather about infants, because he relied on observation and on the interview technique, which depended on verbal responses. Newer techniques requiring nonverbal responses—sucking, looking, heart-rate changes, reaching, and head turning—have shown that infants and young children are more competent than Piaget proposed (Flavell, 1992). For example, there are some signs that awareness of object permanence may begin as early as 3½ months (Baillargeon & DeVos, 1991). And whereas Piaget claimed that deferred imitation begins in the preoperational stage, Meltzoff (1988) has demonstrated that even 9-month-olds are able to imitate actions they have observed as much as 24 hours earlier.

Other studies have shown that preoperational children are able to take the perspective of another. For example, 4-year-old children can adjust their speech when talking to 2-year-olds (Shatz & Gelman, 1973), and they can understand the emotions of characters in a story (Ford, 1979).

Thatcher and others (1987) have noted periodic spurts in the development of the cerebral cortex that seem to coincide with Piaget's stages. Investigators have repeatedly confirmed Piaget's observations, but not all agree with his conclusions (Case, 1985). For instance, some researchers believe that a limitation in short-term memory capacity might explain why preoperational and concrete operational children can deal only with problems that are concrete and physically present (Harris & Bassett, 1975).

Few developmental psychologists believe that cognitive development takes place in the general stagelike fashion proposed by Piaget. If it did, children's cognitive functioning would be similar across all cognitive tasks and content areas (Flavell, 1992). Neo-Piagetians believe that while there are important general properties in cognitive development, there is also more variability in how children perform on certain tasks than Piaget described (Case, 1992). This variability results from expertise children acquire in different content areas through extensive practice and experience (Flavell, 1992). Even adults who use formal operational reasoning fall back on concrete operational reasoning when they approach a task outside their area of expertise.

Cross-cultural studies have affirmed the universality of the types of reasoning and the sequence of stages formulated by Piaget. But cross-cultural research has also revealed differences in the rates of cognitive development in various domains. Whereas Piaget's subjects began to acquire the concept of conservation between ages 5 and 7, Australian Aboriginal children show this change between the ages of 10 and 13 (Dasen, 1994). Yet the Aboriginal children function at the concrete operations stage earlier on spatial tasks than on quantification (counting) tasks, while the reverse is true for Western children. This difference makes sense in light of the high value Aborigines place on spatial skills and the low premium they place on quantification. In the Australian desert, moving from place to place hunting, gathering, and searching for water, Aborigines have few possessions and rarely count things. Their language has words for numbers up to five, and their word for "many" applies to anything above five.

It is fair to say that Piaget has stimulated more research in developmental psychology than any other theorist in recent times (Beilin, 1992). And Piaget's work has had a profound impact on the fields of psychology and education. His influence has led teachers to arrange richer learning environments in which children gain knowledge and improve cognitive skills through exploration and discovery.

Vygotsky's Sociocultural View of Cognitive Development

> **?** *In Vygotsky's view, what purpose does the private speech of children serve?*

In developing cognitive competence, according to Piaget's view, children are relatively solitary explorers, internally motivated to formulate and test their ideas in the real world. But Russian psychologist Lev Vygotsky (1934/1986) strongly rejected Piaget's individualistic view and offered his own theory that each individual's quest for cognitive growth and development is forged within a sociocultural environment.

Vygotsky maintained that human infants come equipped with basic skills such as perception, the ability to pay attention, and certain capacities of memory not unlike those of many other animal species. During the first 2 years of life, these skills grow and develop naturally through direct experiences and interactions with the child's sociocultural world. In due course, children develop the ability mentally to represent objects, activities, ideas, people, and relationships in a variety of ways, but primarily through language (speech). With their new ability to represent ideas, activities, and so on through speech, children are often observed "talking to themselves." Vygotsky believed that talking to oneself—private speech—is a key component in the child's cognitive development. Through private speech, children can specify the components of a problem and verbalize steps in a process to help them work through puzzling activities and situations. As young children develop greater competence, private speech fades into barely audible mumbling and muttering, and finally becomes simply thinking silently.

Vygotsky saw a strong connection among social experience, speech, and cognitive development. He also maintained that a child's readiness to learn resides within a zone of proximal (or potential) development. This zone, according to Vygotsky, is a range of cognitive tasks that the child cannot yet perform alone but can learn to perform with the instruction, help, and guidance of a parent, teacher, or more advanced peer. Laura Berk (1994) explains it well: "As children engage in cooperative dialogues with more mature partners, they take the language of these dialogues, make it part of their private speech, and use this speech to organize their independent efforts in the same way" (p. 256).

Vygotsky believed that private speech is a key component in a child's cognitive development.

Followers of Vygotsky advocate the use of an instructional technique known as scaffolding. Scaffolding is a procedure in which a teacher or parent adjusts the quality and degree of help or instruction to fit the child's present level of ability or performance. In scaffolding, more direct instruction is given, at first, for unfamiliar tasks (Maccoby, 1992). But as the child shows increasing competence, the scaffolder (teacher or parent) gradually withdraws from direct and active teaching, and the child may continue toward independent mastery of the task.

Contemporary researchers have found widespread evidence to support many of Vygotsky's ideas (Berk, 1994).

Memory Check 8.4

1. Which statement reflects Piaget's thinking about the cognitive stages?
   a. All people pass through the same stages but not necessarily in the same order.
   b. All people progress through the stages in the same order but not at the same rate.
   c. All people progress through the stages in the same order and at the same rate.
   d. Very bright children sometimes skip stages.

2. Three-year-old Danielle says "Airplane!" when she sees a helicopter for the first time. She is using the process Piaget called (assimilation/accommodation).

3. Four-year-old Kendra rolls a ball of clay into a sausage shape to make "more" clay. Her actions demonstrate that she has *not* acquired the concept of:
   a. reversibility.
   b. animism.
   c. centration
   d. conservation.

4. Not all individuals reach the stage of formal operations. (true/false)

5. Match the stage with the relevant concept.
   ____ 1) abstract thought
   ____ 2) conservation, reversibility
   ____ 3) object permanence
   ____ 4) egocentrism, centration

   a. concrete operations
   b. sensorimotor stage
   c. formal operations
   d. preoperational stage

6. Vygotsky believed that children's private speech slowed their cognitive growth. (true/false)

Answers: 1. b 2. assimilation 3. d 4. true 5. 1) c; 2) a; 3) b; 4) d 6. false

Language Development

At birth, the infant's only means of communication is crying, but at age 17, the average high school graduate has a vocabulary of 80,000 words (Miller & Gildea, 1987). From age 18 months to 5 years the child acquires about 14,000 words, an amazing average of 9 new words per day (Rice, 1989).

But children do much more than simply add new words to their vocabulary. In the first 5 years of life, they also acquire an understanding of the way words are put together to form sentences (syntax) and the way language is used in social situations. Children acquire most of their language without any formal teaching and discover the rules of language on their own—a truly remarkable feat.

The Stages of Language Development: The Orderly Progression of Language

What are the stages of language development from cooing through the acquisition of grammatical rules?

Infants begin to communicate long before they utter their first words. During their first few months, they communicate distress or displeasure through crying, although this is not actually their intent (Shatz, 1983). The cry is simply their innate reaction to an unpleasant internal state, such as hunger, thirst, discomfort, or pain. Intentional or not, the cry usually gets results from a parent or caretaker who is motivated to relieve the baby's discomfort and end the auditory assault.

Cooing and Babbling During the second or third month, infants begin cooing—repeatedly uttering vowel sounds such as "ah" and "oo." Even at this young age, the mother and infant carry on conversations that consist of each vocalizing in turn, and the infant moving in synchrony with the mother's voice.

At about 6 months, infants begin **babbling**. They utter **phonemes**—the basic speech sounds of any language, which form words when combined. Consonant-vowel combinations are repeated in a string, like "ma-ma-ma" or "ba-ba-ba." During the first part of the babbling stage, infants babble all the basic speech sounds that occur in all the languages of the world. Language up to this point

babbling: Vocalization of the basic speech sounds (phonemes), which begins between 4 and 6 months.

phonemes: The basic speech sounds in any language that, when combined, form words.

seems to be biologically determined, because all babies throughout the world, even deaf children, vocalize this same range of speech sounds.

At about 8 months, babies begin to focus attention on those speech sounds (phonemes) common to their native tongue and on the rhythm and intonation of the language. Gradually they cease making the sounds not found in their native language. At about 1 year, a French-speaking child's babbling sounds like French, and an English-speaking child's babbling sounds like English (Levitt & Wang, 1991). Deaf children who are exposed to sign language from birth babble manually. That is, they make the hand movements that represent the phonemes in sign language (Petitto & Marentette, 1991).

The One-Word Stage At about 1 year, the babbling stage gives way to the one-word stage, and infants utter their first real words. The first words usually represent objects that move or those that infants can act upon or interact with. Early words usually include food, animals, and toys—"cookie," "mama," "dada," "doggie," and "ball," to name a few (Nelson, 1973).

Sometimes infants use one-word sentences, called holophrases, in which the same word is used to convey different meanings depending on the context. "Cookie" can mean "This is a cookie," "I want a cookie," or, if the child is looking down from a high chair, "The cookie is on the floor."

From 13 to 18 months of age, children markedly increase their vocabulary (Woodward et al., 1994), and by 2 years it consists of about 270 words (Brown, 1973). Initially a child's understanding of words differs from that of an adult. On the basis of some shared feature and because they lack the correct word, children may apply a word to a broader range of objects than is appropriate. This is known as **overextension**. For example, any man may be called "dada," any four-legged animal, "doggie." **Underextension** occurs, too, when children fail to apply a word to other members of the class. Their poodle is a "doggie," but the German shepherd next door is not.

The Two-Word Stage and Telegraphic Speech Between 18 and 20 months, when the vocabulary is about 50 words, children begin to put nouns, verbs, and adjectives together in two-word phrases and sentences. At this stage children depend to a great extent on gesture, tone, and context to convey their meaning (Slobin, 1972). Depending on intonation, their sentences may indicate questions, statements, or possession. Children adhere to a rigid word order. You might hear "mama drink," "drink milk," or "mama milk," but not "drink mama," "milk drink," or "milk mama."

At about 2½ years, short sentences are used, which may contain three or more words. Labeled **telegraphic speech** by Roger Brown (1973), these short sentences follow a rigid word order and contain only essential content words, leaving out plurals, possessives, conjunctions, articles, and prepositions. Telegraphic speech reflects the child's understanding of syntax—the rules governing how words are ordered in a sentence. When a third word is added to a sentence, it usually fills in the word missing from the two-word sentence (for example, "Mama drink milk").

Suffixes, Function Words, and Grammatical Rules After using telegraphic speech for a time, children gradually begin to add modifiers to make words more precise. Suffixes and function words—pronouns, articles, conjunctions, and prepositions—are acquired in a fixed sequence, although the rate of acquisition varies (Brown, 1973; Maratsos, 1983).

Children pick up grammatical rules intuitively and apply them rigidly. **Overregularization** is the kind of error that results when a grammatical rule is misapplied to a word that has an irregular plural or past tense (Kuczaj, 1978). Thus, children who have learned and correctly used words such as "went,"

overextension: The act of using a word, on the basis of some shared feature, to apply to a broader range of objects than appropriate.

underextension: Restricting the use of a word to only a few, rather than to all, members of a class of objects.

telegraphic speech: Short sentences that follow a strict word order and contain only essential content words.

overregularization: The act of inappropriately applying the grammatical rules for forming plurals and past tenses to irregular nouns and verbs.

TABLE 8.2 Language Development during the First 3 Years of Life

Age	Language Activity
2–3 months	Cooing sounds when infant is alone; infant responds with smiles and cooing when talked to.
20 weeks	Various vowel and consonant sounds mixed in with cooing.
6 months	Babbling; baby will utter phonemes of all languages.
8 months	Focus on the phonemes, rhythm, and intonation of native tongue.
12 months	Single words; baby mimics sounds, understands some words.
18–20 months	Two-word sentences; vocabulary of about 50 words; overextension common.
24 months	Vocabulary of about 270 words; suffixes and function words are acquired in a fixed sequence.
30 months	Telegraphic speech.
36 months	Acquisition of grammar rules; overregularization common.

"came," and "did" incorrectly apply the rule for past tenses and begin to say "goed," "comed," and "doed." What the parent sees as a regression in speech actually means that the child has acquired a grammatical rule (Marcus et al. 1992).

Table 8.2 provides a summary of the early stages of language development.

Theories of Language Development: How Do We Acquire It?

There is no disagreement among theorists that children's learning of language is a truly amazing feat. But theorists do disagree about *how* children are able to accomplish such a feat. Several theories have been proposed to explain language acquisition. Some theories emphasize the role of learning and experience (nurture); some propose a biological explanation, emphasizing maturation (nature); and others suggest an interaction between maturation and experience. "There is currently no consensus of support for any one of them" (Rice, 1989, p. 150).

How do learning theory and the nativist position explain the acquisition of language?

Learning Theory   Learning theorists have long maintained that language is acquired in the same way that other behaviors are acquired—as a result of learning through reinforcement and imitation. B. F. Skinner (1957) asserted that language is shaped through reinforcement. He claimed that parents selectively criticize incorrect speech and reinforce correct speech through praise, approval, and attention. Thus the child's utterances are progressively shaped in the direction of grammatically correct speech. Others believe that children acquire vocabulary and sentence construction mainly through imitation (Bandura, 1977a).

There are some problems, however, with learning theory as the sole explanation for language acquisition. Imitation cannot account for patterns of speech such as telegraphic speech or for systematic errors such as overregularization. Children do not hear telegraphic speech in everyday life, and "I comed" and "He goed" are not forms commonly used by parents.

There are also problems with reinforcement as an explanation for language acquisition. First, parents seem to reward children more for the content of the utterance than for the correctness of the grammar (Brown et al., 1968). And parents are much more likely to correct them for saying something untrue than for making a grammatical error. Regardless, correction has little impact on a child's grammar. But reinforcement still plays an important part in language learning. Responsiveness to infants' vocalizations increases the amount of vocalization, and reinforcement can help children with language deficits improve (Whitehurst et al., 1989).

The Nativist Position Noam Chomsky (1957) believes that language ability is largely innate, and he has proposed a very different theory. Chomsky (1968) maintains that the brain contains a language acquisition device (LAD), which enables children to acquire language and discover the rules of grammar easily and naturally. Language develops in stages that occur in a fixed order and appear at about the same time in most normal children—babbling at about 6 months, the one-word stage at about 1 year, and the two-word stage at 18 to 20 months. Deaf children exposed to sign language from birth proceed along the same schedule (Meier, 1991; Petitto & Marentette, 1991). Lenneberg (1967) claims that biological maturation underlies language development in much the same way that it underlies physical and motor development.

Very young infants do seem to have an innate mechanism that allows them to perceive and differentiate phonemes present in any language (Eimas, 1985). But by the end of the first year, their power to distinguish between speech sounds that do not differentiate words in their own language is greatly reduced (Kuhl et al., 1992). This is why adults whose native tongue is Japanese have so much difficulty discriminating between the *r* and *l* sounds in English.

The nativist position is better able than learning theory to account for the fact that children throughout the world go through the same basic stages in language development. It can account, too, for the similarity in errors that they make when they are first learning to form plurals, past tenses, and negatives—errors not acquired through imitation or reinforcement. However, there are several aspects of language development that the nativist position cannot explain.

Nature and Nurture One's native language, after all, is acquired in a social setting, and experience must exert some influence on development (Bohannon & Warren-Leubecker, 1989). You remember Robert, in our opening story, who could not speak, but whose oral utterances were more like those of the monkeys he lived with. He vocalized what he heard in his own social setting.

Parents can facilitate language acquisition by adjusting their speech to their infant's level of development. Reading to children and with them supports language development. Parents should comment and expand on what the child says and encourage the child to say more by asking questions. According to Rice (1989), "Most children do not need to be taught language, but they do need opportunities to develop language" (p. 155).

Unfortunately, parents from lower socioeconomic classes tend to talk to their children less, to expose them to a less diverse vocabulary, and to discourage them from talking more often (Walker et al., 1994). This disadvantage in language experience not only slows early language development (Hart & Risley, 1992) but may impact negatively on later intellectual development (Walker et al., 1994).

Memory Check 8.5

1. Match the linguistic stage with the example.
   ____ 1) "ba-ba-ba"
   ____ 2) "He eated the cook-ies."
   ____ 3) "Mama see ball"
   ____ 4) "oo," "ah"
   ____ 5) "kitty," meaning a lion
   ____ 6) "ball" meaning "look at the ball"

   a. telegraphic speech
   b. holophrase
   c. overregularization
   d. babbling
   e. overextension
   f. cooing

2. Learning theory is better able than the nativist position to account for how language development can be encouraged. (true/false)

3. The nativist position does *not* suggest that:
   a. language ability is largely innate.
   b. language is acquired in stages that occur in a fixed order.
   c. reinforcement and imitation are the primary factors influencing language acquisition.
   d. most normal children around the world acquire language in the same stages and at the same ages.

4. Which explanation best accounts for the early stages of babbling and telegraphic speech?
   a. reinforcement   c. cognitive mapping
   b. imitation   d. the nativist position

Answers: 1. 1) d; 2) c; 3) a; 4) f; 5) e; 6) b 2. true 3. c 4. d

Socialization of the Child

To function effectively and comfortably in society, we must come to know the patterns of behavior considered to be desirable and appropriate. The process of learning socially acceptable behaviors, attitudes, and values is called **socialization**. Although parents have the major role in socialization, peers, school, the media, and religion are all important influences as well.

Erikson's Theory of Psychosocial Development

What is Erikson's theory of psychosocial development?

Erik Erikson proposed the only major theory of development to include the entire life span. He was the first to stress the part that society and individuals themselves play in their own personality development, rather than focusing exclusively on the influence of parents.

According to Erikson, individuals progress through eight **psychosocial stages** during the life span. Each stage is defined by a conflict involving the individual's relationship with the social environment that must be resolved satisfactorily in order for healthy development to occur. The stages are named for a "series of alternative basic attitudes," which result depending on how the conflict is resolved (Erikson, 1980). Erikson believed that a healthy personality depends on acquiring the appropriate basic attitudes in the proper sequence. Although failure to resolve a conflict impedes later development, resolution may occur at a later stage and reverse any damage done previously.

socialization: The process of learning socially acceptable behaviors, attitudes, and values.

psychosocial stages: Erikson's eight developmental stages through the life span, each defined by a conflict that must be resolved satisfactorily in order for healthy personality development to occur.

Stage 1: Basic Trust versus Basic Mistrust (Ages Birth to 1 Year)

During the first stage, **basic trust versus basic mistrust**, infants develop a sense of trust or mistrust depending on the degree and regularity of care, love, and affection they receive from the mother or primary caregiver. Erikson (1980) considered "basic trust as the cornerstone of a healthy personality" (p. 58).

Stage 2: Autonomy versus Shame and Doubt (Ages 1 to 3 Years)

During the second stage, **autonomy versus shame and doubt**, children are developing their physical and mental abilities and want to do things for themselves. They begin to express their will or independence and develop a "sudden violent wish to have a choice" (Erikson, 1963, p. 252). "No!" becomes one of their favorite words. Erikson believes that parents must set appropriate limits, but at the same time facilitate the child's desire for autonomy by encouraging appropriate attempts at independence. If parents are impatient or overprotective, they may make children feel shame and doubt about their efforts to express their will and explore their environment.

Stage 3: Initiative versus Guilt (Ages 3 to 6 Years)

In the third stage, **initiative versus guilt**, children go beyond merely expressing their autonomy and begin to develop initiative. Enjoying their new locomotor and mental powers, children initiate play and motor activities and ask questions.

> If the child is made to feel that his motor activity is bad, that his questions are a nuisance and that his play is silly and stupid, then he may develop a sense of guilt over self-initiated activities in general that will persist through later life stages. (Elkind, 1970, pp. 87, 89)

If appropriate attempts at initiative are encouraged and inappropriate attempts are handled firmly but sensitively, children will leave this stage with a sense of initiative that will form "a basis for a high and yet realistic sense of ambition and independence" (Erikson, 1980, p. 78).

Stage 4: Industry versus Inferiority (Ages 6 Years to Puberty)

During the fourth stage, **industry versus inferiority**, children develop enjoyment and pride in making things and doing things.

> When children are encouraged in their efforts to make, do, or build practical things . . . , are allowed to finish their products, and are praised and rewarded for the results, then the sense of industry is enhanced. But parents who see their children's efforts at making and doing as "mischief," and as simply "making a mess," help to encourage in children a sense of inferiority. (Elkind, 1970, pp. 89–90)

The encouragement of teachers as well as parents is important for a positive resolution of this stage.

Review and Reflect Table 8.2 (on page 312) describes Erikson's first four stages. Erikson's next four stages, which cover adolescence through adulthood, are discussed in Chapter 9.

The Parents' Role in the Socialization Process

The parents' role in the socialization process consists of the examples they set, their teachings, and their approach to discipline. Parents are usually more successful if they are loving, warm, nurturant, and supportive (Maccoby & Martin, 1983). In fact, a longitudinal study that followed individuals from age 5 to age 41 revealed that "children of warm, affectionate parents were more likely to be socially accomplished adults who, at age 41, were mentally healthy, coping adequately, and psychosocially mature in work, relationships, and generativity" (Franz et al., 1991, p. 593).

basic trust versus basic mistrust: Erikson's first stage (ages birth to 1 year), when infants develop trust or mistrust based on the quality of care, love, and affection provided.

autonomy versus shame and doubt: Erikson's second stage (ages 1 to 3 years), when infants develop autonomy or shame based on how parents react to their expression of will and their wish to do things for themselves.

initiative versus guilt: Erikson's third stage (ages 3 to 6 years), when children develop a sense of initiative or guilt depending on how parents react to their initiation of play, their motor activities, and their questions.

industry versus inferiority: Erikson's fourth stage (ages 6 years to puberty), when children develop a sense of industry or inferiority based on how parents and teachers react to their efforts to undertake projects.

In Erikson's fourth stage—industry versus inferiority—children enjoy and take pride in making things.

Review and Reflect 8.2 *Erikson's Psychosocial Stages of Development*

Stage	Ages	Description
Trust vs. mistrust	Birth to 1 year	Infant learns to trust or mistrust depending on the degree and regularity of care, love, and affection from mother or primary caregiver.
Autonomy vs. shame and doubt	1 to 3 years	Children learn to express their will and independence, to exercise some control, and to make choices. If not, they experience shame and doubt.
Initiative vs. guilt	3 to 6 years	Children begin to initiate activities, to plan and undertake tasks, and to enjoy their developing motor and other abilities. If not allowed to initiate or if made to feel stupid and considered a nuisance, they may develop a sense of guilt.
Industry vs. inferiority	6 years to puberty	Children develop industriousness and feel pride in accomplishing tasks, making things, and doing things. If not encouraged, or if rebuffed by parents and teachers, they may develop a sense of inferiority.
Identity vs. role confusion	Adolescence	Described in Chapter 9.
Intimacy vs. isolation	Young adulthood	
Generativity vs. stagnation	Middle adulthood	
Ego integrity vs. despair	Late adulthood	

Families are dysfunctional when the roles are reversed, and the children nurture and control their parents (Maccoby, 1992).

To be effective, socialization must ultimately result in children coming to regulate their own behavior. The attainment of this goal is undermined when parents control their children's behavior by asserting power over them (Maccoby, 1992).

> *What are the three parenting styles discussed by Baumrind, and which did she find most effective?*

Parenting Styles: What Works and What Doesn't Diane Baumrind (1971, 1980, 1991) has identified three parenting styles—the authoritarian, the authoritative, and the permissive. She related these styles to different patterns of behavior in predominantly white, middle-class children.

Authoritarian Parents **Authoritarian parents** make the rules, expect unquestioned obedience from their children, punish misbehavior (often physically), and value obedience to authority. Rather than giving a rationale for a rule, authoritarian parents consider "because I said so" a sufficient reason for obedience. Parents using this parenting style tend to be uncommunicative, unresponsive, and somewhat distant. Baumrind (1967) found preschool children disciplined in this manner to be withdrawn, anxious, and unhappy.

If the goal of discipline is to have children internalize parental standards, the authoritarian approach leaves much to be desired. Parental failure to provide a rationale for rules makes it hard for children to see any reason for following them. Saying "Do it because I said so" or "Do it or you'll be punished" may succeed in making the child do what is expected when the parent is present, but it is ineffective when the parent is not around. The authoritarian style has been associated with low intellectual performance and lack of social skills, and it is particularly harmful to boys (Maccoby & Martin, 1983).

authoritarian parents:
Parents who make arbitrary rules, expect unquestioned obedience from their children, punish transgressions, and value obedience to authority.

Authoritative Parents **Authoritative parents** set high but realistic and reasonable standards, enforce limits, and at the same time encourage open communication and independence. They are willing to discuss rules and supply rationales for them. Knowing why the rules are necessary makes it easier for children to internalize them and to follow them, whether in the presence of their parents or not. Authoritative parents are generally warm, nurturant, supportive, and responsive, and they show respect for their children and their opinions. Their children are the most mature, happy, self-reliant, self-controlled, assertive, socially competent, and responsible. The authoritative parenting style is associated with higher academic performance, independence, higher self-esteem, and internalized moral standards in middle childhood and adolescence (Lamborn et al., 1991; Steinberg et al., 1989).

Permissive Parents Although rather warm and supportive, **permissive parents** make few rules or demands and usually do not enforce those that are made. They allow children to make their own decisions and control their own behavior. Children raised in this manner are the most immature, impulsive, and dependent, and they seem to be the least self-controlled and self-reliant.

Permissive parents also come in the indifferent, unconcerned, uninvolved variety (Maccoby & Martin, 1983). This parenting style is associated with drinking problems, promiscuous sex, delinquent behavior, and poor academic performance in adolescents.

Parenting Style and Children's Self-Esteem Stanley Coopersmith (1968) studied 10- to 12-year-old middle-class boys and followed them through early adulthood. He found that boys with high self-esteem were successful socially and academically and had parents who "demanded high standards of behavior and were strict and consistent in enforcement of the rules" (p. 99). These parents had good communication with their children and showed interest in their activities and friends. They tended to use rewards and to refrain from using corporal punishment or withdrawal of love to discipline their children.

Coopersmith (1968) found that children with low self-esteem had permissive parents, and "they took the absence of definitely stated rules and limits for their behavior as a sign of lack of parental interest in them" (p. 100). Coopersmith concludes, "It appears that the development of independence and self-reliance is fostered by a well-structured, demanding environment rather than by largely unlimited permissiveness and freedom to explore in an unfocused way" (p. 106).

Many of these values go a long way in explaining the academic success of Southeast Asian immigrants, as described in the World of Psychology section.

authoritative parents: Parents who set high but realistic standards, reason with the child, enforce limits, and encourage open communication and independence.

permissive parents: Parents who make few rules or demands and allow children to make their own decisions and control their own behavior.

World of Psychology

Cultural Values and Academic Achievement

Fleeing the political chaos and economic ruin in the aftermath of the Vietnam War, Southeast Asian refugees came by the thousands to find a better life in the United States. These Vietnamese, Laotian, Cambodian, and other immigrants, known as "boat people," knew little of Western culture and spoke little or no English when they reached America. For the most part, these refugees were not the advantaged elite but common people, and "often they came with nothing more than the clothes they wore" (Caplan et al., 1992).

continued

How well are these children doing in American schools? Educators are astonished by their outstanding school performance. Caplan and others (1992) gathered data on 6,750 Southeast Asian immigrants living in five urban areas—Boston, Chicago, Houston, Seattle, and Orange County, California. They randomly selected 200 families, including 536 school-age children who were about evenly distributed in grades 1 through 11. All the children attended schools located in low-income, urban areas, but nearly 80 percent performed at the A to B level in overall school achievement. They did even better in mathematics, where almost half of them maintained an A average.

Was the students' stunning academic success limited to comparisons in the local schools they attended? No. Their performance was exceptional even when compared to nationwide norms for U.S. students. On the California Achievement Test in math, half the children in the study scored in the top 25 percent of test takers, and 27 percent scored in the top 10 percent of U.S. students nationwide. Their language and reading skills were only slightly below the national average, even though English was not their native tongue.

What explains this remarkable school performance? Cultural values and traditions of the refugees, especially the role of central importance played by the family, strongly influenced school performance. Both parents and students named the love of learning most often as the value that contributed most to academic success. Parents of successful students placed relatively low value on seeking fun and excitement or material possessions, but a higher value on work and study. The parents had high standards for their children, and the older children took an amazing amount of responsibility in helping their younger siblings with their homework. Every weeknight, the entire household cooperated to see that the children learned their assignments. And the children spent between 2½ and 3 hours daily on homework, twice as much as their American classmates.

The most successful families did not reject their values and traditions in favor of the American "melting pot" but held fast to them. Yet the values and traditions that these immigrants honored and practiced are not culturally unique to the Asian people. In fact, some members of virtually every racial and ethnic group we could name hold cultural and family values very similar to those of the successful Asian boat people.

European immigrants who came to America brought strong family values, a belief in hard work, and a respect for education. Jewish culture and tradition place a high value on learning, which contributes to their academic success. And African Americans nurtured by these same cultural values—respecting family and learning—thrive academically. "Reginald Clark of the Claremont Graduate School documented the outstanding achievement of low-income African American students in Chicago whose parents supported the school and teachers and structured their children's learning environment at home" (Caplan et al., 1992, p. 42).

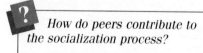

How do peers contribute to the socialization process?

Peer Relationships

Infants begin to show an interest in each other at a very young age. At only 6 months of age they already demonstrate an interest in other infants by looking, reaching, touching, smiling, and vocalizing (Vandell & Mueller, 1980). Friendships begin to develop by 3 or 4 years, and relationships with peers become increasingly important. By middle childhood, membership in a peer group is central to a child's happiness. Peer groups are usually composed of children of the same race, sex, and social class (Schofield & Francis, 1982).

The peer group serves a socializing function by providing models of behavior, dress, and language. It is a continuing source of both reinforcement for appropriate behavior and punishment for deviant behavior. The peer group also provides an objective measure against which children can evaluate their own traits and abilities—how smart or how good at sports they are. In their peer groups children learn how to get along with age-mates—how to share and cooperate, develop social skills, and regulate aggression.

Physical attractiveness is a major factor in peer acceptance even in children as young as 3 to 5 years, although it seems to be more important for girls than for boys (Krantz, 1987; Langlois, 1985). Negative traits are often attributed to unattractive children. Athletic ability and academic success in school are also valued by the peer group. The more popular children are usually energetic, happy, cooperative, sensitive, and thoughtful. Popular children have social skills that lead to positive social outcomes and facilitate the goals of their peers. But they are also able to be assertive and aggressive when the situation calls for it (Newcomb et al., 1993). Also, popular children tend to have parents who use an authoritative parenting style (Dekovic & Janssens, 1992).

Low acceptance by peers is an important predictor of later mental health problems (Kupersmidt et al., 1990). Most often excluded from the peer group are neglected children, who are shy and withdrawn, and rejected children, who typically exhibit aggressive and inappropriate behavior and who are likely to start fights (Dodge, Cole, et al., 1990). Children abused at home tend to be unpopular with their classmates, who typically view them as aggressive and uncooperative (Salzinger et al., 1993). Rejection by peers is linked to unhappiness, alienation, and poor achievement, and in middle childhood with delinquency and dropping out of school (Kupersmidt & Coie, 1990; Parker & Asher, 1987).

Television as a Socializing Agent: Does It Help or Hinder?

? *What are some of the positive and negative effects of television?*

Television is a powerful force on young children, affecting their "knowledge, beliefs, attitudes, and behavior, for good or ill" (Huston et al., 1989, p. 424). By high school graduation, students have spent an average of 22,000 hours watching television—approximately twice the number of hours they have spent in school. By the time they reach age 70, today's teenagers will have watched more than 7 years of television (Cooke, 1992). Children with lower IQs and from low-income families tend to watch most (Huston et al., 1989). Figure 8.5 (on page 316) shows the average number of hours each day American children spend watching television.

The socializing effect of television begins before that of schools, religious institutions, and peers. Television *can* be an effective educational medium. "Mister Rogers' Neighborhood" has been found to increase prosocial behavior, imaginative play, and task persistency in preschoolers (Stein & Friedrich, 1975). Preschool children watching "Sesame Street" learn letters and number skills (Cook et al., 1975). Viewing "Sesame Street" at ages 3 and 4 has been associated with larger vocabularies and better prereading skills at age 5 (Rice et al., 1987, 1990).

But television has its downside. Most studies indicate that TV violence and aggression lead to aggressive behavior in children and teenagers (Comstock, 1990; Eron, 1982). Television also shapes the child's view of the world, and heavy viewers perceive the world as a "mean and scary place" (Rubinstein, 1983). Children's

FIGURE 8.5

Children's Average Daily TV Viewing Time

Research spanning 20 years reveals that American children spend many hours each day watching television. Children aged 10 to 12 average 4 hours or more daily. (From Liebert et al., 1989.)

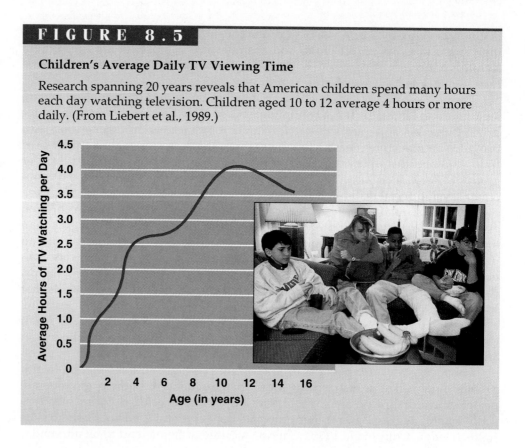

preferences and beliefs are easily manipulated by television (Huston et al., 1989), and it socializes children to be active consumers. TV programs often promote racial and sexual stereotypes and stereotypic views of the elderly and the mentally ill.

Racial and ethnic minorities make up more than 30 percent of our population, but they are underrepresented on television. Of the 19,000 speaking parts in over 1,300 TV programs from 1981 to 1991, 13 percent were played by minorities on prime time and 5 percent on children's programming (Jackson, 1994). And when minority children do appear on children's programs, it is usually not with white children. But the problem does not end there. Minorities on television are often cast as criminals or victims of crime, rather than in parts where they could serve as role models. They are more likely to be cast in lower-class jobs and are rarely in professional or executive roles. And there are few Hispanics, Asian Americans, or Native Americans appearing on national newscasts as anchors, reporters, newsmakers, or as those cited as authorities.

Much of children's commercial programming is marked by rapid activity and change and an "intense auditory and visual barrage" (Wright & Huston, 1983, p. 837). Singer and Singer (1979) suggest that such programming can lead to a shortened attention span. Others contend that television "promotes passive rather than active learning, induces low-level cognitive processing, and takes away time and energy from more creative or intellectually stimulating activities" (Wright and Huston, 1983, p. 835).

We have seen that many factors contribute to human development. And for all of life, from conception onward, it is the interplay of nature and nurture that drives and shapes us. In the next chapter we continue our exploration of human development, moving from adolescence through old age.

Memory Check 8.6

1. According to Erikson, if the basic conflict of a given stage is *not* resolved satisfactorily:
   a. one will not enter the next stage.
   b. development at the next stage will be adversely affected.
   c. one will be permanently damaged regardless of future experiences.
   d. one will revert to the previous stage.

2. Match the psychosocial stage with the appropriate phrase.
   ____ 1) needs regular care and love
   ____ 2) initiates play and motor activities, asks questions
   ____ 3) strives for sense of independence
   ____ 4) undertakes projects, makes things

   a. basic trust versus mistrust
   b. industry versus inferiority
   c. initiative versus guilt
   d. autonomy versus shame and doubt

3. Match the parenting style with the approach to discipline:
   ____ 1) expecting unquestioned obedience
   ____ 2) setting high standards, giving rationale for rules
   ____ 3) setting few rules or limits

   a. permissive
   b. authoritative
   c. authoritarian

4. Which is *not* an effect of television on children?
   a. reducing racial and sexual stereotypes
   b. shortening attention span
   c. taking time away from more worthwhile activities
   d. increasing aggressive behavior through exposure to TV violence

5. The peer group usually has a negative influence on social development. (true/false)

Answers: 1.b 2.1)a 2)c 3)d 4)b 3.1)c 2)b 3)a 4.a 5.false

APPLICATIONS · APPLICATIONS · APPLICATIONS

What Kind of Care Is Best for Your Child?

To work or not to work is *not* the question for well over half of all women with children in the United States. Seventy percent of women with young children, many of whom are single parents, must work to support their families (Hoffman, 1989). By comparison, in 1950 only 12 percent of mothers with young children were in the workforce.

Where do these millions of American preschool children go while their parents work? About 51 percent are cared for by grandparents or other relatives. Another 26 percent are enrolled in day care centers, 19 percent are in family day care homes, and 4 percent stay at home with a sitter (Hofferth, 1992).

Finding the best possible day care is a critical issue for many parents. Before exploring what parents should look for when searching for day care, let's try to answer a question that has perplexed both researchers and parents: How does day care affect children's development?

The Effects of Day Care on a Child's Development

It is difficult to make generalizations about the effect of day care, because there are many variables involved, including the quality of the care and the child's age, gender, temperament, and family background. Nevertheless, hundreds of studies have been undertaken to explore what effects, if any, day care has on children.

Belsky and Rovine (1988) found that infants exposed to more than 20 hours of nonmaternal care per week were at somewhat higher risk for insecure infant–mother attachment if they were male, had unresponsive mothers, and were considered by their mothers to have a difficult temperament. Clarke-Stewart (1989) found 47 percent of infants with extensive early nonmaternal care had secure attachments to their mothers, compared to 53 percent of infants who were cared for by their mothers. Curiously, almost all of the infants in day care who had

continued

insecure attachments were boys (Belsky & Rovine, 1988).

Despite these somewhat negative findings, a number of researchers have found that good-quality nonmaternal care has no adverse effects on children's development (Clarke-Stewart, 1989; Phillips et al., 1987). In fact, some researchers have reported that children in high-quality early day care were more competent socially in grade school than those who entered child care later (Andersson, 1989, 1992; Field, 1991; Howes, 1990). And children in early child care were found to be more assertive than those who enter later (Scarr & Eisenberg, 1993).

While good-quality care can have positive effects, low-quality care can negatively affect the adjustment of infants, with boys being more vulnerable than girls. Poor-quality care also poses a greater risk to children from highly stressed home environments or father-absent homes (Gamble & Zigler, 1986).

What can we conclude about the effects of day care on children's development? Scarr and Eisenberg (1993) reviewed research spanning some 20 years and came to the following conclusions:

1. In general, most children are not affected significantly by nonmaternal care when the care is of a reasonable quality.
2. If there are negative effects, they are more likely to be emotional.
3. If there are positive effects, they are more likely to be social.
4. In most cases, cognitive development is affected either positively or not at all.
5. Higher levels of aggression seem to be more common for children in day care, but these levels are within the normal range.

Although research on the effects of day care continues, two facts are indisputable: "Bad care is never good for any child, and good day care is all too hard to find" (Shell, 1988, p. 74). So how does one go about finding good day care for a preschool-age child?

Finding the Right Day Care Setting for Your Child

It seems clear that the ratio of children to caregivers in a day care setting should be low; that is, there should be enough adults so that each child gets the attention he or she needs. The National Association for the Education of Young Children recommends that each adult caregiver be responsible for no more than four infants, eight 2- to 3-year-olds, or ten 4- to 5-year olds. Others suggest ratios of one adult per three infants or one adult per four toddlers. In addition, the caregivers should be trained in early childhood education or developmental psychology. Try to find out how long the caregivers have been employed at the center. A high rate of staff turnover makes it difficult for children to develop stable, affectionate relationships with their caregivers.

If you are permitted to observe the center's operations for an hour or two (and beware of a center that doesn't allow you to do so), you can find out a lot about the quality of care. As you watch, ask yourself these questions:

- Does the center provide a safe, clean environment? Are dangerous objects out of reach?
- Is there enough play space, both indoors and outdoors? Is the play equipment in good condition? Are all equipment and materials readily available and appropriate for children?
- How well are the children supervised when they use play equipment, go up and down stairs, or use sharp objects like scissors?
- Does the center promote good health habits? Do the children and caregivers wash their hands before eating? Is a first aid kit readily available?
- Is the food served to children nutritious and appetizing?

- Are there separate areas for meals and rest?

In addition to a safe, clean environment, the interactions between caregivers and children are important. As you observe, ask yourself these questions:

- Do the caregivers stimulate children to ask questions and solve problems? Are curiosity and creativity encouraged?
- Do the caregivers attempt to improve children's language skills?
- Does the schedule provide time for active play, quiet play, naps, snacks, and meals? Is it flexible enough to meet each child's needs?
- Are children taught to respect both themselves and others?

- Are children encouraged to cooperate when working and playing together?
- Do the caregivers behave in a positive manner, giving praise and answering children's questions? Do they avoid commands, criticism, and reprimands?

You can find out a lot about a day care center just by looking at the children's faces. Do they seem happy with their activities? Do they smile at their caregivers? If the children look bored or unhappy, or if there is any evidence of physical punishment, keep searching.

Thinking Critically

Evaluation

Evaluate Erikson's first four stages of psychosocial development, explaining what aspects of the theory seem most convincing and least convincing. Support your answer.

Point/Counterpoint

Using your knowledge of both the learning theory and the nativist position on language development, prepare an argument in favor of each position and a counterargument against each.

Psychology in Your Life

Using Baumrind's scheme, classify the parenting style your mother and/or father used in rearing you.

a. Cite examples of techniques they used that support your classification.
b. Do you agree with Baumrind's conclusions about the effects of that parenting style on children? Why or why not?

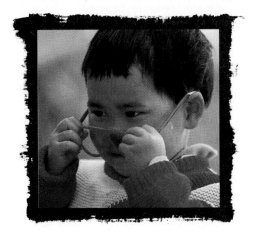

Chapter Summary and Review

Developmental Psychology: Basic Issues and Methodology

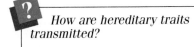 *What are two types of studies developmental psychologists use to investigate age-related changes?*

To investigate age-related changes, developmental psychologists use the longitudinal study and the cross-sectional study.

Heredity and Prenatal Development

How are hereditary traits transmitted?

Hereditary traits are transmitted by genes, which are located on each of our 23 pairs of chromosomes.

When are dominant or recessive genes expressed in a person?

When there are alternate forms of a gene for a specific trait, the dominant gene will be expressed. A recessive gene is expressed when it is paired with another recessive gene.

 What are the three stages of prenatal development?

The three stages of prenatal development are the period of the zygote, the period of the embryo, and the period of the fetus.

What are some negative influences on prenatal development, and during what time is their impact greatest?

Some common hazards in the prenatal environment include certain prescription drugs and nonprescription drugs, psychoactive drugs, poor maternal nutrition, and maternal infections and illnesses. Their impact is greatest during the first trimester.

Key Terms

developmental psychology (p. 284)
nature–nurture controversy (p. 284)
longitudinal study (p. 285)
cross-sectional study (p. 285)
genes (p. 285)
chromosomes (p. 285)
sex chromosomes (p. 286)
dominant gene (p. 287)
recessive gene (p. 287)

period of the zygote (p. 287)
prenatal (p. 287)
embryo (p. 287)
fetus (p. 288)
identical (monozygotic) twins (p. 288)
fraternal (dizygotic) twins (p. 288)
teratogens (p. 289)
critical period (p. 289)
fetal alcohol syndrome (p. 289)
low-birth-weight baby (p. 290)
preterm infant (p. 290)

Perceptual Development and Learning in Infancy

 What are the perceptual abilities of the newborn?

All of the newborn's senses are functional at birth, and he or she already shows preferences for certain odors, tastes, sounds, and visual configurations.

 What types of learning occur in the first few days of life?

Newborns are capable of habituation, and they can acquire new responses through classical and operant conditioning and observational learning.

? *What is the primary factor influencing attainment of the major motor milestones?*

Maturation is the primary factor influencing attainment of the major motor milestones.

Key Terms

neonate (p. 291)
reflexes (p. 291)
visual cliff (p. 292
habituation (p. 292)
maturation (p. 293)

Emotional Development in Infancy

? *What is temperament, and what are the three temperament types identified by Thomas, Chess, and Birch?*

Temperament refers to an individual's characteristic way of responding to the environment. The three temperament types are easy, difficult, and slow-to-warm-up.

? *What did Harlow's studies reveal about maternal deprivation and attachment in infant monkeys?*

Harlow found that the basis of attachment in infant monkeys is contact comfort, and that monkeys raised with surrogates showed normal learning ability but abnormal social, sexual, and emotional behavior.

? *According to Bowlby, when does the infant have a strong attachment to the mother?*

The infant has usually developed a strong attachment to the mother at age 6 to 8 months.

? *What are the three attachment patterns identified by Ainsworth?*

Ainsworth identified three attachment patterns: secure, ambivalent, and avoidant attachment.

? *What are the typical differences in the ways mothers and fathers interact with their children?*

Mothers tend to spend more time caretaking, and fathers spend more time playing with their children.

Key Terms

temperament (p. 294)
attachment (p. 295)
surrogate (p. 295)
separation anxiety (p. 296)
stranger anxiety (p. 297)

Piaget's Theory of Cognitive Development

? *What were Piaget's claims regarding his stages of cognitive development?*

Piaget claimed that intellect develops in four stages, each representing a qualitatively different form of reasoning and understanding. He believed the stages to be universal and to occur in an invariant sequence, although the rate at which children progress through them might vary.

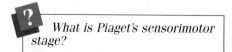

? *What is Piaget's sensorimotor stage?*

During the sensorimotor stage (ages birth to 2 years), infants gain knowledge and understanding of the world through their senses and motor activities. The major accomplishment of the stage is object permanence.

? *What cognitive limitations characterize a child's thinking during the preoperational stage?*

Children at the preoperational stage (ages 2 to 7 years) are increasingly able to represent objects and events mentally, but they exhibit egocentrism and centration, and they have not developed the concepts of reversibility and conservation.

? *What cognitive abilities do children acquire during the concrete operations stage?*

When working on concrete problems, children at the concrete operations stage (ages 7 to 11 or 12 years) become able to decenter their thinking and to understand the concepts of reversibility and conservation.

? *What new capability characterizes the formal operations stage?*

At the formal operations stage (ages 11 or 12 years and beyond) adolescents are able to apply logical thinking to abstract problems and hypothetical situations.

Key Terms

schemas (p. 298)
assimilation (p. 298)
accommodation (p. 299)
sensorimotor stage (p. 299)
object permanence (p. 299)
preoperational stage (p. 300)
conservation (p. 300)
centration (p. 301)
reversibility (p. 301)
concrete operations stage (p. 301)
formal operations stage (p. 303)

Vygotsky's Sociocultural View of Cognitive Development

? *In Vygotsky's view, what purpose does the private speech of children serve?*

Private speech is a key component in children's cognitive development and, in the form of self-guided talk, helps children to direct their actions and solve problems.

Language Development

? *What are the stages of language development from cooing through the acquisition of grammatical rules?*

The stages of language development are cooing (age 2 to 3 months), babbling (beginning at age 6 months), single words (about 1 year), two-word sentences (age 18 to 20 months), and telegraphic speech (age 2½ years), followed by the acquisition of grammatical rules.

> **?** *How do learning theory and the nativist position explain the acquisition of language?*

Learning theory suggests that language is acquired through imitation and reinforcement. The nativist position suggests that language ability is largely innate, because it is acquired in stages that occur in a fixed order at the same ages in most normal children throughout the world.

Key Terms

babbling (p. 306)
phonemes (p. 306)
overextension (p. 307)
underextension (p. 307)
telegraphic speech (p. 307)
overregularization (p. 307)

Socialization of the Child

> **?** *What is Erikson's theory of psychosocial development?*

Erikson believed that individuals progress through eight psychosocial stages during the life span, and each stage is defined by a conflict with the social environment, which must be resolved. The four stages in childhood are basic trust versus basic mistrust (ages birth to 2 years), autonomy versus shame and doubt (ages 1 to 3 years), initiative versus guilt (ages 3 to 6 years), and industry versus inferiority (ages 6 years to puberty).

> **?** *What are the three parenting styles discussed by Baumrind, and which did she find most effective?*

The three parenting styles discussed by Baumrind are the authoritarian, the permissive, and the authoritative; she found authoritative to be best.

> **?** *How do peers contribute to the socialization process?*

The peer group serves a socializing function by modeling and reinforcing behaviors it considers appropriate, by punishing inappropriate behavior, and by providing an objective measure against which children can evaluate their own traits and abilities.

> **?** *What are some of the positive and negative effects of television?*

Television can increase prosocial behavior and improve prereading and number skills, but it can lead to a shortened attention span, take time away from more worthwhile activities, promote racial and sexual stereotypes, and result in aggressive behavior through exposure to TV violence.

Key Terms

socialization (p. 310)
psychosocial stages (p. 310)
basic trust versus basic mistrust (p. 310)
autonomy versus shame and doubt (p. 311)
initiative versus guilt (p. 311)
industry versus inferiority (p. 311)
authoritarian parents (p. 312)
authoritative parents (p. 313)
permissive parents (p. 313)

9

ADOLESCENCE AND ADULTHOOD

CHAPTER OUTLINE

Adolescence: Physical and Cognitive Development

Physical Development during Adolescence: Growing, Growing, Grown

Cognitive Development in Adolescence: Piaget's Formal Operations Stage

Adolescence: Moral and Social Development

Kohlberg's Theory of Moral Development

Parental Relationships: Their Quality and Influence

The Peer Group

Sexuality and Adolescence: The Drive Turns On

Part-Time Jobs for Adolescents: A Positive or a Negative?

Erikson's Psychosocial Theory: Adolescence through Adulthood

Identity versus Role Confusion: Erikson's Stage for Adolescence

Intimacy versus Isolation: Erikson's Stage for Early Adulthood

Pioneers: Erik Homburger Erikson

Generativity versus Stagnation: Erikson's Stage for Middle Adulthood

Ego Integrity versus Despair: Erikson's Final Stage

Erikson's Theory: Does Research Support It?

Early and Middle Adulthood

Physical Changes in Adulthood

Intellectual Capacity during Early and Middle Adulthood

Lifestyle Patterns in Adulthood

Personality and Social Development in Middle Age

Theories of Adulthood

Levinson's Seasons of Life

Reinke, Ellicott, and Harris: The Life Course in Women

Life Stages: Fact or Fiction?

Later Adulthood

Physical Changes in Later Adulthood

Cognitive Development in Later Adulthood

Personality and Social Development in Later Adulthood

World of Psychology: Culture, Race, and Care for the Elderly

Terminal Illness and Death

Applications: Teenage Pregnancy

Thinking Critically

Chapter Summary and Review

The sun had barely made its way over the horizon of the California desert town of Loma Linda on this beautiful day in 1988. Finishing her breakfast and pulling the 25-pound backpack onto her shoulders, Hulda Crooks set off at 6:00 A.M. to climb the highest mountain in the United States (outside of Alaska). Mt. Whitney soars 14,494 feet, and Hulda was no stranger to the mountain—she had climbed it 23 times before. "I've learned the trees and shrubs," she said. "It's like going back to see an old friend" (Innerviews, 1988, p. 64).

Hulda claimed many other "old friends" as well. She climbed California's San Gorgonio Mountain (11,502 feet) 30 times and conquered 97 different peaks, including Japan's 12,388-foot Mt. Fuji. When not busy climbing, Hulda worked at Loma Linda University doing health research and touring the country giving lectures on diet, exercise, health, and fitness.

Many other people have climbed the same mountains as Hulda. But the amazing thing is that Hulda climbed her first mountain at the age of 66. And when she stood at the top of

Mt. Fuji, she was 91 years old, the oldest woman ever to climb it. When she passed 90, Hulda admitted that she had slowed down a bit. "I can tell I'm not 75 anymore," she said (quoted in Mills, 1987, p. 61). But even in her 90s Hulda would take a 15-minute hike 6 days a week and spring up and down 60 steep steps from 5 to 15 times. Even people 70 years younger had trouble keeping up with Hulda, who often left fellow hikers young enough to be her great-grandchildren huffing and puffing.

Born in 1896, Hulda lived nearly 93 rich, full, active years before she died. But she never really got old. Jim Perry, director of the Loma Linda Lopers, the hiking club to which Hulda belonged, once said, "The package looks like it's had some wear, but inside there's an 18-year-old girl" (Reed & Fischer, 1984, p. 90).

Development is a lifelong process, as Hulda Crooks so ably proved every day of her long life. This chapter continues the study of human development, from adolescence through adulthood and old age. We will consider the ways in which we change over time and the ways in which we remain much the same. We will trace physical, cognitive, social, and personality development from adolescence to the end of life. We begin by entering the developmental world of the adolescent.

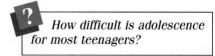

How difficult is adolescence for most teenagers?

Adolescence: Physical and Cognitive Development

If you were to walk up to the average man on the street, grab him by the arm and utter the word "adolescence," it is highly probable—assuming he refrains from punching you in the nose—that his associations to this term will include references to storm and stress, tension, rebellion, dependency conflicts, peer-group conformity, black leather jackets, and the like. (Bandura, 1964, p. 224)

Is this view of adolescence supported by research? The answer might surprise you. **Adolescence** is the developmental stage that spans the period from the end of childhood to the beginning of adulthood. We do not go to sleep one night as a child and awaken as an adult the next morning, at least not in contemporary American society. But some cultures have designed elaborate ceremonies known as rites of passage or puberty rites, which publicly mark the passage from childhood to adulthood. At the end of the ceremony, the young person becomes an "instant adult," ready to assume adult responsibilities and to marry.

The concept of adolescence did not exist until psychologist G. Stanley Hall first wrote about it in his book by that name in 1904. He portrayed this stage in life as one of "storm and stress," the inevitable result of biological changes occurring during the period. Anna Freud (1958), daughter of Sigmund Freud, even

adolescence: The developmental stage that begins at puberty and encompasses the period from the end of childhood to the beginning of adulthood.

324

considered a stormy adolescence a necessary part of adolescent development. But Hall and Freud were wrong.

Compelling evidence now suggests that adolescence is not typically stormy and difficult (Peterson, 1988). Although adolescence poses a great risk to healthy development for about one-fourth of teenagers, for at least one-half of them the period is marked by healthy development (Takanishi, 1993). In a study of 20,000 adolescents, Offer and others (1981) found that average adolescents "function well, enjoy good relationships with their families and friends, and accept the values of the larger society" (p. 116).

Children at highest risk for a troubled adolescence seem to be those who have a tendency toward depression or aggressive behavior or who come from particularly negative environments, such as those filled with family conflict (Buchanan et al., 1992). According to Ebata (1987), adolescent boys who experience turmoil are likely to have had difficulties before they reached adolescence, whereas girls are more likely to experience psychological difficulties for the first time in adolescence. Albert Bandura (1964) warns that expecting the teenage years to be difficult may become a self-fulfilling prophecy.

Contrary to popular belief, adolescence is not stormy and difficult for most teenagers.

Physical Development during Adolescence: Growing, Growing, Grown

Adolescence begins with the onset of **puberty**—a period of rapid physical growth and change that culminates in sexual maturity (Rice, 1992). Although the average onset of puberty is age 10 for girls and age 12 for boys, the normal range extends from age 7 to age 14 for girls and from 9 to 16 for boys (Chumlea, 1982). Every person's individual timetable for adolescence is influenced primarily by heredity, although environmental factors also exert some influence.

puberty: A period of rapid physical growth and change that culminates in sexual maturity.

The Physical Changes of Puberty: Flooding Hormones Jump-Start Growth   Puberty begins with a surge in hormone production, which in turn causes a number of physical changes. The most startling change during puberty is the marked acceleration in growth known as the **adolescent growth spurt**. Who doesn't remember that time in life when the girls were towering over boys of the same age? On the average, the growth spurt occurs from age 10½ to 13 in girls and about 2 years later in boys, from age 12½ to 15 (Tanner, 1961). Because various parts of the body grow at different rates, the adolescent often has a lanky, awkward appearance. Girls finally attain their full height between ages 16 and 17, and boys, between ages 18 and 20 (Roche & Davila, 1972).

During puberty the reproductive organs in both sexes mature, and **secondary sex characteristics** appear—those physical characteristics not directly involved in reproduction that distinguish the mature male from the mature female. In girls the breasts develop and the hips round; in boys the voice deepens, and facial and chest hair appears; and in both sexes there is growth of pubic and underarm (axillary) hair.

The major landmark for females is **menarche**—the onset of menstruation—which occurs at an average age of 12½, although from 10 to 15½ is considered within the normal range (Hill, 1980). Some recent research suggests that environmental stress, such as parental divorce or conflict, is related to an earlier onset of menarche (Belsky et al., 1991; Wierson et al., 1993).

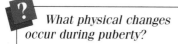

What physical changes occur during puberty?

adolescent growth spurt: A period of rapid physical growth that peaks in girls at about age 12 and in boys at about age 14.

secondary sex characteristics: Those physical characteristics that are not directly involved in reproduction but distinguish the mature male from the mature female.

menarche (men-AR-kee): The onset of menstruation.

The Timing of Puberty: Early and Late Maturation   Probably at no other time in life does physical appearance have such a strong impact on self-image and self-esteem as during adolescence. Girls want to be slim and sexy; boys want to be tall, broad-shouldered, and muscular. The timing of puberty can have impor-

What are the psychological effects of early and late maturation for boys and girls?

tant psychological consequences, coming as it does at a time when a sense of security is gained from being like other members of the peer group.

Early- and Late-Maturing Boys Early maturation in males seems to bestow important advantages and enhanced status in the peer group (Mussen & Jones, 1957; Peterson, 1987). Early-maturing boys, taller and stronger than their classmates, have an early advantage in sports and capture admiring glances from the girls. They are likely to feel confident, secure, independent, and happy and to be more successful academically as well (Blyth et al., 1981; Peterson, 1987). Early maturers are also viewed more favorably by adults. They are perceived as being more attractive and are given more responsibility and freedom than their less physically mature counterparts (Jones & Bayley, 1950).

Judged as less attractive by both peers and adults, late-maturing boys are often at a disadvantage socially and athletically. They are self-conscious about their size and lack the physical traits of manliness—a deep voice and a developing beard. To make matters worse, they are often teased by their peers and treated like "kids."

Early- and Late-Maturing Girls The social advantages and disadvantages of early and late maturation are less clear for girls. Early-maturing girls, who may tower over their peers, feel more self-conscious about their developing bodies and their size. In addition, they have to deal with the sexual advances of older boys before they are emotionally or psychologically mature (Clausen, 1975; Peterson, 1987). By later adolescence, when their peers have caught up, early maturers tend to be shorter and heavier than later maturers and, therefore, are more likely to be unhappy with their physical appearance (Simmons et al., 1983).

Late-maturing girls often experience considerable stress when they fail to develop physically along with their peers. But there is a compensation for the late-maturing girl. Eventually she is likely to be taller and slimmer than her early-maturing age mates.

Cognitive Development in Adolescence: Piaget's Formal Operations Stage

What cognitive abilities develop during the formal operations stage?

The most striking achievement in cognitive development during adolescence is the ability to think abstractly. Jean Piaget (1972; Piaget & Inhelder, 1969) believed that young people typically enter the final stage of cognitive development, the **formal operations stage**, at age 11 or 12, when they become able to use logical reasoning in abstract situations. Remember that according to Piaget, preadolescents are able to apply logical thought processes only in concrete situations. With the attainment of full operational thinking, adolescents are able to attack problems by systematically testing hypotheses and drawing conclusions through deductive reasoning.

Were you mystified by the x's and y's of algebra? When high school students develop formal operational thinking, they are able to unravel the mysteries of algebra and to decipher analogies and metaphors in English literature. With formal operations comes the ability to explore the world of ideas, to look at religion and moral values in a new light, and to consider different philosophies and political systems. Formal operational thinking enables adolescents to think hypothetically; they can think of what *might* be. Given this new ability, it is not surprising that they begin to conceive of "perfect" solutions to the world's problems.

Formal operational thought does not develop automatically, and it may be virtually absent in some primitive cultures (Dasen, 1972). Siegler (1991) claims that it is rare to find high school or college students in the United States who can solve Piagetian formal operations tasks without training. One longitudinal study of American adolescents and adults concluded that only 30 percent of the subjects attained formal operations (Kuhn et al., 1977). Not only do many people fail to show formal operational thinking, but those who do attain it usually apply it

formal operations stage: Piaget's final stage of cognitive development, characterized by the ability to use logical reasoning in abstract situations.

only in those areas where they are most proficient (Ault, 1983; Martorano, 1977). Some studies suggest that even very intelligent, well-educated adults think best when thinking concretely (Neimark, 1975). Now, according to John Flavell (1992), adults appear less competent, and infants and young children more competent, than developmental psychologists once believed.

Adolescent Egocentrism: On Center Stage, Unique, and Indestructible

David Elkind (1967, 1974) claims that the early teenage years are marked by adolescent egocentrism, which takes two forms—the imaginary audience and the personal fable. Do you remember, as a teenager, picturing how your friends would react to the way you looked when you made your grand entrance at a big party? At this stage of life, it never occurred to us that most of the other people at the party were preoccupied not with us, but with the way *they* looked and the impression *they* were making. This **imaginary audience** of admirers (or critics) that adolescents conjure up exists only in their imagination; "but in the young person's mind, he/she is always on stage" (Buis & Thompson, 1989, p. 774).

Teenagers also have an exaggerated sense of personal uniqueness and indestructibility that Elkind calls the **personal fable**. They cannot fathom that anyone has ever felt as deeply as they feel or loved as they love. Elkind suggests that this compelling sense of personal uniqueness may make many adolescents believe they are somehow indestructible and protected from the misfortunes that befall others, such as unwanted pregnancies, auto accidents, or drug overdoses. Belief in the personal fable may account for much of the risk taking during adolescence.

Quadrel and others (1993) dispute Elkind's explanation for adolescent risk taking. They found that both high-risk adolescents (from group homes or juvenile centers) and middle-class, low-risk adolescents actually perceived themselves as *more* likely to experience certain negative events—injury in an auto accident, alcohol dependency, mugging, and so forth—than did adults. Apparently adolescents are willing to engage in high-risk behaviors *in spite of* the risks involved, perhaps because of peer pressure, or because the pleasure outweighs the risk. According to Bjorklund & Green (1992), risk taking may even have some positive consequences. It may enable adolescents to "experiment with new ideas and new tasks and generally behave more independently. Many of these experiences will be adaptive for adult life and for making the transition to adulthood" (p. 49).

Adolescents frequently engage in high-risk behaviors even though they understand the risks involved. What underlying factors might explain this risk taking?

imaginary audience: A belief of adolescents that they are or will be the focus of attention in social situations and that others will be as critical or approving as they are of themselves.

personal fable: An exaggerated sense of personal uniqueness and indestructibility, which may be the basis of risk taking common during adolescence.

Memory Check 9.1

1. Adolescence is a stormy period for most teenagers. (true/false)

2. The secondary sex characteristics:
   a. are directly involved in reproduction.
   b. appear at the same time in all adolescents.
   c. distinguish mature males from mature females.
   d. include the testes and the ovaries.

3. Which of the following provides the most advantages?
   a. early maturation in girls
   b. early maturation in boys
   c. late maturation in girls
   d. late maturation in boys

4. The ability to apply logical reasoning in abstract situations characterizes Piaget's formal operations stage. (true/false)

5. The teenager's personal fable includes all of the following *except* a:
   a. sense of personal uniqueness.
   b. belief in being indestructible and protected from misfortunes.
   c. belief that no one has ever felt so deeply before.
   d. feeling that he or she is always on stage.

Answers: 1. false 2. c 3. b 4. true 5. d

A dolescence: Moral and Social Development

Kohlberg's Theory of Moral Development

How do we develop our ideas of right and wrong? As children, do we acquire our moral values from our parents, from attending church or temple, from our peer group, and from other societal influences? Most of us would agree that all these forces can influence our moral values. But Lawrence Kohlberg (1981, 1984, 1985) believed, as did Piaget before him, that moral reasoning is closely related to cognitive development and that it, too, evolves in stages.

Kohlberg (1969) studied moral development by presenting a series of moral dilemmas to male subjects from the United States and other countries. Read one of his best-known dilemmas, and *Try It!*

In Europe a woman was near death from a special kind of cancer. There was one drug that the doctors thought might save her. It was a form of radium that a druggist in the same town had recently discovered. The drug was expensive to make, but the druggist was charging ten times what the drug cost him to make. He paid $200 for the radium and charged $2,000 for a small dose of the drug. The sick woman's husband, Heinz, went to everyone he knew to borrow the money, but he could only get together $1,000, which is half of what it cost. He told the druggist that his wife was dying, and asked him to sell it cheaper or let him pay later. But the druggist said, "No, I discovered the drug, and I am going to make money from it." So Heinz got desperate and broke into the man's store to steal the drug for his wife. (Colby, Kohlberg, et al., 1983, p. 77)

What moral judgment would you make about the dilemma? Should Heinz have stolen the drug? Why or why not?

 What are Kohlberg's three levels of moral reasoning?

preconventional level: Kohlberg's lowest level of moral reasoning, based on the physical consequences of an act; "right" is whatever avoids punishment or gains a reward.

conventional level: Kohlberg's second level of moral reasoning, in which right and wrong are based on the internalized standards of others; "right" is whatever helps or is approved of by others, or whatever is consistent with the laws of society.

Levels of Moral Reasoning Kohlberg was less interested in whether his subjects judged Heinz's behavior (as described in the *Try It!*) right or wrong than in the *reasons* for their responses. He found that moral reasoning could be grouped into three levels, with each level having two stages.

The Preconventional Level At the first level of moral reasoning, the **preconventional level**, moral reasoning is governed by the standards of others rather than one's own internalized standards of right and wrong. An act is judged good or bad based on its physical consequences. In Stage 1 "right" is whatever avoids punishment; in Stage 2 "right" is whatever is rewarded, benefits the individual, or results in a favor being returned. "You scratch my back and I'll scratch yours" is the thinking common at this stage. Children through age 10 usually function at the preconventional level (see Figure 9.1).

The Conventional Level At the second level of moral reasoning, the **conventional level**, the individual has internalized the standards of others and judges right and wrong in terms of those standards. At Stage 3, sometimes called the "good boy–nice girl" orientation, "good behavior is that which pleases or helps others and is approved by them" (Kohlberg, 1968, p. 26). At Stage 4 the orientation is toward "authority, fixed rules, and the maintenance of the social order. Right behavior consists of doing one's duty, showing respect for authority, and maintaining the given social order for its own sake" (p. 26). Kohlberg believed

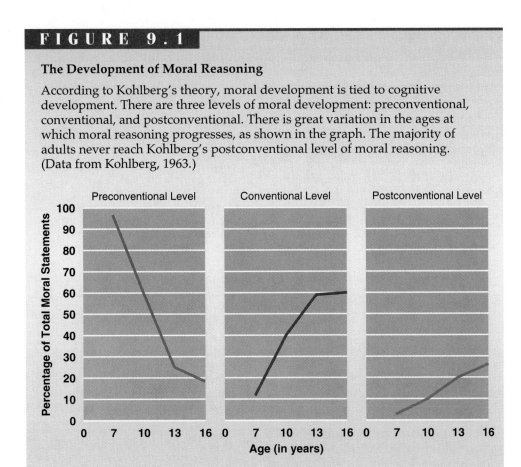

FIGURE 9.1

The Development of Moral Reasoning

According to Kohlberg's theory, moral development is tied to cognitive development. There are three levels of moral development: preconventional, conventional, and postconventional. There is great variation in the ages at which moral reasoning progresses, as shown in the graph. The majority of adults never reach Kohlberg's postconventional level of moral reasoning. (Data from Kohlberg, 1963.)

that a person must function at Piaget's concrete operations stage to reason morally at the conventional level.

✳ **The Postconventional Level** Kohlberg's highest level is the **postconventional level**, which requires the ability to think at Piaget's stage of formal operations. Postconventional reasoning is most often found among middle-class, college-educated people. At this level, people do not simply internalize the standards of others. Instead, they weigh moral alternatives, realizing that at times the law may conflict with basic human rights. At Stage 5 the person believes that laws are formulated to protect both society and the individual and should be changed if they fail to do so. At Stage 6, the universal-ethical-principle orientation, ethical decisions are based on universal ethical principles, which emphasize respect for human life, justice, equality, and dignity for all people. People who reason morally at Stage 6 believe that they must follow their conscience even if it results in a violation of the law.

Could this kind of moral reasoning provide a convenient justification for doing anything a person feels like doing at the time? Not according to Kohlberg, who insisted that an action must be judged in terms of whether it is right and fair from the perspective of everyone involved. In other words, the person must be convinced that the action would be proper even if he or she had to change positions with any individual, from the most favored to the least favored, in the society. Later Kohlberg had second thoughts about this sixth stage and was unsure whether it exists except as a matter of theoretical speculation (Levine et al., 1985).

Review and Reflect Table 9.1 summarizes Kohlberg's six stages of moral development.

postconventional level: Kohlberg's highest level of moral reasoning, in which moral reasoning involves weighing moral alternatives; "right" is whatever furthers basic human rights.

 **and Reflect** 9.1 *Kohlberg's Stages of Moral Development*

Level	Stage
Level I: Preconventional Level (Ages 4–10) Moral reasoning is governed by the standards of others; an act is good or bad depending on its physical consequences—whether it is punished or rewarded.	**Stage 1** The stage where that which avoids punishment is right. Children obey out of fear of punishment. **Stage 2** The stage of self-interest. What is right is that which benefits the individual or gains a favor in return. "You scratch my back and I'll scratch yours."
Level II: Conventional Level (Ages 10–13) The child internalizes the standards of others and judges right and wrong according to those standards.	**Stage 3** The morality of mutual relationships. The "good boy–nice girl" orientation. Child acts to please and help others. **Stage 4** The morality of the social system and conscience. Orientation toward authority. Morality is doing one's duty, respecting authority, and maintaining the social order.
Level III: Postconventional Level (After age 13, at young adulthood, or never) Moral conduct is under internal control; this is the highest level and the mark of true morality.	**Stage 5** The morality of contract; respect for individual rights and laws that are democratically agreed on. Rational valuing of the wishes of the majority and welfare of the people. Belief that society is best served if citizens obey the law. **Stage 6** The highest stage of the highest social level. The morality of universal ethical principles. The person acts according to internal standards independent of legal restrictions or opinions of others.

The Development of Moral Reasoning Kohlberg claimed that we progress through moral stages one stage at a time in a fixed order. We do not skip stages, and if movement occurs, it is to the next higher stage. Postconventional reasoning is not possible, Kohlberg said, until people fully attain Piaget's level of formal operations. They must be able to think in terms of abstract principles and be able to think through and apply ethical principles in hypothetical situations (Kohlberg & Gilligan, 1971; Kuhn et al., 1977). Attaining a high level of cognitive development, however, does not guarantee advanced moral reasoning.

> **?** *What do cross-cultural studies reveal about the universality of Kohlberg's theory?*

Research on Kohlberg's Theory In a review of 45 studies of Kohlberg's theory conducted in 27 countries, Snarey (1985) found support for the virtual universality of Stages 1 through 4, and for the invariant sequence of these stages in all groups studied. Although extremely rare, Stage 5 was found in almost all samples from urban or middle-class populations and absent in all of the tribal or village folk societies studied.

One controversy concerns a possible male sex bias in Kohlberg's stages. Kohlberg indicated that the majority of women remain at Stage 3, while most men attain Stage 4. Do men typically attain a higher level of moral reasoning than women? Carol Gilligan (1982) asserts that Kohlberg's theory is sex-biased. Not only did Kohlberg fail to include females in his original research, Gilligan points out, but he limited morality to abstract reasoning about moral dilemmas. And, at his highest level, Stage 6, Kohlberg emphasized justice and equality but not mercy, compassion, love, or concern for others. Gilligan suggests that females, more than males, tend to view moral behavior in terms of compassion, caring, and concern for others. Thus, she agrees that the content of moral reasoning differs between the sexes, but she contends that males and females do not differ in the complexity of their moral reasoning. Although Kohlberg's theory does emphasize rights and justice over concern for others, researchers, nevertheless, have found females to score as high as males in their moral reasoning (Walker, 1989).

Finally, some critics claim that Kohlberg's theory has a built-in liberal bias and is culture-bound, favoring Western middle-class values (Simpson, 1974; Sullivan, 1977). Yet Snarey (1985), in a review of 45 studies, found that samples from India, Israeli kibbutzim, Taiwan, and Turkey "ranked higher than parallel groups from the United States at one or more points in the life cycle" (p. 228).

In a cross-cultural study of the moral reasoning of adults and children from India and the United States, Miller and Bersoff (1992) found great differences between the two cultures. The postconventional moral reasoning common in India stressed interpersonal responsibilities over justice obligations. In contrast, Americans emphasized a personal or rights-oriented view over individual responsibilities to others: Our world would be more just if each of us, without fail, got exactly what we deserved—no more, no less. But would such a world be more moral? Are mercy and compassion less moral than objective, emotionless justice?

Some critics point out that moral reasoning and moral behavior are not one and the same. Kohlberg readily acknowledged that people can be capable of making mature moral judgments yet fail to live morally. But, said Kohlberg (1968), "The man who understands justice is more likely to practice it" (p. 30). Regardless of whether we agree with Kohlberg's theory, most of us would agree that moral reasoning and moral behavior are critically important aspects of human development. Moral individuals make moral societies.

Parental Relationships:
Their Quality and Influence

Some research indicates that teens at puberty begin to distance themselves from their parents and that conflict increases, particularly with the mother (Paikoff & Brooks-Gunn, 1991). But despite all the talk about the generation gap, most adolescents have good relationships with their parents (Atkinson, 1988).

Bachman (1987) found that over 70 percent of high school seniors believed their personal values were either "very similar" or "mostly similar" to those of their parents. In a study of more than 18,000 adolescents, Curtis (1975) found that adolescents value their parents' advice even more than that of their friends, particularly on educational and occupational goals, or questions about religion, politics, morality, and the use of hard drugs (Marcia, 1980). But on questions of dress, hairstyles, music, sex, tobacco, and alcohol, peer opinions carry more weight. The conventional notion that conflict between parent and child is healthy has not been supported. In fact, high conflict is related to drug abuse, dropping out of school, early pregnancy and marriage, running away, suicide attempts, and the development of psychiatric disorders (Peterson, 1988).

Parental influence is greatest when there is a good parent-child relationship. "Adolescents fare more poorly in families that respond to their development either by throwing up their hands and relinquishing control or cracking down too much" (Eccles et al., 1993, p. 99).

Most adolescents have good relationships with their parents.

> **?** *What outcomes are often associated with the authoritative, authoritarian, and permissive parenting styles?*

The Three Parenting Styles Revisited Of the three parenting styles discussed in Chapter 8—authoritative, authoritarian, and permissive—the authoritative parenting style is most effective and the permissive least effective for adolescents (Baumrind, 1991; Steinberg et al., 1994). In a study of about 2,300 adolescents, those with permissive parents were more likely to use alcohol and drugs and to have conduct problems and less likely to be engaged in school than were those with authoritative or authoritarian parents (Lamborn et al., 1991). The authoritarian style was related to more psychological distress and less self-reliance and self-confidence in adolescents. The authoritative parenting style was associated with psychosocial competence for adolescents of all racial and ethnic groups, and with academic success for white middle-class youth (Steinberg et al., 1994). Adolescents with authoritative parents benefit even further when their friends' parents are also authoritative (Fletcher et al., 1995). But the authoritative style was not found to be associated with high academic achievement in African American and Asian American adolescents (Steinberg, 1992). Why?

Steinberg (1992) suggests that white middle-class students benefit both from an authoritative parenting style and from peer support for academic achievement. And although Asian American adolescents typically have authoritarian parents, several factors may explain why they outperform other groups academically. First, academic achievement is highly valued by both their family and their peers, and second, they believe strongly that academic excellence is a prerequisite for future occupational success. But African American and Hispanic adolescents typically lack peer support for academic excellence and are less likely to see it as necessary for their occupational future. In fact, according to Steinberg (1992), "African American students are more likely than others to be caught in a bind between performing well in school and being popular among their peers" (p. 728). Thus, when peer values and norms do not support academic pursuits, the peer influences often negate parental influence.

> **?** *What are some of the useful functions of the adolescent peer group?*

The Peer Group

At a time when adolescents feel the need to become more independent from their parents, friends become a vital source of emotional support and approval. Adolescents usually choose friends of the same sex and race (Clark & Ayers, 1992), who have similar values, interests, and backgrounds (Duck, 1983; Epstein, 1983).

Interactions with peers are critical while young people are fashioning their identities. Adolescents can try out different roles and observe the reactions of their friends to their behavior and their appearance. The peer group provides teenagers with a standard of comparison for evaluating their own assets as well as a vehicle for developing social skills (Berndt, 1992).

For males and females, popularity within the peer group is based largely on good looks and personality. For boys, athletic ability is often an important factor in popularity with both sexes (Savin-Williams, 1980). And conformity appears to be another important ingredient in popularity for both sexes (Sebald, 1981).

Sexuality and Adolescence: The Drive Turns On

Before the 1960s the surging sex drive of adolescents was held in check primarily because most societal influences—parents, religious leaders, the schools, and the media—were all preaching the same message: Premarital sex was wrong. Then sexual attitudes began to change. In a 1969 national survey by Gallup, 68 percent of adults in the United States believed that premarital sex was wrong; but by 1991, the number had dropped to 40 percent (Hugick & Leonard, 1991b).

According to the Centers for Disease Control (1991), the incidence of premarital intercourse among high school students is 60.8 percent for males and 48 per-

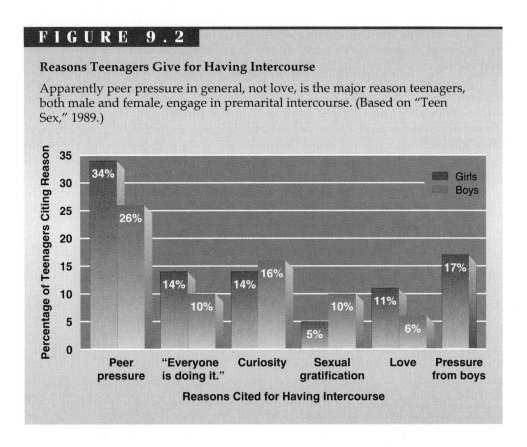

FIGURE 9.2

Reasons Teenagers Give for Having Intercourse

Apparently peer pressure in general, not love, is the major reason teenagers, both male and female, engage in premarital intercourse. (Based on "Teen Sex," 1989.)

cent for females. "Black students were significantly more likely than white or Hispanic students to ever have had intercourse (72.3 percent, 51.6 percent, and 53.4 percent, respectively)" (p. 885). Sonestein and others (1991) report that the typical pattern for males and females is serial monogamy—"a pattern of monogamous relationships that follow one another" (p. 166). Early premarital intercourse is associated with an increased risk of pregnancy (Morgan et al., 1995) and sexually transmitted diseases, and a higher number of sexual partners.

Teens who tend to be less experienced sexually are those who live with both biological parents, who attend religious services frequently, and whose parents are neither too permissive nor too strict in their discipline and rules (White & DeBlassie, 1992). Ostrov and others (1985) found early intercourse less prevalent among adolescents with above-average academic achievement and whose parents had a harmonious relationship. Figure 9.2 shows reasons given by teenage boys and girls for having intercourse.

Part-Time Jobs for Adolescents: A Positive or a Negative?

For several decades it was assumed that adolescents benefit from part-time jobs, because they develop a work ethic, earn money, and become better prepared to enter the world of work. According to national surveys, about two-thirds of high school juniors and seniors are employed part-time during the school year, and half of these seniors work more than 20 hours each week (Steinberg et al., 1993). Several very large studies indicate that for teenagers the consequences of working more than 15 to 20 hours weekly are primarily negative. In a study of more than 70,000 high school seniors, Bachman and Schulenberg (1993) found working long hours was "positively correlated with smoking cigarettes, drinking alcohol, using illicit drugs, interpersonal aggression, theft, victimization, trouble with

In general, what is the impact of adolescents working more than 15 to 20 hours a week during the school year?

police, arguments with parents, lack of sleep, and lack of exercise" (p. 230). Furthermore, rather than "earn and save," the typical pattern was one of "earn and spend."

In a study of 1,800 high school students, Steinberg and others (1993) found that working students spent less time on homework and had poorer class attendance. They were more likely to cheat, to copy homework, and to select less demanding classes and easier teachers to preserve their grade-point average. Also, students who worked long hours were more likely to have used drugs and to have lacked interest in school even before their employment. And their intensive work schedule made their existing problems worse.

Memory Check 9.2

1. Match Kohlberg's level of moral reasoning with the rationale for engaging in a behavior.

   ___ 1) to avoid punishment or gain a reward
   ___ 2) to ensure that human rights are protected
   ___ 3) to gain approval or to follow the law

   a. conventional
   b. preconventional
   c. postconventional

2. Most teenagers have good relationships with their parents. (true/false)

3. For adolescents, the most effective parenting style is the _____; the least effective is the _____.
   a. authoritative; authoritarian
   b. authoritarian; permissive
   c. authoritative; permissive
   d. permissive; authoritarian

4. For most adolescents, the peer group serves some useful functions. (true/false)

5. Overall, the impact of working long hours during high school is positive. (true/false)

Answers: 1. 1) b 2) c 3) a 2. true 3. c 4. true 5. false

Erikson's Psychosocial Theory: Adolescence through Adulthood

identity versus role confusion: Erikson's fifth psychosocial stage, when adolescents need to establish their own identity and to form values to live by; failure can lead to an identity crisis.

In Chapter 8 we presented the first four stages of Erik Erikson's psychosocial theory of development. Recall that his was the only major theory of development to include the entire life span, and he was the first to stress the part that society and individuals themselves play in their own personality development. Also, keep in mind that each of Erikson's stages is built around a conflict that involves the individual's relationship with the social environment. If healthy development is to occur, the conflict at each stage must be resolved satisfactorily. The stages themselves are named for the two opposite basic attitudes that may be formed, depending on how the conflicts are resolved. To preserve the continuity of the theory, we will present the remaining four stages together. Erikson's eight stages are described in Review and Reflect Table 9.2.

? *How did Erikson explain the fifth psychosocial stage— identity versus role confusion?*

Identity versus Role Confusion: Erikson's Stage for Adolescence

Erikson's fifth stage of psychosocial development, **identity versus role confusion**, is the developmental struggle of adolescence. "Who am I?" becomes the critical question at this stage, as adolescents seek to establish their identity and find values to guide their lives (Erikson, 1963). Now for the first time, adolescents are seriously looking to the future and considering an occupational identity—

Review and Reflect 9.2 *Erikson's Psychosocial Stages of Development*

Stage	Ages	Description
Trust vs. mistrust	Birth to 1 year	Infant learns to trust or mistrust depending on the degree and regularity of care, love, and affection from mother or primary caregiver.
Autonomy vs. shame and doubt	1 to 3 years	Children learn to express their will and independence, to exercise some control, and to make choices. If not, they experience shame and doubt.
Initiative vs. guilt	3 to 6 years	Children begin to initiate activities, to plan and undertake tasks, and to enjoy developing motor and other abilities. If not allowed to initiate or if made to feel stupid and considered a nuisance, they may develop a sense of guilt.
Industry vs. inferiority	6 years to puberty	Children develop industriousness and feel pride in accomplishing tasks, making things, and doing things. If not encouraged, or if rebuffed by parents and teachers, they may develop a sense of inferiority.
Identity vs. role confusion	Adolescence	Adolescents must make the transition from childhood to adulthood, establish an identity, develop a sense of self, and consider a future occupational identity. Otherwise, role confusion can result.
Intimacy vs. isolation	Young adulthood	Young adults must develop intimacy—the ability to share with, care for, and commit themselves to another person. Avoiding intimacy brings a sense of isolation and loneliness.
Generativity vs. stagnation	Middle adulthood	Middle-aged people must find some way of contributing to the development of the next generation. Failing this, they may become self-absorbed, personally impoverished, and reach a point of stagnation.
Ego integrity vs. despair	Late adulthood	Individuals review their lives, and if they are satisfied and feel a sense of accomplishment, ego integrity will result. If dissatisfied, they may sink into despair.

what they will choose as their life's work. Erikson (1968) believed that "in general it is the inability to settle on an occupational identity which most disturbs young people" (p. 132). The danger at this stage, he said, is that of role confusion—not knowing who you are or where you belong.

Erikson used the term *identity crisis* to portray the disturbance adolescents experience in forging an identity. But research does not support the notion that most young people experience a crisis (Blyth & Traeger, 1983). Erikson may have been projecting onto all adolescents in general the difficulties he experienced in forming his own identity. Although Erikson (1980) considered establishing an identity to be the focus of adolescence, he recognized that "identity *formation* neither begins nor ends with adolescence: it is a lifelong development" (p. 122).

Intimacy versus Isolation: Erikson's Stage for Early Adulthood

Erikson contended that if healthy development is to continue into adulthood, it is necessary for the young adult to establish intimacy in a relationship. This sixth stage of psychosocial development he called **intimacy versus isolation**. For Erikson, intimacy means the ability of young adults to share with, care for, make sacrifices for, and commit themselves to another person. He believed that avoiding intimacy results in a sense of isolation and loneliness.

intimacy versus isolation: Erikson's sixth psychosocial stage, when the young adult must establish intimacy in a relationship in order to avoid feeling a sense of isolation and loneliness.

? *What is Erikson's psychosocial task for early adulthood?*

PIONEERS *Erik Homburger Erikson (1902–1994)*

Erik Erikson was a personality theorist whose writings won him a Pulitzer Prize and whose books continue to sell by the thousands. Yet he had neither an M.D. nor a Ph.D. in psychology. In fact, he didn't have any kind of university degree at all.

Erikson originated the concept *identity crisis*, and in real life he had to resolve a monumental crisis of his own. Born in Frankfurt, Germany, to Danish parents, Erikson did not know his biological father, who left before he was born. Not long afterward Erikson's mother married Dr. Theodore Homburger, and Erikson was raised as Erik Homburger. He did not learn that Dr. Homburger was not his real father until many years later. In fact, Erikson did not take his biological father's last name until he was 37 years old. Yet Erikson did not resent his mother and stepfather for what he termed their "loving deception."

Erikson experienced other crises about who and what he was during childhood. When he started school, Erikson thought of himself as German, but the German children shunned him because he was Jewish. Yet he fared no better with his Jewish classmates, who rejected him because, as a tall, blond Dane, he was not very Jewish in appearance. Since he did not seem to fit in very well, it is not surprising that he disliked school and made only average grades.

After he finished school, Erikson was not sure what he wanted to do or to be, and so he wandered around "trying to find himself." Eventually he went to Vienna, met Freud, and became fascinated with Freud's psychoanalytic theory. He entered Freud's institute and began training in psychoanalysis, studying mainly with Freud's daughter, Anna. After completing his training in 1933, Erikson married and came with his wife to the United States. He set up a practice working with children in Boston.

Erikson entered Harvard to study for his Ph.D. in psychology. But he soon dropped out to accept a position at Yale teaching at the medical school and working with both disturbed and normal children. Interested in the development of children from diverse cultures, he conducted studies with children from two different Native American tribes, as well as with other American children in Massachusetts and California. He returned to Harvard in the 1960s.

Erikson distinguished himself as a psychoanalyst and personality theorist, and throughout his long life he remained prolific, productive, and influential. Even in his 90s, Erikson continued with his wife Joan (an artist and an author in her own right) to make scholarly contributions. They both served as models of the successful resolution of the eight stages of life that he proposed. Erikson died in 1994 at the age of 92.

---

generativity versus stagnation: Erikson's stage for middle age, when people become increasingly concerned with guiding the next generation rather than stagnating.

What changes did Erikson believe are essential for healthy personality development in middle age?

Erikson (1980) argued that young adults must establish their own identity before true intimacy is possible. He said, "The condition of a true twoness is that one must first become oneself" (p. 101). Several studies support Erikson's notion that a stable identity is a necessary prerequisite for an intimate relationship (Tesch & Whitbourne, 1982; Vaillant, 1977).

Generativity versus Stagnation: Erikson's Stage for Middle Adulthood

Erikson's seventh psychosocial stage is called **generativity versus stagnation**. Erikson (1980) claimed that in order for mental health to continue into middle adulthood, individuals must develop generativity—an "interest in establishing and guiding the next generation" (p. 103).

> The person begins to be concerned with others beyond his immediate family, with future generations and the nature of the society and world in which those generations will live. Generativity does not reside only in parents; it can be found in any individual who actively concerns himself with the welfare of

young people and with making the world a better place for them to live and work. (Elkind, 1970, p. 112)

People who do not develop generativity become self-absorbed and "begin to indulge themselves as if they were their own one and only child" (Erikson, 1980, p. 103). Personal impoverishment and a sense of stagnation often accompany such self-absorption. We enlarge ourselves when we have concern for others.

Ego Integrity versus Despair: Erikson's Final Stage

Psychosocial development continues into later adulthood, but its course is usually an extension of the former life pattern. In Erikson's eighth stage, **ego integrity versus despair**, the outcome depends primarily on whether a person has resolved the conflicts at previous stages (Erikson et al., 1986). Those who have a sense of ego integrity believe their life has had meaning. They look back on their life with satisfaction and a sense of accomplishment, and do not have major regrets.

> At the other extreme is the individual who looks back upon his life as a series of missed opportunities and missed directions; now in the twilight years he realizes that it is too late to start again. For such a person the inevitable result is a sense of despair at what might have been. (Elkind, 1970, p. 112)

Erikson's Theory: Does Research Support It?

Whitbourne and others (1992) studied subjects of three different age groups to measure change over a 22-year period from early to middle adulthood. Their research supported Erikson's claim that a favorable resolution of the psychosocial crisis at one stage depends on the successful resolution of earlier crises. However, the researchers found subjects often continued to show changes associated with previous stages, particularly industry versus inferiority.

In a cross-sectional study of young, midlife, and older adults, McAdams and others (1993) found that compared to younger and older adults, middle-aged adults express more generative concern—a conscious concern for "having a positive and enduring impact on the next generation" (p. 227). But these adults' concerns were not matched with actions, because they did not engage in significantly more behaviors that would foster this end.

ego integrity versus despair: Erikson's stage for old age, when people look back on their lives with satisfaction or with major regrets.

? *What is the key to a positive resolution of Erikson's eighth psychosocial stage—ego integrity versus despair?*

According to Erikson, in middle adulthood people develop generativity—an interest in guiding the next generation.

Memory Check 9.3

1. Which of the following was *not* identified by Erikson as a developmental task in his psychosocial stage for adolescence?
   a. forming an intimate relationship
   b. planning for an occupation
   c. forming an identity
   d. finding values to live by

2. Erikson claimed that an interest in guiding the next generation is necessary for good mental health in:
   a. adolescence.   c. middle age.
   b. young adulthood.   d. old age.

3. Erikson believed the main task in young adulthood is to:
   a. develop generativity.
   b. forge an identity.
   c. start a family.
   d. form an intimate relationship.

4. According to Erikson, older people who feel they did not reach many of their goals or contribute positively to others will experience:
   a. stagnation.   c. isolation.
   b. despair.   d. inferiority.

Answers: 1. a 2. c 3. d 4. b

Early and Middle Adulthood

For years, developmental psychologists focused almost exclusively on childhood and adolescence. But today many are studying the changes that occur during that long period of some 40 to 45 years known as adulthood. Adulthood is generally divided into three parts—young or early adulthood (ages 20 to 40 or 45), middle adulthood (ages 40 or 45 to 65), and late adulthood (after age 65 or 70). These ages are only approximate, because there are no biological or psychological events that neatly define the beginning or ending of a period. Bernice Neugarten, one of the most respected researchers in adult development, has said, "We seem to be moving in the direction of what might be called an age-irrelevant society; and it can be argued that age, like race or sex, is diminishing in importance as a regulator of behavior" (Neugarten & Hagestad, 1976, p. 52).

Obviously, some things change; but in many ways older adults remain much the same as in their earlier years. For most adults (younger and older), love provides the primary source of satisfaction, followed by work (Baum & Stewart, 1990).

Physical Changes in Adulthood

> **?** *What are the physical changes associated with middle age?*

Opinions vary about what period should be called the "prime of life," but it is clear that the *physical* prime of life occurs early. Most people in their 20s and 30s enjoy good general health and vitality, but the decade of the 20s is the period of top physical condition, when physical strength, reaction time, reproductive capacity, and manual dexterity all peak. During the 30s, there is a slight decline in these physical capacities, which is barely perceptible to most people other than professional athletes.

Middle-aged people often complain about a loss of physical vigor and endurance. But such losses have to do less with aging than with exercise, diet, and health habits. Some fine professional athletes, such as star pitcher Nolan Ryan and heavyweight champion George Foreman, were competing into their 40s. One unavoidable change in the mid- to late 40s is **presbyopia**, a condition in which the lenses of the eyes no longer accommodate adequately for near vision, and reading glasses or bifocals are required for reading.

In middle age, people are more susceptible to diseases, especially life-threatening ones. Heart disease is responsible for 30 percent—and cancer, 26 percent—of all deaths among men between ages 45 and 54 (U.S. Bureau of the Census, 1994). Cancer, usually of the breast, accounts for about 44 percent of the deaths of women in this age group. Consequently, during middle age, people become more aware of their mortality and may begin to restructure life "in terms of time-left-to-live rather than time-since-birth" (Neugarten, 1968, p. 97). By the time we reach 50, as one researcher has put it, "We must accept that life's seesaw has tipped; that there are now more yesterdays than tomorrows" (Vaillant, 1977, p. 233).

The major biological event for women during middle age is **menopause**—the cessation of menstruation, which occurs between ages 45 and 55 and signifies the end of reproductive capacity. The most common symptom associated with menopause and the sharp decrease in the level of estrogen is hot flashes—sudden feelings of being uncomfortably hot. Some women also experience symptoms such as anxiety, irritability, mood swings, or depression, but most find menopause less upsetting than they had anticipated (Jackson et al., 1991; Matthews et al., 1990). Men experience a gradual decline in their testosterone level from its peak at about age 20 until 60. During late middle age, men experience a decline in reproductive capability, called the male climacteric.

presbyopia (prez-bee-O-pee-uh): A condition, occurring in the mid to late 40s, in which the eyes' lenses no longer accommodate adequately for near vision, and reading glasses or bifocals are required for reading.

menopause: The cessation of menstruation, occurring between ages 45 and 55 and signifying the end of reproductive capacity.

Intellectual Capacity during Early and Middle Adulthood

Conventional wisdom has held that intellectual ability reaches its peak in the late teens or early 20s, and that it's all downhill after that. Fortunately, conventional wisdom is wrong. It is true that younger people do better on tests requiring speed or rote memory. But on tests measuring general information, vocabulary, reasoning ability, and social judgment, older subjects usually do better than younger ones because of their greater experience and education (Horn, 1982). Adults actually continue to gain knowledge and skills over the years, particularly when they lead intellectually challenging lives.

Schaie (1994) analyzed data from the Seattle Longitudinal Study, which assessed the intellectual abilities of some 5,000 subjects. Many of the subjects were tested six times over the course of 35 years. Schaie found that in five areas—verbal meaning, spatial orientation, inductive reasoning, number, and word fluency—subjects showed modest gains from young adulthood to the mid-40s (see Figure 9.3). Decline did not occur, on average, until after age 60, and even then the decline was modest until the 80s. Half of the subjects, even at age 81, showed no decline over the previous 7 years. The study also revealed several gender differences. Females performed better on tests of verbal meaning and inductive reasoning, while males tended to do better on tests of number and spatial orientation. The only ability found to show a continuous decline from the mid-20s to the 80s was perceptual speed.

Dennis (1968) looked at the productivity of 738 persons who had lived at least 79 years and had attained eminence as scholars or in the sciences or the arts. For almost every one, the decade of the 40s was most productive. Historians, philosophers, and literary scholars enjoyed high productivity from the 40s all the way through the 70s. Scientists were highly productive from their 40s through their

> **?** *In general, can adults look forward to an increase or a decrease in intellectual performance from their 20s to their 60s?*

FIGURE 9.3

Age Differences in Performance on Tests of Five Mental Abilities

This graph shows the average scores of subjects in the Seattle Longitudinal Study on tests of five mental abilities. Subjects were tested six times over a period of 35 years and showed gains through young adulthood until their mid-40s. Very little decline occurred until after age 60. (Based on Schaie, 1994.)

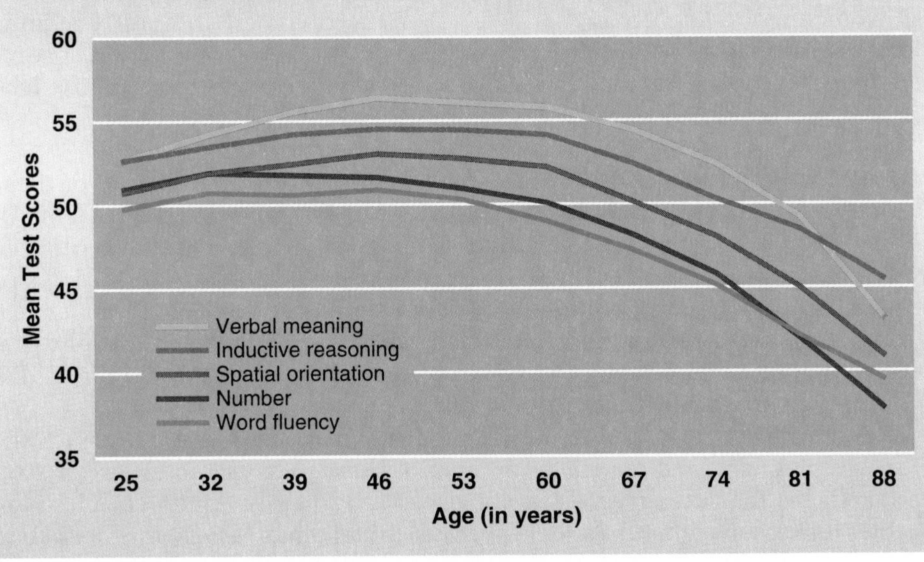

Legend:
- Verbal meaning
- Inductive reasoning
- Spatial orientation
- Number
- Word fluency

Y-axis: Mean Test Scores (35 to 60)
X-axis: Age (in years) — 25, 32, 39, 46, 53, 60, 67, 74, 81, 88

60s, but showed a significant decline in productivity in their 70s. Those in the arts peaked earliest and showed a dramatic decline in their 70s. But, of course, the researchers did not interview Michelangelo, Pablo Picasso, Georgia O'Keeffe, Duke Ellington, Irving Berlin, and many others who were artistically potent and vital into their 70s, 80s, and 90s. Fortunately, middle age is not a time in life when we dry up and deteriorate physically, mentally, or in any other way.

Lifestyle Patterns in Adulthood

Is the "average household" in the United States still headed by a married couple? Yes, for more than two-thirds of the population. The majority of people (67 percent) live in a household headed by a married couple who may or may not have children under age 18 (U.S. Bureau of the Census, 1994). Figure 9.4 illustrates the percentages of the U.S. population living in various household arrangements. Let us consider some of these lifestyle patterns.

Singles: Playing the Field   About 24 percent of males and 19 percent of females over age 18 are single (U.S. Bureau of the Census, 1994). Some people believe that if unburdened by a spouse, they will be able to pursue their careers and their interests and have a more interesting and exciting life. Yet the happiest singles seem to be those who have relationships that provide emotional support.

Some single people who want a relationship choose living together rather than making the commitment of marriage. The U.S. Bureau of the Census (1994) labels them "unmarried couples." From 1970 to 1993 there was a thirteenfold increase in cohabitation for people under age 25. Such arrangements usually last 1 or 2 years, with one-third of the couples marrying and the rest breaking up. Surprisingly, the divorce rate among these couples is higher than the divorce rate for couples who did not live together before marriage (DeMaris & Rao, 1992).

Marriage: Tying the Knot   Despite the growing alternatives to marriage, 67 percent of men and 77 percent of women in the United States either are married or have been married. Though the institution of marriage is still alive and well, men and women are waiting longer to tie the knot. Since 1970, the average age at first marriage has increased by 3 years, to 25.5 years for males and 23.7 for females (U.S. Bureau of the Census, 1994).

In a review of 93 studies, Wood and others (1989) found that married people report much higher levels of well-being than unmarried people, and that married women report slightly higher levels than married men. In a study relating marital status to level of happiness, Campbell (1976) found that married people were most happy, followed by the widowed, separated, or divorced. Those who had never been married were the least happy.

Divorce: Untying the Knot   According to a 1989 Gallup poll, half of those who have ever been married have experienced severe marital problems or divorce, and 26 percent have been divorced at least once (Colasanto & Shriver, 1989). The reasons given for the divorce were basic personality differences or incompatibility (47 percent); infidelity (17 percent); a drug or alcohol problem (16 percent); disputes about money, family, or children (10 percent); and physical abuse (5 percent). People aged 35 to 54 experienced the most severe marital discord, and those over age 55, the least.

The marriages most likely to fail are teenage marriages, those in which the bride was pregnant, and marriages of people whose parents had divorced. And the marriages that do survive are not necessarily happy. Many couples stay together for reasons other than love—because of religious beliefs, for the sake of the children, for financial reasons, or out of fear of facing the future alone.

? *What are some of the trends in lifestyle patterns in young adulthood?*

FIGURE 9.4

Household Arrangements among U.S. Population

Although U.S. households headed by married couples have decreased over the last several decades, 67 percent of the population lives in such households. About 14 percent live alone or with non–family members. (Data from U.S. Bureau of the Census, 1994.)

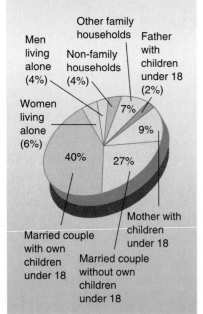

But even for the "miserable marrieds," divorce does not always solve their problems. "Alcoholism, drug abuse, depression, psychosomatic problems, and accidents are more common among divorced than nondivorced adults" (Hetherington et al., 1989, pp. 307–308). Yet most people who do get divorced are not soured on the institution of marriage, because the majority of them do remarry.

Parenthood: Passing Along the Genes According to a 1990 Gallup poll, 90 percent of Americans over age 40 have had children, and despite the difficult task of raising them, only 7 percent say they wish they had never had children (Gallup & Newport, 1990d).

> **?** *What effect does parenthood have on marital satisfaction?*

Even though most couples want children, satisfaction with marriage does tend to decline after the birth of the first child (Belsky et al., 1989; Cowan & Cowan, 1992). Women in general find the period of child rearing the least satisfying time of marriage. The problem centers mainly on the division of work— who does what. Even though men are helping with children more than in the past, child care still generally ends up being primarily the responsibility of the woman. Unless she holds very traditional views of sex roles, a woman's dissatisfaction after the birth of the first child often relates to the discrepancy between how much help with child care and housework she had expected from her husband and how much help she actually receives (Hackel & Ruble, 1992). Glass and Fujimoto (1994) found that time spent in housework was related to an increase in depression for both husbands and wives. Several studies have revealed that when husbands in dual-earner families *do* help with child care, they show a decline in mental health (Rosenfield, 1992), a more negative view of their marriage, and an increase in marital conflict (Crouter et al., 1987).

By 1975 about 37 percent of all married women with children under age 6 and almost 45 percent of those with children under age 18 held part-time or full-time jobs outside the home. Now, almost 58 percent of the women who give birth enter the labor force before the child is a year old (U.S. Bureau of the Census, 1994). Figure 9.5 (on page 342) shows the percentage of married women in the labor force according to the age of their youngest child.

Remaining Childless: No Bundles of Joy Some couples are choosing not to have children, leaving themselves free to devote their time, energy, and money to pursuing their own interests and careers. A few studies indicate that such couples are happier and find their marriages more satisfying than couples with children (Campbell, 1975). However, this same sense of satisfaction may not continue into middle and old age, when couples may wonder if their decision to remain childless was a good one. A 1990 Gallup poll found that only about 4 percent of Americans are "antichildren"—that is, they don't have any, they don't want any, or they are glad they never had any children (Gallup & Newport, 1990c). In spite of the tremendous emotional and financial investment children require, most parents find their children provide a major source of satisfaction and meaning in their lives and that the investment has been a good one.

Parenthood can cause stress and conflict in a marriage, but it is also immensely satisfying for most couples.

Career Choice: A Critical Life Decision Probably no other part of life is so central to identity and self-esteem as a person's occupation or profession, with the possible exception of motherhood for some women. Our career often becomes a basic part of our definition of self and a major factor in the way others define us. A career can define our lifestyle—the friends we choose, the neighborhood we live in, our habits, and even our ideas and opinions. And job satisfaction affects our general life satisfaction.

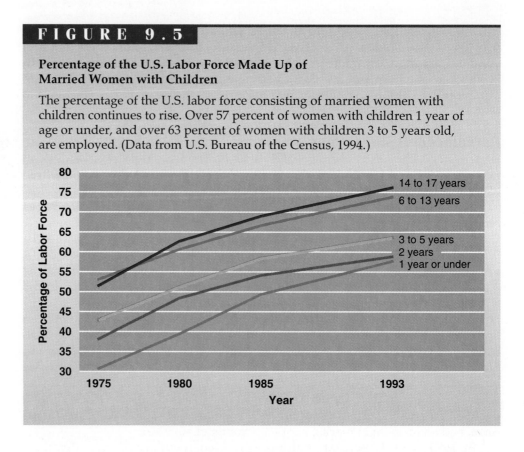

FIGURE 9.5

Percentage of the U.S. Labor Force Made Up of Married Women with Children

The percentage of the U.S. labor force consisting of married women with children continues to rise. Over 57 percent of women with children 1 year of age or under, and over 63 percent of women with children 3 to 5 years old, are employed. (Data from U.S. Bureau of the Census, 1994.)

Although the majority of Americans seem satisfied with their jobs, job satisfaction is higher for the middle-aged than for the young adult (Kohut & DeStefano, 1989). A 1991 Gallup poll revealed that 75 percent of American workers would continue to work even if it were not a financial necessity, and more than 50 percent would continue in their present job (Hugick & Leonard, 1991b).

One of the most profound changes in employment patterns has been the tremendous increase of women in the workplace. In 1993 women made up 45.3 percent of the labor force (U.S. Bureau of the Census, 1994). But women are not rushing into the workplace primarily to find self-fulfillment. Most are there out of economic necessity, even though women earn, on average, only about 77 percent of what men earn (Famighetti, 1994). In spite of lower pay, sex discrimination, and fewer opportunities for advancement, most women with jobs find them enjoyable and express higher self-esteem than do full-time homemakers (Baruch et al., 1983; Hoffman, 1979). And contrary to what one might expect, in middle-class, dual-career couples, positive and negative job experiences have similar effects on the mental health of men and women (Barnett et al., 1993).

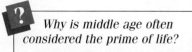

Why is middle age often considered the prime of life?

Personality and Social Development in Middle Age

Many people consider middle age the prime of life. Researcher Bernice Neugarten (1968) states that society "may be oriented towards youth," but it is "controlled by the middle-aged" (p. 93). People aged 40 to 60 are the decision makers in industry, government, and society. Neugarten found that very few at this age "express a wish to be young again" (p. 97). As one of her subjects said, "There is a difference between wanting to *feel* young and wanting to *be* young" (p. 97).

Reaching middle age, men and women begin to express personality characteristics they had formerly suppressed. Men generally become more nurturant and women more assertive. For many women, middle age is a time of increased freedom.

Wink and Helson (1993) found that after children leave home, most women work at least part-time and tend to experience an increase in self-confidence and a heightened sense of competence and independence. Contrary to the conventional notion of the empty nest syndrome—that parents feel empty and depressed when their children grow up and leave home—most parents seem to be happier when their children are on their own. Parents have more time and money to pursue their own goals and interests. "For the majority of women in middle age, the departure of teenage children is not a crisis, but a pleasure. It is when the children do *not* leave home that a crisis occurs (for both parent and child)" (Neugarten, 1982, p. 163). For most people, an empty nest is a happy nest!

Memory Check 9.4

1. During which decade do people reach their peak physically?
   a. teens   b. 20s   c. 30s   d. 40s

2. From the 20s to the 40s, intellectual performance tends to:
   a. increase.   c. remain the same.
   b. decrease.   d. show continuous fluctuation.

3. The majority of people in the United States live in households headed by a married couple. (true/false)

4. The highest levels of life satisfaction are reported by _____; the lowest levels by _____.
   a. singles; married people
   b. married people; the widowed
   c. married people; singles
   d. married people; divorced people

5. Most middle-aged people have difficulty adjusting when their children grow up and leave home. (true/false)

Answers: 1. b   2. a   3. true   4. c   5. false

Theories of Adulthood

Many psychologists have tried to learn how we change and develop through life, and some have attempted to identify stages of adult development.

Levinson's Seasons of Life

Daniel Levinson formulated a stage theory of adult development based on extensive interviews of 40 men between the ages of 35 and 45. They were "hourly workers in industry, business executives, university biologists and novelists"—who were diverse in racial, ethnic, and religious origins and in social class (Levinson et al., 1978). Although the life of each subject was unique, an underlying pattern and sequence of stages were common to all of them. Levinson identified four eras, or seasons, in the life cycle: preadulthood (childhood and adolescence), early adulthood, middle adulthood, and late adulthood. Subjects went through stable periods lasting from 6 to 10 years. During these periods they made certain key choices that formed the basis of their **life structure**—the basic pattern of their life at a given time, including their relationships and activities.

Between these stable 6- to 10-year periods were transitional periods lasting 4 to 5 years. During these transitional periods individuals would review and eval-

? *How is Levinson's concept of life structure related to his proposed stages of development?*

life structure: Levinson's term for the basic pattern of one's life at any given time, including one's relationships and activities and the significance they have for the individual.

uate their life and existing life structure. A transitional period may result in minor changes in the life structure or in drastic changes, such as divorce, remarriage, changing jobs or occupations, or moving to another part of the country. When a transitional period is particularly difficult, it is called a crisis.

Following are descriptions of some of Levinson's proposed stages:

- *Early Adult Transition* (ages 17 to 22): During this period of transition between adolescence and early adulthood, young people begin to separate psychologically from parents and other aspects of the preadult world in preparation for entry into the adult world.

- *Entering the Adult World* (ages 22 to 28): Young adults typically choose an occupation, form love relationships, marry and have a family, and try to turn their dream of the kind of life they want into a reality.

- *Age 30 Transition* (ages 28 to 33): This period is a time for modifying the first adult life structure and creating "the basis for a more satisfactory structure within which to complete the era of early adulthood" (1978, p. 58).

- *Settling Down* (ages 33 to 40): Adults build a second life structure and anchor themselves more firmly in family or community. They seek to advance in their occupation and climb the ladder of success.

- *Midlife Transition* (ages 40 to 45): During this transition period people develop "a heightened awareness of . . . mortality and a desire to use the remaining time more wisely" (1978, p. 192). Some people make few external changes, while others make drastic ones involving "divorce, remarriage, major shifts in occupation and lifestyle" (p. 194). Levinson reported that 80 percent of his subjects experienced a moderate or severe **midlife crisis**.

- *Middle Adult Era* (ages 45 to 60): Now senior members in their own world, individuals feel a responsibility for "the development of the current generation of young adults who will soon enter the dominant generation" (Levinson, 1986, p. 6).

- *Late Adult Transition* (ages 60 to 65): A final transition into late adulthood brings a person to the last rung of Levinson's developmental ladder.

Although his first study included only men, Levinson later studied 45 women. His findings convinced him that his theory was applicable to females as well. On the basis of his research and that of others, Levinson now claims that his theory "holds for men and women of different cultures, classes, and historical epochs" (Levinson, 1986, p. 8).

Reinke, Ellicott, and Harris: The Life Course in Women

Reinke and others (1985) interviewed 124 middle-class women aged 30 to 60 to gain information about their marriage, family, employment, life satisfactions and dissatisfactions, and life changes. Like Levinson, the researchers found major transitional periods in which subjects seemed to reappraise their life and consider changes. Some of these changes were related to specific chronological ages, but the researchers believe that women's development is examined most profitably in relation to six phases in the family cycle: (1) the *no children phase*, (2) the *starting a family–preschool phase*, (3) the *school age phase*, (4) the *adolescent phase*, (5) the *launching phase* (beginning when the first child leaves home and ending when the last child leaves), and (6) the *postparental phase*.

Changes were reliably associated with each of the family-cycle phases, regardless of whether women had experienced major transitions. Women experiencing a major transition at the family–preschool phase were more likely to report changes in themselves, and marital separation or divorce. The 40 percent reporting a transition at the launching phase became more introspective and assertive, but very few experienced the empty nest syndrome. One-third of the

What did Reinke, Ellicott, and Harris's study of middle-class women reveal about major transitional periods in the life cycle?

midlife crisis: A period of turmoil usually occurring in a person's 40s and brought on by an awareness of one's mortality; characterized by a reassessment of one's life and a decision to make changes, either drastic or moderate, in order to make the remaining years better.

subjects had major transitions during the postparental phase, when they experienced decreased inner stability, but the transition usually ended with increased life satisfaction.

Life Stages: Fact or Fiction?

Not all researchers accept the notion of stages in adult development. Some, like Neugarten (1982), seek to develop a greater understanding of the changes that occur during the life span, rather than looking for universals and attempting to make predictions. "Adults change far more, and far less predictably, than the oversimplified stage theories suggest. . . . Choices and dilemmas do not sprout forth at ten-year intervals" (p. 162).

Neugarten warns against assuming that Levinson's findings apply to all adults. Remember that the subjects studied by Levinson and Reinke and colleagues were almost all middle or upper-middle class. Levinson found that 80 percent of his subjects experienced a midlife crisis, but for many people in our country and around the world, life is one long crisis. For someone facing chronic unemployment, a midlife crisis that involved choosing to change a job or vocation would be considered a luxury. Changing one's life structure to allow more time for a hobby or avocation is a concern for people who already enjoy the necessities of life.

Memory Check 9.5

1. Levinson claims that as people make the transition from one era in the life cycle to another, they reexamine and modify their:
   a. life maps.   c. lifestyles.
   b. personal schemas.   d. life structures.

2. Levinson found that the transition most likely to cause a crisis was the:
   a. early adult transition.   c. midlife transition.
   b. age 30 transition.   d. late adult transition.

3. Reinke and others believe that the best way to examine life changes in a woman's life is in relation to:
   a. changes in her marital status.
   b. phases in the family cycle relating to her children.
   c. alternating stable and transitional periods.
   d. young adulthood, middle adulthood, and older adulthood.

Answers: 1. d 2. c 3. b

Later Adulthood

Age 65 or 70 is generally considered the beginning of old age, and 12.6 percent of the U. S. population is now over age 65 (U.S. Bureau of the Census, 1994). What are your perceptions of life after 65? Before reading further, complete the *Try It!* on page 346 by answering *true* or *false* to the statements about older adults.

Physical Changes in Later Adulthood

As you learned in Chapter 3, the elderly lose some of their sensory capacity. With advancing age, they typically become more farsighted and have increasingly impaired night vision (Long & Crambert, 1990). They suffer hearing loss in the higher frequencies and often have difficulty following a conversation when there is competing background noise (Slawinski et al., 1993). And they may have difficulty with balance because of a deterioration in the vestibular senses.

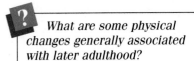

What are some physical changes generally associated with later adulthood?

Are the following statements true (T) or false (F)?

___ 1. Older adults tend to express less satisfaction with life in general than younger adults do.

___ 2. A lack of money is a serious problem for most people over age 65.

___ 3. Marital satisfaction declines in old age.

___ 4. Mandatory retirement forces most workers out of jobs before they are ready to leave.

___ 5. The majority of retirees do not adjust well to retirement.

___ 6. A large percentage of individuals over age 85 end up in nursing homes or institutions.

Answers: All of the statements are false!

Older bodies generally slow down. The brain takes longer to process information, and reaction time is slower (Butler, 1968). There is a decline in heart, lung, kidney, and muscle function, and older adults typically have less energy and stamina. Joints become stiffer, and bones lose calcium and become more brittle, increasing the risk of fractures from falls.

About 80 percent of senior citizens in the United States have one or more chronic conditions such as arthritis, rheumatism, heart problems, or high blood pressure. For both males and females, the three leading causes of death are heart disease, cancer, and stroke. But the good news is that in spite of all of these changes, the vast majority of people over age 65 consider their health good. One-half of those aged 75 to 84 and more than one-third of those over 85 do not have to curb their activities because of health problems (Toufexis, 1988).

An interesting study of the "oldest old"—those over 95—reveals that they are often in better mental and physical condition than those 20 years younger (Perls, 1995). They often remain employed and sexually active through their 90s and carry on "as if age were not an issue" (p. 70). How do they do it? They appear to have a genetic advantage that makes them particularly resistant to the diseases that kill or disable most people at younger ages.

Are there personality characteristics that predict longevity? Would optimism and a sense of humor be good predictors? Friedman and others (1993, 1995) examined data from Terman's 7-decade longitudinal study (discussed in Chapter 7) and found that the childhood personality traits in males that best predicted a long life were conscientiousness, dependability, and truthfulness. Optimism and cheerfulness in childhood were inversely related to longevity. Why? Optimists, the researchers believe, are more likely to be careless and to engage in unhealthy behaviors. The researchers also found that parental divorce during childhood and

FIGURE 9.6

Where Older Americans Live

This graph shows the percentages of males and females in two age groups who live at home independently, who live at home but need the help of another person, and who live in nursing homes. (Data from Schneider & Guralnik, 1990.)

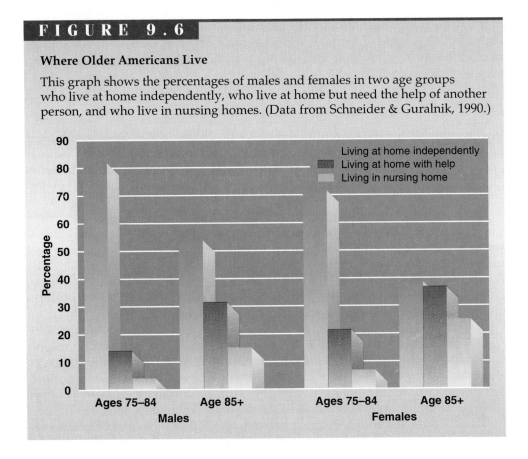

unstable marriage patterns during adulthood were associated with shorter life spans.

One of the greatest fears among the elderly is that they will spend their last years in a nursing home. Yet, even among those 85 and older, this "greatest fear" comes to pass for only 15 percent of males and 25 percent of females. Figure 9.6 shows the percentages of older males and females who live independently at home, at home with help, or in nursing homes.

Fitness and Aging Men and women in their 60s and 70s who exercise properly and regularly can have the energy and fitness of someone 20 to 30 years younger (deVries, 1986). Recent research suggests that physical exercise even enhances the performance of older adults on tests of reaction time, working memory, and reasoning (Clarkson-Smith & Hartley, 1990). "People rust out faster from disuse than they wear out from overuse" (Horn & Meer, 1987, p. 83). In a recent study, 100 frail nursing-home residents, average age 87, exercised their thigh and hip muscles vigorously on exercise machines for 45 minutes three times a week. At the end of 10 weeks, they had increased their stair-climbing power by 28.4 percent and their walking speed by 12 percent, and four were able to exchange their walkers for a cane (Fiatarone et al., 1994). For most of us, the chance to remain fit and vigorous as we age lies within our power. Even strenuous physical activity is not out of the question for people in their 70s and 80s. Remember Hulda Crooks, who was climbing mountains at age 92.

Sex and the Senior Citizen Masters and Johnson (1966) studied the sexual response in older men and women and found that regular sexual relations are necessary to maintain effective sexual performance. In a survey of adults aged 80 to 102 who were not taking medication, 70 percent of the men and 50 percent

Older adults who stay fit and active have a better chance of remaining healthy.

of the women admitted fantasizing about intimate sexual relations often or very often. But 63 percent of the men and 30 percent of the women were doing more than fantasizing—they were still having sex (McCarthy, 1989). And remember, they were between 80 and 102.

Cognitive Development in Later Adulthood

Intellectual decline in late adulthood is *not* inevitable. Older adults who keep mentally and physically active tend to retain their mental skills as long as their health is good (Meer, 1986). They do well on tests of vocabulary, comprehension, and general information, and their ability to solve practical problems is generally higher than that of young adults.

Researchers often distinguish between two types of intelligence (Horn, 1982). **Crystallized intelligence**—one's verbal ability and accumulated knowledge— tends to increase over the life span. **Fluid intelligence**—abstract reasoning and mental flexibility—peaks in the early 20s and declines slowly as people age. The rate at which people process information also slows gradually with age (Hertzog, 1991; Lindenberger et al., 1993). This explains, in part, why older adults perform more poorly on tests requiring speed.

Is it accurate to equate old age with forgetfulness? In laboratory memory tasks, older people do as well or almost as well as younger people on recognition tasks (Hultsch & Dixon, 1990) and on recall of information in their areas of expertise (Charness, 1989). But in tasks requiring speed of processing in short-term memory or recall of items that hold no particular meaning for them, younger subjects do significantly better than older subjects (Verhaeghen et al., 1993).

Two of the most common and annoying age-related memory complaints are being unable to recall a name or to think of a word needed in a conversation (Lovelace & Twohig, 1990). Researchers have also noted some decline in *prospective* memory—remembering to perform an action in the future, such as mailing a letter or taking medicine (Hultsch & Dixon, 1990). Whatever the differences, memory failures in older adults are judged to be a more serious problem than the same memory failures in younger people (Erber et al., 1990).

Several factors are positively correlated with good cognitive functioning in the elderly. They are education (Anstey et al., 1993), a complex work environment, a long marriage to an intelligent spouse, and a higher income (Schaie, 1990). But intellectual functioning can be hampered by physical problems (Manton et al., 1986) or by psychological problems such as depression. Those who continue to function at the highest levels are usually those with more education (Zabrucky et al., 1987) because they are the most likely to stay mentally active, read, and use a variety of cognitive skills. Women generally show less decline than men, and people with a high degree of intellectual functioning tend to live longer (Neugarten, 1976).

Alzheimer's Disease and Other Types of Dementia **Senile dementia**, or senility, is a state of severe mental deterioration marked by impaired memory and intellect, as well as by altered personality and behavior. Moderate to severe dementia is found in 4 to 6 percent of those aged 65 and older (Gatz & Pearson, 1988) and in about 25 percent of those over 85. Sometimes people who are over-medicated or who are suffering from depression have symptoms that mimic those of senility, but the symptoms usually go away when the condition is treated. True senility is caused by physical deterioration of the brain. It can result from such conditions as cerebral arteriosclerosis (hardening of the arteries in the brain), chronic alcoholism, and irreversible damage by a series of small strokes.

About 50 to 60 percent of all cases of senility result from Alzheimer's disease. In **Alzheimer's disease** there is a progressive deterioration of intellect and per-

---

What happens to mental ability in later adulthood?

crystallized intelligence: Aspects of intelligence, including verbal ability and accumulated knowledge, that tend to increase over the life span.

fluid intelligence: Aspects of intelligence involving abstract reasoning and mental flexibility, which peak in the early 20s and decline slowly as people age.

senile dementia: A state of mental deterioration caused by physical deterioration of the brain and characterized by impaired memory and intellect and by altered personality and behavior; senility.

Alzheimer's disease (ALZ-hye-merz): An incurable form of dementia characterized by progressive deterioration of intellect and personality, resulting from widespread degeneration of brain cells.

What is Alzheimer's disease?

sonality that results from widespread degeneration of brain cells. At present, about 4 million people in the United States suffer from this incurable disorder (Fackelmann, 1995). At first, its victims show a gradual impairment in memory and reasoning, and in their efficiency in carrying out everyday tasks. Many have difficulty finding their way around in familiar locations. As the disorder progresses, Alzheimer's patients become confused and irritable, tend to wander away from home, and become increasingly unable to care for themselves. Eventually their speech becomes unintelligible, and they become incontinent (unable to control bladder and bowel functions). If they live long enough, they will reach a stage where they do not respond when spoken to and no longer recognize even their spouse or children.

It is normal for the numbers of neurons to decline in old age. But compared to nondemented people of similar age, Alzheimer's patients in one study averaged 68 percent fewer neurons in parts of the the hippocampus, the area of the brain important in the formation and retention of memories (West et al., 1994). The photo compares a normal brain with that of an Alzheimer's patient. When autopsies are performed on Alzheimer's patients, the cerebral cortex and particularly the hippocampus are found to contain dead neurons clogged with twisted stringy masses (called neurofibrillary tangles) and surrounded by plaques (Pennisi, 1994). A consistent characteristic of Alzheimer's disease is the excessive amounts of amyloid beta protein in the brain, which forms the core of the plaques (Mullan & Crawford, 1993; Selkoe, 1993).

Age and a family history of Alzheimer's disease are the two risk factors that have been consistently associated with the disorder (Farrer & Cupples, 1994; Payami et al., 1994). About 5 percent of Alzheimer's victims have the early-onset type, which begins in the 40s and has been linked to a gene on chromosome 14 (Barinaga, 1995).

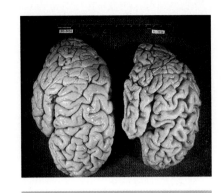

The brain of an Alzheimer's patient (right) has a much smaller volume than a normal adult brain (left).

Social Development and Adjustment in Later Adulthood

Would you say that people are more satisfied with their marriages and with life in general when they are young adults or when they are over 65? It may surprise you to learn that in several major national surveys life satisfaction and feelings of well-being were about as high in older as in younger adults (Inglehart, 1990) (see Figure 9.7 on page 350). Life satisfaction appears to be most strongly related to good health. And to maintain a sense of well-being, people need at least a minimum level of companionship and social activity (Thompson & Heller, 1990), as well as a feeling of control over their life (Rowe & Kahn, 1987). For men, life satisfaction in old age is linked to happiness in career and marriage (Mussen et al., 1982; Sears, 1977). This is consistent with Freud's definition of mental health as the ability to love and work. Levenson and others (1993) found that older couples tended to be happier in their marriages than middle-aged couples, experiencing less conflict and more sources of pleasure than their younger counterparts.

Much has been said about the elderly poor. About 13 percent of older Americans live below the poverty line, and among them a disproportionately high number of African Americans (33 percent) and Hispanics (22 percent) (U.S. Bureau of the Census, 1994). But many adults in the 65-plus group live comfortably. With homes that are paid for and no children to support, people over 65 tend to view their financial situation more positively than do young adults.

Yet there is a grim side to old age. Many losses occur: Health inevitably declines, friends die, and some who do not wish to retire must do so because of company policies or for health reasons. Eventually one

People with Alzheimer's disease, which affects an estimated 4 million Americans, function best in a stable, structured environment.

FIGURE 9.7

Age and Life Satisfaction

Surveys including subjects from many nationalities reveal that levels of life satisfaction and happiness remain much the same and relatively high (approximately 80 percent) throughout life. (Data from Inglehart, 1990.)

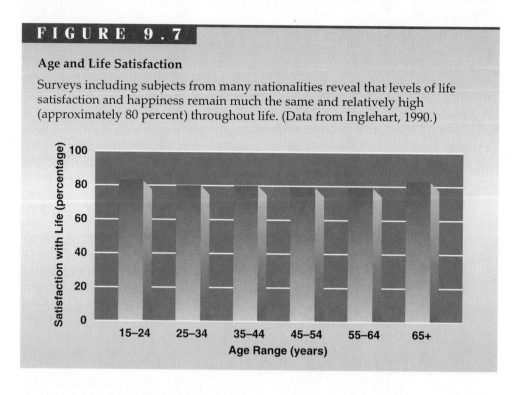

spouse dies, and if the other lives long enough, he or she will be increasingly dependent on others. When life becomes more burdensome than enjoyable, an older person can fall victim to depression, a major problem affecting about 15 percent of the elderly. And depression can be deadly. White males over age 75 have the highest suicide rate of any age group in our society (Roybal, 1988).

Retirement: Leaving the World of Work   To many people, retirement marks the end of middle age and the beginning of old age. Younger people tend to see retirement as a time when people are forced to leave their jobs and are "put out to pasture"—an event that is seen as leading to premature death. But most retirees are happy to leave the world of work. In spite of the change in the mandatory retirement age from 65 to 70 in 1978, fewer than 12.5 percent of people over age 65 remain in the workforce. Generally the people most reluctant to retire are those who are better educated, hold high-status jobs with a good income, and find fulfillment in their work. Bosse and others (1991) found that only 30 percent of retirees reported finding retirement stressful, and of those who did, most were likely to be in poor health and have financial problems.

Losing a Spouse: The Hardest Blow   For most people, losing a spouse is the most stressful event in a lifetime, and more women than men experience this loss. In 1989, 48.7 percent of women over age 65 had lost a spouse compared with only 14 percent of men. There were only about 67.8 males for every 100 females aged 65 and older (U.S. Bureau of the Census, 1994). Both widows and widowers are at a greater risk for health problems and have a higher mortality rate than their age mates who are not bereaved (Kaprio et al., 1987).

Losing a spouse leaves a great void in the life of the survivor, and depression is a likely reaction (Norris & Murrell, 1990). Gone is one's best friend, companion, and lover. Not only must surviving spouses endure the grief process alone, but they must restructure their lives—home life, daily routine, and social life. Widowhood seems to be more emotionally distressing for men than women (Umberson et al., 1992). Women experience more financial strain, but men have the strain of managing the household.

World of Psychology

Culture, Race, and Care for the Elderly

Every weekday morning on the "Today" show, Willard Scott features women and men across the United States who are among the oldest of the old, usually 100 years or older. Living past 100 is not as rare as in decades past. The fastest-growing segment of our population consists of those 85 and older (Thomas, 1992). Are there racial, cultural, and gender differences in the ways older family members are viewed, treated, and cared for?

Older African Americans as well as older Asian and Hispanic Americans are more likely to live with and be cared for by their adult children than are other elderly Americans. African Americans are more likely than whites to regard elderly persons with respect and to feel that children should help their older parents (Mui, 1992).

Multigenerational households are by no means commonplace among most racial groups in the United States. Only about 18 percent of older parents live in the same household with one of their adult children (Crimmins & Ingegneri, 1990). And even in these multigenerational households, it is more often the case that adult children move into the elderly parent's home than that the parent comes to live with one of the children. For the most part, older Americans have a strong preference for maintaining their independence and living in their own home, although they and their adult children express a desire to live near each other (Bengtson et al., 1990).

The living arrangements of American families are not typical of other countries around the world. In many Latin American countries, the majority of elderly people do live in the same household with younger generations in an extended family setting (De Vos, 1990). And in Korea, 80 percent of the elderly are cared for by family members (Sung, 1992). Economic and social necessity often dictate living arrangements.

Are elderly family members accorded less respect and viewed as more of a burden to adult children and grandchildren in the United States than in non-Western cultures? Popular opinion holds that the elderly in Asian cultures are venerated, highly esteemed, and accorded great respect by family members and the culture in general. It is true that non-Western cultures (Japan, for example) have carried forward traditions of long standing that value older family members. Three-generation households have been the rule rather than the exception among the Japanese. How do attitudes toward providing care for aged relatives differ between the two cultures?

Elaine Brody and others (1984) studied the attitudes of three generations of American women on providing care for their aged relatives. Her study was replicated with a comparable sample of three generations of Japanese women in Tokyo (Campbell & Brody, 1985). Women's attitudes were studied because the care of aged relatives is typically provided by female family members in both countries. The studies yielded some surprising findings. The American women expressed a stronger sense of obligation toward elderly members of their family, such as helping them with household chores, than the Japanese women did. The American women also expressed

continued

stronger agreement that their aged parents should be able to look to them for help.

Campbell and Brody (1985) suggest that the difference in attitudes may be explained by cultural differences in the way that help is provided to older family members. Daughters typically care for their elderly parents in the United States. In Japan, daughters-in-law most often care for elderly family members, who are more likely to live in the home of their oldest son. Attitudes between daughters and parents are likely to be more positive than attitudes between daughters-in-law and their husband's parents.

Brody and others (1992) found that married daughters experienced less strain and less depression resulting from parent care than those who were single, divorced, or widowed. Also, the burden of care is perceived as lighter if the care is provided because of a strong attachment rather than because of a sense of obligation (Cicirelli, 1993).

Terminal Illness and Death

One of the developmental tasks for the elderly is to accept the inevitability of their own death and to prepare themselves for it. At no time does this become more critical than when people face a terminal illness.

According to Kübler-Ross, what stages are experienced by terminally ill patients as they come to terms with death?

Kübler-Ross on Death and Dying: The Final Exit   Elisabeth Kübler-Ross (1969) interviewed some 200 terminally ill people and found they shared common reactions to their impending death. In her book *On Death and Dying* she identifies five stages most subjects went through in coming to terms with death.

In the first stage, denial and isolation, most patients react to the initial awareness of their terminal illness with shock and disbelief. When denial can no longer be maintained, it gives way to the second stage, anger, which is marked by feelings of anger, rage, resentment, and envy of those who are young and healthy. "Why me?" is the question that rages inside. In the third stage, bargaining, the person attempts to postpone death for a specific period of time in return for a promise of "good behavior." An individual may offer God some special service or a promise to live a certain kind of life in exchange for an opportunity to attend a child's wedding or a grandchild's graduation. Eventually the bargaining stops, giving way to the fourth stage, depression. This stage brings a great sense of loss—physical loss, loss of money due to expensive treatments, loss of ability to function in a job or in the role of mother, father, husband, or wife. The depression takes two forms—depression over past losses and over impending losses.

If enough time remains, patients usually reach the final stage, acceptance, in which they are neither depressed nor angry about their fate. They stop struggling against death and are able to contemplate its coming without fear or despair. Kübler-Ross claims that the family also goes through stages similar to those experienced by the patient. She believes the "goal should always be to help the patient and his family face the crisis together in order to achieve acceptance of this final reality simultaneously" (p. 173).

Other researchers acknowledge that Kübler-Ross's proposed stages often do occur, but they deny their universality and their invariant sequence (Butler & Lewis, 1982). Each person is unique. We should not expect the reactions of all the terminally ill to conform to some rigid sequence of stages; nor should we dismiss their anguish as merely a stage they are going through.

Death and dying are not pleasant subjects, but remember that life itself is a terminal condition, and each day of life should be treasured like a precious gift. Hulda Crooks, in addressing the elderly, would tell them: "We should be role models to show young people that life is worth living to the last breath" (Innerviews, 1988, p. 64). And what a role model she was!

Memory Check 9.6

1. Which of the following statements is true about adults over 65?
   a. They are considerably less satisfied with life than young adults are.
   b. Their financial situation is considerably worse than that of younger adults.
   c. Most retirees are happy to be retired.
   d. A large percentage of adults over 85 end up in nursing homes.

2. Alzheimer's disease is curable if diagnosed in its very earliest stages. (true/false)

3. Compared to older adults who are mentally and physically active, younger adults do better on:
   a. tests requiring speed.
   b. comprehension tests.
   c. general information tests.
   d. practical problem solving.

4. According to Kübler-Ross, the first stage experienced by terminally ill patients in coming to terms with death is _____; the last stage is _____.
   a. anger; depression
   b. denial; depression
   c. bargaining; acceptance
   d. denial; acceptance

Answers: 1. c 2. false 3. a 4. d

APPLICATIONS · APPLICATIONS · APPLICATIONS

Teenage Pregnancy

The United States has a higher incidence of pregnancy among 15- to 19-year-olds than any other developed country (Brozan, 1985). There are some 10 million adolescent girls in the United States, and each year about 10 percent of them, approximately 1 million, become pregnant (Alan Guttmacher Institute, 1991). About 40 percent of the pregnancies are terminated by abortion (Cullari & Mikus, 1990), and 13 percent by miscarriage (Hayes, 1987). Only 5 percent of teenage mothers put their babies up for adoption (Wallis, 1985). Nearly 70 percent of all teenage mothers are unmarried (Children's Defense Fund, 1991), and among African American teenagers 92 percent of births are out-of-wedlock (National Research Council, 1993). Of those teens who become pregnant, 31 percent find themselves in the same condition again within 2 years (Alan Guttmacher Institute, 1991). These figures are staggering when we consider that only 15 percent of babies were born to unwed mothers in 1960 (Children's Defense Fund, 1991). Why the dramatic increase in out-of-wedlock births? One reason is that the stigma attached to unwed motherhood has largely disappeared. In fact, some unmarried teens today actually want to get pregnant.

The Consequences for Mother and Child

Among girls who give birth before age 18 and choose to keep their babies, half will never complete high school. As a group, their earning power will be about half that of girls who did not have babies at this early age (National Research Council, 1993), and many will eventually have to go on welfare (Brooks-Gunn & Furstenberg, 1986). About one-third of pregnant teenagers marry their baby's father, but the divorce rate for these marriages is two to three times higher than the national average.

Early pregnancy can have serious physical consequences. Teenage mothers are 60 percent more likely than women in their 20s to suffer complications or death during pregnancy or delivery. Pregnant teens are more likely to come from poor backgrounds and less likely to receive early prenatal medical care and adequate nutrition. As a result, they are twice as likely to give birth to premature or low-birth-weight infants than

continued

are mothers who are over 18. Moreover, their babies have a higher mortality rate and are at greater risk for poor health and emotional and educational problems (Furstenberg et al., 1989). Because teenage mothers are more likely to be single parents living in poverty, their children often lack economic security, attention, and discipline.

Teenage mothers often are unable to attend school because there is no one to care for the baby. They also face economic barriers. Although the majority of teenage mothers have some work experience, they find it difficult to earn enough to support themselves and pay for child care.

Relatively little research has focused on teenage fathers. A few studies have revealed that many young fathers want to play a part in the lives of the mother and child, but also want to complete their education and find a good job. They therefore experience stresses similar to those affecting the mother. A teenage father is more likely to marry the mother of his child if he can find a job that provides enough income to support a family. However, few such jobs are available to young people who have not completed high school.

Preventing Pregnancy and Cultural Contradictions

A majority of sexually active American teenagers are aware of the consequences of sexual activity, but do not take responsibility for preventing them. Many sexually active girls between the ages of 15 and 19 do not use contraception at all, while many others use it only occasionally. Why?

Some teens feel guilty about their sexual activity; to them, planning to have sex seems more wrong than simply letting it happen spontaneously. Some find it too embarrassing to buy contraceptives, and others believe contraceptives interfere with sexual pleasure. In addition, many sexually active teenagers greatly underestimate the risk of getting pregnant. As a result, 62 percent of those

who are sexually active and fail to use contraceptives do become pregnant (Zelnik et al., 1979).

American teenagers lack sufficient information about reproduction and contraception, and they are not taught from an early age about the consequences of sexual behavior. Parents are divided on the question of sex education in schools. Some favor it; others fear that teaching children about sex will encourage them to engage in sexual activities. Moreover, certain contradictions in American culture may contribute to the problem of teenage pregnancy. Scores of magazine articles and TV programs focus on sex and casual sexual activity, and yet there is little frank discussion of sexual behavior in homes and schools. Thus, teenagers are led to desire sex but not taught much about how to control their desires or prevent the consequences of sexual behavior if they engage in it.

Advocating Abstinence

In the 1990s, a growing number of teens are discovering the "pleasures of abstinence." And thousands of them across the United States are taking the pledge "No sex before marriage." One of the new virginity movements is an organization known as "True Love Waits." Participating teens sign a pledge card and vow to remain virgins until marriage. In the summer of 1994, 22,000 of these young people marched on Washington, D.C., and planted 200,000 abstinence pledge cards on the Washington Mall, their own and those of other True Love Waits teens across the nation (Ingrassia, 1994).

Even teens who have not waited but have had sexual experiences can have what one abstinence advocacy program, Sex Respect, calls "secondary virginity." Sex Respect and other abstinence programs have been

severely criticized by many sex educators and others. But they have had an impact. Today, approximately 90 percent of sex education courses include abstinence as an option in their curriculum (Ingrassia, 1994). And several high-profile media, rock, and sports stars have publicly announced their virginity—including actress Cassidy Rae of "Models Inc.," MTV star Kennedy, Tori Spelling of "Beverly Hills 90210," rock star Juliana Hatfield, and NBA star A. C. Green, who launched an athletes-for-abstinence campaign.

Whether motivated by fear (of pregnancy or sexually transmitted diseases, including AIDS), by religious conviction, or by the desire to resist peer pressure, a growing number of teens have decided to postpone sex until the time is right for them.

In the United States today, there are basically two competing schools of thought on how best to deal with teenage sex and its consequences (White & DeBlassie, 1992). One view accepts teen sex as inevitable and focuses on how to prevent its negative consequences through condom distribution and other birth control measures. The other view holds that teens can be taught to avoid or delay sexual intercourse until they are older. Furthermore, its proponents strive to help teens understand reasons for their sexual desires and learn how to deal with them.

Thinking Critically

Evaluation

In your opinion, do Erikson's psychosocial stages for adolescence and early adulthood accurately represent the major conflicts of these periods of life? Why or why not?

Point/Counterpoint

Levinson has suggested a theory of adult development, for both men and women, that includes stages and transitional periods occurring at certain chronological ages. Reinke, Ellicott, and Harris have suggested a stage theory for women that revolves around phases in the family cycle. Prepare an argument supporting each of the following positions:

a. Levinson's theory is superior to that of Reinke, Ellicott, and Harris in explaining development in women.
b. Reinke, Ellicott, and Harris's theory is superior to Levinson's in explaining development in women.

Psychology in Your Life

Think back to your junior high school and high school years. To what degree do you believe early or late maturation affected how boys and girls were treated by their peers, their parents, or their teachers? Did early or late matu-

ration affect their adjustment? Explain your answer.

Chapter Summary and Review

Adolescence: Physical and Cognitive Development

 How difficult is adolescence for most teenagers?

Although about one-fourth of teenagers experience a troubled adolescence, for at least half, it is a period of healthy development and good relationships with family and friends.

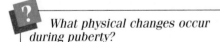 *What physical changes occur during puberty?*

Puberty is characterized by the adolescent growth spurt, further development of the reproductive organs, and the appearance of the secondary sex characteristics. The major event for girls is menarche, and for boys, the first ejaculation.

What are the psychological effects of early and late maturation for boys and girls?

Early maturation provides enhanced status for boys, because of their early advantage in sports and greater attractiveness to girls. Late maturation puts the male at a disadvantage in these areas and results in a lack of confidence that may persist into adulthood. The effects for girls are less clear-cut.

What cognitive abilities develop during the formal operations stage?

During the formal operations stage, adolescents develop the ability to think abstractly, to attack problems by systematically testing hypotheses, to draw conclusions through deductive reasoning, and to think hypothetically.

Key Terms

adolescence (p. 324)
puberty (p. 325)
adolescent growth spurt (p. 325)
secondary sex characteristics (p. 325)
menarche (p. 325)
formal operations stage (p. 326)
imaginary audience (p. 327)
personal fable (p. 327)

Adolescence: Moral and Social Development

 What are Kohlberg's three levels of moral reasoning?

At Kohlberg's preconventional level, moral reasoning is based on the physical consequences of an act—"right" is whatever averts punishment or brings a reward. At the conventional level, right and wrong are based on the internalized standards of others—"right" is whatever helps or is approved of by others, or whatever is consistent with the laws of society. Postconventional moral reasoning involves weighing moral alternatives—"right" is whatever furthers basic human rights.

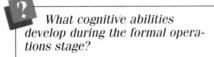 *What do cross-cultural studies reveal about the universality of Kohlberg's theory?*

Cross-cultural studies support the universality of Kohlberg's Stages 1 through 4 as well as their invariant sequence. Stage 5 was found in almost all of the urban or middle-class samples but was absent in tribal and village folk societies.

 What outcomes are often associated with the authoritative, authoritarian, and permissive parenting styles?

Authoritative parenting is most effective and is associated with psychosocial competence in all groups and with academic success in white middle-class youth. Adolescents with authoritarian parents are typically the most psychologically distressed and least self-reliant and self-confident. Permissive parenting is least effective and is often associated with adolescent drug use and conduct problems.

What are some of the useful functions of the adolescent peer group?

The adolescent peer group (usually composed of teens of the same sex and race and similar social background) provides a vehicle for developing social skills and a standard of comparison against which teens' attributes can be evaluated.

In general, what is the impact of adolescents working more than 15 to 20 hours a week during the school year?

Working long hours negatively affects schoolwork, promotes an "earn and spend" pattern, and is associated with drug use and conduct problems.

Key Terms

preconventional level (p. 328)
conventional level (p. 328)
postconventional level (p. 329)

Erikson's Psychosocial Theory: Adolescence through Adulthood

How did Erikson explain the fifth psychosocial stage—identity versus role confusion?

In this stage adolescents seek to establish their identity and find values to guide their lives. Difficulty at this stage can result in an identity crisis.

What is Erikson's psychosocial task for early adulthood?

In Erikson's sixth stage, intimacy versus isolation, young adults must establish intimacy in a relationship to avoid a sense of isolation and loneliness.

What changes did Erikson believe are essential for healthy personality development in middle age?

Erikson's seventh stage, generativity versus stagnation, occurs during middle age. To avoid stagnation, individuals must develop generativity—an interest in establishing and guiding the next generation.

What is the key to a positive resolution of Erikson's eighth stage—ego integrity versus despair?

Erikson's psychosocial stage for old age is a time for reflection. People look back on their lives with satisfaction and a sense of accomplishment or have major regrets about mistakes and missed opportunities.

Key Terms

identity versus role confusion (p. 334)
intimacy versus isolation (p. 335)
generativity versus stagnation (p. 336)
ego integrity versus despair (p. 337)

Early and Middle Adulthood

What are the physical changes associated with middle age?

Physical changes associated with middle age are a need for reading glasses, a greater susceptibility to life-threatening diseases, and the end of reproductive capacity (menopause) in women and a declining reproductive capacity in men.

In general, can adults look forward to an increase or a decrease in intellectual performance from their 20s to their 60s?

Although younger people tend to do better on tests requiring speed or rote memory, adults' intellectual performance shows modest gains until the mid-40s. A modest decline occurs from the 60s to the 80s. Scholars, scientists, and those in the arts are usually most productive in their 40s.

What are some of the trends in lifestyle patterns in young adulthood?

About 68 percent of the population of the United States lives in households headed by a married couple with or without children under 18. Couples are waiting longer to have children, and 60 percent of married women with children under age 6 hold full-time or part-time jobs outside the home.

What effect does parenthood have on marital satisfaction?

Even though most couples want children, satisfaction with marriage, particularly in women, tends to decline after children arrive. This decline can be explained in part by the unequal workload carried by mothers employed outside the home.

Why is middle age often considered the prime of life?

The decision makers in our society are usually aged 40 to 60. When children grow up and leave home, parents have more time and money to pursue their own goals and interests.

Key Terms

presbyopia (p. 338)
menopause (p. 338)

Theories of Adulthood

How is Levinson's concept of life structure related to his proposed stages of development?

According to Levinson's stage theory of adult development, all people go through a fixed set of stages. During transitional periods individuals review and evaluate their lives and their life structure (the basic design of their life). During stable periods they make choices that form the basis of a revised life structure and then proceed to pursue their goals within it.

What did Reinke, Ellicott, and Harris's study of middle-class women reveal about major transitional periods in the life cycle?

Reinke, Ellicott, and Harris found that middle-class women go through major transitional periods that can be related more easily to phases in the family cycle than to chronological age.

Key Terms

life structure (p. 343)
midlife crisis (p. 344)

Later Adulthood

What are some physical changes generally associated with later adulthood?

In addition to obvious changes in appearance, physical changes generally associated with later adulthood include a decline in sensory capacity and in heart, lung, kidney, and muscle function along with an increase in the number of chronic conditions such as arthritis, heart problems, and high blood pressure.

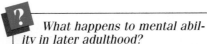

What happens to mental ability in later adulthood?

Crystallized intelligence shows no significant age-related decline; fluid intelligence does decline. Although older adults perform tasks more slowly, those who keep mentally and physi-

cally active can usually maintain their necessary mental skills as long as their health holds out.

What is Alzheimer's disease?

Alzheimer's disease is an incurable form of dementia characterized by a progressive deterioration of intellect and personality, resulting from widespread degeneration of brain cells.

According to Kübler-Ross, what stages are experienced by terminally ill patients as they come to terms with death?

Kübler-Ross maintains that terminally ill patients go through five stages in coming to terms with death: denial, anger, bargaining, depression, and acceptance.

Key Terms

crystallized intelligence (p. 348)
fluid intelligence (p. 348)
senile dementia (p. 348)
Alzheimer's disease (p. 348)

10

MOTIVATION AND EMOTION

CHAPTER OUTLINE

Introduction to Motivation

Theories of Motivation

Instinct Theories of Motivation

Drive-Reduction Theory: Striving to Keep a Balanced Internal State

Arousal Theory: Striving for an Optimal Level of Arousal

Maslow's Hierarchy of Needs: Putting Our Needs in Order

The Primary Drives: Hunger and Thirst

Thirst: We All Have Two Kinds

The Biological Basis of Hunger: Internal Hunger Cues

Other Factors Influencing Hunger: External Eating Cues

Understanding Body Weight: Why We Weigh What We Weigh

Dieting: A National Obsession

Social Motives

The Need for Achievement: The Drive to Excel

Fear of Success

The What and Why of Emotions

Motivation and Emotion: What Is the Connection?

The Components of Emotions: The Physical, the Cognitive, and the Behavioral

Theories of Emotion: Which Comes First, the Thought or the Feeling?

The Polygraph: Lie Detector or Emotion Detector?

The Expression of Emotion

The Range of Emotion: How Wide Is It?

The Development of Facial Expressions in Infants: Smiles and Frowns Come Naturally

World of Psychology: Facial Expressions for the Basic Emotions— A Universal Language

Cultural Rules for Displaying Emotion

Emotion as a Form of Communication

Experiencing Emotion

The Facial-Feedback Hypothesis: Does the Face Cause the Feeling?

Emotion and Rational Thinking

World of Psychology: Gender Differences in Experiencing Emotion

Love: The Strongest Emotional Bond

Applications: Eating Disorders—The Tyranny of the Scale

Thinking Critically

Chapter Summary and Review

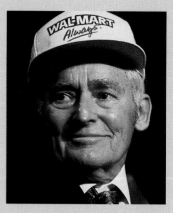

Picture a wheeler-dealer in grand fashion, a tycoon with a capital T, a champion of conspicuous consumption with an insatiable appetite for all things material—bigger, faster, more. Have you got the picture? You are looking at Donald Trump. At the peak of his power in 1989, Trump owned gambling casinos and hotels in New Jersey and grand hotels, housing units, and Trump Tower in New York—an empire valued at hundreds of millions of dollars.

How did Trump get his start? He was child of privilege. His father, Fred, amassed a $40 million fortune as a real estate developer. Through the 1970s and 1980s, Donald Trump was able to spin those millions into a billion plus. Then his troubles began to mount. An extramarital affair with model Marla Maples caused his wife Ivana to divorce him. His bankers and other investors lost confidence in his grand schemes and in his ability to repay his loans. Falling on hard times in the early 1990s, Trump owed more than he owned—nearly a billion dollars more. Passing a beggar on the sidewalks of New York whose "contribution" box sat nearby, Trump is said to have remarked, "See that man? He is 945 million dollars richer than I am."

But Trump came back. Motivated to extract his empire from debt, he wooed other wealthy investors as partners in his enterprises and took a new partner in his personal life, marrying Marla Maples in 1994. By the mid-1990s Donald Trump had a new wife, a new baby, and new financial partners and was rapidly retiring the debt on his billion-dollar empire.

A study in excess and exaggeration, Donald Trump has always enjoyed flaunting his wealth and bragging about his conquests. His way of life has been one of the most flamboyant "lifestyles of the rich and famous." What motivates him?

Now meet a very different person. This man would rise early every morning and have a simple breakfast with his wife in their small-town home in the hilly Ozark region of Arkansas. He would climb into his beat-up 1978 Ford pickup truck and drive a few miles to his work.

This man, a child of poverty, worked his way though the University of Missouri by selling newspapers and found a job as a management trainee at a J.C. Penney store in Iowa. Then came World War II, and in 1942 he was drafted. After the war, he scraped together enough money to open his own small store in rural Arkansas, but he had to close it in 1951 when the building owner would not renew his lease.

He started all over again, and years passed before he began to achieve success in business. When someone remarked about the extent of his growing wealth, he replied, "Aw, it's only paper. All I've got is a pickup truck and some stock in Wal-Mart."

Have you heard of this man, and do you know how much "paper" he was talking about? Sam Walton built a merchandising empire with his Wal-Mart stores, and the "paper" he so casually dismissed was worth more than $20 billion in 1992 and is still growing. But Walton was not just another billionaire. Twice as wealthy as the second-richest person on the 1988 *Forbes 400* list of the 400 wealthiest people, Walton split his billions with his wife and their four children in 1989. He wanted to escape the "embarrassment" of being called the richest person in America.

Sam Walton was obviously not motivated primarily by the things that money can buy. Richest of the rich in America, he lived a simple, frugal lifestyle—no mansions, no yachts, no fleet of superjets or limousines. Only $20 billion worth of paper—and a pickup truck. Sam Walton died in 1992.

Psychologists have always been interested in why people do the things they do. What made the lifestyles of Donald Trump and Sam Walton so different? What motivated them? More importantly, what motivates us?

? *What is the difference between intrinsic and extrinsic motivation?*

Introduction to Motivation

In our study of **motivation**, we will look at the underlying processes that initiate, direct, and sustain behavior in order to satisfy physiological and psychological needs. At any given time our behavior might be explained by one or a combination of **motives**—needs or desires that energize and direct behavior toward a goal. Motives can arise from an internal need, such as when we are hun-

TABLE 10.1 Intrinsic and Extrinsic Motivation

	Description	Examples
Intrinsic motivation	An activity is pursued as an end in itself because it is enjoyable and rewarding.	A person anonymously donates a large sum of money to a university to fund scholarships for deserving students. A child reads several books each week because reading is fun.
Extrinsic motivation	An activity is pursued to gain an external reward or to avoid an undesirable consequence.	A person agrees to donate a large sum of money to a university for the construction of a building, provided it will bear the family name. A child reads two books each week to avoid losing television privileges.

gry and are motivated to find something to eat. In this case we are pushed into action from within. Other motives originate from outside ourselves, as when some external stimulus, or **incentive**, pulls or entices us to act. After finishing a huge meal, some people yield to the temptation of a delicious dessert. At times like this, it is the enticement of the external tempter, not the internal need for food, that moves us.

The intensity of our motivation, which depends on the number and the strength of the motives involved, has a bearing on the effort and the persistence with which we pursue our goals. Sometimes we pursue an activity as an end in itself simply because it is enjoyable, not because any external reward is attached to it. This type of motivation is known as **intrinsic motivation**. On the other hand, when we engage in activities not because they are enjoyable, but in order to gain some external reward or to avoid some undesirable consequence, we are pulled by **extrinsic motivation**. If you are working hard in this course solely because you find the subject interesting, then your motivation is intrinsic. But if you are studying only to meet a requirement or to satisfy some other external need, your motivation is extrinsic. In real life, the motives for many activities are both intrinsic and extrinsic. You may love your job, but you would probably be motivated to leave if your salary, an important extrinsic motivator, were taken away. Table 10.1 gives examples of intrinsic and extrinsic motivation.

What do the experts say about the motives behind our behavior? Let's consider some theories of motivation.

Theories of Motivation

Do we do the things we do because of our inherent nature—the inborn, biological urges that push us from within? Or, do we act because of the incentives that pull us from without? Obviously both forces influence us, but theories of motivation differ in the relative power they attribute to each. The most thoroughly biological theories of motivation are the instinct theories.

motivation: The process that initiates, directs, and sustains behavior to satisfy physiological or psychological needs.

motives: Needs or desires that energize and direct behavior toward a goal.

incentive: An external stimulus that motivates behavior (examples: money, fame).

intrinsic motivation: The desire to perform an act because it is satisfying or pleasurable in and of itself.

extrinsic motivation: The desire to perform an act to gain a reward or to avoid an undesirable consequence.

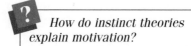

How do instinct theories explain motivation?

instinct: An inborn, unlearned, fixed pattern of behavior that is characteristic of an entire species.

instinct theory: The notion that human behavior is motivated by certain innate tendencies, or instincts, shared by all individuals.

drive-reduction theory: A theory of motivation suggesting that a need creates an unpleasant state of arousal or tension called a drive, which impels the organism to engage in behavior that will satisfy the need and reduce tension.

What is the drive-reduction theory of motivation?

drive: A state of tension or arousal brought about by an underlying need, which motivates one to engage in behavior that will satisfy the need and reduce the tension.

homeostasis: The tendency of the body to maintain a balanced internal state with regard to oxygen level, body temperature, blood sugar, water balance, and so forth.

Instinct Theories of Motivation

Scientists have learned much about instincts by observing animal behavior. Spiders instinctively spin their intricate webs without having *learned* the technique from other spiders. It is neither a choice they make nor a task they learn, but an **instinct**—an inborn, unlearned, fixed pattern of behavior that is characteristic of an entire species. An instinct does not improve with practice, and an animal will perform it the same way even if it has never seen another member of its species. Even when their web-spinning glands are removed, spiders still perform the complex spinning movements and then lay their eggs in the imaginary web they have spun. So instincts explain much of animal behavior.

But can human motivation be explained by **instinct theory**—the notion that human behavior is motivated by certain innate, unlearned tendencies or instincts that are shared by all individuals? The idea of attributing human as well as animal behavior to instincts was not seriously considered until Charles Darwin, in his *Origin of Species* (1859), suggested that humans evolved from lower animals. The notion of the continuity of the species paved the way for the application of the concept of instinct to explain human behavior.

Later, William James (1890) claimed that human behavior is even more instinctive than the behavior of other animals. Another instinct theorist, William McDougall (1908), said that instincts were "the prime movers of all human activity," and he identified what he considered to be 17 instincts. Even Sigmund Freud believed that instincts motivated much of human behavior, but he considered instinctive sexual and aggressive urges to be the prime motivators.

Instinct theory was widely accepted by psychologists and others for the first 20 or 30 years of this century. Over the course of those decades, the list of instincts expanded until thousands of instincts were being proposed to explain human behavior. Common experience alone suggests that human behavior is too richly diverse, and often too unpredictable, to be considered fixed and invariant across our species. Most present-day psychologists reject instinct theory as an explanation of human motivation.

Drive-Reduction Theory: Striving to Keep a Balanced Internal State

Another major attempt to explain motivation, human and otherwise, is the **drive-reduction theory**, or the drive theory, which was popularized by Clark Hull (1943). According to Hull, all living organisms have certain biological needs that must be met if they are to survive. A need gives rise to an internal state of tension or arousal called a **drive,** and we are motivated to reduce it. For example, when we are deprived of food or go too long without water, our biological need causes a state of tension, in this case the hunger or thirst drive. We become motivated to seek food or water to reduce the drive and satisfy our biological need.

Drive-reduction theory is derived largely from the biological concept of **homeostasis**—the tendency of the body to maintain a balanced, internal state in order to ensure physical survival. Body temperature, blood sugar, water balance, oxygen—in short, everything required for physical existence—must be maintained in a state of equilibrium, or balance. When this state is disturbed, a drive is created to restore the balance, as shown in Figure 10.1. But drive theory cannot fully account for the broad range of human motivation.

It is true that we are sometimes motivated to reduce tension, as the drive-reduction theory states, but often we are just as motivated to increase it. Why do people seek activities that actually create a state of tension—hang-gliding, horror movies, and bungee-jumping? Why do animals and humans alike engage in exploratory behavior when it does not serve to reduce any primary drive?

FIGURE 10.1

Drive-Reduction Theory

Drive-reduction theory is based on the biological concept of homeostasis—the body's natural tendency to maintain a state of internal balance, or equilibrium. When the equilibrium becomes disturbed (as when we are thirsty and need water), a drive (internal state of arousal) emerges. Then the organism is motivated to take action to satisfy the need, thus reducing the drive and restoring equilibrium.

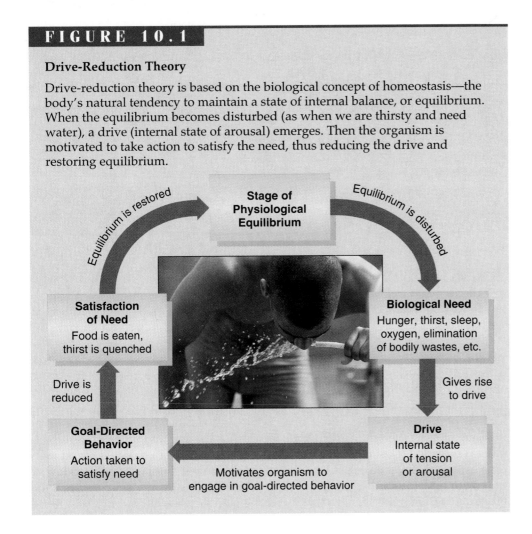

Arousal Theory: Striving for an Optimal Level of Arousal

Arousal theory can answer some of the puzzling questions that drive-reduction theory cannot answer. **Arousal** refers to a person's state of alertness and mental and physical activation. It ranges from no arousal (as in the comatose), to moderate arousal (when we are pursuing normal day-to-day activities), to high arousal (when we are excited and highly stimulated).

Unlike drive-reduction theory, **arousal theory** does not suggest that we are always motivated to reduce arousal or tension. Arousal theory states that we are motivated to maintain an optimal level of arousal. If arousal is less than the optimal level, we do something to stimulate it; if arousal exceeds the optimal level, we seek to reduce the stimulation.

Biological needs, such as the need for food and water, increase our arousal. But we also become aroused when we encounter new stimuli or when the intensity of stimuli is increased, as with loud noises, bright lights, or foul odors. And of course, certain kinds of drugs—stimulants such as caffeine, nicotine, amphetamines, and cocaine—also increase arousal.

Our level of arousal affects how we feel. Some researchers claim that emotional feelings are negative at both extremes of the arousal continuum, and that people generally feel better when their arousal level is somewhere in the middle (Berlyne, 1971). Others disagree and suggest that we are not emotionally happi-

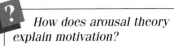
How does arousal theory explain motivation?

arousal: A state of alertness and mental and physical activation.

arousal theory: A theory suggesting that the aim of motivation is to maintain an optimal level of arousal.

Review and Reflect 10.1 *Theories of Motivation*

Theory	View	Example
Instinct theory	Behavior is the result of innate, unlearned tendencies. (This view has been rejected by most modern psychologists.)	Two people fighting because of their aggressive instinct.
Drive-reduction theory	Behavior results from the need to reduce an internal state of tension or arousal.	Eating to reduce hunger.
Arousal theory	Behavior results from the need to maintain an optimal level of arousal.	Climbing a mountain for excitement; listening to classical music for relaxation.

est in the middle of the arousal continuum, but at high arousal when we want stimulation, and at low arousal when we want peace and serenity.

Review and Reflect Table 10.1 summarizes three major motivation theories that we have discussed: instinct theory, drive-reduction theory, and arousal theory.

Stimulus Motives: Increasing Stimulation When arousal is too low, **stimulus motives,** such as curiosity and the motives to explore, to manipulate objects, and to play, cause us to increase stimulation. Stimulus motives are found in other animals as well as in humans. Young monkeys will play with mechanical puzzles for long periods just for the stimulation of doing so (Harlow, 1950). Rats will explore intricate mazes when they are neither thirsty nor hungry and when no reinforcement is provided (Dashiell, 1925). According to Berlyne (1960), rats will spend more time exploring novel objects than familiar objects. So will humans. Children love to play with new toys and to open presents to see what is inside. Adults, too, enjoy tinkering with interesting, new objects, working on puzzles, and exploring.

Arousal and Performance There is often a close link between arousal and performance. According to the **Yerkes–Dodson law,** performance on tasks is best when arousal level is appropriate to the difficulty of the task. We tend to perform better on simple tasks when arousal is relatively high. Tasks of moderate difficulty are best accomplished when our arousal is moderate; complex or difficult tasks when arousal is lower (see Figure 10.2). But performance suffers when arousal level is either too high or too low for the task. You may have experienced too much or too little arousal when taking an exam. Perhaps your arousal was so low that your mind was sluggish and you didn't finish the test; or you might have been so keyed up that you couldn't remember much of what you had studied.

Individual Differences in Arousal: Too Much for One Is Too Little for Another We differ in the level of arousal we normally prefer. Some of us are sensation seekers, who love the thrill of new experiences and adventure. Sensation seekers are willing, even eager, to take risks. They are easily bored and experience little fear or uncertainty (McCourt et al., 1993). Other people are the opposite: They enjoy the routine and the predictable, avoid risk, and fare best when arousal is relatively low.

On tests that measure sensation seeking, people vary greatly in their scores. There may be gender and cultural differences in sensation-seeking tendencies. Some researchers have found that males tend to score higher than females, and white Americans tend to score higher than African Americans (Zuckerman, 1979).

stimulus motives: Motives that cause us to increase stimulation and that appear to be unlearned (examples: curiosity and the need to explore, manipulate objects, and play).

Yerkes–Dodson law: The principle that performance on tasks is best when the arousal level is appropriate to the difficulty of the task—higher arousal for simple tasks, moderate arousal for tasks of moderate difficulty, and lower arousal for complex tasks.

FIGURE 10.2

The Yerkes-Dodson Law

The optimal level of arousal varies according to the difficulty of the task. Arousal levels should be relatively high for simple tasks, moderate for moderately difficult tasks, and lower for difficult tasks.

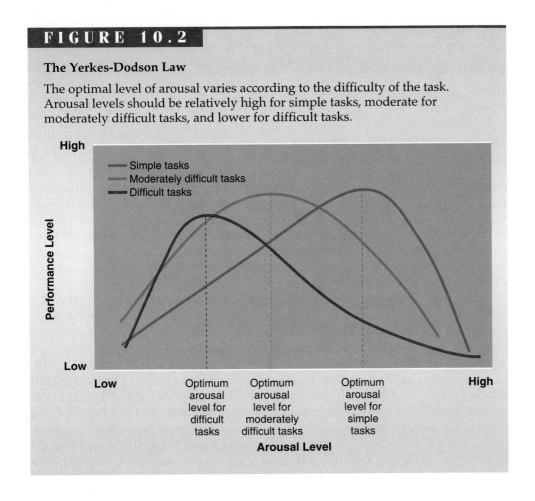

Sometimes arousal can be too low for too long for anyone, even for those who would score lowest on the scale.

The Effects of Sensory Deprivation: Sensory Nothingness How would you like to be paid to do absolutely nothing? In an early experiment Bexton and others (1954) at McGill University gave student volunteers this opportunity when they studied the effects of **sensory deprivation**—a condition in which sensory stimulation is reduced to a minimum or eliminated.

Students had to lie motionless in a specially designed sensory deprivation chamber in which sensory stimulation was severely restricted. They wore translucent goggles that reduced visual input to a diffused light. Their hands were placed in cotton gloves, and cardboard cuffs were placed over their lower arms, preventing the sensation of touch. The only sound they heard was the hum of an air conditioner through a foam-rubber headpiece. The subjects could eat, drink, and go to the bathroom when they wanted to. Occasionally they would take tests of motor and mental function. Otherwise they were confined to their sensationless prison.

Did they enjoy the experience? Hardly! Half the subjects quit the experiment after the first 2 days. Eventually the remaining subjects became irritable, confused, and unable to concentrate. They began to have visual hallucinations. Some began to hear imaginary voices and music and felt as if they were receiving electric shocks or being hit by pellets. Their performance on motor and cognitive tasks deteriorated, and none of the subjects said they liked the experiment.

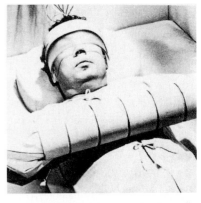

Sensory stimulation is reduced to a minimum for participants in sensory deprivation experiments.

sensory deprivation: A condition in which sensory stimulation is reduced to a minimum or eliminated.

Other studies using milder forms of sensory deprivation, known as sensory restriction, have produced some beneficial effects. Positive results range from improved concentration (Lilly, 1956) to better control over cigarette smoking (Suedfeld, 1990) and other addictions (Borrie, 1991). Some studies have shown that sensory restriction has beneficial effects for autistic children (Harrison & Barabasz, 1991).

Maslow's Hierarchy of Needs: Putting Our Needs in Order

Humans have a variety of needs or motives. Clearly some needs are more critical to sustaining life than others. We could live without self-esteem, but obviously we could not live long without air to breathe, water to drink, or food to eat.

Abraham Maslow (1970) proposed a **hierarchy of needs** (Figure 10.3) to account for the range of human motivation. He placed physiological needs such as food and water at the base of the hierarchy, stating that these needs must be adequately satisfied before higher ones can be considered.

If our physiological needs (for water, food, sleep, sex, and shelter) are adequately met, then the motives at the next higher level (the safety and the security needs) will come into play. When these needs are satisfied, we climb another level to satisfy our needs to belong and to love and be loved. Maslow believed that failure to meet the belonging and love needs deprives individuals of acceptance, affection, and intimacy and is the most prominent factor in human adjustment problems. Still higher in the hierarchy are the needs for self-esteem and the esteem of others. These needs involve our sense of worth and competence, our need to achieve and be recognized for it, and our need to be respected.

At the top of Maslow's hierarchy is the need for **self-actualization**, the need to actualize or realize our full potential. People may reach self-actualization

> *How does Maslow's hierarchy of needs account for human motivation?*

hierarchy of needs: Maslow's theory of motivation, in which needs are arranged in order of urgency ranging from physical needs to security needs, belonging needs, esteem needs, and finally the need for self-actualization.

self-actualization: The development of one's full potential; the highest need on Maslow's hierarchy.

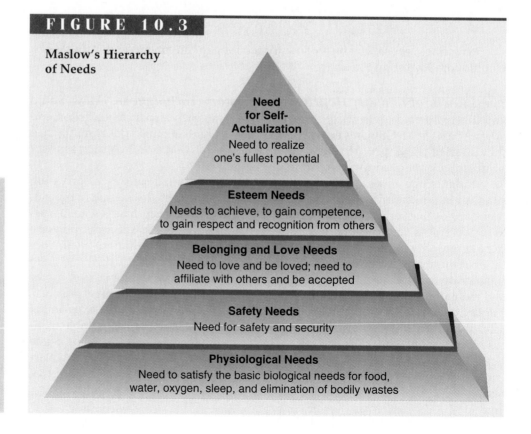

FIGURE 10.3

Maslow's Hierarchy of Needs

Need for Self-Actualization
Need to realize one's fullest potential

Esteem Needs
Needs to achieve, to gain competence, to gain respect and recognition from others

Belonging and Love Needs
Need to love and be loved; need to affiliate with others and be accepted

Safety Needs
Need for safety and security

Physiological Needs
Need to satisfy the basic biological needs for food, water, oxygen, sleep, and elimination of bodily wastes

through achievement in virtually any area of life's work. But the surest path to self-actualization is one in which a person finds significant and consistent ways to serve and contribute to the well-being of humankind.

Although Maslow's hierarchy of needs has been a popular notion, appealing to many, it has not been verified by empirical research. The steps on the hierarchy cannot be said to be invariant, or the same for all people (Wahba & Bridwell, 1976). It is well known that in some people the desire for success and recognition is so strong that they are prepared to sacrifice safety, security, and personal relationships to achieve it. A few people are willing to sacrifice their very lives for others or for a cause to which they are committed. Perhaps they, too, have a hierarchy, but one in which the order of needs is somewhat different. You will learn more about Maslow when we discuss humanistic psychology in Chapter 12.

Memory Check 10.1

1. When you engage in an activity in order to gain a reward or to avoid an unpleasant consequence, your motivation is (intrinsic, extrinsic).

2. In its original form, drive-reduction theory focused primarily on which of the following needs and the drives they produce?
   a. cognitive   c. biological
   b. psychological   d. emotional

3. Which theory suggests that human behavior is motivated by certain innate, unlearned tendencies that are shared by all individuals?
   a. arousal theory   c. Maslow's theory
   b. instinct theory   d. drive-reduction theory

4. According to arousal theory, people seek _____ arousal.
   a. minimized   c. decreased
   b. increased   d. optimal

5. According to Maslow's hierarchy of needs, which needs must be satisfied before a person will try to satisfy the belonging and love needs?
   a. safety and self-actualization needs
   b. self-actualization and esteem needs
   c. physiological and safety needs
   d. physiological and esteem needs

Answers: 1. extrinsic 2. c 3. b 4. d 5. c

The Primary Drives: Hunger and Thirst

The drive-reduction theory suggests that motivation is based largely on the **primary drives**, those which are unlearned and which seek to satisfy biological needs. Two of the most important primary drives are thirst and hunger.

Thirst: We All Have Two Kinds

Thirst is a basic biological drive, for all animals must have a continuous supply of fluid. Adequate fluid is critical because the body itself is about 75 percent water. Without any intake of fluids, we can survive only about 4 or 5 days.

But how do we know when we are thirsty? When we have a dry mouth and throat, or a powerful urge to drink? Yes, but thirst is more complex than that. There are two types of thirst. One type (extracellular thirst) occurs when fluid is lost from the body tissues rather than from the body cells. If you are exercising heavily or doing almost anything in hot weather, you will perspire and lose bodily fluid. Bleeding, vomiting, and diarrhea also rob your body of fluid. Extracellular fluid

? *Under what kinds of conditions do the two types of thirst occur?*

primary drive: A state of tension or arousal arising from a biological need; one not based on learning.

A rat whose satiety center has been destroyed can weigh up to six times as much as a normal rat.

?
What are the roles of the lateral hypothalamus and the ventromedial hypothalamus in the regulation of eating behavior?

lateral hypothalamus (LH): The part of the hypothalamus that supposedly acts as a feeding center and, when activated, signals an animal to eat; when the LH is destroyed, the animal refuses to eat.

ventromedial hypothalamus (VMH): The part of the hypothalamus that presumably acts as a satiety center and, when activated, signals an animal to stop eating; when the area is destroyed, the animal overeats, becoming obese.

?
What are some of the body's hunger and satiety signals?

loss takes fluid from the surrounding tissues, rather than from the body's cells. Perhaps you have heard that it is not a good idea to drink a cold beer or any other type of alcohol to quench your thirst on a very hot day. Alcohol increases extracellular fluid loss. This is why most people awaken with a powerful thirst after drinking heavily the night before.

Another type of thirst (intracellular thirst) involves the loss of water from inside the body cells. When we eat a lot of salty food, the water–sodium balance in the blood and in the tissues outside the cells is disturbed. The salt cannot readily enter the cells, so the cells release some of their own water to restore the balance. As the body cells become dehydrated, thirst is stimulated so that we drink to increase the water volume (Robertson, 1983). This might explain why salted peanuts and pretzels are provided at so many bars free of charge.

The Biological Basis of Hunger: Internal Hunger Cues

Hunger is a biological drive operating in all animals, and food is the substance that satisfies or reduces the hunger drive. You may have thought that the whole matter was very simple—when we get hungry we eat, and when we feel full we stop. But what happens in the body to make us feel hungry, and what causes satiety—the feeling of being full or satisfied?

The Role of the Hypothalamus: Our Feeding and Satiety Centers

Researchers have found two areas of the hypothalamus that are of central importance in regulating eating behavior and thus affect the hunger drive (Steffens et al., 1988). The **lateral hypothalamus (LH)** acts in part as a feeding center to excite eating. Stimulating the feeding center causes animals to eat even when they are full (Delgado & Anand, 1953). When the feeding center is destroyed, animals initially refuse to eat (Anand & Brobeck, 1951).

The **ventromedial hypothalamus (VMH)** presumably acts as a satiety center, and when active, it inhibits eating (Hernandez & Hoebel, 1989). If the satiety center is electrically stimulated, animals stop eating (Duggan & Booth, 1986). If the VMH is surgically removed, animals soon eat their way to gross obesity (Hetherington & Ranson, 1940; Parkinson & Weingarten, 1990). One rat whose satiety center was destroyed weighed nearly six times as much as a normal rat. In human terms this would be like a 150-pound person ballooning up to 900 pounds.

The immediate effect of gorging to obesity or refusing to eat altogether did occur with the destruction of a rat's VMH or LH. Nevertheless, some time after the surgery, the rats began to establish more normal eating patterns. But the obese rats continued to maintain an above-average body weight, and the noneating rats eventually established a below-average body weight (Hoebel & Teitelbaum, 1966). Some researchers believe that destruction of the VMH causes animals to lose the ability to adjust their metabolism and thereby stabilize their body weight (Vilberg & Keesey, 1990).

Other organs and substances in the body also play a role in our feelings of hunger and satiety.

The Role of the Stomach: Hunger Pangs

The fullness of the stomach affects our feeling of hunger. The stomach has a capacity of about 1 pint when empty and stretches to hold 2½ pints when full (Avraham, 1989). Generally, the more full or distended the stomach, the less hunger we feel (Pappas et al., 1989).

Stomach Contractions How do you know when you are hungry? Do you have stomach contractions called hunger pangs? In a classic experiment, Cannon and Washburn (1912) demonstrated a close correlation between stomach contractions and the perception of hunger. But their discovery does not necessarily mean that the sensation of hunger is caused by stomach contractions. Humans and other animals continue to experience hunger even when it is impossible for them to feel stomach contractions. Human cancer and ulcer patients who have had their entire stomach removed still report feeling hunger pangs (Janowitz & Grossman, 1950).

If animals and humans without stomachs continue to experience hunger and satiety, then there must be still other hunger and satiety signals. The search for these signals moved from the stomach to the blood, because the bloodstream is the means of transporting the products of digestion to the cells of the body.

Other Hunger and Satiety Signals Templeton and Quigley (1930) found that the blood of an animal that has eaten its fill is different from the blood of an excessively hungry animal. In one study, blood was taken from a very hungry dog and from a dog that had recently eaten. The blood taken from each dog was used as a transfusion to be given to the other. After the transfusions, the dog that had previously eaten began having stomach contractions even though its stomach was full. When the hungry dog that had been experiencing stomach contractions received the blood transfusion, its stomach contractions stopped.

The question is: What was in the blood that signaled hunger or satiety? Researchers began investigating factors such as the blood levels of glucose—a simple sugar remaining after carbohydrates have been digested.

Glucose and Hunger Blood levels of glucose are monitored by nutrient detectors in the liver that send this information to the brain (Friedman et al., 1986). Hunger is stimulated when the brain receives the message that blood levels of glucose are low.

Insulin Levels in the Blood Insulin, a hormone produced by the pancreas, chemically converts glucose into energy that is usable by the cells. Elevations in insulin cause an increase in hunger, in food intake, and in a desire for sweets (Rodin et al., 1985). Chronic oversecretion of insulin stimulates hunger and often leads to obesity.

Satiety Signals Released from the Gastrointestinal Tract Some of the substances secreted by the gastrointestinal tract during digestion are released into the blood and act as satiety signals (Flood et al., 1990). The hormone cholecystokinin (CCK) is one satiety signal that causes us to limit the amount of food we eat during a meal (Woods & Gibbs, 1989). A deficiency of CCK may be involved in bulimia nervosa, a disorder in which people go on eating binges, consuming immense quantities of food, only to purge the body of the food by self-induced vomiting (Lydiard et al., 1993).

We are pushed to eat not only by our internal hunger drive. There are also external factors that stimulate hunger.

Other Factors Influencing Hunger: External Eating Cues

What are some nonbiological factors that influence what and how much we eat?

Smell that coffee brewing. Look at that mouthwatering chocolate cake. Apart from our internal hunger, there are external factors influencing what, where, and how much we eat. Sensory cues such as the taste, smell, and appearance of food stimulate the appetite. For many the hands of the clock alone, signaling mealtime, are enough to prompt a quest for food. Even eating with other people tends to stimulate us to eat more than when we are eating alone (de Castro & de Castro, 1989).

Just the sight of mouth-watering foods can make us want to eat, even when we aren't actually hungry.

What are some factors that account for variations in body weight?

Susceptibility to External Eating Cues: Can You Resist Them?   Are we all equally susceptible to such external eating cues? Stanley Schachter and colleagues suggested that overweight people are overly responsive to these external cues and are therefore more likely to overeat (Schachter & Gross, 1968). Normal-weight individuals, on the other hand, were thought to be more affected by internal rather than external cues, eating when they are actually in need of food. But later studies show that the degree of external or internal responsiveness was not strongly correlated with the degree of overweight (Rodin, 1981).

However, external cues *can* trigger internal processes that motivate a person to eat. The sight and smell of appetizing food can trigger the release of insulin, particularly in those who are externally responsive (Rodin et al., 1977). Even in rats, environmental cues previously associated with food cause an increase in insulin level (Detke et al., 1989). For some individuals, "simply seeing and thinking about food" can cause an elevated level of insulin, and such people have a greater tendency to gain weight (Rodin, 1985).

The Palatability of Food: Tempting Tastes   How good a particular food tastes—that is, how palatable the food is—seems to work somewhat independently of hunger and satiety in determining how much we eat (Rogers, 1990). Otherwise, most of us would refuse the pie after eating a big Thanksgiving dinner. This can explain why dieters are often tempted to go off their diets not in response to hunger alone, but in response to the sight and smell of palatable food (Rogers & Hill, 1989).

Foods that are sweet and high in fat tend to stimulate the human appetite (Ball & Grinker, 1981), even when the sweetness is provided by artificial sweeteners (Blundell et al., 1988; Tordoff, 1988). In fact, even artificially sweetened chewing gum has been found to increase hunger (Tordoff & Alleva, 1990).

All cultures have their own particular preferences when it comes to food. Which are better—biscuits or bagels, egg-drop soup or creole gumbo, chicken curry or chicken and dumplings? You might say it is a matter of taste, but researchers say that taste itself is largely a matter of culture.

Figure 10.4 summarizes the factors that stimulate and inhibit eating.

Understanding Body Weight: Why We Weigh What We Weigh

Pencil-thin models seen in television commercials and fashion magazines have come to represent the ideal body for many American women. But most of these models have only 10 to 15 percent body fat, far below the 22 to 26 percent considered normal for women (Brownell, 1991). Fat has become a negative term, even though some body fat is necessary. Men need 3 percent and women, 12 percent, just for survival. And in order for a woman's reproductive system to function properly, she must maintain 20 percent body fat.

Extremes in either fatness or thinness can pose health risks. An abnormal desire for thinness can result in eating disorders such as the self-starvation in anorexia nervosa and the pattern of binging and purging found in bulimia nervosa (see the Applications section at the end of the chapter). At the other extreme are the 34 million Americans suffering from obesity—excessive fatness—with its increased risk of high blood pressure, coronary heart disease, stroke, and cancer (Whelan & Stare, 1990).

In 1994 the third in a series of studies—the National Health and Nutrition Examination Surveys—was published, bearing the bad news that for all racial and ethnic groups combined, a full one-third of American adults aged 20 and older are overweight (Kuczmarski et al., 1994). Overweight for men is defined as

FIGURE 10.4

Factors That Inhibit and Stimulate Eating

Both biological and environmental factors combine to inhibit or to stimulate eating.

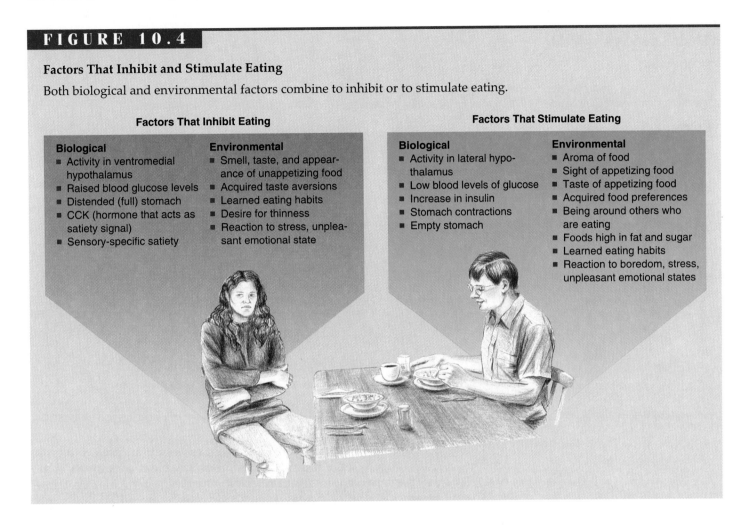

Factors That Inhibit Eating

Biological
- Activity in ventromedial hypothalamus
- Raised blood glucose levels
- Distended (full) stomach
- CCK (hormone that acts as satiety signal)
- Sensory-specific satiety

Environmental
- Smell, taste, and appearance of unappetizing food
- Acquired taste aversions
- Learned eating habits
- Desire for thinness
- Reaction to stress, unpleasant emotional state

Factors That Stimulate Eating

Biological
- Activity in lateral hypothalamus
- Low blood levels of glucose
- Increase in insulin
- Stomach contractions
- Empty stomach

Environmental
- Aroma of food
- Sight of appetizing food
- Taste of appetizing food
- Acquired food preferences
- Being around others who are eating
- Foods high in fat and sugar
- Learned eating habits
- Reaction to boredom, stress, unpleasant emotional states

24 percent above their desirable weight; for women, 20 percent above. Adults in the United States are now 8 percent heavier than they were in 1976. Figure 10.5 (on page 372) shows the prevalence of overweight for non-Hispanic white, non-Hispanic black, and Mexican American males and females of various age groups.

Although both excessive thinness and obesity result from a long-term imbalance between energy intake and energy expenditure, the cause is not necessarily insufficient or excessive food intake. Obesity is usually caused by a combination of factors that include heredity, metabolic rate, activity level, number of fat cells, and eating habits.

The Role of Genetic Factors in Body Weight Adoption and twin studies reveal the strong influence of genes on body size (Stunkard et al., 1990). And genes are particularly likely to be involved when obesity begins before age 10 (Price et al., 1990). Across all weight classes, from very thin to very obese, children adopted from birth tend to resemble their biological parents more than their adoptive parents in body size. In adoptees, thinness seems to be even more influenced by genes than is obesity (Costanzo & Schiffman, 1989). Also, people may inherit their resting metabolic rate, their tendency to store surplus calories primarily as muscle or fat, and even the pattern of where fat is deposited (Bouchard et al., 1990). Nevertheless, considerable evidence suggests that "childhood eating behavior influences whether the inherited tendency towards obesity is realized" (Sims, 1990, p. 1522).

FIGURE 10.5

Some Ethnic and Gender Differences in Prevalence of Overweight

The prevalence of overweight varies somewhat among non-Hispanic white, non-Hispanic black, and Mexican American males and females of various age groups. (From Kuczmarski et al., 1994.)

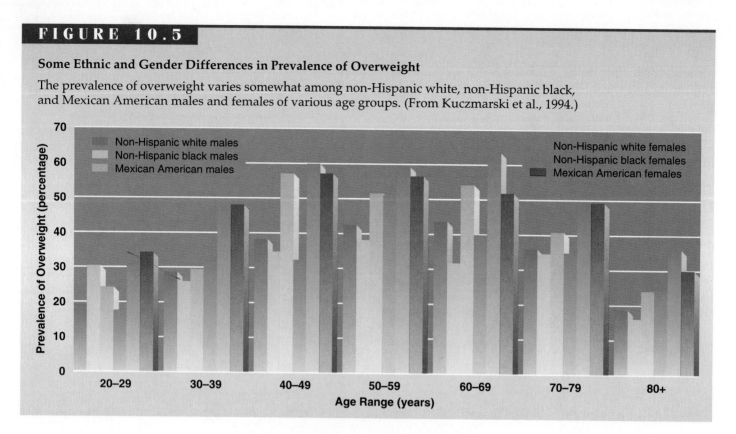

Researchers have discovered a gene in rats that when mutated leads to gross obesity—a gain of up to three times the rats' normal weight (Friedman et al., 1994). Rats that have two copies of the obesity gene lack a particular protein— one that suppresses appetite, increases metabolic rate, and regulates fat stores (Pelleymounter et al., 1995). When obese rats were injected with this protein, they lost 30 percent of their body weight within 2 weeks. Even normal rats had a 12-percent weight loss (Halaas et al., 1995). Researchers hope that the protein will have similar effects in humans, yielding an effective weight-loss treatment.

Metabolic Rate: Burning Energy—Slow or Fast Metabolism refers to all the physical and chemical processes that are carried out in the body to sustain life. And food is the source of energy required to carry out these processes. The rate at which the body burns calories to produce energy is called the **metabolic rate**. Physical activity uses up only about one-third of our energy intake; the other two-thirds is consumed by the maintenance processes that keep us alive. When there is an imbalance between energy intake (how much we eat) and output (how much energy we use), our weight changes. If our calorie intake exceeds our daily energy requirement, we gain weight. If our daily energy requirement exceeds our caloric intake, we lose weight.

metabolic rate (meh-tuh-BALL-ik): The rate at which the body burns calories to produce energy.

fat cells: Numbering 30 to 40 billion, cells that serve as storehouses for liquefied fat in the body; with weight loss, they decrease in size but not in number.

Fat-Cell Theory: Tiny Storage Tanks for Fat Fat-cell theory proposes that fatness is related to the number of **fat cells** in the body. It is estimated that each of us has between 30 and 40 billion fat cells (adipose cells) and that the number is determined by both our genes and our eating habits (Grinker, 1982). Fat cells serve as storehouses for liquefied fat. When we lose weight, we do not lose the fat cells themselves. We lose the fat that is stored in them, and the cells simply shrink (Dietz, 1989).

Researchers once believed that all the fat cells a person would ever have were formed early in life. This is no longer the accepted view. When people overeat beyond the point at which the fat cells reach their capacity, the number of fat cells continues to increase (Rodin & Wing, 1988).

Set-Point Theory: Thin/Fat Thermostat Set-point theory suggests that humans and other mammals are genetically programmed to carry a certain amount of body weight (Keesey, 1988). **Set point** is affected by the number of fat cells in the body and by metabolic rate, both of which are influenced by the genes (Gurin, 1989). Yet people with a genetic propensity to be thin can become very fat indeed if they continually overeat, because over the years they will develop a high set point for body fat.

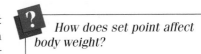 *How does set point affect body weight?*

According to set-point theory, an internal homeostatic system functions to maintain set-point weight, much as a thermostat works to keep temperature near the point at which it is set. Whether we are lean, overweight, or average, when our weight falls below our set point, our appetite increases. When weight climbs above set point, appetite decreases so as to restore the original weight.

According to set-point theory, our rate of energy expenditure is adjusted to maintain the body's set-point weight (Keesey & Powley, 1986). When people gain weight, metabolic rate increases (Dietz, 1989). But when they restrict calories to lose weight, the metabolic rate lowers, causing the body to burn fewer calories and thus make further weight loss more difficult. Increasing the amount of physical activity is the one method recommended for lowering the set point so that the body will store less fat.

Dieting: A National Obsession

At any given time, one out of five adults in the United States is on some kind of reducing diet, but a far larger number—51 percent of women and 43 percent of men—perceive themselves as overweight (Gallup & Newport, 1990a). According to Rodin (1992), the struggle for "the perfect body is like most wars, a costly one—emotionally and physically, to say nothing of financially. It leaves most of us feeling frustrated, ashamed, and defeated" (p. 59). Most diets do produce an initial weight loss—but not once and for all (Serdula et al., 1993; Wadden, 1993). In fact, 95 percent of those who diet do not maintain the weight loss (Williams, 1986).

Why Diets Don't Work To lose weight, a person must decrease calorie intake, increase exercise, or do both. Unfortunately, most people who are trying to lose weight focus only on cutting calories. At first, when overweight people begin to diet and cut their calories, they do lose weight, and fairly quickly if they are on a starvation diet. But as the calorie restriction continues, the rate of weight loss begins to decrease. After an initial shedding of pounds, the dieter's metabolic rate slows down as if to conserve the remaining fat store because fewer calories are being consumed (Weigle et al., 1988).

Why is it almost impossible to maintain weight loss by cutting calories alone?

What can overweight people do to reach their desired weight? Reasonable calorie restriction must be coupled with increased exercise and activity to counteract the body's tendency toward a lower metabolic rate when fewer calories are consumed (Blair, 1993). Starvation diets are self-defeating in the long run. When calories are too severely restricted, even exercise cannot reverse the body's drastic lowering of metabolism and its natural tendency to conserve remaining fat (Ballor et al., 1990). Therefore, women should consume at least 1,000 calories a day, and men 1,500 calories a day, unless they are under a doctor's supervision.

Some encouraging news for overweight exercisers is that the more they weigh, the more calories they burn during exercise compared to a thinner person. And exercise does not increase the appetite. Sometimes exercise alone, without a restriction in diet, can result in weight loss (Frey-Hewitt et al., 1990).

Yo-Yo Dieting Many dieters go through repeated cycles of weight gain and loss, a phenomenon called weight cycling or yo-yo dieting (Brownell, 1988). Some experts suggest that with frequent dieting the body becomes an increasingly effi-

set point: The weight the body normally maintains when one is trying neither to gain nor to lose weight (if weight falls below the normal level, appetite increases and metabolic rate decreases; if weight is gained, appetite decreases and metabolic rate increases so that the original rate is restored).

cient energy conserver, causing the person to lose weight more slowly and regain it more quickly with each succeeding weight cycle (Archambault et al., 1989).

Changing Eating Habits: A Long-Term Solution Dieting is not a long-term solution to the problem of being overweight. Many people believe that once the weight is lost, the diet is no longer necessary and old eating habits can be resumed. But because the old habits caused much of the weight problem, returning to those habits is a sure-fire formula for weight gain. People who return to their old eating habits are rather like compulsive spenders who have their credit cards taken away until their bills are paid. If they resume their old spending habits, the bills will pile up again.

Some evidence suggests that successful weight loss involves more than simply counting calories. It seems that calories eaten in the form of fat are more likely to be stored as body fat than calories eaten as carbohydrates. Miller and others (1990) found that even when obese and thin people have the same caloric intake, thin subjects derive about 29 percent of their calories from fats, while the obese average 35 percent from fat. The composition of the diet may have as much to do with weight gain as the amount of food eaten and the lack of exercise. Counting and limiting the grams of fat may be more beneficial than counting calories to help a person achieve and maintain a desirable body weight. Low-fat diets are healthier, too!

Memory Check 10.2

1. Body cells lose water and become dehydrated when an individual:
   a. perspires heavily.
   b. consumes too much salt.
   c. has diarrhea or vomiting.
   d. drinks too much alcohol.

2. The lateral hypothalamus (LH) acts as a (feeding, satiety) center; the ventromedial hypothalamus (VMH) acts as a (feeding, satiety) center.

3. All of the following are hunger signals *except*:
   a. activity in the lateral hypothalamus.
   b. low levels of glucose in the blood.
   c. the hormone CCK.
   d. high insulin level.

4. Foods that are sweet and high in fat tend to stimulate the appetite. (true/false)

5. Which factor is *most* responsible for how fast your body burns calories to produce energy?
   a. calories consumed   c. eating habits
   b. fat cells   d. metabolic rate

6. According to set-point theory, the body works to (increase, decrease, maintain) body weight.

7. Fat cells never decrease in number. (true/false)

8. Adopted children are more likely to be very thin or obese if their (biological, adoptive) parents are very thin or obese.

9. Increased exercise during dieting is important to counteract the body's tendency to:
   a. increase the fat in the fat cells.
   b. increase the number of fat cells.
   c. lower its metabolic rate.
   d. raise its metabolic rate.

Answers: 1. b 2. feeding, satiety 3. c 4. true 5. d 6. maintain 7. true 8. biological 9. c

What is Murray's contribution to the study of motivation?

social motives: Motives acquired through experience and interaction with others.

Social Motives

Do you have a strong need to be with other people (affiliation) or a need for power or achievement? These needs are three examples of **social motives**, which we learn or acquire through social and cultural experiences. Each of us differs in the strength of various social motives and in the priorities we assign to them. Our highest aspirations, the professions we choose, the partners we are drawn to, and the methods we use to achieve our sense of importance result primarily from our social motives.

In 1938 Henry Murray identified and defined a list of social motives, or needs, such as the need for achievement, recognition, affiliation, dominance, or order. Murray believed that people have social motives in differing degrees. To investigate the strength of various needs, Murray (1938) developed the **Thematic Apperception Test (TAT)**, which consists of a series of pictures of ambiguous situations. Subjects are asked to write a story about each picture—to describe what is going on in the picture, what the person or persons pictured are thinking about, what they may be feeling, and what is likely to be the outcome of the situation. The stories are presumed to reveal the subject's needs and the strength of those needs. (The TAT has also been used as a more general personality test, as described in Chapter 12.)

The Need for Achievement: The Drive to Excel

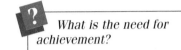

? *What is the need for achievement?*

What explains why Donald Trump seems driven to build an empire? What motivated Sam Walton to bring Wal-Mart stores to happy shoppers in thousands of cities and towns all over the United States? Certainly not biological needs that must be satisfied or drives that must be reduced. Both men were driven by the same social motive, the need for achievement, although they chose to satisfy it in very different ways.

The **need for achievement** (abbreviated *n* Ach) is included on Murray's list of needs. Murray (1938) defined the need for achievement as the motive "to accomplish something difficult. . . . To overcome obstacles and attain a high standard. To excel one's self. To rival and surpass others. To increase self-regard by the successful exercise of talent" (p. 164). The need for achievement, rather than being satisfied with accomplishment, seems to grow as it is fed, not to diminish.

The need for achievement has been researched more vigorously than any other of Murray's needs, and researchers David McClelland and John Atkinson have conducted many of these studies (McClelland et al., 1953; McClelland, 1958, 1961, 1985). Unfortunately, the subjects in these studies have been almost exclusively male.

People with a high need for achievement can overcome even serious disabilities in their efforts to succeed.

To assess achievement motivation, McClelland and Atkinson had subjects view four to six ambiguous pictures from the Thematic Apperception Test and then write stories about them. The content of the subjects' stories was analyzed for references to achievement. Subjects who consistently included achievement themes were scored as being high in achievement motivation. On the basis of a meta-analysis of 105 research studies, Spangler (1992) found support for the TAT as a valid measure of the achievement motivation.

Atkinson's Theory of Achievement Motivation: When Do We Try?

Atkinson (1964) proposed a theory of achievement motivation to explain when people will try to accomplish certain goals. He suggests that when we approach any situation, there are two conflicting factors—our hope for success and our fear of failure. Motivation to avoid failure can cause us to work harder at a task to try to ensure success, or it can cause us to avoid the task altogether.

Whether you strive for a goal depends on three factors: (1) the strength of your need to achieve, (2) your expectation of success, and (3) the incentive value of success or failure at a particular activity (how much you value success in the activity and how distressed you would be if you failed at it). For example, whether you try to achieve an A in psychology will depend on how important

Thematic Apperception Test (TAT): A projective test consisting of drawings of ambiguous human situations, which the subject describes; thought to reveal inner feelings, conflicts, and motives.

need for achievement (*n* Ach): The need to accomplish something difficult and to perform at a high standard of excellence.

an A is to you, whether you believe an A is possible, and how much pride you will feel if you do get an A as opposed to how upset you will be if you do not.

Complete the *Try It!*—which describes a game that is said to reveal high or low achievement motivation.

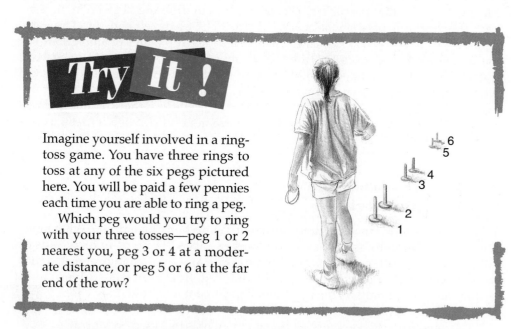

Try It!

Imagine yourself involved in a ring-toss game. You have three rings to toss at any of the six pegs pictured here. You will be paid a few pennies each time you are able to ring a peg.

Which peg would you try to ring with your three tosses—peg 1 or 2 nearest you, peg 3 or 4 at a moderate distance, or peg 5 or 6 at the far end of the row?

> **?** *What are some characteristics shared by people who are high in achievement motivation?*

Characteristics of Achievers: Successful People Possess Them

McClelland and others (1953) found that high achievers differ from low achievers in several ways. People with a high *n* Ach tend to set goals of moderate difficulty. They pursue goals that are challenging yet attainable with hard work, ability, determination, and persistence. Goals that are too easy, those anyone can reach, offer no challenge and hold no interest, because success would not be rewarding (Atkinson, 1958; French, 1955). Impossibly high goals and high risks are also not pursued, because they offer little chance of success and are considered a waste of time. People high in *n* Ach enjoy taking moderate risks in situations that depend on their ability, but they are not gamblers. To become wealthy, businesspeople high in achievement motivation often take moderate risks, ones at which they can succeed, rather than very high risks offering little or no chance of success.

People with low *n* Ach, the researchers claim, are not willing to take chances when it comes to testing their own skills and abilities. They are motivated more by their fear of failure than by their hope and expectation of success. This is why they set either ridiculously low goals, which anyone can attain, or else impossibly high goals (Geen, 1984). After all, who can fault a person for failing to reach a goal that is impossible for almost anyone?

In view of this description, which peg in the ring-toss game in the *Try It!* would people low in achievement motivation try for? If you guessed peg 1 or 2, or peg 5 or 6, you are right. People low in achievement motivation are likely to stand right over peg 1 so they can't possibly fail. Or they may toss the rings at peg 6, hoping that they might be lucky. But failing that, no one can blame them for not attaining a nearly impossible goal. A chance to win a few cents is certainly no incentive for people with a high need for achievement, so they tend to toss their rings at peg 3 or 4, an intermediate distance that offers some challenge. Where did you choose to stand?

People with high n Ach see their success as a result of their own talents, abilities, persistence, and hard work (Kukla, 1972). They typically do not credit luck or the influence of other people for their successes, or blame luck or others for their failures. When people with low n Ach fail, they usually give up quickly and attribute failure to their lack of ability. They believe that luck or fate, rather than effort and ability, is responsible for accomplishment (Weiner, 1974).

Some research indicates that a high or a low need for achievement becomes a fairly stable component of personality (Kagan & Moss, 1962), although the motive may find different expression as people age (Veroff, 1978). In a young person, the need for achievement may be expressed as a need to excel in school. Neumann and others (1988) found that high achievement motivation is related to college students' accomplishments and grades.

In adulthood those high in n Ach are often drawn to business, sometimes starting their own, and to other occupations and professions in which their own efforts can result in high achievement. According to McClelland, it is primarily the achievement motive rather than the profit motive that drives entrepreneurs. They are interested in profits and personal income mainly because it serves as a measure of their competence. Money becomes a symbol of success.

But what about those who want to be achievers, who dream of being rich and famous, yet who are not willing to put forth the effort to achieve it? The person with high n Ach does not fit this picture. People high in achievement motivation may indeed be dreamers, but they are "doers" as well.

Developing Achievement Motivation: Can We Learn It? If achievement motivation, like the other social motives, is primarily learned, how is it learned? Some experts believe that child-rearing practices and values in the home are important factors in developing achievement motivation (McClelland & Pilon, 1983). Parents can foster n Ach if they give their children responsibilities, stress independence when the children are young, and praise them sincerely for genuine accomplishments. Birth order appears to be related to achievement motivation, with first-born and only children showing higher n Ach than younger siblings (Falbo & Polit, 1986). Younger siblings, however, tend to be more sociable and likable than first-born or only children, and this has its rewards too.

Do some people lack achievement motivation because they fear success?

Fear of Success

Have you ever purposely done less than your best to avoid being called a "brain"? Are there some people who are actually afraid of success, or are there other reasons why people prefer to conceal their abilities and lower their performance?

Researcher Matina Horner (1969) conducted an early study on fear of success. She found that women seem to have a "motive to avoid success," which she defined as "the fear that success in competitive achievement situations will lead to negative consequences such as unpopularity and the loss of femininity" (p. 38). In follow-up studies, however, researchers found that men reveal as much fear of success as women (Kearney, 1984; Tresemer, 1977).

One study by Balkin (1987) reports that fear of success in female college students was related to whether their close friends attended college. Of those whose friends attended college, only 10 percent showed fear of success, compared to 42 percent of the subjects with few or no close friends attending college. Such results led Balkin to speculate that fear of success might involve the "fear of disapproval and rejection from significant others, namely, family and friends" (p. 40). Balkin suggests that the same explanation could apply to males.

Memory Check 10.3

1. Social motives are, for the most part, unlearned. (true/false)

2. According to Atkinson, which of the following is *not* a major factor in determining whether a person high in *n* Ach approaches a goal?
   a. the strength of the need for achievement
   b. the expectation of success
   c. how much pride would result from achieving the goal as opposed to how upsetting failure would be
   d. the financial reward attached to the goal

3. Which statement is *not* true of people high in *n* Ach?
   a. They set very high goals for which success will be extremely difficult to obtain.
   b. They set goals of moderate difficulty.
   c. They attribute their success to their talents, abilities, and hard work.
   d. They are likely to choose careers as entrepreneurs.

Answers: 1. false 2. d 3. a

The What and Why of Emotions

Motivation and Emotion: What Is the Connection?

Motivation does not occur in a vacuum. Much of our motivation to act is fueled by our emotional state. In fact, the root of the word **emotion** means "to move," indicating the close relationship between motivation and emotion. The emotion disgust, for example, motivates us to avoid contamination, disease, and illness. Observing the emotion of sadness in another often elicits our feelings of empathy and may motivate us to acts of altruism (helping behavior). Interest motivates exploration, play, and learning, and anger motivates aggressive actions of defense or protection. Fear motivates us either to flee to escape danger or to perform protective behaviors that provide security and safety (Izard, 1992). And among the positive emotions, happiness motivates us to continue performing pleasant activities. Furthermore, emotions enable us to communicate our feelings and intentions more effectively than just words alone and thus make it more likely that others will respond to us. But what, precisely, are emotions?

What are the three components of emotion?

The Components of Emotions: The Physical, the Cognitive, and the Behavioral

Nothing more than feelings. Is that what emotions are? We may say that we feel lonely or sad, happy or content, embarrassed or afraid. We normally describe emotions in terms of feeling states, but psychologists study emotions according to their three components—the physical, the cognitive, and the behavioral.

The physical component is the physiological arousal (the internal body state) that accompanies the emotion. Without the physiological arousal, we would not feel the emotion in all its intensity. The surge of powerful feeling we know as emotion is due largely to the physiological arousal we experience.

The cognitive component—the way we perceive or interpret a stimulus or situation—determines the specific emotion we feel. If you are home alone and the wind is banging a tree limb on your roof, you may become fearful if you perceive the knocking and the banging as a burglar trying to break into your house.

emotion: A feeling state involving physiological arousal, a cognitive appraisal of the situation arousing the state, and an outward expression of the state.

An emotional response to an imaginary threat is every bit as p[...] response to a real threat. Perceptions make it so. Have you ever work[...] up into a frenzy before a first date, a job interview, or an oral presentati[...] of your classes? Then your thinking was contributing to your emotional[...]

The behavioral component of emotions is the outward expression of t[...] tions. Our facial expressions, gestures, body posture, and tone of voice ste[...] and convey the emotions we are feeling within. Some of the facial expre[...] that accompany emotion are innate and are the same across cultures. But s[...] of our emotional expressions are more influenced by our culture and its rules[...] displaying emotion.

Theories of Emotion: Which Comes First, the Thought or the Feeling?

There is no doubt that we react to certain experiences with emotion. For example, if you think you are making a fool of yourself in front of your friends, the emotion you feel is embarrassment, which triggers a physiological response that may cause you to blush. This type of reaction seems logical—it seems to fit our everyday experience. But is this sequence of events the course that an emotional experience really follows? Not according to psychologist William James.

The James–Lange Theory American psychologist William James (1884) argued that the sequence of events in an emotional experience is exactly the reverse of what our subjective experience tells us. James claimed that first an event causes physiological arousal and a physical response. Only then do we perceive or interpret the physical response as an emotion. In other words, saying something stupid causes us to blush, and we interpret our physical response, blushing, as an emotion, embarrassment. James (1890) went on to suggest that "we feel sorry *because* we cry, angry *because* we strike, afraid *because* we tremble" (p. 1066). See Figure 10.6 (on page 380).

According to the James–Lange theory, what sequence of events occurs when we experience an emotion?

At about the same time that James proposed his theory, a Danish physiologist and psychologist, Carl Lange, independently formulated nearly the same theory. Hence, we have the **James–Lange theory** of emotion (Lange & James, 1922). The theory suggests that different patterns of arousal in the autonomic nervous system produce the different emotions we feel, and that the physiological arousal appears before the emotion is perceived.

If the physical arousal itself were the sole cause of what we know as emotion, however, there would have to be a distinctly different set of physical changes associated with each emotion. Otherwise we wouldn't know whether we were sad, embarrassed, frightened, or happy.

The Cannon–Bard Theory An early theory of emotion that challenged the James–Lange theory is the Cannon–Bard theory. Walter Cannon (1927), who did pioneering work on the fight-or-flight response and the concept of homeostasis, pointed out that we often feel an emotion before we notice the physiological state of our bodies. Furthermore, Cannon claimed that the bodily changes caused by each of the emotions are not sufficiently distinct to allow people to distinguish one emotion from another.

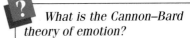

What is the Cannon–Bard theory of emotion?

Cannon presented his own theory, which was later expanded on by one of his students, Philip Bard (1934). Known as the **Cannon–Bard theory**, it suggests that the following chain of events occurs when we feel an emotion: (1) Emotion-provoking stimuli are received by the senses and are then relayed to the thalamus in the brain. (2) The thalamus passes its information in two different directions at the same time—up to the cerebral cortex, which gives us the con-

FIGURE 10.6

The James–Lange Theory of Emotion

The James–Lange theory of emotion is the exact opposite of what our subjective experience tells us. If an angry dog growls at you, the James–Lange interpretation is: The dog growls, your heart begins to pound, and only by observing that your heart is pounding do you conclude that you must be afraid.

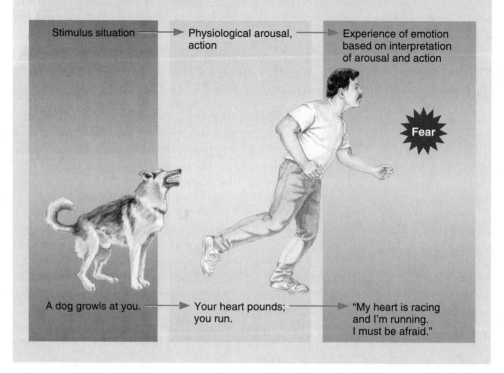

Stimulus situation → Physiological arousal, action → Experience of emotion based on interpretation of arousal and action

Fear

A dog growls at you. → Your heart pounds; you run. → "My heart is racing and I'm running. I must be afraid."

scious mental experience of the emotion, and down to the internal organs of the body, which produce the physiological state of arousal. In other words, our feelings of emotion occur at about the same time that we experience physiological arousal. One does not cause the other.

Later research corrected some of the details of the Cannon-Bard theory. Instead of the thalamus, the hypothalamus apparently starts the process of physical arousal, while other areas of the limbic system are involved in the feeling or the experience of an emotion.

The Schachter–Singer Theory Stanley Schachter believed that the early theories of emotion left out a critical component—our own cognitive interpretation of why we become aroused. Schachter and Singer (1962) proposed a two-factor theory. According to the **Schachter–Singer theory**, two things must happen in order for a person to feel an emotion: (1) The person must first experience physiological arousal. (2) Then there must be a cognitive interpretation or explanation of the physiological arousal so that the person can label it as a specific emotion. Thus, a true emotion can occur only if we are physically aroused and can find some reason for it. Schachter concluded that when people are in a state of physiological arousal but do not know why they are aroused, they tend to label the state as an emotion that is appropriate to their situation at the time.

Review and Reflect Table 10.2 summarizes the three major theories of emotion: James–Lange, Cannon–Bard, and Schachter–Singer.

? *According to the Schachter–Singer theory, what two factors must occur in order for us to experience an emotion?*

Schachter–Singer theory: A two-stage theory stating that for an emotion to occur, there must be (1) physiological arousal and (2) an explanation for the arousal.

Review and Reflect 10.2 Theories of Emotion

Theory	View	Example
James–Lange theory	An event causes physiological arousal. We experience an emotion only *after* we interpret the physical response.	You are walking home late at night and hear footsteps behind you. Your heart pounds and you begin to tremble. You interpret these physical responses as *fear*.
Cannon–Bard theory	An event causes a physiological *and* an emotional response simultaneously. One does not cause the other.	You are walking home late at night and hear footsteps behind you. Your heart pounds, you begin to tremble, and you feel afraid.
Schachter–Singer theory	An event causes physiological arousal. We must then be able to identify a reason for the arousal in order to label the emotion.	You are walking home late at night and hear footsteps behind you. Your heart pounds and you begin to tremble. You know that walking alone at night can be dangerous, and so you feel afraid.

Attempts to replicate the findings of Schachter and Singer have failed to support their theory (Marshall & Zimbardo, 1979). Some studies reveal that people experiencing unexplained arousal find it unpleasant rather than neutral as Schachter and Singer suggest (Leventhal & Tomarken, 1986). Also, the notion that arousal is general rather than specific has been questioned by later researchers who have identified some distinctive patterns of arousal for some of the basic emotions (Ekman et al., 1983; Schwartz et al., 1981). Do you suppose there is a distinctive pattern of arousal that is associated with lying?

The Polygraph: Lie Detector or Emotion Detector?

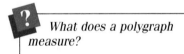

What does a polygraph measure?

Picture yourself in this situation. You are delighted that your application for a job with the federal government has survived the initial screening. Your job interview goes well, too, and you are informed that the job requires a security clearance. If you pass a series of tests, you are hired.

When you arrive to take your first test, you are directed to a small room where a man is seated at a table with a computer monitor and other machinery you have never seen before. As you are seated in a chair facing away from the computer, an assistant explains that you will be asked a series of questions. Then they attach electrodes to the tips of your fingers, strap a tube across your chest and over your heart, and another tube around your upper waist at your diaphragm. Already you feel like a condemned murderer being readied for execution, as a blood pressure cuff is placed around your left upper arm and is pumped up tight. You are ready for a **polygraph**, or lie detector, test. Now the questions begin.

You are asked three different types of questions: irrelevant questions ("Did you eat breakfast this morning?"), control questions ("Did you ever steal anything?"), and relevant questions ("Did you give any false information on your job application?"). The assumption in this line of questioning is that subjects who lied on their application form will have a stronger emotional response to the relevant question than to the control question. But subjects who were truthful on the application form will register a stronger emotional response to the control question ("Did you ever steal anything?"). Could the polygraph indicate you are

polygraph: A device designed to pick up changes in heart rate, blood pressure, respiration rate, and galvanic skin response that typically accompany the anxiety that occurs when a person lies.

The polygraph can detect only the physiological changes associated with a person's emotional arousal.

telling the truth if you are lying? And could it indicate you are lying if you are telling the truth? The answer is yes to both questions.

The polygraph is really not a lie detector. It can detect only physiological changes associated with emotional arousal. It cannot distinguish lying from fear, sexual arousal, anxiety, anger, or general emotional arousal. The assumption is that when people lie, they feel anxious, and their anxiety causes physiological changes in blood pressure, heart rate, breathing, and perspiration.

In the past, lie detector tests were used primarily by law enforcement officers, but then they found their way into business and industry to screen prospective employees and to control employee theft. Until 1988 more than 1 million tests a year were given in the United States (Holden, 1986a). Then Congress passed the Employee Polygraph Protection Act of 1988, which prohibits most polygraph testing outside the government.

How accurate is the polygraph? In one series of studies of actual criminal suspects, 20 percent of the innocent suspects—one out of every five—were pronounced guilty of lying on the polygraph test (Saxe et al., 1985). Other experts say the percentage of innocent people falsely accused of lying is considerably higher, with as many as one out of three innocent people labeled as a liar, as Figure 10.7 illustrates (Kleinmuntz & Szucko, 1984). "Lives of innocent people have been damaged, perhaps unalterably, by false positives on lie detection tests" (Bashore & Rapp, 1993, p. 4). What about guilty people? One out of four who lied on the polygraph test were judged to be telling the truth.

Is it possible to beat the lie detector? Inveterate, or habitual, liars—those who lie easily without any emotional disturbance or physiological arousal—are more likely to come across as telling the truth. It has been suggested that failure to pay close attention, or being distracted during the questioning, also lowers physiological responses. In one study, volunteer subjects distracted themselves by counting backward by sevens throughout the examination, and they were able to lie without being detected more often than when they were not using a distraction

FIGURE 10.7

The Unreliability of Polygraph Tests

Polygraph tests are far from infallible. In one study, one out of four guilty people were judged innocent and one out of three innocent people were judged guilty. People who can lie easily often show little physical arousal and therefore may come across as telling the truth.

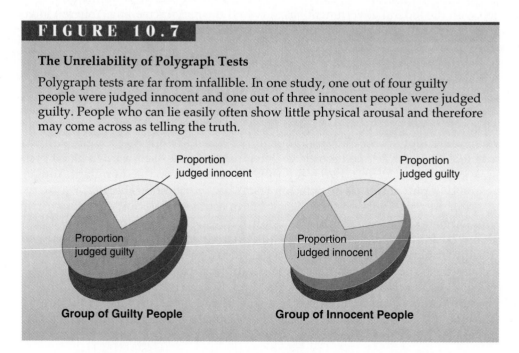

(Waid et al., 1981). Lykken (1981) found that increasing arousal by tensing muscles and thinking about something exciting during neutral questions could also alter the results. Apparently even taking tranquilizers before the test can reduce the physiological response that usually accompanies lying.

The word is out about lie detectors, and their less than satisfactory reliability has led to more restrictions in their use. Today evidence from the polygraph is not admissible in more than half the states in the United States (Lykken, 1985).

Memory Check 10.4

1. According to the text, emotions have all of following *except* a _____ component.
   a. physical   c. sensory
   b. cognitive   d. behavioral

2. Which theory of emotion holds that we feel a true emotion only when we become physically aroused and can identify some cause for the arousal?
   a. Schachter–Singer theory   c. Cannon–Bard theory
   b. James–Lange theory   d. arousal theory

3. Which theory of emotion suggests that we would feel fearful *because* we were shaking?
   a. Schachter–Singer theory   c. Cannon–Bard theory
   b. James–Lange theory   d. arousal theory

4. Which theory suggests that our feeling of emotion and our physiological response to an emotional situation occur at about the same time?
   a. Schachter–Singer theory   c. Cannon–Bard theory
   b. James–Lange theory   d. arousal theory

5. The polygraph measures:
   a. lies.   c. honesty.
   b. integrity.   d. arousal.

Answers: 1. c 2. a 3. b 4. c 5. d

The Expression of Emotion

Expressing emotions comes as naturally to humans as breathing. No one has to be taught how to smile or frown, or how to express fear, sadness, surprise, or disgust. And the facial expressions of the basic emotions are much the same in cultures all over the world.

The Range of Emotion: How Wide Is It?

 What are basic emotions?

How many emotions are there? The number of emotions people list depends on their culture, the language they speak, and other factors. Two leading researchers on emotion, Paul Ekman (1993) and Carroll Izard (1992), insist that there are a limited number of basic emotions. **Basic emotions** are unlearned and universal; that is, they are found in all cultures, are reflected in the same facial expressions, and emerge in children according to their own biological timetable of development. Fear, anger, disgust, surprise, joy or happiness, and sadness or distress are usually considered basic emotions. Izard (1992, 1993) suggests that there are distinct neural circuits that underlie each of the basic emotions, while Levenson and others (1990) point to specific autonomic nervous system activity associated with the basic emotions. Panksepp (1992) believes there is strong evidence for emotional systems in the brain that, at a minimum, underlie rage, fear, expectancy, and panic. Not all researchers, however, subscribe to the notion of basic emotions (Turner & Ortony, 1992).

In studying the range of emotion, Ekman (1993) suggests considering emotions as families. Clearly there are gradients, or degrees, of intensity within a sin-

basic emotions: Emotions that are found in all cultures, that are reflected in the same facial expressions across cultures, and that emerge in children according to their biological timetable (examples: anger, disgust, happiness, sadness, distress).

gle emotion. A person could experience fear, for example, in various degrees, from being mildly uneasy to being afraid, scared, or terrified. The anger family could range from annoyed to irritated, angry, livid, and finally enraged. Furthermore, if perceived as a family, anger should also include various forms of its expression, according to Ekman (1993). Resentment, for example, is a form of anger "in which there is a sense of grievance" (p. 386). Other forms are indignation and outrage, which characterize anger about the mistreatment of someone (ourselves or others). Vengefulness is anger that retaliates, or gets revenge for an injustice or misdeed by another. And in its most intense form, anger may be expressed as blind rage, in which a person loses control, goes berserk, and may commit brutal atrocities against the target of the rage.

It takes little imagination to picture the facial expression of annoyance being quite different from the facial expression of rage, but can you imagine 60 different facial expressions for the different types and intensities of anger? Ekman and Friesen identified 60 anger expressions, with subtle differences, but all sharing the basic properties of the face of anger (Ekman, 1993). Just as there are many words in our vocabulary to describe the variations in the range of any emotion, there are subtle distinctions in the facial expression of a single emotion that convey its intensity.

How do we learn to express our emotions? Or do we learn? There is considerable evidence that the basic emotions (fear, anger, sadness, happiness, disgust, and surprise), or the facial expressions we make when we feel them, are biologically rather than culturally determined.

The Development of Facial Expressions in Infants: Smiles and Frowns Come Naturally

How does the development of facial expressions of different emotions in infants suggest a biological basis for emotional expression?

Facial expressions of emotions develop naturally, just as do the motor skills of crawling and walking, according to the biological timetable of maturation. Carroll Izard (1990) claims that "the facial expressions of pain and the emotions of interest, enjoyment, surprise, sadness, anger, disgust, and fear are present at birth or by about 7 months of age" (p. 492).

Another strong indication that the facial expressions of emotion are biologically determined, rather than learned, results from research on children who were blind and deaf since birth. Their smiles and frowns, laughter and crying, and facial expressions of anger, surprise, and pouting were the same as those of children who could hear and see (Eibl-Eibesfeldt, 1973).

Although recent studies have contributed much to our understanding of facial expressions, the biological connection between emotions and facial expressions was proposed many years ago, as described in the World of Psychology section.

World of Psychology

Facial Expressions for the Basic Emotions— A Universal Language

The relationship between emotions and facial expressions was first studied by Charles Darwin (1872/1975). He believed that the facial expression of emotion was an aid to survival, because it enabled people, before they developed language, to communicate their internal states and react to emergencies. Darwin maintained that most of the emotions we feel and the facial expressions that convey them are genetically inherited and characteristic of the entire human species. To test his belief, he asked missionaries and people of different cultures around the world to record the facial expressions that accompany the basic emotions. Based on those data, he concluded that facial expressions were similar across cultures. Modern researchers agree that Darwin was right.

Convincing evidence that the facial expressions of emotion are universal was provided by Ekman and Friesen (1971). They showed photographs portraying facial expressions of the primary emotions—sadness, surprise, happiness, anger, fear, and disgust—to members of the Fore tribe in a remote area in New Guinea. The Fore people were able to identify the emotional expressions of happiness, sadness, anger, and disgust, although they had difficulty distinguishing fear and surprise.

In later research Ekman and others (Ekman, 1982; Ekman & Friesen, 1975; Ekman et al., 1987) used subjects from the United States, Argentina, Japan, Brazil, and Chile, who viewed photographs showing the same basic emotions. Could people from widely diverse cultures name the emotions conveyed by the facial expressions of Americans? Yes, to an amazing degree. Ekman (1992) believes that research results provide strong support for a biological explanation of facial expression. More recently, Russell (1994) reviewed 11 cross-cultural studies spanning a period of 12 years (1980–1992), and all of the studies concluded that the human face reveals emotions that are universally recognized.

Other recent research finds evidence for universality, as Darwin and Ekman and others did, but evidence for cultural variations as well. Scherer and Wallbott (1994) found massive overlap in the patterns of emotional experiences reported across cultures in 37 different countries on five continents. They also found important cultural differences in the ways in which emotions are elicited and regulated, and in how they are socially shared. Such findings remind us that, while we acknowledge and appreciate our cultural differences and the great diversity we find within the human population, we are, after all, one species. And our facial expressions of basic emotion are much the same around the world.

Try Ekman's test and see if you can identify the faces of emotion in the *Try It!*

Look carefully at the six photographs on the right. Which basic emotion is portrayed in each?

Match the number of the photograph with the basic emotion it portrays:

a. Happiness   d. Anger
b. Sadness   e. Surprise
c. Fear   f. Disgust

Answers: 1. d 2. c 3. f 4. e 5. a 6. b

1. _____

2. _____

3. _____

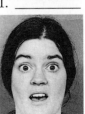
4. _____

5. _____

6. _____

Cultural Rules for Displaying Emotion

While the facial expressions of the basic emotions are much the same in cultures around the world, each culture can have very different **display rules**—cultural rules that dictate how emotions should generally be expressed and where and when their expression is appropriate (Ekman, 1993; Ekman & Friesen, 1975; Scherer & Wallbott, 1994). Often society's display rules expect us to give evidence of certain emotions that we may not actually feel. We are expected to be sad at funerals, to hide our disappointment when we lose, and to refrain from making

facial expressions of disgust if the food we are served tastes bad to us. In one study, Cole (1986) found that 3-year-old girls, when given an unattractive gift, smiled nevertheless. They had already learned a display rule and signaled an emotion they very likely did not feel. Davis (1995) found that among first to third graders, girls were better able to hide disappointment than boys were.

Different cultures, neighborhoods, and even families may have very different display rules. Display rules in Japanese culture dictate that expression of negative emotions must be disguised when others are present (Ekman, 1972). In many societies in the West, women are expected to smile often, whether they feel happy or not. And in East Africa, young males from traditional Masai society are expected to appear stern and stony-faced and to "produce long, unbroken stares" (Keating, 1994). So, if we are to comply with display rules, it appears that much of our communication of emotion is not authentic, not truly felt.

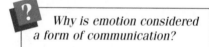

Each culture has its own set of display rules concerning the expression of emotion. In Japan, people do not smile for wedding portraits. What other examples of display rules can you cite?

Most of us learn display rules very early and abide by them most of the time. Yet we may not be fully aware that the rules we have learned dictate where, when, how, and even how long certain emotions should be expressed.

You will learn more about reading emotions and detecting the probable motives of others when we explore nonverbal behavior—the language of facial expressions, gestures, and body positions—in Chapter 16.

? *Why is emotion considered a form of communication?*

Emotion as a Form of Communication

The ways in which we feel and express emotions actually represent a form of communication. Emotions enable us to communicate our feelings, intentions, and needs more effectively than just words alone and thus make it more likely that others will respond to us. And researchers maintain that not only are we biologically wired to convey certain emotion signals but there is evidence that we are biologically predisposed to read and interpret them as well (Dimberg, 1990; Oatley & Jenkins, 1992).

Communicating emotions can motivate action by others. If we communicate sadness or distress, then people close to us are likely to be sympathetic and try to help us. Emotional expressions allow infants to communicate their feelings and needs before they are able to speak. In an early study Katherine Bridges (1932) observed emotional expression in Canadian infants over a period of months. She reported that the first emotional expression to appear is that of distress, which occurs at 3 weeks. In survival terms, the expression of distress enables helpless newborns to get the attention of their caretakers so that their needs can be met.

display rules: Cultural rules that dictate how emotions should be expressed, and when and where their expression is appropriate.

Do you feel happier when you are around others who are happy? You may already know that emotions are contagious. Infants will usually begin to cry when they hear another infant cry. Your own emotional expressions can infect others with the same emotion. Mothers seem to know this intuitively when they display happy expressions to infect their babies with happy moods (Keating, 1994). Researchers have found that mothers in many cultures—Trobriand Island, Yanomamo, Greek,

German, Japanese, and American—attempt to regulate the moods of their babies through facial communication of emotions (Kanaya et al., 1989; Keller et al., 1988; Termine & Izard, 1988).

From an evolutionary perspective, the ability to interpret various states instantly and reliably and then emulate them has survival value. In many species, if a single member of the group or herd senses a predator and communicates the emotion of fear, the other members also become afraid, preparing them to flee for their lives.

We perceive the emotions of others, from as early as our first year of life, and use this information to guide our own behavior. Infants pay close attention to the facial expressions of others, especially their mother. And when they are confronted with an ambiguous situation, they use the mother's emotion as a guide to whether they should approach or avoid the situation. This phenomenon is known as social referencing (Klinnert et al., 1983).

Memory Check 10.5

1. Which of the following is *not* true of the basic emotions?
   a. They are reflected in distinctive facial expressions.
   b. They are found in all cultures.
   c. There are several hundred known to date.
   d. They are unlearned.

2. Which of the following is *not* one of the emotions represented by a distinctive facial expression?
   a. happiness   c. surprise
   b. hostility   d. sadness

3. Facial expressions associated with the basic emotions develop naturally according to a child's own biological timetable of maturation. (true/false)

4. All of the following are true of display rules *except* that they:

   a. are the same in all cultures.
   b. dictate when and where emotions should be expressed.
   c. dictate what emotions should not be expressed.
   d. often cause people to display emotions they do not feel.

5. Which of the following statements is *not* true about emotion as a form of communication?
   a. Emotions communicate our feelings better than just words alone.
   b. Emotions communicate our intentions.
   c. Emotions are often contagious.
   d. Infants under 1 year of age are unable to use the emotions of others to guide their behavior.

Answers: 1. c 2. b 3. true 4. a 5. d

Experiencing Emotion

How are expressions of emotion related to our experience of emotion? Some researchers go so far as to suggest that the facial expression alone can actually produce the experience.

The Facial-Feedback Hypothesis: Does the Face Cause the Feeling?

What is the facial-feedback hypothesis?

Researcher Sylvan Tomkins (1962, 1963), like Darwin, agreed that facial expressions of the basic emotions are genetically programmed. But Tomkins went a step further. He claimed that the facial expression itself—that is, the movement of the facial muscles producing the expression—triggers both the physiological arousal and the conscious feeling associated with the emotion. The notion that the mus-

facial-feedback hypothesis: The idea that the muscular movements involved in certain facial expressions trigger the corresponding emotions (for example, smiling makes us happy).

cular movements involved in certain facial expressions produce the corresponding emotion is called the **facial-feedback hypothesis** (Izard, 1971, 1977, 1990; Strack et al., 1988).

In an extensive review of research on the facial-feedback hypothesis, Adelmann and Zajonc (1989) found impressive evidence to support the association between facial expression and the subjective experience of an emotion. In addition, they found considerable support for the notion that simply the act of making the facial expression can initiate the subjective feeling of the emotion.

The Simulation of Facial Expressions: Put On a Happy Face   Nearly 125 years ago Darwin wrote, "Even the simulation of an emotion tends to arouse it in our minds" (1872/1965, p. 365). Ekman and colleagues (1983) put this notion to the test using 16 subjects (12 professional actors and 4 scientists). The subjects were guided to contract specific muscles in the face so that they could assume the facial expressions of six basic emotions—surprise, disgust, sadness, anger, fear, and happiness. They were never actually told to smile, frown, or put on an angry face, however.

The subjects were hooked up to electronic instruments, which monitored physiological changes in heart rate, galvanic skin response (to measure perspiring), muscle tension, and hand temperature. Measurements were taken as the subjects made each facial expression. The subjects were also asked to imagine or relive six experiences in which they had felt each of the six emotions.

Ekman reported that a distinctive physiological response pattern emerged for the emotions of fear, sadness, anger, and disgust, whether the subjects relived one of their emotional experiences or simply made the corresponding facial expression. In fact, in some cases the physiological measures of emotion were greater when the actors and scientists made the facial expression than when they imagined an actual emotional experience (Ekman et al., 1983). The researchers found that both anger and fear accelerate heart rate, while fear produces colder fingers than does anger.

Do you think that making particular facial expressions will affect your emotions? A simple experiment you can try alone or with friends or classmates is described in the *Try It!*

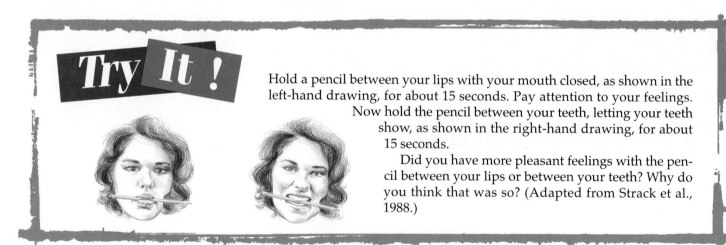

Hold a pencil between your lips with your mouth closed, as shown in the left-hand drawing, for about 15 seconds. Pay attention to your feelings. Now hold the pencil between your teeth, letting your teeth show, as shown in the right-hand drawing, for about 15 seconds.

Did you have more pleasant feelings with the pencil between your lips or between your teeth? Why do you think that was so? (Adapted from Strack et al., 1988.)

In the *Try It!* activity, when you held a pencil between your teeth, you activated the facial muscles used to express happiness. When you held it between your lips, you activated the muscles involved in the expression of anger.

Controlling Our Facial Expressions to Regulate Our Feelings   If facial expressions can activate emotions, is it possible that intensifying or weakening a facial expression might intensify or weaken the corresponding feeling state? In 1872 Darwin wrote:

> The free expression by outward signs of an emotion intensifies it. On the other hand, the repression . . . of all outward signs softens our emotions. He who gives way to violent gestures will increase his rage; he who does not control the signs of fear will experience fear in greater degree. (p. 365)

Izard (1990) believes that learning to self-regulate emotional expression can enable us to gain control over our emotions. We can learn to change the intensity of an emotion by inhibiting, weakening, or amplifying its expression. Or we might change the emotion itself by simulating the expression of another emotion. Izard proposes that this approach to the regulation of emotion might be a useful adjunct to psychotherapy.

Regulating or modifying an emotion by simulating an expression of its opposite may be effective if the emotion is not unusually intense. What is it about intense emotional states that makes them so difficult to control or regulate?

Emotion and Rational Thinking

Have you ever been so "swept away" by emotion that your ability to reason logically deserted you, and you did something you later regretted? Could there be a negative correlation between emotional intensity and objective, rational thinking? The proposition has been posed this way: As emotion intensifies, rational thinking decreases.

Intense emotional states are frequently described in phrases that suggest these states are devoid of rational thinking—"insanely jealous," "blinded by love," "frozen with fright," "consumed by passion," "burning with envy," "seething with anger." The framers of the legal system in the United States apparently believed that strong emotion often obliterates the ability to act rationally. Crimes of passion, for example, in which murder is committed in the "heat" of passion, are usually punished less severely than premeditated (first-degree) murders, committed in "cold" blood. In more common experience we say that love is blind. Blind to what? Faults and blemishes in the object of our affection? When consumed by sexual passion, people often yield to the emotion, act without caution, and suffer unwelcome consequences.

Can you think of examples that would suggest that rational thinking lessens as emotional states intensify? Do the *Try It!*

Try It!

List as many news events as you can that seem to support the notion that when people are consumed by emotion, rational thinking can decrease or disappear with disastrous consequences.

Event	Extreme Emotion
_____	_____
_____	_____
_____	_____
_____	_____

Some dramatic examples of how extreme emotional states can diminish rational thinking and result in tragedy are major depression leading to suicide, and rage resulting in spouse abuse, child abuse, or murder.

Emotional experience is a central part of human existence. But do we all, male and female alike, experience our emotions in identical ways? The World of Psychology section addresses this question.

World of Psychology

Gender Differences in Experiencing Emotion

Do females and males differ significantly in the ways they experience their emotions? Do women tend to be more intensely emotional than men? Some research suggests that the answer to both questions may be yes.

What emotion would you feel first if you were betrayed or criticized harshly by another person? When asked to respond to this hypothetical situation, male subjects were more likely to report they would feel angry, and females were more likely to say they would feel hurt, sad, or disappointed (Brody, 1985). Of course, both males and females express anger, but not always in the same way or toward the same aspects of a situation. Women experience far more anger than men when their partner is sexually aggressive. Men, on the other hand, experience greater anger than women when their partner withholds sex (Buss, 1991).

In the emotional experience of jealousy, too, researchers have found consistent differences between the sexes. Men more than women experience jealousy over suspicions or evidence of sexual infidelity (Buss, 1991). Women, though, are more likely than men to be jealous over a partner's emotional attachment and commitment to another, and over the loss of attention, time, and resources from the relationship (Teismann & Mosher, 1978; White & Mullen, 1989).

But the most puzzling gender difference found in emotional experience is the following: In surveys of happiness, women report greater happiness and life satisfaction than men report (Wood et al., 1989). Paradoxically, women also report more sadness than men, are twice as likely to report being depressed, and admit to greater fear than men (Scherer et al., 1986). How can women be both happier and sadder than men? Another gender difference may explain it. Researchers have found sex differences in the intensity of emotional response. Grossman and Wood (1993) tested male and female subjects for the intensity of emotional responses on five basic emotions—joy, love, fear, sadness, and anger. They found that "women reported more intense and more frequent emotions than men did, with the exception of anger" (p. 1013).

More joy, more sadness, more fear, more love! But these were self-reports. How do we know that the female subjects actually *felt* four of the five emotions more intensely than the males? The researchers also measured physiological arousal. The subjects viewed slides depicting the various emotions while they were hooked up to an electromyogram to measure tension in the facial muscles. The researchers found that "women not only reported more intense emotional experience than men, but they also generated more extreme physiological reactions" (p. 1020). Other researchers agree that, in general, women respond with greater emotional intensity than men and thus can experience both greater joy and greater sorrow (Fujita et al., 1991).

Love: The Strongest Emotional Bond

The emotion of love comes in many varieties. And although we often use the term rather loosely or casually—"I love ice cream," "I love to dance"—the emotion of love is usually experienced as a deep and abiding affection. We feel love for our parents, for our sisters and brothers, for our children, and ideally for our friends and neighbors and for other fellow humans. There is also love of country and love of learning. There seems to be a virtually endless list of people, things, and situations that may produce in humans the emotion of love.

But the variety of love most written about by poets, most set to music by composers, and most longed for by virtually all of us is—romantic love. How many components are there to this thing we call love?

Romantic Love: Lost in Each Other When we say we have "fallen" in love, it is probably romantic love we have fallen into. Romantic love (sometimes called passionate love) is an intense emotional response to another person, coupled with sexual arousal and a tremendous longing for that person. But when the passion fades, couples may find that they do not have the similar backgrounds, attitudes, values, and interests that often form the basis for a more enduring relationship. Fortunately, there is more to love than passion, important though it is. In fact, passion may be only one of three parts of an ideal love relationship.

Sternberg's Theory of Love: Three Components, Seven Types Robert Sternberg (1986b, 1987), whose triarchic theory of intelligence was discussed in Chapter 7, proposes a **triangular theory of love**. Its three components are intimacy, passion, and commitment. Sternberg explains intimacy as "those feelings in a relationship that promote closeness, bondedness, and connectedness" (1987, p. 339). Passion refers to those drives in a loving relationship "that lead to romance, physical attraction, [and] sexual consummation" (1986b, p. 119). The decision/commitment component consists of (1) a short-term aspect—the decision that one person loves another—and (2) a long-term aspect—a commitment the person makes to maintaining that love over time.

Sternberg proposes that these three components, singly and in various combinations, produce seven different kinds of love:

- *Liking* has only one of the love components—intimacy. In this case, liking is not used in a trivial sense. Sternberg says that this intimate liking characterizes true friendships, in which we feel a bondedness, a warmth, and a closeness with another person but not intense passion or a long-term commitment.

- *Infatuated love* consists solely of passion and is often what we feel as "love at first sight." But without the intimacy and the decision/commitment components of love, infatuated love may disappear suddenly.

- *Empty love* consists of the decision/commitment component without intimacy or passion. Sometimes a stronger love deteriorates into empty love—the commitment remains, but the intimacy and passion have died. In cultures in which arranged marriages are common, relationships often begin as empty love.

- *Romantic love* is a combination of intimacy and passion. Romantic lovers are bonded emotionally (as in liking) and physically through passionate arousal.

- *Fatuous love* has the passion and the decision/commitment components but not the intimacy. This type of love can be exemplified by a whirlwind courtship and marriage in which a commitment is motivated largely by passion without the stabilizing influence of intimacy.

- *Companionate love* consists of intimacy and commitment. This type of love is often found in marriages in which the passion has gone out of the relationship, but a deep affection and commitment remain.

- *Consummate love* is the only type that has all three components—intimacy, decision/commitment, and passion. **Consummate love** is the most complete form of love, and it represents the ideal love relationship for which many people strive but which apparently few achieve. Sternberg cautions that maintaining a consummate love may be even harder than achieving it.

How does Sternberg's triangular theory of love account for the different kinds of love?

triangular theory of love: Sternberg's theory that three components—intimacy, passion, and decision/commitment—singly and in various combinations produce seven different kinds of love.

consummate love: According to Sternberg's theory, the most complete form of love, consisting of three components—intimacy, passion, and decision/commitment.

FIGURE 10.8

Sternberg's Triangular Theory of Love

Sternberg identifies three components of love—passion, intimacy, and commitment—and shows how the three, singly and in various combinations, produce seven different kinds of love. Consummate love, the most complete form of love, has all three components. (Based on Sternberg, 1986.)

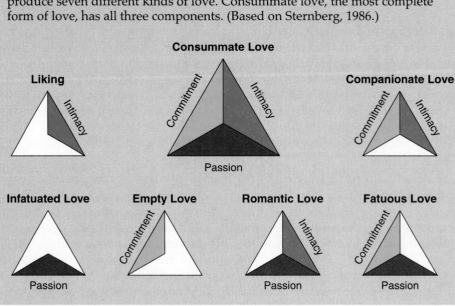

Figure 10.8 depicts Sternberg's triangular theory of love. Sternberg stresses the importance of translating the components of love into action. "Without expression," he warns, "even the greatest of loves can die" (1987, p. 341).

Love in all its fullness, its richness, and its power is such an intense and consuming human experience that researchers find it hard to capture. It is almost too personal to be viewed and studied with passionless objectivity. And we believe that love, the strongest emotional bond, is the most satisfying human experience imaginable for those fortunate enough to find it.

Memory Check 10.6

1. The idea that making a happy, sad, or angry face can actually trigger the physiological response and feeling associated with the emotion is called the:
   a. emotion production theory.
   b. emotion control theory.
   c. facial-feedback hypothesis.
   d. facial expression theory.

2. Heightened emotion tends to facilitate rational thinking. (true/false)

3. Some research supports the notion that women tend to experience emotions more intensely than men. (true/false)

4. Which of the following is *not* one of the central components of love, according to Sternberg's triangular theory?
   a. compatibility   c. commitment
   b. passion   d. intimacy

5. What is the complete form of love, according to Sternberg?
   a. romantic love   c. companionate love
   b. fatuous love   d. consummate love

Answers: 1. c 2. false 3. true 4. a 5. d

Eating Disorders— The Tyranny of the Scale

Imagine this: The thought of even the slightest layer of fat on your body repels you. You have been dieting and exercising strenuously for months, but you still feel fat, even though your friends comment that you're nothing but skin and bones. And you're unbelievably hungry: Your dreams and daydreams are all about food—delicious food, lots of it, elegantly served. You leaf through cookbooks, go grocery shopping, and prepare meals whenever you get a chance, but when you sit down to eat you merely play with your food, because if you ate it you might get fat.

Now imagine this: Driven by an uncontrollable urge, you buy a dozen packages of cookies, some soda, perhaps a box of doughnuts. You take them to your room, lock the door, and start eating them. Once you've started, you can't stop—you gorge yourself on cookies and doughnuts until you feel as if you're about to explode. At that point you are overcome with disgust and anger at yourself. You run to the bathroom and thrust your fingers down your throat to get rid of the excess volume of food you have consumed.

These two scenarios are not as unusual as you might think. They represent two surprisingly common eating disorders: anorexia nervosa and bulimia nervosa. What causes these disorders, and how can they be treated?

Anorexia Nervosa

Although there are some similarities between them, anorexia and bulimia are very different disorders. *Anorexia nervosa* is characterized by an overwhelming, irrational fear of gaining weight or becoming fat, compulsive dieting to the point of self-starvation, and excessive weight loss. Some

anorexics lose as much as 20 to 25 percent of their original body weight. Anorexia typically begins in adolescence, and 90 percent of those afflicted are females (American Psychiatric Association, 1994). About 1 percent of females between ages 12 and 40 suffer from this disorder (Brotman, 1994).

Anorexia often begins with dieting, perhaps in reaction to a gain in weight after the onset of menstruation. Gradually the dieting develops into an obsession. Anorexic individuals continue to feel hunger and are strangely preoccupied with food. They spend inordinate amounts of time thinking about food, reading recipes, shopping for food, preparing it, and watching other people eat, although they may eat only the smallest portions themselves.

Anorexic individuals also have a gross distortion in the perception of their body size. No matter how emaciated they become, they continue to perceive themselves as fat. In fact, they have been found to overestimate their body size by as much as 31 percent (Penner et al., 1991). They are so obsessed with their weight that frequently they not only starve themselves but also exercise relentlessly and excessively in an effort to accelerate their weight loss. Among young women, progressive and significant weight loss eventually results in amenorrhea (cessation of menstruation). Anorexics also become weak and highly susceptible to infection. They may experience low blood pressure, impaired heart function, dehydration, electrolyte disturbances, and/or sterility (American Psychiatric Association, 1993a).

Unfortunately as many as 20 percent of those suffering from anorexia nervosa eventually die of starvation or complications from organ damage (Brotman, 1994). One casualty of the battle with anorexia and bulimia was gymnast Christy Heinrich (shown in the photo), who died in 1994 at the age of 22.

Causes and Treatment of Anorexia

It is difficult to pinpoint the cause of this disorder. Most anorexic individuals are well-behaved children and good students (Vitousek & Manke, 1994). Some investigators believe that young women who refuse to eat are attempting to control a portion of their lives, which they may feel unable to control in other respects.

Anorexia is very difficult to treat. Most anorexics are steadfast in their refusal to eat; some actually starve themselves to death while insisting that nothing is wrong with them. The main thrust of treatment efforts, therefore, is to get the anorexic to gain weight. The patient may be admitted to a hospital, fed a controlled diet, and given rewards and privileges for small gains in weight and increased food intake. The treat-

ment usually includes some type of psychotherapy—cognitive-behavioral therapy, family therapy, psychodynamic therapy, group therapy,

continued

and/or a self-help group. (All these types of therapy are discussed in Chapter 15.) Antidepressant drugs may be used if a patient shows symptoms of depression or obsessive-compulsive disorder.

Bulimia Nervosa

Up to 50 percent of anorexics also develop symptoms of *bulimia nervosa*, a chronic disorder characterized by repeated and uncontrolled episodes of binge eating, often in secret (American Psychiatric Association, 1993a). An episode of binge eating has two main features: (1) the consumption of much larger amounts of food than most people would eat during the same period of time, and (2) a feeling that one cannot stop eating or control the amount eaten. Binges—which generally involve foods that are rich in carbohydrates, such as cookies, cake, and candy—are frequently followed by purging: self-induced vomiting and/or the use of large quantities of laxatives and diuretics. Bulimics may also engage in excessive dieting and exercise. Athletes are especially susceptible to this dis-

order. Many bulimics are average in size and purge after an eating binge simply to maintain their weight.

Bulimia nervosa can cause a number of health problems. The stomach acid in vomit eats away at the teeth and may cause them to rot, and the delicate balance of body chemistry is destroyed by excessive use of laxatives and diuretics. The bulimic may have a perpetually sore throat as well as a variety of other symptoms, including dehydration, swelling of the salivary glands, kidney damage, and hair loss. The disorder also has a strong emotional component; the bulimic person is aware that the eating pattern is abnormal and feels unable to control it. Depression, guilt, and shame often accompany the binges and subsequent purging.

Bulimia nervosa tends to appear in the late teenage years and affects about 1 in 25 women during their lifetime (Kendler et al., 1991). An even larger number of young women regularly binge and purge, but not frequently enough to warrant the diagnosis of bulimia nervosa (Drewnowski et al., 1994). And contrary to the notion that bulimia is confined primarily to white, upper-

middle-class young women, in a survey of high school students, Smith and Krejci (1991) found even higher rates of binge eating among Native Americans and Hispanics. And about 10 to 15 percent of all bulimics are males (Carlat & Camargo, 1991).

Bulimia, like anorexia, is difficult to treat. Cognitive-behavioral therapy has been used successfully to help bulimics modify their eating habits and their abnormal attitudes about body shape and weight (Fairburn et al., 1993; Wilson & Fairburn, 1993). Certain antidepressant drugs have been found to reduce the frequency of binge eating and purging and to result in significant attitudinal change (Agras et al., 1994; Goldbloom & Olmsted, 1993). A combination of medication and cognitive-behavioral therapy seems to be the most effective approach (Agras et al., 1992).

If you or someone you know show signs of suffering from either of these disorders, you can get help by contacting the American Anorexia/Bulimia Association at 418 E. 76th St., New York, NY 10021 (212–734–1114), or Anorexics, Bulimics Anonymous, National Service Office, P.O. Box 47573, Phoenix, AZ 85068 (602–861–3295).

Thinking Critically

Evaluation

1. In your view, which theory or combination of theories best explains motivation: drive-reduction theory, arousal theory, or Maslow's hierarchy of needs? Which theory do you find least convincing? Support your answers.
2. Using what you have learned about body weight and dieting, select any well-known weight-loss plan (for example, Weight Watchers, Jenny Craig, Slim Fast) and evaluate it, explaining why it is or is not an effective way to lose weight and keep it off.

Point/Counterpoint

Present a convincing argument for each of these positions:

a. Polygraph testing should not be allowed in the legal system or in business and industry.
b. Polygraph testing should be allowed in the legal system and in business and industry.

Psychology in Your Life

Which level of Maslow's hierarchy (shown in Figure 10.3 on page 366) provides the strongest motivation for your behavior in general? Give specific examples to support your answer.

Chapter Summary and Review

Introduction to Motivation

? *What is the difference between intrinsic and extrinsic motivation?*

With intrinsic motivation, an act is performed because it is satisfying or pleasurable in and of itself; with extrinsic motivation, an act is performed to bring a reward or to avert an undesirable consequence.

Key Terms

motivation (p. 360)
motives (p. 360)
incentive (p. 361)
intrinsic motivation (p. 361)
extrinsic motivation (p. 361)

Theories of Motivation

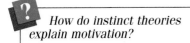

? *How do instinct theories explain motivation?*

Instinct theories suggest that human behavior is motivated by certain innate, unlearned tendencies, or instincts, which are shared by all people.

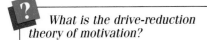

? *What is the drive-reduction theory of motivation?*

Drive-reduction theory suggests that a biological need creates an unpleasant state of arousal or tension called a drive, which impels the organism to engage in behavior that will satisfy the need and reduce tension.

? *How does arousal theory explain motivation?*

Arousal theory suggests that the aim of motivation is to maintain an optimal level of arousal. If arousal is less than optimal, we engage in activities that stimulate arousal; if arousal exceeds the optimal level, we seek to reduce stimulation.

? *How does Maslow's hierarchy of needs account for human motivation?*

Maslow's hierarchy of needs arranges needs in order of urgency—from physical needs (food, water, air, shelter) to security needs, belonging and love needs, esteem needs, and finally the need for self-actualization (developing to one's full potential) at the top of the hierarchy. Theoretically, the needs at the lower levels must be satisfied adequately before a person will be motivated to fulfill the higher needs.

Key Terms

instinct (p. 362)
instinct theory (p. 362)
drive-reduction theory (p. 362)
drive (p. 362)
homeostasis (p. 362)
arousal (p. 363)
arousal theory (p. 363)
stimulus motives (p. 364)
Yerkes–Dodson law (p. 364)
sensory deprivation (p. 365)
hierarchy of needs (p. 366)
self-actualization (p. 366)

The Primary Drives: Hunger and Thirst

? *Under what kinds of conditions do the two types of thirst occur?*

One type of thirst results from a loss of bodily fluid that can be caused by perspiration, vomiting, bleeding, diarrhea, or excessive intake of alcohol. Another type of thirst results from excessive intake of salt, which disturbs the water–sodium balance.

? *What are the roles of the lateral hypothalamus and the ventromedial hypothalamus in the regulation of eating behavior?*

The lateral hypothalamus (LH) apparently acts as a feeding center—when it is activated, it signals the animal to eat; when it is destroyed, the animal refuses to eat. The ventromedial hypothalamus (VMH) evidently acts as a satiety center—when it is activated, it signals the animal to stop eating; when it is destroyed, the animal overeats, becoming obese.

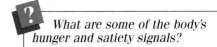

? *What are some of the body's hunger and satiety signals?*

Some biological hunger signals are stomach contractions, low blood glucose levels, and high insulin levels. Some satiety signals are a full stomach, high blood glucose levels, and the presence in the blood of other satiety substances (such as CCK), secreted by the gastrointestinal tract during digestion.

? *What are some nonbiological factors that influence what and how much we eat?*

External eating cues such as the taste, smell, and appearance of food, the variety of food offered, as well as the time of day, can cause people to eat more food than they actually need.

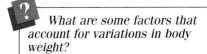

? *What are some factors that account for variations in body weight?*

Variations in body weight are influenced by heredity, metabolic rate, activity level, number of fat cells, and eating habits.

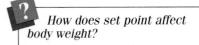

? *How does set point affect body weight?*

Set-point theory suggests an internal homeostatic system that functions to maintain body weight by adjusting appetite and metabolic rate.

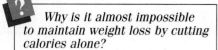 *Why is it almost impossible to maintain weight loss by cutting calories alone?*

It is almost impossible to maintain weight loss by cutting calories alone because the dieter's metabolic rate slows down to compensate for the lower intake of calories. Exercise both prevents the lowering of metabolic rate and burns up additional calories.

Key Terms

primary drive (p. 367)
lateral hypothalamus (LH) (p. 368)
ventromedial hypothalamus (VMH) (p. 368)
metabolic rate (p. 372)
fat cells (p. 372)
set point (p. 373)

Social Motives

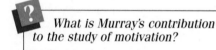 *What is Murray's contribution to the study of motivation?*

Murray defined a list of social motives, or needs, and developed the Thematic Apperception Test (TAT) to assess a person's level of these needs.

 What is the need for achievement?

The need for achievement (*n* Ach) is the need to accomplish something difficult and to perform at a high standard of excellence.

 What are some characteristics shared by people who are high in achievement motivation?

People high in achievement motivation enjoy challenges and like to compete. They tend to set goals of moderate difficulty, are more motivated by hope of success than fear of failure, attribute their success to their ability and hard work, and are most often drawn to business, frequently becoming entrepreneurs.

Key Terms

social motives (p. 374)
Thematic Apperception Test (TAT) (p. 375)
need for achievement (*n* Ach) (p. 375)

The What and Why of Emotions

What are the three components of emotions?

An emotion is a feeling state that involves physiological arousal, a cognitive appraisal of the situation arousing the emotion, and outward expression of the emotion.

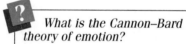 *According to the James–Lange theory, what sequence of events occurs when we experience an emotion?*

According to the James–Lange theory, environmental stimuli produce a physiological response, and then our awareness of this response causes the emotion.

What is the Cannon–Bard theory of emotion?

The Cannon–Bard theory suggests that emotion-provoking stimuli received by the senses are relayed to the thalamus, which simultaneously passes the information to the cortex, giving us the mental experience of the emotion, and to the internal organs, producing physiological arousal.

According to the Schachter–Singer theory, what two factors must occur in order for us to experience an emotion?

The Schachter–Singer theory states that for an emotion to occur (1) there must be physiological arousal, and (2) the person must perceive some reason for the arousal in order to label the emotion.

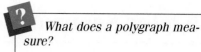 *What does a polygraph measure?*

A polygraph monitors changes in heart rate, blood pressure, respiration rate, and galvanic skin response, which typically accompany the anxiety that occurs when a person lies.

Key Terms

emotion (p. 378)
James-Lange theory (p. 379)
Cannon-Bard theory (p. 379)
Schachter-Singer theory (p. 380)
polygraph (p. 381)

The Expression of Emotion

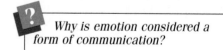 *What are basic emotions?*

The basic emotions (happiness, sadness, disgust, etc.) are those that are unlearned and that are reflected in the same facial expressions in all cultures.

How does the development of facial expressions of different emotions in infants suggest a biological basis for emotional expression?

The facial expressions of different emotions develop in a particular sequence in infants and seem to be the result of maturation rather than learning. The same sequence occurs even in children who have been blind and deaf since birth.

Why is emotion considered a form of communication?

Emotions enable us to communicate our feelings, intentions, and needs more effectively than just words alone and thus make it more likely that others will respond to us.

Key Terms

basic emotions (p. 383)
display rules (p. 386)

Experiencing Emotion

What is the facial-feedback hypothesis?

The facial-feedback hypothesis suggests that the muscular movements involved in certain facial expressions trigger the corresponding emotion (for example, smiling makes us happy).

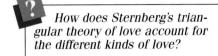

How does Sternberg's triangular theory of love account for the different kinds of love?

In his triangular theory of love, Sternberg proposes that, singly and in various combinations, three components—intimacy, passion, and decision/commitment—produce seven different kinds of love—infatuated, empty, romantic, fatuous, companionate, and consummate love, as well as liking.

Key Terms

facial-feedback hypothesis (p. 388)
triangular theory of love (p. 391)
consummate love (p. 391)

11

HUMAN SEXUALITY AND GENDER

CHAPTER OUTLINE

What Makes a Male, a Male and a Female, a Female?

The Sex Chromosomes: X's and Y's

The Sex Hormones: Contributing to Maleness and Femaleness

Gender-Role Development

Environmental Influences on Gender Typing

Psychological Theories of Gender-Role Development

Adjustment and Gender Typing: Feminine, Masculine, or Androgynous?

Gender Differences: Fact or Myth?

Gender Differences in Aggression: The Clearest Difference

Gender Differences in Cognitive Abilities

World of Psychology: Gender Stereotyping—Who Wins? Who Loses?

Sexual Attitudes and Behavior

The Kinsey Surveys: The First In-Depth Look at Sexual Behavior

Sexual Attitudes and Behavior Today: After the Sexual Revolution

Sexual Desire and Arousal: Factors That Drive the Sex Drive

Pornography: The Researchers' View

Homosexuality

The Causes of Homosexuality: Physiological or Psychological?

Research Findings on the Developmental Experiences of Homosexuals

Social Attitudes toward Homosexuals: From Celebration to Condemnation

Sexual Dysfunctions and Treatment

Sexual Desire Disorders: From Disinterest to Aversion

Sexual Arousal Disorders

Orgasmic Disorders

Sexual Pain Disorders

Sex Therapy: There Is Help

Sexually Transmitted Diseases: The Price of Casual Sex

The Bacterial Infections

Genital Herpes: An Incurable Viral Infection

Acquired Immune Deficiency Syndrome (AIDS)

Protection against Sexually Transmitted Diseases: Minimizing Risk

Applications: Protecting Yourself from Rape

Thinking Critically

Chapter Summary and Review

Walter Fay Cannon was born into a prominent family in Durham, North Carolina, in 1925. A bright, academically talented youth, Cannon was accepted at Princeton University in 1941 when he was only 16 years old. He joined the United States Navy to serve during the last 1½ years of World War II; then he returned to Princeton and graduated in 1946. At Harvard, Cannon, the bright scholar, finished his Ph.D. and began a distinguished career. He was a university professor; an accomplished poet, writer, and historian; and finally a brilliant curator at the Smithsonian Institution in Washington, D.C., where he served until 1979.

But Walter Cannon had a secret life, which was revealed only a few years before his death in 1981. He felt like and believed that he was a woman in a man's body. Though acknowledging himself as a man, Cannon had always used his body as a woman, in homosexual encounters at Princeton, in the Navy, and throughout his life.

Cannon's wish to be female became even more compelling during his last years at the Smithsonian. He insisted on being called Faye rather than Walter and began carrying a purse, one colleague recalls. In 1976 Cannon began showing up for work dressed as a woman. This was a particular embarrassment to the officials at the Smithsonian, because Cannon was

responsible for showing visiting dignitaries around the institution. Needless to say, this eccentric behavior was not consistent with the image the Smithsonian expected of its scholars, and Cannon's early retirement was "arranged" in 1979.

Cannon did not think of himself as gay but referred to himself as a "male woman." After taking hormone treatments, he had a sex-change operation in February 1981. Now she was Susan Faye Cannon, 56 years old, in rapidly failing health and great pain.

Susan was found dead in her home from acute codeine intoxication in early November of 1981. An excerpt from Cannon's obituary notice in the *Princeton Alumni Weekly* reads: "Three months before she died, she called and told a classmate that it had been demonstrated conclusively that genetically he had always been a woman. She was very glad, because she had always suspected it and, in more recent years, known it to be a fact" (quoted in Latham & Grenadier, 1982, p. 65).

Was he, Walter Cannon, a man, or was she, Susan Cannon, a woman? Clearly Walter had the physical body of a man, but he felt like and believed that he was a woman in a man's body. You will learn how such a condtion could occur when you read about the roles the sex chromosomes and the sex hormones play in the physical formation of males and females.

Let's start at the beginning and consider all of the processes leading up to the very first announcement a parent makes—"It's a girl!" or "It's a boy!"

? *What are the biological factors that determine whether a person is male or female?*

What Makes a Male, a Male and a Female, a Female?

The Sex Chromosomes: X's and Y's

gender (JEN-der): One's biological sex—male or female.

sex chromosomes: The pair of chromosomes that determines the sex of a person (XX in females and XY in males).

gonads: The sex glands; the ovaries in females and the testes in males.

The first determiner of **gender**, or biological sex, is the **sex chromosomes**, which are XX in females and XY in males. A female's eggs all carry the X sex chromosome, but sperm cells in the male can carry either an X or a Y chromosome. If a Y-bearing sperm cell unites with the egg, which always carries an X chromosome, the developing embryo will be XY—a male. If a sperm cell carrying an X chromosome fertilizes the egg, the result will be XX—a female.

But this does not mean that being a male or a female is completely set at conception. Conception is only the beginning of the series of events spelling the difference between males and females. At 6 weeks after conception, the primitive **gonads** (sex glands) are the same in the male and the female. During the 7th week, however, if the Y chromosome is present, the gonads develop into primitive testes. If no Y chromosome is present, the gonads develop into ovaries about 12 weeks after conception. But the story does not end here.

The Sex Hormones: Contributing to Maleness and Femaleness

In the male embryo, the primitive testes produce and secrete **androgens**, the male sex hormones that cause the male **genitals**—the penis, testes, and scrotum—to develop. If androgens are not present, female genitals—the ovaries, uterus, and vagina—will develop (Breedlove, 1994). In other words, the presence or absence of androgens determines whether male or female genitals—**primary sex characteristics**—develop. A genetic male (XY) can develop female genitals if androgens are absent, and a genetic female (XX) can develop male genitals if too much androgen is present. Could this be what Cannon had referred to when she told a classmate that "genetically he had always been a woman"?

Androgens affect more than just the development of the genitals. The presence or absence of androgens in the fetus determines whether a part of the brain, the hypothalamus, becomes male- or female-differentiated (Swaab & Hofman, 1995). The hypothalamus, through its control of the pituitary gland, plays a major part in controlling the production and release of the sex hormones.

At puberty the hypothalamus sends a signal to the pituitary, which in turn sets in motion the maturing of the internal and external genitals and the appearance of the **secondary sex characteristics**. These are the physical characteristics associated with sexual maturity—pubic and underarm hair in both sexes, breasts in females, and facial and chest hair and a deepened voice in males.

Gender-Role Development

Why is it that:

- By age 15 to 26 months, children already exhibit clear preferences for toys considered appropriate for their gender?
- By age 2½ years, children already have formed stereotypes concerning what boys and girls do and do not do, and what they like and dislike?
- By age 2 to 3 years, children already consider some jobs to be for men and others for women?

What are the prevailing cultural stereotypes about masculine and feminine **gender roles**—those behaviors associated with males or females? Traditionally, males have been expected to be strong, dominant, independent, competitive, assertive, logical, decisive, confident, and unemotional; females have been expected to be warm, nurturant, caring, sensitive, supportive, emotional, passive, submissive, and dependent.

Environmental Influences on Gender Typing

How do people acquire the traits, behaviors, attitudes, preferences, and interests that the culture considers appropriate for their gender? This process, called **gender typing**, begins at birth, and parents, peers, teachers, television, and other influences play a powerful role in promoting it.

The Parents' Role: Pink and Blue Blankets and Gender-Typed Toys

Albert Bandura (1969b) describes how parents attempt to influence the gender-role development of their children:

> Sex-role differentiation usually commences immediately after birth, when the baby is named and both the infant and the nursery are given the blue or pink treatment depending upon the sex of the child. Thereafter, indoctrination into

androgens: Male sex hormones.

genitals (JEN-uh-tulz): The internal and external reproductive organs.

primary sex characteristics: The internal and external reproductive organs; the genitals.

secondary sex characteristics: The physical characteristics that are not directly involved in reproduction but that develop at puberty and are associated with sexual maturity.

gender roles: Cultural expectations about the behavior appropriate to each gender.

gender typing: The process by which individuals acquire the traits, behaviors, attitudes, preferences, and interests that the culture considers appropriate for their gender.

? *What is gender typing, and what are the environmental factors that contribute to it?*

masculinity and femininity is diligently promulgated by adorning children with distinctive clothes and hair styles, selecting sex-appropriate play materials and recreational activities, promoting associations with same-sex playmates, and through non-permissive parental reactions to deviant sex-role behavior. (p. 215)

Mothers tend to make fewer distinctions in the way they interact with their children based on gender. Fathers, on the other hand, play a more active role in gender typing (Block, 1978; Power, 1985). Fathers typically encourage their sons to be competent, to achieve and compete, to be assertive, and to control their emotions. Daughters are reinforced for being affectionate, nurturant, and obedient (Lamb, 1981). Boys are punished more than girls, and girls are treated with more

warmth and gentleness. Boys are encouraged to engage in large muscle activities and to be more independent than girls (Fagot, 1982; Maccoby & Jacklin, 1974a).

If fathers and mothers play different roles in the gender typing of their children, what happens when children are raised in single-parent homes headed by the mother? The effects of father absence seem to be most pronounced in boys under age 5 (Stevenson & Black, 1988). Father-present boys are more stereotypically gender-typed than father-absent boys and more likely to choose masculine toys and activities. But, by the time they reach adolescence, father-absent boys are more stereotypically gender-typed and more aggressive than father-present boys.

Father absence appears to have little or no effect on the gender typing of girls (Stevenson & Black, 1988). Father-absent girls tend to be slightly less feminine, but this might be the effect of having mothers who are less stereotypically feminine (Kurdek & Siesky, 1980).

Gender-role differentiation begins early in life when girls and boys learn to engage in activities that are considered typically female or male. What influences help shape their behavior?

Other Influences on Gender Typing   Peers also play an important role in enforcing conformity to gender-role stereotypes. The reaction of peers to the selection of a gender-inappropriate toy can be strong indeed.

Parents, peers, and teachers put much stronger pressure on boys to avoid feminine activities, such as playing with dolls and dishes and dressing up in mother's clothes, than they put on girls to avoid masculine activities. Sissies are ostracized, while tomboys are tolerated. Carol Martin (1990) suggests that adults react more negatively to cross-gender behavior in boys because they fear that boys may be less likely to outgrow it.

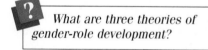 *What are three theories of gender-role development?*

Psychological Theories of Gender-Role Development

Three psychological theories are currently used to explain, in part, how gender-role development occurs—social learning theory, cognitive developmental theory, and gender-schema theory.

Social Learning Theory: Observation, Imitation, and Reinforcement

According to **social learning theory**, observation, imitation, and reinforcement are the mechanisms that explain gender typing (Mischel, 1966). Children are usually reinforced for imitating behaviors considered appropriate for their gender. When behaviors are not appropriate (a boy puts on lipstick, or a girl puts on shaving cream and attempts to shave), children are quickly informed, often in a tone of reprimand, that boys or girls do not do that. As a result of reinforcement and

social learning theory: A theory that explains the process of gender typing in terms of observation, imitation, and reinforcement.

punishment, children are led to engage in gender-appropriate behavior. They need not have knowledge about gender to acquire gender-typed preferences.

Parents are not the only ones who serve as models and dispense reinforcers. Children learn gender-appropriate behaviors from television, peers, teachers, and books. They observe the actions of others and the consequences of those actions. Even the praise or scorn others receive for gender-appropriate or inappropriate actions can provide memorable lessons in what to do and not to do.

Children are particularly influenced by the gender roles depicted in the popular media. Men and women are commonly portrayed in traditional occupational roles on television (Remafedi, 1990; Signorielli, 1990). Advertisements further reinforce gender-role stereotypes. And not only are males portrayed as more competent in various TV series, but 91 percent of the news experts on television are male, as well as 79 percent of the TV news reporters (Evan, 1991). Study gender roles on television for yourself in the *Try It!*

Take an informal sample of 20 television commercials. Record how many males and females are represented (include voiceovers) and briefly describe the role of each. Pay attention to which characters are perceived as leaders or experts, and which are perceived as helpless, passive. or sexy. Do any patterns emerge? If so, what conclusions can you draw from the patterns?

Cognitive Developmental Theory: Understanding Gender in Stages

Cognitive developmental theory, proposed by Lawrence Kohlberg (1966; Kohlberg & Ullian, 1974) suggests that children play an active role in their own gender typing, but that an understanding of gender is a prerequisite. According to Kohlberg, children go through a series of stages in acquiring the concept of gender. Between ages 2 and 3, children acquire **gender identity**—their sense of being a male or a female. Between ages 4 and 5, children acquire the concept of gender stability—awareness that boys are boys and girls are girls for a lifetime. Finally, between ages 6 and 8, children understand gender constancy—that gender does not change regardless of the activities people engage in or the clothes they wear. Moreover, according to Kohlberg, when children realize their gender is permanent, they are motivated to seek out same-sex models and learn to act in ways considered appropriate for their gender. Cross-cultural studies reveal that Kohlberg's stages of gender identity, gender stability, and gender constancy occur in the same order in cultures as different as those in Samoa, Kenya, Nepal, and Belize (Munroe et al., 1984).

Although attaining gender constancy is a necessary part of gender-role development, children have a great deal of gender-role knowledge long before they attain it (Levy & Carter, 1989; Serbin & Sprafkin, 1986). Gender constancy may be acquired between 6 and 8 years, but Kohlberg's theory fails to explain why many gender-appropriate behaviors and preferences are observed in children as young as age 2 or 3 (Jacklin, 1989; Martin & Little, 1990).

cognitive developmental theory: A theory suggesting that when children realize their gender is permanent, they are motivated to seek out same-sex models and learn to act in ways considered appropriate for their gender.

gender identity: One's sense of being a male or a female.

Gender-Schema Theory: Forming Gender Stereotypes Gender-schema **theory**, proposed by Sandra Bem (1981), combines elements of both social learning and cognitive developmental theory. Like social learning theory, gender-schema theory suggests that young children are motivated to pay attention to and behave in a way consistent with gender-based standards and stereotypes of the culture. Like cognitive developmental theory, gender-schema theory stresses that children begin to use gender as a way to organize and process information. But it holds that this process occurs earlier, when gender identity rather than gender constancy is attained (Bem, 1985). According to Martin and Little (1990), "Once children can accurately label the sexes, they begin to form gender stereotypes and their behavior is influenced by these gender-associated expectations" (p. 1438). They develop strong preferences for peers of the same sex and for sex-appropriate toys and clothing. Fagot and others (1992) found gender labeling and gender stereotyping to occur in children 2 to 3 years old.

Children learn which activities and traits are most important for males and females and then evaluate themselves in relation to those traits. They first learn the characteristics appropriate to their own sex, and later those appropriate to the opposite sex (Martin et al., 1990). To a large extent, their own self-concepts and self-esteem depend on the match between their abilities and behaviors and the cultural definition of what is desirable for their gender.

Adjustment and Gender Typing: Feminine, Masculine, or Androgynous?

Traditionally, masculinity and femininity have been considered opposite ends of a continuum. But must we think of masculine traits and feminine traits as mutually exclusive? Must an individual be either independent, competent, and assertive or nurturant, sensitive, and warm? Sandra Bem (1974, 1977) proposed that "masculine" and "feminine" characteristics are separate and independent dimensions of personality rather than opposite ends of a continuum. A person can be high or low on one or both dimensions. **Androgyny** is a combination of the desirable male and female characteristics in one person, who is said to be androgynous. People who are low on both "masculine" and "feminine" dimensions are labeled undifferentiated. There is some evidence that African American women are more androgynous than white women (Binion, 1990).

Some researchers claim that androgynous individuals have a wider range of possible behavioral characteristics at their disposal. Consequently, such individuals are said to be better equipped to meet the challenges of the work world and their personal relationships (Bem, 1975). Is this true? Are androgynous persons better adjusted than those who adopt a more traditional masculine or feminine role consistent with their gender? There is some evidence that a combination of positive masculine traits *and* positive feminine traits in males is correlated with success in intimate relationships (Coleman & Ganong, 1985). But research suggests that for both males and females, masculine traits are most strongly associated with self-esteem and adjustment (Aubé & Koestner, 1992). Jones and others (1978) found that "the more adaptive, flexible, unconventional, and competent patterns of responding occurred among more masculine subjects independent of their gender" (p. 311). To the extent that androgynous people possess the desired masculine traits, they are likely to be better adjusted and have higher self-esteem than people who are feminine or undifferentiated. Males displaying feminine interests and behaviors and the undesirable feminine traits (e.g., submissiveness, gullibility, and so on) are found to have the lowest self-esteem (O'Heron & Orlofsky, 1990; Pryor, 1994).

Do good adjustment and high self-esteem seem to be related to masculine traits, feminine traits, or androgyny?

---

gender-schema theory: A theory suggesting that young children are motivated to attend to and behave in ways consistent with gender-based standards and stereotypes of the culture.

androgyny (an-DROJ-uh-nee): A combination of the desirable male and female characteristics in one person.

Memory Check 11.1

1. The sex chromosomes in a male are _____; the sex chromosomes in a female are _____.
   a. XX; XY b. YY; XX c. XX; YY d. XY; XX

2. The Y sex chromosome must be present for the testes to develop; the ovaries will develop if the Y chromosome is absent. (true/false)

3. If androgens are not present, the female genitals will develop regardless of whether the sex chromosomes are XY or XX. (true/false)

4. What is the process by which individuals acquire the traits, behaviors, attitudes, preferences, and interests that the culture considers gender appropriate?
   a. gender stereotyping   c. gender constancy
   b. sexual enculturation   d. gender typing

5. In the family, the mother usually plays the major role in gender typing. (true/false)

6. Which theory of gender-role development explains the process of gender typing in terms of observation, imitation, and reinforcement?
   a. gender-schema theory
   b. androgyny theory
   c. social learning theory
   d. cognitive developmental theory

7. Good adjustment and high self-esteem are associated with masculine traits in both males and females. (true/false)

Answers: 1. d 2. true 3. true 4. d 5. false 6. c 7. true

Gender Differences: Fact or Myth?

To a remarkable degree throughout recorded history and in the vast majority of cultures around the world, gender has defined destiny. Even in the United States, women did not have the right to vote in national elections until 1920. Why do issues of gender continue to mark our lives so profoundly?

Males and females are indeed different, but in what ways and to what degree? To address this question, Eleanor Maccoby and Carol Jacklin (1974a) examined 1,600 studies on gender differences and published their results in *The Psychology of Sex Differences.* They found evidence that males were generally more aggressive and had a slight advantage in mathematics and spatial skills, while females had a slight advantage in verbal ability. They also refuted some long-standing, unfounded beliefs about gender differences, such as the notion that girls are more sociable or suggestible than boys, less analytical, better at rote learning and repetitive tasks, and lower in self-esteem or achievement motivation.

Gender Differences in Aggression: The Clearest Difference

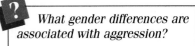

What gender differences are associated with aggression?

Most researchers agree that greater physical aggression in males is one of the most consistent and significant differences observed in comparative studies of gender (Bogard, 1990; Harris, 1992). And these differences have been found in virtually every culture where aggressive behavior has been studied. Such an observation is hardly surprising. We need only consider the number of men in prison for violent crimes compared to the number of women.

Greater aggression can usually be observed in boys from the time they are 2 to 2½ years old. They are more likely than girls to engage in mock fighting and rough-and-tumble play and to have aggressive fantasies (Maccoby & Jacklin, 1974b). But females can be aggressive, too. They may be even more likely than males to use *indirect* forms of aggression, such as gossip, spreading rumors, and rejecting, ignoring, or avoiding the target of aggression (Björkqvist et al., 1992). Females seem to feel more guilt and anxiety about engaging in aggressive behavior and to feel more fear that they will be the target of retaliation (Eagly & Steffen, 1986).

The male sex hormone testosterone has long been suspected as the guilty substance promoting aggression. Gender differences in aggression have been linked to testosterone levels in a number of animal studies, especially with rats and primates (Maccoby & Jacklin, 1980). Gladue (1991) found that both heterosexual and gay men with higher blood levels of testosterone were more likely to engage in physical and verbal aggression than men with lower blood levels.

Gender Differences in Cognitive Abilities

> **?** *For what cognitive abilities are there proven gender differences?*

For many years researchers believed that, on average, females were superior in verbal skills and males were superior in mathematics and spatial skills. What does research say about cognitive differences and gender?

Gender Differences in Verbal Ability: Is One Sex Better with Words?
Maccoby and Jacklin (1974a) reported that girls performed better overall than boys in verbal abilities. But over recent decades, the gender differences in tests of general verbal ability have virtually disappeared. Using meta-analysis, researchers Janet Hyde and Marcia Linn (1988) examined 165 studies reporting test results on verbal ability for approximately 1.5 million males and females. They found no significant gender differences in verbal ability. Analyzing test results from large, nationally representative samples, Hedges and Nowell (1995) found that males were more likely than females to perform poorly in reading comprehension and writing.

Gender Differences in Math Ability: Do Males Have the Edge? In one of the largest studies conducted to date on gender differences in mathematics, Hyde and others (1990) performed a meta-analysis of 100 studies, which together represented test results for more than 3 million subjects. They found no significant gender difference in the understanding of mathematical concepts among the various age groups. Although females did slightly better in mathematical problem solving in elementary and middle school, males scored moderately higher in high school and college. Benbow and Stanley (1980, 1983) found a significant male superiority in a select segment of the population—the brightest of the bright in mathematics ability. There were twice as many boys as girls scoring above 500 on the SAT, and 13 times as many scoring above 700.

Parents often expect boys to do better than girls in math (Lummis & Stevenson, 1990). Such expectations may become a self-fulfilling prophecy, leading girls to lack confidence in their math ability and to decide not to pursue advanced math courses (Eccles & Jacobs, 1986). A report by the American Association of University Women Education Foundation provided evidence that many science teachers and some math teachers, as well, tend to pay noticeably more attention to boys than to girls (Chira, 1992). Such treatment may discourage girls with math or science aptitude from choosing careers in these areas.

Gender Differences in Spatial Ability Researchers have found that, in general, males tend to perform somewhat better than females on tests of spatial skills (Kimura, 1992; Linn & Hyde, 1989; Linn & Peterson, 1985). This gender difference has been found on some but not all of the various spatial tasks, and the difference is so small that only about "5 percent of it at most can be accounted for on the basis of sex" (Fausto-Sterling, 1985, p. 33).

Gender differences are revealed most often on mental rotation tasks, in which three-dimensional figures must be mentally rotated quickly and accurately (Casey

One of the most consistent and significant gender differences found by researchers is that males show higher levels of physical aggression.

FIGURE 11.1

Problem-Solving Tasks Favoring Women and Men

(a) A series of problem-solving tasks on which women generally do better than men. (b) Tasks on which men do better. (From Kimura, 1992.)

Women tend to perform better than men on tests of perceptual speed, in which subjects must rapidly identify matching items—for example, pairing the house on the far left with its twin:

In addition, women remember whether an object, or a series of objects, has been displaced:

On some tests of ideational fluency—for example, those in which subjects must list objects that are the same color—and on tests of verbal fluency—in which participants must list words that begin with the same letter—women outperform men:

Limp, Livery, Love, Laser, Liquid, Low, Like, Lag, Live Lug, Light, Lift, Liver, Lime, Leg, Load, Lap, Lucid ...

Women do better on precision manual tasks—that is, those involving fine motor coordination—such as placing the pegs in holes on a board:

And women do better than men on mathematical calculation tests:

77	$14 \times 3 - 17 + 52$
43	$2(15+3) + 12 - \dfrac{15}{3}$

(a)

Men tend to perform better than women on certain spatial tasks. They do well on tests that involve mentally rotating an object or manipulating it in some fashion, such as imagining turning this three-dimensional object:

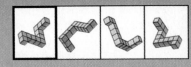

or determining where the holes punched in a folded piece of paper will fall when the paper is unfolded:

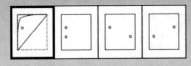

Men also are more accurate than women in target-directed motor skills, such as guiding or intercepting projectiles:

They do better on disembedding tests, in which they have to find a simple shape, such as the one on the left, once it is hidden within a more complex figure:

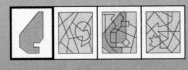

And men tend to do better than women on tests of mathematical reasoning:

1,100	If only 60 percent of seedlings will survive, how many must be planted to obtain 660 trees?

(b)

et al., 1995). Figure 11.1 shows problem-solving tasks, some of which are more easily solved by females, others by males.

The following World of Psychology section considers some of the possible social consequences of gender stereotyping.

World of Psychology

Gender Stereotyping— Who Wins? Who Loses?

A majority of the people on the planet are female, yet around the world women are vastly underrepresented in positions of power. As we have seen, gender stereotypes define males as decisive, aggressive, unemotional, logical, and ambitious. These qualities are perceived by many men and women alike as precisely the "right stuff" for leaders, decision makers, and power people at all levels of society. But women, too, can be strong, bold, and decisive leaders—like former British Prime Minister Margaret Thatcher, Golda Meir of Israel, and Indira Ghandi of India. Yet in 1995, only 8 of the 100 U.S. senators and 48 of the 435 members of the House of Representatives were women.

Today, 99 percent of men and 98 percent of women *say* that women should receive equal pay for equal work (Newport, 1993). Yet the average female worker in the United States is paid only 77 cents for every dollar paid to a male worker (Famighetti, 1994). And women are more likely to hold low-paying, low-status jobs. Figure 11.2 shows the male–female earnings gap in six different occupational fields.

FIGURE 11.2

The Male–Female Earnings Gap

The earnings gap between males and females varies from one occupation to another, as indicated by the six occupational groups shown here. In sales, women make 42 percent less than men. In occupations typically held by females, the earnings gap is smaller. Female registered nurses make 1 percent less than their male counterparts. The percentage of females in each occupational group is shown at the bottom of the chart. (Based on Saltzman, 1991.)

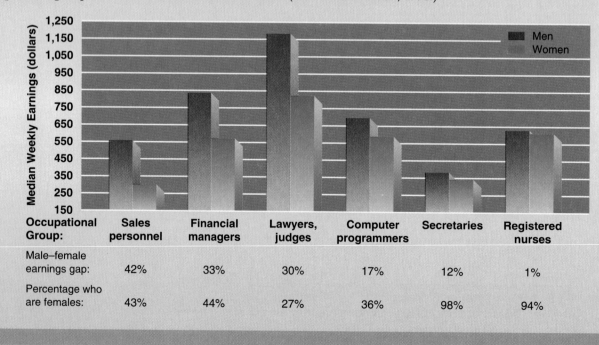

Occupational Group:	Sales personnel	Financial managers	Lawyers, judges	Computer programmers	Secretaries	Registered nurses
Male–female earnings gap:	42%	33%	30%	17%	12%	1%
Percentage who are females:	43%	44%	27%	36%	98%	94%

TABLE 11.1 Average Earnings of Full-Time Female Workers as a Percentage of Those of Men in Ten Industrialized Countries (Nonagricultural Activities), 1980 and 1988

Country	Earnings Ratio (1980)	Earnings Ratio (1988)
Australia	85.9	87.9
Denmark	84.5	82.1
France	79.2	81.8*
Netherlands	78.2	76.8
Belgium	69.4	75.0
West Germany	72.4	73.5
United Kingdom	69.7	69.5†
United States	66.7‡	70.2
Switzerland	67.6	76.4
Japan	53.8	50.7

*1987 data   †1984 data   ‡1983 data

Source: Renzetti & Curran, 1992, p. 192.

Wage discrimination against women is not confined to the United States. Of the ten industrialized nations shown in Table 11.1, Australia has the smallest wage gap between men and women (88 cents to female workers for every dollar paid male workers). Japan has the widest wage gap, with women paid, on the average, only about half as much as men (International Labour Office, 1990).

In 1991 a U.S. Department of Labor study concluded that a barrier described as a "glass ceiling" prevents women from advancing to top management positions in corporate America. Morrison and Von Glinow (1990) define the glass ceiling as "a barrier so subtle that it is transparent, yet so strong that it prevents women and minorities from moving up in the management hierarchy" (p. 200).

Why are there so few women in upper-management, power positions in corporate America? Several explanations have been offered. Many corporate leaders define a good manager as tough, decisive, logical, and unemotional—the male stereotype. People who point to the deficiencies in women claim that their personality traits and attitudes make them less suited for upper management. Yet a considerable body of research refutes this notion (Morrison & Von Glinow, 1990). Nevertheless, the mere perception of deficiencies, if held by the dominant corporate leaders, is sufficient to produce bias and discrimination.

The structure of the organization may present another problem for female managers. A few women among so many men in a management group are highly visible and likely to be viewed as "tokens" by the dominant group (Kanter, 1977). Tokenism is a subtle form of discrimination in which persons are hired or promoted primarily because they represent a specific group or category rather than strictly on the basis of their qualifications.

Paradoxically, some women may be helping to keep the glass ceiling in place. A 1993 Gallup poll revealed that women are even more likely than men to express a preference for a male boss, by 44 to 33 percent (Moore & Gallup, 1993).

The negative effect that women experience due to gender stereotyping in the workplace is not as bad as in decades past, but it is still a major problem for many women.

Memory Check 11.2

1. Maccoby and Jacklin found no differences between boys and girls in sociability, self-esteem, analytical ability, and achievement motivation. (true/false)

2. The largest gender differences are found in:
   a. spatial skills.
   b. verbal skills.
   c. mathematical problem solving.
   d. physical aggression.

3. In which area is there no longer a gender difference?
   a. spatial skills   c. math skills
   b. verbal skills   d. physical aggression

4. Some researchers believe that males are more aggressive than females because of the effects of:
   a. acetylcholine.   c. testosterone.
   b. norepinephrine.   d. estrogen.

Answers: 1. true 2. d 3. b 4. c

Sexual Attitudes and Behavior

Few would disagree that society's attitudes about sexual behavior are more liberal now than in decades past. In the 1940s and 1950s, virtually all societal institutions officially frowned upon sex before marriage. Sex was not considered an appropriate subject for serious investigation, nor was it discussed openly in polite society. But that began to change when Alfred Kinsey came on the scene.

? *What were the famous Kinsey surveys?*

The Kinsey Surveys: The First In-Depth Look at Sexual Behavior

In the 1940s Alfred Kinsey and his associates undertook a monumental survey that helped to bring the subject of sex out in the open. They interviewed thousands of men and women about their sexual behaviors and attitudes, and their results were published in a two-volume report—*Sexual Behavior in the Human Male* and *Sexual Behavior in the Human Female*. The public was stunned by what Kinsey's subjects said they had done and were doing. It appeared that a lot of Americans had a head start on the sexual revolution way back in the 1940s and 1950s. And there was a great gulf between what people were practicing in private and what they were admitting openly.

Kinsey's interviews revealed the following:

- About 50 percent of the females and nearly 90 percent of the males reported having sexual intercourse, **coitus**, before marriage.
- Over 40 percent of the college-educated couples said they engaged in oral sex.
- The majority of women and virtually all males reported that they had masturbated.
- About 26 percent of the married women and half of the married men admitted having had extramarital affairs.

But was Kinsey's study valid? Was it scientific? People attacked the findings for a variety of reasons. It is true that Kinsey's sample was not broadly representative. He reported no information on African Americans. Elderly people, rural people, and those with only grade school educations were underrepresented; Protestants, the college educated, the middle class, and urban populations were overrepresented.

Have sexual attitudes and behavior changed much since Kinsey's surveys half a century ago?

coitus: Penile-vaginal intercourse.

Sexual Attitudes and Behavior Today: After the Sexual Revolution

In 1994 the most comprehensive survey of sexual behavior since Kinsey was published. *The Social Organization of Sexuality* by Laumann and others (1994) is believed to be the most valid and reliable survey of its kind to date. The findings were based on interviews of a nationwide representative sample composed of 3,432 males and females aged 18 to 59. The major findings are summarized below and in Figure 11.3.

- Married people have sex more frequently and are more likely to have orgasms than noncohabiting men and women.

- On average, over the course of a lifetime, men have six sex partners and women have two.

- Almost 75 percent of men and 85 percent of women reported that they had been faithful to their spouses.

- Fifty-four percent of men and 19 percent of women reported thinking about sex every day or several times a day; 4 percent of men and 14 percent of women reported either never thinking of sex or thinking of it less than once a month.

- Twenty-seven percent of men and 8 percent of women said they masturbated at least once a week during the previous 12 months; 37 percent of men and 58 percent of women said they had not masturbated.

- Although 5.3 percent of men and 3.5 percent of women reported having had a homosexual encounter since age 18, only 2.8 percent of men and 1.4 percent of women identified themselves as homosexual or bisexual.

- Of women, 22.8 percent reported having been forced to do something sexually they did not want to do, while only 2.8 percent of men reported forcing a woman to engage in a sexual act.

Throughout all age groups in the United States today, men report having had more different sex partners and express a more permissive attitude toward casual premarital sex than women (Oliver & Hyde, 1993). Women associate sex with love and marriage more than men do, and it may be true that women give more of themselves emotionally to the sexual union.

In the decades before the 1960s, young men and women were less free to say yes to their sexual desires. People were constrained by virtually all of society's institutions and by the most formidable restraint of all—fear of pregnancy. But today, fear of pregnancy is less a factor because of the pill and other contraceptive methods, and abortion is legal. Peer pressure ("everybody's doing it"), films, tele-

FIGURE 11.3

Some Results of a 1994 U.S. Sex Survey

Contrary to what is generally portrayed in the media, most Americans are having sex a few times a month or less. Of the respondents to the survey, 83 percent reported having either one or no sex partner during the past 12 months.

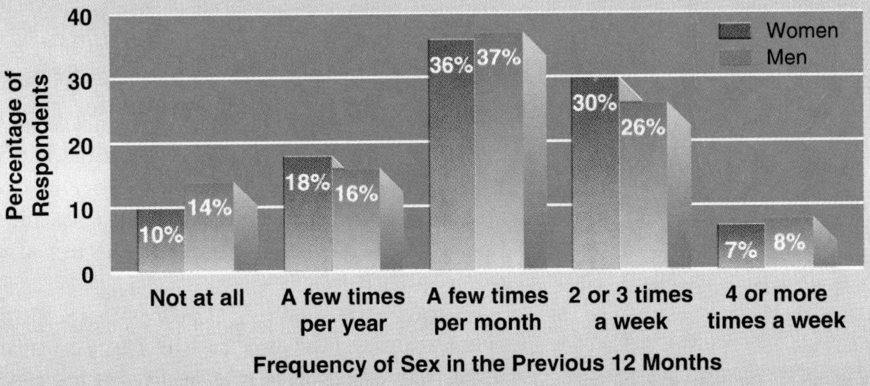

Bar chart. Y-axis: Percentage of Respondents (0 to 40). X-axis: Frequency of Sex in the Previous 12 Months. Legend: Women, Men.

Category	Women	Men
Not at all	10%	14%
A few times per year	18%	16%
A few times per month	36%	37%
2 or 3 times a week	30%	26%
4 or more times a week	7%	8%

vision, magazines, advertisements, song lyrics—all these sources of influence have combined to make it difficult for young people to say no to their sexual desires.

In a sense, then, the societal pressures that decades ago made it hard to say yes to sex have been traded for pressures that today make it just as hard to say no. Sexual freedom prevails only when we are equally free to say yes or no.

Sexual Desire and Arousal: Factors That Drive the Sex Drive

Masters and Johnson and the Human Sexual Response Cycle Kinsey conducted the first major survey of sexual behavior, but what if the act of intercourse could be monitored right in the laboratory? Wouldn't this be more scientific than simply relying on self-reports? These were the questions asked by sex researchers Dr. William Masters and Virginia Johnson. To answer them, they planned and conducted the first laboratory investigations of the human sexual response in 1954. They monitored their volunteer subjects, who engaged in the sex act while connected to sophisticated (for the 1960s) electronic sensing devices.

Masters and Johnson (1966) concluded that the human sexual response is quite similar for males and females. Two major physiological changes occur in both sexes—the flow of blood into the genitals (and breasts in females) and an increase in neuromuscular tension.

Both males and females experience a **sexual response cycle** with four phases: (1) the excitement phase, (2) the plateau phase, (3) the orgasm, and (4) the resolution phase. Masters and Johnson studied over "10,000 complete cycles of sexual response" in 382 women and 312 men (1966, p. 15). They found that these phases apply not only to sexual intercourse but also to other types of sexual activity.

The Excitement Phase The **excitement phase** is the beginning of the sexual response. It can be triggered by direct physical contact as well as by psychological arousal—thoughts, emotions, and a variety of sensory stimuli. For both partners, muscular tension increases, heart rate quickens, and blood pressure rises. As additional blood is pumped into the genitals, the male's penis becomes erect and the female feels a swelling of the clitoris. Vaginal lubrication occurs as the inner two-thirds of the vagina expands and the inner lips of the vagina enlarge. In women especially, the nipples harden and stand erect.

The Plateau Phase After the excitement phase, the couple enters the **plateau phase**, when excitement continues to mount. Blood pressure and muscle tension increase still more, and breathing becomes heavy and more rapid. The man's testes swell, and drops of liquid, which could contain live sperm cells, may drip from the penis during this phase. The outer part of the woman's vagina swells as the increased blood further engorges the area. The clitoris withdraws under the clitoral hood, its skin covering, and the breasts become engorged with blood. Excitement builds steadily for both partners during the plateau phase.

The Orgasm Phase The **orgasm phase**, the shortest of the stages, is the very peak of the experience—the highest point of sexual pleasure—marked by a sudden discharge of accumulated sexual tension. Involuntary muscle contractions may seize the entire body during orgasm, as the genitals throb with rhythmic contractions.

Orgasm is a two-stage experience for the male. First is his awareness that ejaculation is near and that he can do nothing to stop it; second is the ejaculation itself, when semen is released from the penis in forceful spurts.

The experience of orgasm in women builds in much the same way as for men. Marked by powerful, rhythmic contractions, the female's orgasm usually lasts

---

? *According to Masters and Johnson, what are the four phases of the human sexual response cycle?*

Virginia Masters and William Johnson were pioneers in the study of the human sexual response.

sexual response cycle: The four phases—excitement, plateau, orgasm, and resolution—that Masters and Johnson found are part of the human sexual response in both males and females.

excitement phase: The first stage in the sexual response cycle, characterized by an erection in males and a swelling of the clitoris and vaginal lubrication in females.

plateau phase: The second stage of the sexual response cycle, during which muscle tension and blood flow to the genitals increase in preparation for orgasm.

orgasm phase: The third phase in the sexual response cycle, marked by rhythmic muscular contractions and a sudden discharge of accumulated sexual tension.

longer than that of the male. About 40 to 50 percent of women regularly experience orgasm during intercourse (Wilcox & Hager, 1980). Although the vaginal orgasm and clitoral orgasm may feel different, say Masters and Johnson, the actual physiological response in the female is the same.

The Resolution Phase The orgasm period gives way to the **resolution phase**, a tapering-off period, when the body returns to its unaroused state. Men experience a refractory period in the resolution phase, during which they cannot have another orgasm. The refractory period may last only a few minutes for some men, but much longer—many hours—for others. Women do not have a refractory period and may, if restimulated, experience another orgasm right away.

The Role of Hormones in Sexual Desire and Arousal: Sexual Substances In most animal species, sexual activity does not occur unless the female is "in heat." Thus, most animals behave sexually in response to hormones, odors, and biologically determined sexual cycles. But human sexual desire can be aroused at practically any time, independent of the rhythmic biological cycles. And humans engage in far more sex than is required to continue the species.

The sex glands themselves manufacture hormones—**estrogen** and **progesterone** in the ovaries, and androgens in the testes. The adrenal glands in both sexes also produce small amounts of these hormones. Females have considerably more estrogen and progesterone than males do, so these are known as the female sex hormones. Males have considerably more androgens—the male sex hormones. **Testosterone**, the most important androgen, influences the development and maintenance of male sex characteristics as well as sexual motivation.

Testosterone and Sexual Desire Males must have a sufficient level of testosterone in order to maintain sexual interest and have an erection. It is more than coincidence that at puberty, when testosterone levels increase dramatically, sexual thoughts and fantasies, masturbation, and nocturnal emissions also increase significantly. Udry and colleagues (1985) found that adolescents with high blood levels of testosterone spend more time thinking about sex. Thus, they are more likely to engage in masturbation, coitus, or other sexual activity than their counterparts with lower levels of testosterone.

As men age, the level of testosterone declines, and usually there is also a decline in sexual interest and activity, although there is not a one-to-one correspondence between them (Byrne, 1982). Some researchers predict that synthetic testosterone will soon be prescribed to counteract these effects (Hoberman & Yesalis, 1995). Castration (removal of the testes, which produce 95 percent of the male's androgens) usually lowers sexual desire and activity dramatically.

Females, too, need small amounts of androgens circulating in the bloodstream to maintain sexual interest and responsiveness. But hormones and other biological processes are not the only factors that drive sexual arousal. Psychological factors are important, as well, in producing and maintaining sexual arousal.

Psychological Factors in Sexual Arousal: It All Begins in the Mind Psychological factors play a large role in sexual arousal. Part of the psychological nature of sexual behavior stems from those preferences and practices we have learned from our culture. What is perceived as sexually attractive in the male and the female in one culture may differ dramatically from the standards of attractiveness in other cultures. In the United States movie stars and models are often regarded as the ultimate in sexual desirability.

Sometimes, as a result of conditioning, men and women find certain stimuli sexually arousing (Dekker & Everaerd, 1989; O'Donohue & Plaud, 1994). The stimuli might be specific settings (a romantic candlelight dinner, a walk on the beach in the evening), certain music, particular objects or articles of clothing, or even the scent of a certain perfume or after-shave.

> **?** *What are the male and female sex hormones, and how do they affect sexual desire and activity in males and females?*

resolution phase: The final stage of the sexual response cycle, during which the body returns to an unaroused state.

estrogen (ES-truh-jen): A female sex hormone that promotes the secondary sex characteristics in females and controls the menstrual cycle.

progesterone (pro-JES-tah-rone): A female sex hormone that plays a role in the regulation of the menstrual cycle and prepares the lining of the uterus for possible pregnancy.

testosterone (tes-TOS-tah-rone): The most powerful androgen secreted by the testes and adrenal glands in males and by the adrenal glands in females; influences the development and maintenance of male sex characteristics and sexual motivation; associated with male aggressiveness.

Men and women differ in the ways they become sexually aroused. Men are more aroused by what they see; visual cues like watching a woman undress are likely to arouse them. But tender, loving touches coupled with verbal expressions of love arouse women more readily than visual stimulation. Men can become aroused almost instantly, while arousal for women is more likely to be a gradual, building process.

Men are more likely to seek out sexual stimulation and arousal in magazines such as *Playboy*, in X-rated movies, and in adult bookstores. Both males and females often use sexual fantasy to increase arousal. Ellis and Symons (1990) suggest that men's fantasies primarily reflect lust, while in women's fantasies lust is secondary to love. "Women tend to imagine themselves as objects of male passion . . . while men tend to imagine women as responsive, lusty objects" (p. 550). Hsu and others (1994) found that males are more likely than females to fantasize about sexual activities they have never engaged in.

While sexual fantasy may grow out of sexual desire, at other times fantasy is used to heighten sexual desire or to increase passion (Friday, 1980). Sue (1979) found that over 60 percent of male and female college students admitted to having erotic fantasies during intercourse. The reasons they gave for doing so were to facilitate arousal, to imagine activities they do not engage in with their partner, or to increase the partner's attractiveness. They may fantasize about something morally unacceptable to them or unattainable, like having sex with an old boyfriend or girlfriend, a movie star, or some other celebrity (Crépault et al., 1977; Crépault & Couture, 1980). Many people would feel insulted if they knew their mate needed to fantasize them out of the picture in order to gain sexual satisfaction.

Sexuality and Commitment: Where the Best Sex Is Found The physiology of the sex act is certainly important, but there is much more to sex than the physical response. Today many people view sex as a casual recreational activity, and often it has little to do with love. Masters and Johnson have been accused of reducing the sex act to its clinical, physical components, but their book *The Pleasure Bond* (1975) argues strongly against separating the physical act of sex from the context of love and commitment. They are critical of those who "consider the physical act of intercourse as something in and of itself, a skill to be practiced and improved . . . an activity to exercise the body, or a game to be played." "To reduce sex to a physical exchange," they say, "is to strip it of richness and subtlety and, even more important, ultimately means robbing it of all emotional value." In Masters and Johnson's view it is a couple's "total commitment, in which all sense of obligation is linked to mutual feelings of loving concern, [that] sustains a couple sexually over the years" (1975, p. 268).

Pornography: The Researchers' View

Pornography has become a lucrative industry in the United States, reaping about $4 to 6 billion a year. Over half a million people, the majority of whom are middle-aged and middle-class males, view pornography regularly.

There are degrees of pornography. Soft-core pornography depicts nudity and sexual acts short of intercourse. Hard-core pornography, the type commonly seen in X-rated videos, depicts very explicit sex acts, leaving little or nothing to the imagination. Women are often presented as sex objects to be degraded and dehumanized. Violent or aggressive pornography, such as slasher films, portrays women in powerless positions, as victims of aggression and violence ranging from beatings and rape to dismemberment and murder.

Psychological factors, including feelings of love and commitment, play an important role in sexual arousal.

? *What have researchers discovered about the effects of pornography on its viewers?*

pornography: Books, pictures, films, or videos used to increase sexual arousal; hard-core pornography has very explicit depictions of various sex acts.

What does research say about the effects of pornography?

Violent Pornography A number of laboratory studies indicate that the frequent viewing of violent pornography tends to desensitize the regular viewer to violent and degrading sexual practices. Several researchers have found that men who repeatedly view violent rape scenes may become desensitized to the horror and reality of rape and have less compassion for rape victims (Donnerstein & Linz, 1984; Linz et al., 1984, 1988; Zillmann & Bryant, 1982). And "pornography that portrays sexual aggression as pleasurable for the victim increases the acceptance of the use of coercion in sexual relations" (Koop, 1987, p. 945).

Other researchers find that exposure to violent pornography leads many people to accept the **rape myth**—the unfounded belief that women who are raped ask for it, deserve it, and often enjoy it (Malamuth, 1984). Check (1984) found that after watching degrading or violent pornography, male subjects were more likely to admit that they would pressure or even rape a woman if they could be sure they would get away with it.

According to Fisher and Grenier (1994), some studies report that viewing violent pornography had no effect on whether men (1) increased their acceptance of the rape myth (Linz et al., 1988), (2) reported a likelihood that they would rape someone (Malamuth & Ceniti, 1986), or (3) expressed negative attitudes toward women or endorsed interpersonal violence against them (Demare et al., 1988). But the weight of evidence falls clearly on the side of researchers who have found that violent pornography is associated with negative attitudes and behaviors against women. After reviewing numerous studies of violent and nonviolent pornography, Linz (1989) said, "Every study that has included a 'slasher' condition has found antisocial effects resulting from exposure to these films" (p. 74).

Nonviolent Pornography Researchers are more evenly divided on the question of the potentially harmful effects of nonviolent pornography. Linz (1989), who strongly contends that violent pornography produces antisocial effects, has found no significant negative influences that can be attributed to nonviolent pornography. Padgett and others (1989) found no relationship between repeated exposure to nonviolent pornography and negative male attitudes toward women or increased acceptance of the rape myth.

Yet other researchers have reported negative effects of nonviolent pornography. Zillmann & Weaver (1989) contend that when women are portrayed as sexually permissive and promiscuous, men become less sympathetic toward women who are victims of sexual aggression. Some studies reveal that people may come to value their partner and relationship less after exposure to erotic sexual material. Male college students who agreed to view sexually explicit films showing highly attractive females reported being less pleased with their wives or girlfriends than were control groups of college men who did not view such materials (Kenrick & Gütierres, 1980; Weaver et al., 1984). Also, people may feel disappointed with their own sexual performance after comparing it to the performance portrayed by actors. Citing evidence from a series of other studies, Zillmann (1989) also concluded that repeated exposure to pornography that portrays spontaneous, promiscuous sex devoid of responsibility, obligation, and mutual love serves to weaken a commitment to traditional values.

Most research shows that violent pornography is associated with negative attitudes and behaviors toward women.

rape myth: The unfounded belief that women who are raped ask for it, deserve it, or enjoy it.

Memory Check 11.3

1. Who conducted the first major surveys of sexual attitudes and behaviors of American males and females?
   a. Alfred Kinsey
   b. Masters and Johnson
   c. George Gallup
   d. Maccoby and Jacklin

2. Which of the following statements about the human sexual response cycle is false?
   a. It consists of four phases.
   b. It occurs in sexual intercourse and can occur in other types of sexual activity.
   c. It is quite different in males and females.
   d. It was researched by Masters and Johnson.

3. Androgens, estrogen, and progesterone are present in both males and females. (true/false)

4. Testosterone plays a role in maintaining sexual interest in males and females. (true/false)

5. Which of the following is *not* cited in the text as an effect of repeated exposure to violent pornography?
   a. Individuals may become less repelled by violent and degrading sexual practices.
   b. Some men admit a greater willingness to force women to engage in sex.
   c. Some people become more accepting of the rape myth.
   d. Men become more aware of the horror of rape and are more sympathetic to rape victims.

Answers: 1. a 2. c 3. true 4. true 5. d

What is meant by sexual orientation?

Homosexuality

We have said a great deal about the human sexual response and sexual arousal, but we have not considered **sexual orientation**—the direction of an individual's sexual preference, erotic feelings, and sexual activity. In heterosexuality, the human sexual response is oriented toward members of the opposite sex; in homosexuality, toward those of the same sex; and in bisexuality, toward members of both sexes.

Homosexuality has been reported in all societies throughout recorded history (Carrier, 1980; Ford & Beach, 1951). Kinsey and his associates (1948, 1953) estimated that 4 percent of the male subjects had nothing but homosexual relations throughout life, and about 2 to 3 percent of the female subjects had been in mostly or exclusively lesbian relationships. Fay and others (1989) estimate that from 3.3 to 6.2 percent of the adult male population have had adult homosexual contacts. Gay and lesbian rights groups, however, claim that about 10 percent of the U.S. population is predominantly homosexual. Averaging the findings from a number of studies, Diamond (1993) found that 5.5 percent of males and 2.5 percent of females had had at least one homosexual encounter since adolescence. Notably, all estimates suggest that homosexuality is at least twice as prevalent in males as in females.

Until recent years, most homosexuals kept their sexual orientation a secret rather than risk shame and discrimination. But now more homosexuals are "coming out," preferring to acknowledge and express their sexual orientation rather than having to lead a double life (Gorman, 1991).

sexual orientation: The direction of one's sexual preference—toward members of the opposite sex (heterosexuality), toward one's own sex (homosexuality), or toward both sexes (bisexuality).

What are the various biological factors that have been suggested as possible causes of homosexuality?

The Causes of Homosexuality: Physiological or Psychological?

What causes homosexuality? Psychologists continue to debate whether homosexuality is biologically fixed or acquired through learning and experience. Some experts suggest that a homosexual orientation is learned (Gagnon & Simon, 1973; Masters & Johnson, 1979). Others believe that biological factors largely determine sexual orientation (Bailey & Pillard, 1994; Isay, 1989; LeVay, 1993). Still others lean toward an interaction—the theory that both nature and nurture play a part (Byne, 1994; Breedlove, 1994; Friedman & Downey, 1993). Could hormones play a role?

Researchers have failed to show consistent differences in sex-hormone levels between homosexual and heterosexual adults (Griffiths et al., 1974; Meyer-Bahlburg, 1977). The effect of treating gay men with male sex hormones has been to increase sexual desire—not for the opposite sex but for members of their own sex.

Some have suggested that abnormal levels of androgens during prenatal development might influence sexual orientation (Collaer & Hines, 1995). Too much or too little androgen at critical periods of brain development might masculinize or feminize the brain of the developing fetus, making a homosexual orientation more likely (Berenbaum & Snyder, 1995). A few studies have revealed an increase in the incidence of lesbianism among females who had been exposed prenatally to synthetic estrogen (Meyer-Bahlburg et al., 1995) or to an excess of androgens (Ehrhardt et al., 1968; Money & Schwartz, 1977).

Definitive answers to nature–nurture questions are always elusive, but some recent research suggests that biological factors play a part in homosexuality.

The LeVay Study: Homosexuality and a Tiny Speck in the Hypothalamus

Neuroscientist Simon LeVay (1991) reported that an area in the hypothalamus governing sexual behavior is about twice as large in heterosexual men as in homosexual men. This part of the hypothalamus, no larger than a grain of sand, is about the same size in heterosexual females as in homosexual males. Figure 11.4 shows the location of the hypothalamus.

Do LeVay's findings make a strong case for a biological cause of homosexuality? No. LeVay admits that his research offers no direct evidence that the brain differences he found cause homosexuality (LeVay & Hamer, 1994). The brain differences LeVay observed could be the cause or the consequence of sexual

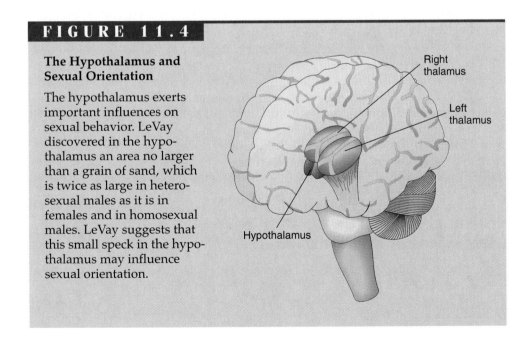

FIGURE 11.4

The Hypothalamus and Sexual Orientation

The hypothalamus exerts important influences on sexual behavior. LeVay discovered in the hypothalamus an area no larger than a grain of sand, which is twice as large in heterosexual males as it is in females and in homosexual males. LeVay suggests that this small speck in the hypothalamus may influence sexual orientation.

orientation, or of variables as yet unidentified that may interact with the brain differences and sexual orientation.

Homosexuality: Is There a Genetic Connection? In researching the influence of heredity on sexual orientation, Bailey and Pillard (1991) studied gay males who had twin brothers. They found that 52 percent of the gay identical twins and 22 percent of the gay fraternal twins had a gay twin brother. Of the gay twins who had adoptive brothers, however, only 11 percent shared a homosexual orientation. In a similar study, Whitam and others (1993) found that 66 percent of the identical twins and 30 percent of the fraternal twins of gay males studied were also gay. Such studies indicate a substantial genetic influence on sexual orientation, but suggest that nongenetic influences are at work as well.

According to Bailey and Benishay (1993), "female homosexuality appears to run in families" (p. 277). They found that 12.1 percent of their lesbian subjects had a sister who was homosexual, compared to 2.3 percent of heterosexual female subjects. Bailey and others (1993) report that in a study of homosexual females, 48 percent of the homosexual females' identical twins, 16 percent of their fraternal twins, 14 percent of their nontwin biological sisters, and 6 percent of their adopted sisters were also lesbian. Bailey and Pillard (1994) claim that, according to their statistical analysis, the heritability of sexual orientation is about 50 percent.

Hamer and others (1993) found that brothers of their gay subjects had a 13.5 percent chance of also being gay. Furthermore, male relatives on the subjects' mother's side of the family, but not on the father's side, had a significantly higher rate of homosexuality. This led the researchers to suspect that a gene influencing sexual orientation might be located on the X chromosome, the sex chromosome contributed by the mother. After studying the DNA on the X chromosomes of 40 pairs of gay brothers, the researchers found that 33 of the pairs carried matching genetic information on the end tip of the X chromosome. But an exact gene has not been identified from among the several hundred genes carried within that end tip. And precisely how the gene might influence sexual orientation is not known (LeVay & Hamer, 1994). These researchers conclude that homosexuality is the result of an interaction of biological, psychological, and social influences.

Do the findings of LeVay, Hamer and others, and Bailey and Pillard provide convincing evidence that homosexuality is caused by biological factors? Not for many critics of the studies cited. Byne and Parsons (1993, 1994; Byne, 1993) insist that LeVay's findings have not been replicated. And even though a particular area in the hypothalamus may differ in size in heterosexual and homosexual males, there is no proof that the area is responsible for sexual orientation. In response to the genetic studies, the critics say that, in the absence of studies of identical twins reared *apart*, the influence of environment cannot be ruled out as the cause of a higher incidence of homosexuality in certain families. Furthermore, they suggest that if one or more genes are involved, they may not be genes directly influencing sexual orientation. Rather, they could be genes affecting personality or temperament that could influence how people react to environmental stimuli (Byne, 1994). We will explore early developmental influences on homosexuality next.

What does the study by Bell, Weinberg, and Hammersmith reveal about the developmental experiences of homosexuals?

Research Findings on the Developmental Experiences of Homosexuals

Some evidence suggests that sexual orientation, whether homosexual or heterosexual, is established by early childhood (Marmor, 1980; Money, 1987).

The Bell, Weinberg, and Hammersmith Study Bell, Weinberg, and Hammersmith (1981) conducted extensive face-to-face interviews with 979 homosexual subjects (293 women, 686 men) and 477 heterosexual controls. The researchers questioned the subjects about their childhood, adolescence, and sexual experiences in an attempt to discover developmental factors associated with homosexuality. The researchers found no single condition of family life that in and of itself appeared to be a factor in either homosexual or heterosexual development. The only experience common to homosexuals was that as children they did not feel they were like others of their sex, and for this reason the researchers assume a biological predisposition.

Early Effeminate Behavior in Boys: What Does It Mean? Some researchers have suggested that boys and girls who do not show typical gender-role behavior, but rather are seen as sissies or tomboys, may be more likely to be homosexual (Green, 1985, 1987; Green & Money, 1961). Zuger (1990) believes that, in many cases, early and extreme effeminate behavior in boys is an early stage of homosexuality. Such effeminate behavior might include a boy's cross-dressing, expressing the desire to be a girl or insisting that he is in fact a girl, and/or preferring girls as playmates and girls' games over boys' games and sports. Boys with these effeminate characteristics often are very close to their mother but spend little time with their father (Zuger, 1990).

This early effeminate pattern is not characteristic of all gay males by any means. But Saghir and Robins (1973) found that two-thirds of their gay male subjects perceived themselves as effeminate during childhood, and 70 percent of lesbians said they were tomboys. Using meta-analysis, Bailey and Zucker (1995) found that cross-gender behavior could be a predictor of homosexuality for both females and males.

Social Attitudes toward Homosexuals: From Celebration to Condemnation

The American Psychiatric Association considered homosexuality a mental disorder until 1973, but now views it as such only if the individual considers it a problem. Lesbians and gay men appear to be as healthy psychologically as their heterosexual counterparts (Strickland, 1995).

Nevertheless, some people in our society could be considered homophobic. **Homophobia** is an intense, irrational hostility toward or fear of homosexuals; in its extreme form homophobia can result in ridicule, beatings, and even murder (Greer, 1986).

In 1992 and 1993 Gallup polls, men expressed more negative attitudes toward homosexuality than women did. Forty-five percent of male respondents believed gays should "stay in the closet"; only 30 percent of female respondents expressed such a belief (Moore, 1993). Thirty-four percent of males, compared to 42 percent of females, considered homosexuality an acceptable lifestyle (Hugick, 1992).

Marsiglio (1993) found that 89 percent of heterosexual males aged 15 to 19 viewed sex between two males as "disgusting," and only 12 percent felt that they could be friends with a gay person. Hispanic males were more likely to say that they would befriend a gay male. The variable most predictive of positive attitudes toward gay males, according to Herek and Glunt (1993), was whether the person reported interpersonal contact with gay men.

homophobia: An intense, irrational hostility toward or fear of homosexuals.

Memory Check 11.4

1. The direction of one's sexual preference—toward members of the opposite sex or those of one's own sex—is termed:
   a. sexual role.
   c. sexual leaning.
   b. sexual identification.
   d. sexual orientation.

2. Statistics suggest that homosexuality is twice as common in males as in females. (true/false)

3. Which of the following factors has the *least* research support as a biological explanation of homosexuality?
   a. genetic factors
   b. variations in adult levels of androgens and estrogen
   c. abnormally high or low levels of androgens during prenatal development
   d. structural differences in an area of the hypothalamus in gay males

4. Which of the following did Bell, Weinberg, and Hammersmith's study reveal about their homosexual subjects?
   a. They were likely to have been seduced or molested by adult homosexuals.
   b. As adolescents, they did not have the normal opportunities for dating.
   c. As children, they did not feel that they were like others of their gender.
   d. As children, they had disturbed relationships with their parents.

Answers: 1. d 2. true 3. b 4. c

sexual dysfunction: A persistent or recurrent problem that causes marked distress and interpersonal difficulty and that may involve any or some combination of the following: sexual desire, sexual arousal or the pleasure associated with sex, or orgasm.

hypoactive sexual desire disorder: A sexual dysfunction marked by little or no sexual desire or interest in sexual activity.

◆Sexual Dysfunctions and Treatment

Like the course of true love, the course of sexual function is not always smooth. Although most people experience sexual problems some of the time, a sizable number of men and women are consistently plagued with sexual dysfunctions, which deny or lower the pleasures of sex. A **sexual dysfunction** is a persistent or recurrent problem that may involve any or some combination of the following: sexual desire, sexual arousal or the pleasure associated with sex, or orgasm. Sexual dysfunctions cause much distress and interpersonal difficulty. The most widely used system for classifying these dysfunctions is found in the American Psychiatric Association's *Diagnostic and Statistical Manual of Mental Disorders-IV* (DSM-IV) (1994). This manual groups sexual dysfunctions into four main categories: sexual desire disorders, sexual arousal disorders, orgasmic disorders, and sexual pain disorders.

Sexual Desire Disorders: From Disinterest to Aversion

? *What are two sexual desire disorders and their defining features?*

Disorders of sexual desire involve either a lack of sexual desire and/or an aversion to genital sexual contact. About 30 percent of people who see sex therapists complain of little or no sexual desire or interest in sexual activity. This condition is known as **hypoactive sexual desire disorder** (Schover & LoPiccolo, 1982). Such people may be unreceptive to the sexual advances of their partner, or they may participate in spite of their lack of desire. Loss of desire or lack of interest could stem from depression, emotional stress, marital dissatisfaction, or repeated unsuccessful attempts at intercourse (difficulty maintaining arousal or achieving orgasm). In men who are middle-aged and older, a decline in sexual interest may be related to a decline in testosterone levels that occurs as men age.

A more severe problem is **sexual aversion disorder**—an "aversion to and active avoidance of genital contact with a sexual partner" (American Psychiatric Association, 1994, p. 499). People with this condition experience emotions ranging from anxiety or fear to disgust when confronted with a sexual situation. In some cases, a sexual aversion stems from a sexual trauma such as rape or incest.

Sexual Arousal Disorders

Sexual arousal disorders are characterized by a persistent inability to attain or maintain psychophysiological arousal until the completion of sexual activity.

Female Sexual Arousal Disorder A woman with **female sexual arousal disorder** may not feel sexually aroused in response to sexual stimulation, or she may be unable to achieve or sustain "an adequate lubrication-swelling response to sexual excitement" (American Psychiatric Association, 1994, p. 500). The problem may stem from the trauma of rape or childhood sexual abuse, from resentment toward one's partner, or from vaginal dryness due to reduced estrogen production.

Male Erectile Disorder: Ready, Willing, and Unable A common sexual dysfunction reported in men is **male erectile disorder**—the repeated inability to have or sustain an erection firm enough for coitus. This disorder (more widely known as impotence or erectile dysfunction) can take different forms: the inability to have an erection at all, having one but losing it, or having a partial erection that is not adequate for intercourse. Some men have firm erections under some conditions but not under others (as with one sexual partner but not with another, or during masturbation but not during intercourse).

The term *erectile disorder* does not apply to the failures all males have on occasion as a result of fear or anxiety, physical fatigue, illness, or drinking too much alcohol. About 10 percent of American men suffer from chronic erectile dysfunction, with the percentages rising to 18 percent at age 55, 30 percent at age 65, and 55 percent at age 75 (Church, 1989).

Male erectile disorder may be physical or psychological in origin. Over 50 percent of the cases are due to physical causes, which include diabetes, alcoholism, and drugs such as amphetamines, barbiturates, tranquilizers, and blood pressure medication (Church, 1989). When the cause is physical, the problem usually develops gradually over a period of months or years, and the man *always* has difficulty achieving an erection, in all circumstances (Lizza & Cricco-Lizza, 1990). But if a man awakens to find himself with an erection, even occasionally, he can usually rule out a physical cause.

Resentment, guilt, fear, or anxiety are psychological factors that are suspected when the symptoms of male erectile disorder come on suddenly or when they occur in some circumstances but not in others (Lizza & Cricco-Lizza, 1990). The most common cause is performance anxiety. When a man fails repeatedly to achieve an erection, his worst psychological enemy is the fear that he will not be able to get an erection when he most wants one.

Orgasmic Disorders

Three disorders involve a persistent and recurrent problem at the orgasm stage of the sexual response cycle. They are female orgasmic disorder, male orgasmic disorder, and premature ejaculation.

What are the sexual arousal disorders and their defining features?

sexual aversion disorder: A sexual desire disorder characterized by an aversion to or a desire to avoid genital contact with a sexual partner.

female sexual arousal disorder: A sexual dysfunction in which a woman may not feel sexually aroused in response to sexual stimulation or may be unable to achieve or sustain "an adequate lubrication-swelling response to sexual excitement."

male erectile disorder: The repeated inability to have or sustain an erection firm enough for coitus; erectile dysfunction, or impotence.

What are the three orgasmic disorders and the defining features of each?

Female Orgasmic Disorder   The most common sexual dysfunction in women is **female orgasmic disorder**—the persistent inability to reach orgasm or a delay in reaching orgasm despite adequate sexual stimulation. Some women have never been able to reach orgasm; others who were formerly orgasmic no longer can achieve orgasm. Some women are able to have orgasms only under certain circumstances or during certain types of sexual activity, while others have orgasms only from time to time. Women with this disorder may be disinterested in sex, or they may still find it exciting, satisfying, and enjoyable.

"Once a female learns how to reach orgasm, it is uncommon for her to lose that capacity, unless poor sexual communication, relationship conflict, a traumatic experience (e.g., rape), a mood disorder, or a general medical condition intervenes" (American Psychiatric Association, 1994, p. 505).

Male Orgasmic Disorder   In **male orgasmic disorder** there is an absence of ejaculation, or ejaculation occurs only after strenuous effort over an extremely prolonged period. Sometimes both partners may nearly collapse from exhaustion before the male finally reaches orgasm or gives up. The delay in or absence of ejaculation usually occurs during intercourse, rather than during manual or oral stimulation or during masturbation. Suspected causes are alcoholism or drug use (illicit or prescription), an overly strict religious background, stressful or traumatic life situations, or fear of impregnating one's partner (Kaplan, 1974).

Premature Ejaculation   Probably the most common sexual dysfunction, **premature ejaculation** is a condition in which the male ejaculates too soon—before he is ready and usually long before his partner is ready. This condition sometimes results when a man feels hostility toward his partner. It may also have its origins in early sexual experiences that called for quick ejaculation, such as hurried masturbation or fast, impersonal sexual release with a prostitute.

Sexual Pain Disorders

Dyspareunia, genital pain associated with sexual intercourse, can occur in both males and females, although it is much more common in women. Inadequate lubrication is the major cause in females, although vaginal infections, sexually transmitted diseases, and various psychological factors may also be involved.

Vaginismus is a sexual dysfunction in which involuntary muscle contractions tighten and even close the vagina, making intercourse painful or impossible. The problem may stem from a rigid religious upbringing in which sex was looked on as sinful and dirty. It may also stem from past experiences of extremely painful intercourse or from a fear of men, rape, or other traumatic experiences associated with intercourse (Kaplan, 1974).

The sexual dysfunctions are summarized in Review and Reflect Table 11.1.

Sex Therapy: There Is Help

In most cases, chronic sexual dysfunctions do not just go away, but there is help for people who suffer from sexual problems. Since the 1950s, a number of sex therapy techniques have been developed. Therapies based on behavioral psychology teach patients to replace their old self-defeating attitudes and behaviors with more adaptive ones. In 1959 Masters and Johnson began their innovative approach to sex therapy, in which the couple rather than the individual is treated.

female orgasmic disorder: The persistent inability of a woman to reach orgasm, or a delay in reaching orgasm despite adequate sexual stimulation.

male orgasmic disorder: A sexual dysfunction in which there is an absence of ejaculation, or in which ejaculation occurs only after strenuous effort over an extremely prolonged period.

premature ejaculation: An orgasmic disorder in which the male ejaculates too soon—before he is ready, and usually long before his partner is ready.

dyspareunia (dis-PAH-roo-nee-yah): A sexual pain disorder marked by genital pain associated with sexual intercourse, occurring in both males and females.

vaginismus (VAJ-ah-NIZ-mus): A sexual pain disorder in which involuntary muscle contractions create a tightening and closing of the vagina, making intercourse painful or impossible.

Review and Reflect 11.1 Sexual Dysfunctions According to the DSM-IV

Sexual Desire Disorders

Hypoactive sexual desire disorder	Little or no sexual desire or interest in sexual activity.
Sexual aversion disorder	An aversion to genital contact with a sexual partner.

Sexual Arousal Disorders

Female sexual arousal disorder	Inability to feel sexually aroused or to lubricate sufficiently in response to sexual stimulation.
Male erectile disorder	The repeated inability to have or sustain an erection firm enough for coitus; impotence.

Orgasmic Disorders

Female orgasmic disorder	The persistent inability to reach orgasm or delay in reaching orgasm despite adequate sexual stimulation.
Male orgasmic disorder	An absence of ejaculation, or ejaculation only after strenuous effort over an extremely prolonged period.
Premature ejaculation	Ejaculation that occurs too soon—before the man is ready and usually long before his partner is ready.

Sexual Pain Disorders

Dyspareunia	Genital pain associated with sexual intercourse.
Vaginismus	Tightening and closing of the vagina, caused by involuntary muscle contractions, which makes intercourse painful or impossible.

Source: Adapted from American Psychiatric Association, 1994.

Biological treatments can be useful for dysfunctions caused by medical conditions. One effective treatment for male erectile disorder is self-injection into the tissue of the penis of a drug that causes the blood vessels to dilate and fill with blood (Wagner & Kaplan, 1992). This technique has enabled thousands of American men to get and sustain an erection.

Memory Check 11.5

Match the appropriate description with each sexual disorder.

_____ 1) male erectile disorder   a. inability to reach orgasm

_____ 2) vaginismus   b. inability to control ejaculation

_____ 3) premature ejaculation   c. lack of sexual interest

_____ 4) female orgasmic disorder   d. inability to have or maintain an erection

_____ 5) female sexual arousal disorder   e. an involuntary closing of the vagina

_____ 6) hypoactive sexual desire disorder   f. inability to feel sexually excited and to lubricate sufficiently

Answers: 1.d 2.e 3.b 4.a 5.f 6.c

? *What are the major bacterial and viral infections known as sexually transmitted diseases?*

Sexually Transmitted Diseases: The Price of Casual Sex

Sexually transmitted diseases (STDs) are infections spread primarily through sexual contact. The incidence of many sexually transmitted diseases has increased dramatically since the early 1970s. This can be explained in part by more permissive attitudes toward sex and an increase in sexual activity among young people, some of whom have sexual contact with multiple partners (Turner et al., 1995) Another factor is the greater use of nonbarrier methods of contraception such as the pill. Barrier methods, such as condoms and vaginal spermicide, provide some protection against STDs.

Some of the serious sexually transmitted diseases are bacterial infections such as chlamydia, gonorrhea, and syphilis, which are curable; and viral infections such as genital herpes and AIDS, which are not curable.

Each year about 12 million Americans contract a sexually transmitted disease (Tanfer, 1994), and 56 million Americans—one in five—already have been infected with an incurable STD-causing virus other than HIV (Barringer, 1993). Minority populations in U.S. inner cities are experiencing an epidemic in STDs, as are people in developing countries (Piot & Islam, 1994). Worldwide, 250 million people contract STDs each year (Quinn, 1994).

The Bacterial Infections

? *Why do chlamydia and gonorrhea pose a greater threat to women than to men?*

Chlamydia: Little Known But Widespread Many people have never heard of **chlamydia**—an infection that affects 4 million people in the United States every year (Stein, 1991). Today 10 percent of all college students have chlamydia, and it is highly infectious. Women have a 70 percent risk of contracting chlamydia from an infected man in any single sexual encounter; men have a 25 to 50 percent risk in a single encounter.

Men with chlamydia are likely to have symptoms that alert them to the need for treatment, but they suffer no adverse reproductive consequences from the infection. Women, on the other hand, typically have only mild symptoms or no symptoms at all when chlamydia begins in the lower reproductive tract. Therefore, the infection often goes untreated and spreads to the upper reproductive tract, where it can cause **pelvic inflammatory disease (PID)**. PID often produces scarring of tissue in the fallopian tubes, which can result in infertility or ectopic pregnancy—a pregnancy in which the fertilized ovum is implanted outside of the uterus (Temmerman, 1994; Weström, 1994). Fortunately, chlamydia can be cured with antibiotics, which should be given to both partners.

sexually transmitted diseases (STDs): Infections that are spread primarily through intimate sexual contact.

chlamydia (klah-MIH-dee-uh): The most common bacterial STD found in both sexes, and one that can cause infertility in females.

pelvic inflammatory disease (PID): An infection in the female pelvic organs, which can result from untreated chlamydia or gonorrhea and can cause pain, scarring of tissue, and even infertility or ectopic pregnancy.

gonorrhea (gahn-ah-REE-ah): An STD that, in males, causes a puslike discharge from the penis; if untreated, females can develop pelvic inflammatory disease and possible infertility.

Gonorrhea: An Old STD Makes a Comeback There were about 501,000 cases of **gonorrhea** reported in 1992 (U.S. Bureau of the Census, 1994). A woman having intercourse one time with an infected partner runs a 50 percent risk of contracting gonorrhea (Platt et al., 1983); a male has a 20 to 25 percent chance of developing gonorrhea after one such exposure.

Within the first 2 weeks after contracting gonorrhea, 95 percent of men develop a discharge from the penis and painful urination (Schwebke, 1991a). Most seek treatment and are cured. If there are no symptoms present or if the individual does not seek treatment within 2 to 3 weeks, the infection may spread to the internal reproductive organs and eventually cause sterility. The bad news for women is that 50 to 80 percent of women who contract gonorrhea do not have early symptoms. The infection spreads from the cervix through the other internal reproductive organs, causing inflammation and scarring. About 20 percent of women with untreated gonorrhea develop pelvic inflammatory disease with its risk of sterility and ectopic pregnancy (Schwebke, 1991a). Gonorrhea can be cured with antibiotics (Levine et al., 1994).

Syphilis: Another Old STD Makes a Comeback About 113,000 cases of **syphilis** were reported in the United States in 1992 (U.S. Bureau of the Census, 1994). The rate is particularly high "among inner city ethnic groups of low socio-economic status" (Schwebke, 1991b, p. 44). Syphilis has been linked to the use of illicit drugs, particularly crack, because addicts often exchange sex for drugs (Gunn et al., 1995).

Left untreated, syphilis progresses in predictable stages. In the primary stage, a painless sore, or chancre (pronounced "shanker"), appears where the syphilis spirochete—the microorganism that causes syphilis—entered the body. This sore may go unnoticed, but even without treatment it will heal.

In the second stage—secondary syphilis—a painless rash appears on the body, usually accompanied by a fever, sore throat, loss of appetite, fatigue, and headache. Again, without treatment these symptoms eventually disappear. Then the spirochetes enter the various tissues and organs of the body, where they may be inactive for anywhere from several years to a lifetime. About 30 to 50 percent of people with syphilis who remain untreated enter the final and terrible third stage, in which blindness, paralysis, heart failure, mental illness, and death result.

Pregnant women with any stage of syphilis will infect the fetus. But syphilis can be stopped at any point in its development, except in the final stage, with strong doses of penicillin (Levine et al., 1994).

Genital Herpes: An Incurable Viral Infection

Each year there are 500,000 new cases of **genital herpes** in the United States (Davies, 1990). Already more than 30 million Americans have this incurable virus (Catotti et al., 1993).

Genital herpes can be caused by two forms of the herpes simplex virus. The type 1 virus usually causes oral herpes—cold sores and fever blisters in the mouth—but as a result of oral sex may produce blisters on the genitals. The type 2 virus generally produces 80 to 90 percent of the cases of genital herpes and is transmitted through direct contact with infected genitals (Peter et al., 1982).

In genital herpes, painful blisters form on the genitals (or around the anus in homosexual men), fill with pus, and then burst, leaving open sores. It is at this point that a person is most contagious. After the blisters heal, the virus travels up nerve fibers to an area around the base of the spinal cord, where it remains in a dormant state but can flare up anew at any time. The first herpes episode is usually the most severe (Apuzzio, 1990); recurrent attacks are typically milder and briefer. Although genital herpes is most contagious during an outbreak, it can be transmitted even when an infected person has no symptoms (Dawkins, 1990).

A survey of over 2,940 people with genital herpes revealed that its impact can be "serious and long-lasting," leaving people depressed, fearing rejection, and feeling isolated (Catotti et al., 1993).

Acquired Immune Deficiency Syndrome (AIDS)

There is no sexually transmitted disease that generates more fear or has more devastating consequences than **acquired immune deficiency syndrome (AIDS)**. Although the first case was diagnosed in this country in 1981, there is still no cure for AIDS and no vaccine to protect against it. By the end of 1993, almost 350,000 cases of AIDS and 218,000 deaths from AIDS had been reported to the Centers for Disease Control (1994).

syphilis (SIF-ih-lis): An STD that progresses through three stages; if untreated, it can eventually be fatal.

genital herpes (HER-peez): An STD caused by the herpes simplex virus (usually type 2) that results in painful blisters on the genitals; presently incurable, usually recurring, and highly contagious during outbreaks.

acquired immune deficiency syndrome (AIDS): A devastating and incurable illness that is caused by HIV and progressively weakens the body's immune system, leaving the person vulnerable to opportunistic infections that usually cause death.

Why is genital herpes particularly upsetting to those who have it?

What happens to a person from the time of infection with HIV to the development of full-blown AIDS?

Greg Louganis, winner of an Olympic gold medal for diving in 1988, announced in 1995 that he is HIV-positive.

AIDS is caused by **HIV**, the **human immunodeficiency virus**, often referred to as the AIDS virus. About 17 million people worldwide are infected with HIV (Cohen, 1994). When a person is first infected, HIV enters the bloodstream. This initial infection usually causes no symptoms, and the immune system begins to produce HIV antibodies. It is these antibodies that are detected in the AIDS test. Individuals then progress to the asymptomatic carrier state, in which they experience no symptoms whatsoever and thus can unknowingly infect others.

HIV attacks the immune system until it becomes essentially nonfunctional. The diagnosis of AIDS is made when the immune system is so damaged that victims develop rare forms of cancer or pneumonia or other so-called opportunistic infections. Such infections would not usually affect people with a normal immune response, but in those with a very impaired immune system, these infections can be serious and even life-threatening. At this point patients typically experience progressive weight loss, weakness, fever, swollen lymph nodes, and diarrhea, and 25 percent have a rare cancer that produces reddish purple spots on the skin. Other infections develop as the immune system weakens further.

Before developing a full-blown case of AIDS, some people develop less severe immune-system symptoms such as unexplained fevers, chronic diarrhea, and weight loss. The average time from infection with HIV to advanced AIDS is about 10 years, but this time span may range from as short as 2 years to as long as 15 years or more (Nowak & McMichael, 1995). The disease progresses faster in smokers, in the very young, in people over 50, and apparently, in women. AIDS also progresses faster in those with repeated exposures to the virus and in those who were infected by someone in an advanced stage of the disease.

Currently researchers are testing drugs on people infected with HIV, and early detection of HIV infection can lead to life-prolonging medical intervention. The drug AZT is used to treat AIDS patients in an attempt to lessen their symptoms and prolong their lives.

How is AIDS transmitted?

HIV (human immunodeficiency virus): The virus that causes AIDS.

The Transmission of AIDS   Researchers believe that HIV is transmitted primarily through the exchange of blood, semen, or vaginal secretions during sexual contact or when IV (intravenous) drug users share contaminated needles or syringes (Des Jarlais & Friedman, 1994). In the United States about 25 percent of those with AIDS are IV drug users (Centers for Disease Control and Prevention, 1994). An estimated 50 percent of IV drug users are infected with HIV, whereas 20 percent of gay men carry the virus ("AIDS and Mental Health," 1994).

The rate of AIDS among gay men is high because many gay men have multiple sex partners, and because gay men are likely to have anal intercourse. Anal intercourse is more dangerous than coitus, because rectal tissue often tears during penetration, offering a ready entry of HIV into the bloodstream.

It is a mistake to view AIDS as a disease confined to homosexuals, however. In Africa, where AIDS is believed to have originated, it strikes men and women equally, and their heterosexual activity is believed to be the primary means of transmission (Abramson & Herdt, 1990). AIDS is transmitted more easily from infected men to women than vice versa (Hutman, 1990).

There is also a 30 to 50 percent risk that babies born to mothers with HIV will be infected (Krajick, 1988). The blood-bank industry claims that the chance of acquiring HIV from a blood transfusion is now 1 in 40,000 (Gorman, 1988).

Figure 11.5 summarizes the means of transmission for AIDS cases in the United States.

The Psychological Impact of HIV Infection and AIDS   Consider the devastating psychological impact—the anxiety, fear, and depression—on learning that one is infected with HIV. A death sentence, alone, is traumatic enough, with one's time left to live measured in a few years, but there is more. Added to the fear of rapidly declining health when full-blown AIDS arrives is the ugly stigma paralleled by few other diseases in history. The heroic young teenager Ryan White, a hemophiliac, contracted AIDS through a blood transfusion. He died of AIDS in 1990 and was not spared the stigma of AIDS in life or even in death. Vandals spray-painted "FAG" on his grave.

What are the psychological effects on people who struggle to cope with this fearsome plague? The reaction to the news that one is HIV-positive is frequently a state of shock, bewilderment, confusion, or disbelief. Stress reactions to the news are typically so common and so acute that experts strongly recommend pretest counseling so that those who do test positive may know in advance of the consequences (Maj, 1990). Another common reaction is anger—anger at past or present sexual partners, family members, health care professionals, or society in general. Often the response includes guilt, a sense that one is being punished for homosexuality or drug abuse. Other patients exhibit denial, ignoring medical advice and continuing to act as if nothing has changed in their lives. Then, of course, there is fear—of death, of mental and physical deterioration, of rejection by friends, family, or co-workers, of sexual rejection, of abandonment.

To cope psychologically, AIDS patients and those infected with HIV need education and information about the disease. They can be helped by psychotherapy, self-help groups, and medications such as antidepressants and antianxiety drugs. Self-help groups and group therapy may serve as a substitute family for some patients. An ever-present concern voiced by patients in psychotherapy is whether to tell others, and if so, what to tell them and how. Patients may feel a compelling need to confide in others and, at the same time, to conceal their condition.

Protection against Sexually Transmitted Diseases: Minimizing Risk

There are only two foolproof ways for people to protect themselves from becoming infected with a sexually transmitted disease through intimate sexual contact. The first is obvious—abstain from sexual contact. The second is to have a mutually faithful (monogamous) relationship with a partner free of infection. Anything short of these two courses of action will place a person at risk.

Discharges, blisters, sores, rashes, warts, odors, or any other unusual symptoms are warning signs of sexually transmitted diseases. Yet we know that many

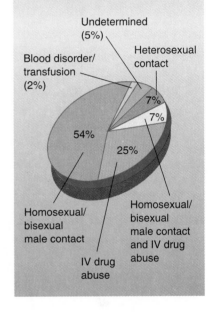

FIGURE 11.5

How HIV Was Transmitted in Adult/Adolescent AIDS Cases Reported in the United States

The primary means of transmission of HIV is through homosexual/bisexual male contact (54 percent). IV drug abuse (sharing needles) accounts for 25 percent of the AIDS cases in the United States. (Data from Centers for Disease Control and Prevention, 1994.)

What are the most effective methods of protection against sexually transmitted diseases?

people who have no visible symptoms carry STDs. And what we don't know *can* hurt us. People who choose to practice risky sex cannot be safe but can reduce the risks by using a latex condom along with a spermicide such as an intravaginal contraceptive foam, jelly, or cream.

The potential for risky sexual behavior is increased when people are under the influence of alcohol and other drugs (Leigh & Stall, 1993). People are putting themselves at risk for AIDS when they have multiple sex partners or if they have sex with prostitutes, IV drug users, or anyone carrying HIV. This potential risk was dramatically demonstrated by basketball star Magic Johnson when he announced that he had tested positive for HIV. Several recent studies reveal that most young people, even those engaging in high-risk behavior, are ignoring the warnings about AIDS (Yam, 1995a). Despite intense efforts to promote the use of condoms, more than half of sexually active college students still do not use condoms regularly, if at all (DeBuono et al., 1990).

Not only is it wise to have regular medical checkups, but people who fear that they might have been exposed to an STD should go to a doctor or clinic to be tested. Many STDs are easily treated, and serious complications can be avoided if the treatment is prompt. Obviously, anyone who has an STD should tell his or her partner so that the partner can be checked and treated.

STDs were curable until herpes and AIDS came on the scene. But today engaging in sexual intimacy with multiple partners or casual acquaintances is indeed a dangerous way to satisfy the sex drive. Much has been written in recent decades about the joy of sex. It is true that the pleasures sex brings to life are many; but chlamydia, gonorrhea, syphilis, herpes, and AIDS are not among them.

Memory Check 11.6

1. Which STD causes painful blisters on the genitals and is usually recurring, highly contagious during outbreaks, and incurable?
   a. syphilis
   b. chlamydia
   c. genital herpes
   d. gonorrhea

2. Which of the following STDs, if left untreated, can eventually be fatal?
   a. syphilis
   b. gonorrhea
   c. genital herpes
   d. chlamydia

3. The two STDs most likely to cause infertility and ectopic pregnancy are:
   a. syphilis and gonorrhea.
   b. syphilis and chlamydia.
   c. genital herpes and chlamydia.
   d. chlamydia and gonorrhea.

4. Since symptoms of STDs are usually more readily apparent in males, males are more likely to seek treatment and be cured. (true/false)

5. HIV eventually causes a breakdown in the _____ system.
   a. circulatory
   b. vascular
   c. immune
   d. respiratory

6. The incidence of AIDS in the United States is highest among:
   a. homosexuals and IV drug users.
   b. homosexuals and hemophiliacs.
   c. homosexuals and bisexuals.
   d. heterosexuals and homosexuals.

Answers: 1. c 2. a 3. d 4. true 5. c 6. a

APPLICATIONS • APPLICATIONS • APPLICATIONS

Protecting Yourself from Rape

Rape is the ultimate sexual outrage. FBI statistics reveal that between 1978 and 1988, rape increased four times faster than other crimes, and that a woman is raped about every 6 minutes. But those are only the *reported* rapes. According to some estimates, as many as 90 percent of rapes are not reported (Gibbs, 1991).

Acquaintance Rape: The Shocking Facts

When we hear that someone has been raped, most of us picture a stranger stalking a woman on a dark, deserted street or breaking into her bedroom. But the majority of all rapes are committed by a man the woman knows—in the act of acquaintance, or date, rape.

For the rapes reported in 1990, only 22 percent of the perpetrators were strangers. The incidence is similar for both African American and white women (Wyatt, 1992).

Many unreported rapes are committed right on college campuses. Koss and others (1987) conducted a study of the incidence of rape in a national sample consisting of 3,187 female and 2,972 male students from 32 colleges and universities. In their sample, 27.5 percent of the women reported having been the target since age 14 of one or more sexual acts that met the legal definition of rape. Among the college men, 7.7 percent admitted committing and/or attempting to commit such acts.

Who Rapes?

Some researchers claim that a macho attitude about women and sex, while not necessarily leading to rape, does apparently relate to a greater toler-

ance of rape and the sexual exploitation of women. In one survey, 175 male college sophomores were asked how often they had used any of 33 acts of sexual coercion, from verbal pressure to actual physical force. Of those male sophomores, 75 percent admitted they had encouraged a date to use alcohol or drugs for the specific purpose of having sex with her; 69 percent had used some type of verbal coercion; over 40 percent had used anger; 13 percent had threatened to use force; and 20 percent said they had used force to get sex (Mosher & Anderson, 1987). According to the legal definition, many of these 175 college sophomores had actually committed rape. How are attitudes about rape formed?

Attitudes about Rape

Kanin and others (1987) studied the attitudes of 355 unmarried college students (155 men and 200 women) toward rape. Then they related the number of different sexual partners each subject had had to the number of years in prison he or she believed a convicted rapist should serve. For both men and women, as the number of sexual partners increased, the number of years recommended for the sentence of a rapist significantly decreased. Furthermore, over 71 percent of the men and 55 percent of the women expressed a surprising opinion: They said that if a woman had previously engaged in any form of sexual intimacy with a man, it could not be considered rape if that man later forced her to have sex with him. Similarly, a survey of high school students revealed a surprising

number of conditions under which both sexes agreed that it was permissible for a man to force a woman to have sexual intercourse (Mahoney, 1983). Another study revealed that when rape victims were dressed provocatively, they were judged to be more responsible for the rape (Cassidy & Hurrell, 1995). But, under any circumstances, if sexual intercourse is forced on a woman against her will, it is rape.

Effects of Rape on the Victim

The effects of rape on the victim vary widely, but some are quite serious—even life-threatening. Almost 20 percent of rape victims—nearly one in five—admit to attempting suicide, a rate eight times higher than that of nonvictims ("Female Victims," 1984). The effects of rape can be just as devastating to a victim whether the rapist was an acquaintance or a stranger, and a victim can suffer for years (Katz, 1991; Koss, 1993; Parrot, 1990). A National Victims' Center report (1992) concluded that the fear of

continued

being injured or killed is about as common among women raped by husbands or dates as among those raped by total strangers.

How to Avoid Acquaintance Rape

The following suggestions can help women avoid acquaintance rape.

- Know the men you date, and avoid those who show a lack of respect for women.
- Avoid risky situations and settings on a first date, and be sure to tell someone where you are.
- Remember that accepting a date with someone does not obligate you to engage in any sexual activity.
- Set sexual limits, communicate them to your date, and be emphatic in refusing to be pressured to go beyond those limits.

- Avoid drinking too much or mixing drinks; alcohol and drugs are often contributing factors in date rape.
- Trust your instincts. If a situation does not feel right to you, change it or get away from it. Don't worry about what others might think.
- Do not send signals that can be misinterpreted by your date. Some men assume that if a woman drinks too much, invites a date into her apartment or room, or goes to his apartment, this signals that she is willing to have sex.
- If you are in danger, don't hesitate to run or scream.

What to Do If You Are Raped

In her book *Sex on Your Terms*, Elizabeth Powell (1996) suggests the following actions should you be raped:

- Don't change anything about your body—don't wash or even comb

your hair. Leave your clothes as they are. You could destroy evidence.
- Report the incident to police. You may prevent another woman from being assaulted, and you will be taking charge, starting on the path from victim to survivor.
- Ask a relative or friend to take you to a hospital; if you can't, get an ambulance or a police car. If you call the hospital, tell them why you are requesting an ambulance so that they can send someone trained in rape crisis.
- Seeking help is an assertive way to show you're worth it. Get medical help; injuries of which you are unaware may be detected. Insist that written or photographic documentation of your condition be made. You may decide to prosecute and you will need evidence.

Thinking Critically

Evaluation

What are some of the potential problems with information about sexual behavior and attitudes derived from surveys?

Point/Counterpoint

List the most persuasive arguments you can think of to justify each of the following:

a. In the 1990s it is easier to be a man than a woman.

b. In the 1990s it is easier to be a woman than a man.

Psychology in Your Life

Mary has sex with several partners, and she takes birth control pills to prevent pregnancy. She believes that she is careful in her choice of partners and that condoms are therefore not necessary in her case. Has Mary overlooked anything that could put her at risk?

Chapter Summary and Review

What Makes a Male, a Male and a Female, a Female?

What are the biological factors that determine whether a person is male or female?

At conception the sex chromosomes are set—XY in males and XX in females. The primitive gonads develop into testes if the Y chromosome is present or into ovaries if it is absent. If sufficient levels of androgens are present, male genitals develop; if not, female genitals develop.

Key Terms

gender (p. 400)
sex chromosomes (p. 400)
gonads (p. 400)
androgens (p. 401)
genitals (p. 401)
primary sex characteristics (p. 401)
secondary sex characteristics
    (p. 401)

Gender-Role Development

What is gender typing, and what are the environmental factors that contribute to it?

Gender typing is the process by which people acquire the traits, behaviors, attitudes, preferences, and interests that the culture considers appropriate for their biological sex. Parents, peers, the school, and the media each play a role in gender typing.

What are three theories of gender-role development?

Three theories of gender-role development are social learning theory, cognitive developmental theory, and gender-schema theory.

Do good adjustment and high self-esteem seem to be related to masculine traits, feminine traits, or androgyny?

Masculine traits appear to be related to better adjustment and high self-esteem in both males and females.

Key Terms

gender roles (p. 401)
gender typing (p. 401)
social learning theory (p. 402)
cognitive developmental theory
    (p. 403)
gender identity (p. 403)
gender-schema theory (p. 404)
androgyny (p. 404)

Gender Differences: Fact or Myth?

What gender differences are associated with aggression?

The most consistent and significant gender difference is that males tend to be more physically aggressive than females. Females are more likely to use indirect aggression.

For what cognitive abilities are there proven gender differences?

Males are slightly better at some spatial skills, and in high school and college males perform somewhat better in mathematical problem solving. The female advantage in verbal ability has virtually disappeared.

Sexual Attitudes and Behavior

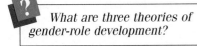

What were the famous Kinsey surveys?

In the 1940s and 1950s Alfred Kinsey and associates conducted the first ma-

jor surveys of the sexual attitudes and behaviors of American men and women.

According to Masters and Johnson, what are the four phases of the human sexual response cycle?

The sexual response cycle consists of four phases: the excitement phase, the plateau phase, the orgasm phase, and the resolution phase.

What are the male and female sex hormones, and how do they affect sexual desire and activity in males and females?

The female sex hormones are estrogen and progesterone; the male sex hormones are the androgens, the most important of which is testosterone. Testosterone affects sexual interest and the ability to have an erection in males, and small amounts are necessary for females to maintain sexual interest and responsiveness.

What have researchers discovered about the effects of pornography on its viewers?

Researchers have found that frequent viewing of violent pornography often desensitizes men to violent and degrading sex practices and to the horror of rape, as well as increasing their acceptance of the rape myth and possibly their willingness to force women to engage in sex. There is less agreement about the effects of nonviolent pornography.

Key Terms

coitus (p. 410)
sexual response cycle (p. 412)
excitement phase (p. 412)
plateau phase (p. 412)
orgasm phase (p. 412)

resolution phase (p. 413)
estrogen (p. 413)
progesterone (p. 413)
testosterone (p. 413)
pornography (p. 414)
rape myth (p. 415)

Homosexuality

> **?** *What is meant by sexual orientation?*

Sexual orientation refers to the direction of a person's sexual preference—toward members of the opposite sex (heterosexuality), toward one's own sex (homosexuality), or toward both sexes (bisexuality).

> **?** *What are the various biological factors that have been suggested as possible causes of homosexuality?*

The biological factors suggested as possible causes of homosexuality are (1) abnormal levels of androgens during prenatal development, which could masculinize or feminize the brain of the developing fetus; (2) structural differences in an area of the hypothalamus of homosexual men; and (3) genetic factors.

> **?** *What does the study by Bell, Weinberg, and Hammersmith reveal about the developmental experiences of homosexuals?*

In comparing homosexuals to heterosexual controls, Bell, Weinberg, and Hammersmith were unable to trace differences between the two groups to problems in parental relationships. The only commonality was that as children, homosexuals did not feel that they were like others of their sex.

Key Terms

sexual orientation (p. 416)
homophobia (p. 419)

Sexual Dysfunctions and Treatment

> **?** *What are two sexual desire disorders and their defining features?*

Hypoactive sexual desire disorder is characterized by little or no sexual desire or interest; sexual aversion disorder, by an aversion to genital contact with a sexual partner.

> **?** *What are the sexual arousal disorders and their defining features?*

A woman with female sexual arousal disorder may not feel sexually aroused or lubricate sufficiently in response to sexual stimulation. Male erectile disorder, or impotence, involves the repeated inability to have or sustain an erection firm enough for coitus.

> **?** *What are the three orgasmic disorders and the defining features of each?*

Female orgasmic disorder is the persistent inability of a woman to reach orgasm or a delay in reaching orgasm despite adequate sexual stimulation. In male orgasmic disorder there is an absence of ejaculation, or it occurs only after strenuous effort over a prolonged period. In premature ejaculation the male ejaculates before he is ready, and usually long before his partner is ready.

Key Terms

sexual dysfunction (p. 420)
hypoactive sexual desire disorder (p. 420)
sexual aversion disorder (p. 421)
female sexual arousal disorder (p. 421)
male erectile disorder (p. 421)
female orgasmic disorder (p. 422)
male orgasmic disorder (p. 422)
premature ejaculation (p. 422)
dispareunia (p. 422)
vaginismus (p. 422)

Sexually Transmitted Diseases: The Price of Casual Sex

> **?** *What are the major bacterial and viral infections known as sexually transmitted diseases?*

The major sexually transmitted diseases are chlamydia, gonorrhea, and syphilis (all curable bacterial infections), and genital herpes and AIDS (viral infections and presently not curable).

> **?** *Why do chlamydia and gonorrhea pose a greater threat to women than to men?*

Chlamydia and gonorrhea pose a particular threat to women because they, unlike men, typically have no symptoms or very mild symptoms, making prompt treatment less likely. If the infection spreads, it may result in infertility or ectopic pregnancy.

> **?** *Why is genital herpes particularly upsetting to those who have it?*

Genital herpes causes painful blisters on the genitals, is usually recurring and highly contagious during outbreaks, and is incurable.

> **?** *What happens to a person from the time of infection with HIV to the development of full-blown AIDS?*

When a person is initially infected with HIV, the body begins to produce HIV antibodies, eventually detectable in a blood test. For a period of time the victim is without symptoms, but HIV gradually renders the immune system nonfunctional. The diagnosis of AIDS is made when the person succumbs to various opportunistic infections.

How is AIDS transmitted?

AIDS is transmitted primarily through the exchange of blood or semen during sexual contact or through the sharing of contaminated needles and syringes among IV drug users.

What are the most effective methods of protection against sexually transmitted diseases?

Abstinence or a monogamous relationship with a partner free of infection is the only foolproof way to protect yourself from acquiring an STD through intimate sexual contact. Failing this, avoid sex with multiple or anonymous partners, be on the lookout for symptoms of these diseases in a potential partner, and use a latex condom with a spermicide.

Key Terms

sexually transmitted diseases (STDs) (p. 424)
chlamydia (p. 424)
pelvic inflammatory disease (PID) (p. 424)
gonorrhea (p. 424)
syphilis (p. 425)
genital herpes (p. 425)
acquired immune deficiency syndrome (AIDS) (p. 425)
HIV (human immunodeficiency virus) (p. 426)

12

PERSONALITY THEORY AND ASSESSMENT

CHAPTER OUTLINE

Sigmund Freud and Psychoanalysis

The Conscious, the Preconscious, and the Unconscious: Levels of Awareness

The Id, the Ego, and the Superego: Warring Components of the Personality

Pioneers: Sigmund Freud

Defense Mechanisms: Protecting the Ego

The Psychosexual Stages of Development: Centered on the Erogenous Zones

Freud's Explanation of Personality

Evaluating Freud's Contribution

The Neo-Freudians

Carl Gustav Jung

Alfred Adler: Overcoming Inferiority

Karen Horney: Champion of Feminine Psychology

Pioneers: Karen Horney

Trait Theories

Gordon Allport: Personality Traits in the Brain

Raymond Cattell's 16 Personality Factors

Hans Eysenck: Stressing Two Factors

The Five-Factor Theory of Personality: The Big Five

Evaluating the Trait Perspective

World of Psychology: Personality and Culture

Learning Theories and Personality

The Behaviorist View of B. F. Skinner

The Social-Cognitive Theorists: Expanding the Behaviorist View

Humanistic Personality Theories

Abraham Maslow: The Self-Actualizing Person

Carl Rogers: The Fully Functioning Person

Evaluating the Humanistic Perspective

Personality: Is It in the Genes?

The Twin Study Method: Studying Identical and Fraternal Twins

The Shared and Nonshared Environment

The Adoption Method

Personality Assessment

Observation, Interviews, and Rating Scales

Personality Inventories: Taking Stock

Projective Tests: Projections from the Unconscious

Personality Theories: A Final Comment

Applications: Is There Really a Sucker Born Every Minute?

Thinking Critically

Chapter Summary and Review

435

What makes us the way we are? Are the personality characteristics we exhibit influenced more markedly by our genes or by the environment in which we live, grow, and develop? Environments can be strikingly different. Consider the two environments described in the next two paragraphs.

Oskar Stohr was raised as a Catholic by his grandmother in Nazi Germany. As part of Hitler's youth movement, Oskar was expected to be an obedient Nazi. Book burnings, military parades, hatred of Jews, and the raised right hand with the greeting "Heil Hitler" were all part of Oskar's early environment. How did this environment affect his personality?

Jack Yufe, the same age as Oskar, was raised by his Jewish father on the island of Trinidad. Far removed from the goose-stepping storm troopers in Nazi Germany, Jack enjoyed all of the educational advantages and social supports of a middle-class Jewish upbringing. How did Jack's environment affect his personality?

Though raised in starkly different environments, Oskar and Jack are amazingly alike. They have quick tempers, are domineering toward women, enjoy surprising people by faking sneezes in elevators, and flush the toilet before using it. They both read magazines from back to front, store rubber bands on their wrists, like spicy foods and sweet liqueurs, and dip buttered toast in their coffee.

The list is much longer, but there is a good reason for the similarities between Oskar and Jack. They are identical twins. They were separated shortly after birth when their father took Jack with him to the island of Trinidad, and their maternal grandmother raised Oskar in Germany.

Researchers at the Minnesota Center for Twin and Adoption Research are studying the effects of genetics and environment on identical twins reared apart. When Oskar and Jack first arrived at the center to take part in the study, they looked almost exactly alike physically, and both of them were wearing double-breasted blue shirts with epaulets, identical neatly trimmed mustaches, and wire-rimmed glasses. How powerfully the genes influence personality!

Joan Gardiner and Jean Nelson are another pair of identical twins in the Minnesota study. They were also raised apart, but their environments did not differ so markedly. Joan's adoptive mother and Jean's adoptive father were sister and brother, so the twins were together quite often.

Like Oskar and Jack, Joan and Jean have many similarities and a few differences. But one difference between the twins is so unusual that researchers are especially intrigued by it. Joan is musical; Jean is not. Although her adoptive mother was a piano teacher, Jean does not play. But Joan, whose adoptive mother was not a musician, plays piano very well—so well, in fact, that she has performed with the Minnesota Symphony Orchestra. Joan's mother made her practice piano several hours every day, while Jean's mother allowed her to pursue whatever interests she chose. Duplicate genes but musical differences—how do the researchers explain it?

David Lykken of the Minnesota Center suggests that both twins have the same genetic musical capability, but the reason one played and the other did not shows the effects produced by the environment. How powerfully the environment influences personality!

personality: A person's unique and stable pattern of characteristics and behaviors.

psychoanalysis (SY-co-ah-NAL-ih-sis): Freud's term for his theory of personality and his therapy for treating psychological disorders.

We often hear it said that no two people are exactly alike, that each of us is unique. When most people talk about someone's uniqueness, they are referring to the personality. **Personality** is defined as an individual's unique and stable pattern of characteristics and behaviors. And personalities are indeed different—consider Mother Theresa and Madonna, Howard Stern and Billy Graham, Eddie Murphy and Bill Cosby. What makes these people so different?

There are a number of theories that attempt to account for our personality differences and explain how we come to be the way we are. This chapter explores some of the major personality theories, and the variety of tests and inventories used to assess personality.

To what two aspects of Freud's work does the term psychoanalysis apply?

Sigmund Freud and Psychoanalysis

Most textbooks begin their exploration of personality theory with Sigmund Freud, and for good reason. Freud created one of the first and most controversial personality theories. Using information gained from the treatment of his patients and from his own life experiences, Freud developed the theory of **psychoanalysis**. When you hear the term *psychoanalysis*, you may picture a psychiatrist treating a troubled patient on a couch. But psychoanalysis is much more than that. The term refers not only to a therapy for treating psychological disorders but also to a personality theory.

Freud's theory of psychoanalysis is neither the extension of an earlier theory nor a reaction against one. It is largely original, and it was revolutionary and shocking to the 19th- and early 20th-century European audience to which it was introduced. The major components of Freud's theory, and perhaps the most controversial, are (1) the central role of the sexual instinct, (2) the concept of infantile sexuality, and (3) the dominant part played by the unconscious in moving and shaping our thoughts and behavior. Freud's theory assumes a psychic determinism, the view that there is a cause for our every thought, idea, feeling, action, or behavior. Nothing happens by chance or accident; everything we do and even everything we forget to do has a cause behind it.

A married man vacationing alone in Hawaii sends his wife a postcard and writes, "Having a wonderful time! Wish you were her." The husband, no doubt, would protest that he was writing hurriedly and accidentally left off the *e*. His wife might suspect otherwise, and Freud would agree. The "her" was no accident. It was a Freudian slip. Slips of the tongue, slips of the pen, and forgetting appointments—incidents we often call accidental—are not accidental at all, according to Freud (1901/1960).

Like all of us, Freud was partly a product of his environment. Read the Pioneers box to learn what kind of environment helped to shape Sigmund Freud.

The Conscious, the Preconscious, and the Unconscious: Levels of Awareness

Freud believed that there are three levels of awareness in consciousness: the conscious, the preconscious, and the unconscious. The **conscious** consists of whatever we are aware of at any given moment—a thought, a feeling, a sensation, or a memory. When we shift our attention or our thoughts, there is a change in the content of the conscious.

Freud's **preconscious** is very much like long-term memory. It contains all the memories, feelings, experiences, and perceptions that we are not consciously thinking about at the moment, but that may be brought to consciousness. Where did you go to high school? In what year were you born? This information resides in your preconscious but can easily be brought to consciousness.

The most important of the three levels is the **unconscious**, which Freud believed to be the primary motivating force of our behavior. The unconscious holds memories that once were conscious but were so unpleasant or anxiety-provoking that they were repressed (involuntarily removed from consciousness). The unconscious also contains all of the instincts (sexual and aggressive), wishes, and desires that have never been allowed into consciousness. Freud traced the roots of psychological disorders to these impulses and repressed memories.

The Id, the Ego, and the Superego: Warring Components of the Personality

In 1920, when he was nearly 65 years old, Freud (1923/1961) proposed a new conception of the personality, one that contained three systems—the id, the ego, and the superego. These systems do not exist physically; they are only concepts, or ways of looking at personality.

The **id** is the only part of the personality that is present at birth. It is inherited, primitive, inaccessible, and completely unconscious. The id contains (1) the life instincts, which are the sexual instincts and the biological urges such as hunger and thirst, and (2) the death instinct, which accounts for our aggressive and destructive

conscious (KON-shus): The thoughts, feelings, sensations, or memories of which we are aware at any given moment.

preconscious: The thoughts, feelings, and memories that we are not consciously aware of at the moment but that may be brought to consciousness.

unconscious (un-KON-shus): For Freud, the primary motivating force of behavior, containing repressed memories as well as instincts and wishes that have never been conscious.

 What are the three levels of awareness in consciousness?

What are the roles of the id, the ego, and the superego?

id (IHD): The unconscious system of the personality, which contains the life and death instincts and operates on the pleasure principle.

PIONEERS   *Sigmund Freud (1856–1939)*

Sigmund Freud was born in 1856, the first of seven surviving children of Jakob and Amalie Freud. Freud resented sharing his mother's attention with his brothers and sisters, but he was her favorite child. He was the only one to have his own room, and he had the only oil lamp—the others used candles. When his sister's piano playing disturbed his studies, the piano was removed from the house. Freud later spoke of the inestimable advantage of being his mother's favorite.

As a youth, Freud was an outstanding student and proficient in eight languages. At age 17 he entered the University of Vienna to study medicine. After completing his degree, Freud began a career in biological research, which lasted only a year. He had fallen in love with Martha Bernays and wanted to marry her; since the research position paid so poorly, he decided to practice medicine instead.

In April 1886 Freud opened a private practice in Vienna, treating psychological disorders. He and Martha were married 5 months later. In their life together, the couple had three sons and three daughters; one daughter, Anna, became a renowned psychoanalyst. Although Freud was a towering figure in psychology, at the time of his marriage he stood "five feet seven inches tall and weighed just over 126 pounds" (Jones, 1953, p. 151).

For about 10 years Freud suffered from a neurosis, so he began his own psychoanalysis in 1897. This provided much of the material for his major work *The Interpretation of Dreams* (1900/1953a), which sold a mere 600 copies in 8 years and brought Freud only $209 in royalties.

Freud's office was connected to his home. He would see patients all day and then write in his study until 1:00 A.M. or later each night. His practice grew, with patients coming from all over eastern Europe and Russia. By 1922 Freud had developed a worldwide reputation, and his books had been translated into many languages.

For years Freud smoked about 20 large cigars daily. Probably as a result of this habit, in 1923 he developed cancer of the jaw, which required 33 operations over the course of his life. With much of his palate and inner jaw cut away, Freud had to wear a large metal device in his mouth to form a separation between his mouth and nasal cavities. The device caused him great pain, made his speech defective, and made eating difficult. Recurring infections caused nearly total deafness on the side where his jaw had been cut away.

Freud, being Jewish, was a prominent target for the Nazis, who held a public burning of his books in 1933. By 1938 Germany had conquered Austria, and Freud's home in Vienna was invaded by a Nazi gang. His daughter Anna was arrested although later released. Friends begged Freud to take his family and leave Vienna.

Finally, after the intervention of some high-ranking diplomats and the payment of a substantial sum of money, Freud moved to London with his family in 1938. He died there one year later.

---

pleasure principle: The principle by which the id operates to seek pleasure, avoid pain, and obtain immediate gratification.

libido (lih-BEE-doe): Freud's name for the psychic or sexual energy that comes from the id and provides the energy for the entire personality.

ego (EE-go): In Freudian theory, the rational, largely conscious system of personality, which operates according to the reality principle.

impulses (Freud, 1933/1965). The id operates according to the **pleasure principle**; that is, to seek pleasure, avoid pain, and gain immediate gratification of its wishes. The id is the source of the **libido**, the psychic energy that fuels the entire personality; yet the id cannot act on its own. It can only wish, image, fantasize, demand.

The **ego** is the logical, rational, realistic part of the personality. The ego evolves from the id and draws its energy from the id. One of the ego's functions is to satisfy the id's urges. But the ego, which is mostly conscious, acts according to the reality principle. It must consider the constraints of the real world in determining appropriate times, places, and objects for gratification of the id's wishes. The art of the possible is its guide, and sometimes compromises must be made— a McDonald's hamburger instead of steak or lobster.

When the child is age 5 or 6, the **superego**—the moral component of the personality—is formed. The superego has two parts: (1) The "conscience" consists of all the behaviors for which we have been punished and about which we feel guilty; (2) the "ego ideal" contains the behaviors for which we have been praised and rewarded and about which we feel pride and satisfaction. At first the superego reflects only the parents' expectations of what is good and right, but it expands over time to incorporate teachings from the broader social world. In its

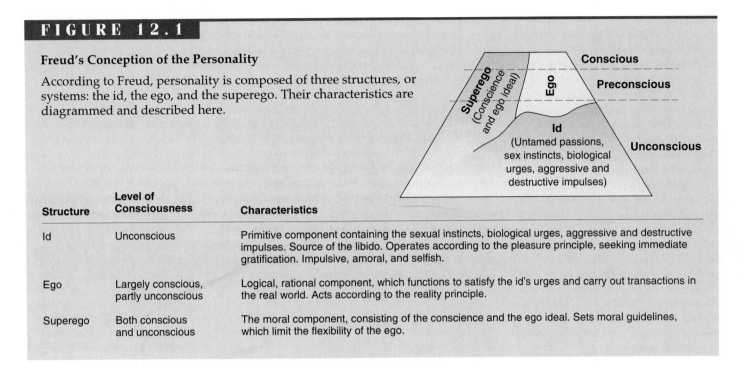

FIGURE 12.1

Freud's Conception of the Personality

According to Freud, personality is composed of three structures, or systems: the id, the ego, and the superego. Their characteristics are diagrammed and described here.

Structure	Level of Consciousness	Characteristics
Id	Unconscious	Primitive component containing the sexual instincts, biological urges, aggressive and destructive impulses. Source of the libido. Operates according to the pleasure principle, seeking immediate gratification. Impulsive, amoral, and selfish.
Ego	Largely conscious, partly unconscious	Logical, rational component, which functions to satisfy the id's urges and carry out transactions in the real world. Acts according to the reality principle.
Superego	Both conscious and unconscious	The moral component, consisting of the conscience and the ego ideal. Sets moral guidelines, which limit the flexibility of the ego.

quest for moral perfection, the superego sets moral guidelines that define and limit the flexibility of the ego.

Figure 12.1 describes the three systems of the personality.

Defense Mechanisms: Protecting the Ego

All would be well if the id, the ego, and the superego had compatible aims. But the id's demands for sensual pleasure are often in direct conflict with the superego's desire for moral perfection. At times the ego needs some way to defend itself against the anxiety created by the excessive demands of the id, by the harsh judgments of the superego, or by the sometimes threatening conditions in the environment. Often the ego can relieve anxiety by solving its problems rationally and directly. When it cannot do so, it must resort to irrational defenses against anxiety called defense mechanisms. Freud's daughter Anna (1966), also a psychoanalyst, contributed much to our understanding of defense mechanisms.

A **defense mechanism** is a technique used to defend against anxiety and to maintain self-esteem, but it involves self-deception and the distortion of reality. We use defense mechanisms to protect ourselves from failure and from guilt-arousing desires or actions. Defense mechanisms are like painkillers. They lessen the pain of anxiety, but they do not cure the problem; and if they are to work, they must be unconscious. All of us use defense mechanisms to some degree; it is only their overuse that is considered abnormal. But there is a price to be paid. Psychic energy is required to keep defenses in place—energy that could be used more profitably in other ways.

Repression: Out of Mind, Out of Sight According to Freud, **repression** is the most important and the most frequently used defense mechanism, and it is present to some degree in all other defense mechanisms. Repression operates in two ways: (1) It can remove painful or threatening memories, thoughts, ideas, or perceptions from consciousness and keep them in the unconscious; (2) it can prevent unconscious but disturbing sexual and aggressive impulses from breaking into consciousness.

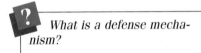

What is a defense mechanism?

superego (sue-per-EE-go): The moral system of the personality, which consists of the conscience and the ego ideal.

defense mechanism: An unconscious, irrational means used by the ego to defend against anxiety; involves self-deception and the distortion of reality.

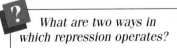

What are two ways in which repression operates?

repression: Involuntarily removing an unpleasant memory or barring disturbing sexual and aggressive impulses from consciousness. (page 439)

What are some other defense mechanisms?

projection: Attributing one's own undesirable thoughts, impulses, traits, or behaviors to others.

denial: Refusing to acknowledge consciously the existence of danger or a threatening condition.

rationalization: Supplying a logical, rational, socially acceptable reason rather than the real reason for an action.

regression: Reverting to a behavior characteristic of an earlier stage of development.

reaction formation: Denying an unacceptable impulse, usually sexual or aggressive, by giving strong conscious expression to its opposite.

displacement: Substituting a less threatening object for the original object of an impulse.

sublimation: Rechanneling sexual or aggressive energy into pursuits that society considers acceptable or admirable.

Even though repressed, the memories lurk in the unconscious and exert an active influence on personality and behavior. In fact, Freud (1933/1965) said repressed memories are "virtually immortal; after the passage of decades, they behave as though they had just occurred" (p. 74). This is why repressed traumatic events of childhood can cause psychological disorders (neuroses) in adults. Freud believed that the way to cure such disorders is to bring the repressed material back to consciousness. This was what he tried to accomplish through his therapy, psychoanalysis (see Chapter 15).

Other Defense Mechanisms: Excuses, Substitutions, and Denials

There are several other defense mechanisms that we may use from time to time. We use **projection** when we attribute our own undesirable impulses, thoughts, personality traits, or behavior to others, or when we minimize the undesirable in ourselves and exaggerate it in others. Projection allows us to avoid acknowledging our unacceptable traits and thereby to maintain our self-esteem, but it seriously distorts our perception of the external world. A sexually promiscuous husband or wife may accuse the partner of being unfaithful. A dishonest businessman may think everyone is out to cheat him.

Denial is a refusal to acknowledge consciously or to believe that a danger or a threatening condition exists. Smokers use denial when they refuse to admit that cigarettes are a danger to their health. Many people who abuse alcohol and drugs deny that they have a problem. Yet denial is sometimes useful as a temporary means of getting through a crisis until a more permanent adjustment can be made, such as when people initially deny the existence of a terminal illness.

Rationalization occurs when we unconsciously supply a logical, rational, or socially acceptable reason rather than the real reason for an action or event. Rationalization can be used to justify past, present, or future behaviors or to soften the diappointment connected with not attaining a desired goal. When we rationalize, we make excuses for, or justify, our failures and mistakes. A student who did not study and then failed a test might complain, "The test was unfair." An ineffective teacher may blame students for their low grades, claiming that they are unmotivated and lazy.

Sometimes, when frustrated or anxious, we may use **regression** and revert to behavior that might have reduced anxiety at an earlier stage of development. A 5-year-old child with a new baby sister or brother may regress and suck her thumb, wet her pants, or drag a blanket around the house. An adult may have a temper tantrum, rant and rave, or throw things.

Reaction formation is at work when people express exaggerated ideas and emotions that are the opposite of their disturbing, unconscious impulses and desires. In reaction formation the conscious thought or feeling masks the unconscious one. Unconscious hatred may be expressed as love and devotion, cruelty as kindness. A former chain smoker becomes irate and complains loudly at the faintest whiff of cigarette smoke. A reaction formation may be suspected when a behavior is extreme, excessive, and compulsive. Reaction formation can be viewed as a barrier unconsciously erected to prevent a person from acting on an unacceptable impulse.

Displacement occurs when we substitute a less threatening object or person for the original object of a sexual or aggressive impulse. If your boss makes you angry, you may take out your hostility on your boyfriend or girlfriend.

With **sublimation**, we rechannel sexual or aggressive energy into pursuits or accomplishments that society considers acceptable or even praiseworthy. An aggressive person may rechannel the aggression and become a football or hockey player, a boxer, a surgeon, or a butcher. Freud viewed sublimation as the only completely healthy ego defense mechanism. In fact, Freud (1930/1962) considered all advancements in civilization to be the result of sublimation.

Review and Reflect Table 12.1 summarizes the defense mechanisms.

Review and Reflect 12.1 Defense Mechanisms

Defense Mechanism	Description	Example
Repression	Involuntarily removing an unpleasant memory from consciousness or barring disturbing sexual and aggressive impulses from consciousness.	Jill forgets a traumatic incident from childhood.
Projection	Attributing one's own undesirable traits or impulses to another.	A very lonely divorced woman accuses all men of having only one thing on their mind.
Denial	Refusing to acknowledge consciously the existence of danger or a threatening situation.	Amy is severely injured when she fails to take a tornado warning seriously.
Rationalization	Supplying a logical, rational reason rather than the real reason for an action or event.	Fred tells his friend that he didn't get the job because he didn't have connections.
Regression	Reverting to a behavior characteristic of an earlier stage of development.	Susan bursts into tears whenever she is criticized.
Reaction formation	Expressing exaggerated ideas and emotions that are the opposite of disturbing, unconscious impulses and desires.	A former purchaser of pornography, Bob is now a tireless crusader against it.
Displacement	Substituting a less threatening object for the original object of an impulse.	After being spanked by his father, Bill hits his baby brother.
Sublimation	Rechanneling sexual and aggressive energy into pursuits that society considers acceptable or even admirable.	Tim goes to a gym to work out when he feels hostile and frustrated.

Memory Check 12.1

1. Psychoanalysis is both a theory of personality and a therapy for the treatment of psychological disorders. (true/false)

2. Freud considered the (conscious, unconscious) to be the primary motivating force of our behavior.

3. The part of the personality that would make you want to eat, drink, and be merry is your:
   a. id.   b. ego.   c. superego.   d. ego ideal.

4. You just found a gold watch in a darkened movie theater. Which part of your personality would urge you to turn it in to the lost and found?
   a. id.   b. ego.   c. superego.   d. ego ideal.

5. The part of the personality that must determine the most appropriate ways and means of satisfying your biological urges is the:
   a. id.   b. ego.   c. superego.   d. ego ideal.

6. Defense mechanisms are used only by psychologically unhealthy individuals. (true/false)

7. Match the example with the corresponding defense mechanism.
   ____ 1) sublimation
   ____ 2) repression
   ____ 3) displacement
   ____ 4) rationalization

   a. forgetting a traumatic childhood experience
   b. supplying a logical reason for arriving late
   c. creating a work of art
   d. venting anger on a friend or spouse after getting a speeding ticket from a police officer

Answers: 1. true 2. unconscious 3. a 4. c 5. b 6. false 7. 1) c 2) a 3) d 4) b

What are the psychosexual stages, and why did Freud consider them so important in personality development?

psychosexual stages: A series of stages through which the sexual instinct develops; each stage is defined by an erogenous zone that becomes the center of new pleasures and conflicts.

fixation: Arrested development at a psychosexual stage occurring because of excessive gratification or frustration at that stage.

oral stage: Freud's first psychosexual stage (birth to 1 or $1\frac{1}{2}$ years), in which sensual pleasure is derived mainly through stimulation of the mouth.

anal stage: Freud's second psychosexual stage (ages 1 or $1\frac{1}{2}$ to 3 years), in which the child derives sensual pleasure mainly from expelling and withholding feces.

phallic stage: Freud's third psychosexual stage (ages 3 to 5 or 6 years), during which sensual pleasure is derived mainly through touching the genitals, and the Oedipus complex arises.

What is the Oedipus complex?

Oedipus complex (ED-uh-pus): Occurring in the phallic stage, a conflict in which the child is sexually attracted to the opposite-sex parent and feels hostility toward the same-sex parent.

The Psychosexual Stages of Development: Centered on the Erogenous Zones

The sex instinct, Freud said, is the most important factor influencing personality; but it does not just suddenly appear full-blown at puberty. It is present at birth and then develops through a series of **psychosexual stages**. Each stage centers around a particular erogenous zone, a part of the body that provides pleasurable sensations and around which a conflict arises (1905/1953b; 1920/1963b). If the conflict is not resolved without undue difficulty, the child may develop a **fixation**. This means that a portion of the libido (psychic energy) remains invested at that stage, leaving less energy to meet the challenges of future stages. Over-indulgence at a stage may leave a person unwilling psychologically to move on to the next stage. But too little gratification may leave the person trying to make up for previously unmet needs. Freud believed that certain personality characteristics develop as a result of difficulty at one or another of the stages.

The Oral Stage (Birth to 12 or 18 Months) During the **oral stage**, the mouth is the primary source of an infant's sensual pleasure, which Freud (1920/1963b) considered to be an expression of infantile sexuality. The conflict at this stage centers on weaning. Too much or too little gratification may result in an oral fixation—an excessive preoccupation with oral activities such as eating, drinking, smoking, gum chewing, nail biting, and even kissing. (Freud's 20-cigars-a-day habit probably qualifies as an oral fixation, according to his theory.) Freud claimed that difficulties at the oral stage can result in personality traits such as either excessive dependence, optimism, and gullibility (tendency to "swallow" anything) or extreme pessimism, sarcasm, hostility, and aggression.

The Anal Stage (1 or $1\frac{1}{2}$ to 3 Years) During the **anal stage**, children derive sensual pleasure from expelling and withholding feces. But a conflict arises when toilet training begins, because this is one of the parents' first attempts to have children withhold or postpone gratification. When parents are harsh in their approach, children may rebel openly, defecating whenever and wherever they please. This may lead to an anal expulsive personality—someone who is sloppy, irresponsible, rebellious, hostile, and destructive. Other children may defy their parents and gain attention by withholding feces. They may develop anal retentive personalities, gaining security through what they possess and becoming stingy, stubborn, rigid, excessively neat and clean, orderly, and precise (Freud, 1933/1965). Do these patterns remind you of Felix and Oscar of the old TV series "The Odd Couple"?

The Phallic Stage (3 to 5 or 6 Years) During the **phallic stage**, children learn that they can get pleasure by touching their genitals, and masturbation is common. They become aware of the anatomical differences in males and females and may begin to play "Doctor."

The conflict that develops at this stage is a sexual desire for the parent of the opposite sex and a hostility toward the same-sex parent, a conflict Freud called the **Oedipus complex** (after the central character in the Greek tragedy *Oedipus Rex*, by Sophocles). "Boys concentrate their sexual wishes upon their mother and develop hostile impulses against their father as being a rival" (1925/1963a, p. 61). But the young boy eventually develops castration anxiety—an intense fear that his father might retaliate and harm him by cutting off his penis, the offending organ (1933/1965). This fear becomes so intense, Freud believed, that the boy usually resolves the Oedipus complex by identifying with his father and repressing his sexual feelings for his mother. With identification, the child takes on his father's behaviors, mannerisms, and superego standards, and in this way the superego develops (Freud, 1930/1962).

Girls experience a similar internal Oedipal conflict that is often referred to as the Electra complex, although Freud did not use that term. When young girls discover they have no penis, they develop "penis envy," Freud claimed, and they turn to their father because he has the desired organ (1933/1965). They feel sexual desires for him and develop jealousy and rivalry toward their mother. But eventually girls, too, experience anxiety as a result of their hostile feelings. They repress their sexual feelings toward the father and identify with the mother, leading to the formation of their superego (Freud, 1930/1962).

According to Freud, failure to resolve these conflicts can have serious consequences for both boys and girls. Freud thought that tremendous guilt and anxiety could be carried over into adulthood and cause sexual problems, great difficulty relating to members of the opposite sex, and even homosexuality.

The Latency Period (5 or 6 Years to Puberty) Following the stormy phallic stage, the **latency period** is one of relative calm. The sex instinct is repressed and temporarily sublimated in school and play activities, hobbies, and sports.

The Genital Stage (from Puberty On) In the **genital stage**, the focus of sexual energy gradually shifts to the opposite sex for the vast majority of people, culminating in heterosexual love and the attainment of full adult sexuality. Freud believed that the few who reach the genital stage without having fixations at earlier stages, can achieve the state of psychological health that he equated with the ability to love and work.

Review and Reflect Table 12.2 (on page 444) provides a summary of Freud's psychosexual stages.

Freud's Explanation of Personality

According to Freud, personality is almost completely formed at age 5 or 6, when the Oedipal conflict is resolved and the superego is formed. He believed that there are two primary sources of influence on personality: (1) the traits that develop because of fixations at any of the psychosexual stages, and (2) the relative strengths of the id, the ego, and the superego. In psychologically healthy people, there is a balance among the three components. If the id is too strong and the superego too weak, people will take pleasure and gratify desires, no matter who is hurt or what the cost, and not feel guilty. But a tyrannical superego will leave people with perpetual guilt feelings, unable to enjoy sensual pleasure.

Evaluating Freud's Contribution

Freud's theory is so comprehensive (he wrote more than 24 volumes) that its elements must be evaluated separately. His beliefs that women are inferior to men sexually, morally, and intellectually and that they suffer penis envy seem ridiculous today. Also, research contradicts Freud's notion that personality is almost completely formed by age 5 or 6. However, we are indebted to him for emphasizing the influence of early childhood experiences on later development.

Critics charge that much of Freud's theory defies scientific testing. How, they ask, can a conceptual framework based on Freud's analysis of his own life and the case histories of his disturbed patients provide a theory of personality generalizable to the larger population? The most serious flaw critics find is that Freud's theory interprets and explains behavior after the fact and lacks the power to predict behavior (Stanovich, 1989). In too many cases, any act of

Freud believed that a fixation at the anal stage, resulting from harsh parental pressure, could lead to an anal retentive personality—characterized by excessive stubbornness, rigidity, and neatness.

? *According to Freud, what are the two primary sources of influence on the personality?*

latency period: The period following Freud's phallic stage (ages 5 or 6 years to puberty), in which the sex instinct is largely repressed and temporarily sublimated in school and play activities.

genital stage: Freud's final psychosexual stage (from puberty on), in which for most people the focus of sexual energy gradually shifts to the opposite sex, culminating in the attainment of full adult sexuality.

Review and Reflect 12.2 *Freud's Psychosexual Stages of Development*

Stage		Erogenous Zone	Conflicts/Experiences	Adult Traits Associated with Problems at This Stage
Oral (birth to 12–18 months)		Mouth	Weaning Oral gratification from sucking, eating, biting	Optimism, gullibility, dependency, pessimism, passivity, hostility, sarcasm, aggression
Anal (12–18 months to 3 years)		Anus	Toilet training Gratification from expelling and witholding feces	Excessive cleanliness, orderliness, stinginess, messiness, rebelliousness, destructiveness
Phallic (3 to 5–6 years)		Genitals	Oedipal conflict Sexual curiosity Masturbation	Flirtatiousness, vanity, promiscuity, pride, chastity
Latency (5–6 years to puberty)		None	Period of sexual calm Interest in school, hobbies, same-sex friends	
Genital (puberty onward)		Genitals	Revival of sexual interests Establishment of mature sexual relationships	

behavior or even no act of behavior at all can be interpreted to support Freud's theory.

Even so, some research in neuroscience and psychology supports the notions of unconscious mental processing (Shevrin & Dickman, 1980). Motley (1985) conducted research that indicates that the unconscious is sometimes at work in Freudian slips, to our embarrassment; but he finds that most slips of the tongue should be attributed to misfirings in the brain and its verbal mechanisms. Research also finds evidence for repression, especially of memories related to feelings of fear and self-consciousness (Davis & Schwartz, 1987).

As we have seen, Freud believed that his concepts of the unconscious and the principles by which it operated were his most important work. In fact the primary aim of psychoanalysis is to bring unconscious thoughts, wishes, and desires to consciousness. Leading scholars today do not dispute the existence of unconscious processes (Loftus & Klinger, 1992). However, they do not see the unconscious as envisioned by Freud, and they disagree as to how sophisticated or simple it might be (Epstein, 1994; Erdelyi, 1992; Greenwald, 1992).

Freud is a towering figure in the world of psychology, but today he does not loom as large as in decades past. There are very few strict Freudians left, and for most psychoanalysts, Freud's techniques constitute only a part of their therapeutic arsenal. Sigmund Freud has been both worshipped and ridiculed, but his standing as a pioneer in psychology cannot be denied.

Memory Check 12.2

1. According to Freud, the sex instinct arises at (birth, puberty).

2. Which of the following lists presents Freud's psychosexual stages in the order in which they occur?
   a. anal; oral; genital; phallic
   b. genital; anal; oral; phallic
   c. oral; phallic; anal; genital
   d. oral; anal; phallic; genital

3. Excessive concern with cleanliness and order could indicate a fixation at the _____ stage.
   a. oral   b. anal   c. phallic   d. genital

4. When a young boy develops sexual feelings toward his mother and hostility toward his father, he is said to have a conflict called the _____.

5. According to Freud, which of the following represents a primary source of influence on our personality?
   a. our heredity
   b. life experiences after we begin school
   c. the relative strengths of our id, ego, and superego
   d. the problems we experience during adolescence

Answers: 1. birth 2. d 3. b 4. Oedipus complex 5. c

The Neo-Freudians

Several personality theorists, referred to as neo-Freudians, started their careers as followers of Freud but began to disagree on certain basic principles of psychoanalytic theory. They modified aspects of the theory and presented their own original ideas about personality. We will discuss Carl Jung (analytical psychology), Alfred Adler (individual psychology), and Karen Horney.

Carl Gustav Jung

Carl Jung (1875–1961) differed with Freud on many major points. He did not consider the sexual instinct to be the main factor in personality; nor did he believe that the personality is almost completely formed in early childhood. For

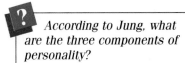

According to Jung, what are the three components of personality?

Carl Gustav Jung (1875–1961)

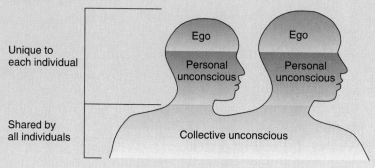

What are five archetypes that Jung believed have a major influence on the personality?

Jung (1933), middle age was an even more important period for personality development. He also disagreed with Freud on the basic structure of personality.

Jung's View of the Personality: A Different View of the Unconscious Jung conceived of the personality as consisting of three parts: the ego, the personal unconscious, and the collective unconscious. He saw the ego as the conscious component of personality, which carries out our normal daily activities. Like Freud, he believed the ego to be secondary in importance to the unconscious.

The **personal unconscious** develops as a result of one's own experience and is therefore unique to each person. It contains all the experiences, thoughts, and perceptions accessible to the conscious, as well as repressed memories, wishes, and impulses. The personal unconscious resembles a combination of Freud's preconscious and unconscious.

The **collective unconscious** is the deepest and most inaccessible layer of the unconscious. Jung thought that the universal experiences of humankind throughout evolution are transmitted to each of us through the collective unconscious. This is how he accounted for the similarity of certain myths, dreams, symbols, and religious beliefs in cultures widely separated by distance and time.

Figure 12.2 provides a summary of Jung's conception of the personality.

Archetypes: Unconscious Predispositions The collective unconscious contains what Jung called archetypes. An **archetype** is an inherited tendency to respond to universal human situations in particular ways. Jung would say that

personal unconscious: In Jung's theory, the layer of the unconscious containing all of the thoughts and experiences that are accessible to the conscious, as well as repressed memories and impulses.

collective unconscious: In Jung's theory, the most inaccessible layer of the unconscious, which contains the universal experiences of humankind transmitted to each individual.

archetype (AR-keh-type): Existing in the collective unconscious, an inherited tendency to respond in particular ways to universal human situations.

FIGURE 12.2

Jung's Conception of Personality

Like Freud, Carl Jung saw three components in personality. The ego and the personal unconscious are unique to each individual. The collective unconscious is shared by all people and accounts for the similarity of myths and beliefs in diverse cultures.

Structure	Characteristics
Ego	The conscious component of personality; carries out normal daily activities.
Personal unconscious	The component containing all the individual's memories, thoughts, and feelings that are accessible to consciousness, and all repressed memories, wishes, and impulses; similar to a combination of Freud's preconscious and unconscious.
Collective unconscious	The most inaccessible layer of the unconscious, shared by all people; contains the universal experiences of humankind throughout evolution, as well as the archetypes.

the tendency of people to believe in a god, a devil, evil spirits, and heroes, or to have a fear of the dark or of snakes, all result from inherited archetypes.

Jung named several archetypes that exert a major influence on the personality: the persona, the shadow, the anima and animus, and the self. The persona is the public face we show to the world—"a kind of mask, designed on the one hand to make a definite impression on others, and, on the other, to conceal the true nature of the individual" (Jung, 1966, p. 192). The persona is consistent with the roles we play, and it helps us function socially. It presents no problem as long as people remain aware that it consists of the impression they are trying to make and not the real person behind it.

The shadow is a powerful archetype that represents "the 'negative side' of the personality, the sum of all those unpleasant qualities we like to hide" (Jung, 1917/1953, par. 103). To deny our shadow, or to fail to be conscious of it, gives it more power over us. The qualities we condemn most in others may be lurking in our own shadow, unadmitted and unknown.

While Jung saw differences in the psychology of males and females, he believed that we all carry qualities and images of the opposite sex within us, although usually in an underdeveloped state. The *anima* is Jung's term for the "inner feminine figure" within the unconscious of every man, and the *animus*, the "inner masculine figure" within the unconscious of every woman (Jung, 1961, p. 186). Both the masculine and feminine qualities must be consciously acknowledged and integrated for a healthy personality to develop. Jung's work is a forerunner of the more recent research on psychological androgyny (see Chapter 11).

The self represents the full development of the personality and is attained only when the opposing forces within are integrated and balanced. The self encompasses the conscious and the unconscious, the persona, the shadow, the masculine and feminine qualities, and the tendencies toward extraversion and introversion (terms originated by Jung). **Extroversion** (Jung spelled it "extraversion") is the tendency to be outgoing, adaptable, and sociable; **introversion** is the tendency to focus inward and to be reflective, retiring, and nonsocial.

Jung believed that the balancing and integration of these opposing forces of the personality begins in midlife. For some, the beginning of change may be accompanied by a midlife crisis, which Jung himself experienced. Because he emphasized personality development in midlife, many consider Jung the founder of the psychology of adult development (Moraglia, 1994).

Alfred Adler: Overcoming Inferiority

? *What did Adler consider to be the driving force of the personality?*

Alfred Adler (1870–1937) disagreed with most of Freud's basic beliefs; on many points his views were the exact opposite. Adler emphasized the unity of the personality rather than the separate warring components of id, ego, and superego. He believed that our behavior is motivated more by the conscious than by the unconscious and that we are influenced more by future goals than by early childhood experiences.

Unlike Freud, who claimed that sex and pleasure seeking are our primary motives, Adler (1927, 1956) maintained that we are driven by the need to compensate for inferiority and to strive for superiority or significance. For him, feelings of weakness and inferiority are an inevitable experience in every child's early life. Adler himself had felt a particularly keen sense of inferiority as a child. He was small, sickly, and unable to walk until he was 4, because of rickets.

According to Adler (1956), people at an early age develop a "style of life"—a unique way in which the child and later the adult will go about the struggle to achieve superiority. Sometimes inferiority feelings are so strong that they prevent personal development, and Adler originated a term to describe this condition—the "inferiority complex" (Dreikurs, 1953).

extroversion: The tendency to be outgoing, adaptable, and sociable.

introversion: The tendency to focus inward; to be reflective, retiring, and nonsocial.

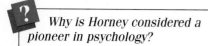

Why is Horney considered a pioneer in psychology?

Karen Horney: Champion of Feminine Psychology

Karen Horney's work centered on two main themes—the neurotic personality (Horney, 1937, 1945, 1950) and feminine psychology (Horney, 1967). She considered herself a disciple of Freud, accepting his emphasis on unconscious motivation and the basic tools of psychoanalysis. However, she disagreed with many of his basic beliefs. She did not accept his division of personality into id, ego, and superego, and she flatly rejected his psychosexual stages and the concepts of the Oedipus complex and penis envy. Furthermore, Horney thought Freud overemphasized the role of the sexual instinct and neglected cultural and environmental influences on personality. While she did stress the importance of early childhood experiences, Horney (1939) believed that personality could continue to develop and change throughout life. Horney argued forcefully against Freud's notion that a woman's desire to have a child and a man are nothing more than a conversion of the unfulfilled wish for a penis.

Horney insisted that, rather than envying the male's penis, women really want the same opportunities, the same rights and privileges society grants to males. Freud did not respond directly to Horney's arguments, but implied that her challenge to his theory was merely a manifestation of her own penis envy. Horney prevailed and continued her pioneering efforts for women. She argued convincingly that women must be free to find their own personal identities, to develop their abilities, and to pursue careers if they choose.

PIONEERS *Karen Horney (1885–1952)*

Karen Horney (HOR-nye) pioneered in the introduction of feminine psychology, a perspective that until her time had been virtually excluded from the world of psychology.

Born Karen Danielsen in a small village near Hamburg, Germany, in 1885, Karen was the second child and first daughter in a financially secure Protestant family. Her Norwegian father was a commercial ship captain who was devoutly religious, stern, and silent. Her mother was Dutch, bright, beautiful, vivacious, a free thinker, and 17 years younger than Captain Danielsen. Young Karen sometimes accompanied her father on long voyages at sea, visiting many ports and observing diverse cultures. This may have influenced her heavy emphasis on social and cultural forces in the formation of personality, rather than the biological forces proposed by Freud.

Karen was more heavily influenced by her mother and spent more time with her because of the long periods when her father was away at sea. An excellent student, Karen decided at age 12 to study medicine. Over the strong objections of her father but with the encouragement of her mother, Karen Danielsen, at age 21, entered

medical school in Berlin. Three years later, in 1909, she married Oscar Horney, a lawyer, and she finished her M.D. degree in 1911 at the age of 26. Karen Horney became a member of the Berlin Psychoanalytic Society and went into analysis with a strict Freudian, Karl Abraham, who praised her with great enthusiasm to Freud. She opened her psychoanalytic practice and became a training analyst for the Berlin Psychoanalytic Institute. Over the next several years, three daughters were born to the Horneys.

While still in Berlin Dr. Horney wrote theoretical articles, several of which were on feminine psychology. All along she had known that her male colleagues did not understand the psychology of women. In 1926 Karen Horney and her husband separated, and in 1932, at the age of 47, she moved to the United States, first to Chicago and two years later to New York. There Horney established her clinical practice and published her first book, *The Neurotic Personality of Our Time*, in 1937.

Karen Horney continued her practice and writing, and untiringly pioneered the cause of feminine psychology. She died in New York in 1952 at the age of 67.

Horney (1945) believed that in order to be psychologically healthy, we all need safety and satisfaction. But these needs can be frustrated in early childhood by parents who are indifferent, unaffectionate, rejecting, or hostile. Such early experiences may cause a child to develop basic anxiety—"the feeling a child has of being isolated and helpless in a potentially hostile world" (p. 41). To minimize this basic anxiety and satisfy the need for safety, children develop coping strategies that form their basic attitude toward life—either moving toward people, moving against people, or moving away from people. Normal people move in all three ways as different situations demand. But a neurotic person will use only one way to reduce anxiety, and will use it excessively and inappropriately.

Horney insisted that, rather than envying the male's penis, as Freud believed, women really want the same opportunities and privileges as men.

If we cannot tolerate ourselves the way we are, said Horney, we may repress all our negative attributes and replace them with an idealized image, perfect and unblemished. As long as this image remains real to us, we feel superior and entitled to make all kinds of demands and claims. Horney (1950) believed that the idealized self brings with it the "tyranny of the should"—unrealistic demands for personal perfection, which "no human being could fulfill" (p. 66). The irrational, neurotic thinking that may spring from the "tyranny of the should" is an important part of Horney's theory. Her influence may be seen in modern cognitive-behavioral therapies, which we explore in Chapter 15.

Memory Check 12.3

1. In Jung's theory, the inherited part of the personality that stores the experiences of humankind is the (collective, personal) unconscious.

2. Match the archetype with its description.

   ____ 1) self
   ____ 2) anima or animus
   ____ 3) shadow
   ____ 4) persona

   a. the dark side of our nature
   b. our public face
   c. the full development of the integrated and balanced personality
   d. the qualities and images of the opposite sex carried within us

3. Who is the personality theorist who believed that our basic drive is to overcome and compensate for inferiority feelings and strive for superiority and significance?

   a. Sigmund Freud
   b. Carl Jung
   c. Alfred Adler
   d. Karen Horney

4. Horney traced the origin of psychological maladjustment to:

   a. the inferiority feelings of childhood.
   b. basic anxiety resulting from the parents' failure to satisfy the child's needs for safety and satisfaction.
   c. excessive frustration or overindulgence of the child at early stages of development.
   d. the failure to balance opposing forces in the personality.

Answers: 1. collective 2. 1) c 2) d 3) a 4) b 3. c 4. b

Trait Theories

What are trait theories of personality?

How would you describe yourself—cheerful, moody, talkative, quiet, shy, friendly, outgoing? When you describe your personality or that of someone else, you probably list several relatively stable and consistent personal characteristics called **traits. Trait theories** are attempts to explain personality and differences between people in terms of their personal characteristics.

trait: A personal characteristic that is used to describe or explain personality.

> ? *How did Allport differentiate between cardinal and central traits?*

Gordon Allport: Personality Traits in the Brain

Gordon Allport (1897–1967) claimed that personality traits are real entities, physically located somewhere in the brain (Allport & Odbert, 1936). We each inherit our own unique set of raw materials for given traits, which are then shaped by our experiences. Traits describe the particular way we respond to the environment and the consistency of that response. If we are shy, we respond to strangers differently than if we are friendly; if we are self-confident, we approach tasks differently than if we feel inferior. Recent research in behavioral genetics supports the notion that certain personality characteristics are influenced by the genes.

> **trait theories:** Theories that attempt to explain personality and differences between people in terms of their personal characteristics. (page 449)
>
> **cardinal trait:** Allport's name for a personal quality that is so strong a part of a person's personality that he or she may become identified with that trait.
>
> **central trait:** Allport's name for the type of trait you would use in writing a letter of recommendation.

Allport (1961) identified two main categories of traits—common traits and individual traits. Common traits are those we share or hold in common with most others in our own culture. The quiet, polite behavior often seen in Asian people is a common trait of those cultures. More important to Allport were three types of individual traits: cardinal, central, and secondary traits.

A **cardinal trait** is "so pervasive and so outstanding in a life that . . . almost every act seems traceable to its influence" (Allport, 1961, p. 365). It is so strong a part of a person's personality that he or she may become identified with or known for that trait. We even describe people who, to some degree, exhibit the cardinal traits of others as being Christlike or a Scrooge, for example.

Central traits are those, said Allport (1961), that we would "mention in writing a careful letter of recommendation" (p. 365). Do the *Try It!* to learn more about central traits.

Which adjectives in this list best describe you? Which characterize your mother or your father? In Allport's terms you are describing your or their central traits.

decisive	outgoing	generous	industrious
funny	inhibited	sloppy	deceptive
intelligent	religious	laid-back	cooperative
disorganized	arrogant	rebellious	reckless
shy	loyal	calm	sad
fearful	competitive	good-natured	honest
jealous	liberal	nervous	happy
controlled	friendly	serious	selfish
responsible	compulsive	humble	organized
rigid	quick	lazy	quiet

We also have secondary traits, but these are less obvious, less consistent, and not as critical in defining our personality as the cardinal and central traits. Secondary traits are such things as food and music preferences and specific attitudes. We have many more secondary traits than cardinal or central traits.

Raymond Cattell's 16 Personality Factors

> ? *How did Cattell differentiate between surface and source traits?*

Raymond Cattell (1950) considered personality to be a pattern of traits providing the key to understanding and predicting a person's behavior. Cattell identified two types: surface traits and source traits. — opposites

> **surface traits:** Cattell's name for observable qualities of personality, such as those used to describe a friend.

If you were asked to describe your best friend, you might say that she is kind, honest, helpful, generous, and so on. These observable qualities of personality Cattell called **surface traits**. (Allport called these qualities central traits.) Using observations and questionnaires, Cattell studied thousands of people, and he found certain clusters of surface traits that appeared together time after time. He thought these were evidence of deeper, more general, underlying personality factors. Using a statistical technique called factor analysis, Cattell tried to identify these factors, which he called source traits.

Source traits make up the most basic personality structure and, according to Cattell, cause behavior. Even though we all possess the same source traits, we do not all possess them in the same degree. Intelligence is a source trait, and every person has a certain amount of it, but obviously not exactly the same amount or the same kind. How intelligent people are can influence whether they pursue a college degree, what profession or job they choose, what type of leisure activities they pursue, and what kind of friends they have.

Cattell found 23 source traits in normal individuals, 16 of which he studied in great detail. Cattell's Sixteen Personality Factor Questionnaire, commonly called the "16 P. F. Test," yields a personality profile (Cattell et al., 1950, 1977). You can chart your own source traits in the *Try It!*

source traits: Cattell's name for the traits that make up the most basic personality structure and cause behavior.

This hypothetical personality profile is based on Cattell's Sixteen Personality Factor Questionnaire. Along each of the 16 dimensions of bipolar traits, circle the point you think would result if you took the 16 P. F. Test.

Reserved	Warm
Concrete	Abstract
Reactive	Emotionally stable
Avoids conflict	Dominant
Serious	Lively
Expedient	Rule-conscious
Shy	Socially bold
Utilitarian	Sensitive
Trusting	Suspicious
Practical	Imaginative
Forthright	Private
Self-assured	Apprehensive
Traditional	Open to change
Group-oriented	Self-reliant
Tolerates disorder	Perfectionistic
Relaxed	Tense

The Cattell Personality Profile can be used to provide a better understanding of a single individual or to compare one person's profile with that of others. When later researchers tried to confirm Cattell's 16 factors, no one could find more than 7 factors, and most found 5 (Digman, 1990).

Hans Eysenck: Stressing Two Factors

British psychologist Hans Eysenck (1990) has always believed that personality is largely determined by the genes, and that environmental influences are slight at best. Although Eysenck claims that three higher-order factors or dimensions are needed to capture the essence of personality, he places particular emphasis on two dimensions—Extroversion (extroversion versus introversion) and Neuroticism (emotional stability versus instability). Extroverts are sociable, outgoing, and active, whereas introverts are withdrawn, quiet, and introspective. (Jung originally introduced the terms *introversion* and *extraversion*.) Emotionally stable people are calm, even-tempered, and often easygoing, while emotionally unstable people are anxious, excitable, and easily distressed.

Eysenck (1981) believes that individual variability on the two dimensions may be partly due to differences in nervous system functioning. He suggests that extroverts have a lower level of cortical arousal than introverts and as a result seek out more stimulation to increase arousal, while introverts are more easily aroused and thus more likely to show emotional instability. Stelmack (1990) sug-

What does Eysenck consider to be the two most important dimensions of personality?

gests that rather than having a higher base rate of arousal, "introverts exhibit greater reactivity to sensory stimulation than extroverts" (p. 293).

What are the Big Five personality dimensions in the five-factor theory as described by McCrae and Costa?

According to the five-factor theory of personality, people who are extroverts are sociable, outgoing, and active. What are some characteristics of introverts?

The Five-Factor Theory of Personality: The Big Five

Today, the most talked-about personality theory is the **five-factor theory**, also known as the Big Five. Each of the five broad personality factors is composed of a constellation of traits. As Goldberg (1993) puts it, the five-factor theory seeks to provide a scientifically accurate framework for organizing the many individual differences that characterize humankind.

Even some of the researchers who accept these five broad dimensions of personality still disagree as to what they should be named. We will describe the Big Five dimensions using the names assigned by Robert McCrae and Paul Costa (1987), the most influential proponents of the five-factor theory:

- *Extroversion.* This dimension contrasts such traits as sociable, outgoing, talkative, assertive, persuasive, decisive, and active with more introverted traits such as withdrawn, quiet, passive, retiring, and reserved.

- *Neuroticism.* People high on Neuroticism are prone to emotional instability. They tend to experience negative emotions and to be moody, irritable, nervous, and prone to worry. Neuroticism differentiates people who are anxious, excitable, and easily distressed from those who are emotionally stable and thus calm, even-tempered, easygoing, and relaxed.

- *Conscientiousness.* This factor differentiates individuals who are dependable, organized, reliable, responsible, thorough, hard-working, and persevering from those who are undependable, disorganized, impulsive, unreliable, irresponsible, careless, negligent, and lazy.

- *Agreeableness.* This factor is composed of a collection of traits that range from compassion to antagonism toward others. A person high on Agreeableness would be a pleasant person, good-natured, warm, sympathetic, and cooperative; while one low on Agreeableness would tend to be unfriendly, unpleasant, aggressive, argumentative, cold, even hostile and vindictive.

- *Openness to Experience.* This factor contrasts individuals who are imaginative, curious, broad-minded, and cultured with those who are concrete-minded and practical, and whose interests are narrow (Hogan et al., 1994).

Researchers from many different traditions have found five factors when they have subjected self-ratings, observer ratings, and peer ratings to factor analysis. Five factors have emerged, as well, from studies in many different languages; across different age groups; with females and males; and in various cultures, including the German, Japanese, Dutch, English, and Filipino (Digman, 1990; McCrae & John, 1992). Still more support for the five-factor theory comes from cross-cultural studies by Paunonen and others (1992) involving subjects from Canada, Finland, Poland, and Germany.

Arguing from the evolutionary perspective, Buss (1991) suggests that humans have evolved who were able to pay attention to, interpret, and act upon these five dimensions of their social world and thus gain a better chance of survival. Others who hold the evolutionary perspective point to long-standing evidence of substantial heritability of some personality factors, Neuroticism and Extroversion, for example.

Costa & McCrae (1985, 1992a, 1995) developed the NEO Personality Inventory (NEO-PI) to measure the Big Five dimensions of personality and, more recently, the NEO Personality Inventory–Revised (NEO-PI-R). Certain patterns of scores on the five dimensions appear to be characteristic of particular psychological disorders (Costa & McCrae, 1992b; Trull & Sher, 1994).

five-factor theory: A trait theory that attempts to explain personality using five broad dimensions, each of which is composed of a constellation of personality traits.

Although growing in acceptance, the five-factor model has its critics. McAdams (1992) argues that the model fails to address "core constructs of personality functioning beyond the level of traits" and to provide "compelling causal explanations for human behavior and experience" (p. 329). Because the five-factor theory operates at a highly general level, knowing how high or low a person scored on the five dimensions would not enable you to predict that person's behavior in a specific situation. But the Big Five may be helpful in predicting general trends of behavior in a wide variety of situations.

Evaluating the Trait Perspective

Do we possess stable and enduring traits that predictably guide the way we will act across time and changing situations? Critics of trait theories say no and maintain that the consistency of our behavior across situations is very low and not predictable on the basis of personality traits. Initially, one of the severest critics of the trait theory was Walter Mischel (1968), who concluded that the situation, not our traits, determines behavior. His position stimulated the person–situation debate—the question of the relative importance of factors within the person and factors within the situation that account for behavior (Rowe, 1987). Mischel (1973, 1977) has modified his original position and now admits that behavior is influenced by both the person *and* the situation. Mischel views a trait as a conditional probability that a particular action will occur in response to a particular situation (Wright & Mischel, 1987).

The weight of evidence supports the view that there are internal traits that strongly influence behavior across situations (Carson, 1989; McAdams, 1992). "Even though situations profoundly affect what people do, people can still manage to preserve their distinctive behavioral styles across situations" (Funder & Colvin, 1991, p. 791). Additional support for trait theory has come from longitudinal studies. McCrae and Costa (1990) studied personality traits of subjects over time and found them to be stable for periods of 3 to 30 years. They concluded that "aging itself has little effect on personality" (Costa & McCrae, 1988, p. 862). According to McCrae (1993), "Stable individual differences in basic dimensions are a universal feature of adult personality" (p. 577).

Many situations in life call forth behavior that is very similar for most of us even when our internal traits differ drastically. Even the most talkative and boisterous among us tend to be quiet during a religious service, a funeral, or other solemn occasions. Characteristic traits, say the trait theorists, determine how we behave *most* of the time, not *all* of the time. Even the most optimistic, happy, and outgoing people have "down" days, fall ill, and frown occasionally.

The World of Psychology section considers cultural differences in personality.

Personality and Culture

There is general agreement that both nature and nurture wield their shared influence in forming and shaping personality. Important among the influences of nurture are the diverse cultures in which humans live and grow.

Hofstede (1980, 1983) analyzed questionnaire responses measuring the work-related values of more than 100,000 IBM employees in 53 countries

continued

around the world. Factor analysis revealed four separate dimensions that Hofstede believed "correspond to core cultural values that influence the form of the social arrangements, institutions, customs, and practices of any given society" (Bochner, 1994, p. 273). One factor, the individualism/collectivism dimension, is of particular interest here.

"Individualist cultures emphasize independence, self-reliance, [and] creativity" (Triandis et al., 1993, p. 368). Individualists "see themselves as more differentiated and separate from others, and place more importance on asserting their individuality" (Bochner, 1994, p. 274). People in collectivist cultures, on the other hand, tend to be more interdependent and define themselves and their personal interests in terms of their group membership.

Hofstede rank-ordered the 53 countries on each of the four dimensions. It should hardly be surprising that the United States ranked as the most individualist country in the sample, followed by Australia, Great Britain, Canada, and the Netherlands. At the other end of the continuum were the most collectivist, or least individualist, countries—Guatemala, Ecuador, Panama, Venezuela, and Colombia, all Latin American countries.

Although, according to Hofstede, the United States ranks first in individualism, there are many distinct minority cultural groups in the United States, which may be decidedly less individualistic.

Native Americans number about 2.1 million, and even within this relatively small cultural group, there are over 200 different tribes, and no single language, religion, or culture (Bennett, 1994). Yet Native Americans have many shared values, such as the importance of family, community, cooperation, and generosity. Native Americans value a generous nature as evidenced by acts of gift giving and helpfulness. Such behaviors bring more honor and prestige than accumulating property and building individual wealth. Taken together, these values are more collectivistic than individualistic in nature.

In stark contrast is the majority American culture, which places more emphasis on individual achievement. High-achieving individuals who rise far above others in any field of endeavor are accorded great honor and prestige in this culture.

Consider the second-largest cultural/ethnic minority group in the United States, the Hispanics, who according to the 1992 census number almost 24.2 million. Although there are significant cultural differences among various Hispanic groups, there are striking similarities as well. The clearest shared cultural value is a strong identification with and attachment to the extended family. Another important value is *simpatía*—the desire for smooth and harmonious social relationships, which include respect for the dignity of others, avoidance of confrontation, and avoidance of words or actions that might hurt the feelings of another (Márin, 1994).

To observe that the Native American and Hispanic cultures value collectivist more than individualist interests does not mean that any one member of these cultures is necessarily less individualistic than any given member of the majority American culture. Moreover, a person could value both orientations, being individualistic at work, for example, and collectivistic in the home and community (Kagitcibasi, 1992).

Many factors converge in the making of personality. Our genes, our environment, our experiences, and our culture are among the many threads that, woven together, yield the tapestry of human personality.

Memory Check 12.4

1. According to Allport, the kind of trait that is a defining characteristic of one's personality is a _____ trait.
   a. common
   b. source
   c. secondary
   d. cardinal

2. According to Cattell, the differences between people are explained by the number of source traits they possess. (true/false)

3. Who claimed that we can best understand personality by assessing people on two major dimensions, Extroversion and Neuroticism?
   a. Hans Eysenck   c. Raymond Cattell
   b. Gordon Allport   d. Carl Jung

4. The text suggests that, according to a growing consensus among trait theorists, there are _____ major dimensions of personality.
   a. 3   b. 5   c. 7   d. 16

Answers: 1. d 2. false 3. a 4. b

Learning Theories and Personality

According to the learning perspective, personality consists of the learned tendencies that have been acquired over a lifetime.

The Behaviorist View of B. F. Skinner

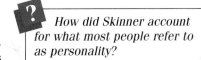

? How did Skinner account for what most people refer to as personality?

B. F. Skinner and other strict behaviorists have an interesting view of personality. They deny that there is any such thing. What we call personality, they believe, is nothing more nor less than a collection of learned behaviors or habits that have been reinforced in the past. Skinner denied that a personality or self initiates and directs behavior. The causes of behavior, he stated, lie outside the person, and they are based on past and present rewards and punishments. Thus, Skinner did not use the term *personality*. He simply described the variables in the environment that shape an individual's observable behavior. Healthy experiences in a healthy environment make a healthy person.

But what about the psychologically unhealthy individual? Skinner (1953) believed that psychologically unhealthy people have been reinforced by the environment for behaving abnormally. For example, an overly dependent person may have been punished by her parents for asserting her independence and reinforced for dependency. To change behavior, then, we must restructure the environment to reinforce normal rather than abnormal behavior. What a contrast to psychoanalytic theory and trait theory, which see internal forces as the major shapers and determiners of behavior.

The Social-Cognitive Theorists: Expanding the Behaviorist View

Much of our behavior can be traced to classical and operant conditioning; but can all of personality, or even all of learning, be explained in this way? Not according to social-cognitive theorists, who consider both the environment *and* personal/cognitive factors in their attempts to understand personality and behavior. Personal/cognitive factors include personal dispositions, feelings, expectancies, perceptions, and cognitions, such as thoughts, beliefs, and attitudes.

? *What are the components that make up Bandura's concept of reciprocal determinism, and how do they interact?*

Albert Bandura's Views on Personality   The chief advocate of the social-cognitive theory is Albert Bandura (1977a, 1986). He maintains that personal/cognitive factors, our behavior, and the external environment all influence each other and are influenced by each other (Bandura, 1989). This mutual relationship Bandura calls **reciprocal determinism** (see Figure 12.3).

Consider how Bandura's concept of reciprocal determinism might work in the following situation: A waiter who normally works in a section of a restaurant where good tippers habitually sit, is reassigned to tables in an area where tips are normally poor. This new environment influences the waiter's beliefs and expectancies (personal/cognitive factors). Now, because he believes that good service will not be appropriately rewarded, his behavior changes. He is inattentive, is not very pleasant, and provides poor service. Consequently, the waiter's attitude and behavior have a reciprocal effect on the customers, influencing their thinking, feelings, and attitudes. And these, in turn, affect their behavior. Not surprisingly, these customers *do* tip poorly.

Try to recall examples in your own life where your thinking, expectancies, and attitudes, your behavior, and external environmental factors worked reciprocally to your benefit—or to your detriment.

One of the personal/cognitive factors Bandura (1977b) considers especially important is self-efficacy. **Self-efficacy** is the perception people hold of their ability to perform competently and successfully in whatever they attempt. And this, Bandura believes, affects how they behave in a variety of situations. People high in self-efficacy will approach new situations confidently and will persist in their efforts because they believe success is likely. People low in self-efficacy, on the other hand, will expect failure and avoid challenges. In a real sense, one's sense of self-efficacy can become a self-fulfilling prophecy.

? *What does Rotter mean by the terms internal and external locus of control?*

Julian Rotter and Locus of Control   Julian Rotter proposes another concept—**locus of control**—which provides additional insight into why people behave as they do. Some of us see ourselves as primarily in control of our behavior and its consequences. This perception Rotter (1966, 1971, 1990) defines as an internal locus of control. Others perceive that whatever happens to them is in the hands of fate, luck, or chance. They exhibit an external locus of control and may claim that it does not matter what they do because "whatever will be, will be." Rotter contends that people with an external locus of control are less likely to change their behavior as a result of reinforcement, because they do not see reinforcers as being tied to their own actions.

reciprocal determinism: Bandura's concept that behavior, personal/cognitive factors, and environment all influence and are influenced by each other.

self-efficacy: A person's belief in his or her ability to perform competently in whatever is attempted.

locus of control: A concept used to explain how people account for what happens in their lives—people with an *internal* locus of control see themselves as primarily in control of their behavior and its consequences; those with an *external* locus of control perceive what happens to be in the hands of fate, luck, or chance.

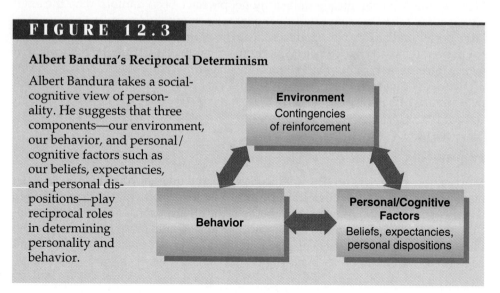

FIGURE 12.3

Albert Bandura's Reciprocal Determinism

Albert Bandura takes a social-cognitive view of personality. He suggests that three components—our environment, our behavior, and personal/cognitive factors such as our beliefs, expectancies, and personal dispositions—play reciprocal roles in determining personality and behavior.

Environment
Contingencies of reinforcement

Behavior

Personal/Cognitive Factors
Beliefs, expectancies, personal dispositions

Evaluating the Social-Cognitive Perspective The social-cognitive perspective cannot be criticized for lacking a strong research base. Yet some of its critics claim that the social-cognitive perspective continues to weigh the situation too heavily. These critics ask: What about unconscious motives or internal dispositions (traits) that we exhibit fairly consistently across many different situations? Other critics point to mounting evidence of a genetic influence on personality, which may explain 40 to 50 percent or more of the variation in personality characteristics (Bouchard, 1994).

> **humanistic psychology:** An approach to psychology that stresses the uniquely human attributes and a positive view of human nature.

Memory Check 12.5

1. According to Skinner, behavior is initiated by inner forces called personality. (true/false)

2. Bandura's concept of reciprocal determinism refers to the mutual effects of:
   a. our behavior, personality, and thinking.
   b. our feelings, attitudes, and thoughts.
   c. our behavior, personal/cognitive factors, and the environment.
   d. classical and operant conditioning and observational learning.

3. Which statement is *not* true of people low in self-efficacy?
   a. They persist in their efforts.
   b. They lack confidence.
   c. They expect failure.
   d. They avoid challenge.

4. Who proposed the concept of locus of control?
   a. B. F. Skinner   c. Hans Eysenck
   b. Albert Bandura   d. Julian Rotter

Answers: 1. false 2. c 3. a 4. d

Humanistic Personality Theories

> **?** *Who were the two pioneers in humanistic psychology, and how did they view human nature?*

Humanistic psychology seeks to give a more complete and positive picture of the human personality than the two other major forces in psychology—behaviorism and psychoanalysis. Humanistic psychologists are critical of psychoanalysis because it is based primarily on Freud's work with patients who were psychologically unhealthy. Moreover, the humanists take issue with behaviorism because of its almost exclusive concern with observable behavior, to the neglect of what is going on inside the person.

But more than simply reacting against psychoanalysis and behaviorism, humanistic psychologists developed their own unique view of human nature, a view that is considerably more flattering. Human nature is seen as innately good, with a natural tendency toward growth and the realization of one's fullest potential. The humanists largely deny a dark or evil side of human nature. They do not believe that we are shaped strictly by the environment or ruled by mysterious unconscious forces. Rather, as creative beings with an active, conscious free will, we can chart our own course in life.

Humanistic psychology is sometimes called the "third force" in psychology. (Behaviorism and psychoanalysis are the other two forces.) The pioneering humanistic psychologists were Abraham Maslow and Carl Rogers.

Abraham Maslow: The Self-Actualizing Person

> **?** *What is self-actualization, and how did Maslow study it?*

For Abraham Maslow (1970), motivational factors were at the root of personality. As we saw in Chapter 10, Maslow constructed his hierarchy of needs, ranging

Abraham Maslow (1908–1970)

from physiological needs at the bottom upward to safety needs, to belonging and love needs, further upward to esteem needs, and finally to the highest need—for self-actualization. **Self-actualization** means developing to one's fullest potential. A healthy person is ever growing and becoming all that he or she can be.

Maslow claimed that if you want to know what makes a healthy personality, you must study people who are healthy. He wrote, "the study of the crippled, stunted, immature, and unhealthy specimens can yield only a cripple psychology." So Maslow studied people he believed were using their talents and abilities to their fullest—in other words, those who exemplified self-actualization. He studied some historical figures, such as Abraham Lincoln and Thomas Jefferson, and figures who made significant contributions during his own lifetime—Albert Einstein, Eleanor Roosevelt, and Albert Schweitzer. After examining the lives of such people, Maslow identified characteristics that self-actualizing persons seem to share.

Maslow found self-actualizers to be accurate in perceiving reality—able to judge honestly and to spot quickly the fake and the dishonest. Self-actualizers are comfortable with life; they accept themselves and others, and nature as well, with good humor and tolerance. Most of them believe they have a mission to accomplish or the need to devote their life to some larger good. Self-actualizers tend not to depend on external authority or other people but seem to be inner-driven, autonomous, and independent. They feel a strong fellowship with humanity, and their relationships with others are characterized by deep and loving bonds. They can laugh at themselves, and their sense of humor, though well developed, never involves hostility or criticism of others. Finally, the most telling mark of self-actualizers are frequently occurring peak experiences—experiences of deep meaning, insight, and harmony within and with the universe.

Maslow concluded that each of us has the capacity for self-actualization. If we apply our talent and energy to doing our best in whatever endeavor we choose, then we, too, can lead creative lives and be self-actualizing.

Carl Rogers: The Fully Functioning Person

> *According to Rogers, why don't all people become fully functioning persons?*

Carl Rogers (1951, 1961), like Freud, developed his theory of personality through insights gained from his patients in therapy sessions. Yet he saw something very different from what Freud and the psychoanalysts observed. Rogers viewed human nature as basically good. If left to develop naturally, he thought, people would be happy and psychologically healthy.

According to Rogers, we each live in our own subjective reality, which he called the phenomenological field. It is in this personal, subjective field (rather than in the objective, real, physical environment) that we act and think and feel. In other words, the way we see it is the way it is—for us. Gradually a part of the phenomenological field becomes differentiated as the self. The self concept emerges as a result of repeated experiences involving such terms as "I," "me," and "mine." With the emerging self comes the need for positive regard. We need such things as warmth, love, acceptance, sympathy, and respect from the people who are significant in our lives. But there are usually strings attached to positive regard from others.

Our parents do not view us positively regardless of our behavior. They set up **conditions of worth**—conditions on which their positive regard hinges. Conditions of worth force us to live and act according to someone else's values rather than our own. In our efforts to gain positive regard, we deny our true self by inhibiting some of our behavior, denying and distorting some of our perceptions, and closing ourselves to parts of our experience. In so doing, we experience stress and anxiety, and our whole self-structure may be threatened.

For Rogers, a major goal of psychotherapy is to enable people to open themselves up to experiences and begin to live according to their own values rather

self-actualization: Developing to one's fullest potential.

conditions of worth: Conditions upon which the positive regard of others rests.

than the values of others in order to gain positive regard. He calls his therapy "person-centered therapy," preferring not to use the term *patient* (Rogers's therapy will be discussed in Chapter 15). Rogers believed that the therapist must give the client **unconditional positive regard**, that is, positive regard no matter what the client says, does, has done, or is thinking of doing. Unconditional positive regard is designed to reduce threat, eliminate conditions of worth, and bring the person back in tune with his or her true self. If successful, the therapy helps the client become what Rogers calls a fully functioning person—one who is functioning at an optimal level and living fully and spontaneously according to his or her own inner value system.

Evaluating the Humanistic Perspective

Humanism has become much more than a personality theory and an approach to therapy. Its influence has spread significantly as a social movement in the schools and in society in general. Some of its severest critics are religious and moral leaders who see the philosophy of humanism as a powerful threat to traditional moral values and the Judeo-Christian ethic. Others charge that an all-consuming personal quest for self-fulfillment can lead to a self-centered, self-serving, self-indulgent personality, lacking moral restraint or genuine concern for others (Campbell & Sprecht, 1985; Wallach & Wallach, 1983).

Humanistic psychologists do not accept such criticisms as valid. By and large, they trust in the inherent goodness of human nature, and their perspective on personality is consistent with that trust. But how do humanists explain the evil we see around us—assaults, murder, rape? Where does this originate? Carl Rogers (1981) replied, "I do not find that this evil is inherent in human nature " (p. 16). Of psychological environments that nurture growth and choice, Rogers said, "I have never known an individual to choose the cruel or destructive path. . . . So my experience leads me to believe that it is cultural influences which are the major factors in our evil behaviors" (p. 16).

Even some humanists disagree about the nature of human nature. In an open letter to Carl Rogers, psychologist Rollo May (1982) wrote, "Who makes up the culture except persons like you and me? . . . The culture is not something made by fate and foisted upon us. . . . The culture is evil as well as good because we, the human beings who constitute it, are evil as well as good" (pp. 12–13).

Though the humanists have been criticized for being unscientific and for seeing, hearing, and finding no evil within the human psyche, they have inspired the study of the positive qualities—altruism, cooperation, love, and acceptance of self and others.

Personality: Is It in the Genes?

Behavioral genetics is a field of research that investigates the relative effects of heredity and environment on behavior and ability.

The Twin Study Method: Studying Identical and Fraternal Twins

An ideal way to assess the relative contribution of heredity and environment to personality is to study identical twins who have been separated at birth and reared apart. When identical twins who were reared apart have strikingly similar traits, as in the case of Oskar and Jack introduced at the beginning of this chapter, it is assumed that heredity has been a major contributor. When twins differ

unconditional positive regard: Unqualified caring and nonjudgmental acceptance of another.

behavioral genetics: The field of research that investigates the relative effects of heredity and environment on behavior and ability.

What has research in behavioral genetics revealed about the influence of the genes and the environment on personality?

heritability: An index of the degree to which a characteristic is estimated to be influenced by heredity.

on a given trait, as with Joan and Jean, the influence of the environment is thought to be greater.

In the Minnesota twin study, Tellegen and others (1988) found that identical twins are quite similar on several personality factors regardless of whether they are raised together or apart. The term **heritability** refers to the degree to which a characteristic is estimated to be influenced by heredity. After studying heritability of traits in 573 adult twin pairs, Rushton and colleagues (1986) found that nurturance, empathy, and assertiveness are substantially influenced by heredity. Even altruism and aggressiveness, traits one would expect to be strongly influenced by parental upbringing, were actually more heavily influenced by heredity.

Twin studies have also revealed a genetic influence on social attitudes such as traditionalism—whether we endorse traditional moral values and follow rules and authority (Martin et al., 1986; Tellegen et al., 1988). There even seems to be a genetic influence on the way people tend to view their environment (Chipuer et al., 1993; Plomin & Bergeman, 1991), on how they perceive life events, particularly controllable ones, and on their sense of well-being (Plomin & Rende, 1991).

More recent evidence from behavioral genetics suggests that the average heritability of the Big Five personality factors is about .41 to .42 (41 to 42 percent), somewhat less than the earlier twin study estimates of around .50 (50 percent) (Bouchard, 1994). Figure 12.4 shows the heritability estimates for the Big Five from the Minnesota studies of twins reared apart and the Loehlin twin studies (Loehlin, 1992).

FIGURE 12.4

Estimated Influence of Heredity and Environment on the Big Five Personality Factors

The Minnesota studies of twins reared apart yield an average heritability estimate of .41 (41 percent) for the Big Five personality factors; the Loehlin twin studies, a heritability estimate of .42 (42 percent). Both studies found the influence of the shared environment to be only about .07 (7 percent). The remaining percentage represents a combination of nonshared environmental influences and measurement error. (Adapted from Bouchard, 1994.)

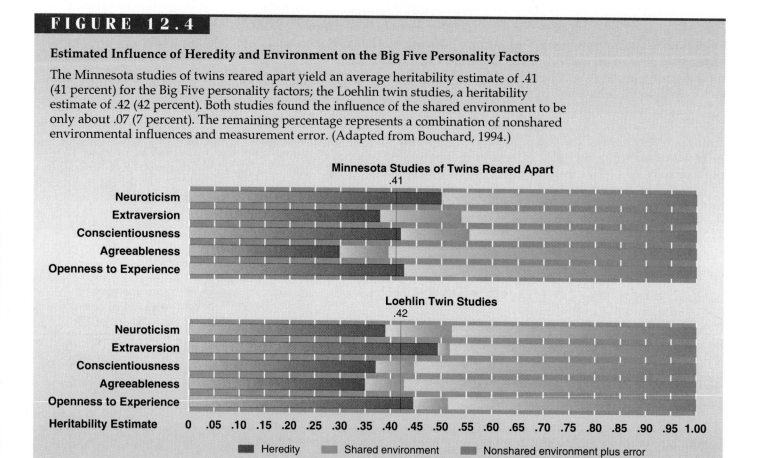

How can heritability estimates vary so much from study to study? The reason is that researchers can only estimate statistically how much variability is due to genetics in a particular group of subjects. And their estimates apply to that sample only. When different researchers find similar heritabilities, however, we come to have more confidence in the findings.

Taken together, these data show that personality factors are significantly influenced by heredity. But even with a heritability estimate as high as .50, the remaining 50 percent of the variance would be attributed to nongenetic (environmental) factors plus measurement error. The behavioral genetics studies, then, leave a great deal of room for environmental forces to shape personality. Plomin and others (1994) claim that "nongenetic factors generally account for as much variance as genetic factors" (p. 1736). So personality is a product of nature *and* nurture working together.

The Shared and Nonshared Environment

Have you ever wondered why siblings raised in the same household often seem to have totally different personalities? To explain why, researchers point out that environmental influences are produced in two different forms: through the shared environment and through the nonshared environment. The shared environment consists of those environmental influences that tend to make family members similar. If the shared environmental influences were high, then we would expect siblings raised in the same household to be more alike than different. But the shared environmental influences on personality are modest at best, about 7 percent (Bouchard, 1994; Loehlin, 1992).

The nonshared environment consists of influences that operate in different ways among children in the same family (Rowe, 1994). These influences "cause family members to differ regardless of whether the locus of influence is the family (such as differential treatment by parents) or outside the family (such as different experiences at school or with peers)" (Plomin & Daniels, 1987, p. 7). Nonshared influences can occur because individual children tend to elicit different responses from their parents for a variety of reasons—their temperament, gender, or birth order, or accidents and illnesses they may have had (Plomin, 1989). Bouchard claims that twins can experience nonshared environmental influences even in the womb if the positioning of the twin embryos in the uterus leads to differences in fetal nutrition (Aldhous, 1992).

We are impressed when similarities are pointed out to us between identical twins separated at birth, but striking similarities are sometimes found even between total strangers. And although several thousand pairs of twins have been studied, most have been raised in middle-class environments. Might the differences between twins have been greater, particularly between identical twins reared apart, if their nonshared environments had differed more drastically?

The Adoption Method

Another method used to disentangle the effects of heredity and environment is to study children adopted shortly after birth. Loehlin and others (1987) assessed the personalities of 17-year-olds who had been adopted at birth and came to this startling conclusion: "Adopted children do not resemble their adoptive family members in personality, despite having lived with them from birth, but they do show a modest degree of resemblance to their genetic mothers, whom they had never known" (p. 968). When the adopted children were compared to other children in the family, the researchers found that the shared family environment had virtually no influence on their personalities. Other researchers studying adopted children have come to the same basic conclusion (Scarr et al., 1981). Loehlin and colleagues (1990) measured change in personality of adoptees over a 10-year period and found that children tended "to change on the average in the direction of their genetic parents' personalities" (p. 221). The prevailing thinking in behavioral genetics, then, is that the shared environment plays a negligible role in the formation of personality (Loehlin et al., 1988), although there have been a few dissenting voices (Rose et al., 1988).

The genetic influences we have been discussing are not the result of one or even a few genes. Rather they involve many genes, each with small effects (Plomin et al., 1994). While these findings indicate that most personality traits are influenced by genes, "behavioral genetic research clearly demonstrates that both nature and nurture are important in human development" (Plomin, 1989, p. 110).

To learn that most psychological traits are significantly heritable does not lessen the value or reduce the importance of environmental factors such as family influences, parenting, and education (Bouchard et al., 1990). Furthermore, Bouchard and colleagues (1990) state that their findings "do not imply that parenting is without lasting effects" (p. 227).

Memory Check 12.6

1. Humanistic psychologists would *not* say that:
   a. human nature is innately good.
   b. human beings have a natural tendency toward self-actualization.
   c. human beings have free will.
   d. researchers' should focus primarily on observable behavior.

2. Which psychologist studied individuals he believed exemplified self-actualization in order to identify characteristics that self-actualizing persons share?
   a. Carl Rogers   c. Abraham Maslow
   b. Gordon Allport   d. Hans Eysenck

3. Which psychologist believed that individuals often do not become fully functioning persons because, in childhood, they fail to receive unconditional positive regard from their parents?
   a. Carl Rogers   c. Abraham Maslow
   b. Gordon Allport   d. Hans Eysenck

4. Many behavioral geneticists believe that personality may be as much as _____ inherited.
   a. 10 to 20 percent   c. 40 to 50 percent
   b. 25 to 35 percent   d. 65 to 75 percent

5. Behavioral geneticists have found that the (shared, nonshared) environment has the greater effect on personality.

6. Children adopted at birth are more similar in personality to their adoptive parents than to their biological parents. (true/false)

Answers: 1. d 2. c 3. a 4. c 5. nonshared 6. false

? *What are the three major methods used in personality assessment?*

Personality Assessment – no

Just as there are many different personality theories, there are many different methods for measuring personality. Various personality tests are used by clinical and counseling psychologists, psychiatrists, and counselors in the diagnosis of patients and in the assessment of progress in therapy. Personality assessment is also used in business and industry to aid in hiring decisions and by counselors for vocational and educational counseling.

Personality assessment methods can be grouped in a few broad categories: (1) observation, interviews, and rating scales, (2) inventories, and (3) projective tests.

Observation, Interviews, and Rating Scales

Observation All of us use observation informally, to form opinions about other people. Psychologists, too, use observation in personality assessment and evaluation in a variety of settings—hospitals, clinics, schools, and workplaces.

Behaviorists, in particular, prefer observation to other methods of personality assessment. Using an observational technique known as behavioral assessment, psychologists can count and record the frequency of particular behaviors. This method is often used in behavior modification programs in settings such as mental hospitals, where psychologists may chart the progress of patients in reducing aggressive acts or other undesirable or abnormal behaviors.

Although much can be learned from observation, it has its shortcomings; it is time-consuming and expensive, and observers must be trained and paid. What is observed may be misinterpreted, and two observers can view the same event and interpret it differently. Probably the most serious limitation is that the very presence of the observer can alter the behavior being observed.

The Interview Another personality assessment technique is the interview. Clinical psychologists and psychiatrists use interviews to help in the diagnosis and treatment of patients. Counselors use the interview to screen applicants for admission to college or other special programs, and employers use it to evaluate job applicants and employees for job promotions.

Interviewers consider not only a person's answers to questions but the person's tone of voice, speech, mannerisms, gestures, and general appearance as well. Professionals use both structured and unstructured interviews in making their assessments. In unstructured situations, the direction the interview will take and the questions to be asked are not all planned beforehand, and so the interview can be highly personalized. But the unstructured interview may be so loose that little objective information is gained. Also, it is hard to compare people unless some of the same questions are asked of everyone.

For this reason interviewers often use a structured interview, in which the content of the questions and even the manner in which they are asked are carefully planned ahead of time. The interviewer tries not to deviate in any way from the structured format so that more reliable comparisons can be made between different subjects.

Rating Scales Sometimes examiners use rating scales to record data from interviews or observations. Rating scales are useful because they provide a standardized format, including a list of traits or behaviors to evaluate. The rating scale helps to focus the rater's attention on all the relevant traits to be considered so that some are not overlooked or others weighed too heavily.

But there are problems with rating scales, too. Often there is low agreement among raters in their evaluation of the same individual. If you have watched Olympic events such as figure skating on television, you have noticed sometimes wide variations in the several judges' scoring of the same performance. One way to overcome this weakness is to train the judges or raters to a point where high agreement can be achieved when rating the same person or event.

Another problem in evaluation is the **halo effect**—the tendency of raters to be excessively influenced in their overall evaluation of a person by one or a few favorable or unfavorable traits. Often traits or attributes that are not even on the rating scale, such as physical attractiveness or similarity to the rater, heavily influence a rater's perception of a subject.

halo effect: The tendency of raters to be excessively influenced in their overall evaluation of a person by one or a few favorable or unfavorable traits.

What is an inventory, and what are the MMPI-2 and the CPI designed to reveal?

Personality Inventories: Taking Stock

There is an objective method for measuring personality, a method in which the personal opinions and ratings of observers or interviewers do not unduly influence the results. This method is the **inventory**, a paper-and-pencil test with questions about an individual's thoughts, feelings, and behaviors, which measures several dimensions of personality and can be scored according to a standard procedure. Psychologists favoring the trait approach prefer the inventory because it reveals where people fall on various dimensions of personality and yields a personality profile. Of the many personality inventories available, none has been more widely used than the Minnesota Multiphasic Personality Inventory.

The MMPI and MMPI-2 The **Minnesota Multiphasic Personality Inventory-2 (MMPI-2)** is a revision of the most popular, the most heavily researched, and the most widely used personality test for screening and diagnosing psychiatric problems and disorders, and for use in psychological research.

There have been more than 115 recognized translations of the MMPI, and it is used in more than 65 countries (Butcher & Graham, 1989). Published in 1943 by researchers McKinley and Hathaway, the MMPI was originally intended to identify tendencies toward various types of psychiatric disorders. McKinley and Hathaway gathered over 1,000 questions about attitudes, feelings, and specific psychiatric symptoms from case histories, textbooks, and other sources (Levitt & Duckworth, 1984). Then they selected groups of psychiatric patients who had been clearly diagnosed with various specific disorders to answer their questions. They also picked a group of normal men and women similar to the psychiatric patients in age, sex, social class, and other such variables, and had them answer the questions. Finally they compared the answers to see whether there were significant differences that would separate the specific psychiatric groups from those considered to be normal. For the final version of the MMPI, 550 items were chosen that were to be answered "true," "false," or "cannot say."

Because the original MMPI had become outdated, the MMPI-2 was published in 1989 (Butcher et al., 1989). Most of the original test items were retained, but some had to be deleted because they were obsolete. New items were added to more adequately cover areas such as alcoholism, drug abuse, suicidal tendencies, eating disorders, and Type A personality. Although the MMPI-2 now has 567 items, updating the items has made it more "user-friendly" and easier for the subject (Butcher & Hostetler, 1990). And new norms were established to reflect national census data and thus achieve a better geographical, racial, and cultural balance (Ben-Porath & Butcher, 1989).

The MMPI-2 provides scores on 4 validity scales and 10 clinical scales, shown in Table 12.1. Here are examples of questions on the test:

I wish I were not bothered by thoughts about sex.
When I get bored I like to stir up some excitement.
In walking I am very careful to step over sidewalk cracks.
If people had not had it in for me, I would have been much more successful.

Scoring the MMPI-2 Scoring the MMPI-2 can be done by computer. A high score on any of the scales does not necessarily mean that a person has a problem or a psychiatric symptom. Rather the psychologist looks at the individual's MMPI profile—the pattern of scores on all the scales. The profile is then compared to the profiles of normal individuals and people with various psychiatric disorders.

But what if someone lies on the test in order to appear mentally healthy? The MMPI-2 has items called the L-scale embedded in the test to provide a check against lying. If you were taking the MMPI-2, how would you answer these questions?

inventory: A paper-and-pencil test with questions about a person's thoughts, feelings, and behaviors, which can be scored according to a standard procedure.

Minnesota Multiphasic Personality Inventory-2 (MMPI-2): A revision of the most extensively researched and widely used personality test; used to screen and diagnose psychiatric problems and disorders.

TABLE 12.1 The Validity and Clinical Scales of the MMPI-2

	Scale Name	Interpretation
Validity Scales	1. Cannot say scale (?)	High scorers are evasive in filling out the questionnaire.
	2. Lie scale (L)	High scorers attempt to present themselves in a very favorable light and possibly tell lies to do so.
	3. Infrequency (F)	High scorers are presenting themselves in a particularly bad way and may well be "faking bad."
	4. Correction (K)	High scorers may be very defensive in filling out the questionnaire.
Clinical Scales	1. Hypochondriasis (Hs)	High scorers reflect an exaggerated concern about their physical health.
	2. Depression (D)	High scorers are usually depressed, despondent, and distressed.
	3. Hysteria (Hy)	High scorers complain often about physical symptoms, with no apparent organic cause.
	4. Psychopathic deviate (Pd)	High scorers show a disregard for social and moral standards.
	5. Masculinity / femininity (Mf)	High scorers show "traditional" masculine or feminine attitudes and values.
	6. Paranoia (Pa)	High scorers demonstrate extreme suspiciousness and feelings of persecution.
	7. Psychasthenia (Pt)	High scorers tend to be highly anxious, rigid, tense, and worrying.
	8. Schizophrenia (Sc)	High scorers tend to be socially withdrawn and to engage in bizarre and unusual thinking.
	9. Hypomania (Ma)	High scorers are highly emotional, excitable, energetic, and impulsive.
	10. Social introversion (S)	High scorers tend to be modest, self-effacing, and shy.

Once in a while I put off until tomorrow what I ought to do today.
I gossip a little at times.
Once in a while, I laugh at a dirty joke.

Most people would almost certainly have to answer "yes" to such questions—unless, of course, they were lying. When a person scores high on the L-scale, the test results are considered to be invalid. Another scale, the F-scale, controls for people who are faking psychiatric illness, as in the case of someone wanting to be judged not guilty of a crime by reason of insanity. Both the L-scale and the F-scale are validity scales. Several recent research studies have found the validity scales in the MMPI-2 effective in detecting subjects who were instructed to fake psychological disturbance or to lie to make themselves appear more psychologically healthy (Austin, 1992; Bagby et al., 1994). Wetter and colleagues (1993) found that even when subjects were given specific information about various psychological disorders, they could not produce profiles like those of people who actually suffered from the disorder.

California Psychological Inventory (CPI): A highly regarded personality test used to assess the normal personality.

projective test: A personality test in which people respond to inkblots, drawings of ambiguous human situations, incomplete sentences, and the like, by projecting their own inner thoughts, feelings, fears, or conflicts onto the test materials.

Rorschach Inkblot Test (ROR-shok): A projective test composed of ten inkblots to which a subject responds; used to reveal unconscious functioning and the presence of psychiatric disorders.

Evaluating the MMPI-2   The MMPI-2 is reliable, easy to administer and score, and inexpensive to use. It is useful in the screening, diagnosis, and clinical description of abnormal behavior, but does not reveal differences among normal personalities very well. The MMPI had often been unreliable for African Americans, women, and adolescents (Levitt & Duckworth, 1984). But this problem has been addressed, and norms have been established for the MMPI-2 that are more representative of the national population today. A special form of the test, the MMPI-A, was developed for adolescents in 1992. The MMPI-A has some items that are especially relevant to adolescents, such as those referring to eating disorders, substance abuse, and problems with school and family.

Because so much research has been conducted using the MMPI, those who revised the test wanted the MMPI-2 to yield comparable results. Some researchers say that the MMPI and MMPI-2 do provide comparable results (Ben-Porath & Butcher, 1989; Hargrave et al., 1994; Harrell et al., 1992). Others have found lower rates of agreement (Edwards et al., 1993; Morrison et al., 1994).

Both the MMPI and MMPI-2 can claim only modest success in predicting a clinical diagnosis. Morrison and others (1994) found that both instruments agreed with the diagnosis made by clinicians only 39 percent of the time. Thus, researchers caution against making diagnoses based exclusively on the MMPI and MMPI-2 (Brems, 1991; Libb et al., 1992). Clinicians should integrate MMPI results with other sources of clinical information before making a diagnosis.

The MMPI-2 is being translated for use in Belgium, Chile, China, France, Hong Kong, Israel, Korea, Italy, Japan, Norway, Russia, Spain, and Thailand (Butcher, 1992). Lucio and others (1994) administered the Mexican (Spanish) version of MMPI-2 to more than 2,100 Mexican college students. They found the profiles of these students "remarkably similar" to profiles of U.S. college students.

The California Psychological Inventory   Are there instruments to assess the personality of a normal person? Yes, the **California Psychological Inventory (CPI)** is a highly regarded personality test developed especially for normal populations aged 13 and older.

Similar to the MMPI, the CPI even has many of the same questions, but it does not include any questions designed to reveal psychiatric illness (Gough, 1987). The CPI is valuable for predicting behavior, and it has been "praised for its technical competency, careful development, cross-validation and follow-up, use of sizable samples and separate sex norms" (Domino, 1984, p. 156). The CPI was revised in 1987, and the revised test should yield "a picture of the subject's life-style and the degree to which his or her potential is being realized" (McReynolds, 1989, p. 101).

Projective Tests: Projections from the Unconscious

? *How do projective tests provide insight into personality, and what are several of the most commonly used projective tests?*

Responses on interviews and questionnaires are conscious responses and, for this reason, are less useful to therapists who wish to probe the unconscious. Such therapists may choose a completely different technique called a projective test. A **projective test** is a personality test consisting of inkblots, drawings of ambiguous human situations, or incomplete sentences for which there are no obvious correct or incorrect responses. People respond by projecting their own inner thoughts, feelings, fears, or conflicts into the test materials. Just as a movie projector projects the images on the film outward and onto a screen, so do we project our inner thoughts, feelings, fears, and conflicts into our analysis and description of inkblots and other vague or ambiguous projective test materials.

The Rorschach Inkblot Test: What Do You See?   One of the oldest and most popular projective tests is the **Rorschach Inkblot Test** developed by Swiss

FIGURE 12.5

An Inkblot Similar to One on the Rorschach Inkblot Test

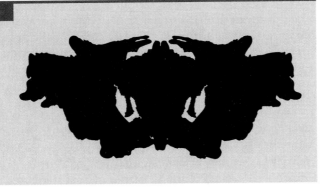

psychiatrist Hermann Rorschach (ROR-shok) in 1921. It consists of 10 inkblots, which the subject is asked to describe (see Figure 12.5).

To develop his test, Rorschach put ink on paper and then folded the paper so that symmetrical patterns would result. Earlier, psychologists had used standardized series of inkblots to study imagination and other variables, but Rorschach was the first to use inkblots to investigate personality. He experimented with thousands of inkblots on different groups of people and found that 10 of the inkblots could be used to discriminate between different diagnostic groups, such as manic depressives, paranoid schizophrenics, and so on. These 10 inkblots—5 black and white, and 5 with color—were standardized and are still widely used.

Administration and Scoring of the Rorschach   The 10 inkblots are shown to the subject, who is asked to tell everything that each inkblot looks like or resembles. The examiner writes down the subject's responses and then goes through the cards again, asking questions to clarify what the subject has reported.

In scoring the Rorschach, the examiner considers whether the subject uses the whole inkblot in the description or only parts of it. The subject is asked whether the shape of the inkblot, its color, or something else prompted the response. The tester also considers whether the subject sees movement, human figures or parts, animal figures or parts, or other objects in the inkblots.

Interpreting the Responses   What difference does it make whether you describe parts or wholes, color or movement, animals or people?

> Using the whole inkblot suggests integration and organization; many small details indicate compulsiveness and over-control. . . . The presence of much poor form, uncommon responses, and confused thinking suggests a psychotic condition. Responsiveness to color is supposed to represent emotionality. . . . Responses mentioning human movement indicate imagination, intelligence, and a rich inner life. (Sundberg, 1977, p. 208)

The main problem with the Rorschach test is that the results are too dependent on the interpretation and judgment of the examiner. One study dramatically calls the reliability of the Rorschach into question (Harrower, 1976). Experts were asked to interpret results of Rorschach tests administered shortly after World War II to 16 Nazi war criminals, including Adolf Eichmann and Hermann Göring. The experts knew whose test results they were interpreting, and they concluded that the responses showed the subjects to be violent and abnormal men. However, another researcher had the same Rorschach responses analyzed by other experts who did not know they were from Nazi war criminals. One expert thought the responses came from a cross-section of middle-class Americans, and another thought the responses might have been made by clergymen.

In response to such criticisms, Exner (1993) has developed a more reliable system of scoring the Rorschach test. It provides some normative data so that the responses of a person taking the test can be compared to those of others with known personality characteristics. Although this is a positive step, reliable interpretation still remains a problem because researchers have found low reliability and validity (Sundberg, 1990; Walsh & Betz, 1990). Perhaps, as Weiner (1994) suggests, the Rorschach should not be considered a personality test at all because it does not measure anything. Rather, it might best be thought of as a method that "generates useful information about personality functioning" (pp. 499–500).

The Thematic Apperception Test: Seeing Ourselves in Scenes of Others

Another projective test is the **Thematic Apperception Test (TAT)** developed by Henry Murray and his colleagues in 1935 (Morgan & Murray, 1935; Murray, 1938). The TAT consists of 1 blank card and 19 other cards showing vague or ambiguous black-and-white drawings of human figures in various situations. "The test is based upon the well-recognized fact that when a person interprets an ambiguous social situation he is apt to expose his own personality as much as the phenomenon to which he is attending" (Morgan & Murray, 1962, p. 531).

If you were tested on the TAT, this is what you would be told:

> This is a test of your creative imagination. I shall show you a picture, and I want you to make up a plot or story for which it might be used as an illustration. What is the relation of the individuals in the picture? What has happened to them? What are their present thoughts and feelings? What will be the outcome? Do your very best. Since I am asking you to indulge your literary imagination, you may make your story as long and as detailed as you wish. (Morgan & Murray, 1962, p. 532)

Interpreting the Results   What does the story you write have to do with your personality or your problems or motives? Murray (1965) stresses the importance of "an element or theme that recurs three or more times in the series of stories" (p. 432). For example, if many of a person's story themes are about illness, sex, fear of failure, aggression, power, interpersonal conflicts, and so on, such a recurring theme is thought to reveal a problem in the person's life. Murray (1965) also claims that the strength of the TAT is "its capacity to reveal things that the patient is unwilling to tell or is unable to tell because he is unconscious of them" (p. 427).

The TAT is time-consuming and difficult to administer and score. Although it has been used extensively in research, it suffers from the same weaknesses as other projective techniques: (1) It relies heavily on the interpretation skills of the examiner, and (2) it may reflect too strongly a person's temporary motivational and emotional state and not get at the more permanent aspects of personality. Because Murray was trained as a Freudian and Jungian analyst, it is not surprising that he developed an instrument to assess unconscious motivation (Triplet, 1992).

The Sentence Completion Method: Filling in the Blanks

Another projective technique, the sentence completion method, may be one of the most valid projective techniques of all. It consists of a number of incomplete sentences to be completed by the subject, such as these:

I worry a great deal about _____.
I sometimes feel _____.
I would be happier if _____.
My mother _____.

In a comprehensive review, Goldberg (1965) summarized 50 validity studies and concluded that sentence completion is a valuable technique appropriate for widespread clinical and research use.

Thematic Apperception Test (TAT): A projective test consisting of drawings of ambiguous human situations, which the subject describes; thought to reveal inner feelings, conflicts, and motives, which are projected onto the test materials.

Review and Reflect 12.3 Three Approaches to Personality Assessment

Method	Examples	Description
Observation and rating	Observation Interviews Rating scales	Performance (behavior) is observed in a specific situation, and personality is assessed based on observation. In interviews, the responses to questions are taken to reveal personality characteristics. Rating scales are used to score or rate subjects on the basis of traits, behaviors, or results of interviews. Assessment is subjective, and accuracy depends largely on the ability and experience of the evaluator.
Inventories	Minnesota Multiphasic Personality Inventory–2 (MMPI-2) California Personality Inventory (CPI)	Subjects reveal their beliefs, feelings, behavior, and/or opinions on paper-and-pencil tests. Scoring procedures are standardized and responses are compared to group norms.
Projective tests	Rorschach Inkblot Test Thematic Apperception Test (TAT) Sentence completion method	Subjects respond to ambiguous test materials and presumably reveal elements of their own personality by what they describe in inkblots, by themes they write about scenes showing possible conflict, or by how they complete sentences. Scoring is subjective, and accuracy depends largely on the ability and experience of the evaluator.

The Value of Projective Tests How effective are projective tests? Research evidence concerning the validity of projective techniques as a whole is very disappointing. Projective tests continue to suffer from a lack of objectivity in scoring and an absence of adequate norms. A survey of directors of clinical training in doctoral programs in psychology revealed that 45 percent predicted a decrease in the use of projective tests in academic settings in the near future (Piotrowski & Zalenski, 1993). Nevertheless, in clinical practice projective tests continue to be a popular and valued diagnostic tool (Archer et al., 1991).

Review and Reflect Table 12.3 summarizes the various personality tests.

Personality Theories: A Final Comment

We have explored the major theories of personality, which are summarized in Review and Reflect Table 12.4 (on page 470). The question might come to mind—which perspective best captures the elusive concept of personality? Some psychologists adhere strictly to single theories and are followers of Freud, for example, or Skinner or Rogers. It is our belief that all of the theories contribute to our knowledge, but that none taken alone can adequately explain the whole of human personality.

Review and Reflect 12.4 Summary of Approaches to Personality

Approach	Associated Theorists	Assumptions about Behavior	Assessment Techniques	Research Methods
Psychoanalytic	Freud	Behavior arises mostly from unconscious conflicts between pleasure-seeking id and moral-perfectionist superego with reality-oriented ego as mediator.	Projective tests to tap unconscious motives; interviews for purposes of analysis.	Case studies.
Trait	Allport Cattell Eysenck McCrae and Costa	Behavior springs from personality traits that may be influenced by both heredity and environment.	Self-report inventories; adjective checklists; inventories.	Analysis of test results for identifying strength of various traits.
Learning behaviorist	Skinner	Behavior is determined strictly by environmental influences.	Direct observation of behavior; objective tests; interviews; rating scales; self-report.	Analysis of observations of behavior; quantifying behaviors; analysis of person–situation interactions.
Social-cognitive	Bandura Rotter	Behavior results from an interaction between internal cognitive factors and environmental influences.		
Humanistic	Maslow Rogers	Behavior springs from the person's own unique perception of reality and conscious choices. Humans are innately good.	Interviews and tests designed to assess the person's self-concept and perceptions of control.	Analysis of the relationship between the person's feelings or perceptions and behavior.

Memory Check 12.7

1. Match the personality test with its description.
   ____ 1) MMPI-2
   ____ 2) Rorschach
   ____ 3) TAT
   ____ 4) CPI

   a. inventory used to diagnose psychopathology
   b. inventory used to assess normal personality
   c. projective test using inkblots
   d. projective test using drawings of ambiguous human situations

2. Dr. X and Dr. Y are both experts in personality assessment. They would be most likely to agree on their interpretation of results from the:
   a. Rorschach.
   b. MMPI-2.
   c. TAT.
   d. sentence completion method.

3. George has an unconscious resentment toward his father. Which test might best detect this?
   a. MMPI-2
   b. CPI
   c. Rorschach
   d. TAT

4. Which of the following items might appear on the MMPI-2?
   a. What is happening in the picture?
   b. Hand is to glove as foot is to _____.
   c. My mother was a good person.
   d. What is your favorite food?

Answers: 1. 1) a 2) c 3) d 4) b 2. b 3. d 4. c

Is There Really a Sucker Born Every Minute?

Scorpio (Oct. 23–Nov. 22): You will start to feel more in control of your life than in recent weeks. You are beginning to understand why several things went wrong. Though you may not be in a position to fix them immediately, you can begin to plan how to do it in the near future. Put your best foot forward, and be gentle in trying to win a point.

Aquarius (Jan. 21–Feb. 19): Your reputation has been up and down several times in the last few months. This week you are poised to make a remarkable comeback. Young Aquarians may receive your first real job offers or start to develop an interest that will eventually lead to a long and satisfying career. (Accurso, 1994, p. 44)

These two horoscopes are products of the "science" of astrology, which is based on the notion that the relative positions of the stars and planets at the time of a person's birth will influence that individual's personality traits and behavior throughout life. Each day a horoscope is published for the 12 signs, that is, for each of the constellations that have traditionally been included in the zodiac—Gemini, Leo, Capricorn, Pisces, and so on.

If you're a Scorpio or an Aquarian, one of these horoscopes applies to you, right? Look again. When you read them carefully, you can see that all horoscopes contain advice and predictions that could apply to almost anyone. People who believe that *their* horoscope applies only to those with the same sign are showing the influence of the Barnum effect, named for the famed circus impresario P. T. Barnum. "Always

have a little something for everybody," Barnum used to say. The same principle operates in popular psychology as in marketing and circus promotion: You can reach the widest possible audience if you present something in such general terms that almost anyone will believe it applies to him or her.

In fact, horoscopes apply to no one. Researchers have found no correlation between the signs of the zodiac and individual personality traits (Gauguelin, 1982). The same can be said about handwriting analysis, or graphology. Graphologists claim to be able to measure personality and predict job success by analyzing handwriting, and graphology is sometimes used in job placement. However, scientific studies have found little connection between the characteristics of a person's handwriting and his or her personality traits or success at a particular job (Beyerstein & Beyerstein, 1992; Dean et al., 1992).

We can see the Barnum effect in action in the "personality tests" often published in popular magazines. Consider some questions from a test purporting to determine whether the reader is a "control freak" (Todd, 1994):

You solicit and follow other people's advice:

a) sometimes, though you usually modify their suggestions a bit.

b) rarely. You generally decide for yourself what to do.

c) almost all the time. But you blame other people when things go wrong.

How do you handle criticism?

a) It freaks you out—you've been accused of getting a little defensive.

b) You ignore it—no one's perfect.

c) You don't always respond well right away, but usually you're able to evaluate any feedback and figure out whether it's justified or not.

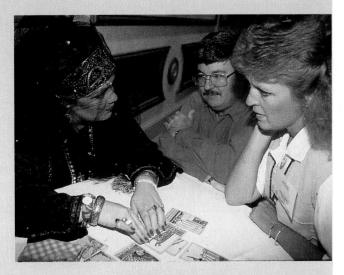

The odds are that for each of these questions you will select the answer that reflects most favorably on you. Even if you select a "negative" answer, the chances are that you are doing so because of a temporary problem, not because you behave that way all the time. The results of such a quiz have little chance of being scientifically accurate. Pop psychology articles in magazines fulfill Barnum's promise of having "a little something for everybody," but the reader who takes them seriously is in danger of illustrating another famous saying attributed to Barnum: "There's a sucker born every minute."

The descriptions of personality that are often published in astrological charts share some of the characteristics of the personality analyses in popular magazines. At first glance,

continued

you might consider the description under your sign wonderfully accurate. But if you look more closely, you'll see that most of the traits contained in the description are desirable ones. Even when the description includes both positive and negative traits you may find it remarkably accurate. Two tendencies related to the Barnum effect are operating here. The first is referred to as the self-serving bias: We are more likely to accept a positive description of ourselves than a negative one. The second tendency is known as the fallacy of positive instances: A person is likely to notice or remember something that matches his or her expectations and not to notice other information that might contradict those expectations. Personality profiles and horoscope charts capitalize on these tendencies by presenting descriptions that are so general that they apply to almost anyone and so flattering that almost anyone will accept them as accurate (French et al., 1991).

By now it should be obvious that the same principles apply to fortune-telling and palmistry. The Barnum effect can be seen in the predictions of fortune-tellers: They have "a little something for everybody"—that is, they contain such general statements that they seem to fit almost anyone. The same goes for the personality assessments palmists offer after examining the lines and folds in the skin of your hand. An observation such as "At times you are extroverted, affable, and sociable, while at other times you are introverted, wary, and reserved" could describe most of the people on this planet.

You can avoid being one of Barnum's "suckers" if you apply critical thinking in evaluating personality profiles, horoscopes, fortunes, and the like. Be alert to vague all-purpose descriptions. Pay attention to the content of the description—notice the negative statements as well as the positive ones. And watch out for flattery disguised as science. This is not to say that you should never read your horoscope or have your fortune told—these activities can be entertaining. But if you do, watch out for the Barnum effect!

Thinking Critically

Evaluation

In your opinion, which personality theory is the most accurate, reasonable, and realistic? Which is the least accurate, reasonable, and realistic? Support your answers.

Point/Counterpoint

Are personality characteristics mostly learned? Or are they mostly transmitted through the genes? Using what you have learned in this chapter and other evidence you can gather, make a case for each position. Support your answers with research and expert opinion.

Psychology in Your Life

Consider your own behavior and personality attributes from the standpoint of each of the theories: psychoanalysis, trait theory, and the learning, humanistic, and genetic perspectives. Which theory or theories best explain your personality? Why?

Chapter Summary and Review

Sigmund Freud and Psychoanalysis

? *To what two aspects of Freud's work does the term psychoanalysis apply?*

Psychoanalysis is the term Freud used for both his theory of personality and his therapy for the treatment of psychological disorders.

? *What are the three levels of awareness in consciousness?*

The three levels of awareness in consciousness are the conscious, the preconscious, and the unconscious.

? *What are the roles of the id, the ego, and the superego?*

The id is the primitive, unconscious part of the personality, which contains the instincts and operates on the pleasure principle. The ego is the rational, largely conscious system, which operates according to the reality principle. The superego is the moral system of the personality, consisting of the conscience and the ego ideal.

? *What is a defense mechanism?*

A defense mechanism is an unconscious, irrational means that the ego uses to defend against anxiety and to maintain self-esteem; it involves self-deception and the distortion of reality.

? *What are two ways in which repression operates?*

Through repression, (1) painful memories, thoughts, ideas, or perceptions are involuntarily removed from consciousness, and (2) disturbing sexual or aggressive impulses are prevented from breaking into consciousness.

? *What are some other defense mechanisms?*

Other defense mechanisms include projection, denial, rationalization, regression, reaction formation, displacement, and sublimation.

? *What are the psychosexual stages, and why did Freud consider them so important in personality development?*

Freud believed that the sexual instinct is present at birth, develops through a series of psychosexual stages, and provides the driving force for thought and activity. The psychosexual stages are the oral stage, anal stage, phallic stage (followed by the latency period), and genital stage.

? *What is the Oedipus complex?*

The Oedipus complex, occurring in the phallic stage, is a conflict in which the child is sexually attracted to the opposite-sex parent and feels hostility toward the same-sex parent.

? *According to Freud, what are the two primary sources of influence on the personality?*

Freud believed that differences in personality result from the relative strengths of the id, the ego, and the superego and from the personality traits that develop as a result of problems during the psychosexual stages.

Key Terms

personality (p. 436)
psychoanalysis (p. 436)
conscious (p. 437)
preconscious (p. 437)
unconscious (p. 437)
id (p. 437)
pleasure principle (p. 438)
libido (p. 438)
ego (p. 438)
superego (p. 438)
defense mechanism (p. 439)
repression (p. 439)
projection (p. 440)
denial (p. 440)
rationalization (p. 440)
regression (p. 440)
reaction formation (p. 440)
displacement (p. 440)
sublimation (p. 440)
psychosexual stages (p. 442)
fixation (p. 442)
oral stage (p. 442)
anal stage (p. 442)
phallic stage (p. 442)
Oedipus complex (p. 442)
latency period (p. 443)
genital stage (p. 443)

The Neo-Freudians

? *According to Jung, what are the three components of personality?*

Jung conceived of the personality as having three parts: the ego, the personal unconscious, and the collective unconscious.

? *What are five archetypes that Jung believed have a major influence on the personality?*

Jung believed that the persona, shadow, anima, animus, and self are five archetypes that exert a major influence on personality.

? *What did Adler consider to be the driving force of the personality?*

Adler claimed that the predominant force of the personality is the drive to overcome and compensate for feelings of weakness and inferiority and to strive for superiority or significance.

? *Why is Horney considered a pioneer in psychology?*

Horney took issue with Freud's sexist view of women and added the feminine dimension to the world of psychology.

Key Terms

personal unconscious (p. 446)
collective unconscious (p. 446)
archetype (p. 446)
extroversion (p. 447)
introversion (p. 447)

Trait Theories

 What are trait theories of personality?

Trait theories of personality are attempts to explain personality and differences between people in terms of their personal characteristics.

How did Allport differentiate between cardinal and central traits?

Allport defined a cardinal trait as a personal quality that is so strong a part of a person's personality that he or she may become identified with that trait or known for it. A central trait is the type you would mention in writing a letter of recommendation.

How did Cattell differentiate between surface and source traits?

Cattell used the term *surface traits* to refer to observable qualities of personality, which you might use in describing a friend. *Source traits* underlie the surface traits, exist in all of us in varying degrees, make up the most basic personality structure, and cause behavior.

What does Eysenck consider to be the two most important dimensions of personality?

Eysenck considers Extroversion (extroversion versus introversion) and Neuroticism (emotional stability versus instability) to be the most important dimensions of personality.

What are the Big Five personality dimensions in the five-factor theory as described by McCrae and Costa?

According to McCrae and Costa, the Big Five factors are Neuroticism, Extroversion, Conscientiousness, Agreeableness, and Openness to Experience.

Key Terms

trait (p. 449)
trait theories (p. 449)
cardinal trait (p. 450)
central trait (p. 450)
surface traits (p. 450)
source traits (p. 451)
five-factor theory (p. 452)

Learning Theories

How did Skinner account for what most people refer to as personality?

B. F. Skinner viewed personality as simply a collection of behaviors and habits that have been reinforced in the past.

What are the components that make up Bandura's concept of reciprocal determinism, and how do they interact?

The external environment, behavior, and personal/cognitive factors are the three components of reciprocal determinism, each influencing and being influenced by the others.

What does Rotter mean by the terms internal and external locus of control?

According to Rotter, people with an internal locus of control see themselves as primarily in control of their behavior and its consequences; those with an external locus of control believe their destiny is in the hands of fate, luck, or chance.

Key Terms

reciprocal determinism (p. 456)
self-efficacy (p. 456)
locus of control (p. 456)

The Humanistic Perspective

Who were the two pioneers in humanistic psychology, and how did they view human nature?

Abraham Maslow and Carl Rogers, the two pioneers in humanistic psychology, believed that human nature is innately good and that people have free will and a tendency toward growth and realization of their potential.

What is self-actualization, and how did Maslow study it?

Self-actualization means developing to one's fullest potential. Maslow studied people who had made significant contributions in their lifetime and who exemplified self-actualization to determine what characteristics they shared.

According to Rogers, why don't all people become fully functioning persons?

Individuals often do not become fully functioning persons because in childhood they did not receive unconditional positive regard from their parents. To gain positive regard, they had to meet their parents' conditions of worth.

Key Terms

humanistic psychology (p. 457)
self-actualization (p. 458)
conditions of worth (p. 458)
unconditional positive regard (p. 459)

Personality: Is It in the Genes?

What has research in behavioral genetics revealed about the influence of the genes and the environment on personality?

Research in behavioral genetics has

revealed that about 40 to 50 percent of personality can be attributed to the genes, and that the environmental influences on personality are mainly from the nonshared environment.

Key Terms

behavioral genetics (p. 459)
heritability (p. 460)

Personality Assessment

> **?** *What are the three major methods used in personality assessment?*

The major methods used in personality assessment are (1) observation, interviews, and rating scales, (2) inventories, and (3) projective tests.

> **?** *What is an inventory, and what are the MMPI-2 and the CPI designed to reveal?*

An inventory is a paper-and-pencil test with questions about a person's thoughts, feelings, and behaviors, which can be scored according to a standard procedure. The MMPI-2 is designed to screen and diagnose psychiatric problems, and the CPI is designed to assess the normal personality.

> **?** *How do projective tests provide insight into personality, and what are some of the most commonly used projective tests?*

In a projective test, people respond to inkblots, drawings of ambiguous human situations, incomplete sentences, and the like by projecting their own inner thoughts, feelings, fears, or conflicts onto the test materials. Examples are the Rorschach Inkblot Test, the Thematic Apperception Test (TAT), and the sentence completion method.

Key Terms

halo effect (p. 463)
inventory (p. 464)
Minnesota Multiphasic Personality Inventory–2 (MMPI-2) (p. 464)
California Psychological Inventory (CPI) (p. 466)
projective test (p. 466)
Rorschach Inkblot Test (p. 466)
Thematic Apperception Test (TAT) (p. 468)

13

HEALTH AND STRESS

477

Many years ago Norman Cousins (1979), who was editor of the *Saturday Review*, was hospitalized and diagnosed as having a rare and crippling disease that destroys the connective tissues of the body. The doctors gave Cousins a grim report and told him that his condition was not reversible. He could not recover. In constant pain, with his body rapidly deteriorating, he faced inevitable death. In response, Cousins decided to leave the hospital, check into a hotel, and take an active part in his own treatment. With the help of a trusted doctor and others, he followed a regimen of vitamin therapy and watched hilarious films—old "Candid Camera" TV shows, Marx Brothers films, and other comedy treats. He reports in his book *Anatomy of an Illness* that the laughter inspired by the films gave him relief from pain, which made it possible for him to sleep for short periods at a time. Cousins continued his laughter therapy for several months, and he didn't grow worse and die. He walked out of his hotel room with his "incurable" disease in remission. Not only that, he lived many additional healthy years and, among many other activities, became a lecturer at the UCLA School of Medicine.

Even though he took advantage of the best conventional medical care available, Cousins added some not-so-conventional components that he believed contributed to his healing. Cousins did not rely on laughter alone to supplement his treatments. He said, "In order to recover I brought a full range of positive emotions into play—love, hope, faith, will to live, festivity, purpose, [and] determination" (Cousins, 1989, p. 22).

Cousins's experience does not suggest that we can laugh all our troubles and illnesses away. Even optimists and humorists get sick and die. But his experience and that of many others suggest that the body is not a completely separate system that falls ill and either recovers or dies apart from psychological and social influences.

? *How do the biomedical and biopsychosocial models differ in their approaches to health and illness?*

biomedical model: A perspective that focuses on illness rather than health, explaining illness in terms of biological factors without regard to psychological and social factors.

biopsychosocial model: A perspective that focuses on health as well as illness and holds that both are determined by a combination of biological, psychological, and social factors.

health psychology: The field concerned with the psychological factors that contribute to health, illness, and recovery.

Two Approaches to Health and Illness

The doctors who diagnosed Norman Cousins's illness and pronounced him incurable were using the best medical knowledge available according to the biomedical model, the predominant view in medicine. The **biomedical model** focuses on illness rather than health. It explains illness in terms of biological factors without considering psychological and social factors that might contribute to the disorder. Professionals who are narrowly committed to the biomedical model can only shake their heads in disbelief when patients like Cousins regain their health with the help of treatments other than conventional medical ones.

Another approach that is gaining serious attention is the **biopsychosocial model** of health and wellness. This approach focuses on health as well as illness, and it holds that both are determined by a combination of biological, psychological, and social factors (Engel, 1977, 1980; Schwartz, 1982). It is this model that most health psychologists endorse and that guides our exploration in this chapter. The biopsychosocial model is depicted in Figure 13.1.

But first, what is **health psychology**? Health psychology is "the field within psychology devoted to understanding psychological influences on how people stay healthy, why they become ill, and how they respond when they do get ill" (Taylor, 1991, p. 6). Health psychologists study psychological factors associated with health and illness, and they promote interventions that foster good health and aid recovery from illness.

Why do people become ill in the modern age? At the beginning of the 20th century, the primary causes of death in the United States were pneumonia and infectious diseases such as diphtheria and tuberculosis. Medical research has virtually conquered these diseases, with the exception of some new strains of tuber-

478

FIGURE 13.1

The Biopsychosocial Model of Health and Wellness

The biopsychosocial model focuses on health as well as illness and holds that both are determined by a combination of biological, psychological, and social factors. Most health psychologists endorse the biopsychosocial model. (From Green & Shellenberger, 1990.)

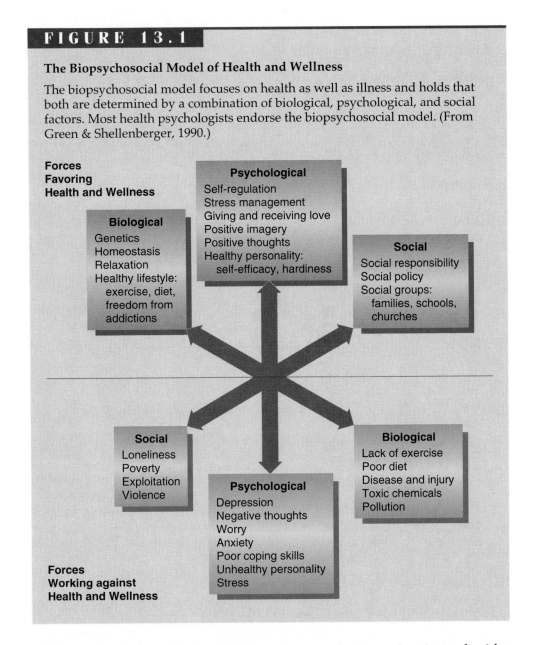

culosis. The health menaces of modern times are diseases related to unhealthy lifestyle and stress—heart attack, stroke, hardening of the arteries, cancer, and cirrhosis of the liver. In this chapter we will discuss stress, disease, and behaviors that promote and compromise health.

Theories of Stress

How would you define stress? Is stress something in the environment? Is it a physiological or psychological reaction that occurs within a person? Is it something we should avoid at all costs? As with most issues in psychology, there are different ways to view stress. Some researchers emphasize the physiological effects of stress, while others focus on the role that our thinking plays in stress. Most psychologists define **stress** as the physiological and psychological response to a condition that threatens or challenges the individual and requires some form of adaptation or adjustment.

stress: The physiological and psychological response to a condition that threatens or challenges a person and requires some form of adaptation or adjustment.

Hans Selye and the General Adaptation Syndrome

An early, classic contribution to stress research was made by Walter Cannon (1932), who described the fight-or-flight response. Cannon discovered that when any threat is perceived by an organism (animal or human), the sympathetic nervous system and the endocrine glands prepare the body to fight the threat or flee from it. Cannon considered the fight-or-flight response wonderfully adaptive, because it helps the organism respond rapidly to threats. He also considered it potentially harmful in the long run, if an organism is not able to fight or flee and experiences prolonged stress and continuing physical arousal (Sapolsky, 1994).

Hans Selye (1907–1982), the researcher most prominently associated with the effects of stress on health, established the field of stress research. Read about his work in the Pioneers box.

PIONEERS   *Hans Selye (1907–1982)*

Hans Selye was born in Vienna, Austria, in 1907, the son of a surgeon. At age 18 he was admitted to medical school at the University of Prague in Czechoslovakia, even though he had a rather undistinguished academic record. But 4 years later, in 1929, he earned his M.D. degree, graduating first in his class and extending his family's medical tradition to five generations. He stayed at the university 2 more years, earning a Ph.D. in organic chemistry in 1931.

Selye spent most of his pioneering career in Canada—at McGill University from 1932 to 1945 and at the University of Montreal from 1945 to 1977. At McGill University Selye conducted research on the effects of sex hormones. In one experiment, he injected rats with hormone-rich extracts of cow ovaries. What happened to the rats? To Selye's amazement, (1) their adrenal glands became swollen, (2) their immune systems were weakened, and (3) they developed bleeding ulcers in their stomachs and intestines. Never before had a hormone been shown to cause such clear physical symptoms. Selye, an excited and elated 28-year-old, thought he might be hot on the trail of discovering a new hormone. But further experiments proved that the same symptoms could be produced by almost anything Selye tried on the rats, including a wide variety of toxic chemicals and exposure to freezing cold temperatures. Even extreme muscle fatigue caused the same symptoms.

It seemed that Selye had not discovered anything at all. He was crushed, and he later admitted, "Suddenly all my dreams of discovering a new hormone were shattered. . . . I became so depressed that for a few days I could not do any work at all. I just sat in my laboratory, brooding" (1956, p. 24). Then brooding gave way to reflection. Selye recalled, "As I repetitiously continued to go over my ill-fated experiments and their possible interpretation, it suddenly struck me that one could look at them from an entirely different angle" (p. 25).

The different angle Selye pursued paved the way for the rest of his life's work. He realized that the body responds in much the same way to all harmful agents (toxic substances, injuries, electric shock) and a host of other stressors. The physical response was so predictable, so general, that Selye named it the "general adaptation syndrome." As a medical student in the 1920s, Selye had been struck by the fact that patients admitted to the hospital with an amazingly wide variety of illnesses all had many of the same physical symptoms. Now he was seeing general symptoms result in rats exposed to a variety of stressors.

Selye was elated with his discovery, but the medical world was skeptical. The notion that organisms react in the same way to a wide range of dangers was completely contrary to the orthodox medical thinking of the day. Against the advice of his colleagues and without the endorsement of the medical research establishment, Selye continued to test his new theories. He prevailed, and within 5 years he proved that the general stress reaction was indeed the body's way of responding to stress.

Although Selye has his critics, his contribution is now widely accepted by researchers around the world. His place as a pioneer in medicine and psychology seems secure.

***The General Adaptation Syndrome: A General Physical Response to
Many Stressors***   Selye knew that all living organisms are constantly confronted with **stressors**—stimuli or events that place a demand on the organism for adaptation or readjustment. Each stressor causes both specific and nonspecific responses. Extreme cold, for example, causes the specific response of shivering. Apart from the specific response, the body makes a common or nonspecific response to a wide variety of stressors. The heart of Selye's concept of stress is the **general adaptation syndrome (GAS)**, his term for the nonspecific response to stress. The syndrome consists of three stages—the alarm stage, the resistance stage, and the exhaustion stage (Selye, 1956). (See Figure 13.2.)

The body's first response to a stressor is the **alarm stage**, when emotional arousal occurs and the defensive forces of the body are prepared to meet the threat. In the alarm stage the sympathetic nervous system, through the release of hormones, mobilizes the body to fight or flee. If the stressor cannot be quickly conquered or avoided, the organism enters the **resistance stage**, characterized by intense physiological efforts to either resist or adapt to the stressor. During the resistance stage the adrenal glands pour out powerful hormones to help the body resist stressors. Resistance may last a long time, but according to Selye, the length of the resistance stage depends both on the strength or intensity of the stressor and on the body's power to adapt.

If the organism finally fails in its efforts to resist, the **exhaustion stage** is reached. Selye (1974) wrote, "The stage of exhaustion after a temporary demand upon the body, is reversible, but the complete exhaustion of all stores of deep adaptation energy is not" (p. 29). If exposure to the stressor continues, all the stores of deep energy are depleted, and disintegration and death follow.

> What is the general adaptation syndrome?

stressor: Any event capable of producing physical or emotional stress.

general adaptation syndrome (GAS): The predictable sequence of reactions (the alarm, resistance, and exhaustion stages) that organisms show in response to stressors.

alarm stage: The first stage of the general adaptation syndrome, when there is emotional arousal and the defensive forces of the body are prepared for fight or flight.

resistance stage: The second stage of the general adaptation syndrome, when there are intense physiological efforts to resist or adapt to the stressor.

exhaustion stage: The final stage of the general adaptation syndrome, occurring if the organism fails in its efforts to resist the stressor.

FIGURE 13.2

The General Adaptation Syndrome

The three stages in Hans Selye's general adaptation syndrome are (1) the alarm stage, during which there is emotional arousal and the defensive forces of the body are mobilized for fight or flight; (2) the resistance stage, in which intense physiological efforts are exerted to resist or adapt to the stressor; and (3) the exhaustion stage, when the organism fails in its efforts to resist the stressor. (Based on Selye, 1956.)

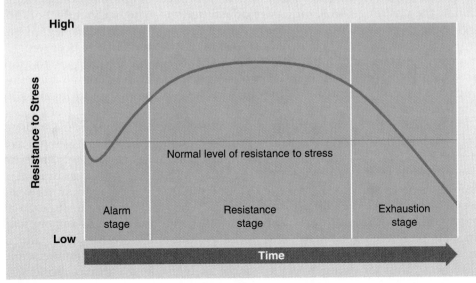

Selye claimed that any event requiring a readjustment, positive or negative, will produce stress in an organism. He did, however, differentiate between the positive and negative aspects of stress. "Eustress" is positive or good stress, including exhilaration, excitement, and the thrill of accomplishment. "Distress" is damaging or unpleasant stress, such as that of frustration, inadequacy, loss, disappointment, insecurity, helplessness, or desperation.

Criticisms of Selye's Theory: A Missing Cognitive Factor Thanks to Selye, the connection between extreme, prolonged stress and certain diseases is now widely accepted by medical experts; but critics point out that Selye's model was primarily formulated from research on laboratory rats. Although there may be some individual variation in the way rats respond to particular stressors, there is infinitely more variation in individual human responses to stress.

The major criticism is directed at Selye's claim that the intensity of the stressor determines one's physical reaction to it. His theory does not provide for a psychological component—how a person perceives and evaluates the stressor. This criticism led to the development of the cognitive theory of stress.

Richard Lazarus's Cognitive Theory of Stress

Richard Lazarus (1966; Lazarus & Folkman, 1984) contends that it is not the stressor itself that causes stress, but a person's perception of the stressor. Because Lazarus emphasizes the importance of perceptions and appraisal of stressors, his is a cognitive theory of stress and coping. To Lazarus (1993), the stress process can be understood in terms of four phases. First, there is a causal agent, either external or internal, that is commonly referred to as stress or the stressor. Second, the mind or the body evaluates the stressor as either threatening or benign. Third, the mind or the body uses coping processes to deal with the stressor. Finally, there is the stress reaction—the "complex pattern of effects on mind and body" (p. 4). Lazarus believes that physiological and psychological stress must be analyzed differently. Selye's model describes how the body copes with physiological stress, while Lazarus's model focuses on how we cope with psychological stressors.

The Cognitive Appraisal of Stressors: Evaluating the Stressor and Considering Your Options According to Lazarus, when people are confronted with a potentially stressful event, they engage in a cognitive process that involves a primary and a secondary appraisal. A **primary appraisal** is an evaluation of the meaning and significance of a situation—whether its effect on our well-being is positive, irrelevant, or negative. An event appraised as negative or stressful could involve (1) harm or loss—damage that has already occurred; (2) threat—the potential for harm or loss; or (3) challenge—the opportunity to grow or to gain. An appraisal of threat, harm, or loss can occur in relation to anything important to us—a friendship, a part of our body, our property, our finances, or our self-esteem.

The same event can be appraised differently by different people. Some students may welcome the opportunity to give an oral presentation in class, seeing it as a challenge and a chance to impress their professor and raise their grade. Other students may feel threatened, fearing that they may embarrass themselves in front of their classmates and lower their grade in the process. Still others may view the assignment as both a challenge and a threat. When we appraise a situation as involving harm, loss, or threat, we have negative emotions such as anxiety, fear, anger, or resentment (Folkman, 1984). A challenge appraisal, on the other hand, is usually accompanied by positive emotions such as excitement, hopefulness, and eagerness. Stress for younger people is more likely to take the form of challenges; for older people, losses and threats are more common (El-Shiekh et al., 1989).

? *What are the roles of primary and secondary appraisal when people are confronted with a potentially stressful event?*

---

primary appraisal: Evaluating the significance of a potentially stressful event according to how it will affect one's well-being—whether it is perceived as irrelevant or as involving harm or loss, threat, or challenge.

When we assess an event as stressful, we engage in a **secondary appraisal**. During secondary appraisal, if we judge the situation to be within our control, we make an evaluation of our available coping resources—physical (health, energy, stamina), social (support network), psychological (skills, morale, self-esteem), material (money, tools, equipment), and time. Then we consider our options and decide how we will deal with the stressor. The level of stress we feel is largely a function of whether our resources are adequate to cope with the threat, and how severely our resources will be taxed in the process.

Figure 13.3 summarizes the Lazarus and Folkman psychological model of stress. There is research support for Lazarus and Folkman's claim that the physiological, emotional, and behavioral reactions to stressors depend partly on whether the stressors are appraised as challenging or threatening. Tomaka and others (1993) found that active coping with stressors appraised as challenging was associated with increased heart rate, better performance, and positive emotions. Active coping with stressors appraised as threatening was related to increased blood pressure, poorer performance, and negative emotional tone.

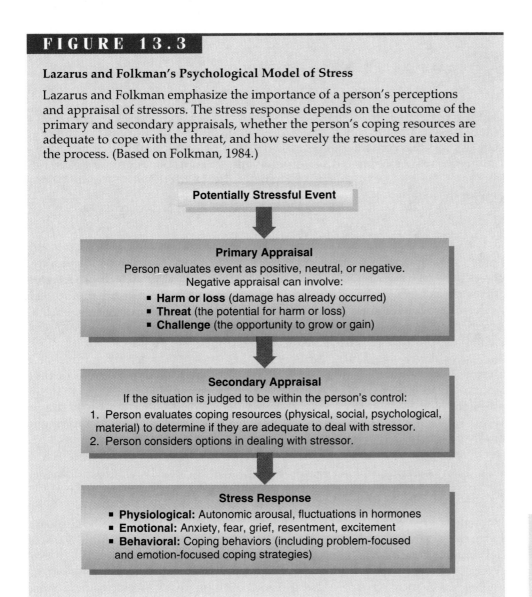

FIGURE 13.3

Lazarus and Folkman's Psychological Model of Stress

Lazarus and Folkman emphasize the importance of a person's perceptions and appraisal of stressors. The stress response depends on the outcome of the primary and secondary appraisals, whether the person's coping resources are adequate to cope with the threat, and how severely the resources are taxed in the process. (Based on Folkman, 1984.)

Potentially Stressful Event

Primary Appraisal
Person evaluates event as positive, neutral, or negative.
Negative appraisal can involve:
- **Harm or loss** (damage has already occurred)
- **Threat** (the potential for harm or loss)
- **Challenge** (the opportunity to grow or gain)

Secondary Appraisal
If the situation is judged to be within the person's control:
1. Person evaluates coping resources (physical, social, psychological, material) to determine if they are adequate to deal with stressor.
2. Person considers options in dealing with stressor.

Stress Response
- **Physiological:** Autonomic arousal, fluctuations in hormones
- **Emotional:** Anxiety, fear, grief, resentment, excitement
- **Behavioral:** Coping behaviors (including problem-focused and emotion-focused coping strategies)

secondary appraisal: Evaluating one's coping resources and deciding how to deal with a stressful event.

Memory Check 13.1

1. The biomedical model focuses on _____; the biopsychosocial model focuses on _____.
   a. illness; illness
   b. health and illness; illness
   c. illness; health and illness
   d. health and illness; health and illness

2. The stage of the general adaptation syndrome marked by intense physiological efforts to adapt to the stressor is the (alarm, resistance) stage.

3. Susceptibility to illness increases during the (alarm, exhaustion) stage of the general adaptation syndrome.

4. During secondary appraisal, we:
   a. evaluate our coping resources and consider options in dealing with the stressor.
   b. determine whether an event is positive, neutral, or negative.
   c. determine whether an event involves loss, threat, or challenge.
   d. determine whether an event causes physiological or psychological stress.

5. Selye focused on the (psychological, physiological) aspects of stress; Lazarus focused on the (psychological, physiological) aspects of stress.

Answers: 1. c 2. resistance 3. exhaustion 4. a 5. physiological; psychological

Sources of Stress: The Common and the Extreme

Some stressors produce temporary stress, while others produce chronic stress—a state of stress that continues unrelieved over time. Chronic health problems, physical handicaps, poverty, and unemployment are sources of chronic stress. The burden of chronic stress is disproportionately heavy for the poor, for minorities, and for the elderly.

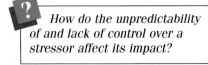
How do approach–approach, avoidance–avoidance, and approach–avoidance conflicts differ?

Choices: Everyday Sources of Stress

Sometimes conflicting motives can be sources of stress. When we must make a choice between two desirable alternatives, known as an **approach–approach conflict**, stress may be the result. Some approach-approach conflicts are minor, such as deciding which movie to see. Others can have major consequences, such as whether to continue building a promising career or to interrupt the career to raise a child. In approach–approach conflicts, both choices are desirable.

In **avoidance–avoidance conflicts** we must choose between two undesirable alternatives. You may want to avoid studying for an exam, but at the same time want to avoid failing the test. **Approach–avoidance conflicts** include both desirable and undesirable features in the same choice. We are simultaneously drawn to and repelled by a choice—wanting to take a wonderful vacation but having to empty a savings account to do so.

How do the unpredictability of and lack of control over a stressor affect its impact?

Unpredictability and Lack of Control: Factors That Increase Stress

Unpredictable stressors are more difficult to cope with than predictable stressors. Laboratory tests have shown that rats receiving electric shocks without warning develop more ulcers than rats given shocks just as often but only after a warning (Weiss, 1972). Likewise, humans who are warned of a stressor before it occurs and have a chance to prepare themselves for it experience less stress than those who cannot predict when a stressor will occur.

Our physical and psychological well-being is profoundly influenced by the degree to which we feel a sense of control over our lives (Rodin & Salovey, 1989). Langer and Rodin (1976) studied the effects of control on nursing-home residents. One group of residents were given some measure of control over their lives, such as choices in arranging their rooms and in the times they could see movies. They showed improved health and well-being and had a lower death rate than another group who were not given control. Within 18 months, 30 percent of the residents given no choices had died compared to only 15 percent of those who had been given some control over their lives. Control is important for cancer patients, too. Some researchers suggest that for cancer patients a sense of control over their daily physical symptoms and emotional reactions may be even more important than control over the course of the disease itself (Thompson et al., 1993).

Several studies suggest that we are less subject to stress when we have the power to do something about it, whether we exercise that power or not. Glass and Singer (1972) subjected two groups of subjects to the same loud noise, but one group was told that they could, if necessary, terminate the noise by pressing a switch. The group that had the control suffered less stress even though they never did exercise the control they were given. Friedland and others (1992) suggest that when people experience a loss of control because of a stressor, they are motivated to try to reestablish control in the stressful situation. Failing this, they often attempt to increase their sense of control in other areas of their lives.

Catastrophic Events and Chronic Intense Stress

Environmental, social, bodily, and emotional stressors are a fact of life for most people, but some people also experience catastrophic events such as plane crashes, fires, or earthquakes. Panic reactions are rare, except in situations such as fires in which people feel that they will survive only if they escape immediately. Many victims of catastrophic events react initially with such shock that they appear dazed, stunned, and emotionally numb. They seem disoriented and may wander about aimlessly, often unaware of their own injuries, attempting to help neither themselves nor others. Following this stage, the victims show a concern for others, and although unable to act efficiently on their own, they are willing to follow the directions of rescue workers. You may have observed these reactions in TV coverage of the Oklahoma City bombing.

As victims begin to recover, the shock is replaced by generalized anxiety. Recovering victims typically have recurring nightmares and feel a compulsive need to retell the event over and over. Reexperiencing the event through dreaming and retelling helps desensitize them to the horror of the experience. Crisis-intervention therapy can provide victims with both coping strategies and realistic expectations about the problems they may face in connection with the trauma.

Posttraumatic Stress Disorder: The Trauma Is Over, but the Stress Remains Posttraumatic stress disorder (PTSD) is a prolonged and severe stress reaction to a catastrophic event (such as a plane crash or an earthquake) or to chronic intense stress (such as occurs in combat or imprisonment as a hostage or POW). Breslau and others (1991) found that 9 percent of a random sample of 1,007 adults aged 20 to 30 in metropolitan Detroit had suffered from posttraumatic stress disorder from a variety of events; 80 percent of the women with PTSD had been raped. The disorder may show up immediately, or it may not occur until 6 months or more after the traumatic experience, in which case it is called delayed posttraumatic stress disorder. More than 400,000 Vietnam veterans were found to suffer from PTSD (Goldberg et al., 1990). The most serious cases have resulted from witnessing brutal atrocities, whether among Vietnam veterans

approach–approach conflict: A conflict arising from having to choose between desirable alternatives.

savoidance–avoidance conflict: A conflict arising from having to choose between two undesirable alternatives.

approach–avoidance conflict: A conflict arising when the same choice has both desirable and undesirable features.

posttraumatic stress disorder (PTSD): A prolonged and severe stress reaction to a catastrophic event or to chronic intense stress.

How do people typically react to catastrophic events?

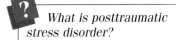

What is posttraumatic stress disorder?

Posttraumatic stress disorder is a reaction to a catastrophic event or to chronic intense stress, such as the ongoing bombing in Sarajevo.

? *What is the difference between problem-focused and emotion-focused coping?*

coping: Efforts through action and thought to deal with demands that are perceived as taxing or overwhelming.

problem-focused coping: A response aimed at reducing, modifying, or eliminating a source of stress.

emotion-focused coping: A response aimed at reducing the emotional impact of the stressor.

(Yehuda et al., 1992), Cambodian refugees (Carlson & Rosser-Horgan, 1991), Holocaust survivors (Kuch & Cox, 1992), or victims of state-sanctioned terrorism and torture (Bloche & Eisenberg, 1993).

People with posttraumatic stress disorder often have flashbacks, nightmares, or intrusive memories in which they feel as though they are actually reexperiencing the traumatic event. They suffer increased anxiety and startle easily, particularly in response to anything that reminds them of the trauma (Green et al., 1985). Many survivors of war or catastrophic events experience survivor guilt because they lived while others died. Some feel that perhaps they could have done more to save others. Extreme combat-related guilt in Vietnam veterans is a risk factor for suicide or preoccupation with suicide (Hendin & Haas, 1991).

Research on 4,042 identical and fraternal twin pairs who were Vietnam veterans suggests a genetic susceptibility to posttraumatic stress symptoms. Identical twins were much more similar than fraternal twins in the posttraumatic stress symptoms they had in response to similar combat experiences (True et al., 1993).

Is there anything that can lessen the stress that follows a major trauma? According to Bloche and Eisenberg (1993), "Belief systems that give life a sense of purpose and meaning can prevent emotional damage" (p. 5).

Coping with Stress

When we encounter stressful situations, we try either to alter or to reinterpret them to make them seem more favorable. **Coping** refers to our efforts through action and thought to deal with demands we perceive as taxing or overwhelming.

Problem-Focused and Emotion-Focused Coping

Coping strategies fall into two categories—problem-focused and emotion-focused (Lazarus & Folkman, 1984). **Problem-focused coping** is direct; it consists of reducing, modifying, or eliminating the source of stress itself. If you are getting a poor grade in history and appraise this as a threat, you may study harder, talk over your problem with your professor, form a study group with other class members, get a tutor, or drop the course.

But what can we do when we face stress that we cannot fight, escape from, avoid, or modify in any way? We can use **emotion-focused coping** to change the way we respond emotionally. Emotion-focused coping may involve reappraising a stressor. If you lose your job, you may decide that it isn't a major tragedy and instead view it as a challenge—an opportunity to find a better job with a higher salary. To cope emotionally, people may use anything from religious faith, wishful thinking, humor, or denial, to alcohol, drugs, or promiscuous sex (Lazarus & DeLongis, 1983). But misguided emotion-focused coping efforts can become additional sources of stress themselves.

Well-functioning people use a combination of problem-focused and emotion-focused coping in almost every stressful situation. Folkman and Lazarus (1980) studied the coping patterns of 100 subjects over a 12-month period and found that both types of coping were used in 98 percent of the 1,300 stressful life events their subjects had confronted. Not surprisingly, problem-focused coping strategies increased in situations subjects appraised as changeable, and emotion-focused coping techniques increased in situations appraised as not changeable.

The two types of coping are summed up well in an ancient prayer you may have heard: "Lord, grant me the strength to change those things that I can change [problem-focused coping], the grace to accept those things that I cannot change [emotion-focused coping], and the wisdom to know the difference."

Religion and Coping with Negative Life Events

According to one of the largest surveys of religious affiliation ever conducted in the United States, more than 92 percent of Americans reported considering themselves religious (Goldman, 1991). Does religious faith help people cope with negative life events? Several studies indicate that in the majority of cases, it does. Koenig and others (1992) studied a large sample of hospitalized elderly men who had been suffering from a range of serious medical problems. They found that religious coping was inversely related to depression. That is, the more these patients turned to religious coping, the less likely they were to be depressed.

McIntosh and others (1993) evaluated 124 parents who had lost a child to sudden infant death syndrome. When evaluated at 3 weeks and at 18 months after the death of their infant, the parents who participated in religious services were better able to cope with their loss. The researchers suggested that religious participation had provided social support, enabled the parents to view death as less threatening, and helped them find meaning in the death.

Finally, Larson and others (1992) conducted a meta-analysis of 38 studies of religious commitment and mental health. For the 50 measures on which the two variables were related, the association was positive in 72 percent of the comparisons, negative in 16 percent, and neutral in 12 percent. When mental health is studied in relation to the dimensions of ceremony, social support, prayer, and relationship with God, 92 percent of the associations are positive.

Memory Check 13.2

1. Rick cannot decide whether to go out or stay home and study for his test. What kind of conflict does he have?
   a. approach–approach conflict
   b. avoidance–avoidance conflict
   c. approach–avoidance conflict
   d. ambivalence–ambivalence conflict

2. Panic is the most common *initial* reaction to a catastrophic event. (true/false)

3. Victims of catastrophic events typically want to talk about their experience. (true/false)

4. Posttraumatic stress disorder is a prolonged and severe stress reaction that results when a number of common sources of stress occur simultaneously. (true/false)

5. What has research shown to increase stress?
   a. predictability of the stressor
   b. unpredictability of the stressor
   c. predictability of and control over the stressor
   d. unpredictability of and lack of control over the stressor

6. Coping aimed at reducing, modifying, or eliminating a source of stress is called (emotion-focused, problem-focused) coping; that aimed at reducing an emotional reaction to stress is called (emotion-focused, problem-focused) coping.

7. People typically use a combination of problem-focused and emotion-focused coping when dealing with a stressful situation. (true/false)

Answers: 1. c 2. false 3. true 4. false 5. d 6. problem-focused; emotion-focused 7. true

? *What was the Social Readjustment Rating Scale designed to reveal?*

Even positive life events, such as getting married, can cause stress.

Evaluating Life Stress: Major Life Changes, Hassles, and Uplifts

There are two major approaches to evaluating life stress and its relation to illness. One approach focuses on major life events, which cause life changes that require adaptation. A second approach focuses on life's daily hassles.

Holmes and Rahe's Social Readjustment Rating Scale: Adding Up the Stress Score

Interested in the relationship between life changes and illness, researchers Thomas Holmes and Richard Rahe (1967) developed the **Social Readjustment Rating Scale (SRRS)**. The SRRS is designed to measure stress by ranking different life events from most to least stressful and assigning a point value to each event. Life events that produce the greatest life changes and require the greatest adaptation are considered the most stressful, regardless of whether the events are positive or negative. The 43 life events range from death of a spouse (assigned 100 stress points), to such items as divorce (73 points), death of a close family member (63 points), marriage (50 points), and pregnancy (40 points), to minor law violations such as getting a traffic ticket (11 points). Add up the number of stress points in your life—complete the *Try It!* on the opposite page.

Holmes and Rahe claim that there is a connection between the degree of life stress and major health problems. After analyzing more than 5,000 medical case histories, they concluded that major life changes often precede serious illness (Rahe et al., 1964). People who score 300 or more on the SRRS, the researchers say, run about an 80 percent risk of suffering a major health problem within the next 2 years. And those who score between 150 and 300 have a 50 percent chance of becoming ill within a 2-year period.

Are Holmes and Rahe's claims justified? Most researchers do not consider a high score on the SRRS a reliable predictor of future health problems (Krantz et al., 1985; McCrae, 1984). The correlations between major life changes and subsequent illness have, in fact, been quite small (Schroeder & Costa, 1984). One of the main shortcomings of the SRRS is that it assigns a point value to each life change without taking into account whether the change is for better or worse. For example, life changes such as divorce, pregnancy, retirement from work, and changing jobs or residences may be either welcome or unwelcome events.

The Hassles of Life: Little Things Stress a Lot

? *What roles do hassles and uplifts play in the stress of life, according to Lazarus?*

Richard Lazarus disagrees with the rationale behind Holmes and Rahe's scale. He contends that life events cannot be assessed and assigned a numerical value for stressfulness without considering their meaning to the individual. Furthermore, he believes that the little stressors, which he calls **hassles**, add up to more stress than major life events.

Daily hassles are the "irritating, frustrating, distressing demands and troubled relationships that plague us day in and day out" (Lazarus & DeLongis, 1983, p. 247). Kanner and others (1981) developed the Hassles Scale to assess various categories of hassles. Unlike the Holmes and Rahe scale, the Hassles Scale takes into account that items may or may not represent stressors and that the amount of stress produced by an item varies from person to person. Consequently, people completing the scale indicate the items that have been a hassle for them and rate the items for severity on a 3-point scale.

 To assess your life in terms of life changes, check all of the events listed that have happened to you in the past year. Add up the points to derive your life stress score. (Based on data from Holmes & Masuda, 1974.)

Rank	Life Event	Life Change Unit Value	Your Scores
1	Death of spouse	100	___
2	Divorce	73	___
3	Marital separation	65	___
4	Jail term	63	___
5	Death of close family member	63	___
6	Personal injury or illness	53	___
7	Marriage	50	___
8	Getting fired at work	47	___
9	Marital reconciliation	45	___
10	Retirement	45	___
11	Change in health of family member	44	___
12	Pregnancy	40	___
13	Sex difficulties	39	___
14	Gain of new family member	39	___
15	Business readjustment	39	___
16	Change in financial state	38	___
17	Death of close friend	37	___
18	Change to different line of work	36	___
19	Change in number of arguments with spouse	35	___
20	Taking out loan for major purchase (e.g., home)	31	___
21	Foreclosure of mortgage or loan	30	___
22	Change in responsibilities at work	29	___
23	Son or daughter leaving home	29	___
24	Trouble with in-laws	29	___
25	Outstanding personal achievement	28	___
26	Wife beginning or stopping work	26	___
27	Beginning or ending school	26	___
28	Change in living conditions	25	___
29	Revision of personal habits	24	___
30	Trouble with boss	23	___
31	Change in work hours or conditions	20	___
32	Change in residence	20	___
33	Change in schools	20	___
34	Change in recreation	19	___
35	Change in church activities	19	___
36	Change in social activities	18	___
37	Taking out loan for lesser purchase (e.g., car or TV)	17	___
38	Change in sleeping habits	16	___
39	Change in number of family get-togethers	15	___
40	Change in eating habits	15	___
41	Vacation	13	___
42	Christmas	12	___
43	Minor violation of the law	11	___
		Total score:	___

uplifts: The positive experiences in life, which can neutralize the effects of many of the hassles.

TABLE 13.1　The Ten Most Common Hassles for College Students

Hassle	Percentage of Times Checked
1. Troubling thoughts about future	76.6
2. Not getting enough sleep	72.5
3. Wasting time	71.1
4. Inconsiderate smokers	70.7
5. Physical appearance	69.9
6. Too many things to do	69.2
7. Misplacing or losing things	67.0
8. Not enough time to do the things you need to do	66.3
9. Concerns about meeting high standards	64.0
10. Being lonely	60.8

Source: "Comparison of Two Modes of Stress Measurement: Daily Hassles and Uplifts versus Major Life Events," by A. D. Kanner, J. C. Coyne, C. Schaefer, and R. S. Lazarus, 1981, *Journal of Behavioral Medicine, 4*, pp. 1–39.

DeLongis and others (1988) studied 75 American couples over a 6-month period and found that daily stress (as measured on the Hassles Scale) related significantly to present and future "health problems such as flu, sore throat, headaches, and backaches" (p. 486). Several studies reveal that scores on the Hassles Scale are better than SRRS scores at predicting illness (DeLongis et al., 1982; Weinberger et al., 1987) and at predicting psychological symptoms such as anxiety and depression (Kanner et al., 1981).

Table 13.1 shows the ten most frequent hassles reported by college students.

According to Lazarus, "a person's morale, social functioning, and health don't hinge on hassles alone, but on a balance between the good things that happen to people—that make them feel good—and the bad" (quoted in Goleman, 1979, p. 52). Fortunately, the **uplifts**, or positive experiences in life, may neutralize or cancel out the effect of many of the hassles. Lazarus and his colleagues also constructed an Uplifts Scale. As with the Hassles Scale, people completing the scale make a cognitive appraisal in determining what they consider an uplift. Items viewed as uplifts by some people may actually be stressors for other people. Kanner and others (1981) found that for middle-aged people, uplifts were often health- or family-related, whereas for college students uplifts often came in the form of having a good time.

Memory　Check 13.3

1. On the Social Readjustment Rating Scale, only negative life changes are considered stressful. (true/false)

2. The Social Readjustment Rating Scale takes account of the individual's perceptions of the stressfulness of the life change in assigning stress points. (true/false)

3. According to Lazarus, hassles typically account for more life stress than major life changes. (true/false)

4. Lazarus's approach to measuring hassles and uplifts considers individual perceptions of stressful events. (true/false)

Answers: 1. false　2. false　3. true　4. true

Health and Disease

Responding to Illness

Health psychologists study the myriad ways in which we respond to illness, and the factors that affect whether we seek treatment. How do people tend to respond to illness?

The Sick Role We have all been sick at one time or another, and most of us do not wish to be again. However, some people seem to take comfort in the "sick role." Sociologist Talcott Parsons (1979) indicated that there are benefits provided by the sick role. The ill person gets attention, sympathy, and concern, which can be very rewarding. Also, little is expected of a person who is sick. Obligations can be postponed and demands can be lifted until the person is well again. The surge in visits to college and university health services when term papers are due and when examinations begin may be partly due to students taking refuge in the sick role. How do we determine whether we are sick enough to seek treatment?

Recognizing and Interpreting Symptoms Headache, stomachache, sore throat, back pain, diarrhea—all are familiar symptoms that can represent nothing serious or something very critical. Often the first signs of serious disorders are common symptoms, familiar to us all. Painful symptoms are typically interpreted as more serious than painless ones. And the more painful the symptom, the more likely we are to interpret it as serious and seek treatment.

Situational factors sometimes affect our tendency to recognize and interpret symptoms. For example, "medical student disease" is common among medical students, who sometimes fear that they may be afflicted with the symptoms of the diseases they are learning about. Psychology students are also subject to letting their imagination run rampant when they study the symptoms of psychological disorders. Be forewarned when you study Chapter 14.

Seeking Treatment When people recognize symptoms and interpret them as potentially serious, they seek treatment—or do they? Several factors determine who is likely to seek treatment and use health services. Gender is one: Women use medical services more frequently than men. The reasons are not clear, and even when visits involving pregnancy and childbirth are factored out, women still seek health services more than men. It has been suggested that women may be more sensitive to bodily changes and detect symptoms more readily than men (Taylor, 1991). Cultural norms and expectations may also partly explain why women seek treatment more than men (Bishop, 1984).

Socioeconomic class is related to seeking treatment because the lower socioeconomic classes have less to spend on health care. The poor are likely to seek treatment only in emergencies and are far less likely than middle- or upper-class people to have a regular physician.

Compliance with Medical Treatment: Following the Doctor's Orders
When we do receive medical treatment, do we always comply with the treatment regimen? Do we take all the medicine prescribed as the doctor instructed, or do we stop taking it when our symptoms disappear? A review of some 250 studies indicates that up to 50 percent of patients fail to follow what the doctor ordered (Adler & Stone, 1984). Even among patients with chronic disorders, at least half do not comply fully with their prescribed treatment regimen (Taylor, 1991). It is even less likely that patients will comply with lifestyle changes that promote better health. In fact, 97 percent of patients do not adhere fully to lifestyle recommendations (Taylor, 1991). Health professionals and researchers have discovered many more effective treatments than people are willing to follow.

sedentary lifestyle: A lifestyle in which a person exercises less than 20 minutes three times a week.

Type A behavior pattern: A behavior pattern marked by a sense of time urgency, impatience, excessive competitiveness, hostility, and anger; considered a risk factor in coronary heart disease.

Type B behavior pattern: A behavior pattern marked by a relaxed, easygoing approach to life; not associated with coronary heart disease.

? *What are the Type A and Type B behavior patterns?*

Type A personalities have a strong sense of time urgency and are impatient, competitive, hostile, and easily angered. Do you know anyone who fits this pattern?

Coronary Heart Disease: The Leading Cause of Death

The leading cause of death in the United States is coronary heart disease, which accounts for approximately 33 percent of all deaths (U.S. Bureau of the Census, 1994). For the heart muscle to survive, it requires a steady, sufficient supply of oxygen and nutrients carried by the blood. Coronary heart disease is caused by the narrowing or the blockage of the coronary arteries—the arteries that supply blood to the heart muscle.

A health problem of modern times, coronary heart disease is largely attributable to lifestyle and is therefore an important field of study for health psychologists. A **sedentary lifestyle**—one with less than 20 minutes of exercise three times per week—is the primary modifiable risk factor contributing to death from coronary heart disease. High levels of stress and job strain have also been associated with increased risk for coronary heart disease and stroke (Rosengren et al., 1991; Siegrist et al., 1990). Other risk factors are high serum cholesterol levels, cigarette smoking, obesity, high blood pressure, and diabetes. Though not modifiable, another important risk factor is a family history of heart disease.

The Type A and Type B Behavior Patterns: In a Hurry or Laid Back

One day cardiologists Meyer Friedman and Ray Rosenman (1974) asked an upholsterer to repair the chairs in their reception room. After inspecting the chairs, the upholsterer asked what kind of practice they had. The doctors explained that they were cardiologists and asked the upholsterer why he wanted to know. " 'Well,' he replied, 'I was just wondering, because it's so peculiar that only the front edges of your chair seats are worn out' " (p. 71).

Apparently most of the heart patients had been literally sitting on the edge of their seats. This discovery led Friedman and Rosenman to wonder if there might be two types of personalities, one related to healthy hearts and one related to heart disease. After extensive research, they concluded that there are two types—the Type A personality, associated with a high rate of coronary heart disease, and the Type B personality, commonly found in persons unlikely to develop heart disease. Are your characteristics more like those of a Type A or a Type B person? Before reading further, complete the *Try It!* on the opposite page and find out.

People with the **Type A behavior pattern** have a strong sense of time urgency and are impatient, excessively competitive, hostile, and easily angered. They are "involved in a *chronic, incessant* struggle to achieve more and more in less and less time," often called the "hurry sickness" (Friedman & Rosenman, 1974, p. 84). Type A's would answer "true" to most or all of the questions in the *Try It!* The Type A person may be a driven executive, a competitive mortician, or a stressed hourly employee and may wear a white collar, a blue collar, or no collar at all.

In helping people change their Type A behavior, Friedman has run into some extreme cases. To avoid wasting time chewing, one man liquefied his food in a blender (Rogers, 1989).

In stark contrast to Type A's, people with the **Type B behavior pattern** are relaxed and easygoing and do not suffer from a sense of time urgency. They are not impatient or hostile and are able to relax without guilt. They play for fun and relaxation rather than to exhibit superiority over others. Yet the Type B individual may be as bright and ambitious as the Type A, and more successful as well. Type B's would answer "false" to most or all of the *Try It!* questions.

Try It! Answer true (T) or false (F) for each of the statements below. (Adapted from Friedman and Rosenman, 1974.)

___ 1. I forcefully emphasize key words in my everyday speech.

___ 2. I usually walk and eat quickly.

___ 3. I get irritated and restless around slow workers.

___ 4. When talking to others, I get impatient and try to hurry them along.

___ 5. I get very irritated, even hostile, when the car in front of me drives too slowly.

___ 6. When others are talking, I often think about my own concerns.

___ 7. I usually think of or do at least two things at the same time.

___ 8. I get very impatient when I have to wait.

___ 9. I usually take command and move the conversation to topics that interest me.

___ 10. I usually feel guilty when I relax and do nothing.

___ 11. I am usually too absorbed in my work to notice my surroundings.

___ 12. I keep trying to do more and more in less time.

___ 13. I sometimes punctuate my conversation with forceful gestures such as clenching my fists or pounding the table.

___ 14. My accomplishments are due largely to my ability to work faster than others.

___ 15. I don't play games just for fun. I play to win.

___ 16. I am more concerned with acquiring things than with becoming a better person.

___ 17. I usually use numbers to evaluate my own activities and the activities of others.

Research on Behavior Pattern and Heart Disease Time urgency, a clear Type A trait, is a factor related to serum cholesterol level, say Friedman and Rosenman (1974). In one study they monitored the serum cholesterol levels in accountants from January through June. Cholesterol levels rose as the income tax deadline approached and then fell after April 15. Later the researchers compared the serum cholesterol levels in Type A and Type B men and women and found higher levels in Type A's of both sexes.

What aspect of the Type A behavior pattern is most clearly linked to coronary heart disease?

Using meta-analysis, Miller and others (1991) found that 70 percent of middle-aged men with coronary heart disease were Type A, while only 46 percent of healthy middle-aged men were. Some researchers speculate that it may not be the whole Type A behavior pattern that leads to heart disease. Dembroski and others (1985) point to anger and hostility as the toxic components. Redford Williams of Duke University Medical School suggests that hostility is the real culprit, particularly a cynical, distrustful attitude (Barefoot et al., 1983; Williams, 1989). Rosenman, too, has come to believe that it is the hostility rather than the "hurry sickness" that really causes the problem. Friedman, on the other hand, disagrees (he and Rosenman are no longer a team) and considers the whole Type A pattern a disorder that needs to be treated.

Male heart-attack survivors are at greater risk for dying from heart disease if they are high in hostility, cynicism, and impatience. But just the opposite may be the case for females. Powell and others (1993) found that among women who have survived a heart attack, those who suppress unpleasant emotions such as anger, resentment, loneliness, and dissatisfaction tend to be at greatest risk of death. Women who died of heart disease were also more likely to be divorced, lacking a college education, and working full-time but earning less than $20,000. Financial and emotional stress and the lack of an intimate relationship appeared to be associated with increased risk of dying of coronary heart disease.

Apparently the effects of stress may enter the bloodstream almost as if they were injected intravenously. Malkoff and others (1993) report that after experimental subjects had experienced laboratory-induced stress, their blood platelets (special clotting cells) released large amounts of a substance that promotes the buildup of plaque in blood vessels and may lead to heart attack and stroke. No changes were found in the blood platelets of unstressed control subjects.

Cancer: A Dreaded Disease

Cancer. The word alone is frightening. Second only to heart disease as the leading cause of death, cancer causes 23.9 percent of deaths in the United States (U.S. Bureau of the Census, 1994). Cancer strikes frequently in the adult population, and about 30 percent of Americans—over 75 million people—will develop cancer at some time in their lives. The young are not spared the scourge of cancer, for it takes the lives of more children aged 3 to 14 than any other disease.

We speak of cancer as a single disease, but actually it is a complicated collection of diseases. It can invade cells in any part of a living organism—humans, other animals, and even plants. It always starts small, because it is a disease of the body's cells. Normal cells in all parts of the body divide, but fortunately they have built-in instructions about when to stop dividing. If they did not, every part of our body would continue to grow as long as we live. Unlike normal cells, cancer cells do not stop dividing. And unless caught in time and destroyed, they continue to grow and spread, eventually killing the organism.

Health psychologists warn that diet, smoking, excessive alcohol consumption, promiscuous sexual behavior, or becoming sexually active in the early teens (especially for females) are all behaviors that increase the risk of cancer. Many cancer patients report more high-stress situations occurring before their cancer was diagnosed.

The 1 million people in the United States who are diagnosed with cancer each year have the difficult task of adjusting to a potentially life-threatening disease and the chronic stressors associated with it. Patients must cope with difficult therapies, "continued emotional distress, disrupted life tasks, social and interpersonal turmoil and fatigue and low energy" (Anderson et al., 1994, p. 390). Patients need more than medical treatment for cancer, say researchers. Their therapy should include help with psychological and behavioral factors that can influence their quality of life. Patients should be free to discuss their fears and anxieties, be given information about their disease and treatment, and be taught coping strategies and relaxation techniques to lower their arousal.

What behaviors and attitudes help cancer patients lessen psychological distress and improve quality of life? Carver and others (1993) found that 3 months and 6 months after surgery, breast-cancer patients who maintained an optimistic outlook, accepted the reality of their situation, and maintained a sense of humor experienced less distress. Patients who used denial—refusal to accept the reality of their situation—and had thoughts of giving up experienced much higher levels of distress. Dunkel-Schetter and others (1992) found that the most effective elements of a strategy for coping with cancer were social support (such as through self-help groups), a focus on the positive, and distraction. Avoidant coping strategies such as fantasizing, denial, and social withdrawal were associated with more emotional distress.

Is there such a thing as a cancer-prone personality? Some researchers claim that people who suppress or hold in their emotions—those who are *too* calm, passive, or apathetic—and people who have a tendency toward depression are more susceptible to developing cancer (Bahnson, 1981; Renneker, 1981).

Even the leading health risk factors are strongly influenced by cultural differences, as you will discover in the following World of Psychology section.

World of Psychology

Health in the United States

The quality of health and the leading health risk factors are not the same for all Americans. They differ among the various cultural and ethnic groups that make up our nation and according to gender and age as well.

African Americans

As the nation's largest minority group, African Americans make up 12.6 percent of the population and are represented in every socioeconomic group from the poorest to the richest. But their overall poverty rate is about 3 times higher than that of the white population. As a result, many African Americans are at higher risk for disease and death and are more likely to suffer from inadequate health care. Their life expectancy has trailed behind that of the total U.S. population throughout the 20th century. African American infants are at twice the risk of death within their first year of life as white infants.

High blood pressure is twice as common in African Americans as in the general population, and the doubly stressing conditions of poverty and racism could contribute to this (Klag et al., 1991). Among African Americans, the rate of AIDS is more than 3 times higher than among whites, and African American women are from 10 to 15 times more likely than white women to contract AIDS (Public Health Service, 1991).

Hispanic Americans

By 1992 Hispanic Americans, the fastest-growing and second-largest minority group, had increased to about 9.5 percent of the total U.S. population. While many Hispanics are immigrants, over 70 percent are native-born Americans. Most Hispanics, about 63 percent, are Mexican Americans.

Obesity and diabetes are more prevalent among Hispanic Americans than among non-Hispanics, and cigarette smoking and alcohol abuse are more common among Hispanic teenagers than among other teenagers, white or black. Hispanic Americans are at high risk of death from accidental injuries (automobile and others), homicide, cirrhosis and other chronic liver diseases, and AIDS (Public Health Service, 1991).

Most migrant farm workers are Hispanic Americans. Such workers endure back-breaking labor and low wages and have an average life expectancy of only 49 years—far below the national average of 75 years (National Migrant Resource Program and Migrant Clinicians Network, 1990).

Asian Americans

Over 8 million Asian Americans comprise the third-largest minority group in the United States. Some 75 percent of Asian Americans are immigrants, among them many refugees, primarily from Southeast Asia (Laos, Cambodia, Vietnam).

Asian Americans born and well established in the United States resemble the total population in terms of health and are better off financially than most other minorities. In stark contrast, however, are Asian immigrant groups such

continued

as Laotians, whose poverty rate is one of the highest in the nation. They and other Asian immigrant subgroups are far more likely to suffer from certain infectious diseases, such as hepatitis B and especially tuberculosis. In fact, the rate of tuberculosis is 40 times higher in Southeast Asian immigrants than in the total population (Public Health Service, 1991).

Native Americans

Native Americans, the smallest of the defined minority groups, number about 2 million. A large proportion of Native Americans die before the age of 45. This fact partly accounts for their statistically low rates of heart disease and cancer, which are more common among older people.

Obesity is common among many Native American tribes and contributes to the prevalence of diabetes. According to the Indian Health Service (1988), over one-fifth of the members of some tribes suffer from diabetes. Alcohol represents a serious risk factor, since cirrhosis of the liver occurs among Native Americans at 3 times the rate for the total U.S. population. About 95 percent of Native American families are affected in some way by alcohol abuse (Rhoades et al., 1987). And alcohol is a leading factor in Native Americans' homicide rate and suicide rate, which are 60 percent higher and 28 percent higher, respectively, than in the total U.S. population (Indian Health Service, 1988).

The Gender Gap in America's Health Care

Significant health disparities also exist that are related neither to poverty nor to racial or ethnic differences (Holloway, 1994). There is a serious gender gap in health care and medical research in the United States. Most medical research, much of it funded by the U.S. government, rejects women as subjects in favor of men. Women are slighted as well in health care and treatment (Rodin & Ickovics, 1990). Physicians are more likely to see women's health complaints as "emotional" in nature rather than due to physical causes (Council on Ethical and Judicial Affairs, AMA, 1991). The American Medical Association released a major report in 1991 revealing that of men and women who received an abnormal reading on a heart scan, 40 percent of the men but only 4 percent of the women were referred for further testing and possible bypass surgery. Women are less likely than men to receive kidney dialysis and 30 percent less likely to receive a kidney transplant (Council on Ethical and Judicial Affairs, AMA, 1991).

The good news is that efforts to erase the gender and race disparities in medical research and treatment are now underway. The National Institutes of Health have created offices of Research on Women's Health and of Minority Programs. Every application for research funding from the National Institutes of Health must now include women and minorities unless there is a good rationale for not doing so. Studies of hypertension and coronary disease in African Americans have been funded. And a study of 60,000 postmenopausal women is examining the effects of estrogen replacement therapy and nutrition on cardiovascular health and the prevention of breast cancer and osteoporosis (Holloway & Yam, 1992). Such efforts are long overdue.

The Immune System: An Army of Cells to Fight Off Disease

Today most researchers do not question the notion that stress and health are closely related (Kiecolt-Glaser & Glaser, 1992). People who experience stress may indeed be more susceptible to coronary heart disease, stroke, and poorer pregnancy outcomes (Adler & Matthews, 1994). But even more ominous is the growing evidence that stress can impair the functioning of the immune system itself.

The immune system, now known to be one of the most complex systems of the body, protects us from infection and disease. An army of highly specialized cells and organs, the immune system works to identify, remember, and search out and destroy bacteria, viruses, fungi, parasites, and any other foreign matter that may enter the body. Cells of the immune system can distinguish instantly between self and nonself. Virtually every cell in your body carries distinctive molecules that mark it as self (Schindler, 1988). Nonself cells also carry their own distinctive molecules, which mark them as foreign invaders to be attacked and destroyed. This is why organ transplants—foreign, or nonself, tissue to the recipient—are rejected by the immune system unless powerful immune-suppressant drugs are administered.

The key components of the immune system are white blood cells known as **lymphocytes**, which include B cells and T cells. B cells are so named because they are produced in the bone marrow. T cells derive their name from the thymus gland (a spongy organ high behind the breastbone) where they grow to maturity (von Boehmer & Kisielow, 1991). B cells carry on their surface large protein molecules known as antibodies. Each B cell carries only one kind of antibody, which is specific to only one type of invading cell. All cells foreign to the body, such as bacteria, viruses, and so on, are known as antigens. When an antigen enters the body, it will eventually confront a B cell whose antibody has a matching receptor. This encounter will chemically stimulate that B cell to divide and immediately begin mass production of its antibody. And B cells are prolific producers. "One B cell can pump out more than 10 billion antibody molecules an hour" (Nossal, 1993, p. 58). The antibodies produced by B cells are highly effective in destroying antigens that live outside the body's cells, such as in the bloodstream and in the fluid surrounding other body tissues (Paul, 1993). But for defeating harmful foreign invaders that have taken up residence inside the body's cells, T cells are critically important.

One class of T cells assists the B cells, and thus these T cells are known as "helper" cells. These attack and defeat bacteria and other parasites living inside the body's cells, beyond the reach of B cells. The other class of T cells, known as "killer" cells, root out and destroy pathogens, such as viruses, that have more deeply invaded the body's cells (Paul, 1993). The killer T cells are indeed deadly. To kill cells infected by bacteria or viruses, they punch holes in the infected cells and release "chemicals that destroy the entire cell" (Janeway, 1993, p. 78).

Other large lymphocytes in the immune system are known as macrophages ("big eaters"). Found throughout the body, macrophages roam around, gobble up infected cells, and digest them. Particles of the digested invading cells are then "presented" to T cells, which recognize and remember them as antigens. The T cells will then find these antigen-marked cells and kill them on contact.

During wartime, when recognition and communication systems fail, troops may attack and kill their own soldiers—a phenomenon referred to as "friendly fire." Likewise, the immune system may turn on healthy self cells or specific organs and attack them, as happens in autoimmune diseases such as juvenile diabetes, multiple sclerosis, rheumatoid arthritis, and lupus.

The most feared disease related to the immune system is AIDS, which is caused by the human immunodeficiency virus (HIV). The virus attacks the helper T cells, gradually but relentlessly weakening the immune system until it is essentially nonfunctional. See Chapter 11 for a detailed discussion of HIV and AIDS.

Stress and the Immune System   Have you heard of a field of study known as **psychoneuroimmunology**? This nine-syllable word names a field of study in which psychologists, biologists, and medical researchers combine their expertise

lymphocytes: The white blood cells that are key components of the immune system—B cells, T cells, and macrophages.

psychoneuroimmunology (sye-ko-NEW-ro-IM-you-NOLL-oh-gee): A field in which psychologists, biologists, and medical researchers study the effects of psychological factors on the immune system.

What are the effects of stress and depression on the immune system?

to learn the effects of psychological factors (emotions, thinking, and behavior) on the immune system (Maier et al., 1994).

Several studies provide evidence that psychological factors, emotions, and stress are related to immune system functioning (O'Leary, 1990). Moreover, the immune system exchanges information with the brain, and what goes on in the brain can apparently influence the immune system for good or ill.

High periods of stress have been correlated with increased symptoms of many infectious diseases, including oral and genital herpes, mononucleosis, colds, and flu (Jemmott & Locke, 1984). Several studies revealed that subjects exposed to cold viruses were more likely to develop colds if they had experienced a greater number of life changes in the previous year (Cohen et al., 1993; Stone et al., 1992). And stress has caused decreased levels of the immune system's B and T cells (Schindler, 1988). Cohen and Williamson (1991) conclude from a review of studies that stress is associated with an increase in illness behaviors—reporting physical symptoms and seeking medical care.

Poor marital relationships, sleep deprivation, even exams and academic pressures have been linked to lowered immune response (Kiecolt-Glaser et al., 1987; Maier & Laudenslager, 1985). Several researchers have reported that severe, incapacitating depression is also related to lowered immune activity (Irwin et al., 1987; Schleifer et al., 1985). For several months after the death of a spouse, the widow or widower suffers weakened immune system function (Schleifer et al., 1983) and is at a higher risk of mortality (Rogers & Reich, 1988).

McNaughton and others (1990) report that immune suppression in the elderly is associated with depressed mood, severe stress, and dissatisfaction with social supports, whereas improved immune functioning is related to the use of problem-focused coping. Rodin (1986) found that nursing-home residents who were given training in coping skills developed fewer illnesses, suffered less deterioration from chronic conditions, and reported less stress than a similar group not given the training. Moreover, physicians have long observed that stress and anxiety can worsen autoimmune diseases. And "if fear can produce relapses [in autoimmune diseases], then even the fear of a relapse may become a self-fulfilling prophecy" (Steinman, 1993, p. 112).

What three personal factors are associated with health and resistance to stress?

Personal Factors Reducing the Impact of Stress and Illness

Researchers have identified three personal factors that may contribute to better health—optimism, psychological hardiness, and social support.

Optimism and Pessimism People who are generally optimistic tend to cope more effectively with stress, and this in turn may reduce their risk of illness (Horowitz et al., 1988). An important characteristic optimists share is that they generally expect good outcomes. And such positive expectations help to make them more stress-resistant than pessimists, who tend to expect bad outcomes. Optimists are more likely to use problem-focused coping, to seek social support, and to find the positive aspects of a stressful situation (Carver et al., 1993; Scheier & Carver, 1992). Pessimists, on the other hand, are more likely to use denial or to focus on their stressful feelings (Scheier et al., 1986). In a study of college students, Scheier and Carver (1985) found that at the end of the semester, optimistic students reported fewer physical symptoms than those who were pessimistic. And another study, of patients who had undergone coronary bypass surgery, revealed that optimists recovered faster during their hospitalization and were able to resume their normal activities sooner after discharge than pessimists (Scheier et al., 1989). Apparently, happy thoughts are healthy thoughts.

Psychological Hardiness: Commitment, Challenge, and Control

Suzanne Kobasa (1979) wondered why some people under great stress succumb to illness while others do not. She studied 670 male executives, who identified stressful life events and symptoms of illness they had suffered in the preceding 3 years. Kobasa then administered personality questionnaires to the 200 executives who had ranked high on both stress and illness and to the 126 who had equally stressful life events but few symptoms of illness. She found high-stress/low-illness male subjects were more immersed in their work and social lives. They enjoyed challenge and had a greater sense of control over events than their high-stress/high illness counterparts. Two years later Kobasa and others (1982) looked again at the same executives. The high-stress/low-illness group remained healthier and retained their attitudes of commitment, challenge, and control—three characteristics that Kobasa collectively called psychological **hardiness**. And hardy individuals, say Roth and others (1989), "may possess a cognitive style such that troubling life events are interpreted less negatively and thereby rendered less harmful" (p. 141).

Social Support: Help in Time of Need

Another factor contributing to better health is **social support** (Cohen, 1988; Kaplan et al., 1994). It can be thought of as support provided, usually in time of need, by a spouse or other family members or by friends, neighbors, colleagues, support groups, or others. Social support can involve tangible support, information, and advice, as well as emotional support. It can also be viewed as the feeling that we are loved, valued, and cared for by those for whom we feel a mutual obligation (Cobb, 1976).

Social support may help encourage health-promoting behaviors and reduce the impact of stress so that people will be less likely to resort to unhealthy methods of coping, such as smoking or drinking (Adler & Matthews, 1994). Broman (1993) found that people having a good relationship with their spouse were less likely to smoke or drink.

Social support has been shown to reduce the impact of stress from unemployment, long-term illness, retirement, and bereavement (Krantz et al., 1985). People with social support recover more quickly from illnesses and lower their risk of death from specific diseases (House et al., 1988). Social support may even increase the probability of surviving a heart attack, help moderate the effects of high blood pressure, and influence the length of survival for those stricken with cancer (Turner, 1983). In a study of 4,775 people over a 9-year period, Berkman and Syme (1979) found that people low in social support were twice as likely to die as those high in social support.

Recent research on natural disasters reveals that initial social support is common but that the support tends to deteriorate, because the needs of victims overwhelm the tangible and emotional resources of friends and family (Kaniasty & Norris, 1993). Similarly, chronic physical or mental illness may deplete the resources and lead to burnout in those supplying care and social support (Schulz & Tompkins, 1990).

In a study of 821 female twin pairs, Kessler and others (1992) found that both genetic and environmental factors appear to influence social support or the perception of social support. For example, personality factors such as neuroticism and extroversion influence a person's tendency to make friends and to perceive them as being supportive. Environmental factors such as frequency of interaction with others will also affect one's perception of social support.

hardiness: A combination of three psychological qualities shared by people who can undergo high levels of stress yet remain healthy: a sense of control over one's life, commitment to one's personal goals, and a tendency to view change as a challenge rather than as a threat.

social support: Tangible support, information, advice, and/or emotional support provided in time of need by family, friends, and others; the feeling that we are loved, valued, and cared for.

A strong social support network can help a person recover faster from an illness.

Memory Check 13.4

1. Recent research suggests that the most toxic component of the Type A behavior pattern is:
   a. hostility.
   c. a sense of time urgency.
   b. impatience.
   d. perfectionism.

2. Most research has pursued the connection between the Type A behavior pattern and:
   a. cancer.
   c. stroke.
   b. coronary heart disease.
   d. ulcers.

3. Lowered immune response has been associated with:
   a. stress.
   c. stress and depression.
   b. depression.
   d. neither stress nor depression.

4. Some research suggests that optimists are more stress-resistant than pessimists. (true/false)

5. Social support tends to reduce stress but is unrelated to health outcomes. (true/false)

6. Which of the following is *not* a dimension of psychological hardiness?
   a. a feeling that adverse circumstances can be controlled and changed
   b. a sense of commitment and deep involvement in personal goals
   c. a tendency to look upon change as a challenge rather than a threat
   d. close, supportive relationships with family and friends

Answers: 1. a 2. b 3. c 4. true 5. false 6. d

 What constitutes an unhealthy lifestyle, and how serious a factor is lifestyle in illness and disease?

Your Lifestyle and Your Health

For most Americans, health enemy number one consists of their own habits. As Figure 13.4 shows, 53.5 percent of all deaths in the United States are attributable to unhealthy behavior or lifestyle (Powell, 1986). What are these unhealthy behaviors? The culprits are all well known—an unhealthy diet (Willett, 1994), overeating, lack of exercise, alcohol or drug abuse, too little sleep, and so on. But the most dangerous unhealthy behavior of all is smoking.

Why is smoking considered the single most preventable cause of death?

Smoking: Hazardous to Your Health

Today some 46 million Americans smoke—a full 26 percent of the adult population (Sherman, 1994). And every day 3,000 more teenagers become regular smokers (Novello, 1990). The Centers for Disease Control (1991) calls smoking "the single most preventable cause of death in the United States." According to current estimates, smoking is directly related to 434,000 deaths annually in the United States (Raloff, 1994). Countless other millions who must breathe smoke-filled air suffer the ill effects of passive smoking. Add to this statistic the suffering of millions from chronic bronchitis, emphysema, and other respiratory diseases; death and injury from fires caused by smoking; and low birth weight and retarded fetal development in babies born to smoking mothers. The American Cancer Society claims that compared to the death rates of nonsmokers, the death rate increases 60 percent for men smoking less than half a pack of cigarettes a day, 90 percent for those smoking one to two packs a day, and 120 percent for those smoking more than two packs a day. Among women who smoke, lung cancer claims more lives than breast cancer. But the risk of cancer, particularly lung cancer, can be greatly reduced if people quit smoking (Chyou et al., 1992).

The risk of passive smoke is significant. The increased risk for lung cancer in nonsmoking adults who live with smokers averages 24 percent. For nonsmokers exposed at work, the increased risk is 39 percent; and those exposed to smoke for at least 2 hours a week in social settings run a 50 percent greater risk for lung cancer (Fontham et al., 1994).

Most smokers acquire the habit during adolescence, when peer pressure is strong. Adolescents tend to emulate the behavior of others to gain social acceptance (Taylor, 1991). And teens with parents and friends who smoke are at greater risk of taking up smoking themselves.

Now for the good news: The percentage of smokers in the U.S. population is declining. There are now about 45 million ex-smokers, and 80 percent of current smokers claim they want to quit, an indication that a strong nonsmoking sentiment is building (Sherman, 1994). Why do adult smokers continue the habit when the majority admit that they would prefer to be nonsmokers? There seems little doubt that smoking is an addiction, and the U.S. Surgeon General declared in 1988 that tobacco is as addictive as cocaine and heroin. Nicotine is a powerful substance that increases the release of acetylcholine, norepinephrine, dopamine, and other neurotransmitters, which improve mental alertness, sharpen memory, and reduce tension and anxiety (Pomerleau & Pomerleau, 1989). According to Parrott (1993), some people smoke primarily to increase arousal, while others smoke primarily to reduce stress and anxiety. Thus smoking becomes a coping mechanism used to regulate moods.

Because smoking is so addictive, smokers have great difficulty breaking the habit. Even so, 90 percent of ex-smokers quit smoking on their own (Novello, 1990). The average smoker makes five or six attempts to quit before finally succeeding (Sherman, 1994). Some aids, such as nicotine gum and the nicotine patch, help many people kick the habit. A meta-analysis involving 17 studies and over 5,000 people revealed that 22 percent of people who used the nicotine patch were smoke-free compared to only 9 percent of those who received a placebo. And 27 percent of those receiving the nicotine patch plus antismoking counseling or support remained smoke-free (Fiore, cited in Sherman, 1994). But even with the patch, quitting is difficult, because the patch only lessens withdrawal symptoms, which typically last 2 to 4 weeks (Hughes, 1992). Half of all relapses occur within the first 2 weeks after people quit, and relapses are most likely when people are experiencing negative emotions or are using alcohol. It takes just one cigarette, sometimes only one puff, to cause a relapse.

Researchers have found smoking rates to be high in people suffering from alcoholism and schizophrenia (Glassman, 1993a). And recently a link has been found between smoking and a history of major depression, both of which are thought to be influenced by genetic factors (Breslau et al., 1993; Kendler, Neale, MacLean, et al., 1993). When smokers try to quit, withdrawal brings on depression in more than 85 percent of those with a history of depression compared to only 20 percent of those with no such history (Glassman, 1993b). Consequently, depressed smokers are much less likely to be successful at quitting (Hall et al., 1993).

Alcohol: A Problem for Millions

Although smoking is directly related to a greater number of deaths, alcohol undoubtedly causes more misery. The health and social costs of alcohol are staggering—fatalities, medical bills, lost work, family problems. According to Rodin and Salovey (1989), alcohol is one of the three main causes of death in modern societies. Some 18 million Americans have a serious drinking problem (Lord et al., 1987), and about 10 million are alcoholics (Neimark et al., 1994). Alcohol abuse and dependence is 3 times more prevalent in males than in females (Grant et al., 1992). Although a higher percentage of white-collar workers use alcohol, the percentage of problem drinkers is higher among blue-collar workers (Harford et al., 1992). For many, alcohol provides a method of coping with life stress they feel powerless to control (Seeman & Seeman, 1992).

Alcohol can damage virtually every organ in the body, but it is especially harmful to the liver and is the major cause of cirrhosis, which kills 26,000 people

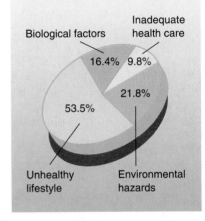

FIGURE 13.4

Factors Contributing to Death before Age 65

The number one factor leading to premature death in the United States is unhealthy lifestyle. Fortunately our own lifestyle is more completely under our control than are any of the other factors contributing to premature death. (Based on Powell et al., 1986.)

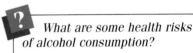

What are some health risks of alcohol consumption?

each year (Neimark et al., 1994). Alcohol can also cause stomach problems—indigestion, nausea, diarrhea, and ulcers. One-half of long-term, heavy drinkers suffer damage to their skeletal muscles, and one-third sustain damage to their heart muscle (Urbano-Marquez et al., 1989). Alcohol increases the risk of many cancers, including cancer of the liver, mouth, throat, tongue, and voice box. Pregnant women should avoid all alcohol because of its potentially disastrous effects on the developing fetus. (See Chapter 8 for a discussion of fetal alcohol syndrome.)

Shrinkage in the cerebral cortex of alcoholics has been found by researchers using magnetic resonance imaging (Jernigan et al., 1991). CT scans also show brain shrinkage in a high percentage of alcoholics, even in young subjects and in those who appear to be intact mentally (Lishman, 1990). Moreover, heavy drinking can cause cognitive impairment (Goldman, 1983) and seizures (Ng et al., 1988). The only good news in recent studies is that some of the effects of alcohol on the brain seem to be partially reversible with prolonged abstinence.

Alcoholism's toll goes beyond the physical damage to the alcoholic. Drunk drivers cause 50 percent of the motor vehicle accidents in the United States (Koshland, 1989), killing 50,000 yearly (Mayer, 1983) and injuring 75,000 more (Nathan, 1983). Alcohol has been implicated in 70 percent of drownings in the United States, in 30 percent of the suicides, and in almost one-third of the rapes, burglaries, and assaults (Desmond, 1987).

Alcoholism: Causes and Treatment The American Medical Association maintains that alcoholism is a disease, and once an alcoholic, always an alcoholic. According to this view, even a small amount of alcohol is believed to cause an irresistible craving for more, leading alcoholics to lose control of their drinking (Jellinek, 1960). Thus, total abstinence is seen as the only acceptable method of treatment. The medical establishment and Alcoholics Anonymous endorse both the disease concept and the total abstinence approach to treatment.

Some studies suggest a genetic factor in alcoholism and lend support to the disease model. According to Goodwin (1985), about one-half of hospitalized alcoholics have a family history of alcohol abuse. Adoption studies have revealed that "sons of alcoholics were three or four times more likely to be alcoholic than were sons of nonalcoholics, whether raised by their alcoholic biologic parents or by nonalcoholic adoptive parents" (Goodwin, 1985, p. 172).

A large study by McGue and others (1992) involving 356 pairs of identical and fraternal twins revealed a substantial genetic influence for males when the first symptoms of alcoholism appear before age 20. And a study of 1,000 pairs of female identical and fraternal twins by Kendler, Neale, and others (1994) found that alcoholism in women is 50 to 60 percent heritable, a rate similar to that for male alcoholics.

Is alcoholism a disease? Some experts reject the disease concept and contend that alcoholism can take various forms and have various causes (Pattison, 1982). Even in people who are genetically predisposed, researchers caution against overlooking the environmental contribution to alcoholism (Searles, 1988). Family and cultural influences are apparently the dominant factors in men whose drinking problems appear after adolescence.

Some experts stress the role of behavioral, social, and cultural factors in alcoholism and advocate various approaches to treatment. One approach—cue exposure—systematically exposes the problem drinker to cues that have stimulated a craving for alcohol and triggered drinking in the past (Neimark et al., 1994). The person is prevented from drinking in the presence of those cues and gradually becomes less responsive to them.

In another new approach—network therapy—the therapist meets with the alcoholic and a small group of friends and family members at regular intervals (Galanter, 1993). The group focuses on helping the alcoholic face the distorted perceptions and manipulative behaviors that have enabled him or her to deny the drinking problem. The group learns to provide the necessary support to help the drinker develop a drug-free life. It also can present a united front, showing disapproval of the behaviors that lead to relapse.

With behavior therapy, some (not all) problem drinkers can learn the skills necessary to drink socially without losing control (Peele, 1992; Sobell & Sobell, 1978). Advocates of this treatment—**controlled drinking**—generally suggest that it is most successful with younger drinkers who have less serious drinking problems and who are not yet physically dependent on alcohol (Marlatt, 1983; Polich et al., 1981).

Whatever treatment approach is used, social support is essential. It can be provided by friends, family members, therapists, or self-help groups. Alcoholics who have such support are often able to quit on their own, without any formal treatment. The key seems to be to develop the motivation to quit drinking and then to quit with the encouragement and support of others. Abstinence is the surest, solution to alcoholism—the country's foremost drug problem (Nathan, 1992).

Exercise: Keeping Fit Is Healthy

For years medical experts, especially health psychologists, have promoted regular exercise. Yet "only 15 percent of the general population is highly active, and as much as 70 percent of the entire population can be characterized as inactive" (Rodin & Salovey, 1989, p. 554). Many studies show that regular **aerobic exercise** pays rich dividends in the form of physical and mental fitness. Aerobic exercise (such as running, swimming, brisk walking, bicycling, rowing, and jumping rope) is exercise that uses the large muscle groups in continuous, repetitive action and requires increased oxygen intake and increased breathing and heart rates. To improve cardiovascular fitness and endurance and to lessen the risk of heart attack, aerobic exercise should be performed regularly. This means 3 or 4 times a week for 20 to 30 minutes, with additional 5- to 10-minute warm-up and cool-down periods (Alpert et al., 1990; Shepard, 1986). Less than 20 minutes of aerobic exercise 3 times a week has "no measurable effect on the heart," and more than 3 hours per week "is not known to reduce cardiovascular risk any further" (Simon, 1988, p. 3).

Regular aerobic exercise is beneficial for people of all ages. Even preschoolers have been shown to receive cardiovascular benefits from planned exercise (Alpert et al., 1990). At the other end of the age spectrum, regular, planned exercise yields dramatic increases in muscle and bone strength in older people. Exercisers between the ages of 87 and 96 who were on a weight-lifting program for only 2 months showed the same absolute gains in rate of muscular strength as younger people (Allison, 1991). Strenuous workouts would not transform a George Burns into an Arnold Schwarzenegger, but significant increases in muscle strength have been recorded even in people pushing 100.

A large study on the health benefits of physical fitness is compelling enough to convince couch potatoes of all ages to get up and get moving. Steven Blair and colleagues (1989) studied 13,344 men and women of different age groups, 20 years and older. The subjects were tested for physical fitness and then assigned to one of five physical fitness levels based on age, sex, and performance on a treadmill test. Follow-up continued for a little more than 8 years, and during that time 283 subjects (240 men and 43 women) died. And the number of deaths from all causes for both men and women was significantly related to their fitness level.

But there is some encouraging news from this large study. We do not need to become marathon runners or spend several hours a day sweating and grunting in a fitness center in order to enjoy the maximum benefits of health and longevity. Even a daily brisk walk of 30 minutes or more helps to reduce stress and yields the fitness standard associated with a much lower death rate.

According to Brown (1991), "People who are physically fit are less vulnerable to the adverse effects of life stress than are those who are less fit" (p. 560). In

controlled drinking: A behavioral approach to the treatment of alcoholism, designed to teach the skills necessary so that alcoholics can drink socially without losing control.

aerobic exercise (ah-RO-bik): Exercise that uses the large muscle groups in continuous, repetitive action and requires increased oxygen intake and increased breathing and heart rates.

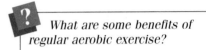

What are some benefits of regular aerobic exercise?

Regular exercise is essential for good health.

a study of 137 stressed male business executives, Kobasa and her colleagues (1982) found that those who exercised had lower rates of illness. The more stress the men suffered, the more important exercise was in the prevention of illness.

In case you are not yet convinced, consider the following benefits. Exercise:

- Increases the efficiency of the heart, enabling it to pump more blood with each beat; reduces the resting pulse rate and improves circulation.
- Raises HDL (the good blood cholesterol) levels, which (1) helps rid the body of LDL (the bad blood cholesterol) and (2) removes plaque buildup on artery walls.
- Burns up extra calories, enabling you to lose weight or maintain your weight.
- Makes bones denser and stronger, helping to prevent osteoporosis in women.
- Moderates the effects of stress.
- Gives you more energy and increases your resistance to fatigue.
- Benefits the immune system by increasing natural killer cell activity (Fiatarone et al., 1988).

Memory Check 13.5

1. Which is the most important factor leading to disease and death?
   a. unhealthy lifestyle
   b. a poor health care system
   c. environmental hazards
   d. genetic disorders
2. Which health-compromising behavior is responsible for the most deaths?
   a. overeating
   b. smoking
   c. lack of exercise
   d. excessive alcohol use

3. (Alcohol, Smoking) damages virtually every organ in the body.

4. To improve cardiovascular fitness, aerobic exercise should be done:
   a. 15 minutes daily.
   b. 1 hour daily.
   c. 20 to 30 minutes daily.
   d. 0 to 30 minutes 3 or 4 times a week

Answers: 1. a 2. b 3. Alcohol 4. d

APPLICATIONS • APPLICATIONS • APPLICATIONS

Managing Stress

Anyone who is alive is subject to stress, but some of us are more negatively affected by it than others.

If stress leaves you fretting and fuming with your muscles in knots, try a few relaxation techniques that might spell relief.

Progressive Relaxation

The fight-or-flight response is our body's way of preparing us to deal with a threat, but if we can neither fight nor flee, we are left with intense physiological arousal, or stress.

There are several relaxation techniques that you can use to calm yourself and relieve muscular tension. Probably the most widely used relaxation technique in the United States is *progressive relaxation* (Rice, 1987). It consists of flexing and then relaxing the different muscle groups throughout the body from the head to the toes. Here's how to do it:

1. Loosen or remove any tight-fitting clothing, take off your shoes, and situate yourself comfortably in an armchair with your arms resting on the chair's arms. Sit straight in the chair, but let your head fall forward so that your chin rests

comfortably on your chest. Place your feet flat on the floor with your legs slightly apart in a comfortable position.

2. Take a deep breath. Hold it for a few seconds, and then exhale slowly and completely. Repeat several times. Notice the tension in your chest as you hold the breath, and the relaxation as you let the breath out.

3. Flex the muscles in your right upper arm (in your left arm if you are left-handed). Hold the muscles as tight as you can for about 10 seconds. Observe the feeling of tension. Now relax the muscles

completely and observe the feeling of relaxation. Repeat the flexing and the relaxing several times. Then do the same with the other arm.

4. After completing the opening routine with your arms, use the same procedure, tensing and then relaxing a group of muscles, starting with the muscles in the forehead. Progressively work your way down through all the muscle groups in the body, ending with your feet.

Another excellent relaxation technique is Herbert Benson's relaxation response, described in Chapter 4 (on page 144).

Managing Mental Stress

Many of us stress ourselves almost to the breaking point by our own thinking. When we become angry, hostile, fearful, worried, and upset by things we think are going to happen, we cause our hearts to pound and our stomachs to churn. How often have you done this to yourself only to find that what you had imagined never actually materialized? The next time you begin to react to something you *think* will happen, stop yourself. Remember all the times you have become upset about things that never came to pass. Learn to use your own thinking to reduce stress, not create it. Give your body a break!

Stress-Inoculation Training. *Stress-inoculation training*, a program that was designed by Donald Meichenbaum (1977), helps people cope with stressors that are troubling them. Test anxiety, stress over personal and social relationships, and some types of per-

formance anxiety have been successfully treated with stress inoculation. Individuals are taught to recognize their own negative thoughts ("I'll never be able to do this" or "I'll probably make a fool of myself"), and to replace negative thoughts with positive ones. They learn how to talk to themselves using positive coping statements to dispel worry and provide self-encouragement. Here are some examples of these coping statements (adapted from Meichenbaum, 1975):

Preparing for the Stressor

"I can come up with a plan to handle the problem."

"I refuse to worry about it. Worry doesn't help anything."

Facing or Confronting the Stressor

"If I take one step at a time, I know I can handle this situation."

"I will take a few slow, deep breaths and relax."

Coping with the Stressor

"If I feel fear, I will simply pause."

"I will keep my mind focused on the present, on what is happening now, and just concentrate on what I have to do."

When the Coping Attempt Is Finished

"This was easier than I thought it would be."

"I am really making progress."

Taking a Breather. To counteract the shallow, rapid breathing that occurs when you are stressed, you need to take deep, abdominal breaths. To learn how, place one hand on your chest and the other on your abdomen. Practice inhaling in such a way that your abdomen, not your chest, rises. Once you are able to accomplish this, you are ready to learn how to "take a breather" to counteract stress.

1. Slowly exhale through your mouth to remove the stale air from your lungs. Repeat until your lungs feel empty.

2. Inhale through your nose until your abdomen (not your lungs)

begins to rise, hold for 5 seconds, and then exhale.

3. Repeat four or five times whenever you feel tense and irritable.

Working Off Stress. Often when you are stressed, your body is reacting with the fight-or-flight response in a situation where you can neither fight nor flee. What can you do? Blow off steam physically by exercising or engaging in physical work (raking leaves, gardening, or cleaning the house). Physical activity provides a "flight" outlet for your mental stress.

Turning Pain into Laughter. You may have been told after you have had a major hassle or mishap that some day you would look back and laugh about it. And it is true that much of what we laugh about has an element of pain. Kathleen Passanisi suggests that "humor is pain removed from pain," and that a key to our well-being is to shorten the time between experiencing the pain and being able to laugh at it (quoted in M. Harris, 1993, p. 1C).

Other Stress-Reducing Measures

Here are some additional suggestions for reducing the negative effects of stress.

- Engage in regular exercise.
- Eat a balanced diet and get enough sleep.
- Use caffeine in moderation.
- Make time for relaxation and activities you enjoy.
- Rely on social support to moderate the effects of stress.
- Don't expect perfection from yourself or from other people.
- If you suffer from "hurry sickness," slow down.
- Learn patience.
- Don't respond to stress with behaviors that will increase stress in the long run, such as overeating, drinking, or using drugs.

Thinking Critically

Evaluation

In your view, which is more effective for evaluating stress—the Social Readjustment Rating Scale or the Hassle Scale? Explain the advantages and disadvantages of each.

Point/Counterpoint

Prepare two arguments—one supporting the position that alcoholism is a genetically inherited disease, and the other supporting the position that alcoholism is not a medical disease but results from learning.

Psychology in Your Life

Choose several stress-producing incidents from your own life and explain what problem-focused and emotion-focused coping strategies you used. From the knowledge you have gained in this chapter, list other coping strategies that might have been more effective.

Chapter Summary and Review

Two Approaches to Health and Illness

How do the biomedical and biopsychosocial models differ in their approaches to health and illness?

The biomedical model focuses on illness rather than on health and explains illness in terms of biological factors. The biopsychosocial model focuses on health as well as on illness and holds that both are determined by a combination of biological, psychological, and social factors.

Key Terms

biomedical model (p. 478)
biopsychosocial model (p. 478)
health psychology (p. 478)

Theories of Stress

What is the general adaptation syndrome?

The general adaptation syndrome is the predictable sequence of reactions that organisms show in response to stressors. It consists of the alarm stage, the resistance stage, and the exhaustion stage.

What are the roles of primary and secondary appraisal when people are confronted with a potentially stressful event?

Lazarus maintains that when we are confronted with a potentially stressful event, we engage in a cognitive appraisal process consisting of (1) a primary appraisal, to evaluate the relevance of the event to our well-being (whether it will be positive; will be irrelevant; or will involve harm or loss, threat, or challenge); and (2) a secondary appraisal to determine how we will cope with the stressor.

Key Terms

stress (p. 479)
stressor (p. 481)
general adaptation syndrome (GAS) (p. 481)
alarm stage (p. 481)
resistance stage (p. 481)
exhaustion stage (p. 481)
primary appraisal (p. 482)
secondary appraisal (p. 483)

Sources of Stress: The Common and the Extreme

How do approach–approach, avoidance–avoidance, and approach–avoidance conflicts differ?

In an approach–approach conflict, we must decide between equally desirable alternatives; in an avoidance–avoidance conflict, between two undesirable alternatives. In an approach–avoidance conflict, we are both drawn to and repelled by a choice.

How do the unpredictability of and lack of control over a stressor affect its impact?

Stressors that are unpredictable and uncontrollable are more stressful than those that are predictable and controllable.

How do people typically react to catastrophic events?

Victims of catastrophic events are initially dazed and stunned. When they begin to recover from the shock, they typically experience anxiety, nightmares, and a compulsive need to recount the event over and over.

What is posttraumatic stress disorder?

Posttraumatic stress disorder (PTSD) is a prolonged, severe stress reaction to a catastrophic event.

Key Terms

approach–approach conflict (p. 484)
avoidance–avoidance conflict (p. 484)
approach–avoidance conflict (p. 484)
posttraumatic stress disorder (PTSD)
(p. 485)

Coping with Stress

What is the difference between problem-focused and emotion-focused coping?

Problem-focused coping is a response aimed at reducing, modifying, or eliminating the source of stress; emotion-focused coping is aimed at reducing the emotional impact of the stressor.

Key Terms

coping (p. 486)
problem-focused coping (p. 486)
emotion-focused coping (p. 486)

Evaluating Life Stress: Major Life Changes, Hassles, and Uplifts

What was the Social Readjustment Rating Scale designed to reveal?

The SRRS assesses stress in terms of life events that necessitate life change. Holmes and Rahe found a relationship between degree of life stress (as measured on the scale) and major health problems.

What roles do hassles and uplifts play in the stress of life, according to Lazarus?

According to Lazarus, daily hassles typically cause more stress than major life changes. The positive experiences in life—the uplifts—can neutralize the effects of many of the hassles.

Key Terms

Social Readjustment Rating Scale
(SRRS) (p. 488)

hassles (p. 488)
uplifts (p. 490)

Health and Disease

What are the Type A and Type B behavior patterns?

The Type A behavior pattern, often cited as a risk factor for coronary heart disease, is characterized by a sense of time urgency, impatience, excessive competitive drive, hostility, and easily aroused anger. The Type B behavior pattern is characterized by a relaxed, easygoing approach to life.

What aspect of the Type A behavior pattern is most clearly linked to coronary heart disease?

Hostility is the aspect of the Type A pattern most clearly linked to coronary heart disease.

What are the effects of stress and depression on the immune system?

Both stress and depression have been associated with lowered immune response, and stress has been linked with increased symptoms of various infectious diseases.

What three personal factors are associated with health and resistance to stress?

Personal factors related to health and resistance to stress are optimism, psychological hardiness, and social support.

Key Terms

sedentary lifestyle (p. 492)
Type A behavior pattern (p. 492)
Type B behavior pattern (p. 492)
lymphocytes (p. 497)
psychoneuroimmunology (p. 497)

hardiness (p. 499)
social support (p. 499)

Your Lifestyle and Your Health

What constitutes an unhealthy lifestyle, and how serious a factor is lifestyle in illness and disease?

Slightly over 50 percent of all deaths in this country can be attributed to unhealthy lifestyle factors, which include smoking, overeating, an unhealthy diet, too much coffee or alcohol, drug abuse, and/or too little exercise and rest.

Why is smoking considered the single most preventable cause of death?

Smoking is considered the single most preventable cause of death because it is directly related to 434,000 deaths each year, including deaths from heart disease, cancer, lung disease, and stroke.

What are some health risks of alcohol consumption?

Alcohol damages virtually every organ in the body, including the liver, stomach, skeletal muscles, heart, and brain; and it is involved in over 50 percent of motor vehicle accidents.

What are some benefits of regular aerobic exercise?

Regular aerobic exercise reduces the risk of cardiovascular disease, increases muscular strength, moderates the effects of stress, makes bones denser and stronger, and helps one maintain a desirable weight.

Key Terms

controlled drinking (p. 503)
aerobic exercise (p. 503)

14

PSYCHOLOGICAL DISORDERS

CHAPTER OUTLINE

What Is Abnormal?

Perspectives on the Causes and Treatment of Psychological Disorders

Defining and Classifying Psychological Disorders

Anxiety Disorders: When Anxiety Is Extreme

Generalized Anxiety Disorder

Panic Disorder

Phobias: Persistent, Irrational Fears

Obsessive Compulsive Disorder

Somatoform and Dissociative Disorders

Somatoform Disorders: Physical Symptoms with Psychological Causes

Dissociative Disorders: Mental Escapes

Schizophrenia

The Symptoms of Schizophrenia: Many and Varied

Types of Schizophrenia

The Causes of Schizophrenia

Mood Disorders

Depressive Disorders and Bipolar Disorder: Emotional Highs and Lows

Causes of Major Depressive Disorder and Bipolar Disorder

World of Psychology: Suicide and Gender, Race, and Age

Other Psychological Disorders

Personality Disorders: Troublesome Behavior Patterns

Sexual and Gender Identity Disorders

Applications: Depression—Bad Thoughts, Bad Feelings

Thinking Critically

Chapter Summary and Review

509

It was early in January, and Sybil Dorsett was working with other students in the chemistry lab at Columbia University in New York. Suddenly the loud crash of breaking glass made her heart pound and her head throb. The room seemed to be whirling around, and the acrid smell of chemicals filled the air, stinging her nostrils.

That smell—so like the old drugstore back in her native Wisconsin—and the broken glass—like a half-forgotten, far-off memory at home in her dining room when she was a little girl. Again Sybil heard the accusing voice, "You broke it." Frantically she seized her chemistry notes, stuffed them into her brown zipper folder, and ran for the door with all eyes—those of the professor and the other students—following her in astonishment.

Sybil ran down the long, dark hall on the third floor of the chemistry building, pushed the elevator button, and waited. Seconds seemed like hours.

The next thought that entered Sybil's awareness was that of clutching for her brown folder, but it was gone. Gone, too, were the elevator she was waiting for and the long, dark hallway. She found herself walking down a dark, deserted street in a strange city. An icy wind whipped her face, and thick snowflakes filled the air. This wasn't New York. Where could she be? And how could she have gotten here in the

few seconds between waiting for the elevator and now? Sybil walked on, bewildered, and finally came to a news-stand, where she bought a local paper. She was in Philadelphia. The date on the newspaper told her that five days had passed since she stood waiting for the eleva-tor. Where had she been? What had she done?

A victim of sadistic physical abuse since early childhood, Sybil had experienced blackouts—missing days, weeks, and even longer periods, which seemed to have been taken from her life. Unknown to Sybil, other, very different personali-ties emerged during those periods to take control of her mind and body. Sixteen separate selves, 14 female and 2 male, lived within Sybil, each with different talents and abil-ities, emotions, ways of speaking and acting, moral values, and ambitions.

After many years of working with a talented psychiatrist, Sybil's 16 personalities were integrated into one. At last she was herself alone. (Adapted from Schreiber, 1973.)

What you have just read is not fiction. These and even stranger experiences are part of the real-life story of Sybil Isabel Dorsett, who suffered from an unusual phenomenon, dissociative identity disorder, better known as multiple personal-ity. Her life story, told in the book *Sybil*, and the life story of Chris Sizemore, told in *The Three Faces of Eve*, are two of the best-known cases of this disorder.

How can we know whether *our* behavior is normal or abnormal? At what point do our fears, thoughts, mood changes, and actions move from normal to mentally disturbed? This chapter explores many psychological disorders, their symptoms, and their possible causes. But first let us ask the obvious question: What is abnormal?

> *What criteria might be used to differentiate normal from abnormal behavior?*

What Is Abnormal?

Virtually everyone would agree that Sybil's behavior is abnormal. But most abnor-mal behavior is not so extreme and clear-cut. There are not two clearly distinct kinds of human beings—one kind always mentally healthy and well adjusted, and another kind always abnormal and disturbed. Behavior lies along a continuum, with most of us fairly well adjusted and experiencing only occasional maladap-tive thoughts or behavior. At one end of the continuum are the unusually men-tally healthy; at the other end are the seriously disturbed, like Sybil.

But where along the continuum does behavior become abnormal? There are several questions we might ask in determining what behavior is abnormal.

- *Is the behavior considered strange within the person's own culture?* What is considered normal and abnormal in one culture will not necessarily be considered so in another.

510

The culture generally defines what behaviors are acceptable. But even within the same culture, conceptions about what is normal can change from time to time.

- *Does the behavior cause personal distress?* When people experience considerable emotional distress without any life experience that warrants it, they may be diagnosed as having a psychological or mental disorder. Some people may be sad and depressed, some anxious; others may be agitated or excited, and still others frightened, or even terrified by delusions and hallucinations. But not all persons with psychological disorders feel distress. Some are perfectly comfortable, even happy with the way they are and the way they feel.

- *Is the behavior maladaptive?* Some experts believe that the best way to differentiate between normal and abnormal behavior is to consider whether the behavior is adaptive or maladaptive, that is, whether it leads to healthy or impaired functioning. Maladaptive behavior interferes with the quality of people's lives and can cause a great deal of distress to family members, friends, and co-workers.

Abnormal behavior is defined by each culture. For example, homelessness is considered abnormal in some cultures and completely normal in others.

- *Is the person a danger to self or others?* Another consideration is whether people are a danger to themselves or others. To be committed to a mental hospital, a person must be judged both mentally ill and a danger to self or others.

- *Is the person legally responsible for his or her acts?* Often the term *insanity* is used to label those who behave abnormally, but mental health professionals do not use this term. It is a legal term used by the courts to declare people not legally responsible for their acts. Mass murderer Jeffrey Dahmer was ruled legally responsible for his acts, yet his behavior was clearly abnormal.

Perspectives on the Causes and Treatment of Psychological Disorders

Several different perspectives on psychological disorders attempt to explain their causes and to recommend the best methods of treatment. The earliest explanation of psychological disorders was that disturbed people were possessed by evil spirits or demons. The five current perspectives are the biological, psychodynamic, learning, cognitive, and humanistic perspectives.

What are five current perspectives that attempt to explain the causes of psychological disorders?

The Biological Perspective   The biological perspective views abnormal behavior as a symptom of an underlying physical disorder. Just as doctors look for an organic cause of physical illness, those who hold the biological view believe that psychological disorders have a physical cause, such as genetic inheritance, biochemical abnormalities or imbalances, structural abnormalities within the brain, and/or infection. Consequently, those holding the biological view generally favor biological treatments, which may include drugs, electroconvulsive therapy (shock treatment), or psychosurgery.

There are two points to keep in mind as you read this chapter. First, even when there is strong evidence of a genetic factor in a psychological disorder, people do not inherit the disorder directly. They inherit a predisposition toward the disorder. Whether they actually develop the disorder will depend on other conditions in their lives. Second, when certain structural or biochemical abnormalities are associated with a psychological disorder, there is the possibility that such abnormalities could be the result rather than the cause of the disorder.

The Psychodynamic Perspective   Where does the psychodynamic perspective look for the cause of psychological disorders? Originally proposed by Freud, the psychodynamic perspective maintains that psychological disorders stem from early childhood experiences and unresolved, unconscious conflicts, usually of a sexual or aggressive nature. The cause assumed by the psychodynamic approach also suggests the cure—psychoanalysis—which Freud developed to uncover and resolve such unconscious conflicts.

The Learning Perspective   According to the learning perspective, psychological disorders are not symptoms of an underlying disorder; the behavioral symptoms are themselves the disorder. Get rid of the symptoms (the abnormal behavior), and the problem is solved. Many abnormal behaviors are thought to be learned and sustained in the same way as any other behavior. According to this view, people who exhibit abnormal behavior either are victims of faulty learning or have failed to learn appropriate patterns of thinking and acting. Behavior therapists use learning principles to eliminate distressing behavior and to establish new, more appropriate behavior in its place.

The Cognitive Perspective   The cognitive perspective suggests that faulty thinking or distorted perceptions can contribute to some types of psychological disorders. For example, negative thinking is intimately involved in depression and anxiety. Treatment consistent with this perspective is aimed at changing thinking and perceptions, which presumably will lead to a change in behavior.

The Humanistic Perspective   The humanistic perspective views human nature as inherently good and rational and as naturally moving toward self-actualization (the fulfillment of each person's potential). According to this view, psychological disorders result when a person's natural tendency toward self-actualization is blocked (Maslow, 1970; Rogers, 1961). Remove the psychological blocks, and the person can move toward self-actualization.

Review and Reflect Table 14.1 summarizes the perspectives on psychological disorders. Which of these perspectives is correct? There are many psychological disorders with a variety of causes, and none of these theories has tried to explain them all. Each view suggests an emphasis on different methods of treatment, all of which have been shown to work in some cases with some disorders. In fact, many of these methods are combined in practice. Each perspective has its place in the description, analysis, and treatment of certain psychological disorders.

Although mental health professionals often disagree about the causes of abnormal behavior and the best treatments, there is less disagreement about diagnosis. A standard set of criteria has been established and is used by the majority of mental health professionals to diagnose psychological disorders.

Review and Reflect 14.1 *Perspectives on Psychological Disorders*

Perspective	Cause of Psychological Disorders	Treatment
Biological perspective	A psychological disorder is a symptom of an underlying physical disorder caused by a structural or biochemical abnormality in the brain, by genetic inheritance, or by infection.	Diagnose and treat like any other physical disorder. Drugs, electroconvulsive therapy, or psychosurgery
Psychodynamic perspective	Psychological disorders stem from early childhood experiences; unconscious sexual or aggressive conflicts; imbalance among id, ego, and superego.	Bring disturbing repressed material to consciousness and help patient work through unconscious conflicts. Psychoanalysis
Learning perspective	Abnormal thoughts, feelings, and behaviors are learned and sustained like any other behaviors; or there is a failure to learn appropriate behaviors.	Use classical and operant conditioning and modeling to extinguish abnormal behaviors and to increase adaptive behavior. Behavior therapy, behavior modification
Cognitive perspective	Faulty and negative thinking can cause psychological disorders.	Change faulty, irrational, and/or negative thinking. Beck's cognitive therapy, rational-emotive therapy
Humanistic perspective	Psychological disorders result from blocking of normal tendency toward self-actualization.	Increase self-acceptance and self-understanding; help patient become more inner-directed. Client-centered therapy, Gestalt therapy

Defining and Classifying Psychological Disorders

 What is the DSM-IV?

In 1952 the American Psychiatric Association published a manual providing a diagnostic system for describing and classifying psychological disorders. Over the years the manual has been revised several times. In 1994 the most recent edition appeared—the *Diagnostic and Statistical Manual of Mental Disorders (Fourth Edition)*, commonly known as the **DSM-IV**. It contains descriptions of about 290 specific psychological disorders and lists criteria that must be met in order to make a particular diagnosis. The *DSM-IV*, the most widely accepted diagnostic system in the United States, is used by researchers, therapists, mental health workers, and most insurance companies. It enables professionals to speak the same language when diagnosing, treating, researching, and conversing about a variety of psychological disorders. Review and Reflect Table 14.2 (on page 514) summarizes the major categories of disorders in the *DSM-IV*.

You have heard the terms *neurotic* and *psychotic* used in relation to mental disturbances. Before 1980 the American Psychiatric Association grouped psychological disorders into two broad, general categories labeled neuroses and psychoses (plurals of neurosis and psychosis). Although now obsolete, the term **neurosis** was applied to disorders that cause people considerable personal distress and some

DSM-IV: The *Diagnostic and Statistical Manual of Mental Disorders (Fourth Edition)*, a manual published by the American Psychiatric Association, which describes about 290 mental disorders and their symptoms.

neurosis (new-RO-sis): An obsolete term for a disorder causing personal distress and some impairment in functioning but not causing loss of contact with reality or violation of important social norms.

Review and Reflect 14.2   _Major DSM-IV Categories of Mental Disorders_

Disorder	Symptoms	Examples
Anxiety disorders	Disorders characterized by anxiety and avoidance behavior.	Panic disorder Social phobia Obsessive compulsive disorder Posttraumatic stress disorder
Somatoform disorders	Disorders in which physical symptoms are present that are psychological in origin rather than due to a medical condition.	Hypochondriasis Conversion disorder
Dissociative disorders	Disorders in which one handles stress or conflict by forgetting important personal information or one's whole identity, or by compartmentalizing the trauma or conflict into a split-off alter personality.	Dissociative amnesia Dissociative fugue Dissociative identity disorder
Schizophrenia and other psychotic disorders	Disorders characterized by the presence of psychotic symptoms including hallucinations, delusions, disorganized speech, bizarre behavior, or loss of contact with reality.	Schizophrenia, disorganized type Schizophrenia, paranoid type Schizophrenia, catatonic type Delusional disorder, jealous type
Mood disorders	Disorders characterized by periods of extreme or prolonged depression or mania or both.	Major depressive disorder Bipolar disorder
Personality disorders	Disorders characterized by long-standing, inflexible, maladaptive patterns of behavior beginning early in life and causing personal distress or problems in social and occupational functioning.	Antisocial personality disorder Histrionic personality disorder Narcissistic personality disorder Borderline personality disorder
Substance-related disorders	Disorders in which undesirable behavioral changes result from substance abuse, dependence, or intoxication.	Alcohol abuse Cocaine abuse Cannabis dependence
Disorders usually first diagnosed in infancy, childhood, or adolescence	Disorders that include mental retardation, learning disorders, communication disorders, pervasive developmental disorders, attention-deficit and disruptive behavior disorders, tic disorders, and elimination disorders.	Conduct disorder Autistic disorder Tourette's disorder Stuttering
Eating disorders	Disorders characterized by severe disturbances in eating behavior.	Anorexia nervosa Bulimia nervosa

Source: Based on _DSM-IV_ (American Psychiatric Association, 1994).

psychosis (sy-CO-sis): A severe psychological disorder, marked by loss of contact with reality and a seriously impaired ability to function.

impairment in functioning, without causing them to lose contact with reality or to violate important social norms. In contrast, a **psychosis** is a more serious disturbance that greatly impairs the ability to function in everyday life. It can cause people to lose touch with reality, possibly suffer from delusions and/or hallucinations, and sometimes require hospitalization. The term _psychosis_ is still used by mental health professionals.

Memory Check 14.1

1. It is relatively easy to differentiate normal behavior from abnormal behavior. (true/false)

2. The *DSM-IV* is a manual published by the American Psychiatric Association that is used to:
   a. diagnose psychological disorders.
   b. explain the causes of psychological disorders.
   c. outline treatments for various psychological disorders.
   d. assess the effectiveness of treatment programs.

3. Match the perspective with its suggested cause of abnormal behavior.
   ____ 1) faulty learning
   ____ 2) unconscious, unresolved conflicts
   ____ 3) blocking of the natural tendency toward self-actualization
   ____ 4) genetic inheritance or biochemical or structural abnormalities in the brain
   ____ 5) faulty thinking

   a. psychodynamic
   b. biological
   c. learning
   d. humanistic
   e. cognitive

Answers: 1. false 2. a 3. 1) c 2) a 3) d 4) b 5) e

Anxiety Disorders: When Anxiety Is Extreme

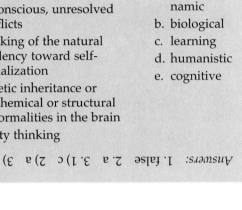

When is anxiety normal, and when is it abnormal?

The most commonly occurring psychological disorders (other than substance abuse disorders) are the **anxiety disorders**. **Anxiety** is a vague, general uneasiness or feeling that something bad is about to happen. It may be associated with a particular situation or object, or may be free-floating—not associated with anything specific. None of us is a stranger to anxiety. We have all felt it.

Some anxiety is normal and appropriate. Imagine driving on a highway late at night and noticing that your gas tank is on empty. The anxiety you would feel in this situation is normal anxiety—a response to a real danger or threat. Normal anxiety would prompt you to take useful action—to look for a gas station. But anxiety serves no useful purpose and is abnormal if it is all out of proportion to the seriousness of the situation, if it does not soon fade once the danger is past, or if it occurs in the absence of real danger (Goodwin, 1986).

Psychological disorders characterized by severe anxiety are generalized anxiety disorder, panic disorder, phobias, and obsessive compulsive disorder.

Generalized Anxiety Disorder

How many people do you know who are chronic worriers? **Generalized anxiety disorder** is the diagnosis given to those who experience *excessive* anxiety and worry, which they find difficult to control. They may be unduly worried about their finances, their own health or that of family members, their performance at work, or their ability to function socially. Their excessive anxiety may cause them to feel tense, tired, and irritable, and to have difficulty concentrating and sleeping. Other symptoms may include trembling, palpitations, sweating, dizziness, nausea, diarrhea, or frequent urination. About 5.1 percent of the population will suffer from generalized anxiety disorder at some time in their lives—3.6 percent of men and 6.6 percent of women (Kessler et al., 1994). Kendler and others (1992b) estimate the heritability of generalized anxiety disorder to be about 30 percent. Previously thought of as a mild disorder, generalized anxiety disorder is now considered to lessen substantially the quality of life for those who suffer from it

anxiety disorders: Psychological disorders characterized by severe anxiety (e.g., panic disorder, phobias, general anxiety disorder, obsessive compulsive disorder).

anxiety: A generalized feeling of apprehension, fear, or tension that may be associated with a particular object or situation or may be free-floating, not associated with anything specific.

generalized anxiety disorder: An anxiety disorder in which people experience excessive anxiety or worry that they find difficult to control.

(Massion et al., 1993; Wittchen et al., 1994). But, as troubling as this disorder is, it is less severe than panic disorder.

Panic Disorder

? *What are the symptoms of panic disorder?*

panic attack: An attack of overwhelming anxiety, fear, or terror.

panic disorder: An anxiety disorder in which a person experiences recurrent unpredictable attacks of overwhelming anxiety, fear, or terror.

phobia (FO-bee-ah): A persistent, irrational fear of an object, situation, or activity that the person feels compelled to avoid.

agoraphobia (AG-or-uh-FO-bee-uh): An intense fear of being in a situation where immediate escape is not possible or help is not immediately available in case of incapacitating anxiety.

> Mindy Markowitz is young, attractive, and successful. An art director for a trade magazine, she came seeking treatment for panic attacks she had suffered over the past year. Now occurring as often as two or three times a day, the panic attacks would appear, seemingly out of nowhere, as a sudden, intense wave of terrible fear, sometimes during the day and sometimes at night, waking her from sleep. During the attacks Mindy would begin to tremble, feel nauseated, and sweat profusely. She "feels as though she is gagging," she said, but even worse is the horrible fear that "she will lose control and do something crazy, like run screaming into the street." (Spitzer et al., 1989, p. 154)

During **panic attacks**—attacks of overwhelming anxiety, fear, or terror—people commonly report that their heart is pounding, they tremble or shake uncontrollably, and they feel as if they are choking or smothering. Some say they are afraid they are going to die or are "going crazy" (Lipschitz, 1988).

Mindy Markowitz was diagnosed with **panic disorder**—a disorder characterized by recurrent, unpredictable panic attacks that cause apprehension about the occurrence and consequences of further attacks. This apprehension can lead people to avoid situations that have been associated with previous panic attacks. About 2 percent of men and 5 percent of women in the United States suffer from panic disorder (Kessler et al., 1994).

The biological perspective sheds some light on panic disorder. PET scans reveal that even in a nonpanic state, many panic-disorder patients show a greatly increased blood flow to parts of the right hemisphere of the limbic system—the part of the brain involved in emotion (Reiman et al., 1989). And family and twin studies suggest that genetic factors play a role in panic disorder (Crowe, 1990).

High life stress, particularly significant losses or threatening events, may be the precipitating factor in the first panic attack (Faravelli & Pallanti, 1989). And once people have had an attack, they may develop extreme anxiety about the possibility that it will happen again (Gorman et al., 1989). Clark (1988) offers a cognitive theory suggesting that panic attacks are associated with a catastrophic misinterpretation of bodily sensations. Roth and others (1992) suggest that when panic-disorder patients know a stressor is coming, their anticipatory anxiety may set the stage for a panic attack.

Panic disorder can have significant social and health consequences. Panic-disorder patients have an elevated risk of suicide (Massion et al., 1993) and are at increased risk for abuse of alcohol and other drugs.

Phobias: Persistent, Irrational Fears

? *What are the characteristics of the three categories of phobias?*

People suffering from a **phobia** experience a persistent, irrational fear of some specific object, situation, or activity that poses no real danger (or whose danger is blown all out of proportion). Phobics realize their fear is irrational, but they nevertheless feel compelled to avoid the feared object or situation. There are three classes of phobias—agoraphobia, social phobia, and specific phobia.

Agoraphobia The phobia most likely to drive people to seek professional help is **agoraphobia**. Agoraphobics have an intense fear of being in a situation where immediate escape is not possible or where help would not be available if the person should become overwhelmed by anxiety or experience a panic attack or panic-like symptoms. In some cases a person's entire life must be planned around avoiding feared situations such as busy streets, crowded stores, restaurants, or public transportation. An agoraphobic often will not leave home unless accompanied by a friend or family member and, in severe cases, not even then.

Although agoraphobia can occur without panic attacks, it typically begins during the early adult years with repeated panic attacks (Horwath et al., 1993). The intense fear of having another attack causes the person to avoid any place or situation where previous attacks have occurred. Some researchers believe that agoraphobia is actually an extreme form of panic disorder (Sheehan, 1983).

People are at greater risk of developing agoraphobia when other family members have it—the closer the relative, the higher the risk (Rosenbaum et al., 1994). Some agoraphobics have been treated successfully with psychotherapy (Marks, 1987a, 1988); others have responded well to antidepressants (Mavissakalian, 1990).

People with agoraphobia have an intense fear of public places and are often reluctant to leave home.

Social Phobia Sufferers of **social phobia** are intensely afraid of any social or performance situation in which they might embarrass or humiliate themselves in front of others—where they might shake, blush, sweat, or in some other way appear clumsy, foolish, or incompetent. They may fear eating, talking, writing, or doing anything else that would cause people to think poorly of them. Can you imagine being unable to cash a check, use a credit card, or even take notes or a written exam in class because you feared writing in front of other people?

Social phobia affects about 13.3 percent of the population at some time during their lives—11.1 percent of males and 15.5 percent of females (Kessler et al., 1994), and genetic factors appear to play a role (Fyer, 1993; Kendler et al., 1992b). Although less debilitating than agoraphobia, social phobia in its extreme form can seriously affect people's performance at work, prevent them from advancing in their careers or pursuing an education, and severely restrict their social lives (Judd, 1994; Ross, 1993). And often those with social phobia turn to alcohol and tranquilizers to lessen their anxiety in social situations (Kushner et al., 1990).

Specific Phobia Specific phobia—a marked fear of a specific object or situation—is a catchall category for any phobias other than agoraphobia and social phobia. This type usually begins in childhood or adolescence (Emmelkamp, 1988). The categories of specific phobias, in order of frequency of occurrence, are (1) situational phobias (fear of elevators, airplanes, enclosed places, public transportation, tunnels, bridges); (2) fear of the natural environment (storms, water, heights); (3) blood–injection–injury phobia (seeing blood or injury, receiving an injection); and (4) animal phobias (dogs, snakes, insects, mice) (American Psychiatric Association, 1994). Two types of situational phobia, claustrophobia (fear of closed spaces) and acrophobia (fear of heights), are the specific phobias treated most often by therapists. The *Try It!* on page 518 will introduce you to some others.

People with specific phobias usually fear the same things others fear, but their fears are greatly exaggerated. To be considered a phobia, a fear must cause great distress or interfere with a person's life in a major way.

Faced with the object or situation they fear, phobics experience intense anxiety, even to the point of shaking or screaming. They will go to great lengths to avoid the feared object or situation. Some people with blood–injection–injury phobia will not seek medical care even if it is a matter of life and death (Marks, 1988). And those with a severe dental phobia will actually let their teeth rot rather than visit the dentist.

social phobia: An irrational fear and avoidance of social situations in which people believe they might embarrass or humiliate themselves by appearing clumsy, foolish, or incompetent.

specific phobia: A marked fear of a specific object or situation; a catchall category for any phobia other than agoraphobia and social phobia.

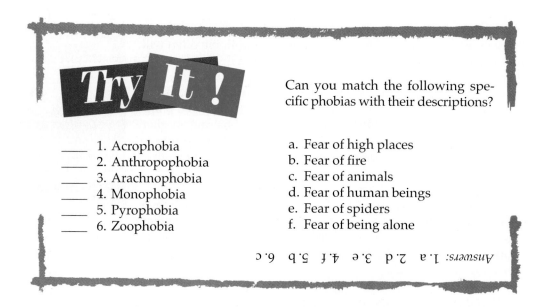

Try It !

Can you match the following specific phobias with their descriptions?

_____ 1. Acrophobia
_____ 2. Anthropophobia
_____ 3. Arachnophobia
_____ 4. Monophobia
_____ 5. Pyrophobia
_____ 6. Zoophobia

a. Fear of high places
b. Fear of fire
c. Fear of animals
d. Fear of human beings
e. Fear of spiders
f. Fear of being alone

Answers: 1.a 2.d 3.e 4.f 5.b 6.c

Figure 14.1 shows the percentages of males and females who have suffered from phobias and other anxiety disorders during their lifetime.

? What do psychologists see as probable causes of phobias?

Causes of Phobias   Most specific and social phobias probably result from learning (Thyer et al., 1985). Frightening experiences set the stage for phobias, although not all phobics recall the experience producing the phobia. A person with a dog phobia may be able to trace its beginning to a painful dog bite (Beck & Emory, 1985). Or a person humiliated by performing poorly in front of others may develop a social phobia (Rosenbaum et al., 1994).

FIGURE 14.1

Lifetime Prevalence of Anxiety Disorders

The percentages of males and females in the United States who have suffered from various anxiety disorders during their lifetime are based on the findings of the National Comorbidity Survey. (Data from Kessler et al., 1994.)

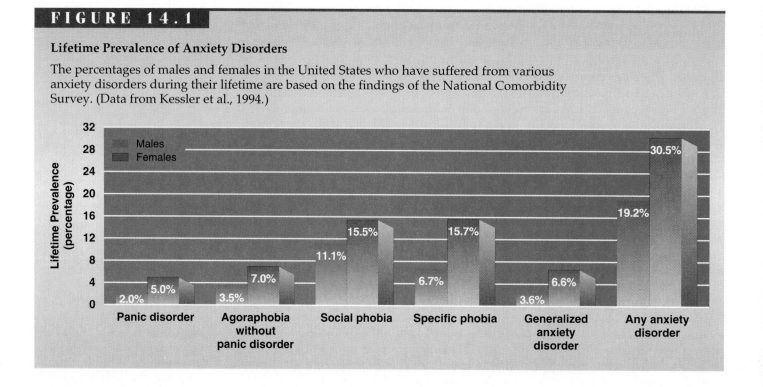

Phobias may be acquired, as well, through observational learning. For example, children who hear their parents talk about frightening experiences with the dentist or with bugs or snakes or thunderstorms may develop similar fears themselves. In many cases phobias are acquired through a combination of conditioning and observational learning (Merckelbach et al., 1989, 1991; Milgrom et al., 1995).

Genes appear to play a role in all classes of phobias. And people are at three times the risk of developing a phobia if a close relative suffers from one (Fyer et al., 1993).

From the psychodynamic perspective, people develop phobias primarily as a defense against the anxiety they feel when sexual or aggressive impulses threaten to break into consciousness. If the anxiety can be displaced onto a feared object and if that object can be avoided, then there is less chance that the disturbing impulse will break through. For example, a single person who has strong repressed sexual urges may develop a fear of going out at night as an unconscious defense against acting on these urges.

Obsessive Compulsive Disorder

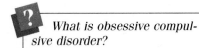
What is obsessive compulsive disorder?

What is wrong with people who are endlessly counting, checking, or performing other time-consuming rituals over and over? What causes some people to wash their hands 100 times a day until they are raw and bleeding? The answer is **obsessive compulsive disorder (OCD)**, another form of anxiety disorder in which people suffer from recurrent obsessions or compulsions, or both.

Obsessions If you have ever had a tune or the words of a song run through your mind over and over without being able to stop it, you have experienced obsessive thinking in a mild form. But imagine how miserable you would be if every time you touched something you thought you were being contaminated, or if the thought of stabbing your mother kept popping into your mind. **Obsessions** are persistent, recurring, involuntary thoughts, images, or impulses that invade consciousness and cause a person great distress.

People with obsessions might worry about contamination or about whether they performed a certain act, such as turning off the stove or locking the door (Insel, 1990). Other types of obsessions center upon aggression, religion, or sex. One minister reported obsessive thoughts of running naked down the church aisle and shouting obscenities at his congregation.

Do people ever act on their obsessive thoughts? It is extremely rare for people actually to carry out their obsessive thoughts (Marks, 1978b). Yet many people are so horrified by their obsessions that they think they are losing their mind.

Compulsions A person with a **compulsion** feels literally compelled to repeat certain acts or perform specific rituals over and over. The individual knows such acts are irrational and senseless but cannot resist performing them without experiencing an intolerable buildup of anxiety—anxiety that can be relieved only by yielding to the compulsion. Many of us have engaged in compulsive behavior like stepping over cracks on the sidewalk, counting stairsteps, or performing little rituals from time to time. The behavior becomes a psychological problem only if the person cannot resist performing it, if it is very time-consuming, and if it interferes with the person's normal activities and relationships with others.

Compulsions usually involve cleanliness, counting, checking, or touching objects (de Silva & Rachman, 1992). Sometimes compulsive acts or rituals resemble magical thinking and must be performed faithfully to ward off some danger.

obsessive compulsive disorder (OCD): An anxiety disorder in which a person suffers from obsessions and/or compulsions.

obsession: A persistent, recurring, involuntary thought, image, or impulse that invades consciousness and causes great distress.

compulsion: A persistent, irresistible, irrational urge to perform an act or ritual repeatedly.

People with OCD do not enjoy the time-consuming rituals—the endless counting, checking, or cleaning. They realize that their behavior is not normal; but they simply cannot help themselves, as shown in the following example.

> Mike, a 32-year-old patient, performed checking rituals that were preceded by a fear of harming other people. When driving, he had to stop the car often and return to check whether he had run over people, particularly babies. Before flushing the toilet, he had to check to be sure that a live insect had not fallen into the toilet, because he did not want to be responsible for killing a living thing. At home he repeatedly checked to see that the doors, stoves, lights, and windows were shut or turned off. . . . Mike performed these and many other checking rituals for an average of 4 hours a day. (Kozak et al., 1988, p. 88)

Are there many Mikes out there, or is his case unusual? Mike's checking compulsion is quite extreme, but apparently about 2 to 3 percent of the U.S. population (over 4 million people) suffer from obsessive compulsive disorder (Jenike, 1989). Fairly similar rates have been reported in studies in Canada, Puerto Rico, Germany, Korea, and New Zealand (Weissman et al., 1994).

About 70 percent of people in treatment for OCD have both obsessions and compulsions. But surveys of OCD in the general population reveal that 50 percent of the cases involve obsessions only, 34 percent compulsions only, and 16 percent both obsessions and compulsions (Weissman et al., 1994). When both occur together, the compulsion usually serves to relieve the anxiety caused by the obsession. All age groups with this disorder—children, adolescents, and adults—show strikingly similar thoughts and rituals (Swedo et al., 1989).

Causes of Obsessive Compulsive Disorder For many years obsessive compulsives were seen as extremely insecure people who viewed the world as threatening and unpredictable. Ritualistic behavior was thought to be their method of imposing some order, structure, and predictability on their world. From the psychodynamic perspective, obsessive compulsive behavior protects people from recognizing the real reasons for their anxiety—repressed hostility or unacceptable sexual urges. Without quite knowing why, a person might perform compulsive acts to undo or make amends for unconscious forbidden wishes, such as compulsive hand washing to atone for "dirty thoughts."

Some evidence points to a biological basis for obsessive compulsive disorder in some people, and several twin and family studies suggest that a genetic factor may be involved (Rasmussen & Eisen, 1990). PET scans of OCD patients have revealed abnormally high rates of glucose consumption in two brain regions involved in emotional reactions—the orbitofrontal cortex (the part of the frontal lobes just above the eye sockets) and the cingulate cortex (a part of the limbic system) (Rauch et al., 1994).

The most significant finding seems to be that many OCD patients have an imbalance in levels of the neurotransmitter serotonin (Barr et al., 1992). Such patients are often helped by an antidepressant medication, which restores the balance of serotonin (Murphy & Pigott, 1990), and in turn lessens activity in the orbitofrontal cortex (Swedo et al., 1992). But because the drug treatment does not work for all OCD patients, some researchers suggest that OCD may have several different causes (Goodman et al., 1989).

Most people with OCD never get treatment, because they know their symptoms are bizarre, and they are afraid to seek help for fear other people will think they are "crazy" (Rasmussen & Eisen, 1992).

Memory Check 14.2

1. Match the psychological disorder with the example.

___ 1) René refuses to eat in front of others for fear her hand will shake.

___ 2) John is excessively anxious about his health and his job, even though there is no concrete reason for it.

___ 3) Betty has been housebound for 4 years.

___ 4) Jackson gets hysterical when a dog approaches him.

___ 5) Laura has incapacitating attacks of anxiety that come on her suddenly.

___ 6) Max repeatedly checks his doors, windows, and appliances before he goes to bed.

a. panic disorder
b. agoraphobia
c. specific phobia
d. generalized anxiety disorder
e. social phobia
f. obsessive compulsive disorder

2. Anxiety serves no useful function. (true/false)

3. Most phobias result from frightening experiences and observational learning. (true/false)

4. Obsessive compulsive disorder appears to be caused primarily by psychological rather than biological factors. (true/false)

Answers: 1. 1) e 2) d 3) b 4) c 5) a 6) f 2. false 3. true 4. false

Somatoform and Dissociative Disorders

> **?** *What are two somatoform disorders, and what symptoms do they share?*

Somatoform Disorders: Physical Symptoms with Psychological Causes

The **somatoform disorders** involve bodily symptoms that cannot be explained by known medical conditions (the word *soma* means "body"). Although their symptoms are psychological in origin, patients are sincerely convinced that they spring from real physical disorders. People with somatoform disorders are not consciously faking illness to avoid work or other activities. Two types of somatoform disorders are hypochondriasis and conversion disorder.

Hypochondriasis People with **hypochondriasis** are overly concerned about their health and believe that their bodily symptoms are a sign of some serious disease. Yet their symptoms are not usually consistent with known physical disorders, and even when a medical examination reveals no physical problem, they are not convinced. Hypochondriacs may "doctor shop," going from one physician to another, seeking confirmation of their worst fears. Unfortunately, hypochondriasis is not easily treated, and there is usually a poor chance for recovery.

Conversion Disorder: When Thoughts and Fears Can Paralyze A man is suddenly struck blind, or an arm, a leg, or some other part of his body becomes

somatoform disorders (so-MAT-uh-form): Disorders in which physical symptoms are present that are due to psychological rather than physical causes.

hypochondriasis (HI-puh-kahn-DRY-uh-sis): A somatoform disorder in which persons are preoccupied with their health and convinced they have some serious disorder despite reassurance from doctors to the contrary.

paralyzed. Extensive medical tests find nothing wrong—no physical reason that could possibly cause the blindness or the paralysis. How can this be?

A diagnosis of **conversion disorder** is made when there is a loss of motor or sensory functioning in some part of the body that is not due to a physical cause but that solves a psychological problem. A person may become blind, deaf, or unable to speak or may develop a paralysis in some part of the body. Many of Freud's patients suffered from conversion disorder, and he believed that they unconsciously developed a physical disability to help resolve an unconscious sexual or aggressive conflict.

Modern-day psychologists think that conversion disorder can act as an unconscious defense against any intolerable anxiety situation that the person cannot otherwise escape. For example, a soldier who desperately fears going into battle might escape the anxiety by developing a paralysis or some other physically disabling symptom.

You would expect normal persons to show great distress if they suddenly lost their sight or hearing or became paralyzed. But this is not true of many patients with conversion disorder; they seem to exhibit a calm and cool indifference to their symptoms, called "la belle indifference." Furthermore, many seem to enjoy the attention, sympathy, and concern their disability brings them.

Conversion disorder is two to ten times more common in women than in men and is seen more often in people with limited medical knowledge (American Psychiatric Association, 1994).

Dissociative Disorders: Mental Escapes

Day in and day out we are consciously aware of who we are, and we are able to recall important events in our lives. Our memories, our identity, our consciousness, and our perception of the environment are integrated. But in response to unbearable stress, some people develop a **dissociative disorder** and lose this integration. Their consciousness becomes dissociated from their identity or their memories of important personal events, or both. Dissociative disorders provide a mental escape from intolerable circumstances. Three types of dissociative disorders are dissociative amnesia, dissociative fugue, and dissociative identity disorder (commonly known as multiple personality).

Dissociative Amnesia: "Who Am I?" Amnesia is a complete or partial loss of the ability to recall personal information or identify past experiences that cannot be attributed to ordinary forgetfulness or substance use. Popular books, movies, and TV shows have used amnesia as a central theme in which, usually after a blow to the head, characters cannot remember who they are or anything about their past. But in **dissociative amnesia**, no physical cause is present. Instead a traumatic experience—a psychological blow, so to speak—or an unbearable anxiety situation causes the person to escape by "forgetting." Patients with dissociative amnesia can have a loss of memory of specific periods of their life or a complete loss of memory for their entire identity. For example, if a soldier experienced the trauma of watching his best friend blown apart on the battlefield, he might protect himself from that trauma by developing some form of dissociative amnesia. Yet such people do not forget everything. They forget only items of personal reference such as their name, their age, and where they live, and they may fail to recognize their parents, other relatives, and friends. But they do not forget how to read and write or solve problems, and their basic personality structure remains intact.

Dissociative Fugue: "Where Did I Go and What Did I Do?" Even more puzzling than dissociative amnesia is **dissociative fugue**. In a fugue state, peo-

---

What are dissociative amnesia and dissociative fugue?

conversion disorder: A somatoform disorder in which a loss of motor or sensory functioning in some part of the body has no physical cause but solves some psychological problem.

dissociative disorders: Disorders in which, under stress, one loses the integration of consciousness, identity, and memories of important personal events.

dissociative amnesia: A dissociative disorder in which there is a loss of memory for limited periods in one's life or for one's entire personal identity.

dissociative fugue (FEWG): A dissociative disorder in which one has a complete loss of memory for one's entire identity, travels away from home, and may assume a new identity.

ple not only forget their identity, they also leave the scene and travel away from home. Some take on a new identity that is usually more outgoing and uninhibited than their former identity. The fugue state may last for hours, days, or even months. The fugue is usually a reaction to some severe psychological stress, such as a natural disaster, a serious family quarrel, a deep personal rejection, or military service in wartime.

For most people, recovery from dissociative fugue is rapid, although they may have no memory of the initial stressor that brought on the fugue state. And when people recover from the fugue, they often have no memory of events that occurred during the episode.

Dissociative Identity Disorder: Multiple Personality

In **dissociative identity disorder**, two or more distinct, unique personalities exist in the same individual, as in the case of Sybil, described at the beginning of this chapter. In 50 percent of the cases, there are more than 10 different personalities (Sybil had 16). The change from one personality to another often occurs suddenly and usually during stress.

What are some of the identifying symptoms of dissociative identity disorder?

The host personality is the one in control of the body the largest percentage of time (Kluft, 1984). The alternate, or alter, personalities may differ radically in intelligence, speech, accent, vocabulary, posture, body language, hairstyle, taste in clothes, manners, and even handwriting. And incredibly, within the same individual, the alter personalities may differ in gender, age, and even sexual orientation. Almost all people with this disorder have "a number of child and infant personalities" (Putnam, 1992, p. 34). Some alters may be right-handed; others left-handed. Some may need different prescription glasses, have specific food allergies, or show different responses to alcohol or medications (Putnam et al., 1986). And there are usually promiscuous alters who act on forbidden impulses (Putnam, 1992).

Many multiple personality patients report hearing voices in their head and sometimes the sounds of crying or screaming or laughter. For this reason, they have often been misdiagnosed as schizophrenic.

In 80 percent of the cases of dissociative identity disorder, the host personality does not know of the alters, but the alters have varying levels of awareness of each other (Putnam, 1989, p. 114). The host and alter personalities commonly show amnesia for certain periods of time or for important events in their life such as their graduation or wedding. There is the common complaint of "lost time"—periods for which a given personality has no memory because he or she was not in control of the body.

Causes of Dissociative Identity Disorder

Dissociative identity disorder usually begins in early childhood but is rarely diagnosed before adolescence (Vincent & Pickering, 1988). About 90 percent of the treated cases have been women (Ross et al., 1989), and more than 95 percent of the patients reveal early histories of severe physical and/or sexual abuse (Putnam, 1992; Ross et al., 1990). The splitting off of separate personalities is apparently a way of coping with the intolerable abuse.

How can we account for the 5 percent of multiple personality patients who were not abused? The psychodynamic perspective suggests that alternate personalities may come forth to express forbidden sexual or aggressive impulses that would be unacceptable to the original personality.

The Incidence of Dissociative Identity Disorder

There is no general consensus on the incidence of dissociative identity disorder. Some clinicians believe that it is extremely rare or nonexistent (Chodoff, 1987; Thigpen & Cleckley, 1984). Skeptics suggest that patients may simply assume the role of a person with multiple personalities to explain their deviant behavior and have the role reinforced

dissociative identity disorder: A dissociative disorder in which two or more distinct personalities occur in the same person, each taking over at different times; also called multiple personality.

by the therapist (McHugh, 1993). Or therapists may be uncovering personalities in gullible patients for financial gain (Aldridge-Morris, 1989).

Other clinicians believe that the disorder is even more common than reported and claim that it is widely misdiagnosed and underdiagnosed (Bliss & Jeppsen, 1985; Kluft, 1993). Dramatic increases in the number of cases have been reported in the last decade in the United States (Putnam & Loewenstein, 1993). And cases are also being reported in Puerto Rico (Martinez-Taboas, 1991) and in a number of other countries—Canada (Ross et al., 1991), Switzerland (Modestin, 1992), the Netherlands (Boon & Draijer, 1993), and 11 other countries outside of North America (Coons et al., 1991).

Memory Check 14.3

1. Match the psychological disorder with the example.

____ 1) Mark is convinced he has some serious disease although his doctors can find nothing physically wrong.

____ 2) David was found far away from his hometown, calling himself by another name and having no memory of his past.

____ 3) Theresa suddenly loses her sight, but doctors can find no physical reason for the problem.

____ 4) Larry has no memory of being in the boat with other family members the day his older brother drowned.

____ 5) Nadine has no memory for blocks of time in her life and often finds clothing in her closet that she cannot remember buying.

a. dissociative identity disorder
b. dissociative fugue
c. dissociative amnesia
d. hypochondriasis
e. conversion disorder

2. Somatoform disorders have physiological rather than psychological causes. (true/false)

3. Dissociative disorders are psychological in origin. (true/false)

Answers: 1. 1) d 2) b 3) e 4) c 5) a 2. false 3. true

Schizophrenia

Most of us can imagine being anxious, fearful, or depressed; we can picture ourselves having an obsession or a compulsion. But schizophrenia is so far removed from our common, everyday experience that it is all but impossible for us to imagine what it is like to be schizophrenic. Consider the case of Eric, whose normal childhood and youth turned into a nightmare when he lost touch with reality during his senior year in high school.

Now in his thirties, he lives in his parents' wood-paneled basement. Usually sitting with a blanket covering his head, Eric is oblivious to the normal world. His world consists of the voices he hears inside his head and the visual hallucinations he takes to be real. Eric insists that he talks to God and to Satan, and at times he believes that he is Jesus Christ. If he refuses to take his antipsychotic medication, he is likely to become violent, and two times he has tried to take his own life. "His parents live in fear of what tomorrow will bring as they muddle through discouraging todays. There is seldom a moment without stress, an hour with peace of mind." (Bartimus, 1983, p. D1)

Schizophrenia is the most serious of the psychological disorders. It affects about 1 person in 100, and one-half of all the mental hospital beds in this country are occupied by schizophrenic patients. Schizophrenia usually begins in adolescence or early adulthood, although it can appear later in life. It is probably the most devastating of all the psychological disorders because of the social disruption and misery it causes to the people who suffer from it and their families. "One should never underestimate the depth of their pain, even though the illness itself may diminish their ability to convey it" (Keith, 1993, p. 1617).

The Symptoms of Schizophrenia: Many and Varied

Any given individual with schizophrenia may have one or more of its major symptoms, yet there is not one single symptom or brain abnormality shared by all people with the disorder. For this reason, some researchers consider schizophrenia not one illness but a group of related disorders (Heinrichs, 1993).

The symptoms of schizophrenia are classified into two categories—positive symptoms and negative symptoms.

Positive Symptoms Positive symptoms are *not* so named because they are desirable. Rather, they are the abnormal behaviors that occur in people with schizophrenia. Positive symptoms include hallucinations, delusions, disorganized thinking and speech, and grossly disorganized or bizarre behavior (McGlashan & Fenton, 1992).

Hallucinations One of the clearest symptoms of schizophrenia is the presence of **hallucinations**—imaginary sensations. Schizophrenic patients may see, hear, feel, taste, or smell strange things in the absence of any stimulus in the environment, but hearing voices is the most common type of hallucination. Patients may think they hear the voice of God or Satan, the voices of family members or friends, unknown voices, and even their own voice broadcasting aloud what they are thinking. Most often the voices accuse or curse the patients or engage in a running commentary on their behavior. Sometimes the voices are menacing and order patients to kill someone or take their own life.

Several researchers, using computerized brain-imaging techniques, have found increased activity in Broca's area when schizophrenics reported they were hearing voices (Cleghorn et al., 1992; McGuire et al., 1993). This suggests that the voices may be simply the person's own inner speech, not recognized as such. Tiihonen and others (1992) report that auditory hallucinations stimulate the primary auditory cortex much like real sounds do.

Visual hallucinations, less common than auditory hallucinations, are usually in black and white and commonly take the form of friends, relatives, God, Jesus, or the devil. Schizophrenics also may experience exceedingly frightening and painful bodily sensations and feel they are being beaten, burned, or sexually violated. One schizophrenic complained that "spiders were crawling all through his heart and vessels, eating his brain, and . . . crawling on his skin" (Salama & England, 1990, p. 86).

Delusions Imagine how upset you would be if you believed that your every thought was being broadcast aloud for everyone to hear. What if you were convinced that some strange agent was stealing your thoughts or inserting other

> ? *What are some of the major positive and negative symptoms of schizophrenia?*

schizophrenia (SKIT-suh-FREE-nee-ah): A severe psychological disorder characterized by loss of contact with reality, hallucinations, delusions, inappropriate or flat affect, some disturbance in thinking, social withdrawal, and/or other bizarre behavior.

hallucination: A sensory perception in the absence of any external sensory stimulus; an imaginary sensation.

thoughts in your head? These are examples of **delusions**—false beliefs not generally shared by others in the culture. Usually patients cannot be persuaded that their beliefs are false, even in the face of strong evidence.

Delusions may take different forms. Schizophrenics with **delusions of grandeur** may believe they are a famous person (the President or Jesus Christ, for example) or a powerful or important person who possesses some great knowledge, ability, or authority. Those with **delusions of persecution** have the false notion that some person or agency is trying to harass, cheat, spy on, conspire against, injure, kill, or in some other way harm them.

Disturbances in the Form of Thought or Speech Schizophrenia is often marked by a disturbance in the form of thought. Most common is loosening of associations, when a person does not follow one line of thought to completion, but on the basis of vague connections shifts from one subject to another.

> I am writing on paper. The pen I am using is from a factory called 'Perry & Co.' This factory is in England. . . . The city of London is in England. I know this from my school-days. Then, I always liked geography. My last teacher in that subject was . . . a man with black eyes. I also like black eyes. There are also blue and gray eyes and other sorts, too. I have heard it said that snakes have green eyes. All people have eyes. There are some, too, who are blind. (Bleuler, 1950, p. 17)

The speech of schizophrenics is often difficult or even impossible to understand. The content of the message may be extremely vague, or the person may invent words or use them inappropriately (Chaika, 1985).

Grossly Disorganized Behavior Grossly disorganized behavior can include such things as childlike silliness, inappropriate sexual behavior (masturbating in public), disheveled appearance, and peculiar dress. There may also be unpredictable agitation, including shouting and swearing, and unusual or inappropriate motor behavior, including strange gestures, facial expressions, or postures.

Inappropriate Affect Schizophrenics may display **inappropriate affect**; that is, their facial expressions, tone of voice, and gestures may not reflect the emotion that would be expected under the circumstances. A person might cry when watching a TV comedy and laugh when watching a news story showing bloody bodies at the scene of a fatal automobile accident.

Negative Symptoms Negative symptoms of schizophrenia represent a loss of or a deficiency in thoughts and behaviors that are characteristic of normal functioning. Negative symptoms may include social withdrawal, apathy, loss of motivation, lack of goal-directed activity, very limited speech, slowed movements, and poor hygiene and grooming (McGlashan & Fenton, 1992). Some schizophrenic patients show flat affect—practically no emotional response at all. They may speak in a monotone, have blank and emotionless facial expressions, and act and move more like robots than humans. Schizophrenics with negative symptoms seem to have the poorest outcomes (Belitsky & McGlashan, 1993; Fenton & McGlashan, 1994).

Schizophrenics tend to withdraw from normal social contacts and retreat into their own world. They have difficulty relating to people, and often their functioning is too impaired for them to hold a job or even to care for themselves.

Brain Abnormalities in Some Schizophrenics Several abnormalities in brain structure and function have been found in schizophrenic patients (Andreasen, 1988; Cannon & Marco, 1994). PET scans have revealed abnormally low neural activity in the frontal lobes (Winn, 1994). Other studies have revealed a

---

delusion: A false belief, not generally shared by others in the culture, that cannot be changed despite strong evidence to the contrary.

delusion of grandeur: A false belief that one is a famous person or one who has some great knowledge, ability, or authority.

delusion of persecution: An individual's false belief that a person or group is trying in some way to harm him or her.

inappropriate affect: A symptom common in schizophrenia in which a person's behavior (including facial expression, tone of voice, and gestures) does not reflect the emotion that would be expected under the circumstances; for example, a person laughs at a tragedy, cries at a joke.

catatonic schizophrenia (KAT-uh-TAHN-ik): A type of schizophrenia characterized by complete stillness or stupor and/or periods of great agitation and excitement; patients may assume an unusual posture and remain in it for long periods.

disorganized schizophrenia: The most serious type of schizophrenia, marked by inappropriate affect, silliness, laughter, grotesque mannerisms, and bizarre behavior.

decreased volume of the hippocampus (Bogerts, 1993), the amygdala (Breier et al., 1992), and the thalamus (Andreasen et al., 1994). In many schizophrenics, the ventricles—fluid-filled cavities in the brain—are larger than in the normal brain (Lieberman et al., 1992; Zipursky et al., 1992). This particular abnormality was found in the brain of John Hinckley, Jr., the man who tried to assassinate Ronald Reagan.

Types of Schizophrenia

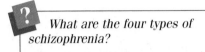

What are the four types of schizophrenia?

Even though various symptoms are commonly shared by schizophrenics, certain features distinguish one type of schizophrenia from another. The four types of schizophrenia are catatonic, disorganized, paranoid, and undifferentiated.

Persons with **catatonic schizophrenia** may display complete stillness and stupor, or great excitement and agitation. Frequently they alternate rapidly between the two. They may become frozen in a strange posture or position, as shown in the photograph, and remain there for hours without moving.

Disorganized schizophrenia, the most serious type, tends to occur at an earlier age than the other types and is marked by extreme social withdrawal, hallucinations, delusions, silliness, inappropriate laughter, grimaces, grotesque mannerisms, and other bizarre behavior. These patients show flat or inappropriate affect and are frequently incoherent. They often exhibit obscene behavior, may masturbate openly, and swallow almost any kind of object or material. Disorganized schizophrenia results in the most severe disintegration of the personality (Beratis et al., 1994), and its victims have the poorest chance of recovery (Fenton & McGlashan, 1991; Kane, 1993).

People with **paranoid schizophrenia** usually suffer from delusions of grandeur or persecution. They may be convinced that they have an identity other than their own—that they are the President, the Virgin Mary, or God—or that they possess great ability or talent. They may feel that they are in charge of the hospital or on a secret assignment for the government. Paranoid schizophrenics often show exaggerated anger and suspiciousness. If they have delusions of persecution and feel that they are being harassed or threatened, they may become violent in an attempt to defend themselves against their imagined persecutors. Usually the behavior of the paranoid schizophrenic is not so obviously disturbed as that of the catatonic or disorganized type, and the chance for recovery is better (Fenton & McGlashan, 1991; Kendler et al., 1984).

Undifferentiated schizophrenia is the general catchall category used when schizophrenic symptoms either do not conform to the criteria of any schizophrenia type or conform to more than one type.

A person with catatonic schizophrenia may become frozen in an unusual position, like a statue, for hours at a time.

The Causes of Schizophrenia

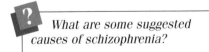

What are some suggested causes of schizophrenia?

During the 1950s and 1960s, many psychiatrists and some researchers pointed to unhealthy patterns of communication and interaction in the entire family as the breeding ground for schizophrenia (Bateson et al., 1956; Lidz et al., 1965). But unhealthy family interaction patterns could be the *result* rather than the *cause* of schizophrenia. There is no convincing evidence to justify pointing the finger of blame at parents or other family members (Johnson, 1989; Torrey, 1983).

On the other hand, research evidence continues to mount that suggests a biological factor in many cases of schizophrenia.

Genetic Inheritance Schizophrenia does tend to run in families, and genetic factors play a major role (Gottesman, 1991; Kendler & Diehl, 1993; Kendler, McGuire, et al., 1993). The chance of a person in the United States developing

paranoid schizophrenia (PAIR-uh-noid): A type of schizophrenia characterized by delusions of grandeur or persecution.

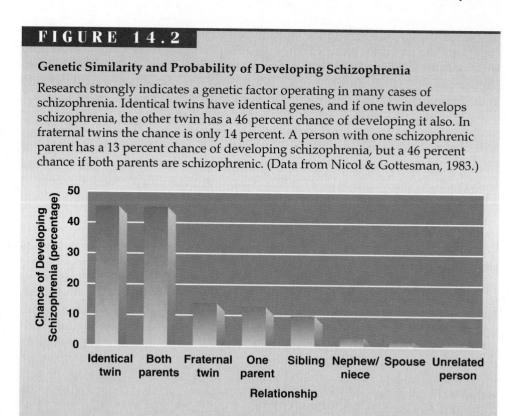

FIGURE 14.2

Genetic Similarity and Probability of Developing Schizophrenia

Research strongly indicates a genetic factor operating in many cases of schizophrenia. Identical twins have identical genes, and if one twin develops schizophrenia, the other twin has a 46 percent chance of developing it also. In fraternal twins the chance is only 14 percent. A person with one schizophrenic parent has a 13 percent chance of developing schizophrenia, but a 46 percent chance if both parents are schizophrenic. (Data from Nicol & Gottesman, 1983.)

schizophrenia is about 1 in 100 (Jeste, 1994). However, people with one schizophrenic parent have about a 13 percent chance of developing the disorder; those with two schizophrenic parents have roughly a 46 percent chance. If one identical twin develops schizophrenia, the other twin has about a 46 percent chance of having it as well (Nicol & Gottesman, 1983). Figure 14.2 shows how the chance of developing schizophrenia varies with the degree of relationship to a schizophrenic person. Still more evidence for a genetic factor comes from adoption studies showing that adoptees have ten times the risk of developing schizophrenia if their biological parent rather than their adoptive parent is schizophrenic (Kendler et al., 1994; Kety et al., 1994).

Exactly what is the genetic connection? According to genetic theorists, what is inherited is not schizophrenia itself, but a predisposition or tendency to develop it (Zubin & Spring, 1977). According to the **diathesis–stress model**, schizophrenia develops when there is *both* a genetic predisposition toward the disorder (diathesis) and more stress than a person can handle (Fowles, 1992). The excessive stress can occur in the womb or during childhood, adolescence, or adulthood.

Some researchers now believe that a virus or injury during the second trimester of prenatal development can result in the development of the disorder in a genetically susceptible person (Bracha et al., 1992; Stabenau & Pollin, 1993). Disturbances in prenatal brain development can interfere with the normal migration of neurons to their proper destination in the brain (Akbarian et al., 1993; Winn, 1994).

Schizophrenics are particularly vulnerable to stress, and whether predisposed people develop the disorder may depend on their life circumstances (Fowles, 1992; Johnson, 1989). Torrey and Bowler (1990) have data suggesting that schizophrenia is more common in highly urbanized areas of the United States than in rural areas. They speculate that the cause is the greater stress of city life coupled with higher exposure to pollutants, toxins, and infectious diseases.

diathesis–stress model: The idea that people with a constitutional predisposition (diathesis) toward a disorder, such as schizophrenia, may develop the disorder if they are subjected to sufficient environmental stress.

Excessive Dopamine Activity Abnormal activity in the brain's dopamine systems is common in many schizophrenics (Winn, 1994). Much of the dopamine activity occurs in the limbic system, which is involved in human emotions (Davis et al., 1991). Drugs that are effective in reducing the symptoms of schizophrenia block dopamine action (Iverson, 1979; Torrey, 1983), although about one-third of the patients do not show improvement with such drugs (Wolkin et al., 1989).

Three more dopamine receptors have been discovered recently, bringing the known total to five. Drugs are being developed whose action is aimed at specific dopamine receptors (Taubes, 1994). But many questions still remain about the causes of schizophrenia. Most likely many factors play an interactive role—genetic predispositions, biochemical processes, environmental conditions, and life experiences.

Memory Check 14.4

1. Match the symptom of schizophrenia with the example.
   - ____ 1) Joe believes he is Moses.
   - ____ 2) Elena thinks her family is spreading rumors about her.
   - ____ 3) Peter hears voices cursing him.
   - ____ 4) Marco laughs at tragedies and cries when he hears a joke.

   a. delusions of grandeur
   b. hallucinations
   c. inappropriate affect
   d. delusions of persecution

2. There is substantial research evidence for all of the following having roles as causes of schizophrenia *except*:
   a. genetic factors.
   b. stress in people predisposed to the disorder.
   c. excessive dopamine activity.
   d. unhealthy family interaction patterns.

3. Match the subtype of schizophrenia with the example:
   - ____ 1) Louise stands for hours in the same strange position.
   - ____ 2) Ron believes the CIA is plotting to kill him.
   - ____ 3) Harry makes silly faces, laughs a lot, and masturbates openly.
   - ____ 4) Sue has the symptoms of schizophrenia but does not fit any one type.

   a. paranoid schizophrenia
   b. disorganized schizophrenia
   c. catatonic schizophrenia
   d. undifferentiated schizophrenia

Answers: 1.1) a 2) d 3) b 4) c 2. d 3.1) c 2) a 3) b 4) d

◈ Mood Disorders

Mood disorders involve moods or emotions that are extreme and unwarranted. In the most serious disorders, mood ranges from the depths of severe depression to the heights of extreme elation. Mood disorders fall into two broad categories—depressive disorders and bipolar disorders.

Depressive Disorders and Bipolar Disorder: Emotional Highs and Lows

Major Depressive Disorder It is normal to feel blue, sad, or depressed in response to many of life's common experiences—death of a loved one, divorce, loss of a job, or an unhappy ending to a long-term relationship. Major depression, however, is not normal. People with **major depressive disorder** feel an overwhelming sadness, despair, and hopelessness, and they usually lose their ability

mood disorders: Disorders characterized by extreme and unwarranted disturbances in feeling or mood.

major depressive disorder: A mood disorder marked by feelings of great sadness, despair, guilt, worthlessness, and hopelessness.

What are the symptoms of major depressive disorder?

People experiencing major depression feel overwhelming sadness, despair, and hopelessness.

to experience pleasure. They may have changes in appetite, weight, or sleep patterns, loss of energy, and difficulty in thinking or concentrating. Body movements and speech may be so slowed that some depressed people seem to be doing everything in slow motion. Others experience the opposite extreme and are constantly moving and fidgeting, wringing their hands, and pacing. Depression can be so severe that its victims suffer from delusions or hallucinations. It is the most common of all serious mental disorders and strikes people of all social classes, cultures, and nations around the world.

In the United States, about 21.3 percent of women and 12.7 percent of men have had a major depressive episode at some time in their lives (Kessler et al., 1994). This higher rate for women has also been found in Canada, Germany, and New Zealand (Weissman et al., 1993). In recent years there has been an increase in depression in adolescents, particularly in adolescent girls, and perhaps in Native Americans and homosexual young people as well (Petersen et al., 1993). Studies have also revealed high rates of mood disorders in writers and artists (Jamison, 1995; Richards, 1992; Schildkraut et al., 1994).

Some people suffer only one major depressive episode, but 50 to 60 percent will have a recurrence. Risk of recurrence is greatest for females (Winokur et al., 1993), for those with an onset of depression before age 20 (Giles et al., 1989), and for those with a family history of mood disorders (Akiskal, 1989). Recurrences may be frequent or infrequent, and for 20 to 35 percent of patients, the episodes are chronic, lasting two years or longer. Recurring episodes tend to be increasingly more severe and long-lasting (Greden, 1994; Maj et al., 1992). According to the American Psychiatric Association (1994), one year after their initial diagnosis of major depressive disorder, 40 percent of patients are without symptoms; 40 percent are still suffering from major depression; and 20 percent are depressed, but not enough to warrant a diagnosis of major depression. Slightly less than one-half of those hospitalized for major depressive disorder are fully recovered after one year (Keitner et al., 1992). Unfortunately, about 80 percent of those suffering from depression never even receive treatment (Holden, 1986b). About 15 percent of people with major depressive disorder commit suicide (Coppen, 1994). To learn more about suicide, read the World of Psychology section on page 534.

Many people suffer from a milder form of depression called dysthymia, which is nonetheless chronic (lasting 2 years or longer). People with dysthymia suffer from depressed mood but have fewer of the associated symptoms common in major depressive disorder.

Seasonal Depression Many people find that their moods seem to change with the seasons (Kasper et al., 1989). But people suffering from **seasonal affective disorder (SAD)**, experience a significant depression that tends to come and go with the seasons (Wehr & Rosenthal, 1989). There is a spring/summer depression that remits in winter, but the most common type, winter depression, seems to be triggered by light deficiency. During the winter months, when the days are shorter, some people become very depressed and tend to sleep and eat more, gain weight, and crave carbohydrates (Rosenthal et al., 1986; Wurtman & Wurtman, 1989). However, during the spring and summer months, they are in higher spirits, become more energetic, and claim to function better (Wehr et al., 1986).

Reasoning that the obvious difference between the seasons was the amount and intensity of light, Rosenthal and colleagues (1985) exposed patients with winter depression to bright light, which simulated the longer daylight hours of summer. After several days of the light treatment, most of the subjects improved.

seasonal affective disorder (SAD): A mood disorder in which depression comes and goes with the seasons.

FIGURE 14.3

Seasonal Mood Changes

Normally mood fluctuates with the seasons. People typically report feeling best during May and June and worst during January and February. People with seasonal affective disorder (SAD) experience wider mood fluctuations—higher highs in June, July, and August and lower lows in December, January, and February. The winter depression of seasonal affective disorder seems to be related to the light deficiency during the short winter days. An effective treatment is light therapy. (After Wurtman & Wurtman, 1989.)

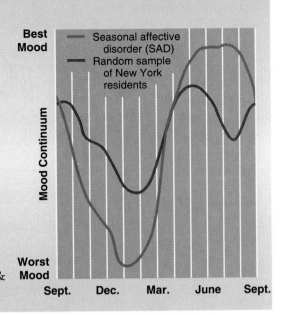

Figure 14.3 shows the difference in mood fluctuations between seasonal-affective-disorder patients and a random sample of New York residents.

Bipolar Disorder Another type of mood disorder is **bipolar disorder**, in which patients experience two radically different moods—extreme highs called manic episodes (or mania) and the extreme lows of major depression—usually with relatively normal periods in between. A **manic episode** is marked by excessive euphoria, inflated self-esteem, wild optimism, and hyperactivity. During a manic episode people are wound up and full of energy. They frantically engage in a flurry of activity, rarely sleep, and talk loud and fast, skipping from one topic to another.

What is wrong with being euphoric, energetic, and optimistic? Obviously nothing, as long as it is warranted. But people in a manic state have temporarily lost touch with reality and frequently have delusions of grandeur along with their euphoric high. Their high-spirited optimism is not merely irrational, it is delusional. They may go on wild spending sprees or waste large sums of money on grand get-rich-quick schemes. If family members try to stop them or talk them out of their irrational plans, they are likely to become irritable, hostile, enraged, or even dangerous. Quite often patients must be hospitalized during manic episodes to protect them and others from the disastrous consequences of their poor judgment.

The excessive euphoria, boundless energy, and delusions of grandeur are all apparent in this manic episode of Edward O, a 27-year-old high school teacher:

> One day Edward O's behavior suddenly became bizarre. He charged into the principal's office and outlined his plan for tearing down the school building and having his students rebuild it from the ground up over the weekend. The school principal called the police and had Edward taken to a hospital. There Edward paced up and down for two days, would not sleep or eat, and spoke excitedly about his plans to take over administration of the hospital. On the third day he demanded paper and pens and, in a frenzy, wrote 100 letters, one to each U.S. senator. He cursed the pens for not writing faster and threw them against the wall, demanding new ones. When staff members tried to stop him, Edward flew into a rage, so they decided to let him "run out of steam." After the fourth day he collapsed, totally exhausted. (Adapted from Goldenberg, 1977)

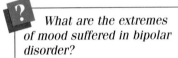

What are the extremes of mood suffered in bipolar disorder?

bipolar disorder: A mood disorder in which one has manic episodes alternating with periods of depression, usually with relatively normal periods in between.

manic episode (MAN-ik): A period of extreme elation, euphoria, and hyperactivity, often accompanied by delusions of grandeur and by hostility if activity is blocked.

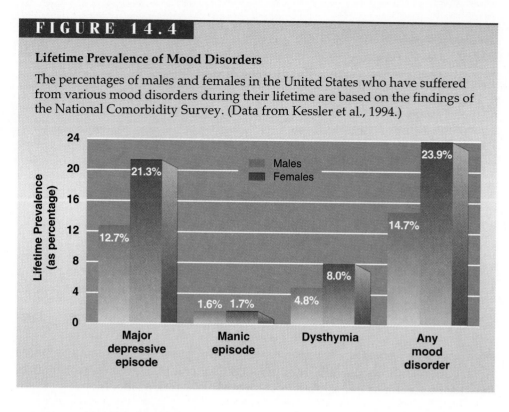

FIGURE 14.4

Lifetime Prevalence of Mood Disorders

The percentages of males and females in the United States who have suffered from various mood disorders during their lifetime are based on the findings of the National Comorbidity Survey. (Data from Kessler et al., 1994.)

Bipolar disorder is much less common than major depressive disorder, and the lifetime prevalence rates are about the same for males (1.6 percent) and females (1.7 percent) (Kessler et al., 1994). Unfortunately, some 89 percent of those with bipolar disorder have recurrences (Winokur et al., 1994), and in 60 to 70 percent of the cases, the manic episodes either directly precede or follow major depressive episodes. The good news is that 70 to 80 percent of the patients return to normal after an episode (American Psychiatric Association, 1994). But some are "rapid cyclers"—experiencing four or more episodes per year. And like depression, bipolar disorder can follow a seasonal pattern (Faedda et al., 1993).

Figure 14.4 shows the percentages of American females and males who have suffered from manic episodes and other mood disorders during their lifetime.

Causes of Major Depressive Disorder and Bipolar Disorder

What are some suggested causes of major depressive disorder and bipolar disorder?

The biological and cognitive perspectives offer some insight into the causes of mood disorders and suggest treatments that have proven helpful to many people suffering from these disorders.

The Biological Perspective Biological factors such as genetic inheritance and abnormal brain chemistry play a major role in bipolar disorder and major depressive disorder. PET scans have revealed abnormal patterns of brain activity in both of these disorders (Drevets et al., 1992; George et al., 1993).

The Role of Genetic Inheritance Does depression tend to run in families? Apparently so, because people who have relatives with mood disorders are at higher risk of developing mood disturbances, and this risk is due to shared genetic factors rather than shared environmental factors (Kendler et al., 1992d). Based on a study of 1,721 identical and fraternal female twins, Kendler, Neale, Kessler, and others (1993) estimated the heritability of major depression to be

70 percent and the contribution of environment to be 30 percent. A person is three times more likely to develop depression if a close relative has had an early onset of depression and if the depression was recurring rather than a single episode (Bland et al., 1986).

Adoption studies have shown that among adult adoptees who had developed depression, there was 8 times more major depression and 15 times more suicide in biological than in adoptive family members (Wender et al., 1986). And the genetic link is even stronger for bipolar disorder than for depression. The odds of developing bipolar disorder are 24 times greater in persons who have **first-degree relatives** (parents, children, or siblings) with the disorder (Weissman, Gershon, et al., 1984).

The Role of Serotonin and Norepinephrine   We all know that substances can alter mood—alcohol, caffeine, other uppers and downers, and a host of additional psychoactive substances. Researchers now know that our moods are also altered and regulated by our own biochemicals, and norepinephrine and serotonin are two neurotransmitters thought to play important roles in mood disorders. Both are localized in the limbic system and the hypothalamus, parts of the brain that help regulate emotional behavior. Too little norepinephrine is associated with depression, and too much is related to mania (Schildkraut, 1970). Amphetamines, which cause an emotional "high," are reported to stimulate the release of both serotonin and norepinephrine.

An important unanswered question remains. Do these biochemical differences in the brain *cause* psychological changes or *result* from them? Theorists who emphasize psychological causes see biochemical changes as results, not causes, of mood disorders.

The Cognitive Perspective

Cognitive explanations hold that depression results from distortions in thinking. According to Beck (1967, 1991), depressed individuals view themselves, their world, and their future all in negative ways. They see their interactions with the world as defeating—a series of burdens and obstacles that usually end in failure. Depressed persons believe they are deficient, unworthy, and inadequate, and they attribute their perceived failures to their own physical, mental, or moral inadequacies. Finally, according to the cognitive theory, depressed patients believe that their future holds no hope. They may reason: "Everything always turns out wrong." "I never win." "Things will never get better." "It's no use."

In a review of a number of studies, Haaga and others (1991) did indeed find that depression is related to distortions in thinking. The cognitive perspective has much to offer that we can apply in our daily lives. Read the Applications section at the end of this chapter to learn more.

The Psychodynamic Explanation

Psychodynamic theorists propose another cause for mood disorders. They suggest that when people cannot effectively express aggressive or negative feelings, they may turn those feelings inward (repress them) and thus experience depression.

Stress

Even though heredity is the best predictor of depression over a lifetime, Kendler, Kessler, and others (1995) found stressful life events such as getting divorced or losing a job to be the best short-term predictors of depression, and for those who are genetically predisposed, the risk is much greater. The vast majority of first episodes of depression strike after major life stress (Brown et al., 1994; Frank et al., 1994). Yet recurrences of depression, at least in people who are biologically predisposed, often occur without significant life stress (Brown et al., 1994).

first-degree relatives: A person's parents, children, or siblings.

Women raising children in conditions of extreme poverty are at higher risk of developing depression.

Why are women so much more likely to suffer from depression than men? Are they somehow more biologically predisposed? Are they subject to more life stress than men? The National Task Force on Women and Depression suggests that the higher rate of depression in women is largely due to social and cultural factors. In fulfilling their many roles—mother, wife, lover, friend, daughter, neighbor—women are likely to put the needs of others ahead of their own. Having young children poses a particular risk, and women suffer other stresses disproportionately, such as poverty and physical and sexual abuse. In fact, Pribor and Dinwiddie (1992) found an alarming incidence of depression, 88.5 percent, among female incest victims.

Stressful life events may leave some people simply feeling bad, but others become clinically depressed. What accounts for the difference? Our genes? Brain chemistry? Early childhood experiences? Or is it the way we interpret life events, whether optimistic or pessimistic? There is some evidence to suggest that each explanation may play a part in the puzzle of depression.

Some depressed people commit the ultimate act of desperation—suicide. What are some of the risk factors for suicide, and what can we do to help prevent a person from committing suicide? Read the following World of Psychology section to find out.

World of Psychology

Suicide and Gender, Race, and Age

On April 5, 1994, Kurt Cobain, lead singer of the rock group Nirvana, commited suicide by shooting himself. He was 27 years old. Why would any person commit this final act of desperation?

Who Commits Suicide?

There were almost 31,000 suicides reported in the United States in 1991, and more than 80 percent were males (U.S. Bureau of the Census, 1994). Why do so many

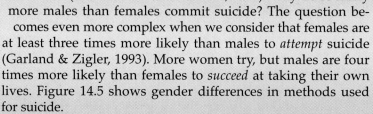

more males than females commit suicide? The question becomes even more complex when we consider that females are at least three times more likely than males to *attempt* suicide (Garland & Zigler, 1993). More women try, but males are four times more likely than females to *succeed* at taking their own lives. Figure 14.5 shows gender differences in methods used for suicide.

According to some accounts, up to 40 percent of those who attempt suicide will try again, and 10 to 14 percent will eventually succeed (Garland & Zigler, 1993). White males of all age groups have the highest suicide rate, 1.8 times higher than the rate among African American males.

Who Is at Highest Risk for Suicide?

Older Americans are at far greater risk for suicide than younger people. White males aged 85 and over have the highest recorded suicide rate, which in 1991 reached 75.1 suicides for every 100,000 people in that age group (U.S. Bureau

FIGURE 14.5

Gender Differences in Methods Used for Suicide

Males who commit suicide are far more likely to use firearms (65.1 percent) than any other method. Hanging and strangulation is a very distant second at 15.1 percent. Although females, too, are most likely to use firearms (39.8 percent), poisoning (36.9 percent) is a very close second. (Data from U.S. Bureau of the Census, 1994.)

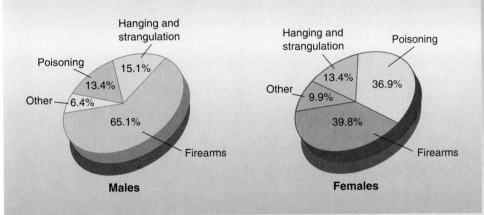

of the Census, 1994). This is more than six times the average national suicide rate of 12.2 per 100,000. Poor general health, serious illness, loneliness (often due to the death of a spouse), and decline in social and economic status are conditions that may push many older Americans, especially those aged 75 and over, to commit suicide (Rich et al., 1991).

For teenagers and young adults aged 15 through 24, suicide is now the third leading cause of death, with accidents ranking first and homicides second (U.S. Bureau of the Census, 1994). For college students, however, suicide ranks second. According to Garland and Zigler (1993), 6 to 13 percent of adolescents and 10.4 percent of college students have made a suicide attempt.

The rate of suicide among 15- to 19-year-olds has nearly doubled over the last few decades, an increase that may be due to increases in alcohol and drug abuse (Berman & Schwartz, 1990), psychiatric disorders (Runeson, 1989), antisocial behavior (Shafii et al., 1985), and disturbed home life (Holinger et al., 1987). In addition, an underlying psychiatric condition or a precipitating circumstance such as the breakup of a relationship, family conflict, a disciplinary crisis, or school problems may push a teenager "over the edge" (Heikkinen et al., 1993). There is also an elevated risk of suicide among adolescents who have been in trouble with the police or incarcerated (Brent et al., 1993).

Regardless of age group, suicide rates are lowest for married persons (Smith et al., 1988) and lower in women who have children (Hoyer & Lund, 1993). And the suicide rate is highest for persons who have made a previous suicide attempt (Beck et al., 1990). People suffering from psychiatric disorders, particularly depression, schizophrenia, panic disorder, and alcoholism or drug abuse, are at higher risk (Lesage et al., 1994; Mościcki, 1995). In fact, 70 percent of suicides are associated with depression (Coppen, 1994). Figure 14.6 (on page 536) shows the differences in U.S. suicide rates according to race, gender, and age.

continued

FIGURE 14.6

Differences in Suicide Rate According to Race, Gender, and Age

In every age group the suicide rate is highest for white males and second highest for black males. The general conclusion is that males are more likely to commit suicide than females, and whites are more likely than blacks. Suicide rates indicated by asterisks (*) are too low to be statistically reliable. (Data from U.S. Bureau of the Census, 1994.)

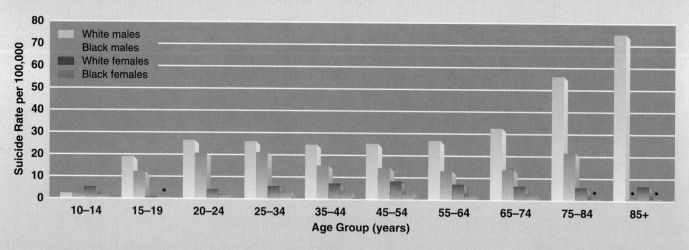

Preventing Suicide

Although there are cultural differences in the rates, the methods used, and the reasons for committing suicide, the warning signs are very similar across racial, gender, and age groups.

Most suicidal persons communicate their intent; in fact, about 90 percent of them leave clues (Shneidman, 1994). They may communicate verbally: "You won't be seeing me again." "You won't have to worry about me any more." "Life isn't worth living." They may leave behavioral clues, such as giving away their most valued possessions; withdrawing from friends, family, and associates; taking unnecessary risks; showing personality changes; acting and looking depressed; and losing interest in favorite activities. These warning signs should always be taken seriously. Suicidal individuals need compassion, emotional support, and the opportunity to express the feelings and problems that are the source of their psychological pain.

Hopelessness is a common characteristic of suicidal individuals (Beck et al., 1993). Proposing solutions or alternatives that could lessen hopelessness may lower the likelihood of suicide. Most people contemplating suicide are not totally committed to self-destruction. This may explain why many potential victims leave warnings or use less lethal means in attempted suicide.

But we should not be amateur psychologists if we are dealing with a suicidal person. Probably the best service you can render is to encourage the person to get professional help. There are 24-hour-a-day suicide hotlines all over the country. A call might save a life.

Memory Check 14.5

1. Monteil has periods in which he is so depressed that he becomes suicidal. At other times he is energetic and euphoric. He would probably receive the diagnosis of:
   a. dysthymia.
   b. seasonal mood disorder.
   c. bipolar disorder.
   d. major depressive disorder.

2. Match the theory of depression with the proposed cause.
   ___ 1) negative thoughts about oneself, the world, and one's future
   ___ 2) a deficiency of serotonin and norepinephrine
   ___ 3) turning resentment and hostility inward
   ___ 4) a family history of depression

   a. psychodynamic theory
   b. cognitive theory
   c. genetic theory
   d. biochemical theory

3. Stress appears to be unrelated to depression. (true/false)

4. The suicide rate is lower for:
   a. males than for females.
   b. African Americans than for whites.
   c. the elderly than for teenagers.
   d. people who suffer psychological disorders than for those who do not.

Answers: 1. c 2. 1) b 2) d 3) a 4) c 3. false 4. b

Other Psychological Disorders

Personality Disorders: Troublesome Behavior Patterns

Do you know people who are impossible to get along with—people who always seem to be at odds with themselves, their environment, their family, and others? Such people may have a **personality disorder**—a long-standing, inflexible, maladaptive pattern of behaving and relating to others, which usually begins early in childhood or adolescence (Widiger et al., 1988). They tend to have problems in their social relationships and at work, and may experience personal distress as well. Some people with personality disorders know that their behavior causes problems in their lives, yet they seem unable to change. But more commonly, they are self-centered and do not see themselves as responsible for their difficulties. Instead, they tend to blame other people or situations for their problems.

The *DSM-IV* lists ten categories of personality disorders; five are explained briefly in Table 14.1 (on page 538). Of particular interest is antisocial personality disorder.

Antisocial Personality Disorder Too often we read or hear about people who commit horrible crimes and show no remorse whatsoever. After raping and nearly beating to death a young woman jogging in New York's Central Park, one of her attackers calmly stated, "She was nothing." Another happily claimed, "It was fun!" Baffled, we ask ourselves how a person could do such a thing. Many

What characteristics are shared by most people with personality disorders?

personality disorder: A continuing, inflexible, maladaptive pattern of inner experience and behavior that causes great distress or impaired functioning and differs significantly from the patterns expected in the person's culture.

TABLE 14.1 Examples of *DSM-IV* Categories of Personality Disorders

Type of Disorder	Symptoms
Paranoid	Person is highly suspicious, untrusting, guarded, hypersensitive, easily slighted, lacking in emotion; holds grudges.
Antisocial personality	Person shows callous disregard for the rights and feelings of others; is manipulative, impulsive, selfish, aggressive, irresponsible, reckless; is willing to break the law, lie, cheat, or exploit others for personal gain, without remorse; fails to hold job.
Histrionic	Individual seeks attention and approval; is overly dramatic, self-centered, shallow; is demanding, manipulative, easily bored, suggestible; craves excitement; often, is attractive and sexually seductive.
Narcissistic	Person has exaggerated sense of self-importance and entitlement and is self-centered, arrogant, demanding, exploitive, envious; craves admiration and attention; lacks empathy.
Borderline	Individual is unstable in mood, behavior, self-image, and social relationships; has intense fear of abandonment; exhibits impulsive and reckless behavior, inappropriate anger; makes suicidal gestures and performs self-mutilating acts.

Source: Based on the *DSM-IV* (American Psychiatric Association, 1994).

of these people may have what psychologists call antisocial personality disorder. Ted Bundy, the infamous serial killer executed in 1990, was thought to have antisocial personality disorder.

People with **antisocial personality disorder** have a "pervasive pattern of disregard for, and violation of, the rights of others that begins in childhood or early adolescence and continues into adulthood" (American Psychiatric Association, 1994, p. 645). As children they lie, steal, vandalize, initiate fights, skip school, run away from home, and may be physically cruel to others. By early adolescence they usually drink excessively, use drugs, and engage in promiscuous sex. And in adulthood they cannot keep a job, act as a responsible parent, honor financial commitments, or obey the law.

Many antisocial types are intelligent and may seem charming and very likable at first. They are good con men, and they are more often men—as many as 5.8 percent of the U.S. male population, compared to less than 1.3 percent of the female population (Kessler et al., 1994). Checkley (1941), one of the first to study antisocial personality, revealed that persons with the disorder seem to lack the ability to love or feel loyalty and compassion toward others. They do not appear to have a conscience and feel little or no guilt or remorse no matter how cruel or despicable their actions might be (Hare, 1985).

Although the *DSM-IV* does not include the following characteristics, some experts believe that antisocial types fail to experience anxiety as normal people do. They seem fearless, oblivious to danger to themselves and unconcerned about the possible, even likely, consequences of their actions; and they appear to be unable to profit from experience (Chesno & Kilmann, 1975; Hare, 1970). Several adoption studies strongly indicate a genetic factor in antisocial personality disorder (Loehlin et al., 1988).

Years ago people with antisocial personality disorder were referred to as psychopaths or sociopaths. Con men, quack doctors, impostors, and today many drug pushers, pimps, delinquents, and criminals could be diagnosed as having this disorder. Some come to the attention of the authorities; others do not.

antisocial personality disorder: A disorder marked by lack of feeling for others; selfish, aggressive, irresponsible behavior; and willingness to break the law, lie, cheat, or exploit others for personal gain.

sexual dysfunction: A persistent or recurrent problem that causes marked distress and interpersonal difficulty and that may involve any or some combination of the following: sexual desire, sexual arousal or the pleasure associated with sex, or orgasm.

FIGURE 14.7

Lifetime Prevalence of Psychiatric Disorders

The percentages of males and females in the United States who suffer from various psychiatric disorders during their lifetime are based on the findings of the National Comorbidity Survey. Almost 50 percent of the respondents interviewed in this large national survey suffered from at least one psychiatric disorder in their lifetime. Males and females had about the same rate for experiencing some type of disorder. Males had higher rates for substance abuse and dependence and antisocial personality disorder. Females had higher rates for anxiety disorders and mood disorders. (Data from Kessler et al., 1994.)

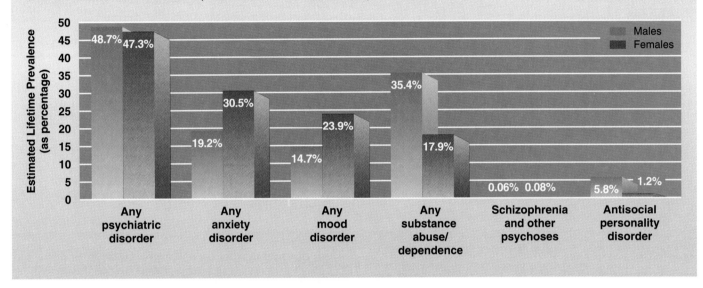

Figure 14.7 shows the estimated lifetime prevalence in the United States of antisocial personality disorder and other disorders we have discussed.

Sexual and Gender Identity Disorders

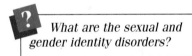

What are the sexual and gender identity disorders?

Most psychologists define sexual disorders as those that are destructive, guilt- or anxiety-producing, compulsive, or a cause of discomfort or harm to one or both parties involved. The *DSM-IV* has two categories of sexual disorders: sexual dysfunctions (discussed in Chapter 11) and paraphilias. As Chapter 11 explained, **sexual dysfunctions** are persistent, recurrent, and distressing problems involving sexual desire, sexual arousal, or the pleasure associated with sex or orgasm. **Paraphilias** are disorders in which recurrent sexual urges, fantasies, or behaviors involve children, other nonconsenting partners, nonhuman objects, or the suffering or humiliation of the individual or the partner. To be diagnosed as having a paraphilia, the person must experience considerable psychological distress or an impairment in functioning in an important area of his or her life. **Gender identity disorders** involve a problem accepting one's identity as male or female; children either express a desire to be or insist that they are the other gender. They show a preference for the clothes, games, pastimes, and playmates of the opposite sex.

Table 14.2 (on page 540) shows a number of the sexual disorders listed in the *DSM-IV*. Please note that homosexuality is *not* considered a sexual disorder.

As we have seen, there are a variety of mental disorders with a range of causes from the biological or genetic to life events and one's environment. As you will see in Chapter 15, there are a variety of treatments as well.

paraphilia: A sexual disorder in which sexual urges, fantasies, and behavior generally involve children, other nonconsenting partners, nonhuman objects, or the suffering and humiliation of one or one's partner.

gender identity disorders: Disorders characterized by a problem accepting one's identity as male or female.

TABLE 14.2 *DSM-IV* **Categories of Sexual Disorders**

Type of Disorder	Symptoms
Paraphilias	Disorders in which recurrent sexual urges, fantasies, and behavior involve nonhuman objects, children, other nonconsenting persons, or the suffering or humiliation of the individual or his/her partner.
Fetishism	A disorder in which sexual urges, fantasies, and behavior involve an inanimate object, such as women's undergarments or shoes.
Pedophilia	A disorder in which sexual urges, fantasies, and behavior involve sexual activity with a prepubescent child or children.
Exhibitionism	A disorder in which sexual urges, fantasies, and behavior involve exposing one's genitals to an unsuspecting stranger.
Voyeurism	A disorder in which sexual urges, fantasies, and behavior involve watching unsuspecting people naked, undressing, or engaging in sexual activity.
Sexual masochism	A disorder in which sexual urges, fantasies, and behavior involve being beaten, humiliated, bound, or otherwise made to suffer.
Sexual sadism	A disorder in which sexual urges, fantasies, and behavior involve inflicting physical or psychological pain and suffering on another.
Other paraphilias	Disorders in which sexual urges, fantasies, and behavior involve, among other things, animals, feces, urine, corpses, filth, or enemas.
Sexual dysfunctions	Disorders involving low sexual desire; the inability to attain or maintain sexual arousal; a delay or absence of orgasm; premature ejaculation; or genital pain associated with sexual activity.

Source: Based on the *DSM-IV* (American Psychiatric Association, 1994).

Memory Check 14.6

1. Which statement is true of personality disorders?
   a. Personality disorders usually begin in adulthood.
   b. Persons with these disorders usually realize their problem.
   c. Personality disorders typically cause problems in social relationships and at work.
   d. Persons with these disorders typically seek professional help.

2. Tim lies, cheats, and exploits others without feeling guilty. His behavior best fits the diagnosis of _____ personality disorder.
   a. avoidant   c. antisocial
   b. histrionic   d. narcissistic

3. (Sexual dysfunctions, Paraphilias) are disorders in which sexual urges, fantasies, and behaviors involve children, other nonconsenting partners, or nonhuman objects.

Answers: 1. c 2. c 3. Paraphilias

APPLICATIONS • APPLICATIONS • APPLICATIONS

Depression— Bad Thoughts, Bad Feelings

Did you know that you can cause your own moods? Consider these thoughts: "I'll never pass this course." "He/she would never go out with me." "I can't do anything right." "I'm a failure." How do these thoughts make you feel?

When it comes to physical health and well-being, you have probably heard it said that "You are what you eat." To a large extent, in the area of mental health, "You are what you think." Depression and other forms of mental misery can be fueled by our negative or irrational thoughts—especially self-evaluations that include the words "never" or "always."

Depression is so widespread that it is often called the common cold of psychological problems. Everyone feels "down" or "blue" once in a while, but depression goes beyond such feelings. According to the American Psychiatric Association (1994), the most frequent symptoms of depression are:

- Feeling depressed, sad, hopeless, empty, or tearful most of the time
- Losing interest and pleasure in most of your activities
- Feeling tired or without energy for no reason most of the time
- Feeling worthless or inappropriately guilty most of the time
- Difficulty concentrating and making decisions
- Change in appetite—either eating more or less than usual

- Having difficulty sleeping or sleeping much more than usual

The Cognitive Approach to Depression

Many psychologists and psychiatrists take a cognitive approach to depression and believe that in many cases, negative and irrational thinking are directly responsible for a depressed mood. David Burns (1980) goes so far as to say:

All your moods are created by your "cognitions," or thoughts. . . . You *feel* the way you do right now because of the *thoughts you are thinking at this moment.* . . . The moment you have a certain thought and believe it, you will experience an immediate emotional response. Your thought actually *creates* the emotion. (pp. 11–12)

continued

One step toward healthy thinking is to recognize and avoid the following five cognitive traps.

Cognitive Trap 1: The "Tyranny of the Should." One certain path to unhappiness is to set unrealistic, unachievable standards for yourself. Karen Horney (1950) called this cognitive trap the "tyranny of the should." Unrealistic and unachievable standards are characterized by such words as *always, never, all, everybody*, and *everything*. Have you ever been tyrannized by any of these *shoulds*?

I "should always be the perfect friend, lover, spouse, parent, student, teacher, [or] employee."

I "should be able to endure everything" and "like everybody."

I "should never feel hurt" and "should always be calm."

I "should know, understand, and foresee everything."

I "should be able to solve all of my problems and the problems of others in no time."

I "should never be tired or fall ill." (Adapted from Horney, 1950, pp. 64–66.)

Cognitive Trap 2: Negative, "What If" Thinking. Much of our unhappiness stems from a preoccupation with what might be. These are examples of "what if" thinking: "What if she/he turns me down?" "What if I lose my job?" "What if I flunk this test?" "What if I can't pay my bills?" And if a "what if" comes to pass, the third cognitive trap may be sprung.

Cognitive Trap 3: Making Mountains Out of Molehills. A molehill becomes a mountain when a single negative event is perceived as catastrophic or allowed to become a definition of total worth. "I failed this test" might become "I'll never pass

this course," "I'll never graduate from college," "I'm too dumb to be in college," or "I'm a failure."

Cognitive Trap 4: The Perfection–Failure Dichotomy. Only on the rarest occasions can anyone's performance be considered absolutely perfect or a total failure. In reality, outcomes will fall somewhere on a continuum between these two extremes. But people who fall into this cognitive trap judge anything short of perfection as total failure.

Cognitive Trap 5: Setting Impossible Conditions for Happiness. Don't let your happiness hinge on perfection in yourself and others. Not everyone will love you or even like you, approve of you, or agree with you. If any of these are conditions upon which your happiness depends, you are setting the stage for disappointment or even depression.

Developing Healthier Thinking Habits

If negative or irrational thoughts are part of your habitual repertoire, you need to develop healthier thinking habits. Albert Ellis developed rational-emotive therapy to help people change irrational thinking. One technique he recommends is to write down negative thoughts when they occur and then write a rational substitute for that thought. (You will read more about Ellis's approach in Chapter 15.) Here are a few suggestions that may help you:

- Instead of thinking "It would be *the end of everything* if I lost my job!" think "I would not want to lose my job, but I could find another."

- Instead of thinking "I am a *failure* because this turned out so badly" substitute "I am embarrassed about how this turned out, but I'll do better the next time."

The next time you notice yourself entertaining negative thoughts or self-doubts, write them down and analyze them objectively and unemotionally. But don't go to the opposite extreme and substitute equally distorted positive thinking or mindless "happy talk." Self-delusion in either direction is not healthy.

Your goal should be to monitor your thinking and to systematically make it less distorted, more rational, more accurate, and more logical. We must live in the "real" world, and in order to enjoy happiness and mental health, we must think realistically. When our expectations, goals, and desires are unrealistic and unachievable, we are setting ourselves up for unhappiness, disappointment, and misery.

Depression is a complex psychological disorder with both physiological and psychological causes. All depression cannot be controlled simply by a change in thinking. If symptoms such as those listed at the beginning of this section persist, seek professional treatment.

Thinking Critically

Evaluation

Some psychological disorders are more common in women (depression, agoraphobia, and simple phobia), and some are more common in men (antisocial personality disorder and substance abuse and dependence). Give some possible reasons why such gender differences exist in the prevalence of these disorders. Support your answer.

Point/Counterpoint

There is continuing controversy over whether specific psychological disorders are chiefly biological in origin (nature) or result primarily from learning and experience (nurture). Select any two disorders from this chapter and prepare arguments for both the nature and nurture positions for both disorders.

Psychology in Your Life

Formulate a specific plan for your own life that will help you to recognize and avoid the five cognitive traps that contribute to unhealthy thinking. You might enlist the help of a friend to monitor your negative statements.

Chapter Summary and Review

What Is Abnormal?

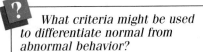 What criteria might be used to differentiate normal from abnormal behavior?

Behavior might be considered abnormal if it deviates radically from what is considered normal in one's own culture, if it leads to personal distress or impaired functioning, or if it results in one's being a danger to self and/or others.

 What are five current perspectives that attempt to explain the causes of psychological disorders?

Five current perspectives on the causes of abnormal behavior are (1) the biological perspective, which views it as a symptom of an underlying physical disorder; (2) the psychodynamic perspective, which maintains that it is caused by unconscious, unresolved conflicts; (3) the learning perspective, which claims that it is learned and sustained in the same way as other behavior; (4) the cognitive perspective, which suggests that it results from faulty thinking; and (5) the humanistic perspective, which views it as a result of the blocking of one's natural tendency toward self-actualization.

 What is the DSM-IV?

The *DSM-IV*, published by the American Psychiatric Association, is the system most widely used in the United States to diagnose psychological disorders.

Key Terms

DSM-IV (p. 513)
neurosis (p. 513)
psychosis (p. 514)

Anxiety Disorders: When Anxiety Is Extreme

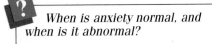 When is anxiety normal, and when is it abnormal?

Anxiety—a generalized feeling of apprehension, fear, or tension—is healthy if it is a response to a real danger or threat, and it is unhealthy if it is inappropriate or excessive.

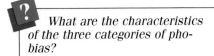 What are the symptoms of panic disorder?

Panic disorder is marked by recurrent, unpredictable panic attacks—attacks of overwhelming anxiety, fear, or terror, during which people experience palpitations, trembling or shaking, choking or smothering sensations, and the feeling that they are going to die or lose their sanity.

What are the characteristics of the three categories of phobias?

The three categories of phobias are (1) agoraphobia, fear of being in situations where escape is impossible or help is not available in case of incapacitating anxiety; (2) social phobia, fear of social situations where one might be embarrassed or humiliated by appearing clumsy or incompetent; and (3) specific phobia, a marked fear of a specific object or situation and a catchall category for all phobias other than agoraphobia or social phobia.

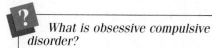
What do psychologists believe are some probable causes of phobias?

Phobias result primarily from frightening experiences or through observational learning. Genes may also play a role.

What is obsessive compulsive disorder?

Obsessive compulsive disorder is characterized by obsessions (persistent, recurring, involuntary thoughts, images, or impulses that cause great distress) and/or compulsions (persistent, irresistible, irrational urges to perform an act or ritual repeatedly).

Key Terms

anxiety disorders (p. 515)
anxiety (p. 515)
generalized anxiety disorder (p. 515)
panic attack (p. 516)
panic disorder (p. 516)
phobia (p. 516)
agoraphobia (p. 516)
social phobia (p. 517)
specific phobia (p. 517)
obsessive compulsive disorder (OCD) (p. 519)
obsession (p. 519)
compulsion (p. 519)

Somatoform and Dissociative Disorders

What are two somatoform disorders, and what symptoms do they share?

Somatoform disorders involve bodily symptoms that cannot be explained by known medical conditions. Hypochondriasis involves a persistent fear that bodily symptoms are the sign of some serious disease, and conversion disorder involves a loss of motor or sensory functioning in some part

of the body, such as paralysis or blindness.

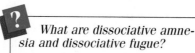
What are dissociative amnesia and dissociative fugue?

People with dissociative amnesia have a loss of memory for limited periods of their life or for their entire personal identity. In dissociative fugue people forget their entire identity, travel away from home, and may assume a new identity somewhere else.

What are some of the identifying symptoms of dissociative identity disorder?

Dissociative identity disorder (often called multiple personality) is one in which two or more distinct, unique personalities occur in the same person, each taking over at different times. Most patients are female and victims of early, severe physical and/or sexual abuse, and they typically complain of periods of "lost time."

Key Terms

somatoform disorders (p. 521)
hypochondriasis (p. 521)
conversion disorder (p. 522)
dissociative disorder (p. 522)
dissociative amnesia (p. 522)
dissociative fugue (p. 522)
dissociative identity disorder (p. 523)

Schizophrenia

What are some of the major positive and negative symptoms of schizophrenia?

The positive symptoms of schizophrenia are abnormal behaviors and characteristics including hallucinations, delusions, disorganized thinking and speech, bizarre behavior, and inappropriate affect. The negative symptoms represent deficiencies in thoughts and behavior and include social with-

drawal, apathy, loss of motivation, very limited speech, slowed movements, flat affect, and poor hygiene and grooming.

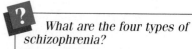
What are the four types of schizophrenia?

The four types of schizophrenia are catatonic, disorganized, paranoid, and undifferentiated schizophrenia.

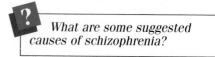
What are some suggested causes of schizophrenia?

Some suggested causes of schizophrenia are a genetic predisposition, sufficient stress in people who are predisposed to the disorder, and excessive dopamine activity in the brain.

Key Terms

schizophrenia (p. 525)
hallucination (p. 525)
delusion (p. 526)
delusion of grandeur (p. 526)
delusion of persecution (p. 526)
inappropriate affect (p. 526)
catatonic schizophrenia (p. 527)
disorganized schizophrenia (p. 527)
paranoid schizophrenia (p. 527)
diathesis–stress model (p. 528)

Mood Disorders

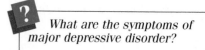
What are the symptoms of major depressive disorder?

Major depressive disorder is characterized by feelings of great sadness, despair, guilt, worthlessness, hopelessness, and, in extreme cases, suicidal intentions.

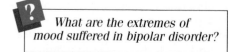
What are the extremes of mood suffered in bipolar disorder?

Bipolar disorder is a mood disorder in which a person suffers from manic episodes (periods of extreme elation, euphoria, and hyperactivity) alternating with major depression, usually with relatively normal periods in between.

What are some suggested causes of major depressive disorder and bipolar disorder?

Some of the proposed causes are (1) a genetic predisposition; (2) an imbalance in the neurotransmitters norepinephrine and serotonin; (3) a tendency to turn hostility and resentment inward rather than expressing it; (4) distorted and negative views of oneself, the world, and the future; and (5) stress.

Key Terms

mood disorders (p. 529)
major depressive disorder (p. 529)
seasonal affective disorder (SAD) (p. 530)

bipolar disorder (p. 531)
manic episode (p. 531)
first-degree relatives (p. 533)

Other Psychological Disorders

What characteristics are shared by most people with personality disorders?

People with personality disorders have longstanding, inflexible, maladaptive patterns of behavior that cause problems in their social relationships and at work and often cause personal distress. Such people seem unable to change and blame others for their problems.

What are the sexual and gender identity disorders?

Three categories of sexual disorders are sexual dysfunctions (problems with sexual desire, sexual arousal, or orgasm); paraphilias (needing unusual or bizarre objects, conditions, or acts for sexual gratification); and gender identity disorders (having a problem accepting one's identity as male or female).

Key Terms

personality disorder (p. 537)
antisocial personality disorder (p. 538)
sexual dysfunction (p. 539)
paraphilia (p. 539)
gender identity disorders (p. 539)

15

THERAPIES

CHAPTER OUTLINE

Insight Therapies

Psychodynamic Therapies:
Freud Revisited

The Humanistic and Existential
Therapies

Therapies Emphasizing
Interaction with Others

**Behavior Therapy:
Unlearning the Old,
Learning the New**

Behavior Modification
Techniques Based on Operant
Conditioning

Therapies Based on Classical
Conditioning

Therapies Based on
Observational Learning
Theory: Just Watch *This!*

**Cognitive Therapies: It's the
Thought That Counts**

Rational-Emotive Therapy:
Human Misery—The Legacy
of False Beliefs

Beck's Cognitive Therapy:
Overcoming "the Power of
Negative Thinking"

The Biological Therapies

Drug Therapy: Pills for
Psychological Ills

Electroconvulsive Therapy: The
Controversy Continues

Psychosurgery: Cutting to Cure

**Therapies and Therapists:
Many Choices**

Evaluating the Therapies:
Do They Work?

Mental Health Professionals:
How Do They Differ?

Selecting a Therapy: Finding
One That Fits

**World of Psychology: Therapy
and Race, Ethnicity, and Gender**

**Applications: Finding
a Therapist**

Thinking Critically

Chapter Summary and Review

Bill, a 21-year-old college student, suffers from a debilitating phobia, an intense fear of any kind of sudden loud noise—fireworks, gunshots, cars backfiring, and especially the sound of popping balloons. His fear of the sound of balloons bursting has extended to balloons themselves, and now he cannot bear to touch or even stand within several feet of a balloon.

One day two people lead Bill into a small room that is filled with 100 large balloons of every imaginable color. Already Bill is visibly shaking, and he huddles near the door. One person stands close to Bill, while the other person explains that he will now begin popping the balloons. While some 50 balloons are popped with a pin, Bill shakes uncontrollably. Tears stream down his face, he turns pale, and his legs shake so hard that a chair has to be provided so he can sit down. The remaining balloons are popped, making even more frightening sounds as the person steps on them. This upsets Bill even more, but he must endure the popping of another 250 balloons before he is allowed to leave. And he must return for the next 2 days for still more balloon popping.

What is going on here? Torture? An initiation? A sadistic ritual? No! It is a therapy session. Bill is undergoing treatment for his phobia, and the therapists are using a rapid treatment technique known as flooding. Flooding is a form of behavior therapy in which the patient agrees to be instantly and totally

immersed in the feared situation or surrounded by the feared object—in Bill's case, balloons.

Although Bill was doing well in college—he maintained a respectable "B" average—he hardly had a social life at all. Because of his phobia, Bill avoided all social situations where even the remotest possibility existed that balloons might be present—parties, dances, weddings, athletic events, concerts. But he did have a girlfriend, and it was she who referred him to the therapists who treated his phobia.

During the course of the 3 days, Bill became progressively less fearful in the presence of balloons and was even able to join in stepping on hundreds of balloons and popping them. After a 1-year follow-up, Bill reported that he experienced no distress in the presence of balloons and no longer avoided situations where he might encounter them. In fact, according to his girlfriend, balloons were on the table at one formal event they attended, yet it didn't bother Bill. Neither was he ill at ease when he sat relatively near a fireworks display on the Fourth of July. (Adapted from Houlihan et al., 1993.)

psychotherapy: The treatment for psychological disorders that uses psychological rather than biological means and primarily involves conversations between patient and therapist.

insight therapy: Any type of psychotherapy based on the notion that psychological well-being depends on self-understanding.

Surely Bill would agree that 3 rather torturous days of flooding therapy was a small price to pay to be free of his debilitating phobia. And flooding is only one of the many effective therapies you will learn about in this chapter.

What comes into your mind when you hear the word *psychotherapy*? Many people picture a patient on a couch talking to a gray-haired, bearded therapist who has a heavy accent. But that picture is hopelessly out of date, as you will see. **Psychotherapy** uses psychological rather than biological means to treat emotional and behavioral disorders, and it usually involves a conversation between the patient (often called a client) and the therapist. But psychotherapy has grown and changed enormously since its beginnings in the days of Freud, more than 100 years ago. Now it seems that there is a therapy for every trouble, a technique for every taste—over 450 different psychotherapies (Karasu, 1986). Today, for the most part, the couch has been replaced by a comfortable chair, and instead of years of treatment, psychotherapy is usually relatively brief, averaging about 18 sessions among private therapists (Goode, 1987). Furthermore, psychotherapy in the modern age is not completely dominated by men, as more women are becoming therapists. We have come a long way since the days of Sigmund Freud.

In this chapter we will explore insight therapies, which use talk, thought, reasoning, understanding, and analysis to treat psychological problems. Next we will look at behavior therapies, which are based on principals of learning theory. Finally, we will examine biological therapies—drug therapy, electroconvulsive therapy, and psychosurgery.

Insight Therapies

Some forms of psychotherapy are collectively referred to as **insight therapies** because their assumption is that our psychological well-being depends on self-understanding—understanding of our thoughts, emotions, motives, behavior, and coping mechanisms. The major insight therapies are psychoanalysis, person-centered therapy, existential therapy, and Gestalt therapy.

Psychodynamic Therapies: Freud Revisited

Freud originally proposed the psychodynamic perspective on abnormal behavior, which maintains that the cause of psychological disorders lies in early childhood experiences and in unresolved, unconscious conflicts, usually of a sexual or aggressive nature. **Psychoanalysis**, the treatment approach developed by Freud, was the first formal psychotherapy, and it was the dominant influence in psychotherapy in the 1940s and 1950s. The goals of psychoanalysis are to uncover repressed memories and to bring to consciousness the buried, unresolved conflicts believed to lie at the root of a person's problem.

Freud's famous couch was used by his patients during psychoanalysis.

Psychoanalysis: From the Couch of Freud Freudian psychoanalysis uses four basic techniques: free association, analysis of resistance, dream analysis, and analysis of transference.

? What are the four basic techniques of psychoanalysis, and how are they used to help disturbed patients?

Free Association The central technique of psychoanalytic therapy is **free association**, in which the patient is asked to reveal whatever thoughts, feelings, or images come to mind no matter how trivial, embarrassing, or terrible they might appear. Freud believed that free association allows important unconscious material to surface, such as repressed memories, threatening impulses, and traumatic episodes of childhood.

The patient lies comfortably on a couch, with the analyst sitting out of the patient's view. This setting is presumed to minimize distractions that might interfere with the patient's free flow of thoughts and speech. The analyst pieces together the free-flowing associations, explains their meaning, and helps patients gain insight into the thoughts and behavior that are troubling them.

Analysis of Resistance How do you think you would react if an analyst told you to express *everything* that came into your mind? Would you try to avoid revealing certain painful or embarrassing thoughts? Freud's patients did, and he called this **resistance**. Freud (1920/1963b) said:

> The patient attempts to escape from it by every possible means. First he says nothing comes into his head, then that so much comes into his head that he can't grasp any of it. . . . He betrays it by the long pauses which occur in his talk. At last he admits that he really cannot say something, he is ashamed to. (p. 254)

If the patient hesitates, balks, or becomes visibly upset about any topic, the analyst assumes the topic is emotionally significant for him or her. Freud also pointed out other forms of resistance, such as "forgetting" appointments with the analyst or arriving late.

Dream Analysis Freud believed that areas of emotional concern repressed in waking life are sometimes expressed in symbolic form in dreams. He called dreams "the royal road to the unconscious" because they often convey hidden meanings and identify important repressed thoughts, memories, and emotions.

psychoanalysis (SY-ko-uh-NAL-ul-sis): The psychotherapy that uses free association, dream analysis, and analysis of resistance and transference to uncover repressed memories, impulses, and conflicts thought to cause psychological disorders.

free association: A psychoanalytic technique used to explore the unconscious by having patients reveal whatever thoughts or images come to mind.

resistance: In psychoanalytic therapy, the patient's attempts to avoid expressing or revealing painful or embarrassing thoughts or feelings.

transference: An intense emotional situation occurring in psychoanalysis, when one comes to behave toward the analyst as one had behaved toward a significant figure from the past.

person-centered therapy: A nondirective, humanistic therapy in which the therapist creates a warm, accepting climate, freeing clients to be themselves and releasing their natural tendency toward positive growth.

self-actualization: Developing to one's fullest potential.

Analysis of Transference   Freud claimed that at some point during psychoanalysis, the patient inevitably begins to react to the analyst with the same feelings and attitudes that were present in another significant relationship—usually with the mother or father. This reaction he called **transference**.

> In every analytic treatment there arises . . . an intense emotional relationship between the patient and the analyst. . . . It can be of a positive or of a negative character and can vary between the extremes of a passionate, completely sensual love and the unbridled expression of an embittered defiance and hatred. (Freud, 1925/1963a, p. 71)

Transference allows the patient to relive or reenact troubling experiences from the past with the analyst as parent substitute. Then the unresolved childhood conflicts can be replayed in the present, but this time with a parent figure who does not reject, provoke guilt, or punish as the actual parent did.

Psychodynamic Therapy Today: The New View   Traditional psychoanalysis can be a long and costly undertaking. Patients attend four or five therapy sessions per week for 2 to 4 years. But by the mid-1980s, only about 2 percent of people undergoing psychotherapy chose classical psychoanalysis (Goode, 1987). And today the number appears to be steadily declining (Grünbaum, 1994). Psychoanalysis is most suitable for those with average or higher intelligence who are not severely disturbed but are interested in extensive self-exploration.

Although some psychoanalysts practice traditional psychoanalysis, many practice brief psychodynamic therapy, which is also aimed at gaining insight into unconscious conflicts. The therapist and patient decide on the issues to explore at the outset rather than waiting for them to emerge in the course of treatment. The therapist assumes a more active role and places more emphasis on the present than in traditional psychoanalysis. Brief psychodynamic therapy may require only one or two visits per week for as few as 12 to 20 weeks (Altshuler, 1989). In a meta-analysis of 11 well-controlled studies, Chrits-Christoph (1992) found brief psychodynamic therapy to be as effective as other psychotherapies.

Criticisms of Psychoanalytic Therapy   Traditional psychoanalysis has been criticized for its emphasis on the unconscious and the past and its virtual neglect of the conscious and the present. Furthermore, the focus on unconscious motives as the major determinants of behavior minimizes patients' responsibility for their behavior and their choices. And from a practical standpoint, research does not suggest that the tremendous cost of psychoanalysis yields results superior to briefer, less costly therapy.

The Humanistic and Existential Therapies

Based on a more optimistic and hopeful picture of human nature and human potential, humanistic and existential therapies stand in stark contrast to psychoanalysis. Individuals are viewed as unique and basically self-determining, with the ability and freedom to lead rational lives and make rational choices. Humanistic and existential therapists encourage personal growth and seek to teach clients how to fulfill their potential and to take responsibility for their behavior and for what they become in life. The focus is primarily on current relationships and experiences.

?   *What are the role and the goal of the therapist in person-centered therapy?*

Person-Centered Therapy: The Patient Becomes the Person   **Person-centered therapy**, developed by Carl Rogers (1951), is based on the humanistic view of human nature. According to this view, people are innately good and if allowed to develop naturally, they will grow toward **self-actualization**—the realization of their inner potential.

If people grow naturally toward self-actualization, then why is everyone not self-actualized? The humanistic perspective suggests that psychological disorders result when a person's natural tendency toward self-actualization is blocked. Rogers (1959) insisted that individuals themselves block their natural tendency toward growth and self-actualization when they act in ways inconsistent with their true self in order to gain the positive regard of others.

In person-centered therapy (formerly called client-centered therapy), the focus is on conscious thoughts and feelings. The therapist attempts to create a warm, accepting climate in which clients are free to be themselves so that their natural tendency toward growth can be released. Person-centered therapy is a **nondirective therapy**; that is, the direction of the therapy sessions is controlled by the client. The therapist acts as a facilitator of growth, giving understanding, support, and encouragement rather than proposing solutions, answering questions, or actively directing the course of therapy. Rogers rejected all forms of therapy that cast the therapist in the role of expert and clients in the role of patients who expect the therapist to tell them something or prescribe something that "cures" their problem.

According to Rogers, there are only three conditions required of therapists. First, they must have unconditional positive regard for, or total acceptance of, the client, regardless of the client's feelings, thoughts, or behavior. In this atmosphere of unconditional positive regard, clients will feel free to reveal their weakest points, to relax their defenses, and to begin to accept and value themselves. Second, therapists' feelings toward their clients must be genuine, or congruent—no facade, no putting up a professional front. Third, therapists must have empathy with the clients—the ability to put themselves in the clients' place. Therapists must show that they comprehend the clients' feelings, emotions, and experiences, and that they understand and see the clients' world as the clients see it. When clients speak, the therapist follows by restating or reflecting back their ideas and feelings. In this way clients begin to see themselves more clearly and eventually resolve their own conflicts and make positive decisions about their lives.

The following is an excerpt from a 21-year-old woman's first session of person-centered therapy.

> *Therapist:* I really know very little as to why you came in. Would you like to tell me something about it?
> *Client:* It is a long story. I can't find myself. Everything I do seems to be wrong. . . . If there is any criticism or anyone says anything about me I just can't take it. . . .
> *Therapist:* You feel things are all going wrong and that you're just crushed by criticism.
> *Client:* Well, it doesn't even need to be meant as criticism. It goes way back. In grammar school I never felt I belonged. . . .
> *Therapist:* You feel the roots go back a long way but that you have never really belonged, even in grammar school. (Rogers, 1977, p. 199)

In the 1940s and 1950s, person-centered therapy enjoyed a strong following among psychologists. And by the early 1980s, a survey of 400 psychologists and counselors revealed that Carl Rogers was considered the most influential figure in counseling and psychotherapy (Smith, 1982).

Gestalt Therapy: Getting in Touch with Your Feelings

Gestalt therapy, developed by Fritz Perls (1969), emphasizes the importance of clients fully experiencing, in the present moment, their feelings, thoughts, and actions and then

nondirective therapy: An approach in which the therapist acts to facilitate growth, giving understanding and support rather than proposing solutions, answering questions, or actively directing the course of therapy.

Gestalt therapy: A therapy originated by Fritz Perls and emphasizing the importance of clients fully experiencing, in the present moment, their feelings, thoughts, and actions and taking personal responsibility for their behavior.

Carl Rogers (at upper right) facilitates discussion in a therapy group.

What is the major emphasis in Gestalt therapy?

directive therapy: An approach to therapy in which the therapist takes an active role in determining the course of therapy sessions and provides answers and suggestions to the patient.

taking responsibility for them. Perls maintains that many of us block out aspects of our experience and are often not aware of how we really feel.

Gestalt therapy is a **directive therapy**, one in which the therapist takes an active role in determining the course of therapy sessions. The well-known phrase "getting in touch with your feelings" is an ever-present objective of the Gestalt therapist, who helps, prods, or badgers clients to experience their feelings as deeply and genuinely as possible and then admit responsibility for them.

Perls suggests that those of us who are in need of therapy carry around a heavy load of unfinished business, which may be in the form of resentments or conflicts with parents, siblings, lovers, employers, or others. If not resolved, these conflicts are carried forward into our present relationships. One method for dealing with unfinished business is the "empty chair" technique. The client imagines, for example, that a wife, husband, father, or mother sits in the empty chair and proceeds to tell the chair what he or she truly feels about that person. Then the client will trade places and sit in the empty chair and role-play what the imagined person's response would be to what the client has said.

The goal of Gestalt therapy is not merely to relieve symptoms, but to help clients achieve a more integrated self and become more authentic and self-accepting. In addition, they must learn to assume personal responsibility for their behavior rather than blame society, past experiences, parents, or others.

Existential Therapy: Finding Meaning in Life Existential therapy helps people deal with the issues that are part of the human condition—finding meaning in life, finding values that are worth living and even dying for. The existential point of view tries to deal with alienation, the feeling that we are disconnected from the rest of the world, that we don't fit in, that we are lonely and stand apart.

The existential therapist stresses that we have both the freedom and the responsibility to choose the kind of person we want to become. Because each of us is unique, we must find our own personal meaning in our existence.

Memory Check 15.1

1. In psychoanalysis the technique whereby a patient reveals every thought, idea, or image that comes to mind is called _____; the patient's attempt to avoid revealing certain thoughts is called _____.
   a. transference; resistance
   b. free association; transference
   c. revelation; transference
   d. free association; resistance

2. What is the directive therapy that emphasizes the importance of the client fully experiencing, in the present moment, his or her thoughts, feelings, and actions?
   a. person-centered therapy
   b. Gestalt therapy
   c. existential therapy
   d. psychoanalytic therapy

3. What is the nondirective therapy developed by Carl Rogers in which the therapist creates a warm, accepting climate so that the client's natural tendency toward positive change can be released?
   a. person-centered therapy
   b. Gestalt therapy
   c. existential therapy
   d. psychoanalytic therapy

4. Which therapy presumes that the cause of the patient's problems are repressed memories, impulses, and conflicts?
   a. person-centered therapy
   b. Gestalt therapy
   c. existential therapy
   d. psychoanalytic therapy

Answers: 1. d 2. b 3. a 4. d

Therapies Emphasizing Interaction with Others

Some therapies look not only at the individual's internal struggles but also at interpersonal relationships.

Interpersonal Therapy: Short Road to Recovery Interpersonal therapy (IPT) is a brief psychotherapy that has proven very effective in the treatment of depression (Elkin et al., 1989; Klerman et al., 1984). IPT is designed specifically to help patients cope with four types of problems commonly associated with major depression:

> ? *What four problems commonly associated with major depression is interpersonal therapy designed to treat?*

1. *Unusual or severe responses to the death of a loved one.* The therapist and patient discuss the patient's relationship with the deceased person and feelings (such as guilt) that may be associated with the death. The therapist tries to help the patient release the past and develop an active interest in the present.

2. *Interpersonal role disputes.* Depression is often associated with mutually incompatible expectations about roles or responsibilities between patients and their spouses, children, parents, friends, co-workers, or employers. These may be a source of conflict, resentment, and even hostility in which neither party discusses the problem openly and honestly or really tries to understand the other's point of view. The therapist helps the patient to understand what is at stake for those involved and to explore options for bringing about change. If the problem involves a family member, it is often helpful for that person also to attend a therapy session.

3. *Difficulty in adjusting to role transitions such as divorce, career change, and retirement.* Role transitions may involve a loss, such as a life change resulting from an illness or injury or the loss of a job. Other role transitions involve positive events, such as marriage, a new baby, or a promotion. Patients are helped to see the change not as a threat but as a challenge and an opportunity for growth that they can master.

4. *Deficits in interpersonal skills.* Some people lack the skills to make friends and to sustain intimate relationships. Such deficits may lead to loneliness, isolation, and depression. Through role-playing and analysis of the patient's communication style, the therapist tries to help the patient develop the interpersonal skills necessary to initiate and sustain relationships.

Interpersonal therapy is brief, consisting of 12 to 16 weekly sessions. A large study conducted by the National Institute of Mental Health found IPT to be an effective treatment even for severe depression and one with a low dropout rate (Elkin et al., 1989). Research also indicates that patients who recover from major depression can enjoy a longer period without relapse when they continue with monthly sessions of IPT (Frank et al., 1991).

Family therapists pay attention to the dynamics of the family unit—how members communicate, act toward each other, and view each other.

Family and Marital Therapy: Healing Our Relationships Even the best of families sometimes have problems, and there are therapists of all types who specialize in treating the troubled family. Families who come to therapists include those with troubled or troublesome teenagers, alcoholic parents, abusive family situations, or other problems. In **family therapy**, parents and children enter therapy as a group with one or more family therapists (called conjoint therapy). Sometimes therapists work with only one or a few family members at a time.

The therapist pays attention to the dynamics of the family unit—how family members communicate, how they act toward one another, and how they view each other. Is there a power struggle? Are unreasonable demands being made? The goal of the therapist is to help the family reach agreement on certain changes that will help heal the wounds of the family unit, improve communication patterns, and create more understanding and harmony within the group.

Marriages often have problems, too. Nearly half of the couples who decide to tie the knot will later decide to untie it. Some therapists work with married couples. They may help them resolve their difficulties and stay together; or they

interpersonal therapy (IPT): A brief psychotherapy designed to help depressed people understand their problems in interpersonal relationships and develop more effective ways to improve them.

family therapy: Therapy based on the assumption that an individual's problem is caused and/or maintained in part by problems within the family unit, and so the entire family is involved in therapy.

may work to ease the emotional turmoil if ending an irretrievably broken marriage is the best answer for the couple.

Family therapy can be beneficial in the treatment of schizophrenic patients. Patients are more likely to relapse if their family members express emotions, attitudes, and behaviors that involve criticism, hostility, or emotional overinvolvement (a pattern labeled high in expressed emotion, or high EE) (Falloon, 1988; Jenkins & Karno, 1992). Family therapy can help other family members modify their behavior toward the patient.

What are some advantages of group therapy?

Group Therapy: Helping One at a Time, Together Group therapy really took root in the military more than 50 years ago, during World War II. The armed services ran short of therapists and tried to handle more patients with group therapy. Besides being less expensive than individual therapy, group therapy has other advantages. It gives the individual a sense of belonging and an opportunity to express feelings, to get feedback from other members, and to give and receive help and emotional support. Learning that others also share their problems leaves people feeling less alone and ashamed. The American Psychiatric Association (1993b) has endorsed group therapy as particularly useful for depression associated with bereavement or chronic illness.

Psychodrama, originated by J. L. Moreno (1959), is a technique used by many group therapists. If you entered group therapy based on this approach, you would act out your problem situation or relationship with the assistance and participation of other group members. Sometimes you would play the part of the person who is a problem in your life, a technique called role reversal. You might take the role of your parent, boyfriend, girlfriend, or spouse and in this way gain some understanding of the other person's feelings. When group members act out their own frustrations and role-play the frustrations of others, they gain insight into their problems and troubling relationships.

Group Help of a Different Sort Many Americans seek help for their problems from sources other than mental health professionals. Some are attending encounter groups, and millions of others are getting support from self-help groups.

Encounter Groups: Where Anything Goes Although not technically considered therapy, **encounter groups** claim to promote personal growth and self-knowledge and to improve personal relationships through intense emotional encounters with other group members. Groups are composed of 10 to 20 people who meet with a leader or leaders over a period of several weeks or months. Marathon encounter groups, which meet for 18 to 48 hours, provide a particularly intense form of encounter experience.

Encounter group participants are encouraged to become more open and let down their defenses so that they can reveal themselves to others and allow others to reach them. Group members are urged to express honestly their feelings about themselves and others. Not all exchanges are verbal. Relating to others nonverbally in the form of hugging, holding, massaging, and touching may be encouraged, to help group members "peel off their hangups" (Harper, 1975, p. 93).

Sometimes more is peeled off than just hangups—all is bared at nude encounters. How successful are these encounters? Are there any dangers involved? Some studies indicate that about one-third of the participants benefit from the experience, one-third are unaffected, and one-third have negative effects (Lieberman et al., 1973). Although encounter group leaders generally agree that their groups are not appropriate for disturbed individuals, often little is done to screen applicants. About 8 to 10 percent of encounter group participants have significant negative effects from the experience (Hartley et al., 1976).

group therapy: A form of therapy in which several clients (usually 7–10) meet regularly with one or two therapists to resolve personal problems.

psychodrama: A group therapy in which one group member acts out personal problem situations and relationships, assisted by other members, to gain insight into the problem.

encounter group: An intense emotional group experience designed to promote personal growth and self-knowledge; participants are encouraged to let down their defenses and relate honestly and openly to one another.

Self-Help Groups: Let's Do It Ourselves   A special type of group offering help for specific problems is the self-help group. Unlike other group therapy approaches we have discussed, self-help groups usually are not led by professional therapists. They are simply groups of people who share a common problem and meet to give and receive support. About 12 million people in the United States participate in roughly 500,000 self-help groups.

One of the oldest and best-known self-help groups is Alcoholics Anonymous, which claims 1.5 million members worldwide. Other self-help groups patterned after Alcoholics Anonymous have been formed to help individuals overcome many other addictive behaviors, from overeating (Overeaters Anonymous) to gambling (Gamblers Anonymous). There are self-help groups for people with a variety of physical and mental illnesses, and groups to help people deal with crises, from divorce and bereavement to victimization. In addition, there are groups to help relatives and friends of people having such problems.

Self-help groups offer comfort because people can talk about their problems with others who have "been there" and learn that their painful emotional reactions are normal. They can exchange useful information, discuss their coping strategies, and gain hope by seeing people who are coping with the same problems successfully. Lieberman (1986), after reviewing a number of studies of self-help groups, concluded that the results tend to be positive. For problems such as alcoholism and obesity, self-help groups are often as effective as psychotherapy (Zilbergeld, 1986). Jacobs and Goodman (1989) even claim that "the self-help group is becoming a serious rival to psychotherapy as a major method for coping with mental health problems" (p. 544).

> **behavior therapy:** A treatment approach employing the principles of operant conditioning, classical conditioning, and/or observational learning theory to eliminate inappropriate or maladaptive behaviors and replace them with more adaptive responses.

Memory Check 15.2

1. Which depressed person would be *least* likely to be helped by interpersonal therapy (IPT)?
   a. Kirk, who is unable to accept the death of his wife
   b. Martha, who has been depressed since she was forced to retire
   c. Sharon, who was sexually abused by her father
   d. Tony, who feels isolated and alone because he has difficulty making friends

2. Which of the following is *not* true of group therapy?
   a. It allows people to get feedback from other members.
   b. It allows individuals to receive help and support from other members.
   c. It is not conducted by trained therapists.
   d. It is less expensive than individual therapy.

3. Encounter groups may not be beneficial for people with a serious emotional disturbance. (true/false)

4. Self-help groups are generally ineffective, because they are not led by professionals. (true/false)

Answers: 1. c   2. c   3. true   4. false

Behavior Therapy: Unlearning the Old, Learning the New

What is behavior therapy?

Behavior therapy is a treatment approach consistent with the learning perspective on psychological disorders—that abnormal behavior is learned. According to the behaviorists, unless people are suffering from some physiological disorder, such as brain pathology, those who seek therapy need it for one of two reasons: (1) they have learned inappropriate or maladaptive responses, or (2) they never had the opportunity to learn appropriate behavior in the first place. Instead of viewing the maladaptive behavior as a symptom of some underlying disorder, the behavior therapist sees the behavior itself as the disorder. If a person comes to a therapist with a fear of flying, that fear of flying is seen as the problem.

Behavior therapy uses the principles of operant conditioning, classical conditioning, and/or observational learning theory to eliminate inappropriate or maladaptive behaviors and replace them with more adaptive responses. Sometimes this approach is referred to as **behavior modification.** The goal is to change the troublesome behavior, not to change the individual's personality structure or to search for the origin of the problem behavior. "Behavior therapy is educational rather than 'healing' " (Thorpe & Olson, 1990, p. 15). The therapist's role is active and directive.

> ? *How do behavior therapists modify behavior using operant conditioning techniques?*

Behavior Modification Techniques Based on Operant Conditioning

Behavior modification techniques based on operant conditioning seek to control the consequences of behavior. Undesirable behavior is eliminated by withholding or removing reinforcement for the behavior. Behavior therapists also seek to reinforce any desirable behavior in order to increase its frequency, and they use reinforcement, as well, to shape entirely new behaviors. The process works best when it is applied consistently. Institutional settings such as hospitals, prisons, and school classrooms are well suited to these techniques, because they provide a restricted environment where the consequences (or contingencies) of behavior can be more strictly controlled.

behavior modification: The systematic application of learning principles to help a person eliminate undesirable behaviors and/or acquire more adaptive behaviors; also called behavior therapy.

token economy: A behavioral technique used to encourage desirable behaviors by reinforcing them with tokens that can be exchanged later for desired objects, activities, and/or privileges.

time out: A behavioral technique, used to decrease the frequency of undesirable behavior, that involves withdrawing an individual from all reinforcement for a period of time.

stimulus satiation (say-she-A-shun): A behavioral technique in which a patient is given so much of a stimulus that it becomes something the patient wants to avoid.

Token Economies: What Would You Do for a Token? Some institutions use behavior modification programs called **token economies** that reward appropriate behavior with tokens such as poker chips, play money, gold stars, or the like. These tokens can later be exchanged for desired goods (candy, gum, cigarettes) and/or privileges (weekend passes, free time, participation in desirable activities). Sometimes individuals are fined a given number of tokens for undesirable behavior. Such programs are used in institutional settings such as hospitals, prisons, and schools. For decades mental hospitals have successfully used token economies with chronic schizophrenics to improve their self-care skills and social interaction (Ayllon & Azrin, 1965, 1968). Patients tend to perform chores when reinforced but not when reinforcement is discontinued. Schizophrenic symptoms such as delusions and hallucinations, of course, are not affected.

Time Out: All Alone with No Reinforcers Another effective method used to eliminate undesirable behavior, especially in children and adolescents, is **time out** (Brantner & Doherty, 1983). The principle is simple. Children are told in advance that if they engage in certain undesirable behaviors, they will be removed calmly from the situation and will have to pass a period of time (usually no more than 15 minutes) in a place containing no reinforcers (no television, books, toys, friends, and so on). Theoretically, the undesirable behavior will stop if it is no longer followed by attention or any other positive reinforcers.

Stimulus Satiation: Too Much of a Good Thing Another behavior modification technique, **stimulus satiation**, attempts to change problem behaviors by giving people too much of whatever they find reinforcing. The idea is that the reinforcer will lose its attraction and become something to be avoided.

The stimulus satiation technique was used successfully with a 47-year-old chronic schizophrenic woman who, during her 9 years of hospitalization, would collect and hoard large numbers of towels.

> At the beginning of treatment, the nurses would bring a towel to the patient in her room several times throughout the day, and without any comment, simply hand it to her. "The first week she was given an average of 7 towels daily, and by the third week this number was increased to 60." (Ayllon, 1977, p. 358)
>
> At first, she seemed to enjoy folding and stacking her towels, but finally, when the patient had 625 towels in her room, she could stand it no longer and began saying to the nurses: "Don't give me no more towels. I've got enough." "Take them towels away. . . . I can't sit here all night and fold towels." (p. 359)
>
> Stimulus satiation was working well. Within a few weeks the patient was angrily demanding, "Get these dirty towels out of here." And finally after taking hundreds of towels out of her room, she remarked to the nurse, in desperation, "I can't drag any more of these towels, I just can't do it." (p. 359)

During the following 12 months, no more than one or two towels could be found in the patient's room.

The Effectiveness of Operant Approaches: Do They Work? Behavior therapies based on operant conditioning have been particularly effective in modifying some behaviors of seriously disturbed people (Paul & Lentz, 1977). Although these techniques do not presume to cure schizophrenia, autism, or mental retardation, they can increase the frequency of desirable behaviors and decrease the frequency of undesirable behaviors. Sometimes modifying some of the more extreme and bizarre behaviors enables family members to accept and care for the patient themselves.

Behavior modification techniques can also be used by people who want to break bad habits such as smoking and overeating or to develop good habits such as a regular exercise regime. If you want to modify any of your behaviors, devise a reward system for desirable behaviors, and remember the principles of shaping. Reward gradual changes in the direction of your ultimate goal. If you are trying to develop better eating habits, don't try to change a lifetime of bad habits all at once. Begin with a small step such as substituting frozen yogurt for ice cream. Set realistic weekly goals with a likelihood of success.

Therapies Based on Classical Conditioning

Some behavior therapies are based mainly on the principles of classical conditioning, which can account for how we acquire many of our emotional reactions. In Chapter 5 you learned how Little Albert came to fear the white rat when it was presented along with a frightening, loud noise. In classical conditioning, a neutral stimulus—some object, person, or situation that initially does not elicit any strong positive or negative emotional reaction—is paired with either a very positive or a very negative stimulus. Then, after conditioning, the strong feeling toward the positive or negative stimulus transfers to the original, neutral stimulus.

Therapies based on classical conditioning can be used to rid people of fears and other undesirable behaviors. We will discuss four types of therapy based primarily on classical conditioning: systematic desensitization, flooding, exposure and response prevention, and aversion therapy.

> **?** *What behavior therapies are based on classical conditioning?*

> **?** *How do therapists use systematic desensitization to rid people of fears?*

Systematic Desensitization: Overcoming Fears One Step at a Time
Have you ever been both afraid and relaxed at the same time? Psychiatrist Joseph

systematic desensitization:
A behavior therapy, used to treat phobias, that involves training clients in deep muscle relaxation and then having them confront a graduated series of anxiety-producing situations (real or imagined) until they can remain relaxed while confronting even the most feared situation.

flooding: A behavioral therapy used to treat phobias, during which clients are exposed to the feared object or event (or asked to imagine it vividly) for an extended period until their anxiety decreases.

Wolpe (1958, 1973) came to the conclusion that these two responses are incompatible; that is, one inhibits the other. On the basis of this idea, Wolpe developed a therapy to treat fears and phobias. He reasoned that if he could get people to relax and stay relaxed while they thought about a feared object, person, place, or situation, they could conquer their fear or phobia.

In Wolpe's therapy, **systematic desensitization**, clients are trained in deep muscle relaxation. Then they confront a hierarchy of fears—a graduated series of anxiety-producing situations, either *in vivo* (in real life) or in imagination—until they can remain relaxed even in the presence of the most feared situation. The therapy can be used for everything from fear of animals to claustrophobia, test anxiety, and social and other situational fears.

What do you fear most? Many college students would say that they fear speaking in front of a group. If that were your fear and you went to a behavior therapist who used systematic desensitization, this is what would happen. First the therapist would ask you to identify the fear causing your anxiety and everything connected with it. Then all the aspects of the fear would be arranged on a hierarchy from least to most anxiety-producing.

After the hierarchy was prepared, you would be taught deep muscle relaxation, progressively relaxing parts of your body until you achieved a completely relaxed state. During the actual desensitization procedure, you would be asked to picture, as vividly as possible, the least fear-producing item on your hierarchy—for example, reading in the syllabus that the presentation will be assigned. When you were able to remain relaxed while visualizing this item, the therapist would have you move one step up the hierarchy and picture the next item—having your professor assign the oral presentation. This procedure would be followed until you reached the top of the hierarchy and could remain calm and relaxed while you imagined vividly the most fear-producing stimulus—actually making your presentation in class. If, during the desensitization process, anxiety should creep in as you imagined items on the hierarchy, you would signal the therapist. The therapist would instruct you to stop thinking about that item. You would then clear your mind, come back to a state of complete relaxation, and begin again. Try creating your own hierarchy in the *Try It!* on the facing page.

How effective is systematic desensitization? Many experiments, demonstrations, and case reports confirm that systematic desensitization is a highly successful treatment for eliminating fears and phobias in a relatively short time (Kalish, 1981; Rachman & Wilson, 1980). It has proved effective for specific problems like test anxiety, stage fright, and anxiety related to sexual disorders such as impotence and frigidity. Wolpe (1981) claims that skilled behavior therapists using systematic desensitization report marked improvement in about 80 percent of their patients. And desensitization seems to be about equally effective whether it is carried on in real-life settings or in one's imagination (James, 1985).

The critical element in systematic desensitization is the patient's exposure to the feared stimulus. Even the relaxation, an important part of Wolpe's treatment, is apparently not essential. But relaxation does help to keep especially fearful patients from jumping up and running away from the fear-provoking stimulus.

There are several other therapies used to treat phobias and obsessive compulsive disorder that have exposure as the key therapeutic element.

What is flooding?

Flooding: Confronting Our Fears All at Once **Flooding** is a behavior therapy used in the treatment of phobias. It involves exposing clients to the feared object or event (or asking them to vividly imagine it) for an extended period until their anxiety decreases. Flooding is almost the opposite of systematic desensitization. The person is exposed to the fear all at once, not gradually and certainly

Use what you have learned about systematic desensitization to create a step-by-step approach to help someone overcome a fear of making a class presentation. The person's hierarchy of fears begins with reading in the syllabus that an oral presentation will be assigned and culminates in actually making the oral presentation. Fill in successive steps, according to a possible hierarchy of fears, that will lead to the final step. One set of possible solutions appears below.

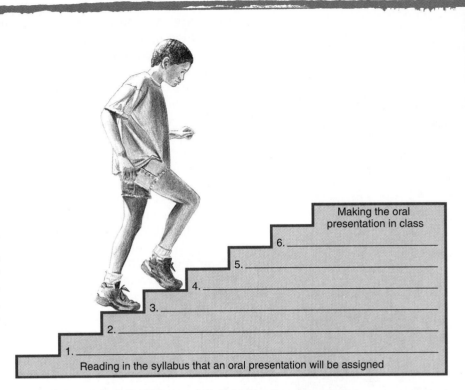

Answer: (1) Being assigned the oral presentation and given a due date. (2) Preparing the oral presentation. (3) Practicing the oral presentation one week before it is due. (4) Practicing the oral presentation the night before it is due. (5) Waiting to give the presentation. (6) Walking to the front of the room to give the presentation.

not in a state of relaxation. An individual with a fear of heights, for example, might have to go onto the roof of a tall building and remain there until the fear subsided. A person with a cat phobia might be told: "Visualize the cat all over you, perhaps scratching you, its eyes right up against yours, its hair all over you" (Sheehan, 1983, pp. 158–159).

What is the key to success in flooding? It is not that a person must be scared to death in order for flooding to work. The key to success is keeping the patients in the feared situation long enough to see that none of the dreaded consequences they fear actually come to pass (Marks, 1978a). If the exposure is too brief, anxiety simply intensifies, and patients get worse instead of better. Flooding sessions typically last from 30 minutes to 2 hours and should not be terminated until patients are markedly less afraid than they were at the beginning of the session. Additional sessions are required until the fear response is extinguished or reduced to an acceptable level. Rarely are more than six treatment sessions needed (Marshall & Segal, 1988).

In vivo flooding, the real-life experience, works faster and is more effective than simply imagining the feared object, and it should be used whenever possible (Chambless & Goldstein, 1979; Marks, 1972). Flooding may be quite painful for the patient, as it was for Bill in our opening story. And it is certainly not the treatment of choice for phobics with a weak heart. But flooding often works where other therapies have failed and works faster as well.

> **?** *How does exposure and response prevention help people with obsessive compulsive disorder?*

exposure and response prevention: A behavior therapy that exposes obsessive compulsive disorder patients to stimuli generating increasing anxiety; patients must agree not to carry out their normal rituals for a specified period of time after exposure.

Cigarette smoking can be reduced or eliminated through aversion therapy.

> **?** *How does aversion therapy rid people of a harmful or undesirable behavior?*

aversion therapy: A behavior therapy in which an aversive stimulus is paired with an undesirable behavior until the behavior becomes associated with pain and discomfort.

Exposure and Response Prevention: Cutting the Tie That Binds Fears and Rituals **Exposure and response prevention** has been successful in treating obsessive compulsive disorder (Foa, 1995; Jenike & Rauch, 1994). The therapy consists of two components. The first involves *exposure*—exposing patients to objects or situations they have been avoiding because they trigger obsessions and compulsive rituals. The second component is *response prevention*, in which patients agree to resist performing their compulsive rituals for progressively longer periods of time.

Initially the therapist identifies the thoughts, objects, or situations that trigger the compulsive ritual. For example, touching a doorknob, a piece of unwashed fruit, or garbage might ordinarily send people with a fear of contamination to the nearest bathroom to wash their hands. Patients undergoing exposure and response prevention therapy are gradually exposed to stimuli that they find more and more distasteful and anxiety-provoking. They must agree not to perform the normal ritual (hand washing, bathing, or the like) for a specified period of time after exposure. Gradually patients learn to tolerate the anxiety evoked by the various "contaminants."

A typical treatment course—about 10 sessions over a period of 3 to 7 weeks—can bring about considerable improvement in 60 to 70 percent of patients (Jenike, 1990). The therapy is quite effective for patients suffering from compulsions only or for obsessions coupled with compulsions, but less effective for obsessions only (Baer, 1993). And patients treated with exposure are less likely to relapse after treatment than those treated only with drugs (Greist, 1992). O'Sullivan and others (1991) found that 6 years after exposure treatment, 38 percent of the former patients had maintained their gains, and an additional 12 percent had improved still further.

It appears that behavior therapy can even produce physical changes in the brain. PET scans show that the therapy brings about reductions in the abnormal brain activity associated with obsessive compulsive disorder (Baxter et al., 1992).

Systematic desensitization, flooding, and exposure help people to stop avoiding feared objects or situations. But what if the person's problem is just the opposite—bad habits, addictions, and other such behaviors that *should* be avoided? What type of therapy exists to help people break bad habits, overcome addictions, and learn to avoid situations that trigger harmful behavior, Aversion therapy is designed to do just that.

Aversion Therapy: Making Us Sick to Make Us Better **Aversion therapy** is used to rid clients of a harmful or socially undesirable behavior by pairing it with a painful, sickening, or otherwise aversive stimulus. Electric shock, emetics (which cause nausea and vomiting), or other unpleasant stimuli are paired with the undesirable behavior time after time until a strong negative association is formed and the person comes to avoid that behavior, habit, or substance. Treatment continues until the bad habit loses its appeal because it becomes associated with pain or discomfort.

Smokers treated with aversion therapy are asked to smoke so rapidly and continuously—a puff every 6 to 8 seconds—that smoking becomes extremely distasteful. Although rapid smoking is an effective technique in getting people to quit smoking (Tiffany et al., 1986), only about 50 percent of smokers who try this technique quit permanently (Hall et al., 1984). Because in rare cases cardiac complications can occur with rapid smoking, this technique should be carried out *only* in a medical setting (Thorpe & Olson, 1990).

Sometimes alcoholics are given a nausea-producing substance such as Antabuse, which reacts violently with alcohol and causes people to retch and vomit until their stomach is empty. Obviously the aversion therapist cannot show up at the alcoholic's house every morning with a bottle of Antabuse, but nausea-based aversion therapy has produced abstinence rates of approximately 60 percent 1 year after treatment (Elkins, 1991).

It is even possible to eliminate a harmful or socially undesirable behavior simply by having a patient mentally associate it with some unpleasant or disgusting thought or image. Maletzky (1974) has reported success with exhibitionists, who experienced sexual satisfaction by flashing their genitals to women on the street. Maletzky tells about one patient whom he instructed to imagine the sexually deviant activity the patient found exciting and pleasurable. At the height of the patient's imagined pleasure, the therapist would describe a scene so vivid and sickening that the patient became violently ill and vomited all over himself. The therapist strengthened the technique by adding a foul-smelling substance to the revolting verbal description. At the end of a 12-month period, not one of the patients had been arrested for exposing himself, and none reported the deviant sexual urges and fantasies of the past.

Therapies Based on Observational Learning Theory: Just Watch *This!*

> ? *How does participant modeling help people overcome fears?*

A great deal of what we learn in life, we learn from watching others and then copying or imitating the behaviors modeled for us. Much positive behavior is learned this way; but so are bad habits, aggressive behaviors, and fears or phobias. Therapies derived from the work of Albert Bandura on observational learning are based on the belief that people can overcome fears and acquire social skills through modeling.

For example, therapists have effectively treated fears and phobias by having clients watch a model (on film or in real life) responding to a feared situation in appropriate ways with no dreaded consequences. Usually the model approaches the feared object in gradual steps. Bandura (1967) describes how nursery school children lost their fear of dogs after watching a film depicting a child who was not afraid of dogs first approach a dog, then play with it, pet it, and so on. Modeling films have been used to reduce the fears of children preparing for surgery (Melamed & Siegel, 1975) and to reduce children's fear of the dentist (Shaw & Thoresen, 1974).

The most effective type of therapy based upon observational learning theory is called **participant modeling** (Bandura, 1977a; Bandura et al., 1975, 1977). Here the model not only demonstrates the appropriate response in graduated steps, but the client attempts to imitate the model step by step, while the therapist gives encouragement and support. This technique provides the additional benefit of exposure to the feared stimulus.

Most simple phobias, such as fear of snakes, can be extinguished after only a few hours of modeling therapy with client participation.

Suppose you had a snake phobia and your therapist used participant modeling. First she would calmly approach the snake's cage and encourage you to do the same. Then the therapist would show you how easy it is to handle a snake while it is in the cage. She would urge you to touch it, perhaps suggesting how surprised you will be to find that the snake does not feel at all slimy. Next she could remove the snake from the cage and have you observe her holding it for a period of time with no adverse results. In this manner your behavior would gradually imitate hers until you reached the point of actually holding the snake.

Most specific phobias can be extinguished in only 3 or 4 hours of modeling therapy when the client participates. Participant modeling has proved more effective in curing snake phobias than simple observation of a filmed or live model, and more effective than systematic desensitization (Bandura et al., 1969). In fact, in one study 92 percent of the subjects completely lost their fear of snakes.

participant modeling: A behavior therapy in which an appropriate response is modeled in graduated steps and the client attempts each step, encouraged and supported by the therapist.

Memory Check 15.3

1. Techniques based on (classical, operant) conditioning try to change behavior by reinforcing desirable behavior and removing reinforcers for undesirable behavior.

2. Behavior therapies based on classical conditioning are used mainly to:
   a. shape new, more appropriate behaviors.
   b. rid people of fears and undesirable behaviors or habits.
   c. promote development of social skills.
   d. demonstrate appropriate behaviors.

3. Exposure and response prevention is a treatment for people with:
   a. panic disorder.
   b. phobias.
   c. generalized anxiety disorder.
   d. obsessive compulsive disorder.

4. Match the description with the therapy.
   ____ 1) flooding
   ____ 2) aversion therapy
   ____ 3) systematic desensitization
   ____ 4) participant modeling

   a. practicing deep muscle relaxation during gradual exposure to feared object
   b. imagining painful or sickening stimuli associated with undesirable behavior
   c. being exposed directly to feared object without relaxation
   d. imitating a model responding appropriately in feared situation

Answers: 1. operant 2. b 3. d 4. 1) c 2) b 3) a 4) d

Cognitive Therapies: It's the Thought That Counts

We have seen that behavior therapies based on classical and operant conditioning and modeling are effective in eliminating many types of troublesome behavior. But what if the problem is in our thinking, attitudes, false beliefs, or poor self-concept? There are therapies for these problems as well. **Cognitive therapies,** based on the cognitive perspective, assume that maladaptive behavior can result from irrational thoughts, beliefs, and ideas, which the therapist tries to change. When cognitive therapy is combined with behavioral techniques such as relaxation training or exposure, it is called cognitive-behavioral therapy.

The emphasis in cognitive therapies is on conscious rather than unconscious processes and on the present rather than the past. We will explore two types of cognitive therapy—rational-emotive therapy and Beck's cognitive therapy.

Rational-Emotive Therapy: Human Misery—the Legacy of False Beliefs

What is the aim of rational-emotive therapy?

Picture this scenario: Harry received two free tickets to a Saturday-night concert featuring his favorite group. Filled with excitement, Harry called Sally, whom he had dated a couple of times, to ask her to share the evening with him. But she turned him down with some lame excuse like "I have to do my laundry." He was stunned and humiliated. "How could she do this to me?" he wondered. As the week dragged on, he became more and more depressed.

What caused Harry's depression? Sally turning him down? Not according to Albert Ellis (1961, 1977, 1993), a clinical psychologist who developed **rational-emotive therapy** in the 1950s. Rational-emotive therapy is based on Ellis's ABC theory. The A refers to the *activating event*, the B to the person's *belief* about the event, and the C to the emotional *consequence* that follows. Ellis claims that it is

FIGURE 15.1

The ABCs of Albert Ellis's Rational Emotive Therapy

Rational emotive therapy teaches clients that it is not the activating event (A) that causes the upsetting consequences (C). Rather, it is the client's beliefs (B) about the activating event. Irrational beliefs cause emotional distress, according to Albert Ellis. Rational emotive therapists help clients identify their irrational beliefs and replace them with rational ones.

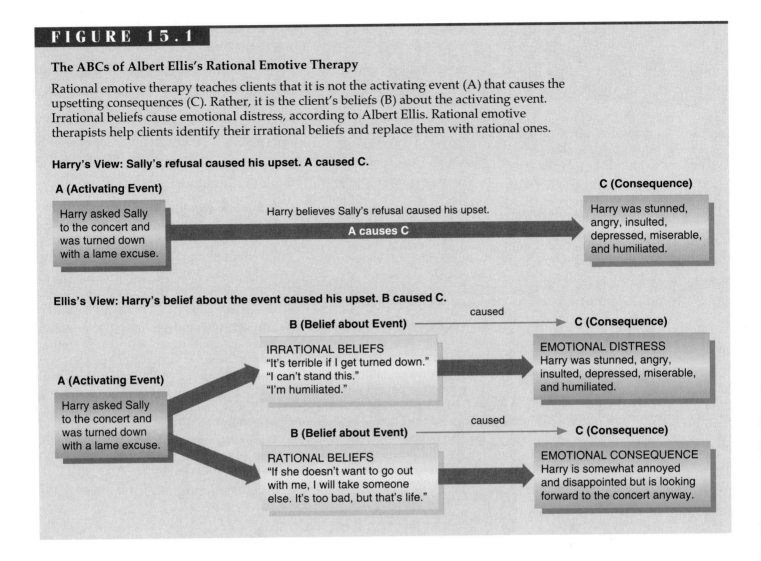

not the event itself that causes the emotional consequence, but rather it is the person's belief about the event. In other words, A does not cause C; B causes C. If the belief is irrational, then the emotional consequence can be extreme distress, as illustrated in Figure 15.1.

"Everyone should love me!" "I must be perfect!" Reality does not conform to these and other irrational beliefs, and people who hold them are doomed to frustration and unhappiness. Irrational beliefs cause people to see an undesirable event as a catastrophe rather than as a disappointment or an inconvenience, leading them to say "I can't stand this" rather than "I don't like this." Irrational beliefs cause people to feel depressed, worthless, or enraged instead of simply disappointed or annoyed. Even worse, they go on to feel "anxious about their anxiety" and "depressed about their depression" (Ellis, 1987, p. 369).

Rational-emotive therapy is a directive, confrontational form of psychotherapy designed to challenge clients' irrational beliefs about themselves and others. As clients begin to replace irrational beliefs with rational ones, their emotional reactions become more appropriate, less distressing, and more likely to lead to constructive behavior. Try challenging an irrational belief of your own in the *Try It!* on page 564.

cognitive therapy: Any therapy designed to change maladaptive behavior by changing the person's irrational thoughts, beliefs, and ideas.

rational-emotive therapy: A directive, confrontational therapy designed to challenge and modify the irrational beliefs thought to cause personal distress; developed by Albert Ellis.

Use what you have learned about Albert Ellis's rational-emotive therapy to identify—and perhaps even eliminate—an irrational belief that *you* hold about yourself.

First, identify an irrational belief, preferably one that causes some stress in your life. For example, maybe you feel that you must earn all A's in order to think of yourself as a good person.

Ask yourself the following questions, and write down your answers in as much detail as possible.

- Where does this belief come from? Can you identify the time in your life when it began?

- Why do you think this belief is true? What evidence can you think of that "proves" your belief?

- Can you think of any evidence to suggest that this belief is false? What evidence contradicts your belief? What other people do you know who do not cling to this belief?

- How does holding this belief affect your life, both negatively and positively?

- How would your life be different if you stopped holding this belief? What would you do differently?

Most clients in rational-emotive therapy are seen individually, once a week, for 5 to 50 sessions. In stark contrast to person-centered therapists (and most other therapists, for that matter), "rational-emotive therapists do not believe a warm relationship between counselee and counselor is a necessary or a sufficient condition for effective personality change" (Ellis, 1979, p. 186). In Ellis's view, "Giving a client RET with a good deal of warmth, approval and reassurance will tend to help this client 'feel better' rather than 'get better'" (p. 194).

One meta-analysis of 28 studies showed that patients receiving rational-emotive therapy did better than those receiving no treatment or placebo, and about the same as those receiving systematic desensitization (Engles et al., 1993).

? *How does Beck's cognitive therapy help people overcome depression and anxiety disorders?*

Beck's Cognitive Therapy: Overcoming "The Power of Negative Thinking"

"In order to be happy, I have to be successful in whatever I undertake."
"To be happy, I must be accepted (liked, admired) by all people at all times."
"My value as a person depends on what others think of me."
"If people disagree with me, it means they don't like me."

Aaron T. Beck

If you agree with all of these statements, you probably spend a good part of your time upset and unhappy. Psychiatrist Aaron T. Beck (1976) claims that much of the misery of depressed and anxious people can be traced to **automatic thoughts**—unreasonable but unquestioned ideas that rule the person's life. Beck (1991) believes that depressed persons hold "a negative view of the present, past, and future experiences" (p. 369). They tend to view themselves as "deficient, defective, and/or undeserving"; their environment as "unduly demanding, depriving, and/or rejecting"; and their future as "without promise, value, or meaning" (Karasu, 1990a, p. 138). These persons notice only negative, unpleasant things and jump to upsetting conclusions. Anxious people expect the worst; they catastrophize and at the same time underestimate their coping ability.

The goal of **Beck's cognitive therapy** is to help patients stop their negative thoughts as they occur, and replace them with more objective thoughts. The focus is on the present rather than on the past, and no attempt is made to uncover hidden meanings in the patients' thoughts and responses. After challenging patients' irrational thoughts, the therapist sets up a plan and guides patients so that their own experience can provide actual evidence in the real world to refute their false beliefs. Patients are given homework assignments, such as keeping track of automatic thoughts and the feelings evoked by them and substituting more rational thoughts.

Beck's cognitive therapy is brief, usually lasting only 10 to 20 sessions, and is therefore less expensive than many other types of therapy (Beck, 1976). This therapy has been researched extensively and is reported to be highly successful in the treatment of mild to moderately depressed patients (Dobson, 1989; Thase et al., 1991). There is some evidence that depressed people who have received Beck's cognitive therapy are less likely to relapse than those who have been treated with antidepressant drugs (Evans et al., 1992).

Beck's cognitive therapy has proven to be effective for treating panic disorder (Pollack et al., 1994). In panic disorder, if patients misinterpret bodily sensations associated with anxiety as a sign of mental or physical collapse, their anxiety builds and causes panic (Michelson et al., 1990). Cognitive therapy teaches them to change their catastrophic interpretations of these symptoms and thereby prevent the symptoms from escalating into panic. Recent studies have shown that after 3 months of cognitive therapy, about 90 percent of patients with panic disorder are panic-free (Robins & Hayes, 1993). Not only does cognitive therapy have a low dropout rate and a low relapse rate, but often patients continue to improve even after treatment is completed (Öst & Westling, 1995). Also, cognitive therapy has proved effective for generalized anxiety disorder (Beck, 1993), OCD (Oppen et al., 1995), cocaine addiction (Carroll et al., 1994), bulimia, and, when coupled with exposure, social phobia (Heimberg, 1993).

automatic thoughts: Unreasonable and unquestioned ideas that rule a person's life and lead to depression and anxiety.

Beck's cognitive therapy: A brief therapy for depression and anxiety, which helps people recognize their automatic thoughts and replace them with more objective thoughts.

biological therapy: A therapy that is based on the assumption that most mental disorders have physical causes; treatments include drug therapy, ECT, and psychosurgery.

Memory Check 15.4

1. Cognitive therapists believe that, for the most part, emotional disorders:
   a. have physical causes.
   b. result from unconscious conflicts and motives.
   c. result from faulty and irrational thinking.
   d. result from environmental stimuli.

2. The goal of Beck's cognitive therapy is best described as helping people:
   a. develop effective coping strategies.
   b. replace automatic thoughts with more objective thoughts.
   c. develop an external locus of control.
   d. develop realistic goals and aspirations.

3. Rational-emotive therapy is a nondirective therapy that requires a warm, accepting therapist. (true/false)

4. Beck's cognitive therapy has proved very successful in the treatment of:
   a. depression and mania.
   b. schizophrenia.
   c. fears and phobias.
   d. anxiety disorders and depression.

Answers: 1. c 2. b 3. false 4. d

The Biological Therapies

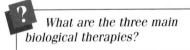

What are the three main biological therapies?

Professionals who favor the biological perspective, the view that psychological disorders are symptoms of underlying physical disorders, usually favor a **biological therapy**. The three treatment categories that make up the biological therapies are drug therapy, electroconvulsive therapy, and psychosurgery.

Drug Therapy: Pills for Psychological Ills

The favorite and by far the most frequently used biological treatment is drug therapy. Now capable of relieving the debilitating symptoms of schizophrenia, depression, bipolar disorder, and some anxiety disorders, modern drug therapy has had a tremendous impact on the treatment of psychological disorders.

> **?** *How do antipsychotic drugs help schizophrenic patients?*

Antipsychotic Drugs Throughout the long course of history, efforts to treat schizophrenia have been woefully inadequate. Mental hospitals confined many patients to locked wards, and padded cells, straitjackets, and other restraints were widely used. Then, shortly after the introduction of antipsychotic drugs in 1955, the picture suddenly changed. The breakthrough in drug therapy, coupled with the federal government's effort to reduce involuntary hospitalization of mental patients, enabled many schizophrenics who had been locked in mental institutions to be discharged into the community. In fact the mental hospital patient population decreased from about 559,000 in 1955, when the drugs were introduced, to slightly over 100,000 by 1990, as shown in Figure 15.2.

Antipsychotic drugs, or neuroleptics (sometimes called major tranquilizers), are drugs prescribed mainly for schizophrenia to control severe psychotic symptoms, such as hallucinations, delusions, and other disorders in thinking. They are also effective in reducing restlessness, agitation, and excitement. You may have heard of these drugs under their brand names—Thorazine, Stelazine, Compazine, and Mellaril. These drugs apparently work by inhibiting the activity of the neurotransmitter dopamine. But many patients are not helped by them, and others show only slight or modest improvement in symptoms. Even among patients who are helped, many stop taking the drugs because of their very unpleasant side effects—restless pacing and fidgeting, muscle spasms and cramps, and a shuffling gait. The long-term use of neuroleptics carries a high risk of the most severe side effect, tardive dyskinesia—almost continual twitching and jerking movements of the face and tongue, and squirming movements of the hands and trunk (Glazer et al., 1993).

Several newer "atypical" neuroleptics are now being used. They are referred to as atypical neuroleptics because they affect certain dopamine receptors differently than do standard neuroleptics, and they also block serotonin receptors (Michels & Marzuk, 1993). One such drug, clozapine, has been found to help patients who have benefited too little or not at all from standard neuroleptics (Breier et al., 1994; Meltzer, 1995). About 10 percent of patients who take clozapine find the results so dramatic that it is almost like being reborn (Wallis & Willwerth, 1992).

> **antipsychotic drugs:** Drugs used to control severe psychotic symptoms, such as the delusions and hallucinations of schizophrenics; also known as neuroleptics or major tranquilizers.

FIGURE 15.2

Decrease in Patient Populations in State and County Mental Hospitals (1950–1990)

State and county mental hospital patient populations peaked at approximately 560,000 in 1955. In that year the antipsychotic drugs were introduced. Coupled with the federal government's efforts to reduce involuntary hospitalization of mental patients, these drugs caused a dramatic decrease in the patient population—down to about 100,000 in 1990.

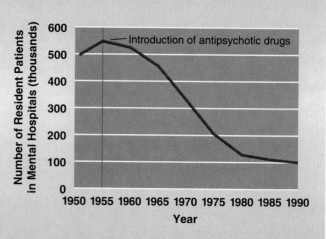

Clozapine produces fewer side effects than standard neuroleptics, and patients taking it are less likely to develop tardive dyskinesia (Kane et al., 1993). However, clozapine is extremely expensive, and without careful monitoring it can cause a fatal blood defect in 1 or 2 percent of patients who take it. An even more recent breakthrough, risperidone, appears to be safe (Marder & Meibach, 1994). It has produced no fatalities and has fewer side effects than standard neuroleptics (Owens, 1994). Yet another advantage is that risperidone is much more effective than other neuroleptics in treating the negative symptoms of schizophrenia—apathy, emotional unresponsiveness, and social withdrawal (Schooler, 1994).

Schizophrenics who were hospitalized in the past could expect to stay for weeks or months. Now, thanks to the antipsychotics, the average stay of such patients is usually a matter of days. But even though antipsychotic drugs help two-thirds of the patients, they do not cure schizophrenia. The drugs reduce and control many of the major symptoms so that patients are able to function, but most patients must continue to take them in order to avoid relapse (Gilbert et al., 1995).

Antidepressant Drugs Not long after the antipsychotic drugs came on the scene, the **antidepressants** were introduced. Antidepressants act effectively as mood elevators for people who are severely depressed and are also helpful in the treatment of certain anxiety disorders.

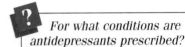

For what conditions are antidepressants prescribed?

Imbalances in the neurotransmitters serotonin and norepinephrine often accompany symptoms of depression. The tricyclic antidepressants, which include amitriptyline (Elavil) and imipramine (Tofranil), work against depression by blocking the reuptake of norepinephrine and serotonin into the axon terminals, thus enhancing their action in the synapses. The tricyclics are the drug treatment of first choice for major depression (Nelson, 1991), proving effective for over 60 percent of depressed patients (Karasu, 1990b). Imipramine is also effective in relieving the symptoms of generalized anxiety disorder (Rickels, Downing et al., 1993) and panic disorder and agoraphobia (Clum et al., 1993). In fact, Aronson (1987) found that 88 percent of panic disorder patients who could tolerate the drug stopped having panic attacks.

But tricyclics can have some unpleasant side effects—sedation, dizziness, nervousness, fatigue, dry mouth, forgetfulness, and weight gain (American Psychiatric Association, 1993b). According to Noyes and others (1989), progressive weight gain (an average of more than 20 pounds) is the main reason people stop taking tricyclics, in spite of relief from distressing psychological symptoms.

A new category of antidepressants known as serotonin-selective reuptake inhibitors (SSRIs) block the reuptake of serotonin, increasing its effect at the synapses (Greden, 1994). SSRIs include such drugs as fluoxetine (sold as Prozac) and clomipramine (Anafranil). By 1994 more than 10 million people had used Prozac (Barondes, 1994); now more than 1 million prescriptions are being written for it each month, making it the most widely used antidepressant (Mauro, 1994). Prozac's popularity is due not to greater effectiveness than the tricyclics but to milder side effects (Pen et al., 1994). But Prozac can cause sexual dysfunction, although normal sexual functioning returns when the drug is discontinued.

Prozac has proven to be an effective treatment for less severe depression, with 50 to 60 percent of patients showing improvement (Nelson, 1991). It is also effective in the treatment of obsessive compulsive disorder, which has been associated with a serotonin imbalance (Rapoport, 1989). With an adequate trial of Prozac, the large majority of OCD patients are at least moderately better, and some become symptom-free. But about 30 percent have little or no response to the drug (Rasmussen et al., 1993; Tollefson et al., 1994).

antidepressants: Drugs that are prescribed to treat depression and some anxiety disorders.

Monoamine Oxidase Inhibitors (MAO Inhibitors) Another line of treatment for depression is the monoamine oxidase inhibitors. By blocking the action of an enzyme that breaks down norepinephrine and serotonin in the synapses, MAO inhibitors increase the availability of norepinephrine and serotonin. These drugs (sold under the names of Marplan, Nardil, and Parnate) are usually prescribed for depressed patients who do not respond to other antidepressants (Thase et al., 1992). They are also effective in treating panic disorder (Sheehan & Raj, 1988) and social phobia (Marshall et al., 1994). But MAO inhibitors have many of the same unpleasant side effects as tricyclic antidepressants, and patients taking MAO inhibitors must avoid certain foods or run the risk of stroke.

? *How does lithium help patients with bipolar disorder?*

Lithium: A Natural Salt That Evens Moods **Lithium,** a naturally occurring salt, is considered a wonder drug for bipolar disorder, and it is said to begin to quiet the manic state within 5 to 10 days. This is an amazing accomplishment, because the average episode, if untreated, lasts about 3 to 4 months. The proper maintenance dose of lithium will usually even out the moods of the patient and reduce the number and severity of episodes of both mania and depression (Prien et al., 1984). Combined results of six studies show that patients who discontinue lithium are 6.3 times more likely to have a recurrence than those who keep taking the drug (Suppes et al., 1991). Careful and continuous monitoring of the lithium level in the patient's system is absolutely necessary, however, to guard against lithium poisoning and permanent damage to the nervous system (Schou, 1989).

The Minor Tranquilizers The family of minor tranquilizers called benzodiazepines includes, among others, the well-known drugs sold as Valium and Librium and the newer high-potency benzodiazepine Xanax (pronounced ZAnax). Used primarily to treat anxiety, benzodiazepines are prescribed more often than any other class of psychoactive drugs (Medina et al., 1993).

Xanax, the largest selling psychiatric drug, appears to be particularly effective in relieving anxiety and depression. Xanax is effective in the treatment of panic disorder, and it works faster and has fewer side effects than antidepressants (Ballenger et al., 1993; Jonas & Cohon, 1993). After 4 weeks of treatment, 60 to 70 percent of patients are panic-free (Klerman, 1992). But there is a downside to Xanax. Many patients, after they are panic-free, find themselves unable to discontinue the drug because they experience moderate to severe withdrawal symptoms, including severe anxiety (Otto et al., 1993). Furthermore, if patients do discontinue treatment, relapse is likely (Rickels et al., 1993).

? *What are some of the problems with drug therapy?*

Some Problems with Drug Therapy So far, one might conclude that drug therapy is the simplest and possibly the most effective way of treating schizophrenia, depression, panic disorder, and obsessive compulsive disorder. There are, however, a number of potential problems with the use of drugs. Antipsychotics and antidepressants have side effects that can be unpleasant enough that a number of patients stop treatment before they have a reduction in symptoms. Other patients discontinue treatment even if they believe the drugs are helping to relieve their psychological distress.

Antipsychotics, antidepressants, and lithium do not cure psychological disorders, so patients usually experience a relapse if they stop taking the drugs when their symptoms lift. Maintenance doses of antidepressants following a major depression reduce the probability of recurrences (Maj et al., 1992; Thase, 1992). Maintenance doses are usually required with anxiety disorders as well, or symptoms are likely to return (Rasmussen et al., 1993).

People who have not been helped by drug therapy may have been given too low a dosage for too short a period of time (Keller, 1989). When the same drugs are administered in the same dose to different people, there can be a 40-fold difference in blood levels of the antipsychotics (Torrey, 1983) and a 30-fold difference in blood levels of the tricyclics (Preskorn, 1993). This means that the correct

lithium: A drug used in bipolar disorder to control the symptoms in a manic episode and to even out the mood swings and reduce recurrence of future manic or depressive states.

dose for one patient may be too much or too little for another patient. "Many 'nonresponders' to antidepressant drugs may become responders with a higher dosage and/or longer duration of treatment" (Joyce & Paykel, 1989, p. 94).

The main problem with antidepressants is that they are relatively slow-acting. In addition, more often than not, depressed patients have to try several different antidepressants before finding one that is effective. A severely depressed patient would need at least 2 to 6 weeks to obtain relief, and 30 percent don't respond at all. This can be too risky for suicidal patients. If suicide is an imminent danger, antidepressant drugs are not the treatment of choice. In such cases many experts consider electroconvulsive therapy the preferred treatment.

Electroconvulsive Therapy: The Controversy Continues

? *For what purpose is electroconvulsive therapy (ECT) used, and what is its major side effect?*

Electroconvulsive therapy (**ECT**), or electric shock, was introduced as a treatment for mental disorders by two Italian physicians, Cerletti and Bini, in 1938. ECT was widely used as a treatment for several mental disorders until the introduction of the antipsychotic and antidepressant drugs in the 1950s. ECT developed a bad reputation, partly because it was misused and overused in the 1940s and 1950s. Often it was misused simply to make troublesome patients easier to handle, and some patients received hundreds of shock treatments. Today electroconvulsive therapy is used mainly as a treatment for severe depression, but also results in marked improvement or remission in 80 percent of manic patients who have not been helped by lithium (Mukherjee et al., 1994).

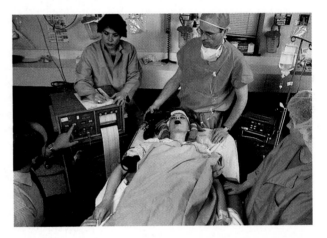

If you were to have electroconvulsive therapy, what could you expect? Two electrodes would be placed on your head, and a mild electric current would be passed through your brain for 1 or 2 seconds. Immediately after the shock was administered, you would lose consciousness and experience a seizure lasting about 30 seconds to 1 minute. Apparently the seizure is necessary if ECT is to have any effect. The complete ECT procedure takes about 5 minutes, and medical complications following the procedure are said to be rare (Abrams, 1988). Usually there is no pain associated with the treatment, and patients have no memory of the experience when they wake up. Normally ECT is given three times per week for 2 to 4 weeks (Sackeim, 1985).

In electroconvulsive therapy a mild electric current is passed through the brain for 1–2 seconds, causing a brief seizure.

Although ECT can cut depression short, it is not a cure. Experts think that the seizure temporarily changes the biochemical balance in the brain, which in turn results in a lifting of depression. ECT causes the release of beta endorphins from the pituitary (Young et al., 1991).

The Side Effects of ECT Some psychiatrists and neurologists have spoken out against the use of ECT, claiming that it causes pervasive brain damage and memory loss (Breggin, 1979; Friedberg, 1977). But advocates of ECT say that claims of brain damage are based on animal studies in which dosages of ECT were much higher than those now used in human patients. No structural brain damage from ECT has been revealed in studies where MRI or CT scans were compared before and after a series of treatments (Devanand et al., 1994).

Even advocates of ECT acknowledge that there are side effects, the most disturbing of which is memory loss. The memory loss appears to result from a temporary disruption of memory consolidation that, in most cases, lasts for only a few weeks. Some patients have a spotty memory loss of events that happened before ECT (Sackeim et al., 1993; Squire, 1986). But in a few patients the memory loss may last longer than 6 months (Sackeim, 1992).

electroconvulsive therapy (ECT): A treatment in which an electric current is passed though the brain, causing a seizure; usually reserved for the severely depressed who are either suicidal or unresponsive to other treatment.

The severity of the memory loss varies from person to person but seems to depend, in part, on how ECT is administered. A different type of electrical current (brief-pulse current) became widely used in the 1980s. It requires less current overall and causes less memory loss. For many years the electric current was passed through both cerebral hemispheres (called bilateral ECT). Recent studies show that ECT can be effective and memory problems reduced if (1) a standard dose of current is administered to the right hemisphere only, a procedure known as unilateral ECT (Rosenberg & Pettinati, 1984), or (2) bilateral ECT is administered with just enough current to cause a seizure (Sackeim et al., 1986).

While its pros and cons continue to be hotly debated, ECT seems to be making a comeback. About 100,000 people receive ECT each year (Squire, 1987). According to the National Institute of Mental Health (1985), a majority of psychiatrists believe that there is a legitimate place for ECT in the treatment of severely depressed patients who are suicidal or who have not been helped by any other therapy.

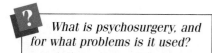

What is psychosurgery, and for what problems is it used?

Psychosurgery: Cutting to Cure

An even more drastic procedure than ECT is **psychosurgery**—brain surgery performed strictly to alleviate serious psychological disorders, such as severe depression, severe anxiety, or obsessions, or to provide relief from unbearable chronic pain. Psychosurgery is *not* the same as other brain surgery performed to correct a physical problem, such as removing a tumor or blood clot.

In the 1930s experimental brain surgery was performed to calm abnormally excitable animals. The first such surgical procedure for human patients was developed by Portuguese neurologist Egas Moniz in 1935 to treat severe phobias, anxiety, and obsessions. In his technique, the **lobotomy**, surgeons severed the neural connections between the frontal lobes and the deeper brain centers involved in emotion. But no brain tissue was removed. At first the procedure was considered a tremendous contribution, and it won for Moniz the Nobel Prize in Medicine in 1949. Not everyone considered it a contribution, however. One of Moniz's lobotomized patients curtailed the surgeon's activities by shooting him in the spine, leaving him paralyzed on one side.

Neurosurgeons performed tens of thousands of frontal lobotomies in the United States and elsewhere from 1935 until 1955. But eventually it became apparent that this treatment was no cure-all. Although the surgery was effective in calming many of the patients, it often left them in a severely deteriorated condition. Apathy, impaired intellect, loss of motivation, and a change in personality kept many from resuming a normal life.

In the mid-1950s, when antipsychotic drugs came into use, psychosurgery virtually stopped. Since that time there has been a "second wave" of psychosurgical procedures that are far less drastic than the lobotomies of decades past. In some of the most modern procedures, there is less intellectual impairment because, rather than conventional surgery, electric currents are delivered through electrodes to destroy a much smaller, more localized area of brain tissue. In one procedure, called a cingulotomy, electrodes are used to destroy the cingulum, a small bundle of nerves connecting the cortex to the emotional centers of the brain. The cingulotomy has been helpful for some extreme cases of obsessive compulsive disorder (Baer et al., 1995; Jenike & Rauch, 1994).

But even today the results of psychosurgery are still not predictable, and for better or for worse, the consequences are irreversible. For this reason, the procedure is considered experimental and absolutely a treatment of last resort.

psychosurgery: Brain surgery to treat some severe, persistent, and debilitating psychological disorder or severe chronic pain.

lobotomy: A psychosurgery technique in which the nerve fibers connecting the frontal lobes to the deeper brain centers are severed.

Memory Check 15.5

1. For the most part, advocates of biological therapies assume that psychological disorders have a physical cause. (true/false)

2. Match the disorder with the drug most often used for its treatment.

   ____ 1) panic disorder and agoraphobia
   ____ 2) schizophrenia
   ____ 3) bipolar disorder
   ____ 4) depression
   ____ 5) obsessive compulsive disorder

   a. lithium
   b. antipsychotic
   c. antidepressant

3. Medication that relieves the symptoms of schizophrenia is thought to work by blocking the action of:
   a. serotonin.
   b. dopamine.
   c. norepinephrine.
   d. epinephrine.

4. Which of the following is *not* true of drug therapy for psychological disorders?
   a. It is often difficult to determine the proper dose.
   b. Drugs often have unpleasant side effects.
   c. Patients often relapse if they stop taking the drugs.
   d. Drugs are usually not very effective.

5. For which disorder is ECT typically used?
   a. severe depression
   b. schizophrenia
   c. anxiety disorders
   d. panic disorder

6. The major side effect of ECT is tardive dyskinesia. (true/false)

7. Psychosurgery techniques are now so precise that the exact effects of the surgery can be predicted in advance. (true/false)

Answers: 1. true 2. 1) c 2) b 3) a 4) c 5) c 3. b 4. d 5. a 6. false 7. false

Therapies and Therapists: Many Choices

Evaluating the Therapies: Do They Work?

How effective is psychotherapy? Several hundred studies have compared the effectiveness of several psychotherapies against no treatment at all. What do these studies show on average? Researchers Smith, Glass, and Miller (1980) tried to answer this question by reanalyzing 475 studies, which involved 25,000 patients. Using meta-analysis, they were able to combine the findings of the studies and compare various psychotherapies against no treatment. They concluded that "the average person who receives therapy is better off at the end of it than 80 percent of the persons who do not" (p. 87). Figure 15.3 (on page 572) shows the comparative effectiveness of various psychotherapies as reported by Smith and others (1980). Although this study revealed that psychotherapy is better than no treatment, it did not indicate that one type of therapy was clearly more effective than another. In other words the different types of therapy—behavioral, psychodynamic, and cognitive—appeared to be more or less equally effective. Moreover, neither the length of treatment nor the therapists' years of experience appeared to be related to the effectiveness of treatment.

Hans Eysenck (1994) takes issue with the conclusion that Smith and others (1980) reached in their meta-analysis. According to Eysenck's analysis of the data, psychodynamic, person-centered, Gestalt, and rational-emotive therapies were not significantly more effective than a placebo treatment. He found them to be significantly less effective than systematic desensitization, flooding, behavior modification, and other cognitive therapies.

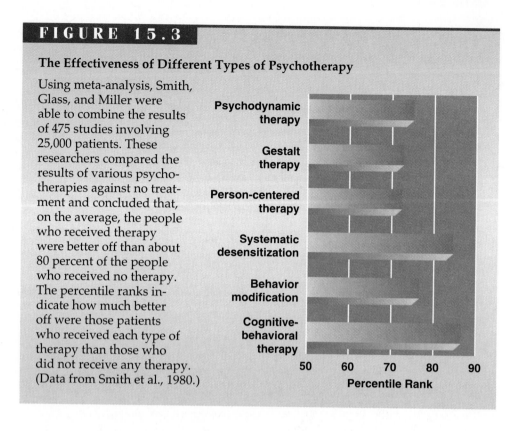

FIGURE 15.3

The Effectiveness of Different Types of Psychotherapy

Using meta-analysis, Smith, Glass, and Miller were able to combine the results of 475 studies involving 25,000 patients. These researchers compared the results of various psychotherapies against no treatment and concluded that, on the average, the people who received therapy were better off than about 80 percent of the people who received no therapy. The percentile ranks indicate how much better off were those patients who received each type of therapy than those who did not receive any therapy. (Data from Smith et al., 1980.)

An even larger meta-analysis—which was a combined study of 302 other meta-analyses—revealed that psychological, educational, and behavioral treatment generally had "a strong, dramatic pattern of positive overall effects" (Lipsey & Wilson, 1993).

All these findings have led some researchers to suggest that it may be the strength of the relationship between the therapist and the patient that accounts for the effectiveness of treatment, rather than the specific techniques of the various therapies (Pilkonis et al., 1984). Furthermore, it could be the common elements that virtually all therapies share (for example, the patient–therapist relationship, "acceptance and support of the patient," "the opportunity to express emotions," and so forth) rather than their differences that account for success (Altshuler, 1989, p. 311).

Mental Health Professionals: How Do They Differ?

? *What different types of mental health professionals conduct psychotherapy?*

According to one of the most comprehensive studies of the use of mental health services in the United States, 22.8 million people sought help for substance use and mental health problems during a recent 1-year period (Narrow et al., 1993). Troubled people turned to a variety of sources for help. As shown in Figure 15.4, 37.5 percent of all visits to professional or volunteer sources were made to psychiatrists, clinical psychologists, psychiatric social workers, and other trained mental health counselors. Who are these mental health professionals, and for what problems are their services most appropriate?

For serious psychological disorders, a clinical psychologist or psychiatrist is the best source of help. A **clinical psychologist** specializes in the assessment, treatment, and/or research of psychological problems and behavioral disturbances, and usually has a Ph.D. in clinical psychology. Clinical psychologists use various types of psychotherapy to treat a variety of psychological disorders and adjustment problems.

clinical psychologist: A psychologist, usually with a Ph.D., whose training is in the diagnosis, treatment, or research of psychological and behavioral disorders.

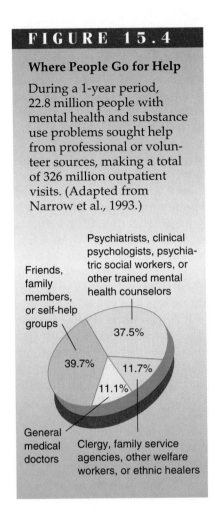

FIGURE 15.4

Where People Go for Help

During a 1-year period, 22.8 million people with mental health and substance use problems sought help from professional or volunteer sources, making a total of 326 million outpatient visits. (Adapted from Narrow et al., 1993.)

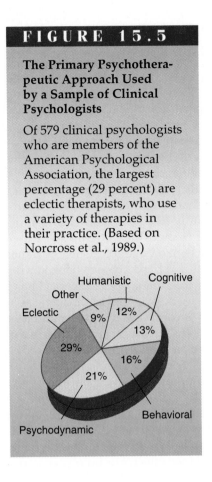

FIGURE 15.5

The Primary Psychotherapeutic Approach Used by a Sample of Clinical Psychologists

Of 579 clinical psychologists who are members of the American Psychological Association, the largest percentage (29 percent) are eclectic therapists, who use a variety of therapies in their practice. (Based on Norcross et al., 1989.)

A **psychiatrist** is a medical doctor with a specialty in the diagnosis and treatment of mental disorders. Psychiatrists can prescribe drugs and other biological treatments, and many also provide psychotherapy. A **psychoanalyst** is usually, but not always, a psychiatrist with specialized training in psychoanalysis from a psychoanalytic institute.

For clients with other psychological problems, such as adjustment disorders, substance abuse, and marital or family problems, the choice of mental health professionals widens and includes counseling psychologists, counselors, and psychiatric social workers. A counseling psychologist usually has a Ph.D. in clinical or counseling psychology or a doctor of education degree (Ed.D.) with a major in counseling. A counselor typically has a master's degree in psychology or counselor education. Often employed by colleges and universities, counseling psychologists and counselors help students with personal problems and/or test or counsel them in academic or vocational areas. A psychiatric social worker usually has a master's degree in social work (MSW) with specialized training in psychiatric problems, and may practice psychotherapy.

The entire range of mental health professionals may be found in private practice, in social agencies, or in hospital or clinic settings. Although there are over 450 types of therapy (Karasu, 1986), there is a trend in psychotherapy toward eclecticism—toward incorporating techniques from many different therapies as appropriate, rather than practicing only one type of therapy exclusively. Figure 15.5 shows the percentages of clinical psychologists practicing various types of psychotherapy.

psychiatrist: A medical doctor with a specialty in the diagnosis and treatment of mental disorders.

psychoanalyst (SY-ko-AN-ul-ist): A professional, usually a psychiatrist, with special training in psychoanalysis.

? *What therapy, if any, has proved to be the most effective in treating psychological disorders?*

Selecting a Therapy: Finding One That Fits

Is one therapy really better, on average, than other therapies? It seems obvious that we should ask which therapy, if any, is likely to be best for a specific person with a particular disorder, under the given circumstances. Therapists do not treat "average" persons; they treat people individually, and some therapies are more effective than others for treating certain disorders.

Insight therapies are often more effective for general feelings of unhappiness and interpersonal problems. Various types of behavior therapy are usually best for people with a specific problem behavior they want to change, such as a fear, phobia, bad habit, or some socially undesirable behavior. Specific phobias are successfully treated with flooding and systematic desensitization. Social phobia is better treated with cognitive-behavioral therapy (Heimberg, 1993) or high-potency benzodiazepines such as Xanax (Marshall et al., 1994). Tricyclic antidepressants and high-potency benzodiazepines often relieve the symptoms of panic disorder (Klerman, 1992; Mavissakalian & Perel, 1995). Cognitive-behavioral therapy also works well for panic disorder, and patients are less likely to relapse when therapy is complete than are patients treated with drugs alone (Pollack et al., 1994; Robins & Hayes, 1993). Obsessive compulsive disorder is best treated with exposure and response prevention (Foa, 1995) and/or the new antidepressants known as SSRIs (Griest et al., 1995; Jenike & Rauch, 1994).

For depression, a variety of treatments have proved successful—tricyclic antidepressants, SSRIs, MAO inhibitors, cognitive therapy, and interpersonal therapy (American Psychiatric Association, 1993b). ECT is often effective for severely depressed people for whom other treatments have not worked and for suicidal individuals who need immediate help and cannot wait for the standard treatments to take effect. For bipolar disorder, lithium is the treatment of choice.

Conventional antipsychotics (neuroleptics) are prescribed for people suffering from schizophrenia. When these drugs are not effective or the patient cannot tolerate the side effects, atypical neuroleptics such as clozapine and resperidone are often helpful (Breier et al., 1994; Marder & Meilbach, 1994). There is a general consensus that antipsychotics are best for controlling the psychotic symptoms of schizophrenia, but "family counseling, supportive therapy, rehabilitation programs and aid in solving problems of daily life can be crucially important" adjuncts to drug therapy (Baldessarini, 1988, p. 6).

Although drugs provide relief for people with many psychiatric disorders, they do not cure. Relapse is likely when the drugs are discontinued. For many disorders, psychotherapy provides relief from symptoms and a lower likelihood of relapse after termination of treatment. Many mental health professionals see value in combining drug therapy and psychotherapy for disorders such as depression, obsessive compulsive disorder, panic disorder, and agoraphobia. A considerable number of patients respond to a combination of cognitive-behavioral therapy, exposure, and drugs (Mattick et al., 1990).

Review and Reflect Table 15.1 provides a summary and comparison of major approaches to therapy.

In evaluating the outcomes of various therapies, it is not only the technique specific to a particular brand of therapy but also the individual therapist's ability to establish a rapport with the patient that, in large measure, will determine the outcome. But today psychologists are becoming increasingly aware that multicultural factors—the patient's race, ethnicity, and gender—can strongly influence the patient–therapist relationship. Learn more about this issue in the following World of Psychology section (on page 576).

Review and Reflect 15.1 Summary and Comparison of Major Approaches to Therapy

Type of Therapy	Perceived Cause of Disorder	Goals of Therapy	Methods Used	Primary Disorders Treated
Psycho-analysis	Unconscious sexual and aggressive urges or conflicts; fixations; weak ego.	Help patient bring disturbing, repressed material to consciousness and work through unconscious conflicts; strengthen ego functions.	Psychoanalyst analyzes and interprets dreams, free associations, resistances, and transference.	General feelings of unhappiness; unresolved problems from childhood.
Person-centered therapy	Blocking of normal tendency toward self-actualization; incongruence between real and desired self; overdependence on positive regard of others.	Increase self-acceptance and self-understanding; help patient become more inner-directed; increase congruence between real and desired self; enhance personal growth.	Therapist shows empathy, unconditional positive regard, and genuineness, and reflects client's expressed feelings back to client.	General feelings of unhappiness; interpersonal problems.
Behavior therapy	Learning of maladaptive behaviors or failure to learn appropriate behaviors.	Extinguish maladaptive behaviors and replace with more adaptive ones; help patient acquire needed social skills.	Therapist uses methods based on classical and operant conditioning and modeling, which include systematic desensitization, flooding, exposure and response prevention, aversion therapy, and reinforcement.	Fears, phobias, panic disorder, obsessive compulsive disorder, bad habits.
Cognitive therapy	Irrational and negative assumptions and ideas about self and others.	Change faulty, irrational, and/or negative thinking.	Therapist helps client identify irrational and negative thinking and substitute rational thinking.	Depression, anxiety, panic disorder, general feelings of unhappiness.
Biological therapies	Underlying physical disorder caused by structural or biochemical abnormality in the brain; genetic inheritance.	Eliminate or control biological cause of abnormal behavior; restore balance of neurotransmitters.	Physician prescribes drugs such as antipsychotics, antidepressants, lithium, or tranquilizers; ECT or psychosurgery.	Schizophrenia, depression, bipolar disorder, anxiety disorders.

World of Psychology

Therapy and Race, Ethnicity, and Gender

There is a growing awareness that psychotherapists need to consider multicultural variables such as race, ethnicity, and gender in diagnosing and treating psychological disorders (Bernal & Castro, 1994). The American Psychological Association (1993) has issued "Guidelines for Providers of Psychological Services to Ethnic, Linguistic, and Culturally Diverse Populations." And for the first time, the American Psychiatric Association's *Diagnostic and Statistical Manual of Mental Disorders (Fourth Edition) (DSM-IV)* reflects an awareness that a failure to consider ethnic and cultural differences can result in misdiagnosis of psychological problems. The manual, used by mental health professionals in diagnosing mental disorders, now provides a section headed "Specific Culture, Age, and Gender Features" for most psychological disorders and a description of disorders specific to particular cultures. Finally, the National Institute of Mental Health has become interested in the part that cultural factors play in the use of mental health services and in the effectiveness of different therapeutic approaches. Nevertheless, most graduate students in clinical and counseling psychology are not adequately trained to work with minority clients (Allison et al., 1994; Bernal & Castro, 1994).

When the cultures of the therapist and patient (client) differ markedly, behavior that is normal for the patient can be misinterpreted as abnormal by the therapist (Lewis-Fernandez & Kleinman, 1994). But despite efforts to train more members of ethnic minorities as mental health professionals, the numbers of such professionals are still extremely low (Vargas & Willis, 1994).

Psychologists Sue and Sue (1990) identified four cultural barriers that hinder effective counseling: cultural values, social class, language, and nonverbal communication (gestures, facial expressions, and the like). For example, "an Asian American client who values restraint of strong feelings may be viewed by a counselor as repressed, inhibited, or unassertive." Even worse, "counseling strategies and techniques may force the client to violate strong cultural values and dictates" (Sue, 1994, p. 293).

There is dramatic evidence that language can pose a problem in both diagnosis and treatment. When a group of Puerto Rican patients took the Thematic Apperception Test (TAT) in English, their pauses and the choices of words they used to describe the TAT pictures were interpreted as an indication of

continued

psychological problems. In fact, their "problems" were not psychological at all but were problems with the language, which was not the patients' native tongue (Suarez, 1983). A group of Mexican Americans interviewed in English were perceived as having more disorders in thinking and more emotional disorders than when they were interviewed in Spanish (Martinez, 1986).

Nonverbal behavior does not have the same meaning for all cultural and ethnic groups. Making direct eye contact, which is presumed by many in the U.S. majority culture to connote honesty, interest, and self-confidence, is a gesture of disrespect among many Native Americans. The misinterpretation of this and other nonverbal communications helps partly to explain why so many Native Americans (over 50 percent) never return to non–Native American therapists after the first visit (Heinrich et al., 1990).

There are also significant racial differences in optimal therapeutic doses of some drugs used to treat mental disorders, including schizophrenia and bipolar disorder. Researcher Ken-Ming Lin discovered that a 2-milligram dose of the neuroleptic drug halperidol relieved symptoms of schizophrenia in Asian patients, whereas 10 times that dose was required for white American patients (Holden, 1991).

There are gender differences in the effectiveness of some drugs as well. According to Yonkers and others (1992), "Young women seem to respond better to and require lower doses of antipsychotic agents and benzodiazepines than men" (p. 587). In spite of the differences, research to establish the dosage of drugs has been conducted largely on men, even though women use the drugs more often than men.

In therapy, one size does *not* fit all.

Memory Check 15.6

1. What is true regarding the effectiveness of therapies?
   a. All are equally effective for any disorder.
   b. Specific therapies have proved effective in treating particular disorders.
   c. Insight therapies are consistently best.
   d. Therapy is no more effective than no treatment for emotional and behavioral disorders.

2. One must have a medical degree to become a:
   a. clinical psychologist.
   b. psychoanalyst.
   c. psychiatrist.
   d. clinical psychologist, psychiatrist, or psychoanalyst.

3. Match the problem with the most appropriate therapy.
   ____ 1) eliminating fears, bad habits
   ____ 2) schizophrenia
   ____ 3) general unhappiness, interpersonal problems
   ____ 4) severe depression

   a. behavior therapy
   b. insight therapy
   c. drug therapy

Answers: 1. b 2. c 3. 1) a 2) c 3) b 4) c

Finding a Therapist

Your friend has been "down in the dumps" for several weeks. She hasn't been going to class and is in danger of failing many of her courses. She spends a lot of time in her room, lying on the bed or gazing out the window, and she doesn't seem to be eating very much. When you ask her, "What's the matter?" she turns away without answering. You try to persuade her to go to the student health center, but she responds angrily, saying it wouldn't do any good and you should mind your own business. You're afraid her condition is becoming serious, but you don't seem able to convince her to seek help.

People are often embarrassed to seek professional help or are afraid that friends and relatives will think less of them if they do. Sometimes they are afraid of the therapy itself or afraid that seeking help means there is something fundamentally wrong with them. There is no reason for such feelings. Going to a psychotherapist when you are feeling anxious or depressed is no different from going to a doctor when you are feeling sick. If you have a problem that has made you unhappy for a significant length of time, you should seek help—especially if you feel overwhelmed by your problem, and your friends or relatives have suggested that you seek help.

This is not to imply that whenever you feel sad or worried about something you should go to a psychiatrist. Often, simply talking to a good friend who is willing to listen can cheer you up when you're feeling down or help you cope with day-to-day problems. There are times, however, when a sympathetic ear is not enough. Then you need the help of a trained professional—a clinical or counseling psychologist, psychiatrist, psychiatric social worker, or mental health counselor. All are trained and licensed to work with people who are experiencing mental and emotional difficulties.

(However, only psychiatrists, who are also medical doctors, can prescribe medication.)

According to the National Institute of Mental Health, there are three basic signs indicating that a person may be in need of professional help:

1. Is the person acting differently than usual?
2. Does the person complain of episodes of extreme, almost uncontrollable, anxiety or "nervousness"?
3. Does the person become aggressive, rude, and abusive over minor incidents?

Where to Turn for Help

Suppose that a friend agrees to seek help or that you feel you need therapy yourself. How would you go about finding a therapist? Don't just go to any therapist who happens to be nearby. Professional training and academic credentials are important, but they do not guarantee that you will receive high-quality treatment. A good place to start in searching for a therapist is to ask family members, friends, your doctor, or your psychology professor for recommendations. Another place to look is the psychology department or counseling center at your college or the psychiatry department of a local hospital or medical school. Many cities also have community mental health centers and human service agencies that can provide recommendations. In addition, some companies have employee assistance programs that offer counseling to employees or will refer them to an appropriate therapist.

Choosing a Therapist

In considering a particular therapist, you should ask about his or her educational background, supervised experience, types of therapy practiced, length of treatment, and fees. The therapist must be professionally trained to listen in a supportive fashion and to help you understand and

interpret your thoughts and feelings. Bear in mind that many states place no restrictions on the use of the title "therapist." People who call themselves therapists may not actually be qualified to provide the kind of therapy you need. You can usually find out about a therapist's credentials by simply asking.

Take your time when choosing a therapist. A "good" therapist is one who is able to create an atmosphere of acceptance and sympathy. Because the relationship between client and therapist is an extremely important ingredient of successful therapy, it is essential to have a therapist whom you like and trust. The first step is to arrange for a brief consultation. If, during that initial interview, you find that you do not feel comfortable with the therapist, you should say so. Usually the therapist will be willing to recommend someone else.

For more information about finding a therapist, you can contact the following organizations:

American Psychological Association
750 First Street, NE
Washington, DC 20002-4242

American Psychiatric Association
1400 K Street, NW
Washington, DC 20005

National Association for Mental Health
1800 North Kent Street
Rosslyn, VA 22209

Cost and Other Considerations

Private therapists, of course, receive fees for their services that are comparable to those received by doctors, dentists, and other professionals. Some health insurance plans cover those fees; others do not. If you have insurance that covers psychotherapy, check to make sure your policy covers the type of therapy you will be receiving. Also note any restrictions contained in the policy, such as limits on the number of sessions allowed.

Group therapy tends to be less expensive than individual therapy because the cost is shared among several people. You can also receive less expensive therapy at public facilities such as community mental health centers. These are usually supported by tax revenues and therefore can charge clients on a sliding scale, that is, according to their ability to pay. The services of a student counseling center are usually provided free or at a low cost.

Most forms of therapy that have been shown to be successful (for example, cognitive therapy for depression) do not require more than 20 sessions. Lengthy therapy is more expensive and has not been shown to be more effective than brief therapy. In a study of 854 psychotherapy out-patients, Kopta and others (1994) found that 50 percent had recovered after 2.5 months of therapy (11 sessions) and 75 percent had recovered after 58 sessions. Howard and others (1986) found that the greatest benefits of psychotherapy are gained within the first 6 months. See Figure 15.6.

You may be concerned about confidentiality. Confidentiality is fundamental to the client–therapist relationship. Moreover, under guidelines established by professional associations and federal and state laws, the client has the right to control access to information about his or her treatment and the release of records for insurance or other purposes.

Of course, what we said earlier about taking your time when choosing a therapist doesn't apply in a crisis. In such a situation it is essential to get help immediately. In most communities you can call a hotline and receive counseling at any time, day or night. If the crisis is nonviolent in nature, you can call a mental health center or go to a hospital emergency room. If the crisis is more urgent—for example, if a friend is threatening to commit suicide—call the police.

FIGURE 15.6

The Number of Psychotherapy Sessions and Patient Improvement

About 75 percent of patients undergoing psychotherapy improve within 6 months (26 weekly sessions). After 1 year (52 sessions), some 80 percent of patients show improvement, and with 2 years of therapy, a little over 90 percent have improved. (After Howard et al., 1986.)

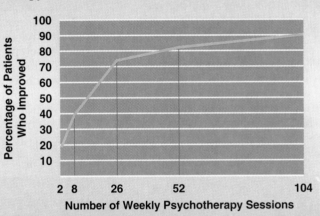

Thinking Critically

Evaluation

What are the major strengths and weaknesses of the following approaches to therapy: psychoanalysis, person-centered therapy, behavior therapy, cognitive therapy, and drug therapy?

Point/Counterpoint

From what you have learned in this chapter, prepare a strong argument to support each of these positions:

a. Psychotherapy is generally superior to drug therapy in the treatment of psychological disorders.

b. Drug therapy is generally superior to psychotherapy in the treatment of psychological disorders.

Psychology in Your Life

In selecting a therapist for yourself or advising a friend or family member, what are some important questions you would ask a therapist to determine whether he or she would be a good choice?

Chapter Summary and Review

Insight Therapies

What are the four basic techniques of psychoanalysis, and how are they used to help disturbed patients?

The four basic techniques of psychoanalysis are free association, analysis of resistance, dream analysis, and analysis of transference. They are used to uncover the repressed memories, impulses, and conflicts presumed to be the cause of the patient's problems.

What are the role and the goal of the therapist in person-centered therapy?

Person-centered therapy is a nondirective therapy in which the therapist provides a climate of unconditional positive regard where clients are free to be themselves so that their natural tendency toward positive growth will be released.

What is the major emphasis in Gestalt therapy?

Gestalt therapy emphasizes the importance of clients fully experiencing, in the present moment, their feelings, thoughts, and actions, and taking personal responsibility for their behavior.

What four problems commonly associated with major depression is interpersonal therapy designed to treat?

Interpersonal therapy (IPT) is designed to help depressed patients cope with severe responses to the death of a loved one, interpersonal role disputes, difficulties in adjusting to role transitions, and deficits in interpersonal skills.

What are some advantages of group therapy?

Group therapy is less expensive than individual therapy and gives people an opportunity to express feelings and get feedback from other members, and to give and receive help and emotional support.

Key Terms

psychotherapy (p. 548)
insight therapy (p. 549)
psychoanalysis (p. 549)
free association (p. 549)
resistance (p. 549)
transference (p. 550)
person-centered therapy (p. 550)
self-actualization (p. 550)
nondirective therapy (p. 551)
Gestalt therapy (p. 551)
directive therapy (p. 552)
interpersonal therapy (IPT) (p. 553)
family therapy (p. 553)
group therapy (p. 554)
psychodrama (p. 554)
encounter group (p. 554)

Behavior Therapy: Unlearning the Old, Learning the New

What is behavior therapy?

Behavior therapy is a treatment approach that employs the principles of operant conditioning, classical conditioning, and/or observational learning theory to replace inappropriate or maladaptive behaviors with more adaptive responses.

How do behavior therapists modify behavior using operant conditioning techniques?

Operant conditioning techniques involve the withholding of reinforcment to eliminate undesirable behaviors, as in time out, or the use of reinforcement to shape or increase the frequency of desirable behaviors, as in token economies.

What behavior therapies are based on classical conditioning?

Behavior therapies based on classical conditioning are systematic desensitization, flooding, exposure and response prevention, and aversion therapy.

How do therapists use systematic desensitization to rid people of fears?

Therapists using systematic desensitization train clients in deep muscle relaxation and then have them confront a series of graduated anxiety-producing situations, either real or imagined, until they can remain relaxed even in the presence of the most feared situation.

What is flooding?

With flooding, clients are exposed to the feared object or event or asked to imagine it vividly for an extended period until their anxiety decreases and they realize that none of the dreaded consequences come to pass.

How does exposure and response prevention help people with obsessive compulsive disorder?

In exposure and response prevention, people with OCD are exposed to the anxiety-generating stimuli but gradually increase the time before they begin their compulsive rituals and thus learn to tolerate their anxiety.

How does aversion therapy rid people of a harmful or undesirable behavior?

Aversion therapy pairs the unwanted behavior with an aversive stimulus until the bad habit becomes associated with pain or discomfort.

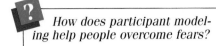 *How does participant modeling help people overcome fears?*

In participant modeling, an appropriate response is modeled in graduated steps and the client is asked to imitate each step with the encouragement and support of the therapist.

Key Terms

behavior therapy (p. 555)
behavior modification (p. 556)
token economy (p. 556)
time out (p. 556)
stimulus satiation (p. 556)
systematic desensitization (p. 558)
flooding (p. 558)
exposure and response prevention (p. 560)
aversion therapy (p. 560)
participant modeling (p. 561)

Cognitive Therapies: It's the Thought That Counts

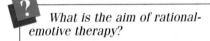 *What is the aim of rational-emotive therapy?*

Rational-emotive therapy is a directive form of therapy designed to challenge and modify the client's irrational beliefs, which are believed to be the cause of personal distress.

How does Beck's cognitive therapy help people overcome depression and anxiety disorders?

Beck's cognitive therapy helps people overcome depression and anxiety disorders by pointing out the irrational thoughts causing them misery and by helping them learn other, more realistic ways of looking at themselves and their experience.

Key Terms

cognitive therapy (p. 562)
rational-emotive therapy (p. 562)
automatic thoughts (p. 564)
Beck's cognitive therapy (p. 564)

The Biological Therapies

What are the three main biological therapies?

The three main biological therapies are drug therapy, ECT, and psychosurgery.

How do antipsychotic drugs help schizophrenic patients?

Antipsychotic drugs control the major symptoms of schizophrenia by inhibiting the activity of dopamine.

For what conditions are antidepressants prescribed?

Antidepressants are prescribed for depression, generalized anxiety disorder, panic disorder, agoraphobia, and obsessive compulsive disorder.

How does lithium help patients with bipolar disorder?

Lithium is used to control the symptoms in a manic episode and to even out the mood swings in bipolar disorder.

What are some of the problems with drug therapy?

Some problems are the drugs' unpleasant or dangerous side effects, the difficulty in establishing the proper dosages, and the fact that relapse is likely if the drug therapy is discontinued.

For what purpose is electroconvulsive therapy (ECT) used and what is its major side effect?

ECT is a treatment of last resort for people with severe depression, and it is most often reserved for those for whom suicide is an imminent danger. Some memory loss is its major side effect.

 What is psychosurgery, and for what problems is it used?

Psychosurgery is brain surgery performed strictly to relieve some severe, persistent, and debilitating psychological disorder; it is considered experimental and highly controversial.

Key Terms

biological therapy (p. 565)
antipsychotic drugs (p. 566)
antidepressants (p. 567)
lithium (p. 568)
electroconvulsive therapy (ECT) (p. 569)
psychosurgery (p. 570)
lobotomy (p. 570)

Therapies and Therapists: Many Choices

What different types of mental health professionals conduct psychotherapy?

Professionals trained to conduct psychotherapy fall into these categories: clinical psychologists, counseling psychologists, counselors, psychiatrists, psychoanalysts, and psychiatric social workers.

What therapy, if any, has proved to be the most effective in treating psychological disorders?

Although, overall, no one therapeutic approach has proved generally superior, specific therapies have proven effective in treating particular disorders.

Key Terms

clinical psychologist (p. 572)
psychiatrist (p. 573)
psychoanalyst (p. 573)

16

SOCIAL PSYCHOLOGY

CHAPTER OUTLINE

Introduction to Social Psychology

Social Perception

Impression Formation: Sizing Up the Other Person

Attribution: Our Explanation of Behavior

Attraction

Factors Influencing Attraction: Magnets That Draw Us Together

Romantic Attraction

Mate Selection: The Mating Game

Conformity, Obedience, and Compliance

Conformity: Going Along with the Group

Obedience: Following Orders

Compliance: Giving In to Requests

Group Influence

The Effects of the Group on Individual Performance

The Effects of the Group on Decision Making

Social Roles

Attitudes and Attitude Change

Attitudes: Cognitive, Emotional, and Behavioral Patterns

Persuasion: Trying to Change Attitudes

Prejudice and Discrimination

The Roots of Prejudice and Discrimination

World of Psychology: Discrimination in the Workplace

Combating Prejudice and Discrimination

Prejudice: Is It Increasing or Decreasing?

Prosocial Behavior: Behavior That Benefits Others

The Bystander Effect: The More Bystanders, the Less Likely They Are to Help

People Who Help in Emergencies

Aggression: Intentionally Harming Others

Biological Factors in Aggression: Genes, Hormones, and Brain Damage

Aggression in Response to Frustration: Sometimes but Not Always

Aggression in Response to Aversive Events: Pain, Heat, Noise, and More

The Social Learning Theory of Aggression: Learning to Be Aggressive

Applications: Nonverbal Behavior—The Silent Language

Thinking Critically

Chapter Summary and Review

Sunday mornings were usually quiet and peaceful in this college town, but not this particular Sunday morning. The scream of sirens split the air as the city police conducted a surprise mass arrest, rounding up nine male college students. The students were searched, handcuffed, read their constitutional rights, and hauled off to jail. Here they were booked and fingerprinted, then transported to "Stanford County Prison." At the prison each student was stripped naked, searched, deloused, given a uniform and a number, and placed in a cell with two other prisoners. All of this was more than sufficiently traumatic, but then there were the guards in their khaki uniforms, wearing reflector sunglasses that made eye-to-eye contact impossible and carrying clubs that resembled small baseball bats.

The prisoners had to get permission from the guards for the most simple, routine matters, such as writing a letter, smoking a cigarette, or even using the toilet. And the guards were hard—severe in the punishments they imposed. Prisoners were made to do pushups while the guards sometimes stepped on them or forced another prisoner to sit on them. Some prisoners were placed in solitary confinement. (Adapted from Zimbardo, 1972.)

But wait a minute! Something is wrong with this little scenario. People are not arrested, charged, and thrown into prison without a trial. What happened? In truth the guards were not guards and the prisoners were not prisoners. All were college students who had been selected to participate in a 2-week experiment on prison life conducted by Philip Zimbardo and colleagues (1973) at Stanford University. Guards and prisoners were selected randomly from a final pool of volunteers who had been judged mature, healthy, psychologically stable, law-abiding citizens. Those who were to be prisoners were not aware of their selection until they were "arrested" on that quiet Sunday morning.

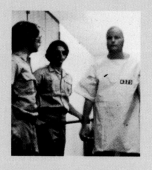

This was only an experiment, but it became all too real—to the guards and especially to the prisoners. How could some of the guards, though mild-mannered pacifists as students, so quickly become sadistic, heartless tormentors in their new role? As one guard remembered it, surprised at his own behavior, he made prisoners clean the toilets with their bare hands and virtually viewed them as cattle. The prisoners fell into their roles quickly as well. How could autonomous, self-respecting students allow themselves to become debased and subservient in their captivity, to suffer physical and mental abuse, and to behave as if they were real prisoners? The experiment was to be run for 2 weeks but had to be called off after only 6 days.

"Only an experiment"—but do the roles we play in real life affect our behavior so dramatically? We will explore this and many other interesting questions in our study of social psychology.

Introduction to Social Psychology

Social psychology is the area of study that attempts to explain how the actual, imagined, or implied presence of others influences the thoughts, feelings, and behavior of individuals. No human being lives in a vacuum, alone and apart from other people. We are truly social animals, and our social nature—how we think about, respond to, and interact with other people—provides the territory that social psychology explores. Research in social psychology yields some surprising and provocative answers to puzzling human behavior, from the atrocious to the altruistic.

This chapter explores social perception—how we form impressions of other people, and how we try to understand why they behave as they do. What are the factors involved in attraction? What draws us to other people, and how do friendships and romantic relationships develop? We will look at factors influencing conformity and obedience, and we'll examine groups and their influence on performance and decision making. We will also discuss attitudes and learn how they can be changed, and then we will explore prejudice and discrimination. Finally,

social psychology: The study of how the actual, imagined, or implied presence of others influences the thoughts, the feelings, and the behavior of individuals.

584

we will look at the conditions under which people are likely to help each other (prosocial behavior) and hurt each other (aggression).

To start, let us consider how social psychologists conduct their studies. You may have seen the TV show "Candid Camera," which shows people "caught in the act of being themselves." Secretly videotaped by a hidden camera, ordinary individuals caught in various social situations provide the humorous, sometimes hilarious, material for the show. This is precisely what researchers in social psychology must do in most of their studies—catch people in the act of being themselves. For this reason deception has traditionally played a prominent part in their research. To accomplish this deception, the researcher often must use one or more **confederates**—people who pose as subjects in a psychology experiment but who are actually assisting the experimenter. The term **naive subject** refers to an actual subject who has agreed to participate but is not aware that deception is being used to conceal the real purpose of the experiment. You will see why it is often necessary to conceal the purpose of an experiment as you read about the classic studies in social psychology.

confederate: Someone posing as a subject in an experiment but who is actually assisting the experimenter.

naive subject: A subject who has agreed to participate in an experiment but is not aware that deception is being used to conceal its real purpose.

ocial Perception

We spend a significant portion of our lives in contact with other people. Not only do we form impressions of others, but we also attempt to understand why they behave as they do.

Impression Formation: Sizing Up the Other Person

When we meet people for the first time, we start forming impressions about them right away, and, of course, other people are busily forming impressions of us. Naturally we notice the obvious attributes first—gender, race, age, dress, and how physically attractive or unattractive someone appears to us. Physical attractiveness, as shallow as it might seem, has a definite impact on first impressions. Beyond noticing physical appearance, we may wonder: What is her occupation? Is he married? Answers to our questions, combined with a conscious or an unconscious assessment of the person's verbal and nonverbal behavior, all play their part in forming a first impression. Our own moods also play a part—when we are happy, our impressions of others are usually more positive than when we are unhappy (Forgas & Bower, 1987). First impressions are powerful and can color many of the later impressions we form about people.

What first impression have you formed of the person shown here?

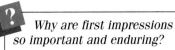 *Why are first impressions so important and enduring?*

First Impressions: Put Your Best Foot Forward—First If we gave you a list of a certain individual's characteristics or traits and asked you to write your impressions of the person, would it matter which traits were listed first? Solomon Asch (1946) gave one group of subjects the following list of traits: intelligent, industrious, impulsive, critical, stubborn, and envious. He then asked the subjects to write their impression of the person. Asch gave another group the same list but in reverse order. The subjects who responded to the list with the positive traits first gave more favorable evaluations than subjects whose list began with the negative traits.

Why should our first impressions be so important? A number of studies reveal that our overall impression or judgment of another person is influenced more by the first information we receive about the person than by information that comes later (Luchins, 1957; Park, 1986). This phenomenon is called the **primacy effect**. It seems that we attend to initial information more carefully, and once an impres-

primacy effect: The tendency for an overall impression of another to be influenced more by the first information that is received about that person than by information that comes later.

attribution: An inference about the cause of our own or another's behavior.

situational attribution: Attribution of a behavior to some external cause or factor operating in the situation; an external attribution.

dispositional attribution: Attribution of one's own or another's behavior to some internal cause such as a personal trait, motive, or attitude; an internal attribution.

sion is formed, it provides the framework through which we interpret later information. Any information that is consistent with the first impression is likely to be accepted, thus strengthening the impression. Information that does not fit with the earlier information is more likely to be disregarded.

Remember, any time you list your personal traits or qualities, always list your most positive qualities first. It pays to put your best foot forward—first.

Expectancies: Seeing What We Expect to See Sometimes our expectations about how other persons will act in a situation become a self-fulfilling prophecy and actually influence the way they do act. Expectations may be based on a person's gender, age, racial or ethnic group, social class, role or occupation, personality traits, past behavior, relationship to us, and so on. Once formed, our expectancies affect how we perceive the behavior of others, what we pay attention to, and what we ignore. But rarely do we consider the possibility that our expectations may also color our own attitude, manner, and treatment of that person in such a way that we ourselves partly bring about the very behavior we expect (Jones, 1986; Miller & Turnbull, 1986).

Attribution: Our Explanation of Behavior

? *What is the difference between a situational attribution and a dispositional attribution for a specific behavior?*

Why do people (ourselves included) do the things they do? To answer this question, we make **attributions**—that is, we assign or attribute causes to explain the behavior of others and to explain our own behavior as well. We are particularly interested in the causes when behaviors are unexpected, when goals are not attained (Weiner, 1985), and when actions are not socially desirable (Jones & Davis, 1965).

Although we can actually observe behavior, we usually can only infer its cause or causes. Whenever we try to determine why we or someone else behaved in a certain way, we can make a **situational attribution** (an external attribution) and attribute the behavior to some external cause or factor operating within the situation. After failing an exam, we might say, "The test was unfair" or "The professor didn't teach the material well." Or we might make a **dispositional attribution** (an internal attribution) and attribute the behavior to some internal cause such as a personal trait, motive, or attitude. We might attribute a poor grade to our own lack of ability or to a poor memory.

? *How do the kinds of attributions we tend to make about ourselves differ from those we make about other people?*

Attributional Biases: Different Attributions for Ourselves and Others
There are basic differences in the way we make attributions about our own behavior and that of others (Jones, 1976, 1990; Jones & Nisbett, 1971). We tend to use situational attributions to explain our own behavior, because we are aware of factors in the situation that influenced us to act as we did. Also, being aware of our past behavior, we know whether our present actions are typical or atypical.

When we try to explain the behavior of other people, however, we focus more on them personally than on the factors operating within the situation. Not knowing how they have behaved in different situations in the past, we assume a consistency in their behavior. Thus we are likely to attribute the behavior to some personal quality. The tendency to overemphasize internal factors and underemphasize situational factors when we explain other people's behavior is so fundamental, so commonplace, that it has been named the **fundamental attribution error** (Ross, 1977).

fundamental attribution error: The tendency to overemphasize internal causes and underemphasize situational factors when explaining the behavior of others.

In the United States, the plight of the homeless and of people on welfare is often attributed to laziness, an internal attribution, rather than to factors in their situation that might explain their condition. The fundamental attribution error is not universal, however. In India, for example, middle-class adults tend to make situational attributions for deviant behavior, attributing it to "role, status, or caste, and kin structures" rather than to internal dispositions (Pepitone & Triandis, 1987, p. 492).

There is one striking inconsistency in the way we view our own behavior—the self-serving bias. We use the **self-serving bias** when we attribute our successes to internal or dispositional causes and blame our failures on external or situational causes (Baumgardner et al., 1986; Brown & Rogers, 1991). If we interview for a job and get it, it is probably because we have the right qualifications. If someone else gets the job, it is probably because he or she knew the right people. The self-serving bias allows us to take credit for our successes and shift the blame for our failures to the situation.

self-serving bias: Our tendency to attribute our successes to dispositional causes, and our failures to situational causes.

proximity: Geographic closeness; a major factor in attraction.

Memory Check 16.1

1. Which of the following statements about first impressions is *false*?
   a. We usually pay closer attention to early information than to later information we receive about a person.
   b. Early information forms a framework through which other information is interpreted.
   c. First impressions often serve as self-fulfilling prophecies.
   d. The importance of first impressions is greatly overrated.

2. We tend to make _____ attributions to explain our own behavior and _____ attributions to explain the behavior of others.
   a. situational; situational
   b. situational; dispositional
   c. dispositional; situational
   d. dispositional; dispositional

3. The tendency of people to overemphasize dispositional causes and underemphasize situational causes when they explain the behavior of others is called the:
   a. fundamental attribution error.
   b. false consensus error.
   c. self-serving bias.
   d. external bias error.

4. Attributing Mike's poor grade to his lack of ability is a dispositional attribution. (true/false)

Answers: 1. d 2. b 3. a 4. true

Attraction

Think for a moment about the people you consider to be your closest friends. What causes you to like or even love one person yet ignore or react negatively to someone else? What factors influence interpersonal attraction—the degree to which we are drawn to or like another?

Factors Influencing Attraction: Magnets That Draw Us Together

Some of the factors influencing attraction are within the situation and some are within the person.

Proximity: Close to You One major factor influencing our choice of friends is physical **proximity**, or geographic closeness. If you live in an apartment complex, you are probably more friendly with people who live next door or only a few doors away (Festinger et al., 1950). The same is true in a dormitory (Priest & Sawyer, 1967). What about the people you like best in your classes? Do they sit next to you or not more than a seat or two away?

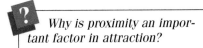

Why is proximity an important factor in attraction?

mere-exposure effect: The tendency of people to develop a more positive evaluation of some person, object, or other stimulus with repeated exposure to it.

Why is proximity so important? It is much less trouble to make friends or even fall in love with people who are close at hand. Physical proximity also increases the frequency of interaction, and mere exposure to people, objects, and circumstances usually increases our liking for them (Zajonc, 1968). The **mere-exposure effect** is the tendency to feel more positively toward stimuli with repeated exposure. People, food, songs, and styles become more acceptable the more we are exposed to them. Advertisers rely on the positive effects of repeated exposure to increase our liking for products and even for political candidates.

There are exceptions to the mere-exposure effect, however. If our initial reaction to a person is highly negative, frequent exposure can make us feel even more negatively toward the person (Swap, 1977). In addition, those who value privacy may react less favorably when proximity results in repeated contacts with people (Larson & Bell, 1988).

Liking through Association: A Case of Classical Conditioning Our own mood and emotions, whether positive or negative, can influence how much we are attracted to people we meet (Cunningham, 1988). And sometimes we develop positive or negative feelings toward others simply because they are present when very good or very bad things happen to us. Through classical conditioning, other people can become associated with the pleasant or unpleasant event and the resulting good or bad feelings may rub off on them (Riordan & Tedeschi, 1983).

Reciprocal Liking: Liking Those Who Like Us Suppose you were at a party last weekend and met several people, including Maria and Bill. Today you learned that Maria found you the most fascinating person at the party, but Bill thought you were a nerd. Would this information cause you to have positive feelings for Maria and anger toward Bill?

Curtis and Miller (1986) falsely led subjects to believe that another person either liked or disliked them after an initial encounter. This false information became a self-fulfilling prophecy. When the subjects met the person again, those who believed they were liked "self-disclosed more, disagreed less, expressed dissimilarity less, and had a more positive tone of voice and general attitude than subjects who believed they were disliked" (p. 284). These positive behaviors, in turn, actually caused the other person to view them positively. The moral of this story seems easy to grasp: If you want others to like you, like them first!

? *How important is physical attractiveness in attraction?*

Attractiveness: Good Looks Attract Although people are quick to deny that mere physical appearance is the main factor that attracts them to someone initially, a substantial body of evidence indicates that it is. People of all ages have a strong tendency to prefer physically attractive people. Even 6-month-old infants, when given the chance to look at a photograph of an attractive or an unattractive woman, man, or infant, will spend more time looking at the attractive face (Langlois et al., 1991). More than 2,000 years ago Aristotle said, "Beauty is a greater recommendation than any letter of introduction." Apparently, it still is.

What constitutes physical beauty? Researchers Langlois and Roggman (1990) found that physical beauty consists not of rare physical qualities but of facial features that are approximately the mathematical average of the features in a given general population. The researchers averaged the individual features of 4, 8, 16, and 32 faces, and then had a computer generate composites of the averaged features. The larger the group that was averaged, the more attractive the computer-generated composite face. A more recent study suggests that exaggerations of some averaged features, in particular larger eyes, were considered most attractive by groups of Japanese and British subjects (Perrett & May, 1994).

But as you are well aware, physical attractiveness extends beyond facial features. In another study, males aged 25 to 85 were shown line drawings of women who varied according to relative waist and hip measurements. Men of all ages preferred low waist-to-hip ratios (Singh, 1993).

Why is physical attractiveness so important? When people have one trait or quality that we either admire or dislike very much, we often assume that they also have other admirable or negative traits—a phenomenon known as the **halo effect** (Nisbett & Wilson, 1977; Thorndike, 1920). Dion and others (1972) found that people generally attribute other favorable qualities to those who are attractive. Attractive people are seen as more exciting, personable, interesting, and socially desirable than unattractive people.

Feingold (1992) conducted several meta-analyses that shed more light on the relationship between physical attractiveness and certain personality characteristics and social behaviors. One meta-analysis confirmed that positive characteristics are, indeed, attributed to physically attractive people. Feingold also reported a most intriguing finding. He discovered a positive correlation between a person's *self-rated* physical attractiveness and many attributes—self-esteem, popularity with the opposite sex, social comfort, extroversion, mental health, and sexual experience. The moral of this story seems to be that if we believe we are physically attractive, others will also perceive us as attractive. This finding may explain why some people you remember from high school may have been very popular and had high self-esteem even though they were less attractive physically than others in the class.

Other than "believing" we are physically attractive, what else can we do to increase our attractiveness to others? Try smiling more. A study by Reis and others (1990) revealed that smiling increases the perceived attractiveness of others and makes them appear more sincere, sociable, and competent.

Eagly and others (1991) analyzed 76 studies of the physical attractiveness stereotype. They found that physical attractiveness has its greatest impact on judgments of popularity and sociability and less impact on judgments of adjustment and intellectual competence. They did find one negative, however. Attractive people are perceived as more vain and less modest than less attractive people.

Research suggests that job interviewers are more likely to recommend highly attractive people (Dipboye et al., 1975), and that attractive people have their written work evaluated more favorably (Landy & Sigall, 1974). Even the evaluation of the attractiveness of a person's voice is affected by the person's physical appearance (Zuckerman et al., 1991).

Being attractive is an advantage to children and adults, to males and females; but according to some studies, women's looks contribute more to how they are judged on other personal qualities than do men's looks (Bar-Tal & Saxe, 1976; Feingold, 1990). Physical attractiveness seems to have its greatest impact in the context of romantic attraction, particularly in initial encounters (Hatfield & Sprecher, 1986; Feingold, 1988).

Does this mean that unattractive people don't have a chance? Fortunately not. Eagly and her colleagues (1991) suggest that the impact of physical attractiveness is strongest in the perception of strangers. But once we get to know people, other qualities assume more importance. In fact, as we come to like people, they begin to look more attractive to us, while people with undesirable personal qualities begin to look less attractive.

Similarity: A Strong Basis of Attraction　　To sum up research on attraction, the saying "Birds of a feather flock together" is more accurate than "Opposites attract." Beginning in elementary school, people are more likely to pick friends of the same age, gender, race, and socioeconomic class. These sociological variables continue to influence the choice of friends through college and later in life. Choosing

halo effect: The tendency to infer generally positive or negative traits in a person as a result of observing one major positive or negative trait.

The halo effect—the attribution of other favorable qualities to those who are attractive—helps explain why physical attractiveness is so important.

Are people, as a rule, more attracted to those who are opposite or to those who are similar to them?

friends who are similar to us could be related to proximity—the fact that we tend to come into contact with people who are more similar to us in a variety of ways.

Liking people who have similar attitudes begins early in childhood and continues throughout life in both sexes (Griffitt et al., 1972). We are likely to choose friends and lovers who have similar views on most things that are important to us. Similar interests and attitudes toward leisure-time activities make it more likely that time spent together is rewarding. Not only is similarity in attitudes an important ingredient in attraction (Newcomb, 1956), but people often have negative feelings toward others whose attitudes differ from their own (Byrne et al., 1986; Smeaton et al., 1989). People who share our attitudes validate our judgments; those who disagree with us suggest the possibility that we are wrong and arouse negative feelings in us. It is similarities, then, not differences, that usually stimulate liking and loving.

Romantic Attraction

The Matching Hypothesis: Peas in a Pod

> Moderately attractive, unskilled, unemployed, 50-year-old divorced man with 7 children seeks beautiful, wealthy, exciting woman between ages of 20 and 30 for companionship, romance, and possible marriage. No smokers or drinkers, please.

Can you imagine reading this ad in the personals column of your newspaper? Even though most of us may be attracted to handsome or beautiful people, the **matching hypothesis** suggests that we are likely to end up with someone similar to ourselves in attractiveness and other assets (Berscheid et al., 1971; Feingold, 1988; Walster & Walster, 1969). Furthermore, couples mismatched in attractiveness are more likely to end the relationship (Cash & Janda, 1984).

It has been suggested that we estimate our social assets and realistically expect to attract someone with approximately equal assets. In terms of physical attractiveness, some people might consider a movie star or supermodel to be the ideal man or woman, but they do not seriously consider the ideal to be a realistic, attainable possibility. Fear of rejection keeps many people from pursuing those who are much more attractive than they are. But instead of marrying an extremely handsome man, a very beautiful woman may sacrifice physical attractiveness for money and social status. Extremely handsome men have been known to make similar "sacrifices."

What about same-sex friendships? The matching hypothesis is generally applicable in same-sex friendships (Cash & Derlega, 1978), although it is more true of males than of females (Feingold, 1988). A person's perceived attractiveness seems to be affected in part by the attractiveness of his or her friends (Geiselman et al., 1984).

Mate Selection: The Mating Game

Robert Winch (1958) proposes that men and women tend to choose mates with needs and personalities that are complementary rather than similar to their own. Winch sees complementary needs not necessarily as opposite, but as needs that supply what the partner lacks. A talkative person may seek a quiet mate who prefers to listen.

The weight of research, however, does not support this notion. By and large it seems to be similarity in needs that attracts (Buss, 1984; Phillips et al., 1988). Similarity in personality as well as "physical characteristics, cognitive abilities, age, education, religion, ethnic background, attitudes and opinions, and socioeconomic status" all play a role in marital choice (O'Leary & Smith, 1991, p. 196).

matching hypothesis: The notion that people tend to have spouses, lovers, or friends who are approximately equivalent in social assets such as physical attractiveness.

What's more, similarity in needs and in personality appears to be related to marital success as well as to marital choice (O'Leary & Smith, 1991). Similarities wear well.

If you were to select a marriage partner, what qualities would attract you? Complete the *Try It!* to evaluate your own preferences.

Try It!

In your choice of a mate, which qualities are most and least important to you? Rank these 18 qualities of a potential mate from most important (1) to least important (18) to you.

___ Ambition and industriousness
___ Chastity (no previous sexual intercourse)
___ Desire for home and children
___ Education and intelligence

___ Emotional stability and maturity
___ Favorable social status or rating
___ Good cooking and housekeeping skills
___ Similar political background
___ Similar religious background
___ Good health
___ Good looks
___ Similar education
___ Pleasing disposition
___ Refinement/neatness
___ Sociability
___ Good financial prospects
___ Dependable character
___ Mutual attraction/love

How do your selections compare with those of men and women from 33 countries and 5 major islands around the world? Generally men and women across cultures rate these four values as most important in mate selection: (1) mutual attraction/love, (2) dependable character, (3) emotional stability and maturity, and (4) pleasing disposition (Buss et al., 1990). Aside from these first four values, however, women and men differ somewhat in the attributes they prefer. According to Buss (1994), "Men prefer to mate with beautiful young women, whereas women prefer to mate with men who have resources and social status" (p. 239). These preferences, he claims, have been adaptive in human evolutionary history. To a male, beauty and youth suggest health and fertility—the best opportunity for reproductive success. To a female, resources and social status provide security for her and her children.

Memory Check 16.2

1. Match each term with a description at the left.

___ 1) Brian sees Susan at the library often and begins to like her.

___ 2) Liane assumes that because Boyd is handsome, he must be popular and sociable.

___ 3) Alan and Carol are going together and are both very attractive.

a. matching hypothesis
b. halo effect
c. mere-exposure effect

2. Physical attractiveness is a very important factor in initial attraction. (true/false)

3. People are usually drawn to those who are more opposite than similar to themselves. (true/false)

Answers: 1. 1) c 2) b 3) a 2. true 3. false

conformity: Changing or adopting an attitude or behavior to be consistent with the norms of a group or the expectations of others.

norms: The attitudes and standards of behavior expected of members of a particular group.

What did Asch find in his famous experiment on conformity?

FIGURE 16.1

Asch's Classic Study of Conformity

If you were one of eight subjects in the Asch experiment who were asked to pick the line (1, 2, or 3) that matched the standard line shown above them, which line would you choose? If the other subjects all chose line 3, would you conform and answer line 3? (Based on Asch, 1955.)

Standard Line

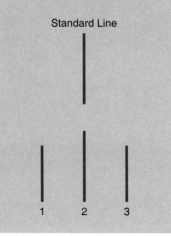

Conformity, Obedience, and Compliance

Conformity: Going Along with the Group

To conform or not to conform—that is not the question for most of us. Rather, the question is, to *what* will we conform? **Conformity** is changing or adopting a behavior or an attitude in order to be consistent with the norms of a group or the expectations of other people. **Norms** are the standards of behavior and the attitudes that are expected of members of the group. Some conformity is necessary if we are to have a society at all. We cannot drive on any side of the street we please, park any place we want, or drive as fast as we choose when in a hurry.

Because we need other people, we must conform to their expectations, to some extent, in order to have their esteem, their love, or even their company. It is easy to see why people conform to norms and standards of groups that are important to them, such as their family, peer group, social group, or team. But to an amazing degree, people also conform to the majority opinion, even when they are among a group of strangers.

Asch's Experiment: The Classic on Conformity The best-known experiment on conformity was conducted by Solomon Asch (1951, 1955), who designed the simple test shown in Figure 16.1. Look at the standard line, and then pick the line—1, 2, or 3—that is the same length. Did you pick line 2? Can you imagine any circumstances in which a person might tell the experimenter that either line 1 or line 3 matched the standard line? This is exactly what happened in Asch's classic experiment, even with tests so simple that subjects could pick the correct line over 99 percent of the time.

Eight male subjects were seated around a large table and were asked, one by one, to tell the experimenter which of the three lines matched the standard line as in Figure 16.1. But only one of the eight was an actual subject; the others were confederates assisting the experimenter. There were 18 trials—18 different lines to be matched. During 12 of these trials, the confederates all gave the same wrong answer, which of course puzzled the naive subject. Would the subject continue to believe his eyes and select the correct line, or would he feel pressure to conform to the group selections and give the wrong answer himself?

Asch found that 5 percent of the subjects conformed to the incorrect, unanimous majority *all* of the time, 70 percent conformed *some* of the time, but 25 percent remained completely independent and were *never* swayed by the group.

Asch wondered how group size would influence conformity. Varying the experiment with groups of 2, 3, 4, 8, and 10–15, he found that the tendency to "go along" with the majority opinion was in full force even when there was a unanimous major-

In this scene from Asch's experiment on conformity, all but one of the "subjects" were really confederates of the experimenter. They deliberately chose the wrong line to try to influence the naive subject (second from right) to go along with the majority.

ity of only 3 confederates. Surprisingly, unanimous majorities of 15 produced no higher conformity rate than did those of 3. Asch also discovered that if just one other person voices a dissenting opinion, the tendency to conform is not as strong. When just one confederate in the group disagreed with the incorrect majority, the naive subjects' errors dropped drastically, from 32 percent to 10.4 percent.

Other research on conformity reveals that people of low status are more likely to conform than those of high status (Eagly, 1987); but, contrary to the conventional wisdom, women are no more likely to conform than men (Eagly & Carli, 1981). And conformity is even greater if the sources of influence are perceived as belonging to one's own group (Abrams et al., 1990).

Obedience: Following Orders

Some obedience is necessary if civilized society is to function, but unquestioned obedience can cause humans to commit unbelievably horrible acts. One of the darkest chapters in human history was due to the obedience of officials in Nazi Germany in carrying out Adolph Hitler's orders to exterminate Jews and other "undesirables." The civilized world was stunned and sickened by the revelations of the Nazi death camps, and nearly everyone wondered what type of person could be capable of committing such atrocities. Stanley Milgram, a young researcher at Yale University in 1961, wondered, too. He designed a study to investigate how far ordinary citizens would go to obey orders, even if obedience meant the injury or possible death of a fellow human being.

The Milgram Study: The Classic on Obedience Back in the 1960s, an advertisement appeared in newspapers in New Haven, Connecticut, and other communities near Yale University.

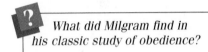

What did Milgram find in his classic study of obedience?

> **Wanted:** Volunteers to serve as subjects in a study of memory and learning at Yale University.

Many people responded to the ad, and 40 male subjects between the ages of 20 and 50 were selected, among them "postal clerks, high school teachers, salesmen, engineers, and laborers" (Milgram, 1963, p. 372). Yet no experiment on memory and learning was to take place. Instead, a staged drama was planned in which only one actual subject at a time would participate. Imagine that you are one of the naive subjects selected for the experiment.

The researcher actually wants to know how far you will go in obeying orders to administer what you believe to be increasingly painful electric shocks to a "learner" who misses questions on a test. The cast of characters is as follows:

> *The Experimenter:* A 31-year-old high school biology teacher dressed in a gray laboratory coat who assumes a stern and serious manner.
> *The Learner:* A pleasant, heavyset accountant about 50 years of age (an accomplice of the experimenter).
> *The Teacher:* You—the only naive member of the cast.

The experimenter leads you and the learner into one room, where the learner is then strapped into an electric-chair apparatus. You, the teacher, are delivered a sample shock of 45 volts, which stings you and is supposedly for the purpose of testing the equipment and showing you what the learner will feel. The learner complains of a heart condition and says that he hopes the electric shocks will not be too painful. The experimenter admits that the stronger shocks will hurt but hastens to add, "Although the shocks can be extremely painful, they cause no permanent tissue damage" (p. 373).

Then the experimenter takes you to an adjoining room, out of sight of the learner. The experimenter seats you in front of an instrument panel (shown in the

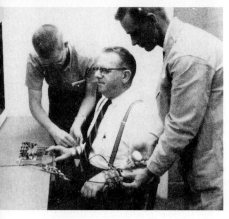

At top is the shock generator used by Milgram in his famous experiment. Below is the learner (actually an accomplice) being strapped into his chair by the experimenter and the unsuspecting participant.

photograph here), on which 30 lever switches are set horizontally. The first switch on the left, you are told, delivers only 15 volts, but each successive switch is 15 volts stronger than the last—30 volts, 45 volts, and so on up to the last switch, which carries 450 volts. The instrument panel has verbal designations ranging from "Slight Shock" to "Danger: Severe Shock."

The experimenter explains that you are to read a list of word pairs to the learner and then test his memory. When the learner makes the right choice, you go on to the next pair. If the learner misses a question, you are to flip a switch and shock him, moving one switch to the right—delivering 15 additional volts—each time he misses a question. The learner does well at first but then begins missing about three out of every four questions. You begin pulling the switches, which you believe are delivering stronger and stronger shocks for each incorrect answer. When you hesitate, the experimenter urges you, "Please continue" or "Please go on." If you still hesitate, the experimenter orders you, "The experiment requires that you continue," or more strongly, "You have no other choice, you *must* go on" (p. 374).

At the 20th switch, 300 volts, the learner pounds on the wall and screams, "Let me out of here, let me out, my heart's bothering me, let me out!" (Meyer, 1972, p. 461). From this point on, the learner answers no more questions. Alarmed, you protest to the experimenter that the learner, who is pounding the wall frantically, does not want to continue. The experimenter answers, "Whether the learner likes it or not, you must go on" (Milgram, 1963, p. 374). Even if the learner fails to respond, you are told to count that as an incorrect response and shock him again.

Do you continue? If so, you flip the next switch—315 volts—and only groans are heard from the learner. You look at the experimenter, obviously distressed, your palms sweating, your heart pounding. The experimenter states firmly, "You have no other choice, you *must* go on" (p. 374). If you refuse at this point, the experiment is ended. Would you refuse, or would you continue to shock a silent learner nine more times until you delivered the maximum of 450 volts?

How many of the 40 subjects do you think obeyed the experimenter to the end—450 volts? Not a single subject stopped before the 20th switch, supposedly 300 volts, when the learner began pounding the wall. Amazingly, 26 subjects—65 percent of the sample—obeyed the experimenter to the bitter end, as shown in Figure 16.2. But this experiment took a terrible toll on the subjects. "Subjects were observed to sweat, tremble, stutter, bite their lips, groan, and dig their fingernails into their flesh. These were characteristic rather than exceptional responses to the experiment" (p. 375).

Variations of the Milgram Study   Would the same results have occurred if the experiment had not been conducted at a famous university like Yale? The same experiment was carried out in a three-room office suite in a run-down building identified by a sign, "Research Associates of Bridgeport." Even there, 48 percent of the subjects administered the maximum shock compared to 65 percent in the Yale setting (Meyer, 1972).

Milgram (1965) conducted a variation of the original experiment in which each trial included three teachers, two of whom were confederates and the other, a naive subject. One confederate was instructed to refuse to continue after 150 volts, and the other confederate after 210 volts. In this situation 36 out of 40 naive subjects (90 percent) defied the experimenter before the maximum shock could be given, compared with only 14 subjects in the original experiment (Milgram, 1965). In Milgram's experiment, as in Asch's conformity study, the presence of another person who *refused to go along* gave many of the subjects the courage to defy the authority.

FIGURE 16.2

The Results of Milgram's Classic Experiment on Obedience

In his classic study, Stanley Milgram showed that a large majority of his subjects would obey authority even if obedience caused great pain or was life-threatening to another. Milgram reported that 87.5 percent of the subjects continued to administer what they thought were painful electric shocks of 300 volts to a victim who complained of a heart condition. Amazingly, 65 percent of the subjects obeyed authority to the bitter end and continued to deliver what they thought were dangerous, severe shocks to the maximum of 450 volts. (Data from Milgram, 1963.)

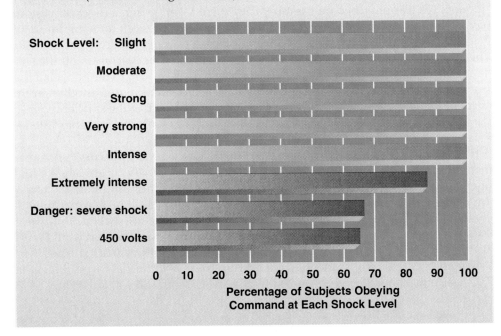

compliance: Acting in accordance with the wishes, the suggestions, or the direct request of another person.

foot-in-the-door technique: A strategy designed to secure a favorable response to a small request at first, with the aim of making the subject more likely to agree later to a larger request.

Compliance: Giving In to Requests

There are many times when people act, not out of conformity or obedience, but in accordance with the wishes, suggestions, or direct requests of another person. This type of action is called **compliance**. Almost daily we are confronted with people who make requests of one sort or another. Do we comply with requests and yield to appeals? Often the answer is yes, and several techniques have been used to gain our compliance.

The Foot-in-the-Door Technique: Upping the Ante One strategy, the **foot-in-the-door technique**, is designed to gain a favorable response to a small request first. The intent is to make the subject more likely to agree later to a larger request (the request that was desired from the beginning). In one study a researcher claiming to represent a consumers' group called a number of homes and asked whether the subjects would mind answering a few questions about the soap products they used. Then a few days later, the same person called those who had agreed to the first request and asked if he could send five or six of his assistants to conduct an inventory of the products in their home. The researcher told the subjects that the inventory would take about 2 hours, and that the inventory team would have to search all drawers, cabinets, and closets in the house. Would you agree to such an imposition?

What are three techniques used to gain compliance?

door-in-the-face technique: A strategy in which someone makes a large, unreasonable request with the expectation that the person will refuse but will then be more likely to respond favorably to a smaller request at a later time.

low-ball technique: A strategy to gain compliance by making a very attractive initial offer to get a person to agree to an action and then making the terms less favorable.

Nearly 53 percent of the foot-in-the-door group agreed to this large request, compared to 22 percent of a control group who were contacted only once with the large request (Freedman & Fraser, 1966). A review of many studies on the foot-in-the-door approach suggests that it is highly effective (Beaman et al., 1983; DeJong, 1979). But, strangely enough, exactly the opposite approach will work just as well.

The Door-in-the-Face Technique: An Unreasonable Request First With the **door-in-the-face technique**, a large, unreasonable request is made first. The expectation is that the person will refuse but will then be more likely to respond favorably to a smaller request later (the request that was desired from the beginning). In one of the best-known studies on the door-in-the-face technique, college students were approached on campus. They were asked to agree to serve without pay as counselors to juvenile delinquents for 2 hours each week for a minimum of 2 years. As you would imagine, not a single person agreed (Cialdini et al., 1975). Then the experimenters countered with a much smaller request, asking if the students would agree to take a group of juveniles on a 2-hour trip to the zoo. Half the students agreed, a fairly high compliance rate. The researchers used another group of college students as controls, asking them to respond only to the smaller request, the zoo trip. Only 17 percent agreed when the smaller request was presented alone.

The Low-Ball Technique: Not Telling the Whole Truth Up Front Another method used to gain compliance is the **low-ball technique**. A very attractive initial offer is made to get people to commit themselves to an action, and then the terms are made less favorable. College students were asked to enroll in an experimental course for which they would receive credit. But they were low-balled: Only after the students had agreed to participate were they informed that the class would meet at 7:00 A.M. But 55 percent of the low-balled group agreed to participate anyway. When another group of students were told up front that the class would meet at 7:00 A.M., only about 25 percent agreed to take the class (Cialdini et al., 1978).

Memory Check 16.3

1. Match the compliance technique with the appropriate example.

   ____ 1) Julie agrees to sign a letter supporting an increase in taxes for road construction. Later she agrees to make 100 phone calls urging people to vote for the measure.

   a. door-in-the-face technique
   b. low-ball technique
   c. foot-in-the-door technique

   ____ 2) Rick refuses a phone request for a $24 donation to send four needy children to the circus but does agree to give $6.

   ____ 3) Linda agrees to babysit for her next-door neighbors and then is informed that their three nephews will be there, too.

2. What percentage of the subjects in the original Asch study never conformed to the majority's unanimous incorrect response?

   a. 70 percent   c. 25 percent
   b. 33 percent   d. 5 percent

3. What percentage of the subjects in Milgram's original obedience experiment administered what they thought was the maximum 450-volt shock?

   a. 85 percent   c. 45 percent
   b. 65 percent   d. 25 percent

Answers: 1. 1) c 2) a 3) b 2. c 3. b

Group Influence

The Effects of the Group on Individual Performance

Our performance on tasks can be enhanced or impaired by the mere presence of others, and the decisions we reach as part of a group can be quite different from those we would make if we were acting alone.

Social Facilitation: Performing in the Presence of Others In certain cases our individual performance can be either helped or hindered by the mere physical presence of others. The term **social facilitation** refers to any effect on performance, whether positive or negative, that can be attributed to the presence of others. Research on this phenomenon has focused on two types of effects: (1) **audience effects**—the impact of passive spectators on performance; and (2) **coaction effects**—the impact on performance caused by the presence of other people engaged in the same task.

In one of the first studies in social psychology, Norman Triplett (1898) looked at coaction effects. He had observed in official bicycle records that bicycle racers pedaled faster when they were pedaling against other racers than when they were racing against the clock. Was this pattern of performance peculiar to competitive bicycling? Or was it part of a more general phenomenon in which people would work faster and harder in the presence of others than when performing alone? Triplett set up a study in which he told 40 children to wind fishing reels as quickly as possible under two conditions—(1) alone, or (2) in the presence of other children performing the same task. He found that the children worked faster when other reel turners were present than when they performed alone.

Later studies on social facilitation found just the opposite effect—that the presence of others, whether coacting or just watching, could hurt or diminish individual performance. Robert Zajonc (1965; Zajonc & Sales, 1966) proposed an explanation for these seemingly contradictory effects. He reasoned that we become aroused by the presence of others and that arousal facilitates the dominant response—the one most natural to us. On simple tasks and on tasks at which we are skilled, the dominant response is the correct one (performing effectively). However, on tasks that are difficult or tasks we are first learning, the incorrect response (making a mistake) would be dominant. This reasoning accounts for the repeated findings that, in the presence of others, performance improves on tasks that people do easily, but suffers on difficult tasks (Michaels et al., 1982). See Figure 16.3 (on page 598).

Other researchers have suggested that it is concern over the observers' evaluation of us that affects performance, particularly if we expect a negative evaluation (Sanna & Shotland, 1990).

Social Loafing: Not Pulling Our Weight in a Group Effort What happens in cooperative tasks when two or more people are working together? Do they increase their effort or slack off? Researcher Bibb Latané used the term **social loafing** for the tendency of people to exert less effort when working with others on a common task than when they are working alone. Social loafing occurs in situations where no one person's contribution to the group can be identified and individuals are neither praised for a good performance nor blamed for a poor one (Williams et al., 1981).

In one experiment, Latané and others (1979) asked male students to shout and clap as loudly as possible, first alone and then in groups. In groups of two,

? *Under what conditions does social facilitation have either a positive or a negative effect on performance?*

social facilitation: Any positive or negative effect on performance due to the presence of others, either as an audience or as co-actors.

audience effects: The impact of passive spectators on performance.

coaction effects: The impact on performance caused by the presence of others engaged in the same task.

social loafing: The tendency to put forth less effort when working with others on a common task than when working alone.

? *What is social loafing, and what factors lessen or eliminate it?*

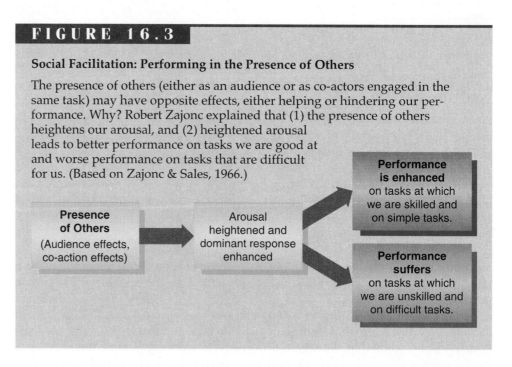

FIGURE 16.3

Social Facilitation: Performing in the Presence of Others

The presence of others (either as an audience or as co-actors engaged in the same task) may have opposite effects, either helping or hindering our performance. Why? Robert Zajonc explained that (1) the presence of others heightens our arousal, and (2) heightened arousal leads to better performance on tasks we are good at and worse performance on tasks that are difficult for us. (Based on Zajonc & Sales, 1966.)

Presence of Others (Audience effects, co-action effects) → **Arousal** heightened and dominant response enhanced → **Performance is enhanced** on tasks at which we are skilled and on simple tasks.

Performance suffers on tasks at which we are unskilled and on difficult tasks.

Social loafing is people's tendency to exert less effort when working with others on a common task, such as pedaling a multi-person cycle.

individuals made only 71 percent of the noise they had made alone; in groups of four, each person put forth 51 percent of his solo effort; and with six persons each made only a 40 percent effort.

Harkins and Jackson (1985) found that social loafing disappeared when subjects in a group were led to believe that each person's output could be monitored and his or her performance evaluated. Even the possibility that the group performance may be evaluated against some standard can be sufficient to eliminate the loafing effect (Harkins & Szymanski, 1989). When group size is relatively small and group evaluation is important, some members will even expend extra effort if they know that some of their co-workers are either unwilling, unreliable, or incompetent (Williams & Karau, 1991). Social loafing is not likely to occur when participants can evaluate their own individual contribution (Szymanski & Harkins, 1987), when they are personally involved in the outcome, when they feel that the task is challenging (Brickner et al., 1986), when they are working with close friends or teammates (Karau & Williams, 1993).

Social loafing is apparently not peculiar to any single culture but is typical of the human species. Some 50 studies conducted in places as diverse as Taiwan, Japan, Thailand, India, and the United States confirm that social loafing is evident when people are performing cooperative tasks (Gabrenya et al., 1983).

The Effects of the Group on Decision Making

The group can have profound and predictable effects on decision making, depending on the group's attitudes before a discussion begins.

? *How are the initial attitudes of group members likely to affect group decision making?*

Group Polarization: When Group Decisions Become More Extreme It is commonly believed that groups tend to make more moderate, conservative decisions than individuals make, but some research in social psychology tells us otherwise.

Group discussion often causes members of a group to shift to a more extreme position in whatever direction the group was leaning initially—a phenomenon known as **group polarization** (Isenberg, 1986; Lamm, 1988). The group members, it seems, will decide to take a greater risk if they were leaning in a risky direction to begin with, but they will shift toward a more cautious position if they were, on the average, somewhat cautious at the beginning of the discussion (Myers & Lamm, 1975). Myers and Bishop (1970) found that as a result of group polarization, group discussions of racial issues can either increase or decrease prejudice.

Why, then, aren't all group decisions either very risky or very cautious? The reason is that the members of a group do not always all lean in the same direction at the beginning of a discussion. When subgroups within a larger group hold opposing views, compromise rather than polarization is the likely outcome (Vinokur & Burnstein, 1978).

Groupthink: When Group Cohesiveness Leads to Bad Decisions Group cohesiveness refers to the degree to which group members are attracted to the group and experience a feeling of oneness. **Groupthink** is the term social psychologist Irving Janis (1982) applies to the decisions often reached by overly cohesive groups. When a tightly knit group is more concerned with preserving group solidarity and uniformity than with objectively evaluating all possible alternatives in decision making, individual members may hesitate to voice any dissent. The group may also discredit opposing views from outsiders and begin to believe it is invulnerable and incapable of making mistakes. Even plans bordering on madness can be hatched and adopted when groupthink prevails.

To guard against groupthink, Janis suggests that the group encourage an open discussion of alternative views and encourage the expression of any objections and doubts. He further recommends that outside experts sit in and challenge the views of the group. Finally, at least one group member should take the role of devil's advocate whenever a policy alternative is evaluated.

So, to summarize, the mere presence of others can increase arousal and thereby affect individual performance, can induce social loafing on a group task, and can even influence the decisions we reach. But groups exert an even more powerful influence on individuals through their prescribed social roles.

Social Roles

The group is indispensable to human life. We are born into a family group, a culture, a racial and ethnic group, and usually a religious group. And as we grow and mature, there are many other groups that we may choose to join, such as social groups and professional groups.

Shakespeare compared the world to a stage on which players enter and exit, playing their many roles. The analogy has held down through the years whenever the nature of roles in social interaction is discussed. **Roles** are the behaviors considered appropriate for individuals occupying certain positions within a group.

Roles are useful because they tell us beforehand how people are likely to act toward us in many situations, even people we have never met before. If you have ever been stopped for speeding by a police officer, you were at that moment unwillingly cast in the role of speeder, and you had few doubts about the role the officer would play. But both you and the police officer assume many different roles in life—family roles, social roles, work roles, and so on—and your behavior can differ dramatically as you shift from role to role.

Roles can indeed shape human behavior, even to an alarming degree. Zimbardo's prison study, which introduced this chapter, makes this point quite dramatically. This study helps us to understand how college students can assume, during some fraternity initiations, roles that are reminiscent of those of Zimbardo's guards and prisoners.

group polarization: The tendency of members of a group, after group discussion, to shift toward a more extreme position in whatever direction they were leaning initially—either more risky or more cautious.

groupthink: The tendency for members of a very cohesive group to feel such pressure to maintain group solidarity and to reach agreement on an issue that they fail adequately to weigh available evidence or to consider objections and alternatives.

roles: The behaviors considered to be appropriate for individuals occupying certain positions within the group.

Memory Check 16.4

1. Which of the following statements regarding the effects of social facilitation is true?
   a. Performance improves on all tasks.
   b. Performance worsens on all tasks.
   c. Performance improves on easy tasks and worsens on difficult tasks.
   d. Performance improves on difficult tasks and worsens on easy tasks.

2. Social loafing is most likely to occur when:
   a. individual output is monitored.
   b. individual output is evaluated.
   c. a task is challenging.
   d. individual output cannot be identified.

3. When group polarization occurs following group discussion, the group will decide to take a greater risk:
   a. if members were leaning in a cautious direction to begin with.
   b. if members were leaning in a risky direction to begin with.
   c. if members were leaning in different directions to begin with.
   d. regardless of the initial position of the members.

4. What occurs when members of a very cohesive group are more concerned with preserving group solidarity than with evaluating all possible alternatives in making a decision?
   a. groupthink
   b. group polarization
   c. social facilitation
   d. social loafing

Answers: 1. c 2. d 3. b 4. a

Attitudes and Attitude Change

Attitudes: Cognitive, Emotional, and Behavioral Patterns

What are the three components of an attitude?

What is your attitude toward abortion? Gun control? Premarital sex? An **attitude** is a relatively stable evaluation of a person, object, situation, or issue. Most of our attitudes have three components: (1) a cognitive component—our thoughts and beliefs about the attitudinal object; (2) an emotional component—our feelings toward the attitudinal object; and (3) a behavioral component—how we are predisposed to act toward the object (Breckler, 1984). Figure 16.4 shows the three components of an attitude.

Attitudes enable us to appraise people, objects, and situations, and provide structure and consistency to our social environment (Fazio, 1989). Attitudes also help us process social information (Pratkanis, 1989), guide our behavior (Sanbonmatsu & Fazio, 1990), and influence our social judgments and decisions (Jamieson & Zanna, 1989).

How do we form our attitudes? Some of our attitudes are acquired through firsthand experience with people, objects, situations, and issues. Others are acquired vicariously. When we hear parents, family, friends, and teachers express positive or negative attitudes toward certain issues or people, we may take the same attitudes as our own. The mass media, including advertising, influence our attitudes and reap billions of dollars annually for their efforts. As you might expect, however, the attitudes that we form through our own direct experience are stronger than those we acquire vicariously, and they are also more resistant to change (Wu & Shaffer, 1987).

The attitudes of older people tend to be more stable over time than those of younger people (Alwin et al., 1991). But the lack of change seems to result from

attitude: A relatively stable evaluation of a person, object, situation, or issue.

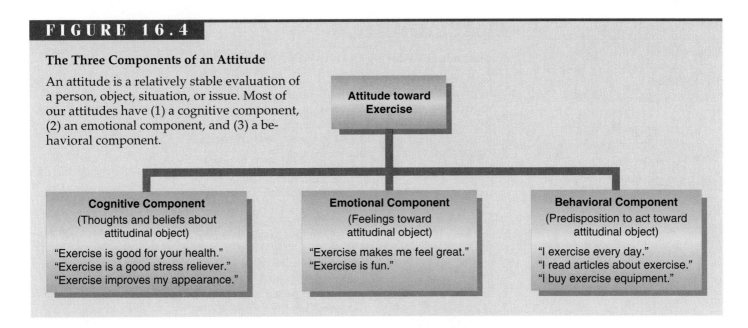

FIGURE 16.4

The Three Components of an Attitude

An attitude is a relatively stable evaluation of a person, object, situation, or issue. Most of our attitudes have (1) a cognitive component, (2) an emotional component, and (3) a behavioral component.

Attitude toward Exercise

Cognitive Component
(Thoughts and beliefs about attitudinal object)

"Exercise is good for your health."
"Exercise is a good stress reliever."
"Exercise improves my appearance."

Emotional Component
(Feelings toward attitudinal object)

"Exercise makes me feel great."
"Exercise is fun."

Behavioral Component
(Predisposition to act toward attitudinal object)

"I exercise every day."
"I read articles about exercise."
"I buy exercise equipment."

limited exposure to change-inducing experiences, not the inability or unwillingness to change (Tyler & Schuller, 1991).

The Relationship between Attitudes and Behavior The general consensus among social scientists initially was that attitudes govern behavior (Allport, 1935). But toward the end of the 1960s, one study after another failed to reveal a strong relationship between what people reported they believed on attitude measurement scales and their actual behavior. Attitudes seemed to predict observed behavior only about 10 percent of the time (Wicker, 1969).

Why aren't attitude measures better predictors of behavior? Attitude measures may often be too general to predict specific behaviors. People may express strong attitudes toward protecting the environment and conservation of resources, yet not take their aluminum cans to a recycling center or join carpools. But when attitude measures correspond very closely to the behavior of interest, they actually become good predictors of behavior (Ajzen & Fishbein, 1977). Finally, attitudes are better predictors of behavior if they are strongly held, are readily accessible in memory (Fazio & Williams, 1986), and vitally affect our interests (Sivacek & Crano, 1982).

Cognitive Dissonance: The Mental Pain of Inconsistency If we discover that some of our attitudes are in conflict with others or that they are not consistent with our behavior, we are likely to experience an unpleasant state. Leon Festinger (1957) called this **cognitive dissonance**. We usually try to reduce the dissonance by changing our behavior or our attitude, or by somehow explaining away the inconsistency or reducing its importance (Aronson, 1976; Festinger, 1957).

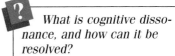 *What is cognitive dissonance, and how can it be resolved?*

Smoking is a perfect situation for cognitive dissonance. What are smokers to do? The healthiest, but perhaps not the easiest, way to reduce cognitive dissonance is to change the behavior—quit smoking. Another way is to change the attitude—to convince themselves that smoking is not as dangerous as it is said to be. Smokers can also tell themselves that they will stop smoking long before any permanent damage is done, or that medical science is advancing so rapidly that a cure for cancer is just around the corner. Figure 16.5 (on page 602) illustrates the methods a smoker can use to reduce cognitive dissonance.

cognitive dissonance: The unpleasant state that can occur when people become aware of inconsistencies between their attitudes or between their attitudes and their behavior.

persuasion: A deliberate attempt to influence the attitudes and/or behavior of another.

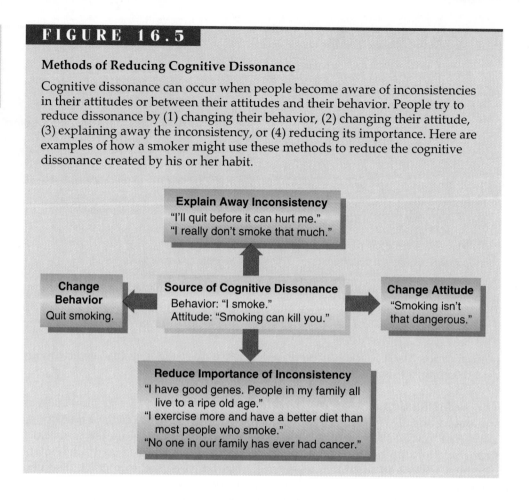

FIGURE 16.5

Methods of Reducing Cognitive Dissonance

Cognitive dissonance can occur when people become aware of inconsistencies in their attitudes or between their attitudes and their behavior. People try to reduce dissonance by (1) changing their behavior, (2) changing their attitude, (3) explaining away the inconsistency, or (4) reducing its importance. Here are examples of how a smoker might use these methods to reduce the cognitive dissonance created by his or her habit.

Explain Away Inconsistency
"I'll quit before it can hurt me."
"I really don't smoke that much."

Change Behavior
Quit smoking.

Source of Cognitive Dissonance
Behavior: "I smoke."
Attitude: "Smoking can kill you."

Change Attitude
"Smoking isn't that dangerous."

Reduce Importance of Inconsistency
"I have good genes. People in my family all live to a ripe old age."
"I exercise more and have a better diet than most people who smoke."
"No one in our family has ever had cancer."

Researchers have found that if people voluntarily make a statement or take a position that is counter to what they believe, they will experience cognitive dissonance because of the inconsistency. To resolve this dissonance, they are likely to change their belief to make it more consistent with their behavior (Festinger & Carlsmith, 1959).

Justifying a Sacrifice Following Festinger's work, Aronson and Mills (1959) found broader applications for the cognitive dissonance theory. They reasoned that the more people have to sacrifice, give up, or suffer to become a member of an organization, say a fraternity or sorority, the more positive their attitudes are likely to become toward the group—in order to justify their sacrifice. Members of cults are often required to endure hardships and make great sacrifices, such as severing ties with their families and friends and turning over their property and possessions to the group. Such extreme sacrifice can then be justified only by a strong and radical defense of the cult, its goals, and its leaders.

What are the four elements in persuasion?

Persuasion: Trying to Change Attitudes

Persuasion is a deliberate attempt to influence the attitudes and/or the behavior of another person. Attempts at persuasion are pervasive parts of our work experience, social experiences, and even family life.

Researchers have identified four elements in persuasion: (1) the source of the communication (who is doing the persuading), (2) the audience (who is being persuaded), (3) the message (what is being said), and (4) the medium (the means by which the message is transmitted).

The Source: Look Who's Talking

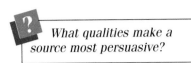

What qualities make a source most persuasive?

Some factors that make the source (the communicator) more persuasive are credibility, attractiveness, and likability. Credibility refers to how believable a source is. A credible communicator is one who has expertise (knowledge of the topic at hand) and trustworthiness (truthfulness and integrity). The influence of a credible source is even greater if the audience knows the communicator's credentials beforehand. Moreover, we attach greater credibility to sources who have nothing to gain from persuading us or, better yet, who seem to be arguing against their own best interest. For example, arguments against pornography are more persuasive if they are made by a source known to be generally opposed to censorship.

In matters that involve our own personal tastes and preferences rather than issues, attractive people and celebrities can be very persuasive (Chaiken, 1979). Movie and TV stars, athletes, and even unknown but attractive fashion models have long been used by advertisers to persuade us to buy certain products. Likable, down-to-earth, ordinary people who are perceived to be similar to the audience are sometimes even more effective persuaders than famous experts, attractive models, or movie stars. Political candidates attempt to appear more likable and more like the voters when they don hard hats and visit construction sites and coal mines, kiss babies, and pose with farmers.

The Audience and the Message

Persuaders must consider the nature of their audience before they attempt to use persuasion. In general, people with low intelligence are easier to persuade than those who are highly intelligent (Rhodes & Wood, 1992). Research evidence suggests that a one-sided message (where only one side of a message is given) is usually most persuasive if the audience is not well informed on the issue, is not overly intelligent, or is already in agreement with the point of view. A two-sided approach (where both sides of an issue are mentioned) works best when the audience is well informed on the issue, is fairly intelligent, or is initially opposed to the point of view. The two-sided approach will usually sway more people than a one-sided appeal (Hovland et al., 1949; McGuire, 1985).

Persuasion is a deliberate attempt to influence the attitudes and/or behavior of another person. What tactics do you use when trying to persuade others?

A message can be well reasoned, logical, and unemotional ("just the facts"); a message can be strictly emotional ("scare the hell out of them"); or it can be a combination of the two. Which type of message works best? Arousing fear seems to be an effective method for persuading people to adopt healthier attitudes and behaviors (Robberson & Rogers, 1988). One review of many studies on fear and persuasion covering various issues—antismoking presentations, seatbelt safety campaigns, and appeals urging regular chest X rays—reported that high-fear appeals were more effective than low-fear appeals (Higbee, 1969). Fear appeals are most effective when the presentation outlines definite actions the audience can take to avoid the feared outcomes (Leventhal et al., 1965).

Another important factor in persuasion is repetition. The more often a product or a point of view is presented, the more people will be persuaded to buy it or embrace it. Advertisers apparently believe in the mere-exposure effect, for they repeat their message over and over (Bornstein, 1989).

Memory Check 16.5

1. Which of the following is *not* one of the three components of an attitude?
   a. cognitive component
   b. emotional component
   c. physiological component
   d. behavioral component

2. All of the following are ways to reduce cognitive dissonance *except*:
   a. changing an attitude.
   b. changing a behavior.
   c. explaining away the inconsistency.
   d. strengthening the attitude and behavior.

3. People who have made a great sacrifice to join a group usually decrease their liking for the group. (true/false)

4. Credibility relates most directly to the communicator's:
   a. attractiveness.   c. likability.
   b. expertise and trustworthiness.   d. personality.

5. With a well-informed audience, two-sided messages are more persuasive than one-sided messages. (true/false)

6. High-fear appeals are more effective than low-fear appeals if they provide definite actions that people can take to avoid dreaded outcomes. (true/false)

Answers: 1. c 2. d 3. false 4. b 5. true 6. true

Prejudice and Discrimination

Increasing cultural diversity is a fact of life in the modern world. And the United States is among the most culturally diverse nations in the world. Can we learn to live and work peacefully with our fellow Americans, no matter what racial, ethnic, cultural, or other differences exist among us? The answer is a conditional yes—if we can learn how to combat prejudice and discrimination.

The Roots of Prejudice and Discrimination

What is the difference between prejudice and discrimination?

Prejudice consists of attitudes (usually negative) toward others based on their gender, religion, race, or membership in a particular group. Prejudice involves beliefs and emotions (not actions) that can escalate into hatred. **Discrimination** consists of behavior—actions (usually negative) toward members of a group. Many Americans have experienced prejudice and discrimination—minority racial groups (racism), women (sexism), the elderly (ageism), the handicapped, homosexuals, religious groups, and others. What are the roots of prejudice and discrimination?

The Realistic Conflict Theory: When Competition Leads to Prejudice

One of the oldest explanations offered for the genesis of prejudice is competition among various social groups who must struggle against each other for scarce resources—good jobs, homes, schools, and so on. Commonly called the **realistic conflict theory**, this view suggests that as competition increases, so does prejudice, discrimination, and hatred among the competing groups. Some historical evidence supports the realistic conflict theory. Prejudice and hatred were high between the American settlers and the Native Americans who struggled over land during the westward expansion. The multitudes of Irish and German immigrants who came to the United States in the 1830s and 1840s felt the sting of prejudice and hatred from other Americans who were facing economic scarcity. As many nations around the world experience hard economic times in the late 1990s, will we see an increase in prejudice and discrimination? The realistic conflict the-

prejudice: Negative attitudes toward others based on their gender, religion, race, or membership in a particular group.

discrimination: Behavior, usually negative, directed toward others based on their gender, religion, race, or membership in a particular group.

realistic conflict theory: The notion that prejudices arise when social groups must compete for scarce resources and opportunities.

ory predicts that we will. But prejudice and discrimination are attitudes and actions too complex to be explained solely by economic conflict and competition. What are some other causes?

Us versus Them: Dividing the World into In-Groups and Out-Groups

Prejudice can also spring from the distinct social categories into which we divide our world—*us versus them* (Turner et al., 1987). An **in-group** is a social group with a strong feeling of togetherness and from which others are excluded. College fraternities and sororities often exhibit strong in-group feelings. The **out-group** consists of individuals or groups specifically identified by the in-group as not belonging. Us-versus-them thinking can lead to excessive competition, hostility, prejudice, discrimination, and even war.

Some leaders have achieved great national solidarity—a collective in-group feeling—by creating hatred for another group or nation (the out-group). The leaders of Iran achieved strong national in-group sentiments by casting the United States in the role of the despised out-group—"the great Satan." During the Gulf War most Americans and our allied nations, including some Arab nations, became the in-group, and Saddam Hussein and the nation of Iraq were perceived as the out-group. But groups need not be composed of different races, religions, nations, or any other particular category for in-group/out-group hostility to develop.

The Robber's Cave Experiment A famous study by Sherif and Sherif (1967) shows how in-group/out-group conflict can escalate into prejudice and hostility rather quickly, even between groups that are very much alike. The researchers set up their experiment at the Robber's Cave summer camp. Their subjects were 22 bright, well-adjusted, 11- and 12-year-old white middle-class boys from Oklahoma City. Divided into two groups and housed in separate cabins, the boys were kept apart for all their daily activities and games. During the first week, in-group solidarity, friendship, and cooperation developed within each of the groups. One group called itself the *Rattlers*; the other group took the name *Eagles*.

During week two of the study, competitive events were purposely scheduled so that the goals of one group could be achieved "only at the expense of the other group" (Sherif, 1958, p. 353). The groups were happy to battle each other, and intergroup conflict quickly emerged. Name-calling began, fights broke out, and accusations were hurled back and forth. During the third week of the experiment, the researchers tried to put an end to the hostility and to turn rivalry into cooperation. They simply brought the groups together for pleasant activities such as eating meals and watching movies. "But far from reducing conflict, these situations only served as opportunities for the rival groups to berate and attack each other. . . . They threw paper, food and vile names at each other at the tables" (Sherif, 1956, pp. 57–58).

Finally, the last stage of the experiment was set in motion. The experimenters manufactured a series of crises that could be solved only if all the boys combined their efforts and resources and cooperated. The water supply, sabotaged by the experimenters, could be restored only if all the boys worked together. After a week of several activities requiring cooperation, cut-throat competition gave way to cooperative exchanges. Friendships developed between groups, and before the end of the experiment, peace was declared. Working together toward shared goals had turned hostility into friendship.

The Social Learning Theory: Acquiring Prejudice through Modeling and Reinforcement

According to the social learning theory, attitudes of prejudice and hatred are learned in the same way that other attitudes are learned. If children hear their parents, teachers, peers, and others openly express prejudices toward different racial, ethnic, or cultural groups, they may be quick to learn such attitudes. And if parents, peers, and others reward children with smiles and

What is meant by the terms in-group and out-group?

Even in the 1990s, prejudice and racial hatred thrive in the United States. What theory explains the rise of hate groups like these neo-Nazis?

in-group: A social group with a strong sense of togetherness and from which others are excluded.

out-group: A social group specifically identified by the in-group as not belonging.

How does prejudice develop, according to the social learning theory?

approval for parroting their own prejudices (operant conditioning), children may learn these prejudices even more quickly.

Oldenburg (1990) cites evidence that the seeds of prejudice are often sown very early. At a preschool class in California, a 4-year-old Korean American boy sat down in the class circle beside a 4-year-old, blond, blue-eyed boy who yelled, "Don't touch me, Chinese!" A hush fell over the class, but teacher Kay Taus knew how to handle the situation. She asked the Korean American child if the remark hurt his feelings. He admitted that it did. The teacher told the children that it was not right to make fun of a person from any race, and she continued to press her point about hurt feelings. Her lesson took root. Some months later she observed the blond boy telling some children who were pulling up the corners of their eyes to stop it because their actions hurt the feelings of Chinese children.

Social Cognition: Natural Thinking Processes Can Lead to Prejudice

Emotion- and learning-based views help explain how prejudice develops. But a more recent view suggests that social cognition plays a role in giving birth to prejudice. **Social cognition** refers to the ways in which we typically process social information—the natural thinking processes we use to notice, interpret, and remember information about our social world. The very processes we use to simplify, categorize, and order our world are the same processes by which we distort it. So prejudice may arise not only from heated negative emotions and hatred toward other social groups, but also from cooler cognitive processes that govern how we think and process social information (Linville et al., 1989).

One way people simplify, categorize, and order their world is by using stereotypes. **Stereotypes** are widely shared beliefs about the characteristics of members of various social groups (racial, ethnic, religious), which include the assumption that *they* are usually all alike. Macrae and colleagues (1994) suggest that we apply stereotypes in our interactions with others because doing so requires less mental energy than trying to understand people as individuals. This enables us to apply our mental resources to other activities. Research by Anderson and others (1990) showed that subjects could process information more efficiently and answer questions faster when they were using stereotypes.

Do you use stereotypes in your thinking? To find out, complete the *Try It!*

> ? *What are stereotypes?*

social cognition: Mental processes that people use to notice, interpret, understand, remember, and apply information about the social world and that enable them to simplify, categorize, and order their world.

stereotypes: Widely shared beliefs about the characteristic traits, attitudes, and behaviors of members of various social groups (racial, ethnic, religious) and including the assumption that *they* are usually all alike.

Can you list characteristics for each of the following groups?

African Americans
White, male top-level executives
Native Americans
Homosexuals
Hispanic Americans
Members of fundamentalist religious groups
Jews
Arabs
Italians
Germans

Do you believe that African Americans are good athletes and musicians but are not ambitious and industrious? Or that to be white is to be racist and filled with hatred toward blacks or other minorities? Are females nurturant and noncompetitive, while males are strong and dominant and make the best leaders? All these beliefs are stereotypes. Once developed, stereotypes strongly influence the way we attend to and evaluate incoming information about specific groups.

Consequently the stereotypes we hold can powerfully affect the ways we react to and make judgments about persons in various groups.

In the *Try It!*, how many group characteristics could you list? If we can list traits thought to represent any group, we are probably demonstrating stereotypic thinking. We know that not *all* members of a group possess the same traits or characteristics, but we tend to use stereotypic thinking nonetheless.

Some research has revealed that social stereotypes involve more than overgeneralization about the traits or characteristics of members of certain groups (Judd et al., 1991). People tend to perceive more diversity, more variability, within the groups to which they belong (in-groups), but they see more similarity among members of other groups (out-groups) (Ostrom et al., 1993). Whites see more diversity among themselves but more sameness within groups of African Americans or Asians. This tendency in thinking can extend from race to gender to age or any other category of persons. Another study showed that young college students believed there was much more variability or diversity in 100 of their group than in a group of 100 elderly Americans, whom the students perceived to be much the same (Linville et al., 1989). What about the elderly subjects? They perceived even more variability within their own group and less variability among 100 college students. Age stereotypes can be even more pronounced and negative than gender stereotypes (Kite et al., 1991).

Stereotypes can be positive or negative, but all are distortions of reality. And stereotypic thinking can result in discrimination, as the World of Psychology section reveals.

World of Psychology

Discrimination in the Workplace

Research conducted at Princeton University by Word and others (1974) indicates that stereotypic thinking can govern our expectancies. And often what we expect is what we get, regardless of whether our expectancies are high or low. Subjects for one study were white undergraduates who were to interview white and African American job applicants (actually confederates of the experimenters). The researchers secretly videotaped the interviews and studied the tapes to see if the student interviewers had treated the African American and white applicants differently. The researchers found substantial differences in the interviews based on the race of the applicants. The interviewers spent less time with the African American applicants, maintained a greater physical distance from them, and generally were less friendly and outgoing. During interviews with applicants, the interviewers' speech deteriorated—they made more errors in grammar and pronunciation.

In a follow-up study the same researchers trained white confederates to copy the two different interview styles used in the first study. The confederates then used the different styles to interview a group of white job applicants. These interviews were videotaped as well, and later a panel of judges evaluated the tapes. The judges agreed that applicants who were subjected to the interview style for African Americans were more nervous and performed more poorly than applicants interviewed according to the "white" style. The experimenters concluded that as a result of the interview style they experienced, the

continued

African American confederates from the first study were not given the opportunity to demonstrate their skills and qualifications to the best of their ability. Thus they were subjected to a subtle form of discrimination in which their performance was hampered by the expectancies of the original interviewers.

Discrimination is also evident after the job interviews have been completed and people take their positions in the workplace. How do women and minorities fare in the world of work in the 1990s? Even though federal legislation forbids hiring, promoting, laying off, or awarding benefits to workers on the basis of sex, race, color, national origin, or religion, studies continue to show discrimination exists (Renzetti & Curran, 1992). A considerable body of research refutes the notion that gender and race deficiencies explain why so few women and minorities are in upper management (Morrison & Von Glinow, 1990). Nevertheless, the mere perception of deficiencies, if held by the dominant corporate leaders, is sufficient to produce bias and discrimination.

Morrison and Von Glinow (1990) claim that "discrimination occurs in part because of the belief by white men that women and people of color are less suited for management than white men" (p. 202). The dominant group's belief that customers, employees, and others are more comfortable dealing with or working for white male managers may lead to discrimination. In such cases these managers may be less willing to promote women and minorities to sensitive, responsible management positions.

Tokenism is a subtle form of discrimination in which persons are hired or promoted primarily because they represent a specific group or category rather than strictly on the basis of their qualifications. Female and minority employees may be perceived by the white majority as "tokens," especially as they move up in the ranks of management. But "tokens" are interchangeable. If placed in a position solely to meet a company's affirmative action goals, one token is as good as another as long as he or she represents the *right* category. No matter how eminently qualified an employee may be, if the employee perceives that he or she is a token, the individual suffers and so does the organization.

? *What is reverse discrimination?*

reverse discrimination:
Giving special treatment or higher evaluations to individuals from groups that have been the target of discrimination.

Reverse Discrimination: Bending Over Backward to Be Fair Another subtle form of discrimination is **reverse discrimination**. It occurs when people bend over backward to treat members of specific groups that have been the target of discrimination more favorably than if they were not members of those particular groups. Those who practice reverse discrimination may be earnestly trying to show that they are not prejudiced. But reverse discrimination is not genuine, and it insults the dignity of the group to which it is directed. It assumes that the other group is indeed inferior and capable only of achieving a lower standard.

A study by Fajardo (1985) clearly illustrates reverse discrimination. A group of teachers (all of whom were white) were asked to grade essays that were identified as having been written by either African American or white students. The researchers had purposely written the essays to be poor, low average, high average, or excellent in quality. If white teachers were practicing reverse discrimination, they would rate the essays they believed were written by African American students higher than those supposedly written by white students. This is exactly what happened, especially when the quality of the essays was in the average range.

Reverse discrimination may benefit people in the short run, but it deceives them and creates false hopes, setting them up for greater disappointment and failure in the long run. Students and workers alike need and deserve objective evaluation of their work and their progress.

Combating Prejudice and Discrimination

Given that prejudice and discrimination may grow from many roots, are there effective ways to reduce them? Many experts believe there are. One way is through education. To the extent that prejudice is learned, it can also be unlearned. We saw how Kay Taus taught her students that prejudice hurts the feelings of others, and how effectively she helped a 4-year-old boy to become more sensitive to the feelings of Asian children. Sustained educational programs designed to increase teachers' and parents' awareness of the damage caused by prejudice and discrimination can be very effective (Aronson, 1990).

What are several strategies for reducing prejudice and discrimination?

Direct Contact: Bringing Diverse Groups Together Prejudice separates us from those of other racial, ethnic, religious, and social groups. Can we reduce our prejudices and stereotypic thinking by increasing our contact and interaction with others from diverse groups? Yes, according to the **contact hypothesis**.

Increased contacts with members of groups about which we hold stereotypes can teach us that *they* are not all alike. But the contact hypothesis works to reduce prejudice *only* under certain conditions. In fact, if people from diverse groups are simply thrown together, prejudice and even hostility are likely to increase rather than decrease, as we learned from Sherif's Robber's Cave experiment. We also learned from Sherif the conditions under which intergroup contact reduces prejudice, and his findings have been confirmed and extended by others (Aronson, 1990; Finchilescu, 1988).

The contact hypothesis will work to reduce prejudice most effectively under the following conditions:

- Interacting groups should be approximately equal in social and economic status and in their ability on the tasks to be performed.
- The intergroup contact must be cooperative (not competitive) in nature, and work should be confined to shared goals.
- The contact should be informal, so friendly interactions develop more easily and group members get to know each other individually.
- The contact situation should be one in which conditions favor group equality.
- The individuals involved should perceive each other as typical members of the groups to which they belong.

Us versus Them: Extending the Boundaries of Narrowly Defined Social Groups Our tendency to separate ourselves into social categories (in-groups and out-groups) creates an us-versus-them mentality. This mentality heightens prejudice, stereotypic thinking, and discrimination—our group (our college, our country, our race, our religion) is better than theirs. But the boundary lines between us and them are not eternally fixed. If such boundaries can be extended, prejudice and in-group/out-group conflict can be reduced. We saw in Sherif's study that the Rattlers and the Eagles became a larger *us* group when they were brought together to work cooperatively on shared goals.

If your college or university wins the state championship in a competitive event, then in-state rival colleges and universities will often join your *us* group as you represent the state in national competition. Many researchers have shown that working cooperatively, rather than in competition, reduces us-versus-them bias and prejudice (Gaertner et al., 1990; Wright et al., 1990).

Prejudice: Is It Increasing or Decreasing?

Few people would readily admit to being prejudiced. Gordon Allport (1954), a pioneer in research on prejudice, said, "Defeated intellectually, prejudice lingers

contact hypothesis: The notion that prejudice can be reduced through increased contact among members of different social groups.

emotionally" (p. 328). Even those who are sincerely intellectually opposed to prejudice may still harbor some prejudiced feelings (Devine, 1989b).

Is there any evidence that prejudice is decreasing in our society? According to some researchers, we are not making much progress toward reducing prejudice and discrimination (Crosby et al., 1980; Gaertner & Dovidio, 1986). But Devine and her colleagues (1991) are more optimistic. Their research suggests, "Many people appear to be in the process of prejudice reduction" (p. 829).

Gallup polls reveal that whites in the United States are becoming more racially tolerant than they were in decades past (Gallup & Hugick, 1990). When whites were asked in 1990 whether they would move if African Americans were to move next door to them, 93 percent said no compared to 65 percent 25 years earlier. Even if African Americans were to move into their neighborhood in great numbers, 68 percent of whites still said they would not move.

School integration, which in the past created a storm of controversy, seems to be less of an issue for most whites today. Only 10 percent of Gallup's white respondents said they would object to sending their children to an integrated school in which up to one-half of the children were African American. Also, the majority of African Americans polled (two-thirds) believed that their children have the same opportunity as white children to get a good education.

Marked differences in opinions about equality of job opportunities, availability of housing, and other racial attitudes still exist. When asked whether the quality of life for African Americans has gotten better, stayed the same, or gotten worse over the last 10 years, 46 percent of African Americans and 62 percent of whites believed conditions had improved. Twenty-five percent of both races believed the quality of life had stayed the same. But 23 percent of African Americans, compared to only 6 percent of whites, believed the quality of life was worse now than it was 10 years ago.

We can make things better for all by examining our own attitudes and actions, and then by using what we have learned here and elsewhere to combat prejudice and discrimination in ourselves. Prejudice has no virtues. It immediately harms those who feel its sting and ultimately harms those who practice it.

Memory Check 16.6

1. Match the example on the left with the term on the right.

　＿＿＿ 1) José was promoted because the firm needed one Hispanic manager.

　＿＿＿ 2) Darlene thinks all whites are racists.

　＿＿＿ 3) Betty's salary is $5,000 less than that of her male counterpart.

　＿＿＿ 4) Bill can't stand Jews.

　＿＿＿ 5) To make his black employees feel good, Mr. Jones, who is white, gave them higher bonuses than he gave his white employees.

    a. stereotypic thinking
    b. discrimination
    c. reverse discrimination
    d. prejudice
    e. tokenism

2. From the in-group perspective, out-group members are often liked as individuals. (true/false)

3. The social learning theory suggests that prejudice develops and is maintained through:
　a. competition and ambition.
　b. us-versus-them thinking.
　c. modeling and reinforcement.
　d. genetic inheritance.

4. Researchers have found that bringing diverse social groups together almost always decreases hostility and prejudice. (true/false)

Answers: 1. 1) e 2) a 3) b 4) d 5) c 2. false 3. c 4. false

Prosocial Behavior: Behavior That Benefits Others

Kitty Genovese was returning home alone late one night. But this was no ordinary night. Nearly 40 of her neighbors who lived in the apartment complex nearby watched as she was attacked and stabbed, but they did nothing. The attacker left. Kitty was still screaming, begging for help, and then . . . he returned. He dragged her around, stabbing her again while her neighbors watched. Some of them turned off their bedroom lights to see more clearly, pulled up chairs to the window, and watched. Someone yelled, "Leave the girl alone," and the attacker fled again. But even then, no one came to her aid. A third time the attacker returned, more stabbing and screaming, and they watched. Finally, Kitty Genovese stopped screaming. When he had finally killed her, the attacker fled for the last time. (Adapted from Rosenthal, 1964.)

This actual event might not seem so unusual today, but it was a rare occurrence back in the early 1960s. So rare, in fact, that people wondered how her neighbors could have been so callous and cold-hearted, to do nothing but watch as Kitty Genovese begged for help that never came. Social psychologists Bibb Latané and John Darley looked deeper for an explanation. Perhaps certain factors in the situation itself would help explain why so many people just stood or sat there.

The Bystander Effect: The More Bystanders, the Less Likely They Are to Help

If you were injured or ill and needed help, would you feel safer if one or two other people were near, or if a large crowd of onlookers were present? You may be surprised to learn of the **bystander effect**: As the number of bystanders at an emergency increases, the probability that the victim will receive help from them decreases, and the help, if given, is likely to be delayed.

Why should this be? Darley and Latané (1968a) set up a number of experiments to study helping behavior. In one study, subjects were placed one at a time in a small room and told that they would be participating in a discussion group by means of an intercom system. It was explained that because personal problems were being discussed, a face-to-face group discussion might be inhibiting. Some subjects were told that they would be communicating with only one other subject, some believed that two other participants would be involved, and some were told that five other people would participate. There really were no other subjects in the study, only the prerecorded voices of confederates assisting the experimenter.

Shortly after the discussion began, the voice of one confederate was heard over the intercom calling for help, indicating that he was having an epileptic seizure. Of the subjects who believed that they alone were hearing the victim, 85 percent went for help before the end of the seizure. When subjects believed that one other person heard the seizure, 62 percent sought help. But when they believed that four other people were aware of the emergency, only 31 percent tried to get help before the end of the seizure. Figure 16.6 (on page 612) shows how the number of bystanders affects both the number of people who try to help and the speed of response.

Latané and Darley suggest two possible explanations for the bystander effect—diffusion of responsibility and the influence of apparently calm bystanders.

Diffusion of Responsibility: An Explanation for the Bystander Effect

When bystanders are present in an emergency, they generally feel that the responsibility for helping is shared by the group, a phenomenon known as **diffusion of responsibility**. Consequently each person feels less compelled to act than if she

> **?** *What is the bystander effect, and what factors have been suggested to explain why it occurs?*

bystander effect: The fact that as the number of bystanders at an emergency increases, the probability that the victim will receive help decreases, and help, if given, is likely to be delayed.

diffusion of responsibility: The feeling among bystanders at an emergency that the responsibility for helping is shared by the group, so each person feels less compelled to act than if he or she alone bore the total responsibility.

Why do people often ignore someone who is unconscious on the sidewalk? Diffusion of responsibility is one possible explanation.

prosocial behavior:
Behavior that benefits others, such as helping, cooperation, and sympathy.

FIGURE 16.6

The Bystander Effect

In their intercom experiment, Darley and Latané showed that the more people a subject believed were present during an emergency, the longer it took the subject to respond and help a person in distress. (Data from Darley & Latané, 1968a.)

(Left graph: Percentage of Subjects Trying to Help vs. Number of Apparent Bystanders — 85% at 1, 62% at 2, 31% at 5.)

(Right graph: Seconds Elapsed before Subjects Tried to Help vs. Number of Apparent Bystanders — 52 at 1, 93 at 2, 166 at 5.)

or he were alone and felt the total responsibility. Kitty Genovese's neighbors were aware that other people were watching because they saw lights go off in the other apartments. They did not feel that the total responsibility for action rested only on their shoulders, or they may have thought that "somebody else must be doing something" (Darley & Latané, 1968a).

The Influence of Apparently Calm Bystanders: When Faces Deceive

Sometimes real emergencies occur in rather ambiguous situations. Bystanders may not be sure if an actual emergency exists. At the risk of appearing foolish, they often hesitate to react with alarm until they are sure that intervention is appropriate (Clark & Word, 1972). So the bystanders may stand there watching other calm-appearing bystanders and conclude that nothing is really wrong and no intervention is necessary (Darley & Latané, 1968b).

More than a few people have died while many potential helpers stood and watched passively because of the bystander effect. Picture an orthopedic surgeon's large waiting room in which eight patients are waiting to see the doctor. In one chair a middle-aged man sits slumped over, yet he does not appear to be sleeping. His position resembles that of a person who is unconscious. If you were a patient in such a setting, would you check on the man's condition or just continue sitting?

This was the actual scene one of the authors entered a few years ago as a patient. She sat down and immediately noticed the man slumped in his chair. She scanned the faces of the other waiting patients but saw no sign of alarm or even concern. Was there really no emergency, or was this a case of the bystander effect? Knowing that the reaction of onlookers is a poor indicator of the seriousness of a situation, she quickly summoned the doctor, who found that the man had suffered a heart attack. Fortunately, the doctor's office was attached to a large hospital complex, and almost immediately a hospital team appeared and rushed the victim to the emergency room.

People Who Help in Emergencies

There are many kinds of **prosocial behavior**—behavior that benefits others, such as helping, cooperation, and sympathy. Prosocial impulses arise early in life.

Researchers agree that children respond sympathetically to companions in distress at least by their second birthday (Hay, 1994; Kochanska, 1993). The term **altruism** is usually reserved for behavior aimed at helping others that requires some self-sacrifice and is not performed for personal gain. What motivates us to help or not to help in an emergency? Batson and colleagues (1989) believe that we help out of empathy—the ability to feel what another feels.

Cultures vary in their norms for helping others—that is, their social responsibility norms. According to Miller and others (1990), people in the United States tend to feel an obligation to help family, friends, and even strangers in life-threatening circumstances, but only family in moderately serious situations. In contrast, in India the social responsibility norm extends to strangers whose needs are only moderately serious or even minor.

In spite of the potentially high costs of helping, we have heard accounts of people who have risked their lives to help others. During World War II, thousands of Christians risked their lives to protect Jews from extermination in Nazi Germany. Are there common factors that might explain such uncommon risks in the service of others? A study of 406 of these rescuers revealed that they did not consider themselves heroes, and that different motives led to their altruistic behavior. Some rescuers were motivated by strong convictions about how human beings should be treated; others, by empathy for the particular person or persons they rescued (Fogelman & Wiener, 1985; Oliner & Oliner, 1988). Still others were acting based on norms of their family or social group that emphasized helping others.

In what conditions or circumstances might a person be more likely to receive help? People are more likely to receive help if they are physically attractive (Benson et al., 1976), if they are perceived by potential helpers as similar to them (Dovidio, 1984), and if they are not considered responsible for their plight (Schmidt & Weiner, 1988). Potential helpers are more likely to help if they have specialized training in first aid or police work, if they are not in a hurry, if they have been exposed to a helpful model (Bryan & Test, 1967), if they are in a positive mood (Carlson et al., 1988), and if the weather is good (Cunningham, 1979).

altruism: Behavior aimed at helping another, requiring some self-sacrifice and not designed for personal gain.

Memory Check 16.7

1. The bystander effect is influenced by all of the following *except*:
   a. the number of bystanders.
   b. the personalities of bystanders.
   c. whether the bystanders appear calm.
   d. whether the situation is ambiguous.

2. Altruism is one form of prosocial behavior. (true/false)

3. As the number of bystanders to an emergency increases, the probability that the victim will receive help decreases. (true/false)

4. In an ambiguous situation, a good way to determine if an emergency exists is to look at the reactions of other bystanders. (true/false)

Answers: 1. b 2. true 3. true 4. false

Aggression: Intentionally Harming Others

We humans have a long history of **aggression**—intentionally inflicting physical or psychological harm on others. Consider the tens of millions of people killed by other humans in wars and even in times of peace. In 1992, in the United States alone, there were almost 24,000 homicides, 109,000 reported rapes, 672,000 rob-

aggression: The intentional infliction of physical or psychological harm on another.

beries, and 1.13 million assaults (U.S. Bureau of the Census, 1994). And each year 3 to 4 million women are victimized by violence (Biden, 1993).

What causes aggression? One of the earliest explanations of aggression was the instinct theory—that human beings, along with other animal species, are genetically programmed for such behavior. Sigmund Freud believed that humans have an aggressive instinct that can be turned inward as self-destruction or outward as aggression or violence toward others. Nobel Prize–winning researcher in animal behavior Konrad Lorenz (1966) claimed that aggression springs from an inborn fighting instinct common in many animal species. Most social psychologists, however, consider human behavior too complex to attribute to instincts.

Biological Factors in Aggression: Genes, Hormones, and Brain Damage

? What biological factors are thought to be related to aggression?

While rejecting the instinct theory of aggression, many psychologists do concede that biological factors are involved. Twin and adoption studies have revealed a genetic link for criminal behavior (DiLalla & Gottesman, 1991). In a study of 573 pairs of adult twins, Rushton and others (1986) reported that aggressive behavior in identical twins showed a correlation of .40 compared to a correlation of only .20 in fraternal twins. Cloninger and others (1982) found that adoptees with a criminal biological parent were 4 times as likely as members of the general population to commit crimes, while adoptees with a criminal adoptive parent were at twice the risk of committing a crime. But adoptees with both a criminal biological and a criminal adoptive parent were 14 times as likely to commit crimes.

Men are more physically aggressive than women, and the male hormone testosterone is thought to be involved. A correlation between high testosterone level and aggressive behavior has been found in both adolescent (Olweus, 1987) and adult males (Archer, 1991; Dabbs & Morris, 1990). Violent behavior has also been linked to low levels of the neurotransmitter serotonin (Brown & Linnoila, 1990; Burrowes et al., 1988).

Brain damage, brain tumors, and temporal lobe epilepsy have all been related to aggressive and violent behavior (Mednick et al., 1988). A study of 15 death row inmates revealed that all had histories of severe head injuries (Lewis et al., 1986). Alcohol and aggression are also frequent partners. A meta-analysis of 30 experimental studies indicates that alcohol is related to aggression (Bushman & Cooper, 1990). People who are intoxicated commit the majority of murders, spouse beatings, stabbings, and instances of physical child abuse.

Aggression in Response to Frustration: Sometimes, But Not Always

? What is the frustration–aggression hypothesis?

frustration: Interference with the attainment of a goal, or the blocking of an impulse.

frustration–aggression hypothesis: The hypothesis that frustration produces aggression.

scapegoating: Displacing aggression onto minority groups or other innocent targets not responsible for the frustrating situation.

Does **frustration**—the blocking of an impulse, or interference with the attainment of a goal—lead to aggression? The **frustration–aggression hypothesis** suggests that frustration produces aggression (Dollard et al., 1939; Miller, 1941). If a traffic jam delayed you and you were frustrated, what would you do—lean on your horn, shout obscenities out of your window, or just sit patiently and wait? Frustration doesn't always cause aggression, but it is especially likely to if it is intense and seems to be unjustified (Doob & Sears, 1939; Pastore, 1950). Berkowitz (1988) points out that even if frustration is justified and not aimed specifically at us, it can cause aggression if it arouses negative emotions.

Aggression in response to frustration is not always aimed at the people causing it. If the preferred target is too threatening or not available, the aggression may be displaced. For example, children who are angry with their parents may take out their frustrations on a younger sibling. Sometimes minorities and others who have not been responsible for a frustrating situation become targets of displaced aggression, a practice known as **scapegoating** (Koltz, 1983).

Aggression in Response to Aversive Events: Pain, Heat, Noise, and More

> **?** *What kinds of aversive events and unpleasant emotions have been related to aggression?*

Aggression in response to frustration is only one special case of a broader phenomenon—aggression resulting from unpleasant or aversive events in general, says a leading researcher on aggression, Leonard Berkowitz (1988, 1989). People often become aggressive when they are in pain (Berkowitz, 1983) or are exposed to loud noise, foul odors (Rotton et al., 1979), and even irritating cigarette smoke. Extreme heat has been linked to aggression in several studies (Anderson, 1989; Anderson & DeNeve, 1992).

These and other studies lend support to the cognitive–neoassociationistic model proposed by Berkowitz (1990). He suggests that anger and aggression result from aversive events and from unpleasant emotional states like sadness, grief, and depression. "The core notion in this model is that negative affect is the basic source of anger and angry aggression" (Berkowitz, 1990, p. 494). Negative emotions (affect) tend to activate angry feelings, thoughts, and memories, as well as tendencies toward aggression or escape. The cognitive component of Berkowitz's model occurs when the angered person makes an appraisal of the aversive situation and makes attributions about the motives of the people involved. As a result of the cognitive appraisal, the initial anger reaction can be intensified or reduced or suppressed. This process will make it either more or less likely that a person will act on the aggressive tendency.

Several studies suggest that aggressive adolescents tend to attribute hostile intentions to others in certain social encounters, leading them to believe retaliation with aggression is appropriate (Dodge, Price, et al., 1990; Fondacaro & Heller, 1990).

The Social Learning Theory of Aggression: Learning to Be Aggressive

> **?** *According to social learning theory, what causes aggressive behavior?*

The social learning theory of aggression holds that people learn to behave aggressively by observing aggressive models and by having their aggressive responses reinforced (Bandura, 1973). It is well known that aggression is higher in groups and subcultures that condone violent behavior and accord high status to aggressive members. A leading advocate of the social learning theory of aggression, Albert Bandura (1976), claims that aggressive models in the subculture, the family, and the media all play a part in increasing the level of aggression in our society.

Children learn to behave aggressively by observing aggressive models, often their parents.

Abused children certainly experience aggression and see it modeled day after day. "One of the most commonly held beliefs in both the scholarly and popular literature is that adults who were abused as children are more likely to abuse their own children" (Widom, 1989b, p. 6). There is some truth to this belief. On the basis of original research and an analysis of 60 other studies, Oliver (1993) concludes that one-third of people who are abused go on to become abusers, one-third do not, and the final third may become abusers if the social stress in their lives is sufficient.

Most abusive parents, however, were not abused as children (Widom, 1989b). Although abused and neglected children are at higher risk of becoming delinquent, criminal, or violent, the majority do not (Widom, 1989a). Several researchers suggest that the higher risk for aggression may not be due solely to an abusive family environment but may be partly influenced by the genes (DiLalla & Gottesman, 1991). Some abused children become withdrawn and isolated rather than aggressive (Dodge, Bates, et al., 1990).

The Media and Aggression: Is There a Connection? Bandura (1976) claims that "the modern child has witnessed innumerable stabbings, beatings, stompings, stranglings, muggings, and less blatant but equally destructive forms of cruelty before he has reached kindergarten age" (p. 125). But is there a causal link between viewing aggressive acts and committing them? Some studies say no (Freedman,

1984; Milavsky et al., 1982), but the overwhelming evidence reveals a relationship between TV violence and viewer aggression (Pearl et al., 1982; Rubinstein, 1983). Some research indicates that adults and children as young as nursery school age show higher levels of aggression after they view media violence (Geen, 1978; Liebert et al., 1989). A study of 840 10-year-old children in Finland revealed that the more TV violence children watched, the more likely they were to have aggressive fantasies and engage in aggression (Viemerö & Paajanen, 1992).

In a longitudinal study of 600 7- to 9-year-old boys launched in 1960, subjects were reinterviewed at age 19 and again at age 30 (Eron, 1987). Subjects who were most aggressive at age 8 were still aggressive at ages 19 and 30, many of them showing antisocial behavior ranging from traffic violations to criminal convictions and aggressiveness toward their spouses and children (Huesmann et al., 1984). Did media influence play a part? "One of the best predictors of how aggressive a young man would be at age 19 was the violence of the TV programs he preferred when he was 8 years old" (Eron, 1987, p. 438). And the more frequently the subjects had watched TV violence at that age, "the more serious were the crimes for which they were convicted by age 30" (p. 440).

A review of 28 studies of the effects of media violence on children and adolescents revealed that "media violence enhances children's and adolescents' aggression in interactions with strangers, classmates, and friends" (Wood et al., 1991, p. 380). Media violence may lead to aggression by activating information related to aggression in memory (Bushman & Geen, 1990). It may stimulate physiological arousal, lower inhibitions, cause unpleasant feelings, and decrease sensitivity to violence and make it more acceptable to people (Wood et al., 1991).

Black and Bevan (1992) administered an aggression inventory to moviegoers attending violent and nonviolent movies. Higher aggression scores were found for moviegoers attending violent movies (both before and after the movie) than for moviegoers attending nonviolent movies. Are violent episodes of TV shows in which the "good guys" finally get the "bad guys" less harmful? Not according to Berkowitz (1964), who claims that justified aggression is the type most likely to encourage the viewer to express aggression.

Can we reduce aggression in our society? Not by letting off steam vicariously through watching aggression or violence in sports or the media, and not by engaging in aggressive but nonviolent behavior (Berkowitz, 1964; Josephson, 1987). The best hope is to find ways to reduce aggression in families, eliminate reinforcement for aggression, and remove excessive violence from the media (Eron, 1980).

Memory Check 16.8

1. The social learning theory of aggression emphasizes all of the following *except* that:
   a. aggressive responses are learned from the family, the subculture, and the media.
   b. aggressive acts are learned through modeling.
   c. most aggression results from frustration.
   d. when aggressive responses are reinforced, they are more likely to continue.

2. Pain, extreme heat, loud noise, and foul odors have all been associated with an increase in aggressive responses. (true/false)

3. Social psychologists generally believe that aggression stems from an aggressive instinct. (true/false)

4. According to the frustration–aggression hypothesis, frustration _____ leads to aggression.
   a. always   b. often   c. rarely   d. never

5. The weight of research suggests that media violence probably is related to increased aggression. (true/false)

6. Research tends to support the notion that a person can drain off aggressive energy by watching others behave aggressively in sports or on television. (true/false)

Answers: 1. c 2. true 3. false 4. b 5. true 6. false

Nonverbal Behavior— The Silent Language

He that has eyes to see and ears to hear may convince himself that no mortal can keep a secret. If his lips are silent, he chatters with his fingertips; betrayal oozes out of him at every pore.

—Sigmund Freud

There is some truth to the old saying "It's not what you say, it's how you say it." When we speak, what emotional impact does the verbal message alone, the words themselves, have on our listeners? Very little, according to Albert Mehrabian (1968). He claims that the emotional impact of a communication is influenced only slightly (about 7 percent) by the verbal message itself. More than 5 times as powerful is what he calls the vocal message—tone of voice, pronunciation, stress on words, vocal inflections, and the length and frequency of pauses—which provides 38 percent of the impact. If you were 30 minutes late for class and your professor said in a sarcastic tone, "We're so happy that you could join us today," would you believe the vocal message (the sarcastic tone) or the verbal message?

The most powerful effect of all comes, not from the verbal or the vocal message, but from *nonverbal behavior*—facial expressions, gestures, posture, and so on—which provides an amazing 55 percent of the emotional impact of a message. If the nonverbal behavior and the verbal message do not match, which one do we believe? Almost every time, the nonverbal message comes across as the real one. Figure 16.7 shows the relative effects of the verbal, vocal, and nonverbal components of a message.

Communicating Feelings through Nonverbal Cues

Nonverbal behavior reveals a great deal about how we feel about others

and how others feel about us. It can communicate anger, liking, love, happiness, sadness, anxiety, impatience, deception, and difference in status among people. But it is important to avoid attributing meaning to an isolated clue apart from its context.

We are best at reading nonverbal behavior that signals anger and a possible threat to our well-being. Cold stares will make almost anyone tense and uncomfortable.

Whether we are aware or not, our nonverbal behavior often reveals our attitudes to others. Encountering people or objects we like, we tend to move closer to them, lean toward them, and look directly at them. Our pupils dilate as if to take in more of them. The opposite occurs when we confront something or someone we dislike. Our pupils constrict, we tend to stand away or look away, and we often assume a closed position with arms and/or legs crossed.

Two people who are romantically involved cannot easily conceal their feelings. Their nonverbal behavior usually sends a clear message. They often gaze into each other's eyes and generally position themselves closer to each other than do friends or acquaintances. They exchange touches, lean toward one another, and often mirror each other's body language. When two people meet at a party and find each other attractive, they usually communicate their feelings to each other, although often unconsciously. Dilated pupils, extended eye contact, bodies leaning toward each other, and preening behavior— stroking the hair, readjusting the clothes—are all signs of interest.

We communicate far more than our likes and dislikes through our nonverbal behavior. We communicate our self-esteem or lack thereof. We reveal whether we are relaxed or ill at ease. And our gestures even signal our social status relative to the person with whom we are interacting.

Touch can be a sign of warmth and intimacy, a sign of sexual inter-

FIGURE 16.7

Getting the Message Across

Researcher Albert Mehrabian claims that most (55 percent) of the emotional impact of a communication comes from nonverbal behavior (facial expressions, gestures, posture). Another large proportion (38 percent) of the emotional impact is provided by the vocal message (tone of voice, vocal inflection, pauses). The verbal message (actual words) carries only 7 percent of the emotional impact. (Data from Mehrabian, 1968.)

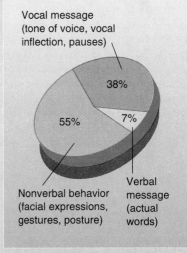

est, or a means of conveying higher status (Major et al., 1990). Higher-status persons are more likely to touch lower-status persons than vice versa (Henley, 1973). In nonintimate settings, men are more likely to touch women than the reverse (Major et al., 1990).

Although people often think they are expert in detecting deception, this is usually not the case. According to authority Paul Ekman, even professionals such as judges and law enforcement officials are no more expert

continued

than anyone else at detecting lies (Goleman, 1991). In his book *Telling Lies*, Ekman (1985) states that failure to look you in the eye is not necessarily a sign of lying but can indicate that a person is uncomfortable under scrutiny. More telling cues are overly long smiles, frowns, or looks of disbelief. Genuine expressions don't last longer than 4 or 5 seconds. Furthermore, genuine smiles are usually symmetrical in contrast to the lopsided, phony smile. True feelings often slip through in the form of fleeting microexpressions that are quickly replaced by the expression meant to deceive (Ekman et al., 1988). In deception there are discrepancies among the verbal, vocal, and nonverbal messages. Finally, when people are lying, they often have more pauses in their speech and begin sentences, stop, then begin again (Stiff et al., 1989).

Ambady and Rosenthal (1993) conducted a study that shows just how powerful nonverbal behavior can be in contributing to our impressions of people. Subjects were asked to rate college teachers based on silent video clips totaling less than 30 seconds in length. Reacting to the nonverbal behavior alone, these subjects' ratings accurately predicted the ratings of students who interacted with the teachers for an entire semester.

Gestures: Different Meanings in Different Countries

When traveling in another country, most tourists find a phrase book indispensable, and some even make an effort to learn another language. But even if tourists learn to speak a foreign language like natives, few will recognize that the gestures they use in communicating may convey something entirely different in another country.

Ekman and colleagues (1984) relate this dramatic illustration of how our gestures can get us into trouble in different cultures. Several years ago, an American tourist learned that the "A-okay" gesture (the thumb and forefinger in a circle) is not a positive signal in all cultures. After a wonderful dinner in Naples, Italy, the American, wishing to thank his waiter for fine food and expert service, flashed a big smile and the A-okay sign. The stunned waiter turned pale and rushed to the restaurant manager, and the two of them discussed excitedly whether they should call the police and have the American arrested for obscene and vulgar behavior in a public place.

Why did the tourist's complimentary gesture cause such an uproar? The A-okay gesture is not a friendly one in all cultures. In Turkey and Greece it signals a lewd, insulting sex-

ual invitation, and in France and Belgium it conveys the message "You are worth zero." In parts of southern Italy (including Naples), the gesture is even more offensive and insulting. The smiling American tourist had unwittingly called his waiter a name that is a crude and vulgar reference to the anal opening.

In ancient Rome, when the gladiators battled each other to the death, the emperor gave a signal to the gladiator who held his sword at the opponent's throat. The emperor's "thumbs-up" sign meant "Let him live." The "thumbs-down" sign meant "Finish the job." Today in the United States and in most Western European countries, the thumbs-up sign means "all right." We see truck drivers, airline pilots, and other people use it as a positive gesture. But in northern Greece and parts of southern Italy, the thumbs-up sign is an obscene gesture that expresses the same sentiment to them as if someone were to raise a middle finger in front of your face.

Ironically, if we are trying to communicate with people who speak a different language, we are even more likely to use an abundance of gestures. Gestures are powerful communication tools, but travelers should be careful when using them in cultures other than their own.

Thinking Critically

Evaluation

Many Americans were surprised when the majority of people in the Soviet Union rejoiced at the downfall of the Communist system. Using what you have learned about attribution bias and conformity, explain why many Americans had mistakenly believed that the Soviet masses preferred Communism.

Point/Counterpoint

Prepare a convincing argument supporting each of these positions:

a. Aggression results largely from biological factors (nature).
b. Aggression is primarily learned (nurture).

Psychology in Your Life

Review the factors influencing impression formation and attraction discussed in this chapter. Prepare a dual list of behaviors indicating what you should and should not do if you wish to make a better impression on other people and to increase their liking for you.

Chapter Summary and Review

Introduction to Social Psychology

Key Terms

social psychology (p. 584)
confederate (p. 585)
naive subject (p. 585)

Social Perception

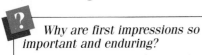

Why are first impressions so important and enduring?

First impressions are important because we attend more carefully to the first information we receive about a person; and because, once formed, an impression acts as a framework through which later information is interpreted.

What is the difference between a situational attribution and a dispositional attribution for a specific behavior?

An attribution is our inference about the cause of our own or another's behavior. In making situational attributions, we attribute the cause of behavior to some factor in the environment. With dispositional attributions, the inferred cause is internal—some personal trait, motive, or attitude.

How do the kinds of attributions we tend to make about ourselves differ from those we make about other people?

We tend to overemphasize dispositional factors when making attributions about the behavior of other people, and to overemphasize situational factors in explaining our own behavior.

Key Terms

primacy effect (p. 585)
attribution (p. 586)
situational attribution (p. 586)

dispositional attribution (p. 586)
fundamental attribution error (p. 586)
self-serving bias (p. 587)

Attraction

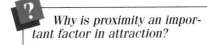

Why is proximity an important factor in attraction?

Proximity influences attraction because it is easier to develop relationships with people close at hand. Also, proximity increases the likelihood of repeated contacts, and mere exposure tends to increase attraction (the mere-exposure effect).

How important is physical attractiveness in attraction?

Physical attractiveness is a major factor in attraction for people of all ages. People attribute positive qualities to those who are physically attractive—a phenomenon called the halo effect.

Are people, as a rule, more attracted to those who are opposite or to those who are similar to them?

People are generally attracted to those who have similar attitudes and interests, and who are similar in economic status, race, and age.

Key Terms

proximity (p. 587)
mere-exposure effect (p. 588)
halo effect (p. 589)
matching hypothesis (p. 590)

Conformity, Obedience, and Compliance

What did Asch find in his famous experiment on conformity?

In Asch's classic study on conformity, 5 percent of the subjects went along

with the incorrect, unanimous majority all the time; 70 percent went along some of the time; and 25 percent remained completely independent.

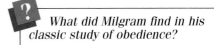

What did Milgram find in his classic study of obedience?

In Milgram's classic study of obedience, 65 percent of the subjects obeyed the experimenter's orders to the end of the experiment and administered what they believed to be increasingly painful shocks to the learner up to the maximum of 450 volts.

What are three techniques used to gain compliance?

Three techniques used to gain compliance are the foot-in-the-door technique, the door-in-the-face technique, and the low-ball technique.

Key Terms

conformity (p. 592)
norms (p. 592)
compliance (p. 595)
foot-in-the-door technique (p. 595)
door-in-the-face technique (p. 596)
low-ball technique (p. 596)

Group Influence

Under what conditions does social facilitation have either a positive or a negative effect on performance?

When others are present, either as an audience or as coactors, one's performance on easy tasks is usually improved, but performance on difficult tasks is usually impaired.

What is social loafing, and what factors lessen or eliminate it?

Social loafing is the tendency of people to put forth less effort when they are working with others on a common task than when working alone. It is less likely to occur when individual output can be monitored or when people are highly involved with the outcome.

> ❓ *How are the initial attitudes of group members likely to affect group decision making?*

Following group discussions, group decisions usually shift to a more extreme position in whatever direction the members were leaning toward initially—a phenomenon known as group polarization.

Key Terms

social facilitation (p. 597)
audience effects (p. 597)
coaction effects (p. 597)
social loafing (p. 597)
group polarization (p. 598)
groupthink (p. 599)
roles (p. 599)

Attitudes and Attitude Change

> ❓ *What are the three components of an attitude?*

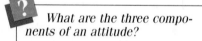

An attitude usually has a cognitive, an emotional, and a behavioral component.

> ❓ *What is cognitive dissonance, and how can it be resolved?*

Cognitive dissonance is an unpleasant state that can occur when we become aware of inconsistencies between our attitudes or between our attitudes and our behavior. We can resolve cognitive dissonance by rationalizing away the inconsistency or by changing the attitude or the behavior.

> ❓ *What are the four elements in persuasion?*

The four elements in persuasion are the source, the audience, the message, and the medium.

> ❓ *What qualities make a source most persuasive?*

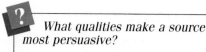

Persuasive attempts are most successful when the source is credible (expert and trustworthy), attractive, and likable.

Key Terms

attitude (p. 600)
cognitive dissonance (p. 601)
persuasion (p. 602)

Prejudice and Discrimination

> ❓ *What is the difference between prejudice and discrimination?*

Prejudice consists of attitudes (usually negative) toward others based on their gender, religion, race, or membership in a particular group. Discrimination consists of actions against others based on the same factors.

> ❓ *What is meant by the terms in-group and out-group?*

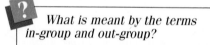

An in-group is a social group with a strong sense of togetherness and from which others are excluded; an out-group consists of individuals or groups specifically identified by the in-group as not belonging.

> ❓ *How does prejudice develop, according to the social learning theory?*

According to this theory, prejudice is learned in the same way as other attitudes—through modeling and reinforcement.

> ❓ *What are stereotypes?*

Stereotypes are widely shared beliefs about the characteristics of members of various social groups (racial, ethnic, religious), including the assumption that *they* are usually all alike.

> ❓ *What is reverse discrimination?*

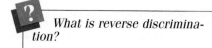

Reverse discrimination involves giving special treatment or higher evaluations to members of a group that has been the target of prejudice and discrimination.

> ❓ *What are several strategies for reducing prejudice and discrimination?*

Several strategies for reducing prejudice include (1) arranging appropriate educational experiences for children, (2) providing situations where diverse social groups can interact under certain favorable conditions, and (3) extending the boundaries of narrowly defined social groups.

Key Terms

prejudice (p. 604)
discrimination (p. 604)
realistic conflict theory (p. 604)
in-group (p. 605)
out-group (p. 605)
social cognition (p. 606)
stereotypes (p. 606)
reverse discrimination (p. 608)
contact hypothesis (p. 609)

Prosocial Behavior: Behavior That Benefits Others

> ❓ *What is the bystander effect, and what factors have been suggested to explain why it occurs?*

The bystander effect means that as the number of bystanders at an emergency increases, the probability that the victim will receive help decreases, and help, if given, is likely to be delayed. The bystander effect may be due in part to diffusion of responsibility or, in ambiguous situations, to the assumption that no emergency exists.

Key Terms

bystander effect (p. 611)
diffusion of responsibility (p. 611)
prosocial behavior (p. 612)
altruism (p. 613)

Aggression: Intentionally Harming Others

? *What biological factors are thought to be related to aggression?*

Biological factors thought to be related to aggression are a genetic link in criminal behavior, high testosterone levels, low levels of serotonin, and brain damage.

? *What is the frustration–aggression hypothesis?*

The frustration–aggression hypothesis holds that frustration produces aggression and that this aggression may be directed at the frustrater or displaced onto another target, as in scapegoating.

? *What kinds of aversive events and unpleasant emotions have been related to aggression?*

Aggression has been associated with aversive conditions such as pain, heat, loud noise, and foul odors, and with unpleasant emotional states such as sadness, grief, and depression.

? *According to social learning theory, what causes aggressive behavior?*

According to social learning theory, people acquire aggressive responses by observing aggressive models in the family, the subculture, and the media, and by having aggressive responses reinforced.

Key Terms

aggression (p. 613)
frustration (p. 614)
frustration–aggression hypothesis (p. 614)
scapegoating (p. 614)

17

APPLIED PSYCHOLOGY

CHAPTER OUTLINE

Industrial/Organizational Psychology: Psychology Goes to Work

Personnel Selection, Training, and Appraisal

Work Motivation

Stress in the Workplace

Human Factors Psychology: Getting Along with Machines and Appliances

Safe Design: Preventing Injuries in the Workplace

Good Design: Features That Won't Defeat Us

Environmental Psychology: The Psychology of Our Surroundings

Noise: More Than Just Annoying

Personal Space: How Close Is Too Close?

World of Psychology: Variations in Personal Space

Territorial Behavior: Protecting Areas We Define as Ours

Density and Crowding: There Is a Difference

The Effects of Crowding: Too Many People, Too Little Space

Architectural Design: More Than Just a Matter of Aesthetics

Forensic Psychology: Psychology Goes to Court

The Role of Psychologists in the Legal System

Mock-Jury Research: Studying the Deliberation Process

Sports Psychology: More Than Playing Games

Relaxation, Concentration, and Visualization

Expert Performance

Consumer Psychology: Psychology Goes to Market

Assessing Consumer Preferences

Testing and Observing

Applications: Sexual Harassment

Thinking Critically

Chapter Summary and Review

In the late 1950s the city of St. Louis launched a bold new venture through which extremely low-income residents could at last move into new high-rise apartments. With federal assistance the city built 33 highrise apartment buildings, known as the Pruitt-Igoe Housing Project. But the bold new venture proved to be an urban disaster, and the urban dream became a nightmare. Vandalism, crime, prostitution, and drug dealing flourished in what should have been a model community. What went wrong?

Experts studied the Pruitt-Igoe problem, and one of them, Oscar Newman (1972), concluded that poor architectural design had played an important role in facilitating the deviant behavior (crime, vandalism, and so on) that soon doomed the project. Each of the 33 buildings had 11 floors with a single elevator shaft in the center and extremely long corridors that isolated the residents. Pruitt-Igoe never became a com-

munity where the people mingled freely and made friendships, because the residents of the 2,800 apartments were housed row on row as in strip motel rooms and stacked 11 floors deep.

Most of the buildings had to be demolished in the 1970s. But many remained standing for years, empty, abandoned, in mute testimony to failed high hopes, poor architectural design, and hasty planning that ignored important principles of psychology. Perhaps the Pruitt-Igoe story would have had a happier ending if applied psychologists—architectural psychologists, in particular—had been included in the planning stages of the project.

applied psychology: The branch of psychology that applies the methods and knowledge of the discipline to investigate and solve practical, everyday human problems.

There is great diversity in the ways psychology is applied to serve the vast array of human wants and needs. **Applied psychology** is the branch of psychology that applies the methods and knowledge of the discipline to solve practical, everyday human problems. We will see how psychologists apply their knowledge in the workplace, in the design of our machines and tools, in the architectural design of the buildings we occupy, and in the way we use (and misuse) our environment. We will also consider the part psychologists play in our legal system, in competitive and recreational sports, and in the way we consume products and respond to advertising.

We first look at applied psychology in the workplace, where we examine the broad range of activities industrial/organizational psychologists perform.

? *What are some of the activities of industrial/ organizational psychologists?*

Industrial/Organizational Psychology: Psychology Goes to Work

In 1995 the United States was ranked as the most competitive economy in the world and as the number one exporter. Modern American manufacturers have developed production methods among the most sophisticated ever known and are turning out goods that are envied all over the world (Zuckerman, 1995).

But there is a challenging question. Can the United States maintain its competitive advantage over other industrialized nations, yet maintain work settings that are satisfying and safe for workers, both physically and psychologically? Increasingly business, industry, and government are turning to industrial/organizational psychologists for expert assistance. **Industrial/organizational psychology** (I/O psychology) is a specialty that focuses on the relationship between the workplace or organization and the worker. The field encompasses such areas as organizational design, decision making, work motivation, job satisfaction, communication, leadership, and personnel selection, training, and evaluation.

industrial/organizational psychology: The specialty that focuses on the relationship between the workplace or work organization and the worker.

Personnel Selection, Training, and Appraisal

Organizations need employees with the necessary skills and abilities to function well in specific positions. I/O psychologists play an important role in helping organizations select and train employees and appraise their performance.

Personnel Selection Of critical interest to business and industry is personnel selection—the procedures used in the hiring and promotion of employees. These procedures usually involve interviews and often include testing as well. Aptitude tests are used to assess particular skills that are relevant to the job, such as mechanical, clerical, verbal, or numerical skills. Interest tests such as the *Strong-Campbell Interest Inventory* and the *Kuder Occupational Interest Survey* yield a profile of the job applicant's interests. This profile is then compared to profiles of people who are successful in a variety of occupations. The idea behind the tests is that people with certain interests tend to be happy and successful in certain occupations.

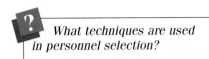

What techniques are used in personnel selection?

To select more competent executives, some organizations test applicants using sophisticated assessment centers that simulate the types of situations and problems confronted in upper-management and executive positions (Coutts, 1991). Job applicants are observed and evaluated as they perform in these simulated work situations. Some organizations also provide job previews—realistic views of the nature of the job presented to applicants through brochures, films, and so on.

Organizations need to hire people who not only have the required skills and ability but who will also enjoy their work and be productive. The fit between the person and the organization is significantly related to performance, job attitude, and turnover (O'Reilly, 1991).

Personnel selection is critically important to employers, who must choose the applicant who best fits the job description.

Personnel Training Even though personnel selection procedures are designed to identify people who already have the skills, knowledge, and ability to fill specific jobs, additional training is often needed. I/O psychologists help to plan a variety of training programs. For some jobs, day-to-day, on-the-job training is sufficient. For others, well-planned training programs are required to develop the necessary expertise. For university graduates in some highly technical fields, continuous training is necessary, because much of their knowledge is obsolete in 4 to 5 years (Coutts, 1991).

Added to the rapid obsolescence of technical knowledge is the obsolescence of ways of doing business in today's global economy. With the passage of the North American Free Trade Agreement (NAFTA) and the General Agreement on Tariffs and Trade (GATT), U.S. business and industry, whether ready or not, must function in a world-spanning global economy. So the role of I/O psychologists in U.S. business and industry has expanded enormously, from local and national to global in scope.

Appraising Employee Performance: A Sensitive Issue A great deal is at stake in employee evaluation—whether a person will get a raise, how much that raise will be, and whether the person will be promoted or even fired. Performance appraisal is an evaluation process, occurring annually or semiannually, in which employees are rated and given feedback on their performance. If performance appraisal is done properly, employees are likely to feel they have been treated fairly and objectively, and will be aware of the areas in which they need to improve. I/O psychologists help organizations develop more objective criteria for evaluating specific jobs—criteria that will be acceptable to both managers and employees. And they help supervisors develop skill in delivering criticism constructively so as to help employees improve their performance without destroying their motivation.

What is performance appraisal, and why is it important?

work motivation: The conditions and processes responsible for the arousal, direction, magnitude, and maintenance of effort one puts forth in one's job.

Work Motivation

Work motivation can be thought of as "the conditions and processes that account for the arousal, direction, magnitude, and maintenance of effort in a person's job" (Katzell & Thompson, 1990, p. 144). Two of the most effective ways to increase employee motivation and improve performance are reinforcement and goal setting.

What is work motivation, and what are two effective techniques for increasing it?

job enrichment: Techniques used to make jobs more interesting, satisfying, and attractive.

To use reinforcement, I/O psychologists help design behavior modification techniques to increase performance and productivity. Reinforcers or incentives include bonuses, recognition awards, praise, time off, posting of individual performance, better offices, more impressive titles, and/or promotions. Companies may discourage ineffective behaviors through such measures as docking employees for missing work.

A second technique for increasing performance is goal setting. Establishing specific, difficult goals leads to higher levels of performance than simply telling people to do their best in the absence of assigned goals (Locke & Latham, 1990). An organization can enhance employees' commitment to goals (1) by having them participate in the goal setting; (2) by making goals specific, attractive, difficult, and attainable; (3) by providing feedback on performance; and (4) by rewarding the employees for attaining the goals (Katzell & Thompson, 1990).

? *What factors are closely related to job satisfaction?*

Job Satisfaction and Performance A survey of 1,500 U. S. workers revealed that the aspects of a job they considered most rewarding were interesting work, good pay, sufficient resources and authority, and friendly and cooperative co-workers (Survey Research Center, University of Michigan, 1971). As important as it is, increased job satisfaction does not typically result in better work performance (Coutts, 1991). But job satisfaction is apparently related to lower absenteeism (F. J. Smith, 1977) and lower turnover. Table 17.1 summarizes the factors influencing job satisfaction.

I/O psychologists help many companies redesign jobs to make them more interesting, satisfying, and attractive—an approach termed **job enrichment**. For example, assembly-line workers might become involved in the production of a whole item instead of repeating the same single task, hour after hour, day after day. In addition, workers might be given a greater voice in how their work will be accomplished. Research suggests that job enrichment improves worker attitudes but not necessarily job performance (Locke et al., 1981; Stone, 1986).

To increase work motivation, job satisfaction, and performance, employers must do more than accentuate the positives in the workplace with rewards and incentives. They must also eliminate the negatives, especially high levels of stress.

TABLE 17.1　Factors Influencing Job Satisfaction

Interesting work

Good pay

Sufficient resources and authority

Friendly, cooperative co-workers

Sufficient recognition

Opportunities for advancement

Good relationships with supervisors

Control over manner in which work is completed

Input in decisions affecting work

Job security

Stress in the Workplace

Hans Selye, the pioneer in stress research, called stress the "spice of life," because within limits it can provide the challenges that make life interesting and enable us to grow. But we all know that too many people find their jobs a source of extraordinary stress. Assembly-line workers and piece-goods workers must endure boring and repetitive jobs; doctors, nurses, and emergency ambulance personnel must deal with life and death on a daily basis. Even workers who hold more ordinary jobs can be subject to extraordinary stress—the salesperson struggling to reach a quota, the manager fretting over the bottom line for the upcoming quarterly financial report. And employees in any field working under managers who hassle or threaten them may suffer from excessive work-related stress.

? *For people to function effectively and find satisfaction on the job, what nine variables should fall within their comfort zone?*

Variables in Work Stress Everyone in the workplace is subject to certain amounts of job-related stress, but the amount and sources of stress differ, depending upon the type of job and the kind of organization. Albrecht (1979) suggests that if people are to function effectively and find satisfaction on the job, the following nine variables must fall within their comfort zone (see Figure 17.1):

■ *Workload.* An overload of work—too much to do and too little time to do it in—causes people to feel anxious, frustrated, and unrewarded. Interestingly, just the opposite—work underload—produces the same feelings.

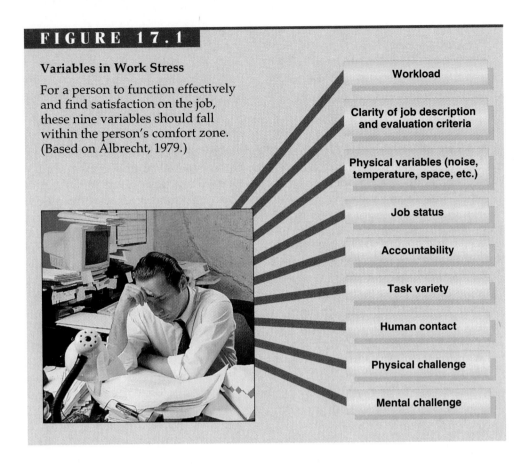

FIGURE 17.1

Variables in Work Stress

For a person to function effectively and find satisfaction on the job, these nine variables should fall within the person's comfort zone. (Based on Albrecht, 1979.)

- Workload
- Clarity of job description and evaluation criteria
- Physical variables (noise, temperature, space, etc.)
- Job status
- Accountability
- Task variety
- Human contact
- Physical challenge
- Mental challenge

- *Clarity of job description and evaluation criteria.* The lack of a clearly defined role or confusion about performance criteria often causes anxiety and stress in workers. At the other extreme, a too rigidly defined role may leave too little room for creativity or individual initiative and may result in worker stress.

- *Physical variables.* Temperature, noise, humidity, pollution, and amount of work space should fall within a person's comfort zone. Being confined to a desk or having to work in fatiguing positions can also create stress.

- *Job status.* Extremes in job status can produce stress. People with very low status—garbage collectors, janitors—may feel psychological discomfort. At the other extreme, those with celebrity status—movie stars, recording artists, sports figures—often cannot handle the stress that fame brings.

- *Accountability.* Accountability has to do with the relationship between the perceived importance of the job and the amount of control a person has over its outcome. Accountability underload occurs when workers perceive their jobs as meaningless. Extreme overload occurs when people have responsibility for the physical or psychological well-being of others but only a limited degree of control, such as air-traffic controllers and emergency-room nurses and doctors.

- *Task variety.* Jobs can be deadly boring, repetitive, and monotonous, as in much factory work. To function well, people need a comfortable amount of variety and stimulation.

- *Human contact.* Some workers have virtually no human contact on the job (forest-fire lookouts); others have almost continuous contact with others (welfare and employment-office workers). People vary greatly in how much interaction they enjoy or even tolerate. Too much or too little human contact can prove very stressful.

Helping workers cope with job stress is a major goal of I/O psychologists.

decision latitude: The degree to which employees have the opportunity to exercise initiative and use their skills to control their working conditions.

- *Physical challenge.* Jobs range from physically demanding (construction work, professional sports) to those requiring no physical activity. Some jobs (fire fighting, police work) involve physical risk as well.

- *Mental challenge.* Jobs that tax people beyond their mental capability or training cause feelings of inadequacy and frustration. Yet jobs that require too little mental challenge are also frustrating.

Decision Latitude: A Critical Factor in Job Stress
Whether occupational stress is the spice of life or the kiss of death depends largely on the amount of decision latitude a job offers (Levi, 1990). **Decision latitude** refers to the degree to which employees may exercise initiative and use their skills to control their working conditions. Jobs high in workload with little latitude or control in the pace and manner in which the work will be completed are highly stressful (Karasek & Theorell, 1990). According to Sauter and others (1990), machine-paced assembly workers report "the highest levels of anxiety, depression, and irritation, as well as more frequent somatic [bodily] complaints" (p. 1150).

In contrast are jobs like those of executives and professionals where high demand is coupled with a high degree of control over how the work will be done. In this case high demand is likely to be viewed as challenging and rewarding. Jobs with low stress have a high degree of control paired with a low psychological workload; examples include scientist and forester (see Figure 17.2).

How much stress have you experienced in jobs you have had? Rate your stress in the *Try It!*

What are the sources of stress in a job you have now or have had in the past? Rate the job by indicating whether there is or was too little, too much, or about the right amount of each of the job dimensions listed. (Adapted from Albrecht, 1979.)

Job Dimension	Too Little	About Right	Too Much
Workload	_____	_____	_____
Decision latitude	_____	_____	_____
Clarity of job description	_____	_____	_____
Task variety	_____	_____	_____
Mental challenge	_____	_____	_____
Physical demand	_____	_____	_____
Human contact	_____	_____	_____
Job status	_____	_____	_____
Job security	_____	_____	_____

What are some of the psychological and health consequences of job stress?

Psychological and Health Consequences of Job Stress
Job stress can have a variety of consequences. Perhaps the most frequent is reduced effectiveness on the job. But stress can also lead to absenteeism, tardiness, accidents, substance abuse, and lower morale (J. C. Smith, 1993). Workers who are experiencing

FIGURE 17.2

The Relationship of Demand and Control to Job Stress

Jobs that are low in decision latitude—that is, those that are high in demand and low in control, such as assembly-line work—are highly stressful.

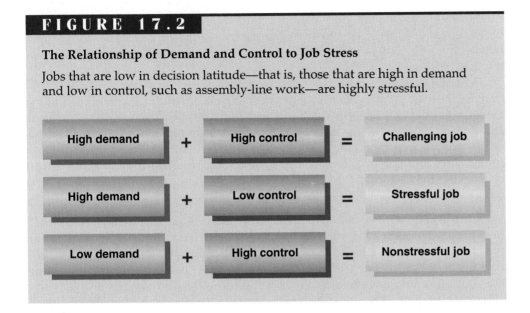

stress often become alienated from their co-workers and may also suffer from headaches, exhaustion, back problems, insomnia, and indigestion. Stress can even lead to more serious illnesses, such as depression, high blood pressure, or cardiovascular disease.

Burnout When job stress is intense and unrelieved, many people suffer from **burnout**, a condition in which they become pessimistic, dissatisfied, inefficient on the job, and debilitated psychologically. Energy reserves are depleted, resistance to illness is lowered, and interest in work wanes. In the final stages of burnout, people may be unable to function. "Job burnout is not a symptom of work stress, it is the end of unmanaged work stress" (Rice, 1987, p. 223). A strong relationship exists between number of hours worked per week and the likelihood of burnout. Workers putting in 80 or more hours per week generally run a much higher risk of depleting their energy stores.

What is burnout?

Combating Work Stress: Some Help from Business and Industry
Employers should not conclude that employee stress is not their problem, for they pay for it in absenteeism, high turnover, and low productivity. With the help of I/O psychologists, many corporations are beginning to address the problem.

What strategies are some industries adopting to combat work stress?

Worksite Stress Management Interventions Some companies are setting up worksite stress management interventions, which may include exercise, meditation, or relaxation to help employees cope with stress (Ivancevich et al., 1990). Or interventions may be cognitive approaches aimed at changing irrational responses to stressors or at improving time management and goal setting. Other interventions involve changes in the sources of job stress. For example, companies may redesign jobs, change organizational structure, improve working conditions, provide better job training, improve personnel selection and placement, or seek ways to improve co-worker relations.

burnout: The result of intense, unrelieved, and unmanaged job stress; a condition in which an individual becomes pessimistic, dissatisfied, inefficient on the job, and debilitated psychologically.

Policies Responsive to Families Because of the ever-increasing presence of dual-worker families and single parents in the workforce, more corporations are implementing policies that are responsive to families. These include mater-

job sharing: Employment in which two employees share one full-time job.

flextime: A flexible work schedule in which a worker may begin the day several hours earlier or later than the usual work day or working longer days and "bank" the hours so as to be able to take time off later.

nity and parental leaves, provision for child care, and flexibility in work schedules (Zedeck & Mosier, 1990). Some companies are giving assistance that ranges from providing payment for child care as part of a benefits program to on-site day-care centers.

Alternative work schedules are attractive options for some workers. These may include job sharing, permanent part-time employment (sometimes having career potential and benefits), or flextime. In **job sharing**, two people share one full-time job (Kahne, 1985; Olmsted, 1977). **Flextime** refers to flexible work schedules—workers may begin the day several hours earlier or later than usual or work longer days and "bank" the hours so as to be able to take time off later. Instead of working five 8-hour days, many nurses are now opting for three or four long days each week.

Employee Fitness and Wellness Programs Employee fitness and wellness programs in the workplace are on the rise. Some of these health promotion programs are informational, designed to raise employee awareness about the dangers of unhealthy habits. Other programs feature health screening at the worksite and more intensive health education efforts. But the most comprehensive employee fitness and wellness programs increase the availability of healthy foods in company cafeterias and provide worksite fitness centers where employees can use the latest exercise equipment (Conrad, 1987).

Unfortunately, most employees do not participate in fitness and wellness programs. About 15 to 30 percent of white-collar workers and only 3 to 5 percent of blue-collar workers participate (Gebhardt & Crump, 1990). But among white-collar workers, the fitness and wellness programs have proved beneficial to both employees and companies, in the form of lower health care costs, fewer injuries, lower employee turnover, and reduced absenteeism. Apparently, company-sponsored programs that directly benefit employee health and fitness are compatible with a healthier company bottom line.

Memory Check 17.1

1. Industrial/organizational psychologists are interested in all of the following activities *except*;
   a. personnel selection.
   b. work motivation.
   c. job training and evaluation.
   d. marketing industrial products.

2. If good personnel selection procedures have been used, there is usually no need for personnel training. (true/false)

3. According to the text, two of the most effective ways I/O psychologists improve employee motivation and performance are:
   a. reinforcement and goal setting.
   b. counseling and guidance.
   c. evaluation and feedback.
   d. training and evaluation.

4. Which of the following is most related to job satisfaction?
   a. good relations with supervisors.
   b. opportunities for advancement.
   c. interesting work.
   d. job security.

5. Job enrichment is primarily concerned with improved worker productivity. (true/false)

6. In general, an assembly-line worker suffers more stress than a business executive because:
   a. the workload is higher.
   b. the workload is lower.
   c. the decision lattitude is higher.
   d. the decision lattitude is lower.

Answers: 1. d 2. false 3. a 4. c 5. false 6. d

Human Factors Psychology: Getting Along with Machines and Appliances

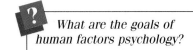

What are the goals of human factors psychology?

In a modern technological society, we use a variety of machines and appliances every day. Many of them are user-friendly, so natural and simple to operate that we hardly give them a second thought. Others may baffle, challenge, or anger us because their design is illogical, unhandy, cumbersome, and complex. Do you push on doors that are meant to be pulled? Have you ever been in an unfamiliar automobile and had difficulty finding the handle to open the door? Have you wasted money in copying machines because you weren't sure which buttons to push? If you answered yes to any of these questions, you are probably not to blame. You may have been the victim of poorly designed machines.

The design of the tools and machines we use has psychological consequences, and an important applied field of psychology is human factors psychology. **Human factors psychology,** also known as ergonomics, is a specialty concerned with designing and modifying machines and work environments to make them more compatible with human sensory, perceptual, cognitive, and motor capabilities. The ultimate goal is to make machines safer and easier to use. To accomplish it, human factors psychologists must possess a highly sophisticated knowledge of human capabilities and limitations (Sanders & McCormick, 1993).

human factors psychology: A specialty concerned with designing and modifying machines and work environments to make them safer, easier to use, and more compatible with human sensory, perceptual, cognitive, and motor capabilities; also called ergonomics.

Safe Design: Preventing Injuries in the Workplace

Human factors psychologists design work equipment so that muscles, tendons, ligaments, and joints are not subject to undue stress, which could eventually lead to permanent damage. They may be asked to study the equipment and movement involved in a job if factory workers, office workers, or others are suffering some work-related musculoskeletal problem (Heron, 1991).

Work-related musculoskeletal disorders, known as cumulative trauma disorders (CTDs), can affect muscles, joints, and tendons. An increasingly common CTD is carpal tunnel syndrome, characterized by the swelling of tendons in the wrist. The condition results in searing pain and tingling and numbness in the hands. Data entry personnel are especially vulnerable to carpal tunnel syndrome, with reported cases nearing 200,000 each year in the United States.

The Institute of Ergonomics and Rehabilitation at the Barnes-Washington University Medical Center in St. Louis was established to help prevent job-related injuries. The institute helps companies make adjustments in the movement patterns of workers and in the ways workers interact with materials, equipment, and machines (King, 1993). Dr. Judith Heusner, an occupational physician at the institute, maintains that for employers, learning how to redesign or rearrange a work station is far less expensive than paying extended worker's compensation claims or settling lawsuits. An analogy she uses is that it is far better to build a fence at the top of a cliff than to have an ambulance waiting to pick up victims at the bottom (King, 1993).

Good Design: Features That Won't Defeat Us

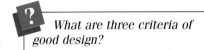

What are three criteria of good design?

Donald A. Norman (1988), a leading expert in human factors psychology, admits to fighting a losing battle with the objects in his home, car, and office. For those of us fighting the same battle, there is some good news. According to Norman

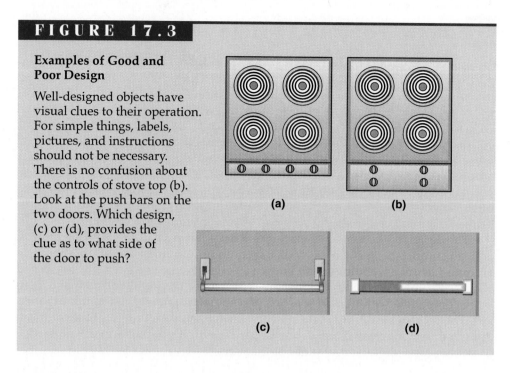

FIGURE 17.3

Examples of Good and Poor Design

Well-designed objects have visual clues to their operation. For simple things, labels, pictures, and instructions should not be necessary. There is no confusion about the controls of stove top (b). Look at the push bars on the two doors. Which design, (c) or (d), provides the clue as to what side of the door to push?

(1995), the failure is in the design of the objects rather than in us. In fact, many of the accidents involving vehicles (airplanes, trains, automobiles) and machinery (even in nuclear power plants) that are blamed on *human error* may be partly due to poor design.

Norman outlines three criteria of good design. First, in well-designed devices, a button or control operates one function only. That explains why single shower knobs that control two functions have flash-frozen or nearly scalded many of us before we could adjust the water temperature. Second, well-designed machines should provide feedback so that we know the immediate result of any action that is taken, like the click that we hear when we hit a key on most computer keyboards. Our VCRs give us trouble because we press buttons but usually don't know what has happened as a result of our actions. Finally, Norman asserts that well-designed objects have visual clues to their operation, a property he calls "visibility." Labels, pictures, or instructions should not be required for simple things. Turning on the desired burner on the stove should not pose a challenge for us. The controls for the burners should be arranged in a pattern that corresponds to the placement of the burners—that is, for most stoves, in a square rather than in a straight line, as shown in Figure 17.3.

Many years ago, safety engineers designed antilock brakes to prevent automobile accidents caused by skidding on wet or icy pavements. The new brakes worked well and should have reduced skid-related accidents, but they did not. Why? The brakes were designed to be operated by applying steady pressure to the pedal. This is exactly the opposite of the action drivers were using to prevent skidding—delicately pumping and releasing the brake pedal. Although mechanically sound, the brakes failed to prevent skidding because of human factors—drivers continued to pump and release their new brakes. Was the answer to retrain more than 10 million drivers to use their antilock brakes properly? No. Human factors engineers had a better solution—to redesign the brakes so that pumping them *is* the correct response (Miller, 1994). Human factors psychologists do not try to make people fit machines; they design machines to fit people.

Memory Check 17.2

1. Psychologists who are *primarily* involved in designing or modifying machines and work environments to make them safer and easier to use are _____ psychologists.

   a. industrial/organizational   c. human factors

   b. consumer   d. forensic

2. Another term for human factors psychology is (ergonomics, I/O psychology).

3. Human factors psychologists consider the _____ effects of poorly designed equipment on the worker.

   a. psychological   c. psychological and physical

   b. physiological   d. aesthetic

4. Human error leading to industrial accidents is often the result of poorly designed equipment. (true/false)

5. In a well-designed machine, a single button or control does the work of many. (true/false)

Answers: 1. c   2. ergonomics   3. c   4. true   5. false

Environmental Psychology: The Psychology of Our Surroundings

How annoying a noise is depends on how loud it is, whether it is predictable or unpredictable, and whether it can be controlled.

Environmental psychology is a specialty concerned with the effect that environments (both natural and constructed) and individuals have on each other. Environmental psychologists are interested in the psychological effects of adverse environmental conditions such as pollution, the weather, overpopulation, crowding, noise, temperature, odors, and other conditions in the world around us. They are also concerned with human behaviors that contribute to environmental problems and with finding ways to encourage people to change these behaviors. How do noise, crowding, temperature, our use of space, the design of our buildings, and other environmental factors affect us psychologically?

Noise: More Than Just Annoying

Why do many people find a whisper in a movie theater more annoying than loud music at a concert? The answer lies in the definition of noise. Noise is not simply loud sound; it is unwanted sound. How annoying a noise is depends on its volume, whether it is predictable or unpredictable, and whether we can control it. The most disturbing noise is loud, unpredictable, and uncontrollable. A noise is even more annoying if we perceive that it is unnecessary, hazardous, or caused by others who are unconcerned about how it affects us.

Some researchers claim that noise pollution is related to high blood pressure and that in children it is linked to distractibility and diminished persistence at tasks (Cohen et al., 1980). Children continuously exposed to high levels of noise in their schools or apartment buildings were found to have impaired auditory discrimination (Cohen et al., 1973) and lower reading achievement (Bronzaft, 1981; Cohen et al., 1986).

? *What are some of the negative psychological effects associated with noise pollution?*

environmental psychology: The specialty concerned with how environments (both natural and constructed) affect individuals.

personal space: An area surrounding us, much like an invisible bubble, that we consider ours and that we use to regulate how closely others can interact with us.

 What is personal space?

Other studies have shown that introverts (reflective, retiring, nonsocial types) and extroverts (outgoing, adaptable, sociable people) respond differently to noise. Introverts generally prefer a quiet environment (Standing et al., 1990). They show an increase in arousal under noisy conditions, whereas arousal in extroverts decreases or is unchanged. Furthermore, reading comprehension was found to decrease in introverts who were subjected to noise but not in extraverts (Daoussis & McKelvie, 1986; Standing et al., 1990). People have various reactions to noise, but *all* people are annoyed when others invade their personal space.

Personal Space: How Close Is Too Close?

Personal space is an area surrounding us, much like an invisible bubble, which we consider part of us and use to regulate how closely others can interact with us. Our personal space serves to protect our privacy and to regulate our level of intimacy with others. It also serves a communication function, in that it determines whether intimate sensory cues like smell and touch will be exchanged or communication will be restricted to nonintimate verbal or visual channels. The size of our personal space varies according to the person or persons with whom we are interacting and the nature of the interaction. It also varies by gender and culture, as the World of Psychology section explains.

Variations in Personal Space

Edward T. Hall (1966), the leading researcher on personal space, maintained that a need for personal space seems to be inborn in most animal species. For humans in general, Hall named four different types of social contact and the typical personal space distances that match them:

- *Intimate distance* (from touching to 18 inches). Reserved for intimate contacts, lovers, family members, and close friends.
- *Personal distance* (18 inches to 4 feet). Used in everyday interactions with people we know—friends or colleagues.
- *Social distance* (4 to 12 feet). For transacting business and communicating with strangers.
- *Public distance* (more than 12 feet). The typical distance in formal settings—between a professor and a class, a speaker and an audience.

Most people have a distinctly unpleasant feeling when their personal space is invaded. If standing, they will often step back to reestablish their space; but when this is not possible, they change their body orientation and/or reduce their amount of eye contact.

Can you imagine how uncomfortable you would feel if you were in the front of a crowded elevator and the next person to enter did not turn around to face the front, but instead stood face to face with you? The fact that people face forward in a crowded elevator makes the space invasion tolerable.

We usually position ourselves closer to people we perceive as similar to us in age, race, sexual orientation, and status than to those we perceive as different on these dimensions. There are gender differences in personal space preferences; pairs of females generally interact at closer distances than pairs of males (Aiello, 1987).

Personal space preferences vary greatly from culture to culture. Arabs, Hispanics, Greeks, and the French are typically comfortable with small interaction distances, while Americans, the English, the Swedish, and other Northern Europeans prefer a larger personal space (Aiello, 1987; Hall, 1966).

Personal space preferences can cause misunderstanding when people from different cultures interact. Americans traveling in Arab countries come face to face with cultural differences in personal space preferences. During conversations, Arabs stand much closer to each other than Americans do. An American speaking with an Arab tries to re-establish a comfortable personal space by backing away. This offends Arabs, who perceive Americans to be unfriendly, distant, and aloof. Consequently, Americans unwittingly insult their Arab hosts, and the Arab hosts unwittingly invade the space of their American visitors.

Territorial Behavior: Protecting Areas We Define as Ours

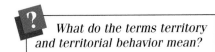

What do the terms territory and territorial behavior mean?

People not only protect their personal space, but also protect what they consider to be their **territory**—an area they define as permanently or temporarily their own. A primary territory is one that is considered to belong to an individual or group, such as a home or office. A secondary territory is one that an individual occupies regularly but shares with others, such as an assigned seat in a classroom. A public territory is one that a person occupies temporarily, for example, a seat in a library or movie theater or a space at the beach.

What would you do if someone moved your coat and books from a table in the library and sat in the area you had staked out for yourself? Just as we react negatively to invasions of our personal space, we don't like invasions into our territory. Most animal species mark off their territory with scent markings, and people, too, engage in **territorial behavior**. Humans mark off their territory to establish control and defend it against unwelcome intrusions. We may mark our homes with fences and hedges, our office doors with nameplates, our spaces at the beach with beach towels or blankets.

territory: An area defined by a person as temporarily or permanently his or her own.

territorial behavior: Marking off a territory in an effort to establish control over it and defend it against unwelcome intrusions.

density: A measure referring to the number of people occupying a unit of space.

Density and Crowding: There Is a Difference

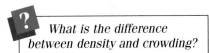

What is the difference between density and crowding?

Most psychologists draw a distinction between **density**—the number of people occupying a defined physical space—and crowding. **Crowding** is subjective and refers to the perception that there are too many people in a defined space. A hermit would probably feel crowded if one other person was anywhere in sight.

Psychologists further differentiate between social density and spatial density (Baum & Valins, 1977), and a sense of crowding is affected by both. Social density increases as the number of people in a fixed space increases. If five relatives came to live in your house for several weeks, social density would increase and you might feel crowded. Conversely, social density decreases as the number of people in a fixed space decreases. With spatial density, the number of people remains constant, but the space they occupy increases or decreases. If you have ever taken a family vacation in a car, you have felt the effects of increasing spatial density. Figure 17.4 (on page 636) illustrates the difference between social density and spatial density.

crowding: A subjective perception that there are too many people in a defined space.

The Effects of Crowding: Too Many People, Too Little Space

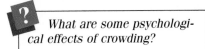

What are some psychological effects of crowding?

Sometimes it is enjoyable and exciting to be densely packed with other people at a sports event, a concert, or a party. But what if the crowd followed you home

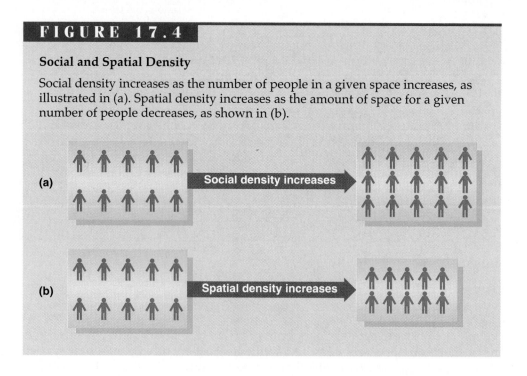

FIGURE 17.4

Social and Spatial Density

Social density increases as the number of people in a given space increases, as illustrated in (a). Spatial density increases as the amount of space for a given number of people decreases, as shown in (b).

Whether or not you feel crowded depends on the setting—waiting in a crowded airport terminal can be stressful, but being a part of the crowd at a sporting event may not be.

architectural psychology: A specialty concerned with the effects that buildings and the surrounding space have on mood and behavior.

and you could not escape to your own private world even for a moment? In many parts of the world, people have little or no privacy. They must live under continuously crowded conditions, where day and night they are subjected to the sights, the sounds, and the smells of too many other people.

What are the psychological effects of crowding? Comparing records from four state prisons, Paulus and others (1988) found that death rates, suicides, disciplinary actions, and psychological problems resulting in psychiatric commitment all increased as the prison population increased. The more inmates per cell, the greater the number of problems. But we must keep in mind that a prison is an atypical environment with an atypical population.

Crowding often leads to higher physiological arousal, and males typically experience its effects more negatively than females do. The effects of crowding also vary across cultures and situations. Researchers have studied its effects on such diverse populations as male heads of households in India and middle-class male and female college students in the United States (Evans & Lepore, 1993). In both of these studies psychological distress was linked to household crowding. Compared to their uncrowded counterparts, people who lived in crowded residences for at least 8 months tended to withdraw socially from others in their crowded living conditions. And this social withdrawal generalized to others in the outside world. Subjects from crowded households were less likely to give support to someone in need and less likely to accept support from others than were subjects from uncrowded households (Evans & Lepore, 1993). Why? The researchers concluded that people from crowded environments may simply tune out social stimuli in order to cope with the social overload they experience living under crowded conditions.

Architectural Design: More Than Just a Matter of Aesthetics

Architectural psychology is a specialty concerned with the effects that buildings and the surrounding space have on mood and behavior (Gifford, 1991). As we

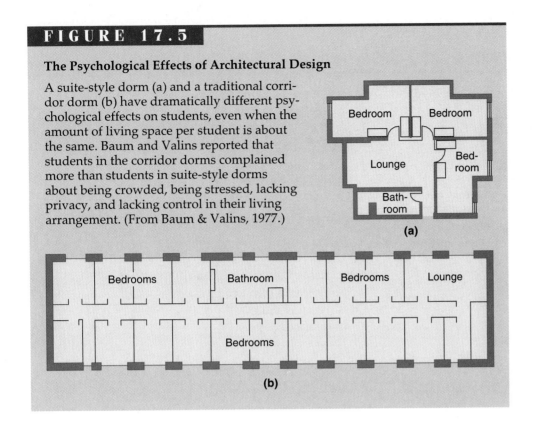

FIGURE 17.5

The Psychological Effects of Architectural Design

A suite-style dorm (a) and a traditional corridor dorm (b) have dramatically different psychological effects on students, even when the amount of living space per student is about the same. Baum and Valins reported that students in the corridor dorms complained more than students in suite-style dorms about being crowded, being stressed, lacking privacy, and lacking control in their living arrangement. (From Baum & Valins, 1977.)

saw at the beginning of this chapter, the Pruitt-Igoe housing project in St. Louis was doomed to failure even before the buildings were built. The serious architectural design flaws actually facilitated the behaviors (isolation, vandalism, crime, and so on) that the buildings were constructed to prevent. Architectural design has significant psychological and social effects in any environment, even in dormitories on the campuses of colleges and universities.

Researchers Baum and Valins (1977, 1979) studied the psychological effects on students of two very different campus dormitory arrangements at the State University of New York at Stony Brook. One type was the traditional corridor dorm, and the other consisted of clusters of suites (see Figure 17.5). The number of students per unit of space was about the same in both types of dormitories, but the psychological effects were dramatically different. Students in the corridor dormitories complained of more stress, the feeling of being crowded, lack of privacy, lack of control in their living situation, and more unsolicited social contacts than students in the suite dormitories. Also, students in the corridor dorms visited the campus health clinic with various complaints more often than did their fellow students in the suite dormitories.

But colleges and universities cannot afford to demolish all of their traditional corridor dorms and build new dorms with clusters of suites. Is there any way to solve the problem? Yes—and a very simple and inexpensive one, according to Baum and Davis (1980), who did a follow-up study of a simple architectural modification of the corridor dorm. Students in the modified dorm reported feeling less crowded and experiencing less stress than students in the traditional corridor dorm. Also, they were happier and enjoyed more friendly social interactions than their fellow students in the traditional dorm.

Environmental psychologists have shown that our surroundings—the environments where we live, work, and play—have profound psychological effects.

Memory Check 17.3

1. Noise can be harmful even if it is not loud enough to damage our hearing. (true/false)

2. Which of the following statements is *not* true of our personal space?
   a. It functions to protect our privacy and regulate intimacy.
   b. How much personal space we require is affected by our culture, race, gender, and personality.
   c. The size of our personal space is fixed.
   d. Invasions of our personal space are usually perceived as unpleasant.

3. Marking off an area in order to establish control over it and defend it against unwelcome intrusions is called:
   a. personal space behavior.
   b. territorial behavior.
   c. area protection behavior.
   d. space facilitation behavior.

4. Which of the following is an objective concept that is measurable?
   a. density
   b. crowding
   c. territorial behavior
   d. noise pollution

5. The text cited all of the following as effects of crowding on humans *except*:
   a. less willingness to give social support.
   b. increased physiological arousal.
   c. social withdrawal.
   d. depression.

Answers: 1. true 2. c 3. b 4. a 5. d

Forensic Psychology: Psychology Goes to Court

Forensic psychology is a law-related specialty in which psychologists serve in the legal justice system as consultants to lawyers and police departments and as expert witnesses. The legal system in the United States operates according to centuries of legal thought and tradition. The assumptions are that the accused must be presumed innocent until proven guilty, that citizens are guaranteed a fair and impartial trial, and that justice is blind (totally unprejudiced). But psychologists and other scientists continue to present growing evidence that justice is not as blind as the ideal tradition would have us believe.

Much of the research described in Chapter 16 on forming initial impressions, conformity, attitudes, and group decision making can be applied in the legal system. Members of the jury, and judges too, can be swayed by a defendant's appearance, dress, attractiveness, gender, race, social class, and many other personal and social attributes. You learned in Chapter 16 that physical attractiveness is an advantage that extends to virtually every aspect of human existence. And the courtroom is no exception.

Physically attractive defendants are more likely to be found not guilty than unattractive defendants (Michelini & Snodgrass, 1980). And attractive witnesses are likely to be more believable to jurors than unattractive ones. In one study, subjects who viewed photographs of adults identified as sex offenders rated the least attractive persons as more dangerous and more likely to commit future crimes than the offenders who were attractive or average looking (Esses & Webster, 1988). The attractiveness stereotype extends across cultures, as evidenced by one study in which both Chinese and American subjects judged attractive defendants more favorably than unattractive ones (Wuensch et al., 1993). But being physically

forensic psychology: A law-related specialty in which psychologists are involved in the legal justice system either as expert witnesses or as consultants to police, attorneys, defendants, judges, juries, or the penal system.

attractive can work against a defendant if attractiveness is considered instrumental in the commission of a crime, as in the case of a handsome male defendant accused of wooing and swindling an aging widow out of her life savings.

Interest in forensic psychology reached an all-time high in 1995 with the O. J. Simpson trial. Many elements of psychological intrigue in the Simpson case captured the interest of most Americans, some of whom slipped into the role of amateur psychologist. How do real forensic psychologists apply the research, principles, and practices of psychology in the legal system?

The Role of Psychologists in the Legal System

Psychologists are playing an increasingly influential role in the legal system as consultants to law-enforcement officials and attorneys and as researchers. Forensic psychologists are often heavily involved in the investigative process long before a suspect is arrested. They assist in developing psychological profiles of suspects in murder cases and other crimes. And in many cases the psychological profiles prove to be highly accurate, especially in cases involving serial killers such as Ted Bundy.

Psychologists may also be called on as expert witnesses to evaluate the mental state of defendants and comment on their potential for future violent behavior (Faust & Ziskin, 1988). Or they may testify on such matters as the reliability of eyewitness testimony (Kassin et al., 1989) or of lie detector tests. Psychologists sometimes assist attorneys in the jury selection process as well.

Often there is great drama in the courtroom, where justice for the accuser and freedom or even life itself for the accused hang in the balance. A jury must be selected to hear the case and reach a decision, and lawyers for the prosecution and defense are allowed to disqualify a certain number of prospective jurors before the case is tried. Today lawyers routinely turn to psychologists for help in determining which jurors might be helpful or harmful to their case. Psychologists also analyze the nonverbal behavior of prospective jurors in an effort to determine their attitudes toward the defendant and the case.

Psychologists may collect demographic data on prospective jurors—about the neighborhoods where they live and their social class, age, race, political party, occupation, amount of education, religious affiliation, and so on. Sometimes probabilities of whether a juror will be more likely to decide for acquittal or conviction can be computed from such demographic data and from attitude surveys on how a prospective juror's neighbors feel about a case to be tried (Hofer, 1991). However, a great deal of evidence suggests that such information about jurors (their age, gender, political ideology, education, occupation, and so on) does not reliably predict how they will vote (MacCoun, 1989).

Psychologists also conduct research that is applied to the criminal justice system. One example of such research is investigation of eyewitness testimony, which we studied in Chapter 6. Another important line of research relates to how juries make decisions.

Mock-Jury Research: Studying the Deliberation Process

How can the deliberation process be studied when juries weigh the evidence behind closed doors? Psychologists conduct studies using a **mock jury** in which subjects are selected randomly to act as jurors and reach a verdict in a simulated legal trial (MacCoun, 1989).

One of the first findings in mock-jury research, still commonly found today, is that many jurors tend to form early opinions about the defendant's guilt or innocence before all of the evidence is presented. This happens in spite of judges'

What role do forensic psychologists play in the legal system?

mock jury: A group of research subjects who are selected randomly to act as jurors and reach a verdict in a simulated legal trial.

sports psychology: A specialty concerned with helping competitive athletes develop the mental and emotional skills necessary to facilitate their maximal competitive performance potential, and with helping people in recreational athletic programs attain greater physical, emotional, and mental benefits.

instructions to withhold judgment until all the facts are in (MacCoun, 1989). Jurors, just like the rest of us, find it hard to lay aside their attitudes, biases, and stereotypic thinking when weighing evidence. If an attorney mentions inadmissible evidence such as a defendant's prior behavior or conviction and the jurors are instructed by the judge to disregard the comment, can they? Not easily, and often it affects their decisions (Sales & Hafemeister, 1985). During the O. J. Simpson trial, one of the jurors reportedly asked Judge Lance Ito to repeat the admonition he made to the jury on the previous day because "I forgot what you told us to ignore."

Ultimately, the jury must reach a verdict and it must be unanimous. What you learned about group polarization and conformity in Chapter 16 sheds some light on the jury deliberation process. What happens if some jurors, a minority, disagree with the majority on the first ballot? Kalven and Zeisel (1966) conducted posttrial interviews with 146 juries that were initially split. And only 7 of the 146 juries moved to the initial minority position. Noting how accurately the majority position on the first ballot predicts the final verdict, the researchers compared the jury deliberation process to the process of developing an exposed film. "It brings out the picture, but the outcome is predetermined" (p. 489).

Not only are psychologists involved in issues such as innocence or guilt, life or death in the legal system, they are on the scene even in the games we play.

? *What do sports psychologists do?*

Sports Psychology: More Than Playing Games

The pitcher is on the mound; the batter is at the plate. The fans are cheering, excitement builds, and you are ready to settle back and enjoy America's favorite pastime. "Play ball!" yells the umpire, and the game begins. But few people are aware of the multitude of activities going on behind the scenes. Obviously the players, coaches, managers, team doctors, trainers, and other assistants have been hard at work. But in many cases, so have psychologists.

Sports psychology is a specialty concerned with improving sports performance and making participation in sports more beneficial. Sports psychologists work with a wide range of clients, from world-class teams and players to average citizens who are interested in physical activity for health reasons or simply for recreation and enjoyment (Durkin, 1991). Some sports psychologists concentrate on community-based athletic and recreation programs. They may teach both adults and children how to gain maximum physical, mental, and emotional benefits from various recreation experiences. They also help people select (and stick to) weight-control and exercise programs. The work of sports psychologists may involve identifying the conditions that facilitate learning motor skills and teaching people how to develop those skills.

Sports psychologists also help coaches develop effective teaching and human relations techniques. Through task analysis, psychologists analyze the many complex skills athletes must perform, and break those skills down into their smallest parts. Then they may assist in developing better teaching and training techniques, which coaches may use in teaching the skills of the game.

Player attitude is another area of critical importance in the stressful and competitive world of sports. Sports psychologists are worth many times their salary when they can help team members develop and maintain winning attitudes

Sports psychologists try to help athletes improve their performance.

and a strong team spirit. According to Singer (1993), sports psychology is "emerging at a rapid rate all over the globe as a legitimate sport science and a profession capable of offering valuable services" (p. 10).

Relaxation, Concentration, and Visualization

Sports psychologists work with world-class and professional athletes to help them develop the mental and emotional skills necessary to reach their maximal competitive performance potential. Because professional athletes are already physically prepared, often the difference between an average and a top performance is due primarily to mental and emotional factors.

Sports psychologists train athletes in relaxation, concentration, and visualization. Learning to concentrate and relax is not simple. According to Durkin (1991), "Learning to concentrate is one of the most difficult mental training tasks that the athlete faces. . . . It may often take an athlete up to a year just to learn to relax and to concentrate" (p. 160). Once athletes master relaxation and concentration, they are taught visualization techniques: They vividly imagine themselves flawlessly performing the actual movements they will later execute in real life. They may also visualize themselves blocking out the crowd noises and other distractions. Through visualization, athletes may improve their concentration, their timing and many other aspects of actual performance.

Try a concentration and visualization exercise yourself in the *Try It!*

Imagine an orange. Do you see it inside your head? Or do you picture it on a screen in front of you? Time yourself and try to hold an image of the orange for one minute. After a few seconds, other thoughts and images will creep in, and your image of the orange will come and go. This is why developing the skill of concentration is so important. People trained in concentration can hold an image as long as they wish.

Now relax and focus your concentration by trying to visualize the orange this way: Imagine the orange again, but do something with it. Slowly remove the peel. Then break it into sections. View the sections clearly and see the juice squirting out as you separate them. Imagine how the orange smells. Now place a section in your mouth. Feel it on your tongue. Try to taste the orange section. If you notice saliva flowing, you are on the right track in learning how to visualize. (After Durkin, 1991.)

You may wonder what visualization has to do with athletics. Sports psychologists have found that athletes skilled in visualization can actually improve their performance by practicing it mentally. In addition to their long hours of physical training and active practice, world-class athletes also use relaxation and visualization techniques in preparation for their performances (Ungerleider, 1992).

Relaxation, concentration, and visualization are important elements involved in helping players achieve **peak performance**. Peak performance involves a psychological state akin to an altered state of consciousness accompanied by a subjective sense that the athlete is operating in a slow-motion time frame (Browne & Mahoney, 1984). In this state, athletes are concentrating with great intensity, totally

peak performance:
Occasions when athletes achieve their top performance and during which they are totally focused, insensitive to pain and fatigue, and filled with a sense of power.

focused, oblivious to their surroundings, and not distracted in any way. They are insensitive to pain and fatigue, and filled with a sense of power and total control.

The psychological state of peak performance is related to profound changes in the brain (Allman, 1992). At the moment the peak performance state begins, the brain's left hemisphere produces an abundance of alpha waves (indicating a relaxed, trancelike state), while two specific areas in the right hemisphere show bursts of increased activity. It appears then, that the athlete attains the peak performance state by relaxing the verbal, analytical left hemisphere of the brain and, at the same time, arousing areas of the right hemisphere responsible for sustained concentration. The trancelike "flow" of the peak performance state is experienced not only by competitive athletes but by musicians and others who must be simultaneously relaxed and concentrating with great intensity if they are to perform at their peak.

But what sets truly great expert performers, who seem to perform routinely at their peak, apart from other competitive athletes?

Expert Performance

Michael Jordan flies through the air on the court, soars upward, and hangs suspended in midair, as if to defy the law of gravity. When fans watch Jordan and others capable of stunning, expert performance, their tendency is to assume that it all just "came naturally." But this is not the case.

Ericsson and Charness (1994) found that those who reach the lofty heights of expert performance in any endeavor do so after long years of sustained, systematic practice. The capabilities required for expert performance in any sport are so complex that mastering them demands about 10 years of virtually full-time work and preparation. This translates into thousands of hours of practice.

Americans, in particular, seem to attribute expert performance primarily to inborn talent or ability. But such an attribution minimizes what researchers have learned about how elite performers attained their levels of excellence. The researchers maintain that deliberate, regular practice, sustained over many years, is the primary ingredient that enables expert performers to soar past the limitations of average performance (Ericsson & Charness, 1994).

Not all of us are sports fans, but we are all consumers. And here, too, psychologists play an important role—in measuring, predicting, and influencing what, when, and how much we buy.

> **?** *What is the purpose of consumer psychology?*

Consumer Psychology: Psychology Goes to Market

All of us are consumers, and it seems that we are bombarded incessantly with commercial messages on television and radio, on billboards, and in newspapers and magazines. What kind of car do you drive, what brand of jeans do you wear, and why? Consumer psychologists are interested in such questions, and they know much more about your buying behavior than you might imagine (Tybout & Artz, 1994).

The purpose of the applied specialty **consumer psychology** is to study, measure, predict, and influence consumer behavior. Some consumer psychologists work for companies that sell products to consumers; others are employed by private organizations or government agencies responsible for consumer education and protection (Sommer & Shutz, 1991).

consumer psychology: A specialty concerned with studying, measuring, predicting, and influencing consumer behavior.

Assessing Consumer Preferences

Consumer psychologists use their knowledge of basic psychological processes to answer such questions as "How does a label acquire name recognition?" "What kinds of colors and patterns have pleasant associations?" (Sommer & Shutz, 1991, pp. 197–198). Consumer psychologists may conduct market research by surveying representative samples of targeted consumer groups and asking them questions about product preferences: What do they like or dislike about certain products? Why do they choose to buy one product rather than an other? What types of advertising influence them most? Consumer psychologists also conduct blind taste tests like the old "Pepsi Challenge," where people were asked to taste Pepsi and Coke in unmarked containers and tell which one they preferred.

Another technique is to form **focus groups**, in which a small number of consumers representing targeted populations (for example, young women or retired persons) are brought together to evaluate product samples and to respond to demonstrations. Sometimes consumer panels are formed, consisting of members of target consumer groups selected according to age, background, education, and other variables. Panel members may be asked to evaluate potential new brand names and rate them according to how exciting, how easy to remember, and how appealing they are to specific age groups. Consumer panels may be reassembled on repeated occasions so that consumer psychologists can learn how responses and preferences change over time (Sommer & Shutz, 1991).

Testing and Observing

Consumer psychologists are also interested in the laboratory testing of products to answer such questions as these: "Is this new paper towel stronger and more absorbent than competing brands?" "How many hours will this ballpoint pen write without running dry?"

Have you ever been observed by a consumer psychologist? You might have been. Often consumer psychologists systematically observe shoppers in stores and shopping malls to learn more about how they make buying decisions. Investigative work is the specialty of some consumer psychologists who are employed by government agencies. They may pose as customers in investigations of consumer fraud. For example, a researcher may take an automobile or VCR that needs only a minor repair to several places of business, asking for a diagnosis and repair estimate.

Consumer psychologists have always paid attention to targeted audiences—children, adolescents, young adults, retired persons. But today they are advising advertisers to acknowledge the increasing diversity in the U.S. population. You will see more advertising models with disabilities (Roberts & Miller, 1992). What motivates such ads? Advertisers know that there are millions of people in the United States with disabilities, and they are reaching out to touch them all.

Consumer psychology has been around for decades, but probably the first person to apply psychology systematically to advertising and consumer behavior was John B. Watson, the founder of behaviorism. When Watson's academic career at Johns Hopkins University ended in 1920, he accepted a position with the J. Walter Thompson advertising agency in New York. More than 75 years ago, he created product images that still exist today—the purity of Johnson's baby powder, the good flavor of Maxwell House coffee ("Good to the last drop"), and the strength of Scott paper towels, among others. Watson knew that sex sells and that products associated with beauty, virility, and sex appeal will move. We have come a long way in advertising and consumer psychology since the days of Watson, but the psychology that moved consumers then still moves them today.

focus group: A small number of consumers representing targeted populations who are brought together to evaluate products and respond to demonstrations.

Memory Check 17.4

1. Forensic psychology is:
   a. a law-related specialty.
   b. a business-related specialty.
   c. an advertising-related specialty.
   d. an engineering-related specialty.

2. When working with competitive athletes, sports psychologists are concerned primarily with the physical skills necessary for a top performance. (true/false)

3. The skills of relaxation and concentration can be learned quickly with the help of a good sports psychologist. (true/false)

4. Which is *not* a purpose of consumer psychology?
   a. to test new products
   b. to develop new products
   c. to influence consumer behavior
   d. to investigate consumer fraud

Answers: 1. a 2. false 3. false 4. b

APPLICATIONS · APPLICATIONS · APPLICATIONS

Sexual Harassment

There has always been sexual harassment in the workplace. But such harassment was in the national spotlight when law professor Anita Hill made public accusations against U.S. Supreme Court Justice Clarence Thomas in connection with his Senate confirmation hearings in 1991.

What Is Sexual Harassment?

There are so many varying concepts as to what constitutes sexual harassment on the job that it is not easy to define. First, let's clarify what sexual harassment is *not*. Sexual harassment should be distinguished from flirting with someone, asking for a date, flattery, and other similar behavior. Sexual harassment lacks the elements of mutual choice found in normal relationships (Charney & Russell, 1994). The Equal Employment Opportunities Commission (1980) issued the following guidelines on workplace sexual harassment, which have become a widely accepted standard:

Unwelcome sexual advances, requests for sexual favors, and other verbal or physical conduct of a sexual nature constitute sexual harassment when 1) submission to such conduct is made either explicitly or implicitly a term or condition of an individual's employment, 2) submission to or rejection of such conduct by an individual is used as a basis for employment decisions affecting such individual, or 3) such conduct has the purpose or effect of unreasonably interfering with an individual's work performance or creating an intimidating, hostile, or offensive working environment. (pp. 74676–74677)

Sexual harassment in the workplace may take many forms, from mild to moderate to severe. In the most extreme form, a supervisor makes the conditions of employment, a raise, a promotion, or other opportunities contingent upon an employee's compliance with sexual demands. Though we are more sensitive to it today, there is nothing new about sexual harassment. Stories of the "casting couch" in Hollywood have been circulated since film-making began. Other less severe forms of sexual harassment consist of unwelcome sexual remarks, lewd sexual comments or jokes, and sexual touch-

ing or deliberate brushing or rubbing against an intended victim.

How Prevalent Is Sexual Harassment?

The most reliable data to date on the prevalence of sexual harassment in the workplace were provided in a study by the U.S. Merit System Protection Board (1981, 1988). This study is an extremely well-designed random-sample survey of 24,000 U.S. federal employees conducted in 1981 and updated in 1988. The study reports that 42 percent of the women and 15 percent of the men surveyed said that they had been sexually harassed during the 2-year period prior to the survey.

In a recent survey conducted by the Harvard Business Review, two-thirds of the men interviewed believed that reports of sexual harassment were exaggerated (Castro, 1992). But a survey by *Working Woman* magazine revealed that over 90 percent of the Fortune 500 companies had recorded employee complaints of sexual harassment, and over one-third of the companies had had sexual harassment lawsuits filed against them (Sandross, 1988).

Sexual harassment is also a problem on the college campus. According to the most comprehensive review of prevalence data available, between 20 and 30 percent of female undergraduates have been sexually harassed while attending college (Charney & Russell, 1994). The rates are said to be higher for graduate students.

Not everyone who has been sexually harassed reports it. Consequently, experts today believe that as many as 50 percent of women in the United States experience some form of sexual harassment on the campus, in the workplace, or elsewhere (Fitzgerald, 1993). And it does not appear that the incidence of sexual harassment has decreased (Ingrassia, 1993).

In the vast majority of cases, women are the victims of sexual harassment, and men are the harassers. A survey of medical residents who had been sexually harassed found that among female victims, 96 percent of the harassers were male, and among male victims, 55 percent of their harassers were male (Komaromy et al., 1993).

What to Do about Sexual Harassment

If you were being sexually harassed by an employer, fellow worker, professor, or student, how would you handle it? Here are some practical suggestions adapted from *Sex on Your Terms* by Elizabeth Powell (1996):

- *Maintain a strictly professional, businesslike manner.* Do not respond personally to acts of sexual harassment. Often a harasser seeks to get a personal, emotional response from his victims, and sometimes to shock, embarrass, or humiliate them. Let the harasser know that your relationship with him is strictly business, and that sexual talk or activity is not part of the business.

- *Don't be alone with the harasser.* If the harasser asks or tries to coerce you to join him for lunch, for drinks, or in some other personal setting, refuse firmly and professionally.

- *Have a talk with the harasser.* If you can't avoid the harasser and he keeps coming on to you, it may help to talk directly with him about the situation. Point out his acts of sexual harassment and tell him directly how his behavior makes you feel and that it must stop immediately.

- *Find support from friends, co-workers, or others you can trust for emotional support and advice.* Surveys indicate that more than 90 percent of sexual harassment victims suffer emotional distress (Charney & Russell, 1994). Victims are less likely to suffer emotional distress with a support group to help, but even then, some people may need professional counseling.

- *File a formal complaint if the harasser refuses to stop.* The law now requires companies (even relatively small ones) to respond to sexual harassment complaints. Large organizations and most colleges and universities have a designated professional to handle such complaints.

- *Seek legal advice if all else fails.* Sexual harassment is against the law, and you can take legal action against the harasser, or even against the company or institution that allowed the harassment to continue.

Thinking Critically

Evaluation

Suppose you have been hired by a company to develop two questionnaires as part of a stress evaluation study. Draw up a 15-item questionnaire to assess the stressfulness of a job and a 10-item questionnaire to evaluate the company's efforts to reduce stress for its employees.

Point/Counterpoint

Based on what you have learned in this chapter about the role psychologists play in the legal system, list the most convincing arguments you can to support each of these positions:

a. People are more likely to get a fair trial as a result of the work of psychologists.
b. People are less likely to get a fair trial as a result of the work of psychologists.

Psychology in Your Life

Drawing on what you have learned in this chapter, consider all aspects of the physical environment where your psychology class meets or where you presently live. Describe in detail why the environment is or is not psychologically satisfying and conducive to learning.

Chapter Summary and Review

Industrial/Organizational Psychology: Psychology Goes to Work

 What are some of the activities of industrial/organizational psychologists?

Industrial/organizational psychologists work to improve personnel selection, training, and evaluation; to increase worker motivation, satisfaction, and performance; and to improve organizational design, communication, and decision making.

What techniques are used in personnel selection?

Procedures used in personnel selection include interviews; assessment centers; and standardized aptitude, personality, and interest tests.

What is performance appraisal, and why is it important?

Performance appraisal is an evaluation process, occurring annually or semi-annually, in which employees are rated and given feedback on their performance. If performance appraisal is done properly, employees know where they need improvement; if it is done poorly, motivation and morale suffer.

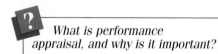 *What is work motivation, and what are two effective techniques for increasing it?*

Work motivation can be thought of as the conditions and processes responsible for the direction, magnitude, and maintenance of one's effort at work. Two effective techniques for increasing work motivation are reinforcement and goal setting.

 What factors are closely related to job satisfaction?

Factors closely associated with job satisfaction are interesting work, good pay, sufficient resources and authority, and compatible co-workers.

For people to function effectively and find satisfaction on the job, what nine variables should fall within their comfort zone?

Nine variables that should fall within a worker's comfort zone are workload, clarity of job description and evaluation criteria, physical variables, job status, accountability, task variety, human contact, physical challenge, and mental challenge.

What are some of the psychological and health consequences of job stress?

Job stress can cause serious illness, such as depression, high blood pressure, and cardiovascular disease; it can also cause problems such as headaches, exhaustion, back problems, insomnia, and indigestion. Other consequences may include absenteeism, reduced productivity, tardiness, accidents, substance abuse, low morale, and alienation from co-workers.

 What is burnout?

Burnout is the result of intense, unrelieved, and unmanaged job stress; in this condition a person becomes pessimistic, dissatisfied, inefficient on the job, and debilitated psychologically.

What strategies are some industries adopting to combat work stress?

Some companies are setting up worksite stress management interventions to help workers deal with stress or to change aspects of the job situation that are sources of job stress. Other measures are maternity and parental leaves, provision for day care, and flexible schedules.

Key Terms

applied psychology (p. 624)
industrial/organizational psychology (p. 624)
work motivation (p. 625)
job enrichment (p. 626)
decision latitude (p. 628)
burnout (p. 629)
job sharing (p. 630)
flextime (p. 630)

Human Factors Psychology: Getting Along with Machines and Appliances

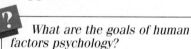 *What are the goals of human factors psychology?*

Human factors psychology is concerned with designing and modifying machines and work environments to make them safer, easier to use, and more compatible with the user's sensory, perceptual, cognitive, and motor capabilities.

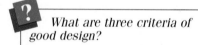 *What are three criteria of good design?*

Well-designed objects should have controls that handle only one function, provide immediate feedback for each action taken, and have visual clues to their operation (visibility).

Key Terms

human factors psychology (p. 631)

Environmental Psychology: The Psychology of Our Surroundings

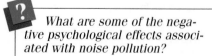 *What are some of the negative psychological effects associated with noise pollution?*

Noise pollution has been linked to high blood pressure. And in children, noise pollution is associated with distractibility, less willingness to persist at tasks, impaired auditory discrimination, lower reading achievement, and increased arousal.

 What is personal space?

Personal space is the area surrounding us that we consider part of us and that we use to regulate how closely others can interact with us. The size of our personal space varies depending on the nature of the interaction; the persons with whom we are interacting; and factors such as our culture, gender, and personality characteristics.

 What do the terms territory and territorial behavior mean?

A territory is an area we define as permanently or temporarily our own. Territorial behavior relates to the strategies we use to establish control of our territory and to defend it against unwelcome intrusions.

 What is the difference between density and crowding?

Density is an objective measure of the number of people occupying a defined

physical space. Crowding is subjective and refers to the perception that there are too many people in a defined space.

 What are some psychological effects of crowding on humans?

Some reported effects include social withdrawal, less willingness to give or receive social support, and increased physiological arousal.

Key Terms

environmental psychology (p. 633)
personal space (p. 634)
territory (p. 635)
territorial behavior (p. 635)
density (p. 635)
crowding (p. 635)
architectural psychology (p. 636)

Forensic Psychology: Psychology Goes to Court

 What role do forensic psychologists play in the legal system?

Forensic psychologists serve as expert witnesses during trials and as consultants to lawyers and police departments; they conduct research on aspects of the judicial process; and they develop psychological profiles of criminals.

Key Terms

forensic psychology (p. 638)
mock jury (p. 639)

Sports Psychology: More Than Playing Games

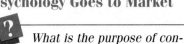 *What do sports psychologists do?*

Sports psychologists help competitive athletes develop the mental and emotional skills necessary for maximal competitive performance, and they help people in recreational athletic programs attain greater physical, emotional, and mental benefits.

Key Terms

sports psychology (p. 640)
peak performance (p. 641)

Consumer Psychology: Psychology Goes to Market

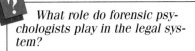 *What is the purpose of consumer psychology?*

The purpose of consumer psychology is to study, measure, predict, and influence consumer behavior.

Key Terms

consumer psychology (p. 642)
focus group (p. 643)

Appendix

Statistical Methods

Comedian Tim Conway, who appeared on the Carol Burnett show many years ago, once did a humorous skit as an inept sports announcer. Reporting the daily baseball scores, he said, "And now here are the scores in the National League—6 to 4, 3 to nothing, 2 to 1, 8 to 3, and 5 to 2." Conway's report of baseball scores may have been humorous, but it was not very informative. Numbers alone tell us very little.

Psychologists must deal with mounds of data in conducting their studies. The data they compute would be just as meaningless as Tim Conway's baseball scores unless there were some methods available to organize and describe the data. Fortunately, there are such methods. Statistics, a branch of mathematics, enables psychologists and other scientists to organize, describe, and draw conclusions about the quantitative results of their studies. We will explore the two basic types of statistics that psychologists use—descriptive statistics and inferential statistics.

Descriptive Statistics

Descriptive statistics are statistics used to organize, summarize, and describe data. Descriptive statistics include measures of central tendency, variability, and relationship.

Measures of Central Tendency

A **measure of central tendency** is a measure or score that describes the center or middle of a distribution of scores. The most widely used and the most familiar measure of central tendency is the mean, which is short for arithmetic mean. The **mean** is the arithmetic average of a group of scores. One computes the mean by adding up all the single scores and dividing the sum by the number of scores.

Carl is a student who sometimes studies and does well in his classes, but occasionally he procrastinates and fails a test. Table A.1 shows how Carl performed on the seven tests in his psychology class last semester. Carl computes his mean score by adding up all his test scores and dividing the sum by the number of tests. Carl's mean, or average, is 80.

TABLE A.1   Carl's Psychology Test Scores

Test 1	98
Test 2	74
Test 3	86
Test 4	92
Test 5	56
Test 6	68
Test 7	86
Sum:	560

Mean: $560 \div 7 = 80$

TABLE A.2   Annual Income for 10 People

Subject	Annual Income	
1	$1,000,000.	
2	$50,000.	
3	$43,000.	
4	$30,000.	
5	$28,000.	
6	$26,000.	$27,000. ← Median
7	$22,000.	
8	$22,000.	← Mode
9	$16,000.	
10	$10,000.	
Sum:	$1,247,000.	

Mean: $1,247,000. ÷ 10 = $124,700.

Median: $27,000.

Mode: $22,000.

The mean is an important and widely used statistical measure of central tendency, but it can be misleading when a group of scores contains one or several extreme scores. For example, in one group of 10 people, the mean annual income last year was $124,700.00. In this case, the figure for the mean income alone covers up more than it reveals. Table A.2 lists the annual incomes of the 10 people in rank order. When a million-dollar income is averaged with several other, more modest incomes, the mean does not provide a true picture of the group.

Therefore, when one or a few individuals score far above or below the middle range of a group, a different measure of central tendency should be used. The **median** is the middle value or score when a group of scores are arranged from highest to lowest. When there are an odd number of scores, the score in the middle is the median. When there are an even number of scores, the median is the average of the two middle scores.

In the 10 incomes arranged from highest to lowest in Table A.2, the median is $27,000, which is the average of the middle incomes, $28,000 and $26,000. The median income—$27,000—is a truer reflection of the comparative income of the group than is the $124,700 mean. It is important to select the measure of central tendency that most accurately reflects the group being studied.

Another measure of central tendency is the mode. The **mode** is easy to find, because it is the score that occurs most frequently in a group of scores. The mode of the annual-income group is $22,000.

Describing Data with Tables and Graphs

A researcher tested 100 students for recall of 20 new vocabulary words. The students were tested 24 hours after they had memorized the list. The raw scores

descriptive statistics: Statistics used to organize, summarize, and describe information gathered from actual observations.

measure of central tendency: A measure or score that describes the center or middle of a distribution of scores (examples: the mean, the median, and the mode).

mean: The arithmetic average of a group of scores; one calculates the mean by adding up all the single scores and dividing the sum by the number of scores.

median: The middle value or score when a group of scores are arranged from highest to lowest.

mode: The score that occurs most frequently in a group of scores.

(number of words recalled), arranged from lowest to highest, for the 100 students are as follows.

2	4	4	5	5	6	6	6	6	7
7	7	7	7	7	7	7	8	8	8
8	8	8	8	8	8	8	9	9	9
9	9	9	9	9	9	9	10	10	10
10	10	10	10	10	10	10	10	10	10
11	11	11	11	11	11	11	11	11	11
11	11	12	12	12	12	12	12	12	12
12	12	12	13	13	13	13	13	13	13
13	13	14	14	14	14	14	14	14	14
15	15	15	15	15	16	16	16	17	19

We can tell from the raw data that one student remembered only 2 words (the lowest score) and that one student remembered 19 words (the highest score). We can also observe that the most frequently occurring score, the mode, is 10.

The researcher organized the scores in a **frequency distribution**—an arrangement showing the frequency, or number of scores that fall within equal-sized class intervals. To organize the 100 test scores, the researcher decided to use intervals of two points each. (A different class interval—three points, for example—could have been chosen instead.) Finally, the frequency (number of scores) within each two-point interval was tallied. Table A.3 presents the resulting frequency distribution.

The researcher then made a histogram, a more graphic representation of the frequency distribution. A **histogram** is a bar graph that depicts the frequency or number of scores within each class interval in the frequency distribution. The intervals are plotted along the horizontal axis, and the frequency of scores in each interval is plotted along the vertical axis. Figure A.1 shows the histogram for the 100 test scores.

Another common method for representing frequency data is the **frequency polygon**. As in a histogram, class intervals are plotted along the horizontal axis

frequency distribution: An arrangement showing the frequency, or number of scores that fall within equal-sized class intervals.

histogram: A bar graph that depicts the frequency or number of scores within each class interval in a frequency distribution.

frequency polygon: A line graph that depicts the frequency or number of scores within each class interval in a frequency distribution.

TABLE A.3　Frequency Distribution of 100 Vocabulary Test Scores

Class Interval	Tally of Scores in Each Class Interval	Number of Scores in Each Class Interval (Frequency)
1–2	I	1
3–4	II	2
5–6	IIII I	6
7–8	IIII IIII IIII II	18
9–10	IIII IIII IIII IIII III	23
11–12	IIII IIII IIII IIII III	23
13–14	IIII IIII IIII II	17
15–16	IIII III	8
17–18	I	1
19–20	I	1

FIGURE A.1

A Frequency Histogram

Vocabulary test scores from the frequency distribution in Table A.3 are plotted here in the form of a frequency histogram. Class intervals of 2 points each appear on the horizontal axis. Frequencies of the scores in each class interval are plotted on the vertical axis.

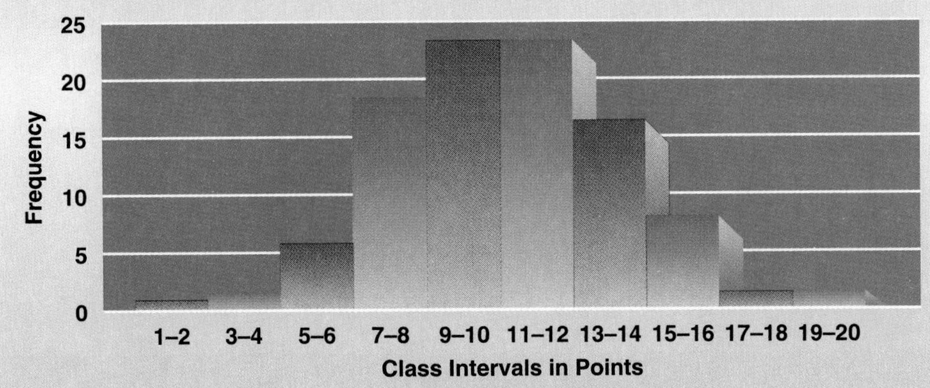

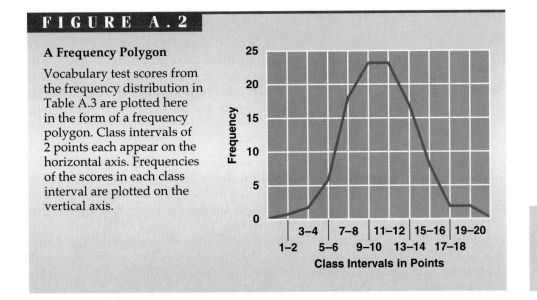

and the frequencies are plotted along the vertical axis. However, in a frequency polygon, a point is placed at the middle (midpoint) of a class interval so that its vertical distance above the horizontal axis shows the frequency of that interval. Lines are drawn to connect the points, as shown in Figure A.2. The histogram and the frequency polygon are simply two different ways of presenting data.

Measures of Variability

Researchers usually need more information than measures of central tendency can provide. Often they need to measure the **variability** of a set of scores—how much the scores spread out, away from the mean. There can be tremendous dif-

FIGURE A.2

A Frequency Polygon

Vocabulary test scores from the frequency distribution in Table A.3 are plotted here in the form of a frequency polygon. Class intervals of 2 points each appear on the horizontal axis. Frequencies of the scores in each class interval are plotted on the vertical axis.

variability: How much the scores in a distribution spread out, away from the mean.

TABLE A.4 Comparison of Range and Standard Deviation for Two Small Groups of Scores Having Identical Means and Medians

Group I			Group II		
Test	Score		Test	Score	
1	99		1	83	
2	99		2	82	
3	98		3	81	
4	80	←Median	4	80	←Median
5	72		5	79	
6	60		6	79	
7	52		7	76	
Sum:	560		Sum:	560	

Mean: $\dfrac{560}{7} = 80$ Mean: $\dfrac{560}{7} = 80$

Median: 80   Median: 80

Range: $99 - 52 = 47$ Range: $83 - 76 = 7$

Standard deviation: 18.1   Standard deviation: 2.14

ferences in variability even when the mean and the median of two sets of scores are exactly the same, as you can see in Table A.4.

Both groups in Table A.4 have a mean and a median of 80. However, the scores in Group II cluster tightly around the mean, while the scores in Group I vary widely from the mean. Just looking at the data is not sufficient for determining variability. Fortunately researchers have statistical techniques available for measuring variability with great precision.

The Range   The simplest measure of variability is the **range**—the difference between the highest and lowest scores in a distribution of scores. Table A.4 reveals that Group I has a range of 47, indicating high variability, while Group II has a range of only 7, or low variability. Unfortunately the range is as limited as it is simple. It tells us the difference between the lowest score and the highest score but nothing about the scores in between. A more sophisticated measure of variability is the standard deviation.

The Standard Deviation   The **standard deviation** is a descriptive statistic reflecting the average amount that scores in a distribution deviate or vary from their mean. The larger the standard deviation, the greater the variability in a distribution of scores. Refer to Table A.4 and note the standard deviations for the two distributions of test scores. In Group I the relatively large standard deviation of 18.1 reflects the wide variation in that distribution. By contrast, the small standard deviation of 2.14 in Group II indicates that the variation is low, and we can see that the scores cluster tightly around the mean.

range: The difference between the highest score and the lowest score in a distribution of scores.

standard deviation: A descriptive statistic reflecting the average amount that scores in a distribution vary or deviate from their mean.

The Normal Curve

Psychologists and other scientists use descriptive statistics most often in connection with an important type of frequency distribution known as the normal curve, pictured in Figure A.3. The **normal curve** is a symmetrical, bell-shaped theoretical curve that represents how scores are normally distributed in a population.

If a large number of people are measured on any of a wide variety of traits, the majority of scores will fall near the mean of the distribution. There will be progressively fewer and fewer scores toward the extremes either above or below the mean. Even our small distribution of the 100 test scores in the histogram in Figure A.1 would be roughly bell-shaped if we applied a curve to it. With increasingly larger numbers of scores in a distribution, the shape of the curve will more strongly resemble the ideal normal curve. On most variables we could measure (height or IQ score, for example), the great majority of values will cluster in the middle, with fewer and fewer people measuring extremely low or high on these variables. The normal distribution with its bell-shaped curve is a potent statistical concept with many very useful, practical applications.

Using the properties of the normal curve and knowing the mean and the standard deviation of a normal distribution, we can tell where any score stands (how high or low) in relation to all the other scores in the distribution. Look again at Figure A.3. You will note that slightly over 68 percent of the scores in a normal distribution fall within 1 standard deviation of the mean (34.13 percent within 1 standard deviation above the mean, and 34.13 percent within 1 standard deviation below the mean). Almost 95.5 percent of the scores in a normal distribution lie between 2 standard deviations above and below the mean. Theoretically the tails of the bell-shaped curve extend indefinitely, never touching the base line of

FIGURE A.3

The Normal Curve

The normal curve is a symmetrical, bell-shaped curve that represents how scores are normally distributed in a population. Slightly over 68 percent of the scores in a normal distribution fall within 1 standard deviation above and below the mean. Almost 95.5 percent of the scores lie between 2 standard deviations above and below the mean, and about 99.75 percent fall between 3 standard deviations above and below the mean.

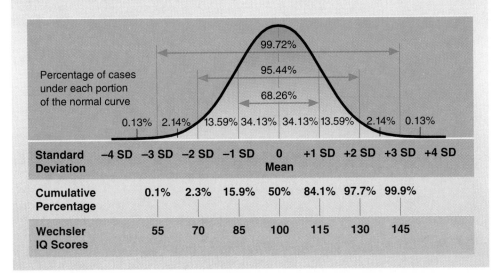

normal curve: A symmetrical, bell-shaped frequency distribution that represents how scores are normally distributed in a population; most scores fall near the mean, and fewer and fewer scores occur in the extremes either above or below the mean.

the curve. Yet the vast majority of scores in a normal distribution, almost 99.75 percent, fall between 3 standard deviations above and below the mean.

On the Wechsler intelligence scales, the mean IQ is 100 and the standard deviation is 15. Thus, 99.72 percent of the population would have an IQ score within 3 standard deviations above and below the mean, ranging from an IQ of 55 to an IQ of 145. We noted that the highest IQ score ever recorded was an unbelievable 230 on the Stanford–Binet Intelligence Scale, scored by Marilyn vos Savant. To plot her score on the normal curve, we would have to count $8\frac{1}{2}$ standard deviations above the mean, so far up the right tail of the curve that her score would be in a standard deviation of its own. The nearest competing score of 210 was almost 7 standard deviations above the mean.

The statistical methods we have discussed so far, the measures of central tendency and the measures of variation, are designed to consider only one variable, such as test scores. What if we are interested in knowing whether two or more different variables are related to each other? The descriptive statistic used to show relationships between variables is the correlation coefficient.

The Correlation Coefficient

A **correlation coefficient** is a number that indicates the degree and direction of relationship between two variables. Correlation coefficients can range from +1.00 (a perfect positive correlation) to .00 (no correlation) to −1.00 (a perfect negative correlation). (See Figure A.4.) A **positive correlation** indicates that two variables

correlation coefficient: A numerical value indicating the strength and direction of relationship between two variables, which ranges from +1.00 (a perfect positive correlation) to −1.00 (a perfect negative correlation).

positive correlation: A relationship between two variables in which both vary in the same direction.

FIGURE A.4

Understanding Correlation Coefficients

Correlation coefficients can range from −1.00 (a perfect negative correlation) through .00 (no correlation) to +1.00 (a perfect positive correlation). As the arrows indicate, a negative correlation exists when an increase in one variable is associated with a decrease in the other variable, and vice versa. A positive correlation exists when both variables tend to either increase or decrease together.

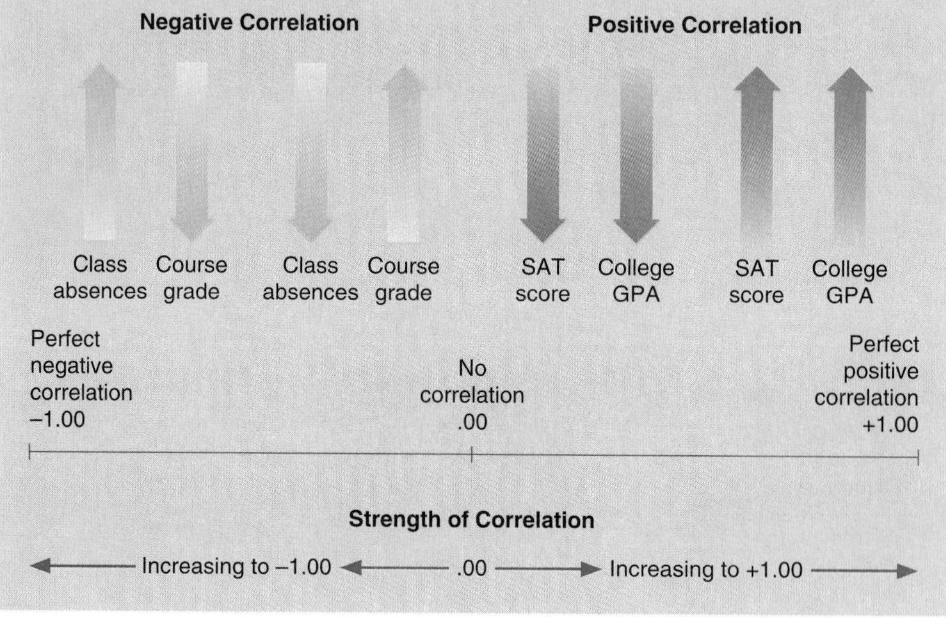

vary in the same direction. An increase in one variable is associated with an increase in the other variable, or a decrease in one variable is associated with a decrease in the other. There is a positive correlation between the number of hours students spend studying and their college grades. The more hours they study, the higher their grades are likely to be.

A **negative correlation** means that an increase in one variable is associated with a decrease in the other variable. As we pointed out in Chapter 1, there is a negative correlation between cigarette smoking and life expectancy. When cigarette smoking increases, the number of years the smoker lives tends to decrease, and vice versa. There may be a negative correlation between the number of hours you spend watching television and studying. The more hours you spend watching TV, the fewer hours you may spend studying, and vice versa.

The sign + or − merely tells whether the two variables vary in the same or opposite directions. (If no sign appears, the correlation is assumed to be positive.) The number in a correlation coefficient indicates the relative *strength* of the relationship between two variables—the higher the number, the stronger the relationship. For example, a correlation of −.70 is higher than a correlation of +.56; a correlation of −.85 is just as strong as one of +.85. A correlation of .00 indicates that no relationship exists between the variables. IQ and shoe size are examples of two variables that are not correlated.

Table A.5 shows the measurements of two variables—high school GPA and college GPA for 11 college students. Most college and university admissions officers use high school grades along with standardized tests and other criteria to predict academic success in college.

Looking at the scores in Table A.5, we can observe that 6 of the 11 students had a higher GPA in high school, while 5 of the students had a higher GPA in college. A clearer picture of the actual relationship is shown by the scatterplot in

TABLE A.5 High School and College GPAs for 11 Students

Student	High School GPA (Variable X)	College GPA (Variable Y)
1	2.0	1.8
2	2.2	2.5
3	2.3	2.5
4	2.5	3.1
5	2.8	3.2
6	3.0	2.2
7	3.0	2.8
8	3.2	3.3
9	3.3	2.9
10	3.5	3.2
11	3.8	3.5

negative correlation: A relationship between two variables in which an increase in one variable is associated with a decrease in the other variable.

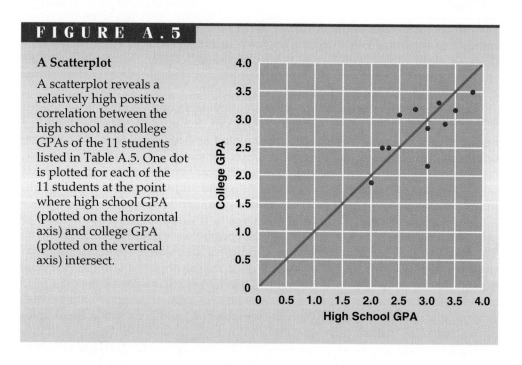

FIGURE A.5

A Scatterplot

A scatterplot reveals a relatively high positive correlation between the high school and college GPAs of the 11 students listed in Table A.5. One dot is plotted for each of the 11 students at the point where high school GPA (plotted on the horizontal axis) and college GPA (plotted on the vertical axis) intersect.

Figure A.5. High school GPA (variable X) is plotted on the horizontal axis, and college GPA (variable Y) is plotted on the vertical axis.

One dot is plotted for each of the 11 students at the point where high school GPA, variable X, and college GPA, variable Y, intersect. For example, the first student's high school and college GPAs intersect at 2.0 on the horizontal (x) axis and at 1.8 on the vertical (y) axis. The scatterplot in Figure A.5 reveals a relatively high correlation between high school and college GPAs because the dots cluster near the diagonal line. It also shows that the correlation is positive because the dots run diagonally upward from left to right. The correlation coefficient for the high school and college GPAs of these 11 students is .71. If the correlation were perfect (1.00), all the dots would fall exactly on the diagonal line.

A scatterplot shows whether a correlation is low, moderate, or high and whether it is positive or negative. Scatterplots that run diagonally up from left to right reveal a positive correlation. Scatterplots that run diagonally down from left to right indicate a negative correlation. The closer the dots are to the diagonal line, the higher the correlation. The scatterplots in Figure A.6 depict a variety of correlations.

We have pointed out elsewhere that correlation does not demonstrate cause and effect. Even a perfect correlation (+1.00 or −1.00) does not mean that one variable causes or is caused by the other. Correlation shows only that two variables are related.

Not all relationships between variables are positive or negative. The relationships between some variables are said to be curvilinear. A curvilinear relationship exists when two variables correlate positively (or negatively) up to a certain point and then change direction. For example, there is a positive correlation between physical strength and age up to about 40 or 45 years of age. As age increases from childhood to middle age, so does the strength of handgrip pressure. But beyond middle adulthood, the relationship becomes negative, and increasing age is associated with decreasing handgrip strength. Figure A.6(d) shows a scatterplot of this curvilinear relationship.

FIGURE A.6

A Variety of Scatterplots

Scatterplots moving diagonally up from left to right as in (a) indicate a positive correlation. Scatterplots moving diagonally down from the left to right as in (c) indicate a negative correlation. The more closely the dots cluster around the diagonal line, the higher the correlation. Scatterplot (b) indicates no correlation. Scatterplot (d) shows a curvilinear relationship that is positive up to a point and then becomes negative. Age and strength of handgrip have a curvilinear relationship: Handgrip increases in strength up to about age 40 and then decreases with continued aging.

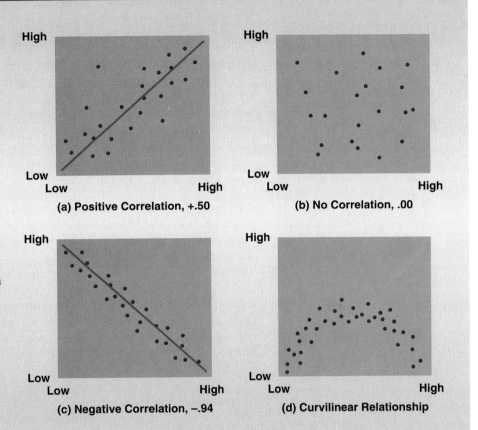

(a) Positive Correlation, +.50

(b) No Correlation, .00

(c) Negative Correlation, −.94

(d) Curvilinear Relationship

Inferential Statistics

We have learned that measures of central tendency, variability, and correlation are important in describing characteristics of data and in describing relationships between sets of data. Often, however, investigators wish to make inferences beyond the relatively small groups of subjects they actually measure. **Inferential statistics** allow researchers (1) to make inferences about the characteristics of the larger population from their observations and measurements of a sample, and (2) to derive estimates of how much faith or confidence can be placed in those inferences.

In statistical theory a **population** is the entire group that is of interest to researchers—the group to which they wish to apply their findings. For example, a population could be all the registered voters in the United States, all the members of a religious denomination or political party, and so on. On a smaller scale, a population might consist of all the female students, the entire senior class, or all the psychology professors at your college or university. A population need not consist of persons. It can be all the chihuahuas in California, all the automobile tires manufactured in the United States, or all the oranges grown in Florida in a given year. In short, a population is all members of any group a researcher may define for study.

Usually researchers cannot directly measure and study the entire population of interest, because the population may be extremely large or inaccessible, or studying the whole population may be too costly in time and money. But thanks to inferential statistical methods, we can make inferences about a large population from

inferential statistics: Statistical procedures that allow researchers (1) to make inferences about the characteristics of the larger population from their observations and measurements of a sample, and (2) to derive estimates of how much confidence can be placed in those inferences.

population: The entire group of interest to researchers and to which they wish to generalize their findings; the group from which a sample is selected.

sample: The portion of any population that is selected for study and from which generalizations are made about the entire population.

random sample: A sample of subjects selected in such a way that every member of the population has an equal chance of being included in the sample; its purpose is to obtain a sample that is representative of the population of interest.

the direct observations of a relatively small sample selected from that population. A **sample** is the part of a population that is selected and studied. For researchers to draw conclusions about the larger population, the sample must be representative; that is, its characteristics must mirror those of the larger population. (See Chapter 1 for more information about representative samples.)

A **random sample** is selected in such a way that every member of the population has an equal chance of being included in the sample. To accomplish this, researchers must have a list of all members of the population. Then the sample is selected using a chance procedure such as pulling names out of a hat or using a table of random numbers generated by a computer.

Statistical Significance

Assume that a random sample of 200 psychology students was selected from the population of students at your college or university. Then the 200 students are randomly assigned to either the experimental group or the control group of 100 students each. Random assignment is accomplished by a chance procedure such as drawing names out of a hat. The experimental group is taught psychology with innovative learning materials for one semester. The control group receives the traditional instruction. At the end of the semester, researchers find that the mean test scores of the experimental group are considerably higher than those of the control group. Can the researchers conclude that the innovative learning program worked? No, not until they can show that the experimental results were not simply due to chance.

The researchers must use inferential statistical procedures to be confident that the results they observe are real (not chance occurrences). Tests of statistical significance yield an estimate of how often the experimental results could have occurred by chance alone. The estimates derived from tests of statistical significance are stated as probabilities. A probability of .05 means that the experimental results would be expected to occur by chance no more than 5 times out of 100. The .05 level of significance is usually required as a minimum for researchers to conclude that their findings are statistically significant. Often the level of significance reached is even more impressive, such as the .01 level. The .01 level means that the probability is no more than 1 in 100 that the results occurred by chance.

The inferences researchers make are not absolute. They are based on probability, and there is always a possibility, however small, that experimental results could occur by chance. For this reason replication of research studies is recommended.

References

Note: Bracketed numbers following references indicate chapter(s) in which they are cited.

Abbott, N. J., & Raff, M. C. (1991). Preface. *Annals of the New York Academy of Sciences, 633,* xiii–xv. [2]

Abramov, I., & Gordon, J. (1994). Color appearance: On seeing red—or yellow, or green, or blue. *Annual Review of Psychology, 45,* 451–485. [3]

Abrams, D., Wetherell, M., Cochrane, S., Hogg, M. A., & Turner, J. C. (1990). Knowing what to think by knowing who you are: Self-categorization and the nature of norm formation, conformity and group polarization. *British Journal of Social Psychology, 29*(Pt. 2), 97–119. [16]

Abrams, R. (1988). *Electroconvulsive therapy.* New York: Oxford University Press. [15]

Abramson, P., & Herdt, G. (1990). The assessment of sexual practices relevant to the transmission of AIDS: A global perspective. *Journal of Sex Research, 27,* 215–232. [11]

Accurso, L. (1994, November 1). Your lucky stars. *Soap Opera Weekly,* p. 44. [12]

Adams, J. M. (1991, August 5). The clearest message may be: "Buy this tape." *Boston Globe,* pp. 37–40. [3]

Adelmann, P. K., & Zajonc, R. B. (1989). Facial efference and the experience of emotion. *Annual Review of Psychology, 40,* 249–280. [10]

Ader, D. N., & Johnson, S. B. (1994). Sample description, reporting, and analysis of sex in psychological research: A look at APA and APA division journals in 1990. *American Psychologist, 49,* 216–218. [1]

Ader, R. (1985). CNS immune systems interactions: Conditioning phenomena. *Behavioral and Brain Sciences, 9,* 760–763. [5]

Ader, R., & Cohen, N. (1982). Behaviorally conditioned immunosuppression and murine systemic Lupus erythematosus. *Science, 215,* 1534–1536. [5]

Ader, R., & Cohen, N. (1993). Psychoneuroimmunology: Conditioning and stress. *Annual Review of Psychology, 44,* 53–85. [5]

Adler, A. (1927). *Understanding human nature.* New York: Greenberg. [12]

Adler, A. (1956). In H. L. Ansbacher & R. R. Ansbacher (Eds.), *The individual psychology of Alfred Adler: A systematic presentation in selections from his writings.* New York: Harper & Row. [12]

Adler, N., & Matthews, K. (1994). Health psychology: Why do some people get sick and some stay well? *Annual Review of Psychology, 45,* 229–259. [13]

Adler, N., & Stone, G. (1984). Psychology and the health system. In J. Ruffini (Ed.), *Advances in medical social science.* New York: Gordon & Breach. [13]

Aggleton, J. P. (1993). The contribution of the amygdala to normal and abnormal emotional states. *Trends in Neurosciences, 16,* 328–333. [2]

Agras, W. S., Rossiter, E. M., Arnow, B., Schneider, J. A., Telch, C. F., Raeburn, S. D., Bruce, B., Perl, M., & Koran, L. M. (1992). Pharmacologic and cognitive-behavioral treatment for bulimia nervosa: A controlled comparison. *American Journal of Psychiatry, 149,* 82–87. [10]

Agras, W. S., Rossiter, E. M., Arnow, B., Telch, C. F., Raeburn, S. D., Bruce, B., & Koran, L. M. (1994). One-year follow-up of psychosocial and pharmacologic treatments for bulimia nervosa. *Journal of Clinical Psychiatry, 55,* 179–183. [10]

AIDS and Mental Health—Part II. (1994). *Harvard Mental Health Letter, 10*(8), 1–4. [11]

Aiello, J. R. (1987). Human spatial behavior. In D. Stokols & I. Altman (Eds.), *Handbook of environmental psychology* (Vol. 1, pp. 505–531). New York: Wiley-Interscience. [17]

Ainsworth, M. D. S. (1973). The development of infant-mother attachment. In B. Caldwell & H. Ricciuti (Eds.), *Review of child development research* (Vol. 3). Chicago: University of Chicago Press. [8]

Ainsworth, M. D. S. (1979). Infant-mother attachment. *American Psychologist, 34,* 932–937. [8]

Ainsworth, M. D. S., Blehar, M. C., Walters, E., & Wall, S. (1978). *Patterns of attachment.* Hillsdale, NJ: Erlbaum. [8]

Aitkin, L. (1990). *The auditory cortex: Structural and functional bases of auditory perception.* London: Chapman & Hall. [2]

Ajzen, I., & Fishbein, M. (1977). Attitude-behavior relations: A theoretical analysis and review of empirical research. *Psychological Bulletin, 84,* 888–918. [16]

Akbarian, S., Bunney, W. E., Potkin, S. G., Wigal, S. B., Hagman, J. O., Sandman, C. A., & Jones, E. G. (1993). Altered distribution of nicotinamide-adenine dinucleotide phosphate-diaphorase cells in frontal lobe of schizophrenics implies disturbances of cortical development. *Archives of General Psychiatry, 50,* 169–177. [14]

Åkerstedt, T. (1988). Sleepiness as a consequence of shift work. *Sleep, 11,* 17–34. [4]

Åkerstedt, T. (1990). Psychological and psychophysiological effects of shift work. *Scandinavian Journal of Work and Environmental Health, 16,* 67–73. [4]

Akiskal, H. S. (1989). New insights into the nature and heterogeneity of mood disorders. *Journal of Clinical Psychiatry, 50*(5, Suppl.), 6–10. [14]

Alan Guttmacher Institute. (1991). *Facts in brief.* New York: Author. [9]

Albert, M. L., & Helm-Estabrooks, N. (1988). Diagnosis and treatment of aphasia: Part II. *Journal of the American Medical Association, 259,* 1205–1210. [2]

Alberts, M. J., Bertels, C., & Dawson, D. V. (1990). An analysis of time of presentation after stroke. *Journal of the American Medical Association, 263,* 65–68. [2]

Albrecht, K. (1979). *Stress and the manager: Making it work for you.* Englewood Cliffs, NJ: Prentice-Hall. [17]

Aldhous, P. (1992). The promise and pitfalls of molecular genetics. *Science, 257,* 164–165. [12]

Aldridge-Morris, R. (1989). *Multiple personality disorder: An exercise in deception.* London: Lawrence Erlbaum Associates. [14]

Allen, B. P. (1994). *Personality theories.* Boston: Allyn & Bacon. [10]

Allison, K. W., Crawford, I., Echemendia, R., Robinson, L., & Knepp, D. (1994). Human diversity and professional competence: Training in clinical and counseling psychology revisited. *American Psychologist, 49,* 792–796. [15]

Allison, M. (1991, February). Improving the odds. *Harvard Health Letter, 16,* pp. 4–6. [13]

Allman, W. F. (1992, August 3). The mental edge. *U.S. News & World Report,* pp. 50–56. [17]

Allport, G. W. (1935). Attitudes. In C. Murchison (Ed.), *Handbook of social psychology.* Worcester, MA: Clark University Press. [16]

Allport, G. W. (1954). *The nature of prejudice.* Reading, MA: Addison-Wesley. [16]

Allport, G. W. (1961). *Pattern and growth in personality.* New York: Holt, Rinehart & Winston. [12]

Allport, G. W., & Odbert, J. S. (1936). Trait names: A psycho-lexical study. *Psychological Monographs, 47*(1, Whole No. 211), 1–171. [12]

659

Alpert, B., Field, T., Goldstein, S., & Perry, S. (1990). Aerobics enhances cardiovascular fitness and agility in preschoolers. *Health Psychology, 9,* 48–56. [13]

Altamura, A. C., & Percudani, M. (1993). The use of antidepressants for long-term treatment of recurrent depression: Rationale, current methodologies, and future directions. *Journal of Clinical Psychiatry, 54*(8, Suppl.), 29–37. [14]

Altshuler, K. Z. (1989). Will the psychotherapies yield different results? A look at assumptions in therapy trials. *American Journal of Psychotherapy, 43,* 310–320. [15]

Alwin, D. F., Cohen, R. L., & Newcomb, T. M. (1991). *Attitude persistence and change over the lifespan.* Madison: University of Wisconsin Press. [16]

Ambady, N., & Rosenthal, R. (1993). Half a minute: Predicting teacher evaluations from thin slices of nonverbal behavior and physical attractiveness. *Journal of Personality and Social Psychology, 64,* 431–441. [16]

American Psychiatric Association. (1993a). Practice guideline for eating disorders. *American Journal of Psychiatry, 150,* p. 212–228. [10]

American Psychiatric Association. (1993b). Practice guideline for major depressive disorder in adults. *American Journal of Psychiatry, 150*(4, Suppl.), 1–26. [14, 15]

American Psychiatric Association. (1994). *Diagnostic and statistical manual of mental disorders* (4th ed.). Washington DC: Author. [10, 11, 14]

American Psychological Association. (1984). *Survey of the use of animals in behavioral research at U. S. universities.* Washington, DC: Author. [1]

American Psychological Association (1992a). *Demographic characteristics of APA members by membership status, 1991.* Washington, DC: Office of Demographic, Employment, and Educational Research, APA Education Directorate. [1]

American Psychological Association (1992b). Ethical principles of psychologists and code of conduct. *American Psychologist, 47,* 1597–1611. [1]

American Psychological Association. (1993). Guidelines for providers of psychological services to ethnic, linguistic, and culturally diverse populations. *American Psychologist, 48,* 45–48. [15]

Anand, B. K., & Brobeck, J. R. (1951). Hypothalamic control of food intake in rats and cats. *Yale Journal of Biological Medicine, 24,* 123–140. [10]

Anastasi, A. (1982). *Psychological testing* (5th ed.). New York: Macmillan. [12]

Anderson, B. L., Kiecolt-Glaser, J. K., & Glaser, R. (1994). A biobehavioral model of cancer stress and disease course. *American Psychologist, 49,* 389–404. [13]

Anderson, C. A. (1989). Temperature and aggression: Ubiquitous effects of heat on occurrence of human violence. *Psychological Bulletin, 106,* 74–96. [16]

Anderson, C. A., & DeNeve, K. M. (1992). Temperature, aggression, and the negative affect escape model. *Psychological Bulletin, 111,* 347–351. [16]

Anderson, M. J., Petros, T. V., Beckwith, B. E., Mitchell, W. W., & Fritz, S. (1991). Individual differences in the effect of time of day on long-term memory access. *American Journal of Psychology, 104,* 241–255. [4]

Anderson, S. M., Klatzky, R. L., & Murray, J. (1990). Traits and social stereotypes: Efficiency differences in social information processing. *Journal of Personality and Social Psychology, 59,* 192–201. [16]

Andersson, B-E. (1989). Effects of public day-care—A longitudinal study. *Child Development, 60,* 857–866. [8]

Andersson, B-E. (1992). Effects of day-care on cognitive and socioemotional competence of thirteen-year-old Swedish schoolchildren. *Child Development, 63,* 20–36. [8]

Andreasen, N. C. (1988). Brain imaging: Applications in psychiatry. *Science, 239,* 1381–1388. [14]

Andreasen, N. C., Arndt, S., Swayze, V., II, Cizadlo, T., Flaum, M., O'Leary, D., Ehrhardt, J. C., & Yuh, W. T. C. (1994). Thalamic abnormalities in schizophrenia visualized through magnetic resonance image averaging. *Science, 266,* 294–298. [14]

Andreasen, N. C., & Black, D. W. (1991). *Introductory textbook of psychiatry.* Washington, DC: American Psychiatric Press. [4]

Andreasen, N. C., Cohen, G., Harris, G., Cizaldo, T., Parkkinen, J., Rezai, K., & Swayze, V. W. (1992). Image processing for the study of brain structure and function: Problems and programs. *Journal of Neuropsychiatry and Clinical Neurosciences, 4,* 125–133. [2]

Annett, M. (1985). *Left, right hand and brain: The right shift theory.* London: Lawrence Erlbaum Associates. [2]

Anstey, K., Stankov, L., & Lord, S. (1993). Primary aging, secondary aging, and intelligence. *Psychology and Aging, 8,* 562–570. [9]

Apgar, V., & Beck, J. (1982). A perfect baby. In H. E. Fitzgerald & T. H. Carr (Eds.), *Human Development 82/83* (pp. 66–70). Guilford, CT: Dushkin. [8]

Apuzzio, J. J. (1990, February). A patient guide: Genital herpes. *Medical Aspects of Human Sexuality, 24,* 15–16. [11]

Archambault, C. M., Czyzewski, D., Cordua y Cruz, G. D., Foreyt, J. P., & Mariotto, M. J. (1989). Effects of weight cycling in female rats. *Physiology and Behavior, 46,* 417–421. [10]

Archer, J. (1991). The influence of testosterone on human aggression. *British Journal of Social Psychology, 82*(Pt. 1), 1–28. [16]

Archer, R. P., Maruish, M., Imhof, E. A., & Piotrowski, C. (1991). Psychological test usage with adolescent clients: 1990 survey findings. *Professional Psychology: Research and Practice, 22,* 247–252. [12]

Arkin, A. M. (1981). *Sleep talking: Psychology and psychophysiology.* Hillsdale, NJ: Lawrence Erlbaum Associates. [4]

Armstrong, B. G., McDonald, A. D., & Sloan, M. (1992). Cigarette, alcohol, and coffee consumption and spontaneous abortion. *American Journal of Public Health, 82,* 85–87. [8]

Aronson, E. (1976). Dissonance theory: Progress and problems. In E. P. Hollander & R. C. Hunt (Eds.), *Current perspectives in social psychology* (4th ed., pp. 316–328). New York: Oxford University Press. [16]

Aronson, E. (1990). Applying social psychology to desegregation and energy conservation. *Personality and Social Psychology Bulletin, 16,* 118–132. [16]

Aronson, E., & Mills, J. (1959). The effect of severity of initiation on liking for a group. *Journal of Abnormal and Social Psychology, 59,* 177–181. [16]

Aronson, T. A. (1987). A naturalistic study of imipramine in panic disorder and agoraphobia. *American Journal of Psychiatry, 144,* 1014–1019. [15]

Asch, S. E. (1946). Forming impressions of personality. *Journal of Abnormal and Social Psychology, 41,* 258–290. [16]

Asch, S. E. (1951). Effects of group pressure upon the modification and distortion of judgments. In H. Guetzkow (Ed.), *Groups, leadership, and men.* Pittsburgh, PA: Carnegie Press. [16]

Asch, S. E. (1955). Opinions and social pressure. *Scientific American, 193,* 31–35. [16]

Atkinson, J. W. (1958). Towards experimental analysis of human motivation in terms of motives, expectancies, and incentives. In J. W. Atkinson (Ed.), *Motives in fantasy, action, and society* (pp. 288–305). Princeton, NJ: Van Nostrand. [10]

Atkinson, J. W. (1964). *An introduction to motivation.* Princeton, NJ: Van Nostrand. [10]

Atkinson, R. (1988). *The teenage world: Adolescent self-image in ten countries.* New York: Plenum Press. [9]

Atkinson, R. C., & Shiffrin, R. M. (1968). Human memory: A proposed system and its controlled processes. In K. W. Spence & J. T. Spence (Eds.), *The psychology of learning and motivation* (Vol. 2, pp. 89–195). New York: Academic Press. [6]

Aubé, J., & Koestner, R. (1992). Gender characteristics and adjustment: A longitudinal study. *Journal of Personality and Social Psychology, 63,* 485–493. [11]

Aubert, G. (1992). Alternative therapeutic approaches in sleep apnea syndrome. *Sleep, 15,* S69–S72. [4]

Ault, R. L. (1983). *Children's cognitive development* (2nd ed.). Oxford: Oxford University Press. [9]

Austin, J. S. (1992). The detection of fake good and fake bad on the MMPI-2. *Educational and Psychological Measurement, 52*, 669–674. [12]

Avraham, R. (1989). *The digestive system.* New York: Chelsea House. [10]

Axelsson, A., & Jerson, T. (1985). Noisy toys: A possible source of sensorineural hearing loss. *Pediatrics, 76*, 574–578. [3]

Ayllon, T. (1977). Intensive treatment of psychotic behaviour by stimulus satiation and food reinforcement. In S. J. Morse & R. I. Watson, Jr. (Eds.), *Psychotherapies: A comparative casebook* (pp. 355–362). New York: Holt, Rinehart & Winston. [15]

Ayllon, T., & Azrin, N. H. (1965). The measurement and reinforcement of behavior of psychotics. *Journal of the Experimental Analysis of Behavior, 8*, 357–383. [5, 15]

Ayllon, T., & Azrin, N. (1968). *The token economy: A motivational system for therapy and rehabilitation.* New York: Appleton-Century-Crofts. [5, 15]

Azrin, N. H., & Holz, W. C. (1966). Punishment. In W. K. Honig (Ed.), *Operant behavior: Areas of research and application.* New York: Appleton-Century-Crofts. [5]

Bach-y-Rita, P., & Bach-y-Rita, E. W. (1990). Biological and psychosocial factors in recovery from brain damage in humans. *Canadian Journal of Psychology, 44*, 148–165. [2]

Bachman, J. G. (1987, July). An eye on the future. *Psychology Today*, pp. 6–8. [9]

Bachman, J. G., & Schulenberg, J. (1993). How part-time work intensity relates to drug use, problem behavior, time use, and satisfaction among high school seniors: Are these consequences or merely correlates? *Developmental Psychology, 29*, 220–235. [9]

Baddeley, A. (1990). *Human memory.* Boston, MA: Allyn & Bacon. [6]

Baddeley, A. (1992). Working memory. *Science, 255*, 556–559. [6]

Baddeley, A. D. (1982). *Your memory: A user's guide.* New York: Macmillan. [6]

Baer, L. (1993). Behavior therapy for obsessive compulsive disorder in the office-based practice. *Journal of Clinical Psychiatry, 54*(6, Suppl.), 10–15. [15]

Baer, L., Rauch, S. L., Ballantine, T., Jr., Martuza, R., Cosgrove, R., Cassem, E., Giriunas, I., Manzo, P. A., Dimino, C., & Jenike, M. A. (1995). Cingulotomy for intractable obsessive-compulsive disorder. *Archives of General Psychiatry, 52*, 384–392. [15]

Bagby, R. M., Rogers, R., & Buis, T. (1994). Detecting malingered and defensive responding on the MMPI-2 in a forensic inpatient sample. *Journal of Personality Assessment, 62*, 191–203. [12]

Bahnson, C. B. (1981). Stress and cancer: The state of the art. *Psychosomatics, 22*, 207–220. [13]

Bahrick, H. P., Bahrick, P. O., & Wittlinger, R. P. (1975). Fifty years of memory for names and faces: A cross-sectional approach. *Journal of Experimental Psychology: General, 104*, 54–75. [6]

Bailey, J. M., & Benishay, D. S. (1993). Familial aggregation of female sexual orientation. *American Journal of Psychiatry, 150*, 272–277. [11]

Bailey, J. M., & Pillard, R. C. (1991). A genetic study of male sexual orientation. *Archives of General Psychiatry, 48*, 1089–1096. [11]

Bailey, J. M., & Pillard, R. C. (1994). The innateness of homosexuality. *Harvard Mental Health Letter, 10*(7), 4–6. [11]

Bailey, J. M., Pillard, R. C., Neale, M. C., & Agyei, Y. (1993). Heritable factors influence sexual orientation in women. *Archives of General Psychiatry, 50*, 217–223. [11]

Bailey, J. M., & Zucker, K. J. (1995). Childhood sex-typed behavior and sexual orientation: A conceptual analysis and quantitative review. *Developmental Psychology, 31*, 43–55. [11]

Baillargeon, R., & DeVos, J. (1991). Object permanence in young infants: Further evidence. *Child Development, 62*, 1227–1246. [8]

Baker, T. B. (1988). Models of addiction: Introduction to the special issue. *Journal of Abnormal Psychology, 97*, 115–117. [4]

Baldessarini, R. J. (1988, September). Update on antipsychotic agents. *Harvard Medical School Mental Health Letter, 5*, pp. 4–6. [15]

Balkin, J. (1987). Contributions of friends to women's fear of success in college. *Psychological Reports, 61*, 39–42. [10]

Ball, C. G., & Grinker, J. A. (1981). Overeating and obesity. In S. J. Mule (Ed.), *Behavior in excess* (pp. 194–220). New York: The Free Press. [10]

Ballenger, J. C., Pecknold, J., Rickels, K., & Sellers, E. M. (1993). Medication discontinuation in panic disorder. *Journal of Clinical Psychiatry, 54*(10, Suppl.), 15–21. [15]

Ballor, D. L., Tommerup, L. J., Thomas, D. P., Smith, D. B., & Keesey, R. E. (1990). Exercise training attenuates diet-induced reduction in metabolic rate. *Journal of Applied Physiology: Respiratory, Environmental, and Exercise Physiology, 68*, 2612–2617. [10]

Bandura, A. (1964). The stormy decade: Fact or fiction? *Psychology in the Schools, 1*, 224–231. [9]

Bandura, A. (1967). Behavioral psychotherapy. *Scientific American, 216*, 78–82. [15]

Bandura, A. (1969a). *Principles of behavior modification.* New York: Holt, Rinehart & Winston. [5]

Bandura, A. (1969b). Social learning theory and identificatory processes. In D. A. Goslin (Ed.), *Handbook of socialization theory and research* (pp. 213–262). Chicago: Rand McNally. [11]

Bandura, A. (1973). *Aggression: A social learning analysis.* Englewood Cliffs, NJ: Prentice-Hall. [16]

Bandura, A. (1976). On social learning and aggression. In E. P. Hollander & R. C. Hunt (Eds.), *Current perspectives in social psychology* (4th ed., pp. 116–128). New York: Oxford University Press. [16]

Bandura, A. (1977a). *Social learning theory.* Englewood Cliffs, NJ: Prentice-Hall. [5, 8, 12, 15]

Bandura, A. (1977b). Self-efficacy: Toward a unifying theory of behavioral change. *Psychological Review, 84*, 191–215. [12]

Bandura, A. (1986). *Social functions of thought and action: A social-cognitive theory.* Englewood Cliffs, NJ: Prentice-Hall. [5]

Bandura, A. (1989). Social cognitive theory. *Annals of Child Development, 6*, 1–60. [12]

Bandura, A., Adams, N. E., & Beyer, J. (1977). Cognitive processes mediating behavioral change. *Journal of Personality and Social Psychology, 35*, 125–139. [15]

Bandura, A., Blanchard, E. B., & Ritter, B. J. (1969). The relative efficacy of desensitization and modeling therapeutic approaches for inducing behavioral, affective and attitudinal changes. *Journal of Personality and Social Psychology, 13*, 173–199. [15]

Bandura, A., Jeffery, R. W., & Gajdos, E. (1975). Generalizing change through participant modeling with self-directed mastery. *Behaviour Research and Therapy, 13*, 141–152. [15]

Bandura, A., Ross, D., & Ross, S. A. (1961). Transmission of aggression through imitation of aggressive models. *Journal of Abnormal and Social Psychology, 63*, 575–582. [5]

Bandura, A., Ross, D., & Ross, S. A. (1963). Imitation of film-mediated aggressive models. *Journal of Abnormal and Social Psychology, 66*, 3–11. [5]

Bar-Tal, D., & Saxe, L. (1976). Perceptions of similarly and dissimilarly attractive couples and individuals. *Journal of Personality and Social Psychology, 33*, 772–781. [16]

Barber, T. X. (1962). Hypnotic age regression: A critical review. *Psychosomatic Medicine, 24*, 181–193. [4]

Barber, T. X. (1970, July). Who believes in hypnosis? *Psychology Today*, pp. 20–27, 84. [4]

Bard, P. (1934). The neurohumoral basis of emotional reactions. In C. A. Murchison (Ed.), *Handbook of general experimental psychology.* Worcester, MA: Clark University Press. [10]

Barefoot, J. C., Dahlstrom, W. D., & Williams, R. B. (1983). Hostility, CHD incidence, and total mortality: A 25-year follow-up study of 255 physicians. *Psychosomatic Medicine, 45*, 59–63. [13]

Barinaga, M. (1995). New Alzheimer's gene found. *Science, 268*, 1845–1846. [9]

Barnett, R. C., Marshall, N. L., Raudenbush, S. W., & Brennan, R. T. (1993). Gender and the relationship between job experiences and psychological distress: A study of dual-earner couples. *Journal of Personality and Social Psychology, 64,* 794–806. [9]

Barnier, A. J., & McConkey, K. M. (1992). Reports of real and false memories: The relevance of hypnosis, hypnotizability, and context of memory test. *Journal of Abnormal Psychology, 101,* 521–527. [4]

Barondes, S. H. (1994). Thinking about Prozac. *Science, 263,* 1102–1103. [15]

Barr, H. M., & Streissguth, A. P. (1991). Caffeine use during pregnancy and child outcome: A 7-year prospective study. *Neurotoxicology and Teratology, 13,* 441–448. [8]

Barr, L. C., Goodman, W. K., Price, L. H., McDougle, C. J., & Charney, D. S. (1992). The serotonin hypothesis of obsessive compulsive disorder: Implications of pharmacologic challenge studies. *Journal of Clinical Psychiatry, 53*(4, Suppl.), 17–28. [14, 15]

Barrett, J., Lack, L., & Morris, M. (1993). The sleep-evoked decrease of body temperature. *Sleep, 16,* 93–99. [4]

Barringer, F. (1993, April 1). Viral sexual diseases are found in 1 of 5 in U.S. *The New York Times,* pp. A1, B9. [11]

Barron, F., & Harrington, D. M. (1981). Creativity, intelligence, and personality. *Annual Review of Psychology, 32,* 439–476. [7]

Bartimus, T. (1983, March 1). One man's descent into schizophrenia. *St. Louis Post-Dispatch,* pp. D1, 7. [14]

Bartlett, F. C. (1932). *Remembering: A study in experimental and social psychology.* London: Cambridge University Press. [6]

Bartoshuk, L. (1989). Taste: Robust across the age span? *Annals of the New York Academy of Sciences, 561,* 65–75. [3]

Bartoshuk, L. M., & Beauchamp, G. K. (1994). Chemical senses. *Annual Review of Psychology, 45,* 419–449. [3, 8]

Bartoshuk, L. M., Fast, K., Karrer, T. A., Marino, S., Price, R. A., & Reed, D. A. (1992). PROP supertasters and the perception of sweetness and bitterness. *Chemical Senses, 17,* 594 (Abstract). [3]

Bartoshuk, L., Rifkin, B., Marks, L. E., & Bars, P. (1986). Taste and aging. *Journal of Gerontology, 41,* 51–57. [3]

Baruch, G., Barnett, R., & Rivers, C. (1983). *Lifeprints.* New York: McGraw-Hill. [9]

Bashore, T. R., & Rapp, P. E. (1993). Are there alternatives to traditional polygraph procedures? *Psychological Bulletin, 113,* 2–22. [10]

Bass, E., & Davis, L. (1988). *The courage to heal.* New York: Harper & Row. [6]

Bateson, G. (1982). Totemic knowledge in New Guinea. In U. Neisser (Ed.), *Memory observed: Remembering in natural contexts.* San Francisco: W. H. Freeman. [6]

Bateson, G., Jackson, D. D., Haley, J., & Weakland, J. (1956). Toward a theory of schizophrenia. *Behavioral Science, 1,* 214–264. [14]

Batson, C. D., Batson, J. G., Griffitt, C. A., Barrientos, S., Brandt, J. R., Sprengelmeyer, P., & Bayly, M. J. (1989). Negative-state relief and the empathy-altruism hypothesis. *Journal of Personality and Social Psychology, 56,* 922–933. [16]

Baum, A., & Davis, G. E. (1980). Reducing the stress of high-density living: An architectural intervention. *Journal of Personality and Social Psychology, 38,* 471–481. [17]

Baum, A., & Valins, S. (1977). *Architecture and social behavior: Psychological studies of social density.* Hillsdale, NJ: Erlbaum. [17]

Baum, A., & Valins, S. (1979). Architectural mediation of residential density and control: Crowding and the regulation of social contact. In L. Berkowitz (Ed.), *Advances in experimental social psychology* (Vol. 12). New York: Academic Press. [17]

Baum, S. K., & Stewart, R. B., Jr. (1990). Sources of meaning through the life-span. *Psychological Reports, 67,* 3–14. [9]

Baumgardner, A. H., Heppner, P. P., & Arkin, R. M. (1986). Role of causal attribution in personal problem solving. *Journal of Personality and Social Psychology, 50,* 636–643. [16]

Baumrind, D. (1967). Child care practices anteceding three patterns of preschool behavior. *Genetic Psychology Monographs, 75,* 43–88. [8]

Baumrind, D. (1971). Current patterns of parental authority. *Developmental Psychology Monographs, 4*(1, Pt. 2). [8]

Baumrind, D. (1980). New directions in socialization research. *American Psychologist, 35,* 639–652. [8]

Baumrind, D. (1985). Research using intentional deception: Ethical issues revisited. *American Psychologist, 40,* 165–174. [1]

Baumrind, D. (1991). The influence of parenting style on adolescent competence and substance use. *Journal of Early Adolescence, 11,* 56–95. [8]

Baxter, L. R., Jr., Schwartz, J. M., Bergman, K. S., Szuba, M. P., Guze, B. H., Mazziotta, J. C., Alazraki, A., Selin, C. E., Ferng, H-K., Munford, P., & Phelps, M. E. (1992). Caudate glucose metabolic rate changes with both drug and behavior therapy for obsessive-compulsive disorder. *Archives of General Psychiatry, 49,* 681–689. [15]

Beaman, A. L., Cole, C. M., Preston, M., Klentz, B., & Steblay, N. M. (1983). Fifteen years of foot-in-the-door research: A meta-analysis. *Personality and Social Psychology Bulletin, 9,* 181–196. [16]

Beck, A. T. (1967). *Depression: Causes and treatment.* Philadelphia: University of Pennsylvania Press. [14]

Beck, A. T. (1976). *Cognitive therapy and the emotional disorders.* New York: New American Library. [14, 15]

Beck, A. T. (1991). Cognitive therapy: A 30-year retrospective. *American Psychologist, 46,* 368–375. [15]

Beck, A. T. (1993). Cognitive therapy: Past, present, and future. *Journal of Consulting and Clinical Psychology, 61,* 194–198. [15]

Beck, A. T., Brown, G., Berchick, R. J., Stewart, B. L., & Steer, R. A. (1990). Relationship between hopelessness and ultimate suicide: A replication with psychiatric outpatients. *American Journal of Psychiatry, 147,* 190–195. [14]

Beck, A. T., & Emery, G. (with R. L. Greenberg). (1985). *Anxiety disorders and phobias: A cognitive perspective.* New York: Basic Books. [14]

Beck, A. T., Steer, R. A., Beck, J. S., & Newman, C. F. (1993). Hopelessness, depression, suicidal ideation, and clinical diagnosis of depression. *Suicide and Life-Threatening Behavior, 23,* 139–145. [14]

Becker, M., Warr-Leeper, G. A., & Leeper, H. A., Jr. (1990). Fetal alcohol syndrome: A description of oral motor, articulatory, short-term memory, grammatical, and semantic abilities. *Journal of Communication Disorders, 23,* 97–124. [8]

Beidler, L. M., & Smallman, R. L. (1965). Renewal of cells within taste buds. *Journal of Cell Biology, 27,* 263–272. [3]

Beilin, H. (1992). Piaget's enduring contribution to developmental psychology. *Developmental Psychology, 28,* 191–204. [8]

Békésy, G. von (1957). The ear. *Scientific American, 197,* 66–78. [8]

Belitsky, R., & McGlashan, T. H. (1993). The manifestations of schizophrenia in late life: A dearth of data. *Schizophrenia Bulletin, 19,* 683–685. [14]

Bell, A. P., Weinberg, M. S., & Hammersmith, S. K. (1981). *Sexual preference: Its development in men and women.* Bloomington: Indiana University Press. [11]

Bell, J. (1991). *Evaluating psychological information: Sharpening your critical thinking skills.* Boston: Allyn & Bacon. [1]

Belsky, J., & Rovine, M. J. (1988). Nonmaternal care in the first year of life and the security of infant-parent attachment. *Child Development, 59,* 157–167. [8]

Belsky, J., Rovine, M., & Fish, M. (1989). The developing family system. In M. Gunnar (Ed.), *Minnesota symposium on child psychology: Vol. 22. Systems and development.* Hillsdale, NJ: Erlbaum. [9]

Belsky, J., Steinberg, L., & Draper, P. (1991). Childhood experience, interpersonal development, and reproductive strategy: An evolutionary theory of socialization. *Child Development, 62,* 647–670. [9]

Bem, S. L. (1974). The measurement of psychological androgyny. *Journal of Consulting and Clinical Psychology, 42,* 155–162. [11]

Bem, S. L. (1975). Sex role adaptability: One consequence of psychological androgyny. *Journal of Personality and Social Psychology, 31,* 634–643. [11]

Bem, S. L. (1977). On the utility of alternative procedures for assessing psychological androgyny. *Journal of Consulting and Clinical Psychology, 45,* 196–205. [11]

Bem, S. L. (1981). Gender schema theory: A cognitive account of sex typing. *Psychological Review, 88,* 354–364. [11]

Bem, S. L. (1985). Androgyny and gender schema theory: A conceptual and empirical integration. In T. B. Sonderegger (Ed.), *Nebraska symposium on motivation: Psychology of gender* (Vol. 32, pp. 179–226). Lincoln: University of Nebraska Press. [11]

Ben-Porath, Y. S., & Butcher, J. N. (1989). The comparability of MMPI and MMPI–2 scales and profiles. *Psychological Assessment: A Journal of Consulting and Clinical Psychology, 1,* 345–347. [12]

Benbow, C. P., & Stanley, J. C. (1980). Sex differences in mathematical ability: Fact or artifact? *Science, 210,* 1262–1264. [11]

Benbow, C. P., & Stanley, J. C. (1983). Sex differences in mathematical reasoning ability: More facts. *Science, 222,* 1029–1031. [2, 11]

Bendich, A., & Keen, C. L. (1993). Influence of maternal nutrition on pregnancy outcome: Public policy issues: Introduction to Part V. *Annals of the New York Academy of Sciences, 678,* 284–285. [8]

Bengtson, V., Rosenthal, C., & Burton, L. (1990). Families and aging: Diversity and heterogeneity. In R. H. Binstock & L. K. George (Eds.), *Handbook of aging and the social sciences* (3rd ed., pp. 263–287). San Diego: Academic Press. [9]

Bennett, S. K. (1994). The American Indian: A psychological overview. In W. J. Lonner & R. Malpass (Eds.), *Psychology and culture* (pp. 35–39). Boston: Allyn & Bacon. [12]

Bennett, W., & Gurin, J. (1982). The dieter's dilemma. New York: Basic Books. [10]

Bennett, W. I. (1990, November). Boom and doom. *Harvard Health Letter, 16,* pp. 1–4. [3]

Benson, H. (1975). *The relaxation response.* New York: Avon. [4]

Benson, P. L., Karabenick, S. A., & Lerner, R. M. (1976). Pretty pleases: The effects of physical attractiveness, race, and sex on receiving help. *Journal of Personality and Social Psychology, 12,* 409–415. [16]

Beratis, S., Gabriel, J., & Holdas, S. (1994). Age at onset in subtypes of schizophrenic disorders. *Schizophrenia Bulletin, 20,* 287–296. [14]

Berenbaum, S. A., & Snyder, E. (1995). Early hormonal influences on childhood sex-typed activity and playmate preferences: Implications for the development of sexual orientation. *Developmental Psychology, 31,* 31–42. [11]

Berk, L. E. (1994). Why children talk to themselves. *Scientific American, 271,* 78–83. [8]

Berkman, L. F., & Syme, S. L. (1979). Social networks, host resistance, and mortality: A nine-year followup study of Alameda County residents. *American Journal of Epidemiology, 109,* 184–204. [13]

Berkowitz, L. (1964). The effects of observing violence. *Scientific American, 210,* 35–41. [16]

Berkowitz, L. (1983). Aversively stimulated aggression: Some parallels and differences in research with animals and humans. *American Psychologist, 38,* 1135–1144. [16]

Berkowitz, L. (1988). Frustrations, appraisals, and aversively stimulated aggression. *Aggressive Behavior, 14,* 3–11. [16]

Berkowitz, L. (1989). Frustration-aggression hypothesis: Examination and reformulation. *Psychological Bulletin, 106,* 59–73. [16]

Berkowitz, L. (1990). On the formation and regulation of anger and aggression: A cognitive-neoassociationistic analysis. *American Psychologist, 45,* 494–503. [16]

Berlin, B., & Kay, P. (1969). *Basic color terms: Their universality and evolution.* Berkeley: University of California Press. [7]

Berlyne, D. E. (1960). *Conflict, arousal, and curiosity.* New York: McGraw-Hill. [10]

Berlyne, D. E. (1971). *Aesthetics and psychobiology.* New York: Appleton-Century-Crofts. [10]

Berman, A. L., & Schwartz, R. H. (1990). Suicide attempts among adolescent drug users. *American Journal of Diseases of Children, 144,* 310–314. [14]

Bernal, M. E., & Castro, F. G. (1994). Are clinical psychologists prepared for service and research with ethnic minorities? Report of a decade of progress. *American Psychologist, 49,* 797–805. [15]

Berndt, T. J. (1992). Friendship and friends' influence in adolescence. *Current Directions in Psychological Science, 1,* 156–159. [9]

Bernstein, I. L. (1985). Learned food aversions in the progression of cancer and its treatment. *Annals of the New York Academy of Sciences, 443,* 365–380. [5]

Bernstein, I. L., Webster, M. M., & Bernstein, I. D. (1982). Food aversions in children receiving chemotherapy for cancer. *Cancer, 50,* 2961–2963. [5]

Berquier, A., & Aston, R. (1992). Characteristics of the frequent nightmare sufferer. *Journal of Abnormal Psychology, 101,* 246–250. [4]

Berreby, D. (1994, January/February). Figures of speech: The rise and fall and rise of Chomsky's linguistics. *The Sciences,* pp. 44–49. [7]

Berscheid, E., Dion, K., Walster, E., & Walster, G. W. (1971). Physical attractiveness and dating choice: A test of the matching hypothesis. *Journal of Experimental Social Psychology, 7,* 173–189. [16]

Bexton, W. H., Herron, W., & Scott, T. H. (1954). Effects of decreased variation in the sensory environment. *Canadian Journal of Psychology, 8,* 70–76. [10]

Beyerstein, B., & Beyerstein, D. (Eds.). (1992). *The write stuff: Evaluations of graphology.* Buffalo, NY: Prometheus Books. [12]

Biden, J. (1993). Violence against women: The congressional response. *American Psychologist, 48,* 1059–1061. [16]

Billiard, M., Pasquiré-Magnetto, V., Heckman, M., Carlander, B., Besset, A., Zachariev, Z., Eliaou, J. F., & Malafosse, A. (1994). Family studies in narcolepsy. *Sleep, 17,* S54–S59. [4]

Binion, V. J. (1990). Psychological androgyny: A Black female perspective. *Sex Roles, 22,* 487–507. [11]

Bishop, G. D. (1984). Gender, role, and illness behavior in a military population. *Health Psychology, 3,* 519–534. [13]

Bjork, D. W. (1993). *B. F. Skinner: A life.* New York: Basic Books. [5]

Bjorklund, D. F., & Green, B. L. (1992). The adaptive nature of cognitive immaturity. *American Psychologist, 47,* 46–54. [9]

Björkqvist, K., Lagerspetz, K. M. J., & Kaukiainen, A. (1992). Do girls manipulate and boys fight? Developmental trends in regard to direct and indirect aggression. *Aggressive Behavior, 18,* 117–127. [11]

Black, S. L., & Bevan, S. (1992). At the movies with Buss and Durkee: A natural experiment on film violence. *Aggressive Behavior, 18,* 37–45. [16]

Blair, S. N. (1993). Evidence for success of exercise in weight loss and control. *Annals of Internal Medicine, 119,* 702–706. [10]

Blair, S. N., Kohl, H. W., III, Paffenbarger, R. S., Jr., Clark, D. G., Cooper, K. H., & Gibbons, L. W. (1989). Physical fitness and all-cause mortality: A prospective study of healthy men and women. *Journal of the American Medical Association, 262,* 2395–2401. [13]

Blanck, P. D., Bellack, A. S., Rosnow, R. L., Rotheram-Borus, M. J., & Schooler, N. R. (1992). Scientific rewards and conflicts of ethical choices in human subjects research. *American Psychologist, 47,* 959–965. [1]

Bland, R. C., Newman, S. C., & Orn, H. (1986). Recurrent and nonrecurrent depression: A family study. *Archives of General Psychiatry, 43,* 1085–1089. [14]

Blau, A. (1946). *The master hand.* New York: American Ortho-Psychiatric Association. [2]

Bleuler, E. (1950). *Dementia praecox, or the group of schizophrenias.* (J. Zinkin & N. D. C. Lewis, Trans.). New York: International Universities Press, 1950. (Original work published 1911). [14]

Bliss, E. L., & Jeppsen, E. A. (1985). Prevalence of multiple personality among inpatients and outpatients. *American Journal of Psychiatry, 142,* 250–251. [14]

Bloche, M. G., & Eisenberg, C. (1993). The psychological effects of state-sanctioned terror. *Harvard Mental Health Letter, 10*(5), 4–6. [13]

Block, J. H. (1978). Another look at sex differentiation in the socialization of mothers and fathers. In J. Sherman & F. L. Denmark (Eds.), *Psychology of women: Future directions of research* (pp. 29–87). New York: Psychological Dimensions. [11]

Bloom, F. E., Lazerson, A., & Hofstadter, L. (1985). *Brain, mind, and behavior.* New York: W. H. Freeman. [2]

Bloomer, C. M. (1976). *Principles of visual perception.* New York: Van Nostrand Reinhold. [3]

Blundell, J. E., Rogers, P. J., & Hill, A. J. (1988). Uncoupling sweetness and calories: Methodological aspects of laboratory studies on appetite control. *Appetite, 11*(Suppl.), 54–61. [10]

Blyth, D. A., Simmons, R. G., Bulcroft, R., Felt, D., VanCleave, E. F., & Bush, D. M. (1981). The effects of physical development on self-image and satisfaction with body-image for early adolescent males. In R. G. Simmons (Ed.), *Research in community and mental health* (Vol. 2). Greenwich, CT: JAI Press. [9]

Blyth, D. A., & Traeger, C. M. (1983). The self-concept and self-esteem of early adolescents. *Theory into Practice, 22,* 91–97. [9]

Bochner, S. (1994). Cross-cultural differences in the self concept: A test of Hofstede's individualism/collectivism distinction. *Journal of Cross-Cultural Psychology, 25,* 273–283. [12]

Bogard, N. (1990). Why we need gender to understand human violence. *Journal of Interpersonal Violence, 5,* 132–135. [11]

Bogen, J. E., & Vogel, P. J. (1963). Treatment of generalized seizures by cerebral commissurotomy. *Surgical Forum, 14,* 431. [2]

Bogerts, B. (1993). Recent advances in the neuropathology of schizophrenia. *Schizophrenia Bulletin, 19,* 431–445. [14]

Bohannon, J. N., III. (1988). Flashbulb memories for the Space Shuttle disaster: A tale of two theories. *Cognition, 29,* 179–196. [6]

Bohannon, J. N., & Warren-Leubecker, A. (1989). Theoretical approaches to language acquisition. In J. B. Gleason (Ed.), *The development of language* (pp. 167–223). Columbus, OH: Merrill. [8]

Bolles, R. C., & Fanselow, M. S. (1982). Endorphins and behavior. *Annual Review of Psychology, 33,* 87–101. [3]

Bonnet, M. H. (1991). The effect of varying prophylactic naps on performance, alertness and mood throughout a 52-hour continuous operation. *Sleep, 14,* 307–315. [4]

Boon, S., & Draijer, N. (1993). Multiple personality disorder in The Netherlands: A clinical investigation of 71 patients. *American Journal of Psychiatry, 150,* 489–494. [14]

Bootzin, R. R., & Perlis, M. L. (1992). Nonpharmacologic treatments of insomnia. *Journal of Clinical Psychiatry, 53*(6, Suppl.), 37–41. [4]

Borg, E., & Counter, S. A. (1989). The middle-ear muscles. *Scientific American, 261,* 74–80. [3]

Borke, H. (1973). The development of empathy in Chinese and American children between 3 and 6 years of age: A cross-cultural study. Developmental Psychology, 9, 102–108. [8]

Bornstein, M. H., & Marks, L. E. (1982, January). Color revisionism. *Psychology Today,* pp. 64–73. [8]

Bornstein, R. F. (1989). Exposure and affect: Overview and meta-analysis of research, 1968–1987. *Psychological Bulletin, 106,* 265–289. [16]

Borod, J. C. (1992). Interhemispheric and intrahemispheric control of emotion: A focus on unilateral brain damage. *Journal of Consulting and Clinical Psychology, 60,* 339–348. [2]

Borrie, R. A. (1991). The use of restricted environmental stimulation therapy in treating addictive behaviors. *International Journal of the Addictions, 25,* 995–1015. [10]

Bosse, R., Aldwin, C. M., Levenson, M. R., & Workman-Daniels, K. (1991). How stressful is retirement? *Journal of Gerontology, 46,* 9–14. [9]

Bouchard, C., Tremblay, A., Despres, J-P., Nadeau, A., Lupien, P. J., Theriault, G., Dussault, J., Moorjani, S., Pinault, S., & Fournier, G. (1990). The response to long-term overfeeding in identical twins. *New England Journal of Medicine, 322,* 1477–1482. [10]

Bouchard, T. J., Jr. (1994). Genes, environment, and personality. *Science, 264,* 1700–1701. [12]

Bouchard, T. J., Jr., Lykken, D. T., McGue, M., Segal, N. L., & Tellegen, A. (1990). Sources of human psychological differences: The Minnesota study of twins reared apart. *Science, 250,* 223–228. [7, 10]

Bouchard, T. J., Jr., Lykken, D. T., McGue, M., Segal, N. L., & Tellegen, A. (1991). IQ and heredity: Response. *Science, 252,* 191–192. [7]

Bouchard, T. J., Jr., & McGue, M. (1981). Familial studies of intelligence: A review. *Science, 212,* 1055–1058. [7]

Bouchard, T. J., Jr., & McGue, M. (1990). Genetic and rearing environmental influences on adult personality: An analysis of adopted twins reared apart. *Journal of Personality, 58,* 263–292. [12]

Bovbjerg, D. H., Redd., W. H., Jacobsen, P. B., Manne, S. L., Taylor, K. L., Surbone, A., Crown, J. P., Norton, L., Gilewski, T. A., Hudis, C. F., Reichman, B. S., Kaufman, R. J., Currie, V. E., & Hakes, T. B. (1992). An experimental analysis of classically conditioned nausea during cancer chemotherapy. *Psychosomatic Medicine, 54,* 623–637. [5]

Bower, B. (1988). Epileptic PET probes. *Science News, 133,* 280–281. [2]

Bower, G. H. (1973, October). How to . . . uh . . . remember! *Psychology Today,* pp. 63–70. [6]

Bower, G. H. (1992). How might emotions affect learning? In S-A. Christianson (Ed.). *Handbook of emotion and memory* (pp. 3–31). Hillsdale, NJ: Erlbaum. [6]

Bower, G. H., Thompson-Schill, S., & Tulving E. (1994). Reducing retroactive interference: An interference analysis. *Journal of Experimental Psychology: Learning, Memory, and Cognition, 20,* 51–66. [6]

Bowlby, J. (1951). Maternal care and mental health. *World Health Organization Monograph* (Serial No. 2). [8]

Bowlby, J. (1969). *Attachment and loss* (Vol. 1). New York: Basic Books. [8]

Bracha, H. S., Torrey, E. F., Gottesman, I. I., Bigelow, L. B., & Cunniff, C. (1992). Second-trimester markers of fetal size in schizophrenia: A study of monozygotic twins. *American Journal of Psychiatry, 149,* 1355–1361. [14]

Bradshaw, J. L. (1989). *Hemispheric specialization and psychological function.* New York: Wiley. [2]

Bransford, J., Sherwood, R., Vye, N., & Rieser, J. (1986). Teaching thinking and problem solving. *American Psychologist, 41,* 1078–1089. [7]

Brantner, J. P., & Doherty, M. A. (1983). A review of time out: A conceptual and methodological analysis. In S. Axelrod & J. Apsche (Eds.), *The effects of punishment on human behavior* (pp. 87–132). New York: Academic Press. [15]

Braungart, J. M., Plomin, R., DeFries, J. C., & Fulker, D. W. (1992). Genetic influence on tester-rated infant temperament as assessed by Bayley's Infant Behavior Record: Nonadoptive and adoptive siblings and twins. *Developmental Psychology, 28,* 40–47. [8]

Bray, G. A. (1992a). Drug treatment of obesity. *American Journal of Clinical Nutrition, 55,* 538S–544S. [2]

Bray, G. A. (1992b). Pathophysiology of obesity. *American Journal of Clinical Nutrition, 55,* 488S–494S. [10].

Brazelton, T. B., Tronick, E., Adamson, L., Als, H., & Wise, S. (1975). Early mother-infant interaction. *In Parent-Infant Interaction, Ciba Symposium 33.* Amsterdam: Assoc. Science Publ. [8]

Breckler, S. J. (1984). Empirical validation of affect, behavior, and cognition as distinct attitude components. *Journal of Personality and Social Psychology, 47,* 1191–1205. [16]

Breedlove, S. M. (1994). Sexual differentiation of the human nervous system. *Annual Review of Psychology, 45,* 389–418. [11]

Breggin, P. R. (1979). *Electroshock: Its brain-disabling effects.* New York: Springer. [15]

Breier, A., Buchanan, R. W., Elashef, A., Munson, R. C., Kirkpatrick, B., & Gellad, F. (1992). Brain morphology and schizophrenia: A magnetic resonance imaging study of limbic, prefrontal cortex, and caudate structures. *Archives of General Psychiatry, 49,* 921–926. [14]

Breier, A., Buchanan, R. W., Kirkpatrick, B., Davis, O. R., Irish, D., Summerfelt, A., & Carpenter, W. T., Jr. (1994). Effects of clozapine on positive and negative symptoms in outpatients with schizophrenia. *American Journal of Psychiatry, 151,* 20–26. [15]

Brems, C. (1991). Depression and personality disorder: Differential diagnosis with the MMPI. *Journal of Clinical Psychology, 47,* 669–675. [12]

Brent, D. A., Perper, J. A., Moritz, G., Baugher, M., Roth, C., Baugher, M., Roth, C., Balach, L., & Schweers, J. (1993). Stressful life events, psychopathology, and adolescent suicide: A case control study. *Suicide and Life-Threatening Behavior, 23,* 179–187. [14]

Breslau, N., Davis, G. C., Andreski, P., & Peterson, E. (1991). Traumatic events and posttraumatic stress disorder in an urban population of young adults. *Archives of General Psychiatry, 48,* 216–222. [13]

Breslau, N., Kilbey, M. N., & Andreski, P. (1993). Nicotine dependence and major depression: New evidence from a prospective investigation. *Archives of General Psychiatry, 50,* 31–35. [13]

Bretherton, I. (1992). The origins of attachment theory: John Bowlby and Mary Ainsworth. *Developmental Psychology, 28,* 759–775. [8]

Brewer, W., & Nakamura, G. (1984). The nature and functions of schemas. In R. Wyer & T. Srull (Eds.), *Handbook of social cognition* (Vol. 3). Hillsdale, NJ: Erlbaum. [6]

Brickner, M. A., Harkins, S. G., & Ostrom, T. M. (1986). Effects of personal involvement: Thought-provoking implications for social loafing. *Journal of Personality and Social Psychology, 51,* 763–769. [16]

Bridges, K. M. B. (1932). Emotional development in early infancy. *Child Development, 3,* 324–341. [10]

Brigham, J. C., & Wolfskeil, M. P. (1983). Opinions of attorneys and law enforcement personnel on the accuracy of eyewitness identifications. *Law and Human Behavior, 7,* 337–349. [6]

Broadbent, D. E. (1958). *Perception and communication.* New York: Pergamon Press. [6]

Brody, E. M., Johnson, P. T., & Fulcomer, M. C. (1984). What should adult children do for elderly parents? Opinions and preferences of three generations of women. *Journal of Gerontology, 39,* 736–746. [9]

Brody, E. M., Litvin, S. J., Hoffman, C., & Kleban, M. H. (1992). Differential effects of daughters' marital status on their parent care experiences. *The Gerontologist, 32,* 58–67. [9]

Brody, G., Pillegrini, A., & Sigel, I. (1986). Marital quality and mother-child and father-child interactions with school-aged children. *Developmental Psychology, 22,* 291–296. [8]

Brody, L. R. (1985). Gender differences in emotional development: A review of theories and research. *Journal of Personality, 53,* 102–149. [10]

Broman, C. L. (1993). Social relationships and health-related behavior. *Journal of Behavioral Medicine, 16,* 335–350. [13]

Bronstein, P. (1984). Differences in mothers' and fathers' behaviors toward children: A cross-cultural comparison. *Developmental Psychology, 20,* 995–1003. [8]

Bronzaft, A. L. (1981). The effect of a noise abatement program on reading ability. *Journal of Environmental Psychology, 1,* 215–222. [17]

Brooks-Gunn, J., & Furstenberg, F. F., Jr. (1986). The children of adolescent mothers: Physical, academic, and psychological outcomes. *Developmental Review, 6,* 224–251. [9]

Brotman, A. W. (1994). What works in the treatment of anorexia nervosa? *Harvard Mental Health Letter, 10*(7), 8. [10]

Brou, P., Sciascia, T. R., Linden, L., & Lettvin, J. Y. (1986). The colors of things. *Scientific American, 255,* 84–91. [3]

Brown, G. L., & Linnoila, M. I. (1990). CSF serotonin metabolite (5-HIAA) studies in depression, impulsivity, and violence. *Journal of Clinical Psychiatry, 51*(Suppl.), 42–43. [16]

Brown, G. W., Harris, T. O., & Hepworth, C. (1994). Life events and endogenous depression: A puzzle reexamined. *Archives of General Psychiatry, 51,* 525–534. [14]

Brown, J. D. (1991). Staying fit and staying well: Physical fitness as a moderator of life stress. *Journal of Personality and Social Psychology, 60,* 555–561. [13]

Brown, J. D., & Rogers, R. J. (1991). Self-serving attributions: The role of physiological arousal. *Personality and Social Psychology Bulletin, 17,* 501–506. [16]

Brown, R. (1973). *A first language: The early stages.* Cambridge, MA: Harvard University Press. [8]

Brown, R., Cazden, C., & Bellugi, U. (1968). The child's grammar from I to III. In J. P. Hill (Ed.), *Minnesota symposium on child psychology* (Vol. 2, pp. 28–73). Minneapolis: University of Minnesota Press. [8]

Brown, R., & Kulik, J. (1977). Flashbulb memories. *Cognition, 5,* 73–99. [6]

Brown, R., & McNeil, D. (1966). The "tip of the tongue" phenomenon. *Journal of Verbal Learning and Verbal Behavior, 5,* 325–337. [6]

Brown, R. J., & Donderi, D. C. (1986). Dream content and self-reported well-being among recurrent dreamers, past-recurrent dreamers, and nonrecurrent dreamers. *Journal of Personality and Social Psychology, 50,* 612–623. [4]

Browne, M. A., & Mahoney, M. J. (1984). Sport psychology. *Annual Review of Psychology, 35,* 605–625. [17]

Brownell, K. (1988, January). Yo-yo dieting. *Psychology Today,* pp. 20–23. [10]

Brownell, K. (1991). Dieting and the search for the perfect body: Where physiology and culture collide. *Behavior Therapy, 22,* 1–12. [10]

Brozan, N. (1985, March 13). U.S. leads industrialized nations in teenage births and abortions. *The New York Times,* pp. 1, 22. [9]

Bruner, J. S., Goodnow, J. J., & Austin, G. A. (1956). A study of thinking. New York: Wiley. [7]

Bryan, J. H., & Test, M. A. (1967). Models and helping: Naturalistic studies in aiding behavior. *Journal of Personality and Social Psychology, 6,* 400–407. [16]

Buchanan, C. M., Eccles, J. S., & Becker, J. B. (1992). Are adolescents the victims of raging hormones? Evidence for activational effects of hormones on moods and behavior at adolescence. *Psychological Bulletin, 111,* 62–107. [9]

Buchholz, E. S., & Korn-Bursztyn, C. (1993). Children of adolescent mothers: Are they at risk for abuse? *Adolescence, 28,* 361–382. [9]

Buck, L., & Axel, R. (1991). A novel multigene family may encode odorant receptors: A molecular basis for odor recognition. *Cell, 65,* 175–187. [3]

Buckhout, R. (1979). The mistaken seven: Eyewitness identification in the case of Delaware v. Father Bernard T. Pagano. *Social Action and the Law, 5,* 35–44. [6]

Buckhout, R., Eugenio, P., Licitra, T., Oliver, L., & Kramer, T. H. (1981). Memory, hypnosis, and evidence: Research on eyewitnesses. *Social Action and the Law, 7,* 67–72. [6]

Buckingham, H. W., Jr., & Kertesz, A. (1974). A linguistic analysis of fluent aphasics. *Brain and Language, 1,* 29–42. [2]

Budiansky, S., Carey, J., Wellborn, S. N., & Silberner, J. (1987, June 29). Taking the pain out of pain. *U.S. News & World Report,* pp. 50–57. [3]

Buis, J. M., & Thompson, D. N. (1989). Imaginary audience and personal fable: A brief review. *Adolescence, 24,* 773–781. [9]

Buonomano, D. V., & Merzenich, M. M. (1995). Temporal information transformed into a spatial code by a neural network with realistic properties. *Science, 267,* 1028–1030. [7]

Burke, A., Heuer, F., & Reisberg, D. (1992). Remembering emotional events. *Memory and Cognition, 20,* 277–290. [6]

Burns, D. D. (1980). *Feeling good: The new mood therapy.* New York: William Morrow. [12, 13]

Burrowes, K. L., Hales, R. E., & Arrington, E. (1988). Research on the biologic aspects of violence. *Psychiatric Clinics of North America, 11,* 499–509. [16]

Burtt, H. E. (1932). An experimental study of early childhood memory. *Journal of Genetic Psychology, 40,* 287–295. [6]

Bushman, B. J., & Cooper, H. M. (1990). Effects of alcohol on human aggression: An integrative research review. *Psychological Bulletin, 107,* 341–354. [4, 16]

Bushman, B. J., & Geen, R. G. (1990). Role of cognitive-emotional mediators and individual differences in the effects of media violence on aggression. *Journal of Personality and Social Psychology, 58,* 156–163. [16]

Busnel, M. C., Granier-Deferre, C., & Lecanuet, J. P. (1992). Fetal audition. *Annals of the New York Academy of Sciences, 662,* 118–134. [8]

Buss, D. M. (1984). Marital assortment for personality dispositions: Assessment with three different data sources. *Behavioral Genetics, 14,* 111–123. [16]

Buss, D. M. (1991). Evolutionary personality psychology. *Annual Review of Psychology, 42,* 459–491. [10, 12]

Buss, D. M. (1994). The strategies of human mating. *American Scientist, 82*, 238–249. [16]

Buss, D. M., Abbott, M., Angleitner, A., Asherian, A., Biaggio, A., Blanco-Villasenor, A., Bruchon-Schweitzer, M., et al. (1990). International preferences in selecting mates: A study of 37 cultures. *Journal of Cross-Cultural Psychology, 21*, 5–47. [16]

Butcher, J. N. (1992, October). International developments with the MMPI–2. *MMPI–2 News & Profiles, 3*, 4. [12]

Butcher, J. N., Dahlstrom, W. G., Graham, J. R., Tellegen, A., & Kaemmer, B. (1989). *Manual for the restandardized Minnesota Multiphasic Personality Inventory: MMPI–2. An administrative and interpretive guide.* Minneapolis: University of Minnesota Press. [12]

Butcher, J. N., & Graham, J. R. (1989). *Topics in MMPI–2 interpretation.* Minneapolis: Department of Psychology, University of Minnesota. [12]

Butcher, J. N., & Hostetler, K. (1990). Abbreviating MMPI item administration: What can be learned from the MMPI for the MMPI–2? *Psychological Assessment: A Journal of Consulting and Clinical Psychology, 2*, 12–21. [12]

Butler, R., & Lewis, M. (1982). *Aging and mental health* (3rd ed.). St. Louis: Mosby. [9]

Butler, R. N. (1968). The facade of chronological age: An interpretive summary. In B. L. Neugarten (Ed.), *Middle age and aging* (pp. 235–242). Chicago: University of Chicago Press. [9]

Buysse, D. J., Reynolds, C. F., III, Monk, T. H., Hoch, C. C., Yeager, A. L., & Kupfer, D. J. (1991). Quantification of subjective sleep quality in healthy elderly men and women using the Pittsburgh Sleep Quality Index (SPQI). *Sleep, 14*, 331–338. [4]

Byne, W. (1993). Human sexual orientation: The biologic theories reappraised. *Archives of General Psychiatry, 50*, 228–239. [11]

Byne, W. (1994). The biological evidence challenged. *Scientific American, 270*, 50–55. [11]

Byne, W., & Parsons, B. (1993). Human sexual orientation: The biologic theories reappraised. *Archives of General Psychiatry, 50*, 228–239. [11]

Byne, W., & Parsons, B. (1994). Biology and human sexual orientation. *Harvard Mental Health Letter, 10*(8), 5–7. [11]

Byrne, D. (1982). Predicting human sexual behavior. In A. G. Kraut, *The G. Stanley Hall Lecture Series* (Vol. 2). Washington, DC: American Psychological Association. [11]

Byrne, D., Clore, G. L., & Smeaton, G. (1986). The attraction hypothesis: Do similar attitudes affect anything? *Journal of Personality and Social Psychology, 51*, 1167–1170. [16]

Caine, S. B., & Koob, G. F. Modulation of cocaine self-administration in the rat through D-3 dopamine receptors. (1993). *Science, 260*, 1814–1816. [4]

Camp, D. S., Raymond, G. A., & Church, R. M. (1967). Temporal relationship between response and punishment. *Journal of Experimental Psychology, 74*, 114–123. [5]

Campbell, A. (1975, May). The American way of mating: Marriage si, children only maybe. *Psychology Today*, pp. 37–43. [9]

Campbell, A. (1976). Subjective measures of well-being. *American Psychologist, 31*, 117–124. [9]

Campbell, D. T., & Sprecht, J. C. (1985). Altruism: Biology, culture, and religion. *Journal of Social and Clinical Psychology, 3*, 33–42. [12]

Campbell, R., & Brody, E. M. (1985). Women's changing roles and help to the elderly: Attitudes of women in the United States and Japan. *The Gerontologist, 25*, 584–592. [9]

Campbell, S. S. (1985). Spontaneous termination of ad libitum sleep episodes with special reference to REM sleep. *Electroencephalography & Clinical Neurophysiology, 60*, 237–242. [4]

Campos, J. J., Langer, A., & Krowitz, A. (1970). Cardiac responses on the visual cliff in prelocomotor human infants. *Science, 170*, 196–197. [8]

Cannon, T. D., & Marco, E. (1994). Structural brain abnormalities as indicators of vulnerability to schizophrenia. *Schizophrenia Bulletin, 20*, 89–102. [14]

Cannon, W. B. (1927). The James-Lange theory of emotions: A critical examination as an alternative theory. *American Journal of Psychology, 39*, 106–112. [10]

Cannon, W. B. (1932). *The wisdom of the body.* New York: Norton. [13]

Cannon, W. B., & Washburn, A. L. (1912). An explanation of hunger. *American Journal of Physiology, 29*, 441–454. [10]

Capaldi, E. J. (1978). Effects of schedule and delay of reinforcement on acquisition speed. *Animal Learning and Behavior, 6*, 330–334. [5]

Caplan, N., Choy, M. H., & Whitmore, J. K. (1992). Indochinese refugee families and academic achievement. *Scientific American, 266*, 36–42. [7, 8]

Carlat, D. J., & Camargo, C. A. (1991). Review of bulimia nervosa in males. *American Journal of Psychiatry, 148*, 831–843. [10]

Carlson, E. B., & Rosser-Hogan, R. (1991). Trauma experiences, post-traumatic stress, dissociation, and depression in Cambodian refugees. *American Journal of Psychiatry, 148*, 1548–1551. [13]

Carlson, M., Charlin, V., & Miller, N. (1988). Positive mood and helping behavior: A test of six hypotheses. *Journal of Personality and Social Psychology, 55*, 211–229. [16]

Carlson, N. R. (1994). *Physiology of behavior* (5th ed.). Boston: Allyn & Bacon. [2, 3]

Carrier, J. (1980). Homosexual behavior in cross-cultural perspective. In J. Marmor (Ed.), *Homosexual behavior* (pp. 100–122). New York: Basic Books. [11]

Carroll, K. M., Rounsaville, B. J., Nich, C., Gordon, L. T., Wirtz, P. W., & Gawin, F. (1994). One-year follow-up of psychotherapy and pharmacotherapy for cocaine dependence: Delayed emergence of psychotherapy effects. *Archives of General Psychiatry, 51*, 989–997. [15]

Carskadon, M. A., & Dement, W. C. (1989). Normal human sleep: An overview. In M. H. Kryger, T. Roth, & W. C. Dement (Eds.), *Principles and practice of sleep medicine* (pp. 3–13). Philadelphia: W. B. Saunders. [4]

Carskadon, M. A., & Rechtschaffen, A. (1989). Monitoring and staging human sleep. In M. H. Kryger, T. Roth, & W. C. Dement (Eds.), *Principles and practice of sleep medicine* (pp. 665–683). Philadelphia: W. B. Saunders. [4]

Carson, R. C. (1989). Personality. *Annual Review of Psychology, 40*, 227–248. [12]

Carver C. S., Pozo, C., Harris, S. D., Noriega, V., Scheier, M. F., Robinson, D. S., Ketcham, A. S., Moffat, F. L., Jr., & Clark, K. C. (1993). How coping mediates the effect of optimism on distress: A study of women with early stage breast cancer. *Journal of Personality and Social Psychology, 65*, 375–390. [13]

Case, R. (1985). *Intellectual development: Birth to adulthood.* Orlando, FL: Academic Press. [8]

Case, R. (Ed.). (1992). *The mind's staircase: Exploring the conceptual underpinnings of children's thought and knowledge.* Hillsdale, NJ: Erlbaum. [8]

Casey, M. B., Nuttall, R., Pezaris, E., & Benbow, C. P. (1995). The influence of spatial ability on gender differences in mathematics college entrance test scores across diverse samples. *Developmental Psychology, 31*, 697–705. [11]

Cash, T. F., & Derlega, V. J. (1978). The matching hypothesis: Physical attractiveness among same-sexed friends. *Personality and Social Psychology Bulletin, 4*, 240–243. [16]

Cash, T. F., & Janda, L. H. (1984, December). The eye of the beholder. *Psychology Today*, pp. 46–52. [16]

Cassidy, L., & Hurrell, R. M. (1995). The influence of victim's attire on adolescents' judgments of date rape. *Adolescence, 118*, 319–323. [11]

Castro, J. (1992, January 20). Sexual harassment: A guide. *Time*, p. 37. [17]

Catlin, F. I. (1986). Noise-induced hearing loss. *American Journal of Otology, 7*, 141–149. [3]

Catotti, D. N., Clarke, P., & Catoe, K. E. (1993). Herpes revisited: Still a cause of concern. *Sexually Transmitted Diseases, 20*(2), 77–80. [11]

Cattell, R. B. (1950). *Personality: A systematic, theoretical, and factual study.* New York: McGraw-Hill. [12]

Cattell, R. B., Eber, H. W., & Tatsuoka, M. M. (1977). *Handbook for the 16 personality factor questionnaire.* Champaign, IL: Institute of Personality and Ability Testing. [12]

Cattell, R. B., Saunders, D. R., & Stice, G. F. (1950). *The 16 personality factor questionnaire.* Champaign, IL: Institute of Personality and Ability Testing. [12]

Cavallero, C., Cicogna, P., Natale, V., Occhinonero, M., & Zito, A. (1992). Slow wave sleep dreaming. *Sleep, 15,* 562–566. [4]

Centers for Disease Control. (1991). Tobacco use among high school students—United States, 1990. *Morbidity and Mortality Weekly Report, 40,* 617–619. [13]

Centers for Disease Control. (1992). Sexual behavior among high school students—United States, 1990. *Morbidity and Mortality Weekly Report, 40*(51, 52), 885–888. [9]

Centers for Disease Control and Prevention. (1994). *HIV/AIDS Surveillance Report, 5*(4), 1–33. [11]

Chaika, E. (1985, August). Crazy talk. *Psychology Today,* pp. 30–35. [14]

Chaiken, S. (1979). Communicator physical attractiveness and persuasion. *Journal of Personality and Social Psychology, 37,* 1387–1397. [16]

Chambless, D. L., & Goldstein, A. J. (1979). Behavioral psychotherapy. In R. J. Corsini (Ed.), *Current psychotherapies* (2nd ed., pp. 230–272). Itasca, IL: F. E. Peacock. [15]

Chance, P. (1986, October). Life after head injury. *Psychology Today,* pp. 62–69. [2]

Changeux, J-P. (1993). Chemical signaling in the brain. *Scientific American, 269,* 58–62. [2]

Charness, N. (1989). Age and expertise: Responding to Talland's challenge. In L. W. Poon, D. C. Rubin, & B. A. Wilson (Eds.), *Everyday cognition in adulthood and old age.* New York: Cambridge University Press. [9]

Charney, D. A., & Russell, R. C. (1994). An overview of sexual harassment. *American Journal of Psychiatry, 151,* 10–17. [17]

Chase, M. H., & Morales, F. R. (1990). The atonia and myoclonia of active (REM) sleep. *Annual Review of Psychology, 41,* 557–584. [4]

Check, J. V. P. (1984). *The effects of violent and nonviolent pornography.* (Department of Supply and Services Contract No. 05SV 19200–3–0899). Ottawa, Ontario: Canadian Department of Justice. [11]

Checkley, H. (1941). *The mask of sanity.* St. Louis: Mosby. [14]

Chesno, F. A., & Killman, P. R. (1975). Effects of stimulation on sociopathic avoidance learning. *Journal of Abnormal Psychology, 84,* 144–150. [14]

Children's Defense Fund. (1991). *The adolescent and young adult fact book.* Washington, DC: Author. [9]

Chipuer, H. M., Plomin, R., Pedersen, M. L., McClearn, G. E., & Nesselroade, J. R. (1993). Genetic influence on family environment: The role of personality. *Developmental Psychology, 29,* 110–118. [12]

Chira, S. (1992, February 12). Bias against girls is found rife in schools, with lasting damage. *The New York Times,* pp. A1, A23. [11]

Chodoff, P. (1987). More on multiple personality disorder. *American Journal of Psychiatry, 144,* 124. [14]

Chomsky, N. (1957). *Syntactic structures.* The Hague: Mouton. [8]

Chomsky, N. (1968). Language and mind. New York: Harcourt, Brace & World. [8]

Christianson, S-Å. (1992). Emotional stress and eyewitness memory: A critical review. *Psychological Bulletin, 112,* 284–309. [6]

Christmas, J. T. (1992). The risks of cocaine use in pregnancy. *Medical Aspects of Human Sexuality, 26*(2), 36–43. [8]

Chumlea, W. C. (1982). Physical growth in adolescence. In B. B. Wolman (Ed.), *Handbook of developmental psychology.* Englewood Cliffs, NJ: Prentice-Hall. [9]

Church, P. (1989, September). Impotence, Part 1: Evaluation. *Harvard Medical School Health Letter, 14,* pp. 4–6. [11]

Church R. M. (1963). The varied effects of punishment on behavior. *Psychological Review, 70,* 369–402. [5]

Chyou, P. H., Nomura, A. M. Y., & Stemmermann, G. N. (1992). A prospective study of the attributable risk of cancer due to cigarette smoking. *American Journal of Public Health, 82,* 37–40. [13]

Cialdini, R. B., Cacioppo, J. T., Basset, R., & Miller, J. A. (1978). Low-ball procedure for producing compliance: Commitment then cost. *Journal of Personality and Social Psychology, 36,* 463–476. [16]

Cialdini, R. B., Vincent, J. E., Lewis, S. K., Catalan, J., Wheeler, D., & Darby, B. L. (1975). Reciprocal concessions procedure for inducing compliance: The door-in-the-fact technique. *Journal of Personality and Social Psychology, 31,* 206–215. [16]

Cicirelli, V. G. (1993). Attachment and obligation as daughters' motives for caregiving behavior and subsequent effect on subjective burden. *Psychology and Aging, 8,* 144–155. [9]

Cipolli, C., Bolzani, R., Cornoldi, C., De Beni, R., & Fagioli, I. (1993). Bizarreness effect in dream recall. *Sleep, 16,* 163–170. [4]

Cipolli, C., & Poli, D. (1992). Story structure in verbal reports of mental sleep experience after awakening in REM sleep. *Sleep, 15,* 133–142. [4]

Clark, D. M. (1988). A cognitive model of panic attacks. In S. Rachman & J. D. Maser (Eds.), *Panic: Psychological perspectives* (pp. 71–89). Hillsdale, NJ: Erlbaum. [14]

Clark, D. M., & Teasdale, J. D. (1982). Diurnal variation in clinical depression and accessibility of memories of positive and negative experiences. *Journal of Abnormal Psychology, 91,* 87–95. [6]

Clark, M. L., & Ayers, M. (1992). Friendship similarity during early adolescence: Gender and racial patterns. *Journal of Psychology, 126,* 393–405. [9]

Clark, R. D., III, & Word, L. E. (1972). Why don't bystanders help? Because of ambiguity? *Journal of Personality and Social Psychology, 24,* 392–400. [16]

Clarke-Stewart, K. A. (1989). Infant day care: Maligned or malignant? *American Psychologist, 44,* 266–273. [8]

Clarkson-Smith, L., & Hartley, A. A. (1990). Structural equation models of relationships between exercise and cognitive abilities. *Psychology and Aging, 5,* 437–446. [9]

Clausen, J. (1975). The social meaning of differential physical and sexual maturation. In D. Dragastin & G. Elder (Eds.), *Adolescence in the life cycle* (pp. 25–47). Washington, DC: Hemisphere Press. [9]

Clavadetscher, J. E., Brown, A. M., Ankrum, C., & Teller, D. Y. (1988). Spectral sensitivity and chromatic discriminations in 3- and 7-week-old human infants. *Journal of the Optical Society of America, 5,* 2093–2105. [8]

Clayton, K. N. (1964). T-maze choice learning as a joint function of the reward magnitudes for the alternatives. *Journal of Comparative and Physiological Psychology, 58,* 333–338. [5]

Cleghorn, J. M., Franco, S., Szechtman, B., Kaplan, R. D., Szechtman, H., Brown, G. M., Nahmias, C., & Garnett, E. S. (1992). Toward a brain map of auditory hallucinations. *American Journal of Psychiatry, 149,* 1062–1069. [14]

Cloninger, C. R., Sigvardsson, S., Bohman, M., & von Knorring, A. L. (1982). Predispositions to petty criminality in Swedish adoptees, II. Cross-fostering analysis of gene-environment interaction. *Archives of General Psychiatry, 39,* 1242–1249. [16]

Clum, G. A., Clum, G. A., & Surls, R. (1993). A meta-analysis of treatments for panic disorder. *Journal of Consulting and Clinical Psychology, 61,* 317–326. [15]

Coe, W. C., & Sarbin, T. R. (1977). Hypnosis from the standpoint of a contextualist. *Annals of the New York Academy of Sciences, 296,* 2–13. [4]

Cohen, C. (1986). The case for the use of animals in biomedical research. *New England Journal of Medicine, 315,* 865–870. [1]

Cohen, D. (1979). *J. B. Watson: The founder of behaviourism.* London: Routledge & Kegan Paul. [5]

Cohen, J. (1994). Basic research comes to the fore as clinical results lag. *Science, 265,* 1028–1029. [11]

Cohen, M. S., & Bookheimer, S. Y. (1994). Localization of brain function using magnetic resonance imaging. *Trends in Neurosciences, 17,* 268–277. [2]

Cohen, S. (1988). Psychosocial models of the role of social support in the etiology of physical disease. *Health Psychology, 7,* 269–297. [13]

Cohen, S., Evans, G. W., Krantz, D. S., & Stokols, D. (1980). Physiological, motivational, and cognitive effects of aircraft noise on children. *American Psychologist, 35,* 231–243. [17]

Cohen, S., Evans, G. W., Stokols, D., & Krantz, D. S. (1986). *Behavior, health, and environmental stress.* New York: Plenum. [17]

Cohen, S., Glass, C. D., & Singer, J. E. (1973). Apartment noise, auditory discrimination, and reading ability in children. *Journal of Experimental Social Psychology, 9,* 407–422. [17]

Cohen, S., Tyrrell, D. A. J., & Smith, A. P. (1993). Negative life events, perceived stress, negative affect, and susceptibility to the common cold. *Journal of Personality and Social Psychology, 64,* 131–140. [13]

Cohen, S., & Williamson, G. M. (1991). Stress and infectious disease in humans. *Psychological Bulletin, 109,* 5–54. [13]

Colasanto, D., & Shriver, J. (1989, May). Mirror of America: Middle-aged face marital crisis. *Gallup Report,* No. 284, 34–38. [9]

Colby, A., Kohlberg, L., Gibbs, J., & Lieberman, M. (1983). A longitudinal study of moral judgment. *Monographs of the Society for Research in Child Development, 48*(1–2, Serial No. 200). [9]

Cole, J. O., & Chiarello, R. J. (1990). The benzodiazepines as drugs of abuse. *Journal of Psychiatric Research, 24,* 135–144. [4]

Cole, P. M. (1986). Children's spontaneous control of facial expression. *Child Development, 57,* 1309–1321. [10]

Coleman, J. (1980). Friendship and the peer group in adolescence. In J. Adelson (Ed.), *Handbook of adolescent psychology.* New York: Wiley. [9]

Coleman, M., & Ganong, L. H. (1985). Love and sex role stereotypes: Do macho men and feminine women make better lovers? *Journal of Personality and Social Psychology, 49,* 170–176. [11]

Collaer, M. L., & Hines, M. (1995). Human behavioral sex differences: A role for gonadal hormones during early development? *Psychological Bulletin, 118,* 55–107. [11]

Collins, R. L. (1970). The sound of one paw clapping: An inquiry into the origins of left handedness. In G. Lindzey & D. B. Thiessen (Eds.), *Contributions to behavior-genetic analysis—the mouse as prototype.* New York: Meredith Corporation. [2]

Collins, W. A., & Gunnar, M. R. (1990). Social and personality development. *Annual Review of Psychology, 41,* 387–416. [8, 10]

Colón, I., & Wuollet, C. A. (1994). Homeland, gender and Chinese drinking. *Journal of Addictive Diseases, 13,* 59–67. [4]

Comstock, G. (1990). Television violence: Is there enough evidence that it is harmful? *Harvard Mental Health Letter, 6*(1), 8. [8]

Condon, W. S., & Sander, L. W. (1974). Neonatal movement is synchronized with adult speech: Interactional participation and language acquisition. *Science, 183,* 99–101. [8]

Conrad, P. (1987). Who comes to worksite wellness programs? A preliminary review. *Journal of Occupational Medicine, 29,* 317–320. [17]

Conrad, R. (1964). Acoustic confusions in immediate memory. *British Journal of Psychology, 55,* 75–84. [6]

Constanzo, P. R., & Schiffman, S. S. (1989). Thinness—not obesity—has a genetic component. *Neuroscience and Biobehavioral Reviews, 13,* 55–58. [13]

Cook, M., Mineka, S., Wolkenstein, B., & Laitsch, K. (1985). Observational conditioning of snake fear in unrelated rhesus monkeys. *Journal of Abnormal Psychology, 94,* 591–610. [5]

Cook, T. D., Appleton, H., Conner, R. F., Shaffer, A., Tamkin, G., & Weber, S. J. (1975). *Sesame Street revisited.* New York: Russell Sage. [8]

Cooke, P. (1992, December/January). TV or not TV. *In Health,* pp. 33–43. [8]

Coons, P. M., Bowman, E. S., Kluft, R. P., & Milstein, V. (1991). The cross-cultural occurrence of MPD: Additional cases from a recent survey. *Dissociation, 4,* 124–128. [14]

Cooper, L. A., Shepard, R. N. (1984). Turning something over in the mind. *Scientific American, 251,* 106–114. [7]

Cooper, S. (1987). The fetal alcohol syndrome. *Journal of Child Psychology and Psychiatry, 28,* 223–227. [8]

Coopersmith, S. (1967). The antecedents of self-esteem. San Francisco: W. H. Freeman. [8]

Coppen, A. (1994). Depression as a lethal disease: Prevention strategies. *Journal of Clinical Psychiatry, 55*(4, Suppl.), 37–45. [14]

Corballis, M. C. (1989). Laterality and human evolution. *Psychological Review, 96,* 492–509. [2]

Coren, S. (1989). Left-handedness and accident-related injury risk. *American Journal of Public Health, 79,* 1–2. [2]

Coren, S., & Halpern, D. F. (1991). Left-handedness: A marker for decreased survival fitness. *Psychological Bulletin, 109,* 90–106. [2]

Coren, S., & Porac, C. (1977). Fifty centuries of right-handedness: The historical record. *Science, 198,* 631–632. [2]

Coren, S., Porac, C., & Ward, L. M. (1979). *Sensation and perception.* New York: Academic Press. [3]

Corina, D. P., Vaid, J., & Bellugi, U. (1992). The linguistic basis of left hemisphere specialization. *Science, 255,* 1058–1060. [2]

Cornell, D., & Cornley, J. E. (1979). Aversive conditioning of campground coyotes in Joshua Tree National Monument. *Wildlife Society Bulletin, 7,* 129–131. [5]

Costa, P. T., Jr., & McCrae, R. R. (1985). *The NEO Personality Inventory.* Odessa, FL: Psychological Assessment Resources. [12]

Costa, P. T., Jr., & McCrae, R. R. (1988). Personality in adulthood: A six-year longitudinal study of self-reports and spouse ratings on the NEO Personality Inventory. *Journal of Personality and Social Psychology, 54,* 853–863. [12]

Costa, P. T., Jr., & McCrae, R. R. (1992a). *NEO-PI-R: Revised NEO Personality Inventory (NEO-PI-R).* Odessa, FL: Psychological Assessment Resources. [12]

Costa, P. T., Jr., & McCrae, R. R. (1992b). Normal personality assessment in clinical practice: The NEO Personality Inventory. *Psychological Assessment, 4,* 5–13. [12]

Costa, P. T., Jr., & McCrae, R. R. (1995). Domains and facets: Hierarchical personality assessment using the Revised NEO Personality Inventory. *Journal of Personality Assessment, 64,* 21–50. [12]

Cotman, C. W., & Lynch, G. S. (1989). The neurobiology of learning and memory. *Cognition, 33,* 201–241. [6]

Council on Ethical and Judicial Affairs, American Medical Association. (1991). Gender disparities in clinical decision making. *Journal of the American Medical Association, 266,* 559–562. [13]

Cousins, N. (1979). *Anatomy of an illness.* New York: Norton. [13]

Cousins, N. (1989, October). Proving the power of laughter. *Psychology Today,* pp. 22–25. [13]

Coutts, L. M. (1991). The organizational psychologist. In R. Gifford (Ed.), *Applied psychology: Variety and opportunity* (pp. 273–299). Boston: Allyn and Bacon. [17]

Cowan, C. P., & Cowan, P. A. (1992, July/August). Is there love after baby? *Psychology Today,* 58–63. [9]

Cowan, N. (1988). Evolving conceptions of memory storage, selective attention, and their mutual constraints within the human information-processing system. *Psychological Bulletin, 104,* 163–191. [6]

Craik, F. I. M., & Lockhart, R. S. (1972). Levels of processing: A framework for memory research. *Journal of Verbal Learning and Verbal Behavior, 11,* 671–684. [6]

Craik, F. I. M., & Tulving, E. (1975). Depth of processing and the retention of words in episodic memory. *Journal of Experimental Psychology: General, 104,* 268–294. [6]

Craik, F. I. M., & Watkins, M. J. (1973). The role of rehearsal in short-term memory. *Journal of Verbal Learning and Verbal Behavior, 12,* 599–607. [6]

Crane, J. (1994). Exploding the myth of scientific support for the theory of Black intellectual inferiority. *Journal of Black Psychology, 20,* 189–209. [7]

Crasilneck, H. B. (1992). The use of hypnosis in the treatment of impotence. *Psychiatric Medicine, 10,* 67–75. [4]

Cravatt, B. F., Prospero-Garcia, O., Siuzdak, G., Gilula, N. B., Henriksen, S. J., Boger, D. L., & Lerner, R. A. (1995). Chemical characterization of a family of brain lipids that induce sleep. *Science, 268,* 1506–1509. [4]

Cravens, H. (1992). A scientific project locked in time: The Terman genetic studies of genius, 1920s–1950s. *American Psychologist, 47,* 183–189. [7]

Craver-Lemley, C., & Reeves, A. (1992). How visual imagery interferes with vision. *Psychological Bulletin, 99,* 633–649. [7]

Crépault, C., Abraham, G., Porto, R., & Couture, M. (1977). Erotic imagery in women. In R. Gemme & C. C. Wheeler (Eds.), *Progress in sexology* (pp. 267–283). New York: Plenum Press. [11]

Crépault, C., & Couture, M. (1980). Men's erotic fantasies. *Archives of Sexual Behavior, 9,* 565–581. [11]

Crespi, L. P. (1942). Quantitative variation of incentive and performance in the white rat. *American Journal of Psychology, 55,* 467–517. [5]

Crick, F., & Koch, C. (1992). The problem of consciousness. *Scientific American, 267,* 152–159. [6]

Crick, F., & Mitchison, G. (1983). The function of dream sleep. Nature, 304, 408–416. [4]

Crick, F., & Mitchison, G. (1995). REM sleep and neural nets. *Behavioural Brain Research, 69,* 147–155. [4]

Crimmins, E. M., & Ingegneri, D. G. (1990). Interaction and living arrangements of older parents and their children: Past trends, present determinants, future implications. *Research on Aging, 12,* 3–35. [9]

Crits-Christoph, P. (1992). The efficacy of brief dynamic psychotherapy: A meta-analysis. *American Journal of Psychiatry, 149,* 151–158. [15]

Crook, T. H., III, & Larrabee, G. J. (1990). A self-rating scale for evaluating memory in everyday life. *Psychology and Aging, 5,* 48–57. [9]

Crosby, F., Bromley, S., & Saxe, L. (1980). Recent unobtrusive studies of black and white discrimination and prejudice: A literature review. *Psychological Bulletin, 87,* 546–563. [16]

Crouter, A. C., Perry-Jenkins, M., Huston, T. L., & McHale, S. M. (1987). Processes underlying father involvement in dual-earner and single-earner families. *Developmental Psychology, 23,* 431–440. [9]

Crowe, L. C., & George, W. H. (1989). Alcohol and human sexuality: Review and integration. *Psychological Bulletin, 105,* 374–386. [4]

Crowe, R. R. (1990). Panic disorder: Genetic considerations. *Journal of Psychiatric Research, 24*(Suppl. 2), 129–134. [14]

Crystal, D. S., Chen, C., Fulligni, A. J., Stevenson, H. W., Hsu, C-C., Ko, H-J., Kitamura, S., & Kimura, S. (1994). Psychological maladjustment and academic achievement: A cross-cultural study of Japanese, Chinese, and American high school students. *Child Development, 65,* 738–753. [7]

Cullari, S., & Mikus, R. (1990). Correlates of adolescent sexual behavior. *Psychological Reports, 66,* 1179–1184. [9]

Cunningham, M. R. (1979). Weather, mood, and helping behavior: Quasi experiments with the sunshine Samaritan. Journal of *Personality and Social Psychology, 37,* 1947–1956. [16]

Cunningham, M. R. (1988). Does happiness mean friendliness? Induced mood and heterosexual self-disclosure. *Personality and Social Psychology Bulletin, 14,* 283–297. [16]

Curtis, R. C., & Miller, K. (1986). Believing another likes or dislikes you: Behaviors making the beliefs come true. *Journal of Personality and Social Psychology, 51,* 284–290. [16]

Curtis, R. L. (1975). Adolescent orientations toward parents and peers: Variations by sex, age, and socioeconomic status. *Adolescence, 10,* 483–494. [9]

Czeisler, C. A., Johnson, M. P., Duffy, J. F., Brown, E. N., Ronda, J. M., & Kronauer, R. E. (1990). Exposure to bright light and darkness to treat physiological maladaptation to night work. *New England Journal of Medicine, 322,* 1253–1259. [4]

Czeisler, C. A., Moore-Ede, M. C., & Coleman, R. M. (1982). Rotating shift work schedules that disrupt sleep are improved by applying circadian principles. *Science, 217,* 460–463. [4]

Dabbs, J. M., Jr., & Morris, R. (1990). Testosterone, social class, and antisocial behavior in a sample of 4,462 men. *Psychological Science, 1,* 209–211. [16]

Dale, N., & Kandel, E. R. (1990). Facilitatory and inhibitory transmitters modulate spontaneous transmitter release at cultured Aplysia sensorimotor synapses. *Journal of Physiology, 421,* 203–222. [6]

Damasio, H., Grabowski, T., Frank, R., Galaburda, A. M., & Damasio, A. R. (1994). The return of Phineas Gage: Clues about the brain from the skull of a famous patient. *Science, 264,* 1102–1105. [2]

Daoussis, L., & McKelvie, S. (1986). Musical preference and the effects of music on a reading comprehension test for extraverts and introverts. *Perceptual and Motor Skills, 62,* 283–289. [17]

Darley, J. M., & Latané, B. (1968a). Bystander intervention in emergencies: Diffusion of responsibility. *Journal of Personality and Social Psychology, 8,* 377–383. [16]

Darley, J. M., & Latané, B. (1968b, December). When will people help in a crisis? *Psychology Today,* pp. 54–57, 70–71. [16]

Darwin, C. (1965). *The expression of emotion in man and animals.* Chicago: University of Chicago Press. (Original work published 1872). [10]

Dasen, P. R. (1972). Cross-cultural Piagetian research: A summary. *Journal of Cross-Cultural Psychology, 3,* 23–29. [9]

Dasen, P. R. (1994). Culture and cognitive development from a Piagetian perspective. In W. J. Lonner & R. Malpass (Eds.), *Psychology and culture* (pp. 145–149). Boston: Allyn & Bacon. [8]

Dashiell, J. F. (1925). A quantitative demonstration of animal drive. *Journal of Comparative Psychology, 5,* 205–208. [10]

Davis, K. L., Kahn, R. S., Ko, G., & Davidson, M. (1991). Dopamine in schizophrenia: A review and reconceptualization. *American Journal of Psychiatry, 148,* 1474–1486. [14]

Davis, P. J., & Schwartz, G. E. (1987). Repression and the inaccessibility of affective memories. *Journal of Personality and Social Psychology, 52,* 155–162. [12]

Davis, S., Butcher, S. P., & Morris, R. G. M. (1992). The NMDA receptor antagonist D-2-amino-5-phosphonopentanoate (D-AP5) impairs spatial learning and LTP in vivo at intracerebral concentrations comparable to those that block LTP in vitro. *Journal of Neuroscience, 12,* 21–34. [6]

Davis, T. L. (1995). Gender differences in masking negative emotions: Ability or motivation? *Developmental Psychology, 31,* 660–667. [10]

Dawkins, B. J. (1990). Genital herpes simplex infections. *Primary Care: Clinics in Office Practice, 17,* 95–113. [11]

Dawson, D., & Campbell, S. S. (1991). Time exposure to bright light improves sleep and alertness during simulated night shifts. Sleep, 14, 511–516. [4]

Dayton, G. O., Jr., Jones, M. H., Aiu, R., Rossen, P. H., Steel, B., & Rose, M. (1964). Developmental study of coordinated eye movements in the human infant. I: Visual acuity in the newborn human: A study based on induced optokinetic nystagmus recorded by electro-oculography. *Archives of Opthalmology, 71,* 865–870. [8]

D'Azevedo, W. A. (1982). Tribal history in Liberia. In U. Neisser (Ed.), *Memory observed: Remembering in natural contexts.* San Francisco: W. H. Freeman. [6]

Dean, G. A., Kelly, I. W., Saklofske, D. H., & Furnham, A. (1992). In B. Beyerstein & D. Beyerstein (Eds.), *The write stuff: Evaluations of graphology.* Buffalo, NY: Prometheus Books. [12]

DeBuono, B. A., Zinner, S. H., Daamen, M., & McCormack, W. M. (1990). Sexual behavior of college women in 1975, 1986, and 1989. *New England Journal of Medicine, 322,* 821–825. [11]

DeCasper, A. J., & Fifer, W. P. (1980). Of human bonding: Newborns prefer their mothers' voices. *Science, 208,* 1174–1176. [8]

DeCasper, A. J., & Spence, M. J. (1986). Prenatal maternal speech influences newborns' perception of speech sounds. *Infant Behavior and Development, 9,* 133–150. [8]

de Castro, J. M., & de Castro, E. S. (1989). Spontaneous meal patterns of humans: Influence of the presence of other people. *Journal of Clinical Nutrition, 50,* 237–247. [10]

Deci, E. L. (1975). *Intrinsic motivation*. New York: Plenum. [5]

Deese, J. (1959). On the prediction of occurrence of particular verbal intrusions in immediate recall. *Journal of Experimental Psychology, 58*, 17–22. [6]

DeJong, W. (1979). An examination of self-perception mediation of the foot-in-the-door effect. *Journal of Personality and Social Psychology, 37*, 2221–2239. [16]

Dekker, J., & Everaerd, W. (1989). Psychological determinants of sexual arousal: A review. *Behaviour Research and Therapy, 27*, 353–364. [11]

Dekovic, M., & Janssens, J. M. A. M. (1992). Parents' child-rearing style and child's sociometric status. *Developmental Psychology, 28*, 925–932. [8]

Delgado, J. M. R. (1969). *Physical control of the mind: Toward a psychocivilized society*. New York: Harper & Row. [2]

Delgado, J. M. R., & Anand, B. K. (1953). Increased food intake induced by electrical stimulation of the lateral hypothalamus. *American Journal of Physiology, 172*, 162–168. [10]

DeLongis, A., Coyne, J. C., Dakof, G., Folkman, S., & Lazarus, R. S. (1982). Relationship of daily hassles, uplifts, and major life events to health status. *Health Psychology, 1*, 119–136. [13]

DeLongis, A., Folkman, S., & Lazarus, R. S. (1988). The impact of daily stress on health and mood: Psychological and social resources as mediators. *Journal of Personality and Social Psychology, 54*, 486–495. [13]

Demare, D., Briere, J., & Lips, H. M. (1988). Violent pornography and self-reported likelihood of sexual aggression. *Journal of Research in Personality, 22*, 140–155. [11]

DeMaris, A., & Rao, K. V. (1992). Premarital cohabitation and subsequent marital stability in the United States: A reassessment. *Journal of Marriage and the Family, 54*, 178–190. [9]

Dembroski, T. M., MacDougall, J. M., Williams, R. B., Haney, T. I., & Blumenthal, J. A. (1985). Components of Type A hostility and anger in relationship to angiographic findings. *Psychosomatic Medicine, 47*, 219–233. [13]

Dement, W., & Kleitman, N. (1957). The relation of eye movements during sleep to dream activity: An objective method for the study of dreaming. *Journal of Experimental Psychology, 53*, 339–346. [4]

Dement, W. C. (1974). *Some must watch while some must sleep*. San Francisco: W. H. Freeman. [4]

Dement, W. C. (1992). The proper use of sleeping pills in the primary care setting. *Journal of Clinical Psychiatry, 53*(12, Suppl.), 50–56. [4]

Dempster, F. N. (1988). The spacing effect: A case study in the failure to apply the results of psychological research. *American Psychologist, 43*, 627–634. [6]

Dennis, W. (1968). Creative productivity between the ages of 20 and 80. In B. L. Neugarten (Ed.), *Middle age and aging* (pp. 106–114). Chicago: University of Chicago Press. [9]

de Silva, P., & Rachman, S. (1992). *Obsessive compulsive disorder: The facts*. Oxford: Oxford University Press. [14]

Des Jarlais, D. C., & Friedman, S. R. (1994). AIDS and the use of injected drugs. *Scientific American, 270*, 82–88. [11]

Desmond, E. W. (1987, November 30). Out in the open: Changing attitudes and new research give fresh hope to alcoholics. *Time*, pp. 80–90. [13]

DeStefano, L., & Colasanto, D. (1990). Unlike 1975, today most Americans think men have it better. *Gallup Poll Monthly*, No. 293, 25–36. [11]

Detke, M. J., Brandon, S. E., Weingarten, H. P., Rodin, J., & Wagner, A. R. (1989). Modulation of behavioral and insulin responses by contextual stimuli paired with food. *Physiology and Behavior, 45*, 845–851. [10]

Deuchar, N. (1984). AIDS in New York City with particular reference to the psycho-social aspects. *British Journal of Psychiatry, 145*, 612–619. [11]

De Valois, R. L., & De Valois, K. K. (1975). Neural coding of color. In E. C. Carterette & M. P. Friedman (Eds.), *Handbook of perception* (Vol. 5). New York: Academic. [3]

Devanand, D. P., Dwork, A. J., Hutchinson, M. S. E., Bolwig, T. G., & Sackeim, H. A. (1994). Does ECT alter brain structure? *American Journal of Psychiatry, 151*, 957–970. [15]

Devine, P. G. (1989). Stereotypes and prejudice: Their automatic and controlled components. *Journal of Personality and Social Psychology, 56*, 5–18. [16]

Devine, P. G., Monteith, M. J., Zuwerink, J. R., & Elliot, A. J. (1991). Prejudice with and without compunction. *Journal of Personality and Social Psychology, 60*, 817–830. [16]

De Vos, S. (1990). Extended family living among older people in six Latin American countries. *Journal of Gerontology: Social Sciences, 45*, S87–94. [9]

deVries, H. A. (1986). *Fitness after 50*. New York: Scribner's. [9]

Diamond, M. (1993). Homosexuality and bisexuality in different populations. *Archives of Sexual Behavior, 22*, 291–310. [11]

Diamond, M. C., Scheibel, A. B., Murphy, G. M., Jr., & Harvey, T. (1985). On the brain of a scientist: Albert Einstein. *Experimental Neurology, 88*, 198–204. [2]

Diamond, M. E., Huang, W., & Ebner, F. F. (1994). Laminar comparison of somatosensory cortical plasticity. *Science, 265*, 1885–1888. [2]

Di Chiara, G., Acquas, E., & Carboni, E. (1992). Drug motivation and abuse: A neurobiological perspective. *Annals of the New York Academy of Sciences, 654*, 207–219. [4]

Dietz, W. H. (1989). Obesity. *Journal of the American College of Nutrition, 8*(Suppl.), 139–219. [10]

Digman, J. M. (1990). Personality structure: Emergence of the five-factor model. *Annual Review of Psychology, 41*, 417–440. [12]

DiLalla, L. F., & Gottesman, I. I. (1991). Biological and genetic contributors to violence—Widom's untold tale. *Psychological Bulletin, 109*, 125–129. [16]

Dimberg, U. (1990). Facial electromyography and emotional reactions. *Psychophysiology, 27*, 481–494. [10]

Dinges, D. F., Whitehouse, W. G., Orne, E. C., Powell, J. W., Orne, M. T., & Erdelyi, M. H. (1992). Evaluating hypnotic memory enhancement (hypermnesia and reminiscence) using multitrial forced recall. *Journal of Experimental Psychology: Learning, Memory & Cognition, 18*, 1139–1147. [4]

Dinges, M. M., & Oetting, E. R. (1993). Similarity in drug use patterns between adolescents and their friends. *Adolescence, 28*, 253–266. [4]

Dion, K., Berscheid, E., & Walster, E. (1972). What is beautiful is good. *Journal of Personality and Social Psychology, 24*, 285–290. [16]

Dion, K. K., & Berscheid, E. (1974). Physical attractiveness and peer perception among children. *Sociometry, 37*, 1–12. [8]

Dionne, V. E. (1988). How do you smell? Principle in question. *Trends in Neurosciences, 11*, 188–189. [3]

Dipboye, R. L., Fromkin, H. L., & Wilback, K. (1975). Relative importance of applicant sex, attractiveness, and scholastic standing in evaluation of job applicant resumes. *Journal of Applied Psychology, 60*, 39–43. [16]

Dobb, E. (1989, November/December). The scents around us. *The Sciences, 29*, 46–53. [3]

Dobbin, M. (1987, October 12). Loud noise from little headphones. *U.S. News & World Report*, pp. 77–78. [3]

Dobie, R. A. (1987, December). Noise-induced hearing loss: The family physician's role. *American Family Physician*, pp. 141–148. [3]

Dobson, K. S. (1989). A meta-analysis of the efficacy of cognitive therapy for depression. *Journal of Consulting and Clinical Psychology, 57*, 414–419. [15]

Dodge, K. A., Bates, J. E., & Pettit, G. S. (1990). Mechanisms in the cycle of violence. *Science, 250*, 1678–1683. [16]

Dodge, K. A., Cole, J. D., Pettit, G. S., & Price, J. M. (1990). Peer status and aggression in boys' groups: Developmental and contextual analyses. *Child Development, 61*, 1289–1309. [8]

Dodge, K. A., Price, J. M., Bachorowski, J. A., & Newman, J. P. (1990). Hostile attributional biases in severely aggressive adolescents. *Journal of Abnormal Psychology, 99*, 385–392. [8, 16]

Dollard, J., Doob, L. W., Miller, N., Mowrer, O. H., & Sears, R. R. (1939). *Frustration and aggression.* New Haven: Yale University Press. [16]

Domino, G. (1984). California Psychological Inventory. In D. J. Keyser & R. C. Sweetland (Eds.), *Test Critiques* (Vol. 1, pp. 146–157). Kansas City: Test Corporation of America. [12]

Donnerstein, E., & Linz, D. (1984, January). Sexual violence in the media: A warning. *Psychology Today,* pp. 14–15. [11]

Doob, L. W., & Sears, R. R. (1939). Factors determining substitute behavior and the overt expression of aggression. *Journal of Abnormal and Social Psychology, 34,* 293–313. [16]

Dovidio, J. F. (1984). Helping behavior and altruism: An empirical and conceptual overview. In L. Berkowitz (Ed.), *Advances in experimental social psychology* (Vol. 17, pp. 361–427). New York: Academic Press. [16]

Doyle, J. A. (1985). *Sex and gender.* Dubuque, IA: Wm. C. Brown [11]

Dreikurs, R. (1953). *Fundamentals of Adlerian psychology.* Chicago: Alfred Adler Institute. [12]

Drevets, W. C., Videen, T. O., Price, J. L., Preskorn, S. H., Carmichael, S. T., & Raichle, M. E. (1992). A functional anatomical study of unipolar depression. *Journal of Neuroscience, 12,* 3628–3641. [14]

Drewnowski, A., Yee, D. K., Kurth, C. L., & Krahn, D. D. (1994). Eating pathology and DSM-III-R bulimia nervosa: A continuum of behavior. *American Journal of Psychiatry, 151,* 1217–1219. [10]

Dryden, J. (1994, September 8). Alcohol use by fathers may affect fetal development. *Washington University Record,* p. 2. [8]

Duck, S. (1983). *Friends for life: The psychology of close relationships.* New York: St. Martin's Press. [9]

Duggan, J. P., & Booth, D. A. (1986). Obesity, overeating, and rapid gastric emptying in rats with ventromedial hypothalamic lesions. *Science, 231,* 609–611. [10]

Dunkel-Schetter, C., Feinstein, L. G., Taylor, S. E., & Falke, R. L. (1992). Patterns of coping with cancer. *Health Psychology, 11,* 79–87. [13]

Durkin, J. (1991). The sport psychologist. In R. Gifford (Ed.), *Applied psychology: Variety and opportunity* (pp. 147–170). Boston: Allyn and Bacon. [17]

Duyme, M. (1988). School success and social class: An adoption study. *Developmental Psychology, 24,* 203–209. [7]

Dworkin, B. R. (1993). *Learning and physiological regulation.* Chicago: University of Chicago Press. [5]

Dywan, J., & Bowers, K. (1983). The use of hypnosis to enhance recall. *Science, 222,* 184–185. [4, 6]

Eagly, A. H. (1987). Sex differences in social behavior: A social-role interpretation. Hillsdale, NJ: Erlbaum. [16]

Eagly, A. H., Ashmore, R. D., Makhijani, M. G., & Longo, L. C. (1991). What is beautiful is good . . . : A meta-analytic review of research on the physical attractiveness stereotype. *Psychological Bulletin, 110,* 109–128. [16]

Eagly, A. H., & Carli, L. (1981). Sex of researchers and sex-typed communications as determinants of sex differences in influence-ability: A meta-analysis of social influence studies. *Psychological Bulletin, 90,* 1–20. [16]

Eagly, A. H., & Steffen, V. J. (1986). Gender and aggressive behavior: A meta-analytic review of the social psychological literature. *Psychological Bulletin, 100,* 309–330. [11]

Ebata, A. T. (1987). *A longitudinal study of psychological distress during early adolescence.* Unpublished doctoral dissertation, Pennsylvania State University. [9]

Ebbinghaus, H. E. (1964). *Memory: A contribution to experimental psychology* (H. A. Ruger & C. E. Bussenius, Trans.). New York: Dover. (Original work published 1885). [6]

Eccles, J. S., & Jacobs, J. E. (1986). Social forces shape math attitudes and performance. *Signs, 11,* 367–389. [11]

Eccles, J. S., Midgley, C., Wigfield, A., Buchanan, C. M., Reuman, D., Flanagan, C., & MacIver, D. (1993). Development during adolescence: The impact of stage-environment fit on young adolescents' experiences in schools and in families. *American Psychologist, 48,* 90–101. [9]

Edmond, S. (1990). When symptom becomes disease. *Harvard Health Letter, 16,* pp. 6–8. [3]

Edwards, D. W., Morrison, T. L., & Weissman, H. N. (1993). The MMPI and MMPI-2 in an outpatient sample: Comparisons of code types, validity scales, and clinical scales. *Journal of Personality Assessment, 61,* 1–18. [12]

Efron, R. (1990). *The decline and fall of hemispheric specialization.* Hillsdale, NJ: Erlbaum. [2]

Egeth, H. E. (1993). What do we *not* know about eyewitness identification? *American Psychologist, 48,* 577–580. [6]

Ehrhardt, A. A., Evers, K., & Money, J. (1968). Influence of androgen and some aspects of sexual dimorphic behavior in women with the late-treated adrenogenital syndrome. *Johns Hopkins Medical Journal, 123,* 115–122. [11]

Eibl-Eibesfeldt, I. (1973). The expressive behavior of the deaf-and-blindborn. In M. von Cranach & I. Vine (Eds.), *Social communication and movement.* New York: Academic Press. [10]

Eich, E., Macaulay, D., & Ryan, L. (1994). Mood dependent memory for events of the personal past. *Journal of Experimental Psychology: General, 123,* 201–215. [6]

Eich, J. E. (1980). The cue dependent nature of state-dependent retrieval. *Memory and Cognition, 8,* 157–173. [6]

Eichenbaum, H., & Otto, T. (1993). LTP and memory: Can we enhance the connection? *Trends in Neurosciences, 16,* 163. [6]

Eimas, P. D. (1985). The perception of speech in early infancy. *Scientific American, 252,* 46–52. [8]

Ekman, P. (1972). Universals and cultural differences in facial expression of emotion. In J. Cole (Ed.), *Nebraska symposium on motivation* (Vol. 19). Lincoln: University of Nebraska Press. [10]

Ekman, P. (1982). *Emotion and the human face* (2nd ed.). New York: Cambridge University Press. [10]

Ekman, P. (1985). *Telling lies: Clues to deceit in the marketplace, marriage, and politics.* New York: Norton. [16]

Ekman, P. (1992). Are there basic emotions? *Psychological Review, 99,* 550–553. [10]

Ekman, P. (1993). Facial expression and emotion. *American Psychologist, 48,* 384–392. [10]

Ekman, P., & Friesen, W. V. (1971). Constants across cultures in the face and emotion. *Journal of Personality and Social Psychology, 17,* 124–129. [10]

Ekman, P., & Friesen, W. V. (1975). *Unmasking the face: A guide to recognizing emotions from facial clues.* Englewood Cliffs, NJ: Prentice-Hall. [10]

Ekman, P., Friesen, W. V., & Bear, J. (1984, May). The international language of gestures. *Psychology Today,* pp. 64–69. [16]

Ekman, P., Friesen, W. V., & O'Sullivan, M. (1988). Smiles when lying. *Journal of Personality and Social Psychology, 54,* 414–420. [16]

Ekman, P., Friesen, W. V., O'Sullivan, M., Chan, A., Diacoyanni-Tarlatzis, I., Heider, K., Krause, R., LeCompte, W. A., Pitcairn, T., Ricci-Bitti, P. E., Scherer, K., Tomita, M., & Tzavaras, A. (1987). Universals and cultural differences in the judgments of facial expressions of emotion. *Journal of Personality and Social Psychology, 53,* 712–717. [10]

Ekman, P., Levenson, R. W., & Friesen, W. V. (1983). Autonomic nervous system activity distinguishes among emotions. *Science, 221,* 1208–1210. [10]

El-Shiekh, M., Klacynski, P. A., & Valaik, M. E. (1989). Stress and coping across the life course. *Human Development, 32,* 113–117. [13]

Elkin, I., Shea, M. T., Watkins, J. T., et al. (1989). National Institute of Mental Health Treatment of Depression Collaborative Research Program: General effectiveness of treatments. *Archives of General Psychology, 46,* 971–982. [15]

Elkind, D. (1967). Egocentrism in adolescence. *Child Development, 38,* 1025–1034. [9]

Elkind, D. (1970, April 5). Erik Erikson's eight ages of man. *The New York Times Magazine,* pp. 25–27, 84–92, 110–119. [8, 9]

Elkind, D. (1974). *Children and adolescents: Interpretive essays on Jean Piaget* (2nd ed.). New York: Oxford University Press. [9]

Elkins, R. L. (1991). An appraisal of chemical aversion (emetic therapy) approaches to alcoholism treatment. *Behaviour Research and Therapy, 29*, 387–413. [15]

Ellis, A. (1961). *A guide to rational living.* Englewood Cliffs, NJ: Prentice-Hall. [15]

Ellis, A. (1977). The basic clinical theory of rational-emotive therapy. In A. Ellis & R. Grieger (Eds.), *Handbook of rational-emotive therapy* (pp. 3–33). New York: Springer. [15]

Ellis, A. (1979). Rational-emotive therapy. In R. J. Corsini (Ed.), *Current psychotherapies* (2nd ed., pp. 185–229). Itasca, IL: F. E. Peacock. [15]

Ellis, A. (1987). The impossibility of achieving consistently good mental health. *American Psychologist, 42*, 364–375. [15]

Ellis, A. (1993). Reflections on rational-emotive therapy. *Journal of Consulting and Clinical Psychology, 61*, 199–201. [15]

Ellis, A., & Harper, R. A. (1975). *A new guide to rational living.* North Hollywood, CA: Wilshire Book Co. [14]

Ellis, A., & Knaus, W. J. (1977). *Overcoming procrastination.* New York: Signet. [5]

Ellis, B. J., & Symons, D. (1990). Sex differences in sexual fantasy: An evolutionary psychological approach. *Journal of Sex Research, 27*, 527–555. [11]

Ellis, H. D. (1984). Practical aspects of face memory. In G. L. Wells & E. F. Loftus (Eds.), *Eyewitness testimony: Psychological perspectives* (pp. 12–37). Cambridge: Cambridge University Press. [6]

Emde, R. N., Plomin, R., Robinson, J., Corley, R., DeFries, J., Fulker, D. W., Reznick, J. S., Campos, J., Kagan, J., & Zahn-Waxler, C. (1992). Temperament, emotion, and cognition at fourteen months: The MacArthur Longitudinal Twin Study. *Child Development, 63*, 1437–1455. [8]

Emmelkamp, P. M. G. (1988). Phobic disorders. In C. G. Last & M. Herson (Eds.), *Handbook of anxiety disorders* (pp. 66–86). New York: Pergamom Press. [14]

Engel, G. L. (1977). The need for a new medical model: A challenge for biomedicine. *Science, 196*, 126–129. [13]

Engel, G. L. (1980). The clinical application of the biopsychosocial model. *American Journal of Psychiatry, 137*, 535–544. [13]

Engen, T. (1982). *The perception of odors.* New York: Academic Press. [3]

Engles, G. I., Garnefski, N., & Diekstra, R. F. W. (1993). Efficacy of rational-emotive therapy: A quantitative analysis. *Journal of Consulting and Clinical Psychology, 61*, 1083–1090. [15]

Epstein, J. (1983). Examining theories of adolescent friendships. In J. Epstein & N. Karweit (Eds.), *Friends in school.* New York: Academic Press. [9]

Epstein, S. (1994). Integration of the cognitive and the psychodynamic unconscious. *American Psychologist, 49*, 709–724. [7, 12]

Equal Employment Opportunities Commission. (1980). Guidelines on discrimination because of sex. *Federal Register, 45*(219), 74676–74677. [17]

Erber, J. T., Szuchman, L. T., & Rothberg, S. T. (1990). Age, gender, and individual differences in memory failure appraisal. *Psychology and Aging, 5*, 600–603. [9]

Erdelyi, M. H. (1992). Psychodynamics and the unconscious. *American Psychologist, 47*, 784–787. [12]

Ericsson, K. A., & Charness, N. (1994). Expert performance: Its structure and acquisition. *American Psychologist, 49*, 725–747. [17]

Erikson, E. H. (1963). *Childhood and society* (2nd ed.). New York: Norton. [8, 9]

Erikson, E. H. (1968). *Identity: Youth and crisis.* New York: Norton. [9]

Erikson, E. H. (1980). *Identity and the life cycle.* New York: Norton. [8, 9]

Erikson, E. H., Erikson, J. M., & Kivnick, H. Q. (1986). *Vital involvement in old age: The experience of old age in our time.* New York: W. W. Norton. [9]

Erlenmeyer-Kimling, L., & Jarvik, L. F. (1963). Genetics and intelligence: A review. *Science, 142*, 1477–1479. [7]

Eron, L. D. (1980). Prescription for reducing aggression. *American Psychologist, 35*, 244–252. [16]

Eron, L. D. (1982). Parent-child interaction, television violence, and aggression of children. *American Psychologist, 37*, 197–211. [8]

Eron, L. D. (1987). The development of aggressive behavior from the perspective of a developing behaviorism. *American Psychologist, 42*, 435–442. [16]

Esses, V. M., & Webster, C. D. (1988). Physical attractiveness, dangerousness, and the Canadian criminal code. *Journal of Applied Social Psychology, 18*, 1017–1031. [17]

Estes, W. K. (1994). *Classification and cognition.* New York: Oxford University Press. [7]

Evan, D. (1991). *The great divide.* New York: Poseidon Press. [11]

Evans, G. W., & Lepore, S. J. (1993). Household crowding and social support: A quasiexperimental analysis. *Journal of Personality and Social Psychology, 65*, 308–316. [17]

Evans, M. D., Hollon, S. D., DeRubeis, R. J., Piasecki, J. M., Grove, W. M., Garvey, M. J., & Tuason, V. B. (1992). Differential relapse following cognitive therapy and pharmacotherapy for depression. *Archives of General Psychiatry, 49*, 802–808. [15]

Ewin, D. M. (1992). Hypnotherapy for warts (Verruca Vulgaris): 41 consecutive cases with 33 cures. *American Journal of Clinical Hypnosis, 35*, 1–10. [4]

Exner, J. E. (1993). *The Rorschach: A comprehensive system: Vol. 1. Basic foundations* (3rd ed.). New York: Wiley.

Eyeferth, K. (1961). Leistungen verschiedener Gruppen von Besatzungskindern in Hamburg-Wechsler Intelligenztest für Kinder (HAWIK). *Archir für die Gesamte Psychologie, 113*, 224–241. [7]

Eysenck, H. J. (1981). *A model for personality.* Berlin: Springer-Verlag. [12]

Eysenck, H. J. (1990). Genetic and environmental contributions to individual differences: The three major dimensions of personality. *Journal of Personality, 58*, 245–261. [12]

Eysenck, H. J. (1994). The outcome problem in psychotherapy: What have we learned? *Behaviour Research and Therapy, 32*, 477–495. [15]

Eysenck, H. J., & Eysenck, S. B. G. (1975). *Manual for the Eysenck Personality Questionnaire.* San Diego: Educational and Industrial Testing Service. [12]

Fackelmann, K. (1995). Mice show Alzeimer brain plaques. *Science News, 147*, 84. [2, 9]

Faedda, G. L., Tondo, L., Teicher, M. H., Baldessarini, R. J., Gelbard, H. A., & Floris, G. F. (1993). Seasonal mood disorders: Patterns of seasonal recurrence in mania and depression. *Archives of General Psychiatry, 50*, 17–23. [14]

Fagot, B. I. (1982). Adults as socializing agents. In T. M. Field (Ed.), *Review of human development.* New York: Wiley. [11]

Fagot, B. I., Leinbach, M. D., & O'Boyle, C. (1992). Gender labeling, gender stereotyping, and parenting behaviors. *Developmental Psychology, 28*, 225–230. [11]

Fairburn, C. G., Jones, R., Peveler, R. C., Hope, R. A., & O'Connor, M. (1993). Psychotherapy and bulimia nervosa. *Archives of General Psychiatry, 50*, 419–428. [10, 15]

Fajardo, D. M. (1985). Author race, essay quality, and reverse discrimination. *Journal of Applied Social Psychology, 15*, 255–268. [17]

Falbo, T., & Polit, D. F. (1986). Quantitative review of the only child literature: Research evidence and theory development. *Psychological Bulletin, 100*, 176–189. [10]

Falloon, I. R. H. (1988). Expressed emotion: Current status. *Psychological Medicine, 18*, 269–274. [15]

Famighetti, R. (Ed). (1994). *The world almanac and book of facts 1995.* New York: Funk & Wagnalls. [9, 11]

Fantz, R. L. (1961). The origin of form perception. *Scientific American, 204*, 66–72. [8]

Faravelli, C., & Pallanti, S. (1989). Recent life events and panic disorder. *American Journal of Psychiatry, 146*, 622–626. [14]

Farbman, A. I. (1992). *Cell biology of olfaction.* New York: Cambridge University Press. [3]

Farrer, L. A., & Cupples, A. (1994). Estimating the probability for major gene Alzheimer disease. *American Journal of Human Genetics, 54,* 374–383. [9]

Faust, D., & Ziskin, J. (1988). The expert witness in psychology and psychiatry. *Science, 241,* 32–35. [17]

Fausto-Sterling, A. (1985). *Myths of gender.* New York: Basic Books. [11]

Faw, H. W. (1990). Memory for names and faces: A fair comparison. *American Journal of Psychology, 103,* 317–326. [6]

Fawcett, J. C. (1992). Intrinsic neuronal determinants of regeneration. *Trends in Neurosciences, 15,* 5–8. [2]

Fay, R. E., Turner, C. F., Klassen, A. D., & Gagnon, J. H. (1989). Prevalence and patterns of same-gender sexual contact among men. Science, 243, 338–348. [11]

Fazio, R. H. (1989). On the power and functionality of attitudes: The role of attitude accessibility. In A. R. Pratkanis, S. J. Breckler, & A. G. Greenwald (Eds.), *Attitude structure and function* (pp. 153–179). Hillsdale, NJ: Erlbaum. [16]

Fazio, R. H., & Williams, C. J. (1986). Attitude accessibility as a moderator of the attitude perception and attitude-behavior relations: An investigation of the 1984 presidential election. *Journal of Personality and Social Psychology, 51,* 505–514. [16]

Feingold, A. (1988). Matching for attractiveness in romantic partners and same-sex friends: A meta-analysis and theoretical critique. *Psychological Bulletin, 104,* 226–235. [16]

Feingold, A. (1990). Gender differences in effects of physical attractiveness on romantic attraction: A comparison across five research paradigms. *Journal of Personality and Social Psychology, 59,* 981–993. [16]

Feingold, A. (1992). Good-looking people are not what we think. *Psychological Bulletin, 111,* 304–341. [16]

Female victims: The crime goes on. (1984). *Science News, 126,* 153. [11]

Fenton, W. S., & McGlashan, T. H. (1991). Natural history of schizophrenia subtypes: I. Longitudinal study of paranoid, hebephrenic, and undifferentiated schizophrenia. *Archives of General Psychiatry, 48,* 969–977. [14]

Fenton, W. S., & McGlashan, T. H. (1994). Antecedents, symptom progression, and long-term outcome of the deficit syndrome in schizophrenia. *American Journal of Psychiatry, 151,* 351–356. [14]

Ferber, R. (1989). Sleepwalking, confusional arousals, and sleep terrors in the child. In M. H. Kryger, T. Roth, & W. C. Dement (Eds.), *Principles and practice of sleep medicine* (pp. 640–642). Philadelphia: W.B. Saunders. [4]

Fernandez, A., & Glenberg, A. M. (1985). Changing environmental context does not reliably affect memory. *Memory and Cognition, 13,* 333–345. [6]

Festinger, L. (1957). *A theory of cognitive dissonance.* Evanston, IL: Row, Peterson. [16]

Festinger, L., & Carlsmith, J. M. (1959). Cognitive consequences of forced compliance. *Journal of Abnormal and Social Psychology, 58,* 203–210. [16]

Festinger, L., Schachter, S., & Back, K. (1950). *Social pressures in informal groups: A study of a housing community.* New York: Harper & Row. [16]

Fiatarone, M. A., Morley, J. E., Bloom, E. T., Benton, D., Makinodan, T., & Solomon, G. F. (1988). Endogenous opioids and the exercise-induced augmentation of natural killer cell activity. *Journal of Laboratory and Clinical Medicine, 112,* 544–552. [13]

Fiatarone, M. A., O'Neill, E. F., Ryan, N. D., Clements, K. M., Solares, G. R., Nelson, M. E., Roberts, S. B., Kehayias, J. J., Lipsitz, L. A., & Evans, W. J. (1994). Exercise training and nutritional supplementation for physical frailty in very elderly people. *New England Journal of Medicine, 330,* 1769–1775. [9]

Field, T. (1991). Quality infant day care and grade school behavior and performance. *Child Development, 62,* 863–870. [8]

Field, T. M., Cohen, D., Garcia, R., & Greenberg, R. (1984). Mother-stranger face discrimination by the newborn. *Infant Behavior and Development, 7,* 19–25. [8]

Fields, H. L. (1978, November). Secrets of the placebo. *Psychology Today,* p. 172. [3]

Finchilescu, G. (1988). Interracial contact in South Africa within the nursing context. *Journal of Applied Social Psychology, 18,* 1207–1221. [16]

Finke, R. A. (1985). Theories relating mental imagery to perception. *Psychological Bulletin, 98,* 236–259. [7]

Fiorito, G., & Scotto, P. (1992). Observational learning in *Octopus vulgaris. Science, 256,* 545–547. [5]

Firestein, S. (1991). A noseful of odor receptors. *Trends in Neurosciences, 14,* 270–272. [3]

Fischbach, G. D. (1992). Mind and brain. *Scientific American, 267,* 48–56. [2, 6]

Fisher, W. A., & Grenier, G. (1994). Violent pornography, antiwoman thoughts, and antiwoman acts: In search of reliable effects. *Journal of Sex Research, 31,* 23–38. [11]

Fitzgerald, L. F. (1993). Sexual harassment: Violence against women in the workplace. *American Psychologist, 48,* 1070–1076. [17]

Flavell, J. H. (1985). *Cognitive development.* Englewood, NJ: Prentice-Hall. [8]

Flavell, J. H. (1992). Cognitive development: Past, present, and future. *Developmental Psychology, 28,* 998–1005. [8, 9]

Fleming, J. D. (1974, July). Field report: The state of the apes. *Psychology Today,* pp. 31–46. [7]

Fletcher, A. C., Darling, N. E., Steinberg, L., & Dornbusch, S. M. (1995). The company they keep: Relation of adolescents' adjustment and behavior to their friends' perceptions of authoritative parenting in the social network. *Developmental Psychology, 31,* 300–311. [9]

Fleury, B. (1992). Sleep apnea syndrome in the elderly. *Sleep, 15,* S39–S41. [4]

Flood, J. F., Silver, A. J., & Morley, J. E. (1990). Do peptide-induced changes in feeding occur because of changes in motivation to eat? *Peptides, 11,* 265–270. [10]

Fluoxetine Bulimia Nervosa Collaborative Study Group. (1992). Fluoxetine in the treatment of bulimia nervosa: A multicenter, placebo-controlled, double-blind trial. *Archives of General Psychiatry, 49,* 139–147. [9]

Flying and alcohol do not mix. (1990, March 19). *Newsweek,* p. 27. [4]

Flynn, J. R. (1980). *Race, IQ, and Jensen.* London: Temple Smith. [7]

Flynn, J. R. (1987a). Massive IQ gains in 14 nations: What IQ tests really measure. *Psychological Bulletin, 101,* 171–191. [7]

Flynn, J. R. (1987b). Race and IQ: Jensen's case refuted. In S. Modgil, & C. Modgil (Eds.), *Arthur Jensen: Consensus and controversy.* New York: Palmer Press. [7]

Foa, E. B. (1995). How do treatments for obsessive-compulsive disorder compare? *Harvard Mental Health Letter, 12*(1), 8. [15]

Fogelman, E., & Wiener, V. L. (1985, August). The few, the brave, the noble. *Psychology Today,* pp. 60–65. [16]

Folkard, S. (1990). Circadian performance rhythms: Some practical and theoretical implications. Philosophical Transactions of the Royal Society of London. Series B: *Biological Sciences, 327,* 543–553. [4]

Folkman, S. (1984). Personal control and stress and coping processes: A theoretical analysis. *Journal of Personality and Social Psychology, 46,* 839–852. [13]

Folkman, S., & Lazarus, R. S. (1980). An analysis of coping in a middle-aged community sample. *Journal of Health and Social Behavior, 21,* 219–239. [13]

Fondacaro, M. R., & Heller, K. (1990). Attributional style in aggressive adolescent boys. *Journal of Abnormal Child Psychology, 18,* 75–89. [16]

Fontham, E. T. H., Correa, P., Reynolds, P., Wu-Williams, A., Buffler, P. A., Greenberg, R. S., Chen, V. W., Alterman, T., Boyd, P., Austin, D. F., & Liff, J. (1994). Environmental tobacco smoke and lung cancer in nonsmoking women: A multicenter study. *Journal of the American Medical Association, 271,* 1752–1759. [13]

Ford, C. S., & Beach, F. A. (1951). *Patterns of sexual behavior.* New York: Harper & Row. [11]

Ford, M. E. (1979). The construct validity of egocentrism. *Psychological Bulletin, 86,* 1169–1188. [8]

Forgas, J. P., & Bower, G. H. (1987). Mood effects on person-perception judgments. *Journal of Personality and Social Psychology, 53,* 53–60. [16]

Forge, A., Li, L., Corwin, J. T., & Nevill, G. (1993). Ultrastructural evidence for hair cell regeneration in the mammalian inner ear. *Science, 259,* 1616–1619. [3]

Fowles, D. C. (1992). Schizophrenia: Diathesis-stress revisited. *Annual Review of Psychology, 43,* 303–336. [14]

Fox, N. A., & Bell, M. A. (1990). Electrophysiological indices of frontal lobe development: Relations to cognitive and affective behavior in human infants over the first year of life. *Annals of the New York Academy of Sciences, 608,* 677–698. [8]

Frackowiak, R. S. J. (1994). Functional mapping of verbal memory and language. *Trends in Neurosciences, 17,* 109–115. [6]

Frank, E., Anderson, B., Reynolds, C. F., III, Ritenour, A., & Kupfer, D. J. (1994). Life events and the research diagnostic criteria endogenous subtype. *Archives of General Psychiatry, 51,* 519–524. [14]

Frank, E., Kupfer, D. J., Wagner, E. F., McEachran, A. B., & Cornes, C. (1991). Efficacy of interpersonal psychotherapy as a maintenance treatment of recurrent depression: Contributing factors. *Archives of General Psychiatry, 48,* 1053–1059. [15]

Franz, C. E., McClelland, D. C., & Weinberger, J. (1991). Childhood antecedents of conventional social accomplishment in midlife adults: A 36-year prospective study. *Journal of Personality and Social Psychology, 60,* 586–595. [8]

Fraser, A. M., Brockert, J. E., & Ward, R. H. (1995). Association of young maternal age with adverse reproductive outcomes. *New England Journal of Medicine, 332,* 1113–1117. [9]

Freedman, J. L. (1984). Effects of television violence on aggressiveness. *Psychological Bulletin, 96,* 227–246. [16]

Freedman, J. L., & Fraser, S. C. (1966). Compliance without pressure: The foot-in-the-door technique. *Journal of Personality and Social Psychology, 4,* 195–202. [16]

Freeman, W. J. (1991). The physiology of perception. *Scientific American, 264,* 78–85. [3]

Freese, A. S. (1977). *The miracle of vision.* New York: Harper & Row. [3]

Freese, A. S. (1980, February). Hypnosis: A weapon against super-medicine, surgery? *Science Digest,* pp. 20–24. [4]

French, C. C., Fowler, M., McCarthy, K., & Peers, D. (1991). Belief in astrology: A test of the Barnum effect. *Skeptical Inquirer, 15,* 166–172. [12]

French, E. G. (1955). Some characteristics of achievement motivation. *Journal of Experimental Psychology, 50,* 232–236. [10]

Freud, A. (1958). *Adolescence: Psychoanalytic study of the child* (Vol. 13). New York: Academic Press. [9]

Freud, A. (1966). *The ego and the mechanisms of defense* (rev. ed.). New York: International Universities Press. [12]

Freud, S. (1922). *Beyond the pleasure principle.* London: International Psychoanalytic Press. [6]

Freud, S. (1953a). The interpretation of dreams. In J. Strachey (Ed. and Trans.), *The standard edition of the complete psychological works of Sigmund Freud* (Vols. 4 and 5). London: Hogarth Press. (Original work published 1900). [12]

Freud, S. (1953b). Three essays on the theory of sexuality. In J. Strachey (Ed. and Trans.), *The standard edition of the complete psychological works of Sigmund Freud* (Vol. 7). London: Hogarth Press. (Original work published 1905). [12]

Freud, S. (1960). Psychopathology of everyday life. In J. Strachey (Ed. and Trans.), *The standard edition of the complete psychological works of Sigmund Freud* (Vol. 6). London: Hogarth Press. (Original work published 1901). [12]

Freud, S. (1961). The ego and the id. In H. Strachey (Ed. and Trans.), *The standard edition of the complete psychological works of Sigmund Freud* (Vol. 19). London: Hogarth Press. (Original work published 1923). [12]

Freud, S. (1962). *Civilization and its discontents* (J. Strachey, Trans.). New York: W.W. Norton. (Original work published 1930). [12]

Freud, S. (1963a). *An autobiographical study* (J. Strachey, Trans.). New York: W.W. Norton. (Original work published 1925). [12, 15]

Freud, S. (1963b). *A general introduction to psycho-analysis* (J. Riviere, Trans.). New York: Simon & Schuster. (Original work published 1920). [12, 15]

Freud, S. (1965). *New introductory lectures on psychoanalysis* (J. Strachey, Trans.). New York: W. W. Norton. (Original work published 1933). [12]

Frey-Hewitt, B., Vranizan, K. M., Dreon, D. M., & Wood, P. D. (1990). The effect of weight loss by dieting or exercise on resting metabolic rate in overweight men. *International Journal of Obesity, 14,* 327–334. [10]

Friday, N. (1980). *Men in love.* New York: Delacorte. [11]

Friedberg, J. M. (1976). *Shock treatment is not good for your brain.* San Francisco: Glide. [15]

Friedland, N., Keinan, G., & Regev, Y. (1992). Controlling the uncontrollable: Effects of stress on illusory perceptions of controllability. *Journal of Personality and Social Psychology, 63,* 923–931. [13]

Friedman, H. S., Tucker, J. S., Schwartz, J. E., Tomlinson-Keasey, C., Martin, L. R., Wingard, D. L., & Criqui, M. H. (1995). Psychosocial and behavioral predictors of longevity: The aging and death of the "Termites." *American Psychologist, 50,* 69–78. [9]

Friedman, H. S., Tucker, J. S., Tomlinson-Keasey, C., Schwartz, J. E., Wingard, D. L., & Criqui, M. H. (1993). Does childhood personality predict longevity? *Journal of Personality and Social Psychology, 65,* 176–185. [9]

Friedman, A. J., Zhang, Y., et al. (1994). Positional cloning of the mouse *obese* gene and its human homologue. *Nature, 372,* 425–432. [10]

Friedman, M., & Rosenman, R. H. (1974). *Type A behavior and your heart.* New York: Fawcett. [13]

Friedman, M. I., Tordoff, M. G., & Ramirez, I. (1986). Integrated metabolic control of food intake. *Brain Research Bulletin, 17,* 855–859. [10]

Friedman, R. C., & Downey, J. (1993). Neurobiology and sexual orientation: Current relationships. *Journal of Neuropsychiatry, 5,* 131–153. [11]

Fujita, F., Diener, E., & Sandvik, E. (1991). Gender differences in negative affect and well-being: The case for emotional intensity. *Journal of Personality and Social Psychology, 61,* 427–434. [10]

Fuligni, A. J., & Stevenson, H. W. (1995). Time use and mathematics achievement among American, Chinese, and Japanese high school students. *Child Development, 66,* 830–842. [7]

Funder, D. C., & Colvin, C. R. (1991). Explorations in behavioral consistency: Properties of persons, situations, and behaviors. *Journal of Personality and Social Psychology, 60,* 773–794. [12]

Furstenberg, F. F., Jr., Brooks-Gunn, J., & Chase-Lansdale, L. (1989). Teenaged pregnancy and childbearing. *American Psychologist, 44,* 313–320. [9]

Fyer, A. J. (1993). Heritability of social anxiety: A brief review. *Journal of Clinical Psychiatry, 54*(12, Suppl.), 10–12. [14]

Fyer, A. J., Mannuzza, S., Chapman, T. F., Liebowitz, M. R., & Klein, D. F. (1993). A direct interview family study of social phobia. *Archives of General Psychiatry, 50,* 286–293. [14]

Gabrenya, W. K., Jr., Latané, B., & Wang, Y-E. (1983). Social loafing in cross-cultural perspective. *Journal of Cross-Cultural Psychology, 14,* 368–384. [16]

Gackenbach, J., & Bosveld, J. (1989, October). Take control of your dreams. *Psychology Today,* pp. 27–32. [4]

Gaertner, S. L., & Dovidio, J. F. (1986). The aversive form of racism. In J. F. Dovidio & S. L. Gaertner (Eds.), *Prejudice, discrimination, and racism* (pp. 61–89). San Diego, CA: Academic Press. [16]

Gaertner, S. L., Mann, J. A., Dovidio, J. F., & Murrell, A. J. (1990). How does cooperation reduce intergroup bias? *Journal of Personality and Social Psychology, 59,* 692–704. [16]

Gaertner, S. L., Mann, J. A., Murrell, A., & Dovidio, J. F. (1989). Reducing intergroup bias: The benefits of recategorization. *Journal of Personality and Social Psychology, 57,* 239–249. [16]

Gagnon, J. H, & Simon, W. (1973). *Sexual conduct: The social origins of human sexuality.* Chicago: Aldine. [11]

Galanter, M. (1993). *Network therapy for alcohol and drug abuse.* New York: Basic Books. [13]

Gallup, G., Jr., & Hugick, L. (1990). Racial tolerance grows, progress on racial equality less evident. *Gallup Poll Monthly,* No. 297, 23–32. [16]

Gallup, G., Jr., & Newport, F. (1990a). The battle of the bulge: Americans continue to fight it. *Gallup Poll Monthly,* No. 303, 23–34. [10]

Gallup, G., Jr., & Newport, F. (1990b). Belief in psychic and paranormal phenomena widespread among Americans. *Gallup Poll Monthly,* No. 299, 35–43. [3]

Gallup, G. H., Jr., & Newport, F. (1990c). Virtually all adults want children, but many of the reasons are intangible. *Gallup Poll Monthly,* No. 297, 8–22. [9]

Galton, F. (1874). *English men of science: Their nature and nurture.* London: Macmillan [7]

Galton, F. (1875). The history of twins as a criterion of the relative powers of nature and nurture. *Journal of the Royal Anthropological Institute, 5,* 391–406. [7]

Gamble, T. J., & Zigler, E. (1986). Effects of infant day care: Another look at the evidence. *American Journal of Orthopsychiatry, 56,* 26–42. [8]

Gannon, L., Luchetta, R., Rhodes, K., Paradie, L., & Segrist, D. (1992). Sex bias in psychological research: Progress or complacency? *American Psychologist, 47,* 389–396. [1]

Garcia, J., & Koelling, A. (1966). Relation of cue to consequence in avoidance learning. *Psychonomic Science, 4,* 123–124. [5]

Gardner, H. (1975). *The shattered mind: The person after brain damage.* New York: Knopf. [2]

Gardner, H. (1981, February). How the split brain gets a joke. *Psychology Today,* pp. 74–78. [2]

Gardner, H. (1983). *Frames of mind: The theory of multiple intelligence.* New York: Basic Books. [7]

Gardner, L. I. (1972). Deprivation dwarfism. *Scientific American, 227,* 76–82. [8]

Gardner, R. A., & Gardner, B. T. (1969). Teaching sign language to a chimpanzee. *Science, 165,* 664–672. [7]

Garland, A. F., & Zigler, E. (1993). Adolescent suicide prevention: Current research and social policy implications. *American Psychologist, 48,* 169–182. [14]

Gastil, J. (1990). Generic pronouns and sexist language: The oxymoronic character of masculine generics. *Sex Roles, 23,* 629–643. [7]

Gates, A. I. (1917). Recitation as a factor in memorizing. *Archives of Psychology, 40.* [6]

Gatz, M., & Pearson, C. G. (1988). Ageism revised and the provision of psychological services. *American Psychologist, 43,* 184–188. [9]

Gauguelin, M. (1982). Zodiac and personality: An empirical study. *The Skeptical Inquirer, 6,* 57–65. [12]

Gawin, F. H. (1991). Cocaine addiction: Psychology and neurophysiology. *Science, 251,* 1580–1586. [4]

Gawin, F. H., & Ellinwood, E. H., Jr. (1988). Cocaine and other stimulants: Actions, abuse, and treatment. *New England Journal of Medicine, 318,* 1173–1182. [4]

Gazzaniga, M. S. (1970). *The bisected brain.* New York: Appleton-Century-Crofts. [2]

Gazzaniga, M. S. (1983). Right hemisphere language following brain bisection: A 20-year perspective. *American Psychologist, 38,* 525–537. [2]

Gazzaniga, M. S. (1989). Organization of the human brain. *Science, 245,* 947–952. [2]

Geary, N. (1987). Cocaine: Animal research studies. In H. I. Spitz & J. S. Rosecan (Eds.), *Cocaine abuse: New directions in treatment and research* (pp. 19–47). New York: Brunner/Mazel. [4]

Gebhardt, D. L., & Crump, C. E. (1990). Employee fitness and wellness programs in the workplace. *American Psychologist, 45,* 262–272. [17]

Geen, R. G. (1978). Some effects of observing violence upon the behavior of the observer. In B. A. Maher (Ed.), *Progress in experimental personality research* (Vol. 8). New York: Academic Press. [16]

Geen, R. G. (1984). Human motivation: New perspectives on old problems. In A. M. Rogers & C. J. Scheier (Eds.), *The G. Stanley Hall lecture series* (Vol. 4). Washington, DC: American Psychological Association. [10]

Geiselman, R. E., Haight, N. A., & Kimata, L. G. (1984). Context effects on the perceived physical attractiveness of faces. *Journal of Experimental Social Psychology, 20,* 409–424. [16]

George, M. S., Ketter, T. A., & Post, R. M. (1993). SPECT and PET imaging in mood disorders. *Journal of Clinical Psychiatry, 54*(11, Suppl.), 6–13. [14]

Geschwind, N. (1979). Specializations of the human brain. *Science, 241,* 180–199. [2]

Geschwind, N., & Behan, P. O. (1982). Left handedness: Association with immune disease, migraine, and developmental learning disorders. *Proceedings of the National Academy of Sciences, 79,* 5097–5100. [2]

Gibbons, A. (1991). Déjà vu all over again: Chimp-language wars. *Science, 251,* 1561–1562. [7]

Gibbs, N. R. (1988, February 22). Grays on the go. *Time,* pp. 66–75. [9]

Gibbs, N. R. (1991, June 3). When is it rape? *Time,* pp. 48–54. [11]

Gibson, E., & Walk, R. D. (1960). The "visual cliff." *Scientific American, 202,* 64–71. [8]

Gifford, R. (1991). The environmental psychologist. In R. Gifford (Ed.), *Applied psychology: Variety and opportunity* (pp. 327–352). Boston: Allyn & Bacon. [17]

Gilbert, P. L., Harris, J., McAdams, L. A., & Jeste, D. V. (1995). Neuroleptic withdrawal in schizophrenic patients: A review of the literature. *Archives of General Psychiatry, 52,* 173–188. [15]

Giles, D. E., Jarrett, R. B., Biggs, M. M., Guzick, D. S., & Rush, A. J. (1989). *Clinical predictors of recurrence in depression. American Journal of Psychiatry, 146,* 764–767. [14]

Gilligan, C. (1982). *In a different voice: Psychological theory and women's development.* Cambridge, MA: Harvard University Press. [9]

Ginty, D. D., Kornhauser, J. M., Thompson, M. A., Bading, H., Mayo, K. E., Takahashi, J. S., & Greenberg, M. E. (1993). Regulation of CREB phosphorylation in the suprachiasmatic nucleus by light and a circadian clock. *Science, 260,* 238–241. [4]

Gladue, B. A. (1991). Aggressive behavioral characteristics, hormones, and sexual orientation in men and women. *Aggressive Behavior, 17,* 313–326. [11]

Glass, D. C., & Singer, J. E. (1972). *Urban stress: Experiments in noise and social stressors.* New York: Academic Press. [13]

Glass, J., & Fujimoto, T. (1994). Housework, paid work, and depression among husbands and wives. *Journal of Health and Social Behavior, 35,* 179–191. [9]

Glassman, A. H. (1993a). Cigarette smoking: Implications for psychiatric illness. *American Journal of Psychiatry, 150,* 546–553. [13]

Glassman, A. H. (1993b). What is the relationship between depression and cigarette smoking? *Harvard Mental Health Letter, 10*(4), 8. [13]

Glazer, W. M., Morgenstern, H., & Doucette, J. T. (1993). Predicting the long-term risk of tardive dyskinesia in outpatients maintained on neuroleptic medications. *Journal of Clinical Psychiatry, 54,* 133–139. [15]

Glickstein, M. (1988). The discovery of the visual cortex. *Scientific American, 259,* 118–127. [2]

Glover, J. A., & Corkill, A. J. (1987). Influence of paraphrased repetitions on the spacing effect. *Journal of Educational Psychology, 79,* 198–199. [6]

Godden, D. R., & Baddeley, A. D. (1975). Context-dependent memory in two natural environments: On land and underwater. *British Journal of Psychology, 66,* 325–331. [6]

Godden, D. R., & Baddeley, A. D. (1980). When does context influence recognition memory? *British Journal of Psychology, 71,* 99–104. [6]

Gold, M. S. (1986). *800-cocaine* (rev.). Toronto: Bantam. [4]

Gold, M. S. (1994). The epidemiology, attitudes, and pharmacology of LSD use in the 1990s. *Psychiatric Annals, 24,* 124–126. [4]

Goldberg, J. (1988). *Anatomy of a scientific discovery.* New York: Bantam. [3]

Goldberg, J., True, W. R., Eisen, S. A., & Henderson, W. G. (1990). A twin study of the effects of the Vietnam War on posttraumatic stress disorder. *Journal of the American Medical Association, 263,* 1227–1232. [13]

Goldberg, L. R. (1993). The structure of phenotypic personality traits. *American Psychologist, 48,* 26–34. [12]

Goldberg, P. A. (1965). A review of sentence completion methods in personality. In B. I. Murstein (Ed.), *Handbook of projective techniques.* New York: Basic Books. [12]

Goldbloom, D. S., & Olmsted, M. P. (1993). Pharmacotherapy of bulimia nervosa with fluoxetine: Assessment of clinically significant attitudinal change. *American Journal of Psychiatry, 150,* 770–774. [10]

Goldenberg, H. (1977). *Abnormal psychology: A social/community approach.* Monterey, CA: Brooks/Cole. [14]

Goldman, A. L. (1991, April 10). Portrait of religion in U.S. holds dozens of surprises. *The New York Times,* pp. A1, A11. [13]

Goldman, M. S. (1983). Cognitive impairment in chronic alcoholics: Some cause for optimism. *American Psychologist, 38,* 1045–1054. [13]

Goldman-Rakic, P. S. (1992). Working memory and the mind. *Scientific American, 267,* 110–117. [6]

Goldsmith, H. H., Buss, A. H., Plomin, R., Rothbart, M. K., Thomas, A., Chess, S., Hinde, R. A., & McCall, R. B. (1987). Roundtable: What is temperament? Four approaches. *Child Development, 58,* 504–529. [8]

Goldstein, A., & Kalant, H. (1990). Drug policy: Striking the right balance. *Science, 249,* 1513–1521. [13]

Goleman, D. (1979, November). Positive denial: The case for not facing reality. *Psychology Today,* pp. 13, 44–60. [13]

Goleman, D. (1991, September 17). Non-verbal cues are easy to misinterpret. *The New York Times,* pp. C1, C9. [16]

Goleman, D., Kaufman, P., & Ray, M. (1992). *The creative spirit.* New York: Dutton. [7]

Gonzalez, R., Ellsworth, P. C., & Pembroke, M. (1993). Response biases in lineups and showups. *Journal of Personality and Social Psychology, 64,* 525–537. [6]

Goode, E. E. (1987, September 28). For a little peace of mine. *U.S. News & World Report,* pp. 98–102. [15]

Goodglass, H. (1993). *Understanding aphasia.* San Diego, CA: Academic Press. [2]

Goodwin, D. W. (1985). Alcoholism and genetics: The sins of the fathers. *Archives of General Psychiatry, 42,* 171–174. [13]

Goodwin, D. W. (1986). *Anxiety.* New York: Oxford University Press. [14, 15]

Gordon, N. P., Cleary, P. D., Parlan, C. E., & Czeisler, C. A. (1986). The prevalence and health impact of shiftwork. *American Journal of Public Health, 76,* 1225–1228. [4]

Gorman, C. (1988, March 21). An outbreak of sensationalism. *Time,* pp. 58–59. [11]

Gorman, E. M. (1991). Anthropological reflections on the HIV epidemic among gay men. *Journal of Sex Research, 28,* 263–273. [11]

Gorman, J. M., Liebowitz, M. R., Fyer, A. J., & Stein, J. (1989). A Neuroanatomical hypothesis for panic disorder. *American Journal of Psychiatry, 146,* 148–161. [14]

Gormezano, I. (1984). The study of associative learning with CS-CR paradigms. In D. L. Alkon & J. Farley (Eds.), *Primary neural substrates of learning and behavioral change* (pp. 5–24). New York: Cambridge University Press. [5]

Gottesman, I. I. (1991). *Schizophrenia genesis: The origins of madness.* New York: W. H. Freeman. [14]

Gough, H. (1987). *California Psychological Inventory: Administrator's Guide.* Palo Alto: Consulting Psychologists Press. [12]

Graeber, R. C. (1989). Jet lag and sleep disruption. In M. H. Kryger, T. Roth, & W. C. Dement (Eds.), *Principles and practice of sleep medicine* (pp. 324–331). Philadelphia: W.B. Saunders. [4]

Graham, S. (1992). "Most of the subjects were white and middle class": Trends in published research on African Americans in selected APA journals, 1970–1989. *American Psychologist, 47,* 629–639. [1]

Grant, B. F., Harford, T. C., Chou, P., Pickering, M. S., Dawson, D. A., Stinson, F. S., & Noble, J. (1991). Prevalence of DSM-III-R alcohol abuse and dependence: United States, 1988. *Alcohol Health & Research World, 15,* 91–96. [13]

Greden, J. F. (1994). Introduction Part III. New agents for the treatment of depression. *Journal of Clinical Psychiatry, 55*(2, Suppl.), 32–33. [2, 14]

Green, B. L., Lindy, J. D., & Grace, M. C. (1985). Post-traumatic stress disorder: Toward DSM-IV. *Journal of Nervous and Mental Disorders, 173,* 406–411. [13]

Green, E., & Green, A. (1977). *Beyond biofeedback.* New York: Dell. [5]

Green, J., & Shellenberger, R. (1990). *The dynamics of health and wellness: A biopsychosocial approach.* Fort Worth: Holt, Rinehart & Winston. [13]

Green, R. (1985). Gender identity in childhood and later sexual orientation: Follow-up of 78 males. *American Journal of Psychiatry, 142,* 339. [11]

Green, R. (1987). *The "sissy boy syndrome" and the development of homosexuality.* New Haven: Yale University Press. [11]

Green, R., & Money, J. (1961). Effeminacy in pubertal boys. *Pediatrics, 27,* 236. [11]

Greenwald, A. G. (1992). New look 3: Unconscious cognition reclaimed. *American Psychologist, 47,* 766–779. [3, 12]

Greenwald, A. G., Spangenberg, E. R., Pratkanis, A. R., & Eskenazi, J. (1991). Double-blind tests of subliminal self-help audiotapes. *Psychological Science, 2,* 119–122. [3]

Greer, W. R. (1986, November 23). Violence against homosexuals rising, groups seeking wider protection say. *The New York Times,* p. 36. [11]

Gregory, R. L. (1978). *Eye and brain: The psychology of seeing* (3rd ed.). New York: McGraw-Hill. [3]

Greist, J. H., & Jefferson, J. W. (1984). *Depression and its treatment.* Washington, DC: American Psychiatric Press. [14, 15]

Greist, J. H., Jefferson, J. W., Kobak, K. A., Katzelnick, D. J., & Serlin, R. C. (1995). Efficacy and tolerability of serotonin transport inhibitors in obsessive-compulsive disorder: A meta-analysis. *Archives of General Psychiatry, 52,* 53–60. [15]

Griffith, R. M., Miyago, O., & Tago, A. (1958). The universality of typical dreams: Japanese vs. Americans. *American Anthropologist, 60,* 1173–1179. [4]

Griffiths, P. D., Merry, J., Browning, M., Eisinger, A. J., Huntsman, R. G., Lord, E. J. A., Polani, P. E., Tanner, J. M., & Whitehouse, R. H. (1974). Homosexual women: An endocrine and psychological study. *Journal of Endocrinology, 63,* 549–556. [11]

Griffitt, W., Nelson, J., & Littlepage, G. (1972). Old age and response to agreement-disagreement. *Journal of Gerontology, 27,* 269–274. [16]

Grinker, J. A. (1982). Physiological and behavioral basis for human obesity. In D. W. Pfaff (Ed.), *The physiological mechanisms of motivation.* New York: Springer-Verlag. [10]

Grochowicz, P., Schedlowski, M., Husband, A., King, M., Hibberd, A., & Bowen, K. (1991). Behavioral conditioning prolongs heart allograft survival in rats. *Brain, Behavior, and Immunity, 5,* 349–356. [5]

Groninger, L. K., & Groninger, L. P. (1980). A comparison of recognition and savings as retrieval measures: A reexamination. *Bulletin of the Psychonomic Society, 15,* 263–266. [6]

Grossman, H. J. (Ed.). (1983). *Manual on terminology and classification in mental retardation.* Washington, DC: American Association on Mental Deficiency. [7]

Grossman, M., & Wood, W. (1993). Sex differences in intensity of emotional experience: A social role interpretation. *Journal of Personality and Social Psychology, 65,* 1010–1022. [10]

Grünbaum, A. (1994). Does psychoanalysis have a future? Doubtful. *Harvard Mental Health Letter, 11*(4), 3–6. [15]

Guilford, J. P. (1967). *The nature of human intelligence.* New York: McGraw-Hill. [7]

Guilford, J. P. (1988). Some changes in the Structure-of-Intellect model. *Educational and Psychological Measurement, 48,* 1–4. [7]

Guilleminault, C. (1993). 1. Amphetamines and narcolepsy: Use of the Stanford database. *Sleep, 16,* 199–201. [4]

Gunn, R. A., Montes, J. M., Toomey, K. E., Rolfs, R. T., Greenspan, J. R., Spitters, C. E., & Waterman, S. H. (1995). Syphilis in San Diego county 1983–1992: Crack cocaine, prostitution, and the limitations of partner notification. *Sexually Transmitted Diseases, 22,* 60–66. [11]

Gupta, D., & Vishwakarma, M. S. (1989). Toy weapons and firecrackers: A source of hearing loss. *Laryngoscope, 99,* 330–334. [3]

Guralnik, J. M., & Simonsick, E. M. (1993). Physical disability in older Americans. *Journals of Gerontology, 48*(Special Issue), 3–10. [9]

Gurin, J. (1989, June). Leaner, not lighter. *Psychology Today,* pp. 32–36. [10]

Gustavson, C. R., Garcia, J., Hankins, W. G., & Rusiniak, K. W. (1974). Coyote predation control by aversive conditioning. *Science, 184,* 581–583. [5]

Gutheil, T. G. (1993). True or false memories of sexual abuse? A forensic psychiatric view. *Psychiatric Annals, 23,* 527–531. [6]

Haaga, D. A. F., Dyck, M. J., & Ernst, D. (1991). Empirical status of cognitive theory of depression. Psychological Bulletin, 110, 215–236. [14]

Haber, R. N. (1980). How we perceive depth from flat pictures. *American Scientist, 68,* 370–380. [3]

Hackel, L. S., & Ruble, D. N. (1992). Changes in the marital relationship after the first baby is born: Predicting the impact of expectancy disconfirmation. *Journal of Personality and Social Psychology, 62,* 944–957. [9]

Hahn, W. K. (1987). Cerebral lateralization of function: From infancy through childhood. *Psychological Bulletin, 101,* 376–392. [2]

Halaas, J. L., Gajiwala, K. S., Maffei, M., Cohen, S. L., Chait, B. T., Rabinowitz, D., Lallone, R. L., Burley, S. K., & Friedman, J. M. (1995). Weight-reducing effects of the plasma protein encoded by the *obese* gene. *Science, 269,* 543–546. [10]

Hales, D. (1981). *The complete book of sleep: How your nights affect your days.* Reading, MA: Addison-Wesley. [4]

Halford, G. S. (1989). Reflections on 25 years of Piagetian cognitive developmental psychology, 1963–1988. *Human Development, 32,* 325–327. [8]

Hall, C. S., & Van de Castle, R. L. (1966). *The content analysis of dreams.* New York: Appleton-Century-Crofts. [4]

Hall, E. T. (1966). *The hidden dimension.* Garden City, NY: Doubleday. [17]

Hall, G. S. (1904). *Adolescence: Its psychology and its relations to physiology, anthropology, sex, crime, religion, and education* (Vol. 1). New York: Appleton-Century-Crofts. [9]

Hall, R. G., Sachs, D. P., Hall, S. M., & Benowitz, N. L. (1984). Two-year efficacy and safety of rapid smoking therapy in patients with cardiac and pulmonary disease. *Journal of Consulting and Clinical Psychology, 52,* 574–581. [15]

Hall, S. M., Muñoz, R. F., Reus, V. I., & Sees, K. L. (1993). Nicotine, negative affect, and depression. *Journal of Consulting and Clinical Psychology, 61,* 761–767. [13]

Halligan, P. W., & Marshall, J. C. (1994). Toward a principled explanation of unilateral neglect. *Cognitive Neuropsychology, 11,* 167–206. [2]

Halpern, D. F., & Coren, S. (1993). Left-handedness and life span: A reply to Harris. *Psychological Bulletin, 114,* 235–241. [2]

Hamer, D. H., Hu, S., Magnuson, V. L., Hu, N., & Pattatucci, A. M. L. (1993). A linkage between DNA markers on the X chromosome and male sexual orientation. *Science, 261,* 321–327. [11]

Hamilton, M. C. (1988). Using masculine generics: Does generic "he" increase male bias in the user's imagery? *Sex Roles, 19,* 785–789. [7]

Hammond, D. C. (1992). Hypnosis with sexual disorders. *American Journal of Preventive Psychiatry & Neurology, 3,* 37–41. [4]

Hancock, L. (1995, March 6). Breaking point. *Newsweek,* pp. 56–59. [17]

Hansel, C. E. M. (1966). *ESP: A scientific evaluation.* New York: Charles Scribner's Sons. [3]

Hansel, C. E. M. (1980). *ESP and parapsychology: A critical reevaluation.* Buffalo, NY: Prometheus. [3]

Hardman, M. L., Drew, C. J., Egan, M. W., & Wolf, B. (1990). *Human exceptionality: Society, school, and family* (3rd ed.). Boston: Allyn and Bacon. [3]

Hare, R. (1985). Comparison of procedures for the assessment of psychopathy. *Journal of Clinical Psychology, 53,* 7–16. [14]

Hare, R. D. (1970). *Psychopathy: Theory and research.* New York: Wiley. [14]

Harford, T. C., Parker, D. A., Grant, B. F., & Dawson, D. A. (1992). Alcohol use and dependence among employed men and women in the United States in 1988. *Alcoholism: Clinical and Experimental Research, 16,* 146–148. [13]

Hargrave, G. E., Hiatt, D., Ogard, E. M., & Karr, C. (1994). Comparison of the MMPI and the MMPI-2 for a sample of peace officers. *Psychological Assessment, 6,* 27–32. [12]

Harkins, S. G., & Jackson, J. M. (1985). The role of evaluation in eliminating social loafing. *Personality and Social Psychology Bulletin, 11,* 456–465. [16]

Harkins, S. G., & Szymanski, K. (1989). Social loafing and group evaluation. *Journal of Personality and Social Psychology, 56,* 941–943. [16]

Harlow, H. F. (1950). Learning and satiation of response in intrinsically motivated complex puzzle performance by monkeys. *Journal of Comparative and Physiological Psychology, 43,* 289–294. [10]

Harlow, H. F. (1953). Motivation as a factor in the acquisition of new responses. In M. R. Jones (Ed.), *Nebraska symposium on motivation.* Lincoln: University of Nebraska Press. [10]

Harlow, H. F. (1959). Love in infant monkeys. *Scientific American, 200,* 68–74. [8]

Harlow, H. F., & Harlow, M. K. (1962). Social deprivation in monkeys. *Scientific American, 207,* 137–146. [8]

Harlow, H. F., Harlow, M. K., and Suomi, S. J. (1971). From thought to therapy: Lessons from a primate laboratory. *American Scientist, 59,* 538–549. [8]

Harlow, J. M. (1848). Passage of an iron rod through the head. *Boston Medical and Surgical Journal, 39,* 389–393. [2]

Harper, R. A. (1975). *The new psychotherapies.* Englewood Cliffs, NJ: Prentice-Hall. [15]

Harrell, T. H., Honaker, M., & Parnell, T. (1992). Equivalence of the MMPI-2 with the MMPI in psychiatric patients. *Psychological Assessment, 4,* 460–465. [12]

Harris, L. J. (1993). Do left-handers die sooner than right-handers? Commentary on Coren and Halpern's (1991) "Left-handedness: A marker for decreased survival fitness." *Psychological Bulletin, 114,* 203–234. [2]

Harris, M. (1993). The best medicine. *West County Journal,* p. 1C. [13]

Harris, N. B. (1992). Sex, race, and experiences of aggression. *Aggressive Behavior, 18,* 201–217. [11]

Harris, P. L., & Bassett, E. (1975). Transitive inference by four year old children. *Developmental Psychology, 11,* 875–876. [8]

Harris, R. A., Brodie, M. S., & Dunwiddie, T. V. (1992). Possible substrates of ethanol reinforcement: GABA and dopamine. *Annals of the New York Academy of Sciences, 654,* 61–69. [4]

Harrison, J. R., & Barabasz, A. F. (1991). Effects of restricted environmental stimulation therapy on the behavior of children with autism. *Child Study Journal, 21,* 153–166. [10]

Harrower, M. (1976, July). Were Hitler's henchmen mad? *Psychology Today,* pp. 76–80. [12]

Hart, B., & Risley, T. R. (1992). American parenting of language-learning children: Persisting differences in family-child interactions observed in natural home environments. *Developmental Psychology, 28,* 1096–1105. [8]

Hartley, D., Roback, H. B., & Abramowitz, S. I. (1976). Deterioration effects in encounter groups. *American Psychologist, 31,* 247–255. [15]

Hartmann, E. (1967). *The biology of dreaming.* Springfield, IL: Charles C Thomas. [4]

Hartmann, E. (1981, April). The strangest sleep disorder. *Psychology Today,* pp. 14–18. [4]

Hartmann, E. (1988). Insomnia: Diagnosis and treatment. In R. L. Williams, I. Karacan, & C. A. Moore (Eds.), *Sleep disorders: Diagnosis and treatment* (pp. 29–46). New York: John Wiley. [4]

Hartmann, E. L. (1973). *The functions of sleep.* New Haven: Yale University Press. [4]

Hartup, W. W. (1989). Social relationships and their developmental significance. *American Psychologist, 44,* 120–126. [8]

Hasselmo, M. E., & Bower, J. M. (1993). Acetylcholine and memory. *Trends in Neurosciences, 16,* 218–222. [2]

Hassett, J. (1980, December). Acupuncture is proving its points. *Psychology Today,* 81–89. [3]

Hatfield, E., & Sprecher, S. (1986). *Mirror, mirror . . . The importance of looks in everyday life.* Albany, NY: State University of New York Press. [16]

Hauri, P. (1982). *The sleep disorders* (2nd ed.). Kalamazoo, MI: Upjohn. [4]

Hauser, M. D. (1993). Right hemisphere dominance for the production of facial expression in monkeys. *Science, 261,* 475–477. [2]

Hawkins, J. D., Catalano, R. F., & Miller, J. Y. (1992). Risk and protective factors for alcohol and other drug problems in adolescence and early adulthood: Implications for substance abuse prevention. *Psychological Bulletin, 112,* 64–105. [4]

Hay, D. F. (1994). Prosocial development. *Journal of Child Psychology and Psychiatry, 35,* 29–71. [16]

Hayes, C. (1951). *The ape in our house.* New York: Harper & Row. [7]

Hayes, C. (Ed.). (1987). *Risking the future: Adolescent sexuality, pregnancy, and childbearing* (Vol. 1.). Washington, DC: National Academy Press. [9]

Hebb, D. O. (1949). *The organization of behavior.* New York: John Wiley & Sons. [6]

Hedges, L. B., & Nowell, A. (1995). Sex differences in mental test scores, variability, and numbers of high-scoring individuals. *Science, 269,* 41–45. [11]

Hefez, A., Metz, L., & Lavie, P. (1987). Long-term effects of extreme situational stress on sleep and dreaming. *American Journal of Psychiatry, 144,* 344–347. [4]

Heikkinen, M., Aro, H., & Lönnqvist, J. (1993). Life events and social support in suicide. *Suicide and Life-Threatening Behavior, 23,* 343–358. [14]

Heilman, K. M., Scholes, R., & Watson, R. T. (1975). Auditory affective agnosia: Disturbed comprehension of affective speech. *Journal of Neurology, Neurosurgery and Psychiatry, 38,* 69–72. [2]

Heimberg, R. G. (1993). Specific issues in the cognitive-behavioral treatment of social phobia. *Journal of Clinical Psychiatry, 54*(12, Suppl.), 38–46. [15]

Heinrich, R. K., Corbine, J. L., & Thomas, K. R. (1990). Counseling Native Americans. *Journal of Counseling and Development, 69,* 128–133. [15]

Heinrichs, R. W. (1993). Schizophrenia and the brain: Conditions for a neuropsychology of madness. *American Psychologist, 48,* 221–233. [14]

Heller, W. (1990, May/June). Of one mind: Second thoughts about the brain's dual nature. *The Sciences, 30,* 38–44. [2]

Hellige, J. B. (1990). Hemispheric asymmetry. *Annual Review of Psychology, 41,* 55–80. [2]

Hellige, J. B. (1993). *Hemispheric asymmetry: What's right and what's left.* Cambridge, MA: Harvard University Press. [2]

Hellige, J. B., Bloch, M. I., Cowin, E. L., Eng, T. L., Eviatar, Z., & Sergent, V. (1994). Individual variation in hemispheric asymmetry: Multitask study of effects related to handedness and sex. *Journal of Experimental Psychology: General, 123,* 235-256. [2]

Hembree, W. C., III, Nahas, G. G., Zeidenberg, P., & Huang, H. F. S. (1979). Changes in human spermatozoa associated with high dose marihuana smoking. In G. G. Nahas & W. D. M. Paton (Eds.), *Marihuana: Biological effects* (pp. 429–439). Oxford: Pergamon Press. [4]

Hendin, H., & Haas, A. P. (1991). Suicide and guilt as manifestations of PTSD in Vietnam combat veterans. *American Journal of Psychiatry, 148,* 586-591. [13]

Hendler, N. H., & Fenton, J. A. (1979). *Coping with pain.* New York: Clarkson N. Potter. [3]

Henley, N. M. (1973). Status and sex: Some touching observations. *Bulletin of the Psychonomic Society, 2,* 91–93. [16]

Henley, N. M. (1989). Molehill or mountain? What we know and don't know about sex bias in language. In M. Crawford & M. Gentry (Eds.), *Gender and thought: Psychological perspectives.* New York: Springer-Verlag. [7]

Hennevin, E., Hars, B., Maho, C., & Bloch, V. (1995). Processing of learned information in paradoxical sleep: Relevance for memory. *Behavioural Brain Research, 69,* 125–135. [4]

Henningfield, J. E., & Ator, N. A. (1986). *Barbiturates: Sleeping potion or intoxicant?* New York: Chelsea House. [4]

Hepper, P. G., Shahidullah, S., & White, R. (1990). Origins of fetal handedness. *Nature, 347,* 431. [2]

Herek, G. M., & Glunt, E. K. (1993). Interpersonal contact and heterosexuals' attitudes toward gay men: Results from a national survey. *Journal of Sex Research, 30,* 239–244. [11]

Herkenham, M. (1992). Cannabinoid receptor localization in brain: Relationship to motor and reward systems. *Annals of the New York Academy of Sciences, 654,* 19–32. [4]

Hernandez, L., & Hoebel, B. G. (1989). Food intake and lateral hypothalamic self-stimulation covary after medial hypothalamic lesions or ventral midbrain 6-hydroxydopamine injections that cause obesity. *Behavioral Neuroscience, 103,* 412–422. [10]

Heron, R. M. (1991). The ergonomist. In R. Gifford (Ed.), *Applied psychology: Variety and opportunity* (pp. 301–325). Boston: Allyn & Bacon. [17]

Herrnstein, R. J., & Murray, C. (1994). *The bell curve: Intelligence and class structure in American life.* New York: Free Press. [7]

Herron, J. (1980). *Neuropsychology of left-handedness.* New York: Academic Press. [2]

Hershenson, M. (1989). *The moon illusion.* Hillsdale, NJ: Erlbaum. [3]

Hertzog, C. (1991). Aging, information processing speed, and intelligence. In K. W. Schaie & M. P. Lawton (Eds.), *Annual Review of Gerontology and Geriatrics* (Vol. 11, pp. 55–79). [9]

Hess, E. H. (1961). Shadows and depth perception. *Scientific American, 204,* 138–148. [3]

Hess, E. H. (1965). Attitude and pupil size. *Scientific American, 212,* 46–54. [3]

Hetherington, A. W., & Ranson, S. W. (1940). Hypothalamic lesions and adiposity in the rat. *Anatomical Record, 78,* 149–172. [10]

Hetherington, E. M., Stanley-Hagan, M., & Anderson, E. R. (1989). Marital transitions: A child's perspective. *American Psychologist, 44,* 303–312. [9]

Higbee, K. L. (1969). Fifteen years of fear arousal: Research on threat appeals: 1953–1968. *Psychological Bulletin, 72,* 426–444. [16]

Higbee, K. L. (1977). *Your memory: How it works and how to improve it.* Englewood Cliffs, NJ: Prentice-Hall. [6]

Hilgard, E. R. (1975). Hypnosis. *Annual Review of Psychology, 26,* 19–44. [4]

Hilgard, E. R., & Hilgard, J. (1975). *Hypnosis in the relief of pain.* Los Altos, CA: William Kaufmann. [3]

Hill, J. P. (1980). *Understanding early adolescence: A framework.* Carrboro, NC: Center for Early Adolescence. [9]

Hilliker, N. A. J., Muehlbach, M. J., Schweitzer, P. K., & Walsh, J. K. (1992). Sleepiness/alertness on a simulated night shift schedule and morningness-eveningness tendency. *Sleep, 15,* 430–433. [4]

Hillman, D. R. (1993). Sleep apnea and myocardial infarction. *Sleep, 16,* S23–S24. [4]

Hingson, R., Alpert, J. J., Day, N., Dooling, E., Kayne, H., Morelock, S., Oppenheimer, E., & Zuckerman, B. (1982). Effects of maternal drinking and marijuana use on fetal growth and development. *Pediatrics, 70,* 539–546. [4]

Hinton, G. E., Dayan, P., Frey, B. J., & Neal, R. M. (1995). The "wake-sleep" algorithm for unsupervised neural networks. *Science, 268,* 1158–1161. [7]

Hoberman, J. M., & Yesalis, C. E. (1995). The history of synthetic testosterone. *Scientific American, 272,* 76–81. [11]

Hobson, J. A. (1988). *The dreaming brain.* New York: Basic Books. [4]

Hobson, J. A. (1989). *Sleep.* New York: Scientific American Library. [4]

Hobson, J. A., & McCarley, R. W. (1977). The brain as a dream state generator: An activation-synthesis hypothesis of the dream process. *American Journal of Psychiatry, 134,* 1335–1348. [2, 4]

Hoebel, B. G., & Teitelbaum, P. (1966). Weight regulation in normal and hypothalamic hyperphagic rats. *Journal of Comparative and Physiological Psychology, 61,* 189–193. [10]

Hofer, P. J. (1991). The lawyer-psychologist. In R. Gifford (Ed.), *Applied psychology: Variety and opportunity* (pp. 245–270). Boston: Allyn & Bacon. [17]

Hofferth, S. L. (1992). The demand for and supply of child care in the 1990s. In A. Booth (Ed.), *Child care in the 1990s: Trends and consequences* (pp. 56–62). Hillsdale, NJ: Erlbaum. [8]

Hoffman, L. (1979). Maternal employment. *American Psychologist, 34,* 859–865. [9]

Hoffman, L. W. (1989). Effects of maternal employment in the two-parent family. *American Psychologist, 44,* 283–292. [8]

Hofstede, G. (1980). *Culture's consequences: International differences in work-related values.* Beverly Hills, CA: Sage. [12]

Hofstede, G. (1983). Dimensions of national cultures in fifty countries and three regions. In J. Deregowski, S. Dzuirawiec, and R. Annis (Eds.), *Explications in cross-cultural psychology.* Lisse: Swets and Zeitlinger.

Hogan, R., Curphy, G. J., & Hogan, J. (1994). What we know about leadership: Effectiveness and personality. *American Psychologist, 49,* 493–504. [12]

Hökfelt, T., Johansson, O., & Goldstein, M. (1984). Chemical anatomy of the brain. *Science, 225,* 1326–1334. [2]

Holden, C. (1986a). Days may be numbered for polygraphs in the private sector. *Science, 232,* 705. [10]

Holden, C. (1986b). Depression research advances, treatment lags. *Science, 233,* 723–726. [14]

Holden, C. (1991). New center to study therapies and ethnicity. *Science, 251,* 748. [15]

Holinger, P. C., Litman, R. E., & Waltzer, H. (1987, September 15). Spotting the potential suicide. *Patient Care, 21,* pp. 62–67. [14]

Holland, J. G. (1992). Obituaries: B. F. Skinner (1904–1990). *American Psychologist, 47,* 665–667. [5]

Holland, J. G., & Skinner, B. F. (1961). *The analysis of behavior.* New York: McGraw-Hill. [5]

Holloway, M. (1991). Rx for addiction. *Scientific American, 264,* 94–103. [4]

Holloway, M. (1994). Trends in women's health: A global view. *Scientific American, 271,* 76–83. [13]

Holloway, M., & Yam, P. (1992). Reflecting differences: Health care begins to address needs of women and minorities. *Scientific American, 266,* 13–18. [13]

Holmes, T. H., & Masuda, M. (1974). Life change and illness susceptibility. In B. S. Dohrenwend & B. P. Dohrenwend (Eds.), *Stressful life events: Their nature and effects.* New York: Wiley. [13]

Holmes, T. H., & Rahe, R. H. (1967). The social readjustment rating scale. *Journal of Psychosomatic Research, 11,* 213–218. [13]

Horgan, J. (1994). Can science explain consciousness? *Scientific American, 271,* 88–94. [4]

Horn, J. (1982). The aging of human abilities. In B. B. Wolman (Ed.), *Handbook of developmental psychology.* Englewood Cliffs, NJ: Prentice-Hall. [9]

Horn, J. C., & Meer, J. (1987, May). The vintage years. *Psychology Today,* pp. 76–90. [9]

Horn, J. L. (1982). The theory of fluid and crystallized intelligence in relation to concepts of cognitive psychology and aging in adulthood.

In F. I. M. Craik & S. Trehub (Eds.), *Aging and cognitive processes* (pp. 201–238). New York: Plenum Press. [9]

Horne, J. (1992). Annotation: Sleep and its disorders in children. *Journal of Child Psychology and Psychiatry, 33,* 473–487. [4]

Horner, M. (1969, November). Fail: Bright women. *Psychology Today,* pp. 36–38, 62. [10]

Horney, K. (1937). *The neurotic personality of our time.* New York: W. W. Norton. [12]

Horney, K. (1939). *New ways in psychoanalysis.* New York: W. W. Norton. [12]

Horney, K. (1945). *Our inner conflicts.* New York: W. W. Norton. [12]

Horney, K. (1950). *Neurosis and human growth.* New York: W. W. Norton. [12, 14]

Horney, K. (1967). *Feminine psychology.* New York: W. W. Norton. [12]

Horowitz, M., Adler, N., & Kegeles, S. (1988). A scale for measuring the occurrence of positive states of mind: A preliminary report. *Psychosomatic Medicine, 50,* 477–483. [16]

Horwath, E., Lish, J. D., Johnson, J., Hornig, C. D., & Weissman, M. M. (1993). Agoraphobia without panic: Clinical reappraisal of an epidemiologic finding. *American Journal of Psychiatry, 150,* 1496–1501. [14]

Hothersall, D. (1984). *History of psychology.* Philadelphia: Temple University Press. [7]

Houlihan, D., Schwartz, C., Miltenberger, R., & Heuton, D. (1993). The rapid treatment of a young man's balloon (noise) phobia using *in vivo* flooding. *Journal of Behavior Therapy and Experimental Psychiatry, 24,* 233–240. [15]

House, J. S., Landis, K. R., & Umberson, D. (1988). Social relationships and health. *Science, 241,* 540–544. [13]

Hovland, C. I., Lumsdaine, A. A., & Sheffield, F. D. (1949). *Experiments on mass communication.* Princeton, NJ: Princeton University Press. [16]

Howard, A., Pion, G. M., Gottfredson, G. D., Flattau, P. E., Oskamp, S., Pfafflin, S. M., Bray, D. W., & Burnstein, A. G. (1986). The changing face of American psychology: A report from the committee on employment and human resources. *American Psychologist, 41,* 1311–1327. [1]

Howard, K. I., Kopta, S. M., Krause, M. S., & Orlinsky, D. E. (1986). The dose-effect relationship in psychotherapy. *American Psychologist, 41,* 159–164. [15]

Howes, C. (1990). Can the age of entry into child care and the quality of child care predict adjustment in kindergarten? *Developmental Psychology, 26,* 292–803. [8]

Hoyer, G., & Lund, E. (1993). Suicide among women related to number of children in marriage. *Archives of General Psychiatry, 50,* 134–137. [14]

Hrushesky, W. J. M. (1994, July/August). Timing is everything. *The Sciences,* 32–37. [4]

Hsu, B., Kling, A., Kessler, C., Knapke, K., Diefenbach, P., & Elias, J. E. (1994). Gender differences in sexual fantasy and behavior in a college population: A ten-year replication. *Journal of Sex & Marital Therapy, 20,* 103–118. [11]

Hubel, D. H. (1963). The visual cortex of the brain. *Scientific American, 209,* 54–62. [3]

Hubel, D. H., & Wiesel, T. N. (1959). Receptive fields of single neurons in the cat's striate cortex. *Journal of Physiology, 148,* 547–591. [3]

Hubel, D. H., & Wiesel, T. N. (1979). Brain mechanisms of vision. *Scientific American, 241,* 130–144. [3]

Hudspeth, A. J. (1983). The hair cells of the inner ear. *Scientific American, 248,* 54–64. [3]

Huesmann, L. R., Eron, L. D., Lefkowitz, M. M., & Walder, L. O. (1984). The stability of aggression over time and generations. *Developmental Psychology, 20,* 1120–1134. [16]

Hughes, J. R. (1992). Tobacco withdrawal in self-quitters. *Journal of Consulting and Clinical Psychology, 60,* 689–697. [13]

Hughes, J. R., Oliveto, A. H., Helzer, J. E., Higgins, S. T., & Bickel, W. K. (1992). Should caffeine abuse, dependence, or withdrawal be added to DSM-IV and ICD–10? *American Journal of Psychiatry, 149,* 33–40. [4]

Hugick, L. (1992). Public opinion divided on gay rights. *Gallup Poll Monthly,* No. 321, 2–6. [11]

Hugick, L., & Leonard, J. (1991a). Job dissatisfaction grows: "Moonlighting" on the rise. *Gallup Poll Monthly,* No. 312, 2–15. [9]

Hugick, L., & Leonard, J. (1991b). Sex in America. *Gallup Poll Monthly,* No. 313, 60–73. [9]

Hull, C. L. (1943). *Principles of behavior.* New York: Appleton-Century-Crofts. [10]

Hultsch, D. F., & Dixon, R. A. (1990). Learning and memory in aging. In J. E. Birren & K. W. Schaie (Eds.), *Handbook of the psychology of aging* (3rd ed., pp. 359–374). San Diego: Academic Press. [9]

Hurley, G. (1988, January). Getting help from helping. *Psychology Today,* pp. 62–67. [15]

Hurvich, L. M., & Jameson, D. (1957). An opponent-process theory of color vision. *Psychological Review, 64,* 384–404. [3]

Huston, A. C., Watkins, B. A., & Kunkel, D. (1989). Public policy and children's television. *American Psychologist, 44,* 424–433. [8]

Hutman, S. (1990, December). AIDS: The year in review. *AIDS Patient Care,* 11–15. [11]

Hyde, J. S., Fenema, E., & Lamon, S. J. (1990). Gender differences in mathematics performance: A meta-analysis. *Psychological Bulletin, 107,* 139–155. [11]

Hyde, J. S., & Linn, M. C. (1988). Gender differences in verbal ability: A meta-analysis. *Psychological Bulletin, 104,* 53–69. [1, 11]

Hyman, A. (1983). The influence of color on the taste perception of carbonated water preparations. *Bulletin of the Psychonomic Society, 21,* 145–148. [3].

Hyman, S. E. (1995). What are second messengers? *Harvard Mental Health Letter, 11*(10), 8. [2]

Indian Health Service. (1988). *Indian health service chart series book.* Washington, DC: U.S. Department of Health and Human Services. [13]

Inglehart, R. (1990). *Culture shift in advanced industrial society.* Princeton, NJ: Princeton University Press. [9]

Ingrassia, M. (1993, October 25). Abused and confused. *Newsweek,* pp. 57–58. [17]

Ingrassia, M. (1994, October 17). Virgin cool. *Newsweek,* pp. 58–69. [9]

Inhelder, B. (1966). Cognitive development and its contribution to the diagnosis of some phenomena of mental deficiency. *Merrill-Palmer Quarterly, 12,* 299–319. [8]

Innerviews. (1988, June/July). *Women's Sports & Fitness,* p. 64. [9]

Insel, T. R. (1990). Phenomenology of obsessive compulsive disorder. *Journal of Clinical Psychiatry, 51*(2, Suppl.), 4–8. [14]

International Labour Office. (1990). *Yearbook of labour statistics.* Geneva: Author. [11]

Intons-Peterson, M. J., & Fournier, J. (1986). External and internal memory aids: When and how often do we use them? *Journal of Experimental Psychology: General, 115,* 267–280. [6]

Irwin, M., Daniels, M., Bloom, E. T., Smith, T. L., & Weiner, H. (1987). Life events, depressive symptoms, and immune function. *American Journal of Psychiatry, 144,* 437–441. [13]

Isabella, R. A., Belsky, J., & von Eye, A. (1989). Origins of infant-mother attachment: An examination of interactional synchrony during the infant's first year. *Developmental Psychology, 25,* 12–21. [8]

Isay, R. A. (1989). *Being homosexual: Gay men and their development.* New York: Farrar, Straus, & Giroux. [11]

Isenberg, D. J. (1986). Group polarization: A critical review and meta-analysis. *Journal of Personality and Social Psychology, 50,* 1141–1151. [16]

Ivancevich, J. M., Matteson, M. T., Freedman, S. M., & Phillips, J. S. (1990). Worksite stress management interventions. *American Psychologist, 45,* 252–261. [17]

Iverson, L. L. (1979). The chemistry of the brain. *Scientific American, 241,* 134–147. [14]

Izard, C. E. (1971). *The face of emotion.* New York: Appleton-Century-Crofts. [10]

Izard, C. E. (1977). *Human emotions.* New York: Plenum Press. [10]

Izard, C. E. (1990). Facial expressions and the regulation of emotions. *Journal of Personality and Social Psychology, 58,* 487–498. [10]

Izard, C. E. (1992). Basic emotions, relations among emotions, and emotion-cognition relations. *Psychological Review, 99,* 561–565. [10]

Izard, C. E. (1993). Four systems for emotion activation: Cognitive and noncognitive processes. *Psychological Review, 100,* 68–90. [10]

Jacklin, C. N. (1989). Female and male: Issues of gender. *American Psychologist, 44,* 127–133. [11]

Jackson, B. B., Taylor, J., & Pyngolil, M. (1991). How age conditions the relationship between climacteric status and health symptoms in African American women. *Research in Nursing and Health, 14,* 1–9. [9]

Jackson, J. (1994, July 25). When will television reflect reality of America today? *Evansville Courier,* p. A7. [8]

Jacobs, G. H. (1993). The distribution and nature of colour vision among the mammals. *Biological Review, 68,* 413–471. [3]

Jacobs, M. K., & Goodman, G. (1989). Psychology and self-help groups: Predictions on a partnership. *American Psychologist, 44,* 536–545. [15]

James, J. E. (1985). Desensitization treatment of agoraphobia. *British Journal of Clinical Psychology, 24,* 133–134. [15]

James, W. (1884). What is an emotion? *Mind, 9,* 188–205. [10]

James, W. (1890). *Principles of psychology.* New York: Holt. [1, 10]

James, W. (1961). *Psychology: The briefer course.* New York: Harper & Row. (Original work published 1892). [6]

Jamieson, D. W., & Zanna, M. P. (1989). Need for structure in attitude formation and expression. In A. R. Pratkanis, S. J. Breckler, & A. G. Greenwald (Eds.), *Attitude structure and function* (pp. 383–406). Hillsdale, NJ: Erlbaum. [16]

Jamison, K. R. (1995). Manic-depressive illness and creativity. *Scientific American, 272,* 62–67. [14]

Janeway, C. A., Jr. (1993). How the immune system recognizes invaders. *Scientific American, 269,* 72–79. [13]

Janis, I. L. (1982). *Groupthink: Psychological studies of policy decisions and fiascoes* (2nd ed.). Boston: Houghton Mifflin. [16]

Janisse, M. P., & Peavler, W. S. (1974, February). Pupillary research today: Emotion in the eye. *Psychology Today,* pp. 60–63. [3]

Janowitz, H. D., & Grossman, M. I. (1950). Hunger and appetite: Some definitions and concepts. *Journal of the Mount Sinai Hospital, 16,* 231–240. [10]

Janowsky, J. S., Shimamura, A. P., & Squire, L. R. (1989). Source memory impairment in patients with frontal lobe lesions. *Neuropsychologia, 27,* 1043–1056. [6]

Jaroff, L. (1993, Nov. 29). Lies of the mind. *Time,* 52–59. [6]

Jarvik, M. E. (1990). The drug dilemma: Manipulating the demand. *Science, 250,* 387–392. [4]

Jaynes, J. (1976). *The origin of consciousness and the breakdown of the bicameral mind.* Boston: Houghton Mifflin. [2]

Jellinek, E. M. (1960). *The disease concept of alcoholism.* New Brunswick, NJ: Hillhouse Press. [13]

Jemmott, J. B., III, & Locke, S. E. (1984). Psychosocial factors, immunologic mediation, and human susceptibility to infectious diseases: How much do we know? *Psychological Bulletin, 95,* 78–108. [13]

Jenike, M. A. (1989). Obsessive-compulsive and related disorders: A hidden epidemic. *New England Journal of Medicine, 321,* 539–541. [14]

Jenike, M. A. (1990, April). Obsessive-compulsive disorder. *Harvard Medical School Health Letter, 15,* pp. 4–8. [15]

Jenike, M. A., & Rauch, S. L. (1994). Managing the patient with treatment-resistant obsessive compulsive disorder: Current strategies. *Journal of Clinical Psychiatry, 55*(3, Suppl.), 11–17. [15]

Jenkins, J. G., & Dallenbach, K. M. (1924). Oblivescence during sleep and waking. *American Journal of Psychology, 35,* 605–612. [6]

Jenkins, J. H., & Karno, M. (1992). The meaning of expressed emotion: Theoretical issues raised by cross-cultural research. *American Journal of Psychiatry, 149,* 9–21. [15]

Jenkins, J. J., Jimenez-Pabon, E., Shaw, R. E., & Sefer, J. W. (1975). *Schuell's aphasia in adults: Diagnosis, prognosis, and treatment* (2nd ed.). Hagerstown, MD: Harper & Row. [2]

Jensen, A. R. (1969). How much can we boost IQ and scholastic achievement? *Harvard Educational Review, 39*, 1–123. [7]

Jensen, A. R. (1985). The nature of the black-white difference on various psychometric tests: Spearman's hypothesis. *Behavioral and Brain Sciences, 8*, 193–263. [7]

Jernigan, T. L., Butters, N., DiTraglia, G., Schafer, K., Smith, T., Irwin, M., Grant, I., Schuckit, M., & Cermak, L. S. (1991). Reduced cerebral grey matter observed in alcoholics using magnetic resonance imaging. *Alcoholism: Clinical and Experimental Research, 15*, 418–427. [13]

Jeste, D. V. (1994). How does late-onset compare with early-onset schizophrenia? *Harvard Mental Health Letter, 10*(8), 8–9. [14]

Johnson, D. L. (1989). Schizophrenia as a brain disease: Implications for psychologists and families. *American Psychologist, 44*, 553–555. [14]

Johnson, J. H., & Sarason, I. G. (1979). Recent developments in research on life stress. In V. Hamilton & D. M. Warburton (Eds.), *Human stress and cognition: An information processing approach* (pp. 205–233). London: Wiley. [13]

Johnston, L. D., O'Malley, P. M., & Bachman, J. G. (1994). *National survey results on drug use from the Monitoring the Future Study, 1975–1993: Vol. 1. Secondary school students.* Rockville, MD: National Institute on Drug Abuse. [4]

Jonas, J. M., & Cohon, M. S. (1993). A comparison of the safety and efficacy of alprazolam versus other agents in the treatment of anxiety, panic, and depression: A review of the literature. *Journal of Clinical Psychiatry, 54*(10, Suppl.), 25–45. [15]

Jones, E. (1953). *The life and work of Sigmund Freud: The formative years and the great discoveries (1856–1900)* (Vol. 1). New York: Basic Books. [12]

Jones, E. E. (1976). How do people perceive the causes of behavior? *American Scientist, 64*, 300–305. [16]

Jones, E. E. (1986). Interpreting interpersonal behavior: The effects of expectancies. *Science, 234*, 41–46. [16]

Jones, E. E. (1990). *Interpersonal perception.* New York: Freeman. [16]

Jones, E. E., & Davis, K. E. (1965). A theory of correspondent inferences: From acts to dispositions. In L. Berkowitz (Ed.), *Advances in experimental social psychology* (Vol. 2, pp. 219–266). New York: Academic Press. [16]

Jones, E. E., & Nisbett, R. E. (1971). *The actor and the observer: Divergent perceptions of the causes of behavior.* New York: General Learning. [16]

Jones, H. B., & Jones, H. C. (1977). *Sensual drugs: Deprivation and rehabilitation of the mind.* Cambridge: Cambridge University Press. [4]

Jones, H. C., & Lovinger, P. W. (1985). *The marijuana question.* New York: Dodd, Mead. [4]

Jones, M. C. (1924). A laboratory study of fear: The case of Peter. *Pedagogical Seminary, 31*, 308–315. [5]

Jones, M. C., & Bayley, N. (1950). Physical maturing among boys as related to behavior. *Journal of Educational Psychology, 41*, 129–148. [9]

Jones, W. H., Chernovetz, M. E. O'C., & Hansson, R. O. (1978). The enigma of androgyny: Differential implications for males and females? *Journal of Consulting and Clinical Psychology, 46*, 298–313. [11]

Josephson, W. L. (1987). Television violence and children's aggression: Testing the priming, social script, and disinhibition predictions. *Journal of Personality and Social Psychology, 53*, 822–890. [16]

Joyce, P. R., & Paykel, E. S. (1989). Predictors of drug response in depression. *Archives of General Psychiatry, 46*, 89–99. [15]

Judd, C. M., Ryan, C. S., & Park, B. (1991). Accuracy in the judgment of in-group and out-group variability. *Journal of Personality and Social Psychology, 61*, 366–379. [16]

Judd, L. L. (1994). Social phobia: A clinical overview. *Journal of Clinical Psychiatry, 55*(6, Suppl.), 5–9. [14]

Jung, C. G. (1933). *Modern man in search of a soul.* New York: Harcourt Brace Jovanovich. [12]

Jung, C. G. (1953). *The psychology of the unconscious* (R. F. C. Hull, Trans.), *Collected works* (Vol. 7). Princeton, NJ: Princeton University Press. (Original work published 1917). [12]

Jung, C. G. (1961). *Memories, dreams, reflections* (R. Winston & C. Winston, Trans.). New York: Random House. [12]

Jung, C. G. (1966). *Two essays on analytical psychology* (R. F. C. Hull, Trans.). Princeton, NJ: Princeton University Press. [12]

Kagan, J., & Moss, A. K. (1962). *Birth to maturity.* New York: Wiley. [10]

Kagitcibasi, C. (1992). A critical appraisal of individualism-collectivism: Toward a new formulation. In U. Kim, H. C. Triandis, and G. Yoon (Eds.), *Individualism and collectivism: Theoretical and methodological issues.* Newbury Park, CA: Sage. [2]

Kahne, H. (1985). *Reconceiving part-time work: New perspectives for older workers and women.* Lanham, MD: Rowman & Allanheld. [17]

Kales, A., Kales, J. D., Soldatos, C. R., Caldwell, A. B., Charney, D. S., & Martin, E. D. (1980). Night terrors: Clinical characteristics and personality patterns. *Archives of General Psychiatry, 37*, 1413–1417. [4]

Kales, J., Tan, T. C., Swearingen, C., et al. (1971). Are over-the-counter sleep medications effective? All-night EEG studies. *Current Therapeutic Research, 13*, 143–151. [4]

Kalish, H. I. (1981). *From behavioral science to behavior modification.* New York: McGraw-Hill. [5, 15]

Kalven, H., & Zeisel, H. (1966). *The American jury.* Boston: Little, Brown. [17]

Kamin, L. J. (1995). Behind the curve [Review of *The Bell Curve: Intelligence and class structure in American life*]. *Scientific American, 272*, 99–103. [7]

Kanaya, Y., Nakamura, C., and Miyake, D. (1989). Cross-cultural study of expressive behavior of mothers in response to their five-month-old infants' different emotion expression. *Research and Clinical Center for Child Development Annual Report, 11*, 25–31. [10]

Kane, J. M. (1993). Understanding and treating psychoses: Advances in research and therapy. *Journal of Clinical Psychiatry, 54*, 445–452. [14]

Kane, J. M., Woerner, M. G., Pollack, S., Safferman, A. Z., & Lieberman, J. A. (1993). Does clozapine cause tardive dyskinesia? *Journal of Clinical Psychiatry, 54*, 327–330. [15]

Kaniasty, K., & Norris, F. H. (1993). A test of the social support deterioration model in the context of natural disaster. *Journal of Personality and Social Psychology, 64*, 395–408. [13]

Kanin, E. J., Jackson, E. C., & Levine, E. M. (1987). Personal sexual history and punitive judgments for rape. *Psychological Reports, 61*, 439–442. [11]

Kanner, A. D., Coyne, J. C., Schaefer, C., & Lazarus, R. S. (1981). Comparison of two modes of stress measurement: Daily hassles and uplifts versus major life events. *Journal of Behavioral Medicine, 4*, 1–39. [13]

Kanter, R. (1977). *Men and women of the corporation.* New York: Basic Books. [11]

Kaplan, G. A., Wilson, T. W., Cohen, R. D., Kauhanen, J., Wu, M., & Salomen, J. T. (1994). Social functioning and overall mortality: Prospective evidence from the Kuopio Ischemic Heart Disease Risk Factor Study. *Epidemiology, 5*, 495–500. [13]

Kaplan, H. S. (1974). *The new sex therapy: Active treatment of sexual dysfunction.* New York: Brunner/Mazel. [11]

Kaprio, J., Koskenvuo, M., & Rita, H. (1987). Mortality after bereavement: A prospective study of 95,647 widowed persons. *American Journal of Public Health, 77*, 283–287. [9]

Karacan, I. (1988). Parasomnias. In R. L. Williams, I. Karacan, & C. A. Moore (Eds.), *Sleep disorders: Diagnosis and treatment* (pp. 131–144). New York: John Wiley. [4]

Karasek, R. A., & Theorell, T. (1990). *Healthy work.* New York: Basic Books. [17]

Karasu, T. B. (1986). The psychotherapies: Benefits and limitations. *American Journal of Psychotherapy, 40*, 324–342. [15]

Karasu, T. B. (1990a). Toward a clinical model of psychotherapy for depression, I: Systematic comparison of three psychotherapies. *American Journal of Psychiatry, 147*, 133–147. [15]

Karasu, T. B. (1990b). Toward a clinical model of psychotherapy for depression, II: An integrative and selective treatment approach. *American Journal of Psychiatry, 147*, 269–278. [15]

Karau, S. J., & Williams, K. D. (1993). Social loafing; a meta-analytic review and theoretical integration. *Journal of Personality and Social Psychology, 65,* 681–706. [16]

Karni, A., Tanne, D., Rubenstein, B. S., Askenasy, J. J. M., & Sagi, D. (1994). Dependence on REM sleep of overnight improvement of a perceptual skill. *Science, 265,* 679–682. [4]

Karrer, T., & Bartoshuk, L. (1991). Capsaicin desensitization and recovery on the human tongue. *Physiological Behavior, 49,* 757–764. [3]

Kasper, S., Wehr, T. A., Bartko, J. J., Gaist, P. A., & Rosenthal, N. E. (1989). Epidemiological findings of seasonal changes in mood and behavior: A telephone survey of Montgomery County, Maryland. *Archives of General Psychiatry, 46,* 823–833. [14]

Kassin, S. M., Ellsworth, P. C., & Smith, V. L. (1989). The "general acceptance" of psychological research on eyewitness testimony: A survey of the experts. *American Psychologists, 44,* 1089–1098. [17]

Kastenbaum, R., & Costa, P. T. (1977). Psychological perspectives on death. *Annual Review of Psychology, 28,* 225–249. [9]

Katz, B. L. (1991). The effects of acquaintance rape on the female victim. In A. Parrot & L. Bechhofer (Eds.), *Acquaintance rape: The hidden crime* (pp. 251–269). New York: Wiley. [11]

Katzell, R. A., & Thompson, D. E. (1990). Work motivation: Theory and practice. *American Psychologist, 45,* 144–153. [17]

Kearney, M. (1984). A comparison of motivation to avoid success in males and females. *Journal of Clinical Psychology, 40,* 1005–1007. [10]

Keating, C. R. (1994). World without words: Messages from face and body. In W. J. Lonner & R. Malpass (Eds.), *Psychology and culture* (pp. 175–182). Boston: Allyn & Bacon. [1]

Keesey, R. E. (1988). The body-weight set point. What can you tell your patients? *Postgraduate Medicine, 83,* 114–118, 121–122, 127. [10]

Keesey, R. E., & Powley, T. L. (1986). The regulation of body weight. *Annual Review of Psychology, 37,* 109–133. [10]

Keith, S. J. (1993). Understanding the experience of schizophrenia. *American Journal of Psychiatry, 150,* 1616–1617. [14]

Keitner, G. I., Ryan, C. E., Miller, I. W., & Norman, W. H. (1992). Recovery and major depression: Factors associated with twelve-month outcome. *American Journal of Psychiatry, 149,* 93–99. [14]

Keller, H., Schlomerich, A., & Eibl-Eibesfeldt, I. (1988). Communication patterns in adult-infant interactions in western and non-western cultures. *Journal of Cross-Cultural Psychology, 19,* 427–445. [10]

Keller, M. B. (1989). Current concepts in affective disorders. *Journal of Clinical Psychiatry, 50,* 157–162. [15]

Kellogg, W., & Kellogg, L. (1933). *The ape and the child.* New York: McGraw-Hill. [7]

Kelly, S. F., & Kelly, R. J. (1985). *Hypnosis: Understanding how it can work for you.* Reading, MA: Addison-Wesley. [4]

Kendler, K. S., & Diehl, S. R. (1993). The genetics of schizophrenia: A current genetic-epidemiologic perspective. *Schizophrenia Bulletin, 19,* 261–285. [14]

Kendler, K. S., & Gruenberg, A. M. (1984). An independent analysis of the Danish Adoption Study of Schizophrenia. *Archives of General Psychiatry, 41,* 555–564. [14]

Kendler, K. S., Gruenberg, A. M., & Kinney, D. K. (1994). Independent diagnoses of adoptees and relatives as defined by DSM-III in the provincial and national samples of the Danish Adoption Study of Schizophrenia. *Archives of General Psychiatry, 51,* 456–468. [14]

Kendler, K. S., Gruenberg, A. M., & Tsuang, M. T. (1984). Outcome of schizophrenic subtypes defined by four diagnostic systems. *Archives of General Psychiatry, 41,* 149–154. [14]

Kendler, K. S., Kessler, R. C., Walters, E. E., MacLean, C., Neale, M. C., Heath, A. C., & Eaves, L. J. (1995). Stressful life events, genetic liability, and onset of an episode of major depression in women. *American Journal of Psychiatry, 152,* 833–842. [14]

Kendler, K. S., MacLean, C., Neale, M., Kessler, R., Heath, A., & Eaves, L. (1991). The genetic epidemiology of bulimia nervosa. *American Journal of Psychiatry, 148,* 1627–1637. [10]

Kendler, K. S., McGuire, M., Gruenberg, A. M., O'Hare, A., Spellman, M., & Walsh, D. (1993). The Roscommon family study: I. Methods,

diagnosis of probands, and risk of schizophrenia in relatives. *Archives of General Psychiatry, 50,* 527–540. [14]

Kendler, K. S., Neale, M. C., Heath, A. C., Kessler, R. C., & Eaves, L. J. (1994). A twin-family study of alcoholism in women. *American Journal of Psychiatry, 151,* 707–715. [13]

Kendler, K. S., Neale, M. C., Kessler, R. C., Heath, A. C., & Eaves, L. J. (1992a). Generalized anxiety disorder in women. *Archives of General Psychiatry, 49,* 267–272. [14]

Kendler, K. S., Neale, M. C., Kessler, R. C., Heath, A. C., & Eaves, L. J. (1992b). The genetic epidemiology of phobias in women. *Archives of General Psychiatry, 49,* 273–281. [14]

Kendler, K. S., Neale, M. C., Kessler, R. C., Heath, A. C., & Eaves, L. J. (1992c). A population-based twin study of major depression in women: The impact of varying definitions of illness. *Archives of General Psychiatry, 49,* 257–266. [14]

Kendler, K. S., Neale, M. C., Kessler, R. C., Heath, A. C., & Eaves, L. J. (1993). The lifetime history of major depression in women: Reliability of diagnosis and heritability. *Archives of General Psychiatry, 50,* 863–870. [14]

Kendler, K. S., Neale, M. C., MacLean, C, J, Heath, A. C., Eaves, L. J., & Kessler, R. C. (1993). Smoking and major depression: A causal analysis. *Archives of General Psychiatry, 50,* 36–43. [13]

Kenrick, D. T., & Gutierres, S. E. (1980). Contrast effects and judgments of physical attractiveness: When beauty becomes a social problem. *Journal of Personality and Social Psychology, 38,* 131–140. [11]

Kerlinger, F. N. (1986). *Foundations of behavioral research* (5th ed.). New York: Holt, Rinehart & Winston. [1]

Kessler, R. C., Kendler, D. S., Heath, A., Neale, M. C., & Eaves, L. J. (1992). Social support, depressed mood, and adjustment to stress: A genetic epidemiologic investigation. *Journal of Personality and Social Psychology, 63,* 257–272. [13]

Kessler, R. C., McGonagle, K. A., Zhao, S., Nelson, C. B., Hughes, M., Eshleman, S., Wittchen, H-U., & Kendler, K. S. (1994). Lifetime and 12-month prevalence of DSM-III-R psychiatric disorders in the United States: Results from the National Comorbidity Survey. *American Journal of Psychiatry, 51,* 8–19. [14]

Kety, S. S., Wender, P. H., Jacobsen, B., Ingraham, L. J., Jansson, L., Faber, B., & Kinney, D. K. (1994). Mental illness in the biological and adoptive relatives of schizophrenic adoptees: Replication of the Copenhagen study in the rest of Denmark. *Archives of General Psychiatry, 51,* 442–455. [14]

Kiecolt-Glaser, J. K., Fisher, L. D., Ogrocki, P., Stout, J., Speicher, C. E., & Glaser, R. (1987). Marital quality, marital disruption, and immune function. *Psychosomatic Medicine, 49,* 13–34. [13]

Kiecolt-Glaser, J. K., & Glaser, R. (1992). Psychoneuroimmunology: Can psychological interventions modulate immunity? *Journal of Consulting and Clinical Psychology, 60,* 569–575. [13]

Kilbride, J. E., & Kilbride, P. L. (1975). Sitting and smiling behavior of Baganda infants. *Journal of Cross-Cultural Psychology, 6,* 88–107. [8]

Kilstrom, J. F. (1985). Hypnosis. *Annual Review of Psychology, 26,* 557–591. [4]

Kim, J. J., & Fanselow, M. S. (1992). Modality-specific retrograde amnesia of fear. *Science, 256,* 675–677. [6]

Kim, S-G., Ashe, J., Hendrich, K., Ellermann, J. M., Merkle, H., Ugurbil, K., & Georgopoulos, A. P. (1993). Functional magnetic resonance imaging of motor cortex: Hemispheric asymmetry and handedness. *Science, 261,* 615–617. [2]

Kim, S-G., Ugurbil, K., & Strick, P. L. (1994). Activation of a cerebellar output nucleus during cognitive processing. *Science, 265,* 949–951. [2]

Kimura, D. (1992). Sex differences in the brain. *Scientific American, 267,* 118–125. [11]

King, G. (1993, Winter). Worker vs. workplace. *Barnes Magazine,* pp. 15–19. [17]

Kingsbury, S. J. (1993). Brief hypnotic treatment of repetitive nightmares. *American Journal of Clinical Hypnosis, 35,* 161–169. [4]

Kinnamon, S. C. (1988). Taste transduction: A diversity of mechanisms. *Trends in Neurosciences, 11,* 491–496. [3]

Kinnunen, T., Zamansky, H. S., & Block, M. L. (1994). Is the hypnotized subject lying? *Journal of Abnormal Psychology, 103*, 184–191. [4]

Kinsella, G., Prior, M. R., & Murray, G. (1988). Singing ability after right- and left-sided brain damage. A research note. *Cortex, 24*, 165–169. [2]

Kinsey, A. C., Pomeroy, W. B., & Martin, C. E. (1948). *Sexual behavior in the human male*. Philadelphia: W. B. Saunders. [11]

Kinsey, A. C., Pomeroy, W. B., Martin, C. E., & Gebhard, P. H. (1953). *Sexual behavior in the human female*. Philadelphia: W. B. Saunders. [11]

Kite, M. E., Deaux, K., & Miele, M. (1991). Stereotypes of young and old: Does age outweigh gender? *Psychology and Aging, 6*, 19–27. [16]

Klag, M. J., Whelton, P. K., Coresh, J., Grim, C. E., & Kuller, L. H. (1991). The association of skin color with blood pressure in U.S. blacks with low socioeconomic status. *Journal of the American Medical Association, 265*, 599–602. [13]

Klatzky, R. L. (1980). *Human memory: Structures and processes* (2nd ed.). New York: W. H. Freeman. [6]

Klatzky, R. L. (1984). *Memory and awareness: An information-processing perspective*. New York: W. H. Freeman. [6]

Kleinmuntz, B., & Szucko, J. J. (1984). A field study of the fallibility of polygraph lie detection. *Nature, 308*, 449–450. [10]

Kleitman, N. (1960). Patterns of dreaming. *Scientific American, 203*, 82–88. [4]

Klerman, G. L. (1992). Treatments for panic disorder. *Journal of Clinical Psychiatry, 53*(3, Suppl.), 14–19. [15]

Klerman, G. L., Weissman, M. N., Rounsaville, B. J., & Chevron, E. S. (1984). *Interpersonal therapy of depression*. New York: Academic Press. [15]

Kleven, M. S., & Seiden, L. S. (1992). Methamphetamine-induced neurotoxicity: Structure activity relationships. *Annals of the New York Academy of Sciences, 654*, 292–301. [4]

Klinnert, M. D., Campos, J. J., Sorce, J. F., Emde, R. N., & Suejda, M. (1983). Emotions as behavior regulators: Social referencing in infancy. In R. Plutchik & H. Kellerman (Eds.), *Emotions in early development: Vol. 2: The emotions* (pp. 57–86). New York: Academic Press. [10]

Kluft, R. P. (1984). An introduction to multiple personality disorder. *Psychiatric Annals, 14*, 19–24. [14]

Kluft, R. P. (1992). Hypnosis with multiple personality disorder. *American Journal of Preventative Psychiatry & Neurology, 3*, 19–27. [4]

Kluft, R. P. (1993). Multiple personality disorder: A contemporary perspective. *Harvard Mental Health Letter, 10*(4), 5–7. [14]

Kobasa, S. (1979). Stressful life events, personality, and health: An inquiry into hardiness. *Journal of Personality and Social Psychology, 37*, 1–11. [13]

Kobasa, S. C., Maddi, S. R., & Kahn, S. (1982). Hardiness and health: A prospective study. *Journal of Personality and Social Psychology, 42*, 168–177. [13]

Koch, C., Zador, A., & Brown, T. H. (1992). Dendritic spines: Convergence of theory and experiment. *Science, 256*, 973–974. [6]

Kochanska, G. (1993). Toward a synthesis of parental socialization and child temperament in early development of conscience. *Child Development, 64*, 325–347. [16]

Koenig, H. G., Cohen, H. J., Blazer, D. G., Pieper, C., Meador, K. G., Shelp, F., Goli, V., & DiPasquale, B. (1992). Religious coping and depression among elderly, hospitalized medically ill men. *American Journal of Psychiatry, 149*, 1693–1700. [13]

Kohlberg, L. (1963). The development of children's orientation toward a moral order: Sequence in the development of moral thought. *Vita Humana, 6*, 11–33. [9]

Kohlberg, L. (1966). A cognitive-developmental analysis of children's sex-role concepts and attitudes. In E. E. Maccoby (Ed.), *The development of sex differences* (pp. 82–173). Stanford, CA: Stanford University Press. [11]

Kohlberg, L. (1968, September). The child as a moral philosopher. *Psychology Today*, pp. 24–30. [9]

Kohlberg, L. (1969). *Stages in the development of moral thought and action*. New York: Holt, Rinehart & Winston. [9]

Kohlberg, L. (1981). *Essays on moral development, Vol. 1. The philosophy of moral development*. New York: Harper & Row. [9]

Kohlberg, L. (1984). *Essays on moral development, Vol. 2. The psychology of moral development*. San Francisco: Harper & Row. [9]

Kohlberg, L. (1985). *The psychology of moral development*. San Francisco: Harper & Row. [9]

Kohlberg, L., & Gilligan, C. (1971). The adolescent as a philosopher: The discovery of the self in a postconventional world. *Daedalus, 100*, 1051–1086. [9]

Kohlberg, L., & Ullian, D. Z. (1974). In R. C. Friedman, R. M. Richart, & R. L. Vande Wiele (Eds.), *Sex differences in behavior* (pp. 209–222). New York: Wiley. [11]

Köhler, W. (1925). *The mentality of apes* (E. Winter, Trans.). New York: Harcourt Brace Jovanovich. [5]

Kohut, A., & DeStefano, L. (1989). Modern employees expect more from their careers: Job dissatisfaction particularly high among the young. *The Gallup Report*, No. 288, 22–30. [9]

Kolodny, R. C., Masters, W. H., & Johnson, V. E. (1979). *Textbook of sexual medicine*. Boston: Little, Brown. [4]

Koltz, C. (1983, December). Scapegoating. *Psychology Today*, pp. 68–69. [16]

Komaromy, M., Bindman, A. B., Haber, R. J., & Sande, M. A. (1993). Sexual harassment in medical training. *New England Journal of Medicine, 328*, 322–326. [17]

Konishi, M. (1993). Listening with two ears. *Scientific American, 268*, 66–73. [3]

Koop, C. E. (1987). Report of the Surgeon General's workshop on pornography and public health. *American Psychologist, 42*, 944–945. [11]

Kopp, C. P., & Kaler, S. R. (1989). Risk in infancy: Origins and implications. *American Psychologist, 44*, 224–230. [8]

Kopta, S. M., Howard, K. I., Lowry, J. L., & Beutler, L. E. (1994). Patterns of symptomatic recovery in psychotherapy. *Journal of Consulting and Clinical Psychology, 62*, 1009–1016. [15]

Korner, A. F., Zeanah, C. H., Linden, J., Berkowitz, R. I., Kraemer, H. C., & Agras, W. S. (1985). The relation between neonatal and later activity and temperament. *Child Development, 56*, 38–42. [8]

Koshland, D. E., Jr. (1989). Drunk driving and statistical mortality. *Science, 244*, 513. [13]

Koss, M., Gidycz, C. A., & Wisniewski, N. (1987). The scope of rape: Incidence and prevalence of sexual aggression and victimization in a national sample of higher education subjects. *Journal of Consulting and Clinical Psychology, 55*, 162–170. [11]

Koss, M. P. (1993). Rape: Scope, impact, interventions, and public policy responses. *American Psychologist, 48*, 1062–1069. [11]

Kosslyn, S. M. (1975). Information representation in visual images. *Cognitive Psychology, 7*, 341–370. [7]

Kosslyn, S. M. (1983). *Ghosts in the mind's machine: Creating and using images in the brain*. New York: Norton. [7]

Kosslyn, S. M. (1988). Aspects of a cognitive neuroscience of mental imagery. *Science, 240*, 1621–1626. [7]

Kosslyn, S. M., (1994). *Image and brain: The resolution of the imagery debate*. Cambridge, MA: MIT Press. [7]

Kosslyn, S. M., & Ochsner, K. N. (1994). In search of occipital activation during visual mental imagery. *Trends in Neurosciences, 17*, 290–292. [7]

Kozak, M. J., Foa, E. B., & McCarthy, P. R. (1988). Obsessive-compulsive disorder. In C. G. Last & M. Herson (Eds.), *Handbook of anxiety disorders* (pp. 87–108). New York: Pergamon Press. [14]

Krajick, K. (1988, May). Private passions & public health. *Psychology Today*, pp. 50–58. [11]

Krantz, D. S., Grunberg, N. E., & Baum, A. (1985). Health psychology. *Annual Review of Psychology, 36*, 349–383. [13]

Krantz, M. (1987). Physical attractiveness and popularity: A predictive study. *Psychological Reports, 60*, 723–726. [8]

Kroger, W. S., & Fezler, W. D. (1976). *Hypnosis and behavior modification: Imagery conditioning*. Philadelphia: J. B. Lippincott. [4]

Kroll, N. E. A., Ogawa, K. H., & Nieters, J. E. (1988). Eyewitness memory and the importance of sequential information. *Bulletin of the Psychonomic Society, 26*, 395–398. [6]

Krosigk, M. von. (1993). Cellular mechanisms of a synchronized oscillation in the thalamus. *Science, 261*, 361–364. [2]

Krueger, W. C. F. (1929). The effect of overlearning on retention. *Journal of Experimental Psychology, 12*, 71–81. [6]

Kübler-Ross, Elisabeth (1969). *On death and dying.* New York: Macmillan. [9]

Kuch, K., & Cox, B. J. (1992). Symptoms of PTSD in 124 survivors of the Holocaust. *American Journal of Psychiatry, 149*, 337–340. [13]

Kuczaj, S. A., III (1978). Children's judgments of grammatical and ungrammatical irregular past-tense verbs. *Child Development, 49*, 319–326. [8]

Kuczmarski, R. J., Flegal, K. M., Campbell, S. M., & Johnson, C. L. (1994). Increasing prevalence of overweight among U.S. adults: The National Health and Nutrition Examination Surveys, 1960 to 1991. *Journal of the American Medical Association, 272*, 205–211. [10]

Kuhl, P. K., Williams, K. A., Lacerda, F., Stevens, K. N., & Lindblom, B. (1992). Linguistic experience alters phonetic perception in infants by 6 months of age. *Science, 255*, 606–608. [8]

Kuhn, D. (1984). Cognitive development. In M. H. Bernstein & M. E. Lamb (Eds.), *Developmental psychology.* Hillsdale, NJ: Erlbaum. [8]

Kuhn, D., Kohlberg, L., Langer, J., & Haan, N. (1977). The development of formal operations in logical and moral judgment. *Genetic Psychology Monographs, 95*, 97–188. [9]

Kukla, A. (1972). Foundations of an attributional theory of performance. *Psychological Review, 79*, 454–470. [10]

Kupersmidt, J. B., & Coie, J. D. (1990). Preadolescent peer status, aggression, and school adjustment as predictors of externalizing problems in adolescence. *Child Development, 61*, 1350–1362. [8]

Kupersmidt, J. B., Coie, J. D., & Dodge, K. A. (1990). Predicting disorder from peer social problems. In S. R. Asher & J. D. Coie (Eds.), *Peer rejection in childhood.* New York: Cambridge University Press. [8]

Kurdek, L. A., & Siesky, A. E. (1980). Sex-role self concepts of single divorced parents and their children. *Journal of Divorce, 3*, 249–261. [11]

Kushner, M. G., Sher, K. J., & Beitman, B. D. (1990). The relation between alcohol problems and the anxiety disorders. *American Journal of Psychiatry, 147*, 685–695. [14]

La Berge, S. P. (1981, January). Lucid dreaming: Directing the action as it happens. *Psychology Today*, pp. 48–57. [4]

Lalonde, R., & Botez, M. I. (1990). The cerebellum and learning processes in animals. *Brain Research Reviews, 15*, 325–332. [2]

Lamar, J. V., Jr. (1986, June 2). Crack: A cheap and deadly cocaine is a spreading menace. *Time*, pp. 16–18. [4]

Lamb, M. E. (1981). The development of father-infant relationships. In M. E. Lamb (Ed.), *The role of the father in child development.* New York: Wiley. [11]

Lamb, M. E. (1987). *The father's role: Cross-cultural perspectives.* Hillsdale, NJ: Erlbaum [8]

Lamb, M. E., & Elster, A. B. (1985). Adolescent mother-infant-father relationships. *Developmental Psychology, 21*, 768–773. [8]

Lamborn, S. D., Mounts, N. S., Steinberg, L., & Dornbusch, S. M. (1991). Patterns of competence and adjustment among adolescents from authoritative, authoritarian, indulgent, and neglectful families. *Child Development, 62*, 1049–1065. [8, 9]

Lamm, H. (1988). A review of our research on group polarization: Eleven experiments on the effects of group discussion on risk acceptance, probability estimation, and negotiation positions. *Psychological Reports, 62*, 807–813. [16]

Landrine, H., Richardson, J. L., Klonoff, E. A., & Flay, B. (1994). Cultural diversity in the predictors of adolescent cigarette smoking: The relative influence of peers. *Journal of Behavioral Medicine, 17*, 331–346. [4]

Landy, D., & Sigall, H. (1974). Beauty is talent: Task evaluation as a function of the performer's physical attractiveness. *Journal of Personality and Social Psychology, 29*, 299–304. [16]

Lang, A. R., Goeckner, D. J., Adesso, V. J., & Marlatt, G. A. (1975). Effects of alcohol on aggression in male social drinkers. *Journal of Abnormal Psychology, 84*, 508–518. [1]

Lange, C. G., & James, W. (1922). *The emotions* (I. A. Haupt, Trans.). Baltimore: Williams and Wilkins. [10]

Lange, R. A., Cigarroa, R. G., Yancy, C. W., Jr., Willard, J. E., Popma, J. J., Sills, M. N., McBride, W., Kim, A. S., & Hillis, L. D. (1989). Cocaine-induced coronary-artery vasoconstriction. *New England Journal of Medicine, 321*, 1557–1562. [4]

Langer, E. J., & Rodin, J. (1976). The effects of choice and enhanced personal responsibility for the aged: A field experiment in an institutional setting. *Journal of Personality and Social Psychology, 34*, 191–198. [13]

Langevin, B., Sukkar, F., Léger, P., Guez, A., & Robert, D. (1992). Sleep apnea syndromes (SAS) of specific etiology: Review and incidence from a sleep laboratory. *Sleep, 15*, S25–S32. [4]

Langlois, J. H. (1985). From the eye of the beholder to behavioral reality: The development of social behaviors and social relations as a function of physical attractiveness. In C. P. Herman (Ed.), *Physical appearance, stigma, and social behavior.* Hillsdale, NJ: Erlbaum. [8]

Langlois, J. H., Ritter, J. M., Roggman, L. A., & Vaughn, L. S. (1991). Facial diversity and infant preferences for attractive faces. *Developmental Psychology, 27*, 79–84. [16]

Langlois, J. H., & Roggman, L. A. (1990). Attractive faces are only average. *Psychological Science, 1*, 115–121. [16]

Larson, D. B., Sherrill, K. A., Lyons, J. S., Craigie, F. C., Thielman, S. B., Greenwold, M. A., & Larson, S. S. (1992). Associations between dimensions of religious commitment and mental health reported in the *American Journal of Psychiatry* and *Archives of General Psychiatry: 1978–1989. American Journal of Psychiatry, 149*, 557–559. [13]

Larson, J. H., & Bell, N. J. (1988). Need for privacy and its effect upon interpersonal attraction and interaction. *Journal of Social and Clinical Psychology, 6*, 1–10. [16]

Latané, B., Williams, K., & Harkins, S. (1979). Many hands make light the work: The causes and consequences of social loafing. *Journal of Personality and Social Psychology, 37*, 822–832. [16]

Latham, A., & Grenadier, A. (1982, October). The ordeal of Walter/Susan Cannon. *Psychology Today*, pp. 64–72. [11]

Lattal, K. A. (1992). B. F. Skinner and psychology: Introduction to the special issue. *American Psychologist, 47*, 1269–1272. [5]

Lauber, J. K., & Kayten, P. J. (1988). Keynote address: Sleepiness, circadian dysrhythmia, and fatigue in transportation system accidents. *Sleep, 11*, 503–512. [4]

Laumann, E. O., Gagnon, J. H., Michael, R. T., & Michaels, S. (1994). *The social organization of sexuality.* Chicago: University of Chicago Press. [11]

Laurent, J., Swerdik, M., & Ryburn, M. (1992). Review of validity research on the Stanford-Binet Intelligence Scale: Fourth Edition. *Psychological Assessment, 4*, 102–112. [7]

Lazarus, R. S. (1966). *Psychological stress and the coping process.* New York: McGraw-Hill. [13]

Lazarus, R. S. (1993). From psychological stress to the emotions: A history of changing outlooks. *Annual Review of Psychology, 44*, 1–21. [13]

Lazarus, R. S., & DeLongis, A. (1983). Psychological stress and coping in aging. *American Psychologist, 38*, 245–253. [13]

Lazarus, R. S., & Folkman, S. (1984). *Stress, appraisal, and coping.* New York: Springer. [13]

LeDoux, J. E. (1993). Emotional memory systems in the brain. *Behavioural Brain Research, 58*, 69–79. [2]

LeDoux, J. E. (1994). Emotion, memory, and the brain. *Scientific American, 270*, 50–57. [2]

Lefebvre, P. P., Malgrange, B., Staecker, H., Moonen, G., & Van De Water, T. R. (1993). Retinoic acid stimulates regeneration of mammalian auditory hair cells. *Science, 260*, 692–695. [3]

Leger, D. (1994). The cost of sleep-related accidents: A report for the National Commission on Sleep Disorders Research. *Sleep, 17*, 84–93. [5]

Leigh, B. C., & Stall, R. (1993). Substance use and risky sexual behavior for exposure to HIV: Issues in methodology, interpretation, and prevention. *American Psychologist, 48*, 1035–1045. [11]

Leiner, H. C., Leiner, A. L., & Dow, R. S. (1993). Cognitive and language functions of the human cerebellum. *Trends in Neurosciences, 16*, 444–447. [2]

Lenneberg, E. (1967). *Biological foundations of language.* New York: Wiley. [8]

Leon, M. (1992). The neurobiology of filial learning. *Annual Review of Psychology, 43*, 337–398. [8]

Lepper, M. R., Greene, D., & Nisbett, R. E. (1973). Undermining children's intrinsic interest with extrinsic rewards: A test of the "overjustification" hypothesis. *Journal of Personality and Social Psychology, 28*, 129–137. [5]

Lesage, A. D., Boyer, R., Grunberg, F., Vanier, C., Morissette, R., Ménard-Buteau, C., & Loyer, M. (1994). Suicide and mental disorders: A case-control study of young men. *American Journal of Psychiatry, 151*, 1063–1068. [14]

Lester, B. M., Hoffman, J., & Brazelton, T. B. (1985). The rhythmic structure of mother-infant interaction in term and preterm infants. *Child Development, 56*, 15–27. [8]

LeVay, S. (1991). A difference in hypothalamic structure between heterosexual and homosexual men. *Science, 253*, 1034–1037. [11]

LeVay, S. (1993). *The sexual brain.* Cambridge, MA: MIT Press. [11]

LeVay, S., & Hamer, D. H. (1994). Evidence for a biological influence in male homosexuality. *Scientific American, 270*, 44–49. [11]

Levenson, R. W., Carstensen, L. L., & Gottman, J. M. (1993). Long-term marriage: Age, gender, and satisfaction. *Psychology and Aging, 8*, 301–313. [9]

Levenson, R. W., Ekman, P., & Friesen, W. (1990). Voluntary facial action generates emotion-specific autonomic nervous system activity. *Psychophysiology, 27*, 363–385. [10]

Leventhal, H., Singer, R. P., & Jones, S. (1965). The effects of fear and specificity of recommendation upon attitudes and behavior. *Journal of Personality and Social Psychology, 2*, 20–29. [16]

Leventhal, H., & Tomarken, A. J. (1986). Emotion: Today's problems. *Annual Review of Psychology, 37*, 565–610. [10]

Levi, L. (1990). Occupational stress: Spice of life or kiss of death? *American Psychologist, 45*, 1142–1145. [17]

Levine, C., Kohlberg, L., & Hewer, A. (1985). The current formulation of Kohlberg's theory and a response to critics. *Human Development, 28*, 94–100. [9]

Levine, D. S. (1988, November/December). Survival of the synapses. *The Sciences, 28*, 46–53. [2]

Levine, W. C., Berg, A. O., Johnson, R. E., Rolfs, R. T., Stone, K. M., Hook, E. W., III, Handsfield, H. H., Holmes, K. K., Islam, M. Q., Piot, P., Brady, W. E., Schmid, G. P., and STD Treatment Guidelines Project Team and consultants. (1994). Development of sexually transmitted diseases treatment guidelines, 1993: New methods, recommendations, and research priorities. *Sexually Transmitted Diseases, 21*(2, Suppl.), S96–S101. [11]

Levinson, D. J. (1986). A conception of adult development. *American Psychologist, 41*, 3–13. [9]

Levinson, D. J., with Darrow, C. N., Klein, E. B., Levinson, M. H., & McKee, B. (1978). *Seasons of a man's life.* New York: Knopf. [9]

Levitt, A. G., & Wang, Q. (1991). Evidence for language-specific rhythmic influences in the reduplicative babbling of French- and English-learning infants. *Language and Speech, 34*, 235–249. [8]

Levitt, E. E., & Duckworth, J. C. (1984). Minnesota Multiphasic Personality Inventory. In D. J. Keyser & R. C. Sweetland (Eds.), *Test critiques* (Vol. 1, pp. 466–472). Kansas City: Test Corporation of America. [12]

Levy, G. D., & Carter, D. B. (1989). Gender-schema, gender constancy, and gender-role knowledge: The roles of cognitive factors in preschoolers' gender-role stereotype attributions. *Developmental Psychology, 25*, 444–449. [11]

Levy, J. (1985, May). Right brain, left brain: Fact and fiction. *Psychology Today,* pp. 38–44. [2]

Levy, J., & Nagylaki, T. (1972). A model for the genetics of handedness. *Genetics, 72*, 117–128. [2]

Lewinsohn, P. M., & Rosenbaum, M. (1987). Recall of parental behavior by acute depressives, remitted depressives, and nondepressives. *Journal of Personality and Social Psychology, 52*, 611–619. [6]

Lewis, D. O., Pincus, J. H., Feldman, M., Jackson, L., & Bard, B. (1986). Psychiatric, neurological, and psychoeducational characteristics of 15 death row inmates in the United States. *American Journal of Psychiatry, 143*, 838–845. [16]

Lewis-Fernández, R., & Kleinman, A. (1994). Culture, personality, and psychopathology. *Journal of Abnormal Psychology, 103*, 67–71. [15]

Libb, J. W., Murray, J., Thurstin, H., & Alarcon, R. D. (1992). Concordance of the MCMI-II, the MMPI, and Axis I discharge diagnosis in psychiatric inpatients. *Journal of Personality Assessment, 58*, 580–590. [12]

Lidz, T., Fleck, S., & Cornelison, A. R. (1965). *Schizophrenia and the family.* New York: International Universities Press. [14]

Lieberman, J., Bogerts, B., Degreef, G., Ashtari, M., Lantos, G., & Alvir, J. (1992). Qualitative assessment of brain morphology in acute and chronic schizophrenia. *American Journal of Psychiatry, 149*, 784–794. [14]

Lieberman, M. (1986). Self-help groups and psychiatry. *American Psychiatric Association Annual Review, 5*, 744–760. [15]

Lieberman, M. A., Yalom, I. D., & Miles, M. B. (1973). *Encounter groups: First facts.* New York: Basic Books. [15]

Liebert, R. M., Sprafkin, J. N., & Davidson, E. S. (1989). *The early window: Effects of television on children and youth* (3rd ed.). New York: Pergamon. [16]

Liebowitz, H., Brislin, R., Perlmutter, L., & Hennessy, R. (1969). Ponzo perspective as a manifestation of space perception. *Science, 166*, 1174–1176. [3]

Liebowitz, H., & Pick, H. (1972). Cross-cultural and educational aspects of the Ponzo perspective illusion. *Perception and Psychophysics, 12*, 430–432. [3]

Lilly, J. C. (1956). Mental effects of reduction of ordinary levels of physical stimuli in intact, healthy persons. *Psychiatric Research Reports, 5*, 1–5. [10]

Lindenberger, U., Mayr, U., & Kliegl, R. (1993). Speed and intelligence in old age. *Psychology and Aging, 8*, 207–220. [9]

Linn, M. C., & Hyde, J. S. (1989). Gender, mathematics, and science. *Educational Researcher, 18*, 17–27. [11]

Linn, M. C., & Peterson, A. C. (1985). Emergence and characterization of sex differences in spatial ability: A meta-analysis. *Child Development, 56*, 1479–1498. [11]

Linn, R. L. (1982). Ability testing: Individual differences, prediction, and differential prediction. In A. K. Wigdor & W. R. Garner (Eds.), *Ability testing: Uses, consequences, and controversies (Part II).* Washington, DC: National Academy Press. [7]

Linton, M. (1979, July). I remember it well. *Psychology Today,* pp. 80–86. [6]

Linville, P. W., Fischer, G. W., & Salovey, P. (1989). Perceived distributions of the characteristics of in-group and out-group members: Empirical evidence and a computer simulation. *Journal of Personality and Social Psychology, 57*, 165–188. [16]

Linz, D. (1989). Exposure to sexually explicit materials and attitudes toward rape: A comparison of study results. *Journal of Sex Research, 26*, 50–84. [11]

Linz, D., Donnerstein, E., & Penrod, S. (1984). The effects of multiple exposures to filmed violence against women. *Journal of Communication, 34*, 130–147. [11]

Linz, D., Donnerstein, E., & Penrod, S. (1988). The effects of long-term exposure to violent and sexually degrading depictions of women. *Journal of Personality and Social Psychology, 55*, 758–768. [11]

Lipschitz, A. (1988). Diagnosis and classification of anxiety disorders. In C. G. Last & M. Herson (Eds.), *Handbook of anxiety disorders* (pp. 41–65). New York: Pergamon Press. [14]

Lipsey, M. W., & Wilson, D. B. (1993). The efficacy of psychological, educational, and behavioral treatment: Confirmation from meta-analysis. *American Psychologist, 48,* 1181–1209. [15]

Lipsitt, L. P. (1990). Learning processes in the human newborn: Sensitization, habituation, and classical conditioning. *Annals of the New York Academy of Sciences, 608,* 113–123. [8]

Lishman, W. A. (1990). Alcohol and the brain. *British Journal of Psychiatry, 156,* 635–644. [13]

Little, R. E., Anderson, K. W., Ervin, C. H., Worthington-Roberts, B., & Clarren, S. K. (1989). Maternal alcohol use during breast-feeding and infant mental and motor development at one year. *New England Journal of Medicine, 321,* 425–430. [8]

Livingstone, M. S. (1988). Art, illusion and the visual system. *Scientific American, 258,* 78–85. [3]

Lizza, E. F., & Cricco-Lizza, R. (1990, October). Impotence—Finding the cause. *Medical Aspects of Human Sexuality, 24,* 30–40. [11]

Lloyd, G. G., & Lishman, W. A. (1975). Effect of depression on the speed of recall of pleasant and unpleasant experiences. *Psychological Medicine, 5,* 173–180. [6]

Locke, E. A., & Latham, G. P. (1990). *A theory of goal setting and task performance.* Englewood Cliffs, NJ: Prentice-Hall. [17]

Locke, E. A., Shaw, K. N., Saari, L. M., & Latham, G. P. (1981). Goal setting and task performance: 1969–1980. *Psychological Bulletin, 90,* 125–152. [17]

Loehlin, J. C. (1992). *The limits of family influence: Genes, experience, and behavior.* New York: Guilford. [12]

Loehlin, J. C., Horn, J. M., & Willerman, L. (1989). Modeling IQ change: Evidence from the Texas Adoption Project. *Child Development, 60,* 993–1004. [7]

Loehlin, J. C., Horn, J. M., & Willerman, L. (1990). Heredity, environment, and personality change: Evidence from the Texas Adoption Project. *Journal of Personality, 58,* 221–243. [12]

Loehlin, J. C., Lindzey, G., & Spuhler, J. N. (1975). *Race differences in intelligence.* San Francisco: Freeman. [7]

Loehlin, J. C., Vandenberg, S., & Osborne, R. (1973). Blood group genes and Negro-White ability comparisons. *Behavior Genetics, 3,* 263–270. [7]

Loehlin, J. C., Willerman, L., & Horn, J. M. (1987). Personality resemblance in adoptive families: A 10-year follow-up. *Journal of Personality and Social Psychology, 53,* 961–969. [12]

Loehlin, J. C., Willerman, L., & Horn, J. M. (1988). Human behavior genetics. *Annual Review of Psychology, 39,* 101–133. [7, 12, 14]

Loftus, E. (1980). *Memory: Surprising new insights into how we remember and why we forget.* Reading, MA: Addison-Wesley. [6]

Loftus, E. F. (1975). Leading questions and the eyewitness report. *Cognitive Psychology, 7,* 560–572. [6]

Loftus, E. F. (1979). *Eyewitness testimony.* Cambridge, MA: Harvard University Press. [6]

Loftus, E. F. (1984, February). Eyewitnesses: Essential but unreliable. *Psychology Today,* pp. 22–27. [6]

Loftus, E. F. (1993a). Psychologists in the eyewitness world. *American Psychologist, 48,* 550–552. [6]

Loftus, E. F. (1993b). The reality of repressed memories. *American Psychologist, 48,* 518–537. [6]

Loftus, E. F. (1994). The repressed memory controversy. *American Psychologist, 49,* 443–445. [6]

Loftus, E. F., & Hoffman, H. G. (1989). Misinformation and memory: The creation of new memories. *Journal of Experimental Psychology: General, 118,* 100–104. [6]

Loftus, E. F., & Klinger, M. R. (1992). Is the unconscious smart or dumb? *American Psychologist, 47,* 761–765. [12]

Loftus, E. F., & Loftus, G. R. (1980). On the permanence of stored information in the human brain. *American Psychologist, 35,* 409–420. [6]

Logue, A. W. (1985). Conditioned food aversion learning in humans. *Annals of the New York Academy of Sciences, 443,* 316–329. [5]

Logue, A. W., Ophir, I., & Strauss, K. R. (1981). The acquisition of taste aversions in humans. *Behaviour Research and Therapy, 19,* 319–333. [5]

Long, G. M., & Crambert, R. F. (1990). The nature and basis of age-related changes in dynamic visual acuity. *Psychology and Aging, 5,* 138–143. [9]

Lorayne, H., & Lucas, J. (1974). *The memory book.* New York: Stein & Day. [6]

Lord, L. J., Goode, E. E., Gest, T., McAuliffe, K., Moore, L. J., Black, R. F., & Linnon, N. (1987, November 30). Coming to grips with alcoholism. *U.S. News & World Report,* pp. 56–62. [13]

Lorenz, K. (1966). *On aggression.* New York: Harcourt, Brace, & World. [16]

Lovaas, I. (1967). A behavior therapy approach to the treatment of childhood schizophrenia. In J. P. Hill (Ed.), *Minnesota symposia on child development* (Vol. 1, pp. 108–159). Minneapolis: University of Minnesota Press. [8]

Lovelace, E. A., & Twohig, P. T. (1990). Healthy older adults' perceptions of their memory functioning and use of mnemonics. *Bulletin of the Psychonomic Society, 28,* 115–118. [9]

Lubin, B., Larsen, R. M., Matarazzo, J. D., & Seever, M. (1986). Psychological assessment services and psychological test usage in private practice and in military settings. *Psychotherapy in Private Practice, 4,* 19–29. [12]

Luchins, A. S. (1957). Experimental attempts to minimize the impact of first impressions. In C. I. Hovland (Ed.), *Yale studies in attitude and communication: Vol. 1. The order of presentation in persuasion* (pp. 62–75). New Haven, CT: Yale University Press. [16]

Lucio, E., Reyes-Lagunes, I., & Scott, R. L. (1994). MMPI-2 for Mexico: Translation and adaptation. *Journal of Personality Assessment, 63,* 105–116. [12]

Lukeman, D., & Melvin, D. (1993). Annotation: The preterm infant: Psychological issues in childhood. *Journal of Child Psychology and Psychiatry, 34,* 837–849. [8]

Lummis, M., & Stevenson, H. W. (1990). Gender differences in beliefs about achievement: A cross-cultural study. *Developmental Psychology, 26,* 254–263. [11]

Lundgren, C. B. (1986, August 20). Cocaine addiction: A revolutionary new treatment. *St. Louis Jewish Light,* p. 7. [4]

Lydiard, R. B., Brewerton, T. D., Fossey, M. D., Laraia, M. T., Stuart, G., Beinfeld, M. C., & Ballenger, J. C. (1993). CSF cholecystokinin octapeptide in patients with bulimia nervosa and in normal comparison subjects. *American Journal of Psychiatry, 150,* 1099–1101. [10]

Lykken, D. T. (1981). A tremor in the blood: *Uses and abuses of the lie detector.* New York: McGraw-Hill. [10]

Lykken, D. T. (1985). The probity of the polygraph. In S. M. Kassin & L. S. Wrightsman (Eds.), *The psychology of evidence and trial procedure.* Beverly Hills, CA: Sage. [10]

Lykken, D. T., Bouchard, T. J., Jr., McGue, M., & Tellegen, A. (1990). The Minnesota Twin Family Registry: Some initial findings. *Acta Geneticae Medicae et Gemellologiae (Rome), 39,* 35–70. [7]

Maas, P. (1994, September 18). The menace of China White. *Parade Magazine,* pp. 4–6. [4]

Maccoby, E. E. (1992). The role of parents in the socialization of children: An historical overview. *Developmental Psychology, 28,* 1006–1017. [8]

Maccoby, E. E., & Jacklin, C. M. (1974a). *The psychology of sex differences.* Stanford, CA: Stanford University Press. [11]

Maccoby, E. E., & Jacklin, C. N. (1974b, December). What we know and don't know about sex differences. *Psychology Today,* pp. 109–112. [11]

Maccoby, E. E., & Jacklin, C. N. (1980). Sex differences in aggression: A rejoinder and reprise. *Child Development, 51,* 964–980.

Maccoby, E. E., & Martin, J. A. (1983). Socialization in the context of the family: Parent-child interaction. In P. H. Mussen (Ed.), *Handbook of child psychology* (4th ed., Vol. 4). New York: John Wiley. [8]

MacCoun, R. J. (1989). Experimental research on jury decision-making. *Science, 244,* 1046–1050. [17]

MacFarlane, A. (1978). What a baby knows. *Human Nature, 1,* 74–81. [8]

Macrae, C. N., Milne, A. B., & Bodenhausen, G. V. (1994). Stereotypes as energy-saving devices: A peek inside the cognitive toolbox. *Journal of Personality and Social Psychology, 66,* 37–47. [16]

Mahoney, E. R. (1983). *Human sexuality.* New York: McGraw-Hill. [11]

Maier, S. F., & Laudenslager, M. (1985, August). Stress and health: Exploring the links. *Psychology Today,* pp. 44–49. [13]

Maj, M. (1990). Psychiatric aspects of HIV–1 infection and AIDS. *Psychological Medicine, 20,* 547–563. [11]

Maj, M., Veltro, F., Pirozzi, R., Lobrace, S., & Magliano, L. (1992). Pattern of recurrence of illness after recovery from an episode of major depression: A prospective study. *Journal of Personality and Social Psychology, 62,* 795–800. [14, 15]

Major, B., Schmidlin, A. M., & Williams, L. (1990). Gender patterns in social touch: The impact of setting and age. *Journal of Personality and Social Psychology, 58,* 634–643. [16]

Malamuth, N. M. (1984). Aggression against women: Cultural and individual causes. In N. M. Malamuth & E. Donnerstein (Eds.), *Pornography and sexual aggression* (pp. 19–52). Orlando, FL: Academic Press. [11]

Malamuth, N. M., & Ceniti, J. (1986). Repeated exposure to violent and nonviolent pornography: Likelihood of raping ratings and laboratory aggression against women. *Aggressive Behavior, 12,* 129–137. [11]

Maletzky, B. M. (1974). "Assisted" covert sensitization in the treatment of exhibitionism. *Journal of Consulting and Clinical Psychology, 42,* 34–40. [15]

Malkoff, S. B., Muldoon, M. F., Zeigler, Z. R., & Manuck, S. B. (1993). Blood platelet responsivity to acute mental stress. *Psychomatic Medicine, 55,* 477–482. [13]

Mandler, J. M. (1990). A new perspective on cognitive development in infancy. *American Scientist, 78*(3), 236–243. [8]

Manton, K. G., Siegler, I. C., & Woodbury, M. A. (1986). Patterns of intellectual development in later life. *Journal of Gerontology, 41,* 486–499. [9]

Maratsos, M. (1983). Some current issues in the study of the acquisition of grammar. In P. H. Mussen (Ed.), *Handbook of child psychology* (Vol. 3). New York: Wiley. [8]

Maratsos, M., & Matheny, L. (1994). Language specificity and elasticity: Brain and clinical syndrome studies. *Annual Review of Psychology, 45,* 487–516. [2]

Marcia, J. (1980). Identity in adolescence. In J. Adelson (Ed.), *Handbook of adolescent psychology.* New York: Wiley. [9]

Marcus, G. F., Pinker, S., Ullman, M., Hollander, M., Rosen, T. J., & Xu, F. (1992). Overregularization in language acquisition. *Monographs for the Society for Research in Child Development, 57*(4, Serial No. 228). [8]

Marder, S. R., & Meibach, R. C. (1994). Risperidone in the treatment of schizophrenia. *American Journal of Psychiatry, 161,* 825–835. [15]

Marín, G. (1994). The experience of being a Hispanic in the United States. In W. J. Lonner & R. Malpass (Eds.), *Psychology and culture* (pp. 23–27). Boston: Allyn & Bacon. [12]

Marks, G. A., Shaffery, J. P., Oksenberg, A., Speciale, S. G., & Roffwarg, H. P. (1995). A functional role for REM sleep in brain maturation. *Behavioural Brain Research, 69,* 1–11. [4]

Marks, I. (1987a). Behavioral aspects of panic disorder. *American Journal of Psychiatry, 144,* 1160–1165. [14]

Marks, I. (1987b). The development of normal fear: A review. *Journal of Child Psychology and Psychiatry, 28,* 667–697. [8]

Marks, I. (1988). Blood-injury phobia: A review. *American Journal of Psychiatry, 145,* 1207–1213. [14]

Marks, I. M. (1972). Flooding (implosion) and allied treatments. In W. S. Agras (Ed.), *Behavior modification.* New York: Little, Brown. [15]

Marks, I. M. (1978a). Behavioral psychotherapy of adult neurosis. In S. Garfield & A. E. Bergin (Eds.), *Handbook of psychotherapy and behavior change* (2nd ed.). New York: Wiley. [15]

Marks, I. M. (1978b). Living with fear: *Understanding and coping with anxiety.* New York: McGraw-Hill. [14]

Marlatt, G. A. (1983). The controlled-drinking controversy: A commentary. *American Psychologist, 38,* 1097–1110. [13]

Marlatt, G. A., & Rohsenow, D. J. (1981, December). The think-drink effect. *Psychology Today,* pp. 60–69, 93. [1]

Marmor, J. (Ed.). (1980). *Homosexual behavior: A modern reappraisal.* New York: Basic Books. [11]

Marshall, G. D., & Zimbardo, P. G. (1979). Affective consequences of inadequately explained physiological arousal. *Journal of Personality and Social Psychology, 37,* 970–988. [10]

Marshall, R. D., Schneier, F. R., Fallon, B. A., Feerick, J., & Liebowitz, M. R. (1994). Medication therapy for social phobia. *Journal of Clinical Psychiatry, 56*(6, Suppl.), 33–37. [15]

Marshall, W. L., & Segal, Z. (1988). Behavior therapy. In C. G. Last & M. Hersen (Eds.), *Handbook of anxiety disorders* (pp. 338–361). New York: Pergamon. [15]

Marsiglio, W. (1993). Attitudes toward homosexual activity and gays as friends: A national survey of heterosexual 15- to 19-year-old males. *Journal of Sex Research, 30,* 12–17. [11]

Martin, C. L. (1990). Attitudes and expectations about children and nontraditional gender roles. *Sex Roles, 22,* 151–155. [11]

Martin, C. L., & Little, J. K. (1990). The relation of gender understanding to children's sex-typed preferences and gender stereotypes. *Child Development, 61,* 1427–1439. [11]

Martin, C. L., Wood, C. H., & Little, J. K. (1990). The development of gender stereotype components. *Child Development, 61,* 1891–1904. [11]

Martin, N. G., Eaves, L. J., Heath, A. C., Jardine, R., Feingold, L. M., & Eysenck, H. J. (1986). Transmission of social attitudes. *Proceedings of the National Academy of Sciences, U.S.A., 83,* 4364–4368. [12]

Martinez, C. (1986). Hispanics: Psychiatric issues. In C. B. Wilkinson (Ed.), *Ethnic psychiatry* (pp. 61–88). New York: Plenum. [15]

Martinez-Taboas, A. (1991). Multiple personality in Puerto Rico: Analysis of fifteen cases. *Dissociation, 4,* 189–192. [14]

Martorano, S. C. (1977). A developmental analysis of performance on Piaget's formal operations tasks. *Developmental Psychology, 13,* 666–672. [9]

Maslow, A. H. (1970). *Motivation and personality* (2nd ed.). New York: Harper & Row. [10, 12, 14]

Massion, A. O., Warshaw, M. G., & Keller, M. B. (1993). Quality of life and psychiatric morbidity in panic disorder and generalized anxiety disorder. *American Journal of Psychiatry, 150,* 600–607. [14]

Masters, J. C. (1981). Developmental psychology. *Annual Review of Psychology, 32,* 117–151. [8]

Masters, W. H., & Johnson, V. E. (1966). *Human sexual response.* Boston: Little, Brown [9, 11]

Masters, W. H., & Johnson, V. E. (1975). *The pleasure bond: A new look at sexuality and commitment.* Boston: Little, Brown. [11]

Masters, W. H., & Johnson, V. E. (1979). *Homosexuality in perspective.* Boston: Little, Brown. [11]

Mathew, R. J., & Wilson, W. H. (1991). Substance abuse and cerebral blood flow. *American Journal of Psychiatry, 148,* 292–305. [4]

Matthews, K. A., Wing, R. R., Kuller, L. H., Meilahn, E. N., Kelsey, S. F., Costello, E. J., & Caggiula, A. W. (1990). Influences of natural menopause on psychological characteristics and symptoms of middle-aged healthy women. *Journal of Consulting and Clinical Psychology, 58,* 345–351. [9]

Matlin, M. W. (1989). *Cognition* (2nd ed.). New York: Holt, Rinehart & Winston. [6]

Matlin, M. W., & Foley, H. J. (1992). *Sensation and perception* (3rd ed.). Boston: Allyn & Bacon. [3]

Matsuda, L., Lolait, S. J., Brownstein, M. J., Young, A. C., & Bonner, T. I. (1990). Structure of a cannabinoid receptor and functional expression of the cloned CDNA. *Nature, 346,* 561–564. [4]

Mattick, R. P., Andrews, G., Hadzi-Pavlovic, D., & Christensen, H. (1990). Treatment of panic and agoraphobia: An integrative review. *Journal of Nervous and Mental Disease, 178,* 567–576. [15]

Mauro, J. (1994, July/August). And Proza for all. *Psychology Today,* 44–48, 80–81. [15]

Mavissakalian, M. (1990). Sequential combination of imipramine and self-directed exposure in the treatment of panic disorder with agoraphobia. *Journal of Clinical Psychiatry, 51,* 184–188. [15]

Mavissakalian, M. R., & Perel, J. M. (1995). Imipramine treatment of panic disorder with agoraphobia: Dose ranging and plasma-level response relationships. *American Journal of Psychiatry, 152,* 673–682. [15]

May, R. (1982). The problem of evil: An open letter to Carl Rogers. *Journal of Humanistic Psychology, 22,* 10–21. [12]

Mayer, W. (1983). Alcohol abuse and alcoholism: The psychologist's role in prevention, research, and treatment. *American Psychologist, 38,* 1116–1121. [4, 13]

McAdams, D. P. (1992). The five-factor model in personality: A critical appraisal. *Journal of Personality, 60,* 329–361. [12]

McAdams, D. P., de St. Aubin, E., & Logan, R. L. (1993). Generativity among young, midlife, and older adults. *Psychology and Aging, 8,* 221–230. [9]

McAneny, L. (1992). Number of drinkers on the rise again. *Gallup Poll Monthly,* No. 317, 43–47. [4]

McCarthy, P. (1989, March). Ageless sex. *Psychology Today,* p. 62. [9]

McCartney, K., Harris, M. J., & Bernieri, F. (1990). Growing up and growing apart: A developmental meta-analysis of twin studies. *Psychological Bulletin, 107,* 226–237. [7]

McCaul, K. D., & Malott, J. M. (1984). Distraction and coping with pain. *Psychological Bulletin, 95,* 516–533. [3]

McClelland, D. C. (1958). Methods of measuring human motivation. In J. W. Atkinson (Ed.), *Motives in fantasy, action and society: A method of assessment and study.* Princeton, NJ: Van Nostrand. [10]

McClelland, D. C. (1985). *Human motivation.* Glenview, IL: Scott, Foresman. [10]

McClelland, D. C., Atkinson, J. W., Clark, R. W., & Lowell, E. L. (1953). *The achievement motive.* New York: Appleton-Century-Crofts. [10]

McClelland, D. C., & Pilon, D. A. (1983). Sources of adult motives in patterns of parent behavior in early childhood. *Journal of Personality and Social Psychology, 44,* 564–574. [10]

McConnell, J. V., Cutler, R. L., & McNeil, E. B. (1958). Subliminal stimulation: An overview. *American Psychologist, 13,* 229–242. [3]

McCourt, W. F., Gurrera, R. J., & Cutter, H. S. G. (1993). Sensation seeking and novelty seeking: Are they the same? *Journal of Nervous and Mental Disease, 181,* 309–312. [10]

McCrae, R. (1984). Situational determinants of coping responses: Loss, threat, and challenge. *Journal of Personality and Social Psychology, 46,* 919–928. [13]

McCrae, R. R. (1993). Moderated analyses of longitudinal personality stability. *Journal of Personality and Social Psychology, 65,* 577–583. [12]

McCrae, R. R., & Costa, P. T., Jr. (1987). Validation of the five-factor model of personality across instruments and observers. *Journal of Personality and Social Psychology, 52,* 81–90. [12]

McCrae, R. R., & Costa, P. T., Jr. (1990). *Personality in adulthood.* New York: Guilford Press. [12]

McCrae, R. R., & John, O. P. (1992). An introduction to the five-factor model and its applications. *Journal of Personality, 60,* 175–215. [12]

McDaniel, M. A., Anderson, D. C., Einstein, G. O., & O'Halloran, C. M. (1989). Modulation of environmental reinstatement effects through encoding strategies. *American Journal of Psychology, 102,* 523–548. [6]

McDonald, A. D., Armstrong, B. G., & Sloan, M. (1992). Cigarette, alcohol, and coffee consumption and prematurity. *American Journal of Public Health, 82,* 87–90. [8]

McDougall, W. (1908). *An introduction to social psychology.* London: Methuen. [10]

McGee, A-M., & Skinner, M. (1987). Facial asymmetry and the attribution of personality traits. *British Journal of Social Psychology, 26,* 181–184. [2]

McGlashan, T. H., & Fenton, W. S. (1992). The positive-negative distinction in schizophrenia: Review of natural history validators. *Archives of General Psychiatry, 49,* 63–72. [14]

McGue, M., Pickens, R. W., & Svikis, D. S. (1992). Sex and age effects on the inheritance of alcohol problems: A twin study. *Journal of Abnormal Psychology, 101,* 3–17. [13]

McGuire, P. K., Shah, G. M. S., & Murray, R. M. (1993). Increased blood flow in Broca's area during auditory hallucinations in schizophrenia. *Lancet, 342,* 703–706. [14]

McGuire, W. J. (1985). Attitudes and attitude change. In G. Lindzey & E. Aronson (Ed.), *Handbook of social psychology* (Vol. 2, 3rd ed.). New York: Random House. [16]

McHugh, P. R. (1993). Multiple personality disorder. *Harvard Mental Health Letter, 10*(3), 4–6. [14]

McIntosh, D. N., Silver, R. C., & Wortman, C. B. (1993). Religion's role in adjustment to a negative life event: Coping with the loss of a child. *Journal of Personality and Social Psychology, 65,* 812–821. [13]

McKellar, P. (1972). Imagery from the standpoint of introspection. In P. W. Sheehan (Ed.), *The function and nature of imagery* (pp. 36–63). New York: Academic Press. [7]

McKelvie, S. J. (1984). Relationship between set and functional fixedness: A replication. *Perceptual and Motor Skills, 58,* 996–998. [7]

McKinley, J. C., & Hathaway, S. R. (1943). The identification and measurement of the psychoneuroses in medical practice: The Minnesota Multiphasic Personality Inventory. *Journal of the American Medical Association, 122,* 161–167. [12]

McNaughton, M. E., Smith, L. W., Patterson, T. L., & Grant, I. (1990). Stress, social support, coping resources, and immune status in elderly women. *Journal of Nervous and Mental Disease, 178,* 460–461. [13]

McReynolds, P. (1989). Diagnosis and clinical assessment: Current status and major issues. *Annual Review of Psychology, 40,* 83–108. [12]

Medina, J. H., Paladini, A. C., & Izquierdo, I. (1993). Naturally occurring benzodiazepines and benzodiazepine-like molecules in brain. *Behavioural Brain Research, 58,* 1–8. [15]

Mednick, S. A., Brennan, P., & Kandel, E. (1988). Predisposition to violence. *Aggressive Behavior, 14,* 25–33. [16]

Mednick, S. A., & Mednick, M. T. (1967). *Examiner's manual, Remote Associates Test.* Boston: Houghton-Mifflin. [7]

Medzerian, G. (1991). *Crack: Treating cocaine addiction.* Blue Ridge Summit, PA: Tab Books. [4, 5]

Meer, J. (1986, June). The age of reason. *Psychology Today,* pp. 60–64. [9]

Mefford, I. N., Baker, T. L., Boehme, R., Foutz, A. S., Ciaranello, R. D., Barchas, J. D., & Dement, W. C. (1983). Narcolepsy: Biogenic amine deficits in an animal model. *Science, 220,* 629–632. [4]

Mehrabian, A. (1968, September). Communication without words. *Psychology Today,* pp. 53–55. [16]

Meichenbaum, D. (1977). *Cognitive behavior modification: An integrative approach.* New York: Plenum. [13]

Meier, R. P. (1991). Language acquisition by deaf children. *American Scientist, 79*(1), 60–70. [8]

Melamed, B. G., & Siegal, L. J. (1975). Reduction of anxiety in children facing hospitalization and surgery by use of filmed modeling. *Journal of Consulting and Clinical Psychology, 43,* 511–521. [15]

Meltzer, H. (1930). Individual differences in forgetting pleasant and unpleasant experiences. *Journal of Educational Psychology, 21,* 399–409. [6]

Meltzer, H. Y. (1995). Clozapine: Is another view valid? *American Journal of Psychiatry, 152,* 821–825. [15]

Meltzoff, A. N. (1988a). Imitation of televised models by infants. *Child Development, 59,* 1221–1229. [8]

Meltzoff, A. N. (1988b). Infant imitation and memory: Nine-month-olds in immediate and deferred tests. *Child Development, 59,* 217–255. [8]

Meltzoff, A. N., & Moore, M. K. (1977). Imitation of facial and manual gestures by human neonates. *Science, 198,* 75–78. [8]

Meltzoff, A. N., & Moore, M. K. (1989). Imitation in newborn infants: Exploring the range of gestures imitated and the underlying mechanisms. *Developmental Psychology, 25,* 954–962. [8]

Melzack, R., & Wall, P. D. (1965). Pain mechanisms: A new theory. *Science, 150,* 971–979. [3]

Melzack, R., & Wall, P. D. (1983). *The challenge of pain.* New York: Basic Books. [3]

Mercer, J. R. (1973). *Labelling the mentally retarded*. Berkeley: University of California Press. [7]

Merckelbach, H., Arntz, A., & de Jong, P. (1991). Conditioning experiences in spider phobics. *Behaviour Research and Therapy, 29*, 333–335. [14]

Merckelbach, H., de Ruiter, C., van den Hout, M. A., & Hoekstra, R. (1989). Conditioning experiences and phobias. *Behaviour Research and Therapy, 27*, 657–662. [14]

Metter, E. J. (1991). Brain-behavior relationships in aphasia studied by positron emission tomography. *Annals of the New York Academy of Sciences, 620*, 153–164. [2]

Meyer, P. (1972). If Hitler asked you to electrocute a stranger, would you? In R. Greenbaum & H. A. Tilker (Eds.), *The challenge of psychology* (pp. 456–465). Englewood Cliffs, NJ: Prentice-Hall. [16]

Meyer-Bahlburg, H. F. (1977). Sex hormones and male homosexuality in comparative perspective. *Archives of Sexual Behavior, 6*, 297–325. [11]

Meyer-Bahlburg, H. F. L., Ehrhardt, A. A., Rosen, L. R., & Gruen, R. S. (1995). Prenatal estrogens and the development of homosexual orientation. *Developmental Psychology, 31*, 12–21. [11]

Michael, R. T., Gagnon, J. H., & Laumann, E. O. (1994). *Sex in America: A definitive survey*. Little, Brown. [11]

Michaels, J. W., Bloomel, J. M., Brocato, R. M., Linkous, R. A., & Rowe, J. S. (1982). Social facilitation and inhibition in a natural setting. *Replications in Social Psychology, 2*, 21–24. [16]

Michelini, R. L., & Snodgrass, S. S. (1980). Defendant characteristics and juridic decisions. *Journal of Research in Personality, 14*, 342–350. [17]

Michels, R., & Marzuk, P. M. (1993). Progress in psychiatry (First of two parts). *New England Journal of Medicine, 329*, 552–560. [15]

Michelson, L., Marchione, K., Greenwald, M., Glanz, L., Testa, S., & Marchione, N. (1990). Panic disorder: Cognitive-behavioral treatment. *Behaviour Research and Therapy, 28*, 141–151. [15]

Middlebrooks, J. C., & Green, D. M. (1991). Sound localization by human listeners. *Annual Review of Psychology, 42*, 135–159. [3]

Milavsky, J. R., Kessler, R., Stipp, H., & Rubens, W. S. (1982). Television and aggression: Results of a panel study. In D. Pearl, L. Bouthilet, & J. Lazar (Eds.), *Television and behavior: Ten years of scientific progress and implications for the eighties* (Vol. 2). Washington, DC: U.S. Government Printing Office. [16]

Milgram, S. (1963). Behavioral study of obedience. *Journal of Abnormal and Social Psychology, 67*, 371–378. [16]

Milgram, S. (1965). Liberating effects of group pressure. *Journal of Personality and Social Psychology, 1*, 127–134. [16]

Milgrom, P., Mancl, L., King, B., & Weinstein, P. (1995). Origins of childhood dental fear. *Behaviour Research and Therapy, 33*, 313–319. [14]

Miller, D. T., & Turnbull, W. (1986). Expectancies and interpersonal processes. *Annual Review of Psychology, 37*, 233–256. [16]

Miller, G. A. (1956). The magical number seven, plus or minus two: Some limits on our capacity for processing information. *Psychological Review, 63*, 81–97. [6]

Miller, G. A., & Gildea, P. M. (1987). How children learn words. *Scientific American, 257*, 94–99. [8]

Miller, I. J., & Reedy, F. E., Jr. (1990). Variations in human taste bud density and taste intensity perception. *Physiological Behavior, 47*, 1213–1219. [3]

Miller, J. G., & Bersoff, D. M. (1992). Culture and moral judgment: How are conflicts between justice and interpersonal responsibilities resolved? *Journal of Personality and Social Psychology, 62*, 541–554. [9]

Miller, J. G., Bersoff, D. M., & Harwood, R. L. (1990). Perceptions of social responsibilities in India and in the United States: Moral imperatives or personal decisions? *Journal of Personality and Social Psychology, 58*, 33–47. [16]

Miller, K. (1994, March 17). Safety quiz: Insurance-claims data don't show advantage of some auto devices. *The Wall Street Journal*, pp. A1, A7. [17]

Miller, L. (1988, February). The emotional brain. *Psychology Today*, pp. 34–42. [2]

Miller, L. (1989, November). What biofeedback does (and doesn't) do. *Psychology Today*, pp. 22–23. [5]

Miller, N. E. (1941). The frustration-aggression hypothesis. *Psychological Review, 48*, 337–342. [16]

Miller, N. E. (1985, February). Rx: Biofeedback. *Psychology Today*, pp. 54–59. [5]

Miller, N. S., & Gold, M. S. (1994). LSD and Ecstasy: Pharmacology, phenomenology, and treatment. *Psychiatric Annals, 24*, 131–133. [4]

Miller, T. Q., Turner, C. W., Tindale, R. S., Posavac, E. J., & Dugoni, B. L. (1991). Reasons for the trend toward null findings in research on Type A behavior. *Psychological Bulletin, 110*, 469–485. [13]

Miller, W. C., Lindeman, A. K., Wallace, J., & Niederpruem, M. (1990). Diet composition, energy intake, and exercise in relation to body fat in men and women. *American Journal of Clinical Nutrition, 52*, 426–430. [13]

Millman, R. B., & Beeder, A. B. (1994). The new psychedelic culture: LSD, Ecstasy, "rave" parties and The Grateful Dead. *Psychiatric Annals, 24*, 148–150. [4]

Mills, J. (1987, November). Life in the nineties: Grandma Whitney's climb to the top. *Women's Sports & Fitness*, p. 61. [9]

Milner, B. (1970). Memory and the medial temporal regions of the brain. In K. H. Pribram & D. E. Broadbent (Eds.), *Biology of memory*. New York: Academic Press. [6]

Milner, B., Corkin, S., & Teuber, H. L. (1968). Further analysis of the hippocampal amnesic syndrome: 14-year follow-up study of H. M. *Neuropsychologia, 6*, 215–234. [6]

Milner, B. R. (1966). Amnesia following operation on the temporal lobes. In C. W. M. Whitty & O. L. Zangwill (Eds.), *Amnesia* (pp. 109–133). London: Butterworth. [6]

Mischel, W. (1966). A social-learning view of sex differences in behavior. In E. E. Maccoby (Ed.), *The development of sex differences* (pp. 56–81). Stanford, CA: Stanford University Press. [11]

Mischel, W. (1968). *Personality and assessment*. New York: Wiley. [12]

Mischel, W. (1973). Toward a cognitive social learning reconceptualization of personality. *Psychological Review, 80*, 252–283. [12]

Mischel, W. (1977). The interaction of person and situation. In D. Magnusson & N. S. Endler (Eds.), *Personality at the crossroads: Current issues in interactional psychology*. Hillsdale, NJ: Lawrence Erlbaum. [12]

Mistlberger, R. E., & Rusak, B. (1989). Mechanisms and models of the circadian timekeeping system. In M. H. Kryger, T. Roth, & W. C. Dement (Eds.), *Principles and practice of sleep medicine* (pp. 141–152). Philadelphia: W. B. Saunders. [4]

Mistry, J., & Rogoff, B. (1994). Remembering in cultural context. In W. J. Lonner & R. Malpass (Eds.), *Psychology and culture* (pp. 139–144). Boston: Allyn & Bacon. [6]

Mitler, M. M., Aldrich, M. S., Koob, G. F., & Zarcone, V. P. (1994). Narcolepsy and its treatment with stimulants. *Sleep, 17*, 352–371. [4]

Mitler, M. M., Carskadon, M. A., Czeisler, C. A., Dement, W. C., Dinges, D. F., & Graeber, R. C. (1988). Catastrophes, sleep, and public policy: consensus report. *Sleep, 11*, 100–109. [4]

Modestin, J. (1992). Multiple personality disorder in Switzerland. *American Journal of Psychiatry, 148*, 88–92. [14]

Monane, M. (1992). Insomnia in the elderly. *Journal of Clinical Psychiatry, 53*(6, Suppl.), 23–28. [4]

Money, J. (1987). Sin, sickness, or status? Homosexual gender identity and psychoneuroendocrinology. *American Psychologist, 42*, 384–399. [11]

Money, J., & Schwartz, M. (1977). Dating, romantic and nonromantic friendships, and sexuality in 17 early-treated adrenogenital females, aged 16–25. In P. A. Lee et al. (Eds.), *Congenital adrenal hyperplasia*. Baltimore: University Park Press. [11]

Monk, T. H. (1989). Circadian rhythms in subjective activation, mood, and performance efficiency. In M. H. Kryger, T. Roth, & W. C. Dement (Eds.), *Principles and practice of sleep medicine* (pp. 163–172). Philadelphia: W. B. Saunders. [4]

Monk, T. H. (1990). Shiftworker performance. *Occupational Medicine: State of the Art Reviews, 5,* 183–198. [4]

Montagu, A. (1962). *The humanization of man.* Cleveland: World. [8]

Moore, D. W. (1993). Public polarized on gay issue. *Gallup Poll Monthly,* No. 331, 30–34. [11]

Moore, D. W., & Gallup, A. (1993). Are women more sexist than men? *Gallup Poll Monthly,* No. 336, 20–21. [11]

Moraglia, G. (1994). C. G. Jung and the psychology of adult development. *Journal of Analytical Psychology, 39,* 55–75. [12]

Moran, M. G., & Stoudemire, A. (1992). Sleep disorders in the medically ill patient. *Journal of Clinical Psychiatry, 53*(6, Suppl.), 29–36. [4]

Moreno, J. L. (1959). Psychodrama. In S. Arieti et al. (Eds.), *American handbook of psychiatry* (Vol. 2). New York: Basic Books. [15]

Morgan, C., Chapar, G. N., & Fisher, M. (1995). Psychosocial variables associated with teenage pregnancy. *Adolescence, 118,* 277–289. [9]

Morgan, C. D., & Murray, H. A. (1935). A method for investigating fantasies: The Thematic Apperception Test. *Archives of Neurology and Psychiatry, 34,* 289–306. [12]

Morgan, C. D., & Murray, H. A. (1962). Thematic Apperception Test. 530–545. In H. A. Murray et al. (Eds.), *Explorations in personality: A clinical and experimental study of fifty men of college age.* New York: Science Editions. [12]

Morgan, C. T., & Morgan, J. D. (1940). Studies in hunger: II. The relation of gastric denervation and dietary sugar to the effect of insulin upon food-intake in the rat. *Journal of Genetic Psychology, 57,* 153–163. [10]

Morin, C. M., Culbert, J. P., & Schwartz, S. M. (1994). Nonpharmacological interventions for insomnia: A meta-analysis of treatment efficacy. *American Journal of Psychiatry, 151,* 1172–1180. [4]

Morrison, A. M., & Von Glinow, M. S. (1990). Women and minorities in management. *American Psychologist, 45,* 200–208. [11, 16]

Morrison, T. L., Edwards, D. W., & Weissman, H. N. (1994). The MMPI and MMPI-2 as predictors of psychiatric diagnosis in an outpatient sample. *Journal of Personality Assessment, 62,* 17–30. [12]

Mościcki, E. K. (1995). Epidemiology of suicidal behavior. *Suicide and Life-Threatening Behavior, 24,* 22–35. [14]

Moscovitch, M., Behrmann, M., & Winocur, G. (1994). Do PETS have long or short ears? Mental imagery and neuroimaging. *Trends in Neurosciences, 17,* 292–294. [7]

Mosher, D. L., & Anderson, R. D. (1987). Macho personality, sexual aggression, and reactions to guided imagery of realistic rape. *Journal of Research in Personality, 20,* 77–94. [11]

Motley, M. T. (1985). Slips of the tongue. *Scientific American, 253,* 116–127. [12]

Mui, A. C. (1992). Caregiver strain among black and white daughter caregivers: A role theory perspective. *The Gerontologist, 32,* 203–212. [9]

Mukherjee, S., Sackeim, H. A., & Schnur, D. B. (1994). Electroconvulsive therapy of acute manic episodes: A review of 50 years' experience. *American Journal of Psychiatry, 151,* 169–176. [15]

Mullan, M., & Crawford, F. (1993). Genetic and molecular advances in Alzheimer's disease. *Trends in Neurosciences, 16,* 398–403. [9]

Mullington, J., & Broughton, R. (1993). Scheduled naps in the management of daytime sleepiness in narcolepsy-cataplexy. *Sleep, 16,* 444–456. [4]

Munroe, R. H., Shimmin, H. S., & Munroe, R. L. (1984). Gender role understanding and sex role preference in four cultures. *Developmental Psychology, 20,* 673–682. [11]

Murphy, D. L., & Pigott, T. A. (1990). A comparative examination of a role for serotonin in obsessive compulsive disorder, panic disorder, and anxiety. *Journal of Clinical Psychiatry, 51*(4, Suppl.), 53–58. [14]

Murphy, E. (1989, July 13–27). Townshend. Tinnitus and rock & roll. *Rolling Stone,* 101. [3]

Murray, H. (1938). *Explorations in personality.* New York: Oxford University Press. [10, 12]

Murray, H. A. (1965). Uses of the Thematic Apperception Test. In B. I. Murstein (Ed.), *Handbook of projective techniques* (pp. 425–432). New York: Basic Books. [12]

Mussen, P., Honzik, M., & Eichorn, D. (1982). Early adult antecedents of life satisfaction at age 70. *Journal of Gerontology, 37,* 315–322. [9]

Mussen, P. H., & Jones, M. C. (1957). Self-conceptions, motivations, and interpersonal attitudes of late- and early-maturing boys. *Child Development, 28,* 243–256. [9]

Myers, D. G., & Bishop, G. D. (1970). Discussion effects on racial attitudes. *Science, 169,* 778–779. [16]

Myers, D. G., & Lamm, H. (1975). The polarizing effect of group discussion. *American Scientist, 63,* 297–303. [16]

Nadon, R., Hoyt, I. P., Register, P. A., & Kilstrom, J. F. (1991). Absorption and hypnotizability: Context effects reexamined. *Journal of Personality and Social Psychology, 60,* 144–153. [4]

Narrow, W. E., Regier, D. A., Rae, D. S., Manderscheid, R. W., & Locke, B. Z. (1993). Use of services by persons with mental and addictive disorders: Findings from the National Institute of Mental Health Epidemiologic Catchment Area Program. *Archives of General Psychiatry, 50,* 95–107. [15]

Nash, M. (1987). What, if anything, is regressed about hypnotic age regression? A review of the empirical literature. *Psychological Bulletin, 102,* 42–52. [4]

Nash, M., & Baker, E. (1984, February). Trance encounters: Susceptibility to hypnosis. *Psychology Today,* pp. 18, 72–73. [4]

Nathan, P. E. (1983). Failures in prevention: Why we can't prevent the devastating effect of alcoholism and drug abuse. *American Psychologist, 38,* 453–467. [13]

Nathan, P. E. (1992). Peele hasn't done his homework—again: A response to "Alcoholism, politics, and bureaucracy: The consensus against controlled-drinking therapy in America." *Addictive Behaviors, 17,* 63–65. [13]

Nathans, J. (1989). The genes for color vision. *Scientific American, 260,* 42–49. [3]

Nathans, J., Davenport, C. M., Maumenee, I. H., Lewis, R. A., Heitmancik, J. F., Litt, M., Lovrien, E., Weleber, R., Bachynski, B., Zwas, F., Klingaman, R., & Fishman, G. (1989). Molecular genetics of human blue cone monochromacy. *Science, 245,* 831–838. [3]

National Institute on Drug Abuse. (1993, April 13). *Annual national high school senior survey.* Rockville, MD: NIDA. [4]

National Institute of Mental Health. (1985, June 10–12). *Consensus development conference statement: Electroconvulsive therapy: Program and abstracts.* Washington, DC: National Institute of Mental Health. [15]

National Migrant Resource Program and the Migrant Clinicians Network. (1990, April). *Migrant and seasonal farmworker, health objectives for the year 2000: Document in progress.* Austin, TX: National Migrant Resource Program. [13]

National Research Council. (1993). *Losing generations: Adolescents in high risk settings.* Washington, DC: National Academy Press. [9]

National Victims Center. (1992, April). *Rape in America: A report to the nation.* Arlington, VA: Author. [11]

Nedergaard, M. (1994). Direct signaling from astrocytes to neurons in cultures of mammalian brain cells. *Science, 263,* 1768–1771. [2]

Neimark, E. (1975). Intellectual development during adolescence. In F. Horowitz (Ed.), *Review of child development research* (Vol. 4). Chicago: University of Chicago Press. [9]

Neimark, E. D. (1981). Confounding with cognitive style factors: An artifact explanation for the apparent nonuniversal incidence of formal operations. In I. Sigel, D. Brodzinsky, & R. Golinkoff (Eds.), *New directions in Piagetian research and theory.* Hillsdale, NJ: Erlbaum. [8]

Neimark, J., Conway, C., & Doskoch, P. (1994, September/October). Back from the drink. *Psychology Today,* 46–53. [13]

Neisser, U. (1967). *Cognitive psychology.* New York: Appleton-Century-Crofts. [6]

Neisser, U., & Harsch, N. (1992). Phantom flashbulbs: False recollections of hearing the news about *Challenger.* In E. Winograd & U. Neisser (Eds.), *Affect and accuracy in recall: Studies of "flashbulb" memories* (pp. 9–31). New York: Cambridge University Press. [6]

Nelson, J. C. (1991). Current status of tricyclic antidepressants in psychiatry: Their pharmacology and clinical applications. *Journal of Clinical Psychiatry, 52,* 193–200. [15]

Nelson, K. (1973). Structure and strategy in learning to talk. *Monographs of the Society for Research in Child Development, 38*(1–2, Serial No. 149). [8]

Nelson, T. O. (1978). Detecting small amounts of information in memory: Savings for nonrecognized items. *Journal of Experimental Psychology: Human Learning and Memory, 4,* 453–468. [6]

Neugarten, B. L. (1968). The awareness of middle age. In B. Neugarten (Ed.), *Middle age and aging* (pp. 93–98). Chicago: University of Chicago Press. [9]

Neugarten, B. L. (1976). *The psychology of aging: An overview. Master lectures on developmental psychology.* Washington, DC: American Psychological Association. [9]

Neugarten, B. L. (1982). Must everything be a midlife crisis? In T. H. Carr & H. E. Fitzgerald (Eds.), *Human development 82/83* (pp. 162–163). (Reprinted from Prime Time, February 1980, 45–48). Guilford, CT: Dushkin. [9]

Neugarten, B. L., & Hagestad, G. (1976). Age and the life course. In H. Binstock & E. Shanas (Eds.), *Handbook of aging and the social sciences.* New York: Van Nostrand Reinhold. [9]

Neumann, Y., Finaly, E., & Reichel, A. (1988). Achievement motivation factors and students' college outcomes. *Psychological Reports, 62,* 555–560. [10]

Newcomb, A. F., Bukowski, W. M., & Pattee, L. (1993). Children's peer relations: A meta-analytic review of popular, rejected, neglected, controversial, and average sociometric status. *Psychological Bulletin, 113,* 99–128. [8]

Newcomb, M. D., & Bentler, P. M. (1989). Substance use and abuse among children and teenagers. *American Psychologist, 44,* 242–248. [4]

Newcomb, M. D., & Felix-Ortiz, M. (1992). Multiple protective and risk factors for drug use and abuse: Cross-sectional and prospective findings. *Journal of Personality and Social Psychology, 63,* 280–296. [4]

Newcomb, T. M. (1956). The prediction of interpersonal attraction. *American Psychologist, 11,* 575–587. [16]

Newell, A., & Simon, H. A. (1972). *Human problem solving.* Englewood Cliffs, NJ: Prentice-Hall. [7]

Newman, O. (1972). Defensible space. New York: Macmillan. [17]

Newport, F. (1993). Americans now more likely to say: Women have it harder than men. *Gallup Poll Monthly,* No. 337, 11–18. [11]

Ng, S. H. (1990). Androcentric coding of *man* and *his* in memory by language users. *Journal of Experimental Social Psychology, 26,* 455–464. [7]

Ng, S. K. C., Hauser, W. A., Brust, J. C. M., & Susser, M. (1988). Alcohol consumption and withdrawal in new onset seizures. *New England Journal of Medicine, 319,* 665–672. [13]

Nguyen, P. V., Abel, T., & Kandel, E. R. (1994). Requirement of a critical period of transcription for induction of a late phase of LTP. *Science, 265,* 1104–1107. [6]

Nickerson, R. S., & Adams, M. J. (1979). Long-term memory for a common object. *Cognitive Psychology, 11,* 287–307. [6]

Nicol, S. E., & Gottesman, I. I. (1983). Clues to the genetics and neurobiology of schizophrenia. *American Scientist, 71,* 398–404. [14]

Nisbett, R. E. (1990). Evolutionary psychology, biology, and cultural evolution. *Motivation and Emotion, 14,* 255–263. [1]

Nisbett, R. E., & Wilson, T. D. (1977). The halo effect: Evidence for unconscious alteration of judgments. *Journal of Personality and Social Psychology, 35,* 250–256. [16]

Nogrady, H., McConkey, K. M., & Perry, C. (1985). Enhancing visual memory: Trying hypnosis, trying imagination, and trying again. *Journal of Abnormal Psychology, 94,* 195–204. [6]

Norcross, J. C., Prochaska, J. O., & Gallagher, K. M. (1989). Clinical psychologists in the 1980s: II. Theory, research, and practice. *Clinical Psychologist, 42,* 45–52. [15]

Nordström, P., Samuelsson, M., Åsberg, M., Träskman-Bendz, L., Åberg-Wistedt, A., Nordin, C., & Bertilsson, L. (1994). CSF 5-HIAA predicts suicide risk after attempted suicide. *Suicide and Life-Threatening Behavior, 24,* 1–9. [2]

Norman, D. A. (1988). *The psychology of everyday things.* New York: Basic Books. [17]

Norman, D. A. (1995). Designing the future. *Scientific American, 273,* 194, 198. [17]

Norris, F. H., & Murrell, S. A. (1990). Social support, life events, and stress as modifiers of adjustment to bereavement by older adults. *Psychology and Aging, 5,* 429–436. [9]

Nossal, G. J. V. (1993). Life, death and the immune system. *Scientific American, 269,* 52–62. [13]

Novello, A. C. (1990). The Surgeon General's 1990 report on the health benefits of smoking cessation: Executive summary. *Morbidity and Mortality Weekly Report, 39* (No. RR–12). [4, 13]

Nowak, M. A., & McMichael, A. J. (1995). How HIV defeats the immune system. *Scientific American, 273,* 58–65. [11]

Noyes, R., Jr., Garvey, M. J., Cook, B. L., & Samuelson, L. (1989). Problems with tricyclic antidepressant use in patients with panic disorder or agoraphobia: Results of a naturalistic follow-up study. *Journal of Clinical Psychiatry, 50,* 163–169. [15]

Oatley, K., & Jenkins, J. M. (1992). Human emotions: Function and dysfunction. *Annual Review of Psychology, 43,* 55–85. [10]

O'Brien, C. P., Childress, A. R., McLellan, A. T., & Ehrman, R. (1992). Classical conditioning in drug-dependent humans. *Annals of the New York Academy of Sciences, 654,* 400–415. [5]

O'Donohue, W., & Plaud, J. J. (1994). The conditioning of human sexual arousal. *Archives of Sexual Behavior, 23,* 321–344. [6]

Offer, D., Ostrov, E., & Howard, K. I. (1981). *The adolescent: A psychological self-portrait.* New York: Basic Books. [9]

O'Heron, C. A., & Orlofsky, J. L. (1990). Stereotypic and nonstereotypic sex role trait and behavior orientations, gender identity, and psychological adjustment. *Journal of Personality and Social Psychology, 58,* 134–143. [11]

Ohzawa, I., DeAngelis, G. C., & Freeman, R. D. (1990). Stereoscopic depth discrimination in the visual cortex: Neurons ideally suited as disparity detectors. *Science, 249,* 1037–1041.

Oldenburg, D. (1990, March 16). Children: Putting down bias: New approach to an age-old problem. *Washington Post,* p. B5. [16]

Olds, D. L., Henderson, C. R., & Tatelbaum, R. (1994). Intellectual impairment in children of women who smoke cigarettes during pregnancy. *Pediatrics, 93,* 221–227. [8]

Olds, J. (1956). Pleasure centers in the brain. *Scientific American, 195,* 105–116. [2]

O'Leary, A. (1990). Stress, emotion, and human immune function. *Psychological Bulletin, 108,* 363–382. [13]

O'Leary, K. D., & Smith, D. A. (1991). Marital interactions. *Annual Review of Psychology, 42,* 191–212. [16]

Oliner, S. P., & Oliner P. M. (1988). *The altruistic personality: Rescuers of Jews in Nazi Europe.* New York: Free Press. [16]

Oliver, J. E. (1993). Intergenerational transmission of child abuse: Rates, research, and clinical implications. *American Journal of Psychiatry, 150,* 1315–1324. [16]

Oliver, M. B., & Hyde, J. S. (1993). Gender differences in sexuality: A meta-analysis. *Psychological Bulletin, 114,* 29–51. [11]

Olmsted, B. (1977). Job sharing—A new way to work. *Personnel Journal, 56,* 78–81. [17]

Olweus, D. (1987). Testosterone and adrenaline: Aggressive antisocial behavior in normal adolescent males. In S. A. Mednick, T. E. Moffitt, & S. A. Stack (Eds.), *The causes of crime: New biological approaches* (pp. 263–282). Cambridge, England: Cambridge University Press. [16]

Orne, M. (1983, December 12). Hypnosis "useful in medicine, dangerous in court." *U.S. News & World Report,* pp. 67–68. [4]

Öst, L-G., & Westling, B. E. (1995). Applied relaxation vs. cognitive behavior therapy in the treatment of panic disorder. *Behavior Research and Therapy, 33,* 145–158. [15]

Ostrom, T. M., Carpenter, S. L., Sedikides, C., & Li, F. (1993). Differential processing of in-group and out-group information. *Journal of Personality and Social Psychology, 64*, 21–34. [16]

Ostrov, E., Offer, D., Howard, K. I., Kaufman, B., & Meyer, H. (1985, May). Adolescent sexual behavior. *Medical Aspects of Human Sexuality, 19*, 28–36. [9]

O'Sullivan, G., Noshirvani, H., Marks, I., Monteiro, W., & Lelliott, P. (1991). Six-year follow-up after exposure and clomipramine therapy for obsessive compulsive disorder. *Journal of Clinical Psychiatry, 52*, 150–155. [15]

Otto, M. W., Pollack, M. H., Sachs, G. S., Reiter, S. R., Meltzer-Brody, S., & Rosenbaum, J. F. (1993). Discontinuation of benzodiazepine treatment: Efficacy of cognitive-behavioral therapy for patients with panic disorder. *American Journal of Psychiatry, 150*, 1485–1490. [15]

Overmeier, J. B., & Seligman, M. E. P. (1967). Effects of inescapable shock upon subsequent escape and avoidance responding. *Journal of Comparative and Physiological Psychology, 67*, 28–33. [5]

Owens, D. G. C. (1994). Extrapyramidal side effects and tolerability of risperidone: A review. *Journal of Clinical Psychiatry, 55*(5, Suppl.), 29–35. [15]

Padgett, V. R., Brislin-Slotz, J. A., & Neal, J. A. (1989). Pornography, erotica, and attitudes toward women: The effects of repeated exposure. *Journal of Sex Research, 26*, 479–491. [11]

Paikoff, R. L., & Brooks-Gunn, J. (1991). Do parent-child relationships change during puberty? *Psychological Bulletin, 110*, 47–66. [9]

Panksepp, J. (1992). A critical role for "affective neuroscience" in resolving what is basic about basic emotions. *Psychological Review, 99*, 554–560. [10]

Pappas, T. N., Melendez, R. L., & Debas, H. T. (1989). Gastric distension is a physiologic satiety signal in the dog. *Digestive Diseases and Sciences, 34*, 1489–1493. [10]

Park, B. (1986). A method for studying the development of impressions of real people. *Journal of Personality and Social Psychology, 51*, 907–917. [16]

Park, K. A., & Waters, E. (1989). Security of attachment and preschool friendships. *Child Development, 60*, 1076–1081. [8]

Parke, R. D. (1977). Some effects of punishment on children's behavior–revisited. In E. M. Hetherington, E. M. Ross, & R. D. Parke (Eds.), *Contemporary readings in child psychology.* New York: McGraw-Hill. [5]

Parke, R. D., O'Leary, S. E., & West, S. (1972). Mother-father-newborn interaction: Effects of maternal mediation, labor and sex of infant. *Proceedings of the American Psychological Association, 7*, 85–86. [8]

Parker, D. E. (1980). The vestibular apparatus. *Scientific American, 243*, 98–111. [3]

Parker, G. H. (1922). *Smell, taste, and allied senses in the vertebrates.* Philadelphia: Lippincott. [3]

Parker, J. G., & Asher, S. R. (1987). Peer relations and later personal adjustment: Are low-accepted children at risk? *Psychological Bulletin, 102*, 357–389. [8]

Parkinson, W. L., & Weingarten, H. P. (1990). Dissociative analysis of ventromedial hypothalamic obesity syndrome. *American Journal of Physiology, 259*, 829–835. [10]

Parrot, A. (1990, April). Date rape. *Medical Aspects of Human Sexuality, 24*, 28–31. [11]

Parrott, A. C. (1993). Cigarette smoking: Effects upon self-rated stress and arousal over the day. *Addictive Behaviors, 18*, 389–395. [13]

Parsons, T. (1979). Definitions of health and illness in light of the American values and social structure. In E. G. Jaco (Ed.), *Patients, physicians and illness: A sourcebook in behavioral science and health.* New York: Free Press. [13]

Partinen, M., Hublin, C., Kaprio, J., Koskenvuo, M., & Guilleminault, C. (1994). Twin studies in narcolepsy. *Sleep, 17*, S13–S16. [4]

Partinen, M., & Telakivi, T. (1992). Epidemiology of obstructive sleep apnea syndrome. *Sleep, 15*, S1–S4. [4]

Pascual-Leone, A., Dhuna, A., Altafullah, I., & Anderson, D. C. (1990). Cocaine-induced seizures. *Neurology, 40*, 404–407. [4]

Pascual-Leone, A., & Torres, F. (1993). Plasticity of the sensorimotor cortex representation of the reading finger in Braille readers. *Brain, 116*, 39–52. [2]

Pastore, N. (1950). The role of arbitrariness in the frustration-aggression hypothesis. *Journal of Abnormal and Social Psychology, 47*, 728–731. [16]

Patterson, D. R., Everett, J. J., Burns, G. L., & Marvin, J. A. (1992). Hypnosis for the treatment of burn pain. *Journal of Consulting & Clinical Psychology, 60*, 713–717. [4]

Pattison, E. M. (1982). The concept of alcoholism as a syndrome. In E. M. Pattison (Ed.), *Selection of treatment for alcoholics.* New Brunswick, NJ: Rutgers Center of Alcohol Studies. [13]

Paul, G. L., & Lentz, R. J. (1977). *Psychosocial treatment of chronic mental patients.* Cambridge, MA: Harvard University Press. [15]

Paul, W. E. (1993). Infectious diseases and the immune system. *Scientific American, 269*, 90–99. [13]

Paulus, P. B., Cox, V. C., & McCain, G. (1988). *Prison crowding: A psychological perspective.* New York: Springer-Verlag. [17]

Paunonen, S. P., Jackson, D. N., Trzebinski, J., & Fosterling, F. (1992). Personality structure across cultures: A multimethod evaluation. *Journal of Personality and Social Psychology, 62*, 447–456. [12]

Pavlov, I. P. (1960). *Conditioned reflexes: An investigation of the physiological activity of the cerebral cortex* (G. V. Anrep, Trans.). New York: Dover. (Original translation published 1927). [5]

Payami, H., Montee, K., & Kaye, J. (1994). Evidence for familial factors that protect against dementia and outweight the effect of increasing age. *American Journal of Human Genetics, 54*, 650–657. [9]

Pearl, D., Bouthilet, L., & Lazar, J. (Eds.). (1982). *Television and behavior: Ten years of scientific progress and implications for the eighties* (Vol. 2). Washington, DC: U.S. Government Printing Office. [16]

Pedersen, D. M., & Wheeler, J. (1983). The Müller-Lyer illusion among Navajos. *Journal of Social Psychology, 121*, 3–6. [3]

Pederson, D. R., Moran, G., Sitko, C., Campbell, K., Ghesquire, K., & Acton, H. (1990). Maternal sensitivity and the security of infant-mother attachment: A Q-sort study. *Child Development, 61*, 1974–1983. [8]

Peele, S. (1984). The cultural context of psychological approaches to alcoholism: Can we control the effects of alcohol? *American Psychologist, 39*, 1337–1351. [4]

Peele, S. (1992). Alcoholism, politics, and bureaucracy: The consensus against controlled-drinking therapy in America. *Addictive Behaviors, 17*, 49–62. [13]

Pelleymounter, M. A., Cullen, M. J., Baker, M. B., Hecht, R., Winters, D., Boone, T., & Collins. (1995). Effects of the *obese* gene product on body weight regulation in *ob/ob* mice. *Science, 269*, 540–543. [10]

Pen, C. L., Levy, E., Ravily, V., Beuzen, J. N., & Meurgey, F. (1994). The cost of treatment dropout in depression: A cost-benefit analysis of fluoxetine vs. tricyclics. *Journal of Affective Disorders, 31*, 1–18. [15]

Penfield, W. (1969). Consciousness, memory, and man's conditioned reflexes. In K. Pribram (Ed.), *On the biology of learning* (pp. 129–168). New York: Harcourt Brace Jovanovich. [6]

Penfield, W. (1975). *The mystery of the mind: A critical study of consciousness and the human brain.* Princeton, NJ: Princeton University Press. [6]

Penner, L. A., Thompson, J. K., & Coovert, D. L. (1991). Size overestimation among anorexics: Much ado about very little? *Journal of Abnormal Psychology, 100*, 90–93. [10]

Pennisi, E. (1994). A molecular whodunit: New twists in the Alzheimer's mystery. *Science News, 145*, 8–11. [9]

Pepitone, A., & Triandis, H. C. (1987). On the universality of social psychological theories. *Journal of Cross-Cultural Psychology, 18*, 471–498. [16]

Perin, C. T. (1943). A quantitative investigation of the delay-of-reinforcement gradient. *Journal of Experimental Psychology, 32,* 37–51. [5]

Perls, F. S. (1969). *Gestalt therapy verbatim.* Lafayette, CA: Real People Press. [15]

Perls, T. T. (1995). The oldest old. *Scientific American, 272,* 70–75. [9]

Perrett, D. I., May, K. A., & Yoshikawa, S. (1994). Facial shape and judgements of female attractiveness. *Nature, 368,* 239–242. [16]

Pert, C. B., Snowman, A. M., & Snyder, S. H. (1974). Localization of opiate receptor binding in presynaptic membranes of rat brain. *Brain Research, 70,* 184–188. [2]

Peter, J. B., Bryson, Y., & Lovett, M. A. (1982, March/April). Genital herpes: Urgent questions, elusive answers. *Diagnostic Medicine, 71–74,* 76–88. [11]

Petersen, A. C., Compas, B. E., Brooks-Gunn, J., Stemmier, M., Ey, S., & Grant, K. E. (1993). Depression in adolescence. *American Psychologist, 48,* 155–168. [14]

Peterson, A. C. (1987, September). Those gangly years. *Psychology Today,* pp. 28–34. [9]

Peterson, A. C. (1988). Adolescent development. *Annual Review of Psychology, 39,* 583–607. [9]

Peterson, I. (1993). Speech for export: Automating the translation of spoken words. *Science News, 144,* 254–255. [7]

Peterson, L. R., & Peterson, M. J. (1959). Short-term retention of individual verbal items. *Journal of Experimental Psychology, 58,* 193–198. [6]

Petitto, L. A., & Marentette, P. R. (1991). Babbling in the manual mode: Evidence for the ontogeny of language. *Science, 251,* 1493–1496. [8]

Phillips, D. A., McCartney, K., & Scarr, S. (1987). Child-care quality and children's social development. *Developmental Psychology, 23,* 537–543. [8]

Phillips, K., Fulker, D. W., Carey, G., & Nagoshi, C. T. (1988). Direct marital assortment for cognitive and personality variables. *Behavioral Genetics, 18,* 347–356. [16]

Piaget, J. (1960). *The child's conception of physical causality.* Patterson, NJ: Littlefield, Adams. [8]

Piaget, J. (1963a). *The child's conception of the world.* Patterson, NJ: Littlefield, Adams. [8]

Piaget, J. (1963b). *Psychology of intelligence.* Patterson, NJ: Littlefield, Adams. [8]

Piaget, J. (1964). *Judgment and reasoning in the child.* Patterson, NJ: Littlefield, Adams. [8]

Piaget, J. (1972). Intellectual evolution from adolescence to adulthood. *Human Development, 15,* 1–12. [9]

Piaget, J., & Inhelder, B. (1969). *The psychology of the child.* New York: Basic Books. [8, 9]

Pilkonis, P. A., Imber, S. D., Lewis, P., & Rubinsky, P. (1984). A comparative outcome study of individual, group, and conjoint psychotherapy. *Archives of General Psychiatry, 41,* 431–437. [15]

Pillemer, D. B. (1990). Clarifying the flashbulb memory concept: Comment on McCloskey, Wible, and Cohen (1988). *Journal of Experimental Psychology: General, 119,* 92–96. [6]

Pinel, J. P. J. (1990). *Biopsychology.* Boston: Allyn & Bacon. [2]

Pinel, J. P. J. (1993). *Biopsychology* (2nd ed.). Boston: Allyn & Bacon. [6]

Pion, G. M., Bramblett, J. P., Jr., & Wicherski, M. (1987). *Preliminary report: 1985 doctorate employment survey.* Washington, DC: American Psychological Association. [1]

Piot, P., & Islam, M. Q. (1994). Sexually transmitted diseases in the 1990s: Global epidemiology and challanges for control. *Sexually Transmitted Diseases, 21*(2, Suppl.), S7–S13. [11]

Piotrowski, C., & Zalenski, C. (1993). Training in psychodiagnostic testing in APA-approved PsyD and PhD clinical psychology programs. *Journal of Personality Assessment, 61,* 374–405. [12]

Platt, R., Rice, P. A., & McCormack, W. M. (1983). Risk of acquiring gonorrhea and prevalence of abnormal adnexal findings among women recently exposed to gonorrhea. *Journal of the American Medical Association, 250,* 3205–3209. [11]

Plomin, R. (1989). Environment and genes: Determinants of behavior. *American Psychologist, 44,* 105–111. [7, 12]

Plomin, R., & Bergeman, C. S. (1991). The nature of nurture: Genetic influence on "environmental" measures. *Behavioral and Brain Sciences, 14,* 373–427. [12]

Plomin, R., Chipuer, H. M., & Loehlin, J. C. (1990). Behavior genetics and personality. In L. A. Pervin (Ed.), *Handbook of personality theory and research* (pp. 225–243). New York: Guilford. [8]

Plomin, R., & Daniels, D. (1987). Why are children in the same family so different from one another? *Behavioral and Brain Sciences, 10,* 1–60. [12]

Plomin, R., DeFries, J. C., & Fulker, D. W. (1988). *Nature and nurture during infancy and early childhood.* New York: Cambridge University Press. [7]

Plomin, R., Owen, M. J., & McGuffin, P. (1994). The genetic basis of complex human behaviors. *Science, 264,* 1733–1739. [7, 8, 12]

Plomin, R., & Rende, R. (1991). Human behavioral genetics. *Annual Review of Psychology, 42,* 161–190. [7, 12]

Polich, J. M., Armor, D. J., & Braiker, H. B. (1981). *The course of alcoholism: Four years after treatment.* New York: Wiley. [13]

Pollack, M. H., Otto, M. W., Kaspi, S. P., Hammerness, P. G., & Rosenbaum, J. F. (1994). Cognitive behavior therapy for treatment-refractory panic disorder. *Journal of Clinical Psychiatry, 55,* 200–205. [15]

Pollack, R. H. (1970). Müller-Lyer illusion: Effect of age, lightness contrast and hue. *Science, 179,* 93–94. [3]

Pomerleau, O. F., & Pomerleau, C. S. (1989). A biobehavioral perspective on smoking. In T. Ney & A. Gale (Eds.), *Smoking and human behavior* (pp. 69–93). New York: Wiley. [13]

Pope, K. S. (1994). Sexual involvement between therapists and patients. *Harvard Mental Health Letter, 11*(2), 5–6. [15]

Porter, F. L., Porges, S. W., & Marshall, R. E. (1988). Newborn pain cries and vagal tone: Parallel changes in response to circumcision. *Child Development, 59,* 495–505. [8]

Postman, L., & Phillips, L. W. (1965). Short-term temporal changes in free recall. *Quarterly Journal of Experimental Psychology, 17,* 132–138. [6]

Potts, N. L. S., Davidson, J. R. T., & Krishman, K. R. R. (1993). The role of nuclear magnetic resonance imaging in psychiatric research. *Journal of Clinical Psychiatry, 54*(12, Suppl.), 13–18. [2]

Powell, E. (1996). *Sex on your terms.* Boston: Allyn & Bacon. [11, 17]

Powell, K. E., Spain, K. G., Christenson, G. M., & Mollenkamp, M. P. (1986). The status of the 1990 objectives for physical fitness and exercise. *Public Health Reports, 101,* 15–21. [13]

Powell, L. H., Shaker, L. A., Jones, B. A., Vaccarino, L. V., Thoresen, C. E., & Pattillo, J. R. (1993). Psychosocial predictors of mortality in 83 women with premature acute myocardial infarction. *Psychosomatic Medicine, 55,* 426–433. [13]

Power, T. G. (1985). Mother- and father-infant play: A developmental analysis. *Child Development, 56,* 1514–1524. [11]

Pratkanis, A. R. (1989). The cognitive representation of attitudes. In A. R. Pratkanis, S. J. Breckler, & A. G. Greenwald (Eds.), *Attitude structure and function* (pp. 71–93). Hillsdale, NJ: Erlbaum. [16]

Premack, D. (1971). Language in chimpanzees. *Science, 172,* 808–822. [7]

Premack, D., & Premack, A. J. (1983). *The mind of an ape.* New York: Norton. [7]

Preskorn, S. H. (1993). Pharmacokinetics of antidepressants: Why and how they are relevant to treatment. *Journal of Clinical Psychiatry, 54*(9, Suppl.), 14–34. [15]

Pribor, E. F., & Dinwiddie, S. H. (1992). Psychiatric correlates of incest in childhood. *American Journal of Psychiatry, 148,* 52–56. [14]

Price, R. A., Cadoret, R. J., Stunkard, A. J., & Troughton, E. (1987). Genetic contributions to human fatness: An adoption study. *American Journal of Psychiatry, 144,* 1003–1008. [10]

Price, R. A., Stunkard, A. J., Ness, R., Wadden, T., Heshka, S., Kanders, B., & Cormillot, A. (1990). Childhood onset (age less than 10) obesity has a high familial risk. *International Journal of Obesity, 14,* 185–195. [10]

Prien, R. F., Kupfer, D. J., Mansky, P. A., Small, J. G., Tuason, V. B., Voss, C. B., & Johnson, W. E. (1984). Drug therapy in the prevention of recurrences in unipolar and bipolar affective disorders. *Archives of General Psychiatry, 41,* 1096–1104. [15]

Priest, R. F., & Sawyer, J. (1967). Proximity and peership: Bases of balance in interpersonal attraction. *American Journal of Sociology, 72,* 633–649. [16]

Prinz, P. N., Vitiello, M. V., Raskind, M. A., & Thorpy, M. J. (1990). Geriatrics: Sleep disorders and aging. *New England Journal of Medicine, 323,* 520–526. [4]

Pryor, J. (1994). Self-esteem and attitudes toward gender roles: Contributing factors in adolescents. *Australian Journal of Psychology, 46,* 48–52. [11]

Public Health Service. (1991). *Healthy people 2000: National health promotion and disease prevention objectives [Summary].* (DHHS Publication No. PHS 91–50213). Washington, DC: U.S. Department of Health and Human Services. [13]

Putnam, F. W. (1989). *Diagnosis and treatment of multiple personality disorder.* New York: Guilford Press. [14]

Putnam, F. W. (1992). Altered states: Peeling away the layers of a multiple personality. *The Sciences, 32,* 30–36. [14]

Putnam, F. W., Guroff, J. J., Silberman, E. K., Barban, L., & Post, R. M. (1986). The clinical phenomenology of multiple personality disorder: Review of 100 recent cases. *Journal of Clinical Psychiatry, 47,* 285–293. [14]

Putnam, F. W., & Loewenstein, R. J. (1993). Treatment of multiple personality disorder: A survey of current practices. *American Journal of Psychiatry, 150,* 1048–1052. [14]

Quadrel, M. J., Fischhoff, B., & Davis, W. (1993). Adolescent (in)vulnerability. *American Psychologist, 48,* 102–116. [9]

Quinn, T. C. (1994). Recent advances in diagnosis of sexually transmitted diseases. *Sexually Transmitted Diseases, 21*(2, Suppl.), S19–S27. [11]

Rabin, M. D., & Cain, W. S. (1984). Odor recognition: Familiarity, identifiability, and encoding consistency. *Journal of Experimental Psychology: Learning, Memory and Cognition, 10,* 316–325. [3]

Rachman, S. J., & Wilson, G. T. (1980). *The effects of psychological therapy* (2nd ed.). New York: Pergamon. [15]

Rahe, R. J., Meyer, M., Smith, M., Kjaer, G., & Holmes, T. H. (1964). Social stress and illness onset. *Journal of Psychosomatic Research, 8,* 35–44. [13]

Raichle, M. E. (1994a). Images of the mind: Studies with modern imaging techniques. *Annual Review of Psychology, 45,* 333–356. [2]

Raichle, M. E. (1994b). Visualizing the mind. *Scientific American, 270,* 58–64. [2]

Rakic, P. (1988). Specification of cerebral cortical areas. *Science, 241,* 170–176. [2]

Raloff, J. (1994). The great nicotine debate: Are cigarette recipes 'cooked' to keep smokers hooked? *Science News, 145,* 314–317. [4, 13]

Ralph, M. R. (1989, November/December). The rhythm maker: Pinpointing the master clock in mammals. *The Sciences, 29,* 40–45 [4]

Randi, J. (1980). *Flim-flam: The truth about unicorns, parapsychology, and other delusions.* New York: Lippincott & Crowell. [3]

Rapoport, J. L. (1989). The biology of obsessions and compulsions. *Scientific American, 260,* 83–89. [15]

Rasmussen, S. A., & Eisen, J. L. (1990). Epidemiology of obsessive compulsive disorder. *Journal of Clinical Psychiatry, 51*(2, Suppl.), 10–13. [14]

Rasmussen, S. A., & Eisen, J. L. (1992). The epidemiology and differential diagnosis of obsessive compulsive disorder. *Journal of Clinical Psychiatry, 53*(4, Suppl.), 4–10. [14]

Rasmussen, S. A., Eisen, J. L., & Pato, M. T. (1993). Current issues in the pharmacologic management of obsessive compulsive disorder. *Journal of Clinical Psychiatry, 54*(6, Suppl.), 4–9. [14, 15]

Rauch, S. L., Jenike, M. A., Alpert, N. M., Baer, L., Breiter, H. C. R., Savage, C. R., & Fischman, A. J. (1994). Regional cerebral blood flow measured during symptom provocation in obsessive-compulsive disorder using oxygen 15–labeled carbon dioxide and positron emission tomography. *Archives of General Psychiatry, 51,* 62–70. [14]

Reed, S., & Fischer, M. A. (1984, January 23). Adventure: Far from being over the hill, Hulda Crooks, at 87, is a real climber. *People Weekly,* pp. 88–90. [9]

Regestein, Q. R., & Monk, T. H. (1991). Is the poor sleep of shift workers a disorder? *American Journal of Psychiatry, 148,* 1487–1493. [4]

Reiman, E. M., Fusselman, M. J., Fox, P. T., & Raichle, M. E. (1989). Neuroanatomical correlates of anticipatory anxiety. *Science, 243,* 1071–1074. [14]

Reinke, B. J., Ellicott, A. M., Harris, R. L., & Hancock, E. (1985). Timing of psychosocial changes in women's lives. *Human Development, 28,* 259–280. [9]

Reis, H. T., Wilson, I. M., Monestere, C., Bernstein, S., Clark, K., Seidl, E., Franco, M., Gioioso, E., Freeman, L., & Radoane, K. (1990). What is smiling is beautiful and good. *European Journal of Social Psychology, 20,* 259–267. [16]

Remafedi, G. (1990). Study group report on the impact of television portrayals of gender roles on youth. *Journal of Adolescent Health Care, 11*(1), 59–61. [11]

Renneker, R. (1981). Cancer and psychotherapy. In J. Goldberg (Ed.), *Psychotherapeutic treatment of cancer patients.* New York: Free Press. [13]

Renzetti, C. M., & Curran, D. J. (1992). *Women, men, and society.* Boston: Allyn & Bacon. [11, 16]

Rescorla, R. A. (1967). Pavlovian conditioning and its proper control procedures. *Psychological Review, 74,* 71–80. [5]

Rescorla, R. A. (1988). Pavlovian conditioning: It's not what you think it is. *American Psychologist, 43,* 151–160. [5]

Restak, R. (1988). *The mind.* Toronto: Bantam. [7]

Restak, R. (1993, September/October). Brain by design. *The Sciences,* 27–33. [4]

Rhoades, E. R., Hammond, J., Welty, T. K., Handler, A. O., & Amler, R. W. (1987). The Indian burden of illness and future health interventions. *Public Health Reports, 102,* 361–368. [13]

Rhodes, N., & Wood, W. (1992). Self-esteem and intelligence affect influenceability: The medicating role of message reception. *Psychological Bulletin, 111,* 156–171. [16]

Rice, F. P. (1992). *Intimate relationships, marriages, and families.* Mountain View, CA: Mayfield. [9]

Rice, M. L. (1989). Children's language acquisition. *American Psychologist, 44,* 149–156. [8]

Rice, M. L., Huston, A. C., Truglio, R., & Wright, J. (1990). Words from "Sesame Street": Learning vocabulary while viewing. *Developmental Psychology, 26,* 421–428. [8]

Rice, P. L. (1987). *Stress and health: Principles and practice for coping and wellness.* Monterey, CA: Brooks/Cole. [17]

Rich, C. L., Warstradt, G. M., Nemiroff, R. A., Fowler, R. D., & Young, D. (1991). Suicide, stressors, and the life cycle. *American Journal of Psychiatry, 148,* 524–527. [14]

Richards, R. (1992). Mood swings and everyday creativity. *Harvard Mental Health Letter, 8*(10), 4–6. [14]

Rickels, K., Downing, R., Schweizer, E., & Hassman, H. (1993). Antidepressants for the treatment of generalized anxiety disorder. *Archives of General Psychiatry, 50,* 884–895. [15]

Rickels, K., Schweizer, E., Weiss, S., & Zavodnick, S. (1993). Maintenance drug treatment for panic disorder II. Short- and long-term outcome after drug taper. *Archives of General Psychiatry, 50,* 61–68. [15]

Riordan, C. A., & Tedeschi, J. T. (1983). Attraction in aversive environments: Some evidence for classical conditioning and negative reinforcement. *Journal of Personality and Social Psychology, 44,* 683–692. [16]

Robberson, M. R., & Rogers, R. W. (1988). Beyond fear appeals: Negative and positive persuasive appeals to health and self-esteem. *Journal of Applied Social Psychology, 18,* 277–287. [16]

Roberts, E., & Miller, A. (1992, February 24). This ad's for you. *Newsweek*, p. 40. [17]

Robertson, G. L. (1983). Thirst and vasopressin function in normal and disordered states of water balance. *Journal of Laboratory and Clinical Medicine, 101,* 351–371. [10]

Robins, C. J., & Hayes, A. M. (1993). An appraisal of cognitive therapy. *Journal of Consulting and Clinical Psychology, 61,* 205–214. [15]

Robinson, F. P. (1941). *Effective behavior.* New York: Harper & Row. [1]

Roche, A. F., & Davila, G. H. (1972). Late adolescent growth in stature. *Pediatrics, 50,* 874–880. [9]

Rock, I., & Palmer, S. (1990). The legacy of Gestalt psychology. *Scientific American, 263,* 84–90. [5]

Rodin, J. (1981). Current status of the internal-external hypothesis for obesity: What went wrong? *American Psychologist, 36,* 361–372. [10]

Rodin, J. (1985). Insulin levels, hunger, and food intake: An example of feedback loops in body weight regulation. *Health Psychology, 4,* 1–24. [10]

Rodin, J. (1986). Aging and health: Effects of the sense of control. *Science, 233,* 1271–1276. [13]

Rodin, J. (1992, January/February). Body image. *Psychology Today,* pp. 56–60. [10]

Rodin, J., & Ickovics, J. R. (1990). Women's health: Review and research agenda as we approach the 21st century. *American Psychologist, 45,* 1018–1034. [13]

Rodin, J., & Salovey, P. (1989). Health psychology. *Annual Review of Psychology, 40,* 533–579. [13]

Rodin, J., Slochower, J., & Fleming, B. (1977). The effects of degree of obesity, age of onset, and energy deficit on external responsiveness. *Journal of Comparative and Physiological Psychology, 91,* 586–597. [10]

Rodin, J., Wack, J., Ferrannini, E., & DeFronzo, R. A. (1985). Effect of insulin and glucose on feeding behavior. *Metabolism, 34,* 826–831. [10]

Rodin, J., & Wing, R. R. (1988). Behavioral factors in obesity. *Diabetes/Metabolism Reviews, 4,* 701–725. [10]

Rodriguez-Trias, H. (1992). Women's health, women's lives, women's rights. *American Journal of Public Health, 82,* 663–664. [13]

Roediger, H. L., III. (1980). The effectiveness of four mnemonics in ordering recall. *Journal of Experimental Psychology: Human Learning and Memory, 6,* 558–567. [6]

Roediger, H. L., III. (1991). They read an article? A commentary on the everyday memory controversy. *American Psychologist, 46,* 37–40. [6]

Roehrich, L., & Kinder, B. N. (1991). Alcohol expectancies and male sexuality: Review and implications for sex therapy. *Journal of Sex and Marital Therapy, 17,* 45–54. [4]

Rogers, C. R. (1951). *Client-centered therapy: Its current practice, implications, and theory.* Boston: Houghton Mifflin. [12, 15]

Rogers, C. R. (1959). A theory of therapy, personality, and interpersonal relationships, as developed in the client-centered framework. In S. Koch (Ed.), *Psychology: A study of a science, Vol. III. Formulations of the person and the social context* (pp. 184–256). New York: McGraw-Hill. [15]

Rogers, C. R. (1961). *On becoming a person: A therapist's view of psychotherapy.* Boston: Houghton Mifflin. [12, 14]

Rogers, C. R. (1977). The case of Mary Jane Tilden. In S. J. Morse & R. I. Watson, Jr. (Eds.), *Psychotherapies: A comparative casebook* (pp. 197–222). New York: Holt, Rinehart & Winston. [15]

Rogers, C. R. (1981). Notes on Rollo May. *Perspectives, 2*(1), 16. [12]

Rogers, J. P. (1989, April). Type A: Healing the spirit. *Psychology Today,* p. 18. [13]

Rogers, M. P., & Reich, P. (1988). On the health consequences of bereavement. *New England Journal of Medicine, 319,* 510–512. [13]

Rogers, P. J. (1990). Why a palatability construct is needed. *Appetite, 14,* 167–170. [10]

Rogers, P. J., & Hill, A. J. (1989). Breakdown of dietary restraint following mere exposure to food stimuli: Interrelationships between restraint, hunger, salivation, and food intake. *Addictive Behaviors, 14,* 387–397. [10]

Rogoff, B., & Mistry, J. (1985). Memory development in cultural context. In M. Pressley & C. Brainerd (Eds.), *The cognitive side of memory development.* New York: Springer-Verlag. [6]

Roland, P. (1992). Cortical representation of pain. *Trends in Neurosciences, 15,* 3–5. [2]

Roland, P. E., & Gulyás, B. (1994). Visual imagery and visual representation. *Trends in Neurosciences, 17,* 281–287. [7]

Rosch, E. H. (1973). Natural categories. *Cognitive Psychology, 4,* 328–350. [7]

Rosch, E. H. (1978). Principles of categorization. In E. H. Rosch & B. Lloyd (Eds.), *Cognition and categorization.* Hillsdale, NJ: Erlbaum. [7]

Rose, R. J., Koskenvuo, M., Kaprio, J., Sarna, S., & Langinvainio, H. (1988). Shared genes, shared experiences, and similarity of personality: Data from 14,288 adult Finnish co-twins. *Journal of Personality and Social Psychology, 54,* 161–171. [12]

Rosekind, M. R. (1992). The epidemiology and occurrence of insomnia. *Journal of Clinical Psychiatry, 53*(6, Suppl.), 4–6. [4]

Rosen, R. C., Rosekind, M., Rosevear, C., Cole, W. E., & Dement, W. C. (1993). Physician education in sleep and sleep disorders: A national survey of U.S. medical schools. *Sleep, 16,* 249–254. [4]

Rosenbaum, J. F. (1990). High-potency benzodiazepines: Emerging uses in psychiatry. *Journal of Clinical Psychiatry, 51*(5, Suppl.), 3. [15]

Rosenbaum, J. F., Biederman, J., Pollock, R. A., & Hirshfeld, D. R. (1994). The etiology of social phobia. *Journal of Clinical Psychiatry, 55*(6, Suppl.), 10–16. [14]

Rosenberg, J., & Pettinati, H. M. (1984). Differential memory complaints after bilateral and unilateral ECT. *American Journal of Psychiatry, 14,* 1071–1074. [15]

Rosenfield, S. (1992). The costs of sharing: Wives' employment and husbands' mental health. *Journal of Health and Social Behavior, 33,* 213–225. [9]

Rosengren, A., Tibblin, G., & Wilhelmsen, L. (1991). Self-perceived psychological stress and incidence of coronary artery disease in middle-aged men. *American Journal of Cardiology, 68,* 1171–1175. [13]

Rosenhan, D. L. (1973). On being sane in insane places. *Science, 179,* 250–258. [3]

Rosenthal, A. M. (1964). *Thirty-eight witnesses.* New York: McGraw-Hill. [16]

Rosenthal, D. (1970). *Genetic theory and abnormal behavior.* New York: McGraw-Hill. [14]

Rosenthal, N. E., Carpenter, C. J., James, S. P., Parry, B. L., Rogers, S. L. B., & Wehr, T. A.. (1986). Seasonal affective disorder in children and adolescents. *American Journal of Psychiatry, 143,* 356–358. [14]

Rosenthal, N. E., Sack, D. A., Carpenter, C. J., et al. (1985). Antidepressant effects of light in seasonal affective disorder. *American Journal of Psychiatry, 142,* 163–170. [14]

Rosenthal, R. (1973, September). The Pygmalion effect lives. *Psychology Today,* pp. 56–63. [1]

Rosenzweig, M. R. (1961). Auditory localization. *Scientific American, 205,* 132–142. [3]

Ross, C. A., Anderson, G., Fleisher, W. P., & Norton, G. R. (1991). The frequency of multiple personality disorder among psychiatric inpatients. *American Journal of Psychiatry, 148,* 1717–1720. [14]

Ross, C. A., Miller, S. D., Reagor, P., Bjornson, L., Fraser, G. A., & Anderson, G. (1990). Structured interview data on 102 cases of multiple personality disorder from four centers. *American Journal of Psychiatry, 147,* 596–601. [14]

Ross, C. A., Norton, G. R., & Wozney, K. (1989). Multiple personality disorder: An analysis of 236 cases. *Canadian Journal of Psychiatry, 34,* 413–418. [14]

Ross, J. (1993). Social phobia: The consumer's perspective. *Journal of Clinical Psychiatry, 54*(12, Suppl.), 5–9. [14]

Ross, J., & Lawrence, K. A. (1968). Some observations on memory artifice. *Psychonomic Science, 13,* 107–108. [6]

Ross, L. (1977). The intuitive psychologist and his shortcomings: Distortions in the attribution process. In L. Berkowitz (Ed.), *Advances in experimental social psychology* (Vol. 10). New York: Academic Press. [16]

Roth, D. L., Wiebe, D. J., Filligim, R. B., & Shay, K. A. (1989). Life events, fitness, hardiness, and health: A simultaneous analysis of proposed stress-resistance effects. *Journal of Personality and Social Psychology, 57*, 136–142. [13]

Roth, W. T., Margraf, J., Ehlers, A., Taylor, B., Maddock, R. J., Davies, S., & Argras, W. S. (1992). Stress test reactivity in panic disorder. *Archives of General Psychiatry, 49*, 301–310. [14]

Rotter, J. B. (1966). Generalized expectancies for internal versus external control of reinforcement. *Psychological Monographs, 80*(1, Whole No. 609). [12]

Rotter, J. B. (1971, June). External control and internal control. *Psychology Today*, pp. 37–42, 58–59. [12]

Rotter, J. B. (1990). Internal versus external control of reinforcement: A case history of a variable. *American Psychologist, 45*, 489–493. [12]

Rotton, J., Frey, J., Barry, T., Milligan, M., & Fitzpatrick, M. (1979). The air pollution experience and physical aggression. *Journal of Applied Social Psychology, 9*, 397–412. [16]

Rovee-Collier, C. (1990). The "memory system" of prelinguistic infants. *Annals of the New York Academy of Sciences, 608*, 517–576. [8]

Rowe, D. (1994). *The limits of family influence: Genes, experience, and behavior*. New York: Guilford. [12]

Rowe, D. C. (1987). Resolving the person-situation debate: Invitation to an interdisciplinary dialogue. *American Psychologist, 42*, 218–227. [12]

Rowe, J. W., & Kahn, R. L. (1987). Human aging: Usual and successful. *Science, 237*, 143–149. [9]

Roybal, E. R. (1988). Mental health and aging: The need for an expanded federal response. *American Psychologist, 43*, 189–194. [9]

Rozin, P., & Zellner, D. (1985). The role of Pavlovian conditioning in the acquisition of food likes and dislikes. *Annals of the New York Academy of Sciences, 443*, 189–202. [5]

Rubenstein, C. (1982, July). Psychology's fruit flies. *Psychology Today*, pp. 83–84. [1]

Rubinstein, E. A. (1983). Television and behavior: Research conclusions of the 1982 NIMH report and their policy implications. *American Psychologist, 38*, 820–825. [8, 16]

Ruggero, M. A. (1992). Responses to sound of the basilar membrane of the mammalian cochlea. *Current Opinion in Neurobiology, 2*, 449–456. [3]

Rumbaugh, D. M. (1977). *Language learning by a chimpanzee: The Lana project*. New York: Academic Press. [7]

Runeson, B. (1989). Mental disorder in youth suicide. DSM-III-R Axes I and II. *Acta Psychiatrica Scandinavica, 79*, 490–497. [14]

Rushton, J. P., Fulker, D. W., Neale, M. C., Nias, D. K. B., & Eysenck, H. J. (1986). Altruism and aggression: The heritability of individual differences. *Journal of Personality and Social Psychology, 50*, 1192–1198. [12, 16]

Russell, J. A. (1994). Is there universal recognition of emotion from facial expression? A review of the cross-cultural studies. *Psychological Bulletin, 115*, 102–141. [10]

Russell, T. G., Rowe, W., & Smouse, A. D. (1991). Subliminal self-help tapes and academic achievement: An evaluation. *Journal of Counseling and Development, 69*, 359–362. [3]

Sackeim, H. A. (1985, June). The case for ECT. *Psychology Today*, pp. 36–40. [15]

Sackeim, H. A. (1992). The cognitive effects of electroconvulsive therapy. In W. H. Moos, E. R. Gamzu, & L. J. Thal (Eds.), *Cognitive disorders: Pathophysiology and treatment*. New York: Marcel Dekker. [15]

Sackeim, H. A., Portnoy, S., Neeley, P., Steif, B. L., Decina, P., & Malitz, S. (1986). Cognitive consequences of low-dosage electroconvulsive therapy. *Annals of the New York Academy of Sciences, 462*, 326–340. [15]

Sackeim, H. A., Prudic, J., Devanand, D. P., Kiersky, J. E., Fitzsimmons, L., Moody, B. J., McElhiney, M. C., Coleman, E. A., & Settembrino,

J. M. (1993). Effects of stimulus intensity and electrode placement on the efficacy and cognitive effects of electroconvulsive therapy. *New England Journal of Medicine, 328*, 839–846. [15]

Saghir, M. T., & Robins, E. (1973). *Male and female sexuality*. Baltimore: Williams and Wilkins. [11]

Sakai, K., & Miyashita, Y. (1994). Visual imagery: An interaction between memory retrieval and focal attention. *Trends in Neurosciences, 17*, 287–289. [7]

Salama, A. A. A., & England, R. D. (1990). A case study: Schizophrenia and tactile hallucinations, treated with electroconvulsive therapy. *Canadian Journal of Psychiatry, 35*, 86–87. [14]

Sales, B. D., & Hafemeister, T. L. (1985). Law and psychology. In E. M. Altmeir & M. E. Meyer (Eds.), *Applied specialties in psychology*. New York: Random House. [17]

Saltzman, A. (1991, June 17). Trouble at the top. *U.S. News & World Report*, pp. 40–48. [11, 17]

Salzinger, S., Feldman, R. S., Hammer, M., & Rosario, M. (1993). The effects of physical abuse on children's social relationships. *Child Development, 64*, 169–187. [8]

Sanbonmatsu, D. M., & Fazio, R. H. (1990). The role of attitudes in memory-based decision making. *Journal of Personality and Social Psychology, 59*, 614–622. [16]

Sanders, M. S., & McCormick, E. J. (1993). *Human factors in engineering and design*. New York: McGraw-Hill. [17]

Sandou, F., Amara, D. A., Dierich, A., LeMeur, M., Ramboz, S., Segu, L., Buhot, M-C., & Hen, R. (1994). Enhanced aggressive behavior in mice lacking 5-HT^{1B} receptor. *Science, 265*, 1875–1878. [2]

Sandross, R. (1988, December). Sexual harassment in the Fortune 500. *Working Woman*, p. 69. [17]

Sanna, L. J., & Shotland, R. L. (1990). Valence of anticipated evaluation and social facilitation. *Journal of Experimental Social Psychology, 26*, 82–92. [16]

Sapolsky, R. M. (1994). *Why zebras don't get ulcers: A guide to stress, stress-related diseases, and coping*. San Francisco: W. H. Freeman. [13]

Savage-Rumbaugh, E. S. (1986). *Ape language*. New York: Columbia University Press. [7]

Savage-Rumbaugh, E. S. (1990). Language acquisition in a nonhuman species: Implications for the innateness debate. *Developmental Psychology, 26*, 599–620. [7]

Savage-Rumbaugh, E. S., Sevcik, R. A., Brakke, K. E., & Rumbaugh, D. M. (1992). Symbols: Their communicative use, communication, and combination by bonobos (Pan paniscus). In L. P. Lipsitt & C. Rovee-Collier (Eds.). *Advances in infancy research* (Vol. 7, pp. 221–278). Norwood, NJ: Ablex. [7]

Savin-Williams, R. (1980). Dominance hierarchies in groups of middle to late adolescent males. *Journal of Youth and Adolescence, 9*, 75–85. [9]

Saxe, L., Dougherty, D., & Cross, T. (1985). The validity of polygraph testing: Scientific analysis and public controversy. *American Psychologist, 40*, 355–366. [10]

Scarr, S., & Eisenberg, M. (1993). Child care research: Issues, perspectives, and results. *Annual Review of Psychology, 44*, 613–644. [8]

Scarr, S., Pakstis, A., Katz, S., & Barker, W. (1977). Absence of a relationship between degree of White ancestry and intellectual skills within a Black population. *Human Genetics, 39*, 69–86. [7]

Scarr, S., Webber, P. L., Weinberg, R. A., & Wittig, M. A. (1981). Personality resemblance among adolescents and their parents in biologically related and adoptive families. *Journal of Personality and Social Psychology, 40*, 885–898. [12]

Scarr, S., & Weinberg, R. (1978). The influence of "family background" on intellectual attainment. *American Sociological Review, 43*, 674–692. [7]

Scarr, S., & Weinberg, R. A. (1986). The early childhood enterprise: Care and education of the young. *American Psychologist, 41*, 1140–1146. [8]

Schab, F. R. (1990). Odors and the remembrance of things past. *Journal of Experimental Psychology: Learning, Memory, and Cognition, 16*, 648–655. [6]

Schachter, S., & Gross, L. P. (1968). Manipulated time and eating behavior. *Journal of Personality and Social Psychology, 10,* 98–106. [10]

Schachter, S., & Singer, J. E. (1962). Cognitive, social, and physiological determinants of emotional state. *Psychological Review, 69,* 379–399. [10]

Schaie, K. W. (1990). Late life potential and cohort differences in mental abilities. In M. Perlmutter (Ed.), *Late life potential* (pp. 43–61). Washington, DC: Gerontological Society. [9]

Schaie, K. W. (1993). Ageist language in psychological research. *American Psychologist, 48,* 49–51. [1]

Schaie, K. W. (1994). The course of adult intellectual development. *American Psychologist, 49,* 304–313. [9]

Scheier, M. F., & Carver, C. S. (1985). Optimism, coping, and health: Assessment and implications of generalized outcome expectancies. *Health Psychology, 4,* 219–247. [13]

Scheier, M. F., & Carver, C. S. (1992). Effects of optimism on psychological and physical well-being: Theoretical overview and empirical update. *Cognitive Therapy and Research, 16,* 201–228. [13]

Scheier, M. F., Matthews, K. A., Owens, J., Magovern, G. J., Sr., Lefebvre, R. C., Abbott, R. A., & Carver, C. S. (1989). Dispositional optimism and recovery from coronary artery bypass surgery: The beneficial effects on physical and psychological well-being. *Journal of Personality and Social Psychology, 57,* 1024–1040. [13]

Scheier, M. F., Weintraub, J. K., & Carver, C. S. (1986). Coping with stress: Divergent strategies of optimists and pessimists. *Journal of Personality and Social Psychology, 51,* 1257–1264. [13]

Scherer, K. R., & Wallbott, H. G. (1994). Evidence for universality and cultural variation of differential emotion response patterning. *Journal of Personality and Social Psychology, 66,* 310–328. [10]

Scherer, K. R., Wallbott, H. G., & Summerfield, A. B. (1986). *Experiencing emotion: A cross-cultural study.* Cambridge, England: Cambridge University Press. [10]

Schiff, M., Duyme, M., Dumaret, A., Stewart, J., & Tomkiewicz, S. (1982). How much could we boost scholastic achievement and IQ scores? A direct answer from a French adoption study. *Cognition, 12,* 165–196. [7]

Schiff, M., & Lewontin, R. (1986). *Education and class: The irrelevance of IQ genetic studies.* Oxford, England: Clarendon. [7]

Schildkraut, J. (1970). *Neuropsychopharmacology of the affective disorders.* Boston: Little, Brown. [14]

Schildkraut, J. J., Hirshfeld, A. J., & Murphy, J. M. (1994). Mind and mood in modern art, II: Depressive disorders, spirituality, and early deaths in the abstract expressionist artists of the New York school. *American Journal of Psychiatry, 151,* 482–488. [14]

Schiller, F. (1993). *Paul Broca: Explorer of the brain.* Oxford: Oxford University Press. [2]

Schindler, L. W. (1988). *Understanding the immune system* (NIH Publication No. 88–529). Washington, DC: Department of Health and Human Services. [13]

Schleifer, S. J., Keller, S. E., Camerino, M., et al. (1983). Suppression of lymphocyte stimulation following bereavement. *Journal of the American Medical Association, 250,* 374–377. [13]

Schleifer, S. J., Keller, S. E., Siris, S. G., Davis, K. L., & Stein, M. (1985). Depression and immunity: Lymphocyte function in ambulatory depressed patients, hospitalized schizophrenic patients, and patients hospitalized for herniorraphy. *Archives of General Psychiatry, 42,* 129–133. [13]

Schmidt, F. L. (1992). What do data really mean? Research findings, meta-analysis, and cumulative knowledge in psychology. *American Psychologist, 47,* 1173–1181. [1]

Schmidt, G., & Weiner, B. (1988). An attributional-affect-action theory of behavior: Replications of judgments of helping. *Personality and Social Psychology Bulletin, 14,* 610–621. [16]

Schmitz, A. (1991, November). How to spot front-page fallacies. *In Health,* pp. 43–45. [1]

Schnapf, J. L., Kraft, T. W., & Baylor, D. A. (1987). Spectral sensitivity of human cone photoreceptors. *Science, 325,* 439–441. [3]

Schneider, E. L., & Guralnik, J. M. (1990). The aging of America: Impact on health care costs. *Journal of the American Medical Association, 263,* 2335–2340. [9]

Schofield, J. W., & Francis, W. D. (1982). An observational study of peer interaction in racially mixed "accelerated" classrooms. *Journal of Educational Psychology, 74,* 722–732. [8]

Schooler, N. R. (1994). Negative symptoms in schizophrenia: Assessment of the effect of risperidone. *Journal of Clinical Psychiatry, 55*(5, Suppl.), 22–28. [15]

Schou, M. (1989). Lithium prophylaxis: Myths and realities. *American Journal of Psychiatry, 146,* 573–576. [15]

Schover, L. R., & LoPiccolo, J. (1982). Treatment effectiveness for dysfunctions of sexual desire. *Journal of Sex and Marital Therapy, 8,* 179–197. [11]

Schreiber, F. R. (1973). *Sybil.* Chicago: Henry Regnery. [14]

Schreurs, B. G. (1989). Classical conditioning of model systems: A behavioral review. *Psychobiology, 17,* 145–155. [5]

Schroeder, D. H., & Costa, P. T., Jr. (1984). Influence of life event stress on physical illness: Substantive effects or methodological flaws? *Journal of Personality and Social Psychology, 46,* 853–863. [13]

Schultz, D. (1975). *A history of modern psychology* (2nd ed.). New York: Academic Press. [5]

Schulz, R., & Tompkins, C. (1990). Life events and changes in social relationships: Examples, mechanisms, and measurement. *Journal of Social and Clinical Psychology, 9,* 69–77. [13]

Schuman, E. M., & Madison, D. V. (1994). Locally distributed synaptic potentiation in the hippocampus. *Science, 263,* 532–536. [6]

Schwartz, G. E. (1982). Testing the biopsychosocial model: The ultimate challenge facing behavioral medicine? *Journal of Consulting and Clinical Psychology, 50,* 1040–1052. [13]

Schwartz, G. E., Weinberger, D. A., & Singer, J. A. (1981). Cardiovascular differentiation of happiness, sadness, anger, and fear following imagery and exercise. *Psychosomatic Medicine, 43,* 343–364. [10]

Schwebke, J. R. (1991a, March). Gonorrhea in the '90s. *Medical Aspects of Human Sexuality, 24,* 42–46. [11]

Schwebke, J. R. (1991b, April). Syphilis in the '90s. *Medical Aspects of Human Sexuality, 25,* 44–49. [11]

Searles, J. S. (1988). The role of genetics in the pathogenesis of alcoholism. *Journal of Abnormal Psychology, 97,* 153–167. [13]

Sears, R. R. (1977). Sources of life satisfactions of the Terman gifted men. *American Psychologist, 32,* 119–128. [9]

Sebald, J. (1981). Adolescents' concept of popularity and unpopularity comparing 1960 with 1976. *Adolescence, 16,* 187–192. [9]

Seeman, M., & Seeman, A. Z. (1992). Life strains, alienation, and drinking behavior. *Alcoholism: Clinical and Experimental Research, 16,* 199–205. [13]

Segal, S. J., & Fusella, V. (1970). Influence of imaged pictures and sounds on detection of visual and auditory signals. *Journal of Experimental Psychology, 83,* 458–464. [7]

Segall, M. H. (1994). A cross-cultural research contribution to unraveling the nativist/empiricist controversy. In J. Lonner & R. Malpass (Eds.), *Psychology and culture* (pp. 135–138). Boston: Allyn & Bacon. [3]

Segall, M. H., Campbell, D. T., & Herskovitz, M. J. (1966). *The influence of culture on visual perception.* Indianapolis: Bobbs-Merrill. [3]

Seidlitz, L., & Diener, E. (1993). Memory for positive versus negative life events: Theories for the differences between happy and unhappy persons. *Journal of Personality and Social Psychology, 64,* 654–664. [6]

Seidman, S. N., & Rieder, R. O. (1995). A review of sexual behavior in the United States. *American Journal of Psychiatry, 151,* 330–341. [9]

Seligman, M. E. P. (1970). On the generality of the laws of learning. *Psychological Review, 77,* 406–418. [5]

Seligman, M. E. P. (1975). *Helplessness: On depression, development and death.* San Francisco: Freeman. [5]

Seligman, M. E. P. (1991). *Learned optimism.* New York: Knopf. [5]

Selkoe, D. J. (1993). Physiological production of the b-amyloid protein and the mechanism of Alzheimer's disease. *Trends in Neurosciences, 16,* 403–409. [9]

Selye, H. (1956). *The stress of life*. New York: McGraw-Hill. [13]

Selye, H. (1974). *Stress without distress*. Philadelphia: Lippincott. [13]

Serbin, L. A., & Sprafkin, C. (1986). The salience of gender and the process of sex-typing in three-to seven-year-old children. *Child Development, 57*, 1188–1209. [11]

Serdula, M. K., Collins, M. E., Williamson, D. F., Anda, R. F., Pamuk, E. P., & Byers, T. E. (1993). Weight control practices of U.S. adolescents and adults. *Annals of Internal Medicine, 119*, 667–671. [10]

Sériès, F., Cormier, Y., La Forge, J., & Desmeules, M. (1992). Mechanisms of the effectiveness of continuous positive airway pressure in obstructive sleep apnea. *Sleep, 15*, S47–S49. [4]

Shafii, M., Carrigan, S., Whittinghill, J. R., & Derrick, A. (1985). Psychological autopsy of completed suicide in children and adolescents. *American Journal of Psychiatry, 142*, 1061–1064. [14]

Sharp, D., Cole, M., & Lave, C. (1979). Education and cognitive development: The evidence from experimental research. *Monographs of the Society for Research in Child Development, 44*(1–2, Serial No. 178). [8]

Shatz, M. (1983). Communication. In P. H. Mussen (Ed.), *Handbook of child psychology* (Vol. 3). New York: Wiley. [8]

Shatz, M., & Gelman, R. (1973). The development of communication skills: Modifications in the speech of young children as a function of listener. *Monographs of the Society for Research in Child Development, 38*(5, Serial No. 152), 1–37. [8]

Shaw, D. W., & Thoresen, C. E. (1974). Effects of modeling and desensitization in reducing dentist phobia. *Journal of Counseling Psychology, 21*, 415–420. [15]

Sheehan, D. V. (1983). *The anxiety disease*. New York: Charles Scribner's Sons. [14, 15]

Sheehan, D. V., & Raj, A. B. (1988). Monoamine oxidase inhibitors. In C. G. Last & M. Hersen (Eds.), *Handbook of anxiety disorders* (pp. 478–506). New York: Pergamon Press. [15]

Shell, E. R. (1988, August). Babies in day care: The controversy over whether nonmaternal care harms infants. *The Atlantic, 262*, pp. 73–74. [8]

Shepard, R.J. (1986). Exercise in coronary heart disease. *Sports Medicine, 3*, 26–49. [13]

Shepard, R. N., & Metzler, J. (1971). Mental rotation of three-dimensional objects. *Science, 171*, 701–703. [7]

Sherif, M. (1956). Experiments in group conflict. *Scientific American, 195*, 53–58. [16]

Sherif, M. (1958). Superordinate goals in the reduction of intergroup conflict. *American Journal of Sociology, 63*, 349–358. [16]

Sherif, M., & Sherif, C. W. (1967). The Robbers' Cave study. In J. F. Perez, R. C. Sprinthall, G. S. Grosser, & P. J. Anastasiou, *General psychology: Selected readings* (pp. 411–421). Princeton, NJ: D. Van Nostrand. [16]

Sherman, C. (1994, September/October). Kicking butts. *Psychology Today*, 41–45. [4, 13]

Shevrin, H., & Dickman, S. (1980). The psychological unconscious: A necessary assumption for all psychological theory? *American Psychologist, 35*, 421–434. [12]

Shneidman, E. (1989). The Indian summer of life: A preliminary study of septuagenarians. *American Psychologist, 44*, 684–694. [7]

Shneidman, E. S. (1995). Clues to suicide, reconsidered. *Suicide and Life-Threatening Behavior, 24*, 395–397. [14]

Shulman, H. G. (1972). Semantic confusion errors in short-term memory. *Journal of Verbal Learning and Verbal Behavior, 11*, 221–227. [6]

Siegler, R. S. (1991). *Children's thinking* (2nd ed.). Englewood Cliffs, NJ: Prentice-Hall. [8, 9]

Siegler, R. S. (1992). The other Alfred Binet. *Developmental Psychology, 28*, 179–190. [7]

Siegrist, J., Peter, R., Junge, A., Cremer, P., & Seidel, D. (1990). Low status control, high effort at work and ischemic heart disease: Prospective evidence from blue-collar men. *Social Science and Medicine, 31*, 1127–1134. [13]

Signorielli, N. (1990). Children, television, and gender roles: Messages and impact. *Journal of Adolescent Health Care, 11*(1), 50–58. [11]

Silva, C. E., & Kirsch, I. (1992). Interpretive sets, expectancy, fantasy proneness, and dissociation as predictors of hypnotic response. *Journal of Personality and Social Psychology, 63*, 847–856. [4]

Simmons, R. G., Blyth, D. A., & McKinney, K. L. (1983). The social and psychological effects of puberty on white females. In J. Brooks-Gunn & A. C. Peterson (Eds.), *Girls at puberty: Biological and psychosocial perspectives*. New York: Plenum. [9]

Simon, H. A. (1974). How big is a chunk? *Science, 183*, 482–488. [6]

Simon, H. B. (1988, June). Running and rheumatism. *Harvard Medical School Health Letter, 13*, pp. 2–4. [13]

Simpson, E. L. (1974). Moral development research. *Human Development, 17*, 81–106. [9]

Sims, E. A. H. (1990). Destiny rides again as twins overeat. *New England Journal of Medicine, 322*, 1522–1524. [10]

Singer, J. L. (1975). Navigating the stream of consciousness: Research on daydreaming and related inner experiences. *American Psychologist, 30*, 727–738. [4]

Singer, J. L., & Singer, D. G. (1979, March). Come back, Mister Rogers, come back. *Psychology Today*, pp. 56–60. [8]

Singer, R. N. (1993). Contemporary perspectives on sport psychology. *Journal of Sports Medicine and Physical Fitness, 33*, 1–12. [17]

Singh, D. (1993). Adaptive significance of female physical attractiveness: Role of waist-to-hip ratio. *Journal of Personality and Social Psychology, 65*, 293–307. [16]

Sivacek, J., & Crano, W. D. (1982). Vested interest as a moderator of attitude-behavior consistency. *Journal of Personality and Social Psychology, 43*, 210–221. [16]

Skinner, B. F. (1938). *The behavior of organisms*. New York: Appleton-Century-Crofts. [5]

Skinner, B. F. (1948a). "Superstition" in the pigeon. *Journal of Experimental Psychology, 38*, 168–172. [5]

Skinner, B. F. (1948b). *Walden two*. New York: Macmillan. [5]

Skinner, B. F. (1953). *Science and human behavior*. New York: Macmillan. [5, 12]

Skinner, B. F. (1957). *Verbal behavior*. New York: Appleton-Century-Crofts. [8]

Skinner, B. F. (1967). Autobiography. In E. G. Boring & G. Lindzey (Eds.), *A history of psychology in autobiography* (Vol. 5, pp. 387–413). New York: Appleton. [5]

Skinner, B. F. (1971). *Beyond freedom and dignity*. New York: Knopf. [5]

Skinner, B. F. (1987). Whatever happened to psychology as the science of behavior? *American Psychologist, 42*, 780–786. [1]

Skinner, B. F. (1988). The operant side of behavior therapy. *Journal of Behavior Therapy and Experimental Psychiatry, 19*, 171–179. [5]

Slamecka, N. J. (1985). Ebbinghaus: Some associations. *Journal of Experimental Psychology: Learning, Memory, and Cognition, 11*, 414–435. [6]

Slawinski, E. B., Hartel, D. M., & Kline, D. W. (1993). Self-reported hearing problems in daily life throughout adulthood. *Psychology and Aging, 8*, 552–561. [9]

Slobin, D. (1972, July). Children and language: They learn the same all around the world. *Psychology Today*, pp. 71–74, 82. [8]

Slotkin, T. A., Lappi, S. E., McCook, E. C., Lorber, B. A., & Siedler, F. J. (1995). Loss of neonatal hypoxia tolerance after prenatal nicotine exposure: Implications for Sudden Infant Death Syndrome. *Brain Research Bulletin, 38*, 69–75. [8]

Smeaton, G., Byrne, D., & Murnen, S. K. (1989). The repulsion hypothesis revisited: Similarity irrelevance or dissimilarity bias? *Journal of Personality and Social Psychology, 56*, 54–59. [16]

Smith, C. (1995). Sleep states and memory processes. *Behavioural Brain Research, 69*, 137–145. [4]

Smith, D. (1982). Trends in counseling and psychotherapy. *American Psychologist, 37*, 802–809. [15]

Smith, F. J. (1977). Work attitudes as predictors of attendance on a specific day. *Journal of Applied Psychology, 62*, 16–19. [17]

Smith, J. C. (1993). *Understanding stress and coping*. New York: Macmillan. [17]

Smith, J. C., Mercy, J. A., & Conn, J. M. (1988). Marital status and the risk of suicide. *American Journal of Public Health, 78,* 78–80. [14]

Smith, J. E., & Krejci, J. (1991). Minorities join the majority: Eating disturbances among Hispanic and Native American youth. *International Journal of Eating Disorders, 10,* 179–186. [10]

Smith, M. L., Glass, G. V., & Miller, T. I. (1980). *The benefits of psychotherapy.* Baltimore, MD: Johns Hopkins University Press. [15]

Smith, P. K. (1979). The ontogeny of fear in children. In W. Sluckin (Ed.), *Fears in animals and man* (pp. 164–168). London: Von Nostrand Reinhold. [8]

Smith, S. M. (1979). Remembering in and out of context. *Journal of Experimental Psychology: Human Learning and Memory, 5,* 460–471. [6]

Smith, S. M., Glenberg, A., & Bjork, R. A. (1978). Environmental context and human memory. *Memory & Cognition, 6,* 342–353. [6]

Snarey, J. R. (1985). Cross-cultural universality of social-moral development: A critical review of Kohlbergian research. *Psychological Bulletin, 97,* 202–232. [9]

Snyder, S. H. (1984, November). Medicated minds. *Science 84,* pp. 141–142. [15]

Sobell, M. B., & Sobell, L. C. (1978). *Behavioral treatment of alcohol problems.* New York: Plenum. [13]

Söderfeldt, B., Rönnberg, J., & Risberg, J. (1994). Regional cerebral blood flow in sign language users. *Brain and Language, 46,* 59–68. [2]

Solomon, P. R., Blanchard, S., Levine, E., Velazquez, E., & Groccia-Ellison, M-E. (1991). Attenuation of age-related conditioning deficits in humans by extension of the interstimulus interval. *Psychology and Aging, 6,* 36–42. [5]

Solso, R. (1991). *Cognitive psychology* (3rd ed.). Boston: Allyn & Bacon. [7]

Sommer, R., & Shutz, H. (1991). The consumer psychologist. In R. Gifford (Ed.), *Applied psychology: Variety and opportunity* (pp. 195–214). Boston: Allyn & Bacon. [17]

Spangler, W. D. (1992). Validity of questionnaire and TAT measures of need for achievement: Two meta-analyses. *Psychological Bulletin, 112,* 140–154. [10]

Spearman, C. (1927). *The abilities of man.* New York: Macmillan. [7]

Spector, I. P., & Carey, M. P. (1990). Incidence and prevalence of the sexual dysfunctions: A critical review of the empirical literature. *Archives of Sexual Behavior, 19,* 389–408. [11]

Sperling, G. (1960). The information available in brief visual presentations. *Psychological Monographs: General and Applied, 74,* Whole No. 498, 1–29. [6]

Sperry, R. W. (1964). The great cerebral commissure. *Scientific American, 210,* 42–52. [2]

Sperry, R. W. (1968). Hemisphere deconnection and unity in conscious experience. *American Psychologist, 23,* 723–733. [2]

Spetch, M. L., Wilkie, D. M., & Pinel, J. P. J. (1981). Backward conditioning: A reevaluation of the empirical evidence. *Psychological Bulletin, 89,* 163–175. [5]

Spezzano, C., & Waterman, J. (1997, December). The first day of life. *Psychology Today,* pp. 110–116. [8]

Spitz, R. A. (1946). Hospitalism: A follow-up report on investigation described in Volume I, 1945. *The Psychoanalytic Study of the Child, 2,* 113–117. [8]

Spitzer, M. W., & Semple, M. N. (1991). Interaural phase coding in auditory midbrain: Influence of dynamic stimulus features. *Science, 254,* 721–724. [3]

Spitzer, R. L., Gibbon, M., Skodol, A. E., Williams, J. B. W., & First, M. B. (1989). *DSM-III-R casebook.* Washington, DC: American Psychiatric Press. [14]

Spooner, A., & Kellogg, W. N. (1947). The backward conditioning curve. *American Journal of Psychology, 60,* 321–334. [5]

Springer, S. P., & Deutsch, G. (1985). *Left brain, right brain* (rev. ed.). New York: W. H. Freeman. [2]

Squire, L. R. (1986). Memory functions as affected by electroconvulsive therapy. *Annals of the New York Academy of Sciences, 462,* 307–314. [15]

Squire, L. R. (1992). Memory and the hippocampus: A synthesis from findings with rats, monkeys, and humans. *Psychological Review, 99,* 195–231. [2, 6]

Squire, L. R., Haist, F., & Shimamura, A. P. (1989). The neurology of memory: Quantitative assessment of retrograde amnesia in two groups of amnesic patients. *Journal of Neuroscience, 9,* 828–839. [6]

Squire, L. R., Knowlton, B., & Musen, G. (1993). The structure and organization of memory. *Annual Review of Psychology, 44,* 453–495. [6]

Squire, L. R., & Zola-Morgan, S. (1991). The medial temporal lobe memory system. *Science, 253,* 1380–1386. [6]

Squire, S. (1987, November 22). Shock therapy's return to respectability. *The New York Times Magazine,* pp. 78–89. [15]

Stabenau, J. R., & Pollin, W. (1993). Heredity and environment in schizophrenia, revisited: The contribution of twin and high-risk studies. *Journal of Nervous and Mental Disease, 181,* 290–297. [14]

Standards of Practice Committee of the American Sleep Disorders Association. (1994). Practice parameters for the use of stimulants in the treatment of narcolepsy. *Sleep, 17,* 348–351. [4]

Standing, L., Lynn, D., & Moxness, K. (1990). Effects of noise upon introverts and extroverts. *Bulletin of the Psychonomic Society, 28,* 138–140. [17]

Stanley, M., & Stanley, B. (1990). Postmortem evidence for serotonin's role in suicide. *Journal of Clinical Psychiatry, 51*(4, Suppl.), 22–28. [14]

Stanovich, K. E. (1989). *How to think straight about psychology* (2 ed.). Glenview, IL: Scott, Foresman. [12]

Stark, E. (1984, October). Answer this question: Responses: To sleep, perchance to dream. *Psychology Today,* p. 16. [4]

Stea, R. A., & Apkarian, A. V. (1992). Pain and somatosensory activation. *Trends in Neurosciences, 15,* 250–251. [2]

Steblay, N. M. (1992). A meta-analytic review of the weapon focus effect. *Law and Human Behavior, 16,* 413–424. [6]

Steffens, A. B., Scheurink, A. J., & Luiten, P. G. (1988). Hypothalamic food intake regulating areas are involved in the homeostasis of blood glucose and plasma FFA levels. *Physiology and Behavior, 44,* 581–589. [10]

Stein, A. H., & Friedrich, L. K. (1975). Impact of television on children and youth. In E. M. Hetherington (Ed.), *Review of child development research* (Vol. 5, pp. 183–256). Chicago: University of Chicago Press. [8]

Stein, A. P. (1991, February). The chlamydia epidemic: Teenagers at risk. *Medical Aspects of Human Sexuality, 25,* 26–33. [11]

Stein, L., Xue, B. G., & Belluzzi, J. D. (1993). Cellular targets of brain reinforcement systems. *Annals of the New York Academy of Sciences, 702,* 41–45. [6]

Steinberg, L. (1992). Ethnic differences in adolescent achievement: An ecological perspective. *American Psychologist, 47,* 723–729. [9]

Steinberg, L., Elman, J. D., & Mounts, N. S. (1989). Authoritative parenting, psychosocial maturity, and academic success among adolescents. *Child Development, 60,* 1424–1436. [8, 9]

Steinberg, L., Fegley, S., & Dornbusch, S. M. (1993). Negative impact of part-time work on adolescent adjustment: Evidence from a longitudinal study. *Developmental Psychology, 29,* 171–180. [9]

Steinberg, L., Lamborn, S. D., Darling, N., Mounts, N. S., & Dornbusch, S. M. (1994). Over-time changes in adjustment and competence among adolescents from authoritative, authoritarian, indulgent, and neglectful families. *Child Development, 65,* 754–770. [9]

Steinman, L. (1993) Autoimmune disease. *Scientific American, 269,* 106–114. [13]

Stelmack, R. M. (1990). Biological bases of extraversion: Psychophysiological evidence. *Journal of Personality, 58,* 293–311. [12]

Stern, L. D. (1981). A review of theories of human amnesia. *Memory & Cognition, 9,* 247–262. [6]

Stern, W. (1914). *The psychological methods of testing intelligence.* Baltimore: Warwick and York. [7]

Sternberg, R. J. (1985a). *Beyond IQ: A triarchic theory of human intelligence.* New York: Cambridge University Press. [7]

Sternberg, R. J. (1985b). Human intelligence: The model is the message. *Science, 230,* 1111–1118. [7]

Sternberg, R. J. (1986a). *Intelligence applied: Understanding and increasing your intellectual skills.* San Diego: Harcourt Brace Jovanovich. [7]

Sternberg, R. J. (1986b). A triangular theory of love. *Psychological Review, 93,* 119–135. [10]

Sternberg, R. J. (1987). Liking versus loving: A comparative evaluation of theories. *Psychological Bulletin, 102,* 331–345. [10]

Sternberg, R. J., & Davidson, J. E. (1982, June). The mind of the puzzler. *Psychology Today,* pp. 37–44. [7]

Stevenson, H. W. (1992). Learning from Asian schools. *Scientific American, 267,* 70–76. [7]

Stevenson, H. W., Chen, C., & Lee, S. Y. (1993). Mathematics achievement of Chinese, Japanese, and American children: Ten years later. *Science, 259,* 53–58. [7]

Stevenson, H. W., Lee, S. Y., Chen, C., Stigler, J. W., Hsu, C. C., & Kitamura, S. (1990). Contexts of achievement. *Monographs of the Society for Research in Child Development, 55*(1–2, Serial No. 221). [7]

Stevenson, H. W., Lee, S. Y., & Stigler, J. W. (1986). Mathematics achievement of Chinese, Japanese, and American children. *Science, 231,* 693–699. [7]

Stevenson, M. R., & Black, K. N. (1988). Paternal absence and sex-role development: A meta-analysis. *Child Development, 59,* 793–814. [11]

Stewart, V. M. (1973). Tests of the "carpentered world" hypothesis by race and environment in America and Zambia. *International Journal of Psychology, 8,* 83–94. [3]

Stiff, J. B., Miller, G. R., Sleight, C., Mongeau, P. L., Garlick, R., & Rogan, R. (1989). Explanations for visual cue primacy in judgments of honesty and deceit. *Journal of Personality and Social Psychology, 56,* 555–564. [16]

Stone, A. A., Bovbjerg, D. H., Neale, J. M., Napoli, A., Valdimarsdottir, H., Cox, D., Hayden, F. G., & Gwaltney, J. M. (1992). Development of the common cold symptoms following experimental rhinovirus infection is related to prior stressful life events. *Behavioral Medicine, 18,* 115–120. [13]

Stone, E. F. (1986). Job scope–job satisfaction and job scope–job performance relationships. In E. A. Locke (Ed.), *Generalizing from laboratory to field settings* (pp. 189–206). Lexington, MA: Lexington Books. [17]

Strack, F., Martin, L. L., & Stepper, S. (1988). Inhibiting and facilitating conditions of facial expressions: A nonobtrusive test of the facial feedback hypothesis. *Journal of Personality and Social Psychology, 54,* 768–777. [10]

Strauch, I., & Meier, B. (1988). Sleep need in adolescents: A longitudinal approach. *Sleep, 11,* 378–386. [4]

Streissguth, A. P., Barr, H. M., Sampson, P. D., Darby, B. L., & Martin, D. C. (1989). IQ at age 4 in relation to maternal alcohol use and smoking during pregnancy. *Developmental Psychology, 25,* 3–11. [8]

Strentz, H. (1986, January 1). Become a psychic and amaze your friends! *Atlanta Journal,* p. 15A. [3]

Strickland, B. R. (1995). Research on sexual orientation and human development: A commentary. *Developmental Psychology, 31,* 137–140. [11]

Strome, M., & Vernick, D. (1989, April). Hearing loss and hearing aids. *Harvard Medical School Health Letter, 14,* pp. 5–8. [3]

Stromeyer, C. F., III. (1970, November). Eidetikers. *Psychology Today,* pp. 76–80. [6]

Stuss, D. T., Gow, C. A., & Hetherington, C. R. (1992). "No longer Gage": Frontal lobe dysfunction and emotional changes. *Journal of Consulting and Clinical Psychology, 60,* 349–359. [2]

Stryer, L. (1987). The molecules of visual excitation. *Scientific American, 257,* 42–50. [3]

Study finds more, younger victims of rape. (1992, April 24). *The Evansville Courier,* p. A3. [11]

Stunkard, A. J., Harris, J. R., Pedersen, N. L., & McClearn, G. E. (1990). The body-mass index of twins who have been reared apart. *New England Journal of Medicine, 322,* 1483–1487. [10]

Suarez, M. G. (1983). *Implications of Spanish-English bilingualism in the TAT stories.* Unpublished doctoral dissertation, University of Connecticut. [15]

Sue, D. (1979). Erotic fantasies of college students during coitus. *Journal of Sex Research, 15,* 299–305. [11]

Sue, D. W. (1994). Asian-American mental health and help-seeking behavior: Comment on Solbert et al. (1994), Tata and Leong (1994), and Lin (1994). *Journal of Counseling Psychology, 41,* 292–295. [15]

Sue, D. W., & Sue, D. (1990). *Counseling the culturally different: Theory and practice.* New York: Wiley. [15]

Sue, S., & Okazaki, S. (1990). Asian-American educational achievements. *American Psychologist, 45,* 913–920. [9]

Suedfeld, P. (1990). Restricted environmental stimulation and smoking cessation: A 15-year progress report. *International Journal of the Addictions, 25,* 861–888. [10]

Sullivan, E. V. (1977). A study of Kohlberg's structural theory of moral development: A critique of liberal social science ideology. *Human Development, 20,* 352–376. [9]

Sullivan, F. J. (1987, May 19). *Testimony before the U.S. House of Representatives Committee on Government Operations, Subcommittee on Human Resources and Intergovernmental Relations, 100th Congress, 1st Session.* Washington, DC: U.S. Government Printing Office. [15]

Sundberg, N. D. (1990). *Assessment of persons* (2nd ed.). Englewood Cliffs, NJ: Prentice-Hall. [12]

Sung, K-T. (1992). Motivations for parent care: The case of filial children in Korea. *International Journal of Aging and Human Development, 34,* 109–124. [9]

Super, C. W. (1981). Behavioral development in infancy. In R. H. Munroe, R. L. Munroe, & B. B. Whiting (Eds.), *Handbook of cross-cultural human development* (pp. 181–269). Chicago: Garland. [8]

Suppes, T., Baldessarini, R. J., Faedda, G. L., & Tohen, M. (1991). Risk of recurrence following discontinuation of lithium treatment in bipolar disorder. *Archives of General Psychiatry, 48,* 1082–1088. [15]

Survey Research Center, University of Michigan. (1971). *Survey of working conditions.* Washington, DC: U.S. Government Printing Office. [17]

Swaab, D. F., & Hofman, M. A. (1995). Sexual differentiation of the human hypothalamus in relation to gender and sexual orientation. *Trends in Neurosciences, 18,* 264–270. [11]

Swain, I. U., Zelazo, P. R., & Clifton, R. K. (1993). Newborn infants' memory for speech sounds retained over 24 hours. *Developmental Psychology, 29,* 312–323. [8]

Swap, W. C. (1977). Interpersonal attraction and repeated exposure to rewarders and punishers. *Personality and Social Psychology Bulletin, 3,* 248–251. [16]

Sweatt, J. D., & Kandel, E. R. (1989). Persistent and transcriptionally-dependent increase in protein phosphorylation in long-term facilitation of Aplysia sensory neurons. *Nature, 339,* 51–54. [6]

Swedo, S. E., Pietrini, P., Leonard, H. L., Schapiro, M. B., Rettew, D. C., Goldberger, E. L., Papoport, S. I., Rapoport, J. L., & Grady, C. L. (1992). Cerebral glucose metabolism in childhood-onset obsessive-compulsive disorder: Revisualization during pharmacotherapy. *Archives of General Psychiatry, 49,* 690–694. [14]

Swedo, S. E., Rapoport, J. L., Leonard, H., Lenane, M., & Cheslow, D. (1989). Obsessive-compulsive disorder in children and adolescents: Clinical phenomenology of 70 consecutive cases. *Archives of General Psychiatry, 46,* 335–341. [14]

Sweller, J., & Levine, M. (1982). Effects of goal specificity on means-end analysis and learning. *Journal of Experimental Psychology: Learning, Memory, and Cognition, 8,* 463–474. [7]

Szymanski, K., & Harkins, S. G. (1987). Social loafing and self-evaluation with a social standard. *Journal of Personality and Social Psychology, 53,* 891–897. [16]

Takahashi, J. S., & Hoffman, M. (1995). Molecular biological clocks. *American Scientist, 83*(2), 156–165. [4]

Takanishi, R. (1993). The opportunities of adolescence—research, interventions, and policy: Introduction to the special issue. *American Psychologist, 48,* 85–87. [9]

Talbot, J. D., Marrett, S., Evans, A. C., Meyer, E., Bushnell, M. C., & Duncan, G. H. (1991). Multiple representations of pain in human cerebral cortex. *Science, 251,* 1355–1358. [2]

Tanfer, K. (1994). Sex and disease: Playing the odds in the 1990s. *Sexually Transmitted Diseases, 21*(2, Suppl.), S65–S72. [11]

Tanner, J. M. (1961). *Education and physical growth.* London: University of London Press. [9]

Tanner, J. M. (1962). *Growth at adolescence* (2nd ed.). Oxford: Blackwell Press. [7]

Tanner, J. M. (1978). *Fetus into man: Physical growth from conception to maturity.* Cambridge, MA: Harvard University Press. [9]

Taubes, G. (1994). Will new dopamine receptors offer a key to schizophrenia? *Science, 265,* 1034–1035. [14]

Taylor, S. E. (1991). *Health psychology* (2nd ed.). New York: McGraw-Hill. [13]

Teasdale, J. D., & Fogarty, S. J. (1979). Differential effects of induced mood on retrieval of pleasant and unpleasant events from episodic memory. *Journal of Abnormal Psychology, 88,* 248–257. [6]

Teasdale, T. W., & Owen, D. R. (1984). Heredity and familial environment in intelligence and educational level: A sibling study. *Nature, 309,* 620–622. [7]

Teen sex: Not for love. (1989, May). *Psychology Today,* p. 10. [9]

Teismann, M. W., & Mosher, D. L. (1978). Jealous conflict in dating couples. *Psychological Reports, 42,* 1211–1216. [10]

Tellegen, A., Lykken, D. T., Bouchard, T. J., Jr., Wilcox, K. J., Segal, N. L., & Rich, S. (1988). Personality similarity in twins reared apart and together. *Journal of Personality and Social Psychology, 54,* 1031–1039. [12]

Temmerman, M. (1994). Sexually transmitted diseases and reproductive health. *Sexually Transmitted Diseases, 21*(2, Suppl.), S55–S58. [11]

Templeton, R. D., & Quigley, J. P. (1930). The action of insulin on the motility of the gastrointestinal tract. *American Journal of Physiology, 91,* 467–474. [10]

Terman, G. W., Shavit, Y., Lewis, J. W., Cannon, J. T., & Liebeskind, J. C. (1984). Intrinsic mechanisms of pain inhibition: Activation by stress. *Science, 226,* 1270–1277. [3]

Terman, L. M. (1925). *Genetic studies of genius, Vol. 1: Mental and physical traits of a thousand gifted children.* Stanford, CA: Stanford University Press. [7]

Terman, L. M., & Oden, M. H. (1947). *Genetic studies of genius, Vol. 4: The gifted child grows up.* Stanford, CA: Stanford University Press. [7]

Terman, L. M., & Oden, M. H. (1959). *Genetic studies of genius, Vol. 5: The gifted group at mid-life.* Stanford, CA: Stanford University Press. [7]

Termine, N. T., & Izard, C. E. (1988). Infants' responses to their mother's expressions of joy and sadness. *Developmental Psychology, 24,* 223–229. [10]

Terry, R. D., & Katzman, R. (1983). Senile dementia of the Alzheimer type. *Annals of Neurology, 14,* 497–506. [9]

Terry, W. S. (1988). Everyday forgetting: Data from a diary study. *Psychological Reports, 62,* 299–303. [6]

Tesch, S. A., & Whitbourne, S. K. (1982). Intimacy and identity status in young adults. *Journal of Personality and Social Psychology, 43,* 1041–1051. [9]

Thase, M. E., (1992). Long-term treatments of recurrent depressive disorders. *Journal of Clinical Psychiatry, 53*(9, Suppl.), 32–44. [15]

Thase, M. E., Frank, E., Mallinger, A. G., Hammer, T., & Kupfer, D. J. (1992). Treatment of imipramine-resistant recurrent depression, III: Efficacy of monoamine oxidise inhibitors. *Journal of Clinical Psychiatry, 53*(1, Suppl.), 5–11. [15]

Thase, M. E., Simons, A. D., Cahalane, J. F., & McGeary, J. (1991). Cognitive behavior therapy of endogenous depression: Part 1: An outpatient clinical replication series. *Behavior Therapy, 22,* 457–467. [15]

Thatcher, R. W., Walker, A., & Guidice, S. (1987). Human cerebral hemispheres develop at different rates and ages. *Science, 236,* 1110–1113. [8]

Thessing, V. C., Anch, A. M., Muehlbach, M. J., Schweitzer, P. K., & Walsh, J. K. (1994). Two- and 4-hour bright-light exposures differentially effect sleepiness and performance the subsequent night. *Sleep, 17,* 140–145. [4]

Thigpen, C. H., & Cleckley, H. M. (1984). On the incidence of multiple personality disorder. *International Journal of Clinical and Experimental Hypnosis, 32,* 63–66. [14]

Thomas, A., Chess, S., & Birch, H. G. (1970). The origin of personality. *Scientific American, 223,* 102–109. [8]

Thomas, J. L. (1992). *Adulthood and aging.* Boston: Allyn & Bacon. [9]

Thompson, L. T., & Best, P. J. (1990). Long-term stability of the place-field activity of single units recorded from the dorsal hippocampus of freely behavior rats. *Brain Research, 509,* 299–308. [2]

Thompson, M. G., & Heller, K. (1990). Facets of support related to well-being: Quantitative social isolation and perceived family support in a sample of elderly women. *Psychology and Aging, 5,* 535–544. [9]

Thompson, S. C., Sobolew-Shubin, A., Galbraith, M. E., Schwankovsky, L., & Cruzen, D. (1993). Maintaining perceptions of control: Finding perceived control in low-control circumstances. *Journal of Personality and Social Psychology, 64,* 293–304. [13]

Thorndike, E. L. (1920). A constant error in psychological ratings. *Journal of Applied Psychology, 4,* 25–29. [16]

Thorndike, E. L. (1970). *Animal intelligence: Experimental studies.* New York: Macmillan. (Original work published 1911). [5]

Thorpe, G. L., & Olson, S. L. (1990). *Behavior therapy: Concepts, procedures, and applications.* Boston: Allyn & Bacon. [15]

Thurstone, L. L. (1938). *Primary mental abilities.* Chicago: University of Chicago Press. [7]

Thyer, B. A., Parrish, R. T., Curtis, G. C., Neese, R. M., & Cameron, O. G. (1985). Ages of onset of DSM-III anxiety disorders. *Comprehensive Psychiatry, 26,* 113–122. [14]

Tiffany, S. T., Martin, E. M., & Baker, T. B. (1986). Treatments for cigarette smoking: An evaluation of the contributions of aversion and counseling procedures. *Behaviour Research and Therapy, 24,* 437–452. [15]

Tiihonen, J., Hari, R., Naukkarinen, H., Rimon, R., Jousmaki, V., & Kajola, M. (1992). Modified activity of the human auditory cortex during auditory hallucinations. *American Journal of Psychiatry, 149,* 255–257. [14]

Todd, A. (1994, July). Are you a control freak? *Mademoiselle,* pp. 114–117. [12]

Togerson, S. (1983). Genetic factors in anxiety disorders. *Archives of General Psychiatry, 40,* 1085–1089. [14]

Tollefson, G. D., Rampey, A. H., Jr., Potvin, J. H., Jenike, M. A., Rush, A. J., Dominguez, R. A., Koran, L. M., Shear, M. K., Goodman, W., & Genduso, L. A. (1994). A multicenter investigation of fixed-dose fluoxetine in the treatment of obsessive-compulsive disorder. *Archives of General Psychiatry, 51,* 559–567. [15]

Tolman, E. C. (1932). *Purposive behavior in animals and men.* New York: Appleton-Century-Crofts. [5]

Tolman, E. C., & Honzik, C. H. (1930). Introduction and removal of reward, and maze performance in rats. *University of California Publications in Psychology, 4,* 257–275. [5]

Tomaka, J., Blascovich, J., Kelsey, R. M., & Leitten, C. L. (1993). Subjective, physiological, and behavioral effects of threat and challenge appraisal. *Journal of Personality and Social Psychology, 65,* 248–260. [13]

Tomkins, S. (1962). *Affect, imagery, and consciousness: The positive effects* (Vol. 1). New York: Springer. [10]

Tomkins, S. (1963). *Affect, imagery, and consciousness: The negative effects* (Vol. 2). New York: Springer. [10]

Tordoff, M. G. (1988). Sweeteners and appetite. In G. M. Williams (Ed.), *Sweeteners: Health effects* (pp. 53–60). Princeton: Princeton Scientific. [10]

Tordoff, M. G., & Alleva, A. M. (1990). Oral stimulation with aspartame increases hunger. *Physiology and Behavior, 47,* 555–559. [10]

Torrey, E. F. (1983). *Surviving schizophrenia: A family manual.* New York: Harper & Row. [14, 15]

Torrey, E. F., & Bowler, A. (1990). Geographical distribution of insanity in America: Evidence for an urban factor. *Schizophrenia Bulletin, 16,* 591–604. [14]

Toufexis, A. (1988, February 22). Older-but coming on strong. *Time,* pp. 76–79. [9]

Travis, J. (1994). Glia: The brain's other cells. *Science, 266,* 970–972. [2]

Treffert, D. A. (1988a). The idiot savant: A review of the syndrome. *American Journal of Psychiatry, 145,* 563–572. [7]

Treffert, D. A. (1988b). An unlikely virtuoso: Leslie Lemke and the story of savant syndrome. *The Sciences, 29,* 26–37. [7]

Tresemer, D. W. (1977). *Fear of success.* New York: Plenum. [10]

Triandis, H. C., McCusker, C., Betancourt, H., Iwao, S., Leung, K., Salazar, J. M., Setiadi, B., Sinha, J. B. P., Touzard, H., & Zaleski, Z. (1993). An etic-emic analysis of individualism and collectivism. *Journal of Cross-Cultural Psychology, 24,* 366–383. [12]

Trimble, J. E. (1994). Cultural variations in the use of alcohol and drugs. In W. J. Lonner & R. Malpass (Eds.), *Psychology and culture* (pp. 79–84). Boston: Allyn & Bacon. [4]

Triplet, R. G. (1992). Henry A. Murray: The making of a psychologist? *American Psychologist, 47,* 299–307. [12]

Triplett, N. (1898). The dynamogenic factors in pacemaking and competition. *American Journal of Psychology, 9,* 507–533. [16]

Trotter, R. J. (1986, August). Three heads are better than one: Profile: Robert J. Sternberg. *Psychology Today,* pp. 56–62. [7]

True, W. R., Rice, J., Eisen, S. A., Heath, A. C., Goldberg, J., Lyons, M. J., & Nowak, J. (1993). A twin study of genetic and environmental contributions to liability for posttraumatic stress symptoms. *Archives of General Psychiatry, 50,* 257–264. [13]

Trull, T. J., & Sher, K. J. (1994). Relationship between the five-factor model of personality and Axis I disorders in a nonclinical sample. *Journal of Abnormal Psychology, 103,* 350–360. [12]

Tulving, E. (1974). Cue-dependent forgetting. *American Scientist, 62,* 74–82. [6]

Tulving, E. (1985). How many memory systems are there? *American Psychologist, 40,* 385–398. [6]

Tulving, E. (1989). Remembering and knowing the past. *American Scientist, 77,* 361–367. [6]

Tulving, E., Kapur, S., Craik, F. I. M., Moscovitch, M., & Houle, S. (1994). Hemispheric encoding/retrieval asymmetry in episodic memory: Positron emission tomography findings. *Proceedings of the National Academy of Sciences, 91,* 2016–2020. [6]

Tulving, E., Schacter, D. L., McLachlan, D. R., & Moscovitch, M. (1988). Priming of semantic autobiographical knowledge: A case study of retrograde amnesia. *Brain and Cognition, 8,* 3–20. [6]

Tulving, E., & Thompson, D. M. (1973). Encoding specificity and retrieval processes in episodic memory. *Psychological Review, 80,* 352–373. [6]

Turner, C. F., Danella, R. D., & Rogers, S. M. (1995). Sexual behavior in the United States, 1930–1990: Trends and methodological problems. *Sexually Transmitted Diseases, 22,* 173–190. [11]

Turner, J. C., Hogg, M. A., Oakes, P. J., Reicher, S. D., & Wetherell, M. S. (1987). *Rediscovering the social group: A self-categorization theory.* Oxford, England: Blackwell. [17]

Turner, R. J. (1983). Direct, indirect, and moderating effects of social support on psychological distress and associated conditions. In H. B. Kaplan (Ed.), *Psychosocial stress: Trends in theory and research* (pp. 105–155). New York: Academic Press. [13]

Turner, T. J., & Ortony, A. (1992). Basic emotions: Can conflicting criteria converge? *Psychological Review, 99,* 566–571. [10]

Tybout, A. M., & Artz, N. (1994). Consumer psychology. *Annual Review of Psychology, 45,* 131–169. [17]

Tyler, T. R., & Schuller, R. A. (1991). Aging and attitude change. *Journal of Personality and Social Psychology, 61,* 689–697. [16]

Tzu-Chin, W., Tashkin, D. P., Djahed, B., & Rose, J. E. (1988). Pulmonary hazards of smoking marijuana as compared with tobacco. *New England Journal of Medicine, 318,* 347–351. [4]

Udry, J. R., Billy, J. O. G., Morris, N. M., Groff, T. R., & Raj, M. H. (1985). Serum androgenic hormones motivate sexual behavior in adolescent boys. *Fertility and Sterility, 43,* 90–94. [11]

Umberson, D., Wortman, C. B., & Kessler, R. C. (1992). Widowhood and depression: Explaining long-term gender differencces in vulnerability. *Journal of Health and Social Behavior, 33,* 10–24. [9]

Underwood, B. J. (1957). Interference and forgetting. *Psychological Review, 64,* 49–60. [6]

Underwood, B. J. (1964). Forgetting. *Scientific American, 210,* 91–99. [6]

Ungerleider, S. (1992, July/August). Visions of victory. *Psychology Today,* pp. 46–53, 83. [17]

U.S. Bureau of the Census (1990). *Statistical abstract of the United States: 1990* (110th ed.). Washington, DC: U.S. Government Printing Office. [9, 11, 17]

U.S. Bureau of the Census (1994). *Statistical abstracts of the United States 1994* (114th ed.). Washington, DC: U.S. Government Printing Office. [8, 9, 13, 14]

U.S. Merit Systems Protection Board. (1981). *Sexual harassment in the federal workplace: Is it a problem?* Washington, DC: U.S. Government Printing Office. [17]

U.S. Merit Systems Protection Board. (1988). *Sexual harassment in the federal workplace: An update.* Washington, DC: U.S. Government Printing Office. [17]

Urbano-Marquez, A., Estruch, R., Navarro-Lopez, F., Grau, J. M., Mont, L., & Rubin, E. (1989). The effects of alcoholism on skeletal and cardiac muscle. *New England Journal of Medicine, 320,* 409–415. [13]

Usy, P-D. (1988, September 23). Chameleons thrive under apartheid. *The New York Times,* p. 27. [17]

Vaillant, G. E. (1977). *Adaptation to life.* Boston: Little, Brown. [9]

van den Hout, M., & Merckelbach, H. (1991). Classical conditioning: Still going strong. *Behavioural Psychotherapy, 19,* 59–79. [5]

Van Lancker, D. (1987, November). Old familiar voices. *Psychology Today,* pp. 12–13. [2]

van Oppen, P., De Haan, E., van Balkom, A. J. L. M., Spinhoven, P., Hoogduin, K., & van Dyck, R. (1995). Cognitive therapy and exposure *in vivo* in the treatment of obsessive compulsive disorder. *Behaviour Research and Therapy, 33,* 379–390. [15]

Vandell, D. L., & Mueller, E. C. (1980). Peer play and friendships during the first two years. In H. C. Foot, A. J. Chapman, & J. R. Smith (Eds.), *Friendship and social relations in children.* New York: Wiley. [8]

Vargas, L. A., & Willis D. J. (1994). Introduction to the special section: New directions in the treatment and assessment of ethnic minority children and adolescents. *Journal of Clinical Child Psychology, 23,* 2–4. [15]

Veleber, D. M., & Templer, D. I. (1984). Effects of caffeine on anxiety and depression. *Journal of Abnormal Psychology, 93,* 120–122. [4]

Vener, K. J., Szabo, S., & Moore, J. G. (1989). The effect of shift work on gastrointestinal (GI) function: A review. *Chronobiologia, 16,* 421–439. [4]

Verhaeghen, P., Marcoen, A., & Goossens, L. (1993). Facts and fiction about memory aging: A quantitative integration of research findings. *Journal of Gerontology, 48,* 157–171. [9]

Veroff, J. (1978). Social motivation. *American Behavioral Scientist, 21,* 706–729. [10]

Viemerö, V., & Paajanen, S. (1992). The role of fantasies and dreams in the TV viewing-aggression relationship. *Aggressive Behavior, 18,* 109–116. [16]

Vilberg, T. R., & Keesey, R. E. (1990). Ventromedial hypothalamic lesions abolish compensatory reduction in energy expenditure to weight loss. *American Journal of Physiology, 258,* 476–480. [10]

Vincent, K. R. (1991). Black/white IQ differences: Does age make the difference? *Journal of Clinical Psychology, 47,* 266–270. [7]

Vincent, K. R. (1993, Fall). On the perfectibility of the human species: Evidence using fixed reference groups. *TCA Journal*, pp. 60–63. [7]

Vincent, M., & Pickering, M. R. (1988). Multiple personality disorder in childhood. *Canadian Journal of Psychiatry, 33*, 524–529. [14]

Viney, W. (1993). *A history of psychology: Ideas and context.* Boston: Allyn & Bacon. [1]

Vinokur, A., & Burnstein, E. (1978). Depolarization of attitudes in groups. *Journal of Personality and Social Psychology, 36*, 872–885. [16]

Vitaterna, M. H., King, D. P., Chang, A-M., Kornhauser, J. M., Lowrey, P. L., McDonald, J. D., Dove, W. F., Pinto, L. H., Turek, F. W., & Takahashi, J. S. (1994). Mutagenesis and mapping of a mouse gene, *Clock*, essential for circadian behavior. *Science, 164*, 719–725

Vitousek, K., & Manke, F. (1994). Personality variables and disorders in anorexia nervosa and bulimia nervosa. *Journal of Abnormal Psychology, 103*, 137–147. [10]

Vogel, G. (1992). Clinical uses and advantages of low doses of benzodiazepine hypnotics. *Journal of Clinical Psychiatry, 53*(6, Suppl.), 19–22. [4]

Vogel, G. W. (1975). A review of REM sleep deprivation. *Archives of General Psychiatry, 32*, 749–761. [4]

Volkow, N. D., & Tancredi, L. R. (1991). Biological correlates of mental activity studied with PET. *American Journal of Psychiatry, 148*, 439–443. [2]

von Boehmer, H., & Kisielow, P. (1991). How the immune system learns about self. *Scientific American, 265*, 74–81. [13]

von Mayrhauser, R. T. (1992). The mental testing community and validity: A prehistory. *American Psychologist, 47*, 244–253. [7]

Vygotsky, L. S. (1986). *Thought and language* (A. Kozulin, Trans.). Cambridge, MA: MIT Press. (Original work published 1934). [8]

Wadden, T. A. (1993). Treatment of obesity by moderate and severe caloric restriction: Results of clinical research trials. *Annals of Internal Medicine, 119*, 688–693. [10]

Wagner, G., & Kaplan, H. S. (1992). *The new injection treatment for impotence: Medical and psychological aspects.* New York: Brunner-Mazel. [12]

Wahba, M. A., & Bridwell, L. G. (1976). Maslow reconsidered: A review of research on the need hierarchy theory. *Organization Behavior and Human Performance, 15*, 212–240. [10]

Waid, W. M., Orne, E. C., & Orne, M. T. (1981). Selective memory for social information, alertness, and physiological arousal in the detection of deception. *Journal of Applied Psychology, 66*, 224–232. [10]

Wakefield, H., & Underwager, R. (1992). Recovered memories of alleged sexual abuse: Lawsuits against parents. *Behavioral Sciences and the Law, 10*, 483–507. [6]

Wald, G. (1964). The receptors of human color vision. *Science, 145*, 1007–1017. [3]

Wald, G., Brown, P. K., & Smith, P. H. (1954). Iodopsin. *Journal of General Physiology, 38*, 623–681. [3]

Walker, D., Greenwood, C., Hart, B., & Carta, J. (1994). Prediction of school outcomes based on early language production and socioeconomic factors. *Developmental Psychology, 65*, 606–621. [8]

Walker, L. (1989). A longitudinal study of moral reasoning. *Child Development, 60*, 157–166. [9]

Walker, L., de Vries, B., & Trevethan, S. D. (1987). Moral stages and moral orientations in real-life and hypothetical dilemmas. *Child Development, 58*, 842–858. [9]

Wallach, H. (1985a). Learned stimulation in space and motion perception. *American Psychologist, 40*, 399–404. [3]

Wallach, H. (1985b). Perceiving a stable environment. *Scientific American, 252*, 118–124. [3]

Wallach, M. A., & Wallach, L. (1983). *Psychology's sanction for selfishness: The error of egoism in theory and therapy.* New York: W. H. Freeman. [12]

Wallis, C. (1984, June 11). Unlocking pain's secrets. *Time*, pp. 58–66. [3]

Wallis, C. (1985, December 9). Children having children. *Time*, pp. 79–90. [9]

Wallis, C., & Willwerth, J. (1992, July 6). Awakenings: Schizophrenia, a new drug brings patients back to life. *Time*, pp. 52–57. [15]

Walsh, J. K., & Engelhardt, C. L. (1992). Trends in the pharmacologic treatment of insomnia. *Journal of Clinical Psychiatry, 53*(12, Suppl.), 10–17. [4]

Walsh, W. B., & Betz, N. E. (1990). *Tests and assessment* (2nd ed.). Englewood Cliffs, NJ: Prentice-Hall. [12]

Walster, E., & Walster, G. W. (1969). The matching hypothesis. *Journal of Personality and Social Psychology, 6*, 248–253. [16]

Warchol, M. E., Lambert, P. R., Goldstein, B. J., Forge, A., & Corwin, J. T. (1993). Regenerative proliferation in inner ear sensory epithelia from adult guinea pigs and humans. *Science, 259*, 1619–1622. [3]

Ward, C. (1994). Culture and altered states of consciousness. In W. J. Lonner & R. Malpass (Eds.), *Psychology and culture* (pp. 59–64). Boston: Allyn & Bacon. [4]

Watson, J. B. (1913). Psychology as the behaviorist views it. *Psychological Review, 20*, 158–177. [1, 5]

Watson, J. B. (1919). *Psychology from the standpoint of a behaviorist.* Philadelphia: Lippincott. [5]

Watson, J. B. (1925). *Behaviorism.* New York: W. W. Norton. [5]

Watson, J. B. (1928). *Psychological care of the infant and child.* New York: W. W. Norton. [5]

Watson, J. B., & Rayner, R. (1920). Conditioned emotional reactions. *Journal of Experimental Psychology, 3*, 1–14. [5]

Weaver, C. A., III. (1993). Do you need a "flash" to form a flashbulb memory? *Journal of Experimental Psychology: General, 122*, 39–46. [6]

Weaver, J. B., Masland, J. L., & Zillmann, D. (1984). Effect of erotica on young men's aesthetic perception of their female sexual partners. *Perceptual and Motor Skills, 58*, 929–930. [11]

Webb, W. B. (1975). *Sleep: The gentle tyrant.* Englewood Cliffs, NJ: Prentice-Hall. [4]

Webb, W. B. (1994). Sleep as a biological rhythm: A historical review. *Sleep, 17*, 188–194. [4]

Webb, W. B., & Campbell, S. S. (1983). Relationships in sleep characteristics of identical and fraternal twins. *Archives of General Psychiatry, 40*, 1093–1095. [4]

Webb, W. B., & Cartwright, R. D. (1978). Sleep and dreams. *Annual Review of Psychology, 29*, 223–252. [4]

Wechsler, D. (1975). Intelligence defined and undefined: A relativistic appraisal. *American Psychologist, 34*, 135–139. [7]

Weekes, J. R., Lynn, S. J., Green, J. P., & Brentar, J. T. (1992). Pseudomemory in hypnotized and task-motivated subjects. *Journal of Abnormal Psychology, 101*, 356–360. [4]

Wehr, T. A., Jacobsen, F. M., Sack, D. A., et al. (1986). Phototherapy of seasonal affective disorder. *Archives of General Psychiatry, 43*, 870–875. [14]

Wehr, T. A., & Rosenthal, N. E. (1989). Seasonality and affective illness. *American Journal of Psychiatry, 146*, 829–839. [14]

Weigle, D. S., Sande, K. J., Iverius, P. H., Monsen, E. R., & Brunzell, J. D. (1988). Weight loss leads to a marked decrease in nonresting energy expenditure in ambulatory human subjects. *Metabolism, 37*, 930–936. [10]

Weinberg, R. A. (1989). Intelligence and IQ: Landmark issues and great debates. *American Psychologist, 44*, 98–104. [7]

Weinberger, M., Hiner, S. L., & Tierney, W. M. (1987). In support of hassles as a measure of stress in predicting health outcomes. *Journal of Behavioral Medicine, 10*, 19–32. [13]

Weiner, B. (Ed.) (1974). *Achievement motivation and attribution theory.* Norristown, NJ: General Learning Press. [10]

Weiner, B. (1985). "Spontaneous" causal thinking. *Psychological Bulletin, 97*, 74–84. [16]

Weiner, I. B. (1994). The Rorschach Inkblot Method (RIM) is not a test: Implications for theory and practice. *Journal of Personality Assessment, 62*, 498–504. [12]

Weingartner, H., Adefris, W., Eich, J. E., & Murphy, D. L. (1976). Encoding-imagery specificity in alcohol state-dependent learning.

Journal of Experimental Psychology: Human Learning and Memory, 2, 83–87. [6]

Weinstein, S. (1968). Intensive and extensive aspects of tactile sensitivity as a function of body part, sex, and laterality. In D. R. Kenshalo (Ed.), *The skin senses.* Springfield, IL: Charles C Thomas. [3]

Weiss, J. M. (1972). Psychological factors in stress and disease. *Scientific American, 226,* 104–113. [13]

Weissman, M. M., Bland, R. C., Canino, G. J., Greenwald, S., Hwu, H-G., Lee, C. K., Newman, S. C., Oakley-Browne, M. A., Rubio-Stipec, M., Wickramaratne, P. J., Wittchen, H-U., & Yeh, E-K. (1994). The cross national epidemiology of obsessive compulsive disorder. *Journal of Clinical Psychiatry, 55*(3, Suppl.), 5–10. [14]

Weissman, M. M., Bland, R., Joyce, P. R., Newman, S., Wells, J. E., & Wittchen, H-U. (1993). Sex differences in rates of depression: Cross-national perspectives. *Journal of Affective Disorders, 29,* 77–84. [14]

Weissman, M. M., Gershon, E. S., Kidd, K. K., et al. (1984). Psychiatric disorders in the relatives of probands with affective disorders: The Yale University-National Institute of Mental Health Collaborative Study. *Archives of General Psychiatry, 41,* 13–21. [14]

Wells, G. L. (1993). What do we know about eyewitness identification? *American Psychologist, 48,* 553–571. [6]

Wender, P. H., Kety, S. S., Rosenthal, D., et al. (1986). Psychiatric disorders in the biological and adoptive families of adoptive individuals with affective disorders. *Archives of General Psychiatry, 43,* 923–929. [14]

Wertheimer, M. (1912). Experimental studies of the perception of movement. *Zeitschrift fur Psychologie, 61,* 161–265. [3]

Wertheimer, M. (1958). Principles of perceptual organization. In D. C. Beardslee & M. Wertheimer (Eds.), *Readings in perception* (pp. 115–135). Princeton, NJ: D. Van Nostrand. [3]

West, M. J., Coleman, P. D., Flood, D. G., & Troncoso, J. C. (1994). Differences in the pattern of hippocampal neuronal loss in normal ageing and Alzheimer's disease. *Lancet, 344,* 769–772. [9]

Weström, L. V. (1994). Sexually transmitted diseases and infertility. *Sexually Transmitted Diseases, 21*(2, Suppl.), S32–S37. [11]

Wetter, M. W., Baer, R. A., Berry, T. R., Robison, L. H., & Sumpter, J. (1993). MMPI-2 profiles of motivated fakers given specific symptom information: A comparison to matched patients. *Psychological Assessment, 5,* 317–323. [12]

Wever, E. G. (1949). *Theory of hearing.* New York: Wiley. [3]

Wheeler, L. R. (1942). A comparative study of the intelligence of East Tennessee mountain children. *Journal of Educational Psychology, 33,* 321–344. [7]

Whelan, E. M., & Stare, F. J. (1990). Nutrition. *Journal of the American Medical Association, 263,* 2661–2663. [10]

Whitam, F. L., Diamond, M., & Martin, J. (1993). Homosexual orientation in twins: A report on 61 pairs and three triplet sets. *Archives of Sexual Behavior, 22,* 187–296. [11]

Whitbourne, S. K., Zuschlag, M. K., Elliot, L. B., & Waterman, A. S. (1992). Psychosocial development in adulthood: A 22-year sequential study. *Journal of Personality and Social Psychology, 63,* 260–271. [9]

White, D. P. (1989). Central sleep apnea. In M. H. Kryger, T. Roth, & W. C. Dement (Eds.), *Principles and practice of sleep medicine* (pp. 513–524). Philadelphia: W. B. Saunders. [4]

White, G. L., & Mullen, P. E. (1989). *Jealousy: Theory, research, and clinical strategies.* New York: Guilford. [10]

White, S. D., & DeBlassie, R. R. (1992). Adolescent sexual behavior. *Adolescence, 27,* 183–191. [9]

Whitehurst, G. J., Fischel, J. E., Caulfield, M. B., DeBaryshe, B. D., & Valdez-Menchaca, M. C. (1989). Assessment and treatment of early expressive language delay. In P. R. Zelazo & R. Barr (Eds.), *Challenges to developmental paradigms: Implications for assessment and treatment* (pp. 113–135). Hillsdale, NJ: Erlbaum. [8]

Whitham, F. L., & Mathy, R. M. (1986). *Male homosexuality in four societies.* New York: Praeger. [11]

Whorf, B. L. (1956). Science and linguistics. In J. B. Carroll (Ed.), *Language, thought, and reality: Selected writings of Benjamin Lee Whorf.* Cambridge, MA: MIT Press. [7]

Wicker, A. W. (1969). Attitudes versus action: The relationship of verbal and overt behavioral responses to attitude objects. *Journal of Social Issues, 25,* 41–78. [16]

Widiger, T. A., Frances, A., Spitzer, R. L., & Williams, J. B. W. (1988). The DSM-III-R personality disorders: An overview. *American Journal of Psychiatry, 145,* 786–795. [14]

Widom, C. S. (1989a). The cycle of violence. *Science, 244,* 160–166. [16]

Widom, C. S. (1989b). Does violence beget violence? A critical examination of the literature. *Psychological Bulletin, 106,* 3–28. [5, 16]

Wierson, M., Long, P. J., & Forehand, R. L. (1993). Toward a new understanding of early menarche: The role of environmental stress in pubertal timing. *Adolescence, 28,* 13–24. [9]

Wilcox, D., & Hager, R. (1980). Toward realistic expectation for orgasmic response in women. *Journal of Sex Research, 16,* 162–179. [11]

Willett, W. C. (1994). Diet and health: What should we eat? *Science, 264,* 532–537. [13]

Williams, K., Harkins, S. G., & Latané, B. (1981). Identifiability as a deterrent to social loafing: Two cheering experiments. *Journal of Personality and Social Psychology, 40,* 303–311. [16]

Williams, K. D., & Karau, S. J. (1991). Social loafing and social compensation: The effects of expectations of co-worker performance. *Journal of Personality and Social Psychology, 61,* 570–581. [16]

Williams, R. (1989, January/February). Curing Type A: The trusting heart. *Psychology Today,* pp. 36–42. [13]

Williams, S. R. (1986). *Essentials of nutrition and diet therapy* (4th ed.). St. Louis: Times Mirror/Mosby. [10]

Wilson, G. T., & Fairburn, C. G. (1993). Cognitive treatments for eating disorders. *Journal of Consulting and Clinical Psychology, 61,* 261–269. [10]

Wilson, M. A., & McNaughton, B. L. (1993). Dynamics of the hippocampal ensemble code for space. *Science, 261,* 1055–1058. [2]

Winch, R. F. (1958). *Mate selection: A study of complementary needs.* New York: Harper & Row. [16]

Wink, P., & Helson, R. (1993). Personality change in women and their partners. *Journal of Personality and Social Psychology, 65,* 597–605. [9]

Winn, P. (1994). Schizophrenia research moves to the prefrontal cortex. *Trends in Neurosciences, 17,* 265–268. [14]

Winokur, G., Coryell, W., Akiskal, H. S., Endicott, J., Keller, M., & Mueller, T. (1994). Manic-depressive (bipolar) disorder: The course in light of a prospective ten-year follow-up of 131 patients. *Acta Psychiatrica Scandinavica, 89,* 102–110. [14]

Winokur, G., Coryell, W., Keller, M., Endicott, J., & Akiskal, H. S. (1993). A prospective follow-up of patients with bipolar and primary unipolar affective disorder. *Archives of General Psychiatry, 50,* 457–465. [14]

Winson, J. (1990). The meaning of dreams. *Scientific American, 263,* 86–96. [4]

Witelson, S. F. (1985). The brain connection: The corpus callosum is larger in left-handers. *Science, 229,* 665–668. [2]

Wittchen, H-U., Zhao, S., Kessler, R. C., Eaton, W. W., & Walsh, D. (1994). DSM-III-R generalized anxiety disorder in the National Comorbidity Survey. *Archives of General Psychiatry, 51,* 355–364. [14]

Witty, P. A., & Jenkins M. D. (1936). Intra-race testing and Negro intelligence. *Journal of Psychology, 1,* 188–191. [7]

Wolfe, L. (1981). *The Cosmo report.* New York: Arbor House. [1]

Wolkin, A., Barouche, F., Wolf, A. P., Rotrosen, J., Fowler, J. S., Shiue, C-Y., Cooper, T. B., & Brodie, J. D. (1989). Dopamine blockade and clinical response: Evidence for two biological subgroups of schizophrenia. *American Journal of Psychiatry, 146,* 905–908. [14]

Wolpe, J. (1958). *Psychotherapy by reciprocal inhibition.* Stanford, CA: Stanford University Press. [15]

Wolpe, J. (1973). *The practice of behavior therapy* (2nd ed.). New York: Pergamon Press. [15]

Wolpe, J. (1981). Behavior therapy versus psychoanalysis: Therapeutic and social implications. *American Psychologist, 36,* 159–164. [15]

Wood, W., Rhodes, N., & Whelan, M. (1989). Sex differences in positive well-being: A consideration of emotional style and marital status. *Psychological Bulletin, 106*, 249–264. [9, 10]

Wood, W., Wong, F. Y., & Chachere, J. G. (1991). Effects of media violence on viewers' aggression in unconstrained social interaction. *Psychological Bulletin, 109*, 371–383. [5, 16]

Woods, J. H., Katz, J. L., & Winger, G. (1987). Abuse liability of benzodiazepines. *Pharmacological Reviews, 39*, 251–413. [4]

Woods, S. C., & Gibbs, J. (1989). The regulation of food intake by peptides. *Annals of the New York Academy of Sciences, 575*, 236–243. [10]

Woodward, A. L., Markman, E. M., & Fitzsimmons, C. M. (1994). Rapid word learning in 13- and 18-month-olds. *Developmental Psychology, 30*, 553–566. [8]

Word, C. O., Zanna, M. P., & Cooper, J. (1974). The nonverbal mediation of self-fulfilling prophecies in interracial interaction. *Journal of Experimental Social Psychology, 10*, 109–120. [16]

Wright, J. C., & Huston, A. C. (1983). A matter of form: Potentials of television for young viewers. *American Psychologist, 38*, 835–843. [8]

Wright, J. C., & Mischel, W. (1987). A conditional approach to dispositional constructs: The local predictability of social behavior. *Journal of Personality and Social Psychology, 53*, 1159–1177. [12]

Wright, S. C., Taylor, D. M., & Moghaddam, F. (1990). Responding to membership in a disadvantaged group: From acceptance to collective protest. *Journal of Personality and Social Psychology, 58*, 994–1003. [16]

Wrong man tried for murder. (1985, October 27). *St. Louis Post-Dispatch*, p. 9A. [6]

Wu, C., & Shaffer, D. R. (1987). Susceptibility to persuasive appeals as a function of source credibility and prior experience with the attitude object. *Journal of Personality and Social Psychology, 52*, 677–688. [16]

Wuensch, K. L., Chia, R. C., Castellow, W. A., Chuang, C-J., & Cheng, B-S. (1993). Effects of physical attractiveness, sex, and type of crime on mock juror decisions: A replication with Chinese students. *Journal of Cross-Cultural Psychology, 24*, 414–427. [17]

Wurtman, R. J., & Wurtman, J. J. (1989). Carbohydrates and depression. *Scientific American, 260*, 68–75. [14]

Wyatt, G. E. (1992). The sociocultural context of African American and white American women's rape. *Journal of Social Issues, 48*, 77–92. [11]

Yam, P. (1995a). Dangerous sex. *Scientific American, 272*, 10–12. [11]

Yam, P. (1995b). James Randi: A skeptically inquiring mind. *Scientific American, 273*, 34–35. [3]

Yanagita, T. (1973). An experimental framework for evaluation of dependence liability in various types of drugs in monkeys. *Bulletin of Narcotics, 25*, 57–64. [4]

Yazigi, R. A., Odem, R. R., & Polakoski, K. L. (1991). Demonstration of specific binding of cocaine to human spermatozoa. *Journal of the American Medical Association, 266*, 1956. [8]

Yehuda, R., Southwick, S. M., & Giller, E. L., Jr. (1992). Exposure to atrocities and severity of chronic posttraumatic stress disorder in Vietnam combat veterans. *American Journal of Psychiatry, 149*, 333–336. [13]

Yonkers, K. A., Kando, J. C., Cole, J. O., & Blumenthal, S. (1992). Gender differences in pharmacokinetics and pharmacodynamics of psychotropic medication. *American Journal of Psychiatry, 149*, 587–595. [15]

Young, E. A., Grunhaus, L., Haskett, R. F., Pande, A. C., Murphy-Weinberg, V., Akil, H., & Watson, S. J. (1991). Heterogeneity in the B-endorphin immunoreactivity response to electroconvulsive therapy. *Archives of General Psychiatry, 48*, 534–539. [15]

Zabrucky, K., Moore, D., & Schultz, N. R., Jr. (1987). Evaluation of comprehension in young and old adults. *Developmental Psychology, 23*, 39–43. [9]

Zajonc, R. B. (1965). Social facilitation. *Science, 149*, 269–274. [16]

Zajonc, R. B. (1968). Attitudinal effects of mere exposure. *Journal of Personality and Social Psychology, Monographs Supplement, 9*(Pt. 2), 1–27. [16]

Zajonc, R. B., & Sales, S. M. (1966). Social facilitation of dominant and subordinate responses. *Journal of Experimental Social Psychology, 2*, 160–168. [16]

Zatorre, R. J., Evans, A. C., Meyer, E., & Gjedde, A. (1992). Lateralization of phonetic and pitch discrimination in speech processing. *Science, 256*, 846–849. [2].

Zedeck, S., & Mosier, K. L. (1990). Work in the family and employing organization. *American Psychologist, 45*, 240–251. [17]

Zelnik, M., Kim, Y. J., & Kantner, J. F. (1979). Probabilities of intercourse and conception among U.S. teenage women, 1971 and 1976. *Family Planning Perspectives, 11*, 177–183. [9]

Zhang, Y., Proenca, R., Maffei, M., Barone, M., Leopold, L., & Friedman, J. M. (1994). Positional cloning of the mouse *obese* gene and its human homologue. *Nature, 372*, 425–432. [10]

Zilbergeld, B. (1986, June). Psychabuse. *Science, 86*, pp. 48–52. [15]

Zillmann, D. (1989). Effects of prolonged consumption of pornography. In D. Zillmann & J. Bryant (Eds.), *Pornography: Research advances and policy considerations* (pp. 127–157). Hillsdale, NJ: Lawrence Erlbaum Associates. [11]

Zillmann, D., & Bryant, J. (1982). Pornography, sexual callousness, and the trivialization of rape. *Journal of Communication, 32*, 10–21. [11]

Zillmann, D., & Weaver, J. B. (1989). Pornography and men's sexual callousness toward women. In D. Zillmann & J. Bryant (Eds.), *Pornography: Research advances and policy considerations* (pp. 95–125).

Zimbardo, P. G. (1972). Pathology of imprisonment. *Society, 9*, 4–8. [16]

Zimbardo, P. G., Haney, C., & Banks, W. C. (1973, April 8). A Pirandellian prison. *The New York Times Magazine*, pp. 38–60. [16]

Zipursky, R. B., Lim, K. O., Sullivan, E. V., Brown, B. W., & Pfefferbaum, A. (1992). Widespread cerebral gray matter volume deficits in schizophrenia. *Archives of General Psychiatry, 49*, 195–205. [14]

Zivin, J. A., & Choi, D. W. (1991). Stroke therapy. *Scientific American, 265*, 56–63. [2]

Zubin, J., & Spring, B. J. (1977). Vulnerability: A new view of schizophrenia. *Journal of Abnormal Psychology, 86*, 103–126. [14]

Zuckerman, M. (1979). *Sensation seeking: Beyond the optimal level of arousal*. Hillsdale, NJ: Erlbaum. [10]

Zuckerman, M., Miyake, K., & Hodgins, H. S. (1991). Cross-channel effects of vocal and physical attractiveness and their implications for interpersonal perception. *Journal of Personality and Social Psychology, 60*, 545–554. [16]

Zuckerman, M. B. (1995, February 27). The glass is half full. *U.S. News & World Report*, p. 80. [17]

Zuger, B. (1990, August). Changing concepts of the etiology of male homosexuality. *Medical Aspects of Human Sexuality, 24*, 73–75. [11]

Glossary

absolute threshold: The minimum amount of sensory stimulation that can be detected 50 percent of the time.

accommodation (cognition): The process by which existing schemas are modified and new schemas are created to incorporate new objects, events, experiences, or information.

accommodation (vision): The changing in shape of the lens as it focuses objects on the retina, becoming more spherical for near objects and flatter for far objects.

acetylcholine: A neurotransmitter that plays a role in learning, memory, and rapid eye movement (REM) sleep and causes the skeletal muscle fibers to contract.

acquired immune deficiency syndrome (AIDS): A devastating and incurable illness that is caused by HIV and progressively weakens the body's immune system, leaving the person vulnerable to opportunistic infections that usually cause death.

action potential: The firing of a neuron that results when the charge within the neuron becomes more positive than the charge outside the cell's membrane.

adolescence: The developmental stage that begins at puberty and encompasses the period from the end of childhood to the beginning of adulthood.

adolescent growth spurt: A period of rapid physical growth that peaks in girls at about age 12 and in boys at about age 14.

adoption method: A method researchers use to study the relative effects of heredity and environment on behavior and ability in children adopted shortly after birth, by comparing them to their biological and adoptive parents.

adrenal glands (ah-DREE-nal): A pair of endocrine glands that release hormones that prepare the body for emergencies and stressful situations and also release small amounts of the sex hormones.

aerobic exercise (ah-RO-bik): Exercise that uses large muscle groups in continuous, repetitive action and requiring increased oxygen intake and increased breathing and heart rates.

afterimage: The visual sensation that remains after a stimulus is withdrawn.

aggression: The intentional infliction of physical or psychological harm on another.

agoraphobia (AG-or-uh-FO-bee-uh): An intense fear of being in a situation where immediate escape is not possible or help is not immediately available in case of incapacitating anxiety.

alarm stage: The first stage of the general adaptation syndrome, when there is emotional arousal and the defensive forces of the body are prepared for fight or flight.

alcohol: A central nervous system depressant.

algorithm: A systematic, step-by-step procedure, such as a mathematical formula, that guarantees a solution to a problem of a certain type if the algorithm is appropriate and executed properly.

alpha wave: The brain wave associated with deep relaxation.

altered state of consciousness: A mental state other than ordinary waking consciousness, such as sleep, meditation, hypnosis, or a drug-induced state.

altruism: Behavior aimed at helping another, requiring some self-sacrifice and not designed for personal gain.

Alzheimer's disease (ALZ-hye-merz): An incurable form of dementia characterized by progressive deterioration of intellect and personality, resulting from widespread degeneration of brain cells.

amnesia: A partial or complete loss of memory resulting from brain trauma or psychological trauma.

amphetamines: A class of CNS stimulants that increase arousal, relieve fatigue, and suppress the appetite.

amplitude: Measured in decibels, the magnitude or intensity of a sound wave, determining the loudness of the sound; in vision the amplitude of a light wave affects the brightness of a stimulus.

amygdala (ah-MIG-da-la): A structure in the limbic system that plays an important role in emotion, particularly in response to aversive stimuli.

anal stage: Freud's second psychosexual stage (ages 1 or $1\frac{1}{2}$ to 3 years), in which the child derives sensual pleasure mainly from expelling and withholding feces.

androgens: Male sex hormones.

androgyny (an-DROJ-uh-nee): A combination of the desirable male and female characteristics in one person.

anterograde amnesia: The inability to form long-term memories of events occurring after a brain injury or brain surgery, although memories formed before the trauma are usually intact.

antidepressants: Drugs that are prescribed to treat depression and some anxiety disorders.

antipsychotic drugs: Drugs used to control severe psychotic symptoms, such as the delusions and hallucinations of schizophrenics; also known as neuroleptics or major tranquilizers.

antisocial personality disorder: A disorder marked by lack of feeling for others; selfish, aggressive, irresponsible behavior; and willingness to break the law, lie, cheat, or exploit others for personal gain.

707

anxiety: A generalized feeling of apprehension, fear, or tension that may be associated with a particular object or situation or may be free-floating, not associated with anything specific.

anxiety disorders: Psychological disorders characterized by severe anxiety (e.g., panic disorder, phobias, general anxiety disorder, obsessive compulsive disorder).

aphasia (uh-FAY-zyah): A loss or impairment of the ability to understand or communicate through the written or spoken word, which results from damage to the brain.

apparent motion: The perception of motion when none is occurring (as in the phi phenomenon or in stroboscopic movement).

applied psychology: The branch of psychology that applies the methods and knowledge of the discipline to investigate and solve practical, everyday human problems.

applied research: Research conducted for the purpose of solving practical problems.

approach–approach conflict: A conflict arising from having to choose between desirable alternatives.

approach–avoidance conflict: A conflict arising when the same choice has both desirable and undesirable features; one in which you are both drawn to and repelled by the same choice.

aptitude test: A test designed to predict a person's achievement or performance at some future time.

archetype (AR-keh-type): Existing in the collective unconscious, an inherited tendency to respond in particular ways to universal human situations.

architectural psychology: A specialty concerned with the effects that buildings and the surrounding space have on mood and behavior.

arousal: A state of alertness and mental and physical activation.

arousal theory: A theory suggesting that the aim of motivation is to maintain an optimal level of arousal.

artificial intelligence: Computer systems that simulate human thinking in solving problems and in making judgments and decisions.

assimilation: The process by which new objects, events, experiences, or information are incorporated into existing schemas.

association areas: Areas of the cerebral cortex that house memories and are involved in thought, perception, learning, and language.

attachment: The strong affectionate bond a child forms with the mother or primary caregiver.

attitude: A relatively stable evaluation of a person, object, situation, or issue.

attribution: An inference about the cause of our own or another's behavior.

audience effects: The impact of passive spectators on performance.

audition: The sensation of hearing; the process of hearing.

authoritarian parents: Parents who make arbitrary rules, expect unquestioned obedience from their children, punish transgressions, and value obedience to authority.

authoritative parents: Parents who set high but realistic standards, reason with the child, enforce limits, and encourage open communication and independence.

automatic thoughts: Unreasonable and unquestioned ideas that rule a person's life and lead to depression and anxiety.

autonomy versus shame and doubt: Erikson's second stage (ages 1 to 3 years), when infants develop autonomy or shame based on how parents react to their expression of will and their wish to do things for themselves.

aversion therapy: A behavior therapy used to rid clients of a harmful or socially undesirable behavior by pairing it with a painful, sickening, or otherwise aversive stimulus until the behavior becomes associated with pain and discomfort.

avoidance–avoidance conflict: A conflict arising from having to choose between equally undesirable alternatives.

avoidance learning: Learning to avoid events or conditions associated with dreaded or aversive outcomes.

axon (AK-sahn): The slender, tail-like extension of the neuron that transmits signals to the dendrites or cell body of other neurons or to the muscles or glands.

babbling: Vocalization of the basic speech sounds (phonemes), which begins between 4 and 6 months.

barbiturates: A class of CNS depressants used as sedatives, sleeping pills, and anesthetics; addictive, and in overdose can cause coma or death.

basic emotions: Emotions that are found in all cultures, that are reflected in the same facial expressions across cultures, and that emerge in children according to their biological timetable (examples: anger, disgust, happiness, sadness, distress).

basic research: Research conducted for the purpose of advancing knowledge rather than for its practical application.

basic trust versus basic mistrust: Erikson's first stage (ages birth to 1 year), when infants develop trust or mistrust based on the quality of care, love, and affection provided.

Beck's cognitive therapy: A brief cognitive therapy for depression and anxiety designed to help people recognize their automatic thoughts and replace them with more objective thoughts.

behavior modification: The systematic application of the learning principles of operant conditioning, classical conditioning, or observational learning to individuals or groups in order to eliminate undesirable behavior and/or encourage desirable behavior; also called behavior therapy.

behavior therapy: A treatment approach employing the principles of operant conditioning, classical conditioning, and/or observational learning theory to eliminate inappropriate or maladaptive behaviors and replace them with more adaptive responses.

behavioral genetics: A field of research that investigates the relative effects of heredity and environment on behavior and ability.

behavioral perspective: A perspective that emphasizes the role of environment in shaping behavior.

behaviorism: The school of psychology founded by John B. Watson that views observable, measurable behavior as the appropriate subject matter for psychology and emphasizes the key role of environment as a determinant of behavior.

beta wave (BAY-tuh): The brain wave associated with mental or physical activity.

binocular depth cues: Depth cues that depend on two eyes working together; convergence and binocular disparity.

binocular disparity: A binocular depth cue resulting from differences between the two retinal images cast by objects at distances up to about 20 feet.

biofeedback: The use of sensitive equipment to give people precise feedback about internal physiological processes so that they can learn, with practice, to exercise control over them.

biological perspective: A perspective that emphasizes the role of biological processes and heredity as the key to understanding behavior.

biological therapy: A therapy, based on the assumption that most mental disorders have physical causes, that attempts to change or influence the biological mechanism involved (e.g., drug therapy, ECT, or psychosurgery).

biomedical model: A perspective that focuses on illness rather than health, explaining illness in terms of biological factors without regard to psychological and social factors.

biopsychosocial model: A perspective that focuses on health as well as illness and holds that both are determined by a combination of biological, psychological, and social factors.

bipolar disorder: A mood disorder in which one has manic episodes alternating with periods of depression, usually with relatively normal periods in between.

bone conduction: The transmission of vibrations along the bones of the skull or face directly to the cochlea.

bottom-up processing: Information processing in which individual components or bits of data are combined until a complete perception is formed.

brainstem: The structure that begins at the point where the spinal cord enlarges as it enters the brain and that includes the medulla, the pons, and the reticular formation.

brightness: The dimension of visual sensation that is dependent on the intensity of light reflected from a surface and that corresponds to the amplitude of the light wave.

brightness constancy: The tendency to see objects as maintaining the same brightness regardless of differences in lighting conditions.

Broca's aphasia (BRO-kuz uh-FAY-zyah): An impairment in the ability physically to produce the speech sounds, or in extreme cases an inability to speak at all; caused by damage to Broca's area.

Broca's area (BRO-kuz): The area in the frontal lobe, usually in the left hemisphere, that controls production of speech sounds.

burnout: The result of intense, unrelieved, and unmanaged job stress; a condition in which an individual becomes pessimistic, dissatisfied, inefficient on the job, and debilitated psychologically.

bystander effect: The fact that as the number of bystanders at an emergency increases, the probability that the victim will receive help decreases, and help, if given, is likely to be delayed.

California Psychological Inventory (CPI): A highlyregarded personality test used to assess the normal personality.

Cannon–Bard theory: The theory that physiological arousal and the feeling of emotion occur simultaneously after an emotion-provoking stimulus is relayed to the thalamus.

cardinal trait: Allport's name for a personal quality that is so strong a part of a person's personality that he or she may become identified with that trait.

case study: An in-depth study of one or a few subjects consisting of information gathered through observation, interview, and perhaps psychological testing.

catatonic schizophrenia (KAT-uh-TAHN-ik): A type of schizophrenia characterized by complete stillness or stupor and/or periods of great agitation and excitement; patientsmay assume an unusual posture and remain in it for long periods.

cell body: The part of the neuron, containing the nucleus, that carries out the metabolic functions of the neuron.

central nervous system (CNS): The brain and the spinacord.

central trait: Allport's name for the type of trait you would use in writing a letter of recommendation.

centration: A preoperational child's tendency to focus on only one dimension of a stimulus and ignore other dimensions.

cerebellum (sehr-uh-BELL-um): The brain structure that executes smooth, skilled body movements and regulates muscle tone and posture.

cerebral cortex (seh-REE-brul KOR-tex): The gray, convoluted covering of the cerebral hemispheres that is responsible for higher mental processes such as language, memory, and thinking.

cerebral hemispheres (seh-REE-brul): The right and left halves of the cerebrum, covered by the cerebral cortex and connected by the corpus callosum.

cerebrum (seh-REE-brum): The largest structure of the human brain, consisting of the two cerebral hemispheres connected by the corpus callosum and covered by the cerebral cortex.

chlamydia (klah-MIH-dee-uh): The most common bacterial STD found in both sexes, and one that can cause infertility in females.

chromosomes: Rod-shaped structures in the nuclei of body cells, which contain all the genes and carry all the hereditary information.

circadian rhythm (sur-KAY-dee-un): Within each 24-hour period, the regular fluctuation from high to low points of certain bodily functions.

classical conditioning: A process through which a response previously made only to a specific stimulus is made to another stimulus that has been paired repeatedly with the original stimulus.

clinical psychologist: A psychologist, usually with a Ph.D., whose training is in the diagnosis, treatment, or research of psychological and behavioral disorders.

coaction effects: The impact on performance caused by the presence of others engaged in the same task.

cocaine: A type of stimulant that produces a feeling of euphoria.

cochlea (KOK-lee-uh): The snail-shaped, fluid-filled organ in the inner ear that contains the hair cells (the sound receptors).

cognitive developmental theory: A theory suggesting that when children realize their gender is permanent, they are motivated to seek out same-sex models and learn to act in ways considered appropriate for their gender.

cognitive dissonance: The unpleasant state that can occur when people become aware of inconsistencies between their attitudes or between their attitudes and their behavior.

cognitive map: A mental representation of an area.

cognitive perspective: A perspective that emphasizes the role of mental processes that underlie behavior.

cognitive processes (COG-nuh-tiv): Mental processes such as thinking, knowing, problem solving, and remembering.

cognitive therapy: Any therapy designed to change maladaptive thoughts and behavior, based on the assumption that maladaptive behavior can result from one's irrational thoughts, beliefs, and ideas.

coitus: Penile-vaginal intercourse.

collective unconscious: In Jung's theory, the most inaccessible layer of the unconscious, which contains the universal experiences of humankind transmitted to each individual.

color blindness: The inability to distinguish some or all colors in vision, resulting from a defect in the cones.

color constancy: The tendency to see objects as maintaining about the same color regardless of differences in lighting conditions.

compliance: Acting in accordance with the wishes, the suggestions, or the direct request of another person.

compulsion: A persistent, irresistible, irrational urge to perform an act or ritual repeatedly.

concept: A label that represents a class or group of objects, people, or events sharing common characteristics or attributes.

concrete operations stage: Piaget's third stage of cognitive development (ages 7 to 11 years), during which a child acquires the concepts of reversibility and conservation and is able to apply logical thinking to concrete objects.

conditioned reflex: A learned reflex rather than a naturally occurring one.

conditioned response (CR): That response that comes to be elicited by a conditioned stimulus as a result of its repeated pairing with an unconditioned stimulus.

conditioned stimulus (CS): A neutral stimulus that, after repeated pairing with an unconditioned stimulus, becomes associated with it and elicits a conditioned response.

conditions of worth: Conditions upon which the positive regard of others rests.

cones: The receptor cells in the retina that enable us to see color and fine detail in adequate light, but that do not function in dim light.

confederate: Someone posing as a subject in an experiment but who is actually assisting the experimenter.

conformity: Changing or adopting an attitude or behavior to be consistent with the norms of a group or the expectations of others.

conscious (KON-shus): Those thoughts, feelings, sensations, or memories of which we are aware at any given moment.

consciousness: The continuous stream of perceptions, thoughts, feelings, or sensations of which we are aware from moment to moment.

conservation: The concept that a given quantity of matter remains the same despite rearrangement or change in its appearance, as long as nothing has been added or taken away.

consolidation: The presumed process, believed to involve the hippocampus, by which a permanent memory is formed.

consolidation failure: Any disruption in the consolidation process that prevents a permanent memory from forming.

consumer psychology: A specialty concerned with studying, measuring, predicting, and influencing consumer behavior.

consummate love: According to Sternberg's theory, the most complete form of love, consisting of three components—intimacy, passion, and decision/commitment.

contact hypothesis: The notion that prejudice can be reduced through increased contact among members of different social groups.

continuous reinforcement: Reinforcement that is administered after every desired or correct response; the most effective method of conditioning a new response.

control group: In an experiment, a group that is similar to the experimental group and is exposed to the same experimental environment but is not exposed to the independent variable; used for purposes of comparison.

controlled drinking: A behavioral approach to the treatment of alcoholism, designed to teach the skills necessary so that alcoholics can drink socially without losing control.

conventional level: Kohlberg's second level of moral reasoning, in which right and wrong are based on the internalized standards of others; "right" is whatever helps or is approved of by others, or whatever is consistent with the laws of society.

convergence: A binocular depth cue in which the eyes turn inward as they focus on nearby objects—the closer an object, the greater the convergence.

conversion disorder: A somatoform disorder in which a loss of motor or sensory functioning in some part of the body has no physical cause but solves some psychological problem.

coping: Efforts through action and thought to deal with demands that are perceived as taxing or overwhelming.

cornea (KOR-nee-uh): The transparent covering of the colored part of the eye that bends light rays inward through the pupil.

corpus callosum (KOR-pus kah-LO-sum): The thick band of nerve fibers that connects the two cerebral hemispheres and makes possible the transfer of information and the synchronization of activity between them.

correlation coefficient: A numerical value that indicates the strength and direction of the relationship between two variables; ranges from +1.00 (a perfect positive correlation) to –1.00 (a perfect negative correlation).

correlational method: A research method used to establish the relationship (correlation) between two characteristics, events, or behaviors.

counseling psychologist: A psychologist who helps people with problems that are considered less severe than those generally handled by a clinical psychologist; often provides vocational or academic counseling; usually works in a nonmedical setting.

crack: The most potent, inexpensive, and addictive form of cocaine, and the form that is smoked.

crash: The feelings of depression, exhaustion, irritability, and anxiety that occur following an amphetamine, cocaine, or crack high.

creativity: The ability to produce original, appropriate, and valuable ideas and/or solutions to problems.

critical period: A period that is so important to development that a harmful environmental influence can keep a bodily structure or behavior from developing normally.

cross-sectional study: A type of developmental study in which researchers compare groups of subjects of different ages on certain characteristics to determine age-related differences.

crowding: A subjective perception that there are too many people in a defined space.

crystallized intelligence: Aspects of intelligence, including verbal ability and accumulated knowledge, that tend to increase over the life span.

CT scan (computerized axial tomography): A brain-scanning technique involving a rotating X-ray scanner and a high-speed computer analysis that produces slice-by-slice, cross-sectional images of the structure of the brain.

culture-fair intelligence test: An intelligence test designed to minimize cultural bias by using questions that will not penalize those whose culture or language differs from that of the urban middle or upper class.

dark adaptation: The eye's increasing ability to see in dim light; results from the recombining of molecules of rhodopsin in the rods and the dilation of the pupils.

decay theory: A theory of forgetting that holds that the memory trace, if not used, disappears with the passage of time.

decibel (DES-ih-bel): A unit of measurement of the intensity or loudness of sound based on the amplitude of the sound wave.

decision latitude: The degree to which employees have the opportunity to exercise initiative and use their skills to control their working conditions.

declarative memory: The subsystem within long-term memory that stores facts, information, and personal life experiences; also called explicit memory.

defense mechanism: An unconscious, irrational means used by the ego to defend against anxiety; involves self-deception and the distortion of reality.

delta wave: The brain wave associated with slow-wave (deep) sleep (Stage 3 and Stage 4 sleep).

delusion: A false belief, not generally shared by others in the culture, that cannot be changed despite strong evidence to the contrary.

delusion of grandeur: A false belief that one is a famous person or one who has some great knowledge, ability, or authority.

delusion of persecution: An individual's false belief that a person or group is trying in some way to harm him or her.

dendrites (DEN-drytes): The branchlike extensions of a neuron that receive signals from other neurons.

denial: Refusing to acknowledge consciously the existence of a danger or a threatening condition.

density: A measure referring to the number of people occupying a unit of space.

dependent variable: The variable that is measured at the end of an experiment and is presumed to vary as a result of manipulations of the independent variable.

depressants: A category of drugs that decrease activity in the central nervous system, slow down bodily functions, and reduce sensitivity to outside stimulation; also called "downers."

depth perception: The ability to see in three dimensions and to estimate distance.

descriptive research methods: Research methods that yield descriptions of behavior rather than causal explanations.

descriptive statistics: Statistics used to organize, summarize, and describe information gathered from actual observations.

developmental psychology: The study of how humans grow, develop, and change throughout the life span.

deviation score: A test score calculated by comparing an individual's score to the scores of others of the same age on whom the test was normed.

diathesis–stress model: The idea that people with a constitutional predisposition (diathesis) toward a disorder, such as schizophrenia, may develop the disorder if they are subjected to sufficient environmental stress.

difference threshold: The smallest increase or decrease in a physical stimulus required to produce a difference in sensation that is noticeable 50 percent of the time.

diffusion of responsibility: The feeling among bystanders at an emergency that the responsibility for helping is shared by the group, so each person feels less compelled to act than if he or she alone bore the total responsibility.

directive therapy: An approach to therapy in which the therapist takes an active role in determining the course of therapy sessions and provides answers and suggestions to the patient.

discrimination (learning): The learned ability to distinguish between similar stimuli so that the conditioned response occurs only to the original conditioned stimulus but not to similar stimuli.

discrimination (social): Behavior, usually negative, directed toward others based on their gender, religion, race, or membership in a particular group.

discriminative stimulus: A stimulus that signals whether a certain response or behavior is likely to be followed by reward or punishment.

disorganized schizophrenia: The most serious type of schizophrenia, marked by inappropriate affect, silliness, laughter, grotesque mannerisms, and bizarre behavior.

displacement (defense mechanism): Substituting a less threatening object for the original object of an impulse.

displacement (memory): The event that occurs when short-term memory is holding its maximum and each new item entering short-term memory pushes out an existing item.

display rules: Cultural rules that dictate how emotions should be expressed, and when and where their expression is appropriate.

dispositional attribution: Attribution of one's own or another's behavior to some internal cause such as a personal trait, motive, or attitude; an internal attribution.

dissociative amnesia: A dissociative disorder in which there is a loss of memory for limited periods in one's life or for one's entire personal identity.

dissociative disorders: Disorders in which, under stress, one loses the integration of consciousness, identity, and memories of important personal events.

dissociative fugue (FEWG): A dissociative disorder in which one has a complete loss of memory for one's entire identity, travels away from home, and may assume a new identity.

dissociative identity disorder: A dissociative disorder in which two or more distinct personalities occur in the same person, each taking over at different times; also called multiple personality.

divergent production: Producing one or more possible ideas, answers, or solutions to a problem rather than a single, correct response.

dominant gene: The gene that is expressed in the individual.

door-in-the-face technique: A strategy in which someone makes a large, unreasonable request with the expectation that the person will refuse but will then be more likely to respond favorably to a smaller request at a later time.

dopamine (DOE-pah-meen): A neurotransmitter that plays a role in learning, attention, and movement; a deficiency of dopamine is associated with Parkinson's disease, and an oversensitivity to it is associated with some cases of schizophrenia.

double-blind technique: An experimental procedure in which neither the subjects nor the experimenter knows who is in the experimental or control groups until after the results have been gathered; a control for experimenter bias.

drive: A state of tension or arousal brought about by an underlying need, which motivates one to engage in behavior that will satisfy the need and reduce the tension.

drive-reduction theory: A theory of motivation suggesting that a need creates an unpleasant state of arousal or tension called a drive, which impels the organism to engage in behavior that will satisfy the need and reduce tension.

drug dependence (physical): A compulsive pattern of drug use in which the user develops a drug tolerance coupled with unpleasant withdrawal symptoms when the drug is discontinued.

drug dependence (psychological): A craving or irresistible urge for a drug's pleasurable effects.

drug tolerance: A condition in which the user becomes progressively less affected by a drug so that larger and larger doses are necessary to maintain the same effect.

DSM-IV: *The Diagnostic and Statistical Manual of Mental Disorders (Fourth Edition)*, a manual published by the American Psychiatric Association, which describes about 290 mental disorders and their symptoms.

dyspareunia (dis-PAH-roo-nee-yah): A sexual pain disorder marked by genital pain associated with sexual intercourse, occurring in both males and females.

ego (EE-go): In Freudian theory, the rational, largely conscious system of personality, which operates according to the reality principle.

ego integrity versus despair: Erikson's stage for old age, when individuals look back on their lives with satisfaction or with major regrets.

eidetic imagery (eye-DET-ik): The ability to retain the image of a visual stimulus several minutes after it has been removed from view.

electroconvulsive therapy (ECT): A treatment in which an electric current is passed though the brain, causing a seizure; usually reserved for the severely depressed who are either suicidal or unresponsive to other treatment.

electroencephalogram (EEG) (ee-lek-tro-en-SEFF-uh-lo-gram): A record of brain-wave activity made by the electroencephalograph.

embryo: The developing human organism during the period (week 3 through week 8) when the major systems, organs, and structures of the body develop.

emotion: A feeling state involving physiological arousal, a cognitive appraisal of the situation arousing the state, and an outward expression of the state.

emotion-focused coping: A response aimed at reducing the emotional impact of the stressor.

encoding: Transforming information into a form that can be stored in short-term or long-term memory.

encoding failure: A cause of forgetting resulting from material never having been put into long-term memory.

encounter group: An intense emotional group experience designed to promote personal growth and self-knowledge; participants are encouraged to let down their defenses and relate honestly and openly to one another.

endocrine system (EN-duh-krin): A system of ductless glands in various parts of the body that manufacture and secrete hormones into the bloodstream or lymph fluids, thus affecting cells in other parts of the body.

endorphins (en-DOOR-fins): Chemicals produced naturally by the brain (the pituitary gland) that reduce pain and positively affect mood.

environmental psychology: The specialty concerned with the effect that environments (both natural and constructed) and individuals

episodic memory (ep-ih-SOD-ik): The subpart of declarative memory that contains memories of personally experienced events.

estrogen (ES-truh-jen): A female sex hormone that promotes the secondary sex characteristics in females and controls the menstrual cycle.

evolutionary perspective: A perspective that focuses on how humans have evolved and adapted behaviors required for survival against various environmental pressures over the long course of evolution.

excitement phase: The first stage in the sexual response cycle, characterized by an erection in males and a swelling of the clitoris and vaginal lubrication in females.

exemplars: The individual instances of a concept that we have stored in memory from our own experience.

exhaustion stage: The final stage of the general adaptation syndrome, occurring if the organism fails in its efforts to resist the stressor.

experimental group: In an experiment, the group of subjects that is exposed to the independent variable, or the treatment.

experimental method: The research method in which researchers randomly assign subjects to groups and control all conditions other than one or more independent vari-

ables, which are then manipulated to determine their effect on some behavioral measure—the dependent variable in the experiment.

experimenter bias: A phenomenon that occurs when the researcher's preconceived notions in some way influence the subjects' behavior and/or the interpretation of experimental results.

exposure and response prevention: A behavior therapy that exposes obsessive compulsive disorder patients to stimuli generating increasing anxiety; patients must agree not to carry out their normal rituals for a specified period of time after exposure.

extinction: The weakening and often eventual disappearance of a learned response (in classical conditioning, the conditioned response is weakened by repeated presentation of the conditioned stimulus without the unconditioned stimulus; in operant conditioning, the conditioned response is weakened by withholding reinforcement).

extrasensory perception (ESP): Gaining awareness of or information about objects, events, or another's thoughts through some means other than the known sensory channels.

extraversion: The tendency to be outgoing, adaptable, and sociable.

extrinsic motivation: The desire to perform an act to gain a reward or to avoid an undesirable consequence.

facial-feedback hypothesis: The idea that the muscular movements involved in certain facial expressions trigger the corresponding emotions (for example, smiling makes us happy).

family therapy: Therapy based on the assumption that an individual's problem is caused and/or maintained in part by problems within the family unit, and so the entire family is involved in therapy.

fat cells: Numbering 30 to 40 billion, cells that serve as storehouses for liquefied fat in the body; with weight loss, they decrease in size but not in number.

feature detectors: Neurons in the brain that respond to specific features of a sensory stimulus (for example, to lines or angles).

female orgasmic disorder: The persistent inability of a woman to reach orgasm, or a delay in reaching orgasm despite adequate sexual stimulation.

female sexual arousal disorder: A sexual dysfunction in which a woman may not feel sexually aroused in response to sexual stimulation or may be unable to achieve or sustain "an adequate lubrication-swelling response to sexual excitement."

fetal alcohol syndrome: A condition, caused by maternal alcohol intake during pregnancy, in which the baby is born mentally retarded, abnormally small, and with facial, organ, and limb abnormalities.

fetus: The developing human organism during the period (week 9 until birth) when rapid growth and further development of the structures, organs, and systems of the body occur.

figure-ground: A principle of perceptual organization whereby the visual field is perceived in terms of an object (figure) standing out against a background (ground).

first-degree relatives: A person's parents, children, or siblings.

five-factor theory: A trait theory that attempts to explain personality using five broad dimensions, each of which is composed of a constellation of personality traits.

fixation: Arrested development at a psychosexual stage occurring because of excessive gratification or frustration at that stage.

fixed-interval schedule: A schedule in which a reinforcer is given following the first correct response after a fixed period of time has elapsed.

fixed-ratio schedule: A schedule in which a reinforcer is given after a fixed number of correct responses.

flashback: The brief recurrence of effects a person has experienced while taking LSD, occurring suddenly and without warning at a later time.

flashbulb memory: An extremely vivid memory of the conditions surrounding one's first hearing the news of a surprising, shocking, or highly emotional event.

flextime: A flexible work schedule in which a worker may begin the day several hours earlier or later than the usual work day or working longer days and "bank" the hours so as to be able to take time off later.

flooding: A behavioral therapy used to treat phobias, during which clients are exposed to the feared object or event (or asked to imagine it vividly) for an extended period until their anxiety decreases.

fluid intelligence: Aspects of intelligence involving abstract reasoning and mental flexibility, which peak in the early 20s and decline slowly as people age.

focus group: A small number of consumers representing targeted populations who are brought together to evaluate products and respond to demonstrations.

foot-in-the-door technique: A strategy designed to secure a favorable response to a small request at first, with the aim of making the subject more likely to agree later to a larger request.

forensic psychology: A law-related specialty in which psychologists are involved in the legal justice system either as expert witnesses or as consultants to police, attorneys, defendants, judges, juries, or the penal system.

formal operations stage: Piaget's fourth and final stage of cognitive development, characterized by the ability to apply logical thinking to abstract problems and hypothetical situations.

fovea (FO-vee-uh): A small area of the retina, $1/50$ of an inch in diameter, that provides the clearest and sharpest vision because it has the largest concentration of cones.

fraternal (dizygotic) twins: Twins, no more alike genetically than ordinary siblings, who develop after two eggs are released during ovulation and fertilized by two different sperm.

free association: A psychoanalytic technique used to explore the unconscious by having patients reveal whatever thoughts or images come to mind.

frequency: Measured in the unit hertz, the number of sound waves or cycles per second, determining the pitch of the sound.

frequency distribution: An arrangement showing the frequency, or number of scores that fall within equalsized class intervals.

frequency polygon: A line graph that depicts the frequency or number of scores within each class interval in a frequency distribution.

frequency theory: The theory that hair cell receptors vibrate the same number of times as the sounds that reach them, thereby accounting for how variations in pitch are transmitted to the brain.

frontal lobes: The lobes that control voluntary body movements, speech production, and such functions as thinking, motivation, planning for the future, impulse control, and emotional responses.

frustration: Interference with the attainment of a goal, or the blocking of an impulse.

frustration–aggression hypothesis: The hypothesis that frustration produces aggression.

functional fixedness: The failure to use familiar objects in novel ways to solve problems because of a tendency to view objects only in terms of their customary functions.

functionalism: An early school of psychology that was concerned with how mental processes help humans and animals adapt to their environments.

fundamental attribution error: The tendency to overemphasize internal causes and underemphasize situational factors when explaining the behavior of others.

gate-control theory: The theory that the pain signals transmitted by slow-firing nerve fibers can be blocked at the spinal gate if fast-firing fibers get their messages to the gate first, or if the brain itself inhibits transmission of the pain messages.

gender (JEN-der): One's biological sex—male or female.

gender identity: One's sense of being a male or a female.

gender identity disorders: Disorders characterized by a problem accepting one's identity as male or female.

gender roles: Cultural expectations about the behavior appropriate to each gender.

gender-schema theory: A theory suggesting that young children are motivated to attend to and behave in ways consistent with gender-based standards and stereotypes of the culture.

gender typing: The process by which individuals acquire the traits, behaviors, attitudes, preferences, and interests that the culture considers appropriate for their gender.

general adaptation syndrome (GAS): The predictable sequence of reactions (the alarm, resistance, and exhaustion stages) that organisms show in response to stressors.

generalization: In classical conditioning, the tendency to make a conditioned response to a stimulus similar to the original conditioned stimulus; in operant conditioning, the tendency to make the learned response to a stimulus similar to the one for which it was originally reinforced.

generalized anxiety disorder: An anxiety disorder in which people experience excessive anxiety or worry that they find difficult to control.

generativity versus stagnation: Erikson's stage for middle age, when the individual becomes increasingly concerned with guiding the next generation rather than becoming and stagnating.

genes: Within the chromosomes, the segments of DNA that are the basic units for the transmission of hereditary traits.

genital herpes (HER-peez): An STD caused by the herpes simplex virus (usually type 2) that results in painful blisters on the genitals; presently incurable, usually recurring, and highly contagious during outbreaks.

genital stage: The final of Freud's psychosexual stages (from puberty on), in which for most people the focus of sexual energy gradually shifts to the opposite sex, culminating in the attainment of full adult sexuality.

genitals (JEN-uh-tulz): The internal and external reproductive organs.

Gestalt (geh-SHTALT): A German word roughly meaning "form" or "pattern."

Gestalt psychology (geh-SHTALT): The school of psychology that emphasizes that individuals perceive objects and patterns as whole units and that the perceived whole is greater than the sum of its parts.

Gestalt therapy: A therapy originated by Fritz Perls and emphasizing the importance of clients fully experiencing, in the present moment, their feelings, thoughts, and actions and taking personal responsibility for their behavior.

g factor: Spearman's term for a general intellectual ability that underlies all mental operations to some degree.

glial cells (GLEE-ul): Cells that help to make the brain more efficient by holding the neurons together, removing waste products such as dead neurons, making the myelin coating for the axons, and performing other manufacturing, nourishing, and clean-up tasks.

gonads: The sex glands; the ovaries in females and the testes in males.

gonorrhea (gahn-ah-REE-ah): An STD that, in males, causes a puslike discharge from the penis; if untreated, females can develop pelvic inflammatory disease and possible infertility.

group polarization: The tendency of members of a group, after group discussion, to shift toward a more extreme position in whatever direction they were leaning initially—either more risky or more cautious.

group therapy: A form of therapy in which several clients (usually 7–10) meet regularly with one or two therapists to resolve personal problems.

groupthink: The tendency for members of a very cohesive group to feel such pressure to maintain group solidarity and to reach agreement on an issue that they fail adequately to weigh available evidence or to consider objections and alternatives.

gustation: The sensation of taste.

habituation: A decrease in response or attention to a stimulus as an infant becomes accustomed to it.

hair cells: Sensory receptors for hearing, found in the cochlea.

hallucination: A sensory perception in the absence of any external sensory stimulus; an imaginary sensation.

hallucinogens (hal-lu-SIN-o-jenz): A category of drugs, sometimes called psychedelics, that alter perception and mood and can cause hallucinations.

halo effect: The tendency of raters to be excessively influenced in their overall evaluation of a person by one or a few favorable or unfavorable traits; the tendency to infer generally positive or negative traits in a person as a result of observing one major positive or negative trait.

hardiness: A combination of three psychological qualities shared by people who can undergo high levels of stress yet remain healthy: a sense of control over one's life, commitment to one's personal goals, and a tendency to view change as a challenge rather than as a threat.

hassles: Little stressors that include the irritating demands and troubled relationships that can occur daily and that, according to Lazarus, cause more stress than do major life changes.

health psychology: The field concerned with the psychological factors that contribute to health, illness, and recovery.

heritability: An index of the degree to which a characteristic is estimated to be influenced by heredity.

heroin: A highly addictive, partly synthetic narcotic derived from morphine.

heuristic (hyu-RIS-tik): A problem-solving method that offers a promising way to attack a problem and arrive at a solution, although it does not guarantee success.

hierarchy of needs: Maslow's theory of motivation, in which needs are arranged in order of urgency ranging from physical needs to security needs, belonging needs, esteem needs, and finally the need for self-actualization.

higher-order conditioning: Occurs when a neutral stimulus is paired with an existing conditioned stimulus, becomes associated with it, and gains the power to elicit the same conditioned response.

hippocampus (hip-po-CAM-pus): A structure in the limbic system that plays a central role in the formation of long-term memories and is involved in the formation of memories of facts, information, and personal experiences.

histogram: A bar graph that depicts the frequency or number of scores within each class interval in a frequency distribution.

HIV (human immunodeficiency virus): The virus that causes AIDS.

homeostasis: The tendency of the body to maintain a balanced internal state with regard to oxygen level, body temperature, blood sugar, water balance, and so forth.

homophobia: An intense, irrational hostility toward or fear of homosexuals.

hormone: A substance manufactured and released in one part of the body that affects other parts of the body.

hue: The property of light commonly referred to as color (red, blue, green, etc.), determined primarily by the wavelength of light reflected from a surface.

human factors psychology: A specialty concerned with designing and modifying machines and work environments to make them safer, easier to use, and more compatible with people's sensory, perceptual, cognitive, and motor capabilities; also called ergonomics.

humanistic perspective: A perspective that emphasizes the importance of an individual's subjective experience as a key to understanding behavior.

humanistic psychology: The school of psychology that focuses on the uniqueness of human beings and their capacity for choice, growth, and psychological health.

hypnosis: A trancelike state of concentrated, focused attention, heightened suggestibility, and diminished response to external stimuli.

hypoactive sexual desire disorder: A sexual dysfunction marked by little or no sexual desire or interest in sexual activity.

hypochondriasis (HI-puh-kahn-DRY-uh-sis): A somatoform disorder in which persons are preoccupied with their health and convinced they have some serious disorder despite reassurance from doctors to the contrary.

hypothalamus (HY-po-THAL-uh-mus): A small but influential brain structure that controls the pituitary gland and regulates hunger, thirst, sexual behavior, body temperature, and a wide variety of emotional behaviors.

hypothesis: A prediction about the relationship between two or more variables.

id (IHD): The unconscious system of the personality, which contains the life and death instincts and operates on the pleasure principle.

identical (monozygotic) twins: Twins with exactly the same genes, who develop after one egg is fertilized by one sperm and the zygote splits into two parts.

identity versus role confusion: Erikson's fifth psychosocial stage, when adolescents need to establish their own identity and to form values to live by; failure can lead to an identity crisis.

illicit drug: An illegal drug.

illusion: A false perception of actual stimuli involving a misperception of size, shape, or the relationship of one element to another.

imagery: The representation in the mind of a sensory experience—visual, auditory, gustatory, motor, olfactory, or tactile.

imaginary audience: A belief of adolescents that they are or will be the focus of attention in social situations and that others will be as critical or approving as they are of themselves.

inappropriate affect: A symptom common in schizophrenia in which a person's behavior (including facial expression, tone of voice, and gestures) does not reflect the emotion that would be expected under the circumstances; for example, a person laughs at a tragedy, cries at a joke.

incentive: An external stimulus that motivates behavior (examples: money, fame).

independent variable: In an experiment, the factor or condition that the researcher manipulates in order to determine its effect on another behavior or condition known as the dependent variable.

industrial/organizational psychology: The specialty that focuses on the relationship between the workplace or work organization and the worker, including areas such as organizational design; decision making; work motivation; job satisfaction; communication; leadership; and personnel selection, training, and evaluation.

industry versus inferiority: Erikson's fourth stage (ages 6 years to puberty), when children develop a sense of industry or inferiority based on how parents and teachers react to their efforts to undertake projects.

infantile amnesia: The relative inability of older children and adults to recall events from the first few years of life.

inferential statistics: Statistical procedures that allow researchers (1) to make inferences about the characteristics of the larger population from their observations and measurements of a sample, and (2) to derive estimates of how much faith or confidence can be placed in those inferences.

in-group: A social group with a strong sense of togetherness and from which others are excluded.

initiative versus guilt: Erikson's third stage (ages 3 to 6 years), when children develop a sense of initiative or guilt depending on how parents react to their initiation of play, their motor activities, and their questions.

innate: Inborn, unlearned.

inner ear: The innermost portion of the ear, containing the cochlea, the vestibular sacs, and the semicircular canals.

insight: The sudden realization of the relationship between elements in a problem situation, which makes the solution apparent.

insight therapy: Any type of psychotherapy based on the notion that psychological well-being depends on self-understanding.

insomnia: A sleep disorder characterized by difficulty falling or staying asleep or by light, restless, or poor sleep, and causing distress and impaired daytime functioning.

instinct: An inborn, unlearned, fixed pattern of behavior that is characteristic of an entire species.

instinct theory: The notion that human behavior is motivated by certain innate tendencies, or instincts, shared by all individuals.

integrity tests: Paper-and-pencil tests used to predict whether prospective employees might be dishonest in positions involving security functions or the handling of money or merchandise.

intelligence quotient (IQ): An index of intelligence originally derived by dividing mental age by chronological age and then multiplying by 100.

interference: Memory loss that occurs because information or associations stored either before or after a given memory hinder our ability to remember it.

interpersonal therapy (IPT): A brief psychotherapy designed to help depressed people understand their problems in interpersonal relationships and develop more effective ways to improve them.

intimacy versus isolation: Erikson's sixth psychosocial stage, when the young adult must establish intimacy in a relationship in order to avoid feeling a sense of isolation and loneliness.

intrinsic motivation: The desire to perform an act because it is satisfying or pleasurable in and of itself.

introversion: The tendency to focus inward; to be reflective, retiring, and nonsocial.

inventory: A paper-and-pencil test with questions about a person's thoughts, feelings, and behaviors, which can be scored according to a standard procedure.

James–Lange theory: The theory that emotional feelings result when we become aware of our physiological response to an emotion-provoking stimulus (for example, we are afraid because we tremble).

job enrichment: Techniques used to make jobs more interesting, satisfying, and attractive.

job sharing: Employment in which two employees share one full-time job.

just noticeable difference (JND): The smallest change in sensation that we are able to detect 50 percent of the time.

kinesthetic sense: The sense providing information about relative position and movement of body parts.

latency period: The period following Freud's phallic stage (ages 5 or 6 years to puberty), in which the sex instinct is largely repressed and temporarily sublimated in school and play activities.

latent learning: Learning that occurs without apparent reinforcement but that is not demonstrated until sufficient reinforcement is provided.

lateral hypothalamus (LH): The part of the hypothalamus that supposedly acts as a feeding center and, when activated, signals an animal to eat; when the LH is destroyed, the animal refuses to eat.

lateralization: The specialization of one of the cerebral hemispheres to handle a particular function.

law of effect: Thorndike's law of learning that states that connections between a stimulus and a response will be strengthened if followed by a satisfying consequence and weakened if followed by discomfort.

learned helplessness: The learned response of resigning oneself passively to aversive conditions, rather than taking action to change, escape, or avoid them; learned through repeated exposure to inescapable or unavoidable aversive events.

learning: A relatively permanent change in behavior, capability, or attitude that is acquired through experience and cannot be attributed to illness, injury, or maturation.

left hemisphere: The hemisphere that controls the right side of the body, coordinates complex movements, and, in 95 percent of people, controls the production of speech and written language.

lens: The transparent structure behind the iris that changes in shape as it focuses images on the retina.

levels-of-processing model: A single memory system model in which retention depends on how deeply information is processed.

libido (lih-BEE-doe): Freud's name for the psychic or sexual energy that comes from the id and provides the energy for the entire personality.

life structure: Levinson's term for the basic pattern of one's life at any given time, including one's relationships and activities and the significance they have for the individual.

limbic system: A group of structures in the brain, including the amygdala and hippocampus, that are collectively involved in emotion, memory, and motivation.

linguistic relativity hypothesis: The notion that the language a person speaks largely determines the nature of that person's thoughts.

lithium: A drug used in bipolar disorder to control the symptoms in a manic episode and to even out the mood swings and reduce recurrence of future manic or depressive states.

lobotomy: A psychosurgery technique in which the nerve fibers connecting the frontal lobes to the deeper brain centers are severed.

locus of control: A concept used to explain how people account for what happens in their lives—people with an internal locus of control see themselves as primarily in control of their behavior and its consequences; those with an external locus of control perceive what happens to be in the hands of fate, luck, or chance.

longitudinal study: A type of developmental study in which the same group of subjects is followed and measured at different ages.

long-term memory: The relatively permanent memory system with a virtually unlimited capacity.

long-term potentiation: A long-lasting increase in the efficiency of neural transmission at the synapses.

low-ball technique: A strategy to gain compliance by making a very attractive initial offer to get a person to agree to an action and then making the terms less favorable.

low-birth-weight baby: A baby weighing less than 5.5 pounds.

LSD (lysergic acid diethylamide): A powerful hallucinogen with unpredictable effects ranging from perceptual changes and vivid hallucinations to states of panic and terror.

lucid dream: A dream during which the dreamer is aware of dreaming and is often able to influence the content of the dream while it is in progress.

lymphocytes: The white blood cells that are key components of the immune system—B cells, T cells, and macrophages.

magnetic resonance imaging (MRI): A diagnostic scanning technique that produces high resolution images of the structures of the brain.

mainstreaming: Educating mentally retarded students in regular rather than special schools by placing them in regular classes for part of the day or having special classrooms in regular schools.

major depressive disorder: A mood disorder characterized by feelings of great sadness, despair, guilt, worthlessness, and hopelessness.

male erectile disorder: The repeated inability to have or sustain an erection firm enough for coitus; erectile dysfunction, or impotence.

male orgasmic disorder: A sexual dysfunction in which there is an absence of ejaculation, or in which ejaculation occurs only after strenuous effort over an extremely prolonged period.

manic episode (MAN-ik): A period of extreme elation, euphoria, and hyperactivity, often accompanied by delusions of grandeur and by hostility if activity is blocked.

marijuana: A hallucinogen with effects ranging from relaxation and giddiness to perceptual distortions and hallucinations.

massed practice: One long learning practice session as opposed to spacing the learning in shorter practice sessions over an extended period.

matching hypothesis: The notion that people tend to have spouses, lovers, or friends who are approximately equivalent in social assets such as physical attractiveness.

maturation: Changes that occur according to one's genetically determined, biological timetable of development.

mean: The arithmetic average of a group of scores; one calculates the mean by adding up all the single scores and dividing the sum by the number of scores.

means-end analysis: A heuristic problem-solving strategy in which the current position is compared with the desired goal, and a series of steps are formulated and taken to close the gap between them.

measure of central tendency: A measure or score that describes the center or middle of a distribution of scores (example: the mean, the median, and the mode).

median: The middle value or score when a group of scores are arranged from highest to lowest.

meditation: A group of techniques that involve focusing attention on an object, a word, one's breathing, or body movement in order to block out all distractions and achieve an altered state of consciousness.

medulla (muh-DUL-uh): The part of the brainstem that controls heartbeat, blood pressure, breathing, coughing, and swallowing.

menarche (men-AR-kee): The onset of menstruation.

menopause: The cessation of menstruation, occurring between ages 45 and 55 and signifying the end of reproductive capacity.

mental retardation: Subnormal intelligence reflected by an IQ below 70 and by adaptive functioning severely deficient for one's age.

mental set: The tendency to apply a familiar strategy to the solution of a problem without carefully considering the special requirements of the problem.

mere-exposure effect: The tendency of people to develop a more positive evaluation of some person, object, or other stimulus with repeated exposure to it.

meta-analysis: A complex statistical procedure researchers use to combine the results from many studies on the same topic in order to determine the degree to which a hypothesis can be supported.

metabolic rate (meh-tuh-BALL-ik): The rate at which the body burns calories to produce energy.

microelectrode: An electrical wire so small that it can be used either to monitor the electrical activity of a single neuron or to stimulate activity within it.

microsleep: A momentary lapse from wakefulness into sleep, usually occurring when one has been sleep deprived.

middle ear: The portion of the ear containing the ossicles, which connect the eardrum to the oval window and amplify the vibrations as they travel to the inner ear.

midlife crisis: A period of turmoil usually occurring in a person's 40s and brought on by an awareness of one's mortality; characterized by a reassessment of one's life and a decision to make changes, either drastic or moderate, in order to make the remaining years better.

Minnesota Multiphasic Personality Inventory-2 (MMPI-2): A revision of the most extensively researched and widely used personality test; used to screen and diagnose psychiatric problems and disorders

mock jury: A group of research subjects who are selected randomly to act as jurors and reach a verdict in a simulated legal trial.

mode: The score that occurs most frequently in a group of scores.

model: The individual who demonstrates a behavior or serves as an example in observational learning.

modeling: Another name for observational learning.

monocular depth cues (mah-NOK-yu-ler): Depth cues that can be perceived by only one eye.

mood disorders: Disorders characterized by extreme and unwarranted disturbances in feeling or mood.

morphemes: The smallest units of meaning in a language.

motivated forgetting: Forgetting through suppression or repression in order to protect oneself from material that is too painful, anxiety- or guilt-producing, or otherwise unpleasant.

motivation: The process that initiates, directs, and sustains behavior satisfying physiological or psychological needs.

motives: Needs or desires that energize and direct behavior toward a goal.

motor cortex: The strip of tissue at the rear of the frontal lobes that controls voluntary body movement.

myelin sheath (MY-uh-lin): The white, fatty coating wrapped around some axons that acts as insulation and enables impulses to travel much faster.

naive subject: A subject who has agreed to participate in an experiment but is not aware that deception is being used to conceal its real purpose.

naloxone: A drug that blocks the action of endorphins.

narcolepsy (NAR-co-lep-see): A serious sleep disorder characterized by excessive daytime sleepiness and sudden, uncontrollable attacks of REM sleep.

narcotics: Derived from the opium poppy, a class of depressant drugs that have pain-relieving and calming effects.

naturalistic observation: A research method in which the researcher observes and records behavior in its natural setting, without attempting to influence or control it.

nature–nurture controversy: The debate concerning the relative influences of heredity and environment on development and on intelligence and other traits.

need for achievement (*n* Ach): The need to accomplish something difficult and to perform at a high standard of excellence.

negative correlation: A relationship between two variables in which an increase in one variable is associated with a decrease in the other variable.

negative reinforcement: The termination of an unpleasant stimulus after a response in order to increase the probability that the response will be repeated.

neonate: Newborn infant up to 1 month old.

neural networks: Computer systems that are intended to mimic the human brain.

neuron (NEW-ron): A specialized cell that conducts impulses through the nervous system and contains three major parts—a cell body, dendrites, and an axon.

neurosis (new-RO-sis): An obsolete term for a disorder causing personal distress and some impairment in functioning but not causing loss of contact with reality or violation of important social norms.

neurotransmitter (NEW-ro-TRANS-mit-er): A chemical that is released into the synaptic cleft from the axon terminal of the sending neuron, crosses the synapse, and binds to appropriate receptor sites on the dendrites or cell body of the receiving neuron, influencing the cell either to fire or not to fire.

nightmare: A very frightening dream occurring during REM sleep.

nondeclarative memory: The subsystem within long-term memory that consists of skills acquired through repetitive practice, habits, and simple classically conditioned responses; also called implicit memory.

nondirective therapy: An approach in which the therapist acts to facilitate growth, giving understanding and support rather than proposing solutions, answering questions, or actively directing the course of therapy.

nonsense syllable: A consonant-vowel-consonant combination that does not spell a word; used to control for the meaningfulness of the material.

norepinephrine: A neurotransmitter affecting eating and sleep; a deficiency of norepinephrine is associated with depression.

normal curve: A symmetrical, bell-shaped frequency distribution that represents how scores are normally distributed in a population; most scores fall near the mean, and fewer and fewer scores occur in the extremes either above or below the mean.

norms (assessment): Standards based on the range of test scores of a large group of people who are selected to provide the bases of comparison for those who take the test later.

norms (behavior): The attitudes and standards of behavior expected of members of a particular group.

NREM dreams: Mental activity occurring during NREM sleep that is more thoughtlike in quality than REM dreams are.

NREM sleep: Non–rapid eye movement sleep, consisting of the four sleep stages and characterized by slow, regular respiration and heart rates, an absence of rapid eye movements, and blood pressure and brain activity that are at a 24-hour low point.

obesity (o-BEE-sih-tee): Excessive fatness; a term applied to men whose body fat exceeds 20 percent of their weight and to women whose body fat exceeds 30 percent of their weight.

object permanence: The realization that objects continue to exist even when they are no longer perceived.

observational learning: Learning by observing the behavior of others and the consequences of that behavior; learning by imitation.

obsession: A persistent, recurring, involuntary thought, image, or impulse that invades consciousness and causes great distress.

obsessive compulsive disorder (OCD): An anxiety disorder in which a person suffers from obsessions and/or compulsions.

occipital lobes (ahk-SIP-uh-tul): The lobes that contain the primary visual cortex, where vision registers, and association areas involved in the interpretation of visual information.

Oedipus complex (ED-uh-pus): Occurring in the phallic stage, a conflict in which the child is sexually attracted to the opposite-sex parent and feels hostility toward the same-sex parent.

olfaction (ol-FAK-shun): The sensation of smell; the process of smell.

olfactory bulbs: Two matchstick-sized structures above the nasal cavities, where smell sensations first register in the brain.

olfactory epithelium: Two 1-inch square patches of tissue, one at the top of each nasal cavity, which together contain about 10 million receptors for smell.

operant conditioning: A type of learning in which the consequences of behavior tend to modify that behavior in the future (behavior that is reinforced tends to be repeated; behavior that is ignored or punished is less likely to be repeated).

opponent–process theory: The theory that certain cells in the visual system increase their firing rate to signal one color and decrease their firing rate to signal the opposing color (red/green, yellow/blue, white/black).

optic nerve: The nerve that carries visual information from the retina to the brain.

oral stage: Freud's first psychosexual stage (birth to 1 or $1\frac{1}{2}$ years), in which sensual pleasure is derived mainly through stimulation of the mouth.

orgasm phase: The third phase in the sexual response cycle, marked by rhythmic muscular contractions and a sudden discharge of accumulated sexual tension.

outer ear: The visible part of the ear, consisting of the pinna and the auditory canal.

out-group: A social group specifically identified by the in-group as not belonging.

overextension: The act of using a word, on the basis of some shared feature, to apply to a broader range of objects than appropriate.

overlearning: Practicing or studying material beyond the point where it can be repeated once without error.

overregularization: The act of inappropriately applying the grammatical rules for forming plurals and past tenses to irregular nouns and verbs.

panic attack: An attack of overwhelming anxiety, fear, or terror.

panic disorder: An anxiety disorder in which a person experiences recurrent unpredictable attacks of overwhelming anxiety, fear, or terror.

paranoid schizophrenia (PAIR-uh-noid): A type of schizophrenia characterized by delusions of grandeur or persecution.

paraphilia: A sexual disorder in which sexual urges, fantasies, and behavior generally involve children, other non-consenting partners, nonhuman objects, or the suffering and humiliation of one or one's partner.

parapsychology: The study of psychic phenomena, including extrasensory

parasomnias: Sleep disturbances in which behaviors and physiological states that normally occur only in the waking state take place during sleep or the transition from sleep to wakefulness (e.g., sleepwalking, sleep terrors).

parasympathetic nervous system: The division of the autonomic nervous system that is associated with relaxation and the conservation of energy and that brings the heightened bodily responses back to normal following an emergency.

parietal lobes (puh-RY-uh-tul): The lobes that contain the somatosensory cortex (where touch, pressure, temperature, and pain register) and other areas that are responsible for body awareness and spatial orientation.

partial reinforcement: A pattern of reinforcement in which some portion, rather than 100 percent, of the correct responses are reinforced.

partial-reinforcement effect: The greater resistance to extinction that occurs when a portion, rather than 100 percent, of the correct responses have been reinforced.

participant modeling: A behavior therapy in which an appropriate response is modeled in graduated steps and the client attempts each step, encouraged and supported by the therapist.

peak performance: Occasions when athletes achieve their top performance and during which they are totally focused, insensitive to pain and fatigue, and filled with a sense of power.

pelvic inflammatory disease (PID): An infection in the female pelvic organs, which can result from untreated chlamydia or gonorrhea and can cause pain, scarring of tissue, and even infertility or ectopic pregnancy.

perception: The process by which sensory information is actively organized and interpreted by the brain.

perceptual constancy: The tendency to perceive objects as maintaining stable properties, such as size, shape, brightness, and color despite differences in distance, viewing angle, and lighting.

perceptual set: An expectation of what will be perceived, which can affect what actually is perceived.

performance appraisal: An evaluation process, occurring annually or semiannually, in which an employee is rated and given feedback on his or her performance.

period of the zygote: Lasting about 2 weeks, the period from conception to the time the zygote attaches itself to the uterine wall.

peripheral nervous system (PNS) (peh-RIF-er-ul): The nerves connecting the central nervous system to the rest of the body.

permissive parents: Parents who make few rules or demands and allow children to make their own decisions and control their own behavior.

person-centered therapy: A nondirective, humanistic therapy in which the therapist creates a warm, accepting climate, freeing clients to be themselves and releasing their natural tendency toward positive growth; developed by Carl Rogers.

personal fable: An exaggerated sense of personal uniqueness and indestructibility, which may be the basis of risk taking common during adolescence.

personal space: An area surrounding us, much like an invisible bubble of space, that we consider ours and that we use to regulate how closely others can interact with us.

personal unconscious: In Jung's theory, the layer of the unconscious containing all of the thoughts and experiences that are accessible to the conscious, as well as repressed memories and impulses.

personality: A person's unique and stable pattern of characteristics and behaviors.

personality disorder: A continuing, inflexible, maladaptive pattern of inner experience and behavior that causes great distress or impaired functioning and differs significantly from the patterns expected in the person's culture.

personnel selection: The procedures used in the hiring and promotion of employees.

persuasion: A deliberate attempt to influence the attitudes and/or behavior of another.

PET scan (positron-emission tomography): A brain-imaging technique that reveals activity in various parts of the brain, based on the amount of oxygen and glucose consumed.

phallic stage: Freud's third psychosexual stage (ages 3 to 5 or 6 years), during which sensual pleasure is derived mainly through touching the genitals, and the Oedipus complex arises.

phi phenomenon: An illusion of movement occurring when two or more stationary lights are flashed on and off in sequence, giving the impression that the light is actually moving from one spot to the next.

phobia (FO-bee-ah): A persistent, irrational fear of an object, situation, or activity that the person feels compelled to avoid.

phonemes: The smallest units of sound in a spoken language—which, when combined, form words.

pituitary gland: The endocrine gland located in the brain and often called the "master gland," which releases hormones that control other endocrine glands and also releases a growth hormone.

placebo (pluh-SEE-bo): Some inert substance, such as a sugar pill or an injection of saline solution, given to the control group in an experiment as a control for the placebo effect.

placebo effect: The phenomenon that occurs when a person's response to a treatment or response on the dependent variable in an experiment is due to expectations regarding the treatment rather than to the treatment itself.

place theory: The theory that sounds of different frequency or pitch cause maximum activation of hair cells at certain locations along the basilar membrane.

plasticity: The ability of the brain to reorganize and compensate for brain damage.

plateau phase: The second stage of the sexual response cycle, during which muscle tension and blood flow to the genitals increase in preparation for orgasm.

pleasure principle: The principle by which the id operates to seek pleasure, avoid pain, and obtain immediate gratification.

polygraph: A device designed to pick up changes in heart rate, blood pressure, respiration rate, and galvanic skin response that typically accompany the anxiety that occurs when a person lies.

population: The entire group of interest to researchers and to which they wish to generalize their findings; the group from which a sample is selected.

pornography: Books, pictures, films, or videos used to increase sexual arousal; hard-core pornography has very explicit depictions of various sex acts.

positive correlation: A relationship between two variables in which both vary in the same direction.

positive reinforcement: A reward or pleasant consequence that follows a response and increases the probability that the response will be repeated.

postconventional level: Kohlberg's highest level of moral reasoning, in which moral reasoning involves weighing moral alternatives; "right" is whatever furthers basic human rights.

posttraumatic stress disorder (PTSD): A prolonged and severe stress reaction to a catastrophic event or to chronic intense stress.

preconscious: The thoughts, feelings, and memories that we are not consciously aware of at the moment but that may be brought to consciousness.

preconventional level: Kohlberg's lowest level of moral reasoning, based on the physical consequences of an act; "right" is whatever avoids punishment or gains a reward.

prejudice: Negative attitudes toward others based on their gender, religion, race, or membership in a particular group.

premature ejaculation: An orgasmic disorder in which the male ejaculates too soon—before he is ready, and usually long before his partner is ready.

prenatal: Occurring between conception and birth.

preoperational stage: Piaget's second stage of cognitive development (ages 2 to 7 years), characterized by rapid development of language and thinking governed by perception rather than logic.

presbyopia (prez-bee-O-pee-uh): A condition, occurring in the mid to late 40s, in which the eyes' lenses no longer accommodate adequately for near vision, and reading glasses or bifocals are required for reading.

preterm infant: An infant born before the 37th week and weighing less than 5.5 pounds; a premature infant.

primacy effect (memory): The tendency to recall the first items on a list more readily than the middle items.

primacy effect (social): The tendency for an overall impression or judgment of another to be influenced more by the first information received about that person than by information that comes later.

primary appraisal: Evaluating the significance of a potentially stressful event according to how it will affect one's well-being—whether it is perceived as irrelevant or as involving harm or loss, threat, or challenge.

primary auditory cortex: The part of the temporal lobes where hearing registers in the cerebral cortex.

primary drive: A state of tension or arousal arising from a biological need; one not based on learning.

primary mental abilities: According to Thurstone, seven relatively distinct abilities that singularly or in combination are involved in all intellectual activities.

primary reinforcer: A reinforcer that fulfills a basic physical need for survival and does not depend on learning (examples: food, water, sleep, termination of pain).

primary sex characteristics: The internal and external reproductive organs; the genitals.

primary visual cortex: The area at the rear of the occipital lobes where vision registers in the cerebral cortex.

problem-focused coping: A response aimed at reducing, modifying, or eliminating a source of stress.

progesterone (pro-JES-tah-rone): A female sex hormone that plays a role in the regulation of the menstrual cycle and prepares the lining of the uterus for possible pregnancy.

projection: Attributing one's own undesirable thoughts, impulses, traits, or behaviors to others.

projective test: A personality test in which people respond to inkblots, drawings of ambiguous human situations, incomplete sentences, and the like, by projecting their own inner thoughts, feelings, fears, or conflicts onto the test materials.

prosocial behavior: Behavior that benefits others, such as helping, cooperation, and sympathy.

prototype: The example that embodies the most common and typical features of a concept.

proximity: Geographic closeness; a major factor in attraction.

psychiatrist: A medical doctor with a specialty in the diagnosis and treatment of mental disorders.

psychoactive drug: A drug that alters normal mental functioning—mood, perception, or thought; if used medically, called a controlled substance.

psychoanalysis (SY-co-ah-NAL-ih-sis): Freud's term for both his theory of personality and his therapy for the treatment of psychological disorders, which uses free association, dream analysis, and analysis of resistance and transference to uncover repressed memories, impulses, and conflicts thought to cause psychological disorder.

psychoanalyst (SY-ko-AN-ul-ist): A professional, usually a psychiatrist, with special training in psychoanalysis.

psychoanalytic perspective (SY-ko-AN-il-IT-ik): A perspective initially proposed by Freud that emphasizes the importance of the unconscious and of early childhood experiences as the keys to understanding behavior and thought.

psychodrama: A group therapy in which one group member acts out personal problem situations and relationships, assisted by other members, to gain insight into the problem.

psycholinguistics: The study of how language is acquired, produced, and used, and how the sounds and symbols of language are translated into meaning.

psychology: The scientific study of behavior and mental processes.

psychoneuroimmunology (sye-ko-NEW-ro-IM-you-NOLL-oh-gee): A field in which psychologists, biologists, and medical researchers study the effects of psychological factors on the immune system.

psychosexual stages: A series of stages through which the sexual instinct develops; each stage is defined by an erogenous zone that becomes the center of new pleasures and conflicts.

psychosis (sy-CO-sis): A severe psychological disorder marked by loss of contact with reality and a seriously impaired ability to function.

psychosocial stages: Erikson's eight developmental stages through the life span, each defined by a conflict that must be resolved satisfactorily in order for healthy personality development to occur.

psychosurgery: Brain surgery to treat some severe, persistent, and debilitating psychological disorder or severe chronic pain.

psychotherapy: The treatment for psychological disorders that uses psychological rather than biological means and primarily involves conversations between patient and therapist.

puberty: A period of rapid physical growth and change that culminates in sexual maturity.

punishment: The removal of a pleasant stimulus or the application of an unpleasant stimulus, which tends to suppress a response.

quality circle: A small group of employees who meet to discuss ways of improving products and job performance.

random assignment: In an experiment, the assignment of subjects to experimental and control groups by using a chance procedure, which guarantees that all subjects have an equal probability of being placed in any of the groups; a control for selection bias.

random sample: A sample of subjects selected in such a way that every member of the population has an equal chance of being included in the sample; its purpose is to obtain a sample that is representative of the population of interest.

range: The difference between the highest score and the lowest score in a distribution of scores.

rape myth: The unfounded belief that women who are raped ask for it, deserve it, or enjoy it.

rational-emotive therapy: A directive, confrontational psychotherapy designed to challenge and modify the clients' irrational beliefs thought to cause their personal distress; developed by Albert Ellis.

rationalization: Supplying a logical, rational, socially acceptable reason rather than the real reason for an action.

reaction formation: Denying an unacceptable impulse, usually sexual or aggressive, by giving strong conscious expression to its opposite.

realistic conflict theory: The notion that prejudices arise when social groups must compete for scarce resources and opportunities.

recall: A measure of retention that requires one to remember material with few or no retrieval cues, as in an essay test.

recency effect: The tendency to recall the last items on a list more readily than those in the middle of the list.

receptor site: A site on the dendrite or cell body of a neuron that will receive only specific neurotransmitters.

recessive gene: A gene that will not be expressed if paired with a dominant gene but will be expressed if paired with another recessive gene.

reciprocal determinism: Bandura's concept that behavior, personal/cognitive factors, and environment all influence and are influenced by each other.

recognition: A measure of retention that requires one to identify material as familiar, or as having been encountered before.

reconstruction: A memory that is not an exact replica of an event but has been pieced together from a few highlights using information that may or may not be accurate.

reflex: An innate, unlearned, automatic response to a particular environmental stimulus (examples: blinking, sucking, grasping).

regression: Reverting to a behavior characteristic of an earlier stage of development.

rehearsal: The act of purposely repeating information to maintain it in short-term memory or to transfer it to long-term memory.

reinforcement: An event that follows a response and increases the strength of the response and/or the likelihood that it will be repeated.

reinforcer: Anything that strengthens a response or increases the probability that it will occur.

relearning method: Measuring retention in terms of the percentage of time or learning trials saved in relearning material compared with the time required to learn it originally; also called the savings method.

reliability: The ability of a test to yield nearly the same score when the same people are tested and then retested on the same test or an alternative form of the test.

REM dreams: Having a dreamlike and storylike quality, the type of dream that occurs almost continuously during each REM period; more vivid, visual, and emotional than an NREM dream.

REM rebound: The increased amount of REM sleep that occurs after REM deprivation; often associated with unpleasant dreams or nightmares.

REM sleep: Sleep characterized by rapid eye movements, paralysis of large muscles, fast and irregular heart rate and respiration rate, increased brain-wave activity, and vivid dreams.

replication: The process of repeating a study with different subjects and preferably a different investigator to verify research findings.

representative sample: A sample of subjects selected from the larger population in such a way that important subgroups within the population are included in the sample in the same proportions as they are found in the larger population.

repression: Removing from one's consciousness disturbing, guilt-provoking, or otherwise unpleasant memories so that one is no longer aware a painful event occurred.

resistance: In psychoanalytic therapy, the patient's attempts to avoid expressing or revealing painful or embarrassing thoughts or feelings.

resistance stage: The second stage of the general adaptation syndrome, during which there are intense physiological efforts to resist or adapt to the stressor.

resolution phase: The final stage of the sexual response cycle, during which the body returns to an unaroused state.

resting potential: The membrane potential of a neuron at rest, about –70 millivolts.

reticular formation: A structure in the brainstem that plays a crucial role in arousal and attention and that screens sensory messages entering the brain.

retina: The tissue at the back of the eye that contains the rods and the cones and onto which the retinal image is projected.

retinal image: The image of objects in the visual field projected onto the retina.

retrieval: The act of bringing to mind material that has been stored in memory.

retrieval cue: Any stimulus or bit of information that aids in the retrieval of particular information from long-term memory.

retrograde amnesia (RET-ro-grade): A loss of memory for events occurring for a period of time preceding a brain trauma that caused a loss of consciousness.

reuptake: The process by which neurotransmitter molecules are taken from the synaptic cleft back into the axon terminal for later use, thus terminating their excitatory or inhibitory effect on the receiving neuron.

reverse discrimination: Giving special treatment or higher evaluations to individuals from groups that have been the target of discrimination.

reversibility: The realization that any change in shape, position, or order of matter can be reversed mentally.

right hemisphere: The hemisphere that controls the left side of the body and that, in most people, is specialized for visual-spatial perception and for interpreting nonverbal behavior.

rods: The light-sensitive receptors in the retina that provide vision in dim light in black, white, and shades of gray.

roles: The behaviors considered to be appropriate for individuals occupying certain positions within the group.

Rorschach Inkblot Test (ROR-shok): A projective test composed of 10 inkblots to which a subject responds; used to reveal unconscious functioning and the presence of psychiatric disorders.

sample: The portion of any population that is selected for study and from which generalizations are made about the entire larger population.

saturation: The degree to which light waves producing a color are of the same wavelength; the purity of a color.

savings score: The percentage of time or learning trials saved in relearning material over the amount of time or number of learning trials required for the original learning.

scapegoating: Displacing aggression onto minority groups or other innocent targets who were not responsible for the frustration causing the aggression.

Schachter–Singer theory: A two-stage theory stating that, for an emotion to occur, there must be (1) physiological arousal and (2) an explanation for the arousal.

schedule of reinforcement: A systematic program for administering reinforcements that has a predictable effect on behavior.

schema: Piaget's term for a cognitive structure or concept used to identify and interpret information; an integrated framework of knowledge and assumptions about people, objects, and events, which affects how we encode and recall information.

schizophrenia (SKIT-suh-FREE-nee-ah): A severe psychological disorder characterized by loss of contact with reality, hallucinations, delusions, inappropriate or flat affect, some disturbance in thinking, social withdrawal, and/or other bizarre behavior.

seasonal affective disorder (SAD): A mood disorder in which depression comes and goes with the seasons.

secondary appraisal: Evaluating one's coping resources and deciding how to deal with a stressful event.

secondary reinforcer: A neutral stimulus that becomes reinforcing after repeated pairings with other reinforcers.

secondary sex characteristics: Those physical characteristics not directly involved in reproduction but distinguishing the mature male from the mature female.

sedentary lifestyle: A lifestyle in which a person exercises less than 20 minutes three times a week.

selection bias: The assignment of subjects to experimental or control groups in such a way that systematic differences among the groups are present at the beginning of the experiment.

self-actualization: Developing to one's fullest potential; the highest need on Maslow's hierarchy.

self-efficacy: A person's belief in his or her ability to perform competently in whatever is attempted.

self-serving bias: Our tendency to attribute our successes to dispositional causes, and our failures to situational causes.

semantic memory: The subpart of declarative memory that stores general knowledge; our mental encyclopedia or dictionary.

semantics: The meaning or the study of meaning derived from morphemes, words, and sentences.

semicircular canals: Three fluid-filled tubular canals in the inner ear that provide information about rotating head movements.

senile dementia: A state of mental deterioration caused by physical deterioration of the brain and characterized by impaired memory and intellect and by altered personality and behavior; senility.

sensation: The process through which the senses pick up visual, auditory, and other sensory stimuli and transmit them to the brain; sensory information that has registered in the brain but has not been interpreted.

sensorimotor stage: Piaget's first stage of cognitive development (ages birth to 2 years), culminating with the development of object permanence and the beginning of representational thought.

sensory adaptation: The process of becoming less sensitive to an unchanging sensory stimulus over time.

sensory deprivation: A condition in which sensory stimulation is reduced to a minimum or eliminated.

sensory memory: The memory system that holds information coming in through the senses for a period ranging from a fraction of a second to several seconds.

sensory receptors: Specialized cells in each sense organ that detect and respond to sensory stimuli—light, sound, odors, etc.—and transduce (convert) the stimuli into neural impulses.

separation anxiety: The fear and distress shown by toddlers when their parent leaves, occurring from 8 to 24 months and reaching a peak between 12 and 18 months.

serial position effect: Upon presentation of a list of items, the tendency to remember the beginning and ending items better than the middle items.

serotonin: A neurotransmitter that plays an important role in regulating mood, sleep, aggression, and appetite; a serotonin deficiency is associated with anxiety, depression, and suicide.

set point: The weight the body normally maintains when one is trying neither to gain nor to lose weight (if weight falls below the normal level, appetite increases and metabolic rate decreases; if weight is gained, appetite decreases and metabolic rate increases so that the original rate is restored).

sex chromosomes: The pair of chromosomes that determines the sex of a person (XX in females and XY in males).

sexual aversion disorder: A sexual desire disorder characterized by an aversion to or a desire to avoid genital contact with a sexual partner.

sexual dysfunction: A persistent or recurrent problem that causes marked distress and interpersonal difficulty and that may involve any or some combination of the following: sexual desire, sexual arousal or the pleasure associated with sex, or orgasm.

sexual orientation: The direction of one's sexual preference—toward members of the opposite sex (heterosexuality), toward one's own sex (homosexuality), or toward both sexes (bisexuality).

sexual response cycle: The four phases—excitement, plateau, orgasm, and resolution—that Masters and Johnson found are part of the human sexual response in both males and females.

sexually transmitted diseases (STDs): Infections that are spread primarily through intimate sexual contact.

shape constancy: The tendency to perceive objects as having a stable or unchanging shape regardless of differences in viewing angle.

shaping: Gradually molding a desired behavior by reinforcing responses that become progressively closer to it; reinforcing successive approximations of the desired response.

short-term memory: The second stage of memory, which holds about seven (a range of five to nine) items for less than 30 seconds without rehearsal; working memory; the mental workspace we use to keep in mind tasks we are thinking about at any given moment.

signal detection theory: The view that detection of a sensory stimulus involves both discriminating a stimulus from background "noise" and deciding whether the stimulus is actually present.

situational attribution: Attribution of a behavior to some external cause or factor operating in the situation; an external attribution.

size constancy: The tendency to perceive objects as the same size regardless of changes in the retinal image.

Skinner box: Invented by B. F. Skinner for conducting experiments in operant conditioning, a soundproof operant conditioning chamber with a device for delivering food and either a bar for rats to press or a disk for pigeons to peck.

sleep apnea: A sleep disorder characterized by periods when breathing stops during sleep and the person must awaken briefly in order to breathe; major symptoms are excessive daytime sleepiness and loud snoring.

sleep cycle: A cycle of sleep lasting about 90 minutes and including one or more stages of NREM sleep followed by a period of REM sleep.

sleep terror: A sleep disturbance in which a person partially awakens from Stage 4 sleep with a scream, dazed and groggy, in a panic state, and with a racing heart.

slow-wave sleep: Stage 3 and Stage 4 sleep; deep sleep.

social cognition: Mental processes that people use to notice, interpret, understand, remember, and apply information about the social world and that enable them to simplify, categorize, and order their world.

social facilitation: Any positive or negative effect on performance due to the presence of others, either as an audience or as co-actors.

socialization: The process of learning socially acceptable behaviors, attitudes, and values.

social learning theory: A theory that explains the process of gender typing in terms of observation, imitation, and reinforcement.

social loafing: The tendency to put forth less effort when working with others on a common task than when working alone.

social motives: Motives acquired through experience and interaction with others.

social phobia: An irrational fear and avoidance of social situations in which people believe they might embarrass or humiliate themselves by appearing clumsy, foolish, or incompetent.

social psychology: The study of how the actual, imagined, or implied presence of others influences the thoughts, the feelings, and the behavior of individuals.

Social Readjustment Rating Scale (SRRS): Holmes and Rahe's stress scale which ranks 43 life events from most to least stressful and assigns a point value to each.

social support: Tangible support, information, advice, and/or emotional support provided in time of need by family, friends, and others; the feeling that we are loved, valued, and cared for.

sociocultural perspective: A perspective that emphasizes social and cultural influences on human behavior and stresses the importance of understanding those influences when we interpret the behavior of others.

somatoform disorders (so-MAT-uh-form): Disorders in which physical symptoms are present that are due to psychological rather than physical causes.

somatosensory cortex (so-MAT-o-SENS-or-ee): The strip of tissue at the front of the parietal lobes where touch, pressure, temperature, and pain register in the cortex.

somnambulism (som-NAM-bue-lism): Sleepwalking that occurs during a partial arousal from Stage 4 sleep.

source traits: Cattell's name for the traits that underlie the surface traits, make up the most basic personality structure, and cause behavior.

specific phobia: A marked fear of a specific object or situation; a catchall category for any phobia other than agoraphobia and social phobia.

spinal cord: An extension of the brain, reaching from the base of the brain through the neck and spinal column, that transmits messages between the brain and the peripheral nervous system.

split-brain operation: An operation, performed in severe cases of epilepsy, in which the corpus callosum is cut, separating the cerebral hemispheres and usually lessening the severity and frequency of grand mal seizures.

spontaneous recovery: The reappearance of an extinguished response (in a weaker form) when an organism is exposed to the original conditioned stimulus following a rest period.

sports psychology: A specialty concerned with helping competitive athletes develop the mental and emotional skills necessary to facilitate their maximal competitive performance potential, and with helping people in recreational athletic programs attain greater physical, emotional, and mental benefits.

Stage 4 sleep: The deepest NREM stage of sleep, characterized by an EEG pattern of more than 50 percent delta waves.

standard deviation: A descriptive statistic reflecting the average amount that scores in a distribution vary or deviate from their mean.

standardization: Establishing norms for comparing the scores of people who will take the test in the future; administering tests using a prescribed procedure.

Stanford–Binet Intelligence Scale: An individually administered IQ test for those aged 2 to 23; Terman's adaptation of the Binet-Simon Scale.

state-dependent memory effect: The tendency to recall information better if one is in the same pharmacological or psychological (mood) state as when the information was encoded.

stereotypes: Widely shared beliefs about the characteristic traits, attitudes, and behaviors of members of various social groups (racial, ethnic, religious) and including the assumption that they are usually all alike.

stimulants: A category of drugs that speed up activity in the central nervous system, suppress appetite, and cause a person to feel more awake, alert, and energetic; also called "uppers."

stimulus (STIM-yu-lus): Any event or object in the environment to which an organism responds; plural is stimuli.

stimulus motives: Motives that cause us to increase stimulation and that appear to be unlearned (examples: curiosity and the need to explore, manipulate objects, and play).

stimulus satiation (say-she-A-shun): A behavioral technique in which a patient is given so much of a stimulus that it becomes something the patient wants to avoid.

storage: The act of maintaining information in memory.

stranger anxiety: A fear of strangers common in infants at about 6 months and increasing in intensity until about 12½ months, and then declining in the second year.

stress: The physiological and psychological response to a condition that threatens or challenges a person and requires some form of adaptation or adjustment.

stressor: Any event capable of producing physical or emotional stress.

stroke: A cardiovascular accident that occurs when the blood supply to the brain is cut off, killing many neurons; the major cause of damage to the adult brain.

structuralism: The first formal school of psychology, aimed at analyzing the basic elements, or structure, of conscious mental experience through the use of introspection.

structure of intellect: The model proposed by Guilford consisting of 180 different intellectual abilities, which involve all of the possible combinations of the three dimensions of intellect—mental operations, contents, and products.

subjective night: The time during a 24-hour period when your body temperature is lowest and when your biological clock is telling you to go to sleep.

sublimation: Rechanneling of sexual or aggressive energy into pursuits that society considers acceptable or admirable.

subliminal perception: Perceiving sensory stimulation that is below the absolute threshold.

subliminal persuasion: Sending persuasive messages below the recipient's level of awareness.

successive approximations: A series of gradual training steps, with each step becoming more like the final desired response.

superego (sue-per-EE-go): The moral system of the personality, which consists of the conscience and the ego ideal.

surface traits: Cattell's name for observable qualities of personality, such as those used to describe a friend.

surrogate: Substitute; someone or something that stands in place of.

survey: A method in which researchers use interviews and/or questionnaires to gather information about the attitudes, beliefs, experiences, or behaviors of a group of people.

sympathetic nervous system: The division of the autonomic nervous system that mobilizes the body's resources during stress, emergencies, or heavy exertion, preparing the body for action.

synapse (SIN-aps): The junction where the axon of a sending neuron communicates with a receiving neuron across the synaptic cleft.

syntax: The aspect of grammar that specifies the rules for arranging and combining words to form phrases and sentences.

syphilis (SIF-ih-lis): An STD that progresses through three stages; if untreated, it can eventually be fatal.

systematic desensitization: A behavior therapy, used to treat phobias, that involves training clients in deep muscle relaxation and then having them confront a graduated series of anxiety-producing situations (real or imagined) until they can remain relaxed while confronting even the most feared situation.

tactile: Pertaining to the sense of touch.

task analysis: Breaking down a job or activity into its smallest component parts so that performance of each part can be analyzed and evaluated and suggestions for improvement can be specific.

taste aversion: The dislike and/or avoidance of a particular food that has been associated with nausea or discomfort.

taste buds: The structures that are composed of 60 to 100 sensory receptors for taste.

telegraphic speech: Short sentences that follow a strict word order and contain only essential content words.

temperament: An individual's behavioral style or characteristic way of responding to the environment.

temporal lobes: The lobes that contain the primary auditory cortex, Wernicke's area, and association areas for interpreting auditory information.

teratogens: Harmful agents in the prenatal environment, which can have a negative impact on prenatal development or even cause birth defects.

territorial behavior: Marking off a territory in an effort to establish control over it and defend it against unwelcome intrusions.

territory: An area defined by a person as temporarily or permanently his or her own.

testosterone (tes-TOS-tah-rone): The most powerful androgen secreted by the testes and adrenal glands in males and by the adrenal glands in females; influences the development and maintenance of male sex characteristics and sexual motivation; associated with male aggressiveness.

thalamus (THAL-uh-mus): The structure, located above the brainstem, that acts as a relay station for information flowing into or out of the higher brain centers.

THC (tetrahydrocannabinol): The principal psychoactive ingredient in marijuana and hashish.

Thematic Apperception Test (TAT): A projective test consisting of drawings of ambiguous human situations, which the subject describes; thought to reveal inner feelings, conflicts, and motives.

theory: A general principle or set of principles that explains how a number of separate facts are related to one another.

timbre (TAM-burr): The distinctive quality of a sound that distinguishes it from other sounds of the same pitch and loudness.

time out: A behavioral technique, used to decrease the frequency of undesirable behavior, that involves withdrawing an individual from all reinforcement for a period of time.

token economy: A behavioral technique used to encourage desirable or socially acceptable behaviors by reinforcing them with tokens that can be exchanged later for desired objects, activities, and/or privileges.

top-down processing: Application of previous experience and conceptual knowledge to first recognize the whole of a perception and thus easily identify the simpler elements of that whole.

trait: A personal characteristic that is used to describe or explain personality.

trait theories: Theories that attempt to explain personality and differences between people in terms of their personal characteristics.

tranquilizer (minor): A central nervous system depressant that calms the user.

transduction: The process by which sensory receptors convert sensory stimulation—light, sound, odors, etc.—into neural impulses.

transference: An intense emotional situation occurring in psychoanalysis when one comes to behave toward the analyst as one had behaved toward a significant figure from the past.

trial and error: An approach to problem solving in which one solution after another is tried in no particular order until a workable solution is found.

trial-and-error learning: Learning that occurs when a response is associated with a successful solution to a problem after a number of unsuccessful responses have been tried.

triangular theory of love: Sternberg's theory that three components—intimacy, passion, and decision/commit-

ment—singly and in various combinations produce seven different kinds of love.

triarchic theory of intelligence: Sternberg's theory that intelligence consists of three parts—the componential, the contextual, and the experiential.

trichromatic theory: The theory of color vision suggesting that there are three types of cones, which are maximally sensitive to red, green, or blue, and that varying levels of activity in these receptors can produce all of the colors.

twin study method: Studying identical and fraternal twins to determine the relative effects of heredity and environment on a variety of characteristics.

Type A behavior pattern: A behavior pattern characterized by a sense of time urgency, impatience, excessive competitive drive, hostility, and easily aroused anger; believed to be a risk factor in coronary heart disease.

Type B behavior pattern: A behavior pattern characterized by a relaxed, easygoing approach to life and not associated with coronary heart disease.

unconditional positive regard: Unqualified caring and nonjudgmental acceptance of another.

unconditioned response (UR): A response that is invariably elicited by the unconditioned stimulus without prior learning.

unconditioned stimulus (US): A stimulus that elicits a specific response without prior learning.

unconscious (un-KON-shus): For Freud, the primary motivating force of behavior, containing repressed memories as well as instincts and wishes that have never been conscious.

underextension: Restricting the use of a word to only a few, rather than to all, members of a class of objects.

uplifts: The positive experiences in life, which can neutralize the effects of many of the hassles.

vaginismus (VAJ-ah-NIZ-mus): A sexual pain disorder in which involuntary muscle contractions create a tightening and closing of the vagina, making intercourse painful or impossible.

validity: The ability of a test to measure what it is intended to measure.

variability: How much the scores in a distribution spread out, away from the mean.

variable-interval schedule: A schedule in which a reinforcer is given after the first correct response following a varying time of nonreinforcement based on an average time.

variable-ratio schedule: A schedule in which a reinforcer is given after a varying number of nonreinforced responses based on an average ratio.

ventromedial hypothalamus (VMH): The part of the hypothalamus that presumably acts as a satiety center and, when activated, signals an animal to stop eating; when the area is destroyed, the animal overeats, becoming obese.

vestibular sense (ves-TIB-yu-ler): Sense that provides information about movement and our orientation in space through sensory receptors in the semicircular canals and the vestibular sacs, which detect changes in the movement and orientation of the head.

visible spectrum: The narrow band of electromagnetic rays, 380–760 nm in length, that are visible to the human eye.

visual cliff: An apparatus used to test depth perception in infants and young animals.

Weber's law: The law stating that the just noticeable difference (JND) for all our senses depends on a proportion or percentage of change in a stimulus rather than on a fixed amount of change.

Wechsler Adult Intelligence Scale (WAIS-R): An individual intelligence test for adults that yields separate verbal and performance (nonverbal) IQ scores as well as an overall IQ score.

Wernicke's aphasia: Aphasia resulting from damage to Wernicke's area, in which the patient's spoken language is fluent, but the content is either vague or incomprehensible to the listener.

Wernicke's area: The language area in the temporal lobe involved in comprehension of the spoken word and in formulation of coherent speech and written language.

withdrawal symptoms: The physical and psychological symptoms (usually the opposite of those produced by the drug) that occur when a regularly used drug is discontinued and that terminate when the drug is taken again.

working backwards: A heuristic strategy in which a person discovers the steps needed to solve a problem by defining the desired goal and working backwards to the current condition.

work motivation: The conditions and processes responsible for the arousal, direction, magnitude, and maintenance of effort one puts forth in one's job.

Yerkes–Dodson law: The principle that performance on tasks is best when arousal level is appropriate to the difficulty of the task—higher arousal for simple tasks, moderate arousal for tasks of moderate difficulty, and lower arousal for complex tasks.

Name Index

Subject Index

Credits

Photos

xxii: Galen Rowell/Mountain Light. **2:** AP Wide World Photo. **5:** C. Steele-Perkins/Magnum Photo. **7:** Billy E. Barnes/Photo Edit. **19:** Tony Freeman/Photo Edit. **20:** Steve Winter/Black Star. **31:** Jeff Greenberg/Photo Edit. **33:** Andy Levin/Photo Researchers Inc. **35:** Galen Rowell/Mountain Light. **38:** Bonnie Kamin. **41:** Biophoto/Photo Researchers Inc. **50:** Bonnie Kamin. **53:** A. Glauberman/Photo Researchers Inc. **56:** Photosynthesis Archives. **59:** Tony Stone Worldwide. **64:** Alexander Tsiaras/Photo Researchers Inc. **65TL:** Tony Stone Worldwide. **65TR:** Dr. Michael Phelps and Dr. John Mazziotta/UCLA School of Medicine. **65B:** Peter Menzel/Material World. **66:** Joseph Nettis/Photo Researchers Inc. **73:** Robert Brenner/Photo Edit. **74:** Bonnie Kaman. **78:** Ben Barnhart/Offshoot. **80:** Charles Gupton/Stock Boston. **83:** Serguel Fedoror/Woodfin Camp and Associates. **92:** T. Farmer/Tony Stone Worldwide. **94:** T. Svensson/The Stock Market. **98:** G. Gardner/The Image Works. **104:** Amy C. Etra/Photo Edit. **106T:** NASA Science Photo Library/Photo Researchers Inc. **106B:** Gerard Vandeystadt/Photo Researchers Inc. **112T:** Bill Horsmon/Stock Boston. **112B:** Ernest Braun/Bonnie Kamin. **116:** The Image Works. **121:** Photo Edit. **122:** Ben Barnhart/Offshoot. **126:** Strauss/Curtis/Offshoot. **128:** Dale E. Boyer/Photo Researchers Inc. **130:** Charles Gupton/Tony Stone Worldwide. **133:** Will & Deni McIntyre/Photo Researchers Inc. **136:** Ed Kashi. **138, 139:** Bohdan Hrynewych/Stock Boston. **142:** Louis Psihoyos/Matrix. **145:** Francoise Sauze, Science Photo Library/Photo Researchers Inc. **147:** Adam Woolfitt/Woodfin Camp and Associates. **148:** Elena Dorfman/Offshoot. **153:** Richard Hutchings/Photo Researchers Inc. **154:** David Austen/Stock Boston. **157:** Esbin Anderson/The Image Works. **158:** Strauss/Curtis/Offshoot. **162:** Michael Newman/Photo Edit. **165:** Courtesy The National Library of Medicine/Photosynthesis Archives. **168:** Tony Freeman/Photo Edit. **171:** Photosynthesis Archives. **172:** Bettmann. **174:** Billy Barnes/Stock Boston. **175:** Richard Hutchings/Photo Edit. **176:** Ed Kashi. **179:** Christopher Johnson/Stock Boston. **180:** Nina Coen/Time Magazine. **184T:** Rick Browne/Stock Boston. **184B:** Leif Skoogfors/Woodfin Camp and Associates. **189:** Klaus Reisihger/Black Star. **197:** Tony Freeman/Photo Edit. **199:** Michael Newman/PhotoEdit. **202:** Galen Rowell/Mountain Light. **204L:** Bettmann. **204R:** Bettmann. **207:** Kent Wood/Photo Researchers. **211R:** Nicholas Desciose/Photo Researchers Inc. **211L:** Barry Iverson/Woodfin Camp and Associates. **221:** Mark Antman/The Image Works. **223:** Bettmann. **224:** Al Francis/AP Wide World Photo. **225:** AP Wide World Photo. **227:** M&E Bernheim/Woodfin Camp and Associates. **239:** Galen Rowell/Mountain Light **242:** Jim Brown/Offshoot. **244L:** Jeffrey Fox/Woodfin Camp and Associates. **244R:** Hank Morgan/Photo Researchers Inc. **247L:** Jim Pickerell. **247M:** A&B Archives. **247R:** F. Baldwin/Photo Researchers Inc. **249:** Photosynthesis Archives. **250:** Lew Merrim/Monkmeyer Press Photo.

253: Cindy Karp/Black Star. **257:** Porterfield/Chickering/Photo Researchers Inc. **259:** Lester Slean/Woodfin Camp and Associates. **260:** Peter Menzel/Material World. **265T:** Jim Simncen/Tony Stone Worldwide. **265B:** Art Wolfe/Tony Stone Worldwide. **275:** CNN. **278:** Kirk McKoy/Material World. **279:** Jim Brown/Offshoot. **282:** Leong Ka Tai/Material World. **284:** Reuters/Bettmann. **288L:** Francis Leroy/Photo Researchers Inc. **288C&R:** Lennart Nilsson/Bonniers. **289:** Jonathan Selig/Tony Stone Worldwide. **292:** Enrico Ferorelli. **296:** Martin Rogers/Stock Boston. **299L&R:** Goodmon/Monkmeyer Press Photo. **301:** Yves De Braine/Black Star. **305:** Myrleen Ferguson/Photo Edit. **308:** Chip Anderson/Tony Stone Worldwide. **311:** Cathlyn Melloan/Tony Stone Worldwide. **314:** Bonnie Kamin. **316:** Jeff Isaac Greenberg/Photo Researchers Inc. **318:** Robert Harbison. **319:** Leong Ka Tai/Material World. **322:** Galen Rowell/Mountain Light. **324:** AP Wide World Photo. **325:** Robert Harbison. **327:** F. Pedrick/The Image Works. **331:** B. Daemmrich/The Image Works. **336:** Olive Pierce/Black Star. **337:** Elizabeth Brooks. **341:** Will & Demi McIntyre/Photo Researchers Inc. **346:** Sotographs/Liaison. **347:** Jayne Kamin. **349T:** Dennis Dickson/Peter Arnold Inc. **349B:** James Wilson/Woodfin Camp and Associates. **351:** Alan Oddie/Photo Edit. **354:** Richard Hutchings/Photo Edit. **355:** Galen Rowell/Mountain Light. **358:** Christina Taccone/Offshoot Stock. **360L:** Lief Skoogfors/Liaison. **360R:** Diana Walker/Liaison. **363:** Anthony Neste. **365:** Courtesy McGill University. **368:** Photosynthesis Archive. **370:** Arthur Beck/Photo Researchers Inc. **375:** Robert Harbison. **382:** Mike Abramson/Woodfin Camp and Associates. **385:** Copyright Paul Eckman 1975. **386:** Robert Isaacs/Photo Researchers Inc. **390:** Russ Schleipman/Offshoot Stock. **393:** AP Wide World Photo. **394:** Christine Taccone/Offshoot. **398:** Penny Gentieu. **400:** Latham, A. & Grenadier, A./*Psychology Today.* **402:** Paul Damien/Tony Stone Worldwide. **406:** Renato Rotolo/Gamma Liaison. **408:** Michael Newman/Photo Edit. **412:** P. Watson/The Image Works. **414:** Robert Harbison. **415:** Ferguson Cate/Photo Edit. **426:** AP Wide World Photo. **429:** B. Daemmrich/The Image Works. **430:** Penny Gentieu. **434:** David Leifer/Offshoot Stock. **438:** Bettmann. **443:** Prettyman/Photo Edit. **446:** Bettmann. **448:** Bettmann. **449:** Larry Kolvoord/The Image Works. **452:** Andy Levin/Photo Researchers Inc. **454:** Robert Brenner/Photo Edit. **458:** Bettmann. **471:** B. Daemmrich/The Image Works. **472:** David Leifer/Offshoot Stock. **476:** Grant Pix/Photo Researchers Inc. **478:** Bettmann. **480:** AP Wide World Photo. **486:** Alexander Boulat/Material World. **488:** David Leifer/Offshoot Stock. **492:** J. Pickerell/The Image Works. **495:** Michael Newman/Photo Edit. **499:** Tony Freeman/Photo Edit. **503:** David Young-Wolff/Photo Edit. **505:** Perlstein/Jerrican/Photo Researchers Inc. **506:** Grant Pix/Photo Researchers Inc. **508:** Contier/The Image Works. **511L:** Robert Harbison. **511R:** Russ Schleipman/Offshoot Stock. **517:** Bonnie Kamin. **527:** Grunnitus/Monkmeyer Press Photo. **530:** Gordon Willitt/Tony Stone Worldwide. **534T:** Wally McNamee/Woodfin Camp and Associates.

Text and Art